the Writer's Handbook 2002

Preface by
Frank McCourt

Edited by Elfrieda Abbe

the Writer books

The Writer Books is an imprint of Kalmbach Trade Press, a division of Kalmbach Publishing Co. These books are distributed to the book trade by Watson-Guptill.

For all other inquiries, including individual orders or details on special quantity discounts for groups or conferences, contact:
Kalmbach Publishing Co.
21027 Crossroads Circle
Waukesha, WI 53187
(800) 533-6644

Visit our website at http://www.writermag.com
Secure online ordering available

Permission to reprint the John Updike interview was graciously given by the interviewer, Leonard Lopate, and by John Updike and his publishers at Knopf; thanks also to the New York Public Library where this public interview was conducted.

"Writing Matters" copyright © 1982, 1998 by Julia Alvarez. Published in SOMETHING TO DECLARE, Algonquin Books of Chapel Hill, 1998. First appeared in a different version in *The Writer*, September 1998. Reprinted by permission of Susan Bergholz Literary Services, New York. All rights reserved.

Printed in the United States of America

01 02 03 04 05 06 07 08 09   10 9 8 7 6 5 4 3 2 1

Publisher's Cataloging-in-Publication
(Provided by Quality Books, Inc.)

The writer's handbook / edited by Elfrieda Abbe ; preface
  by Frank McCourt. — 2002 ed., 66th ed.
    p. cm.
    Includes index.
    ISBN: 0-87116-189-3

    1. Authorship—Handbooks, manuals, etc.
  2. Publishers and publishing. I. Abbe, Elfrieda.

PN137.W73 2001   808'.02
                        QBI01-200672

Art director: Kristi Ludwig
Book layout: Jan Allen

CONTENTS

THE ARTICLES

Professional Development

The Craft of Writing

THE MARKETS

Nonfiction Magazines

Fiction & Poetry Magazines

Book Publishers

Other Markets

Other Resources

PREFACE

Being a writer is a splendid
way to spend one's life

by Frank McCourt

If I hadn't written *Angela's Ashes*, I would have died howling, begging God for another year. When the book was published in 1996, I was 66 and, overnight, an icon for the Social Security set. Reports came in that after discovering my age, ailing senior citizens around the world were leaping from their deathbeds demanding pad and paper to write their memoirs.

So, McCourt, why did it take you so long to write the book?

I was busy. For 30 years I taught high school English in New York, and when you spend your days with American adolescents you have energy for nothing else. Try it.

No. Don't try it. You can't teach in high school and write. Try college. That, for the writer or anyone else, is the greatest racket in the world.

So, I taught and thought and read and discussed everything with my students. I told them stories and that telling sent me back into my childhood.

First there was the talk, and most of that around the fire. In Limerick, back in the forties, friends of my mother would sit with her and gossip and I'd sit on the stairs, out of sight, listening. Sometimes my mother would call out, "Frankie, are you there sitting on the stairs?" and when I'd answer yes she'd tell me get into bed and complain to her friend, "That fella. His ear is always cocked."

She was right: the ear was always cocked. I couldn't get enough of grownup talk because there was always a lowering of voices, a whispering, and that's where all the secrets were. That's when I'd inch down a few steps to the deliciousness of gossip about neighbors: little scandals; hurried departures to England; husbands with a few pints under their belts and how they wouldn't leave you alone. There were shy giggles and exclamations: "God forgive me. Sure we shouldn't be giving scandal like this."

In the slums of Limerick nothing came between us and our lives, no television, no radio. Unlike the high school students I taught years later in New York, we created our own days, had our own adventures, told our own stories. There was no point in staying at home when we could roam city streets and the adjacent countryside. We were street urchins and accustomed to being told Go away, Get out of here, Go home, but while we roamed we talked. Every morning before the bell rang for our first class at school we talked, but not about what we watched on TV the night before. We talked about what we did. We bragged about our fathers, about what we would do when we grew up. We lied and dreamed.

When you have nothing, your dreams are rich and everything is possible.

And what, you're saying to yourself, does all this have to do with writing?

Answer: Everything—because everything has everything to do with writing. How was I to know the itch to write of my childhood would agitate me even into my middle years? How was I to know that when I became a teacher of high school English in New York that my students, after detecting my "brogue," would want to know details of my "miserable childhood"?

I'm circling a little, digressing, when what I want to say is: I've always wanted to be a writer because it's a splendid way to spend one's life. It's not only splendid—but superior. It's godlike.

The godlike part comes from my magical experience with pencil stubs and bits of paper. It will be hard for you, reader out there, to understand how scarce paper was in the lanes of Limerick, and how I saved every scrap for my scribblings, every paper bag, even great sheets of old wallpaper discarded by rich houses. (There was no litter on the streets of Limerick: every scrap of paper was taken home to be burned or, in my case, to be written on.) It was wonderful writing on wallpaper. Once I had scraped off the old plaster I had plenty of space for my epic on the mighty battle between the Irish mythological hero, Cuchulain, and the patron saint of England, St. George. I wasn't too worried about chronology. It was enough that England got its comeuppance so that Ireland could become, once again, a green and pleasant land, though not in my lifetime, not in my lifetime.

I didn't know my stories of paper shortage would so amuse my high school students they would want more. Of course I knew that for many it was a delaying tactic, a way of keeping me from getting to a boring lesson on gerunds or dangling participles and that's where my students won the day. Ignorant of grammar, I was glad of an excuse to travel back to boyhood days.

But what I didn't realize then was that in the telling, I was refining incidents and anecdotes which led to a book called *Angela's Ashes*. My students were intrigued with one story in particular, my experience with a Limerick moneylender, Mrs. Finucane. They're thinking to themselves: This teacher is standing there admitting he wrote threatening letters to his neighbors and even to his own grandmother and that when Mrs. Finucane died he stole money from her for his fare to America.

Wow!

If I know anything about writing or literature of life itself I surely discovered it before those classes at Stuyvesant High School in New York. For 30 years I read the writings of about 11,000 high school students and surely I learned something? Often I read their work in awe and envy, feeling I could never match their talent, especially the ones who followed my advice and sent their work to magazines and newspapers.

Yes, I'm lucky to have had a miserable childhood, a supply of old wall-paper, high school students to urge or goad me on, and enough energy after retiring from teaching to write a memoir and another memoir and who knows what's next. . . .

So here's a word to writers who clutch the brow (thank you, P.G. Wodehouse) and live in despair your work will never see the light of day. During all my days of teaching I scribbled in notebooks *and* tried to write. There's a difference, you see, between scribbling and writing. Scribbling is cool. You're sitting under a tree or on the pot with a notebook in your lap jotting down (or up) random ideas, scenes, characters. For the writer there's nothing like scribbling. Too many books and professors insist on outlines. I say, To hell with the outline. Write what comes.

But when you write, write it hot. (Thank you, D.H. Lawrence.)

What to write about? Once I told my students, "Nothing is significant till you make it significant." I don't want to brag, but I think that was a pretty astute comment, and remember, if you keep your ear cocked, you'll discover treasures of significance.

For your ears are as sacred as anyone else's.

INTRODUCTION

Welcome to a wonderful
community of writers

by Elfrieda Abbe

With this 66th *Writer's Handbook,* I invite you to join a wonderfully diverse, lively and accomplished community of writers—and to participate in one of the most comprehensive writers' workshops available, featuring the best authors of our time. The conversation you'll find here is inspiring and stimulating, covering a wide range of topics from marketing your work, dealing with rejection, and negotiating with editors to crafting great characters and dialogue, researching, and revising, to finding the inspiration, courage, and resolve to keep writing.

Among our conversants are John Updike, Stephen King, Jane Hamilton, Frank McCourt, Joyce Carol Oates, Sue Grafton, Julia Alvarez, Sol Stein, Barbara Delinsky, Anne Perry, Tony Hillerman, Katherine Paterson, and many more successful writers—novelists, educators, journalists, poets—who generously share their ideas, struggles, and suggestions concerning the art and craft of writing.

Each may have a different view of what it means to be successful as a writer and how to get there, but there is a common theme that runs through the discussion: If you want to be a writer, write. Concentrate on the process rather than on the trappings of success. Too often writers fail—or give up—because they haven't embraced the concept of constant improvement.

Updike has written more than 50 books by sticking to a regime of 1,000 words a day, six days a week. He's won the nation's highest writing honors, including two Pulitzer Prizes and the National Book Award, yet he still calls himself "one of the lazier writers."

At the other end of the spectrum, Frank McCourt taught school in New York for 27 years, writing in his free moments, refining his achingly bittersweet stories of his childhood in Limerick, before writing his first book, *Angela's Ashes*. His debut novel, a best-seller around the world, won the 1997 Pulitzer, *Time* Magazine's nonfiction Book of the Year (1996), the National Book Critics Circle Award, and the *Los Angeles Times* Book Award.

Writing is a rigorous, if diverse, step-by-step process. *The Writer's Handbook* gives you an opportunity to learn about that process from some of our foremost authors.

If you want a concise approach to writing success, read Stephen King's "Everything You Need to Know About Writing—In Ten Minutes." Or find out what Sue Grafton has to say about finding precious time to write, or join Maeve Binchy in her writer's study for an insider's view of the writing life.

You'll find practical suggestions and words of wisdom in more than 60 articles that bring you tips and advice in three key areas: Professional Development, The Craft of Writing, and Ideas and Inspiration.

The Writer's Handbook is part of a grand tradition established by *The Writer* when the magazine was founded in 1887 by two *Boston Globe* reporters with the goal of providing writers ("literary workers") with information and inspiration.

Since its earliest days, *The Writer* has featured advice from prominent authors of the day, from Wallace Stegner, William Saroyan, and Daphne du Maurier in the 1930s to poet John Ciardi in the 1970s to John Updike and others in this first decade of the 21st century. Honoring the magazine's roots, we've included a few excerpts from those earlier works in this volume. These gems demonstrate how timeless good advice to writers can be. From Philip Wylie's rant on writers who are fussy about when and where they write to Saroyan's moving letter to a young writer, their words are as valuable today as the day they wrote them.

This is the first *Handbook* in many years that has not been edited by Sylvia Burack. Along with her husband A.S. Burack, who bought the *The Writer* in 1936, she helped shape the editorial direction of the magazine. She was on *The Writer* editorial staff for 60 years, 22 as editor-in-chief. When she retired in 2000, Kalmbach Publishing Co. purchased the magazine and moved it from Boston to Waukesha, Wisconsin, just outside Milwaukee. As the new editor and a writer, I want to thank Sylvia for her dedication to writers and the writing life.

I first read *The Writer's Handbook* in the early days of my own career, when I was freelancing feature articles for magazines and newspapers. On its pages I found valuable advice on how to improve my writing and where I might find markets for it. I found it to be a wonderful writer's companion, connecting me to the wider community of writers, putting me in touch with their concerns and joys, their hopes and dreams, their hard-won insights. It's a pleasure, now, to help continue that legacy with a new edition of the *Handbook*.

Acknowledgments

I am grateful to Books Editor Philip Martin for his knowledge, editorial acumen, and assistance in assembling this volume. Thanks also to many others at Kalmbach Publishing Co. who helped with the preparation of this edition, especially those who helped to assemble the market listings, in particular Jan Allen, Susan Campbell, Sally Laturi, Jeff Reich, Susan Vanselow, Rene Schweitzer, and Mary Graf and her wonderful staff. Thanks also to Mary Algozin for her tireless copy-editing of this thousand-page tome.

All articles are copyright by the original authors, who retain all rights to their work. Most of the articles included here first appeared in the pages of *The Writer* magazine, with a few drawn from other sources, and are used by permission. For any inquiries or questions on further use of this material, contact Permissions Dept., The Writer Books, Kalmbach Publishing Co., at the address given on the copyright page at the front of this book.

We know the publishing world is always in flux, and it is possible that some listings of markets have become outdated. We would greatly appreciate any feedback from readers, with corrections or comments on any markets you found especially useful or less than helpful. Our company has a tradition of outstanding customer service, and we look forward to improving and refining this resource volume in coming years by incorporating your valued feedback.

If you know of new or overlooked markets of significance to aspiring writers that you would like to recommend for future volumes, please forward those ideas to Philip Martin at the mailing address at the front of this book, or by e-mail directly to pmartin@kalmbach.com.

Thanks in advance for your feedback and support, and good writing!

—*Elfrieda Abbe*

SECTION ONE

Professional Development

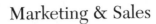

MARKETING DAY

Set aside one day now and then
to vanquish the dread of marketing

by Kathryn Lay

To some writers, "marketing" is an ugly word. Others find it frightening. Still others consider it confusing, frustrating, and intrusive upon their creativity. So how does a writer keep the business side of writing from interrupting the creative flow?

I've found that by setting aside one day a week or month to spend on marketing, I've vanquished the dread of marketing. Because my husband's payday falls on the last Friday of the month, my "Marketing Day" is the last Thursday of the month. Then, on Friday morning, I'm ready to send out my manuscripts.

True marketing involves much more than simply preparing manuscripts for the mail, however. Here are six ways to make the most of your day of marketing:

1. Search for Markets

Spend time reading your market magazines. *The Writer* has a regular section of listings, plus profiles of specific market areas. Do you subscribe to online publications that offer market-listing information and updates? Did you know that the *Writer's Digest* website gives a market of the day, with guidelines?

This is also a good time to study new magazines. Friends will often give me copies of a new magazine they subscribe to or have purchased. Whenever I am in a bookstore, I look over the magazines, and if I see one I am particularly interested in, I'll purchase a copy to study. On Marketing Day, I'll sit back with a soda or cup of tea and study these magazines in hopes of finding ideas to query or stories to send.

2. List Markets for Your Projects

Look over the manuscripts you want to market. Do you know where you will send your work-in-progress? Do you have at least two, and preferably ten, markets for each of your stories, poems, books, or articles? By making a list for each manuscript, I am not at a loss if it is rejected the first time out.

By preparing ahead of time, I am also able to send a returned manuscript on its way again without spending time searching for my next market. When a manuscript sells, I will create a new list for selling reprints of my pieces when they become available again.

3. Update Market Information

Editors come and go, publishers change addresses, houses are swallowed and new ones created, needs and focuses change. If you keep records of markets (You don't? Why not?), you will also need to make changes.

Whenever I hear of an editorial change, I write it on a slip of paper and put it into my market box. On Marketing Day, I go through the changes and record them on the 3x5 cards on which I note potential markets. Whether you keep records in a notebook or on the computer, be prepared to keep correct information.

When a new editor takes charge, or a previous editor moves to a higher position, your cover and query letters should reflect the change. If a magazine changes its policy and accepts only query letters, and I send a full manuscript, I've wasted my time and postage.

4. Create Sparkling Queries

A query or cover letter should be created, not written in a hurry. You are selling yourself and your work. On Marketing Day, I take time to create exciting letters that will best pitch my work to an editor. Are they interesting? Do they come to the point without rambling? Have I found a succinct way to pitch my idea? Is my proposal professional?

I am always surprised when someone tells me that their well-written, exciting article, story, or book has not been sent to a publisher because they don't want to write that query or cover letter. Use your Marketing Day to practice and to learn.

> By setting aside a specific day to work exclusively on marketing, I never feel as if I am interrupting my writing schedule.

5. Study Back Issues, Guidelines, and Catalogs

Do you want to break into *Family Circle*? Read six months to a year of back issues. Find out what they have published, what they haven't, and the focus of their market. Get on the above-mentioned writers' newsletters and look up the hundreds of guidelines waiting to be downloaded from the Web. Some guidelines give specific needs as well as information on monthly columns with openings for freelancers. Send for catalogs by book publishers that publish the type of book you have written.

6. Prepare at Least One Manuscript and One Query

At the end of your Marketing Day, you should be ready to market your work. You have researched, studied, and prepared. Give yourself the reward of at least one manuscript and one query letter that is ready to take to the post office the next day. Tomorrow, you will be ready to let your creative mind flow.

By setting aside a specific day to work exclusively on marketing, I never feel as if I am interrupting my writing schedule. I have come to look forward to these days, and am excited about the possible directions they will lead. Whether you write full- or part-time, you can benefit from a day to tackle the business side of writing. And when guilt over lack of marketing tries to tug you away from writing, you can set those thoughts aside for your next Day of Marketing.

Kathryn Lay keeps 50 manuscripts and queries in the mail at one time, and has sold over 350 short stories and articles and two picture books. Her work has appeared in the anthologies *A Glory of Unicorns, Chicken Soup for the Mother's Soul, Stories for the Family's Heart,* and others.

STAND OUT FROM THE CROWD

Great tips on promoting yourself

by Roberta Beach Jacobson

Do we as writers grab every opportunity to promote ourselves?

Sure, we make certain our queries and submissions are neatly prepared and editors' names correctly spelled. Many of us have designed address stickers on our computer and others carry professional business cards to hand out to potential clients. We have established web sites to show off our clips and we never fail to add that peppy electronic tagline to each e-mail we send.

But what about the next step—doing something so editors or publishers will really take notice of us and remember our names the next time around?

Check your desk drawers and chances are you'll find a variety of colorful pencils or ballpoint pens advertising banks, restaurants, sports teams and clubs. This is only the start of the promotional pitching going on all around us every day.

Look at how the corporate world promotes its various logos on key chains, t-shirts, caps, coasters, bumper stickers, and posters. I'm not suggesting we run out and have our names painted on a race car, but we freelancers could take some lessons from these corporate giants. Although our budgets are considerably smaller, we still have a product to promote to the world—our writing.

Inexpensive Promotion Opportunities

One journalist I know paid to have a logo designed to her specifications, and editors remembered her years later because of her eye-catching business stationary and matching cards. Her initial idea, done on the cheap by a graphics artist student, continues to open door after door.

A freelancer in England opted to include a paper bookmark with each query. Imagine how his pages tagged with a red or purple bookmark catch a new editor's attention. He did the computer work himself and kept his costs minimal.

Calendars are a fairly easy way for writers or photographers to get their names circulated. Shop around and compare prices of print shops. Due to envelope considerations, you must decide early on if the calendars are to be wallet-sized and included with all correspondence, or a larger variety with photos, only to be mailed out with manuscripts. Always be certain to send several calendars at once, so your planned advertisement doesn't just end up adorning the publication's mailroom wall!

We decided mousepads would be the ideal way to get the word out about our new e-zine, and several months before the launch of *Kafenio* we designed an appropriate layout and chose the color scheme. We kept costs to under one dollar each and the items went to prospective readers, writers, and advertisers. Of course, we did not miss the opportunity to selectively include mousepads with our regular queries and manuscripts.

Did we get noticed? Definitely. A few editors even took the time to call and compliment us on our innovative marketing approach.

A word of caution: Whatever item you decide best promotes your work, be it a pen or a calendar, keep your initial costs small. Start out with a hundred or two to test your idea. If you like the results, you can easily reorder more later.

Being caught up in the excitement of a new publicity campaign does not give us a free ride up to the tippy-top of the freelance ladder or mean we can afford to turn sloppy in our work. It just gives us an added marketing push and often this extra bit of attention spells the difference between success and failure.

Sources of Promotional Items:

- Iprint—http://www.iprint.com
Offers mousepads, magnets, calendars, and many other products that you can design yourself online.
- CPI Line—http://www.promobooks.com/dealers.htm
This site offers a state-by-state listing of companies that offer promotional and imprinted products.
- Instant Promotion.com—http://www.logo-motion.com/
- 1Stop Promotional Products—http://store.yahoo.com/1stopshop/
Offers a range of imprinted Bic pen products, plus other promotional items.
- GoPromos.com—www.gopromos.com

Roberta Jacobson writes from Karpathos Island, Greece. She is the co-editor of the e-zine *Kafenio* (http://www.kafenio.com), "Where Europe is only a mouseclick away."

PLOTTING YOUR MARKETING MAP

The more precise your planning, the easier it will be to reach your goal

by Michael Sedge

Like anything done well, marketing your work requires planning. Setting out on a marketing venture without a precise plan is like taking a trip without a map: you can make right turns and left turns, but never seem to reach your final destination. Therefore, the more precise you are in your planning, the easier it will be to reach your goals.

The first factor in any marketing plan is a budget. Without knowing how much you have, or are willing to spend, it is literally impossible to prepare a working strategy. Without assigning money to your plan, what you are in effect doing is dreaming of what you would "like" to do, rather than what is realistically possible. Strange as it may seem, I have worked with many of today's Fortune 500 companies and had the marketing directors say: "Prepare a marketing plan for us, then we'll see if we have the funds to cover it."

Why is money so important? Just as a battle commander with a limited number of soldiers can protect only a certain amount of territory, a marketing director with a restricted budget can only spread the word so far. Let's say, for example, that you plan to do a syndication mailing to editors of 50 travel magazines. The postage alone, if your package is professionally done, could cost over $200. If, after you have purchased stationery and presentation folders, and copied clips of published works to include in the package, you do not have the $200 for postage, what you are doing, in effect, is spinning wheels and dreaming. So be realistic with your goals and your expectations based on your budget.

There are ways to cut costs and still carry out a highly professional marketing operation. Using the Internet is an excellent way to dramatically decrease overhead. Samples of your work can be scanned and transmitted as e-mail attachments, or you can direct potential clients to your web page. This is particularly effective when dealing with editors based in foreign countries. Another method of lowering marketing costs is to create an introductory brochure for your services and products. These can be generated at local print shops for very low cost and, if designed correctly, will fit perfectly into a standard envelope. Be sure, however, that the paper stock used does not exceed the one-ounce, first-class mail weight limit.

Inasmuch as you do not want to waste money, you also do not want to be so tight so as to hinder quality. Keep in mind that after you have made the decision to operate your writing as a business, you must then set aside a fixed amount of funds for marketing purposes. This budget, or lack thereof, will determine how your plan is laid out and executed.

Writers, for the most part, should operate two parallel marketing plans: the first to sell their work; the second to sell themselves. While each area has a specific focus and scope, the two generally overlap. Each time you publish an article or book, you are, in a sense, marketing yourself. Too few writers understand and take advantage of this fact—missing out on the promotional benefits of having their name in print. Those who do profit from this area are often the writers you see on such programs as "Good Morning America" discussing topics that range from childcare and home-financing to world affairs and the president's legal woes.

This morning's "Today" show perfectly illustrated this point. A writer who had recently produced a feature on stock-market trends for *Money Magazine* was advising viewers to ride out Wall Street's current down-swing caused by global economic effects. Given the number of people who watch "Today," there was no doubt more than one book editor or publisher listening to this individual. Some, in fact, may very well have been thinking, Trends on Wall Street . . . that would make a good book. He then may have made a mental note to call the magazine for the writer's telephone number. Such things happen more frequently than one might expect.

While laying out and executing a dual marketing plan, much of the basic logistics may be the same. Stationery, business cards, and samples of published works will be required in both cases.

> Writers, for the most part, should operate two parallel marketing plans: the first to sell their work; the second to sell themselves.

Keep It Simple

There is nothing difficult about a marketing plan, though I've known many corporate directors who like to make it seem so to justify their positions. For me it is a matter of Q+C=S. That is, Query plus Consistency equals Success. I begin by focusing on a target market. Say, for instance, that your goal is to sell two travel articles a month. To achieve this, do your market research, then send out one query a week—always on a different subject, but within the travel theme. At the end of one month, you will have four queries out. At the same time, maintain a list of publications where you can send ideas should they be rejected. To expand your efforts, try sending each query out to five markets around the world (each one targeting a different country).

Eventually, assignments will come in. Don't stop your marketing efforts, though. This is where the "C" or Consistency comes into play. Keep sending out a new query each week. Using this method, I found myself, after three years, with over 250 queries out and more than 20 assignments at any given time. I ultimately stopped using the Q+C=S method because I could not keep up with the work flow—a position I hope you will soon find yourself in.

This same strategy can be applied to book sales as well. In this case, however, you will be sending out one book query a week, followed by a complete proposal. Because, over the past year, I have tried to focus more energy on book writing, I began this systematic method several months ago. Today I have more than 60 queries and 23 book proposals out.

The Q+C=S plan can also be applied to self-promotion. It should, in fact, be incorporated into your marketing of articles, books, and services. If you find it too difficult to maintain the pace—and eventually you should—then divide your efforts between marketing of products and self. For instance, during week one send out queries for articles, and in week two send out self-promotional media kits. Alternating weeks will keep you stimulated and will also allow time for your mind to think of new ideas and markets.

You may be asking why you can't simply do a mass mailing of your media kit. You could. There are several problems with this method, however. First, marketing costs would be immediately high, rather than spread out over a period of time. Second, you might experience a rush of interest and six months later find yourself sitting alone with no work and no media interest in you or what you have to say. For these reasons, your efforts should be precisely targeted and consistent. Don't let a week go by without doing something to sell your work and market yourself.

Though I am always looking for opportunities, I maintain a monthly and annual list to insure that nothing is forgotten. In February, for instance, my list might say:

1) Week One—Query ten newspapers around the world (same query to each) on summer cruises in the Mediterranean.

2) Week Two—Send media kit to ten TV producers; offer to speak on archaeological travel.

3) Week Three—Send book query to ten publishers in New York, topic: Archaeological Travel Guide Series.

4) Week Four—September is back-to-school month, send media kit to ten universities and offer my services as a seminar instructor. Query women's magazines on Living through the Back-to-School Crisis.

This very simple, one-line plan keeps me on track. As ideas and projects come to mind, I add them to the list. The result is a constantly growing, developing market plan that is easy to follow and, if necessary, can be altered based on daily developments.

The key is to have a written "map" to follow on weekly and monthly bases. Ensure that all of your efforts fit the budget you've set aside. And, most important, maintain a consistent plan to sell your work and yourself.

Michael Sedge is author of several books for writers/photographers, including *Successful Syndication*, *Marketing Strategies for Writers*, and *The Photojournalist's Guide to Making Money*. His books are published by Allworth Press and are available on the web at www.allworth.com.

BEATING THE ODDS OF REJECTION

A rejection slip is not a sign that
your writing is poor!

by Dennis E. Hensley

Beginning writers have often shown me their rejected manuscripts to which the editor has attached a small note reading, "Thank you for your manuscript, but this does not meet our current editorial needs." What does that mean? Understandably, these aspiring writers, having studied the market and submitted a competently written article, wonder what had gone wrong.

My first response is that all writers get rejection slips, including me. Pearl Buck received a rejection for one of her short stories the very week she was notified she had won the Nobel Prize for Literature! It's part of the writing business: If you aren't getting rejected, you aren't attempting to break into new markets or explore new writing options.

To risk rejection is to grow. In the long run, it's something positive. Of course, in the short run, it hurts. Writers put their heart and soul on paper. The manuscript becomes their "baby," and nobody wants someone saying, "Your baby has big ears." In essence, that's what a rejection letter sounds like. Since your manuscript cannot get published if you don't submit it, you must risk rejection by sending it out again. But there are better ways of coping with rejection and even of reducing the odds of ever having it happen.

First, a rejection slip isn't necessarily a sign that your writing is poor. A lot of superb manuscripts come across editors' desks that they wish they could publish, but sometimes factors unrelated to the writing make publishing them impossible. The editor may have just accepted a manuscript on the same topic from another author. He may have paid such a large advance on one project, his budget won't allow him to accept any new submissions for a few months. Or she may admire a writer's talent, but her publishing house has decided not to publish textbooks or cookbooks or children's novels any longer. Hence, the decision to reject isn't always related to writing talent.

Sometimes editors' personal lives get in the way. An editor may have a bias against the position an article is taking and reject it; another who agrees with your point of view may accept it. One editor may like the article, but may worry that it might offend one of the magazine's advertisers, so the article gets nixed. The editor may have a headache or may have had a fight with his or her spouse and everything gets rejected that day because of the editor's bad mood. After all, editors are human.

On occasion editors can be wrong in rejecting a manuscript. One editor might be too old to realize the high interest in techno games, so he rejects an article about it. Another editor might not like your staccato, short-sentenced style, so she rejects the manuscript, not realizing that a generation reared on MTV and split-screen images can readily relate to writing such as this. Just because one editor rejects a manuscript, it doesn't mean the topic or the writing style is not worthy of publication. It's a good idea to try your manuscript on several editors.

Understanding what an editor is saying in a rejection letter is also important. If you receive a form rejection slip, it probably means that the publisher has no real interest in your manuscript or in establishing a working relationship with you. But if you receive a rejection slip with a personal note from the editor, take heart. That can mean that while the manuscript is not what the editor needs, you, the writer, have caught the editor's eye. You should feel encouraged to send other material to that publication or publishing house.

On the other hand, don't read more into a rejection letter than is really there. When an editor says, "Thank you for submitting . . . ," don't take it as enthusiasm when it is really just courtesy. Similarly, when an editor writes, "Perhaps you'll have more success with another periodical . . . ," that is not an invitation for you to write back and say, "Please give me a list of those places you thought I should be submitting my manuscript."

A Starting Place for Revisions

Rejection letters are good starting places for manuscript revisions. If two or three editors say that your stories have good plots but weak characters, then retain the plot ideas but work on making your characters more three-dimensional. Likewise, if several editors like your article concepts but say your writing mechanics require too much revision, then learn to do copyediting yourself.

Here are several other suggestions on how to reduce the odds of getting your manuscript rejected:

1. *Let it sit a while*. Don't try to edit your material as soon as you finish writing, because you will be too emotionally attached to it and too familiar with its contents. Let it "cool" for a few days or more, then go back to see if it still seems the best you can make it.

2. *Gauge your timing*. Send Christmas articles in the summer, not in December. Give editors plenty of lead time.

3. *Work your way up*. Before trying to compete in the mass market, get some experience by writing for smaller-circulation trade journals, specialty periodicals, or even your hometown newspaper. Editors of these publications often have more time to help you improve your writing and marketing skills. As you improve, you can expand your market outreach.

4. *Hone your mechanics*. Most editors do not have time to do a thorough copyediting job of your manuscript, then fax or mail it back to you, wait for you to revise and then resubmit it. Instead, sharpen your writing skills so that your manuscripts do not have comma splices, sentence fragments, spelling errors, or grammar problems. If you need help in these areas, have someone in your writing group go over it.

5. *Don't underestimate the impact of the query letter and book proposal*. Too often writers just "dash off" a query letter to obtain a go-ahead for submission from an editor. You may think that even if your query letter isn't very persuasive, it's OK. It's the manuscript that really counts, right? Wrong! The query letter is the equivalent of a job interview. If an editor receives a query letter or book proposal that is weak, poorly written, and unprofessional, the editor will assume the manuscript will be more of the same. So, put as much effort into your query as you do with the manuscript itself.

6. *Know your topic thoroughly*. If you are writing a novel, know the genre. For example, if you want to write a romance, read a lot of romances—both the classics and more contemporary works. If you are writing nonfiction, do exhaustive research. Talk to experts, read whatever is available on the topic, and become something of a walking authority on the topic yourself.

7. *Finally, give networking a try*. Make contacts in the world of publishing by attending writers' conferences and meeting editors face to face. Bring your manuscript and schedule an appointment so that you can talk to an editor about your ideas, current writing projects, and finished works. Weeks later, when you write a query letter, you can begin with, "Thanks again for meeting with me at the summer writers' conference. I've used your suggestions on preparing this article and hope you will find it acceptable." This pre-established relationship with an editor can work in your favor; you are no longer a blank face.

Although getting a rejection letter is never uplifting, it doesn't have to be devastating, either. One of the secrets of coping with both rejection and success

> Just because one editor rejects a manuscript, it doesn't mean the topic or the writing style is not worthy of publication. . . .

is momentum. Keep several manuscripts in the mail at all times. In that way, if a rejection letter comes in, you can comfort yourself with the knowledge that you have four other manuscripts out there that could get accepted any day. (Conversely, if you receive an acceptance, bear in mind that any of the four other manuscripts out there could get rejected.) That being the case, you'd better stay at your typewriter or word processor. This sort of thinking keeps a writer balanced.

Dennis E. Hensley, author and teacher, has been successful writing both fiction and non-fiction. He is the author of six novels, 22 non-fiction books, including, with Holly G. Miller, *Write on Target: A Five-Phase Program for Nonfiction Writers* (The Writer, 1995), and more than 2,700 articles.

Marketing & Sales

THE SIDEBAR SOLUTION

Article add-ons can boost your freelance fees

by Bill Nelson

Wouldn't it be grand if freelance writers could find a magic potion that would make their work:

- Look more professional
- Sell more readily
- Command higher fees
- And, in a time of shrinking editorial holes in many newspapers and magazines, give writers a license to go on for greater lengths?

Well, such an elixir does exist, although many writers remain only dimly aware of its profitable possibilities. We're talking about the miracle of sidebars.

Are you using them at all, or with any degree of regularity, in the articles you submit to magazines and newspapers?

The word sidebar has been floating around journalistic circles a long time, but still hasn't made it into *Webster's* (side*cars*, yes, but side*bars*, no). Nevertheless, they represent a golden opportunity for enterprising—and sometimes wordy—freelance writers.

That insight hit me a decade ago, when I wrote a travel story on the Canary Islands, Spain's "land of eternal spring." A volcanic cluster of islands off northwest Africa, the Canaries are a favorite vacation destination for Europeans—the Hawaii of Europe. There, you find spring-like temperatures all year, as well as mountains, deserts, lush tropical growth and volcanic terrain that often resemble a moonscape.

My article came to a whopping 50 inches and brought a horrified look from the travel editor of the newspaper for which I was writing. "It's good reading," she said, "but the front office has issued a decree that 30 inches should be the maximum length."

"Is there any way around that?" I asked.

"Tell you what," she said, smiling, "Trim your piece to 30 inches, then use your cuts to give me two sidebars to go along with it. That way, we'll keep management happy, and I'll be able to pay you more, besides."

So that's what happened. The main text focused on Tenerife Island, and the two sidebars covered the other tourist-oriented islands and the dearth of English-speaking tourists (in our resort hotel, we heard Spanish, German, Italian, and French spoken, but only rarely, English). A third sidebar told about the topless surprises we found on the beaches where, for many European women, going *au naturel* is the norm.

Thanks to the magic of sidebars, the Canary Islands package earned $500 instead of the usual $300 payment, and was given a dazzling four-story spread far more impressive than I had imagined.

USA Today underscored the sidebar strategy soon afterward, when it gave me an assignment to profile the late master motivator Leo Buscaglia.

"Do a 500-word story on Leo, then give us two or three short sidebars to go with it," an editor said. "Today's readers love sidebars. One might be on how he got started as America's 'love doctor.' Another could be on his penchant for hugs. And the third, well, we'll leave that up to you."

As it turned out, the newspaper used only one sidebar, but the other two helped make the sale.

What type of sidebars might you consider? [See next page.]

THIS IS A SIDEBAR

Read the above, and you no longer need to ask. But by definition, a sidebar is a companion story that appears adjacent to a longer feature story, often in a box or toned in a different typeface to set it apart. The text touches briefly on a subject related to the feature.

Today's readers find these small bites of information irresistible. Sometimes they'll read them before tackling the main feature (caught you skimming this first!).

Some examples of sidebars: I recently read an article on "Rehearsing before a person retires." A sidebar listed five key steps in financial planning to ensure solvency after saying goodbye to the daily rat race.

Another piece on Wisconsin's many bicycle routes carried a sidebar on a relatively new offering, the Gandy Dancer Trail—how could one not be intrigued by the name?

Look for sidebar possibilities each time you write an article.

Useful List

Americans are hooked on lists. *McCall's*, for instance, did a story on how wives could get their husbands more involved in child rearing. A sidebar listed five jobs fathers might do that mothers usually handled, like packing a child's lunch.

Glossary

For example, *Martha Stewart Living* did a story on apple growing, and a sidebar identified three dozen varieties of the fruit. I wrote about Wisconsin's scenic Kettle Moraine area, and a sidebar listed definitions of 10 key terms of glacial handiwork, including drumlins, kettles, kames, and eskers.

You-can-do-it-too Suggestions

Country Journal, for instance, focused on a booming food co-op in New England, and a sidebar gave suggestions on how readers might form their own cooperatives.

Resource List

Another popular sidebar suggests where to go for more information. A New York story on child abuse, for example, ran a sidebar listing treatment centers, self-help groups, and useful books for both children and adults.

Gone are the days when a writer tried to cram everything into one seemingly never-ending article. That no longer works in the era of the *One Minute Manager* and television's 20-second sound bite. Today's time-pressed readers generally appreciate sidebars. These article add-ons—and the organizing of information they require—are something to think about each time you begin to write a story.

As an editor friend confided: "When I get a sidebar along with a manuscript, I know I'm dealing with a professional who's hip to what's going on today."

Bill Nelson is a copy chief and special projects writer for a Wisconsin-based public relations agency and teaches local college writing workshops. This article was first published in *The Writer* magazine in March 2001.

OTHER ARTICLE ADD-ONS
- Listings of related articles or books of interest
- Web site URLs
- Summaries or expansions of key points
- Charts and graphs
- Background information
- Timelines of important events
- Brief articles relevant to primary story
- Professional organizations related to topic

ONE ARTICLE, MANY CHECKS

Selling reprints more than once

by Kelly James-Enger

Want to boost your freelance income overnight? Start selling reprints and you can get paid two times, three times, or even more for the same article.

I've made thousands of dollars on reprint sales in the past couple of years. For example, I sold a story on what secrets brides and grooms should share to *Bridal Guide* for $750; the story ran in November 1998. Within six months, I'd reprinted the story in a women's magazine for $250 and in another bridal publication for $275, bringing my total paycheck for the story to $1275. A dating article that originally sold for $100 has netted another $250 in reprints while a business story that first brought $800 has been reprinted for $250 and $500 during the past year.

Read on to learn how you can snag more than one paycheck for an article:

Step One: Negotiate Better Contracts

You must *own* reprint rights in order to sell them. If you sign work-for-hire or all-rights agreements, you're giving up your right to ever resell the same work in the future. Read publishing contracts carefully before signing them. Some magazines demand a 90-day or 6-month exclusivity provision that precludes you from reprinting the story in any media during that time frame; others may expressly prohibit you from reprinting the story in competing publications.

When selling rights to any work, remember that the fewer rights you sell, the better. For print magazines, the least you can sell is one-time rights (although magazines often want *first* serial rights); most web publications want non-exclusive online rights for a limited period of time. Invest in your future income by negotiating contracts today.

Step Two: Review Your Work

Take a look at the articles to which you currently own rights. Do you have a lot of parenting pieces? Travel stories? Technology articles? Make a list of all available stories, their titles, subject area, word count, and special features like sidebars and quizzes. Write down when reprint rights will be available for stories you're currently working on, and review and update your possible reprint list every three to six months.

Step Three: Scout for Markets

Keeping your available stories in mind, begin looking for potential reprint markets. Because I write mostly health and fitness, diet/nutrition, and bridal and relationship stories, I'm always on the lookout for smaller magazines that cover those subject areas. *Writer's Market* includes listings of magazines that buy reprints. Smaller circulation publications, regional magazines and newspapers, and trade publications all may be interested in previously published material. Check their guidelines to see if they purchase reprinted stories.

Kathy Sena, a freelancer in Los Angeles, has developed a network of regional publications for her parenting and health stories and resells most of the articles she writes. "About 40 percent of my income comes from reprints," says Sena. "The checks aren't that big—maybe $50 or $75 a story—but they add up quickly!"

By calling major newspapers in neighboring states, Melanie McManus, a Madison, Wisconsin, freelancer, found new markets for her regional travel stories. She often resells stories to non-competing publications and has reprinted one story five times.

Finally, don't overlook the Internet—web sites looking for content may be interested in electronic rights to stories, especially if you have a lot of articles in a particular subject area available. I've recently sold web rights to fitness, health, and business stories that originally appeared in print publications.

Step Four: Make Your Pitch

Next, contact your potential reprint markets. If I'm sending only one story, I write the editor a short letter describing the article and why it will appeal to readers; I also note where and when it was published. I close by asking if the editor is interesting in purchasing reprint rights to the story and include a copy of the article.

If I think that the market may be interested in more than one article, I send a letter that includes a story list describing relevant articles by topic and word length, along with several clips. I then follow up by telephone in four to eight weeks to determine if the editor is interested in any stories.

I've made thousands of dollars on reprint sales in the past couple of years.

Step Five: Set Your Price

In some cases, magazines or web sites will offer a set amount for reprint rights; other publications will ask what your usual reprint fee is. Don't set your rates too low, but keep in mind that regional publications usually have smaller budgets and will offer less than national magazines or well-funded web sites.

Step Six: Consider Syndication

Working with a syndicate—an individual or organization that offers reprint rights to your work to various media—is another way to net additional income from previously published work. Syndicates often pay a flat fee for rights to your work for a fixed time period; less frequently, they may share any sales proceeds with you, usually 50/50. While syndicate rates vary, the *L.A. Times* Syndicate paid me $100 to $125 for exclusive worldwide rights for one year to several bridal stories.

I've also worked with two individuals who specialize in selling articles overseas and have made as little as $50 and as much as $250 for reprint rights to a story. The one-man syndicate I currently work with has found markets for my work in Denmark, Malaysia, Singapore, and Australia—and I've made $900 this year on stories he's sold. To find a syndicate, check the syndicate section (found later in this book) or ask for recommendations from other writers.

Step Seven: Keep It Up

Continue to develop your list of reprint markets and consider those potential sales when you accept assignments. For example, I may accept work that pays less than my usual rate if I think I'll be able to sell reprint rights to the story at least once or twice. And don't forget to offer new stories as they become available to your current reprint markets. Invest some time and energy into selling reprints, and you'll be on your way to netting multiple paychecks for every article you write.

Kelly James-Enger is a full-time freelancer whose work has appeared in more than 25 national magazines, including *Woman's Day, Family Circle, Marie Claire,* and *Fitness.* She also leads magazine-writing programs and workshops throughout Illinois.

BARGAIN FOR BETTER RATES

Sometimes it's as simple as asking

by Kelly James-Enger

Your phone rings. Good news—it's a magazine editor who's intrigued by your recent query and wants to assign the story. The two of you discuss word count, deadline, angle, and possible sources. Then she offers you $1 per word—for all rights to the piece.

What do you do? You can accept the assignment, turn it down because she's asking for all rights, or try to negotiate a better deal. While the last option is often the wisest one, I've found that many writers are either afraid to negotiate with editors or would like to, but don't know how to broach the subject.

When I started freelancing full-time four years ago, I accepted whatever editors offered me and signed work-for-hire and all-rights contracts without complaint. (With a work-for-hire agreement, the publisher owns the copyright to the story; with an all-rights agreement, you own the copyright to the story but transfer all rights to the publisher.) I soon realized, though, that every time I did so, I was also giving up any chance of making more money from that particular story by reprinting it.

I started asking for better rates and more writer-friendly contracts instead of automatically agreeing to the editor's offer, and my strategy has paid off. I've made more money on individual stories, and today reprints comprise nearly 10 percent of my income.

Still, negotiating can be stressful, especially when you don't know where to begin. Read on for some strategies that can help to boost your bottom line—without turning off editors.

Set Your Standards

You can't effectively negotiate until you know what you want, what you're willing to concede on and what your absolute bottom line or "walk-away" position is. When I started freelancing, I took on every assignment regardless of pay. I focused on developing relationships with editors, building my portfolio, and improving my writing abilities.

Today, however, I don't write for less than $1 per word, and I usually get more than that. Then, if an editor offers me a story for a lower rate, I say something like, "You know, I'd like to work for you, but I get $1 per word or more for most articles. Can you match that?" Your rate will depend on your experience, whether you've worked with the editor before, and the amount of work that a specific story might require.

Prove Your Worth

If the offer is decent, I usually don't ask for more money the first time I work with an editor. I figure that even if you have hundreds of clips to your name, the editor is taking a chance on you—there are plenty of talented writers who are lazy about deadlines or turn in sloppy copy. After you've done a great job on your first piece, you're in a better position to ask for a higher per-word rate for the next story the publication assigns to you.

I'll often ask for a "raise" on my second or third assignment, using language like, "You've worked with me before, so you know I'll do a good job, meet my deadline, and that the story will fact-check out OK. Considering that, can we bump my rate up?" I used this approach on my third story for a fitness magazine, and the editor raised my rate by 25 cents per word—not bad for a five-minute phone call.

Make Your Case

Being assigned a straightforward story that will require minimal research is one thing. If, however, you're asked to write a piece with a tight deadline or one that will entail significant legwork and time, use these factors as bargaining points.

Last year, an editor I'd worked with before called to assign a 2,000-word piece on oral contraceptives with five sidebars—and then offered $1 per word. I said something like, "I really want to write this piece, but obviously this story is going to take me weeks of research and interviews, especially with all the sidebars. I don't think $1/word is really fair for this particular story. Can you do better than that?" She agreed that the story would require extensive research and bumped the rate to $1.50 per word.

> You can't effectively negotiate until you know what your absolute bottom line or "walk-away" position is.

Back It Up

Rather than just turning down an all-rights contract, explain why you don't want to sign it. In one case, an editor and I had agreed on the basics of a story—a rate of $1 per word, sources and format. Then came the killer—the magazine's all-rights contract. I said, "I'm really excited about this story and I want to work with you, but I usually don't sign all-rights contracts because I make a significant amount of income from reprint rights. How about if we agree that you can have all rights to the piece for a certain period of time, after which they will revert back to me?" She agreed to this compromise, and we used the same contract language for future stories, as well.

Offer an alternative. If the contract asks for more rights than you want to sell, suggest a compromise. Three years ago, a fitness magazine assigned me a story on how to determine your "exercise personality." The editor sent a work-for-hire contract, but I knew the story had definite reprint possibilities. I called the editor and suggested that I sell first North American serial rights, with the provision that I wouldn't write about the same subject for a competing magazine for six months after the piece was published. The editor accepted that language, and I've reprinted that story twice since it first ran.

Ask for more money. On rare occasions, I will sign a work-for-hire contract—if certain circumstances are met. I consider how much time the piece will take, whether it's unlikely to be reprinted, and how much money is being offered.

For example, I recently wrote a short piece on new birth-control developments for a magazine that requires writers to sign work-for-hire agreements. However, the story would only take a few hours to research and write because it was a subject I was familiar with. Because of the nature of the piece, it would immediately become outdated, so reprints weren't likely. And the editor was offering $1.50 per word, certainly a decent rate. Even then, I explained why I usually don't do work-for-hire stories, and asked the editor if she could boost her usual rate. She offered an additional 50 cents per word for the story. I took it.

Know When to Walk Away

Of course, not every negotiation will go the way you want it to. In some instances, an editor may refuse to offer better terms and/or the money you were hoping for. At that point, you must decide whether the money and clip are worth it to you. An editor once offered me $800 for a 1,500-word story that would require a lot of research—and then insisted on an all-rights contract. In that case, I had no qualms about turning down the work. However, If he had offered $3,000 for the same piece, my decision would have been more difficult.

Sure, it's easier to say simply "yes" or "no" to an offer than to negotiate with an editor—but that's not a good reason not to try. Take a deep breath, summon your courage, and ask if the editor can do better.

You can usually find a compromise that will make both of you happy—and pay off in the long run, as well.

Kelly James-Enger is a full-time freelancer whose work has appeared in more than 25 national magazines, including *Woman's Day, Family Circle, Marie Claire,* and *Fitness.* She also leads magazine-writing programs and workshops throughout Illinois.

THE ALL-IMPORTANT QUERY LETTER

Why it makes sense to query

by Steve Weinberg

One of the most important rules for free-lance writers trying to break into a magazine is too frequently violated: When trying to sell an article to an editor unfamiliar with your work, send a query letter. Do not send a complete manuscript.

A few editors buy nonfiction from writers unknown to them on the basis of a completed manuscript. But not many.

So let's discuss why it makes sense to query first, then discuss the elements of successful query letters.

Why Query?

1. *Time is money.* Freelancers who want to make money should not invest months researching and writing a manuscript without an expression of interest from an editor. I have written successful queries after just a few hours of research. Time is precious for editors, too. They rarely want to invest in reading unsolicited manuscripts.

A query letter will help you focus your thoughts. The brevity of the form (one or two pages) will allow you to revise the letter until the phrasing is just right. When the letter reaches its destination, the editor can read it at a convenient moment, mull it over, reread it if necessary.

2. *Query letters can avoid rejections based on the focus or the style, rather than the substance.* The small percentage of editors who take time to read manuscripts because they like the idea frequently find they dislike the approach. Why did the writer use first person instead of omniscient third person? Why did the writer choose a question lead instead of an anecdotal

opening? Rather than guide the unfamiliar writer through a major revision, the editor will just say no.

3. *Editors are too distracted during their work day to hold lengthy conversations by telephone with unfamiliar writers.* Trying to sell articles by telephone almost never works. Besides, editors want to see a writing sample—a query letter can serve as that sample.

The Elements of Successful Query Letters

1. *Queries should be one or two single- or double-spaced pages.* Brevity is mainly for the convenience of the editor, but it benefits writers, too, forcing them to distill their thoughts. A query is not the place for a writer to overwhelm an editor with mastery of the topic's detail. If editors are interested but want to know more, they will ask for more.

2. *Within the brief query letter, the main idea should be described in one sentence if possible, certainly in no more than one paragraph.* That description should be written compellingly, a grabber. It should not be written boringly, as in "This idea has to do with missing persons." Much better:

> Murderers, thousands of them, are walking around free. That is scary enough. Even scarier is that police, prosecutors, and judges have no idea who they are. They are perpetrators of a type of homicide so common, yet so little discussed, that it lacks a commonly accepted label. Let's call it, for now, missing and presumed murdered.

When possible, it is best to write the main idea in the style of the proposed article, as in the previous paragraph from a query letter of mine. A proposed headline usually helps, too.

3. *After the nutshell description, the letter should explain why readers of that magazine are likely to care.* This should be subtle. Hype ("an irresistible topic") will turn off editors. So will preachiness. ("Your magazine must publish this article because of its importance to your readers.") Your query letter should make editors say, "This is irresistible" or "This is really important to my readers."

4. *With the editor clued in to the "what" and "why," it is time to tell the editor the "how" of information gathering.* What sources might consent to be interviewed? What documents can be consulted in libraries, government agencies, or business archives? Are reference books available? If possible, work in a telling anecdote, a case history, or a statistic already in hand—and simultaneously demonstrate your passion for the topic.

5. *Now that the editor knows about the process of information gathering, she or he will be curious about the proposed structure, point of view, timing and*

tone. Will the article be structured chronologically? In cinematic-type scenes? An outline is often the best way to convey the structure.

As for point of view, through whose eyes will the article be told? The author's, in either first person or omniscient third person? The person who is the main subject of the article? A query proposing an article about "capital punishment" is too vague. But telling an editor the article will talk about capital punishment through the executioner's point of view might produce a "go-ahead" or assignment.

About timing: If you include the fact that the number of death-row convicts executed has doubled over the last decade, you have provided the editor with the relevance of your proposed piece.

Moving on to tone, will the article be serious or light? Or downright humorous?

6. *Include something about yourself, such as prior publications, if any; and where you can be contacted by mail, telephone, fax, and/or electronic mail.* Novices worry that if they cannot include previously published articles, it will mean immediate rejection. Not so. Every published writer was at some point unpublished. Furthermore, some editors put little stock in clips, because they cannot tell how much is the result of revision by an editor. For clips, aspiring authors can substitute relevant personal experience, work experience, or academic training.

A caution: Some editors and experienced writers suggest placing personal information in the first paragraph. I disagree. It is the idea that should be emphasized, not the writer who will be researching the idea. Well-known writers might receive assignments on the basis of their names; beginning and intermediate writers rarely do.

7. *Address your query to a specific editor.* Which editor? Perhaps the editor of a particular section or department. Perhaps the managing editor, articles editor, features editor or editor-in-chief.

You may find the name of the appropriate editor in the magazine's masthead. If not, try calling the magazine. (During that call, request a copy of the magazine's guidelines for writers.)

> Include something about yourself, such as prior publications, if any; and where you can be contacted by mail, telephone, and/or e-mail.

What to Leave Out of Query Letters

Omitted from my seven-point list is something that other writers suggest including in query letters-a paragraph about what the magazine's competitors have (or have not) published on the topic. The point is apparently to convince an editor that competing magazines have not run the same story.

I disagree. Most editors do not assume their readers also buy the competitors. So if I have an idea that I want to sell to *The Atlantic Monthly*, I search a few years of its back issues to make sure I am not duplicating. If I find nothing similar, I begin drafting the query. Sure, I will also search back issues of *Harper's, Mother Jones*, and other magazines that might be considered *The Atlantic Monthly*'s competitors. But if I find an article in those publications on my topic, I will not mention it in my query. What I will do is make sure my approach is different enough from what has appeared elsewhere so that my article is advancing knowledge, not duplicating knowledge.

In your query letter, don't mention article length; payment; deadlines (unless the topic is fresh for only a short time, or seasonal); artwork (unless it is a big part of why you should get the assignment); and other contractual terms such as rights.

Editors frequently reject query letters with mistakes in grammar, incorrect punctuation, or misspellings—no matter how good the idea. They are usually unimpressed by college degrees (unless directly relevant to the proposed article), friends of theirs you claim to know, or language filled with pyrotechnics at the expense of clarity. They are not interested in what you think of their magazines, and are especially offended by mini-lectures on how you would improve those magazines.

Simultaneous Submission of Queries?

Whether to submit the same or similar query letters simultaneously to multiple magazines is a topic without one correct answer. Debates within writers' groups and editors' forums over the decades have failed to resolve the matter.

Some freelancers say they are uncomfortable sending multiple queries. They do not want to risk having an editor remember that after making an assignment based on careful consideration, a competitor wound up with the article.

I disagree. Freelancers will starve if they wait for one editor after another to respond. Simultaneous query submissions are smart business. What if two or more editors want you to write for them? My reaction: You should be so lucky.

So now it is time to go forth and submit query letters, simultaneously.

Steve Weinberg is a book author, freelance magazine writer, book reviewer, and editor. He teaches journalism at the University of Missouri. His books include the well-regarded *Reporter's Handbook: An Investigator's Guide to Documents and Techniques.*

A SAMPLE QUERY LETTER

Here are parts of the query letter—with brief explanations inserted—that sold my proposed article about missing persons. I addressed the query to the managing editor at the *ABA* (American Bar Association) *Journal,* based on a conversation with a writer who had already published in the magazine:

MISSING AND PRESUMED MURDERED

[The editor used the headline I suggested. He fleshed it out with this subheadline: When a young Texan vanished, he joined a phenomenon that bedevils prosecutors and police nationwide: How to find justice when they suspect homicide, but have no victim to help prove it.]

> Murderers, thousands of them, are walking around free. That is scary enough. Even scarier is that police, prosecutors, and judges have no idea who they are.

[If that isn't a grabber, what is? Because I hoped it could also serve as the opening paragraph of the actual article, the editor immediately experienced the style I hoped to use.]

> They are perpetrators of a type of homicide so common, yet so little discussed, that it lacks a commonly accepted label. Let's call it, for now, missing and presumed murdered.

[This paragraph expands on the grabber of a lead as well as further demonstrating my style and introducing my informal, but not flippant, tone.]

> The best estimate, based on FBI statistics and anecdotal evidence, is that 21,000 children, teenagers, and adults are missing and presumed murdered. The common denominators are that their bodies remain hidden, with no conviction of perpetrators on the horizon.

[This defines an unfamiliar topic further, plus suggests some of my sources—the FBI and interviews with persons involved in such cases.]

(Continued on next page)

SAMPLE QUERY LETTER, CONTINUED

Probably the best-known case is that of Jimmy Hoffa, who disappeared in 1975. Despite almost immediate notification of the disappearance, hundreds of law enforcement officers, including the best the FBI could offer, failed to find the Teamsters Union leader. Twenty years later, Hoffa is presumed dead. But no body has surfaced, and those responsible remain at large.

[Here I make the unfamiliar familiar by referring to a well-known case. I also further hint at the depth and breadth of my research.]

In the remainder of the query letter, I explained:

• Why readers of that particular magazine would be likely to care (because these cases frustrate the participants in the legal system and cause the citizenry at large to lose faith in that system)

• How I planned to research the article (by gathering FBI and state police statistics; interviewing family members of missing persons, police officers, prosecutors, defense attorneys, and judges; reading trial transcripts; narrating the case of my brother-in-law, missing since 1981, based on notes kept and documents gathered during 14 years of investigating)

• The likely structure of the article (told in sections, beginning with a disappearance, followed by the police investigation, the decision by a prosecutor whether to move forward, the defense strategy in cases involving a specific suspect, the trial and verdict. This is largely a chronological approach, with modifications. Furthermore, each section would begin and end with my brother-in-law's case, which would serve as the connecting thread)

• The point of view (through the thoughts of the investigators, as recounted by them in hindsight and through contemporaneous reports or diaries)

I ended the query with a paragraph about my credentials. I received the assignment soon thereafter. The article appeared in the September 1995 issue of the *ABA Journal*.

FIND A SLANT

The biggest problem with many queries:
they lack an arresting slant

by Howard Scott

Have you ever wondered why your queries aren't hitting? Are rejection letters piling up?

The biggest problem with many queries is that they do not have an arresting slant. A slant isn't the subject; it's the author's particular take on the subject, the central thread that ties the story together. The trick is to come up with a slant that presents the subject in a fresh light and hooks the reader.

A slant is an inherent story, and suggests that an answer or solution exists. Moreover, each slant narrows the subject to suggest a particular audience.

I recently wrote an article for *Nation's Business* on raising prices. My query letter did not read, "Are you interested in seeing an article about raising prices?" Instead, I wrote: "I will focus on how to incur minimum customer resistance to raising prices." Do you see the difference between the two approaches? The first proposal is a subject query. The second proposal is a slant in which I set up an investigatory path, which sets up an expectation, namely, how to achieve minimal customer dissatisfaction, and therefore lose the fewest number of customers to competition.

Consider the harried editor for a moment. He or she receives dozens of proposals every day/week/month. She chooses those few proposals that excite her. Yes, experience and clips count, but if you excite the editor with a "wow, I never thought of that!" slant, your chances are good for a go-ahead on spec.

To create a strong slant, ask yourself these six questions:

1. *Does my slant presuppose a question?* I queried the editor of *The Rotarian* about house-swapping (vacationing by exchanging houses, cars, and information), promising that I would provide a formula to determine who is best suited

to house-swapping and who should never consider the idea. The editor was intrigued with the formula aspect and asked me to spell that part out. If I had just suggested a story about house-swapping, a subject query, she might not have given me the go-ahead. My query made her wonder just what type of person swaps homes. The piece was accepted for publication.

2. Does my slant hint at a useful answer? This is a close cousin to the first question, but there is an important distinction. The good slant asks a question that can be answered. *The Rotarian* editor above felt that the question would deliver a prescriptive answer, which readers could put to immediate use. Make sure your question has an answer that will be useful to the reader.

My query to *Family Life* proposing an article on why ferrets are better pets than rabbits, guinea pigs, mice, or gerbils told the editor that she could expect some factual reasoning on the preferable pet, and that the reader would be able to make an informed decision based on my answers. This was so much better than a query on ferrets as pets, which, in the mind of the editor, wouldn't supply answers.

3. Does the slant sufficiently narrow the topic? You don't want to cover too broad a topic. The reader doesn't learn much, nor is the writer challenged to get down to the essence of the subject. In a more narrowly conceived focus, you must dig beneath the surface for underlying reasons, for explanations, for the story behind the story.

4. Does the slant offer an unusual perspective? The subject matter doesn't have to be unique, but the particular slant should be.

I decided to write an article for *Sky Magazine*, the Delta Airlines in-flight publication, about the Massachusetts Institute of Technology (MIT) Enterprise Forum. The Forum is a monthly get-together of venture capitalists, consultants, and other interested parties that analyze a company, often with the intention of funding the firm. I knew a query on the Enterprise Forum as a profile would not work because *Sky's* articles focus on trends. So I came up with the slant of unusual ways to raise money, calling it "adventure capital." I used the MIT Enterprise Forum as one method; for other examples I found a playwright who raised money by hosting a pre-performance party; and a small business that borrowed equipment from its suppliers to start up. I wove all three examples into the article, drawing from my slant to title the piece "Adventure Capital."

> Can you state the slant in a single sentence? This shows that you have a bona fide concept.

5. Can you state the slant in a single sentence? This shows that you have a bona fide concept. If you can't do so, it means you don't really have an idea, or it's too broad in scope, or it is not well-formulated. If you have to explain your slant in long-winded prose, you probably can't communicate it clearly to the reader.

In the proposal for my article "How to Get Kids

Interested in Bees," which appeared in *Bee Culture* (June 1999), my slant was that kids are naturally interested in insects, thus their curiosity would be piqued by a discussion of the hard science part—bee colonization, bee leadership, flower pollination, etc. My query stated, "Since children are natural insect fans, it's easy to imagine them getting excited about bees," and I proposed to offer several bridge-creating strategies.

6. *Can you restate the slant into a catchy article title?* This tests whether your idea is as concise and as interesting as you think. By creating a catchy title, you can see how your idea stands up, compared to the other articles in the table of contents. Remember, some readers scan the contents page first to see if they want to read an article. Finally, a working title, or handle, helps the editor keep the piece in his mind.

I always thought one reason the *Providence Journal Sunday Magazine* editor gave me a spec go-ahead on an article about being a life-drawing model was my proposed title, "The Naked Truth." When he published the piece, he didn't change my title, which is rare; I imagine that when he received my query, he was captivated by the double entendre aspect of the title.

One final note: No matter how good your queries are, don't expect a 100 percent response. Recently, I sent out 46 queries to 46 trade magazines. The queries were about the tax changes for that calendar year, so all the magazines could use this information. With each query, I included a previously published tax clip and SASE. Eighteen publications, or 39 percent, responded. Five, or 11 percent, gave me an assignment. Those five assignments led to five published pieces.

The moral: Writing is still a numbers game.

Howard Scott, a freelance writer for 20 years, has published more than 1,500 articles and two books. Recent credits include the *Boston Globe*, *Rotarian*, and *Nation's Business*. This piece is condensed from an article, "Query Letters that Work," first published in *The Writer*, March 2000.

E-MAIL AND EDITORS: A PRIMER

E-mail is a wonderful tool, when used in the right way

by Lisa M. Petsche

E-mail is a wonderful time- and money-saving tool for writers. With it you can request writer's guidelines, send queries, submit manuscripts, follow up on queries and submissions, and send invoices.

Editors vary, however, in their receptivity to e-mail communication. Some accept e-queries and e-manuscripts, while others do not. Some may accept manuscripts electronically, but only when they have been solicited. Still others don't accept e-mail submissions from unknown writers, but once you have a relationship with them (i.e., have had an article accepted) you may be invited to submit electronically. On the other hand, many editors of e-zines and Web publications will accept queries and manuscripts only by e-mail.

Finding Writer's Guidelines

To determine what is acceptable to a particular publication's editors, obtain and read the writer's guidelines, which usually indicate acceptable modes of submission. There are numerous online writer's guidelines databases where you can search for the publication you wish to target.

Small publications—especially regional ones—may not be included in even the largest database, however. In that case, use a search engine to try to find a Web presence for the publication.

If you are able to locate a Web site, look for writer's guidelines that you can print for future reference. (Check the site map if you don't see a "Submissions" or "Guidelines" heading on the main menu.)

If you can't find guidelines, look for a "Contact Us" or "Feedback" link. Use it to e-mail the editorial staff to inquire about availability of writers' guidelines and how to obtain them.

Often they can be sent by e-mail. Include your full name and snail mail address, though, in case they must be mailed to you. (Occasionally you may be instructed to request guidelines by mail with a SASE.)

If you can't locate an editorial e-mail link, contact the webmaster instead (the link is usually located at the bottom of the page). Ask how to contact editorial staff by e-mail.

When writer's guidelines include an e-mail address but don't indicate whether electronic queries and submissions are welcome, send a short e-mail to inquire. Do not submit anything electronically—particularly an unsolicited manuscript—unless you know it is welcome.

Projecting a Professional E-image

Most people know the basics of e-mail etiquette, such as "keep it short" and "don't type in capital letters." But there are many other informal do's and don'ts of electronic communication that are worth mentioning. Following them will enhance your image as a professional writer.

Do:

• Make your subject line descriptive to catch the editor's attention and encourage immediate reading.

• Keep initial contacts formal and let the editor set the tone for future communication.

• Use bullets or numbered points if you're including a list of items.

• Write messages that are easy to respond to. If action is required, put it in the subject line, e.g. "Need reply by . . ."

• Take advantage of the spell check feature.

• Be judicious about using the "high importance" notation. If your message is truly urgent, consider using the telephone.

• Check your e-mail frequently for new messages—especially on weekdays. It's worth checking on evenings and weekends too, since an increasing number of editors work from home and have flexible schedules.

Don't:

• Use a background color that is very bright or very dark. The standard white with black lettering works best.

• Bother an editor with frivolous inquiries or premature follow-ups just because it is quick and easy to dash off e-mail messages. Remember, an editor receives dozens if not hundreds of electronic messages per day and won't appreciate unnecessary communication.

• Send attachments unless invited to do so (either through writer's guidelines or personally by the editor). Then, be sure to send the type of file requested (e.g., text file, Word 98, etc.). If an editor indicates that attachments are acceptable but doesn't specify a format, ask first. Otherwise, paste your manuscript into the body of your e-mail message, below your cover letter or introduction. (Be sure to use plain or ASCII text and remove formatting and special characters, such as "smart quotes.")

• Request a receipt unless it's really necessary. Editors may be insulted by the implication that they don't read their mail regularly.

Using e-mail to query and submit material can greatly speed up the process of getting your work accepted—but only if your e-mail presents a courteous, professional image both of your work and of you, the writer.

Lisa M. Petsche is a Canadian freelance writer whose publication credits include: *Canadian Living, Today's Parent, Big Apple Parent, Our Family, Forever Young, The Dollar Stretcher, The Cottage Magazine,* and *The Hamilton Spectator.* This article originally appeared in the Canadian writers' publication *FellowScript.*

THE AUTHOR/EDITOR CONNECTION

You and your editor are a team
striving for the best

by Eve Bunting

At a writers' conference once, I heard an author state: "Make no mistake. The writer and the editor are enemies. He's always on the side of the publisher and not on yours." I was astonished and appalled. This has never been my experience. Never.

As a children's book writer who "publishes around," I have several editors, male and female, young and older. Since I don't work through an agent, my contacts are directly author to editor. I have always been treated fairly and have always had the assurance that we are a team, striving for the best possible book.

This is not to say there have not been disagreements. Of course there have. But with compromise on both sides we have always been able to work a problem out.

To establish and keep a good relationship, there are some things the author should bear in mind.

1. *Be prepared to listen when your editor suggests changes.* Yes, the book is yours. Yes, every word is as perfect as you have been able to make it. But the editor has had a lot of experience, knows what works and what doesn't, and is as anxious as you are for a quality book. But, be prepared to take a stand if you feel you are right. Present your case. Be factual. Be reasonable. Chances are she (I'm using the generic "she" because I have more female editors than male) will come around to your thinking. Be gracious if you are proven wrong. The best editors during discussion will be careful to ask: "Do you agree?" and will often say: "Of course, you have the last word." That may not be exactly true, but it leaves room for further discussion.

2. *Try to realize that your editor is a person who works hard.* Do not burden her with unnecessary questions and complaints. Yes, you want to know how your

book is coming along. It's O.K. to ask. But not every week. When it's finally published, you want to know how it is selling. Call the royalty department. Yes, you are upset that you can't find a copy in your local bookstore. Call the sales department and ask if they know why.

You don't think your work has been promoted with enough enthusiasm? (A lot of us feel that way. I was going to say most of us, but perhaps many authors are totally satisfied. I don't know any of them!) Talk to the Promotions Department to suggest what they might do, as well as what you are willing to do: bookstore signings, school visits, visits to your local library. Perhaps it can be a joint project between you and the publisher.

3. *If you submit a new manuscript to your editor, try not to be irate if she doesn't get back to you right away.* Understand that she has a workload that allows only a small percentage of her time to be spent reading manuscripts—even yours. She has meetings coming out of her ears!

4. *If your editor tells you that your book will not be published this year, and possibly not until the following fall, or the spring after that, bite the bullet.* Publishers' lists fill up, and you have to realize that you are going to have your book scheduled where (a), there is a slot for it, or (b), where the publisher feels it will sell best. There's no point in ranting and raving in your very understandable impatience. Your editor will bless you for not being difficult.

5. *When you are asked to make corrections on a manuscript or galleys, do them promptly.* The editor is making deadlines herself. Being on time can determine whether or not your book makes that list where it's slotted. If your manuscript is not ready, another book may replace yours.

6. *Be absolutely certain of your facts.* An error in a nonfiction book is unforgivable, and it is equally unforgivable in fiction. A reader or reviewer is going to pick up on it. Children's books are particularly open to scrutiny. The embarrassment of an error falls on the editor and copy editor, but yours is the primary accountability. A mistake will not endear you to anyone. In my very first middle-grade novel, I made an incredible blunder: I put the Statue of Liberty in New York Harbor a year before it was actually there! Horrors! No one caught it, except an astute librarian who challenged me on it while I stood at a podium, talking about the book. Double horrors! I will never forget that moment nor the lesson I learned. Since I was a fairly recent immigrant from Ireland, I managed to exclaim, "Oh! Forgive me! I thought that wonderful statue was always there, welcoming the tired and the poor as she welcomed me." That got applause instead of boos! It was corrected in the next printing.

> Try to accept the fact that you are not your editor's only author. She can't give you her undivided attention. . . .

7. *For picture book writers who are not fortunate enough to be able to illustrate their books, the key words are "be reasonable."* Of course, we want the very best artists in the country—in the world—to illustrate our books. Surely, this is not too much to ask! You pine for Trina Schart Hyman. You know she'd do an exquisite job. You lust after Barbara Cooney. Her style would be just perfect for your book. And how about Chris Van Allsburg? But if you are reasonable, you will know that every picture book author wants those illustrators and others equally wonderful, equally famous. The reality is that we are probably not going to get any one of them. It is all right to ask, but don't be aggrieved or petulant if it doesn't happen. Usually the artist is chosen by the editor in consultation with the art department and after much perusal of sample art and already published picture books. They are usually very good at choosing just the right artist. Perhaps they come up with a "first time" artist, and your first reaction is likely to be, "Oh, no! Not for *my* book!" But all wonderful illustrators start somewhere. I personally have discovered the thrill of having newish, relatively unknown artists turn out to be smash hits and lift my books beyond the ordinary to the extraordinary. I thank them. And I thank my editors. They know I trust them.

8. *Try to accept the fact that you are not your editor's only author.* She is juggling four, six, eight other writers and illustrators, too. She can't give you her undivided attention. You may think another author is getting more than her fair share of attention. That may be true. But that author may have paid her dues in many years of good books. One of her books may have made a million dollars for the company. It may have earned a lot of money and prestige-making

WHAT SHOULD AN AUTHOR EXPECT TO GET FROM HER EDITOR?

- As quick a reading of a new manuscript as possible.
- As quick a response as possible.
- Enthusiasm.
- Open-mindedness.
- Support of the book with the sales and publicity departments.
- Attentiveness to your misgivings, if any.
- A commitment to keep in touch. Not to hear what is happening to your book is horrible, and since you would be out of line to bug her, she should be courteous and keep you informed.
- Praise. Insecure as we are, we need a certain amount of TLC.
- The assurance that author and editor are in this together. It's your book.
- To be a person of her word. If she says she'll call, write, see you, then you have the right to assume she is dependable, as you are.

awards. It's been said that 20 percent of a publisher's list supports the other 80 percent. Another author's book and the attention it gets may be making it possible for your book to get published.

9 *If, by unfortunate chance, your editor has to turn down your next manuscript, take a deep breath and swallow your disappointment.* When she says she's sorry, she probably is. An editor does not easily reject a book, especially if she has worked with the author before. It is easier to be the bearer of pleasant news. Your editor may have fought for your book with a publishing committee and lost. Say, "I'm sorry, too. Can you give me any idea why you decided against it?" Listen to what she says. You may want to make changes before you submit it elsewhere. And remember, you may want to try her with another manuscript in the future, so keep that relationship cordial.

10. *Remember that your editor is human.* Show appreciation for her efforts in making your book the thing of beauty that it is. Flowers, candy, or other gifts are unnecessary. A simple thank-you note is sufficient.

So . . . we have a good author/editor relationship, and a good book. Working together, with consideration for one another, we've done it!

Eve Bunting has written an impressive list of children's books, from picture books to novels for the middle grades. She has received many awards and honors including the Golden Kite Award, the Regina Medal, and the Sequoyah Children's Book Award.

HOW I REPRESENT AN AUTHOR'S WORK

The agent as advocate, listener, critic, and friend

by Malaga Baldi

As an agent, my job is to place the author's work with a suitable publisher for a suitable price. I receive a 15 percent commission from the advance offered by the publisher, along with a reimbursement for expenses incurred during the effort. The expenses include xeroxing, messengering, long-distance phone calls, and occasional permission fees. From the day I agree to represent the author, my role is to serve as his or her advocate in contract negotiations and publicity efforts.

Along the way, I wear many different hats. To one author I may serve as a nudge, to another a confidante, and to many simply as a supportive friend. I am also a critic, researcher, legal expert, messenger, diplomat, listener, counselor, and source of publishing information and gossip. I work with writers on developing a presentable submission and make myself available during all aspects of a book's publication.

On the author's behalf I negotiate to keep film, foreign, and other subsidiary rights for our own exploration and exploitation and press for author consultation on and approval of the cover jacket and book title.

The process of deciding which manuscript to represent is exciting and difficult. I try to be as objective as possible in what I receive, but some books leave me uncertain, and those trouble me. I find it difficult to return an interesting manuscript, but realize that it would be far worse to make a half-hearted submission to a publisher. Since it is an uphill battle to place most fiction, or even a splendidly written nonfiction proposal, I find myself asking how good a work is, rather than how commercial the book is or how much money I can get for it. The bottom line at this stage is my enthusiasm for the book. If I am really turned on by a book or a book proposal, I will submit until I place it. I am proud of all the books I have placed.

I believe word of mouth is the best way to look for an agent. Most of my clients have found me this way. Local writers' groups often have names of agents with whom they have established a relationship. Other avenues of information include *Literary Market Place, The Writer,* and the *Writer's Market*. The Association of Authors' Representatives, a national nonprofit organization, has a member list at their website (www.publishersweekly.com/AAR). By reading the acknowledgements in books you admire or books that are similar to yours, you may also find the name of agents who would be interested in your work.

Young and hungry agents may offer the unknown writer a more nurturing, intimate atmosphere than the large agencies provide. When you submit your work to an agent, it is important to make your work easily legible. Double spacing is a must. Some dot matrix printers produce a manuscript that is hard to

COMMONSENSE NUTS & BOLTS

1. *Double space (not 1½ space) your ms.* Type on white paper. One side only. Number your pages. One-inch margin all around.

2. *Use a good printer.*

3. *Do not have your ms. bound.* Keep it loose, in a box or folder.

4. *Do not include a photograph of yourself.* Ever!

5. *Do not send the ms. via FedEx.* It doesn't make anyone read it any faster. Other, less expensive services like UPS, second day air, and overnight Postal Service do provide verification of receipt of your ms. If you want to make sure that your ms. was received, enclose a stamped, self-addressed envelope or send the ms. via "certified mail."

6. *Always enclose an SASE (mailbag or "jiffy").* Make it large enough to secure the safe return of your ms. if it's rejected.

7. *Do not phone to ask if your ms. has been received.*

8. *Be patient.* It takes time to read. Some agents now state that if you haven't heard from them in two months you should feel free to submit to other agents.

9. *Most important.* Write a good book and tell the truth.

xerox. Bound manuscripts are difficult to copy. A loose manuscript inside a box or folder is best. And don't send a photograph of yourself or waste your money on Federal Express—it won't make me read your manuscript any faster. First class mail will suffice. If it makes you feel more secure, use registered or certified mail or enclose a self-addressed stamped postcard.

A cover letter with some biographical information is a good way to personalize the submission. Also enclose a self-addressed stamped envelope to cover the cost of returning the manuscript if it is rejected.

Remember that the process takes time. After an agent reads and accepts a work, it is sent out to appropriate publishers. Agents have no control over how long a publisher holds a manuscript and two months may go by before a publishing house makes a decision. Occasionally even an agent's cover letter won't save the work from being relegated to the slush pile, the pile of unsolicited manuscripts that come without the benefit of an agent.

Many agents now tell potential clients that they should feel free to contact another agent if they do not get a response within two months. I believe the best rule of thumb is to let the agent know what you are doing. If I submit a work to more than one publisher, I tell the editor that I am doing so. I expect the same of an author.

I like to discuss my strategies for selling the book with the author. I also forward copies of rejection letters to the author to let him or her know that the book is being read and considered and what the response is. Truth is, books are seldom sold on the first submission. I have placed several books after 45-plus submissions.

After a book is placed and a contract signed, the production time averages about nine months. Publishers appreciate any enthusiasm and legwork the author can give. All the authors I have worked with have been involved with the publicity and marketing plans for the book.

One must have realistic expectations for this spirited co-venture of author, publisher, and agent. The real fun starts once the contract is signed, not during the initial, often tiresome search for the appropriate house. I mention this since many expectations are dampened by a low advance—say $7,500 for a mystery. Advances for first novels generally run between $10,000 to $20,000, with no advertising budget. Most of my clients work regular jobs while they are writing. The bulk of the work I represent is literary fiction; this means quality fiction, both mid-list books which don't have huge advertising budgets and first-timers. Fiction comprises only 5 percent of all the books published in the United States and the market for first novels is small and extremely competitive. Marketing departments play a major role in decisions about which manuscripts get published. Economic factors, such as conglomerate takeovers, paper costs, budget restraints, and the general economic situation, are all changing the face of publishing.

> Most of my clients work regular jobs while they are writing.

I am often asked whether I would consider a partial manuscript of a first novel. My general response is no. I have only placed one incomplete novel, and it was three-quarters finished and brilliant. It sold on the first submission. But this is rare. A half-finished novel may develop and change during revisions, and early rejection is discouraging to the author. My general policy is to encourage works-in-progress but not to submit them.

On the other hand, a nonfiction proposal sells more readily; often just an outline, introduction, and two sample chapters are sufficient. The length can vary between 50 and 100 pages. An editor will often work closely with an author on a nonfiction proposal and help shape the work into a full-fledged work.

Malaga Baldi has been a literary agent for more than 20 years. She is the sole employee of the Malaga Baldi Literary Agency and loves helping authors and publishers get together.

WHY IS THIS MANUSCRIPT DIFFERENT FROM ALL OTHERS?

To make your manuscript stand out among a large number received by editors and agents it's important to present your work well. Here are some commonsense tips:

1. *All writers should know how important a well written cover letter is when submitting a ms. or nonfiction proposal.* Don't name-drop, but if "somebody" has recommended you, do mention it in the first paragraph. We're all guilty of scanning letters and it should be put up front. Be brief, clear, and make the reader want to read your book or proposal. The most provocative cover letters are those that ask questions.

2. *Sell yourself.* If you have published in magazines, provide clips.

3. *Educate yourself.* Call your favorite publisher for a catalogue. Read the acknowledgements pages of your favorite books. Editors and agents you might want to approach are often mentioned there.

4. *Query first.* Agents and publishing houses have different styles and tastes. Before sending in your Cyberpunk cookbook, find out if they will handle, read, or even consider this type of material. Ask what they prefer. Whether it be the entire ms. synopsis, first three chapters, attached files, e-mail queries . . . if you choose to submit to more than one agent, include this fact in your cover letter.

WHAT DO AGENTS WANT?

The real question:
What do publishers want?

by Nancy Love

Agents say they want new writers, but when you send a query or a proposal, they fire back, "No thanks!" What are you to make of this mixed message? Aside from those agents who really do not welcome new clients, the rest of us need a continuous supply of fresh offerings to submit to publishers, but since we are in the publishing business to sell books, we are constantly trying to select those we think publishers want. The question we ask is: *What do publishers want?*

Death by Mid-list

The conventional wisdom these days is, Publishers do not want mid-list books. The term "mid-list" refers to the place a book has in a publishing house catalogue. It is a book that is not "front-list" (books listed in the first few pages of the catalogue and declared thereby best-seller material), and it is not "back-list" (perennials listed in the back of the catalogue and kept in print season after season). Translation: Only best sellers need apply. That leaves high and dry the nice, little literary or commercial novel with no break-out potential. And what about first novels?

The reality is, mid-list and first novels *do* get published, often by smaller publishing houses, many of which have fine reputations for discriminating taste, and then the authors are poached by the mainstream houses that didn't have the guts to take a chance themselves. Or they are championed by stubborn editors at the larger houses who want to nurture a talented writer or who have enough clout to bulldoze through the disapproval of sales and marketing departments.

Another reality is that it is often easier to get a first novel accepted than a second if the first one bombed. Enter the Dreaded Sales Record. Once you have a sales history documented in bookstore computers everywhere, it will follow you around for the rest of your publishing life, and can be amended only by subsequent successes that balance out the failures, or by changing your name.

One of the dirty little secrets of agentry is that many agents will avoid novels with either of the above potential problems (i.e., a mid-list book or a second book that follows a wipe-out first book), but might be less than candid about sharing these reasons for rejection.

Appetite for Nonfiction

Sure, publishers want front-list nonfiction titles, too, but are more welcoming to a mid-list book that has a potential of being back-listed. Most fiction is here today, gone tomorrow, but a nonfiction title that yields even modest, but steady, revenue may be kept around for a number of years. Many publishers will take on a "small" book they believe will not only earn out, but will generate income in the long run.

But before you rejoice prematurely, remember that today publishers have an insatiable appetite for credentials attached to nonfiction books. Backing by an authority or institution is important, and for some books, essential. A health book needs a genuine medical (doctor, hospital, or health organization) imprimatur, foreword, or co-authorship. A cookbook needs a food establishment tie-in (restaurateur, chef, or TV or print food personality). For large publishers, credentials are a must for an offer of even a minimal advance on a nonfiction book. To really hit pay dirt, you might need more than credentials; it will also help if you have a "platform"—a following or a guaranteed promise of advance sales. In this scenario, the author is not just a gardening authority, but she can also attach the name of the Garden Clubs of America to her book and a promise that the organization will offer it as a premium to their members.

The Agent Connection: Do You Even Want One?

If you write short fiction or articles, academic or textbooks, or poetry, you don't need or want an agent. Often, writers of literary fiction also do better on their own when approaching smaller publishers or college presses that agents may not deal with because of slow response time and low or non-existent advances.

> A nonfiction title that yields even modest, but steady revenue, may be kept around for a number of years.

I know writers of both fiction and nonfiction who—initially, anyhow—like to represent themselves and do well at it. But be prepared to spend a lot of downtime with the nitty-gritty of that process. You might also come out ahead if you have connections and are more comfortable being in control.

Getting in the Agent's Door

What makes the difference?

Agents often specialize. First, research your target. Find out if you are in the right place before you waste your stamp and everyone's time. Use listings in authors' source books. Scan books that are similar to yours for an acknowledgment of an agent. Use the name of the workshop leader or fellow writer who referred you. Go to writers' conferences where you might meet appropriate agents. Collect their cards and use the connection when you are querying.

Winning Queries and Proposals

There are whole books devoted to this subject, so I will stress just a few points:

Queries need to be positive, succinct, yet contain the facts about who you are and what the book is about. A query is like a short story in which every word has to count. A novel can ramble a bit, but short stories and queries don't have that luxury.

There is no excuse for bad spelling or grammar. If you and your computer can't be counted on to proofread, ask a friend to read your work.

Proposals and summaries of novels can be more expansive, but they also should be professionally crafted. Your writing ability and skills are being judged in everything you submit.

There is nothing in a nonfiction proposal more important than a marketing plan. Make suggestions for how the publisher can promote the book, and even more essential, tell the publisher how you can help. Do you have media contacts? Are you an experienced speaker? Do you have lists of newsletters in your field that might review or write about the book? Do you lecture at meetings where the book can be sold or flyers can be distributed? Do you have a website or belong to an organization that does and will promote your book? You get the idea.

Authors frequently respond to a request for this information by saying, "I write the book. That's my job. Selling the book is the job of the publisher." Unfortunately, while that might have been true at one time, it is no longer. Even when large advances are involved, I have discovered that publishers need and expect input from authors, and their cooperation and willingness to pitch in with ideas and commitment.

As an agent, I have to be sensitive to that point of view, so I find myself making decisions on whether or not to take on an author based not only on what she has to say and how well she says it, but on her credentials, her visibility, and on her ability to promote and become involved in publicity. Also, if you are able to put aside some of your advance to pay for publicity and perhaps a publicist, be sure to let the agent know this.

A marketing plan is not usually expected from a novelist, but it is a pleasant and welcome surprise if one is forthcoming. Fiction is promoted, too, by in-store placement, author appearances, book jacket blurbs. Sales of mysteries are helped by authors who are active in such organizations as the Mystery Writers of America (regional branches), Sisters in Crime, and other mystery writer organizations that support their members and boost their visibility. All novelists can start a minor groundswell by making themselves known at local bookstores, by placing items in neighborhood newspapers, and by using other local media.

Some writers have reached out to store buyers with mailings of postcards, book-marks, or reading copies. Signal your readiness to participate, and make known what contacts you have, when you are approaching an agent.

Start out by writing the big, the bold, the grabber novel every agent is going to want. This works only if an author feels that option is viable. I strongly believe a writer has to have a passion for the book she is writing, whether it is fiction or nonfiction, or it probably isn't going to work.

Till Death Do Us Part

You've succeeded in attracting an agent; now what? I would advise waiting until an agent indicates an interest before plunging in with such nuts-and-bolts questions as, What is your commission? Which other writers do you represent? Do you use a contract?

I'm in favor of author-agent contracts, because they spell out the understand-ing and obligations of the two parties, not the least of which is how either one can end the relationship. Basically, unless an agent commits a serious breach, she is on the contract with the publisher for the life of the contract. There should be, however, an agreed-upon procedure for dissolving the author-agent contract.

After all, the author-agent relationship is the business equivalent of a mar-riage. Attracting the partner is just the beginning.

Nancy Love has been an agent for more than 15 years. Prior to that, she was managing editor of *Philadelphia Magazine* and editor-in-chief of *Boston Magazine*. She has written numerous articles for these and other publica-tions. Her agency specializes in nonfiction and mysteries.

HOW TO GET THE MOST FROM THE INTERNET

Improve your writing skills, your writing sales,
and your writing life

by Moira Allen

The Internet has changed the way writers do business—from the way we conduct research to the way we submit material to editors. Using the Web can save writers time and money, give us a break from the isolation that so often accompanies the business of writing, and provide access to resources from around the world—no matter where we live.

Despite what some doomsayers declare, electronic media aren't likely to replace books and magazines anytime soon. They aren't going to destroy our livelihood (even if print publications disappeared tomorrow, writers would still be needed to supply the words that appear online). The Internet is simply another technology—one that offers significant advantages to writers, if we know how to make it work for us. The following tips can help you improve your writing skills, your writing sales—and your writing life.

1. Conduct Research More Effectively

The first reason most writers turn to the Internet is for information: Facts and figures for nonfiction articles, background information for novels and stories.

Internet search engines (such as *Yahoo!*, *Google*, and *Alta Vista*) enable writers to conduct research on a grand scale, or to search out minute details. For example, if you're looking for "everything there is to know" about Roman Britain, a search on that term (in quotes, so that it will be treated as a phrase instead of two separate terms) can take you to archaeological sites posting up-to-the-minute excavation reports, museums offering detailed information on their collections, translations of original documents, "living history" sites that recreate the period online, scholarly reports, journal articles, consumer articles, and more. You might even find an opportunity to go on your own dig!

On the other hand, if you want to conduct more focused research—e.g., details about the "Antonine Wall," the Internet makes that possible as well. Just search on "Antonine Wall" (again, in quotes), and within seconds, you could be examining a detailed, illustrated description of the second-century bathhouse at Bearsden Fort.

If you can't find what you're looking for via a search engine, you may find it in a database. Databases contain vast amounts of information that can't be "searched" by a search engine, but can be accessed (usually for free) directly if you know where to look. *Lycos* offers a list of several thousand searchable databases, while sites like *Direct Search* and *Infomine* let you search databases directly. (By working your way through the Lycos categories, for example, you'll ultimately come to *Romarch*, a leading database on Roman history and archaeology.)

Online bookstores can also aid your research. You may not be able to find the latest British Heritage publication on Roman Britain at your local bookstore, but you *can* find it at *Amazon.com* or *Barnes and Noble*—or, if it's a British pub, you can find it on *Amazon.co.uk* (the British arm of Amazon.com). It's now possible to find books in almost any language online, either through one of the major online bookstores or through one of the dozens of smaller, more specialized electronic book outlets.

2. Locate Experts to Interview

Quite often, your online research will turn up just the person you need for an in-depth interview. Many experts host their own websites; others are often associated with universities, government organizations, and commercial and private agencies. Associations often list directories online, enabling you to locate experts both locally and globally.

If you know the name of the author of a book on the topic you're researching, try searching for that author directly. If no website pops up, visit Amazon.com to see if the author's book listing offers a link to a home page, or an e-mail address. Another option is to look for a directory of author web-pages. (These, however, generally link to fiction rather than nonfiction author pages.)

Once you've located an expert, it's often easiest to make your preliminary request for an interview via e-mail. Some experts prefer to be "interviewed" by e-mail as well; you may also have the option of conducting an interview through an on-line chat session or via free "chat" software such as *AOL Instant Messenger*.

> Quite often, your online research will turn up just the person you need for an in-depth interview.

3. Find New Markets

Today, more and more magazines host websites to supplement their print editions. Many post archives of previously published articles, offering an excellent way for a writer to determine what type of material the magazine prefers—and what subjects have recently been covered.

One way to locate a magazine is to type its name into the "Go To" section of your browser as a URL (e.g., "www.mymagazine.com"). Often, this will take you directly to the magazine's website. If it doesn't, you can try to locate it through a search engine, or through an "electronic newsstand."

Electronic newsstands, such as *Newsdirectory.com*, list thousands of magazines, newspapers, and other media by name, category, and even by country. Newsstands are an excellent way to locate English-language markets in other countries—which can be good places to sell reprints. Newsstands may also provide links to hundreds of newspapers around the world.

Several guideline databases are also available online. *Writer's Digest*, for example, offers guidelines to more than 1500 publishers and magazines online; just type in a keyword or search by topic. Another good source is *The Writers' Guidelines Database*. You can also find databases of specific genre guidelines, such as *The Market List*, a guide to speculative fiction publications.

Finally, if you're looking for electronic publications, you can search through several directories of e-zines—including online publications and e-mail newsletters. The Electronic Journal Mine, for example, allows you to search for e-zines by topic or keyword, while other directories offer alphabetical lists, topical lists, and even lists of e-zines that accept advertising.

4. Contact Editors by E-mail

The majority of magazine editors are now willing to accept queries via e-mail. Some find e-mail faster and easier to respond to than traditional "snail mail"—no envelopes or postage required! Others prefer writers to make "first contact" in the traditional way, but use e-mail to correspond with regular contributors.

To find out whether an editor accepts "e-queries," check the magazine's guidelines online or in *Writer's Market*. If the editor does not specify a preference, send a brief note to the editorial e-mail address asking whether e-mail queries are acceptable. (If you receive no response, assume the answer is no!)

An e-mail query should be just as formal and detailed as a traditional query. The only real difference is that your name, electronic "address," and date are automatically included in the header. (Be sure to add a subject.) Some writers include their snail-mail address, telephone, and/or fax number beneath their signature.

Most publications are also willing to accept solicited manuscripts by e-mail, and an increasing number will also accept unsolicited manuscripts. Most electronic publications insist on receiving queries and submissions by e-mail. Most, however, prefer that submissions be sent within the text of the e-mail itself, rather than as file attachments (especially with growing concerns about computer viruses). Never send an attachment to an editor unless you have confirmed that it will be accepted.

When you submit an article via e-mail that you've composed on a word-processing program, be sure that you have turned off or removed "smart quotes" (curly quotes), as well as any characters that were formed by a combination of keyboard keys (such as a long dash, an ellipsis, etc.). Also, remove all formatting, such as italics or bold. Bold text can be indicated by placing asterisks on each side of the words to be °bolded°, while italics and underlining can be indicated by placing an underline character on each side of the _word_. If these precautions aren't observed, your e-mail is likely to arrive filled with weird doodles—for example, the phrase like ["I won't take it—you have to leave!" he shouted.] is likely to come out looking like [‰I won,t take it‡you have to leave!ʃ he shouted.] This does NOT make an editor's day!

5. Promote Yourself

Most ISPs (Internet Service Providers) offer free webspace as part of your monthly connection package. If yours does not, other sites, such as *Yahoo! Geocities* offer free space for noncommercial sites.

A website offers a writer an unparalleled opportunity to attract new readers, inform readers about the subject nearest your heart, impress editors with "clips," and interact with your audience. If you have a book in print, the Internet offers a host of promotional opportunities that cost absolutely nothing. You can also use your site to offer biographical information to your readers, announce book-signings and conference appearances, or market your writing services.

The cost of developing a website ranges from "free" if you do it yourself (HTML code is not difficult to learn), to several hundred dollars if you pay a professional designer. (For information on creating your own website, try the *Bare Bones Guide to HTML*. Keep in mind that content is the key to a successful site: Snazzy design won't hook readers, but good copy will.

6. Join a Writing Group

If you'd like to "meet" with writers who share your interests or work in the same genre, a good place to start is with an online discussion group. Hundreds of e-mail lists are available, for writers of all interests and levels of experience; members simply post messages to a central address, and those messages are forwarded automatically to the entire list. Other "groups" meet through news-groups—"electronic bulletin boards" that are hosted on the Usenet and are accessed through a news-reader (which usually comes with your browser). Two good places to start hunting for writing discussion lists are *Yahoo! Groups* and *Topica*.

> Do you have a passion for Arthurian legend? A fascination with archaeology? A yen for oriental cooking? No matter what your interest, you'll find a group that shares it. . . .

Nor are your options limited to writing groups. You'll find literally thousands of special interest discussion groups online, addressing every imaginable topic. Do you have a passion for Arthurian legend? A fascination with archaeology? A yen for oriental cooking? No matter what your interest, you'll find a group that shares it (and that may also be an excellent source of information and anecdotes for your research).

Several sites allow you to search for discussion

lists and newsgroups by topic, and also to search for topics of discussion within those groups. Some of the most popular include *CataList, DejaNews,* and *Liszt.*

7. Join a Critique Group

Like writing groups, critique groups bring together writers who share an interest in a particular genre or subject, in this case to review and comment upon one anothers' work. Some groups are open to writers of any level of experience; others prefer to bring together writers of comparable expertise.

Most critique groups operate by e-mail, but offer a website that provides information on membership rules and criteria. Members are usually expected to provide a certain number of critiques per month to remain on the active list (and to be eligible to post their own submissions).

A number of critique groups and sources of critiquing information are listed on the *Writing World* website; these are often hosted through organizations and private websites rather than through groups like Yahoo! or Topica.

8. Take a Class

Dozens of universities and independent organizations offer online writing classes. These classes offer flexibility, the chance to work with established authors, and privacy. Many are less expensive than "real-time" courses, and allow you to "meet" with your professor and do your homework on your own schedule.

While different organizations have different guidelines, the general approach to online coursework is simple. The instructor posts "lectures," reading assignments, and homework assignments on a website. Students turn in writing assignments via e-mail, and receive comments in the same way. Students may also participate in e-mail "discussion sections," or (in some cases) in real-time "chat" sessions.

For less formal instruction, you might want to visit an "OWL" (Online Writing Laboratory). Dozens of university English departments host OWLs, offering handouts on various writing topics, grammar help, exercises, and even one-on-one instruction. *The National Writing Centers Association* offers an extensive directory of OWLS. Or, you can explore the dozens of online grammar tutoring sites, or the hundreds of online dictionaries and glossaries.

9. Join a Club

Many writing associations have gone online, including local clubs and national writing groups. Each of the major genre associations—Horror Writers Association, Mystery Writers of America, Romance Writers of America, and Science Fiction/Fantasy Writers Association—has its own website. Several of these offer extensive resources for members *and* nonmembers, including articles on how to write effectively within the genre, marketing information, links to author pages, and interviews with well-known authors, agent information, and much more. You'll also find organizations for poets, playwrights, screenwriters, editors, technical writers, women writers, minority writers, young writers, and just about any other group you can imagine.

10. Subscribe to a Free Writing Magazine (or Two)

More than a dozen excellent online publications are available for writers—free! A publication is considered a "newsletter" if it is delivered via e-mail, an "e-zine" if you must visit the website to read it. Many online publications offer marketing information that is far more current than anything published in "print." Some of the most popular include *Inscriptions, Writing World, Writer Online, NovelAdvice,* and *Writers Weekly.*

And finally, a word of warning. As you chat with writers, critique submissions, take classes, read articles, and just generally browse the Net, don't forget to leave time for the most important task of all: Writing! The Internet is a useful tool, but it can also become addictive. It's also a far more enjoyable means of procrastination than, say, cleaning your desk. So set yourself a time limit when you start to surf, and once you've reached it, shut down your browser, disconnect your modem, and get back to work!

Resources:

(Note: Links to these and many other online resources can be found at the author's website, http://www.writing-world.com.)

Research – Search engines
Alta Vista—http://www.altavista.com
Google—http://www.google.com
Yahoo!—http://www.yahoo.com
(Yahoo! is actually a directory rather than a search engine; its search engine function is provided by Google.)

Research – Databases
Direct Search—http://gwis2.circ.gwu.edu/~gprice/direct.htm
Infomine—http://infomine.ucr.edu/search.phtml
Lycos Searchable Databases—
http://dir.lycos.com/Reference/Searchable_Databases
Romarch—http://acad.depauw.edu/romarch/

Research – Bookstores
Amazon.com—http://www.amazon.com
Amazon.co.uk—http://www.amazon.co.uk
(Amazon.com also has branches in Germany, Austria, and Japan.)
Barnes and Noble—http://www.barnesandnoble.com

Experts
  Associations and Organizations of Interest to Writers—
  http://www.poewar.com/articles/associations.htm
  Zuzu's Petals Literary Resource: Organizations of Interest to Poets
  and Writers—http://www.zuzu.com/wrt-org.htm
  AOL Instant Messenger—
  http://www.aol.com/aim/promo/73010/aim_download.html

Markets
  The Electronic Journal Mine—http://ejournal.coalliance.org
  Newsdirectory.com—http://www.newsdirectory.com
  Market List—http://www.marketlist.com
  Writer's Digest—http://www.writersdigest.com
  Writers' Guidelines Database—http://mav.net/guidelines/

Promotion – Website hosting/building
  Bare Bones Guide to HTML—http://werbach.com/barebones
  Beginner's Guide to HTML—
  http://www.ncsa.uiuc.edu/General/Internet/WWW/HTMLPrimer.html
  Yahoo! Geocities—http://geocities.yahoo.com/

Groups – Discussion
  CataList—http://www.lsoft.com/lists/listref.html
  DejaNews—http://groups.google.com
  Liszt, the Mailing List Directory—http://www.liszt.com
  Misc. Writing Mailing Lists—http://www.scalar.com/mw/pages/mwmlist.shtml
  Topica—http://www.topica.com
  Yahoo! Groups—http://groups.yahoo.com

Groups – Critique
  Critique Groups—http://www.writing-world.com/links/critique.html

Classes, grammar, dictionaries
  Dictionaries, Glossaries, and Language Resources—
  http://www.writing-world.com/links/dictionaries.html
  Guide to Writing/Grammar Resource Sites—
  http://www.quintcareers.com/writing/general_writing_resources.html
  Links to Writing Classes—http://www.writing-world.com/links/classes.html
  National Writing Centers Association—http://nwca.syr.edu/

Clubs and organizations
  Associations and Organizations of Interest to Writers—
  http://www.poewar.com/articles/associations.htm
  Horror Writers Association—http://www.horror.org
  Mystery Writers of America—http://www.mysterynet.com/mwa/

Organizations of Interest to Poets and Writers—
http://www.zuzu.com/wrt-org.htm
Romance Writers of America—http://www.rwanational.com
Science Fiction/Fantasy Writers Association—http://www.sfwa.org

Publications

Inscriptions—http://www.inscriptionsmagazine.com
NovelAdvice—http://www.noveladvice.com
Writer Online—http://www.novalearn.com/wol/
Writer's Weekly—http://www.writersweekly.com
Writing World—http://www.writing-world.com

Moira Allen has been writing professionally for more than 20 years. More information about online writing resources can be found in her book, *Writing.com: Creative Internet Strategies to Advance Your Writing Career* (Allworth Press, 1999), and her collection of *"1200 Online Resources for Writers,"* available electronically from Booklocker.com. For more writing information, visit her website at http://www.writing-world.com.

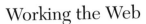

SELLING YOUR WORK ONLINE

Three types of e-publishers

by Emily A. Vander Veer

Stephen King single-handedly catapulted the term "e-publishing" into the mainstream recently when over half a million readers logged onto their computers and downloaded electronic copies of his novella *Riding the Bullet*. While awareness of e-publishing is growing, there's still a lot of misinformation and confusion—not just among writers and readers, but within the e-publishing community itself.

If you're a writer, that confusion can cost you time and money. It can affect your reputation, your copyrights, and your ability to earn revenues from your work far into the future. Whether or not you ultimately choose to publish electronically, it's well worth taking the time to understand this potentially lucrative market.

Technically, e-publishing can refer to any form of publishing in which the text of a manuscript is stored or distributed in digital form. In practice, however, it almost always refers to content aggregation, print-on-demand (POD) publishing or electronic self-publishing. Before you publish online, it's important to know the benefits and risks of each type.

Content Aggregators

Content aggregators, which include e-book and e-zine publishers, are the most common type of e-publisher. These companies solicit manuscripts and then offer them in one or more digital formats. Readers can view manuscripts online (as with e-zines) or download and view them offline. Content aggregators vary widely on the following criteria:

Copyright protection. While some protect authors' copyrights by applying digital encryption, watermarks, passwords, or other security measures to the manuscripts they distribute, most do not. Copyright is virtually impossible to enforce in the absence of such measures.

Electronic format. Content aggregators format manuscripts for display on personal computers, hand-held personal digital assistants, or new e-book devices.

Production standards. Larger content aggregators tend to have attractive, professionally produced Web sites that make finding and downloading e-books and e-articles easy for readers. On the other end of the spectrum are small aggregators with confusing sites that present authors' works in a less-than-positive light.

Editorial standards. Some aggregators accept virtually any manuscript submitted. Others restrict works based only on genre, or screen submissions carefully and select only those that meet their editorial standards.

Rights requested. Some aggregators' standard contracts specify nonexclusive electronic rights, meaning that signed authors can offer their work for sale simultaneously through other content aggregators, through their own Web sites, or through a print publisher. Others specify exclusive rights, up to and including the right to share in any royalties that may be derived from later print publication!

Fees/royalties. Most content aggregators are vanity or subsidy publishers. Instead of paying authors advances, they charge them. In addition to fees for manuscript formatting, some also charge monthly "storage" fees and optional fees for copyediting and online graphics. The total cost to authors can range anywhere from a few dollars to hundreds of dollars. If your manuscript sells, you can expect a royalty of about 40 to 50 percent of the net sales price.

Pros:

• Modest editorial restrictions allow unpublished writers easy access—and seasoned pros the opportunity to try their hands at new genres. "I decided to experiment and post the types of things I haven't gotten paid for in the past," says Judy Pokras, a traditionally published journalist who has contributed several essays to content aggregators that post unedited articles and promise to pay authors based on the number of "hits" each article receives.

• No computer skills are necessary.

Cons:

• While most readers don't mind perusing short pieces on flickering screens, the number willing to pay for and read long manuscripts online is still small. As monitor resolution improves, the e-book market is expected to grow.

• Although most content aggregators say they protect authors' copyrights, few actually do so.

• Even though your manuscript will be listed on an aggregator's Web site, you'll still need to do your own online promotion, just as you would if you were electronically self-publishing.

• Many content aggregators offer little or no up-front compensation.

Print-on-demand (POD) publishers like Xlibris.com and iUniverse.com store manuscripts in electronic form, too. But instead of downloading a "soft" copy, readers order a hard copy. The POD then prints one, ships it to the purchaser, and sends a royalty statement to the author at regular intervals.

Print-on-Demand (POD) Publishers

POD publishers vary based on fees, royalty rates, and the control they exert over titles. For example, some allow authors to set their own prices and provide their own cover art, while others do not.

Pros:
- No computer skills are necessary.
- Since most readers still prefer the familiarity and convenience of a bound book to squinting at a computer screen, your potential audience is bigger than it is with a content aggregator.
- POD publishers can breathe new life into out-of-print titles. "No traditional publishers were showing the slightest interest in reprinting my novels," admits Crawford Kilian, who decided to make seven of his previously published titles available for print-on-demand through iUniverse.com. Sales have been modest, but he's receiving royalty checks once again.
- POD publishers typically take care of all production details, just like a traditional publisher. They'll obtain an ISBN number, a Library of Congress catalog number and a UPC bar code (EAN), all of which you'll need if you plan to sell your book through online stores.

Cons:
- POD publishers charge hefty up-front fees for their services. Essentials like editing and cover design usually cost extra—along with other nice-to-haves. "Maybe I'm spoiled by print publishers, but authors don't get complimentary copies of their POD books," Kilian says.
- PODs don't actively promote titles. Even though your manuscript will be listed on their Web site, you'll still need to do your own online promotion—just as you would if you were electronically self-publishing.

Electronic Self-publishing

By creating and maintaining your own Web site, you can promote, sell, and even distribute your work using the same techniques as a content aggregator. (Choosing to print and mail hard copies of your manuscripts allows you to set up shop as your own POD publisher, too.)

If you are comfortable using a computer, you can use low-cost software to design a Web site that showcases your work and handles credit card sales; or you can pay a Web design firm to produce your site for you. Hosting a site can cost anywhere from nothing to $25 per month.

Pros:

• You retain complete control over the prices and distribution of your work. And you keep the profits. "By keeping my novel on my site, I could name the price I thought was reasonable," says John Michael Scalzi II, who distributed his *Agent to the Stars* using a shareware model. Readers can download the novel from his site (http://scalzi. com/agent/) for free; if they like it, they send Scalzi $1, similar to Stephen King's *The Plant*. Few e-publishers allow authors such flexibility.

• Because few e-publishers aggressively promote authors or even their own sites, self-publishing can be just as effective—if not more so—than signing with a content aggregator or POD publisher.

Cons:

• Self-publishing requires more involvement on your part, from setting up your site to promoting and maintaining it. Still, compared to traditional e-publishing, the demands are modest, as most Web-savvy writers can put together a site quickly. "There was no reason to hire anyone; it's just not that difficult," says Scalzi, who created his own site without the benefit of formal training.

• Some say that e-publishing will revolutionize traditional publishing by changing everything from which writers get published to how readers find, buy, and read books; from opening new worldwide markets to creating new literary forms.

That may be so. However, even if its impact doesn't turn out to be quite that dramatic, e-publishing still represents enormous potential for writers willing to explore it.

Emily Vander Veer specializes in Web-related writing for venues such as Byte and CNET.com. She's also written six books on Web-related topics and has created a writing resource website, www.emilyv.com.

COPYRIGHT ON THE WEB

What you don't know can cost you

by Emily A. Vander Veer

Congratulations!" gushed a friend. "I saw your latest article on XYZ.com, and it's terrific!" At the time, I'd never even visited XYZ.com, much less written for it—but a quick peek proved my friend wasn't mistaken. There, in living color, was the article I'd submitted just days before. The problem was, I'd submitted the piece to a different online publication.

As more and more writers are discovering, the benefits of the Internet—including an explosion of new paying markets, an inexpensive publicity channel, and an efficient, convenient way to conduct research—come with a price. The very technology that makes the Web possible also makes it easy for publishers and individuals to reproduce and distribute a manuscript without the owner's permission. In other words, the Web dramatically increases the threat of copyright violation, whether you write for print, radio, television/film, or online publications.

"I've discovered about 25 unauthorized [Web] reprints in the last year or so," says Amy Gahran, a freelance writer and editor. Like most professional writers who rely on reprints for income, Gahran takes the theft of her property seriously. "This is a business matter, pure and simple. No one ever did me a favor by stealing from me."

Copyright refers, quite literally, to the right to copy an executed work. In the United States, copyright conferral is automatic; the instant you complete a manuscript, you hold the copyright. (Formally registering your manuscript with the U.S. Copyright Office is an optional step that provides additional protection in the event of future litigation.)

But although the Internet doesn't alter the concept of copyright, it does affect the practical matter of tracking violations and enforcing copyrights online. The reason? Works can be obtained, reproduced, and distributed via the Web with startling ease. "Sketching the Future of Copyright in a Networked World," a 1998 report commissioned by the U.S. Copyright Office, refers to this technological free-for-all as "decentralized infringement."

Here are two of the most common examples:

The text of one of your pieces appears on a Web site you never heard of. It takes just minutes to copy the text of an electronically published manuscript (or to scan a printed original) and display that pirated text on a Web site. Amateur Webmasters frequently ignore copyright notices in the mistaken belief that they're doing authors a favor by providing additional "exposure." However, copying a manuscript and reproducing it on a publicly viewable Web site without permission constitutes copyright violation, just as if the article were being reprinted in a traditional print magazine. (Note: Hyperlinks—underlined words that allow visitors to hop from one Web site to another when clicked—allow Web sites to link to the text of an article without actually copying it. Since no copying is involved, a hyperlink from a site to an article does not constitute copyright infringement.)

One or more of your previously published pieces appear in an archived database. Increasingly, both online and print markets are demanding the right to archive material and make it available online, either for free or for a fee—often without offering additional compensation to the author. But in the absence of an explicit transfer of rights, no Web site has the authority to archive your work.

The question of whether electronic archives constitute separate, licensable rights was put to rest by Tasini et al. v. *The New York Times* et al. In September 1999, a three-judge panel of the U.S. Court of Appeals ruled that *The New York Times* and other publishers cannot resell newspaper and magazine articles by means of electronic databases unless they have the freelance authors' express permission.

As the Web has grown, the incidence of copyright violation has increased; and so, predictably, has litigation. While Contentville.com sidestepped a lawsuit earlier this year by agreeing to work with the Publication Rights Clearinghouse (a collective licensing agency administered by the National Writers Union, or NWU), other lawsuits have been brought—including a class-action suit against UnCover, an Internet-based document delivery service.

While lawsuits and pressure from writers' organizations such as the NWU and the American Society of Journalists and Authors (ASJA) appear to be raising the visibility of electronic copyright issues, the wheels of justice are often slow to turn. For awhile, at least, it's up to writers to protect themselves from online theft.

Fortunately, there are several actions you can take to preserve your rights:

1. Understand How Copyright Works

If you don't have a working knowledge of copyright, spend a few minutes online to familiarize yourself with the way copyright works.

Consider formally registering your work with the U.S. Copyright Office (or the office of your country). Doing so conveys rights that may be important if you're ever involved in a copyright-related lawsuit.

2. Know What Rights You're Selling, and to Whom

Many writers begin work on a project only after they've reviewed and signed a written contract; without one, electronic rights are virtually impossible to enforce. In the print world, First North American Serial Rights (FNASR) are assumed in the absence of a contract stating otherwise—but since the Web is limited neither temporally nor geographically, FNASR don't apply. Without benefit of a contract, the rights you assume you're selling may not be the rights an electronic market assumes it's purchasing.

"I sent a couple of sample pieces to the editorial director at a pre-launch dot-com because they were considering using me as an editor," says freelance writer Erica Manfred, who forwarded her work based on a verbal agreement rather than a written contract. "Next thing I know, I find one of my pieces up on their beta site under another name." Because the manuscript was electronically published in its entirety, it was vulnerable to theft by other publishers and individuals for the entire time it was displayed on that Web site. The company subsequently folded, and Manfred never heard back from the director.

3. Log Online Clips

If you contribute to electronic publications, get into the habit of using your browser to print a copy of each electronic clip the day it goes online. When you print a Web page, your browser adds the full Web address of the file and a date to the bottom of the printout, which you can then use to track publication details. This record could be useful during a dispute—especially if the publishing Web site moves or archives your work.

4. Search for Your Byline Online

Once a month or so, try typing your name into a few search engines and online directories. Doing so will display Web sites which have added your name—and possibly your work—directly to the text of their Web sites. Two to try: MetaCrawler.com (a "meta" search engine that searches several popular search engines at once) and DejaNews.com (a directory that searches all newsgroup posts). Also search for your name through online databases such as Lexis-Nexis, www.lexis-nexis.com/lncc. Unfortunately, many online databases require a registration fee.

If you find an article that was posted online without your permission, print out a copy immediately, making sure to note the full Web address and the date.

> Try typing your name into a few search engines . . . doing so will display websites which have added your name. . . .

5. Attempt to Negotiate

Contact any editor, electronic list owner, or e-mail poster who has reproduced your work without your permission, to negotiate payment and/or the removal of your manuscript.

"In all cases but one, I have been able to get my work removed, and in most cases have been able to get payment," says Gahran, who emphasizes that success sometimes requires persistence. "It helps to set a deadline and say, 'If I don't receive my full restitution fee by this date, I will publicize your theft.' "

6. Take It to the Next Level

If contacting the copyright violator directly doesn't work, contact the Internet service provider or Webmaster responsible for hosting the offending site and explain the situation. Most ISPs will shut down a site that's engaging in suspicious practices if you have documentation to prove it.

7. Turn It Over to the Pros

If all else fails, contact a writers' organization or legal counsel. "I joined the NWU," says Caron Golden, a freelancer who discovered that more than 50 articles she originally wrote for *The San Diego Union-Tribune*—and to which she retained full reprint rights—had been included in online databases without her permission. "They (the NWU) are working with me and about 30 other writers to resolve the issue."

8. Stay in the Loop

Online writing communities are often the first to hear about copyright issues such as out-of-court settlements and class-action lawsuits.

COPYRIGHT PRIMER

• Only executed works can be copyrighted. (A novel can be copyrighted; the idea for a novel can not.)

• Copyright is automatic. A writer automatically owns the copyright to a work the second it is completed, even if the work isn't published. Caveat: If you intend to bring a lawsuit, you must first have registered your copyright with the U.S. Copyright Office or another governmental body if you live in another country. In addition, the timing of formal registration (within 90 days of the works' completion, vs. five or more years later) affects the damages you can claim in a lawsuit.

• Reproducing and publicly distributing a manuscript via the Web, e-mail, or any other Internet protocol is considered "publishing" for the purpose of copyright.

• It's always best to have a signed contract in place when you sell your work, so that both parties understand precisely which rights are being granted.

9. Investigate Licensing Agencies

The NWU, ASJA, and other organizations have set up digital licensing and reprint services to track online reprints, collect fees from publishers, and forward those fees on to the rightful copyright owners—much like the music industry fixtures ASCAP (the American Society of Composers, Authors and Publishers) and BMI (Broadcast Music Inc.). While the long-term success of these agencies depends in large part on the participation of publishers, they offer writers an alternative, low-cost way to help preserve copyrights online.

The software and publishing industries recently combined forces to develop a standard, widely implemented document delivery format that's both easy to distribute and impervious to online theft. But until it's successful, it's up to you to protect your own rights in cyberspace.

Emily Vander Veer specializes in Web-related writing for venues such as Byte and CNET.com. She's also written six books on Web-related topics and has created a writing resource website, www.emilyv.com.

SOME USEFUL URLS

• *The U.S. Copyright Office.* Copyright FAQ, instructions, forms—everything you need (www.loc.gov/copyright).

• *The Canadian Intellectual Property Office.* Like the U.S. copyright site, CIPO offers downloadable copyright forms in PDF as well as an extensive FAQ section covering intellectual property issues (http://strategis.ic.gc.ca/sc_mrksv/cipo/cp/cp_main-e.html).

• *The U.K. Patent Office.* Fair use and other copyright basics for authors based in the United Kingdom (www.patent.gov.uk/copy/index.htm).

• *Sketching the Future of Copyright in a Networked World.* This 1998 report, commissioned by the U.S. Copyright Office, explains how copyright works online (PDF file) (www.loc.gov/copyright/docs/thardy.pdf).

• *WhoIs Typing.* an URL into the "whois" interface displays corresponding contact information (useful if you need to track down the owner/contact for a Web site) (www.networksolutions.com/cgi-bin/whois/whois).

• *Online-Writing Discussion List (OWL).* OWL is one of the many online writing communities administered via an e-mail list (www.content-exchange.com/cx/html/owl.htm).

• *ASJA.* The American Society of Journalists and Authors offers breaking news on copyright issues; it also maintains the Authors Registry, a collective licensing agency (www.asja.org).

• *NWU.* The National Writers Union provides current news on copyright issues; it also maintains the Publication Rights Clearinghouse, another collective licensing agency (www.nwu.org).

A SITE OF ONE'S OWN

How to create a writer's Web site and promote yourself

by Roxyanne Young

Once upon a time, a writer's business letterhead listed his or her address, phone number, and maybe a fax number. These days, writers are finding that they also need to list their Web site address. Professional Web sites have become much more than just a trendy calling card, however; they also serve as many writers' primary form of self-promotion.

On a Web site, you can post all of the information you would normally put on book jackets, brochures, and flyers—but much more of it, and with better-quality graphics. In addition, you have the option of changing this information at will, ensuring that it is always current—without incurring printing costs. You can create your own unique work in this digital domain, just as you can on the blank page that faces you at the start of each writing project.

While you may want to enlist the help of a talented Web designer, many Internet Service Providers (ISPs) now offer template tools to create your own Web site. While these tools may limit the complexity of the layout and graphics you can use, they allow you to create a wide variety of looks for your site—from a spiral-bound notebook page for freelance journalists to a shadowy "film noir" feel for mystery writers, to a storybook forest suitable for creators of children's books. The site's look is only the beginning, though. It is content that will draw visitors back time and again.

Besides the usual autobiographical or "meet the author" information, there are many ways to include literary content on professional sites, according to the interests and needs of the individual writer. Here are some suggestions:

• Sample chapters and book-jacket art can promote your upcoming releases or backlist titles. Fans will put their favorite writer's next release date on their calendars months ahead of time. Be sure to get permission before posting any copyrighted content, such as cover art or photographs, online.

• A calendar of book signings, convention dates, and workshop appearances will let readers, teachers, librarians, and booksellers know when you will be in their area, boosting attendance and perhaps book sales at these functions. The organizers are happy. Your fans are happy. And you're happy. It's all good—and all possible through your Web site.

• Writers who make school visits should post their policies, the subjects they cover and fee schedules, along with glowing teacher reviews and thank-you notes from students.

• Freelancers take note: Editors actually do visit a site when you include a Web address with your query letter, so make sure you have a current list of writing credits posted, complete with links to any newspapers, literary journals, magazines, e-zines, or other online publications where your work appears. If your list is rich and varied, all the better.

• Novelists or nonfiction writers with favorable reviews by online publications should include a link to that review prominently placed near the book title with the tagline, "Read a review by . . ."

• Be sure to add links to online booksellers where visitors can purchase your books. As with the review links, make these links prominent, maybe even including a "Buy This Book!" tag in bold letters.

• You may want to include information about other interests in your life that inform your writing, such as scuba diving, hiking, or raising horses. By including links to sites of relevant interest (Civil War sites if your new book is a biography of Robert E. Lee, or an African savanna if you're an adventure travel writer, for example), readers who enjoy your books and articles will learn that your site is a great resource for their continued reading. You might even request that those linked sites reciprocate with a link to your own.

> The site's design is only the beginning. It is content that will draw visitors back time and again.

• If your work could be used in the classroom, offer teacher supplements, lesson plans or interactive games that educators can use.

• Link to sites of writing colleagues and ask that they do the same for you.

• Link to your favorite writing-related sites that offer market information, legal resources, editorial needs, or research. Such links will make your site a directory of sorts for visitors who may come back when they need, say, a recipe for 18th-century mead and know you've got a link to the Society for Creative Anachronism.

• A Frequently Asked Questions (FAQ) page should include answers to the questions you often hear about your work or writing life. Professional tips for aspiring writers are always well received, and if you've got the time to post these questions and answers on a regular basis, it will guarantee repeat traffic to your site.

GREAT AUTHOR SITES

www.sidneysheldon.com—Sidney Sheldon's site is professionally designed, and it shows. Polished, clean navigation easily carries visitors between his bibliography, biography, awards, current projects, and more. The site is packed with information.

www.kingsolver.com—Developed by her publisher, Barbara Kingsolver's site contains the standard biography and bibliography in an easy-to-navigate format. She also has a page where she answers frequently asked questions from readers about *The Poisonwood Bible*.

www.joanholub.com—Holub's whimsical style comes through in her Web site where, besides her biography, books and information on school visits and book-signings, she also has practical classroom tools, activities for teachers, and writing tips for for kids. "I have heard thanks for the Web site activities from many teachers and other educators," Holub says. No doubt, those folks come back again and again to see what new teacher resources she has posted.

www.chucklebait.com—John Scieszka and Lane Smith, creators of *The Stinky Cheese Man, Squids Will Be Squids*, and *The True Story of the Three Little Pigs*, among other wacky children's books, have also created a dynamic site that offers detailed biographies, a list of books complete with sample illustrations, a form to ask questions, and an interactive Rock-Scissors-Paper game. But the great promotional tool here is their e-mail mailing list—visitors sign up to receive updates on this dynamic duo's upcoming releases and special appearances.

www.peggyrathmann.com—Peggy Rathmann's lively illustrations come through bright and clear on her home page, which is a departure from the usual layout. Check out her HamsterTours.com, an interactive tie-in with her book *10 Minutes Till Bedtime*.

www.peaksandvalleys.com—Humorist Cathy Morelli brings Web visitors into her kitchen for a virtual cup of tea and a bit of this and that about being a wife and mother. The site is funny, personable, easy to navigate, and she's got her book of personal essays for sale right there.

• You can offer a newsletter to site visitors who sign up. Send regular e-mail updates to this willing and receptive audience, which will be hungry for news of your release dates and local appearances. More and more ISPs are offering this sort of automated e-mail service, but if yours doesn't, you can still do your own. It will just be a bit more work. Make sure that those who opt in have a way to opt out, too.

Sadly, you can't just build www.yourname.com and expect the world to beat a path to your Web site. It's a great misconception that people (especially people as busy as editors) will be casually surfing the Net and happen across your site. You need to market your Web site just as actively as you do your latest release. Include your Web address on your letterhead, business cards, brochures, and flyers. Notify your publishers so they can include links to your site from theirs. Have your Web address printed in the jacket copy of your newest book or in the bio of your newest article or short story. Every time your name appears professionally, and even personally, in the public eye, make sure your Web address is attached to it.

When constructing the site itself, use META tags (the description of your site's content) and keywords that your readers will likely use when searching for you. Submit your site address to search engines and be sure to follow their rules—you'd be surprised how many folks get banned from search engines because they submit their site every month or use inappropriate search words in their META tags.

While professionally designed Web sites can be cost-prohibitive, with careful planning they don't have to be. And new Web tools are being developed every day to help you take advantage of this medium. In spite of the great opportunities for networking and self-promotion it offers, however, many people are still timid about the Internet. It is definitely worth exploring. Remember that your Web site can become an extension of yourself, a window into your professional and/or personal life, and a great marketing tool.

Roxyanne Young is a San Diego writer and photographer and co-owner of 2-Tier Software, Inc.

SEVEN ROOKIE ERRORS TO AVOID

1. *Text that runs into the margins.* This is a glaring error that is easily fixed by setting the table width.

2. *Graphics that have absolutely nothing to do with the site content.* Sure, that flaming pyramid in the background looks really cool, but does it have anything to do with the books you write? If not, leave it for the gaming sites and find something more appropriate to your subject matter.

3. *The same thing goes for music and other sound files.* It's fairly easy to add sound to your site, but make sure it's relevant and that your visitors have the option to turn it off.

4. *Teeny-tiny text on a busy, textured background.* No one can read this. If you find a great background graphic you like, use it as a border, but leave the space behind the text a solid color. And make your text reasonably large—at least 10 points—so folks can read it easily.

5. *Fonts that belong on an engraved envelope.* Script fonts are beautiful and expressive, especially if you write romance novels, but when you factor in grainy onscreen resolution, they can be very difficult to read. Plus, many browsers don't support these fonts, so they come out as plain text anyway. Make a nameplate graphic with your name in a large script font if you like, but keep the body text in Arial, Helvetica, or Times. All browsers support these.

6. *Navigation that is hard to follow.* I once visited a store site that had all of the navigation at the very bottom of an extremely long home page. I had to scroll down, down, down past several over-large photos and product descriptions to find the navigation buttons. Notice I said that I visited this page only once. Put your site navigation where it is easily accessible—at the top or side—and make sure there is a link back to your home page on all subpages

7. *Broken links.* It's great to offer site visitors more information by linking out to sites that might be of interest to them, but check these periodically to make sure they're still up and running. Sites do go down, and if your links don't work, it makes you look bad.

RECORD KEEPING

Organization is the key to good record-keeping

by Moira Allen

Keeping Records

If you recall the Contentville controversy, where articles showed up unauthorized on that third-party website, you may have begun to ask yourself the same question thousands of other writers are asking: "How can I prove that my work belongs to me? What stands between me and those who seek to make a profit from my writing, without sending so much as a penny my way?"

The answer is "good records." Unfortunately, the creative mind is often not the sort of mind that enjoys administration—such as developing and maintaining good filing systems. I'm constantly amazed by writers who say, "I don't even know if I have a contract with such-and-such publisher."

Fortunately, all you really need to develop a good filing system is a handful of folders or envelopes, a box in which to keep them—and an act of will. The folders or envelopes are for your important papers; the act of will is to ensure that your papers actually find their way into those folders.

What Should I Keep?

Freelance writing is a business. The quick and easy answer to this question, therefore, is that you should keep every file that relates to the running of that business. That includes the following:

Contracts and letters of agreement

Whenever you sell a "work" (an article, story, poem, book, whatever), you should have some sort of written agreement with the purchaser. Sometimes this will be a formal contract; in other cases, it may be little more than a letter saying "Thanks for sending this; yes, we'd love to use it." If you don't receive even that much, create your own letter of agreement specifying the rights you are licensing. For the greatest degree of protection, ask your editor to countersign a copy of this letter and send it back to you.

Such contracts and agreements may be your only evidence, in later years, that you sold (or did *not* sell) a specific set of rights. If you have no record of the terms under which your material was published, it will be very difficult for you to prove the terms of that agreement. (It would be nice to say that in the absence of an agreement, courts assume that you sold First North American Serial Rights, but one can't count on this, especially if the material was sold to an electronic publication or was used electronically by a print publication.)

Keep these contracts *forever*. You don't need a fancy filing system for them; a simple folder marked "contracts" should be enough. If you have lots of contracts, consider investing in an expanding "pocket" folder with alphabetical dividers, so that you can file your contracts by publication name. Never assume that you won't need a copy of that contract in later years; stuff of mine is appearing online that I sold 15 years ago!

Correspondence

Granted, a lot of your writing correspondence looks pretty trivial: "Do you want to buy this article?" "No." Even rejection letters are important, however. If nothing else, they demonstrate to the IRS (in case of an audit) that you really are attempting to conduct a writing business. Acceptance letters are even more important: Often, they spell out the terms of the sale. If so, put them in your "contracts" file.

While it may be tempting to set up alphabetical files for your correspondence, I've never found this necessary. My own system originally consisted of two folders: "Pending" and "Completed." Once a response arrived to a letter in the "pending" file, I'd staple it to my outgoing letter and file both in the "Completed" file. At the end of the year, I'd label the Completed folder for that year (e.g., "Correspondence 2002") and store it in a file box in my closet. When my correspondence became too much for a single folder, I subdivided it into "acceptances," rejections," and "everything else"—all of which get stored in the box at the end of the year. You may never have to touch these files again—but you never know!

Invoices

If you regularly send out invoices to editors, you may want to store these separately from your regular correspondence. As with correspondence, you may also want two folders: One for pending invoices, and one for paid invoices. Again, if you want to subdivide these alphabetically, fine; otherwise, a single "paid" folder will usually suffice for a single year of invoices.

Clips

Rare is the writer whose ego does not require a carefully preserved copy of everything s/he has ever published! This is your "clip" file, and it can be useful in many ways. It is, of course, the source of any "clips" that you send out with queries or proposals. It can become your portfolio if you choose to seek a paid position in the writing industry. It is also your source of reprints; when submitting reprints, it's often better to submit copies of the published article rather than your original manuscript.

Finally, it is your history—the story of your career neatly stored in plastic page-protectors. Gone, thank goodness, are the days when we had to store clips in those dreadful plastic sleeves with the black paper lining—the kind that stuck to the print of newspaper clippings and actually peeled the ink off the paper. Today, you can get acid-free page protectors in any office supply store; use the kind that have an extra strip on the side for binder holes, so that you don't have to punch holes in your clips themselves.

I file my most recent (or important) clips in a leather portfolio; the rest are kept in ordinary three-ring binders.

The page protectors enable you to make photocopies of your clips without removing them from the sleeves. I usually make and store photocopies of newspaper clippings, rather than keeping the originals, which don't age well. I also ask for at least two complimentary copies of any publication in which my work appears, one for the clips and one to keep whole, in a magazine file container.

Manuscripts

Should you keep your old manuscripts forever? A few days ago, I might have said "don't bother." Then I realized, as I contemplated submitting a fairly ancient reprint, that I have only the published version of that article—a version that was butchered by a grammatically challenged editor. Since I no longer have the original, I can't resubmit what I actually wrote—I'm stuck with another editor's hatchet-job.

Fortunately, most of our manuscripts are electronic these days, so we don't have to worry about saving boxes and boxes of published (or unpublished) works. Just be sure to back up your manuscript files on disk periodically, or a computer crash could wipe out your life's work in a blink of an electron.

Keeping Electronic Records

> Never assume that you won't need a copy of that contract in later years; stuff of mine is appearing online that I sold 15 years ago!

That raises another issue: Electronic records. Chances are, most of your writing and much of your correspondence is handled electronically nowadays—you may never even have print copies of much of this material. That's great from the standpoint of saving trees (and space in the back of your closet). However, it does present a risk, in that a computer failure can irretrievably wipe out your most important records. It can also be more difficult to locate important correspondence in a confusion of e-mail folders.

The key to keeping good electronic files is to resist the temptation to purge them. It's very easy to think that you'll never need a particular e-mail record—only to find, months later, that it had a vital bit of information that is now lost to you forever. If nothing else, keep an "archive" folder in your e-mail system that stores copies of every writing-related bit of e-mail you send or receive. (You can also model these archives on your hardcopy files, creating a new archive for each year or even each month.)

Need I mention the importance of *backing up* these files on disk periodically? While I admit that I often fail to practice what I am about to preach, I cannot emphasize enough the importance of making regular backups of *everything* that might be relevant to your writing records.

Unfortunately, backing up everything on floppy disks can be a tedious chore, and disks aren't always reliable; just when you think you have everything nicely saved, you insert a disk and find that the computer suddenly can't read it, or there is a "disk error" in the middle of your most important document. The solution: Invest $300 (or less) in a CD-ROM writer. CDs now cost $1 apiece or less—a small price to pay for the ability to easily back up all your writing files in ten minutes or less, every week or so.

The quickest and easiest way to maintain CD-ROM backup files is to build an "archive" folder on your system that includes aliases to the various other folders that you would like to back up. Rather than manually moving or copying every new article you've written, every bit of correspondence, or every important bit of e-mail, just make aliases that "point" to your correspondence folder, your articles folder, your e-mail folders. Make sure that you instruct your CD-writing program to "resolve aliases," so that when you tell it to back up this master archive, it will automatically retrieve all the folders (and the files in those folders) that you've aliased. This will ensure that each time you back up your system, you'll have your most recent correspondence and the latest versions of everything, without having to "remember" to back up or archive each new item.

Keeping good records isn't just a matter of saving what you're working on today. It's a matter of recognizing that you have no way of knowing what will suddenly become vitally important to you *tomorrow*. It can be so tempting to throw out that e-mail, that unsold article, those old letters. But we are entering an era when an increasing number of threats to our rights (and our livelihood) are coming down the pike—threats we can scarcely anticipate today and probably couldn't have imagined yesterday. Good records are your best (and only) form of self-protection. When in doubt, *don't* throw it out!

Moira Allen has been writing professionally for more than 20 years. More information about online writing resources can be found in her book, *Writing.com: Creative Internet Strategies to Advance Your Writing Career.*

WHY AND HOW TO REGISTER YOUR ARTICLES

by the American Society of Journalists and Authors

First Things First: The One-Paragraph Copyright Primer

As a freelance writer, unless you've signed a work-made-for-hire agreement or otherwise transferred copyright, what you write belongs to you. You need not put a little "c" in a circle on it. You need not register it with the Copyright Office. The work need not even be published for your copyright to take effect. The copyright is yours immediately. If your work appears in a periodical, the publisher owns the copyright in the entire issue as a *collective work*, but not in your individual work. The publisher may print a little © with its company name and file the issue with the Copyright Office, but its protection covers the issue as *an issue,* not the articles within. The copyright in your writing is *yours* unless and until, induced by cash or cowed by threats, you sign it away.

Why Register?

Under the law, if your copyright is infringed, you can't sue unless the work has been registered with the U.S. Copyright Office. You can, of course, wait until there's a problem before you bother filing a registration application. But there's a good reason to file as a matter of routine.

In copyright infringement cases, courts may assess two distinct kinds of damages.

Statutory damages—up to $100,000 if the infringement is judged to be willful—are available only if the work was registered no later than three months after first publication or, where the work was registered later than that, if the infringement begins after registration. ("Publication" means public availability, which may be earlier than the cover date.) In cases where statutory damages apply, the court may also award attorneys' fees.

Actual damages are monetary losses suffered by the infringed party—losses that are likely to be small as well as time-consuming and difficult to prove. What's more, courts are not free to award attorneys' fees in conjunction with actual damages.

So for infringement of articles not registered in time, it is rarely cost-effective to hire a lawyer and sue in federal court. (A suit in small claims court, based on contract rather than copyright, may make sense in such cases.) If you've registered your copyright in time, you're in a better position to inflict pain in a real lawsuit; thus, you have far greater clout.

In short: As a defensive move against infringement—such as unauthorized electronic use of an article—it can be wise to register each magazine and newspaper article you write.

Isn't Registration an Expensive Pain?

Actually, it's neither as costly nor as onerous as you may think. Registration costs $30, but you can gang articles on a single application to save on fees and drudgery. If you're a prolific article writer, the cost per story is quite low. To meet the within-three-months requirement, you need to file four times a year, each time listing your previous three months' published work; thus, four filings and $120 give you maximum protection on a year's output.

How to Do It

To group register, you need two official U.S. Copyright Office forms:

Form TX for nondramatic literary works (the streamlined *Short Form TX* may usually be used for a single work);

Form GR/CP for grouping published works on a single application.

You can obtain the forms directly from the Copyright Office by phoning (202) 707-9100 (available 24 hours a day). Leave a message; wait two to three weeks for the forms to arrive. If you have a computer with Adobe Acrobat Reader, you can download forms from the Copyright Office's Website; see address below. Photocopy them at will, but use a good grade of 8½ x 11 white paper, use both sides of the sheet, and match the layout of the originals. Type or print in black ink.

On Form TX, question 1, if you are registering two or more articles at the same time, enter "See GR/CP, attached." In question 2, under "Nature of Authorship," you should typically enter "Entire Text" or "Co-Author of Entire Text," whichever applies. If you're group-registering: in 3a, use the latest applicable date; in 3b, enter "See GR/CP, attached." In question 4, "Copyright Claimant," is ordinarily the same as the author: you. In question 5, under "Previous Registration," check "No" (remember that registration of the entire issue by the publisher does not constitute specific registration of your work). For most magazine or newspaper articles, ignore question 6.

On Form GR/CP, list articles chronologically, from earliest to latest, numbering the lines consecutively; no more than 12 months may separate the first from the last.

The Copyright Office's separate instruction sheets say that you must include the entire magazine or newspaper section in which each submitted article appeared—but that needn't actually be done. The Office advises that you may instead submit simple tearsheets or even photocopies. Just be sure to include with your application a letter asking that the Office "please accept the enclosed tearsheets (or photocopies) as part of ongoing special relief from the deposit requirement"; the request is routinely granted.

Enclose a check for $30, payable to Register of Copyrights. Mail your application to Register of Copyrights, Library of Congress, Washington, DC 20559-6000. Certified mail, return receipt requested, isn't a bad idea.

Four Frequently Asked Questions

1. How long will it take? Perhaps as long as 16 weeks. If you haven't heard by then, call the number below.

2. When does registration take effect? As soon as the application and supporting materials are received by the Copyright Office.

3. What do you do if an article appears in more than one periodical? Submit any published version, the earlier the better; if different published versions reflect only minor changes, you need not register each version.

4. What about unpublished works? You may also submit the manuscript version(s), but you may not use form GR/CP, nor may you mix published and unpublished works. Unpublished works may be grouped using form TX alone; simply use a descriptive title for the group, such as "unpublished writings, Jan–Mar 2000."

For More Information

Contact the U.S. Copyright office:
Phone: (202) 707-3000, 8:30–5 Eastern time, Monday–Friday
World Wide Web: http://lcweb.loc.gov/copyright

The American Society of Journalists and Authors is the nation's leading organization of independent nonfiction writers. The membership consists of more than 1,000 freelance writers of magazine articles, trade books, and other forms of nonfiction writing.

SECTION TWO

The Craft of Writing

HOW TO FIND TIME TO WRITE WHEN YOU DON'T HAVE TIME TO WRITE

by Sue Grafton

Early in my writing career, I managed to turn out three novels, one right after another, while I was married, raising two children, keeping house, and working full time as a medical secretary. Those novels were never published and netted me not one red cent, but the work was essential. Writing those three books prepared the way for the fourth book, which was published and got me launched as a professional writer. Ironically, now that I'm a "full-time" writer with the entire workday at my disposal, I'm often guilty of getting less work done. Even after 25 years at it, there are days when I find myself feeling overwhelmed . . . far less effective and efficient than I know I could be. Lately, I've been scrutinizing my own practices, trying to determine the techniques I use to help me produce more consistently. The underlying challenge, always, is finding the time to write and sticking to it.

Extracting writing time from the fabric of everyday life is a struggle for many of us. Even people who are technically free to write during an eight-hour day often can't "get around" to it. Each day seems to bring some crisis that requires our immediate attention. Always, there's the sense that tomorrow, for sure, we'll get down to work. We're uncomfortably aware that time is passing and the job isn't getting done, but it's hard to know where to start. How can you fit writing into a schedule that already *feels* as if it's filled to capacity? If you find yourself lamenting that you "never have time to write," here are some suggestions about how to view the problem and, better yet, how to go about solving it.

First of all, accept the fact that you may never have the "leisure" (real or imaginary) to sit down and complete your novel without interruption. Chances are you won't be able to quit your job, abandon your family, and retire to a writers' colony for six weeks of uninterrupted writing every year. And even if you could, that six weeks probably wouldn't get the job done. To be productive, we have to make writing a part of our daily lives. The problem is that we view writing as a luxury, something special to allow ourselves as soon as we've taken care of the countless nagging duties that seem to come first. Well, I've got news for you. It really works the other way. Once you put writing first, the rest of your life will fall into place.

Successful writers disagree about how much time is needed per stint—ranging anywhere from one to ten hours. I feel that two hours is ideal and not impossible to find in your own busy day. One of the first tricks is to make sure you use precious writing time for *writing* and not for the myriad other chores associated with the work.

"Writing" is made up of a number of sub-categories, each of which needs tending to. A professional doesn't just sit down and magically begin to create prose. The process is more complex than that, and each phase requires our attention. Analyzing the process and breaking it down into its components will help you understand which jobs can be tucked into the corners and crevices of your day. In addition to actual composition, writing encompasses the following:

Planning—initiating projects and setting up a working strategy for each.
Research—which includes clipping and filing.
Outlining—once the material has been gathered.
Marketing—which includes query letters, manuscript typing, Xeroxing, trips to the post office.
And finally, *follow-up* for manuscripts in submission.

All of these things take time, but they won't take all of your time, and they shouldn't take your best time. These are clerical details that can be dispatched in odd moments during the day. Delegate as much as possible. Hire someone for these jobs if you can. Have a teen-ager come in one day a week to clip and file. Ask your spouse to drop off a manuscript at the post office on his or her way to work. Check research books out of the library while the kids are at story hour. Use time waiting for a dental appointment or dead time at the Laundromat to jot down ideas and get them organized. Take index cards with you everyplace.

Now take a good look at your day. Feel as if you're already swamped from dawn to dark? Here are some options:

1. Stay up an hour later each night. At night, the phone doesn't ring and the family is asleep. You'll have fewer distractions and no excuses. You won't drop dead if you cut your sleep by an hour. The time spent creatively on projects important to you will give you energy. Eventually, you can think about stretching that one hour to two, but initially, stick to a manageable change and incorporate it thoroughly into your new schedule before tackling more. I used to write from ten at night until midnight or one a.m., and I still find those hours best for certain kinds of work.

2. Get up an hour earlier, before the family wakes. Again, shaving an hour from your sleep will do you no harm, and it will give you the necessary time to establish the habit of daily writing. Anthony Trollope, one of my favorite writers, worked for most of his adult life as a postal clerk, on the job from eight until five every day. His solution was to get up at five a.m. and write 250 words every 15 minutes till eight—three hours. If he finished a book before the time to go to work, he started a new project at once. In his lifetime, he turned out 46 full-length books, most of them while he earned a living in another capacity.

3. If you're employed outside your home, try working en route. British crime writer Michael Gilbert wrote 23 novels . . . all while riding the train to his work as a solicitor. He used the 50-minute transit time to produce 2 to 2½ pages a day, 12 to 15 pages a week. Buses, trains, commuter flights can all represent productive time for you. Use those periods for writing, while you're inaccessible to the rest of the world.

4. What about your lunch hour? Do you go out to lunch every day to "escape" the tensions and pressures of the job? Why not stay at your desk, creating a temporary haven in your own head? Pack a brown bag lunch. It's cheaper, among other things, and if you limit yourself to fruit and raw vegetables, you can get thin while you pile up the pages!

5. Look at your week nights. See if there's a way to snag one for yourself. You'd make the time if you decided to take an adult education class. Invent a course for yourself, called "Writing My Novel At Long Last" and spend three hours a week in the public library. I heard about a writer who finished a book just this way, working only on Tuesday nights.

6. Weekends generally have free time tucked into them. Try Saturday afternoons when the kids are off at the movies, or Sunday mornings when everyone else sleeps late.

Invent a course for yourself, called "Writing My Novel At Long Last" and spend three hours a week in the public library.

7. Revamp your current leisure time. Your schedule probably contains hidden hours that you could easily convert to writing time. Television is the biggest time-waster, but I've also realized that reading the daily paper from front to back takes 90 minutes out of my day! For a while, I convinced myself that I needed to be informed on "current events," but the truth is that I was avoiding my desk, squandering an hour and a half that I desperately needed to complete a manuscript. I was feeling pressured, when all the while, the time was sitting right there in front of me . . . literally. Recently, too, I took a good look at my social calendar. I realized that a dinner party for six was requiring, in effect, two full days of activity . . . time I now devote to my work. I still have friends. I just cut my entertainment plans by a third.

Now.

Once you identify and set aside those newly found hours, it's a matter of tailoring the work to suit the time available. This can be done in four simple steps:

1. Make a list of everything you'd like to write . . . a novel, a short story, a film script, a book review for the local paper, that travel article you outlined during your last trip.

2. Choose three. If you only have one item on your agenda, how lucky you are! If you have more than three projects on your list, keep the remaining projects on a subsidiary list to draw on as you complete the items on your primary list and send them out into the marketplace. I generally like to have one book-length project (my long-term goal) and two smaller projects (an article, a short story . . . short-term goals) on my list.

3. Arrange items on the list in the order of their true priority. Be tough about this. For instance, you might have a short story possibility, an idea you've been toying with for years, but when you come right down to it, it might not seem important enough (or fully developed enough) to place among the top three on your list. My first priority is always the detective novel I'm writing currently. I work on that when I'm at my freshest, saving the smaller projects for the period after my first energy peaks. Having several projects in the works simultaneously is good for you psychologically. If you get stuck on one, you can try the next. As you finish each project, the feeling of accomplishment will spur you to renewed effort on those that remain. In addition, by supplying yourself with a steady stream of new projects, you'll keep your interest level high.

4. Once you select the three projects you want to work on, break the writing down into small, manageable units. A novel isn't completed at one sitting. Mine are written two pages at a time over a period of six to eight months. Assign yourself a set number of pages . . . one or two . . . and then meet your own quota from day to day. Once you've completed two pages, you can let yourself off the hook, moving on to the next task. By doing a limited amount of work on a number of projects, you're more likely to keep all three moving forward. Don't burden yourself with more than you can really handle. Assigning yourself ten pages a day sounds good on the surface, but you'll soon feel so overwhelmed that you'll start avoiding the work and won't get anything done. Remember, it's persistence that counts, the steady hammering away at the writing from day to day, day after day, that produces the most consistent work and the greatest quantity of it.

Essentially, then, all you need to do is this:

Analyze the task.
Scrutinize your schedule.
Tailor the work to fit.

I have one final suggestion, a practice that's boosted my productivity by 50 percent. Start each day with a brief meditation . . . five minutes of mental quiet in which you visualize yourself actually sitting at your desk, accomplishing the writing you've assigned yourself. Affirm to yourself that you'll have a good, productive day, that you'll have high energy, solid concentration, imagination, and enthusiasm for the work coming up. Use these positive messages to block out your anxieties, the self-doubt, the fear of failure that in fact comprise procrastination. Five minutes of quiet will reinforce your new determination and will help you make the dream of writing real.

Sue Grafton is the author of the popular "A-Z" series of mystery novels featuring P.I. Kinsey Millhone, the most recent being *P Is for Peril* (2001). She is also the author of many magazine articles, television scripts, and short stories. This article first appeared in *The Writer*, December 1986.

EVERYTHING YOU NEED TO KNOW ABOUT WRITING SUCCESSFULLY – IN TEN MINUTES

by Stephen King

I. The First Introduction

That's right. I know it sounds like an ad for some sleazy writers' school, but I really am going to tell you everything you need to pursue a successful and financially rewarding career writing fiction, and I really am going to do it in ten minutes, which is exactly how long it took me to learn. It will actually take you twenty minutes or so to read this article, however, because I have to tell you a story, and then I have to write a second introduction. But these, I argue, should not count in the ten minutes.

II. The Story, or, How Stephen King Learned to Write

When I was a sophomore in high school, I did a sophomoric thing which got me in a pot of fairly hot water, as sophomoric didoes often do. I wrote and published a small satiric newspaper called *The Village Vomit*. In this little paper I lampooned a number of teachers at Lisbon (Maine) High School, where I was under instruction. These were not very gentle lampoons; they ranged from the scatological to the downright cruel.

Eventually, a copy of this paper found its way into the hands of a faculty member, and since I had been unwise enough to put my name on it (a fault, some critics would argue, of which I have still not been entirely cured), I was brought into the office. The sophisticated satirist had by that time reverted to what he really was: a fourteen-year-old kid who was shaking in his boots and wondering if he was going to get a suspension . . . what we called a "three-day vacation" in those dim days of 1964.

I wasn't suspended. I was forced to make a number of apologies—they were warranted, but they tasted like dog-dirt in my mouth—and spent a week in detention hall. And the guidance counselor arranged what he no doubt thought of as a more constructive channel for my talents. This was a job—contingent upon the editor's approval—writing sports for the *Lisbon Enterprise*, a twelve-page weekly of the sort with which any small-town resident will be familiar. This editor was the man who taught me everything I know about writing in ten minutes. His name was John Gould—not the famed New England humorist or the novelist who wrote *The Greenleaf Fires*, but a relative of both, I believe.

He told me he needed a sports writer, and we could "try each other out," if I wanted.

I told him I knew more about advanced algebra than I did sports.

Gould nodded and said, "You'll learn."

I said I would at least try to learn. Gould gave me a huge roll of yellow paper and promised me a wage of ½¢ per word. The first two pieces I wrote had to do with a high school basketball game in which a member of my school team broke the Lisbon High scoring record. One of these pieces was a straight piece of reportage. The second was a feature article.

I brought them to Gould the day after the game, so he'd have them for the paper, which came out Fridays. He read the straight piece, made two minor corrections, and spiked it. Then he started in on the feature piece with a large black pen and taught me all I ever needed to know about my craft. I wish I still had the piece—it deserves to be framed, editorial corrections and all—but I can remember pretty well how it went and how it looked when he had finished with it. Here's an example:

> Last night, in the ~~well-loved~~ (gymnasium) of Lisbon High
> School, partisans and Jay Hills fans alike were stunned by
> an athletic performance unequalled in school history: Bob
> Ransom~~, known as "Bullet" Bob for both his size and~~
> ~~accuracy,~~ scored thirty-seven points. He did it with grace
> and speed. . .and he did it with a odd courtesy as well,
> committing only two personal fouls in his ~~knight-like~~ quest
> for a record which has eluded Lisbon *vs basketball team* ~~thinclads~~ since 1953.

When Gould finished marking up my copy in the manner I have indicated above, he looked up and must have seen something on my face. I think *he* must have thought it was horror, but it was not: It was revelation.

"I only took out the bad parts, you know," he said. "Most of it's pretty good."

"I know," I said, meaning both things; yes, most of it was good, and yes, he had only taken out the bad parts. "I won't do it again."

"If that's true," he said, "you'll never have to work again. You can do *this* for a living."

Then he threw back his head and laughed.

And he was right: I *am* doing this for a living, and as long as I can keep on, I don't expect ever to have to work again.

III. The Second Introduction

All of what follows has been said before. If you are interested enough in writing to be a purchaser of this book, you will have either heard or read all (or almost all) of it before. Thousands of writing courses are taught across the United States each year; seminars are convened; guest lecturers talk, then answer questions, and it all boils down to what follows.

I am going to tell you these things again because often people will only listen—really listen—to someone who makes a lot of money doing the thing he's talking about. This is sad but true. And I told you the story above not to make myself sound like a character out of a Horatio Alger novel but to make a point: I saw, I listened, and *I learned*. Until that day in John Gould's little office, I had been writing first drafts of stories that might run 2,500 words. The second drafts were apt to run 3,300 words. Following that day, my 2,500-word first drafts became 2,200-word second drafts. And two years after that, I sold the first one.

So here it is, with all the bark stripped off. It'll take ten minutes to read, and you can apply it right away . . . if you *listen*.

IV. Everything You Need to Know About Writing Successfully

1. *Be talented*

This, of course, is the killer. What is talent? I can hear someone shouting, and here we are, ready to get into a discussion right up there with "What is the meaning of life?" for weighty pronouncements and total uselessness. For the purposes of the beginning writer, talent may as well be defined as eventual success—publication and money. If you wrote something for which someone sent you a check, if you cashed the check and it didn't bounce, and if you then paid the electric bill with the money, I consider you talented.

Now some of you are really hollering. Some of you are calling me one crass money-fixated creep. Nonsense. Worse than nonsense, off the subject. We're not talking about good or bad here. I'm interested in telling you how to get your stuff published, not in critical judgments of who's good or bad. As a rule, the critical judgments come after the check's been spent, anyway. I have my own opinion, but most times I keep them to myself. People who are published steadily and are paid for what they are writing may be either saints or trollops, but they are clearly reaching a great many someones who want what they have. Ergo, they are communicating. Ergo, they are talented. The biggest part of writing successfully is being talented, and in the context of marketing, the only bad writer is one who doesn't get paid. If you're not talented, you won't succeed. And if you're not succeeding, you should know when to quit.

When is that? I don't know. It's different for each writer. Not after six rejection slips, certainly, nor after sixty. But after six hundred? Maybe. After six thousand? My friend, after six thousand pinks, it's time you tried painting or computer programming.

Further, almost every aspiring writer knows when he is getting warmer—you start getting little jotted notes on your rejection slips, or personal letters . . . maybe a commiserating phone call. It's lonely out there in the cold, but there *are* encouraging voices . . . unless there is nothing in your words that warrants encouragement. I think you owe it to yourself to skip as much of the self-illusion as possible. If your eyes are open, you'll know which way to go . . . or when to turn back.

2. *Be neat*

Type. Double-space. Use a nice heavy white paper. If you've marked your manuscript a lot, do another draft.

3. *Be self-critical*

If you *haven't* marked up your manuscript a lot, you did a lazy job.

Only God gets things right the first time. Don't be a slob.

Somewhere along the line, pernicious critics have invested the American reading and writing public with the idea that entertaining fiction and serious ideas do not overlap. This would have surprised Charles Dickens. . . .

4. *Remove every extraneous word*

You want to get up on a soapbox and preach? Fine. Get one, and try your local park. You want to write for money? Get to the point. And if you remove the excess garbage and discover you can't *find* the point, tear up what you wrote and start all over again . . . or try something new.

5. *Never look at a reference book while doing a first draft*

You want to write a story? Fine. Put away your dictionary, your encyclopedias, your World Almanac, and your thesaurus. Better yet, throw your thesaurus into the wastebasket. The only things creepier than a thesaurus are those little paperbacks college students too lazy to read the assigned novels buy around exam time. Any word you have to hunt for in a thesaurus is the wrong word. There are no exceptions to this rule. You think you might have misspelled a word? O.K., so here is your choice: Either look it up in the dictionary, thereby making sure you have it right—and breaking your train of thought and the writer's trance in the bargain—or just spell it phonetically and correct it later. Why not? Did you think it was going to go somewhere? And if you need to know the largest city in Brazil and you find you don't have it in your head, why not write in Miami, or Cleveland? You can check it . . . but *later*. When you sit down to write, *write*. Don't do anything else except go to the bathroom, and only do that if it absolutely cannot be put off.

6. *Know the markets*

Only a dimwit would send a story about giant vampire bats surrounding a high school to *McCall's*. Only a dimwit would send a tender story about a mother and daughter making up their differences on Christmas Eve to *Playboy* . . . but people do it all the time. I'm not exaggerating; I have seen such stories in the slush piles of the actual magazines. If you write a good story, why send it out in an ignorant fashion? Would you send your kid out in a snowstorm dressed in Bermuda shorts and a tank top? If you like science fiction, read science fiction novels and magazines. If you want to write mysteries, read the magazines. And so on. It isn't just a matter of knowing what's right for the present story; you can begin to catch on, after a while, to overall rhythms, editorial likes and dislikes, a magazine's slant. Sometimes your reading can influence the next story, and create a sale.

7. *Write to entertain*

Does this mean you can't write "serious fiction"? It does not. Somewhere along the line pernicious critics have invested the American reading and writing public with the idea that entertaining fiction and serious ideas do not overlap. This would have surprised Charles Dickens, not to mention Jane Austen, John Steinbeck, William Faulkner, Bernard Malamud, and hundreds of others. But your serious ideas must always serve your story, not the other way around. I repeat: If you want to preach, get a soapbox.

8. *Ask yourself frequently, "Am I having fun?"*

The answer needn't always be yes. But if it's always no, it's time for a new project or a new career.

9. *How to evaluate criticism*

Show your piece to a number of people—ten, let us say. Listen carefully to what they tell you. Smile and nod a lot. Then review what was said very carefully. If your critics are all telling you the same thing about some facet of your story—a plot twist that doesn't work, a character who rings false, stilted narrative, or half a dozen other possibles—change it. It doesn't matter if you really like that twist or that character; if a lot of people are telling you something is wrong with your piece, it is. If seven or eight of them are hitting on that same thing, I'd still suggest changing it. But if everyone—or even most everyone—is criticizing something different, you can safely disregard what all of them say.

10. *Observe all rules for proper submission*
Return postage, self-addressed envelope, etc.

11. *An agent? Forget it. For now.*
Agents get 10% to 15% of monies earned by their clients. 15% of nothing is nothing. Agents also have to pay the rent. Beginning writers do not contribute to that or any other necessity of life. Flog your stories around yourself. If you've done a novel, send around query letters to publishers, one by one, and follow up with sample chapters and/or the complete manuscript. And remember Stephen King's First Rule of Writers and Agents, learned by bitter personal experience: You don't need one until you're making enough for someone to steal . . . and if you're making that much, you'll be able to take your pick of good agents.

12. *If it's bad, kill it*
When it comes to people, mercy killing is against the law. When it comes to fiction, it *is* the law.

That's everything you need to know. And if you listened, you can write everything and anything you want. Now I believe I will wish you a pleasant day and sign off.
My ten minutes are up.

Stephen King has kept many a reader enthralled with his tales of mayhem and horror. He has written more than 28 novels, including the recent bestseller *Dreamcatcher*. Many of his stories have been made into movies. He lives in a 25-room house in Bangor, Maine. "People want to know why I . . . write such gross stuff. I tell them I have the heart of a small boy—and I keep it in a jar on my desk." This article first appeared in *The Writer*, July 1986.

THE HOW-TOS OF HOW-TOS

Best tips for selling a well-crafted article

by Linda Slater

I have been writing and selling how-to articles for about 20 years. Most editors are willing to consider a well-crafted article that helps other people learn how to do something well. I have sold many articles and have not been immune to rejection either, so I feel I have been through the School of Hard Knocks several times! Here are my best tips for selling that how-to article:

1. Never give up.
If an article is rejected by *Mother Earth News*, try *Back Home* or *Countryside*. I once sent an article to eight different magazines before it sold. Your article won't be published gathering dust on the shelf.

2. Revise.
If an article is rejected, reread it and see what might make it sparkle. Does it need better, more detailed photographs? Do you need a few more quotes from other, more varied experts? Is the article dated?

3. Read at least ten issues of the magazine you are aiming to sell to.
What style do they favor? Are the articles formal or informal and conversational? Carefully study the photographs. Are the articles 50 percent text and 50 percent photos? Does humor fit this magazine's style? Now you know how to slant your article.

4. Try new markets that had been unknown to you.
I once sent a garden article to a small magazine I found in my doctor's office. I am now the garden editor of that magazine! Risk-taking is healthy for all

writers. You might be surprised where you might sell your article on flyfishing for women. I took a risk once and sent an article on self-esteem to a magazine for large women, *Big Beautiful Woman*, and sold it. Spend ten minutes every day studying market lists on books on writing at your library or at home. You may be amazed at which magazine or newspaper will buy your how-to article.

5. Keep an "idea file" for those days when inspiration won't come.
Several kinds of articles from various publications get me going. For example, I keep a garden idea file, a self-help idea file, and a general human-interest idea file. If I read about a local artist or unusual character, I cut out the article so that I'll remember to try an article similar to that or in more depth about that sub-ject. A news story about a flood or fire might turn into a human-interest piece or an article on flood or fire insurance, with examples of people who have lost everything because they weren't insured.

6. Ask for feedback.
Ask friends or family to read your article and give you good or bad feedback. Is the piece clear and easy to read? Do the photographs help tell the reader how to do something? You will learn from each feedback you receive. Take a deep breath and try it.

7. Stay in touch with local events.
Keep a calendar of local and state fairs, festivals, competitions, and events. Visit some of these events and see whom you can meet and talk to. Take photos of local artists, musicians, crafts-people, and writers. Could you turn any of these interviews into a how-to piece on drawing or painting? Sewing or fishing? Quilting or boating? One woman in my area compiled and self-published a booklet on "How to Compete in Art Fairs and Festivals and Sell Your Work," and sold several thousand copies at art fairs and through the mail. I once took photos of four weavers at a show and sold an article about them to a regional publication, and another time, I did a profile of a woman who paints on gourds and sells them for hundreds of dollars.

> Spend ten minutes every day studying market lists. . . . You may be amazed at which magazine or newspaper will buy your how-to article.

8. Write about your passionate interests.
I am wild about gardening, so I love interviewing area gardeners, talking to people who run nurseries, and telling others how to garden. I make my own herbal teas, so I sent an article on this topic to *Mother Earth News*. They bought it, used it in the magazine, then paid me again when they reprinted it in an anthology. I sold an article to an environ-mental magazine on gardening with my children, and one on how to quit smoking to a health food publication. If you love angels or miracles, you have

the germ of an article idea. (Hint: Anything with the word "soul" in it seems to sell these days!)

9. Solve a problem.

This type of article tells readers how to overcome a problem or solve a dilemma in their everyday lives. It could be about how to take out coffee stains or cleaning the house with non-toxic chemicals, how to catch bass or grow spinach. This kind of article may require some research or interviews with local or national experts. I find that if I have at least five quotes in an article from experts who live all over the country, it has more credibility. I check the library for names of experts in the field and write or call them. Once Joyce Brothers called me back while I was baking cookies and surprised me with her promptness. For ideas, ask your friends or relatives what kinds of problems they are trying to solve. (Hint: Many of my friends are struggling with how to communicate with their teenager and how to pay for their children's college education. Remember, there are 40 million baby boomers now thinking about these problems.)

10. Tailor your article to a specific market.

Check and recheck your article for spelling, grammar, and punctuation. Ask people to proof it, read it, give you feedback. Enclose an SASE, and send your article out! If it is rejected, revise and send it out the next day to another market. Your article will not sell sitting on your desk or waiting for you to make it perfect.

Linda Slater has published more than 100 articles, which have appeared in *The Christian Science Monitor, Mother Earth News, Countryside, Colorado Life,* and elsewhere. She is also an accomplished poet.

WRITING PROFILES OF ORDINARY PEOPLE

Many markets want to hear about non-celebrities

by Fraser Sherman

If you have a fresh new angle on Elvis or Marilyn, Richard Nixon or Leonardo DiCaprio, the world will beat a path to your door.

If you have a fresh new angle—or any angle—on an average citizen, will anyone care? Someone's story may be fascinating, his or her accomplishments commendable, but in this celebrity-fixated world, readers may not think an article on an ordinary person is worth their time.

Yet there are more ordinary people in the world than there are celebrities, and you can talk to them without fighting through press agents and publicists. And there *are* plenty of markets interested in hearing about them; I know, because I've sold assorted profiles of people no one has ever heard of:

- A charter-boat captain who's watched his hometown change from an isolated village to a condo crowded resort
- A local martial-arts teacher
- A Christian clown who uses humor to teach the Gospel
- A military officer turned romance writer

None of these subjects were big names, but I sold articles on all of them. In the process, I learned a few things about finding, marketing, and writing articles about ordinary people—and how you can do it, too.

Where to Find Subjects

Have you ever thought anyone you know (or even anyone in your town) deserved to be profiled? Remember, you're not looking for potentates or

111

superstars, merely for someone with an interesting, colorful story. With that in mind, take another look around you for good profile subjects.

1. *Personal acquaintances.* Ted Raymond, an ex-military officer and retired professional actor who appeared in the movie *The Truman Show,* belongs to the same local theater group I do. When he got the role, I heard all about it.

2. *The newspaper.* Local papers often profile local celebrities, artists, and entrepreneurs still unknown outside your area, but worthy of coverage in national magazines.

3. *Organizations.* Whether you belong to the Kiwanis, Habitat for Humanity, or a local business networking group, you may run into a fellow member doing something remarkable, or hear about him in the group newsletter. Based on a piece in the *Amnesty International* newsletter, I recently submitted a query about a murder victim's son who organized a group to oppose the death penalty.

4. *Local events.* Keep your eye open for book signings, concerts, art exhibits, or plays that might feature someone worth covering. I got an interview with Colonel Merline Lovelace, the romance writer, after meeting her at a local book signing.

When you first hear about a possible subject, you may wonder whether he or she is really interesting enough for an editor to pay you for a profile. If your prospect hooks your interest so much you want to write about him or her, it's worthwhile looking for a suitable market and querying the editor. This doesn't guarantee a sale, or an "on spec" go-ahead (even if the editor agrees with you, he may have handled a similar story just recently), but if your enthusiasm and your query conveys why, it can only help your chances.

Finding a Market

So you've found a subject whose story you're convinced would make a great article. Now, Who's most likely to pay you for it?

1. *Local papers and magazines love to cover local figures—rising stars, retired stars, or just a person who's plain unusual.* I profiled a local comic-book artist, David Dorman (who designed figures for the G.I. Joe toy line during the eighties), for a local magazine, *Emerald Cities*; a fireman who dresses as a clown to teach fire safety for the *Pensacola NewsJournal.* If the publication is open to free-lance work, it's a natural place to start.

2. *Specialized national markets may bite if a person comes within their sphere of interest:* My profile of Ted Raymond ran in *Air Force Times*; my piece on Colonel Lovelace was published in *Military Lifestyle.* The Christian clown act got his profile in a section of *Grit* that covers people helping their community.

3. *If your subject seems so remarkable or memorable he or she merits a national audience, look at major markets such as* Reader's Digest, *women's magazines, etc.* I haven't sold a profile to such topflight markets yet—but I keep trying.

In choosing markets, look at several possibilities. When I profiled Colonel Lovelace, her writing career wasn't distinctive enough for an article in a writers' magazine—but the idea of an air-force officer writing not technothrillers but romances made her unusual enough to catch *Military Lifestyle's* eye.

If you can query more than one market, go ahead: a story about a homeopathic vet might interest a local paper, a pet-care magazine, and a new-age publication. Editors won't usually object, provided the markets are distinct (a profile in *Convention South* won't compete with *Cinefantastique*) and you respect any rights you've already sold.

And of course, the angles should be different. I went into far more detail on Ted Raymond's military career for *Air Force Times* than I would have for a movie magazine. The story on the charter-boat captain I wrote for a local paper included lots of local references which would have been meaningless in a national seniors magazine.

As with any query, make sure you study the target magazine and the writers' guidelines before you actually pitch your idea—and take them seriously. Some business magazines, for instance, will want a profile only if your subject is a rising entrepreneur; others would prefer someone making his or her way in an established corporation. Some magazines don't use profiles of unknowns at all; only world-class movers and shakers interest them.

Finding a Hook

If you're writing about Drew Barrymore, John Grisham, or Stephen Spielberg, readers may put up with a slow start. When writing about ordinary people, readers need to be hooked from the beginning, with one of the following traditional tricks for attention-grabbing openings.

1. *A curious fact.* When I wrote an article on Susan Shaw—marketing head for a college arts center—for the local paper, I opened with "Susan Shaw's job is to market something people don't realize exists." Intriguing enough, I hoped, to make readers keep going for the explanation: Many in our local community don't believe we have such a high-quality arts center around here.

> Your profile needs facts that document your subject's achievements.

2. *The unexpected.* For the article on a local martial-arts teacher, I began with his statement that in martial arts, it's more important to heal people than to hurt them—not the image you get from Bruce Lee and Cynthia Rothrock films.

3. *Irony.* Ted Raymond's role in *The Truman Show,* his biggest ever, came 16 years after he'd given up on his acting career and withdrawn from the actors' unions.

4. *A great anecdote.* An article in *Builder* a few years ago opened with a builder completing the roofing on a 5,000-foot home . . . only to start taking the roof off the same day, because the owner suddenly wanted a second story.

Of course, the rest of your article has to support the opening. The *Builder* anecdote worked because it showed the secret to the contractor's success—his willingness to meet the every whim of his very wealthy clients. If the article had profiled his charity work, the anecdote wouldn't have fit the story.

Focus on What Counts

Many readers will be fascinated learning what Boris Yeltsin or Shania Twain have for lunch; no one gives a hoot what an ordinary joe eats, unless it's opossum souffle. Even after you grab readers with your opening, you must continue to give them reasons to keep reading. In order of importance, readers want:

1. *Facts.* Whether presented as quotes, narrative, or anecdotes, your profile needs facts that document your subject's achievements—the growth of her business, the tortures he suffered in a P.O.W. camp, how many rejections it took before he sold his first novel.

2. *Quotes.* If your subject's words are colorful enough, by all means use them. "My veterinary clinic is open 24 hours a day." doesn't need to be in quotation marks, but "If an animal's hurt anywhere within 100 miles, I'll be there—any time, any animal, any place." certainly should be.

3. *Anecdotes.* A colorful story about selling Porsches or preparing for the Olympics can bring your subject to life for your readers. Focus on the stories that show your subject in action (as a coin collector or a 90-year-old MBA student) or highlight his or her character. The fact that someone proposed ten times before his wife said yes is relevant if you're writing about his 75-year marriage, not if you're writing about his career, unless it shows the same determination that makes him an ace salesman.

4. *Details.* If her lunch menu or his video collection tells us something important or interesting, mention them. When I profiled local cartoonist Peggy Wyatt, she told me how her cartoons sold overseas according to subject (Swiss love cartoons about machinery, South Africans go for gags about taxes); I used that detail in my opening paragraph. It's not only interesting, I hope, but it drives home the fact that Wyatt has been published all around the world.

Details that highlight achievements ("She has books on her shelves in 27 languages, all of which she speaks fluently."), or reveal his character ("To keep himself from slacking off, he wears a three-piece business suit, even when he's alone in his home office.") are far more important than the color of his hair or that he likes to play golf on Sundays.

Wrap It Up

As AP editor Rene J. Cappon once put it, "journalists . . . can never hope to say the last word on any subject." You don't have the space to write a complete biography, so choose the best anecdotes, the most colorful details, but nothing that isn't relevant and interesting. Your goal is to leave readers feeling they've learned *enough*, even if they haven't learned *everything*.

So to that end, ask yourself: if you have backed up whatever claim you made in your lead. Did I tell the story my opening led readers to expect? When I reread your first draft, did you find yourself with leftover questions? ("Dang, I never asked why she chose gator-wrestling to pay for medical school.")? And will your profile convince readers and editors that your subject is worth taking the time to read about?

If the answer to any of these is no, put some more work in. When the answer to all of them is yes, the odds are that a profile of an ordinary person will bring you your next byline.

Fraser Sherman has written for *Air Space and Science, Emergency, Newsweek, Boy's Life,* and many other publications, in addition to serving on the staff of two regional homebuilding magazines, *Foundation* and *Style.* His book on science-fiction and fantasy TV movies, *Cyborgs, Santa Claus, and Satan,* was published in May 2000. This article first appeared in *The Writer,* October 2000.

BEATING THE ANXIETY
OF INTERVIEWS

by Chloe Osborne

You've accepted the challenge of writing an article on a topic you know almost nothing about. Suddenly the anxiety hits: How do you make the article sound convincing? Who can provide reliable information, and perhaps a few quotes?

I faced this problem a few months back, when I submitted a query for an article on the America's Cup. My query was accepted, and I was suddenly left feeling like I had gotten myself into something I couldn't handle. Sure, I'm an avid follower of the America's Cup yachting races, but my knowledge of yachting is far from erudite.

Feeling discouraged, yet under pressure to get those quotes, I visited numerous sites belonging to these individuals' America's Cup teams. Finally, I found an e-mail address for Dennis Conner. I e-mailed a request for an interview, then did the same for Dawn Riley. I was surprised by the quick responses asking for more information, then the speedy agreements to complete online interviews. I was able to assimilate a wealth of information from these two individuals, and my stories became the front-page lead exclusives at the respective publications.

What can you learn from this personal anecdote? First, a lot about the way interviewees react. People enjoy being interviewed. It makes them feel that their advice and experiences are of interest to a wide range of people, and that would make anyone feel special—right? While not everyone will be willing to do an interview with you, there are always many experts who would be more than happy to lend a little of their time to answer your questions.

Making Contacts

How do you get in touch with such people? In this era of technology, most professionals will have e-mail addresses, which can be found at their web sites. If they don't have a web site, you can easily look them up in the online white pages (or yellow pages if they are a business), and call or write to them. Word-of-mouth also works when it comes to contacting professionals. If you mention the article you are writing to enough friends and colleagues, it is likely that someone will say, "Well, I have a friend who is an expert in . . ." This makes finding experts far less daunting than trying to contact the most famous person you can find.

There are many places to find experts, or at least knowledgeable people to help with your article. The Internet is the most comprehensive information resource; simply type appropriate keywords into a search engine to reap a variety of sources to interview. Visit the web sites that come up, and you're likely to find several names, e-mail address, and telephone numbers of experts. If that doesn't work, ProfNet (http://www.profnet.com) is a database created by over 11,000 public relations professionals to provide journalists with links to expert sources. These people are willing to answer questions relating to their expertise.

How do you ask for an interview over the phone? Many people feel anxious when thinking about interviewing someone. The same is true for me, as the more famous my subject is, the more nervous I become. However, there is no need to be fraught with anxiety before an interview. Take a deep breath, pick up the phone and dial the number. When the subject answers, politely introduce yourself and explain who you are and what publication you are writing for, and say that you would like to interview them for your article. Explain the subject matter in as much detail as possible. Try to speak slowly to avoid overwhelming your interviewee, and be informal but respectful.

Choosing an Interview Format

There are three basic ways to conduct an interview these days. Each works well for different types of interviews, so it's up to you to decide which to choose.

The first is the traditional meeting in person. This type of interview is great for obtaining descriptions of the interviewee's reactions as you ask questions, and definitely adds color to an interview. However, if you are located in California and your subject lives in Texas, flying out for a personal interview is likely to cost you a bundle. This is when the telephone comes in handy.

Telephone interviews are wonderful to cover geographical distance, as well as for interviewees who are always on the go. Interviewing people over the phone is also good for getting a mental picture of the personality of your subject, as voice can reveal a lot about a person. Telephone interviews are also great because you can slip in extra questions as you think of them. The long distance costs are about the only downside.

Last but not least are e-mail interviews. The most

> Many people feel anxious when thinking about interviewing someone. The same is true for me . . . the more famous my subject is, the more nervous I become.

contemporary approach, e-mail interviews have good and bad points. Obviously, they are extremely quick to complete, although many interview subjects will procrastinate on replying to your questions, and that can put a stop to fast-paced deadlines. Also, it is usually difficult to ascertain the personality of your subject through e-mail, as text doesn't have quite the animation of a real-life or telephone interview. E-mail interviews are great if your subject works irregular hours, lives far away from you, or is extremely busy and will answer your questions in their few spare minutes of the day.

Bringing Interviews Alive

Many people are nervous during interviews because they know that their words will appear in a magazine or online, and many people will be reading about them. If your interviewee is stiff and short with you, it is possible to bring them out of their shell and make them more animated. Ask them questions about something they are thoroughly interested in, whether it has to do with the interview topic or not. Make these questions easy, and they will pour out information about themselves. This will enable you to ask questions on your topic, and receive a more animated response.

You don't need to know everything to do with the subject about which you are writing. Just a basic knowledge, and an interest in the topic, will suffice. There is an abundance of experts in nearly every field, and if your particular topic is an area in which expertise is not extremely common, chances are that the few experts present will be even more willing to interview with you in order to publicize their field.

While your dream interviews might include Leonardo DiCaprio, Arnold Schwarzenegger, and Demi Moore, you probably won't get these interviews unless you are writing for a high-profile magazine such as *Cosmopolitan* or *GQ*. However, if you are writing an article on, say, the movie *Titanic,* you don't need to interview the lead movie stars. How about contacting a member of the stage crew—someone who is often left out of interviews in favor of the bigger names? Such a person can often provide a unique insight into the filming of the movie that the big names could never give you.

So the next time you worry that you've taken on much more than you can handle, sit back, relax, and hunt down some experts. Chances are that with expert quotes and commentary, you'll wow the editors of the publication, and encourage them to accept your next story idea as well. Good luck!

Chloe Osborne is the editor-in-chief of The O_zon (www.theozon.com) and former Nonfiction Editor of *Deeply Shallow.* Her most recent e-book is "How to Become a Good Public Speaker," available at Booklocker.com (www.booklocker.com/bookpages/cosborne.html).

CROSS-CULTURAL CONNECTIONS

Presenting a more inclusive view

by Aly Colón

Articles and essays published in magazines and newspapers sometimes resemble the character in the movie *Groundhog Day* who faces the same situation day after day after day. He wakes up at the same hour and embarks on the same series of events. The only excitement occurs when he tries to break the spell.

By default, many published stories, essays, interviews, and articles reflect a homogeneous view of the world (often from a primarily white, middle-class, heterosexual perspective). As writers, we need to find ways to break this spell of sameness and to present a broader, more inclusive vision of the world. By expanding our sources for interviews, story ideas, and expertise, and including a wider range of races, cultures, and socioeconomic groups, we enrich our writing and create articles that are more compelling.

'The more complete the picture, the greater the truth," says Keith Woods, who teaches professional journalists at the Poynter Institute for Media Studies. The more variety a writer can draw upon, the richer the content becomes, but finding diverse points of view means you have to make an effort to go outside your routine.

Here are ten questions to ask yourself when you are writing an article:

1. Who else might be affected by this story?

2. In what different way might they be affected?

3. Who might have a different point of view on this topic?

4. Who am I ignoring?

5. How can I challenge my assumptions about who/what I'm writing about?

6. What types of people am I leaving out of the story?

7. Why am I leaving them out?

8. Where can I go to find new sources or subjects for this story?

9. What other frame could I use to tell this story?

10. What would someone of a different race, ethnicity, class, gender, sexual orientation, age, ability, religion, political persuasion, education, or profession add to this story?

DIVERSE READING

Magazine articles

"Making Connections," *Quill* magazine, July/August 2000.

"The Push for Connections: Covering the Untold Stories," *Poynter Report*, Spring 2000.

Books

The Alchemy of Race and Rights: Diary of a Law Professor by Patricia J. Williams, 1991. Personal essays on exclusion, law, race, and rights.

Brotherman: The Odyssey of Black Men in America—An Anthology, edited by Herb Boyd and Robert L. Allen, 1996. Writings from African-American men such as Muhammad Ali and Cornell West.

Growing Up Asian American, edited by Maria Hong, 1993. Stories and essays about Asian-Americans and their experiences.

The Hispanic Condition: Reflections on Culture & Identity in America by Ilan Stavans, 1995. History, culture, and identity of Latinos in the U.S.

In the Spirit of Crazy Horse by Peter Matthiessen, 1992. An examination of Native Americans' struggles with the U.S. government.

Invisibility Blues: From Pop to Theory by Michele Wallace, 1990. Essays centering on the place of black women in American culture.

Roll Down Your Window: Stories of a Forgotten America by Juan Gonzalez, 1995. A collection of neighborhood stories by the *New York Daily News* columnist.

Sister Outsider by Audre Lorde, 1984. A collection of essays and speeches that address race, gender and lesbian issues.

Annie Nakao of the *San Francisco Examiner* suggests stepping out of your usual environment. "Take a tour of your own city to learn about its diversity. Use public transportation and walk around neighborhoods," she writes on the Poynter Institute's Web site.

Expand and nurture your sources, she adds. Reach out to people from different backgrounds who represent varied viewpoints and interests—neighbors, work colleagues, classmates, commuters, grocery store shoppers, church, synagogue, or mosque worshippers. Talk to people. Invite them for a cup of coffee. Eat lunch with them. Seek out their views of the world they live in. Ask them to tell you their stories. Share your stories with them.

Take notes, then or later, about what you learn. Get their names, phone numbers, e-mail addresses. You can follow up with them when you find a story that would benefit from their perspectives and knowledge.

Do the same with people you don't know: in a cab, on a bus, during a walk, on the subway or train, in a restaurant, at a bookstore.

Elizabeth Llorente of *The Record* (Bergen County, N.J.), who wrote about changing neighborhoods in that town, says you can learn a lot about a community at local ethnic dinners, community centers, or schools—places where people often speak more candidly.

Don't make generalizations about people based on their backgrounds, she admonishes. Be sure you contact several sources within a community to accurately represent a "variety of interests and viewpoints."

One of the most important things you can do is listen to people's stories. For example, I started a conversation with the taxi driver who was taking me to the Portland, Oregon, airport. She said she had been in the forefront of counterculture protests in the 1960s and had worked in politics and television. When I asked her how she came to drive a taxi, she hesitated a moment, then told me she was bipolar, which caused dramatic mood swings. Employers found it difficult to deal with her bouts of depression. That conversation presented a unique perspective on several topics, including mental illness.

If we want our writing to be more representative of the world we live in, we need to travel beyond the obvious, mainstream sources of information, observe, ask questions, be open to people from walks of life other than our own, and seek out their untold stories.

Aly Colón is a member of the ethics faculty of the Poynter Institute for Media Studies in St. Petersburg, Florida, and is a regular contributor to *The Writer*. He has a strong journalistic background, with stints at several large newspapers. Ethics and diversity are two of his special professional interests. This article first appeared in *The Writer*, March 2001.

HELPFUL WEB SITES ON DIVERSITY

Online articles on diversity
"The 5 Ws of Journalism from a Diverse Perspective,"
www.poynter.org/dj/tips/diversity/aly.htm
"Reporting on Race," www.poynter.org/ dj/060600.htm
"Diversity Wheel," http://poynter.org/dj/tips/vj/difference.htm
"Reporting Race," www.cjr.org/year/99/5/race.asp

Web sites
International Women's Media Foundation www.iwmf.org
Founded to strengthen the role of women in media around the world.

LatinoLink www.latinolink.com
Contains stories and photographs by Latino journalists from the United
States and Puerto Rico.

Maynard Institute http://www.maynardije.org
Features resources for increasing racial and ethnic diversity in news
coverage, staffing, and business operations.

National Association of Black Journalists www.nabj.org
Founded to promote and communicate the importance of diversity in
newsrooms.

National Video Resources/Viewing Race www.ViewingRace.org
Articles on independent media addressing race, diversity, and tolerance.

Native American Journalists Association www.naja.com
Formed to encourage, inspire, enhance, and empower Native American
communicators. Includes news articles, archives, and links.

News Watch Project http://newswatch.org
A project of the Center for Integration and Improvement of Journalism,
Francisco State University Journalism Department.

Poynter Diversity Resource File www.poynter.org/Research/div.htm
Lists articles and Web sites concerning diversity.

Unity: Journalists of Color www.unityjournalists.org
A coalition of four national minority journalism associations working to
inspire and motivate the nation's media to embrace diversity.

HOW TO RESEARCH AND WRITE NONFICTION FOR CHILDREN

by Susan Goldman Rubin

During the past few years I've discovered the excitement and satisfaction of researching and writing nonfiction for children—and getting it published. Many editors are looking for lively, nonfiction manuscripts ranging in areas from biographies to art, science, nature, history, and social issues. They want books for the youngest children as well as for middle-grade readers and young adults. The field is wide open. Yet many aspiring writers and experienced pros stick to fiction.

According to Steve Mooser, President of the Society of Children's Book Writers and Illustrators (SCBWI), the ratio of all children's books published is about 60 percent fiction to 40 percent nonfiction. So why not give nonfiction a try as a way of breaking in or as a new challenge?

Start by finding a subject that interests you. Perhaps it's a biography of an unsung hero or heroine. Or a historical incident that will be celebrated in the next two or three years. (Remember that it takes at least a year to produce a children's book from the time the contract is signed, and it may take another year to do the research and writing.)

Maybe you have an idea for a book that could fit into an existing series. This happened to me when I proposed my first nonfiction manuscript, a biography of architect Frank Lloyd Wright. I thought it belonged in a young adult series called First Impressions published by Harry N. Abrams; the editor agreed.

For me, finding the subject is a snap. I love art and feel passionate about sharing my enthusiasm with children, but you don't necessarily have to know everything about the subject you choose. In fact, part of the pleasure of writing nonfiction is in learning more about something or someone that you're greatly interested in. When I began researching my Frank Lloyd Wright biography, I wasn't even sure whether he had been born in the United States or Europe! But when our family set out for a repeat visit to Wright's Hollyhock House in Barnsdall Art Park, Los Angeles, I knew then that I wanted to do a book about him.

The next stop was the library to see what had been published and when. *The Subject Guide to Children's Books in Print* (now on the Internet) provides a list of titles and dates of publication. Perhaps a book on your topic came out many years ago and is now outdated. Maybe books on your subject were for an older age group but had never been done as a picture book for young readers. See what's out there and come up with a fresh angle.

"Get the hook and you've got the book," said my editor at Holiday House when I told her I wanted to write more about architecture for middle-grade readers. I dimly remembered hearing in an interior design class that the Eiffel Tower had stirred up controversy when it was first built. Parisians had actually protested! Maybe there were more stories like that. So I came up with the idea for *There Goes the Neighborhood! Ten Buildings People Loved to Hate*. (A catchy title helps, too.) The trick was to find nine other stories like the one about the Eiffel Tower, and to feature different kinds of buildings throughout the world.

It is possible to sell a nonfiction book without having completed it. What you have to do is write the proposal, and sometimes an outline and sample chapters. Caroline Arnold, author of more than 100 nonfiction books for children, calls this stage becoming a "temporary expert."

Include a partial bibliography of the materials you've consulted so far. If you're planning a book illustrated with vintage photographs, or reproductions of art, find out what the pictures may cost. Make some calls and state sample prices in your proposal to reassure your intended publisher that permissions for illustrations will be affordable. Some houses do their own photo research, but I prefer doing it myself.

Unless you already have a publisher who has expressed interest in your project, it's acceptable to send out multiple queries or proposals. Consult the list of book publishers in a recent issue of *The Writer* magazine. See who's looking for nonfiction for the age group you're targeting, and send your proposal to more than one house.

If and when an editor shows serious interest, you have to buckle down and start researching in earnest before even writing your first draft. Read everything you can find about your subject—books, magazine articles, newspaper clippings—whether written for adults or children. The bibliographies of other authors' books often contain good leads for further reading. Look at videos. Listen to CDs. Immerse yourself! Keep a big box for the project and toss in anything you come across that may be useful. It's amazing how newspapers seem to print stories with just the information you need when you're doing a book. And who knows? You may come up with an idea for your next book. Be alert to other possibilities.

Make a list of your sources. Note the libraries from which you borrowed materials so that you can find them again. If you come across quotations that you may want to use, jot down the names of the publications and page numbers. Some authors keep this information on index cards. Others use their computers. I confess to being less well-organized and have suffered for it when frantically searching through my scribbled notes to find sources of quotes.

All of this research is called "secondary." But *primary* research means visiting a site, conducting interviews, and reading letters and diaries.

When I started work on a biography of photographer Margaret Bourke-White, I went to the University of Syracuse to examine their archives. There were more than one hundred boxes of prints, writings, correspondence, notes, personal documents, and memorabilia such as cameras, lenses, and scrapbooks! Where to begin?

Fortunately, I had received a description from the Syracuse archivist of Bourke-White's papers so I had a chance to browse through and make some preliminary choices.

Next I made many phone calls and talked to people who had known Bourke-White: her nephews, who manage her estate; her sister-in-law, who took care of her during the last months of her life; and numerous photographers, reporters, editors, and assistants who worked with her at *Life* magazine. Although most of these interviews amounted to only a few lines of text, they gave me fresh insights into facets of Bourke-White's personality. I even consulted with a professional photographer who set up an old fashioned 8″ x 10″ view camera like the one Bourke-White used so that I could better understand the technical problems she faced when taking pictures.

The research can become absorbing and costly, so it's important to know when to stop researching and start writing. After all, you want to honor the deadline set in your contract and turn in your manuscript on time.

In nonfiction as well as in fiction, the principles of good writing apply: clarity, simplicity, liveliness. Trust your own voice. Write your manuscript as if you're talking directly to the readers. Organize the material into a sequence that makes sense. Follow your outline. If it's a biography, a chronological order works best.

Most nonfiction writers try to use storytelling techniques—that is, they present their information with a beginning, middle, and end. Anecdotes and scenes dramatize events and grab the readers' interest. Quotations help bring characters and situations to life. In writing about architect Philip Johnson's Glass House in New Canaan, Connecticut, for *There Goes the Neighborhood!* I quoted from an interview with him. When I asked Mr. Johnson how he felt when his neighbors criticized his design, he chuckled and said, "I rejoice in rejection."

> The research can become absorbing and costly, so it's important to know when to stop researching and start writing.

When you've completed your manuscript, go over it and see if it flows smoothly. Read it from start to finish. Is it too long? Does it need cutting? Have you repeated certain words, phrases or stylistic devices (such as parentheses) too often? If you're using quotations, have you copied them accurately? Are events presented in correct chronological order?

Your bibliography may include a list of video cassettes, sound recordings, and Websites, as well as the dates of those expensive phone interviews. Place an asterisk next to works suitable for children. Finally, write the introduction. One of my editors says that the best time to do this is after the whole book is done. Only then do you have a clear sense of what you wanted to say and what the book is about. Perhaps it needs a personal note to explain why you decided to write it in the first place.

Now your manuscript is ready to send off. This doesn't mean it's finished. Your editor will be going over it, flagging pages, and asking questions that will send you scurrying back to the library, and studying your original notes in order to come up with the answers. You may disagree with some of the editor's suggestions. It's your book, and you have the right to keep what you feel belongs and omit what you think doesn't fit. But everyone wants the best book possible. As one copyeditor told me after I had to wade through hundreds of her notes and Post-It flags without fainting, "We only want to make *you* look good."

At last the manuscript goes back to the publisher and gets set into type. Meanwhile, you clear your desk, pay your overdue library fines, and start researching your next nonfiction book for children.

Susan Goldman Rubin is an award-winning children's author who writes both fiction and nonfiction. Her biography, *Frank Lloyd Wright*, won a 1996 award from the New York Public Library, and her most recent work, *Margaret Bourke-White: Her Pictures Were Her Life*, recently received a Smithsonian Notable Book for Children Award. Ms. Rubin also teaches at the UCLA Extension Writer's Program.

ADVENTURE TRAVEL WRITING

Take the reader along

by Martha Sutro

Our Camelbaks bulging, we pedaled out onto the Mongolian steppe, each of us choosing one of a dozen dirt tracks threading through the long, waving grass. Five hundred and sixty miles northwest of the markets of Ulan Bator, Mongolia's capital, we had entered the Asian outback from the town of Mörön, the nine of us feeling like the luckiest mountain bikers alive. [Excerpt from "Destinations: Mongolian Heights" by Martha Sutro in *Outside,* July 2000.]

Biking across Mongolia on an assignment for *Outside* magazine was one of the most rigorous and exhilarating experiences I've had. But when it comes to adventure travel writing, the trip itself is only part of a challenging journey that begins with selling your idea to an editor, who probably has hundreds of similar queries, and ends with a glossy feature spread.

While the interest in reading about travel adventures is growing (you'll find dozens of magazines devoted to the subject at your local bookstore), it's not an easy market to break into. Researching and writing such stories also poses unique challenges.

Your level of physical skills should match the assignment. For example, a recent issue of *National Geographic Adventure* featured stories on rafting and scuba diving in Australia and another on climbing to a remote mountaintop hotel in China. Gathering information, interviewing people, and taking notes while you're on a trip often requires special care.

Here are a few things I've learned while writing for *Outside, Women Outside,* and *Sports Illustrated for Women.*

Research Before the Pitch

You've heard it before, but it bears repeating: Do your groundwork before calling an editor, so you can back up your story idea with information. Study the magazine's contents from cover to cover. Libraries and bookstores are a good place to start. Travel guides, especially those with a unique slant, such as the Lonely Planet series, can be excellent resources. Interview people who have gone to the place where you will be traveling.

To prepare for the Mongolian trip, I interviewed people who had worked and traveled there, including a grasslands expert who had headed USAID projects in the Gobi Desert and an old friend who had mountain biked in Mongolia.

When you've done your background research and organize your materials, you're ready to make the pitch. Write a proposal that's clear, informed, and assures the editor that you're the best person for the job. Pitch clearly in the first sentence: "Dear Mark: I'd like to propose a story on the first all-female team to dog-sled to the North Pole."

If you're too slow in getting to the point, the editor might dismiss your idea. Capture the essence of the article in one paragraph and include some of the unusual details you've come across in your research. Perhaps you have a wonderful quote about the destination that can set the tone, or you've learned of a little-known region that you want to explore. Your proposal should demonstrate that you are knowledgeable about travel and the area.

If your idea is rejected, don't give up. It's likely you just won't hear one way or the other. Until you get a "no thanks," you still stand a chance of getting a "yes," so stay in touch.

When I had the opportunity to take a mountain bike excursion in a new national park in Mongolia, I pitched the story to several prestigious adventure magazines. I got a bunch of "maybes," and as the trip's departure date drew closer and closer, I started to see a missed opportunity the size of Africa on my horizon. I pulled out a copy of *Outside,* the magazine I really wanted to write for, looked up editors' names on the masthead, called the editorial number, and went down the list until someone picked up the call. When I finally reached an editor, I watched the clock, knowing I had about 30 seconds to get my idea across. To assure the editor that I could handle the logistics of such a big trip, I mentioned other places I had traveled in Asia and offered to send clips from previous articles. Finally, the editor said "yes."

> "Dear Mark: I'd like to propose a story on the first all-female team to dog-sled to the North Pole."

Throughout the process, I remembered a helpful adage: "You have to increase your rate of failure in order to increase your rate of success." You have to be willing to put yourself out there.

Your research gives you some idea of what you might find on your trip, and the editor outlines what he or she wants, but some of your experiences will be different from anything you imagined.

The *Outside* editor wanted the article to focus on biking conditions across the Mongolian steppe. It was an unexpected September snowstorm that gave me some of the best images of the trip and also clearly conveyed the quality of the bike riding.

> We strung out in Technicolor shapes on the gray and brown hills and spent the first four days in sunny, clear weather. Then, on the afternoon of our fifth day, we left the rolling grasslands and felt the chill of the Saridag Mountains ahead. Melted snow and frost turned our ascent into a slushy mess, and snowflakes soon blanketed our helmets.

Keeping track of sensations, sights, sounds, and atmosphere as you go along will help when you write the story later, but taking notice and gathering background materials in the midst of your adventure isn't always convenient. Packing a few key items helps. Bring a couple of notebooks (I prefer reporter-size or black-and-white composition notebooks), your camera, and a tape recorder. Use the tape recorder to capture sounds, such as music or a crowded marketplace, that will help you relive the experience later, when you are ready to write about it. If you've got a tough laptop computer, bring that too, but not in place of notebooks. Bring extras of everything and plastic bags to protect your notebooks or to store small items you pick up along the way—such as grass and leaf samples, beer labels, and receipts.

Travel reporting is a great training ground for the underrated art of scribbling. The back of an airplane ticket is the perfect place for a string of adjectives describing the tarmac and fog at the airport. A notation on the back of a receipt for a soda jogged my memory of the vendor who sold it to me. A few words to a song can evoke the smell or atmosphere of the place where you heard it.

Keep all your receipts, whether you're intending to use them for reimbursements or not. The names of the places where you stopped can trigger your memory. "Narayan's" printed on a thin, gray receipt recalls the upstairs floor of the famous Katmandu restaurant, its windows open to the noise of rug vendors, traveling climbers, and the pitch of car horns below.

Receipts, scraps of cloth, sometimes a blade or two of grass, coins, strange pamphlets that I can't necessarily read, bus tokens—these are my notes. A couple of cigarettes vividly remind me of a dusty corner of a cafe where two, Mongolian nomads offered me a smoke.

I also note temperatures and temperature changes, the sound of skis on snow in the morning—and then that same sound in the evening, the number of hours I slept at night, what I ate for each meal, which direction the wind blew, and whether that wind rocked four or 20 boats in a harbor. I write in guidebooks (often my notes cover the title page) and on maps. Lists, quotes, vignettes, schedules, recipes, images, hand-drawn maps, and sketches—these are the contents of my trip journals. It usually takes me a day or two to sift through the piles of information I accumulated.

To help me visualize my experiences, I follow a popular practice that I learned from poet friends—writing 10 to 15 images a day. At the end of a long and sometimes very physical day of climbing, rowing, biking, picking cherries, or switching buses five times, the prospect of jotting down a few lines can be more appealing than writing a narrative of the day's events. Here are some notations I made while trekking in Mongolia:

> A lone Mongolian nomad, riding a rickety old one-speed bicycle up the river wash ahead of us, picks his way around four boulders while the trees blow back the wind all around and above him.

> Six oxen pulling a cart loaded with a dismantled yurt. The bridge they're crossing, creaking, and M.C. and I standing beneath them on the river shore, holding our fishing rods in above the current.

Armed with your notes and memorabilia, you need to make one more stop before heading home. Visit a good bookstore and collect some local guidebooks, which will give you a feel for the residents' view of their city or country.

Coming Home and Writing

Once you're home and ready to write, it's the details that give life to your piece and help you recapture on the page your passion for travel and the places you've been. Readers are looking for an experience, not just a list of places. Try to get across the element of mystery and excitement you feel in a foreign setting.

I relish being in a place outside the familiar grid and away from a routine schedule, where every sense is heightened. The mountains seem loftier, the people more complex, the storms more intense than in familiar surroundings.

I try to give the reader an idea of what it's like to be the stranger. When I visit a new country, city or region, I enjoy reinventing myself. As a writer, I try to capture this transforming aspect of travel, and once the story is finished, I'm ready to browse the atlas in search of my next adventure.

Martha Sutro is a teacher and editor in Brooklyn, New York. An accomplished adventure traveler, she has contributed stories to magazines such as *Outside* and *Sports Illustrated for Women*. A recent essay was published in the book *Out on the Wild Blue*.

WRITING FOR COUNTRY MAGAZINES

by Linda Batt

Country life is a popular subject covered by an ever-increasing number of publications, ranging from local newsprint weeklies to glossy national magazines. Somewhere in that range is a market just right for your material, even if you don't live on a ranch in the middle of Montana.

Here are stories you can sell.

1. How-To

Country magazines cover a wide range of practical material. The list of subjects is endless: setting up a kitchen garden, drying herbs, keeping recipes organized, saving energy, reusing plastic grocery bags, marketing strawberries, reducing tick problems, ridding your dog of skunk odor, and so on.

Magazines don't want articles pulled from a book; they want firsthand tried-and-true how-to pieces. If you aren't knowledgeable on a particular subject, you can still write by reporting on someone else who is.

I wrote an article for *Back Home* on growing beans for drying. I'd never even put a seed in the ground, but a friend of mine grew them organically and sold them to local co-op stores. An interview with my friend gave me all the information I needed and an expert to quote. The article had the added benefit of giving my friend some mail-order business.

2. Personal Experiences

If you live in the country or have a country memory, your experience might have sale value. Magazines like *Country, Farm and Ranch Living, Country Woman,* and others often include humorous or touching personal stories.

They can be current happenings or past episodes.

A humorous story I wrote about our Christmas tree choose-and-cut business found its way into a December issue of *Country*. I wrote another story about starting our tree plantation for *Farm and Ranch Living*.

3. Country Characters

Do you know anyone in a rural area doing something heroic, unusual, or artistic? They can become the subject of a manuscript.

Country magazines always like to publish stories about remarkable characters.

For example, Kermit Sexton trains oxen. He lives in the house where he was born and works oxen on his land, just like his father and grandfather did.

At local fairs and festivals, he uses his animals to give a history lesson for youngsters. *Rural Heritage* bought my story on him.

4. Interesting Animals

A unique breed, an animal with an outstanding performance record, a funny "character," the extreme loyalty of a horse or dog, and many other animal tales can be sold in this market.

I wrote a wonderful little piece on Duke, a canine so loved in Shepherdstown, West Virginia, that he was made the official town dog.

5. Crafts and Kitchen Tips

There are entire magazines on country crafts, and almost every general country publication carries at least some tips.

Even *Bee Culture*, a magazine just for beekeepers, prints recipes that use honey.

Some very marketable subjects might cover crafts of a region or recipes from a rural community. Pie-baking for the county fair is a hundred-year-old tradition and a good topic for an article. The women, their recipes and the pride of winning could all go into the mix.

Country magazines often prefer personal articles. If you've studied journalism and had the "I" stamped out of your reporting, you need to relearn the art of telling from the first person.

6. Travel

Articles on unusual country spots to visit can always find a market. I didn't bother to write about the Grand Canyon when I visited, but the out-of-the-way places with some real appeal will always catch an editor's eye. I sold an article to *Northeast Outdoors* on the winter carnival in Saranac Lake, New York. It's a folksy festival in the Adirondack Mountains that's just plain, old-fashioned fun.

Getting Started

You see, even if you live in a large city, you can have a story idea or two that's knee-slapping good. Why not turn those ideas into a manuscript?

Start by reading as many country magazines as you

can find in your local library or at your corner newsstand[or see listings later in this book]. Reading will help you decide on a topic and match the topic to a likely market. Make a list of subjects, and under each subject make a note of the magazines you think might buy the article.

Next, write an article or two. Many freelancers query first and work only on assignment, but trying your hand at a manuscript gets you into the swing of things. Several magazines such as *Country* and *Farm and Ranch Living* won't consider queries. They want to see the completed manuscript, so the practice could end in a first sale.

Adopt the style of the publication. You'll find that writings about rural areas often includes descriptive passages about nature. Helen Henderickson begins an article on hunting wildflowers with: "Winter loosens its icy grip, and spring waits for its cue with silent anticipation." Jo Northrop starts "Cherishables," an article she wrote for *Country Living*, by saying: "Here in North Carolina, when the wind moans at the corners of the house and you're not sure from one minute to the next whether to toss another log on the fire or turn off the heat entirely, you know it's March."

Country magazines often prefer personal articles. If you've studied journalism and had the "I" stamped out of your reporting, you need to relearn the art of telling from the first person. Henderickson's article on wildflowers continues with: "Meeting a new wildflower is much like making a new friend. I like to learn its name and face so I'll recognize it if I see it again."

Northrop talks about filling her mottled brown Rockingham pitcher with spring jonquils before she tells about collecting the pottery. When you open an issue of *Country*, you'll have a hard time finding an article that isn't written in the first person.

Here are the lead sentences to three articles: "I'll never forget the root cellar on our farm." "One of my favorite country things would have to be my mother's apron." "Green and gold flow from our front door out through the widening mouth of a box canyon." This may not always be true, however, so be sure to do your homework.

Whether the article is personal and descriptive or scientific and factual, if you are writing for a country publication, the material ought to be easy to read and understand. Sentence structure should be short and information to the point. John Vogel, editor of the *American Agriculturist*, says his readers are busy and his articles are becoming more condensed. "Tell the reader why the material is important to him and then give him the facts," he advises.

The lead to a recent how-to piece in *American Agriculturist* follows his directions: "Turning sap into syrup and marketing it are jobs many farmers with woodlots don't have time for. But there are two less-involved ways of making a profit from maple trees."

Country publications love anecdotes. Humorous, warm touches often help sell a manuscript. Michael Leisher begins his article in *Country*, "He Discovers the Wave of the Future," with an anecdote about his uncle. Then he continues, "The lesson my uncle taught me that day remains fresh in my mind."

With suggestions for subject and style in mind, it's time to write and send out an article. Adhere to the standard format for manuscripts and write a brief, informal cover letter. Include a stamped, self-addressed envelope, and then sit back and wait for acceptance.

Linda Batt freelances from her farm in Rensselaer Falls, New York. Recently, her work has appeared in *Country, Farm and Ranch Living, Adirondack Life, BackHome,* and *Rural Heritage.*

END PIECES:
HAVING THE LAST WORD

Break into the big time with
a point of view that's all yours

by Ruth Smalley

A rapidly spreading development in magazines is offering a wide-open opportunity to new as well as established writers.

Nonfiction writers yearn to express themselves in creative essays—but often the bread-and-butter articles that sell are "just the facts, ma'am": how-to instructions; profiles of interesting and/or famous personages; and travel advice—from hidden weekend getaways to the lure of the Himalayas. Sometimes they can be personalized; sometimes editors don't want first-person pieces at all.

And yet factual writers do, now and then, have something that needs saying. You may have been told that you need to establish your writing reputation first, and then you can persuade editors and readers to listen to your personal voice. But it's not true. At least it's no longer the only truth. Increasingly, magazine editors are looking for opinion pieces from writers ranging from the well known to the wannabes who have no publishing record.

Where can you find the editor who wants to hear what you have to say about national problems or what a walk in the woods means to you? Almost everywhere.

This phenomenon is the essay page—often the last page or the "end piece"—popular in many periodicals. These usually run to 1,000 words or so and provide the writer with space to express his or her point of view. Here are some examples:

Newsweek led this trend with its standard "My Turn" column, which runs in the front of the magazine. One writer talks about the feelings of personal violation after a robbery. Another asks why people are no longer helping in volunteer groups. Someone comments on lawyers who win millions of dollars for frivolous suits—and keep most of it for themselves. What has happened, asks the

author, to civility? A retired executive ponders a new career that will offer satisfaction instead of power. While the magazine receives over 500 submissions
every month, it's worth trying: pay is $1,000 for each "My Turn" column.

Ladies' Home Journal uses intensely personal memoirs, such as: "How I Had
to Go Through Motherhood to Learn to Forgive and Relate to My Mother," or
"My Roommate's Tidy Closet and the Disaster That Was Mine." One writer
points out that good neighbors, not good fences, lead to tolerance and pleasant
living. Query the "First Person" editor with your column ideas.

Field & Stream's column, "Finally," at 750 to 800 words, is related mostly to
hunting and fishing, sometimes in a humorous vein. One writer spoke about the
thrill of hunting—an outing that leads to delight in nature and needs no trophies
for success. Another celebrated cross-generational delight in fishing.

The magazine is also interested in even shorter how-to pieces (75 to 150
words) and short pieces (up to 500 words) for their "Outdoor Basics" and
"Sportsman's Projects" sections. Other topics of interest are techniques for
hunting and fishing, and natural phenomena. In addition, their "Up Front" page
is open to news, humor, tips, and opinion pieces (25 to 400 words).

American Heritage puts "My Brush with History" right in the front of the
magazine. The editors stress quality writing from people who have experienced
such historical moments as an interaction with President Eisenhower or participation in battles during the Korean war.

They also publish a page toward the back called "Reader's Album" which
spotlights unusual, previously, unpublished old photos (be sure to send copies if
they're irreplaceable). They pay $100 per photo.

Family Fun's "last page"—actually located in the middle of the magazine—is
called "My Great Ideas." Articles here are typically about family interaction: kids
hand-painting a T-shirt for Grandpa, a parent arranging to spend special time
with just one child, a mother getting a friend to teach her child how to juggle.

The emphasis is on humor in *Smithsonian*. Its "Back Page," at 1,000 words or
so, ranges from tales of a mischievous childhood to a family of snorers. One
author bemoans his inability to remember names, and another nostalgically
recalls the old-time advertising signs along the highways of yesterday. Since only
one "Back Page" piece is used each month, the competition is keen. Payment is
$1,000 per article.

Good Housekeeping, currently being redesigned, has a page called "Light
Housekeeping" that features humorous prose and verse; for example, an article
on spoiling your dog even more than you did your kids. Some months feature
cartoons, witty remarks, and the occasional unusual photograph.

Several departments, including "The Better Way" (consumer advice) and
"Profiles" (inspirational women) call for 300 to 600 words and pay $1 per word.

If you like nature and lifestyle writing, *Mother Earth News* is the place for
you. One contributor to its back page, called "Last Laugh," compared
"designer" trees with the good old kind the writer lounged under. Another
described a trip to a county fair harness track.

Other departments include "Country Lore," "Bits & Pieces," Herbs and

Remedies," and "Energy & Environment," all offering downhome, practical information and solutions.

Southern Living considers itself a strictly regional magazine. Its back page, called "Southern Journal," is the only part of the magazine that accepts freelance material.

Articles are on Southern lifestyle and subjects, ranging from romantic literature for teenage girls to the pleasure of watching a night-blooming cereus come into flower. Pieces for "Southern Journal" run 800 words.

Occasionally, you'll find the warning: "We no longer accept unsolicited manuscripts." A few editors told me this isn't completely true. After all, you may be the undiscovered genius they've been waiting for.

So have a go at it. Break into the big time with a point of view that is your own. Eventually, this may give you the credibility to publish that longer feature article you'd like to write for the magazine of your choice.

Ruth Smalley is a columnist for the *Knoxville News-Sentinel* and has written articles for magazines such as *Highways, Coast to Coast, MotorHome, Mature Years,* and *Georgia Journal.* She has also authored several books about Tennessee life and people.

REVISIONS AND REWRITES

Good books are not written, they are rewritten

by Phyllis A. Whitney

Sometimes I think a fiction writer must get a story or novel down on paper before he can discover his true direction. What you may have written—however badly—is never wasted. Seeing it in written form, however rough, will set you on a surer course.

Remember: good books aren't written; they are rewritten. Revision is a key phase of your novel writing.

With short fiction pieces, it's advisable to put them aside and let them "cool" for awhile. Only then can you go back to your own work with a fresh and somewhat objective eye and catch a few of your mistakes. Though you'll never see them all. Fortunately, with a novel, when you've written your way through the last chapter, enough time will have passed so that you can return to the beginning with more objectivity. Though even then you can't be entirely objective.

Here are a few questions to help you check your own work during revision. This short list will help remind you of danger spots to watch for.

1. *Are the time and place of your action always clear?* Not only in the opening scene, where it's very important to orient the reader, but all the way through. Especially at the beginning of a chapter or a new scene.

2. *Are your characters consistent in their behavior?* This may be hard to achieve in the first drafts, when you'll lose track of what has happened earlier. Now you can watch for such detail as you read.

3. *Have you individualized your characters so that they aren't just types?* Is this done all the way through? Although you won't give a full description every

time an actor walks onstage, you do want to jog the reader's memory by repeating touches of description here and there. Readers like to visualize as the story continues.

4. *Have you given your settings some unique details that you refer to as the story goes on?* Just because you've described a room or an outdoor scene at the beginning, don't count on having your reader remember it later in the novel. Touch in a detail or two as a reminder, so that your story does not seem to move in a vacuum.

5. *Are there any characters onstage that you've forgotten about and left standing around without anything to do or say?* If you don't need them, get them off! If you do, use them, so the reader won't wonder what's happened to so-and-so.

6. *Does your main character have a strong drive that will keep building throughout the book?* Or is this character at least resisting something? If he or she wants nothing, or is not being threatened or thwarted, you'll have a weak story.

7. *Is there strong conflict to build interest?* If there is no trouble, no opposition, you have no story.

8. *Is your main character likable or hateable?* A single word can give an effect you never intended. Readers of popular fiction want main characters they can care about—though sometimes it is equally satisfying to watch someone you dislike get his (or her) comeuppance.

9. *Is a minor character steering the story in a wrong direction?* Side roads can intrigue a writer, but if they go nowhere, they'd better come out. In fact, this is the final test for any scene, any character, any ingredient of your story: If it can be dropped out and never missed, then it doesn't belong in the first place. A sound plot is like a Chinese puzzle—you can't leave anything out or the whole will collapse. A poorly plotted novel is like a freight train. Take out a car or two and the train will go right on running. If you can do that in a story, something is wrong.

> Are there any characters onstage that you've forgotten about and left standing around without anything to do or say?

10. *Consider your theme, the point you want to make: Are you preaching and lecturing the reader?* Have you made some sort of statement through your characters and story action without getting up on a soapbox? The author's voice is no longer heard in most of today's fiction. It's there, but it remains behind the scenes.

11. *If the gloom never ends, if threats are carried out too consistently, and there is no touch of hope to hold the reader, he will become discouraged and put the book aside.* The dangling of hope is the carrot to pull him along. So ask yourself if the setbacks are interlaced with hope.

12. *What about logic?* What about the motivation of your characters? Here it is very easy to deceive ourselves. We know that it's necessary to reach a certain point, and sometimes we bend our characters unnaturally to achieve this purpose. I call this "author's logic." Often it is illogical and impossible. If you examine the real motivations of your characters, you may need to figure out some other way to reach your goal. If you push your characters out of character, the reader will be annoyed.

13. *In writing a mystery or suspense novel, it is especially important to pick up every loose end you've dangled and explain it logically.* Readers hate loose ends. In your final reading, list such red herrings or question marks, so that you won't forget to clear them up before the end. Yet such explanation must never wind up in undramatic stretches of solid exposition.

14. *The first time around you can set everything down as roughly as you like.* Polish can come later—the hard part is getting it down. In revising, you will need to look at every word through a magnifying glass, watching for repetitions, for awkward phrasing (my favorite offense), for the wrong word that will give the wrong effect. And at this stage you will cut out the superfluous words as well.

15. *Have you tried for variety in every part of your story?* Variety in characters, of course, and in your action, your scenes. Variety also in the words you use, the length and arrangement of sentences and paragraphs. If you begin most of your sentences with a pronoun, a name, a subject, your writing will become monotonous. Rearrange these phrases.

In the end, it is the attention to hundreds of details that adds up to a successful novel. Don't try to be critical of yourself while you write. Forget the "rules." Lose yourself in the story, and let it flow. During revision you must become the critic. In the first writing, you give your story life. In the second, you get it right.

Phyllis A. Whitney knows revisions and rewrites. Her writing career spans more than 75 years and includes 70 novels and 100 short stories. Her work in the mystery genre has garnered numerous awards, including two Edgar Awards, the Agatha Award, and Grand Master of Mystery Writing. This article is condensed from a chapter in her excellent book on fiction-writing methods, *Guide to Fiction Writing* (*The Writer*, 1988)

Fiction Workshop

CHALLENGE AND IMPROVE YOUR WRITING

Revising your fiction manuscript

by John Dufresne

For every writer, the first draft is an act of discovery; then the real labor begins. Be ruthless. The story should improve with each revision. Make a list of your "obsessions." Challenge your characters to take responsibility for their actions. Read each draft closely, because you must find the solution to the problems in the story itself. You begin to write better than you thought you could. You fix the problem, a new one appears, you persevere, and write on. If you never revise, you never learn to write. You see that the made-up characters you have created have become vivid and intriguing people who live interesting, but often heartbreaking, lives. You begin to resent the time spent away from them.

I write many drafts longhand, because it slows me down, gives me time to think. I change sentences, words, phrases as I write, often recopying the entire annotated draft from the first line to the point at which the corrections get so messy and confusing that I have to stop and make a fresh copy. In this way, I get to feel the rhythm of the prose, hear the tone of the narrative voice.

When I'm finally satisfied that the elements of plot are in place and I think I know what my characters want, I type this draft into the computer. I print it out, then put the copy away for a few days. When I read it again, I immediately begin to tear it apart. What I couldn't see in the heat of writing usually becomes clear now. I see that a story that I thought was good can be made even stronger. I make the changes, wait, reread, and start over.

There are some common stylistic problems that you will want to address in each stage of revision or at some point before the manuscript is finished. The following checklist may help you do that. By "challenge," I mean take out the offending word or phrase, read the piece again, and only if the word or words in question are essential should you put them back in.

1. *Challenge every adverb.* Mark Twain said, "The adverb is the enemy of the verb." Often, what we need are not two words, one qualifying, thus weakening, the other, but one stronger word. Not "He walked unsteadily" but "He staggered." Adverbs modifying verbs of attribution are particularly intrusive and offensive. "'I see the problem,' she said confidently." Show us her confidence; don't tell us.

2. *Challenge every adjective.* Like adverbs, most adjectives are unnecessary. Often the adjectival concept is in the noun. A night is dark, an ache painful, a needle sharp. Color is often redundant, as in blue sky, green grass, and so on. Other adjectives are too conventional to be either vivid or significant, like a tender heart or a sly fox. An adjective should never be simply a decoration; it must always be essential.

3. *Challenge every verb with an auxiliary.* Replace passive voice verbs with active ones that are immediate, clear, and vigorous. "I kissed her" is better than "She was kissed by me"—and shorter. Also, replace progressive forms of verbs with the simple tenses: "I brewed coffee" indicates a more definite time than "I was brewing coffee." (On the other hand, be sure to use the past perfect tense if denoting an action completed before a time in the past: "My mother had already called the plumber by the time I arrived.")

4. *Challenge the first paragraph.* Sometimes the first paragraph helps get the story going, but often it merely introduces the reader to the story we are about to tell. Action may actually begin in the second paragraph.

5. *Challenge the last paragraph.* If the last paragraph unnecessarily summarizes or explains the meaning of the story, cut it out.

By "challenge," I mean take out the offending word or phrase, read the piece again, and only if the word or words in question are essential should you put them back in.

6. *Challenge every line that you love.* Delete every word that is there only for effect, every phrase you think is clever, every sentence for which there is no purpose or point. Your concern must be with the characters and not with your own wit or style. Check your list of "obsessions" and correct them. Watch for your "pet" words—"just," "very," and "that" are common offenders—and delete them if they're not essential. Or perhaps your first-person narrators do too much telling and not enough showing, or you tend to shift tenses needlessly.

7. *Challenge every exclamation point.* Like adverbs, they are intrusive.

8. *Be alert for every cliche or hackneyed word or phrase, every overused or unnecessary modifier.* If you've heard it often, don't use it.

9. *Cut every nonessential dialogue tag.* In a conversation between two people you may need only a single tag:

> "Doris, I'm home," Lefty said.
> "In the kitchen, dear. Did you remember the milk?"
> "Got it right here."

The new paragraphs clearly indicate who is speaking. When you're attributing dialogue, use "said" or "asked." Anything else focuses attention away from the dialogue.

10. *Eliminate those colloquial introductory words in dialogue, like "yes," "no," "well," "oh," etc.* What follows usually tells enough.

11. *Eliminate everything you're not sure of.* If you doubt whether a sentence, word, or behavior belongs, it doesn't.

12. *Read the draft aloud and listen for awkward and repetitious words, inadvertent rhyme, faulty rhythm.*

13. *Proofread for clarity, consistency, grammar, punctuation, economy.* And then proofread again.

Revision is not just a time to edit. It's a time to invent and surprise, to add texture and nuance. In writing fiction, you must be honest and rigorous. You cannot judge your characters or want to say something so much that you manipulate them, twist the plot, or ignore what their reactions and responses would be. You owe it to your characters to do justice to their lives. Revision continues until you feel that you have done all you can to make the story as compelling and honest as possible. Ask yourself if you care enough about these characters to put in the time, energy, and thought it takes to work a story into its best possible shape. If you quit, if you don't revise, then you don't care enough.

John Dufresne is a novel and short-story writer who has won acclaim in both categories. His novel *Louisiana Power & Light* received a *New York Times* Notable Book of the Year award. *The Boston Globe* called it "mordantly funny, insistently aural . . . you want to grab somebody by the elbow [and] say, 'Here, listen to this. . . !'" It is currently being made into a movie. Dufresne teaches at Florida International University. This piece is excerpted from his article "Revising Your Fiction Manuscript," which originally appeared in *The Writer*, November 1993.

THE POWER OF DIALOGUE

by Sol Stein

Dialogue is a language that is foreign to most writers of nonfiction and to many newcomers to fiction writing. It is also a triumphant language. It can make people unknown to the author cry, laugh, and believe lies in seconds. It is succinct, but can carry a great weight of meaning. In a theater, dialogue can draw thunderous applause from people who have paid heavily for the privilege of listening to it. At its best, as in Shakespeare's best, dialogue provides us with memorable—and beautiful—guides to understanding human behavior. Fortunately, the techniques of dialogue can be learned by writers eager to please their readers.

I'm lucky in having started out as a playwright, where the only words the audience hears are dialogue. It had better be good. When I write novels, I am tempted to use dialogue often. The minute characters talk, the reader sees them. And we know readers prefer to see what's happening, rather than to hear about it through narration. Not to be lightly dismissed are those white spaces on the page created by exchanges of dialogue. They make the reader feel the story is moving fast.

Dialogue is meant to be experienced by the reader, not studied. Halting over a line of dialogue can interrupt the reader's experience. It is important to understand that the reader perceives thoughts serially, one at a time, which is why dialogue that builds is so effective when characters fling sentences one after another, each adding to the force of the whole. Dialogue that is short, snappy, and punchy engages other characters as well as the reader.

Life is full of routine exchanges. "How are you?" "I am fine." "How's the family?" All those usual greetings are boring as dialogue, which thrives on surprise and indirection. For example:

> She: Hello there! How are you?
> He: On my way to jail.
> She: Good God, what are you planning to do?
> He: It's done.

This exchange raises more questions than it answers, and that is good. The main purpose of dialogue is to reveal character and to move a story along. The example obviously gets a story going.

Let's look at a simple example of dialogue that reveals character:

> She: I see you're feeling better.
> He: Since when can you see what I feel?
> She: I thought this was going to be a peaceful discussion.
> He: That was yesterday.

With only two lines for each character, it is safe to say that the woman is temperate and wants a harmonious relationship. The man is intemperate, difficult, and quick to anger.

Dialogue is at its best when it is confrontational and adversarial—either or both. Talk is an action. And when talk is tough and combative, it can be much more exciting than physical action. In that excitement, the writer is likely to make a mistake. He will take sides with one of the characters.

Does the writer take sides?

Indeed he does; he takes both sides and gives each its due. And here's a hint: If in a verbal duel you find yourself wedded to the beliefs of one of the characters, try your damnedest to make the other character win the argument. You won't succeed, but you should try to conceal your prejudices. It will make your exchanges far more interesting.

And here's a hint: If in a verbal duel you find yourself wedded to the beliefs of one of the characters, try your damnedest to make the other character win the argument.

Character most reveals itself in dialogue under stress. Stressed characters will blurt things out that they never meant to say. They can also be defensive, as in the following example:

I am not nervous, I just can't stand being called for jury duty. I walk into the courthouse, I think I'm the one that's on trial. For what? I've never even gone through a yellow light.

Characters also reveal themselves when they are angry. Example:

My missus and me been in this jammed waiting room for two solid hours. Not one person has been ushered in. What's the doctor doing? How many patients does a doctor need in his waiting room to satisfy his ego? Our kid, he was supposed to be picked up fifteen minutes ago. I can't phone the sidewalk outside the school, I've got to get out of here and leave the missus to hear the bad news of her tests all alone. Jesus, why can't these stethoscope generals keep appointments like other people?

The aim of dialogue is to create an emotional effect in the reader, and one of the things a writer has to learn is that dialogue may sound artificial when it is coherent and logical. You want thoughts that are loose, words that tumble out. In life, we try to avoid shouting because it shows that we are out of control. And we don't like it when other people shout at us. Someone else's anger makes us uncomfortable. Readers love shouting if the tone is carried by the words rather than by the author telling the reader that a character is shouting.

Shouting can be dramatic if anger is responded to by anger, but perhaps even more dramatic if the anger is met with an attempt to pacify or to resolve, especially if the anger continues. Listen to the supervisor in the following exchange:

"Don't you knock before you come in?"
"I'm sorry, I—"
"Can it. I've heard all the excuses, you blew your last chance, that's it."
"It wasn't my fault. Judy can tell you—"
"I don't want you involving Judy, George, Carey, anybody; it was you who didn't . . . look, I've had enough! Just pack, get your things, and get out of here."

Without the context, readers don't know who did what, but they get a sense of the supervisor's anger, not only from what he says, but also from the looseness of his disjointed comments. What comes across is the strength of his emotion, and to the extent that what he says seems unfair to the other person, the emotion transfers to the reader.

What can you say about the student below?

Teacher: Tell me about yourself.
Student: I'm just a boy.
Teacher: All the boys here are boys. What's different about you?
Student: Nothing, I have a mother and a sister and I do my homework every day.
Teacher: You left out your father.
Student: It's not my fault. He left himself out.
Teacher: Did you forget to mention him?
Student: He took off. He doesn't even phone.
Teacher: Do you know where he is? Can you get in touch?
Student: He isn't anywhere. He could be dead and I wouldn't know!

The boy is trying not to reveal to his teacher or classmates the secret thing that makes him different. When the boy is eventually forced to reveal it, the reader is immediately sympathetic toward him. A character who reveals not enough reveals much.

To sum up, a character reveals himself most readily when under stress, blurting things out, saying things in anger that are normally suppressed, saying not enough, saying too much.

Before you begin writing any new dialogue, know the purpose of the exchange. How will you orchestrate it to make it adversarial? If a conflict between the characters speaking already exists, does the exchange exacerbate that conflict or at least increase the tension between the characters? After completing an exchange, or when revising a scene, check to see if the lines spoken by each character are consistent with that character's background. Weed out any unnecessary words. Loosen stiff sentences. Substitute colloquial expressions for formal ones. And perhaps most important, check to see what's going on between the lines.

Three underused techniques for making dialogue interesting are as follows: showing impatience, conveying a misunderstanding between characters, and differing underlying attitudes that rise to the surface.

As a refresher, let's review some basic guidelines for dialogue:

1. *What counts in dialogue is not what is said but what is meant.*

2. *Whenever possible, dialogue should be adversarial.* Think of dialogue as confrontations or interrogations. Remember, combat can be subtle.

3. *The best dialogue contains responses that are indirect, oblique.*

4. *Dialogue is illogical.* Non sequiturs are fine. So are incomplete sentences, and occasional faulty grammar suited to the character.

5. *Dialogue, compared to actual speech, is terse.* If a speech runs over three sentences, you may be speechifying. In accusatory confrontations, however, longer speeches can increase tension if the accusations build.

6. *The use of misunderstandings and impatience in your characters' dialogue will help increase tension.*

7. *Characters reveal themselves best in dialogue when they lose their cool and blurt things out.*

8. *In life, adversarial or heated exchanges tend to be repetitive; in dialogue, such exchanges build.* In life, adversarial exchanges vent the speakers' emotions; in dialogue, such exchanges are designed to move a story forward.

9. *Avoid dialect.* It makes readers see words on the page and interrupts their feeling them.

10. *In dialogue every word counts.* Be ruthless in eliminating excess verbiage. All talk is first draft. Dialogue is not talk.

Sol Stein founded the book publishing firm of Stein and Day and served as its president and editor-in-chief for more than 25 years. Aside from editing and publishing such noted authors as Elia Kazan, Dylan Thomas, W.H. Auden, David Frost, and others, he is also an award-winning playwright.

THE SUPPORTING CAST IN YOUR NOVEL

by Barbara Delinsky

When I began fiction writing, I didn't have to think about minor characters and their role in a novel. In those days, I wrote 200-page novellas that were too short to allow for minor characters. That changed with my shift into full-length fiction. Suddenly my books were twice as long and twice as deep. They definitely called for a cast of characters that went beyond two or three stars.

So I began adding secondary characters. I had no formal training in creative writing, but common sense told me that the purpose of a supporting cast was to flesh out my hero and heroine by giving them lives independent of one another. To that end, I created parents who had raised those main characters, and siblings with whom they had grown up and competed. I created friends who shaped their early adulthood and former spouses who left them burned. I created children who affected not only their present, but their future.

In doing this, I instinctively applied the same rule that trial-and-error had taught me about fiction writing in general: Just as every scene has to have a purpose, so every character, no matter how minor, has to have a purpose. Tossing in a character solely for the sake of making a book longer is pure filler and unacceptable. Readers see through this ploy in no time flat—and feel cheated.

Looking back, now that I have over 60 full-length books to my credit, I can see method to my madness in creating a supporting cast. Minor characters add richness to a novel, no doubt about that, but there are dozens of ways in which they do so. For simplification's sake, I offer three general categories that describe what the supporting cast contributes: depth, breadth, and movement.

Movement

Let's start with movement, since it is the most obvious of the three. Minor characters are often introduced to propel a plot forward, and in this role, they serve a specific purpose: to provide information or create a complication; as a sounding board, to help a major character work through an emotional dilemma; as an all-out villain whose evil deeds must be answered.

Plots in which minor characters have a role are most often action-driven. Mysteries fall into this category, as do legal thrillers, westerns, science fiction. Of my own recent books, *A Woman's Place* does so, too.

In this first-person novel, the main character, Claire Rafael, is a successful businesswoman whose husband, Dennis, sues her for divorce, demanding sole custody of the children, possession of their house, and huge alimony. Much of the story centers on Claire's fight to regain custody of the children.

Most of the minor characters in *A Woman's Place* are tools for moving the plot forward. Carmen Niko, Claire's lawyer, sets the legal wheels in motion. Judge E. Warren Selwey hears the case and makes decisions that have a direct impact on the plot. Dean Jenovitz is the psychologist whose role it is to interview Claire and Dennis, gain insight into them, and make a custody recommendation to the court. Phoebe Lowe, as Dennis's lawyer and potential significant other, is responsible for many of Dennis's actions, to which Claire must then respond.

Breadth

A Woman's Place is more action-driven than some of my other novels. In *Three Wishes*, which I wrote immediately after it, minor characters serve a very different purpose: They bring breadth to the novel.

By breadth, I mean color—color, atmosphere, backdrop. *Three Wishes* is set in a small town in northern Vermont that itself is a vital part of the story. How to bring out the flavor of this oh-so-crucial-to-the-plot small town? Minor characters. They create the environment in which the major characters operate. Flash O'Neill, who owns the diner where the heroine works, adds the twist of modern chic that sets the tone of the town. Various regulars at the diner describe the businesses that keep the town solvent. Emma McGreevy, Eliot Bonner, and Earl Yarum represent the traditional, old-time triumvirate of power. Dotty Hale is the obligatory gossip; Julia Dean is the newcomer who illustrates the town's capacity for warmth; Verity Greene is the bohemian who pushes the town's limits of trust.

> The purpose of a supporting cast is to flesh out the hero and heroine by giving them lives independent of each other.

These minor characters add breadth to *Three Wishes* in the form of a physical environment, but minor characters can also add emotional breadth. This often takes the form of a sub-plot or two that echo—and hence reinforce—the major theme of the book.

My novel *Coast Road* is the best example I can give of the emotional element. It is the story of Rachel and Jack, artist and architect respectively, who have been divorced for six years, after ten years of marriage. When Rachel is in a near-fatal accident, Jack receives a middle-of-the-night call that brings him to her bedside and puts him in charge of their two teenage daughters. During 16 days of trying to coax Rachel out of her coma, he becomes immersed in an in-depth analysis of not only of his marriage, but of parenthood.

Loyalty—as in fighting for what matters most—emerges as a major theme in this examination. Loyalty is also the theme of several subplots driven by the supporting characters. Just as Jack comes to realize that he wasn't there emotionally for his wife during the later years of their marriage, he finds himself talking about loyalty with his 15-year-old daughter as she straddles a social crossroad; with his 13-year-old daughter, as she cares for her sick cat; and with his ex-wife's best friend as she tries to explain the deepest meaning of friendship. This echoing of the theme among the supporting cast helps Jack understand and resolve his own larger issue of loyalty.

Depth

Coast Road is also a good example of the third type of contribution minor characters can make—depth. Depth is crucial to novels like this that are heavily emotional and largely character-driven. The starring players in such novels must be three-dimensional. The supporting cast is instrumental in making them so.

Each supporting cast member is chosen to illuminate some aspect of the life or personality of a major character. In the case of family members, the illumination has to do with the passage of time. Family members share a history with the major character. Their thoughts and personalities help explain the "why" of the main character's behavior. They offer glimpses of the main character in childhood, adolescence, adulthood, and serve as a mechanism that allows the writer to reach into the past or imagine the future.

But depth has another dimension as well. Here, minor characters help round out a picture of the major characters in the present tense. These would be friends, neighbors, colleagues—all of whom, through words, action, or mere presence, say something about who and what the main character is as the story unfolds.

Again, *Coast Road* is an apt illustration. The female lead lies comatose for nine-tenths of the book. How, then, is her voice heard? This was the challenge I set for myself in writing the book. The answer? Through the supporting cast. Rachel may lie in a coma, but she remains the main character through a depth offered by her daughters, her best friend, her book group, her mother, and, yes, the husband she divorced six years before.

One of the questions I'm most frequently asked is whether I create the plot before the characters, or vice versa. A natural follow-up to that question is whether star players are created before the supporting cast. My answer to both questions is the same: It depends on the novel. The general assumption would be that major characters are created first, and minor characters are added as needed, rather like salt and pepper, for flavor; yes, this is what happens most often. But there are exceptions. I recently finished writing a book with another small-town setting, and I actually had half a dozen members of the supporting cast already chosen, while I was still grappling with the major theme of the book and, hence, the identity of the stars.

Neither way is right or wrong. What is wrong is if a writer gets so hung up on which should come first that he or she is stalled and can't write at all!

A note here on point of view. Some very successful writers brain-hop, relating the innermost thoughts of even the most peripheral minor character. I am uncomfortable doing that. For one thing, I like to write an entire scene from one point of view, that of the character with the most at stake emotionally. For another, I think that introducing so many diverse—and often irrelevant—elements dilutes the effectiveness of the emotions. Since my novels have become known for their emotional impact, this method is working for me. The bottom line is that you must think about what the strength of your book will be, and make point-of-view decisions accordingly.

Making the wrong point-of-view decision is but one of several dangers I would caution you against, where the supporting cast is concerned.

Another is introducing the supporting cast at the outset of the book, before you introduce a main character or two. Readers can be like ducklings. They will imprint on the first character they meet. If that character is a peripheral one, there will be confusion and a delay in their relating to the main character. Too long a delay, and the reader becomes detached emotionally, closes the book, and is lost.

Similarly, if the supporting cast is so much more likable than the leading players that readers don't care about the leading players, they won't read on, you've lost them. If part of your plot makes the good guys look bad for a while, that's fine, but keep in mind that you walk a tightrope. The reader has to care what happens. If your supporting cast can make the reader care enough to keep reading until the major characters pick up the ball, your problem is solved.

Conversely, a minor character who is overly loud, bad, quirky, or glaring may divert the reader's attention from the flow of the plot. I call this the "cauliflower breast" issue, named after a love scene I once read, a beautifully lyrical piece in which the author suddenly likened the heroine's breast to cauliflower. That stopped me short, ice water on any passion I might have imagined. Jarring minor characters can have the same effect. Keep in mind that every minor character must have a role in supporting the major characters. If the jarring has a definite purpose, it may work. If, however, you have simply created a wonderfully weird minor player on the spur of the moment, think twice about it. Such a player may drag the reader too far afield, and might best be saved for its own starring role.

> Readers can be like ducklings. They will imprint on the first character they meet.

Those caveats aside, I can't stress strongly enough the positive role that the supporting cast can play. Alone, a major character is like the right hand picking out single notes on a piano. The notes may have rhythm and a tune; in the hands of a maestro, they may even have feeling and heart. But the tune remains largely one-dimensional until a second player, the left hand, joins in. When that left hand picks out single notes of a complementary theme, you have a pleasant duet. Add chords by either or both hands, and you have a full-bodied song. The supporting cast in a novel supply the notes in those chords. They shouldn't overpower, jar, or bore. Used to their fullest, they turn a song into a song that is beautiful, meaningful, and memorable.

Barbara Delinsky has written and published more than 65 novels since 1980. She started in the field of romance, and then moved into mainstream fiction with such major successes as *For My Daughters, Together Alone, A Woman's Place, Three Wishes,* and *Coast Road.* More than 25 million copies of her books are in print.

CREATING CHARACTERS FOR CHILDREN'S BOOKS

How can I make my protagonist more three-dimensional?

by Lee Wardlaw

Q: I've received several rejection letters on my first middle-grade novel. Each editor commented that I have a good story idea, but that my main character, a 12-year-old girl, is too one-dimensional. What does this mean, and how can I fix it?

A: Sounds like your protagonist is suffering from a severe case of Paper Doll-itis! Meaning, she's all dressed up with no place to go. She may look pretty on the outside, but there's not much on the inside: she's a flat cut-out with no personality, no values, no goals, no problems.

To create an interesting, unique, three-dimensional story, you must have a full understanding of your characters. In other words, you must understand their motivations: the values that move them to action. At the end of a story, you, your readers—and your editor!—should always know why the characters acted as they did. I recommend using a Character Questionnaire, like the one below, to help you flesh out *all* your characters, and to help you explore the possible "whys"—as well as the "whats"—of their personalities. Here are some of the questions you might wish to ask:

A Character Questionnaire

1. *Personal stats:* What is your character's name? Does she like it? Why or why not? Does she have a nickname? Who gave it to her? What is her birthdate and her birthplace? Do these affect her in any way? Dian Curtis Regan, the author of more than 30 books for young readers, wrote a marvelous short novel called *The Class with the Summer Birthdays*, about a third grade girl who never gets to celebrate her special day at school because her birthday is in July.

2. *Personal Appearance:* height, weight, hair color, etc. My novel *Alley Cat* focuses on the self-esteem problems of a high school girl who towers over in the tallest boys at school.

3. *Voice/speech patterns:* Is your character's voice sultry? Squeaky? Husky? Does your main character, perhaps, stutter? Why? Does your character have an exuberance toward life that causes her to ALWAYS SPEAK IN CAPITAL LETTERS? In my novel *101 Ways to Bug Your Parents*, one of the minor characters desperately wants to become a famous French pastry chef, even though he was born in Oklahoma. He speaks constantly in a phony French accent, which has kids rolling in the aisles.

4. *Habits/Gestures:* Does she bite nails? Pick split ends? Have any favorite expressions or slang words?

5. *Dress/style:* Is it preppie? New age? Garage sale? Saks? Heavy metal? What does this character's dress style say about her personality? Why does she dress the way she does?

6. *Description of home:* Physical, mental, emotional atmosphere. Does your character live in a trailer park? Apartment? Home? Is she homeless? How does this affect her?

7. *Parents/siblings:* Personalities and relationships, i.e., how do they get along? Are the parents divorced? Is there a grandparent living in the home?

8. *Educational background (plus worst and best subjects):* My first published book, *Me + Math = Headache*, was popular because the main character constantly flunked math tests.

9. *Work experience and skills:* Does she have an after-school job? Dishing up ice cream or flipping burgers?

10. *Handicaps:* These are not necessarily physical; they can be psychological. In *101 Ways to Bug Your Parents*, one minor character suffers from hiccups 23 hours a day, as a way to get attention from his hectic family.

11. *Hobbies*

12. *Pastimes:* What does your character like to do after school? On Saturdays?

13. *Pets (or is your character allergic to animals?)*

14. *Favorite colors/music/books/movies/TV shows/foods*

15. *Humor:* wry, sarcastic, silly, etc. What makes your character laugh?

16. *Best friend:* Why is this person special? What characteristics do they share? Have they ever had a falling out? What caused it?

17. *Enemy:* Why does the character hate this person, or vice versa?

18. *What is important to this person, and why?*

19. *Basic nature or outlook on life:* Optimistic? Pessimistic? Jealous? Cheerful?

20. *Ambitions/dreams:* What does she want to be when she grows up . . . or what does she want to be or do in the next 15 minutes?

21. *Philosophy of life*

22. *Fears/inhibitions:* Afraid of the dark? Of heights? Too shy to talk to boys?

23. *Heroes:* Whom does the character look up to, and why?

24. *Boyfriend/girlfriend*

25. *Present problem:* How will it get worse? How will it be resolved?

26. *Strongest/weakest character traits (as seen by you, the author, or by the main character, or by her friends)*

27. *Why is your character worth writing about?* (Remember, if *you* don't care about your character, neither will your readers.) How or why is this character different from other similar characters?

28. *Do I like/dislike this character and why?* Will readers react the same way?

29. *Will this character be remembered and why?*

30. *What is something the character has done that she/he is very proud of?* Ashamed of? Embarrassed about?

Last but not least, ask yourself: What does my character want more than anything in the world? Why does she want it? And how will it be attained?

Granted, you're not going to find room in your story for all the answers to these questions. But the more you know about your characters, the more they will become real, live people—to you and to your readers.

Lee Wardlaw is the author of more than 20 books for young readers, ranging from picture books to young adult novels. Winner of seven Reader's Choice Awards, her recent books include: *We All Scream for Ice Cream: The Scoop on America's Favorite Dessert* (HarperCollins); *Saturday Night Jamboree* (picture book, Dial/Penguin Putnam); and *My Life As a Weirdo* (middle-grade novel, Troll).

Fiction Workshop

WRITING THE HISTORICAL MYSTERY

How to accurately put your characters
into a place and time

by Anne Perry

Attending writers' conferences is almost always enjoyable, and at the best of them one may learn a great deal. For me, most of it has come from two sources: One is listening to others, sometimes writers, sometimes editors or agents. The other is in being asked questions, and having to think of the answers. Other people have a great gift for putting their finger on the hole in your argument, or the gap in your self-knowledge. It obliges you to think, and the courtesy that people will listen obliges you to be as honest as you can.

Doing Research

As a writer of historical mysteries, I am most often asked this question: "Where do you do your research?"—to which the answer is mostly in books. Looking at clothes, places, artifacts can be helpful, but they are only the dressing, the props, for a scene. You need to know about people more than things. By all means have the feel, the smell, and the sounds correct. Never use even the most trivial inventions before their time. Note especially those that we take for granted: fabrics, pens and paper, postal systems, forms of heating, transport, spectacles, etc. Medicine is a great key to a period; so is food. It is remarkable how choice and taste have widened with refrigeration and flight, not to mention education and immigration.

But far more than material things, I think one should research beliefs, values, and attitudes of mind. A present-day mind in a period costume is not a historical story. Ask yourself a few questions about the period you are working in. For example, what were political expectations? Had anybody even imagined "one man vote," let alone women's rights? Few people are outraged by lack of what they have not ever imagined having. We take one step of progress at a time. No 1990s consciences in 1890—or 1790!

What did people, particularly women, hope from marriage? And what did they reasonably expect? Again, not 1990s: equality, freedom, or constant romance. But perhaps greater loyalty, to be protected (or suffocated) from certain unpleasant realities.

What medicines were available? But more important, what diseases were endemic, what were the usual sanitary conditions? What knowledge or ignorance was there about infection, childbirth, contraception, even anatomy and physiology?

What were people afraid of? What did they hope for, dream of? What embarrassed them or made them laugh?

Many of the facts you find will be the same as today, which is how you make the readers identify with your characters. Other facts are different—which is where your exploration begins.

How much of your research do you include, and how do you know what to leave out? I think one of my greatest mistakes (which I have now recognized, and, I hope, addressed) was somehow to weave in everything that interested me, and that was far too much.

Anyone who wishes to read a social history will buy one. What a novelist is aiming for is a drama about people who happen to have lived in another time, and possibly another place.

About Plot

The single most important thing I know about plot, again discovered through constructive criticism from others, is that all characters must have a reason for everything they do (and "because the author needs them to" is not a reason). The questions to ask yourself are—"would you do that if you were in their place?" and "why?"

Every scene must have a purpose. "It was a great event in history—I would love to have been there" is not a purpose. It was one of the most consistent mistakes I made. I hope I have learned not to repeat it, but I am still tempted! I can feel myself slither toward the precipice. How can you resist a royal execution, a great betrayal, the meeting of two figures who will become lovers, or enemies who destroy a nation? You had better resist it, if they have nothing to do with your story!

You need to know about people more than things. By all means have the feel, the smell and sounds correct. . . .

Remember Yourself as a Reader

The lesson I learned from someone else and from which I benefit most is to remember yourself as a reader, as well as a writer. What do you enjoy reading? Why? What sort of plots do you like? What sort of characters? What makes you laugh, cry? Why do you have to turn the page? What gives you greatest satisfaction or excitement?

What do you skip over? What irritates you? What makes you feel loved, or cheated, or disappointed?

Think of your favorite books, and why you like them. Is it a compulsive plot that makes sense, complex characters with passion, humor, vulnerability, the power to love, a setting that is used but not obtrusive?

That is what I like, too.

Perhaps that is what we should try to write.

Anne Perry, born in England, now resides in Scotland. From her first published novel decades ago to her more recent works, she imbues her stories with lush characterizations and Victorian atmosphere. Her recent novel *The Whitechapel Conspiracy* stars her popular characters Inspector Thomas Pitt and his wife Charlotte. *Booklist* noted that her historical mysteries have the sweep of Victorian novels with contemporary pacing: "Reading Perry is a bit like reading Thackeray edited by Elmore Leonard."

Fiction Workshop

THE READER
AS PARTNER

by Tony Hillerman

Sometime very early in my efforts to make a living as a writer, I noticed an odd little fact, trivial but useful: People just back from seeing the Rocky Mountains didn't describe the Front Range. They told me about the clump of mountain iris they'd seen blooming through the edge of a dwindling snowbank. Witnesses of a train wreck I interviewed when I was a reporter would describe the women's clothing scattered along the right-of-way and ignore the big picture. The fellow drinking beer after watching the rodeo would talk about the sounds the bulls made coming out the gate—not the derring-do of the champion rider.

I noticed my own brain worked that way, too: It would store a scattering of details in full color and with every stitch showing, but the general scene would be vague and ill-defined. I presumed that this was the way run-of-the-mill men and women remembered things, and thus, it would be useful for writers in the process of converting a scene that exists in our minds into words that would re-create it in the imagination of those who read what we write.

I doubt if there is anything new or original about this thinking or this tactic. Selecting significant details to cause the reader to focus attention exactly where it's wanted was being done with quill pen on papyrus and probably before. Except for those dilettantes of the "art for art's sake" school, every writer is engaged in a joint venture every time he writes. He looks at what's behind his own forehead and translates it into words. At the other end of the crosscut saw, the reader drinks in those words and tries to transmute them back into images.

It's a partnership. We work at it. So does the reader.

But we're getting paid for it, in money, fame (if we're lucky), and in the fun of controlling the process. The reader expects a different reward for the cash and time he or she invests. Even so, that reader is a working member of the team. I always write with some clear notions about those for whom I write. They are, for example, a little more intelligent than I am and have a bit better education. They have good imaginations. They enjoy suspense. They are impatient. They are middle-aged. They are busy. They know very little about the specific subject I'm writing about. They are interested in it only if I can provoke that interest.

Given that, how should I go about my business? For example, how should I describe in physical terms this benign character I am about to introduce in chapter three? Not much, probably, if that character is to be important to the plot, and the reader is to come to know him from repeated meetings. But quite a bit if said character takes the stage only briefly.

Why this odd inversion? Because my intelligent, well-educated, middle-aged, imaginative reader knows from personal experience what various sorts of people look like. Therefore, if you use a character a lot, the reader paints his own portrait. For example, as far as I can remember, I have never given more than the vaguest descriptions of either Joe Leaphorn or Jim Chee, the two Navajo tribal policemen who are often the protagonists in my mystery novels. Yet scores of readers have described them to me. Tall and short, big and little, plump and lean, handsome and homely. The reader's imagination creates the character from his or her own experience, making the policeman look exactly the way he should look. Why should the writer argue with that? Why should the person who is investing money and time in reading my story be denied his role in the creative process?

Minor characters, I think, need more description. The reader is likely to see them only briefly through the eyes of the protagonist. He should be as curious about minor characters as is the viewpoint character—looking for the spot of gravy on the necktie, the nervous twitch at the corner of the eye, the dark roots of the bleached blonde hair, the scar tissue on the left cheek. Our reader won't see this minor actor enough to fit him into any personal mold.

Sometimes, of course, the writer must exercise more control over the image the reader would create. The story line may demand that the reader know the character is burly, has an artificial hand, and that his eyes tend to water if he stands too long reading the sympathy cards in the Hallmark shop. Otherwise, I count on the reader to perform his half of the task with no interference from me. I think he enjoys it more.

> Tall and short, big and little, plump and lean, handsome and homely. The reader's imagination creates the character from his or her own experience. . . .

This notion of the reader as partner in a game of imagination affects how I write in many other ways. For example, there's that hard-to define something that I think of as "mood." It exists in my mind as I write a scene. Sometimes it is merely the mental state of the viewpoint character through whose eyes whatever is happening is seen. But it can be more than that, or even different from that. For example, I may need to send signals to the reader that it is time for nervous anxiety, while the protagonist is still happily remembering that there's nothing left to worry about.

I tend to take on the mood of the scene—writing with lower lip gripped between my teeth when doom is impending, writing with a grin when all is well in chapter nine. I want the reader to join me in this mood. And here I'm on shaky ground. I simply have no way of knowing if my tactics work.

They involve engaging the reader's senses. I interrupt the dialogue or the action to show the reader through the eyes of the protagonist the dust on the windowsill, the grime on the windowpane, the tumbleweeds blowing across the yard, the broken gate creaking in the wind, the spider scurrying toward the center of its web, the stuffed weasel in its frozen leap toward the cowering quail in the taxidermy display. I have the reader notice the odors of old age, of decay, and of air breathed too often in a closed and claustrophobic room. I have him hear the sort of vague sounds that intrude into tired, tense silences. These are the sorts of signals my senses are open to when I am in this certain mood. If they don't contribute to causing it, at least they reflect it. Perhaps the same will be true for the reader.

Another mood. Another set of sensory signals. Take satisfaction-contentment-happiness (what my Navajo characters might call "hozro"). There's the smell of rain in the air (remember, I write mostly about a landscape where rain is all rare and a joyful blessing), the aroma of brewing coffee, the promising voice of distant thunder, the sound of birds, the long view through slanting sunlight of sage and buffalo grass, and the mountains on the horizon, a sense of beauty with room enough and time enough to enjoy it, and the good feeling of fresh-baked bread under the fingertips.

Unless some psychologist can come up with a universal catalogue of which objects/smells/sounds are connected in the mind of Average Human with which mood, neither you nor I will ever know how effective this technique is. My conversations with those who have read my work suggest that sometimes I can make it work, and sometimes I fail. But I am working at it, using my only laboratory animal—myself—as guinea pig.

Someone I meet pleases me. I think I would like them. Why? Well, you know . . . there was just something about him. But specifically, exactly what was it? Go back, you sluggard, and remember. What was it, specifically and exactly, that first caused you to start looking at and listening to this stranger? It was the body language, the expression, that told you he was really and intently listening when you talked to him. Interested in you and in what you were saying. So how can that be described most effectively? And what else was there? The way he said things? The turn of phrase. To defer. Not to interrupt. The tendency not to overdescribe, to presume his listener was intelligent and informed. Whatever it was, isolate it. Remember it. Have it handy the next time you want to introduce this sort of person to the reader.

A scene depresses me, leaves me out of sorts and angry. Why? The coldness of the room, the dim, yellow light, the tarnish on the gold tassel on the rope, the arrogant stare of the hostess, the slick, clammy coolness of the surface of this table. . . . What else?

I awake at night from a bad dream, tense and anxious. Quick. Dissect the mood before it evaporates. Nightmares are rare these days for me. For a man who deals in suspense, fear, and tension, they are too valuable to waste. What was in it and in the darkness around the bed that provokes this uneasiness and anxiety? Specifically, what do you hear, or smell, or feel or see that causes this painful tension?

I have been doing this for years: stripping down people and places, dissecting their looks and their mannerisms, filling the storage bins of imagination with useful parts; doing the same with street scenes, with landscapes, with the weather. When I wrote only nonfiction, such stuff was jotted in my notebook—the telltale details I trained my mind to isolate and collect. The anthropologist squatted on a grassy slope beside an anthill, his callused fingers sifting through those tiny grains ants bring to the surface, frowning in his fierce hope of finding a chip from a Stone Age artifact. The same fingers sorting through the residue left on the sifter-frame over his wheelbarrow, eliminating the gravel, roots, and rabbit droppings, saving the tiny chips flaked from a flint lance point; finding a twig to fish out the angry scorpion and return him to the grass. And that final detail, I hope my reader will agree, does more than put him on the scene with me. It gives him insight into the character of the man who owns the callused fingers.

Tony Hillerman is a past president of the Mystery Writers of America and has received their highest honors, the Edgar and the Grand Master awards. His other honors include the Silver Spur for best novel set in the West, and the Navajo Nation's Special Friend Award. His writing is noted especially for its accurate sense of place, often set in and around Navajo lands in the American Southwest.

Fiction Workshop

SECRETS OF ROMANTIC CONFLICT

External and internal tension
are essential

by Vanessa Grant

Romance is a massive market, with thousands of developing writers struggling to crack it. Those who succeed know how to create and resolve romantic conflict to sustain suspense.

Romance literature tells us that love is the most powerful force in our lives. A story that does not convey this message is not a romance, although it may contain a romantic subplot.

Even romances that end unhappily, like *Casablanca* and *Bridges of Madison County*, show readers how love can help one achieve personal growth. In the best romances, this powerful love-message is inseparable from story conflict and suspense.

What Is Romantic Conflict?

In a romance, falling in love creates problems for both hero and heroine, but ultimately love's power provides the solution. During their romantic journey, characters must experience both internal and external conflict as they struggle to achieve their goals.

Internal conflict is the result of a character's wanting two incompatible things. A hero wants love, yet fears being vulnerable. A heroine must keep a secret, although her moral code demands honesty.

In my novel *Hidden Memories* my heroine Abby has a secret. Her daughter Trish was conceived with Ryan, a stranger she met when she was in shock after her husband's death. Abby knows she should be honest about her daughter's real father, but fears the consequences of telling the truth. She wants to be an honest person, but she wants to hide the truth. Because she can't have both, she struggles inwardly.

165

If your characters don't experience internal conflict, you're telling the reader that the issues in this story aren't important enough to worry about. Internal conflict is essential, but external conflict generates excitement. If your hero and heroine don't experience *external* threats to their goals, they'll spend the book agonizing about the internal struggle and your reader will become impatient. External conflict occurs when characters struggle with each other over opposing goals. When characters with opposing goals have transactions with each other, conflict moves out in the open, becoming visible to readers and other characters.

Whenever a character experiencing internal conflict acts in response to that struggle, it becomes externalized and may create conflict with other characters. Abby's internal conflict, when she acts on it, has the potential to affect Ryan, her daughter, her daughter's grandfather, and her parents.

In Chapter One, Abby tries to hide when she recognizes Ryan across a crowded room. He could expose her secret and throw her life into turmoil. Even before Abby makes the first move in her struggle with this hero, she's fighting with her conscience, Ryan's right to know his child, and her desire to avoid exposure. When Ryan recognizes Abby, his attempt to learn all he can about her threatens to expose her secret even more. She fears he'll learn she has a daughter and realize he's the father. Abby's frightened response to the external conflict generates intensifying internal conflict.

In your novel, external conflict should always intensify the internal conflict.

Ryan wants to know why Abby disappeared after their brief affair. Once he learns she's had his child, he wants to form a strong relationship with his daughter. Because Abby wants to maintain the fiction that Trish is her dead husband's daughter, she can't let him have what he wants. Their opposing goals create both internal and external conflict.

Every step in the external struggle between Ryan and Abby makes Abby's internal conflict worse. Because of her internal conflict, when the external conflict begins, her reactions are instinctive, not logical. Characters experiencing heightened internal conflict often behave irrationally.

Abby is under stress, attacked from outside by Ryan, from inside by her own conscience. She tries to hide, to pretend, to evade. Ryan becomes suspicious. Abby's mother, who likes Ryan, makes things worse when she tries some matchmaking. As Abby and Ryan fall in love, both internal and external conflict skyrocket.

With strong internal conflict and strong interlinking external conflict, the stakes rise. The reader fears it won't work out for these characters. Will Abby drive Ryan away with her inability to live openly with the truth? Will Ryan become angry and leave? The more uncertainty readers feel over the outcome, the more satisfied they will be when hero and heroine come together in the end.

As your story progresses, the conflict must change and develop. Your hero and heroine must

> To create conflict, first give your character an important goal, then have someone oppose that goal. . . .

have trouble getting what they want, they must worry about it, doubting whether their relationship can work. For good reasons, they must offend one another. We all commit offenses against people we love because we're tired, worried, or afraid we're not loved as much as we love. Those are valid emotional reasons arising from our internal conflicts. They generate transactions that are part of external conflict.

In a love story, the conflict eventually develops to make the reader ask: "Do hero and heroine care enough about each other to make the necessary compromises? Can they trust each other enough to reveal their inner selves and commit to a believable, lasting relationship?

How to Create Conflict

Conflict is created when goals meet obstacles. To create conflict, first give your character an important goal, then have someone oppose that goal.

Every strong desire has its corresponding fear. If you combine your character's goal to a fear, you'll achieve a high level of internal conflict when things begin to go wrong. Abby's goal of keeping her secret is attached to her fear of what will happen if the truth becomes known. Her late husband was a famous artist, and although he destroyed Abby's sense of self, the world believed their marriage was idyllic. Now, however, if the truth is exposed, both Abby and her daughter will suffer.

Strong Goals Conceal Strong Fears

By the time Ryan discovers Abby's lie, they are struggling with their own new relationship. The external conflict issues have grown. They are in conflict over Ryan's desire to be acknowledged as Trish's father, Abby's fear of committing to another disastrous relationship, and his insistence that they marry and become a family.

To create conflict in your story, give your character a goal, then ask yourself what fear hides behind that goal. The more powerful the fear, the higher the level of conflict. If your hero's goal is financial power, why is money so important to him? What does he fear? Did he live in severe poverty as a child? Perhaps he vowed never to be poor again. If he fears poverty, intensify the fear by making it personal. Perhaps his baby brother had a disease requiring expensive medical care. The hero worked a paper route, mowed lawns, and dug ditches for extra money, but it wasn't enough. The brother died.

This hero has a deep emotional fear that someone he loves will suffer again, and he won't be able to provide enough. With this fear behind his drive to achieve wealth, any threat to his financial security will create strong internal conflict. If this hero must choose between money and the woman he loves, all his fears about poverty will be aroused, and he'll be thrown into severe conflict. If he chooses money, he'll lose his love and the joy in life. If he chooses love, he'll lose the money and may be unable to keep his love safe. Unless your story is a tragedy, the hero will have to win the battle against his demons and choose love. His struggle will involve pain, suffering, and sacrifice.

From Conflict to Resolution

A good story begins by putting forth a story question in the reader's mind. In a romance novel, the story question is usually, "Will heroine and hero overcome the obstacles to love—their conflict issues—and find happiness?"

In *Hidden Memories*, Abby's opening conflict arises from her internal struggle between honesty and fear. As the story progresses, the conflict changes and develops. When Ryan discovers Trish is his daughter, he wants Abby to marry him so that they can be a family, but she believes their marriage would be a disaster. Abby and Ryan still struggle over their daughter's identity, but a new element has been added: Abby's fear of the pain she risks if she surrenders to her growing love for Ryan and agrees to marry him.

As your story progresses, new problems should continue to emerge as the romantic conflict moves through several stages: beginning, middle, black moment, and ending. Ideally, the beginning of your story will create suspense and curiosity in your reader by showing or hinting at internal or external conflict. If you didn't put conflict in the first page of your manuscript, try beginning the story at a different point.

Here are a few examples from the opening paragraphs of my own stories:

> It couldn't be him!
> Abby had dreamed him in nightmares, dreams suppressed and almost forgotten. A man's head and shoulders glimpsed across a room . . .
> from *Hidden Memories*

> Eight hours was too long. She should have walked right up to Connar and faced him this morning at the exhibition. "Let's talk," she should have said.
> from *Yesterday's Vows*

> "We may have to turn back!" the pilot shouted over the engine noise.
> "Can't you give it a try?" Sarah squinted to see through the windscreen and wished herself back in her Vancouver office.
> from *Nothing Less Than Love*

If you begin your story by tossing your characters into strong conflict—with themselves, each other, or circumstances—you'll be off to a good start. As your story progresses, your characters should face a series of problems that create increasing conflict, thus forcing them to wrestle with the real issue. A satisfying novel pits characters against overwhelming odds, then leaves them to struggle through disaster after disaster until victory is won.

Heroine and hero may have a wonderful time on a date. They may laugh, make love, even get married, but despite their ultimate victories, the problems keep coming until happiness seems impossible. The harder you make life for your characters, the better your readers will like the book. Until you reach the final scene, every transaction must present new problems, or new developments to old problems. Forget everything you ever learned about being nice to people.

To be a good storyteller, you must treat your characters terribly, throwing their worst fears in their faces

In a satisfying romance, the suspense between hero and heroine culminates in a black moment when all seems lost. To be powerful, the black moment must emerge from the personality and fears of your characters, and it must be deeply related to the conflict issue. The more powerful your moment, the more satisfying the resolution.

It is only after the black moment, when hero and heroine realize that they've lost each other, that they can experience the full strength of their love. In the aftermath of the black moment, hero and heroine each realize that their relationship matters more than the convictions they held so rigidly. After this realization, they are willing to make the necessary sacrifice to achieve their happy ending.

Panicked by Ryan's demands for marriage and her own fears, Abby finally succeeds in driving Ryan away, only to realize how bleak life will be without the man she loves. If the conflict is based on your characters' fears and personal history, the sacrifice must be related. The hero who fears poverty must sacrifice the illusion that money can prevent personal loss. Abby, who fears exposure, must embrace truth and risk herself.

To achieve a happy ending, lovers must always sacrifice their need to protect themselves against abandonment. They must allow themselves to become vulnerable, to risk broken hearts and grief, before they can win the prize of true intimacy.

It is only at the end of the romance novel, when hero and heroine make their sacrifices and emerge victorious over the conflicts that threaten their future, that the reader's suspense is ended with the satisfying answer to the story question.

Can this couple overcome the obstacles to love and find a happy ending?

Yes, they can, but it isn't easy.

Vanessa Grant has successfully published 27 romance novels and *Writing Romance*, a critically acclaimed guide for romance writers. She has more than 10 million books in print in 15 languages. Living on the West Coast of Canada, she now divides her time between writing, traveling, lecturing, and her family.

Fiction Workshop

PASSIONATE PROSE

Readers may love sexy novels, but it takes
strong characters to keep the romance alive

by Judith Rosen

Sweet or sultry? Tempestuous or tender? When it comes to writing romance novels, one of the challenges is to create love scenes that capture readers' hearts while teasing their libidos.

Savvy writers finesse a readable balance between sizzle and sensitivity, never losing sight of one key element—romance—which is, after all, why readers pick up the novels in the first place.

Romance novels are one of the most popular genres in publishing. In 1999, they generated more than $1.35 billion in annual sales, according to a study compiled by Libby Hall, past president of the Romance Writers of America, and the Book Industry Study Group.

Bestselling novelists such as Nora Roberts, Tami Hoag, and Sandra Brown have enhanced the market and gained wider recognition for the genre.

At its heart, the romance novel centers on two people falling in love. The story doesn't have to end happily, but it should be optimistic. Within this broad framework, authors have plenty of leeway. A romance can be funny, mysterious, historical, or contemporary—some have a little bit of everything.

Successful writers agree that strong, appealing characters, sensuous writing, and an understanding of how to create sexual tension are the key elements of good romance novels. Writing strong love scenes that are neither too sappy nor too graphic is one of the challenges of the genre.

I talked with seven leading romance writers, with works ranging from funny to tender to sexy, to find out how they capture passion on the page.

In 1993, when journalist Sandra Hill—who has since published 11 romances, including *Truly, Madly Viking* (Love Spell)—started thinking of herself as a novelist, she decided, "I'm not going to just write when the mood hits me." While discipline (she spends at least three hours a day writing) and a computer system have helped, reading other writers was also key to her successful transition.

Hill continues to use her clipping file. "It's never to copy what someone has written," she says. She is more interested in how colleagues use details, "like eyes or the movement of a hand on the small of the back. What does this author do that I liked a lot?" To make sure she gets a well-rounded perspective, she subscribes to *Men's Health* and reads books on sexuality such as William Cane's *The Art of Kissing* (St. Martin's Press). She also recommends buying reference books, including Jean Salter and Candace Shelton's *The Romance Writers' Phrase Book* (Perigee). Although she admits that "it's the hokiest book in the world," she finds that the authors' extensive list of expressions can serve as a springboard for creativity.

Hill prefers writing in silence, but some writers agree with Shakespeare that music is the food of love—and love stories.

Karen Wiesner—who writes for e-publishers Hard Shell Word Factory and Avid Press, and did a monthly column on electronic publishing for Inkspot.com—makes a soundtrack for each of her books, which include the titles *Vows & the Vagabond*, *Fire & Ice*, and *Restless as Rain*.

"Music," she explains, "is such a part of my soul, I have to listen to it while I create. My soundtracks are tailored to selected areas of the book, which really helps me get into the mood. I've often used a snippet of a song to create an entire novel."

Rochelle Alers (*Private Passions*, Arabesque) also likes to create a romantic atmosphere for writing. Spending her days as an administrator for state-funded substance abuse agencies, Alers finds she needs to switch gears before she sits down to write. "I always burn candles," she says. "I also turn on my Zen fountain and play background music. I love movie soundtracks because of the movements—the highs and lows."

No matter how romance writers get started on their five to ten pages a day—a typical goal for many—there's still the problem of writing about the anatomy of love again and again. There are only so many ways to describe sex, not counting crashing waves or arching rainbows.

> I don't write sex scenes to spice things up. I think it's much more about the emotional landscape.
>
> — Eileen Goudge

You have to make the readers care, says Hill. "It's much more important to have sizzling sexual tension than the actual sex." Keeping a love scene fresh "has nothing to do with technique or the kink du jour, it has to do with character."

Wiesner, who chronicles her writing tips in the soon-to-be-published *The Productive Writer* (Avid Press), combines desire and heart-stopping emotional intimacy. "The key is to not get mired in either aspect of it for long. Don't let your characters get so swept away that they're riding on a cloud of the author's purple prose," she says.

Keep It Fresh

"Humor works very well, because it makes the reader laugh," Wiesner notes, and the tenderness eases the tension. In *Fire & Ice*, for example, when the hero and heroine are in the kitchen cooking together, the hero lifts her onto the counter, and they both hear a loud splat when she sits on a tomato.

Originally a painter, Susan Johnson (*Temporary Mistress*, Bantam) says that when she started writing in 1979, her goal was to be "the Henry Miller of romance." Chosen as one of four authors in Kensington's new Brava line of steamy romances, she's definitely a woman who likes to turn up the heat. She owns a Victorian erotica collection and likes to read diaries and memoirs about love affairs past. "For me," she says, "writing sex scenes is very time-consuming. You have to choreograph every move." She also recommends using dialogue to create sexy scenes. Remember Bogey and Bacall's suggestive repartee in *The Big Sleep*? "Keep in mind that this is entertainment," she advises.

Vicky Lewis Thompson, who recently published *That's My Baby* (Harlequin), likes love scenes that seem real—which doesn't necessarily mean graphic. She compares the difficulty of keeping her work fresh—she's written more than 50 books—with keeping her marriage going strong. In both cases, she says, there are still a lot of variables that can affect the outcome. "You've got different people in each book, and you can vary the settings," she remarks. "You don't have to have beds, and you can vary the conflicts. I've been married for 30 years; you have the same kind of challenge. It really does bring out true creativity."

Lately, Thompson has begun turning to books for ideas. She started reading her way through her local bookstore's sexuality section, beginning with Nancy Friday's classic on women's sexual fantasies, *My Secret Garden* (Pocket Books).

But no amount of lusty language can make up for unlikeable characters, she says. "If either is a cad who would turn you off in real life," she says, "then the scene will be yucky."

What makes great sex on the page isn't "so much about zippers flying open, it's about feelings and the little things that happen," says Eileen Goudge (*The Second Silence*, Viking), who is working on a trilogy set in California. In her work, she tries to convey some of life's ironies. An upcoming book features "a 48-year-old woman who falls in love with her youngest daughter's 30-year-old stepson. She's a widow, and he's a painter hunk. So they have this first sex scene, and you think she's going to teach him a thing or two. But he's the one who teaches her."

> When I set up the props for a love scene, or anything else, it's like watching frames of film. I'm aware of the lighting, the weather.

Sense Appeal

"I don't write sex scenes to spice things up," says Goudge, who started her career writing teen romances like the Sweet Valley High series. "I think it's much more about the emotional landscape than body parts bumping up against each other. I had a lot of scenes that were more about what the girl is thinking while he runs his hand up the inseam of her jeans. I really think that's what is more arousing."

Alers appeals to the readers' senses. "Usually," she says, "I can see what is happening in a particular scene. As a writer, I must set the mood so the reader becomes a visual participant. When I set up the props for a love scene, or anything else, it's like watching frames of film. I'm aware of the lighting, the weather. Sometimes I decide to add a storm and use the wind as a character. I can also make use of the time of day—the color of the sky, how shadows play across the objects in a room. It may sound insignificant, but it's important to me and makes a scene more alive, more visual."

In the end, it all boils down to character, says Alers. By knowing her characters intimately before she starts, she doesn't need to rewrite, which is especially important for a writer working two jobs. "I begin every novel with a detailed character dossier," she says, describing her books as character-driven. "These people are very real to me. I create a complete biography, including their positive and negative traits, family composition, what books they read, their financial status, favorite time of day. If you know your characters, they will fill up the blank screen for you."

In *Summer Magic* (Arabesque), she created two emotionally wounded people who share a house for the summer. The woman is a victim of domestic violence, and the man sees his fiance in bed with his best friend. "The plot is very predictable, reminiscent of a teenage summer romance," concedes Alers. "But I managed to create two extraordinary characters." Readers felt the same way, and liked it as much as her Hideaway series.

Susan Elizabeth Phillips agrees that complex characters give romance zest. "You have to be invested in the characters to write sexy. How would these people make love? Is it going to be a funny little romp? Will it drive them apart or bring them together?"

A two-time recipient of the Romance Writers of America's Favorite Book of the Year Award, Phillips made her hardcover debut in January with *This Heart of Mine* (Morrow). She polishes her story and characters with what she calls "texturing, or layering" as she goes along. Each layer adds depth and complexity to the novel.

"I don't work with any kind of synopsis," she says. "I plot as I write. By the time I get to the end of the book, I'm finished."

For Wiesner, building sexual tension between characters begins on the first page. "One of the biggest reasons I think authors have trouble with love scenes is that they don't begin the 'exaggerated awareness' aspect immediately. You have to reveal a character and what she wants, even if it's only a tiny part of the whole picture. When you introduce characters as soul mates, even if they don't know it yet, there has to be an immediate connection."

Remember that in the romance game, say these experts, it takes two to tango. The author's and reader's imaginations work together to create an irresistible read.

With a little discipline and a lot of care taken to get descriptions and feelings right, it's possible to create a romance that's a keeper. There really are happy endings, not just for the hero and heroine, but for the aspiring romance writer as well. And, as the statistics show, it can be profitable to play by the rules of romance.

Judith Rosen, a freelance writer in Cambridge, Massachusetts, is New England correspondent for *Publisher's Weekly* and a former book columnist for the *Boston Herald.*

EDITORS WANT CHARACTERS AND CHEMISTRY

"What romance is, on a lot of levels, is wish fulfillment," says Christopher Keeslar, an editor at Dorchester Publishing Co., which publishes a range of romances—from sweet to hot—under its Leisure Books and Love Spell lines. One of the few men who work with romance writers, he notes that "it wasn't a departure for me, because I grew up reading fantasy and sci-fi." All three genres, he notes, share a sense of heroism, idealism, and fantasy.

He cautions new romance authors against writing "gratuitous love scenes. If you're going to write a romance that's based on sexual exploits, it's difficult to develop the emotional level. Sometimes the best love scenes are implied."

Keeslar says that many writers get bogged down going back and forth describing what each lover feels. "I tend to be a purist when it comes to point of view," he says. "I don't like to see a switch of point of view in a love scene. You might want to write more than one love scene, or break it up. Have one of the characters take a nap, then write from the other's perspective."

Both Kate Duffy, editorial director at Kensington, and Birgit Davis-Todd, senior editor at Harlequin, are looking for spicy romance in their books. The inaugural list for Kensington's trade paperback Brava line includes historical romances by Beatrice Small, Susan Johnson, Thea Divine, and Robin Schone, whose fantasies were showcased two years ago in the Kensington anthology *Captivated.*

Davis-Todd ran a contest last summer for Harlequin's Blaze Temptation line. More than 300 writers answered the call for a ten-page love scene and five-page synopsis. "Contests are a great way of getting an editor's attention," she says. Reading a love scene, "you can get a sense of whether this is a sensual writer." The trick isn't writing a love scene, she says, it's coming up with "great characters, a great plot, and balance."

Fiction Workshop

A WRITER IS A STRANGE CREATURE

by Daphne du Maurier

[This piece is excerpted from the November 1938 issue of *The Writer* (Vol. 51, No. 11).]

It is a strange and rather puzzling thing, that the profession of writing should cause more interest and curiosity in the mind of the layman than any other craft in the world.

The plumber is not questioned as to how he mends his pipe, nor the road mender begged to give an explanation of the whys and wherefores of his pick and shovel, though the skill required is much greater than that of a novelist with his pen. . . . Why should the artist, be he writer, actor, painter, composer, be considered as though he were a species apart from his fellow men . . . living in another world from road menders and plumbers?

. . . The very manner of his working, alone, in a closed room, adds a little spice of glamour. The actor works before his public, the musician plays, even the painter holds court in his studio . . . but the writer, the writer, what does he look like, what does he do, behind that fastened door? It can't be that he just sits down at a desk, at nine o'clock, and opens his typewriter, like any junior clerk?

Alas, for the romantic layman, but such is generally the case. If not the typewriter it is the more modern dictaphone; office hours are kept, nine till one, and two till five; so many thousand words per day can usually be guaranteed, and at five o'clock the manuscript is put away until the following morning. The fallacy still exists, of course, that a sensation of pleasure is experienced by this rare creature, the author. How many people have said to me at one time or another, "How marvelous it must be just to sit down whenever you feel like it and write. I suppose it just pours from you."

Put in this way the act of writing sounds like a hideous form of vice. If only it were true! How nice it would be to lock the door every morning and turn on the tap. . . .

Another error committed by the layman is his or her habit of believing that an author is forever in search of copy. A casual dinner party among friends and someone says, with an arch smile, "I hope you are not going to put us all down in your next book," as though one kept a notebook down the bosom of an evening dress.

. . . Funnily enough, little credit is given to the imagination. It is always supposed that a novel must be based on something that has really happened, and that the more scurrilous parts of the story are but thinly disguised versions of one's own past. "I can't think what made you write about such a dreadful man," I remember someone saying once with a surreptitious glance at my husband, and a look of surprise that he had not the hooked features and gigantic frame of Joss Merlyn in *Jamaica Inn*.

. . . Even my own family have their doubts. "You always seem to write about such unpleasant things, darling. Why not write something cheerful for a change?"

And what can I do but shake my head and sigh and murmur sadly, I will try again. But there it is, the whole crux of this writing business. We do not choose our subjects, they choose themselves. How I should love to write a gay, high-spirited tale, full of wit and humor, every line a gem. What I would give to make people split their sides with mirth. But it does not happen. The laughter will not come. I laugh, I think, as much as most people, and my life is a very happy one, with husband, home, and children. But I go for a walk on a moor and see a twisted tree and a pile of granite stones beside a deep, dark pool, and *Jamaica Inn* is born. . . .

"You'll never be a great writer," said my husband once, "until you write a happy story about happy people." I believe he is right. But I can't do anything about it. They creep so insidiously, these creatures of the imagination, before I am aware, and they fasten themselves upon the bidden places of the mind, and feed there, and take root, and once they are securely lodged I cannot banish them. They must develop and become little men and women and tell their story, and once the story is told they can return to the dust from whence they came, and be remembered no more. And what is the dust from whence they sprang? I cannot say. Nor can any writer unless his tales are true ones and not things of the imagination. . . .

Daphne du Maurier (1907–1989) was an English novelist, biographer, and playwright. She published romantic suspense novels, mostly set on the coast of Cornwall. She is best known, perhaps, for *Rebecca* (1938), filmed by Alfred Hitchcock, and for "The Birds," a short story also made into a movie by Hitchcock.

FOUR TRICKS OF THE POET'S TRADE

by David Kirby

You've probably spent some time wool-gathering and thinking about the future—specifically, your future as a poet. And no doubt you've asked yourself some version of the question, "What do editors really want?"

To answer that question, let's begin by considering what it's like to be an editor right now. Editing a poetry magazine these days is like turning on a fire hydrant. Only it's poems that gush out, not water: Even the littlest magazine receives a half-dozen manuscripts every day, and the big ones like *Poetry* attract tens of thousands of submissions over the course of a year.

The way I see it, the flood of poetry into editorial offices is only going to get stronger. More people are going to school and learning to write well. Too, the economy's booming, and that's going to leave more time for artistic pursuits. Finally, the appearance of new markets every day is going to encourage new talent: Every year there are more listings in *The Directory of Poetry Publishers* (Dustbooks); a recent edition lists 2,336 poetry publishers. And electronic publication is just starting to take off; as more on-line journals appear, and more people acquire Internet service, it won't be long before poetry web pages are as inundated with submissions as the traditional poetry magazines are.

My guess is that, as far as market changes go, the big trend in poetry over the next few years is going to involve not variety but quantity. The development of any significant new type of poetry seems unlikely, because there is already so much variety among the dominant types—free verse, formal poetry, prose poetry, language poetry, performance poetry—and also still much work to be done in these areas. So I'm predicting that the tendency will be not toward some new variety of poem, but toward more of the same—much more.

Where does this leave poets who want to share their work with others but are aware that the competition is ferocious? Let's begin by reminding ourselves that the editors of the world are not our enemies: They love poetry passionately or they wouldn't be the underpaid, overworked people they usually are. And the editors I know are pretty open-minded; they don't care what kind of poetry you write, as long as you write it well. They're simply looking for the best work out there. In fact, they demand it.

But they're overwhelmed. Let's imagine an editor is sitting in his office and looking at a stack of, say, 20 submissions from 20 poets, and it's not even lunchtime yet. Let's also say there are three or four poems in each submission, and that among these 60 to 80 poems are several of yours. How are you going to make your poems stand out? How are you going to get that editor to put the other poems aside and give your work a good, close read?

As a poet, teacher, contest judge, and, mainly, a fan of poetry, I read dozens of poems every week, hundreds every month, and thousands every year, and I can tell you this: A poem either engages my interest immediately or it doesn't. Too, a poem also either sustains that interest or it fails to.

How? There are four very simple tricks of the trade that every poet should know and that any poet can use to write the type of poem that he or she wants to. So let me tell you what they are, and then I have a couple of surprises for you.

I think I can best illustrate my points if we first take a look at a poem of mine that was published in the magazine *Amelia* and later appeared in my book *Saving the Young Men of Vienna*, which won the Brittingham Prize in Poetry:

Fallen Bodies

The night of the Franklinton game
the bus breaks down, the seniors cry
because they will never play football again,
and we all go home with our parents and girlfriends.
Billy Berry lies in the back of my father's Buick,
covered with bruises, unable to lift his right arm,
and tells stories he swears are true:
that apple seeds cure cancer,
that a giant dove hovered over the van
the night his church group
came back from Mexico,
that Hitler left Germany by submarine
after the war and established a haven
in Queen Maud Land, near the South Pole.
The air comes in through windows
that won't quite close
as we drive up the dark highway to Baton Rouge,
through towns where tired old men
sell peaches on the corners of used car lots
or doze in diners that sag by the roadside,
spacecraft cooling in the Louisiana night.

Using "Fallen Bodies" as our text, let's look at the four tricks of the trade that will make your poem stand out from all the others:

1. *The Hook*. What catches the reader's attention and makes this poem different from all others? The answer is something concrete and slightly mysterious; in this instance, it's a broken-down bus and a bunch of unhappy high-school football players. Immediately you get a mental picture, and then you ask, "What next?"

2. *The Voice*. What vocabulary (formal or streetwise), sentence length (long, short, mixed), tonal qualities (wistfulness, confidence, horror, humor) do you want to use to get the effect you desire? In "Fallen Bodies," the voice is world-weary; look at all those negative words and phrases, like "breaks down," "cry," "never," "bruises," "unable," "cancer," "won't quite," "dark," "tired old," "used," and "sag," not to mention the word "night," which occurs in the first and last lines of the poem and one other time as well. Yet this voice is also thoughtful: There are only three sentences in the poem, and each is packed with ideas and images, as though the speaker has composed his thoughts very carefully. So the overall effect is of a world-weary yet philosophical observer.

3. *Saturation*. The first draft of a poem is usually a skinny draft. Fatten it with details: The ones in this poem speak for themselves, from the capsule picture of the defeated team to the outlandish story of Hitler's submarine voyage to the portraits of the old men in the car lots and diners.

4. *The Big Theme*. Whenever I use that phrase, I always capitalize the first letters of the words to remind myself that The Theme must always be Big. A pretty poem can still be a trivial poem, so make sure your poem deals with something of consequence. That doesn't mean you should be obvious about it; you'll always want to present your argument by means of images rather than editorial statements. In the case of "Fallen Bodies," I wanted to say that, even in defeat, one can still see that the world is filled with strange wonders, and this realization can be consoling. Hence my final image: not chrome-and-glass diners per se, but spacecraft that seem to come from another dimension, as if by magic.

And that's it. Once you know what you want to say, you figure out the best way to start, you decide what voice you want to use, you saturate your writing with plenty of details, and you arrange everything so your Big Theme will emerge. You can test this scheme on other poems, your own or someone else's; my guess is that your favorites will all have the four elements I've outlined above and the ones that don't work quite as well will be lacking in one or more areas.

And now for the surprises. The first you've probably guessed already, which is that my four tricks of the trade, which are intended to help you write the poetry of the future, are also characteristic of the great poetry of the past. Take Dante's *Inferno*. It begins with a man getting lost in the woods at night: What a hook! Then there's the poet's voice, which ranges from comic to angry to pity-ing to devout but is, for the most part, simply awestruck at all the bizarre figures in the underworld. As for detail, if giants and harpies and dragons aren't enough, not to mention some of the greatest celebrity sinners of all time, there's Satan himself, frozen in the ice of Hell's basement. And while there's more than one Big Theme (after all, it's a Big Poem), certainly the immortality of true love is the greatest of these.

The second surprise is that the four tricks of the trade essential to any good poem are also indispensable to any piece of good writing. For example, a good novel has a good hook. (What would Moby Dick be without "Call me Ishmael"?) Each hit song has an unmistakable voice; you could play "Somewhere Over the Rainbow" loud and fast, but the version most people remember is the wistful one that Judy Garland sang. Every good play is saturated with details: If Macbeth didn't have all those witches and sword fights, it would just be a dull treatise on Scottish politics. And each of these has its own Big Theme: pride, nostalgia, ambition.

The fact that these four tricks have characterized every good piece of writing, regardless of its genre or the period in which it was written, is especially good news, since it means that, if you use them in your own writing, you will, in effect, "market-proof" your work against any changes in editorial taste that may occur.

Say I'm wrong in my earlier predictions and editors begin to demand some new kind of poetry that we can't even conceive of at the moment. It won't matter, because you'll be writing work that uses four elements that have always worked.

David Kirby is the W. Guy McKenzie Professor of English at Florida State University. He is the recipient of many grants and awards, including the Guy Owen Poetry Prize from *Southern Poetry Review* and the University of Wisconsin's Brittingham Prize in Poetry. He is also the author of *Writing Poetry: Where Poems Come From, and How to Write Them* (The Writer, 1997)

EVERYONE WANTS TO BE PUBLISHED

Does your poem lack "thingness"?

by John Ciardi

At a recent writers' conference I sat in on a last-day session billed as "Getting Published." Getting published was, clearly, everyone's enthusiasm. The hope of getting published will certainly do as one reason for writing. It need not be the only, nor even the best, reason for writing. Yet that hope is always there.

. . . I was, accordingly, in sympathy with the conference members—but I was also torn. For I had just spent days reading a stack of the manuscripts these people had submitted, and I had found nothing that seemed worthy of publication. I sat by, thinking that session on getting published was an exercise in swimming in a mirage. I even suspected a few of those present of drowning in their mirages.

The poems I had read lacked anything that could be called a body of information. The writers seemed to have assumed that their own excited ignorance was a sufficient qualification for the writing of poetry.

I wanted to go back and say to my conferees, "Your poems care nothing about the fact!" Isn't that another way of saying they were conceived in ignorance? Not one of the poets I read had even tried to connect fact A to fact B in a way to make an emotional experience of the connection. The writing lacked *thingness* and a lover's knowledge of thing.

Consider these lines by Stanley Kunitz (the italics are mine):

Winter that *coils* in the thickets now,
Will *glide* from the fields, the *swinging* rain
Be *knotted* with flowers. On every bough
A bird will *meditate* again.

The diction, the rhyming, the rhythmic flow and sustainment are effortless, but how knowledgeably things fall into place! Winter *coils* in the thickets because that snow that lies in shade is the last to melt, thinning down to scrolls of white by the last thaw. Winter will then *glide* from the fields—and what better (continuous, smooth) motion for the run-off of the last melt? The swinging rain (what word could better evoke our sense of April showers?) will then be *knotted* (as if) with flowers while birds (as if) *meditate* on every bough. The rain, of course, will not literally be knotted with flowers, nor will birds, literally, meditate. Yet what seems to be a scientific inaccuracy is of the central power of metaphor. Metaphor may, in fact, be conceived as an exactly felt error.

Metaphor is supposed to state the unknown in terms of the known. It is supposed to say X equals Y. Yet when we say "John is a lion," we do not think of John with a mane, with four clawed paws, nor with a pompon-tipped tail. We extract from "lion" the emotional equivalent we need and let the rest go. The real metaphoric formula is X does-and-does-not-equal Y. Kunitz understands this formula. His knowledge of it is part of his qualification as a master poet.

There is more. More than can be parsed here. But note how the italicized words *hearken* to one another, each later term being summoned (by some knowledge and precision in the poet) by what went before. The italicized words form what I will dare to call a chord sequence by a composer who has mastered musical theory.

The passage, that is to say, is empowered by a body of knowledge of which I could find no trace in the poets I had been reading at the conference. My poets had been on some sort of trip. Their one message was "I feel! I feel!" Starting with that self-assertive impulse (and *thing* be damned), they then let every free association into the poem. They were too ignorant even to attempt a principle of selection.

I do not imply that I know what any given poem's principle of selection ought to be. To find the principle that serves best and to apply it in a way to enchant the reader is the art and knowledge of the poet. Everything in a good poem must be *chosen* into it. Even the accidents. How else could it be when one stroke of the pen will slash a thing out forever? All that has not been slashed out, it follows, is chosen in.

Ignorance, as nearly as I could say it (too late), was what had really stifled the poems I had read. The writers had not cared enough to learn their own art and use their eyes.

. . . But have they earned the right to publication? I ask the question not to answer it. It is every writer's question to ask for himself.

John Ciardi (1916–1986) led an accomplished life in the world of poetry, and was the long-time Poetry Editor for *Saturday Review*.

SECTION THREE

A Conversation with an American Master

Interview

THE WRITING LIFE AND TIMES OF JOHN UPDIKE

America's literary icon may be successful,
but he's not satisfied

by Leonard Lopate

I have had quite a few opportunities to interview John Updike over the years. He has been a guest on my radio show often—enough to have led him to mention the show in one of the Bech stories.

The first time was around 15 years ago, when he was promoting a collection of essays. I must have been feeling my oats, because I chided him for something he had written that I felt pandered too much to anti–New York feelings. He had lived in my city for years, I pointed out, and was too sophisticated to really believe that sort of nonsense.

"You're absolutely right," he responded, "I'll never do it again." In a way, it was typical Updike. Nobody listening would have believed that he actually meant it, and yet it was delivered in such a charming way, I was happy to move on to something else.

Updike is a master of misdirection, avoidance, and deflecting criticism. Sometimes he does it by making a witty, self-deprecating remark he has borrowed from one of his critics. One is not sure just how much irony to read into those jokes. At other times he will answer a question obliquely, but what he is saying turns out to be so interesting and amusing that one feels it would be almost cruel to force him to get back to the subject at hand.

The following interview, conducted before an audience of about 500, was part of the New York Public Library's In the Forum series. Updike is always witty, but he is also one of the most thoughtful people one could hope to talk to. Our conversation touched on many of his works, including the *Rabbit* and *Bech* series, his essays and short stories. He can be admirably honest, a quality that is most evident throughout this conversation.

Every time I talk to John Updike about his life and work, I gain new insights into how I should read him. This exchange was no exception.

Leonard Lopate: The subtitle of *Licks of Love* is *Short Stories and a Sequel, Rabbit Remembered.* Did you think that you were done with the Angstrom family once you'd completed *Rabbit at Rest* or did you know you were going to do this?

John Updike: I certainly thought I was done at the end of *Rabbit at Rest.* The last word is "enough"—we'd all had enough of Rabbit, including himself. I also thought I might not be around in ten years. The books, as some of you may know, were written every ten years, in the ninth year of the decade. I was content to let him rest in the hospital bed where we last saw him, but 1999 came, I was still kicking, and I was troubled by the loose ends in several plots and themes: Was that or was that not his daughter, whom he began to chase in the last two novels of the sequence? I thought maybe it would be nice for my faithful readers if I tied up that loose end and revisited his survivors. I tried to show him as a remembered presence still affecting life, even though he was dead.

Lopate: It also allowed you to talk about one of the juiciest times in American history. Discussing current events has been part of the *Rabbit* series. I can't help but envy the way you have taken the issues of the day and kept them fresh. They don't feel dated. But when you started that, you must have thought: "In ten years, nobody will understand what the heck I've written."

Updike: That might prove to be the case. The first one was written with no special thought of writing a chronicle of Rabbit's or my time, but he does turn on the radio when he's driving south, trying to escape his domestic situation and heading toward an area of freedom, which he identifies as Florida. In fact we all, I think, identify Florida as an area of freedom, and we're all trying to get there one way or another. He just turns on the radio, so a certain stream of 1959 news—including the flight of the Dalai Lama—comes on.

But the next one, *Rabbit Redux,* certainly was set during a year—1969—and a decade full of news. It was hard to keep the news out. Maybe there's more of it in the book than there should be, but it was such an arresting time in the development of this republic and its inner life that I did include some news. The last two sequels also required that there be some news background in them. My theory is that as residents of a nation, we don't live the news, but we do live with it, and it does go on in the background of our lives. In some ways it seeps through so that the various revolutions in taste and sexual mores, which Rabbit notices, in fact are also seeping into his life.

As to the year 1999, I began the book in September and I found that my writing kept overtaking the actual time, so I had to keep stopping to let history, as it were, catch up. The book had a long pause between the opening scene in

September and the Thanksgiving dinner, at which the family discusses the Clinton administration and Clinton's embarrassments and so on. That's the most news-laden part of the book.

Lopate: One of the things that I rarely hear talked about is that you chose to write the *Rabbit* series in the present rather than the past tense. That must present some technical difficulties. Is this the only series you've done that way?

Updike: I've written some short stories in the present tense; it was fairly rare in 1959, when I began *Rabbit, Run*. I'd encountered it in a novel by Joyce Cary, *Mister Johnson*. I was struck by it, because it eliminates that whole slightly tedious historical dimension that fiction is burdened with: the pluperfect, the past tense—"this happened a while ago," and so on. I discovered in writing in the present tense that you suddenly are on the surface of the present, just like a movie. The original title of *Rabbit, Run* was *Rabbit, Run: A Movie*. I meant for the opening sequence of the boys playing basketball around a backboard in an alley to be the background for the title—that's how cinematic my imagination was at that point. I discovered the present tense just cuts out a lot of trouble; I found it the opposite of difficult. I found it was a liberating experience to write in the present tense. It's now become a cliche; everybody writes in the present tense. I can see why it is very alluring, because in some way it rivals the cinematic thing of being there. It's not very reflective; it's not mired in past action. So it was fun to discover the present tense, fun to carry on a series in the present tense about a hero who basically lived in the present, somewhat haphazardly.

Lopate: The *Rabbit* books aren't the only series that you've created: There are the Richard and Joan Maples stories, Olinger stories, the Bech stories. Do you know from the start when you have created certain characters that they are people you'd want to return to?

Updike: Almost invariably, no. I first wrote about Richard and Joan Maples when I was living in New York—my two brief years of Manhattan residence. The story is called "Snowing in Greenwich Village." It presents a young couple living down on West 13th Street and the awkwardness of youthful marriage. Those '50s marriages were generally youthful. It wasn't until I'd moved to New England and the suburbs, perhaps as much as seven or eight years later, that I picked them up again. And once I'd picked them up again, they became like Sherlock Holmes, in that it's easy to revisit characters once you've named them, once you've established their tics and their environment. So to a lazy writer—and I think I am one of the lazier writers—it's very appealing to go where you've already been before and done a lot of groundwork.

> I discovered in writing in the present tense that you suddenly are on the surface of the present, just like a movie.

Henry Bech is a blocked writer when we first see him. I don't like fiction about writers, because I don't think writers are that interesting. You should keep them out of fiction if you possibly can, but I had had some experiences that only a writer would have had—I had them behind the then–Iron Curtain. I tried to invent a writer quite unlike myself: unmarried, Jewish, blocked—I was considered too-little blocked. With these credentials of disparity, I felt free to write about a writer, and the story went pretty well. It even won an O. Henry First Prize. I was in that way encouraged to pick him up again later, and I've continued to do so, being lazy, being thrifty.

Lopate: Recently you told me, "I think I'm finished with Henry," and here he is in this collection, as well. I'm surprised you call him blocked. I remember Bech once asking, "Am I blocked? I've just thought of myself as a slow typist." Well, you're obviously not a slow typist, or don't you type?"

Updike: I don't feel very rapid or prolific to myself. Looking back on the alleged 50 books that I've written, many of them are quite short, some are children's books, some are collections of material that appears in other books, so in a way it's a fraudulent appearance of muchness. Some of the books are sequels, which, again, is a kind of cheating. I feel always on the edge of my last effort, my last invention, my last book. I feel that way sitting here, in fact.

Perhaps I've said everything that I was born to say. I've said it even more than once. When I try to think of what my next novel might be, I keep running into novels I've already written. And as I get further along in the development of the idea in my own mind and get excited about it, I then realize that I published that 20 years ago. In a sense I am blocked, or at least I feel on the bottom of the barrel most of the time.

Lopate: Yet you at least are rumored to write six days a week, 300 to 400 words a day, then you quit to play golf or do something else like that. Now that is pretty steady work. Does that mean that if you're not thinking of a novel, you decide to write an opera libretto or some light verse, or dash off a review for *The New Yorker* or *The New York Review of Books*?

Updike: I try. My father was a teacher, and my grandfather on the other side was a teacher. The effect upon me of watching my father struggle trying to teach algebra to a bunch of kids who didn't want to learn was that I was not going to teach. By the time I was 20, I emerged with a determination not to teach but to make a living as a writer if I could. It was a more innocent world then. In the '50s there were a lot of writers around who were respected as tweedy but useful citizens. They often lived in

> There was an innocent presumption that there would be a place for a diligent writer in the world, so I decided to stake my all on writing.

Connecticut and smoked pipes, but whether they were called Thornton Wilder or Willa Cather, they had a certain place in society. You felt that society needed them. There was an innocent presumption that there would be a place for a diligent writer in the world, so I decided to stake my all on writing. That really is all I do in the morning. I have no excuse not to write.

You mentioned 400 words—which I don't really think is quite enough. I think the quota I set for myself is three pages a day, which is closer to 1,000 words than 400. The idea was basically to do something every day, to advance that particular idea, and in that way you do accumulate quite a lot of manuscript.

Lopate: How many times do you rewrite a particular sentence and/or paragraph? How do you know when to leave it alone?

Updike: It varies. Sometimes you work quite hard at a given section because you have some vision of something magical that might happen here, and the words that are on the page aren't making it happen but you keep fiddling with it, trying to make it happen. In general, though, I think the best writing is often the first flow, because you're in the groove, you're in the rhythm, and so it's with some trepidation that I try to revise myself. One of the charms of the old methods, either by hand or by typewriter, is that the first version was always there. The diabolical thing about writing on a computer is, of course, you erase your first versions as you go along. I try not to write hastily in the hopes that I can fix it later. I think it's important to at least feel you're writing as well as you can as you go along, and to build each sentence or paragraph upon a happy and sound base. To that degree, I'm not one of your great revisers. I've never been one for macrocosmic revision, where you delete characters or turn sections around. I think you should do that kind of work, probably, in your head, when the whole work is still very fluid and hasn't acquired that bogus concreteness of being written down on paper.

Lopate: Have you found writing criticism helpful, or has it been something of a distraction?

Updike: My mother didn't raise me to be a critic. We thought of criticism as a kind of handmaiden to the real arts of poetry and fiction. But The New Yorker, if I may reminisce, in the late '50s, early '60s, seemed to me not to be presenting criticism worthy of the rest of the magazine. I was brash enough to mention this to William Shawn, the editor, who said, "Well, do you think you could do any better?" I must have allowed that I thought I could, because he began to send me books, and I began to review them. I never dreamed of all the reviewing that would be in my future. I became, as others faded away or died out, almost the main reviewer and did an awful lot of reviewing in the '70s and '80s—much more, probably, than was good for me. It kept me in The New Yorker, and my superstition is that it's always good to be in The New Yorker. It compelled me to read a lot of books that otherwise I might not have had the wit to find.

My theory about being an American writer, at a time when I was still forming ideas, was that you are American enough just by being you. One of the few things my father said to me, which actually was helpful later in life, he said while he was making a sandwich—he worked in the college cafeteria when he was a young man. I admired how well he buttered the bread. And he said, "Always butter toward the edges—enough gets in the middle anyway." So I thought that I should butter toward the un-American edges; I read a lot of European, Latin American, and communist-country fiction in those years of trying to shed new light upon the mystery of what fiction is for and how we can make it fresh. So in that sense, reviewing was an education for me. I'm grateful for that, but there comes a point when you wonder if you aren't tired, as a critic; if you haven't unpacked all of your favorites; if you haven't done all of your pets; and if you're just going through the motions. I wonder really how useful a critic I am right now. I still enjoy doing it, but I enjoy it mostly when it's a book I'm really enthusiastic about, or a book that in some way leads to a theory I'm keen to express or test out.

Lopate: You mentioned reminiscing about *The New Yorker*. There are a lot of stories in *Licks of Love* that are reminiscences of fathers and mothers and the small Pennsylvania towns of your youth—memories of being young—triggered by high school reunions, about chance encounters with women who'd been lovers in the past. Is this because you're getting on in years?

Updike: I could have called it *Memory Lane* instead of *Licks of Love*. I think you get kind of doddering in that the past becomes more real to you than the present, and you find your memory turning over. Little shocks occur to you that bring back to life some long-buried tract of your existence, so that almost all of the 12 stories in this book look backward—a lot. But all of the stories seem to be about love in some form. That applied to the title story, "Licks of Love," about a banjo player who goes to the Soviet Union in the mid-'60s and, just by being his irrepressible and charming self, spreads the gospel of freedom and democracy. I was sent on such a mission; I did not play the banjo, but I certainly did do the equivalent of playing the banjo—I read and talked—talked more than I knew I could. It was in the Soviet Union that I discovered that a microphone is, to some extent, a friendly presence to me. I stammered as a boy; I was sort of shy, but in the Soviet Union, I was able to talk at great length about this and that. So, yes, I was there and I wrote this story trying to bring it back. *Licks of Love* sounds lewd, but it's really a very—as indeed my work in general is—a very innocent story.

> I read a lot of European, Latin American, and communist-country fiction in those years of trying to shed new light upon the mystery of what fiction is for and how we can make it fresh.

Lopate: I remember reading one critic who was trying to decide whether some of your books were as pornographic as *Portnoy's Complaint*, and I think he decided that yours weren't, but not by much.

Updike: What is pornography? I think it's an attempt to excite us, and I've seen my works criticized because the descriptions of sex were not exciting but rather depressing. The artistic challenge to me, as I saw it in the late '50s and mid-'60s, was to try to describe sex honestly as a human transaction, as a human event, and try to place it on the continuum of the personality, to write about it freely but not necessarily as an endorsement of sex. I don't think sex really needs an endorsement. Our bodies provide endorsement enough.

I was not hurt when people said that they found the descriptions and couples turned them off, because who knows what lurked in my Puritan heart. Maybe I was trying to turn them off. At any rate, I was trying to look at sexual behavior as slightly extraordinary behavior. Isn't it? We put our careers and our good names at risk for this . . . acrobatic activity. Mark Twain somewhere complains that the people who wrote about heaven never described sex in heaven, and yet it seemed to him that the thing above all on earth—that women and men alike were willing to die for—was sex.

Lopate: Do you feel misunderstood when *Time* puts you on the cover with the caption,"The adulterous society," or when a feminist critic calls you "just a penis with a thesaurus?" Are they confusing you with what you are writing about?

Updike: With a real thesaurus? I was glad that my children by and large weren't reading when that issue of *Time* came out. I didn't feel it was a misstatement. *Couples,* which was the book that prompted this very flattering amount of attention, was about adultery, adultery as, indeed, a mode of disruption, disrupting all those '60s marriages. But it was also a mode of bonding in the absence of pressing claims from state or church or job.

This is talking about the early '60s, that far-off era when men didn't take their work terribly seriously; they didn't work from 7 in the morning until 10 at night. The job was something you did to earn a kind of ticket, but you didn't obsess about it. In the absence of all those claims upon your loyalty, it was natural to make a churchlike entity, at least a tribelike entity, out of your fellow couples. That's what I was trying to describe. It was not just about sex and adultery, it was about bonding in general between young people who had nowhere to look for fun and leadership but to each other. No, I did not feel misrepresented. I mean, the buck stops here. I did write about it.

> My overall thought about the American character . . . is that Americans are learners; maybe they're slower learners than many would wish, but they can accommodate.

Lopate: You've written mostly about middle-class ordinary life. In fact, you once joked that people complained to you that when you wrote *Gertrude and Claudius*, you'd made them into a suburban couple. You've said the American Protestant small-town middle class is where extremes clash and ambiguity restlessly rules. How do extremes clash in the Protestant middle class?

Updike: That was issued at a time in my life when I was more fluent and more abundant with theories, because I was groping my own way, I think, with the *Rabbit* books in mind. What happens in Washington or in Tibet or the race riots in Detroit or Houston or wherever, all this does reverberate in the mind of my middle-class people. Harry Angstrom certainly is aware of his fate being in some tenuous way tied to the fate of the nation. In *Rabbit Redux*, there are all kinds of extreme and experimental and revolutionary slogans and behavior being paraded in front of the poor, helpless middle class with their own children bringing posters of Mao and Che. All of that certainly was a case of the news and extremes turning and entering the middle-class home by the window or even the front door, and that's what I tried to show.

I've had that book criticized as being fantastic and incredible, and I've had an opportunity to re-read it. I found myself still persuaded that this is a useful metaphor of the condition of the country and that Harry, as a representative middle-class man, is being invaded by all kinds of new thoughts, some of which he embraces. My overall thought about the American character as evinced by him is that Americans are learners; maybe they're slower learners than many would wish, but they can accommodate. There's certainly been a lot of changes in social style since I was a boy, in regard to both gender and race—I think we're a much more liberal society. There was a kind of a cruelty that used to be condoned and accepted as part of nature that no longer is accepted and condoned.

Lopate: I'm curious about when you realized that you were going to be more than a writer of light verse and a cartoonist. What do you think Albert Guerard, your writing teacher at Harvard, thought about your prospects in the literary world? Were you one of the writers who people would have spotted as somebody who's going to have the kind of career you've had?

> I enjoyed the writing teachers— they all had something new, they all had a different slant, but in the end, you have to find your own way.

Updike: I was not viewed by the minds who dominated the creative writing part of the English department at Harvard as very promising. I was practical-minded; I did have this very laughably, or certainly un-Harvardian, ambition to be a cartoonist. I graduated slowly from being in love with Disney to being in love with magazine cartoons and, by extension, *The New Yorker* cartoons, which were clearly the best and the most elegant and the funniest. I had this practical hope of actually supporting myself, somehow, by the work of my pen and my imagination. I was never admitted into Archibald MacLeish's most advanced writing course; I was turned down repeatedly. Albert Guerard was a very good sport to admit me—he was the most avant-garde and a modernist. He gave me a good mark in the course, but always I felt that I grudgingly got good marks at Harvard, that the professors' real love was for other students.

Guerard did say of one story that it really frightened him. I didn't think it was frightening; I was trying to describe life in Pennsylvania. It's called "Ace in the Hole," and it was one of my first of several attempts to write about the figure of the former basketball high-school great. "Ace in the Hole" was kind of a preliminary *Rabbit, Run*.

I enjoyed the writing teachers—they all had something new, they all had a different slant, but in the end, you have to find your own way. You can only teach so much about writing. You can do some things about point of view and try to clean up spelling and punctuation, but basically, I think, of all the higher arts it's the most self-taught. You learn through the example of the writers who move and impress you.

Lopate: You were the editor of the *Harvard Lampoon*, at one point.

Updike: I became the president, which was the editor. But there were other talents there, from whom I learned what I was, what I wasn't, and what I could be. In those four years, I went in as a would-be cartoonist but came out a would-be writer, and I think that's more or less the Harvard ethos. Majoring in English did not seem, then, like an eccentric or useless thing to do. It seemed what it was all about in a funny way, and the proven practitioners of the written word, the great modernists—Eliot, Pound, and Joyce—were worth it. They were our saints, and these texts, the idea of producing texts of equal interest, of equal mysteriousness, of equal authenticity, seemed self-evidently worth doing. So having imbibed that message, I did set out to be a writer and found in myself—although I like writing amusingly and I still take pleasure in the amusing writing of others—that there was something tragic or existentially challenged, which opened up another vein.

Lopate: Critic Alfred Kazin once praised you with the observation that you write as if there is no greater pleasure. Is that true?

Updike: You try to write in such a way as to give others pleasure. My belief and the kind of writer I'm attracted to is a writer who gives pleasure—the prose writer who does a little more than what is strictly called for to deliver the image or the facts. I'm not a very fast reader, so I like to open up a book and feel some whiff of poetry or of extra effort or of something inventive going on, so that even read backwards, a paragraph of prose will yield something to the sense. I've just tried to write in a way that would entertain and please me, if I were the reader.

I suppose, yes, I do find it easier to write than some writers, and maybe harder than some others, because I'm aware of the need to write—especially in a time when there are so many alternative claims on our entertainment budget, from the Florida election to all-night TV to blue movies on the Family Channel. All that makes it more urgent than ever that a book be more than just the news, that it be the news plus something extra, some shiver, some rainbow edge to the prose. You can't really control your writer's voice. It's a lot like your hand-writing—you can't stop it. You can try to alter it, but it always comes out as you. My prose tends to come out as me, and I know it turns off people, because I really ask you to read a little slower than maybe you read the newspaper—but my feeling is that's what makes a book different than a newspaper and more lasting.

Lopate: Woody Allen joked about speed-reading *War and Peace* in 20 minutes. He said, "It's about Russia, isn't it?" Part of the fun of reading really good literature is that you do read it slowly, and you do think about what it's saying. You once said that writing makes life less grim.

Updike: The act of writing has a therapeutic dimension, and also an escapist value. I find that the writing time goes by very quickly, once you get into it, that the three hours or whatever that you've allotted to the writing activity to make up your quota goes by in a flash. You look up and it's lunchtime already—it's 1:20, which is about when I quit. It speeds by, whereas even an hour spent raking leaves seems endless. So yes, in some way it enables me to get through life, to get through the day. I feel until I've secreted a certain amount of my ichor, my essence, that I haven't earned the right to enjoy the rest of the hours of the day. So I've built it into my biological budget, and to call it a pleasure is in a way to understate it. It's become a need, a necessity, this wish to deliver your goods.

Proust goes on at characteristic length about the writer's duty to his own inner hieroglyphics. He speaks of a man underwater, groping, finding this pattern, and so it is in yourself. However many books you write, whether it's 15 or 50, this fear that you haven't transcribed honestly your own hieroglyphics, that you haven't found what was in you to say, haunts a writer. Especially after Proust, who wrote that masterpiece about a writer finding at last what he had to say.

Leonard Lopate is host of "New York & Co.," a radio program on WNYC offering a wide-ranging overview of American culture. This excerpt of Lopate's conversation with John Updike, held at the New York Public Library, appeared in *The Writer*, July 2001.

PUBLISHED WORKS OF JOHN UPDIKE

Poetry Collections

The Carpentered Hen (1958)
Telephone Poles and Other Poems (1963)
Verse (1965)
Midpoint and Other Poems (1969)
Tossing and Turning (1977)
Facing Nature (1985)
Collected Poems 1953-1993 (1993)
Americana (2001)

Nonfiction

Assorted Prose (1965)
Picked-Up Pieces (1975)
Hugging the Shore (1983)
Just Looking: Essays on Art (1989)
Self-Consciousness: Memoirs (1989)
Odd Jobs (1991)
Golf Dreams: Writings on Golf (1996)
More Matter: Essays and Criticism (1999)
Humor in Fiction (2000)
On Literary Biography (2000)

Play

Buchanan Dying (1974)

Children's Books

The Magic Flute (1962)
The Ring (1964)
A Child's Calendar (1965)
Bottoms' Dream (1969)
A Helpful Alphabet of Friendly Objects (1995)

PUBLISHED WORKS OF JOHN UPDIKE

Novels

The Poorhouse Fair (1959)
Rabbit, Run (1960)
The Centaur (1963)
Of the Farm (1965)
Couples (1968)
Rabbit Redux (1971)
A Month of Sundays (1975)
Marry Me: A Romance (1976)
The Coup (1978)
Rabbit is Rich (1981)
The Witches of Eastwick (1984)
Roger's Version (1986)
S. (1988)
Rabbit at Rest (1990)
Memories of the Ford Administration (1992)
Brazil (1994)
Rabbit Angstrom: A Tetralogy (1995)
In the Beauty of the Lilies (1996)
Toward the End of Time (1997)
Gertrude and Claudius (2000)

Short Story Collections

The Same Door (1959)
Pigeon Feathers and Other Stories (1962)
Olinger Stories: A Selection (1964)
The Music School (1966)
Bech: A Book (1970)
Museums and Women and Other Stories (1972)
Problems and Other Stories (1979)
Too Far to Go: The Maples Stories (1979)
Bech is Back (1982)
Trust Me (1987)
The Afterlife and Other Stories (1994)
Bech at Bay: A Quasi-Novel (1998)
Licks of Love: Short Stories and a Sequel,
    "Rabbit Remembered" (2000)
The Complete Henry Bech (2001)

SECTION FOUR

More Ideas and Inspiration
from Great Writers

WELCOME TO MY STUDY

How to write a novel that readers won't forget

by Maeve Binchy

As they say in Ireland, a hundred thousand welcomes to my study. Or my half of the study. I share a big, bright room with my husband Gordon Snell, a children's writer, and we find that the discipline of working side by side is a great help.

You can't suddenly turn on the radio, file your nails, or get lost in reading someone else's novel if you have announced that you're going to get 1,200 words done today. It's much easier to fool yourself than to find an excuse to fool someone else. And as writers, we all know we are aching for an excuse not to write. So this is why I'm taking time off from my next book to pause and tell you all the things you should be doing. I was a schoolteacher for eight years, and old habits die hard. Once a bossy schoolmarm, always a bossy schoolmarm.

You want to know how to write a novel. All right, sit up and pay attention. Here we go.

Timing

The secret of the Universe is timing, and it's especially true for writing a novel. Before you start you must decide how long you think it's going to take. Make a realistic timetable, and stick to it. My pages are 250 words each and I think I write five pages a day. A book is around 500 pages, so in theory it should take one hundred days to write a book. But we all know that is madness. We don't write every day; in my case I write four days a week. So that's more like 20 pages a week, and to get 500 pages you have to work for 25 weeks. Good, you say; that's not too bad—about six months. But that's madness, too. You have to plan a book first, and to my mind that takes ten weeks. And when it's finished, you have to spend five more weeks tidying it up before you send it off. So—a total of 40 weeks. How does that sound?

Planning

I think of some emotion, like friendship, betrayal, eagerness for an education, the class system. Then I sit for days thinking of a story with a beginning, middle, and end to hang it on. This is the hardest bit, but it's easier if you remember you don't have to stick to it, it just has to be there, like some kind of scaffolding for putting up a building.

Now make up the main characters—about four or five of them, not a cast of thousands. And when I say make up, do make them up: Don't put your friend, your mother-in-law, your colleague into it. Put yourself in, of course; you can't sue yourself. Also, you're familiar with the way you react, so it's dead easy to write yourself into books. I always put idealized versions of myself in, younger, thinner, more beautiful, nicer, more saintly. (Whenever you find a good, warm, kind-hearted teacher in one of my books, that's me!)

Next, get some pastel-colored paper—I choose pale-green—and write down each character's name and birthday, and draw a picture of where they live. I have found this to be hugely helpful. Whenever I mention someone, I just check the green pages to make sure I don't put her in the wrong house or make her five years younger than she should be!

The last thing to do in the planning phase is to take a piece of pale-pink paper and write down the chapter endings—say things like, "By the end of Chapter Three, we must know what she is going to do about this situation, and she has begun to act on it," or "By the end of Chapter Five he must have discovered the missing money and realized that only one person could have taken it." Otherwise, you could have the next four chapters drifting on and on with someone trying to resolve a situation and the whole audience out there fast asleep.

Now, you're ready to begin writing.

Write Quickly

You probably don't write any better when you write slowly than when you write quickly, so make it speedy. Don't pause for breath, punctuation, too much analysis. Imagine you can hear the people speaking, and try to get it down as quickly as possible. To get dialogue right, listen to everyone, everywhere—eavesdrop, follow people so you can hear what they are saying. To get a scene right for Tara Road, I spent two days watching mothers and teenage daughters buying clothes in a store. Never hang up on a crossed telephone line, watch people in planes and trains, and be vigilant the whole time. When the people in your books speak, try to hear their voices in your head. Don't give them fake Deep South accents, or bad pronunciation, or lisps, but pretend you are listening at the door, and somehow it comes easier. In a conversation between two people, I often put my head on one side when I'm writing what one character is saying, and on the other when the second one is speaking.

Are They Real People?

I usually make most of my characters people that I would like to meet and know, but put a fair sprinkling of rotten apples in, as well. Funnily, people always remember the bad guys, the ones who prove "there ain't no good in men," but there must be strong, brave people as well, people who make the right decisions and don't abandon friends or loves or duty.

If you pretend they are real people, they will become so. I don't say I wonder what I will make Marilyn do here, as if my character were a puppet. Instead I say, "I wonder what she would do here," as if she had a life of her own. It really does work.

If you give your characters lots of clothes and records and hobbies and pets of their own . . . even though you don't mention all these things, somehow they make characters more believable.

I never let all the good people become sickeningly good; I give them a few slightly irritating habits, as everyone in real life has, and the same goes for the villainous ones. They can't be truly bad; they must have some redeeming features, as even the worst people I ever met seem to have.

Is It Any Good?

I have no idea whether anything I write will be of the remotest interest to anyone else. Some mornings when I read what I wrote the previous day I think it's fairly entertaining; other times I think it's pure rubbish. The main thing is not to take any notice, not to get elated or upset, just keep going.

If you write what you know about, you will always be on safe ground. I am very edgy and nervous about going into territories I know nothing about. That's why you don't find much high finance, group sex, or yachting parties in my stories.

And I write exactly as I speak; I don't roll each sentence around and examine it carefully before letting it loose! If you speak in your own voice, you can never be accused of being pretentious or showing off; you can just be yourself, and that's a huge advantage in anybody.

And finally . . .

Keep to your 40 weeks. And remember that when you have finished, that's only the first draft. If you have no publisher yet, then the horrible bit of being rejected starts. But stick with it; those who quit are just leaving the coast clear for those of us who didn't quit. Remember, the really famous writers who were rejected time after time got up, and dusted themselves off, and started again.

If you do have publishers, they will want you to change things here and there. If you trust them, then change what they ask you. My publishers always ask me to change things, and say exactly the same two things to me on every single book. Fourteen books, and I can never remember to put in a physical description of anyone, and I have to do it all at the end. Fourteen books, and I always forget

> I never let all the good people become sickeningly good; I give them a few slightly irritating habits as everyone in real life has . . .

that one thing should lead to another, rather than having lots of incidents flying in formation.

But I have remembered some of the other advice: If you're telling a story, get on with it; don't delay too long, rambling down little byways; and you often learn a lot about the main characters from little things that minor characters say about them. I know things in my own heart, for example, there is nobody really ordinary if you know where to look. We are all the heroes and heroines of our own life story. Stand at a railway station, in a shopping mall, in an airport, and watch the faces. Everyone has some kind of a dream, a hope, a plan. Some may have nightmares and regrets, but there isn't one person out there in that crowd who is uninteresting. Believe that, and you will never be without a plot, a character, or indeed, an interesting life.

Maeve Binchy, Irish author, began her writing career when her father sold a letter (she had written to him) to *The Irish Times* about her life in a Jewish kibbutz. From there, she has gone on to publish three volumes of short stories and ten novels, including *Tara Road, The Copper Beech,* and *Circle of Friends.* This article was first published in *The Writer,* February 2000.

The Writer's Life

WRITING WITH JOY

by Jane Yolen

There are writers who believe that writing is agony, and that's the best anyone can say of it. Gene Fowler's famous words are quoted all the time: "Writing is easy: All you do is sit staring at a blank sheet of paper until the drops of blood form on your forehead." Or Red Smith's infamous creed: "There's nothing to writing. All you do is sit down at a typewriter and open a vein."

But that's a messy way of working! And blood is extremely hard to get off of white paper.

Now, I am one of those people who makes a distinction between being a writer and being an author. A writer puts words on a page. An author lives in story. A writer is conversant with the keyboard, the author with character.

Roland Barthes has said: "The author performs a function; the writer an activity." We are talking here about the difference between desire and obsession; between hobby and life. But in either case, I suggest you learn to write not with blood and fear, but with joy.

Why joy?

It's a personal choice.

First of all, I am not a masochist willing to submit myself day after day to something that brings me pain. And I do mean day after day. Like an athlete or a dancer, I am uncomfortable—and even damaged—by a day away from my work.

Second, one need not have an unhappy life to write tragedy. Or conversely, one need not be deliriously happy all the time to write comedy. (In fact, many stand-up comics admit to being miserable much of the time.) Shakespeare was neither a king nor a fool, not a Moor or a Jew. He never saw a real fairy, and he was never asea in a tempest. His life was somewhere between happy and sad, as are most authors' lives. Yet he could write tragedy, comedy, and all between.

Authors are like actors; we get under the skins of our characters, inhabiting their lives for a while. We just don't have to live on and on with them forever. I have written about dragons, mermaids, angels, and kings. Never met any up close. I have even written a murder mystery, but I did not have to murder someone in order to write it. Still—don't mess with me. After doing my research, I do know how!

Third, writing for a living is much easier than spending a lot of time in a therapist's chair. Cheaper, too. Authors get to parade their neuroses in public disguised as story. If we are lucky, we get paid for doing it. And we get applause as well. As Kurt Vonnegut said: "Writers get to treat their mental illnesses every day."

Writing fiction—and poetry—is a bit like dreaming. You can find out what is troubling you on a deeper level. That one's writing goes out and touches someone else on that same level—though differently—is one of the pieces of magic that attends to art.

But I speak of choosing joy as if it were truly a matter of choice. For some people it is not. For some, agony oils the writing machine.

So—if you find that writing with pain is part of your process, I will not try and talk you out of it. After all, who am I to argue when Susan Sontag proclaims: "You have to sink down to a level of hopelessness and desperation to find the book that you can write." Or when Fran Lebowitz complains: "I just write when fear overtakes me." Or when Georges Simenon confesses: "Writing is not a profession but a vocation of unhappiness."

I may consider them whiners more than writers, but it is simply their way. Just don't ask me to stand by and give them a literary Heimlich maneuver when they get a bit of plot stuck in their throats.

Jane Yolen is the prolific and much-acclaimed author of over 200 books for children and adults. Her books have won the Caldecott Medal, two Nebula Awards, two Christopher Medals, the World Fantasy Award, and the Golden Kite Award, among others. This article appeared in *The Writer,* February 1999.

Writer's Classic

THOUGHTS ON YOUR WORKING METHODS

From a letter to a beginner

by Philip Wylie

Finally, don't, please, get precious about your working methods. There seems to be some sort of pipsqueak tenet on the matter. Writers presumably have to work from one to three a.m. in a room upholstered in red plush, on purple paper, with an old quill that belonged to their Revolutionary ancestor. Half-baked colleagues of mine are constantly touching off little autobiographical notes such as "I do my Hohokus stories on windy afternoons in the cupola of a haunted barn, writing in Chinese characters with an airbrush."

Saints preserve us! You're going to learn how to write—not how to fall into a trance and call up spirits. The more you humor your inadequacies by compensating with phony environment, the tougher your work will become. You have to be in a mood. I grant that. But if you haven't the understanding of yourself to get into any mood when you wish—then don't fool around with the mood business. Be an automobile salesman. I would like you to be able to write as well as you can with pen, pencil, and typewriter, in tree houses, boiler factories, and on subway trains. I insist that you must be able to write with a stomach-ache, a crying baby, a paving drill going—and on a typewriter that has a non-functioning "e" and an inoperable back-spacer. If you want to and need to. Then—for your regular surroundings—any moderately quiet, well-ventilated room with an ordinary typewriter table and chair will be paradisiacal.

You might as well begin correctly in the matter of time, too. Work right after breakfast. Why not? . . .

Philip Wylie (1902–71) was co-author of *When Worlds Collide* (1932), one of the most popular end-of-the-world novels of all time. This letter is excerpted from "Random Thoughts on Writing," *The Writer*, July 1938.

THE JOURNEY INWARD

How do you begin?

by Katherine Paterson

"Do you keep a journal?" No, I answer a bit red-faced, because I know that real writers keep voluminous journals so fascinating that the world can hardly wait until they die to read the published versions. But it's not quite true. I do make journal-like entries in used schoolgirl spiral notebooks, on odd scraps of paper, in fairly anonymous computer files. These notations are all so embarrassing that I am hoping for at least a week's notice to hunt them down and destroy all the bits and pieces before my demise.

I write these entries, you see, only when I can't write what I want to write. If they were collected and published, the reader could logically conclude that I was not only totally inept as a writer but that I lacked integration of personality at best, and at worst, was dangerously depressed.

If I had kept a proper journal, these neurotic passages would be seen in context, but such is not the case. If my writing is going well, why would I waste time talking about it? I'd be doing it. So if these notes survive me, they will give whatever segment of posterity might happen upon them a very skewed view of my mental state.

The reason I am nattering on about this is that I have come to realize that I am not alone. As soon as my books (after years of struggle) began to be published, I started to get questions from people that I had trouble answering in any helpful way: "Do you use a pen and pad or do you write on a typewriter?" (Nowadays, "computer" is always included in this question, but I'm talking about 20 years ago.)

"Whatever works," I'd say. Which was true. Sometimes I wrote first drafts by hand, sometimes on the typewriter; often I'd switch back and forth in an attempt to keep the flow going. The questioner would thank me politely, but, looking back, I know now that I had failed her.

"Do you have a regular schedule every day or do you just write when you feel inspired?" the person would ask earnestly. I am ashamed to say, I would often laugh at this. "If I wrote only when I was inspired," I'd say, "I'd write about three days a year. Books don't get written in three days a year."

Occasionally, the question (and now, I know, all these were the same question) would be framed more baldly. "How do you begin?" "Well," I would say, "you sit down in front of the typewriter, roll in a sheet of paper and . . ."

If I ever gave any of you one of those answers, or if any other writer has ever given you similar tripe, I would like to apologize publicly. I was asked, in whatever disguise, a truly important question, and I finessed the answer into a one-liner.

How *do* you begin? It is not an idle or trick question. It is a cry from the heart.

I know. That's what all those aborted journal notes are about. They are the cry when I simply cannot begin. When no inspiration ever comes, when neither pen, nor pencil, nor typewriter, nor state-of-the-art computer can unloose what's raging about inside me.

So what happens? Well, something must. I've begun and ended over and over again through the years. There are several novels out there with my name on the cover. Somehow I figured out how to begin. Once the book is finished, the memory of the effort dims—until you're trying to begin the next one.

Well, I'm there now. I have to begin again. What have I done those other times? How have I gotten from that feeling of stony hopelessness? How do I break through that barrier as hard as sunbaked earth to the springs of creativity?

Sometimes, I know, I have a conversation with myself on paper:

What's the matter?

What do you mean "what's the matter?" You know perfectly well. I want to write, but I can't think of a thing to say.

Not a single thing?

Not a single thing worth saying.

You're scared what you might say won't be up to snuff? Scared people might laugh at you? Scared you might despise yourself?

Well, it is scary. How do I know there's still anything in here?

You don't. You just have to let it flow. If you start judging, you'll cut off the flow—you've already cut off the flow from all appearances—before it starts.

Grump.

Ah yes, we never learn, do we? Whatever happened to that wonderful idea of getting up so early in the morning that the critic in you was still asleep?

How do I know it will work this time?

You won't know if you don't try. But then, trying is risky, and you do seem a bit timid to me.

You don't know what it's like pouring out your guts to the world.

I don't?

Well, you don't care as much as I do.

> Like a child, pour out what is inside you, not listening to anything but the stream of life within you. . . .

Of course I do. I just happen to know that it is so important to my psychic health to do this that I'm willing to take the risk. You, my friend, seem to want all the creative juices inside you to curdle and poison the whole system.

You're nothing but a two-bit psychologist.

Well, I've been right before.

But how do I begin?

I don't know. Why don't we just get up at five tomorrow, come to the machine and type like fury for an hour and see what happens? Could be fun. Critic won't be up, and we won't ever have to show anybody what we've done.

Now you understand why I have to burn this stuff before I die. My posthumous reputation as a sane person of more than moderate intelligence hangs in the balance. But living writers, in order to keep writing, have to forget about posthumous reputations. We have to become, quite literally, like little children. We have to remember our early griefs and embarrassments. Talk aloud to ourselves. Make up imaginary companions. We have to play.

Have you ever watched children fooling with play dough or fingerpaint? They mess around to see what will emerge, and they fiddle with what comes out. Occasionally, you will see a sad child, one that has decided beforehand what he wants to do. He stamps his foot because the picture on the page or the green blob on the table falls short of the vision in his head. But he is, thankfully, a rarity, already too concerned with adult approval.

The unspoiled child allows herself to be surprised with what comes out of herself. She takes joy in the material, patting it and rolling it and shaping it. She is not too quick to name it. And, unless some grownup interferes, she is not a judge but a lover of whatever comes from her heart through her hands. This child knows that what she has created is marvelous simply because she has made it. No one else could make this wonderful thing because it has come out of her.

What treasures we have inside ourselves—not just joy and delight but also pain and darkness. Only I can share the treasures of the human spirit that are within me. No one else has these thoughts, these feelings, these relationships, these experiences, these truths.

How do I begin? You could start, as I often do, by talking to yourself. The dialogue may help you understand what is holding you back. Are you afraid that deep down inside you are really shallow? That when you take that dark voyage deep within yourself, you will find there is no treasure to share? Trust me. There is. Don't let your fear stop you. Begin early in the morning before that critical adult within wakes up. Like a child, pour out what is inside you, not listening to anything but the stream of life within you. Read Dorothea Brande's classic *On Becoming a Writer*, in which she suggests that you put off for several days reading what you have written in the wee hours. Then when you do read it you may discern a repeated theme pointing you to what you want to begin writing about.

Begin, Anne Lamott suggests in her wonderful book *Bird by Bird*, in the form of a letter. Tell your child or a trusted friend stories from your past. Exploring childhood is almost always an effective wedge into what's inside you. And didn't you mean to share those stories with your children someday anyhow?

While I was in the midst of revising this article, my husband happened to bring home Julia Cameron's book, *The Artist's Way.* Cameron suggests three pages of longhand every morning as soon as you get up. I decided to give the "morning pages" a try and heartily recommend the practice, though these pages, too, will need to be destroyed before I die.

When I was trying to begin the book which finally became *Flip-Flop Girl* (and you should see the anguished notes along the way!), I just began writing down the name of every child I could remember from the fourth grade at Calvin H. Wiley School. Sometimes I appended a note that explained why that child's name was still in my head. Early-morning exercises explored ways the story might go, and I rejected most of them, but out of those fourth-grade names and painful betrayals a story began to grow. Judging from the notes, it was over a year in developing and many more months in the actual writing. But I did begin, and I did finish. There's a bit of courage for the next journey inward.

Now it's your turn. Bon voyage.

Katherine Paterson credits her early years in China as the daughter of missionaries for shaping her love of diversity, respect for culture, and patience in times of difficulty. She is the author of more than 20 books including *Bridge to Terabithia, Jacob I Have Loved, The Great Gilly Hopkins,* and *Flip-Flop Girl,* which have garnered her a number of awards including a National Book Award, Special Edgar Allen Poe Award, a Scott O'Dell Award, and the Hans Christian Anderson Award. This article was first published in *The Writer,* August 1995.

WRITERS: SEE HOW THEY RUN

by Joyce Carol Oates

Running! If there's any activity happier, more exhilarating, more nourishing to the imagination, I can't think of what it might be. The mysterious efflorescence of language seems to pulse in the brain, in rhythm with our feet and the swinging of our arms. Ideally, the runner who's a writer is running through the land- and cityscapes of her fiction, like a ghost in a real setting.

The structural problems I set for myself in writing, in a long, snarled, frustrating, and sometimes despairing morning of work, for instance, I can usually unsnarl by running in the afternoon.

On days when I can't run, I don't feel "myself"; and whoever the "self" is I feel, I don't like nearly so much as the other. And the writing remains snarled in endless revisions.

Writers and poets are famous for loving to be in motion. The English Romantic poets were clearly inspired by their long walks, in all weather: Wordsworth and Coleridge in the idyllic Lake District, for instance. The New England Transcendentalists, most famously Henry David Thoreau, were ceaseless walkers; Thoreau boasted of having "traveled much in Concord," and in his eloquent essay "Walking" acknowledged that he had to spend more than four hours out of doors daily, in motion; otherwise he felt "as if I had some sin to be atoned for."

My favorite prose on the subject is Charles Dickens's "Night Walks." Written with his usual brilliance, this haunting essay seems to hint at more than its words reveal. Dickens associates his terrible night restlessness with what he calls "houselessness": under a compulsion to walk and walk and walk in the darkness and pattering rain.

It isn't surprising that Walt Whitman should have tramped impressive distances, for you can feel the pulse beat of the walker in his slightly breathless, incantatory poems. Henry James also loved to walk for miles in London.

I, too, walked (and ran) for miles in London years ago. Much of it in Hyde Park. Regardless of weather. Living for a sabbatical year with my husband, an English professor, in a corner of Mayfair overlooking Speakers' Corner, I was so afflicted with homesickness for America, and for Detroit, I ran compulsively; not as respite for the intensity of writing but as a function of writing.

As I ran, I was running in Detroit, envisioning the city's parks and streets, avenues and expressways, with such eidetic clarity I had only to transcribe them when I returned to our flat, recreating Detroit in my novel *Do With Me What You Will* as faithfully as I'd recreated Detroit in *Them* when I was living there.

What a curious experience! Without the bouts of running, I don't believe I could have written the novel; yet how perverse, one thinks, to be living in one of the world's most beautiful cities, London, and to be dreaming of one of the world's most problematic cities, Detroit. But of course, writers are crazy. Each of us, we like to think, in her own inimitable way.

Both running and writing are highly addictive activities; both are, for me, inextricably bound up with consciousness. I can't recall a time when I wasn't running, and I can't recall a time when I wasn't writing.

(Before I could write what might be called human words in the English language, I eagerly emulated grown-ups' handwriting in pencil scribbles. My first "novels"—which I'm afraid my loving parents still have in a trunk or a drawer—were tablets of inspired scribbles illustrated by line drawings of chickens, horses, and upright cats. For I had not yet mastered the trickier human form, as I was years from mastering human psychology.)

My earliest outdoor memories have to do with the special solitude of running or hiking in our pear and apple orchards, through fields of wind-rustling corn towering over my head. Through childhood I hiked, roamed, tirelessly explored the countryside: neighboring farms, a treasure trove of old barns, abandoned houses, and forbidden properties of all kinds, some of them presumably dangerous, like cisterns and wells covered with loose boards.

These activities are intimately bound up with storytelling, for always there's a ghost-self, a "fictitious" self, in such settings. For this reason I believe that any form of art is a species of exploration and transgression. (I never saw a "No Trespassing" sign that wasn't a summons to my rebellious blood. Such signs, dutifully posted on trees and fence railings, might as well cry, "Come Right In!")

> The structural problems I set for myself in writing, I can usually unsnarl by running. . . .

To write is to invade another's space, if only to memorialize it. To write is to invite angry censure from those who don't write, or who don't write in quite the way you do, for whom you may seem a threat. Art by its nature is a transgressive act, and artists must accept being punished for it.

If writing involves punishment, at least for some of

us, the act of running even in adulthood can evoke painful memories of having been, long ago, as children, chased by tormentors. (Is there any adult who hasn't such memories? Are there any adult women who have not been, in one way or another, sexually molested or threatened?) That adrenaline rush, like an injection to the heart!

I attended a one-room country schoolhouse in which eight very disparate grades were taught by a single overworked woman. The teasing, pummeling, pinching, punching, mauling, kicking, and verbal abuse that surrounded the relative sanctuary of the schoolhouse simply had to be endured, for in those days there were no protective laws against such mistreatment. I don't believe I was singled out, and I came to see years later that such abuse is generic, not personal. It must prevail through the species; it allows us insight into the experiences of others, a sense of what a more enduring panic, entrapment, suffering, and despair must be truly like. Sexual abuse seems to us the most repellent kind of abuse, and it's certainly the abuse that nourishes a palliative amnesia.

Beyond the lines of printed words in my books are settings in which the books were imagined and without which the books could not exist. Sometime in 1985, for instance, running along the Delaware River south of Yardley, Pennsylvania, I glanced up and saw the ruins of a railroad bridge and experienced in a flash such a vivid, visceral memory of crossing a footbridge beside a similar railroad trestle high above the Erie Canal in Lockport, New York, when I was 12 to 14 years old, that I saw the possibility of a novel. This would become *You Must Remember This*, set in a mythical upstate New York city very like the original.

Yet often the reverse occurs: I find myself running in a place so intriguing to me, amid houses, or the backs of houses, so mysterious, I'm fated to write about these sights, to bring them to life (as it's said) in fiction. I'm a writer absolutely mesmerized by places; much of my writing is a way of assuaging homesickness, and the settings my characters inhabit are as crucial to me as the characters themselves. I couldn't write even a very short story without vividly "seeing" what its characters see.

Stories come to us as wraiths requiring precise embodiments. Running seems to allow me, ideally, an expanded consciousness in which I can envision what I'm writing as a film or a dream. I rarely invent at the typewriter but recall what I've experienced. I don't use a word processor but write in longhand, at considerable length.

By the time I come to type out my writing formally, I've envisioned it repeatedly. I've never thought of writing as the mere arrangement of words on the page but as the attempted embodiment of a vision: a complex of emotions, raw experience.

The effort of memorable art is to evoke in the reader or spectator emotions appropriate to that effort. Running is meditation; more practicably it allows me to scroll through, in my mind's eye, the pages I've just written, proofreading for errors and improvements.

My method is one of continuous revision. While writing a long novel, every day I loop back into earlier sections to rewrite, in order to maintain a consistent, fluid voice. When I write the final two or three chapters of a novel, I write them simultaneously with the rewriting of the opening, so that, ideally at least, the novel is like a river uniformly flowing, each passage concurrent with all the others.

My most recent novel is 1,200 finished manuscript pages, which means many more typed-out pages, and how many miles of running, I dare not guess!

The twin activities of running and writing keep the writer reasonably sane and with the hope, however illusory and temporary, of control.

Joyce Carol Oates has spent the last three decades pouring out novels, short-story collections, poetry volumes, plays, and essays. She has earned numerous awards including the National Book Award, the Rosenthal Award, a Guggenheim Fellowship, and the O. Henry Prize. Oates is presently the Roger S. Berlind Distinguished Professor of Humanities at Princeton University. This article was first published in *The Writer,* August 2000.

A PROFILE
OF SHERMAN ALEXIE

Tough, smart, funny, and not about
to back off from his Indian roots

by Joel McNally

Sherman Alexie was named one of the 20 best writers for the 21st century by the *New Yorker* and one of the 20 best American novelists under the age of 40 by *Granta*. Such recognition gives the author, a Spokane/Coeur d'Alene Indian, the status of a literary insider, but his perspective remains that of an outsider, and that's the way he prefers it.

Alexie, who grew up on a reservation of 1,100 Spokane Indians in Wellpinit, Washington, doesn't complain about his writing being categorized because of his background. He can be fierce, funny, or heartbreaking when writing about race and culture and what it means to be an American Indian. Yet his writing transcends cultural boundaries, appealing to a cross-section of readers who relate to his characters' struggles—but don't call it universal.

When "universal" is used as an adjective of praise in the mainstream media, it means nothing more than writing about the lives of minorities in a way that can be understood by white people, he says.

"Besides, it can be a self-fulfilling prophecy. If you object to being defined by your race and culture, you are saying there is something wrong with writing about your race and your culture. I am not going to let others define me. . . . If I write it, it's an Indian novel. If I wrote about Martians, it would be an Indian novel. If I wrote about the Amish, it would be an Indian novel. That's who I am."

Lynn Cline of Ploughshares wrote that his "work carries the weight of five centuries of colonization, retelling the American Indian struggle to survive, painting a clear, compelling, and often painful portrait of modern Indian life."

When Alexie's first collection of poetry and prose, The *Business of Fancydancing*, was published in 1992, *The New York Times* described him as "one of the major lyric voices of our time." Ever since, the writer has continued to receive critical acclaim.

At 34, Alexie has published nine volumes of poetry, two collections of short stories—*The Lone Ranger and Tonto Fistfight in Heaven* (1993) and *The Toughest Indian in the World* (2000), and two novels—*Reservation Blues* (1995) and *Indian Killer* (1998). He also wrote and produced *Smoke Signals*, an independent film that won the Audience Award and Filmmakers Trophy at the 1998 Sundance Film Festival.

Despite all the acclaim, he knows that Indians sometimes resent him for selling stories of despair on the reservation to the outside world—and that whites can be just as uncomfortable with his portrayals of white oppression or, perhaps worse, the kindly colonialism of self-proclaimed admirers who appropriate Indian culture and spirituality for themselves.

The characters and themes of his writing, in whatever form, come from the reservation, he says. And he sees no reason to look anywhere else for inspiration.

"Every theme, every story, every tragedy that exists in literature takes place in my little community. *Hamlet* takes place on my reservation daily. *King Lear* takes place on my reservation daily. It's a powerful place. I'm never going to run out of stories."

To Indians who complain that he violates tribal taboos by writing about problems on the reservation, Alexie responds just as bluntly:

"I would say no sober Indian has ever objected to the way I have written about life on the reservation. I write about alcoholics because I am a recovering alcoholic. If I extend my family out as far as I possibly can to include a hundred or more people—all but maybe two of them are alcoholics."

Despite his parents' often overwhelming personal problems, they took steps to assure that Alexie had a chance to fulfill the promise he showed from early on as a geeky, bookish kid. They transferred him to a predominantly white high school in nearby Reardan, Washington, where he starred on the basketball team and got the academic courses—unavailable on the reservation—that made it possible for him to attend college.

Some of the saddest stories Alexie writes concern the bright, young hopes of the reservation who embody the tribe's dreams for success against the outside world. These young men all too quickly take their place at the the the bar, drinking themselves unconscious.

Alexie found himself living an Indian cliche. After avoiding alcohol in high school, he fell into the college drinking life and didn't find his way out until he had dropped out of school. He explains both his early resistance to alcohol and his later surrender: "I guess I was just a lot more confident as a 16-year-old than I was as a 19-year-old. I was scared [in college]. Alcohol numbs fears."

The writer, however, reversed all the rock 'n' roll mythology about professional success as a prelude to self-destruction. He quit drinking the day his first book of poetry was accepted for publication by a small independent publisher.

The book that fixed Alexie in the minds of many readers—and within the literary establishment—was *The Lone Ranger and Tonto Fistfight in Heaven.* Alexie says he didn't realize just how much attention the title itself would attract. "The title came to me in a dream, where the Lone Ranger and Tonto got into a fistfight in heaven and the loser had to go to hell. It was the title of a poem first. You can look back now and see how it immediately set the book apart. But I didn't realize at the time how good it really was."

Because Alexie often employs humor and pop-culture icons in his writing, many readers may not remember that the title story in the collection is neither satirical nor about fictional Western heroes. It's about an urban Indian and his white girl-friend struggling against all the demons that are pulling their relationship apart.

Alexie's most enduring creations from *Lone Ranger* were the characters Thomas Builds-the-Fire and Victor Joseph who live on in other works. Any reader who tries to figure out which of the contentious, oil-and-water characters represents Alexie himself—Victor, the too-proud former tribal athlete, or Thomas, the nerdy, comic storyteller who follows him around—is doomed to failure. Alexie says that both characters, along with falling-down drunk Lester Falls-Apart, form an unholy trinity drawn from competing sides of his own personality. "All of my characters are me."

At the same time, Thomas and Victor have expanded into other dimensions, first in Alexie's novel *Reservation Blues,* and then in the film *Smoke Signals,* written by Alexie from one of the stories in *Lone Ranger.* His only preparation for trying the new form was watching a lot of movies. He approached it simply with the attitude, "I'm a writer. Putting words on paper, that's what I do."

Thomas and Victor are now the focus of a growing cult following for *Smoke Signals.* Perhaps their appeal is a result of Alexie's willingness to show characters dealing with personal feelings and the the actors' authentic performances. Alexie says it is difficult even for him to separate the characters he wrote from those created on screen by actors Evan Adams (Thomas) and Adam Beach (Victor).

"My characters are being taken away from me," he says. "It's a collaboration in my head whenever I write about them now. I can no longer picture Thomas without picturing Evan."

Alexie currently is writing a screenplay based on *Reservation Blues,* in which Thomas and Victor, using bluesman Robert Johnson's guitar, market a reservation rock band to the music industry, which is searching for a hot new Indian sound. As the characters continue to evolve, he says, Thomas is becoming more aware of what is going on around him, more clever and manipulative, and Victor is becoming an even bigger jerk.

Alexie uses humor when writing about deadly serious subjects such as racism and genocide. It's a technique he sometimes has to defend at public readings.

> The characters and themes of his writing, in whatever form, come from the reservation, he says. And he sees no reason to look anywhere else for inspiration.

"Just because something is funny doesn't mean it isn't serious. When did it become wrong for literature to entertain people to make a point? There are always going to be people who don't like humor, because people who are funny are sarcastic and irreverent. It makes people nervous."

Clearly, though, the book that made people most nervous—including many critics—was Alexie's least humorous. Written in the genre of a thriller, the novel *Indian Killer* is about a modern urban race war set off by a series of murders in which victims are scalped and ritual owl feathers are left behind. As the novel progresses, the question grows: Does a serial killer actually exist or is one being conjured up out of the fears and resentments of both whites and Indians?

"It was intentionally an angry novel," Alexie says. "I got tired of being accused of being so angry all the time. Well, if you want to see angry, here it is."

Alexie's own disappointment with the novel had nothing to do with critics' charges that it went too far over the top or that it lacked any real heroes or appealing characters. "I just didn't think I wrote the conventional mystery-novel parts well enough."

He still has no qualms about violating an old writing-class maxim: Never write out of revenge, because if you don't like your characters, your readers won't either.

"That's really wimpy. You know, Ahab wasn't a very nice guy, either."

The critics' rap doesn't square with the audience-friendly humor of his public readings, which he's honed into stand-up performance art, or with the way he expresses his beliefs. He openly condemned the American Indian Movement, which he says lost as soon as it picked up a gun.

"I'm anti-violence in all forms. And anti-gun for any reason. The only thing that elevates us above animals is our ability to say no to violence. I don't care what your political reasons are. It's always wrong. I'm not going to hurt anybody for my political beliefs. If that means I get shot, fine. I might die for what I believe in, but I'm not going to kill for it."

The screenplay for *Reservation Blues* is the third that Alexie has written since *Smoke Signals*. He also completed screenplays of *Indian Killer* and Norman MacLean's *Young Men and Fire*, a tale of fighting forest fires in Montana.

So what are Alexie's expectations for *Reservation Blues*, which he would like to direct? "None. I doubt it's going to get made. It's the most conservative business out there. The publication of books is much freer."

As a result, Alexie says he is currently exploring unconventional ways of making movies. "I really can't talk about my next career step in that regard, but let's just say I'm trying to do something very independent. I made a literary career for myself, and I didn't need anybody's permission. I'm attempting to replicate that in the movie world."

Hamlet takes place on my reservation daily. King Lear takes place on my reservation daily. It's a powerful place. I'm never out of stories.

Alexie is always writing. In addition to his screenplays, he is working on a political novel about a U.S. Senate race, and he continually writes poetry. "They all use different sets of muscles, you know. Novels are always the toughest. The analogy I always give is running. Writing a poem is like doing a 100-yard dash. Writing a novel is a marathon. No athlete does both well, and yet there are those of us who are trying. So I guess I'm always in the writing decathlon."

When asked who he admires, he goes out of his way to praise the work of horror writer Stephen King, whose enormous popularity is dismissed by some in the literary establishment.

"I think he's a great writer, I really do. All these academics talk about looking for the Great American Novel. What about a novel by someone like Stephen King, with which not only I—as a skinny, little kid growing up on the rez—but millions of other people could identify? That's amazing."

The other constant in his life is touring and performing. Last summer, he became the first three-time winner of the annual World Heavyweight Championship Poetry Bout, a ten-round exhibition held in Taos, New Mexico.

Because of his interest in performing and movies, Alexie says more and more reviewers jump to odd conclusions about his writing.

"I've gotten such a reputation for performance now, it's hilarious. Even though I'm writing the same, exact stuff I've always written, people automatically make all these assumptions now—'This is just being written as a performance piece.' I made a movie, so now automatically everything I'm writing, I'm thinking about making into a movie."

His motives for performing poetry are simple, he says. "Poetry is meant to be read to people. There are plenty of poems I write that I wouldn't perform because I think they only work on the page. But I don't write poems with that idea in mind. I just write poems. And then, when I go to perform, I look at them and see which ones will work."

Alexie's other motive for performing is obvious to anyone who has seen him. He enjoys it immensely. "Mostly. At least 90 percent of the time. I do wish there were teleportation machines, though."

But to Alexie, traveling to sell books is just part of his job as a writer. "Being an artist, being a writer, does not exclude me from financial responsibility. My publishers pay me a lot of money to write books. I'm going to do all I can to help them get that money back. I simply approach my job professionally. And I'm not going to be arrogant enough, just because I'm an artist, to believe that I'm somehow above the logistics of a job."

Of all the forms in which Alexie works, his preference would be to write poetry, "but I like to eat, too." Commercial pressures often push writers toward novels and screenplays, he says, whether that's what they want to write or not.

"I'm spared from a lot just because I write about Indians, who are noncommercial to begin with. It's hard to sell your soul when nobody's offering."

Joel McNally is an award-winning columnist and former editor of the Milwaukee *Shepherd Express*. He also worked for 27 years as a reporter, feature writer, and satirical columnist for the *Milwaukee Journal*.

ON HAVING WRITTEN A NOVELETTE

by Wallace Stegner

[This piece is excerpted from an article that first appeared in *The Writer*, November 1937.]

It is remarkable what violence the winning of a prize can do to the stability of one's mental life, particularly if the prize is given for an undefined piece of writing loosely called a "novelette." The rub is not so much in producing the story, though that calls for persistent labor and luck and much eating of apples and many difficulties with one's wife when she finds drying apple cores stuck all over her pet rosewood desk. The rub is not there: it comes afterward, when people begin asking you what you have done.

In the beginning, let me be publicly suspicious of people who know in advance exactly what they are going to write; how many characters there will be; how those characters will interact, to the tiniest detail; what the central thesis will be, and how each incident or character will illustrate that thesis; how many chapters or pages or volumes the work will run; and exactly how all the multiple strands of a story shall be woven together. . . .

I, for example, had no idea how long *Remembering Laughter* might turn out to be when I began writing it. I merely sat down hoping that it would emerge somewhere between the contest limits of 15,000 and 35,000 words. When I had been writing for two weeks I still half anticipated having to pad it to get it up above the minimum. All I actually had when I began was a mental acquaintance with three people, a vision of a single event with the possibilities of profound human effects. I also had the mornings until ten-thirty free, I had a fifteen-year-old typewriter named Old Bedlam, and I had a bushel of apples. In the course of six weeks' steady writing I wore out Old Bedlam, the bushel of apples, and my digestive system, and had a completed manuscript of 30,000 words. But I hadn't planned it; when I began I had thought I had a short story that might be padded; when I finished I was hauling back for dear life to keep it from becoming a full-length novel. I still wasn't worried about it, however. It was only after the prize announcement that the trouble began.

Then women's clubs began calling to ask if I would talk on the subject of the new fictional form, the novelette. Friends with an over-supply of intellectual curiosity discovered a yearning to know what a novelette was, technically. How did it differ from the novel? Was it merely a short novel, or was there a structural and intentional difference? Or was it just an expanded short story? Must it have the singleness of impression of the short story, or could it spread itself? . . . I had won a prize. I ought to know.

But I didn't know. I didn't have the least idea.

At last, to escape, we loaded the baby on his long-suffering grandmother and fled to England, where I rode around on a bicycle with a pipe in my teeth (apples were out of season), and thought to find peace.

Now a bicycle is a splendid place to be alone, and the rhythmic exercise of pumping makes a fine physical background for the composition of phrases. The novella-dilemma had gone completely from my mind, and before I knew it I had written two more of them in my head. At least, on the basis of the first one, they looked suspiciously as if they would emerge as "novelettes.". . .

This, as they say, gave me pause. I recalled that James Hilton was said to have written *Goodbye, Mr. Chips* on a bicycle. Perhaps, in my attempted flight, I had put my head into the lion's mouth. I sold the bicycle and came home. . . .

The short story, ancient or modern, has always been handicapped by its brevity. It can X-ray a single phase of character with pitiless brilliance, but it can never create a rounded human being. The moment one begins developing a complete human being in a short story, that story takes on the more leisurely tempo of the novel. . . .

We have come to a point now where definition is demanded, and I said that I couldn't define. But I can guess. I can guess that a novelette is a story whose characters are brought to the full stature of life, but which limits the number of its people as stringently as the short story must. In other words, it is a tale which has received the preliminary drastic selection of the short story, and the full-bodied character development of the novel. . . .

A novelette, I imagine, is a short story stretched just far enough.

Wallace Stegner (1913–1993) is the author of *Crossing to Safety, Angle of Repose*, and other prominent works of American fiction. He spent his life writing and teaching others about writing. His works received a Pulitzer Prize and a National Book Award.

A CONVERSATION WITH JAMES PATTERSON

by Lewis Burke Frumkes

Lewis Burke Frumkes: After much success with his past thrillers *Along Came a Spider, Kiss the Girls, Jack & Jill,* and *When the Wind Blows,* James Patterson has published *Pop Goes the Weasel,* another in the series featuring detective Alex Cross. Jim, tell us how you stumbled across Alex Cross, and how did that evolve?

James Patterson: When I set up the series, I wanted to write books that people couldn't put down, because I didn't find enough of them myself. Second, I was interested in creating a larger-than-life black hero. I just didn't think there were many of those; they tended not to show up in the movies. If you think about Cross, he's an anti-stereotype, he's raising two kids by himself, he has a great relationship with his grandmother. He is a trained psychologist who's also a detective, fearless, a little too obsessive about his work; he's got his downsides, but he's bigger than life. The other part, which I didn't figure out until later, has to do with the whole Cross family, including Alex.

When I was a kid I grew up in upstate New York, and my grandparents had a small restaurant. The cook was a black woman. At one point, when I was about two or three, she was having trouble with her husband, and my parents and grandparents said, "Move in with us." She moved into our house, and she lived with us for about four years. She didn't have any duties in the house, she just worked in the restaurant, but she and I became unbelievably close. I spent incredible amounts of time with her and her family, her aunts and uncles, nephews and nieces, that whole thing. She was like a mother to me. She eventually went back to Detroit, where she was from originally, and that was the closest I had felt to there being a death in the family, we had been so close. But that's where my notion of the Cross family comes from. It comes from her family. I don't believe that I could write convincingly about what goes on on street corners on 110th Street right now. I mean, I can write in a superficial way about it, but I can write about that family. I know that family.

There are two things readers always say about the Alex Cross books. One is that they are hard to put down—you know, I like to try to keep readers on the edge of their seats for the whole six or seven hours they spend with the book—and the second is they like the Cross family. I am constantly being warned that nothing bad must ever happen to anybody in the family, including the cat Rosie. So, I'm very careful with them.

Frumkes: *Pop Goes the Weasel, When the Wind Blows, Jack & Jill*—these titles come from children's nursery rhymes. How do you select them?

Patterson: Well, having a young child helps! We have a big book of nursery rhymes at home. Originally *Along Came a Spider* was called *Remember Maggie Rose*, but my editor didn't think that was a great title. "Along Came a Spider" was the title of one of the sections in the book. Once we went with that, we realized it was a lot easier. It would be easier for people to remember James Patterson, the one who wrote all those books with the nursery-rhyme titles. It also seems to counterpoint nicely against the books, which can be pretty scary.

Frumkes: Absolutely. Jim, you've already said you love page turners, and you write that way; there is nobody that does that better. When you are not writing, whom do you read, and whom did you read who might have influenced you?

Patterson: That question comes up when I am touring, and initially I didn't have an answer because I couldn't think of who had influenced me as a writer. It wasn't mystery writers; I didn't really read mysteries. But when I first started getting involved in literature, the writers who really opened up my world and said to me, people are different, it's not like the way you grew up in the Hudson Valley, were Jean Genet, John Rechy, Beckett. They got me excited about writing, excited about ideas, and probably helped me open my head up so I could create these crazy bad guys. I didn't read a lot of commercial fiction either growing up or in college, but there were two page turners I read—*Day of the Jackal* and *The Exorcist*—that gave me this notion that you can write a book that people can't wait to get back to.

> Jean Genet, John Rechy, Beckett . . . got me excited about writing, excited about ideas, and helped me open my head up so I could create these crazy bad guys.

Frumkes: Most people may not be aware of the fact that you have been very successful in the advertising business. I wonder if you could just briefly talk about that, how you got into advertising, and whether the lessons you used in that field in any way have an impact on how you write.

Patterson: I wanted to write novels, but I thought it was presumptuous to think that I could write them and get them published, so I thought I'd better get a job. I had a friend who had a friend in advertising. I went and talked to her. She was running around her office in a T-shirt, she was funny, she was making a lot of money, and she said, this is easy. So I said, OK, I can do that while I'm trying to write novels. And I got into it, and I found it very nice and eventually as I moved up the ladder I hired only one kind of person, talented and nice to be around. So it was really kind of like a liberal arts environment. Eventually I was chairman of J. Walter Thompson, then I said, Enough! Let's do something else!

Frumkes: And you've just hit it big with these books. Did it surprise you with the first one, how fast it caught on?

Patterson: Yes, it did. I thought we had a good shot because the publisher for *Along Came a Spider* went out and did what they had to do: They had enough books out there—people didn't have to go hunting around in the bookstores and find it on the back shelves; they promoted it very nicely. We were fortunate that people picked it up, and then that they liked the books a lot. I mean, you can sell them one time, but if they don't like the books, that's the end of it.

Frumkes: Jim, do you have favorite words that you either return to more often than other words or that appeal to you more than other words?

Patterson: I haven't thought about it, but probably. In the beginning, I really worried a lot about the sentences in my books. But at some point—and I think it's one of the reasons that I sell a lot of books—I stopped writing sentences and started writing stories. And that's the advice I give to new writers. Sentences are really hard to write. Stories flow. If you've got an idea, the story will flow. Once you have the story down if you want to go back and polish it for the next ten years, you can do that. But don't start with the sentences, you'll just drive yourself crazy. You also will put a lot of sentences down that you ought to take out but you can't because you say, Oh, I love that paragraph! Oh, I love that page! Oh, I love that chapter! But it's not really part of the story and it shouldn't be in there. Write the story.

Frumkes: Along with this wonderful advice, tell us about your habits. Do you write at night, during the day? Do you work on a computer?

Patterson: The main discipline I have is that I write every day. I try to write in the morning because it was my habit when I was in the advertising business. Now I have a lot more time to think about the books, and also if I happen to have some free time, dead time, I just go and write. I do use an outline; outlines are great. If you want to write a novel where plot is important you must outline it first, or you will waste an incredible amount of time and energy. I deviate from the outline; I always change the endings. I never know until I've written the whole thing. To me it's a lot like editing film, which I used to do a lot of in advertising, where I put all the pieces down and say, well let's look at it. It's not a movie, yet it needs something. Fortunately I can go out and reshoot, so to speak, write another chapter without getting the actors back.

Frumkes: Because you are having such an enormous success with the Alex Cross books, there must be terrific pressure on you to turn out similar books. Have you ever entertained the idea of doing what you did with *Miracle on the 17th Green*, of doing something different?

Patterson: I'm involved with a lot of things right now. I'm writing a love story that I am very excited about, it's a really good story. I just couldn't resist it. I'm creating a new series that takes place in San Francisco. It features four women who get involved in solving murders.

Frumkes: That sounds fabulous. It's amazing how you can keep all of it straight. James Patterson's new book, *Pop Goes the Weasel*, is the perfect novel if you want to stay up all night because it's incredible, and you can't put it down.

Lewis Burke Frumkes is host of the "Lewis Burke Frumkes Show" in New York. He is Director of the Marymount Manhattan College Writing Center and author of seven books, including *How to Raise Your I.Q. by Eating Gifted Children* and *The Logophiles' Orgy (Favorite Words of Famous People)*. This interview was first published in *The Writer*, November 2000.

Interview

A CONVERSATION WITH ELMORE LEONARD

by Lewis Burke Frumkes

Lewis Burke Frumkes: I'd like to begin by asking Elmore Leonard to tell us a little bit about how his novel, *Riding the Rap*, differs from any of his other books.

Elmore Leonard: I'm not sure that it is different, because it still has my cast of characters, or at least, the type of characters I like to work with; I spend at least half the time with the antagonist. Every year or so, while I'm writing a book, I get a letter from a friend who's in the business. He says, "Well, has your first chapter become your chapter three yet? Has your main character decided to do anything?" Because I'm so intrigued with the guys who are pulling the crime, whatever it is. I like their attitude. They never get along with each other. You always see that two of them are going to bump heads. You wonder which one might kill the other and be left then for the main character. I'm never sure myself, until I get to the scene where it's going to happen. Then I realize, it's got to be this guy, because my characters have to talk. In fact, they're auditioned. The characters are all auditioned in the early scenes so I can see how important they really are.

Frumkes: So you don't actually plot a novel out in detail before you begin?

Leonard: No, I don't. In *Riding the Rap*, Harry Arno, a character from my previous novel, *Pronto*, disappears. What happened to him? His former girl-friend Joyce asks her new boyfriend Raylan Givens, who's also the U.S. Deputy Marshall, "Would you look for Harry? What do you think happened to him?" Raylan, the lead character, isn't sure he cares what happened to Harry, because

Joyce is so concerned with him, but he starts looking for him. That's the idea: What happened to Harry.

We see that Harry's been abducted, but not in the usual way. This is a scheme that was inspired by the hostage-taking in Beirut. Chip Ganz, the fellow who comes up with the idea, had watched stories on television about the hostage-taking and wondered, "Could there be any money in that? What if I took a hostage, blindfolded him, and chained him to a wall in a filthy basement somewhere?" One of his accomplices says, "But, where are you going to find a filthy basement?" So, they end up holding the hostage in a fairly nice beachfront mansion. The idea is that instead of sending a ransom note to someone, they deal with just the hostage. "You tell us how you can get two million dollars to us without anyone knowing about it. If we like the idea, we'll let you go. If we don't like the idea, you're dead." These are the guys who are into money and manipulative with money. Harry Arno, for example, is a sports bookie. Another guy that they pick up is a savings-and-loan scoundrel who may have thirty million dollars hidden away somewhere—all his investors went broke, that kind of guy.

So, that's the scheme that I start with, and I develop it with different points of view. Among the bad guys, I have three points of view: Chip Ganz and the two fellows who work for him. Then I have Ben Rolins's point of view, Joyce's point of view, and Harry's point of view. So, in movie fashion, I can cut to anyone's point of view at any given time. That's the key—point of view—because I am always writing from the point of view of one of my characters, never from mine. I'm not the omniscient author. I don't know anything. If a character is looking out the window, and there's a reason to describe the weather, it will be as he sees the weather, not as I see the weather, not as I use imagery and fall on my face trying to be poetic in describing the weather. I avoid the difficult things in writing prose.

Frumkes: Do you always write that way?

Leonard: In studying Hemingway, I came upon this technique: letting the dialogue pull the story as much as possible. I've always been interested in dialogue, but I don't know that I work any harder at it than anyone else. I just have a good ear. I don't hang out wherever criminals hang out and listen. There's always the sound of a character. In some cases, it's more pronounced than others, but you never hear me. That's the main thing.

> Point of view. That's the key. I'm always writing from the point of view of one of my characters, never from mine. . . .

Frumkes: Now, it's no accident that you began by writing Westerns, right? The closing scene in *Riding the Rap* is like a Western thriller, with two men who could be called "fast guns" facing each other. It's an incredible scene. What in the Western do you take into the crime novel?

Leonard: Well, when I started writing in the 1950s the market for Westerns was tremendous. Almost all magazines except women's magazines were publishing Western stories, and Western movies were big. But, in the eight Western books and the thirty short stories that I wrote, I never once ended with that face-off in the street where they're going to draw, because that never happened. I would read the accounts in the *Tombstone Epitaph* of shootings. A guy is standing at a bar, and another guy walks in with a pistol, fires at him three or four times, and misses. The guy at the bar turns around, chases him out, and hits him once or twice as the guy's running across the street. That was a gunfight. Why would they stand waiting for somebody to count to three or for a twitch? Why would they do that? These men were not honorable, not like gentlemen in old French duels.

Now, in the climactic situation of *Riding the Rap*, there is a little dishonorability, and the reference, of course, is to Western movies when one character says, "I want to know what it's like to meet a guy like that, like in the movies, and draw."

Frumkes: In *Riding the Rap*, you deal with a psychic, the beautiful Reverend Navarro, who has a gift for reading Tarot. It was an interesting subplot.

Leonard: In a way, she's sort of a central character. A lot of the plot hinges on her. The guys in the book are attracted to her for different reasons. She practices her art—or her con; we are not always sure that she really is psychic. Sometimes she is. When she's talking to someone on the phone at night, and she says, "Turn the light on. I can't see," you wonder, "Hey, wait a minute." Or when she says to Raylan, "You're from West Virginia. No, you're from Kentucky originally, and you were a coal miner." How did she know that? She's holding his hands, but he could have been a dishwasher.

Frumkes: Who were your models when you were first starting out in crime writing?

Leonard: When I began to study writing, I studied Hemingway, Steinbeck, and Richard Bissell—he wrote *7½ Cents*, which became the play *The Pajama Game*. I loved Hemingway for his dialogue, but I realized I did not share his attitude about anything. He took himself and everything else so seriously. A writer's style really comes out of his attitude and how he sees things. So, I had to look around at other writers, including Mark Harris, who wrote *Bang the Drum Slowly*, John Steinbeck, and John O'Hara. I could never get into Faulkner. I could never read *Crime and Punishment*; there seemed to be too many words.

Frumkes: What do you read for pleasure when you're not writing?

Leonard: A book I enjoyed quite a bit was Stephen Hunter's *Dirty White Boys*. I like Pete Dexter. I like Ed McBain. I think you can't touch his police stuff. I like James Lee Burke, Jim Hall, and Carl Hiaasen. I don't read them all the time, but I think they are all pros.

Frumkes: Do you work on a word processor?

Leonard: No, I write in longhand, and then, I put it on the typewriter as I go along. I bought my first electric typewriter a few summers ago. For twenty years or so, I had been using a manual that I'd bought secondhand. Finally, I became tired of changing and hunting for the ribbons.

Frumkes: What's your writing schedule?

Leonard: When I'm writing a novel, I work from 9:30 a.m. to 6:00 p.m. every day and most of Saturday—unless it's summertime. I start a book in January and finish it by May. Then, I don't write anything for several months, and the time just flies by. By fall, I start thinking of the next book. About five years ago, I saw a picture of a female marshall in the paper. She was a good-looking woman in her early thirties, standing in front of a federal building in Miami with a shotgun on her hip. Just looking at this picture, I thought, "That is the next book." It wasn't the next book. I wrote a couple others first, but I kept the clipping. Finally, I used that character in a collection of short stories Otto Penzler put together for Delacorte, called *Out of Sight*. He asked me to write one, and I thought, "Well, I'll try out my female marshall, whose name is Karen Cisco. I'll get to know her in this short story."

Frumkes: What advice would you give to writers just starting out?

Leonard: Read. You read and study what the writer is doing. Find a writer you feel you have a rapport with, and study the paragraphing, study the punctuation, study everything. I think the paragraphing is extremely important. Learn how to paragraph to keep the story flowing. Find out by experimenting how you write most naturally. You may be a traditional prose writer, an omniscient author whose words and descriptions are the most important elements. Or, like me, you hide behind the characters and let them do all the work.

> Find a writer you feel you have a rapport with, and study the paragraphing, study the punctuation, study everything.

Lewis Burke Frumkes is host of the "Lewis Burke Frumkes Show" in New York and Director of the Marymount Manhattan College Writing Center. This interview was first published in *The Writer*, November 1997.

HOW I WRITE

by Anne Rice

Why I Write

I write to be read, to create something that other people will read, care about and enjoy.

When and How Much

I don't have any rules about it. Usually I write on Saturday and Sunday. I start around 1 p.m.—I can't do anything before noon—and write until Mass at 4 p.m., have dinner and then write until 9 or 10 p.m. I often write an entire chapter in a sitting, 15 to 20 pages doubled-spaced. I used to stay up all night, but I don't anymore.

Where I Find Ideas

The best come from my research. I read nonfiction, history, archeology, and some New Age material about people who claim to see ghosts or have had near-death experiences.

Writer's Block

I never had writer's block until the spring of 1999, after I had been in a diabetic coma and almost died. It was very difficult. I had no ideas, no characters. I worked through it by writing *Merrick*.

Advice to Writers

Stick with it no matter who says what. Believe in yourself.
If you determine you are a writer, walk through the world as a writer. Claim that. People will try to tear you down. Ignore them. It takes courage.

Anne Rice, the doyenne of gothic novels, is best known for weaving the visible and supernatural worlds together. Since publishing *Interview with the Vampire* (1982), she has enthralled readers with her haunting stories of vampires, ghosts, and witches. Her books are rich tapestries of history, belief, philosophy, religion, and compelling characters. *Merrick,* Rice's most recent foray into this supernatural world, is her 21st novel.

Don't believe people who tell you that writing can't be taught. You can learn a lot about writing from other writers, from just reading [their] books very carefully. You can learn a lot about technique. It's helped a lot me to read, over and over again, the beginnings of *David Copperfield* and study how Dickens opens those chapters and reveals David's life. They are very, very helpful.

I learned a lot from the French writer Simenon. He would write a book in two weeks. He would lock himself in a room, and he would write for two weeks. They would have to bring his meals to the door, and he would speak to no one. And he had a very spare way of writing. I read him to learn how to do that. Because I tend to write in a rush of words, an abundance of words. But from Simenon, I learned how to use some white space on the page, how to say in one sentence, maybe, the same thing [as] in five.

—Anne Rice (excerpted from a section of her website, www.annerice.com, where she answers questions from her readers about her books and the writing process.)

A LETTER TO A YOUNG TALENTED WRITER

by William Saroyan

[This piece is excerpted from an article in *The Writer*, September 1938.]

First, forget that you are an unpublished writer. Regard yourself, so far as you are concerned, as the only writer in the world. This is very important: it is not pride, not egotism, it is simply a necessary viewpoint for the serious writer. You must believe you alone of all the writers of the world are writing the story of the living.

Remember to be inwardly calm. Remember to look upon all living, evil and good, with a clean eye. Remember to be a part of the world with a pure heart. Remember to be good-humored. Remember to be generous. And remember that in the midst of that which is most tragic there is always the comic, and in the midst of that which is most evil, there is always much good. Remember to relate, in your work, the two extremes: one side and the other. And remember to smile. . . .

I want you to write in a way that no one else in the world has written. Any writer who is a writer can do it. You have a new language within yourself: it may not be developed yet, but it will develop if you make the right beginning. If you do not make the right beginning, you will never be able to write. They will put you down as one who has been influenced by another, and that will be the end. If they do that with your first stories, and your first book, there will never be any freedom from their judgment.

The way not to write like anybody else is to go to the world itself, to life itself, to the senses of the living body, and translate in your own way what you see there, and hear, and smell, and taste, and feel, and imagine, and dream, and do: translate the thing or the act or the thought or the mood into your own language. Remember this. I want you to make the right beginning because, if you make the right beginning, nothing can stop you. . . .

In writing this letter I am not being kind, and I do not want you to feel grateful to me. I don't want you to feel that I am encouraging you . . . You cannot feel indebted to anyone and be a great writer. You've got to be a little mean about the whole business, a little sore, and at the same time objectively generous and tolerant: not generous to anyone in particular, but to the idea, the abstract idea: everything you do you do for yourself, not for another. For living. You've got to be selfish. This isn't pettiness: it has to do with what and how you will write.

. . . After you read this letter I want you to get up and yawn and go for a walk and say to yourself, "To hell with him," and, "To hell with everybody": because only then will you be able to begin. . . .

I can't decide for you whether or not you have got to write, but if anything in the world, war, or pestilence, or famine, or private hunger, or anything, can stop you from writing, then don't write, don't want to write, forget it, be an honest clerk, go to the movies, dream, awake, and sleep like everybody else, because if anything can even begin to keep you from writing you aren't a writer and you'll be in a hell of a mess until you find out. If you are a writer, you'll still be in a mess, but you'll have better reasons. Good wishes and good luck.

William Saroyan (1908–1981) was an internationally renowned writer, playwright, and humanitarian. He was awarded a Drama Critic's Circle Award and the Pulitzer Prize for his play *The Time of Your Life*; but he declined the Pulitzer on the grounds that "commerce should not patronize art. . . ."

A CONVERSATION WITH KAZUO ISHIGURO

The international novelist examines a
chaotic world through the prism of memory

by Lewis Burke Frumkes

As a boy, Kazuo Ishiguro dreamed of being a musician. He eventually sent his songs to music publishers and subsequently learned about rejection, something he hasn't experienced as a writer.

Since writing his first novel, *A Pale View of Hills*, 18 years ago, Ishiguro's work has been critically acclaimed. His novels include *An Artist of the Floating World* (Whitbread Book of the Year, 1986), *Remains of the Day* (Booker Prize for Fiction, 1989), *The Unconsoled* (1995), and *When We Were Orphans* (nominated for a Booker Prize, 2000).

"As soon as I started to write fiction, I almost immediately met with success," says Ishiguro. "The first few stories were published immediately in literary magazines. I was actually encouraged by my publishers, who gave me a contract in advance to finish the novel I was writing. A lot of things happen in life like that."

The author, who was born in Nagasaki, Japan, in 1954, came to England with his parents in 1960. The family had every intention of eventually going back to Japan, but stayed in England, where Ishiguro grew up straddling two worlds.

"I have a sense of having just left without saying goodbye, and of this whole other world just kind of fading away. . . . I have the feeling of this completely alternative person I should have become. There was another life that I might have had, but I'm having this one," says the writer, who considers his work to be international.

He attended the University of Kent at Canterbury and the University of East Anglia in Norwich, where he studied English, philosophy and creative writing.

"I served my creative apprenticeship for writing through the form of songs. I wrote over a hundred songs. I don't think it's such a jump from songs to stories.

I can see when I look at first-time writers that they are going through the same phases I went through as a songwriter. I went through an intensely autobiographical stage, and then moved on to purple prose, very technical but self-indulgent. By the time I was toward the end of my songwriting period, I had found a style. It was very pared-down, simplified writing that was similar to my first short stories. To some extent, that is the style I have stuck with as a writer."

Ishiguro's work often deals with how people are shaped by events or circumstances in their pasts. *A Pale View of Hills* involves a widow in postwar Japan recalling her life in Nagasaki. In *The Remains of the Day* (which was made into an Academy Award–nominated film starring Anthony Hopkins and Emma Thompson), an English butler struggles with the changing class structures of postwar England. *When We Were Orphans* concerns a famous English detective who returns to his birthplace, Shanghai, to solve the mystery of his parents' disappearance many years earlier.

"The maze of human memory—the ways in which we accommodate and alter it, deceive and deliver ourselves with it—is territory that Kazuo Ishiguro has made his own," writes a *Book* magazine critic.

In addition to five novels, Ishiguro has written several short stories. His work has been translated into 28 languages. In 1995, he received the Order of the British Empire for service to literature.

Lewis Burke Frumkes: In *When We Were Orphans*, Christopher Banks, the central character, is a detective who moves to Shanghai. I read that your father was Japanese but lived in Shanghai. Did you spend any time in the city?

Kazuo Ishiguro: I don't know Shanghai firsthand at all. It's a place that I have put together in this book from my association with that city at that time. It was a pre-Communist Shanghai. I learned about it through my father. There were a lot of photos that he had in an album. I couldn't quite believe that people I actually knew, who I always thought of as leading a very sedentary kind of life in England, had lived there. That my grandfather, who I knew as a small child, actually had lived in this wild and exotic place. That is what Shanghai was until the Japanese came, and then later the Communists took over.

This story takes place really between the turn of the century and 1937. That was the heyday of the old Shanghai, where huge fortunes could be made, where different foreign communities lived together: British, American, French, and Japanese. The Chinese—the Communists and the Nationalists—were having an underground war with each other. The Russian refugees from the revolution had settled there. Jews from Europe found refuge there. Many strands of history and international commerce came together in Shanghai.

Frumkes: Within that framework, how did you make the novel historically accurate?

Ishiguro: It wasn't ever my intention to write a historical novel—it was the myth of Shanghai I found interesting. I feel I did sufficient and hard research. I have a pretty large collection of books at home about Shanghai during this period. I found that stuff written there at the time was the most interesting; the guidebooks published gave local histories.

One of the poignant things about books is that they are written by people who assume their community will be here forever. They talk in minute detail about where you can get Italian pastries, where the best tailor might be, or which is a good club. They talk about it as if these things were set in stone. Of course, you know full well when you are holding the book that within a handful of years it would all be wiped out. There's a certain poignancy about that.

Frumkes: Having done so much research on Shanghai, and having written this novel, do you feel like visiting the city, even though it has changed so dramatically?

Ishiguro: I'm only mildly curious. In fact, to some extent I feel that my imaginary cities are in competition with the real cities. The question of research has always been a vexing one for me. In my early writing life, I was writing books set in Japan. Then, too, I had a very ambivalent attitude toward being brought face to face with any kind of solid, real Japan. I had my own imaginary landscape of Japan, Shanghai, England.

For novelists, it is very important that you build that imaginary world in a solid way so that you get to know it. You get to know its peculiarities. You get to know to what extent it veers away from the realistic. You get to know whether it is a comic world, how the people in it behave, the atmosphere. To some extent, you get bogged down with too much information about a historical or real place. It gets in the way of building your world.

There's a big difference between research for a novelist and research for a historian or a travel writer. The nature of what you are trying to do as a writer of fiction is slightly different.

If people want to know about the history of Shanghai, there are very good books that I could point them to. In fact, an author of one of these books told me that I had actually caught it well. I was gratified to know that, because I don't want to distort things, I don't want to mislead people.

Essentially, as a novelist, this is a landscape that I am using for my imaginative purposes. To me, it's location hunting. I have a theme, a story, and I want to put them down where they can best be orchestrated. I needed a place for a childhood with the chaos of the modern world, with war and international issues as well. As long as I had those things, it could be anywhere.

Frumkes: Why did you make Christopher Banks a detective? You could have made him anything and still have looked into his past.

Ishiguro: There are various ways to answer that. One was that I became interested in a certain view of evil that seemed to exist in this genre of fiction—the notion that all the bad things that happen come from a master criminal some-where, that there's a Moriarty figure behind the bad things. The way to conquer them is to become a detective and ferret out the source of evil.

After World War I, it seems to me that there is a kind of a change, certainly in the English detective tradition. I think there is an awareness that evil and suffer-ing don't really work like that. There is a generation that went through the trau-ma of modern warfare and realized that the bad things in life cannot emanate just from some clever evil character. It's something else altogether—chaos.

Frumkes: Christopher Banks has a Kafkaesque experience in his search. It's not always straightforward. It doesn't end with an evil criminal at work.

Ishiguro: It's not straightforward because he is a detective, because that is the view he starts out with. He thinks he can solve all of the bad things that have happened to him. Indeed, he wants to set the clock back and heal something that happened in his childhood. If only he can find the "baddies."

I'm slightly reluctant about calling it Kafkaesque, but it certainly gets surreal and bizarre. In the end, he is trying to fulfill an illogical mission. There is a part of him that refuses to let go of the idea. It takes him a long time to realize that some things remain broken forever. Yes, things get very strange for him. To some extent, it's a journey through his interior.

Frumkes: What kinds of books have inspired you? The opening line about 1923 and somewhere in the middle, when you wrote, "I would not see Sarah Hemmings again . . ." reminded me of Gatsby.

Ishiguro: I find this an interesting thing. There is often an assumption that the writers who you love the most are the ones you are influenced by the most, and that might be true for many writers. I don't think that it is for me. People who I have par-tially read or accidentally come across often influ-ence me. There is some aspect of their writing that intrigues me. I like to write through the filter of memory. I like the atmosphere and the movements of the mind when it is remembering.

Proust is a good example. I've never read the entire novel [*Remembrance of Things Past*]; I've only read the first volume. The overture, the first 60 pages, that's where I got a lot of this stuff about mimicking the movement of memory in somebody's head. I read that between my first and second nov-els—it had a big impact on me. I realized that as a novelist, you did not necessarily have to tell a story by going from one solid, well-built scene to the next.

I realized that as a novelist, you didn't have to tell a story by going from one solid, well-built scene to the next. You could actually mimic the way memory runs through some-one's mind.

You could actually mimic the way memory runs through someone's mind. You can have a fragment of a scene dovetailed into a scene that takes place 30 years later. You don't have to have whole scenes. You can make references to things and come back to them later.

That whole atmosphere and mood—searching through that foggy world of memory to find out who you are, what your history is—fascinates me. That's an example of something I read at a time when I was searching as a writer, and I found it. I'm not a big Proust fan; I've hardly read him. I have to say, though, that he's had a profound influence on me.

Frumkes: What advice would you give to young writers?

Ishiguro: There is a tendency in the writing world today that I think young writers probably have to guard against. There is an environment in which it can be very tempting to not take on full responsibility for your own writing. You can write a bit and then take it to a group or teacher, and then they tell you what to do, and so on. I find this a very dangerous tendency. Writing well is about finding your own voice. There is no way around taking responsibility for your own writing.

There is something about the whole nature of creative writing groups in universities that you have to be very careful about. They can be tremendously encouraging and useful, but you can easily become dependent on other people. You can't write unless you commit.

Lewis Burke Frumkes is host of the "Lewis Burke Frumkes Show" in New York and Director of the Marymount Manhattan College Writing Center. This interview was first published in *The Writer*, May 2001.

A CONVERSATION WITH RUSSELL BANKS

The path to an answered prayer

by Lewis Burke Frumkes

Russell Banks has established himself as one of America's greatest writers. He has written nine critically acclaimed novels, among them *Affliction, Rule of the Bone,* and *Continental Drift.* His short stories have garnered O. Henry and Best American Short Story awards, and two of his books, *Affliction* and *The Sweet Hereafter,* have been made into films.

His newest book, *The Angel on the Roof,* is a collection of 31 stories both old and new. Janet Maslin of *The New York Times* calls the book "a beautifully lucid, frequently wrenching collection. . . . What elevates these stories far above their tacitly heartbreaking events are the vast reserves of compassion and wisdom that Mr. Banks brings to framing tragedy."

Lewis Burke Frumkes: Why did you write *The Angel on the Roof,* and how did you select the stories?

Russell Banks: Well, it's not a complicated story. After I wrote *Cloudsplitter* and finished the publicity tour, I realized that I had given up five, maybe six years of my life for that one book. Then I realized that for the whole decade, I had written four novels without taking a break. My brain felt as though some of the fuses had gone out! I wasn't quite burnt out, but that side of the brain—whatever side of the brain writes novels—was exhausted. So I turned to short stories.

What I used to do was write a novel and then take a year off to write short stories, which would turn into a collection the following year. On re-reading the earlier stories and writing the new stories, I saw that, in fact, I had a deep personal investment, a long-time investment, in the form. I had done work that I really wanted to save. I had done work in my 20s, 30s, and 40s that I thought was good enough, mature enough, and interesting enough to stand alongside the stories I had written in my late 50s—this past year. I also thought it would be interesting to save the best stories, put them with the new stories, and make a different kind of book than I had ever made before.

Frumkes: Why did you call it *The Angel on the Roof*?

Banks: The title is a metaphor. It appears in the introduction as an image, which I tried to find a way to talk about, of what storytelling itself is. What are we doing when we are telling stories? It seemed to me that we are uttering a kind of prayer, and we are uttering it to the angel on the roof.

The angel on the roof is a figure—the Muse, maybe, or a genie, or an angel that makes us better, smarter, more honest than we might be otherwise in the telling of a story. So it refers to the figure, which is a figure of the imagination. All stories seem, in some way, to be prayers to that angel on the roof. The prayer in the introduction is essentially this—very simple but very complex. It's at the heart of the storytelling impulse. The prayer is that I hope you, the stranger, will love me for no good reason. It's for that unconditional love.

A storyteller is always, in some way, asking that of a stranger.

Frumkes: What draws you to the short story format?

Banks: When I started writing, I was just a kid in my early 20s who had fallen in love with poetry. I wanted to be a poet. I had the intelligence, but you probably don't have to be awfully intelligent to be a poet—you have to have the gift. And I didn't have the gift. I had a formal intelligence. I loved form, the excellency of form, the exigencies of form—what it makes you do and say that's unexpected: the way a sonnet can force you to say and see things in a fine language that you couldn't if you weren't working within the restrictions of a sonnet.

A short story has form like that. It is rigorous and binding in many ways. The ways in which it binds you is also the way in which it liberates you. It's a kind of back and forth between confinement or restriction and liberation. It's very exciting for a writer. All poets talk about it, and I think short story writers feel it too. You don't feel it with novels. They have that great big baggy form and there isn't the same kind of restriction. They're not quite as formal in the rigorous sense that a short story is. As a result, it engages language very differently. The need for concision, the sense of a phrase turning the entire meaning of a story on its head—you go in one direction or the other and however you go changes the meaning entirely. It's a very exciting and intense kind of writing.

> What are we doing when we are telling stories? It seemed to me that we are uttering a kind of prayer . . . to the angel on the roof.

Frumkes: Has your love of poetry and your early interest in visual arts influenced the way you write fiction?

Banks: Devoting myself to writing and reading poetry for a number of years has certainly influenced my sense of language as a tangible thing, something with solidity and life outside my thoughts and desires. I like to think it has made my prose more interesting. As for my early experience as a visual artist, yes, that's had an effect on my fiction, I'm sure. It's at the center of my belief that a writer (and reader) must see what's being written and not just hear it.

Frumkes: Several of your novels have been turned into films: *Affliction, The Sweet Hereafter,* and soon, *Continental Drift.* How did you feel about each of those films?

Banks: Well, I'm one of very few writers who really likes the movie adaptation of the novels—so far. Yes, they've won awards, but they have been really interesting movies in their own right. Even if they weren't adaptations of my novels, I would have gone to see Atom Egoyan's *The Sweet Hereafter* or Paul Schrader's *Affliction* and say, "Boy, that was a good movie." I was very lucky in that both Atom and Paul invited me into the process right from the conception, with our arms around each other's shoulders looking at everything step by step, line by line. It was a very intimate and collegial kind of process.

Frumkes: Have you considered writing a screenplay?

Banks: I've written two based on my own novels, *Rules of the Bone* and *Continental Drift,* neither produced yet, and have just finished adapting Jack Kerouac's *On the Road* for Francis Ford Coppola. I love writing screenplays and I think I'm not bad at it. It's nothing like writing fiction, however. A screenplay is mainly a set of instructions, a plan or blueprint, not the thing itself.

Frumkes: In *Affliction,* your most autobiographical novel, the narrator tells the story of his brother's decline because "his story is my ghost life, and I want to exorcise it." You grew up in a broken home with an abusive father. Has writing helped free the demons of your difficult childhood?

Banks: Not so much "free the demons" as free me from them, to let me live a life not controlled by my childhood experiences. But that's not something peculiar to writing. It's the discipline and rigor of the life I've had to live in order to write my stories and novels that have freed me from those demons you mention. If you devote yourself to an art, or to religious study, say, or to scholarship, to anything that requires your constant best attention, you're not likely to suffer from the leftover bad memories of a difficult childhood. They just have no room in your life to play much of a role.

Frumkes: Tell us how your career as a writer has evolved.

Banks: I came out of a blue-collar family in northern New England. We are a kind of rough and hearty breed of people. Hard-drinking, hard-fighting, hard-working. The idea of becoming a writer or artist was very difficult for me to imagine, to apply to myself. I came at it in an awkward, unconventional way. I worked at a variety of jobs; the one I was best at and stayed the longest at was that of a plumber. That's what my father was, that's what my grandfather was. I knew the different fittings because I had worked as a plumber's helper when I was a kid during the summers. So that was the direction I was going when I began to take myself seriously as a writer.

The inevitable conflict got resolved in some ways when I married at age 24. My wife's mother offered to send me to college. I ended up going to the University of North Carolina at Chapel Hill and finding my peers. In a sense, I found my world. By the time I got out [in the late '60s], I was published fairly widely and I began to teach. I liked teaching, and I think I was fairly good at it. So I began to have a new career. Teaching ran sort of parallel to my career as a writer.

Frumkes: You retired from teaching after 16 years in Princeton's Creative Writing Program. Do you miss working with students?

Banks: Definitely. But not so much that I want to return to teaching. When I gave up teaching, it was for me an exchange of the pleasures of the classroom for more time to write. And it wasn't an even exchange, because while I value both, I value my remaining time to write more than I do the pleasures of the classroom.

Frumkes: You have become one of the more successful writers, and deservedly so. You also seem to have kept things in perspective. What has success meant to you?

Banks: Mainly, it's freedom. That's the point. I get to control my time. As you get older, time is of the essence. You really hear the meter running, and you know time is what you need most of all. You need your health, memory, and mind, but to utilize those things you need time. That's what success has provided for me. But this all came to me in the last decade. If this happened when I was a kid, in my 20s or 30s, I think it could have been harmful in many ways. But by the time it arrived, my habits were set, my routines were set, my relation to my work was set, my friendships were set. What am I going to do? I might buy some nice copper-clad cookware or something, but that's about it. It doesn't change your life too much, except for the fact that there is a lot more time.

Frumkes: Are there certain books you'd like to be remembered for?

Banks: Yes. The next one. The unwritten book, the one in which I'm trying to get it right, finally, and actually do get it right. You know, it's impossible for a writer to second-guess how his or her work will be seen in years to come. All one can do is hope that one is given enough time, energy and talent to write one book that will outlive the author. Sadly, the author will never know which—or if he or she has done that already.

It's like not being able to see who shows up at your funeral.

Frumkes: Do you have favorite words, or words that you use frequently in your writing?

Banks: That's a tough question. So many words dazzle me. Looking over my work from earlier years, there are some words that do reappear. They aren't necessarily pretty to the ear, but they are, in my mind, interesting. These words are transformation, reconfiguration, words that suggest starting over, a re-evaluation or a fresh beginning. Those words and concepts show up over and over again in my stories. I think that's a lot of what the stories are about. They are about people who return to a breach in their lives or to betrayal, abandonment or failure, and try to recognize and grasp it. People who try to reconfigure their lives, their futures, as a result of the re-engagement of the past.

Frumkes: That might actually be a theme to *The Angel on the Roof.* What advice would you give to young writers starting out?

Banks: A number of people gave me advice when I was young. There are many things I would say. First of all, don't quit your day job. That's an important one. Also, trust your dreams more than your intelligence. It's very easy to be an intelligent young writer, very hard to be a dreamer who trusts his dreams. I don't mean the dreams that are your fantasies; I mean the dreams that bubble up from your unconscious. Trust the dreams that wake you up in the middle of the night, the ones that stir you and move you in mysterious ways. Which leads to my next bit of advice: Try to penetrate the mysteries.

Lewis Burke Frumkes is host of the "Lewis Burke Frumkes Show" in New York and Director of the Marymount Manhattan College Writing Center. Jeff Reich, managing editor of *The Writer,* contributed to this interview, which was first published in *The Writer,* February 2001.

Interview

A CONVERSATION WITH JANE HAMILTON

Good writing is in the details

by Pegi Taylor

Jane Hamilton has had a meteoric writing career. Her novel, *The Book of Ruth*, won the PEN/Hemingway Foundation award for best first novel in 1989. *A Map of the World*, her second novel, landed on *The New York Times* bestseller list in 1994. Both books, which feature rural women struggling to come to terms with irreparable loss, were chosen by talk-show host Oprah Winfrey for her television book club; in 1999, a film version of *A Map of the World* was released starring Sigourney Weaver.

Hamilton's third novel, *The Short History of a Prince* (1998), was a startling departure from her first two. The protagonist, Walter McCloud, is a gay man in midlife reviewing his adolescence, when he dreamed of dancing in a production of *The Nutcracker*. His ballet teacher forces him to realize he lacked sufficient skills, and his passion for his first male lover is brutally rebuffed. At the same time, Walter's older brother becomes terminally ill.

Hamilton spoke to *The Writer* shortly before embarking on a publicity tour for her fourth novel, *Disobedience*. Her latest work chronicles a year in the life of the Shaw family, as narrated by 17-year-old Henry. The family lives in suburban Chicago, where the father, Kevin, teaches history at a progressive high school. Henry focuses his attention on his sister, 13-year-old Elvira, who takes on the persona of a boy to participate in Civil War reenactments, and their piano-playing mother, Beth, whom Henry discovers is having an affair with a violin maker. Tensions in the family come to a head on the way to a Battle of Shiloh reenactment. Hamilton explores both teenage and middle-age malaise with great sensitivity and humor.

Hamilton lives on an apple orchard in Rochester, Wisconsin, with her husband, Bob Willard, and two teenage children, Ben and Hannah. While writing in her second-floor office at home, she looks out over rolling farmland. She may see a whooping crane, the apple trees in full blossom, or some of their sheep grazing in the pasture. Most days, whether tromping through snow or hidden by cornstalks, she takes a walk through the countryside as a break from writing.

Laughing often, Hamilton speaks with great vitality, but with equal care. She is intensely curious, asking almost as many questions as she answers. A voracious reader with a remarkable memory, she has strong opinions about contemporary fiction and even recites some poetry.

Pegi Taylor: What would you call the most difficult part of writing?

Jane Hamilton: For me, it will probably always be the first draft. This is a quote from someone: "You have to be willing to commit bad words to paper to write anything at all." The sentences don't flow and the details aren't quite right. The first draft is sort of outline-ish, and I wouldn't want anyone to read it.

Taylor: You said in a Random House interview that "The Book of Ruth was fueled by Ruth's voice," and "In *A Map of the World,* I felt propelled by the incidents." What fueled *The Short History of a Prince* and *Disobedience?*

Hamilton: Each book has a kernel that is the starting point and, in a way, its own fuel. In *The Short History of a Prince,* I was interested in capturing that whole ballet school dynamic. That was the kernel and then there were other elements that fell into the story. *The Short History,* in particular, isn't fueled by the voice or the plot. The one who carries it is Walter himself. The plot and voice hang on him. *Disobedience* is a book about voice, and everything is hung on Henry's voice.

Taylor: Your ear for dialog seems at its best in *Disobedience,* from Beth Shaw's women friends ranting about men, to Elvira's teenage friend Hilare mouthing off, to disjointed family conversations at the dinner table. How were you able to handle so many different voices with authenticity?

Hamilton: I did something I'd never done before that was helpful: I read the work chapter by chapter into a tape recorder and then listened to it while driving long distances. It was a strange thing. I felt like I was a fresh reader, a fresh listener. It was probably not the best highway driving I've done. I'd think, "Oh my God, I've got to change that word," and then scribble little notes to myself. But it was very useful, and I would recommend it as a technique for anybody.

Taylor: You've spoken about reading all your novels out loud to your husband. What happens when you read your books to him?

Hamilton: I read the work to Bob when I can go no farther. I read the end of *Disobedience* to him, which I knew wasn't right, and I couldn't quite figure it out. I read it again out loud to myself, but there's something about his presence in the room and hearing the words through his ears that makes it possible to instantly identify a phrase, a sentence, or a scene that doesn't work. There's nothing like reading, something you've made to a specific listener. He knows where everything comes from. It's very gratifying. He laughs and cries in just about all the right places. You can't have more of an experience with a book than that.

Taylor: *Disobedience* includes over a dozen e-mails as part of the text, as well as a few letters. Why did you decide to add this epistolary element to the novel?

Hamilton: I knew there had to be some way for Henry to find out what his mother was up to. It is a device. I didn't suddenly in the middle of it decide to include those e-mails. They were there almost from the very start. They have to reveal what his mother, as well as the lover, is thinking and feeling. Letters can be useful as a revealing tool for all kinds of characters. The reader can understand, in a way Henry can't, what the letters mean.

Taylor: What are you thinking about when you form the initial paragraph of a chapter?

Hamilton: Those beginnings are important because they have to take you into the body of the chapter. They have to seize the reader. Some writers write to please their readers; some writers couldn't care less. I don't write for readers—that is, I try not to worry about whether a reader will be comfortable or pleased—but I do feel it's important to have a good start and to draw the reader in. I'm aware of not having an inert first paragraph.

Taylor: In your syllabus for a fiction-writing course you taught at Carleton College in 1996, you quote Willa Cather: "Art should simplify. That, indeed, is very nearly the whole of the higher artistic process; finding what conventions of form and what detail one can do without and yet preserve the spirit of the whole." Can you give an example of your own simplifying process?

People tend to use too many metaphors. It's very, very rare to have a metaphor that actually works, that has the power to stun.

Hamilton: I wrote a 20-page prologue for *The Short History of a Prince*, and I knew it wasn't interesting to anybody but myself. My editor said I should get rid of it, and I knew she was right. I condensed it down to about four pages. It was distilling the essence-taking the most important things and whittling it down. Sometimes you don't need to write about everything.

Taylor: You plant a powerful image early on in *Disobedience*. Henry has recently discovered his mother's affair and realizes, "To picture my mother a lover, I had at first to break her in my mind's eye, hold her over my knee, like a stick, bust her in two." Can you remember how that image emerged?

Hamilton: Well, I remember thinking that no self-respecting teenage boy would really spend much time thinking about his mother having sex. Children in general don't like to imagine their parents engaged in that activity. So then I began to think, "What does Henry have to do to think about her in that way?" which he actually does quite a bit. The "breaking" seemed like the only possible way, giving him a certain power, making him the master puppeteer.

Taylor: Do you have a particular stance toward the use of metaphorical language?

Hamilton: People tend to use too many metaphors. I've come to this as a reader. When I read I often want to edit on the spot: "unnecessary." It's very, very rare to have a metaphor that actually works, that has the power to stun. I think just from reading enough fiction where metaphors weren't aptly used, I've cut them out myself.

Taylor: You're known as a writer who does extensive revisions. Do you revise in stages, looking for certain aspects like characterization, or do you go after everything at once? Do some parts, like the opening or closing, get more attention than others?

Hamilton: Generally, I'll write the first couple of chapters over and over and over again until I have the momentum to go to the middle. And I'll write that, and then I'll start again at the beginning and go through the middle. And then I'll start again at the beginning and go through the middle. And their I'll take a sprint to the end. And then I'll start over, because the ending changes how the beginning is, and the middle. And then I'll go through it again, and then I'll go through it again, and then I'll go through it again. Then the ending will need attention. I'll start in the middle and go to the end, and then just work the end, the end, the end, the end, the end. And then, usually, I go through it again.

For me the pleasure is going over it, having the details fall into place and hearing it in a different way each time. I have tried to respect the amount of time it takes.

Taylor: In your syllabus for the fiction-writing course, you advised students to "Look at life through your character's eyes as you eat lunch, go to sleep,

> Every detail you include for the character has to be psychologically true to that character. And that's something you can only accomplish with time.

wake up, brush your teeth, walk around campus." What was it like to walk around as teenage Henry for a couple of years?

Hamilton: Well, I had to listen to that awful music. I knew that he was funny initially, had that wry, ironic sensibility, but I didn't know how deeply sad he was going to be. I kept trying to talk him out of it. One of my pet lines is when he says in his ambivalent, wishy-washy jeans way, "In those days my heart, I guess it was, sank more or less, every day." We grew together in that element.

Taylor: In a *Publisher's Weekly* interview, you said the characters in your first two novels were "only warm-ups" for Walter. How were the characters in your prior three novels warm-ups for Henry?

Hamilton: I could not have written this book without first writing about Walter. Walter and Henry are in many senses related. Elvira is sort of a flip side of Walter. She's not comfortable with her gender and her identity. But I think Walter had that same ironic sensibility that Henry has. I think those books are linked in a way that the other two books aren't.

Taylor: The *Library Journal* said your forte was "depicting adolescents left not by villainy but by circumstances on the fringes of family life while they figure out ways to raise themselves." This is true for Henry in *Disobedience*, too. What do you think is the source of this gift?

Hamilton: I've always been interested in adolescence—that time in your life when, in many ways, you're very powerful and yet you know you're essentially powerless. It's a terrible tension, and I find it very compelling.

Taylor: What do you consider most important for creating a fully realized character?

Hamilton: Every detail you include for the character has to be psychologically true to that character. And that's something you can only accomplish with time. You can write something and think it's terrific and really be married to the sentence—and get distracted by the fact that the detail in that lovely sentence doesn't really fit the character. So you have to be very careful. Care and time will prove to you whether those details actually work. God, I've come to agree, is in the details.

Taylor: Place plays a huge role in all your novels. In *Disobedience*, Henry contrasts his teenage years in Illinois with his early childhood in Vermont. At one point, he suddenly feels homesick for Vermont and laments, "I missed the shape in the near and far distance, of mountains, what was so grotesquely absent in the Midwest." All your other novels describe the Midwest's beauty. What did it take to turn a critical eye on this landscape?

Hamilton: I was writing this book and doing a reading at a bookstore in the Midwest when the topic of landscape came up. A woman from West Virginia started talking about how much she missed the mountains and what it felt like to be without them. I was casting about for ways to think about the landscape, and I did borrow things she said that illuminated for me what it really would be like to live without mountains.

Taylor: *Publisher's Weekly* called *A Map of the World* "a piercing picture of domestic relationships under the pressure of calamitous circumstances." The husband and wife, Alice and Howard Goodwin, tell the story in *Map*. Henry relates the calamitous domestic circumstances in *Disobedience*. What opportunities or frustrations did writing about a marriage from a teenage son's point of view afford you?

Hamilton: No one can know what goes on in a marriage. Children can't, although they are as close to it as anybody. I wanted to show what the marriage was as much as possible, but I couldn't do it completely because Henry's telling it. And that did represent a certain challenge. Kevin Shaw gets short shrift in the book; he's the most mysterious character. I probably did fail to have him shine through past Henry's pen. That was a frustration, and one that I was trying to figure out how to fix up to the last minute.

Taylor: Both Henry and his friend Karen witness and describe a crucial scene, where Beth comes to her daughter's aid at a Shiloh reenactment. Henry and Karen evaluate the mother's actions quite differently. Why did you decide to juxtapose these two perceptions? Don't you risk the trustworthiness of Henry as narrator?

Hamilton: All along he's reliable in his unreliability. I first knew what he saw, and then I realized that what he saw was not complete, or that there was a different point of view. Karen came in very handy because I didn't want to have Beth Shaw tell it. I would think the reader would still trust Henry, because what he sees is true to himself and makes sense for him. He doesn't step out of himself to tell it.

Taylor: All of your novels are written in the first person except *The Short History of a Prince*. Why did you write *Disobedience* in the first person?

Hamilton: It's the way it came to me. I tried to write *A Map of the World* in the third person, and I strained for it, even though deep down I knew it didn't serve the book well. Eventually I ditched it and wrote it in the first person. When I wrote a story about Elvira in 1996, it was written in the first person from Henry's point of view. For some reason, I can't say precisely why, he was always the one in charge of the narrative, the filter. It happens at an intuitive level. It's one of the first things that come.

Taylor: In *Disobedience* you write, "Through her music Beth Shaw expressed the typical sentiments of a classical pianist: beauty, the briefness of rapture, and let's not forget sadness, sorrowing, the grandeur of lost passion, lost youth." How does this list compare to what you want to express through your writing?

Hamilton: I'm most interested in trouble and how people relate to each other and themselves as they get through whatever trouble is at hand, whether it's love or lost youth.

Taylor: Henry says, "I got to thinking that maybe treachery is the only interesting story." How does treachery play a part in all your novels?

Hamilton: In order to write anything, the writer has to be in touch with the fact of the dark side. Everybody has the experience of treachery in some way or another. What's interesting is discovering what a character is made of, testing that character by letting him react to treachery that is done to others or to himself.

Taylor: Your editor, Deb Futter, described *Disobedience* as "funny, even devilish at times." Did set out to write a funny novel, or did the characters and plot invite it?

Hamilton: No, I didn't set out for it to be funny, but it was clear to me right away that Henry's sensibilities could amuse me. He looks in his wry way at his sister, so there's lots of comic possibility there. He's just standing back and looking at the whole family dynamic He was wry from the start, but his material is rich.

Taylor: What role does humor play in your writing?

> Every project is imbued with terror. What if you can't get through it? What if it falls apart? What if there isn't anything there? What if you can't figure out how to end it?

Hamilton: Each of the books has funny bits in them—even Alice (*A Map of the World*). I think Alice is funny. Not many people pick up on that, and I feel for her in that regard.

As I get older, I rue things that are overly earnest. There are a couple of novels I've read recently that were written by people in their 20s and they were so very, very earnest. My reaction was that if only they'd waited a few more years, they might have been able to make the books a little funny.

Taylor: You've said in the past that you always know the last lines of your novels from the start. How does having a last line in mind influence your writing?

Hamilton: The last line is merely a beacon; it's a

destination. It doesn't mean that the book is going to be didactic, or that it's the final answer, or that it's the message. It's a place to arrive at. You can get there and realize that's not really what you wanted to say after all. It is merely a marker.

Taylor: What happened to short story Jane? You haven't had a short story in *Harper's* since "Rehearsing 'The Firebird'" came out in June 1990.

Hamilton: I really think I am a novelist. *Disobedience* began as a short story about Elvira, and for the amount of disruption that happened in 15 pages, it wasn't believable, it didn't have any weight. In the story, the parents were divorced after Beth ran off with a worker from 3M. Henry's sensibility and Elvira's quirkiness are the survivors of that story. Somewhere along the line I realized that the story could be about the marriage, instead of the divorce.

I wrote, in about 1987, a story called "Sue Rawson's Swindle" and then another story called "Prince," basically about Walter's dog, but they were just fragments. The stories served as character sketches for *The Short History*. The stories were very small outlines, just as, I suppose, a painter makes a study for a painting. He draws only the hands or the arms and then, later, you get a painting with all the body parts of several nudes.

Taylor: You told *Publisher's Weekly* that you became "paralyzed" while writing *A Map of the World*. This wasn't an issue for your third or fourth novels. Can you imagine a situation when writer's block might strike you again?

Hamilton: Sure. Any day. Each project is imbued with terror. What if you can't get through it? What if it falls apart? What if there isn't anything there? What if you can't figure out how to end it? What if the middle falls flat? What if, what if, what if? What if in the end you really don't have anything to say?

Taylor: What haven't I asked you that I should have?

Hamilton: Oh, the title for *Disobedience*; this is one of the kernels. I got it from A.A. Milne's poem "Disobedience." [Hamilton recites from memory:]

James James
Morrison Morrison
Weatherby George Dupree
Took great
Care of his Mother,
Though he was only three.
James James
Said to his Mother,
"Mother," he said, said he:
"You must never go down to the end of the town,
if you don't go down with me."

James James
Morrison's Mother
Put on a golden gown,
James James
Morrison's Mother
Drove to the end of the town.
James James
Morrison's Mother
Said to herself, said she:
"I can get right down to the end of the town
and be back in time for tea."

I was going to put a little snippet in as an epigraph, but I just didn't want to start the novel with a nursery rhyme. I figured if you knew it, you knew it, and if you didn't, it didn't matter. That poem had such meaning to me, starting with when (my son) Ben came home from D.A.R.E. (the drug education program) and told me I could never have another glass of wine. The child really does not want the parent to have any kind of life that's separate from him. That poem is so perfect.

James James
Morrison Morrison
(Commonly known as Jim)
Told his
Other relations
Not to go blaming him.
James James
Said to his Mother,
"Mother," he said, said he:
"You must never go down to the end of the town
without consulting me."

Pegi Taylor is a Milwaukee writer, educator, and long-time friend of Hamilton's. She has published articles for magazines and websites such as Salon.com. This interview was first published in *The Writer*, January 2001. "Disobedience" is from *When We Were Very Young* by A.A. Milne (copyright E.P. Dutton, reprinted by permission of E.P. Dutton and the Estate of A.A. Milne).

Interview

A CONVERSATION WITH MARTIN AMIS

by Lewis Burke Frumkes

Lewis Burke Frumkes: Martin Amis, one of the finest writers on our side of the Atlantic, has a new book out called *Heavy Water,* published by Harmony Books. Martin, this book is extraordinary, interesting in so many ways. In one of the stories, you have a screenwriter who is writing about three gorgons who have an idea for coming back and opening one of these escort agencies. It was just so hilarious. The stories in *Heavy Water* were written over how many years?

Martin Amis: Actually, 22. The first story is dated 1975, when I was 26. They span that length of time because I write short stories at a reasonably steady rate. So, three stories were stranded back in time, and the rest are actually recent. But there is no design in the book. It's just the old principle of when you've got enough short stories, you just sling them into a book.

Frumkes: Each one is more fun than the other. But, there is one extraordinary story at the end, "What Happened to Me on My Holiday." How did that story originate in your mind?

Amis: Perhaps only once or twice in a writer's life will a short story happen to you, and that story happened to me. It happened to my children, and I wrote the story one morning because it was all there in front of me. But then I decided that it would be too transparent if written in normal English. And so it's written in an 11-year-old's sarcastic, facetious notion of what an American accent sounds like. But, he's using that device as a way to delay his apprehension of death, which is what the story is really about. He's fending off death until the

253

last few lines, when the story reverts to the clarity of English and you feel that the experience is being absorbed.

Frumkes: Michiko Kakutani of *The New York Times,* who's not an easy critic, fell in love with that story. She felt you reached out on so many levels that she was extraordinarily moved by it. . . . Let's turn to Martin Amis the man, the writer, the personality. You are the son of a very successful man. Sometimes having a celebrated forebear must be very difficult, but sometimes it opens all kinds of doors. I don't for a minute mean to suggest that your gifts are not your own; and certainly noted writers from Updike to Bellow have sung your praises. What was it like having Kingsley Amis for a father?

Amis: That's a topic that has been much on my mind, because I've just published a memoir about him and about me and others. It was always a very close relationship, based on humor and good nature and generosity and support. We did have a few spats in the press, but we disagreed more in print than we did around the sitting room. On literary questions, really. What it comes down to is that he felt that the novel should be entertainment, and my novels, I suppose, are more "worked at," more literary than his. He was also a poet, and he had poetry as an avenue on which he could slow things down and be linguistically very precise. I didn't have that outlet, so it all went into my novels. But although he thought my work was pretentious, he did concede that I was the best of a bad lot. You're always likely to scorn the upcoming generation, and it's equally natural to revere your forebears.

Frumkes: When did you start writing?

Amis: Not until I began my first novel. When I went to the university I wrote a few scenes but I wasn't one of those kids who writes an epic poem at the age of 11 and then a series of dramas. I wasn't precocious. But I do think all writers begin to be writers in adolescence. That's the natural time when you write poems and keep a diary and a notebook and begin to explore your own consciousness and yourself. Writers are just the regressives who never grew out of that. I believe a writer needs an element of innocence despite all the supposedly flashy sophistication and gaudiness of "worked-at" prose. There's still a route back to your childhood and adolescence, and a literary man is a) a literary man; b) an angry man; and c) an innocent. It's a necessary component.

Frumkes: You live quite a colorful life. You have been much admired and much criticized and much just the subject of conversation because not only are you at the top of your field as a writer, but you live a sort of international social life. What is the real Martin Amis all about? What is the essence of Martin Amis? How do you respond to the people looking in who paint you in various ways?

Amis: The basic unit is the writer, and that means someone who is most alive when he is alone. I see myself as sitting in my study all day. That is the basic unit in my life—the day in my study in which everything comes. Nurturing a preoccupation. Protecting your solitude. In my case, with five children, there seems to be the permanent battle for solitude.

Frumkes: So you are, to some extent, a family man as well?

Amis: Yes. I'll give you an example: When I was growing up, it was only in the direst emergency that you knocked on the study door of my father, who'd whip around in his chair and say, "What?"—although he was very soft and friendly when he wasn't in his study. It was with trepidation that you approached his door. I'm astonished when my boys wander up into my study without so much as a "May I come in?"

Frumkes: They don't fear you?

Amis: They don't fear me at all. They sort of respect what I do, but there is no aura of un-interruptibility that my father managed to evoke.

Frumkes: How long ago did your father die?

Amis: He died in '95.

Frumkes: So he had an opportunity to see much of your success.

Amis: Oh, yes.

Frumkes: Was he very proud of you?

Amis: I think he was, but he was slightly resentful of being outflanked. A woman came up to him once at a party and asked, "How does it feel to have a son who is more famous than you are?" and he said, "He isn't more famous than I am." And she said, "He is much more famous than you are." My father told that story, but I think with some irritation.

> . . . a literary man is a) a literary man; b) an angry man; and c) an innocent.

Frumkes: As someone who loves language, uses words well, do you have favorite words? Words that crop up more often than other words, or that you am particularly fond of because of euphony or any other reason?

Amis: I have crushes on words. *Quiddity* was showing up more often than it should in my stuff, and my father used to say that I used the word *sweaty* too often. But you have these crushes and then the infatuation passes. But all writers have key words. In Conrad it's *ineffable, terrible,* words of that kind. In Henry James it's words with eight syllables that mean delicate. When you deal in words, you have your preoccupations.

Frumkes: Do you write in longhand? On a computer? On a typewriter? At night? During the day?

Amis: I can work all through the day and it is a wrench sometimes to stop around seven. I don't work at night. I might make notes at night, but when the day is over I need to recuperate for the next day. I always work in longhand and when I get the whole thing written—perhaps not in the right order, and perhaps not sufficiently polished—I type it up and then retype it. But this memoir I've just done is the first book I've written on a computer, and I'm hoping that will eliminate the middle stage. I use my computer only as a sort of advanced typewriter. I don't use any of its functions besides the word count and I seem to have a very provincial computer that underlines, in a squiggly red line, almost every other word I use.

Frumkes: Because they are neologisms?

Amis: Words not recognized by my computer. All foreign cities and all names. I don't want to fall into the trap that I think is there for people who use computers for creative writing that nothing is ever really finished, because it is so easy to go back and rewrite a phrase. My father had a rule: Don't put it down unless it's right, and stay with it until it is right. There's that danger and also the more elusive one, that the cursor is there and the whole thing is humming. It gives you the impression that you're thinking even though you're not.

Frumkes: Whose work inspired you to write? Whose work did you read? Whose work did you love?

Amis: I was very slow to come to literature. I spent my teens reading comics, and then my later teens rereading those comics. But when I did come to it, I came to it whole. It was actually the poets I read hungrily—the romantics, the Victorians, Milton, Shakespeare. I had a good appetite for anthologies. I came to the novel a little later, and then it was in the English tradition.

Frumkes: What do you read now when you're not writing?

Amis: I read Don DeLillo, Saul Bellow, John Updike, Norman Mailer—all the obvious senior Americans.

Frumkes: What about the well-regarded British novelists?

Amis: I read those contemporaries of mine with dread, because you can't get out of it. My two closest novelist friends, Salman Rushdie and Ian McEwan, I read with great pleasure and admiration.

Frumkes: Martin, if you were giving advice to young writers starting out, what would you tell them?

Amis: Two things. I think these are the only useful bits of advice: Write about what you know; don't write tremendously elaborate fantasies. Be specific, be concrete, write about details of life you see, and not necessarily about yourself, but the world. That's more fun. Point two, just get going and keep going. Dismiss anxiety. Just proceed to the end.

Lewis Burke Frumkes is host of the "Lewis Burke Frumkes Show" in New York and Director of the Marymount Manhattan College Writing Center. This interview was first published in *The Writer*, October 2000.

Writer's Classic

THIS QUESTION OF TRUTH

by A. J. Cronin

[This piece is excerpted from an article, "The Writing of a Novel," published in *The Writer,* December 1938.]

I believe there are writers who enjoy writing. For my part, I loathe and abhor it. I enjoy immensely sitting in an easy chair before the fire, closing my eyes and rapturously envisaging the sweep, the drive, the sound, and the fury of the masterpiece—they are all masterpieces at that stage—which I am going to produce. But writing—ah! That is a different pair of shoes! I have none of that grace and facility of composition which I admire so much in others. No sooner am I seated at my desk than I want to get up again, to wander about the room, look at the view, eat apples, suck toffee, smoke. And when at last I take a pen in my hand I am a stammering man striving to be articulate, a muscle-bound juggler longing for cannon balls, compelled to be dexterous with three-penny bits. . . .

The sole satisfaction which one achieves, at this point, is the sense of progress. I do my writing upon two-penny exercise books—those I used [for my novel *The Stars Look Down*] bore a smiling photograph of the handsome young man who was then our Prince of Wales. And my mainstay, the pillar of my sanity, was the growing pile of written-up, besmirked copy-books stacked at the side of my desk. Every one I added caused me to feel that I was easing the burden upon my back. If I counted these books once I counted them a hundred times.

. . . I decided that David Fenwick, my young protagonist, must, in his effort to advance the miner's cause, be elected to Parliament, and that, in Parliament . . . he must be ignominiously defeated. I wished, above everything, to be honest. A true hero of fiction would doubtless have secured justice for the men in a scene of wild and stormy triumph. But reality is a dog which follows closely at my heels. . . . I had no desire to produce a propaganda novel. And so, unhappy and unpalatable though it might be, I resolved to end the book in tragedy.

Maupassant once declared that the vast bulk of the reading public is made up of various groups who exclaim, "Comfort me; amuse me; touch me, make me shudder, make me laugh!" And only a few chosen spirits demand, "Let this show us the truth and nothing but the truth."

Yet it is this question of truth in the novel which seems to me of paramount importance. Of course, nowadays no word is more dangerous than the word truth. To speak it above a whisper is to court the disaster of being mistaken for a politician or a fool. At the mention of the word, people look pointedly away or else they sigh, "Ah! what is Truth?" assume an air of profundity, and then begin to talk about the weather.

In short, the modern idea is that cosmic truth does not matter a button as long as one has money for "the pictures" or a radio set. Nevertheless . . . I feel most strongly that the function of the novelist is to tell the truth, to represent life honestly—not as it should be, but as it is.

A.J. Cronin (1896–1981) grew up in sight of the slag heaps of the west Scottish coalfields. He became a doctor in the valleys of South Wales "where every man is a pitman, predestined from his birth. Life has few illusions for the overworked general practitioner; he sees his fellow-men without their masks." Later he took a job with the British Ministry of Mines, studying pulmonary disabilities, and eventually left the practice of medicine to become a novelist, where he achieved great success.

Interview

A CONVERSATION WITH PATRICIA CORNWELL

by Dorman T. Shindler

Devoted readers of Patricia Cornwell's Kay Scarpetta series may have noticed that the tough, no-nonsense chief medical examiner has been going through something of a midlife crisis. In recent books, the normally secretive Scarpetta opens up to friends and a therapist, becoming more vulnerable. Scarpetta's transformation is no accident, says Cornwell.

"One of the reasons I've not revealed much about her that is personal is because I've been guarded about myself. A lot of what you find out in *The Last Precinct* about what it's like to be Scarpetta—how exposure to such cruelty and tragedy has affected her on a deep level—is true about me. It's part of my development as a writer to try to expand and get deeper."

Though Cornwell, who has a state-of-the-art security system at her home, protects her privacy, she lets her guard down when writing about her alter ego, Scarpetta. Like Scarpetta, Cornwell is a stickler for detail and often comes across as dead serious.

But the author has a lighter side too—a facet of her personality she expresses through a humorous mystery series. Featuring reporter-turned-cop Andy Brazil, Police Chief Judy Hammer, and Deputy Virginia West, the series focuses on the comedy of errors that makes up the main characters' lives, rather than on murder and mayhem. Like Scarpetta, Brazil's background mirrors some of Cornwell's experience. As a reporter for *The Charlotte (North Carolina) Observer*, she often rode along on police patrols, and worked as a volunteer for the Richmond, Virginia, police force. And like Cornwell, Brazil has a politically incorrect sense of humor.

While working as a reporter, Cornwell did some research in the chief medical examiner's office in Richmond. Her fascination with the work resulted in a job there as a computer analyst and part-time "scribe," recording the measurements of wounds on murder victims. That experience led her to write *Postmortem* in 1990, the first in her Scarpetta series and winner of the Edgar, Creasey, Anthony, Prix Roman d'Adventure, and Macavity awards, which are given by the writers and readers of mystery and crime fiction—high marks for a book that was rejected by seven publishers.

Cruel and Unusual, her fourth novel, was awarded Britain's celebrated Gold Dagger for the year's best crime novel. Cornwell has written 16 books, becoming a regular on *The New York Times* bestseller list (recently with *Southern Cross*, featuring Brazil, and *The Last Precinct*, featuring Scarpetta).

Cornwell spoke with me by telephone from her office in Richmond shortly after the release of her latest novel, *The Last Precinct*.

Dorman T. Shindler: In the last two Kay Scarpetta novels, you seem to have been tearing down Scarpetta's emotional walls, forcing her to reveal more of herself. Was that something you had planned to do all along?

Patricia Cornwell: Readers have been telling me for years that they want to know her better. In fact, I have friends who are approached by readers who ask if they know [personal] things about Scarpetta. *The Last Precinct* is a book about secrets, the secrets of the dead, the secrets of the living, and Scarpetta's secrets. If you want to know what it's like to be Scarpetta, well, by God, I'm going to show you. But in doing so, you're going to find out a lot more about what it's like to be me, too. I've decided to take that risk.

> If you want to know what it's like to be Scarpetta, well, by God, I'm going to show you. But in doing so, you're going to find out a lot more about what it's like to be me, too. I've decided to take that risk.

Shindler: You've said that Scarpetta is your alter ego. Does her emotional development parallel your own?

Cornwell: Yes, that's very true. She's under intense scrutiny. She has major security concerns because of what she does and the kinds of people she testifies against in court. She has privacy concerns; she's a very private person. And life does sometimes imitate art. I can understand much better now what it's like to be her than I could have when I was writing *Postmortem*.

Shindler: In *Black Notice* and *The Last Precinct*, Scarpetta goes through big emotional changes, but she also contemplates a career change. Are you trying to take the Scarpetta series in a new direction?

Cornwell: I am going to take it in another direction, but it's not so much that I'm changing her career as that I'm broadening it. She's going to become a private consultant who's hired by the State of Virginia, but she doesn't actually work for the state anymore. As a result, she'll have the freedom to be a consultant on cases that could happen anywhere in the world. One of the things I'm looking forward to is having her get involved in a case that has a victim who's still alive. Medical examiners do, in fact, get called into hospitals to look at people who have been assaulted or badly injured, to interpret what the wounds mean. Is that a bite mark, a belt mark, or what is that?

Shindler: You mentioned research. *The Last Precinct* touches on a recent archaeological dig in Jamestown, Virginia, in which you've recently gotten involved. How did that come about?

Cornwell: You may recall that in the November 2000 issue of *National Geographic,* the cover story was about the mummies of Incan children who had been sacrificed in the Andes. They're the most perfectly preserved mummies ever found and about 500 years old. While I was in Argentina last spring, I got to go up to Salta to see those mummies, see the scientific testing. It was an incredible experience, and it rekindled my interest in archaeology. I've always been interested in it.

Then I found out there was this incredible dig going on in Jamestown, which isn't far from where I live. So I started going down there and participating. Now it's become one of my passions. I'm very involved with Jamestown, both financially and just working with the people. In my next book, *Isle of Dogs,* a follow-up to *Southern Cross,* there's tremendous focus on Jamestown. *Isle of Dogs* is the name of the area in London where John Smith and his men set sail for the New World.

Shindler: You've said that after working in the medical examiner's office, you became even more fascinated with the criminal mind. Do you read widely in the field of true crime writing?

Cornwell: No, I don't read those kinds of books. I tend to stick with the books of the profession. I will read textbooks, written by experts, who might describe psychopathology and deal with sex crimes. But what I don't read are the books where these people retire from their professions and give an account of all their case works. I don't get into that stuff. I'm not interested in it. I'm more interested in what I find out firsthand. I'd rather sit down with a forensic psychiatrist and ask him specific questions than read books; to me, that's secondary research. Most of the books in my library are very complicated, technical books. Of course, most of my knowledge comes from going to the labs or going to the morgue. I'm the chair of the board of the Virginia Institute of Forensic Science and Medicine, so I'm directly involved in these fields in my everyday life, too. I worked in a morgue for six years, have attended as many as 1,000 autopsies. When I was working at the medical examiner's office, I scribed for doctors during their cases. One of the reasons I still go to the morgue a number of times in the year and ride with the police is that I want to show readers the reality of violence.

Shindler: Do you think Americans deal with death differently than in other cultures?

Cornwell: Yes. America is the most violent democracy in the world. It's something that's met with great shock, horror, and mystery when I travel to other countries. They ask, Why are there so many shootings in America? Why does everyone own a gun? I do think there's a striking difference. However, we are seeing more violence everywhere.

Shindler: Do you read much fiction?

Cornwell: No, I don't. I have two favorite fiction writers who I do read. One is John Jakes [On Secret Service]. I love his historical novels, because I learn so much from them. I love Mark Helprin [A Soldier of the Great War]. I think he's the finest writer in the world. I read him just for the sheer beauty of his language, in hopes that it can inspire me to improve my own.

Shindler: When you sit down to write, do you work with an outline?

Cornwell: I don't write from an outline or use note cards. I only use research notes when I'm writing. I write my books the way my characters work their cases, because until they follow the evidence, they don't know what's going to happen, either. The story always takes on its own life. It's as if it tells itself to me, and I simply report on it.

Shindler: Do you have a strict routine for writing? A certain number of hours per day?

Cornwell: I don't write every day. At least four months out of every year I do nothing but research. When I'm in the throes of doing nothing but writing, I'll write 14 to 15 hours a day. The hardest part is the research. Because the entire time I'm trying to take in very technical information, I'm also trying to figure out how I'll use it in the book.

The easiest part is revision, because the story is already there. But my writing is like a relationship. Even when I'm not sitting down doing it, it's with me everywhere I go and in everything I do.

Shindler: Why did you begin the Andy Brazil series?

Cornwell: I like writing the series because I have a "Far Side" sense of humor, and I don't get to use it in the Scarpetta books. It's a different voice that I feel a need to use. I also can poke fun at issues that I couldn't [in a more serious novel] without really offending people. It gives me an opportunity to laugh at myself and, hopefully, for people to laugh at themselves.

Shindler: You recently wrote a children's book, *Life's Little Fable*. What prompted you to do so and how was the experience?

Cornwell: It was fun! I started out as a poet, and it's a rather poetic story. I was inspired to do it because I was speaking to a class of second-graders in Los Angeles, critiquing some stories they had written, and they were all asking if I'd written anything they could read.

When I was flying back from L.A., I decided to write something for kids. So I started working on it on my laptop. Nobody was interested in it, so we produced it ourselves. My company did. We found the artist, I paid to have the artwork done, and then people decided they liked the book. And if readers are interested in it, they can go to my Web site (www.patricia-cornwell.com). I sell autographed copies of it, because you can't get it in stores anymore.

Shindler: When you started out, did you have particular writing icons you wanted to emulate?

Cornwell: No, I really didn't. I came out of a journalistic experience, so I've always enjoyed nonfiction, which is what I read mostly. My writing is pretty much based on my journalistic instincts—to go out and observe, smell, touch, taste, do it yourself and then, to write the story. But I read really fine writers, just to help improve my own writing skills.

> I was devastated when [my first novels] were rejected, but it was such a blessing. It was the best thing that could've happened to me. It would've hurt me badly had they been published because they're not good.

Shindler: Before finally selling *Postmortem*, had you attempted to write other novels?

Cornwell: My first novel I wrote in college. It was really awful. It was my attempt to write a portrait of an artist as a young woman and . . . what a joke! And it's hidden in a box somewhere, where it belongs. Then I wrote three crime novels. I considered them "graduate school." They were my way of learning how to do what I'm doing now, although I was devastated when they were rejected, but it was such a blessing. It was the best thing that could've happened to me. It would've hurt me badly had they been published, because they're not good. They're certainly nothing like what I do now.

My failure as an author in those early days caused me to have to stay at the morgue, because I needed a job. What started out as research became my career. I was there six years. I didn't leave the morgue until I began *Cruel & Unusual*, my fourth book.

Shindler: That's surprising—your first novel was such a critical success.

Cornwell: But I didn't make any money! I only got $6,000 for that book. I spent $1,200 of it on making [publicity] posters. My friends and I taped them up in grocery stores and Laundromats because there was no advertising or promotional budget.

I didn't consider myself a success with *Postmortem* until it started winning all of those awards, but by then it was practically out of print. They printed 10,000 hard copies total: 6,000 in the first printing, and then, I think, two more small printings. That was it. There was a huge word-of-mouth push and it got fabulous reviews. It's kind of an irony that a book that won five awards was kind of the stepchild.

Shindler: Was *The Body Farm* a breakout book in terms of recognition and success?

Cornwell: When I turned that manuscript in, Scribner's really liked it a lot, and I got $20,000 for it. That's when I knew that maybe things were going in a good direction. It wasn't until *The Body Farm* and *From Potter's Field* that the books started going to number one.

I've had a dramatic lifestyle change, and one that I'm lucky to have. I never take it for granted. It's mind-boggling to me. I'm very appreciative of it. I try very hard to do a lot of things for other people, make a difference in other people's lives, to give something back, because I've been so blessed.

I've always wanted to write, just because I love it. My dream was just to get published. I never thought in terms of making money. And I never thought I'd be on a bestseller list or that anybody would know who I am.

Shindler: Do you have any advice for aspiring, struggling writers out there?

Cornwell: Well, first of all, they have to write. You have to write and write and write, just like an athlete has to learn to be excellent in whatever sport he or she undertakes. I recommend having other people read your writing and listen to their reactions.

It's very important that you read other writers who you admire, because you can study what they do and figure out what works and what doesn't work. You should read good writers and bad writers—you need to learn why something works and why something doesn't work. Then, when the day comes that you've got something you want to have published, go to a literary agency.

But don't get discouraged. And most of all, do what you love. Don't write about something just because you think that's the hot ticket of the day. Write about what's inside of you.

Dorman T. Shindler of Kansas City is a regular contributor to the *Dallas Morning News, Bloomsbury Review, Denver Post,* and other publications including *The Writer.* He is currently writing two novels. This interview was first published in *The Writer,* March 2001.

IS IT GOOD ENOUGH
FOR CHILDREN?

by Madeleine L'Engle

Several years ago, when I was teaching a course on techniques of fiction, a young woman came up to me and said, "I do hope you're going to teach us something about writing for children, because that's why I'm taking this course."

"What have I been teaching you?" I asked her.

"Well—writing."

"Don't you write when you write for children?"

"Yes, but—isn't it different?"

No, I assured her, it isn't different. The techniques of fiction are the techniques of fiction, and they hold as true for Beatrix Potter as they do for Dostoevsky.

But the idea that writing for children isn't the same as writing for adults is prevalent indeed, and usually goes along with the conviction that it isn't quite as good. If you're a good enough writer for adults, the implication is, of course, you don't write for children. You write for children only when you can't make it in the real world, because writing for children is easier.

Wrong, wrong, wrong!

I had written several regular trade novels before a publisher asked me to write about Swiss boarding school experiences. Nobody had told me that you write differently when you write for children, so I didn't. I just wrote the best book I possibly could; it was called *And Both Were Young*. After that, I wrote *Camilla*, which was reissued as a Young Adult novel, and then *Meet the Austins*. It's hard today for me to understand that this simple little book had a very hard time finding a publisher, because it's about a death, and how an ordinary family reacts to that death. Death at that time was taboo. Children weren't supposed to know about it. I had a couple of offers of publication if I'd take the death out. But the reaction of the family—children as well as the parents—to the death was the core of the book.

Nowadays what we offer children makes *Meet the Austins* seem pale, and on the whole, I think that's just as well, because children know a lot more than most grown-ups give them credit for. *Meet the Austins* came out of my own family's experience with several deaths. To have tried to hide those deaths from our children would have been blind stupidity. All hiding does is to confuse children and add to their fears. It is not subject matter that should be taboo, but the way it is handled.

A number of years ago—the first year I was actually making reasonable money from my writing—my sister-in-law was visiting us, and when my husband told her how much I had earned that year, she was impressed and commented, "And to think most people would have had to work so hard for that!"

Well, it is work, it's most certainly work; wonderful work, but work. Revision, revision, revision. Long hours spent not only in the actual writing, but in research. I think the best thing I learned in college was how to do research, so that I could go right on studying after I graduated.

Of course, it is not only work; it is work that makes the incomprehensible comprehensible. Leonard Bernstein said that for him music was cosmos in chaos. That is true for writing a story, too. Aristotle wrote that what is plausible and impossible is better than what is possible and implausible.

That means that story must be true, not necessarily factual, but true. This is not easy for a lot of people to understand. When I was a child, one of my teachers accused me of telling a story. She was not complimenting me on my fertile imagination; she was accusing me of telling a lie.

Facts are fine; we need facts. But story takes us to a world that is beyond facts, out on the other side of facts. And there is considerable fear of this world.

The writer Keith Miller told me of a young woman who was determined that her three preschool children were going to grow up in the real world. She was not, she vowed, going to sully their minds with myth, fantasy, fairy tales. They were going to know the truth—and for truth, read fact—and the truth would make them free.

One Saturday, after a week of rain and sniffles, the sun came out, so she piled the children into her little red VW bug and took them to the Animal Farm. The parking lot was crowded, but a VW bug is small, and she managed to find a place for it. She and the children had a wonderful day, petting the animals, going on rides, enjoying the sunshine. Suddenly, she looked at her watch and found it was far later than she realized. She and the children ran to where the VW bug was parked, and to their horror, found the whole front end was bashed in.

Outraged, she took herself off to the ranger's office. As he saw her approach, he laughed and said, "I'll bet you're the lady with the red VW bug."

"It isn't funny," she snapped.

"Now, calm down, lady, and let me tell you what happened. You know the elephant your children had such fun riding? She's a circus-trained elephant, and she was trained to sit on a red bucket. When she saw your car, she just did what she was trained to do and sat on it. Your engine's in the back, so you can drive it home without any trouble. And don't worry. Our insurance will take care of it. Just go on home, and we'll get back to you on Monday."

Slightly mollified, she and the kids got into the car and took off. But she was later than ever, so when she saw what looked like a very minor accident on the road, she didn't stop, but drove on.

Shortly, the flashing light and the siren came along, and she was pulled over. "Lady, don't you know that in this state it's a crime to leave the scene of an accident?" the trooper asked.

"But I wasn't in an accident," she protested.

"I suppose your car came that way," the trooper said, pointing to the bashed-in front.

"No. An elephant sat on it."

"Lady, would you mind blowing into this little balloon?"

That taught her that facts alone are not enough; that facts, indeed, do not make up the whole truth. After that she read fairy tales to her children and encouraged them in their games of Make Believe and Let's Pretend.

I learned very early that if I wanted to find out the truth, to find out why people did terrible things to each other, or sometimes wonderful things—why there was a war, why children are abused—I was more likely to find the truth in story than in the encyclopedia. Again and again I read *Emily of the New Moon*, by Lucy Maud Montgomery, because Emily's father was dying of diseased lungs, and so was mine. Emily wanted to be a writer, and so did I. Emily knew that there was more to the world than provable fact, and so did I. I read fairy tales, the myths of all nations, science fiction, the fantasies and family stories of E. Nesbitt. I read Jules Verne and H.G. Wells. And I read my parents' books, particularly those with lots of conversation in them. What was not in my frame of reference went right over my head.

We tend to find what we look for. If we look for dirt, we'll find dirt, whether it's there or not. A very nice letter I received from a reader said that she found *A Ring of Endless Light* very helpful to her in coming to terms with the death of a friend, but that another friend had asked her how it was that I used dirty words. I wrote back saying that I was not going to reread my book looking for dirty words, but that as far as I could remember, the only word in the book that could possibly be construed as dirty was zuggy, which I'd made up to avoid using dirty words. And wasn't looking for dirty words an ugly way to read a book?

> The techniques of fiction are the techniques of fiction, and they hold as true for Beatrix Potter as they do for Dostoevsky. . . .

One of my favorite books is Frances Hodgson Burnett's *The Secret Garden*. I read it one rainy weekend to a group of little girls, and a generation later to my granddaughters up in an old brass bed in the attic. Mary Lennox is a self-centered, spoiled-rotten little heroine, and I think we all recognize at least a little of ourselves in her. The secret garden is as much the garden of Mary's heart as it is the physical walled garden. By the end of the book, warmth and love and concern for others have come to Mary's heart, when Colin, the sick boy, is able to walk and run again. And Dickon, the gardener's boy, looks at the beauty of the restored garden and says, "It's magic!" But "magic" is one of the key words that has become taboo to today's self-appointed censors, so, with complete disregard of content, they would add *The Secret Garden* to the pyre. I shudder. This attitude is extreme. It is also dangerous.

It comes down to the old question of separate standards, separate for adults and children. The only standard to be used in judging a children's book is: Is it a good book? Is it good enough for me? Because if a children's book is not good enough for all of us, it is not good enough for children.

Madeleine L'Engle is an author who has enjoyed popularity with both children and adults for decades. One of her most beloved children's novels, *A Wrinkle in Time*, won the Newbery Award. She has written fiction, nonfiction, poetry, plays, mysteries, and more. This article was first published in *The Writer,* July 2000.

The Writer's Life

WRITING MATTERS

by Julia Alvarez

One of the questions that always comes up during question-and-answer periods is about the writing life. The more sophisticated, practiced questioners usually ask me, "Can you tell us something about your process as a writer?"

In part, this is the curiosity we all have about each other's "processes," to use the terminology of my experienced questioner. We need to tell, and we also want to know (don't we?) the secret heart of each other's life. Perhaps that is why we love good novels and poems—because we can enter, without shame or without encountering defensiveness or embarrassment, the intimate lives of other people.

But the other part of my questioner's curiosity about the writing life has to do with a sense we all have that if we can only get a hold of the secret ingredients of the writing process, we will become better writers. We will have an easier time of it if we only find that magic pencil or know at which hour to start and at which hour to quit and what to sip that might help us come up with the next word in a sentence.

I always tell my questioners the truth: Listen, there are no magic solutions to the hard work of writing. There is no place to put the writing desk that will draw more words out of you. I had a friend who claimed that an east-west alignment was the best one for writing. The writing would then flow and be more in tune with the positive energies. The north-south alignment would cause blocks as well as bad dreams if your bed was also thus aligned.

See, I tell my questioners, isn't this silly?

But even as I say so, I know I am talking out of both sides of my mouth. I admit that after getting my friend's tip, I lined up my writing desk (and my bed) in the east-west configuration. It wasn't that I thought my writing or my dream life would improve, but I am so impressionable that I was afraid that I'd be thinking and worrying about my alignment instead of my line breaks. And such fretting would affect my writing adversely. Even as recently as this very day, I walk into my study first thing in the morning, and I fill up my bowl of clear water and place it on my desk. And though no one told me to do this, I somehow feel this is the right way to start a writing day.

Of course, that fresh bowl of water sits on my desk on good and bad writing days. I know these little ceremonies will not change the kind of day before me. My daily writing rituals are small ways in which I contain my dread and affirm my joy and celebrate the mystery and excitement of the calling to be a writer.

I use the word calling in the old religious sense: a commitment to a life connected to deeper, more profound forces (or so I hope) than the marketplace, or the academy, or the hectic blur of activity that my daily life is often all about. But precisely because it is a way of life, not just a job, the writing life can be difficult to combine with other lives that require that same kind of passion and commitment—the teaching life, the family life, the parenting life, and so on. And since we writers tend to be intense people, whatever other lives we combine with our writing life, we will want to live them intensely, too. Some of us are better at this kind of juggling than others.

After twenty-five years of clumsy juggling—marriages, friendships, teaching, writing, community work, political work, child caring—I think I've finally figured out what the proper balance is for me. Let me emphasize that this is not a prescription for anyone else. But alas, I'm of the Gerald Ford school of writers who can't chew gum and write iambic pentameter at the same time. I can do two, maybe three intense lives at once: writing and being in a family; writing and teaching and being in a family; writing and teaching and doing political work; but if I try to add a fourth or fifth, I fall apart, that is, the writing stops, which for me is the same thing as saying I fall apart.

But still, I keep juggling, picking up one life and another and another, putting aside the writing from time to time. We have only one life, after all, and we have to live so many lives with it. (Another reason the writing life appeals so much is that you can be, at least on paper, all those selves whose lives you can't possibly live out in the one life you've got.)

Living other lives enriches our writing life. The tension between them can sometimes exhaust us, this is true—but the struggle also makes the hard-won hours at the writing desk all the more precious. And if we are committed to our writing, the way we lead our other lives can make them lives-in-waiting to be writing lives.

For me, the writing life doesn't just happen when I sit at the writing desk. It is a life lived with a centering principle, and mine is this: that I will pay close attention to this world I find myself in. "My heart keeps open house," was the way the poet Theodore Roethke put it in a poem. And rendering in language what one sees through the opened windows and doors of that house is a way of bearing witness to the mystery of what it is to be alive in this world.

This is all very high-minded and inspirational, my questioner puts in, but what about when we are alone at our writing desks, feeling wretchedly anxious, wondering if there is anything in us worth putting down?

Let me take you through the trials and tribulations of a typical writing day. It might help as you also set out onto that blank page, encounter one adventure or mishap after another, and wonder—do other writers go through this?

The answer is probably yes.

Not much has happened at six-twenty or so in the morning when I enter my writing room above the garage. I like it this way. The mind is free of household details, worries, commitments, voices, problems to solve.

My mood entering the room depends on what happened with my writing the day before. If the previous day was a good one, I look forward to the new writing day. If I was stuck or uninspired, I feel apprehensive. In short, I can't agree more with Hemingway's advice that a writer should always end his writing day knowing where he is headed next. It makes it easier to come back to work.

The first thing I do in my study every morning is read poetry (Jane Kenyon, George Herbert, Rita Dove, Robert Frost, Elizabeth Bishop, Rhina Espaillat, Jane Shore, Emily Dickinson . . .). This is the first music I hear, the most essential. Interestingly, I like to follow the reading of poetry with some prose, as if, having been to the heights I need to come back down to earth.

I consider this early-morning reading a combination of pleasure-reading time when I read the works and authors I most love and finger-exercise reading time, when I am tuning my own voice to the music of the English language as played by its best writers. There's an old Yiddish story about a rabbi who walks out in a rich neighborhood and meets a watchman walking up and down. "For whom are you working?" the rabbi asks. The watchman tells him, and then in his turn, he asks the rabbi, "And whom are you working for, rabbi?" The words strike the rabbi like a shaft. "I am not working for anybody just yet," he barely manages to reply. Then he walks up and down beside the man for a long time and finally asks him, "Will you be my servant?" The watchman says, "I should like to, but what would be my duties?"

"To remind me," the rabbi says.

I read my favorite writers to remind me of the quality of writing I am aiming for.

Now, it's time to set out: Pencil poised, I read through the hard copy that I ran off at the end of yesterday's writing day. I used to write everything out by longhand, and when I was reasonably sure I had a final draft, I'd type it up on my old Selectric. But now, I usually write all my prose drafts right out on the computer, though I need to write out my poems in longhand, to make each word by hand.

This is also true of certain passages of prose and certainly true for times when I am stuck in a novel or story. Writing by hand relieves some of the

> The first thing I do in my study every morning is read poetry (Jane Kenyon, George Herbert, Rita Dove, Robert Frost, Elizabeth Bishop, Rhina Espaillat, Jane Shore, Emily Dickinson . . .). This is the first music I hear.

pressure of seeing something tentative flashed before me on the screen with that authority that print gives to writing. "This is just for me," I tell myself, as I scratch out a draft in pencil. Often, these scribblings turn into little bridges, tendrils that take me safely to the other side of silence. When I'm finally on my way, I head back to the computer.

But even my hard copies look as if they've been written by hand. As I revise, I begin to hear the way I want a passage to sound. About the third or fourth draft, if I'm lucky, I start to see the shape of what I am writing, the way an essay will go, a character will react, a poem unfold.

Sometimes if Bill and I go on a long car trip, I'll read him what I am working on. This is a wonderful opportunity to "hear" what I've written. The process of reading my work to someone else does tear apart that beauteous coating of self-love in which my own creation comes enveloped. I start to hear what I've written as it would sound to somebody else.

When I'm done with proofing the hard copy of the story or chapter or poem, I take a little break. This is one of the pleasures of working at home. I can take these refreshing breathers from the intensity of the writing: go iron a shirt or clean out a drawer or wrap up my sister's birthday present.

After my break, I take a deep breath. What I now do is transcribe all my handwritten revisions on to my computer, before I launch out into the empty space of the next section of the story or essay or the chapter in a novel. This is probably the most intense time of the writing day. I am on my way, but I don't know exactly where it is I am going. But that's why I'm writing: to find out.

On the good days, an excitement builds up as I push off into the language, and sentence seems to follow sentence. I catch myself smiling or laughing out loud or sometimes even weeping as I move through a scene or a stanza. Certainly writing seems to integrate parts of me that are usually at odds. As I write, I feel unaccountably whole; I disappear! That is the irony of this self-absorbed profession: The goal finally is to vanish. On bad days, on the other hand, I don't disappear. Instead, I'm stuck with the blank screen before me. I take more and more breaks. I wander out on the deck and look longingly south toward the little spire of the Congregational church and wish another life for myself. Oh, dear, what have I done with my life?

I have chosen it, that's what I've done. So I take several deep breaths and go back upstairs and sit myself down and work over the passage that will not come. As Flannery O'Connor attested: "Every morning between 9 and 12, I go to my room and sit before a piece of paper. Many times, I just sit for three hours with no ideas coming to me. But I know one thing: If an idea does come between 9 and 12, I am there ready for it." The amazing thing for me is that years later, reading the story or novel or poem, I can't tell the passages that were easy to write, the ones that came forth like "greased lightning" from those other passages that made me want to give up writing and take up another life.

On occasion, when all else fails, I take the rest of the day "off." I finish reading the poet or novelist with whom I began the day or I complain to my journal or I look through a picture book of shoes one of my characters might wear. But all the while I am feeling profound self doubt—as if I were one of those cartoon characters who runs off a cliff, and suddenly looks down only to discover, there's no ground beneath her feet!

At the end of the writing day (about two-thirty or three in the afternoon), I leave the room over the garage. I put on my running clothes, and I go for a run. In part, this exercise does make me feel better. But one of the best perks of running has been that it allows me to follow Hemingway's advice. I don't always know where I am headed in my writing at the end of the work day, but after I run, I usually have one or two good ideas. Running helps me work out glitches in my writing and gives me all kinds of unexpected insights. While I run down past the Fields's house, through Tucker Development, down to the route that goes into town, and then back, I've understood what a character is feeling or how I'm going to organize an essay or what I will title my novel. I've also had a zillion conversations with dozens of worrisome people, which is much better than trying to have these conversations with them while I am trying to write. Also, since I am not near a phone, I am not tempted to call them up and actually have it out with them. I've saved a lot of friendships and relationships and spared myself plenty of heartaches this way.

After the run, the rest of the workday is taken up by what I call the writing biz part of being a writer. What this involves, in large part, is responding to the publicity machine that now seems to be a necessary component of being a published writer. Answering mail, returning phone calls, responding to unsolicited manuscripts from strangers or to galleys from editors who would so appreciate my putting in a good word for this young writer or translation or series. Ironically, all this attention can sometimes amount to distraction that keeps me from doing the work that brought these requests to my door in the first place.

I could just ignore these requests. But all along the way, I found helpers who did read my manuscript, did give me a little of their busy day. These are favors I can never pay back, I can only pass on. And so I do try to answer my own mail and read as many galleys by new writers as I possibly can and return phone calls to those who need advice I might be able to give.

> I don't always know where I am headed in my writing at the end of the work day, but after I run, I usually have one or two good ideas.

When I'm finally finished with my writing biz or I've put it aside in the growing pile for tomorrow, I head to town to run errands or see a friend or attend a talk at the college. As the fields and farms give way to houses and lawns, I feel as if I'm reentering the world. After having been so intensely a part of a fictional world, I love this daily chance to connect with the small town I live in, to find out how everybody else is doing.

How's it going? everyone asks me, as if they really want to know all about my writing day.

At the end of a good reading, the audience lingers. It's late in Salt Lake City or Portland or Iowa City.

Outside the bookstore windows, the sky is dark and star-studded. Then, that last hand goes up, and someone in the back row wants to know, "So, does writing really matter?"

This once really happened to me on a book tour. I felt as if I'd just been hit "upside the head," an expression I like so much because it sounds like the blow was so hard, the preposition got jerked around, too. Does writing matter? I sure hope so, I wanted to say. I've published six books. I've spent most of my thinking life, which is now over thirty years, writing. Does writing really matter? It was the hardest, and the best, question I've been asked anywhere.

Let's take out the really, I said. It makes me nervous. I don't really know much of anything, which is why I write, to find things out. Does writing matter?

It matters, of course, it matters. But it matters in such a small, almost invisible way that it doesn't seem very important. In fact, that's why I trust it, the tiny rearrangements and insights in our hearts that art accomplishes. It's how I, anyhow, learned to see with vision and perplexity and honesty and continue to learn to see. How I keep the windows and doors open instead of shutting myself up inside the things I "believe" and have personally experienced. How I move out beyond the safe, small version of my life to live other lives. "Not only to be one self," the poet Robert Desnos wrote about the power of the imagination, "but to become each one."

And this happens not because I'm a writer or, as some questioners put it, "a creative person." I'll bet that even those who aren't writers, those who are concerned with making some sense of this ongoing journey would admit this: that it's by what people have written and continue to write, our stories and creations, that we understand who we are. In a world without any books, we would not be the same kind of critter. "Art is not the world," Muriel Rukeyser reminds us, "but a knowing of the world. It prepares us."

Prepares us for what? I have to admit that I don't really know what it prepares us for. For our work in the world, I suppose. Prepares us to live our lives more intentionally, ethically, richly. A hand shoots up. "You mean to say that if Hitler had read Tolstoy he would have been a better person?"

Let's say that it would have been worth a try. Let's say that if little Hitler had been caught up in reading Shakespeare or Tolstoy and was moved to the extent that the best books move us, he might not have become who he became. But maybe, Tolstoy or no Tolstoy, Hitler would still have been Hitler. We live, after all, in a flawed world of flawed beings. In fact, some very fine writers who have written some lovely things are not very nice people.

> Does writing really matter? It was the hardest, and the best, question I've been asked anywhere.

But I still insist that while writing or entering into the writing of another, they were better people. If for no other reason than they were not out there, causing trouble. Writing is a form of vision, and I agree with that proverb that says, "Where there is no vision, the people perish." The artist keeps that vision alive, cleared of the muck and refuse and junk and little dishonesties that always collect and begin to cloud our view of the world around us.

It is the end of the reading. My readers, who for this brief evening have become real people with questions about my writing life, come forward to have their books signed and offer some new insight or ask a further question. That they care matters. That they are living fuller versions of themselves and of each one because they have read books matters. This is why writing matters. It clarifies and intensifies; it reduces our sense of isolation and connects us to each other.

Julia Alvarez is a poet, essayist, and fiction writer who spent her early childhood in the Dominican Republic. Her first novel, *How the Garcia Girls Lost Their Accents,* won a PEN Oakland Award and was selected as a Notable Book by *The New York Times.* Her second novel, *In the Time of the Butterflies,* was a finalist for the National Book Critics' Award. She has also published books of poetry and books for children. This article appeared in *The Writer,* September 1998.

NONFICTION MAGAZINES

NONFICTION MAGAZINES

The magazines in the following list are in the market for freelance articles in many categories. Unless listings state otherwise, a writer should submit a query first, including a brief description of the proposed article and any relevant qualifications or credits. A few editors want to see samples of published work, if available.

Submit photos or slides only if the editor has specifically requested them. A self-addressed envelope with postage sufficient to cover the return of the manuscript or the answer to a query should accompany all submissions.

All information in these lists comes from query responses from the editors, publishers, and directors and from their published guidelines, but personnel and addresses change, as do requirements. No published listing can give as clear a picture of editorial needs and tastes as a careful study of several issues of a magazine, and writers should never submit material without first thoroughly researching the prospective market. If a magazine is not available in the local library or on the newsstand, write directly to the editor for the price of a sample copy. Many companies also offer a formal set of writers guidelines, available for an SASE (self-addressed, stamped envelope) upon request, or posted on its web site.

While some of the more established markets may seem difficult to break into, especially for the beginner, there are thousands of lesser-known publications where editors will consider submissions from first-time freelancers.

All manuscripts must be typed double-space and submitted with self-addressed envelopes bearing postage sufficient for the return of the material. If a manuscript need not be returned, note this with the submission, and enclose an SASE or a self-addressed, stamped postcard for editorial reply. Use good white paper. Always keep a copy, since occasionally material is lost in the mail. Magazines may take several weeks, or longer, to read and report on submissions. If an editor has not reported on a manuscript after a reasonable length of time, write a brief, courteous letter of inquiry.

Some publishers will accept, and may in fact prefer, work submitted on computer disk, usually noting the procedure and type of disk in their guidelines.

ABILITIES

ABLE NEWSPAPER

P.O. Box 395, Old Bethpage, NY 11804. 516-939-2253. E-mail: ablenews@aol.com. Web site: www.ablenews.com. Monthly. $15/yr. Circ.: 35,000. Suzanne Christy, Editor. **Description:** Newspaper for people with disabilities. **Nonfiction:** News about or for people with disabilities. 500 words, $40. **Art:** Prints, $35. **Queries:** Required. **E-queries:** No. **Unsolicited mss:** Accepts. **Response:** Queries 1 week, submissions 1 month. **Freelance Content:** 40%. **Payment:** On publication.

ACCENT ON LIVING

P.O. Box 700, Bloomington, IL 61701. 309-378-2961. E-mail: acntlvng@aol.com. Web site: www.accentonliving.com. Quarterly. $12/year. Circ.: 21,000. Betty Garee, Editor. **Description:** Provides information about new devices and approaches so people with physical disabilities can enjoy a better lifestyle. **Nonfiction:** Product information helpful to individuals with limited physical mobility. Intelligent articles about physically disabled persons in "normal" living situations. How-to articles on everyday living; up-to-date news; profiles of disabled personalities; 800-1,000 words; $.10/word. **Fillers:** Cartoons (humorous incidents encountered by physically disabled individuals in everyday living; a person in a wheelchair is typical, should be depicted in humorous but normal situations); $20. **Art:** b/w, color (provide captions); prints, disk, electronic (.tif, 300 dpi); $5-$50 (color cover). **Tips:** Don't write for able-bodied audience about being disabled. Use informal, not academic, style. Show individuals with disabilities involved in all aspects of life. Good photos or illustrations helpful. **Queries:** Preferred. **E-queries:** Accepts. **Unsolicited mss:** Accepts. **Response:** Queries 2 weeks, submissions 3 weeks, SASE required. **Freelance Content:** 80%. **Rights:** One-time. **Payment:** On publication.

CLOSING THE GAP

526 Main St., P.O. Box 68, Henderson, MN 56044. 507-248-3294. Web site: www.closingthegap.com. Megan Turek, Managing Editor. **Description:** Focuses on microcomputer products that affects the education, vocation, recreation, mobility, communication, etc., of persons who are handicapped or disabled. **Nonfiction:** Articles, 700-1,500 words. Non-product-related articles also used.

DIALOGUE

P.O. Box 5181, Salem, OR 97304-0181. 800-860-4224. E-mail: blindskl@teleport.com. Web site: www.blindskills.com. Carol McCarl, Editor. **Description:** We want to give readers an opportunity to learn about interesting and successful people who are visually impaired. **Nonfiction:** Articles for visually impaired youth and adults. Career opportunities, educational skills, and recreational activities. 800-1,200 words; pay varies. **Poetry:** To 20 lines. **Queries:** Preferred. **Response:** SASE. **Payment:** On publication.

KALEIDOSCOPE

United Disability Services, 701 S. Main St., Akron, OH 44311-1019. 330-762-9755. E-mail: mshiplett@udsakron.org. Web site: www.udsakron.org. Semi-annual. $5/issue. Circ.: 1,000. Darshan Perusek, Ph.D., Editor-in-Chief. **Description:** Explores the experience of disability through literature and fine arts, from the perspective of individuals, families, health-care professionals, and society. Seeks to challenge and overcome stereotypical, patronizing, sentimental attitudes about disability. Pay $25 and 2 copies. **Fiction:** Character-centered stories, not action pieces. No romance; 5,000 words max. **Nonfiction:** Narratives and articles on experiences and issues of disability; 5,000 words max. **Poetry:** Free verse on disability or written by someone with a disability. Also, short nature poems and light humor; 1-5 poems. **Art:**

35mm color, b/w 8x10 glossy; up to $100. **Tips:** Photos a plus. **Queries:** Not necessary. **E-queries:** Yes. **Unsolicited mss:** Accepts. **Response:** Queries 2 weeks, Submissions 6 months, SASE required. **Freelance Content:** 60%. Rights: 1st serial rights. **Payment:** On publication.

MINDPRINTS
Allan Hancock College, Disabled Student Programs & Services, 800 South College Dr., Santa Maria, CA 93454-6399. 805-922-6696 ext. 3274.
E-mail: htcdsps@sbceo.org. Annual. Free. Circ.: 500. Paul Fahey, Editor. **Description:** Literary journal of short fiction, memoir, poetry, and art for writers with disabilities and writers with an interest in this field. Showcases a variety of talent from this diverse population. **Fiction:** Short-short fiction, flash fiction; 250-750 words. **Nonfiction:** Short memoir, creative nonfiction (often disability-related); 250-750 words. **Poetry:** Rhymed and prose; up to 25 lines. **Art:** b/w photos and artwork. **Queries:** Not necessary. **E-queries:** Yes. **Unsolicited mss:** Accepts; cover letter with bio required. **Response:** 1 week queries, 2-3 months submissions, SASE. **Rights:** One-time. **Payment:** in copies.

WEMEDIA
130 William St., New York, NY 10038. 646-769-2722.
Web site: www.wemedia.com. Monthly. Charles A. Riley II. **Description:** For people with disabilities "celebrating their lives in sports and the arts, spotlighting foreign travel, and dining out in major American cities." **Fiction:** 1,500-2,000 words. **Nonfiction:** Varying lengths; pay varies. **Art:** Photos. **Queries:** Preferred. **Payment:** On publication.

AGRICULTURE & RURAL LIFE

ACRES USA
P.O. Box 91299, Austin, TX 78709. 512-892-4400.
Web site: www.acresusa.com. Fred C. Walters, Editor. **Description:** Articles on sustainable agriculture (technology, case reports, "hands-on" advice). **Nonfiction:** Emphasis on commercial production of quality food without use of toxic chemicals; pays $.05/word. **Payment:** On publication.

AMERICAN BEE JOURNAL
51 N. Second St., Hamilton, IL 62341. 217-847-3324.
Web site: www.dadant.com. Joe M. Graham, Editor. **Description:** Beekeeping for professionals. **Nonfiction:** Articles, pays $.75/column inch. **Art:** Photos. **Queries:** Preferred. **Payment:** On publication.

BACKHOME

Wordsworth Communications, P.O. Box 70, Hendersonville, NC 28793. 828-696-3838. E-mail: backhome@ioa.com. Web site: www.backhomemagazine.com. Bi-monthly. $3.95/$18.97. Circ.: 30,000. Lorna K. Loveless, Editor. **Description:** Do-it-yourself information on sustainable, self-reliant living. Offers information and resources on rural land, mortgage-free building, solar/renewable energy, chemical-free gardening, wholesome cooking, home business, home schooling, small livestock, vehicle and workshop projects, family activities. **Nonfiction:** On self-sufficient, sustainable-living practices, preferably first-person experiences; selling eggs, building a dome home, drying herbs, etc.; 800-3,000 words; $35/printed page. **Art:** To accompany articles; prints, slides; $20/image. **Tips:** Focus not on "dropping out," but on becoming better citizens and caretakers of the planet. Avoid impersonal essays. **Queries:** Not necessary. **E-queries:** Accepts. **Unsolicited mss:** Accepts. **Response:** 2-4 weeks, SASE. **Freelance Content:** 80%. **Payment:** On publication; kill fee offered.

BEE CULTURE

623 W. Liberty St., Medina, OH 44256. 330-725-5624 x3214. E-mail: kim@airoot.com. Web site: www.airoot.com/beeculture. Monthly. $3.95/issue, $20/year. Circ.: 12,000,000. Mr. Kim Flottum, Editor. **Description:** Beekeeping, pollination, gardening with bees, nature. **Nonfiction:** Basic how-to, some profiles of commercial operations; 1,000-2,000 words; $100-$250. **Art:** Slides, b/w prints. **Tips:** Must know bee and commercial beekeeping. Avoid "How I got started in beekeeping." **Queries:** Preferred. **E-queries:** Yes. **Unsolicited mss:** Accepts. **Response:** Queries 1 month, submissions 1-3 months, SASE required. **Freelance Content:** 25%. **Rights:** 1st NA. **Payment:** On publication.

BEEF

7900 International Dr., Suite 300, Minneapolis, MN 55425. 952-851-9329. E-mail: beef@intertec.com. Web site: www.beef-mag.com. 13x/year. Circ.: 101,000. Joe Robal, Editor. **Description:** Informational articles for cattlemen and cattle industy. **Nonfiction:** Articles on feeding, cowherds, stock operations, cattle industry. Pays to $300. **Queries:** Required. **E-queries:** Yes. **Payment:** On acceptance.

BRAHMAN JOURNAL

P.O. Box 220, Eddy, TX 76524-0220. 254-859-5507. Monthly. Circ.: 3,900. Joe Brockett, Editor. **Description:** Covers Brahman breed of beef cattle. **Nonfiction:** About the Brahman breed or people involved with them; 1,500 words; up to $250. **Queries:** Preferred. **E-queries:** No. **Unsolicited mss:** Accepts. **Freelance Content:** 5%. **Rights:** All. **Payment:** On acceptance.

CAPPER'S

Ogden Publications, 1503 S.W. 42nd St., Topeka, KS 66609-1265. 785-274-4300. E-mail: cappers@cjnetworks.com. Web site: www.cappers.com. Bi-weekly. $27.95/year. Circ.: 250,000. Ann Crahan, Editor. **Description:** Focuses on home and family, for readers in the rural Midwest. **Fiction:** Query first, with brief description; $75-$300. **Nonfiction:** Inspirational, nostalgic, family-oriented, travel, human-interest; 700 words max.; $2.50/inch. **Poetry:** Easy to read, down-to-earth themes; 4-16 lines; $10-$15. **Fillers:** Jokes (limit submissions to batches of 5-6; no jokes returned); $2 gift certificate. **Art:** slides, transparencies, prints; include captions; $5-$40. **Queries:** Preferred. **E-Queries:** Yes. **Unsolicited mss:** Accepts. **Response:** Submissions 2-6 months. SASE required. **Freelance Content:** 25%. **Rights:** FNASR. **Payment:** On publication.

THE CATTLEMAN

Texas and Southwestern Cattle Raisers Assn.
1301 W. 7th St., Fort Worth, TX 76102-2660. 817-332-7064.
Web site: www.texascattleraisers.org. Lionel Chambers, Editor. **Description:** For ranchers who raise beef cattle. **Queries:** Preferred.

COUNTRY

Reiman Publications, 5400 S. 60th St., Greendale, WI 53129. 414-423-0270.
E-mail: editor@country-magazine.com. Web site: www.country-magazine.com. Bimonthly. $14.98/year. Circ.: 1,400,000. Jerry Wiebel, Editor. **Description:** Articles and photographs describing the allure of country life today. Mostly reader-written. **Nonfiction:** First-person articles; 500-700 words; $75-$100. **Art:** Good candid color photos. **Tips:** No articles on farm production techniques. **Queries:** Not necessary. **Unsolicited mss:** Accepts. **Response:** 2 months. **Freelance Content:** 90%. **Payment:** On acceptance.

COUNTRY FOLK

HC 77, Box 608, Pittsburgh, MO 65724. 417-993-5944.
E-mail: salaki@country folkmag.com. Web site: www.countryfolkmag.com. Bimonthly. $2.75/issue $15.00/year. Circ.: 6,000. Susan Salaki, Editor. **Description:** True Ozark history stories, old rare recipes, historical photos, and interesting fillers. **Nonfiction:** Ozark history; 1,000-1,200 words; $20-$50. **Poetry:** Standard rhyming; 3 verses max.; 0-$5. **Freelance Content:** 99%.

COUNTRY JOURNAL

98 N. Washington St., Boston, MA 02114. 617-742-5600.
E-mail: countryjournal@primedia.com. Web site: www.countryjournal.com. Bimonthly. $3.50/issue, $21/year. Circ.: 100,000. Toby Lester, Executive Editor. **Description:** A practical, intellectual, general-interest magazine for people living in the country. **Nonfiction:** Helpful, authoritative pieces (how-to projects, small-scale farming, and gardening), for country and small-town residents; up to $1,500. **Columns, Departments:** Reports, profiles, essays, how-to pieces; 50-1,500 words; up to $750. **Queries:** Not necessary. **E-queries:** Yes. **Unsolicited mss:** Accepts. **Response:** Submission 1 month, SASE required. **Freelance Content:** 60%. **Rights:** 1st serial. **Payment:** On acceptance. **Contact:** Submissions Editor.

COUNTRY WOMAN

Reiman Publications, 5925 Country Lane, Greendale, WI 53129. 414-423-0100. E-mail: editors@countrywomanmagazine.com. Web site: www.countrywomanmagazine.com. Bimonthly. $3.50/issue. Circ.: 1,700,000. Kathy Pohl, Executive Editor. **Description:** For women living in the country or interested in country life. Recipes, craft projects, fiction and nostalgia stories, decorating and fashion, profiles of country woman, and poetry. **Fiction:** Wholesome fiction with country perspective or rural theme; 1,000 words; $90-$125. **Nonfiction:** Nostalgia pieces, essays on farm/country life, humorous stories, decorating features, inspirational articles; 750-1,000 words; $50-$75. **Poetry:** Good rhythm and rhyme, seasonal in nature; 12-24 lines; $10-$25. **Art:** Good candid color photos. **Queries:** Not necessary. **Unsolicited mss:** Accepts. **Response:** 2-3 months, SASE required. **Freelance Content:** 90%. **Payment:** On acceptance. **Contact:** Kathleen Anderson, Managing Editor.

DAIRY GOAT JOURNAL

P.O. Box 10, Lake Mills, WI 53551. 920-648-8285. 9x/year. $2.50/$21. Circ.: 7,000. Dave Thompson, Editor. **Description:** For successful dairy-goat owners, youths, about interesting people and practical husbandry ideas. **Nonfiction:** 1,000-1,500 words; $75-$150. **Fillers:** $25-$75. **Art:** b/w prints; $25-$75. **Tips:** Needs practical stories about goats and their owners; about marketing goat cheese and dairy products. Readership in U.S. and over 70 foreign countries. **Queries:** Preferred. **E-queries:** No. **Unsolicited mss:** Accepts. **Response:** 2 weeks, SASE. **Freelance Content:** 50%. **Rights:** All. **Payment:** On acceptance.

FARM AND RANCH LIVING

5400 S. 60th St., Greendale, WI 53129. 414-423-0100. E-mail: editors@farmandranchliving.com. Web site: www.farmandranchliving.com. Bi-monthly. $3.50/issue, $17.98/year. Circ.: 350,000. Nick Pabst, Editor. **Description:** For U.S. and Canadian families that farm or ranch full-time. Focuses on people; includes diaries, humor, rural nostalgia, tractor talk, 4-H, events calendar. **Nonfiction:** Photo—illustrated stories about today's farmers and ranchers; 1,200 words; $75-$150. **Fillers:** Farm-related humor; 100 words; $25-$50. **Tips:** Submit upbeat, positive stories. **Queries:** Not necessary. **E-queries:** Yes. **Unsolicited mss:** Accepts. **Response:** 4 weeks, SASE required. **Freelance Content:** 30%. **Rights:** 1st, one-time. **Payment:** On publication.

FARM INDUSTRY NEWS

7900 International Dr., #300, Minneapolis, MN 55425. 612-851-4609. Web site: www.homefarm.com. Kurt Lawton, Editor. **Description:** For farmers, on new products, machinery, equipment, chemicals, and seeds. **Nonfiction:** Articles; pays $350-$500. **Queries:** Required. **Payment:** On acceptance.

FARM JOURNAL
1500 Market St., 28th Fl., Philadelphia, PA 19102-2181. 215-557-8900.
Web site: www.agweb.com. Sonja Hillgren, Editor. **Description:** On the business of
farming. **Nonfiction:** Articles, 500-1,500 words, with photos; pays $.20-$.50/word.
Queries: Preferred. **Payment:** On acceptance.

FLORIDA GROWER
1555 Howell Branch Rd., Suite C-204, Winter Park, FL 32789. 407-539-6552.
E-mail: flg_edit@meisternet.com. Monthly. Circ.: 15,000. Michael Allen, Editor.
Description: The voice of Florida agriculture, on all aspects of commercial fruit and
vegetable industries. **Nonfiction:** On production or marketing Florida's agricultural
products; 1,400 words; $300. **Queries:** Not necessary. **E-queries:** Yes. **Unsolicited
mss:** Accepts. **Freelance Content:** 20%. **Rights:** All. **Payment:** On publication.

THE FURROW
John Deere Ag. Marketing Ctr., 11145 Thompson Ave.,
Lenexa, KS 66219-2302. 913-310-8300.
8x/year. Circ.: 500,000. Karl Kessler, Senior Editor. **Description:** For John Deere
Dealers. **Tips:** Freelance content limited. **Queries:** Required. **Unsolicited mss:**
Does not accept.

THE LAND
P.O. Box 3169, Mankato, MN 56002-3169. 507-344-6342.
E-mail: kschulz@theland.com. Web site: www.theland.com. Weekly zoned. $20/year.
Circ.: 40,000. Kevin Schulz, Editor. **Description:** Agricultural and rural-life magazine
for Minnesota farm families. **Nonfiction:** On Minnesota agriculture and rural issues,
production, how-tos; 500 words; $35-$60. **Queries:** Preferred. **E-queries:** Yes.
Unsolicited mss: Accepts. **Response:** Queries 3-4 weeks, submissions 1-2 weeks,
SASE. **Freelance Content:** 50%. **Rights:** 1st NA. **Payment:** On acceptance.

THE MAINE ORGANIC FARMER & GARDENER
RR 2, Box 594, Lincolnville, ME 04849. 207-763-3043.
E-mail: jenglish@midcoast.com. Web site: www.mofga.com. Quarterly. $12/year.
Circ.: 5,000. Jean English. **Description:** Published by Maine Organic Farmers and
Gardeners Assn. **Nonfiction:** Organic farming and gardening, environmental issues
relating to food/health, consumer issues, book reviews; 250-2,000 words; $.08/word.
Fillers: Gardening and farming tips; $.08/word. **Art:** Photos with articles. **Tips:**
Avoid rehashing old material, no chemical fertilizers, no potato-flake recipes. Readers
know organic methods, seek new ideas, new crops, new cultivation techniques.
Queries: Preferred. **E-queries:** Yes. **Unsolicited mss:** Accepts. **Response:**
Queries in 2 weeks, submissions in 1 month, SASE. **Freelance Content:** 50%.
Rights: 1st, reprint. **Payment:** On publication.

NATIONAL CATTLEMEN

5420 S. Quebec St., Englewood, CO 80111-1905. 303-694-0305.
Web site: www.beef.org. Curt Olson. **Description:** For the cattle industry.
Nonfiction: Articles, 400-1,200 words; pay varies. **Payment:** On publication.

NEW HOLLAND NEWS

New Holland, N.A., Inc., P.O. Box 1895,
New Holland, PA 17557-0903. 717-393-3821.
Web site: www.newholland.com/na. 8x/year. Gary Martin, Editor. **Description:**
Farm management, rural features for modern farm families. **Fiction:** 1,500 words;
$600-$800. **Nonfiction:** People stories about farm struggles; ways to improve farm
income; 800-1,500 words; $600-$800. **Art:** Transparencies, prints; $500/cover. **Tips:**
No farmer profiles. **Queries:** Preferred. **E-queries:** No. **Unsolicited mss:** Accepts.
Response: Queries 1 month, submissions 2 months, SASE. **Freelance Content:**
100%. **Rights:** 1st NA. **Payment:** On acceptance.

OHIO FARMER

117 W. Main St., #202, Lancaster, OH 43130. 740-654-6500.
Web site: www.farmprogress.com. Tim White, Editor. **Description:** On farming and
rural living in Ohio. **Nonfiction:** Technical articles; pays $50/column. **Payment:** On
publication.

ONION WORLD

P.O. Box 9036, Yakima, WA 98909-9036. 509-248-2452.
E-mail: brent@freshcut.com. Web site: www.onionworld.net. 8x/year. Circ.: 6,000.
D. Brent Clement, Editor. **Description:** On marketing and production, for U.S. and
Canadian onion industries (growers, packers, shippers). **Nonfiction:** On onion production, packing, and shipping businesses; varieties grown, challenges, solutions, etc.;
to 1,500 words; $5/column inch. **Art:** Include photos with article. **Tips:** No meaning-
less drivel. No gardening articles. **Queries:** Preferred. **E-queries:** Yes. **Unsolicited
mss:** Accepts. **Response:** Queries 7 days, submissions 2 weeks, SASE. **Freelance
Content:** 25%. **Rights:** 1st. **Payment:** On publication.

PEANUT FARMER

3000 Highwoods Blvd., Suite 300, Raleigh, NC 27604-1029. 919-872-5040.
E-mail: publisher@peanutfarmer.com. Monthly. $15. Circ.: 19,000. Mary Ann Rood,
Managing Editor. **Description:** For commercial farmers. **Nonfiction:** Production
practices; 500-2,000 words. **Queries:** Preferred. **E-queries:** Yes. **Unsolicited mss:**
Accepts. **Response:** 2 weeks, SASE. **Freelance Content:** 10%. **Rights:** 1st NA.
Payment: On publication.

PENNSYLVANIA FARMER

P.O. Box 4475, Gettysburg, PA 17325. 717-334-4300.
E-mail: jvogel@farmersprogress.com. Web site: www.farmersprogress.com. Monthly.
$21.95. Circ.: 17,000. John R. Vogel, Editor. **Description:** Trade publication for

farmers. **Nonfiction:** On regional farmers and successful farm operations; 500 words; $50. **Columns, Departments:** Country Air; 600-1,200 words; $200-$300. **Art:** with accepted story; $25. **Queries:** Required. **E-queries:** Yes. **Unsolicited mss:** Accepts. **Response:** SASE. **Freelance Content:** 10%. **Rights:** 1st. **Payment:** On publication.

PROGRESSIVE FARMER
2100 Lakeshore Dr., Birmingham, AL 35209. 205-877-6494. Web site: www.progressivefarmer.com. Jack Odle, Editor. **Description:** For farmers. Covers new developments in agriculture; rural communities; personal business issues for farmstead and home office; relationships; worker safety; finances, taxes, and regulations. **Nonfiction:** Articles; to 5 double-spaced pages (3 pages preferred); pays $50-$400. **Queries:** Preferred. **Payment:** On publication.

RURAL HERITAGE
281 Dean Ridge Ln., Gainesboro, TN 38562. 931-268-0655. Web site: www.ruralheritage.com. Bi-monthly. $5.75/$24. Circ.: 4,500. Gail Damerow, Editor. **Description:** Covers modern farming and logging with horses, mules, and oxen. **Nonfiction:** draft animal use, training, implements, etc.; 1,200 words; $.05/word. **Poetry:** humorous, twist of fate, action-oriented; short; $5 min. **Queries:** Preferred. **E-queries:** Yes. **Unsolicited mss:** Accepts. **Response:** Queries 1 week, submissions to 3 month. **Freelance Content:** 90%. **Rights:** 1st serial. **Payment:** On publication.

RURALITE
P.O. Box 558, Forest Grove, OR 97116. 503-357-2105. E-mail: curtis@ruralite.org. Web site: www.ruralite.org. Monthly. $10/yr. Circ.: 287,600. Curtis Condon, Editor. **Description:** For rural electric cooperatives and public power districts in 7 western states; general interest and energy-related. **Nonfiction:** For rural/small-town audiences (OR, WA, ID, WY, NV, northern CA, AK), on rural/urban interests, regional history and celebrations, self-help, profiles; 400-2,000 words; $50-$400. **Art:** 35mm, 2¼; $25-$300. **Tips:** Readership 60% women, 50 years and older. **Queries:** Required. **E-queries:** Yes. **Unsolicited mss:** Does not accept. **Response:** 1-2 months, SASE. **Freelance Content:** 80%. **Payment:** On acceptance.

SHEEP!
P.O. Box 10, Lake Mills, WI 53551. 920-648-8285. Monthly. $21/yr. Circ.: 12,000. Dave Thompson, Editor. **Description:** For sheep and wool farmers across the U.S. and Canada. How-tos, flock owner stories, and industry news. **Nonfiction:** Articles, to 1,500 words, on successful shepherds, woolcrafts, sheep raising, sheep dogs; 800-1,500 words; $80-$125. **Art:** Yes. **Tips:** Especially interested in people who raise sheep successfully as a sideline enterprise. **Queries:** Preferred. **E-queries:** No. **Unsolicited mss:** Accepts. **Response:** 1 month, SASE. **Freelance Content:** 50%. **Payment:** On acceptance.

SMALL FARM TODAY

3903 W. Ridge Trail Rd., Clark, MO 65243-9525. 573-687-3525. E-mail: small farm@socket.net. Web site: www.smallfarmtoday.com. Bi-monthly. $4.95/$23.95. Circ.: 12,000. Ron Maches, Editor. **Description:** A "how-to" magazine of alternative and traditional crops, livestock, and direct marketing, to help farmers make their operations profitable and sustainable. **Nonfiction:** Stories about a specific crop, livestock, or marketing method, with how-to and budget information; 1,000-1,800 words; $.03-$.05/word. **Tips:** Readers prefer alternative sustainable methods over traditional chemical farming. **Queries:** Preferred. **E-queries:** Yes. **Unsolicited mss:** Accepts. **Response:** Queries 2 months, submissions 4 months, SASE. **Freelance Content:** 40%. **Rights:** 1st. **Payment:** On publication.

SMALL FARMER'S JOURNAL

P.O. Box 1627, Dept. 106, Sisters, OR 97759-1627. 541-549-2064. E-mail: farmersjournal.com. Web site: www.smallfarmersjournal.com. Quarterly. $8.50/$30 yr. Circ.: 18,000. Mr. Lynn R. Miller, Editor. **Description:** On practical farming with horses and small family farming. **Nonfiction:** How-tos, humor, practical work-horse information, livestock and produce marketing, gardening, articles for the independent family farm. Pay varies. **Tips:** Write of your own farm experiences. Avoid use of chemicals. **Queries:** Not necessary. **E-queries:** Yes. **Unsolicited mss:** Accepts. **Response:** 3 months, SASE. **Freelance Content:** 50%. **Rights:** 1st. **Payment:** On publication.

SUCCESSFUL FARMING

1716 Locust St., Des Moines, IA 50309-3023. 515-284-2853. Web site: agriculture.com. Monthly. $15 yr. Circ.: 475,000. Loren Kruse, Editor. **Description:** For farmers and ranchers, all sizes and types. **Nonfiction:** About successful family farms/businesses, big and small, that illustrate positive aspects. **Art:** Color transparencies preferred; pay varies. **Tips:** Provide ideas families can take right to the barn, shop, office, home, and heart to add value to their lives. Measure new practices and trends with dollar signs; use examples; use multiple sources. **Queries:** Preferred. **E-queries:** No. **Unsolicited mss:** Accepts. **Response:** Queries 2 days, submissions 1 week, SASE. **Freelance Content:** 20%. **Rights:** All. **Payment:** On acceptance. **Contact:** Gene Johnston, Managing Editor.

WALLACES FARMER

6200 Aurora Ave., Suite 609E, Urbandale, IA 50322-2838. 515-278-7782. E-mail: fholdmeyer@farmprogress.com. Web site: www.wallacesfarmer.com. 15x/year. Circ.: 60,000. Frank Holdmeger, Editor. **Description:** Farming in Iowa; methods and equipment; interviews. **Nonfiction:** Features, 600-700 words. **Queries:** Required. **E-queries:** Yes. **Unsolicited mss:** Accepts. **Freelance Content:** 1%. **Payment:** On acceptance.

THE WESTERN PRODUCER

Box 2500, Saskatoon, Saskatchewan, Canada S7K 2C4. 800-667-6978. Web site: www.producer.com. **Description:** On agricultural and rural subjects, preferably with Canadian slant. **Nonfiction:** Articles, to 800 words (prefer under 600 words); pays from $.23/word. **Art:** Color photos ($50-$100). **Payment:** On publication.

ANIMALS & PETS

AKC GAZETTE

American Kennel Club, 260 Madison Ave., New York, NY 10016. 212-696-8200. Web site: www.akcgazette.com. Mark Roland, Features Editor. **Description:** Official journal for the sport of purebred dogs. **Nonfiction:** Articles, 1,000-2,500 words, for serious breeders, exhibitors, and judges of purebred dogs; pays $250-$600. **Queries:** Preferred. **Payment:** On acceptance.

AMERICAN FARRIERS JOURNAL

P.O. Box 624, Brookfield, WI 53008-0624. 262-782-4480. Web site: www.americanfarriers.com. Frank Lessiter, Editor. **Description:** Articles, 800-2,000 words, on farriery issues, hoof care, tool selection, equine lameness, and horse handling. **Nonfiction:** Pays $.50/published line. **Art:** Pays $13/illustration or photo. **Queries:** Preferred. **Payment:** On publication.

AMERICAN FIELD

542 S. Dearborn St., Suite 1350, Chicago, IL 60605. 312-663-9797. Web site: www.americanfield.com. B.J. Matthys, Managing Editor. **Description:** Short items and anecdotes on hunting dogs and field trials for bird dogs. Yarns on hunting trips, bird-shooting; articles, to 1,500 words, on dogs and field trials, emphasizing conservation of game resources. Pay varies. **Payment:** On acceptance.

ANIMAL PEOPLE

P.O. Box 960, Clinton, WA 98236-0906. 360-579-2505. E-mail: anmlpepl@whidbey.com. Web site: www.animalpeoplenews.org. 10x/year. **Description:** "News for People Who Care About Animals." **Nonfiction:** Articles and profiles, of individuals of positive accomplishment, in any capacity that benefits animals or illustrates the intrinsic value of other species. **Tips:** No fiction or poetry. No stories about atrocities, essays on why animals have rights, or material that promotes animal abuse (hunting, fishing, trapping, and slaughter). **Queries:** Preferred. **Payment:** On acceptance.

ANIMALS

350 S. Huntington Ave., Boston, MA 02130. 617-522-7400. Web site: www.animelsmagazine.com. Quarterly. $15/year. Circ.: 50,000. Paula Abend, Editor. **Description:** Full-color publication with timely, reliable, provocative coverage of wildlife issues, pet-care topics, and animal protection concerns.

Nonfiction: Informative, well-researched articles, to 2,500 words. **Columns, Departments:** Profiles, 800 words, on individuals who work to make life better for animals, wild or domestic, or to save habitat. Reviews, 300-500 words. **Art:** Do not send originals. **Tips:** No personal accounts or favorite pet stories. **Queries:** Required. **E-queries:** No. **Unsolicited mss:** Accepts. **Response:** 6 weeks, SASE required. **Freelance Content:** 90%. **Rights:** NA. **Payment:** On acceptance.

AQUARIUM FISH

P.O. Box 6050, Mission Viejo, CA 92690. 949-855-8822.
Web site: www.animalnetwork.com. Russ Case, Editor. **Description:** On all types of freshwater, saltwater, and pond fish. **Nonfiction:** Articles (with or without color transparencies); 2,000-4,000 words; pay varies. **Tips:** No "pet fish" stories. **Payment:** On publication.

THE BACKSTRETCH

P.O. Box 7065, Louisville, KY 40257-0065. 800-325-3487.
Web site: www.thebackstretch.com. Kevin Baker, Editor. **Description:** Published by United Thoroughbred Trainers of America. **Nonfiction:** Feature articles, with photos, on subjects related to thoroughbred horse racing. **Payment:** On publication.

BIRD TALK

Box 6050, Mission Viejo, CA 92690. 949-855-8822.
Web site: www.animalnetwork.com. Melissa Kauffman, Editor. **Description:** Articles for pet bird owners (care and feeding, training, safety, outstanding personal adventures, exotic birds in their native countries, profiles of celebrities' pet birds, travel to bird parks or shows). **Nonfiction:** Good transparencies a plus; pays to $.10/word. **Queries:** Required. **Payment:** On publication.

BIRDS AND BLOOMS

5925 Country Lane, Greendale, WI 53129. 414-453-0100.
E-mail: editors@birdsandblooms.com. Web site: www.birdsandblooms.com. Bimonthly. Jeff Nowak, Editor. **Description:** For people who love the beauty of their own backyard. Focuses on background birding and gardening. **Nonfiction:** First-person experiences from your own backyard; 200-900 words; $100-$200. **Fillers:** 50-300 words; $50-$75. **Art:** Slides; $75-$300. **Tips:** Write conversationally, include tips to benefit readers, keep stories short and to the point. Submit photos. No bird rescue stories. **Queries:** Not necessary. **E-queries:** Yes. **Unsolicited mss:** Accepts. **Response:** Queries 1-2 months, submissions 2-3 months, SASE. **Freelance Content:** 25%. **Rights:** 1st NA. **Payment:** On publication. **Contact:** Jeff Nowak.

CAT FANCY

P.O. Box 6050, Mission Viejo, CA 92690. 949-855-8822.
E-mail: aluke@fancypubs.com. Web site: www.animalnetwork.com. Monthly. Circ.: 303,000. Amanda Luke, Editor. **Description:** Covers cat care, health, and grooming.

Nonfiction: to 2,500 words; $.20/word. **Queries:** Required. **Response:** SASE required. **Payment:** On publication.

CATS

260 Madison Ave., 8th Fl., New York, NY 10016. 917-256-2200. E-mail: info@catsmag.com. Web site: www.catsmag.com. Monthly. Circ.: 127,000. Beth Adelman, Editor. **Description:** Consumer magazine for cat enthusiasts. **Nonfiction:** All topics of interest to cat owners. Articles on multi-cat households; on advocacy on behalf of domestic and big cats, etc.; 1,500-2,000 words; $15-$500. **Columns, Departments:** Spotlight (profile of a person or cat who has done something extraordinary to benefit humankind or cat kind); Last Meow (humorous piece about the nature of cats and how humans fit into feline world); 1,500-2,000 words. Cat Tales (personal stories of readers and their cats, 800 words); $15-$500. **Tips:** Seeking submissions for Cat Tales, Last Meow, Spotlight, and features. Prefers articles with some specific, practical advice (What can I do today to make my cat's life better?), along with the reasoning behind the advice: What and Why. Don't just rely on your own experience; interview experts. **Queries:** Required. **E-queries:** Yes. **Unsolicited mss:** Accepts. **Response:** 1-2 months. **Rights:** Exclusive (6 months). **Payment:** On publication.

CITY & COUNTRY PETS

P.O. Box 7423, Dallas, TX 75209. 214-368-3658. E-mail: ndegan@aol.com. Web site: www.ccpets.com. Monthly. Free. Nancy Egan, Editor. **Description:** Features articles on dogs, cats, birds, horses, and fish, and their owners. **Nonfiction:** Articles with universal appeal or local focus. Especially needs pieces about pet birds and how to train them; 600-1,000 words; $50. **Tips:** Submit query with complete manuscript by mail. Welcomes new writers. **Queries:** Preferred. **Unsolicited mss:** Accepts. **Response:** SASE required. **Rights:** Nonexclusive.

DOG FANCY

P.O. Box 6050, Mission Viejo, CA 92690-6050. E-mail: Sbiller@fancypubs.com. Web site: www.dogfancy.com. Monthly. Circ.: 286,000. Kim Thornton, Editor. **Description:** On the care and enjoyment of all dogs, purebreds and mixed breeds. Readers are college-educated, middle-class adults interested in dog training, health, behavior, activities, and general care. **Nonfiction:** Well-written, well-researched articles on dog care, health, grooming, breeds, activities, events. 850-1,200 words. Pay varies. **Art:** Quality color slides or photos. **Tips:** No poetry, fiction, or articles in which the dog speaks as if human. Avoid tributes to dogs that have died or to beloved family pets. **Queries:** Preferred. **Freelance Content:** 80%. **Payment:** On publication.

DOG WORLD

Primedia Special Interest Pubs.

500 N. Dearborn Ave., Suite 1100, Chicago, IL 60610. 312-396-0600.

E-mail: dogworld3@aol.com. Web site: www.dogworldmag.com. Monthly. $3.99/$23.70. Circ.: 70,000. Donna Marcel, Editor. **Description:** For breeders, exhibitors, hobbyists, and professionals in kennel operations, veterinary medical research, grooming, legislation, show awards, training and dog sports. **Nonfiction:** 1,500-5,000 words; pay varies. **Columns, Departments:** 1,000 words. **Tips:** Written for the serious enthusiast. Seeking in-depth science, training, and health stories. Only one human-interest piece per issue; no poetry or fiction. **Queries:** Preferred. **E-queries:** Yes. **Unsolicited mss:** Accepts. **Response:** 4-6 months, SASE. **Freelance Content:** 25%. **Rights:** 1st. **Payment:** On publication.

EQUUS

656 Quince Orchard Rd., Suite 600, Gaithersburg, MD 20878. 301-977-3900. Laurie Prinz, Editor. **Description:** On all breeds of horses, covering their health and care as well as the latest advances in equine medicine and research. **Nonfiction:** Articles, 1,000-3,000 words; pays $100-$400. **Tips:** Speak as one horseperson to another. **Payment:** On publication.

FERRETS

Fancy Publications, P.O. Box 6050, Mission Viejo, CA 92690. 949-855-8822. Bimonthly. **Description:** For all ferret lovers.

THE FLORIDA HORSE

P.O. Box 2106, Ocala, FL 34478. 352-732-8858.

Web site: www.thefloridahorse.com. Michael Compton, Editor. **Description:** On Florida thoroughbred breeding and racing. Also veterinary articles, financial articles, topics of general interest to horse owners and breeders. **Nonfiction:** Articles, 1,500 words; pays $200-$300. **Queries:** Preferred. **Payment:** On publication.

FRESHWATER AND MARINE AQUARIUM

144 W. Sierra Madre, Sierra Madre, CA 91024. 800-523-1736.

Web site: www.mag-web.com. Don Dewey. **Description:** For tropical-fish enthusiasts. **Nonfiction:** How-to articles, varying lengths, on basic, semi-technical, and technical aspects of freshwater and marine aquariology; pays $50-$350. **Fillers:** $25-$75.

GOOD DOG!

P.O. Box 10069, Austin, TX 78766-1069. 512-454-6090.

E-mail: judie@gooddogmagazine.com. Web site: www.gooddogmagazine.com. Bimonthly. $12. Judi Becker, Editor. **Description:** Dog news and information, advice on food and nutrition, flea and tick products, behavior problems, training, puppies, breeds, and animal health. **Nonfiction:** Informative, fun to read. No material "written" by the dog; pay varies. **Tips:** Be informative, friendly, expert, fun. Write in third person, unless first person is more appropriate for a humor or opinion piece. **Queries:** Preferred. **Rights:** 1st electronic. **Payment:** On publication.

GUN DOG
6420 Wilshire Blvd., Los Angeles, CA 90048. Web site: www.emapusa.com. Roger Sparks, Editor. **Description:** On bird hunting (how-tos, where-tos, dog training, canine medicine, breeding). **Nonfiction:** Features, 1,000-2,500 words, with photos; $150-$450. **Payment:** On acceptance.

HORSE ILLUSTRATED
P.O. Box 6050, Mission Viejo, CA 92690. 949-855-8822. E-mail: horseillustrated@fancypubs.com. Web site: www.animalnetwork.com/horses. Monthly. $3.50. Circ.: 200,000. Moira C. Harris, Editor. **Description:** For horse owners, covers all breeds, all disciplines. Also, medical care, training, grooming, how-to, and human interest. **Nonfiction:** How-to (horse care/owning horses), training (English and Western), profiles (industry celebrities); 2,000 words or less; $300-$400. **Fillers:** humor. **Art:** Color transparencies, prints; $60-$90; cover, $200. **Tips:** Readers are mostly women, ages 18-40, who ride and show for pleasure and are concerned about well-being of their horses. **Queries:** Preferred. **E-queries:** Yes. **Unsolicited mss:** Accepts. **Response:** Queries 3 weeks, submissions 6 weeks, SASE required. **Freelance Content:** 15-20%. **Rights:** 1st NA. **Payment:** On publication.

HORSE & RIDER
PO Box 4101, 741 Corporate Circle, Suite A, Golden, CO 80401. 720-836-1257. E-mail: hrsenrider@cowles.com. Web site: www.equisearch.com. Monthly. $3.50/issue, $19.95/year. Circ.: 165,000. René E. Riley, Executive Editor. **Description:** For competitive and recreational Western riders. Training articles, stable management, health care tips, safe trail riding practices, consumer advice, and behind-the-scenes coverage of major equine events. **Nonfiction:** How-tos (training, horse care/horsekeeping). Consumer buying advice. Profiles of Western horse show people. 150-2,000 words; $150-$1,000. **Fillers:** Humorous experiences; 150-1,000 words; $150-$1,000. **Columns, Departments:** Real-life horse stories. Trail-riding tips. Training tips. Horsekeeping tips. 150-1,000 words; $0-$1,000. **Queries:** Preferred. **E-queries:** No. **Unsolicited mss:** Accepts. **Response:** 3 months, SASE required. **Freelance Content:** 5-10%. **Rights:** 1st NA. **Payment:** On acceptance.

HORSEMEN'S YANKEE PEDLAR
83 Leicester St., N. Oxford, MA 01537. 508-987-5886. E-mail: info@pedlar.com. Web site: www.pedlar.com. Molly Johns, Editor. **Description:** About horses and horsemen in the Northeast. **Nonfiction:** News and feature-length articles, with photos; pays $2/published inch. **Payment:** On publication.

I LOVE CATS
450 7th Ave., Suite 1701, New York, NY 10123. 212-244-2351. E-mail: Savings@ix.Netcom.com. Web site: www.iluvcats.com. Bimonthly. Circ.:

100,000. Lisa Allmendinger. **Description:** All about cats. **Fiction:** 500-700 words. **Nonfiction:** Features, to 1,000 words; pays $40-$150. **Fillers:** $25. **Art:** Photos. **Tips:** Send us your cat's picture and interesting story and we'll publish it on our site. **Queries:** Preferred. **Payment:** On publication.

MODERN FERRET

Crunchy Concepts, Inc., P.O. Box 1007, Smithtown, NY 11787. 631-981-3574. E-mail: mary@modernferret.com. Web site: http://www.modernferret.com. Monthly. Mary Shefferman, Editor-in-Chief. **Description:** For ferret owners, by ferret owners.

MUSHING

P.O. Box 149, Ester, AK 99725-0149. 907-479-0454. E-mail: editor@mushing.com. Web site: www.mushing.com. Todd Hoener, Editor. **Description:** Dog-driving how-tos, innovations, history, profiles, interviews, and features related to sled dogs. International audience. **Nonfiction:** 1,200-2,000 words. **Columns, Departments:** Competitive and recreational dog drivers; weight pullers, dog packers, and skijorers; 500-1,000 words. **Art:** Photos; $20-$250. **Queries:** Preferred.

PERFORMANCE HORSE

2895 Chad Dr., Eugene, OR 97408. 541-341-6508. Web site: www.performancehorse.com. Monthly. $24.95. Circ.: 15,000. Betsy Lynch, Editor. **Description:** Seeks to help high-level western performance horse breeders, owners, trainers, and competitors to excel in the sports of cutting, reining, and working cow-horses. **Nonfiction:** Training, breeding, management, competitive strategies, how-to; for reining, cutting, and working cow-horse competition; 500-3,000 words; to $500. **Art:** Photos to accompany feature stories and articles; 35mm or larger prints or slides; to $50. **Queries:** Preferred. **E-queries:** Yes. **Unsolicited mss:** Accepts. **Response:** 4-6 weeks, SASE. **Freelance Content:** 80%. **Rights:** 1st NASR. **Payment:** On publication.

PERFORMANCE HORSEMAN

Gum Tree Corner, Unionville, PA 19375. 800-588-7921. Web site: www.performancehorse.com. Joanne Tobey, Editor. **Description:** For the serious western rider, on training, improving riding skills, all aspects of care and management. **Nonfiction:** How-to pieces; pays from $300. **Queries:** Preferred. **Payment:** On acceptance.

PET BUSINESS

233 Park Ave. S., 6th Floor, New York, NY 10003. Oriol Gutierrez, Executive Editor. **Description:** On animals and products found in pet stores (research findings; legislative/regulatory actions; business and marketing tips and trends). **Nonfiction:** Brief, well-documented articles; pays $.10/word, $20/photo. **Payment:** On publication.

PETLIFE

3451 Boston Ave., Ft. Worth, TX 76116. 800-856-2032. Web site: www.petlifeweb.com. Bimonthly. $3.99/$19.99. Circ.: 187,000. Alexis Wilson, Editor. **Description:** Offers a full spectrum of human/pet interaction, on all pets. **Nonfiction:** On pet health-care and nutrition, training, new products, humor, general interests; stories on the human-animal bond. While dogs and cats are main focus, other pets featured on occasion; 100-1,500 words; pay varies. **Columns, Departments:** Pet Health, Vet Perspective, Odd Pets, Celebrity Interviews; 100-1,000 words. **Tips:** Most readers are women. Seeking ways to better care for animal companions; heartwarming stories about human/animal bond. **Queries:** Required. **E-queries:** Yes. **Unsolicited mss:** Does not accept. **Response:** Queries 3-4 weeks, SASE not needed. **Freelance Content:** 80%. **Rights:** Worldwide. **Payment:** On acceptance.

PRACTICAL HORSEMAN

Box 589, Unionville, PA 19375. 610-380-8977. E-mail: Prachorse@aol.com. Mandy Lorraine, Editor. **Description:** How-to articles conveying leading experts' advice on English riding, training, and horse care. **Tips:** Send clips. **Queries:** Preferred. **Payment:** On acceptance.

THE RETRIEVER JOURNAL

Wildwood Press, P.O. Box 968, Traverse City, MI 49685. 231-946-3712. Web site: www.villagepress.com/wildwood. Steve Smith. **Description:** On topics of interest to retriever owners and breeders. **Nonfiction:** Articles, 1,500-2,200 words; pays $250 and up. **Queries:** Preferred.

TROPICAL FISH HOBBYIST

211 W. Sylvania Ave., Neptune, NJ 07753. 732-988-8400. E-mail: editor@tfh.com. Web site: www.tfh.com. Monthly. $3.95/issue. Circ.: 65,000. Ray Hunziker, Editor. **Description:** Covers tropical fish and aquariums. **Nonfiction:** For beginning and experienced tropical and marine fish enthusiasts; 2,500 words; $100-$250. **Fillers:** cartoons (¼ page vertical); $25. **Queries:** Not necessary. **E-queries:** Yes. **Unsolicited mss:** Accepts. **Response:** 60 days, SASE. **Freelance Content:** 50%. **Rights:** All. **Payment:** On acceptance.

THE WESTERN HORSEMAN

P.O. Box 7980, Colorado Springs, CO 80933-7980. 719-633-5524. Web site: www.westernhorseman.com. Pat Close, Editor. **Description:** on care and training of horses; farm, ranch, and stable management; health care and veterinary medicine. **Nonfiction:** Articles, about 1,500 words, with photos; pays to $800. **Payment:** On acceptance.

YOUNG RIDER

Box 8237, Lexington, KY 40533. 859-260-9800. Web site: www.animalnetwork.com. Bimonthly. Lesley Ward. **Description:** About horses and children. **Nonfiction:** No overly sentimental stories, or stories with "goody two-shoes" characters; 1,200 word stories; pays $120. **Art:** Photos. **Tips:** Query or send manuscript. **Queries:** Not necessary. **Payment:** On publication.

ARTS & ARCHITECTURE

(For music, dance, etc., see Performing Arts)

AIRBRUSH ACTION

P.O. Box 2052, 1985 Swarthmore Ave., Lakewood, NJ 08701. 800-876-2472. E-mail: kpriest@idt.net. Web site: www.airbrushaction.com. Bi-monthly. $5.99/issue, $26.95/year. Circ.: 60,000. Kathryn Priest, Editor. **Description:** Showcases innovative airbrush art. Profiles on notable artists, step-by-step "how-to"; columns on T-shirt painting, automotive airbrushing, fingernail design. Also, regular Buyer's Guides with comparisons of airbrush art supplies. **Nonfiction:** Profiles of artists by request only; 1,000-2,000 words; $.15/word. **Queries:** Required. **E-queries:** Yes. **Unsolicited mss:** Accepts. **Response:** 2 weeks, SASE required. **Freelance Content:** 50%. **Rights:** All. **Payment:** On publication.

AMERICAN ART JOURNAL

730 Fifth Ave., New York, NY 10019-4105. 212-541-9600. Annual. Circ.: 2,000. Jayne A. Kuchna, Editor-in-Chief. **Description:** American art of 17th through mid-20th centuries. **Nonfiction:** Scholarly articles; 2,000-10,000 words; $200-$500. **Art:** Photos. **Payment:** On acceptance.

AMERICAN INDIAN ART

7314 E. Osborn Dr., Scottsdale, AZ 85251. 480-994-5445. Roanne P. Goldfein, Editor. **Description:** Detailed articles, on American Indian arts: painting, carving, beadwork, basketry, textiles, ceramics, jewelry, etc. **Nonfiction:** 10-20 double-spaced pages; pay varies. **Queries:** Preferred. **Payment:** On publication.

ARCHITECTURE

770 Broadway, New York, NY 10003. 646654-5766. E-mail: info@architecturemag.com. Web site: www.architecturemag.com. Monthly. $8.95/issue; $55/year. Circ.: 70,000. Reed Kroloff, Editor. **Description:** Architectural design and culture. **Nonfiction:** Articles on architecture, building technology, professional practice; up to 2,000 words; $.50/word. **Queries:** Preferred.

ART & ANTIQUES

2100 Powers Ferry Rd., Atlanta, GA 30339. 770-955-5656. Web site: www.artantiquesmag.com. 11x/year. $5/$39.95. Circ.: 190,000. Barbara S. Tapp, Editor. **Description:** For lovers of fine art and antiques. **Nonfiction:** Research articles, art and antiques in context (interiors), overviews, personal narratives; 150-1,200 words; $1/word. **Tips:** Query with resumé and clips. **Queries:** Preferred. **E-queries:** Yes. **Unsolicited mss:** Accepts. **Response:** Queries 2 weeks, submissions 2 months, SASE not required. **Freelance Content:** 90%. **Payment:** On acceptance. **Contact:** Patti Verbanas, Managing Editor.

ART THOUGHTS JOURNAL

E-mail: mark@artthought.com. Web site: www.artthought.com. Bimonthly. Mark Patro, Editor. **Description:** Online publication discussing artists and their work (painters, sculptors, photographers, filmmakers, etc.). Seeks to broaden understanding about why artists create in the way they do. **Nonfiction:** Seeking art-related articles, essays, and interviews. Focus on the artists themselves and the inspirations for their work; $25-$100. **Queries:** Required. **E-queries:** Yes. **Unsolicited mss:** Accepts. **Response:** 2 weeks. **Rights:** Electronic, archival; author retains print rights. **Payment:** On publication.

ART-TALK

P.O. Box 8508, Scottdale, AZ 85252-8508. 480-948-1799. E-mail: bill4243@aol.com. Bill Macomber. **Description:** A fine-art publication, for the collector. **Nonfiction:** Articles, fillers; pay varies. **Payment:** On acceptance.

ARTIST'S MAGAZINE

1507 Dana Ave., Cincinnati, OH 45207. 513-531-2222. E-mail: tamedit@fw.pubs.com. Web site: www.artistsmagazine.com. Monthly. $3.99/issue, $19.96/year. Circ.: 220,000. Sandra Carpenter, Managing Editor. **Description:** Written by artists for artists. Offers instruction for professional success, on painting techniques, media and materials, design and composition, problem solving, special effects, marketing, and other business topics. **Nonfiction:** Specific art instruction (e.g., "Behind the Scenes," from start to finish: master the elements to improve your watercolor landscapes); 1,200-1,500 words; $300-$500. **Columns, Departments:** Color Corner (e.g., "Paint it Black," get those tubes of black paint out of the closet and use them to improve your paintings); 900-1,200 words; $200-$300. **Art:** Art-related cartoons; $65. **Tips:** Best opportunities include: Artist's Life and Business columns. Must be able to write from the artist's viewpoint, using the language of art. **Queries:** Preferred. **E-queries:** No. **Unsolicited mss:** Accepts. **Response:** 90 days, SASE required. **Freelance Content:** 40-45%. **Rights:** FNASR. **Payment:** On publication. **Contact:** Greg Schaber, Exec. Ed.

ARTS ATLANTIC

145 Richmond St., Charlottetown, P.E.I., Canada C1A 1J1. 902-628-6138. Joseph Sherman, Editor. **Description:** Articles and reviews, 600-3,000 words, on visual, performing, and literary arts primarily in Atlantic Canada. Also, "idea and concept" articles of universal appeal. **Queries:** Preferred.

BLACKLINES

2011 Newkirk Ave., Suite 7D, Brooklyn, NY 11226. 718-703-8000. E-mail: kathleen@blacklines.net. Web site: www.blacklines.net. Quarterly. Carla

Robinson, Managing Editor. **Description:** Features black designers in architecture, interior design, construction, development, and the arts. Challenges traditional ideas and perceptions, offers a context for design and a means to exchange ideas and information. **Tips:** Send cover letter and resumé for consideration, with 2-5 clips that show your ability to interview diverse subjects. **Queries:** Preferred. **E-queries:** Yes. **Unsolicited mss:** Accepts.

BOMB

594 Broadway, Suite 905, New York, NY 10012. 212-431-3943. E-mail: betsy@bombsite.com. Web site: www.bombsite.com. Quarterly. $4.96/$18. Circ.: 20,000. Betsy Sussler, Editor. **Description:** Articles, varying lengths, on artists, musicians, writers, actors, and directors. Some fiction and poetry. **Fiction:** 30 pages max; $100. **Nonfiction:** Will consider conversational interviews, but query first. **Poetry:** 10 pages; $100. **Queries:** Preferred. **E-queries:** Yes. **Unsolicited mss:** Accepts. **Response:** Queries 2 months, submissions 4 months, SASE. **Freelance Content:** 5%. **Rights:** 1st serial. **Payment:** On publication. **Contact:** Susan Sherman, Assoc. Ed.

CAMERA ARTS

P.O. Box 2328, Corrales, NM 87048. 505-899-8054. Web site: www.cameraarts.com. Bimonthly. $24 (U.S.), $40 (Canada and Mexico). Circ.: 18,000. Steve Simmons, Editor. **Description:** The art and craft of photography in the 21st century. **Nonfiction:** Articles on photography. New writers need to send samples of previous work; 1,000-2,000 words; $.25/word. **Art:** Photographs need to be very good; pay varies. **Tips:** Before you write about a photographer, send query with samples of his/her artwork first. **Queries:** Required. **E-queries:** Yes. **Unsolicited mss:** Accepts. **Response:** 2-8 weeks, SASE required. **Freelance Content:** 80%. **Rights:** 1st NA. **Payment:** On publication.

THE COMICS JOURNAL

Fantagraphics, Inc., 7563 Lake City Way NE, Seattle, WA 98115. 206-524-1967. Web site: www.tcj.com. Monthly. $5.95. Circ.: 10,000. **Description:** Covers the comics medium as an art form. An eclectic mix of industry news, interviews, and reviews, for readers worldwide. **Nonfiction:** Comics news, journalism, and criticism; 200-2,000 words; $.07/word. **Queries:** Preferred. **E-queries:** Yes. **Unsolicited mss:** Accepts. **Response:** 1-2 months, SASE. **Freelance Content:** 95%. **Payment:** On publication.

CONTEMPORARY STONE & TILE DESIGN

299 Market St., Suite 320, Saddle Brook, NJ 07663-5312. 201-291-9001. Web site: www.stoneworld.com. Quarterly. Michael Reis. **Description:** On using stone in architecture and interior design. **Nonfiction:** Articles, 1,500 words; $6/column inch. **Art:** Photos, drawings. **Payment:** On publication.

DECORATIVE ARTIST'S WORKBOOK

1507 Dana Ave., Cincinnati, OH 45207-1005. 513-531-2690. E-mail: dawedit@fwpubs.com. Web site: www.decorativeartist.com. Bimonthly. Circ.: 90,000. Anne Hevener, Editor. **Description:** How-to articles on decorative painting. **Nonfiction:** Painting projects only, not crafts; 1,000-1,500 words; $150-$300. **Columns, Departments:** Artist of the Issue (profiles of up-and-coming painters); 500 words; $100-$150. **Queries:** Required. **Payment:** On acceptance.

DOUBLETAKE

55 Davis Square, Somerville, MA 02144. 617-591-9389. E-mail: dtmag@doubletakemagazine.org. Web site: www.doubletakemagazine.org. Quarterly. $10/$24. Circ.: 40,000. Robert Coles, Editor. **Description:** Fiction, poetry, and photo-essays that reveal "extraordinary events and qualities found in everyday lives of Americans and others." **Fiction:** Stories, narrative realism that observes life, quietly but with understanding and compassion. **Nonfiction:** Narrative, with documentary, literary, esthetic, or reportorial excellence. **Poetry:** Yes. **Art:** Photos. **Queries:** Not necessary. **E-queries:** No. **Unsolicited mss:** Accepts. **Response:** 3 months, SASE. **Freelance Content:** 90%. **Rights:** 1st worldwide English-language serial. **Payment:** On acceptance.

FASHION FLASHBACKS

Platform Publishing, P.O. Box 138, San Mateo, CA 94401. 650-344-6977. E-mail: lanajean@best.com. Web site: www.best.com/~lanajean/flashbacks.html. Lanajean Vecchoine, Editor/Publisher. **Description:** Online and in print. Focuses on fashion design and history from 1960-1979. **Nonfiction:** Articles, photos, and press releases about notable events accepted. **Tips:** Include both your e-mail and mailing addresses. **Payment:** in copies.

FIBERARTS

50 College St., Asheville, NC 28801. 828-253-0467. E-mail: editor@fiberartsmagazine.com. Web site: www.fiberartsmagazine.com. 5x/year. $4.50/issue, $22/year. Circ.: 24,000. Sunita Patterson, Editor. **Description:** Covers all fiber-arts: weaving, quilting, embroidery, wearable art, 3-D work, basketry, and more. Readers include professional artists, craftspeople, hobbyists, collectors, curators. **Nonfiction:** Articles and interviews (outstanding artists and craftspeople, trends and issues, exhibitions, business concerns, historic and ethnic textiles); 250-2,000 words; $65-$500. **Columns, Departments:** Profile (1 artist); Reviews (exhibits/books). Commentary; Notable Events (conferences, exhibitions); Art & Technology; 250-500 words; $65-$125. **Art:** 35mm slides; transparencies; b/w glossies; electronic images (if 300 dpi or greater resolution. No color prints. **Tips:** Good visuals key to acceptance. Submit with synopsis, outline, writing samples. Use accessible, not scholarly, writing tone. **Queries:** Preferred. **E-queries:** No. **Unsolicited mss:** Accepts. **Response:** 1 month, SASE required. **Freelance Content:** 90%. **Rights:** 1st NA. **Payment:** On publication.

LOG HOME DESIGN IDEAS

H&S Media, 1620 Lawe St., Ste. 2, Appleton, WI 54915. 920-830-1701. E-mail: editor@athenet.net. Web site: www.loghomeideas.com. **Description:** For people interested in log homes. **Queries:** Preferred.

PETERSEN'S PHOTOGRAPHIC MAGAZINE

6420 Wilshire Blvd., Los Angeles, CA 90048. 323-782-2200. Web site: www.emapusa.com. Ron Leach, Editor. **Description:** On all phases of still photography, for the amateur and advanced photographer. **Nonfiction:** How-tos; pays $125/printed page for articles, with photos. **Payment:** On publication.

POPULAR PHOTOGRAPHY

1633 Broadway, New York, NY 10019. 212-767-6578. Web site: www.popphoto.com. Monthly. Circ.: 450,000. Jason Schneider, Editor. **Description:** For serious amateur photographers. **Nonfiction:** Illustrated how-to articles, 500-2,000 words. **Art:** With all photos, submit technical data (camera used, lens, film, shutter speed, aperture, lighting, etc.) to show how picture was made; pay varies. **Tips:** Interested in new, unusual phases of photography not covered previously. No general articles. **Queries:** Required. **Payment:** On acceptance.

PROFESSIONAL PHOTOGRAPHER

229 Peachtree St. NE, 2200 International Tower, Atlanta, GA 30303. 404-522-8600. Monthly. Circ.: 24,000. **Description:** Since 1907, for professional photographers engaged in all types of photography.

SCULPTURE

International Sculpture Ctr. 1529 18th Street NW, Washington, DC 20036. 202-234-0555. Web site: www.sculpture.org. Glenn Harper. **Description:** Published by International Sculpture Center. Articles on sculpture, sculptors, collections, books, criticism, technical processes, etc. **Nonfiction:** Pay varies. **Queries:** Preferred. **Unsolicited mss:** Accepts.

SOUTHWEST ART

5444 Westheimer, Suite 1440, Houston, TX 77056. 713-296-7000. E-mail: southwest@southwestart.com. Web site: www.southwestart.com. Monthly. $4.99/$32.00. Circ.: 65,000. Margaret L. Brown, Editor. **Description:** For collectors of Western art (about the West or created, exhibited, or sold in the West). Artist profiles, gallery and museum events. **Nonfiction:** On artists, collectors, exhibitions, events, dealers, history, trends in Western American art. Most interested in representational or figurative arts; 1,400 words; $600. **Art:** Slides, transparencies. **Queries:** Preferred. **E-queries:** Yes. **Unsolicited mss:** Accepts. **Response:** Queries/submissions 4 months, SASE. **Freelance Content:** 70%. **Rights:** Exclusive worldwide. **Payment:** On acceptance.

SUNSHINE ARTIST MAGAZINE
Palm House Publishing Co., 2600 Temple Dr., Winter Park, FL 32789-1371. 407-539-1399. Web site: www.sunshineartist.com. Monthly. Circ.: 12,000. **Description:** Covers national outdoor art shows, fairs, festivals. Business focus.

U.S. ART
220 S. Sixth St., Suite 500, Minneapolis, MN 55402. 612-339-7571. E-mail: sgilbert@mspcommunications.com. Monthly. Circ.: 50,000. Sara Gilbert, Editor. **Description:** For collectors of limited-edition art prints. **Nonfiction:** Features and artist profiles; 1,200 words; $300-$450. **Queries:** Required. **Payment:** On acceptance.

WATERCOLOR
770 Broadway, New York, NY 10003. 646-654-5220. Quarterly. M. Stephen Doherty, Editor-in-Chief. **Description:** On watercolor and other water media (gouache, casein, acrylic, etc.). **Nonfiction:** How-to articles, varying lengths; pay varies. **Queries:** Preferred. **Payment:** On publication.

WESTART
P.O. Box 6868, Auburn, CA 95604-6868. 530-885-0969. Semimonthly. Circ.: 4,000. Martha Garcia, Editor-in-Chief. **Description:** Fine arts and crafts. **Nonfiction:** Features, 350-700 words. No hobbies; $.50/column inch. **Art:** Photos. **Queries:** Preferred.

ASSOCIATIONS

AOPA PILOT
421 Aviation Way, Frederick, MD 21701. 301-695-2350. E-mail: pilot@aopa.org. Web site: www.aopa.org. Monthly. $5.00/issue. Circ.: 341, 339. Thomas B. Haines, Editor. **Description:** National general-aviation magazine, published by Aircraft Owners and Pilots Assn. **Fiction:** Detailed, concise, to convey message without overloading (or boring) the reader; length varies. **Art:** 35mm color slides. **Tips:** Include telephone and/or fax numbers, and your AOPA numbers with all submissions. **Queries:** Preferred. **Unsolicited mss:** Accepts. **Payment:** On publication.

CATHOLIC FORESTER
355 Shuman Blvd., P.O. Box 3012, Naperville, IL 60566-7012. 630-983-4900. E-mail: cofpr@aol.com. Web site: www.catholicforester.com. Bimonthly. Circ.: 97,000. Mary Anne File, Editor. **Description:** Full-color, with organizational news, general interest, fiction, and some nonfiction articles for members. Pays $.20/word. **Fiction:** Humor, children, inspirational; 500-1,500 words. **Nonfiction:** Health, fitness, parenting, financial; 500-1,500 words. **Poetry:** Inspirational, religious; 25-50 words. **Queries:** Not necessary. **E-queries:** Yes. **Unsolicited mss:** Accepts.

Response: Submissions 3-6 months, SASE required. **Freelance Content:** 20%. **Rights:** One-time. **Payment:** On acceptance. **Contact:** Patricia Baron.

ELKS

425 W. Diversey Parkway, Chicago, IL 60614-6196. 773-755-4894. E-mail: annai@elks.org. Web site: www.elks.org/elksmag/. 10x/year. Circ.: 1,200,000. Fred D. Oakes, Editor. **Description:** General interest, published by the Elks fraternal organization. Typical reader is over 40, an above-average income, living in a town of 500,000 or less. **Nonfiction:** Authoritative articles (please include sources) for lay person, varied topics: technology, science, sports, history, seasonal; 1,500-2,500 words; $.20/word. **Art:** Cover art; slides, transparencies; $450. **Tips:** No religion, politics, controversial issues. Avoid queries or clips. **Queries:** Not necessary. **E-queries:** Yes. **Unsolicited mss:** Accepts. **Response:** Queries 1 week, submissions 1-6 weeks, SASE required. **Freelance Content:** 30%. **Rights:** One-time NA serial. **Payment:** On acceptance.

HARVARD MAGAZINE

7 Ware St., Cambridge, MA 02138-4037. 617-495-5746. Web site: www.harvardmagazine.com. Bimonthly. $4.95/$30. Circ.: 225,000. John Rosenberg, Editor. **Description:** About Harvard faculty, staff, students, and alumni, also on research and teaching being conducted in this educational community. **Nonfiction:** Profiles; examples of work and research; 800-10,000 words; $300-$2,000. **Queries:** Required. **E-queries:** Yes. **Unsolicited mss:** Accepts. **Response:** 1-2 weeks, SASE. **Freelance Content:** 50%. **Rights:** One-time. **Payment:** On publication.

KIWANIS

3636 Woodview Trace, Indianapolis, IN 46268-3196. 317-875-8755. E-mail: cjonak@kiwanis.org. Web site: www.kiwanis.org. 10x/year. $2/issue. Circ.: 240,000. Chuck Jonak, Managing Editor. **Description:** For Kiwanians, community leaders involved in volunteer service work through their clubs. **Nonfiction:** On home; family; international issues; career and community concerns, and social, health, and emotional needs of youth (especially under age 6). No travel pieces, interviews, profiles. Also, financial planning for younger families; retirement planning for older people; 1,500-2,500; $400-$1,000. **Queries:** Preferred. **E-queries:** Yes. **Unsolicited mss:** Accepts. **Response:** Queries 1-2 weeks, submissions 2-4 weeks, SASE required. **Freelance Content:** 40%. **Rights:** First. **Payment:** On acceptance.

LION

300 22nd St., Oak Brook, IL 60523. 630-571-5466. E-mail: rkleinfe@lionsclub.org. Web site: www.lionsclubs.org. 10x/year. Circ.: 580,000. Robert Kleinfelder, Senior Editor. **Description:** Published by Lion's Club International, reflecting service activities for men and women interested in voluntary community service. **Nonfiction:** Primarily photo stories of Lions' service activities; 50-2,000 words; $300-$400. **Fillers:** Family-oriented humor; 500-1,000 words; $300-

$500. **Art:** Photos. **Tips:** No political, religious, or autobiographical topics. **Queries:** Preferred. **E-queries:** Yes. **Unsolicited mss:** Accepts. **Response:** Queries 1-2 weeks, submissions 2-3 weeks, SASE required for articles. **Freelance Content:** 20%. **Rights:** All. **Payment:** On acceptance.

MANAGERS REPORT
3923 Lake Worth Rd., Suite 209, Lake Worth, FL 33461. 561-687-4700. E-mail: mgrreport@aol.com. Web site: www.managersreport.com. Monthly. $18. Circ.: 10,000. Lisa Pinder, Executive Editor. **Description:** For managers and board members of condominiums, homeowners associations, co-ops and community associations. Motto is "Helping Community Associations Help Each Other." **Nonfiction:** Prefers how-to format, featuring readers and how they resolved problems in their communities; length varies; $25-$150. **Art:** Prefer photos to accompany all stories; $10. **Tips:** Welcomes new writers. **Queries:** Preferred. **E-queries:** Yes. **Unsolicited mss:** Accepts. **Response:** SASE required. **Freelance Content:** 40%. **Rights:** 1st. **Payment:** On acceptance.

MODERN WOODMEN
Modern Woodmen of America, 1701 1st Ave., Rock Island, IL 61201. 309-786-6481. E-mail: jweaver@modern-woodmen.org. Web site: www.modern-woodmen.org. Quarterly. Circ.: 400,000. Gloria Bergh, Editor. **Description:** For members of Modern Woodmen of America, a fraternal life-insurance society. **Fiction:** Stories that promote patriotism, volunteerism, family; 1,000 words; $100-$500. **Nonfiction:** On postive family and community life, community service, patriotism, financial well-being; 1,000; $100-$500. **Tips:** Readers mostly middle-class, with children in the home. **Queries:** Not necessary. **E-queries:** No. **Response:** Queries/submissions 4 weeks. **Freelance Content:** 20%. **Rights:** One-time. **Payment:** On acceptance.

OPTIMIST
4494 Lindell Blvd., St. Louis, MO 63108. 314-371-6000. E-mail: magazine@optimist.org. Web site: www.optimist.org. Dena Hull, Editor. **Description:** On activities of local Optimist Clubs, and techniques for personal and club success. **Nonfiction:** Articles, to 1,000 words; pays from $100. **Queries:** Preferred. **Payment:** On acceptance.

RETIREMENT LIFE
National Assn. of Retired Federal Employees, 606 N. Washington St., Alexandria, VA 22314. 703-838-7760. Web site: www.narfe.org. Monthly. Circ.: 350,000. **Description:** Focuses on issues of interest to retired federal employees.

ROTARIAN
1560 Sherman Ave., Evanston, IL 60201-3698. 847-866-3000. E-mail: prattc@rotaryintl.org. Web site: http://208.240.90.200/pubs/rotarian/. Monthly. Circ.: 514,000. Charles W. Pratt, Editor. **Description:** Personal and busi-

ness interests for Rotary members (international understanding, goodwill and peace, vocational relationships, community life, human relationships). **Nonfiction:** Business, travel, health, education, environment, management and ethics, sciences, sports and adventure. **Columns, Departments:** Executive Health, Book Review, Trends, Manager's Memo, Earth Diary. **Queries:** Preferred. **Unsolicited mss:** Accepts. **Contact:** Cary Silver, managing editor.

TOASTMASTER
Toastmasters International, P.O. Box 9052, Mission Viejo, CA 92690. 949-858-8255. E-mail: pubs@toastmaster.org. Web site: www.toastmaster.org. Monthly, for members. Circ.: 175,000. Suzanne Frey, Editor. **Description:** On public speaking, leadership, and communication skills. **Nonfiction:** Articles on decision-making, leadership, language, interpersonal and professional communication, humor, logical thinking, rhetorical devices, public speaking, profiles of great orators, etc.; 2,000 words; $300 max. **Queries:** Preferred. **E-queries:** Yes. **Unsolicited mss:** Accepts. **Response:** Queries 1 month, submissions 6 weeks, SASE. **Payment:** On acceptance.

VFW
406 W. 34th St., Kansas City, MO 64111. 816-756-3390. E-mail: pbrown@vfw.org. Web site: www.vfw.org. Monthly. $10/yr. Circ.: 1,800,000. Richard K. Kolb, Editor. **Description:** Focuses on military history, issues relating to veterans and the military. **Nonfiction:** Articles on current foreign policy and defense, along with all veterans' issues; 1,000 words. **Tips:** Write with clarity and simplicity, concrete detail and short paragraphs. Use active voice, and avoid flowery prose and military jargon. **Queries:** Preferred. **Unsolicited mss:** Accepts. **Rights:** FNASR. **Payment:** On publication.

WOODMEN
1700 Farnam St., Omaha, NE 68102. 402-342-1890. Web site: www.woodmen.com. Scott J. Darling, Editor. **Description:** On history, insurance, family, health, science, fraternal lodge activities, etc. **Nonfiction:** Articles; pays $.10/word, extra for photos. **Art:** Photos. **Queries:** Preferred. **Payment:** On acceptance.

AUTOMOTIVE

AMERICAN MOTORCYCLIST
American Motorcyclist Assn.
13515 Yarmouth Dr., Pickerington, OH 43147. 614-856-1900. Web site: www.ama-cycle.org. Greg Harrison, Editor. **Description:** Articles and fiction, to 3,000 words, on motorcycling: news coverage, personalities, tours. **Nonfiction:** Pay varies. **Art:** Photos. **Queries:** Preferred. **Response:** SASE required. **Payment:** On publication.

ASPHALT ANGELS

24 Carriage Lane, Scotts Valley, CA 95066. 831-438-7882. Web site: www.thunderpressinc.com. **Description:** For female motorcyclists. **Queries:** Preferred.

AUTO REVISTA

Motorline Media
14330 Midway Rd., Ste 202, Dallas, TX 75244-3514. 972-386-0040. Weekly. Circ.: 40,000. Aaron Esslinger, Editor. **Description:** Spanish-language magazine, devoted to cars.

AUTOMUNDO

2960 SW 8th St., 2nd Fl., Miami, FL 33135. 305-541-4198. Web site: www.automundo.com. Monthly. Circ.: 45,000. Ernesto Lanata, Editor. **Description:** Spanish-language publication for auto fans. Articles on makes, models, scenic drives, the latest technology and more.

CAR AND DRIVER

2002 Hogback Rd., Ann Arbor, MI 48105-9795. 734-971-3600. E-mail: editors@caranddriver.com. Web site: www.caranddriver.com. Monthly. Circ.: 1,300,000. Steve Spence, Managing Editor. **Description:** Profiles unusual people or manufacturers involved in cars and racing. **Nonfiction:** To 2,500 words. **Tips:** Mostly staff-written; query with clips. **Queries:** Required. **Unsolicited mss:** Does not accept. **Freelance Content:** 5%. **Payment:** On acceptance.

CAR CRAFT

6420 Wilshire Blvd., 9th Fl., Los Angeles, CA 90048. 323-782-2000. David Freiburger, Editor. **Description:** Covers high-performance street machines, drag cars, racing events; technical pieces; action photos. **Nonfiction:** Articles and photo-features; pays from $150/page. **Payment:** On publication.

CC MOTORCYCLE NEWS

P.O. Box 808, Nyack, NY 10960-0808. 845-353-6686. E-mail: info@motorcyclenews.cc. Web site: www.motorcyclenews.cc. Annual. Circ.: 60,000. Mark Kalan, Editor. **Description:** Motorcycles news, travel, technology, and entertainment. **Fiction:** About motorcycles or on sport of motorcycling, in a positive manner; 1,200 words; $10. **Nonfiction:** Motorcycle themes; up to 2,500 words; $50-$150. **Poetry:** positive; $10. **Fillers:** Humorous stories; $10. **Columns, Departments:** Technical, about sport of motorcycling; 800 words; $75-$100. **Tips:** Don't submit "I used to ride but . . ." stories. **E-queries:** Yes. **Unsolicited mss:** Accepts. **Response:** 60 days, SASE. **Freelance Content:** 10%. **Rights:** All. **Payment:** On publication.

CYCLE NEWS

3505-M Cadillac Ave., P.O. Box 5084, Costa Mesa, CA 92626. 715-751-7433. Web site: www.cyclenews.com. Jack Mangus, Editor. **Description:** For motorcycle enthusiasts. **Columns, Departments:** Technical articles on motorcycling; profiles and interviews with newsmakers. Pays $2/column inch. **Queries:** Preferred.

CYCLE WORLD

1499 Monrovia Ave., Newport Beach, CA 92663. 949-720-5300. E-mail: cw1edwards@aol.com. David Edwards, Editor-in-Chief. **Description:** News items on motorcycle industry, legislation, trends. **Nonfiction:** Technical and feature articles, 1,500-2,500 words, for motorcycle enthusiasts. Pays $100-$200 per page. **Art:** Photos. **Queries:** Preferred. **Payment:** On publication.

DRIVER

Volkswagen of America, Mail Code 3C03, 3800 Hamlin Rd., Auburn, MI 48326. Web site: www.vw.com/owners/magazine. Marlene Goldsmith, Editor. **Description:** For Volkswagen owners: profiles of well-known personalities; inspirational or human-interest pieces; travel; humor; German travel. **Nonfiction:** Articles, 600-1,200 words; pays $300. **Fillers:** Anecdotes, to 100 words, about Volkswagen owners' experiences; humorous photos of current model Volkswagens. Pays $100. **Art:** Photos. **Queries:** Preferred. **Payment:** On acceptance.

EASYRIDERS

P.O. Box 3000, Agoura Hills, CA 91376-3000. 818-889-8740. Web site: www.easyriders.com. Keith R. Ball, Editor. **Description:** Hard-hitting, rugged fiction, 1,200-2,000 words, that depicts bikers in a favorable light; humorous bent preferred. Pays $.10-$.25/word. **Payment:** On acceptance.

HOT BIKE

774 S. Placentia Ave., Placentia, CA 92670. 714-939-2400. Web site: www.hotbikeweb.com. Howard Kelly, Editor. **Description:** On Harley-Davidson motorcycles (contemporary and antique). Event coverage on high-performance street and track and sport touring motorcycles, with emphasis on Harley Davidsons. Geographical motorcycle features. **Nonfiction:** Articles, 250-2,500 words, with photos; pays $50-$100/printed page. **Payment:** On publication.

HOT ROD

6420 Wilshire Blvd., Los Angeles, CA 90048-5515. 323-782-2000. E-mail: mcgonegr@emapusa.com. Web site: www.hotrod.com. Monthly. $3.99/issue,$11.99/year. Circ.: 850,000. Ro McGonegal, Editor. **Description:** Largest publication for street machines, rods, customs, engine buildups, nostalgia. **Nonfiction:** How-tos and articles on auto mechanics, hot rods, track and drag racing. Photo-features on custom or performance-modified cars; $300-$500/page. **Queries:** Preferred. **E-queries:** Yes. **Unsolicited mss:** Accepts. **Response:** SASE required. **Freelance Content:** 10%. **Rights:** All North American. **Payment:** On acceptance.

MOTOR TREND

6420 Wilshire Blvd., Los Angeles, CA 90048-5515. 323-782-2220.
Web site: www.motortrend.com. C. Van Tune, Editor. **Description:** On autos, auto
history, racing, events, and profiles. **Nonfiction:** Articles, 250-2,000 words, photos
required; pay varies. **Queries:** Preferred. **Payment:** On acceptance.

MOTORCYCLIST

6420 Wilshire Blvd., Los Angeles, CA 90048-5515. 323-782-2000.
Web site: www.emapusa.com. Mitch Boehm, Editor. **Description:** Articles,
1,000-words, with photos. Pays $150-$300/published page. **Payment:** On publication.

OLD CARS WEEKLY

700 East State St., Iola, WI 54990. 715-445-4612.
E-mail: elmorec@krause.com. Web site: www.oldcarsweekly.com. Chad Elmore.
Description: On the hobby of collectible cars and trucks (restoration, researching,
company histories, collector profiles, toys, etc.). **Nonfiction:** Features, to 2,000 words;
pays $.03/word. **Art:** Photos to accompany articles; $5/photo. **Queries:** Preferred.

OPEN WHEEL

3816 Industry Blvd., Lakeland, FL 33811. 863-644-0449.
Web site: www.openwheel.com. Doug Auld, Editor. **Description:** On open-wheel
drivers, races, and vehicles. **Nonfiction:** Articles, to 6,000 words; pays to $400. **Art:**
Photos. **Payment:** On publication.

RIDER

2575 Vista Del Mar Dr., Ventura, CA 93001. 805-667-4100.
E-mail: editor@ridermagazine.com. Monthly. Circ.: 140,000. Mark Tuttle Jr., Editor.
Description: Covers travel, touring, commuting, and camping motorcyclists.
Nonfiction: to 2,000 words; $100-$750. **Art:** Color slides. **Queries:** Required.
Response: SASE. **Payment:** On publication.

ROAD KING

Hammock Publishing
3322 W. End Ave., Suite 700, Nashville, TN 37203. 615-385-9745.
Web site: www.roadking.com. Bimonthly. $15/yr. Circ.: 270,000. Bill Hudgins, Editor-
in-Chief. **Description:** An advocate for the trucking industry and its people.
Nonfiction: New products, trends, services, technical and how-to issues, profiles,
human interest articles; 250-2,000 words; $100-$400. **Fillers:** cartoons, pays $50.
Art: Color (slide, print, digital). **Tips:** Owned by national truckstop chain,
TravelCenters of America; no articles about competitors accepted. **Queries:**
Required. **E-queries:** Yes. **Unsolicited mss:** Accepts. **Response:** Queries 6 weeks,
submissions 4 weeks, SASE. **Freelance Content:** 60%. **Rights:** 1st NA and electronic. **Payment:** On acceptance. **Contact:** Bill Hudgins.

ROAD & TRACK

P.O. Box 1757, 1499 Monrovia Ave., Newport Beach, CA 92663. 949-720-5300. Web site: www.roadandtrack.com. Monthly. Circ.: 740,000. Thomas L. Bryant, Editor. **Description:** For knowledgeable car enthusiasts. **Nonfiction:** Short automotive articles of a "timeless nature"; to 450 words. **Queries:** Required. **Payment:** On publication. **Contact:** Ellida Maki.

STOCK CAR RACING MAGAZINE

5555 Concord Pkwy. S., Suite 326, Harrisburg, NC 28075. E-mail: jewettl@emapusa.com. Web site: www.stockcarracing.com. David Miller, Editor. **Description:** For oval-track enthusiasts. **Nonfiction:** Technical automotive pieces, and profiles of interesting racing personalities. Articles on stock car drivers, races and vehicles; up to 6,000 words; pay varies. **Payment:** On publication.

BUSINESS

ACCESSORIES

185 Madison Ave., New York, NY 10016. 212-686-4412. Marcy Brunch, Editor. **Description:** Illustrated articles, for women's fashion-accessories buyers and manufacturers. **Nonfiction:** Profiles of retailers, designers, manufacturers; articles on merchandising and marketing. Pays $75-$200 (short articles), $200-$500 (features). **Queries:** Preferred. **Payment:** On publication.

ACROSS THE BOARD

845 Third Ave., New York, NY 10022-6679. 212-339-0450. E-mail: ajvogl@conference-board.org. Web site: www.conference-board.org. 10x/year. $4.50/issue. Circ.: 30,000. A.J. Vogl, Assistant to the Editor. **Description:** Deals with business management and social policy issues for senior managers of global companies. **Nonfiction:** Articles; 500-3,500 words; pay varies. **Queries:** Preferred. **E-queries:** Yes. **Unsolicited mss:** Accepts. **Response:** Queries 2-3 weeks. **Freelance Content:** 70%. **Rights:** 1st NA. **Payment:** On acceptance.

ALASKA BUSINESS MONTHLY

501 Northern Lights Blvd., Ste. 100, Anchorage, AK 99503. 907-276-4373. E-mail: info@akbizmag.com. Web site: www.akbizmag.com. Monthly. $3.95/$21.95. Circ.: 10,000. Debbie Cutler, Editor. **Description:** For Alaskans and other audiences interested in the business affairs of the 49th State. Thorough, objective analysis of issues and trends affecting Alaskan businesses. **Art:** 35mm photos; pay varies. **Tips:** Query first, Alaska business topics only. Avoid generalities, need to be specific for this market. **Queries:** Preferred. **E-queries:** Yes. **Unsolicited mss:** Accepts. **Response:** 1 month. **Freelance Content:** 80%. **Rights:** All. **Payment:** On publication.

ALTERNATIVE ENERGY RETAILER

P.O. Box 2180, Waterbury, CT 06722. 800-325-6745.
Web site: www.aer-online.com. Michael Griffin, Editor. **Description:** For retailers of hearth products (appliances that burn wood, coal, pellets, and gas, also accessories and services). **Nonfiction:** Feature articles; interviews with successful retailers, etc.; 1,000 words; pays $200. **Art:** b/w photos. **Queries:** Preferred. **Payment:** On publication.

AMERICAN BANKER ONLINE

One State Street Plaza, New York, NY 10004. 212-803-8200.
Web site: www.americanbanker.com. David Longobardi, Editor-in-Chief. **Description:** Articles, 1,000-3,000 words, on banking and financial services, technology in banking, consumer financial services, investment products. Pay varies. **Queries:** Preferred. **Payment:** On publication.

AMERICAN BICYCLIST

7 Barker St., Paris, Ontario N3L 2H4 Canada. 519-442-7181.
E-mail: news@biketrade.net. Web site: www.biketrade.net. Bimonthly. $40/year. Circ.: 12,500. Rob Jones, Editor. **Description:** For bicycle retailers, wholesalers, and manufacturers. Covers new products, trade show reports, how-to techniques. **Nonfiction:** Articles, 1,500-2,800 words, on sales and repair practices of successful bicycle and moped dealers. Pays from $.09/word, extra for photos. **Art:** Photos. **Queries:** Preferred. **Unsolicited mss:** Accepts.

AMERICAN SALESMAN

320 Valley, Burlington, IA 52601-5513. 319-752-5415.
Monthly. Circ.: 1,500. Teresa Levinson, Editor. **Description:** For company sales reps. Articles on techniques to increase sales (case histories or public-relations articles). **Nonfiction:** Sales seminars, customer service, closing sales, competition, phone usage, managing territory, new sales concepts; 900-1,200 words. **Tips:** Freelance content limited. **Queries:** Preferred. **Unsolicited mss:** Does not accept.

ART BUSINESS NEWS

1 Park Ave., New York, NY 10016. 212-951-6600.
Web site: www.advanstar.com. Julie Macdonald, Editor. **Description:** For art dealers and framers, on trends and events of national importance to the art and framing industry, and relevant business subjects. **Nonfiction:** Articles; 1,000 words; pay varies. **Queries:** Preferred. **Payment:** On publication.

BARRON'S

1155 Avenue of the Americas, New York, NY 10036-6710. 212-597-5984.
Web site: www.barronsmag.com. Edwin A. Finn, Jr., President and Editor. **Description:** Investment-interest articles. **Tips:** Send queries to Richard Rescigno, Managing Ed. **Queries:** Preferred.

BARTENDER

P.O. Box 158, Liberty Corner, NJ 07938. 908-766-6006.
E-mail: armag@aol.com. Web site: www.bartender.com. Quarterly. Jaclyn W. Foley.
Description: On liquor and bartending for bartenders, tavern owners, and owners of restaurants with full-service liquor licenses. **Nonfiction:** Articles, 100-1,000 words; pays $50-$200. **Fillers:** 25-100 words. **Columns, Departments:** 200-1,000 words. **Payment:** On publication.

BICYCLE RETAILER AND INDUSTRY NEWS

310 Broadway, Laguna Beach, CA 92651. 949-376-8131.
Web site: www.bicycleretailer.com. Michael Gamstetter, Editor. **Description:** On employee management, employment strategies, and general business subjects for bicycle manufacturers, distributors, and retailers. **Nonfiction:** Articles, to 1,200 words; pays $.20/word (higher rates by assignment). **Queries:** Preferred. **Payment:** On publication.

BLACK ENTERPRISE

130 Fifth Ave., Fl. 10, New York, NY 10011. 212-242-8000.
Web site: www.blackenterprise.com. Alfred Edmond, Editor-in-Chief. **Description:** Articles on money management, careers, political issues, entrepreneurship, high technology, and lifestyles for black professionals. Also, profiles. **Queries:** Preferred. **Payment:** On acceptance.

BLACK ENTERPRISE FOR TEENS

Earl G. Graves Publishing Co., 130 5th Ave., Fl. 10,
New York, NY 10011. 212-242-8000.
6x/year. Circ.: 4,000. **Description:** For African-American teens interested in business.

BOATING INDUSTRY

National Trade Publications
13 Century Hill Dr., Latham, NY 12110-2197. 518-783-1281.
Web site: www.boating-industry.com. John Kettlewell, Senior Editor. **Description:** On recreational marine products, management, merchandising, and selling, for boat dealers and marina owners/operators. **Nonfiction:** Articles; 1,000-2,500 words; pay varies. **Art:** Photos. **Queries:** Preferred. **Payment:** On publication.

BOX OFFICE

155 South El Molino Ave., Suite 100, Pasedena, CA 91101. 626-396-0250.
E-mail: boxofficeearthlink.net. Web site: www.boxoffice.com. Monthly. $40/yr. Circ.: 8,000. Kim Williamson. **Description:** For movie theater operations. **Nonfiction:** Interview, profiles, new products, technical information, problems/opportunities in movie industry; 500-1,000 words; $.10/word. **Columns, Departments:** Insights on business of movie theaters; 600 words. **Art:** TIFF; $10/photo. **Queries:** Preferred. **E-queries:** Yes. **Unsolicited mss:** Accepts. **Response:** 1 month, SASE. **Freelance Content:** 10%. **Rights:** 1st print, all electronic. **Payment:** On publication.

BUSINESS READER REVIEW
The Business Reader, 409 Yorkshire Dr., Williamsburg, VA 23185. 757-258-4746. E-mail: bizbooks@gte.net. Web site: home1.gte.net/bizbooks. Monthly. Theodore Kinni, Editor. **Description:** Reviews of business management books published in the last 30 days. **E-queries:** Yes. **Unsolicited mss:** Accepts.

BUSINESS START-UPS
2445 McCabe Way, Irvine, CA 92614. E-mail: bsumag@entrepreneur.com. Web site: www.bizstartups.com. Karen E. Spaeder, Editor. **Description:** Entrepreneur's BizStartup.com is an online magazine, for Gen-X entrepreneurs who have started a business recently or plan to soon. **Nonfiction:** How-to, motivational/psychological, trend pieces, sales/marketing, technology, start-up money issues, management; 1,000 words; $400 and up. **Tips:** Send well-written queries with relevant clips. **Queries:** Required. **E-queries:** Yes. **Unsolicited mss:** Does not accept. **Response:** 8-12 weeks, SASE. **Freelance Content:** 10%. **Rights:** FNASR. **Payment:** On acceptance.

CHIEF EXECUTIVE
733 Third Ave., 24th Fl., New York, NY 10017. E-mail: jpdonlan@chiefexecutive.net. Web site: www.chiefexecutive.net. J.P. Donlon, Editor-in-Chief. **Description:** On management, financial, or global business issues of direct concern to CEOs only. **Nonfiction:** Articles, by CEOs; 2,000-2,500 words; pay varies. **Columns, Departments:** 750 words, on investments, corporate finance, technology, Internet, emerging markets. **Queries:** Preferred. **Payment:** On acceptance.

CHRISTIAN RETAILING
600 Rinehart Rd., Lake Mary, FL 32746. 407-333-0600. Web site: www.christianretailing.com. Carol Chapman Stertzer, Editor. **Description:** On new products, trends, or topics related to running a profitable Christian retail store. **Nonfiction:** Features, 1,500-2,300 words; pays $150-$400. **Payment:** On publication.

CLUB MANAGEMENT
107 W. Pacific Ave., St. Louis, MO 63119. E-mail: avincent@finan.com. Web site: www.club-mgmt.com. Bi-monthly. $21.95/yr. Circ.: 16,400. Anne Marie Vincent, Editor. **Description:** For managers of private clubs in U.S. and abroad. Provides executives with information and resources for successful operations. **Nonfiction:** Construction/renovation profiles, insurance, technology, staffing issues, golf-course design and maintenance, special events, maintenance, food/beverage trends, guest-room amenities, spa facilities, outsourcing; 1,500-2,000 words. **Columns, Departments:** Sports, tax, law, management, membership marketing, manager career perspectives, service, beverage/food trends, pools, entertainment; 1,200-1,600 words. **Queries:** Preferred. **E-queries:** Yes. **Unsolicited mss:** Accepts. **Response:** 2-3 weeks, SASE required. **Freelance Content:** 40%. **Rights:** 1st. **Payment:** On publication.

COLORADO BUSINESS

7009 S. Potomac, Englewood, CO 80112. 303-662-5283. E-mail: rschwab@cobizmag.com. Web site: www.cobizmag.com. Monthly. $3.95/issue, $22.97/yr. Circ.: 17,000. Robert Schwab, Editor. **Description:** Covers business in Colorado. Readers are decision-makers at their businesses. **Nonfiction:** On business, personalities, and economic trends. **Queries:** Preferred. **Payment:** On acceptance.

CONVENIENCE STORE NEWS

770 Broadway, 4th Fl., New York, NY 10003-9522. 646-654-7676. Web site: www.csnews.com. John Callanan, Editor-in-Chief. **Description:** For convenience-store owners/operators. **Nonfiction:** Features, news items, 750-1,200 words; pay negotiated. **Art:** Photos; pay varies. **Queries:** Preferred.

CORPORATE GIFT REVIEW

815 Haines St., Jacksonville, FL 32206. Quarterly. $19.95. Circ.: 5,000. Tonya Ringgold, Editor. **Description:** Innovative tips and how-tos on sales, marketing, management, and operations. Focuses on business gifting. Hard data, stats, and research requested. Readers are college-educated, successful business owners. **Tips:** Avoid generalizations, basic content, and outdated theories. **Queries:** Not necessary. **E-queries:** No. **Unsolicited mss:** Accepts. **Response:** 30 days, SASE required. **Freelance Content:** 50%. **Rights:** one-time. **Payment:** On publication.

THE COSTCO CONNECTION

P.O. Box 34088, Seattle, WA 98124-1088. 425-313-8510. Web site: www.costco.com. Anita Thompson. **Description:** About small business and Costco members. **Nonfiction:** Articles, 100-1,200 words; pays to $300-$400. **Queries:** Preferred. **Payment:** On acceptance.

COUNTRY BUSINESS

707 Kautz Rd., St. Charles, IL 60174. 630-377-8000. E-mail: cbiz.Sampler.emmis.com. Web site: www.country-business.com. Bi-monthly. Circ.: 32,000. Susan Wagner, Features Editor. **Description:** For retailers of country gifts and accessories. On trends, giftware markets, and business advice. **Nonfiction:** Business articles on small business management and retail finance, legal, technology, marketing, management, etc.; 800-1,800 words; pay varies. **Queries:** Preferred. **E-queries:** Yes. **Unsolicited mss:** Accepts. **Response:** 4-6 weeks, SASE required. **Freelance Content:** 60%. **Rights:** 1st, all (assignments). **Payment:** On acceptance.

CRAIN'S CHICAGO BUSINESS

740 Rush St., Chicago, IL 60611. 312-649-5411. Web site: www.chicagobusiness.com. **Description:** Business articles about Chicago metro area.

DOTCEO

Web site: www.dotceo.com. Christine Larson, Editor-In-Chief. **Description:** For chief executive officers of dot.com companies. Online and print versions.

EMPLOYEE SERVICES MANAGEMENT

ESM Association, 2211 York Rd., Suite 207, Oak Brook, IL 60523. 630-368-1280. Web site: www.esmassn.org. Renee M. Mula, Editor. **Description:** For human resource and employee service professionals. On recruitment and retention, becoming an employee of choice, work/life issues, employee services, wellness, management, and more. **Nonfiction:** Articles, 1,200-2,500 words. **Payment:** In copies.

ENTREPRENEUR

2445 McCabe Way, Irvine, CA 92614. 949-261-2325. E-mail: entmag@entrepreneur.com. Web site: www.entrepreneurmag.com. Rieva Lesonsky, Editor. **Description:** For small business owners, on all aspects of running a business. **Queries:** Required. **Payment:** On acceptance.

FLORIDA TREND

490 First Ave. S., Petersburg, FL 33701. 727-821-5800. Web site: www.floridatrend.com. Mark R. Howard, Executive Editor. **Description:** On Florida business and businesspeople. **Queries:** Required. **Response:** SASE.

FLORIST

33031 Schoolcraft Rd., Livonia, MI 48105. 800-383-4383. E-mail: bgillis@ftdassociation.org. Web site: www.ftdassociation.org. Monthly. $45/year. Circ.: 20,000. Sallyann Moore, Editor. **Description:** For retail florists. **Nonfiction:** Business-related stories (retail trends, electronic commerce, loss prevention, tax tips, etc.). **Queries:** Required. **E-queries:** Yes. **Unsolicited mss:** Accepts. **Response:** Varies, SASE required. **Freelance Content:** 5% or less. **Rights:** 1st NA. **Payment:** On acceptance.

FLOWERS &

11444 W. Olympic Blvd., Los Angeles, CA 90064. 310-966-3590. Bruce Wright, Editor. **Description:** How-to information for retail florists. **Nonfiction:** Articles, 500-1,500 words; pays $.50/word. **Tips:** Send clips. **Queries:** Preferred. **Payment:** On acceptance.

GIFT BASKET REVIEW

815 Haines St., Jacksonville, FL 32206. 904-634-1902. Web site: www.festivities-pub.com. Monthly. $39.95/yr. Circ.: 15,000. Tonya Ringgold, Editor. **Description:** Covers products, cutting-edge ideas, and up-to-date industry news. **Nonfiction:** Inspiring ideas, professional tips, industry news. **Tips:** Avoid generalizations and basic content. Submit specific tips and how-tos on sales, marketing, management, and operations. Hard data, stats and research appreciated. Readers are college-educated, successful business owners. **Queries:** Not necessary.

E-queries: No. **Response:** Submissions 30 days, SASE required. **Freelance Content:** 50%. **Rights:** One-time. **Payment:** On publication.

GREENHOUSE MANAGEMENT & PRODUCTION

P.O. Box 1868, Fort Worth, TX 76101-1868.
David Kuack, Editor. **Description:** For professional greenhouse growers. **Nonfiction:** How-tos, innovative production or marketing techniques, 500-1,800 words. **Art:** Color slides; $50-$300. **Queries:** Preferred. **Unsolicited mss:** Accepts. **Payment:** On acceptance.

GREYHOUND REVIEW

National Greyhound Assn., Box 543, Abilene, KS 67410-0543. 785-263-4660. E-mail: nga@ojc.net. Web site: www.nga.jc.net. Monthly. $30. Circ.: 3,500. Greg Guccione, Managing Editor. **Description:** For greyhound owners, breeders, trainers, racetrack officials. Covers racing industry; trade news, special events at tracks, medical news. **Nonfiction:** How-to, historical nostalgia, interviews; 1,000-10,000 words; $50-$150. **Art:** Photos, $85-150. **Tips:** No general interest about dogs, pet ownership. **Queries:** Preferred. **E-queries:** Yes. **Unsolicited mss:** Accepts. **Response:** Queries 1 month, SASE required. **Freelance Content:** 80%. **Rights:** 1st. **Payment:** On acceptance. **Contact:** Tim Horan, Editor.

GROWERTALKS

P.O. Box 9, 335 N. River St., Batavia, IL 60510-0009. 630-208-9080. E-mail: beytes@growertalks.com. Web site: www.growertalks.com. Chris Beytes. **Description:** Seeks to help commercial greenhouse growers (not florist/retailers or home gardeners) do their jobs better. Covers trends, successes in new types of production, marketing, business management, new crops, and issues facing the industry. **Nonfiction:** Articles, 800-2,600 words; pay varies. **Queries:** Preferred. **Payment:** On publication.

HARDWARE TRADE

10617 France Ave. S., #225, Bloomington, MN 55431. 952-944-3172. Web site: www.hardwaretrade.com. Patt Patterson, Editor. **Description:** On unusual hardware and home center stores and promotions in the Northwest and Midwest. **Nonfiction:** Articles, 800-1,000 words; no payment offered. **Queries:** Preferred.

HARVARD BUSINESS REVIEW

Harvard Business School Publishing Corp.
60 Harvard Way, Boston, MA 02163. 617-783-7410.
Web site: www.hbsp.harvard.edu. Suzy Wetlaufer, Editor. **Description:** Covers new ideas about management, for senior executives. **Nonfiction:** Request guidelines for authors, or submit written query.

HEARTH & HOME
P.O. Box 2008, Laconia, NH 03247. 603-528-4285.
Richard Wright, Editor. **Description:** Profiles and interviews, with specialty retailers selling both casual furniture and hearth products (fireplaces, woodstoves, accessories, etc.). **Nonfiction:** 1,000-1,800 words; pays $150-$250. **Payment:** On acceptance.

HISPANIC BUSINESS
425 Pine Ave., Santa Barbara, CA 93117-3709.
E-mail: jim.medina@hbinc.com. Web site: www.hispanicbusiness.com. Jim Medina, Managing Editor. **Description:** Features a variety of personalities, political agendas, and fascinating stories. **Nonfiction:** Articles; especially on technology and finance issues; $350 (negotiable). **Tips:** Has an ongoing need for experienced freelance writers.

HISPANIC MARKET NEWS
13014 N. Dale Mabry Hwy. #663, Tampa, FL 33618-2808. 813-264-0560.
Monthly. Circ.: 20,000. **Description:** For people involved with merchandising to the Hispanic markets. In both English and Spanish.

HOBBY MERCHANDISER
225 Gordons Corner Rd., P.O. Box 420, Manalapan, NJ 07726-0420. 800-969-7176.
Web site: www.hobbymerchandiser.com. Monthly. Jeff Troy, Editor-in-Chief. **Description:** For the professional hobby business; also general small-business advice. **Nonfiction:** Articles, 800-1,500 words; pays $75-$200. **Payment:** On publication.

HOME OFFICE COMPUTING
Scholastic, Inc., 180 Freedom Ave., Murfreesboro, TN 37129.
Bernadette Grey, Editor-in-Chief. **Description:** Focuses on microcomputers, software, home office products, and issues affecting small and home businesses. **Nonfiction:** Practical information on how to run a business and use technology effectively (3,000 words). Profiles of small-business owners. Education and entertainment pieces (800-1,500 words) for Family Computing section. **Columns, Departments:** Finance, legal issues, sales and marketing, communications, government; 1,200 words. **Queries:** Preferred. **Unsolicited mss:** Accepts. **Payment:** On acceptance.

HOMEBUSINESS JOURNAL
Steffen Publishing, 9584 Main St., Holland Patent, NY 13354. 800-756-8484.
E-mail: Kim@steffenpublishing.com. Web site: www.homebizjour.com. Bimonthly. $18.96 (U.S.), $34 (Canada). Circ.: 50,000. Kim Lisi, Managing Editor. **Description:** National publication offering quality information and advice for readers in a home business, or seriously interested in such work, to help them thrive and enjoy working at home. **Nonfiction:** Editorials pertaining to home-based business issues; financial, family, health, etc.; ave. 1,000 words; $75. **Tips:** Common mistake is to fail to note the difference in needs between small businesses and home businesses. Welcomes new

writers. **Queries:** Required. **E-queries:** Yes. **Unsolicited mss:** Accepts. **Response:** 3-4 weeks, SASE required. **Rights:** FNASR. **Payment:** On publication.

HUMAN RESOURCE EXECUTIVE

LRP Publications Co., 747 Dresher Rd., Horsham, PA 19044-0980. 215-784-0910. E-mail: dshadovitz@lrp.com. Web site: www.hrexecutive.com. David Shadovitz, Editor. **Description:** Profiles and case stories, for people in the human-resource profession. **Nonfiction:** 1,800-2,200 words; pay varies. **Queries:** Required. **Payment:** On acceptance.

INC.

38 Commercial Wharf, Boston, MA 02110. 617-248-8000. E-mail: editors@inc.com. Web site: www.inc.com. Monthly. $4.00/issue, $20/year. Circ.: 650,000. George Gendron, Editor. **Description:** Focuses on small, rapidly growing, privately held companies. **Nonfiction:** Articles with helpful how-to tips on how readers can grow and manage their companies. **Tips:** Looks for stories not specific to only one industry. Don't write about products; write about managing the company. **Queries:** Preferred. **E-queries:** No. **Unsolicited mss:** Accepts. **Response:** 30 days, SASE required. **Freelance Content:** 3%. **Rights:** 1st serial. **Payment:** On publication.

INDUSTRY WEEK

The Penton Media Building
1300 E. Ninth St., Cleveland, OH 44114-2543. 800-326-4146. E-mail: tvinas@industryweek.com. Web site: www.industryweek.com. Biweekly. Circ.: 233,000. John R. Brandt, Editor-in-Chief. **Description:** Written for a senior-level management audience, *IndustryWeek* delivers powerful editorial on the challenges facing today's companies. **Nonfiction:** Articles on business and management; pay varies. **Columns, Departments:** Executive Briefing, Emerging Technologies, Finance, Economic Trends, Executive Life. **Queries:** Required. **Payment:** On acceptance. **Contact:** Patricia Panchak, Managing Editor.

INSTANT & SMALL COMMERCIAL PRINTER

P.O. Box 7280, Libertyville, IL 60048. 847-816-7900. E-mail: iscpmag@innespub.com. Web site: www.innespub.com. Monthly. $85/year. Circ.: 49,000. Sharon Spielman, Editor. **Description:** Covers small commercial and instant printing market. **Nonfiction:** Case histories, how-tos, technical pieces, small-business management; 1,000-5,000 words; pay negotiable. **Queries:** Preferred. **E-queries:** Yes. **Unsolicited mss:** Accepts. **Response:** 1-6 months, SASE required. **Freelance Content:** 20%. **Payment:** On publication.

IQ

Hachette Filipacchi Magazines
460 West 34th St., 20th Fl., New York, NY 10001. 212-560-2100. E-mail: iq@cisco.com. Web site: www.cisco.com/warp/public/750/iq. Heather Alter,

Editor-in-Chief. **Description:** All about the Internet economy: news, analysis, cutting edge technology reviews, trends, resources, and more.

KIDS' WALL STREET NEWS

WORLD, P.O. Box 1207, Rancho Santa Fe, CA 92067. 760-591-7681. E-mail: emailkwsn@aol.com. Bimonthly. Kate Allen, Editor-in-Chief. **Description:** On money matters and other topics. **Columns, Departments:** Adventure, Sports Arena, Think about This, Money & Banking, to 500 words. **Art:** Photos, graphs, and artwork. **Tips:** Submit material on a Mac format disk, with hard copy. **Payment:** On publication.

LATIN TRADE

Freedom Communications, Inc.
95 Merrick Way, Ste 600, Coral Gables, FL 33134-5311. 305-358-8373. Web site: www.latintrade.com. **Description:** For business persons in Latin America. Covers a wide variety of topics relating to trade, markets, research, technology, and investments.

LONG ISLAND BUSINESS NEWS

2150 Smithtown Ave., Ronkonkoma, NY 11779. 631-737-1700. Web site: www.libn.com. Weekly. Circ.: 11,000. Robert Walzer, Managing Editor. **Description:** Covers news in Nassau and Suffolk counties in New York. **Queries:** Preferred. **E-queries:** Yes. **Response:** 2 weeks, SASE required. **Rights:** One-time. **Payment:** On publication.

MANAGE

2210 Arbor Blvd., Dayton, OH 45439. 937-294-0421. E-mail: nma@nma1.org. Web site: www.nma1.org. Quarterly. Circ.: 35,000. Doug Shaw, Editor. **Description:** Covers human resource development, team building, leadership skills, ethics in the workplace, law, compensation and technology. **Nonfiction:** On management and supervision for first-line and middle managers; 800-1200 words; $.05/word. **Fillers:** Business management/leadership related; 500-600 words. **Queries:** Not necessary. **E-queries:** Yes. **Unsolicited mss:** Accepts. **Response:** Queries 3 weeks, submissions 4 weeks, SASE. **Freelance Content:** 60%. **Rights:** Reprint. **Payment:** On publication.

MARKETING NEWS

American Marketing Assn.
311 S. Wacker Dr., Chicago, IL 60606-2266. 312-542-9000. E-mail: news@ama.org. Web site: www.ama.org. Bi-weekly. $100/yr. Circ.: 30,000. Lisa M. Keefe, Editor. **Description:** Authoritative analysis of news, current trends, and application of developments in marketing profession; also, information on American Marketing Assn. **Nonfiction:** Timely articles on advertising, sales promotion, direct marketing, telecommunications, consumer and business-to-business marketing, and market research; 800-1,200 words; $.75/word. **Tips:** Due to potential

conflict of interest, no news stories written by marketing professionals. **Queries:** Preferred. **E-queries:** Yes. **Unsolicited mss:** Does not accept. **Response:** Queries 6-8 weeks, submissions 2-4 months. **Freelance Content:** 30%. **Rights:** 1st, all media. **Payment:** On acceptance.

THE MEETING PROFESSIONAL
4455 LBJ Freeway, Suite 1200, Dallas, TX 75244. 972-702-3000.
E-mail: publications@mpiweb.org. Web site: www.mpiweb.org. Monthly. $50 U.S., $69 outside U.S. Circ.: 30,000. **Description:** For meeting professionals. **Tips:** Only works with published writers. Submit query by e-mail; send resumé and clips by mail (with SASE). **Queries:** Preferred. **E-queries:** Yes. **Unsolicited mss:** Accepts. **Response:** 2 weeks, SASE required. **Freelance Content:** 50%. **Rights:** All. **Payment:** On acceptance.

MERCADO
1401 W. Flagler St., #206, Miami, FL 33135-2254. 305-649-7711.
Web site: www.mercadousa.com. Monthly. Circ.: 35,000. **Description:** For people interested in learning about and being involved in the Latin American markets.

MODERN PHYSICIAN
740 Rush St., Chicago, IL 60611. 312-649-5324.
E-mail: moddoc@crain.com. Web site: www.modernphysician.com. Biweekly. $45. Circ.: 32,000. Karen Petitte, Editor. **Description:** Covers business and management news for physician executives. **Nonfiction:** Business stories about how medical practices are changing; 1,000-1,500 words; $.50/word. **Tips:** No product or clinical stories. **Queries:** Required. **E-queries:** Yes. **Unsolicited mss:** Accepts. **Response:** Varies, SASE required. **Freelance Content:** 30%. **Rights:** All. **Payment:** On acceptance.

MUTUAL FUNDS
P.O. Box 60001, Tampa, FL 33660.
E-mail: letters@mfmag.com. Web site: www.mfmag.com. **Description:** Seeking writers experienced in covering mutual funds for the print media. Send resumé and clips. **Queries:** Preferred.

NEEDLEWORK RETAILER
P.O. Box 2438, Ames, IA 50010. 515-232-6507.
Web site: yarntree.com/nr.htm. Bimonthly. Megan Chriswisser, Editor. **Description:** For owners and managers of independent needlework retail stores. **Nonfiction:** Profiles of shop owners; articles about a successful store event or promotion, 500-1,000 words; pay varies. **Tips:** No generic business articles. **Payment:** On acceptance.

NETWORK JOURNAL
139 Fulton St., Suite 407, New York, NY 10038. 212-962-3791.
E-mail: tnj@obel.com. Web site: www.tnj.com. Monthly. Circ.: 11,000. Njeru

Waithaka, Editor. **Description:** Small-business, personal finance, and career management for African American small-business owners and professionals. **Nonfiction:** Profiles of entrepreneurs; how-to pieces; articles on sales and marketing, managing a small business and personal finance; 800 to 1,500 words; $75 to $150. **Payment:** On acceptance.

NSGA RETAIL FOCUS

National Sporting Goods Assn.
1601 Feehanville Drive, #300, Mt. Prospect, IL 60056-6035. 847-296-6742.
E-mail: info@nsga.org. Web site: www.nsga.org. Bimonthly. Members only. Circ.: 4,000. Larry Weindruch, Editor. **Description:** For members of National Sporting Goods Assn., with industry news and trends. **Nonfiction:** Articles, 1,000-1,500 words, on industry news and trends, new product information, and management and store operations. Pay varies. **Queries:** Required. **E-queries:** Yes. **Unsolicited mss:** Does not accept. **Response:** Queries 1 week, SASE. **Freelance Content:** 15%. **Rights:** 1st and website. **Payment:** On publication.

PARTY & PAPER RETAILER

107 Mill Plain Rd., Suite 204, Danbury, CT 06811. 203-730-4090.
E-mail: editor@partypaper.com. Web site: www.partypaper.com. Trisha McMahon Drain, Editor. **Description:** Offers employee, management, and retail marketing advice, for party or stationery store owners. Display ideas, success stories; advertising, promotion, financial, and legal advice. **Nonfiction:** Articles, factual, anecdotes appreciated, 1,000-1,500 words; pay varies. **Tips:** Send published clips. **Queries:** Preferred. **Payment:** On publication.

PET BUSINESS

233 Park Ave. S., 6th Floor, New York, NY 10003.
Oriol Gutierrez, Executive Editor. **Description:** On animals and products found in pet stores (research findings; legislative/regulatory actions; business and marketing tips and trends). **Nonfiction:** Brief, well-documented articles; pays $.10/word, $20/photo. **Payment:** On publication.

PET PRODUCT NEWS

P.O. Box 6050, Mission Viejo, CA 92690. 949-855-8822.
E-mail: slogan@fancypubs.com. Web site: www.petproductnews.com. Monthly. Circ.: 23,000. Susan Logan, Editor. **Description:** On pet shops, and pet and product merchandising. **Fiction:** Articles, 1,200-1,500 words, with photos; pays $250 and up; $50 for photos. **Tips:** Prefers query by e-mail. No fiction. **Queries:** Required. **Unsolicited mss:** Does not accept. **Response:** up to 3 months. **Rights:** FNASR. **Payment:** On publication.

PHOTO MARKETING

3000 Picture Pl., Jackson, MI 49201. 517-788-8100.
Web site: www.photomarketing.com. Gary Pageau, Editor. **Description:** For owners

and managers of camera/video stores or photo processing labs. **Nonfiction:** Business articles, 1,000-3,500 words; pays $150-$500, extra for photos. **Queries:** Preferred. **Unsolicited mss:** Does not accept. **Payment:** On acceptance.

POOL & SPA NEWS
4160 Wilshire Blvd., Los Angeles, CA 90010. 323-964-4800. Web site: www.poolspanews.com. .**Description:** For the swimming pool and hot-tub construction, retail, and service industries. **Nonfiction:** Business and how-to articles. **Queries:** Preferred. **Payment:** On publication.

PRO
P.O. Box 803, Fort Atkinson, WI 53538. 920-563-6388. Web site: www.promagazine.com. Noel Brown, Editor-in-Chief. **Description:** On business management for owners of lawn-maintenance firms. **Nonfiction:** Articles, 1,000-1,500 words; pays $150-$250. **Queries:** Preferred. **Payment:** On publication.

QUICK PRINTING
Cygnus Publishing Inc., 445 Broad Hollow Rd., Melville, NY 11747. 631-845-2700. E-mail: quickptg@aol.com. Web site: www.quickprinting.com. Gerald Walsh, Editor. **Description:** For owners and operators of quick print shops, copy shops, and small commercial printers. How to make their businesses more profitable (including photos and figures). Also, articles on using computers and peripherals in graphic arts applications. **Nonfiction:** Articles, 1,500-2,500 words; pays from $150. **Tips:** No generic business articles. **Payment:** On publication.

RELATIONS, INC.
2101 W. State Road 434, Ste. 221, Longwood, FL 32779. 407-949-9300. E-mail: PhilR@iibinc.comLeslieS@iibinc.com. Web site: www.grantdouglas.com. Phil Robertson, Editor. **Description:** Varied topics relating to corporate relations. **Nonfiction:** Articles, 750-1,000 words; pay varies. **Queries:** Required. **E-queries:** Yes. **Unsolicited mss:** Accepts. **Freelance Content:** 20%. **Rights:** One-time. **Contact:** Leslie C. Stone, Managing Editor.

RESTAURANTS USA
1200 17th St. NW, Washington, DC 20036-3097. 202-331-5900. E-mail: jbatty@dineout.com. Web site: www.restaurant.org. Monthly. $125. Circ.: 50,000. Jennifer Batty, Editor. **Description:** For restaurateurs, to help them run their business more competitively. Hot trends, management techniques, cost-saving tips, operational issues. **Nonfiction:** 500-300 words; $50-$600. **Tips:** Need business stories: how to retain employees, management tips, etc. **Queries:** Required. **E-queries:** Yes. **Unsolicited mss:** Accepts. **Response:** 2 months, SASE. **Freelance Content:** 30%. **Rights:** All. **Payment:** On acceptance.

RETAIL SYSTEMS RESELLER

4 Middlebury Blvd., Randolph, NJ 07869. E-mail: kcarson@edgellmail.com. Web site: www.retailsystemsreseller.com. Monthly. Circ.: 20,000. Kathleen Carson, Managing Editor. **Description:** Covers news, products, technology and services for value-added resellers and system integrators selling into the retail channel. Focuses retail point-of-sale and payment processing, extending into backend systems and retail supply chain. **Nonfiction:** 600-1,500 words; $400-$800. **Tips:** Seeking writers who can write for this specific market and know how to dig as a reporter. No syndicated articles or general business ideas. **E-queries:** Yes. **Unsolicited mss:** Accepts. **Response:** 60-90 days, SASE required. **Freelance Content:** 80%. **Rights:** 1st NA. **Payment:** On publication.

REVOLUTION

220 Fifth Ave., 14th Fl., New York, NY 10001. 212-471-8700. E-mail: stovin.hayter@revolutionmagazine.com. Web site: www.reolutionmagazine.com. Stovin Hayter, Editor. **Description:** Seeks to provide senior business people with an understanding of digital media, to evaluate what products and services they can best use in their companies.

SALES & MARKETING MANAGEMENT

Bill Communications, Inc., 770 Broadway, New York, NY 10003. 646-654-7323. Web site: www.salesandmarketing.com. Melinda Ligos, Editor. **Description:** For sales and marketing executives. Seeking practical "news you can use." **Nonfiction:** Features and short articles; pays varies. **Queries:** Preferred. **Payment:** On acceptance.

SAN FRANCISCO BUSINESS TIMES

275 Battery St., Suite 940, San Francisco, CA 94111. 415-989-2522. Web site: www.bizjournals.com/sanfrancisco. Steve Symanovich, Editor. **Description:** Bay area business-oriented articles **Nonfiction:** Limited freelance market; pays $250-$350. **Queries:** Preferred. **Payment:** On publication.

SIGN BUILDER ILLUSTRATED

323 Clifton St., Suite 7, Greenville, NC 27858. 252-355-5806. Web site: www.signshop.com. Bimonthly. Jeff Wooten, Editor. **Description:** On the sign industry. **Nonfiction:** How-to articles and editorials, 1,500-2,500 words; pays $300-$500. **Payment:** On acceptance.

SIGN BUSINESS

P.O. Box 1416, Broomfield, CO 80038. 303-469-0424. Web site: www.nbm.com/signbusiness. Regan Dickinson, Editor. **Description:** For the sign business. **Nonfiction:** Prefers step-by-step, how-to features; pays $150-$300. **Payment:** On publication.

SOFTWARE
40 Speen St., Suite 403, Framingham, MA 01701. 508-875-9555.
Web site: www.softwaremag.com. Monthly. Circ.: 110,000. Colleen Trye, Managing Editor. **Description:** For corporate systems managers and MIS personnel. **Nonfiction:** Features and information on latest software.

SOUVENIRS, GIFTS, AND NOVELTIES
Kane Publications, 7000 Terminal Sq., Suite 210,
Upper Darby, PA 19082. 610-734-2420.
Web site: www.souvenirgiftsnovelties.com. Tony DeMasi, Editor. **Description:** On retailing and merchandising collectible souvenir items for managers at zoos, museums, hotels, airports, and souvenir stores. **Nonfiction:** Articles, 1,500 words; pays $.12/word. **Payment:** On publication.

STOCKBROKER
Grant Douglas Publishing, 2101 W. State Road 434, Ste. 221,
Longwood, FL 32779. 407-949-9300.
E-mail: philr@iibinc.com; leslies@iibinc.com. Web site: www.grantdouglas.com. Quarterly. Circ.: 150,000. Phil Robertson, Editor. **Description:** For stockbrokers and financial advisors. **Nonfiction:** Articles, 750-1,000 words, pay varies. **Queries:** Required. **E-queries:** Yes. **Unsolicited mss:** Accepts. **Freelance Content:** 20%. **Rights:** one-time. **Payment:** On publication. **Contact:** Leslie Stone, Managing Editor.

TANNING TRENDS
3101 Page Ave., Jackson, MI 49203-2254. 800-652-3269.
E-mail: joe@smarttan.com. Web site: www.smarttan.com. Joseph Levy. **Description:** On small businesses and skin care for tanning salon owners. Seeks to help salon owners move to the "next level" of small business ownership. Focuses on business principles, emphasis on public relations and marketing. **Nonfiction:** Scientific pro-tanning articles, "smart tanning" pieces. Query for profiles. Pay varies. **Payment:** On publication.

TEA & COFFEE TRADE JOURNAL
26 Broadway, Floor 9M, New York, NY 10004. 212-391-2060.
Web site: www.teaandcoffee.net. Jane P. McCabe, Editor. **Description:** On issues of importance to the tea and coffee industry. **Nonfiction:** Articles, 3-5 pages; pays $.20/word. **Queries:** Preferred. **Payment:** On publication.

TEXAS TECHNOLOGY
13490 TI Boulevard, Suite 100, Dallas, TX 75243. 972-690-6222.
Web site: www.ttechnology.com. Monthly. $30. Circ.: 480,000. Laurie Kline, Editor. **Description:** Covers news, trends, products, and more. **Nonfiction:** Technology trends, new products information, features on obtaining and retaining employees in high-tech sector; 400-3,000 words; fee negotiable. **Art:** Photos, artwork. **Tips:** Not interested in company or product-specific stories. Seeking stories on trends and general topics to appeal to both business and mainstream audience. Welcomes new

writers! **Queries:** Required. **E-queries:** Yes. **Unsolicited mss:** Accepts. **Response:** 14 weeks, SASE required. **Freelance Content:** 80% . **Rights:** 1st print and electronic. **Payment:** On acceptance.

TEXTILE WORLD
6151 Powers Ferry Rd. NW, Atlanta, GA 30339-2959. 770-618-0427. E-mail: mac_issacs@intertec.com. Web site: www.textileworld.com. Monthly. $57/yr. Circ.: 33,000. McAllister Issacs III, Editor. **Description:** Serves textile executives in their dual roles as technologists and managers. **Nonfiction:** Technical textile articles; 1,500 words; pay negotiable. **Art:** Slides, prints, electronic. **Queries:** Required. **E-queries:** Yes. **Response:** 4 weeks. **Freelance Content:** 5%. **Rights:** All. **Payment:** On publication.

TOURIST ATTRACTIONS AND PARKS
7000 Terminal Sq., Suite 210, Upper Darby, PA 19082. 610-734-2420. Web site: tapmag.com. Scott C. Borowski, Editor-in-Chief. **Description:** On successful management of parks, entertainment centers, zoos, museums, arcades, fairs, arenas, and leisure attractions. **Nonfiction:** Articles, 1,500 words; pays $.12/word. **Queries:** Preferred. **Payment:** On publication.

TRAINING
50 S. Ninth St., Minneapolis, MN 55402. 612-333-0471. E-mail: edit@trainingmag.com. Web site: www.trainingmag.com. Tammy Galvin, Editor. **Description:** For managers of training and development activities in corporations, government, etc. **Nonfiction:** Articles, 1,000-2,500 words; pay varies. **Queries:** Preferred. **Payment:** On acceptance.

TREASURY & RISK MANAGEMENT
52 Vanderbilt Ave. Ste. 514, New York, NY 10017. 212-557-7480. Web site: www.treasuryandrisk.com. 9x/year. Anthony Baldo, Editor. **Description:** On management for corporate treasurers, CFOs, and vice presidents of finance. **Nonfiction:** Articles, 200-3,000 words; pays $.50-$1.00/word. **Tips:** Seeking freelance writers. **Queries:** Preferred. **Payment:** On acceptance.

UPSIDE
731 Market St., 2nd Fl., San Francisco, CA 94103. 415-489-5600. Web site: www.upsidetoday.com. Monthly. Vince Ryan. **Description:** On business and technology. **Nonfiction:** Short articles about computer and technology businesses, profiles of successful business people. **Queries:** Preferred.

VENDING TIMES
1375 Broadway, New York, NY 10018. 212-302-4700. Tim Sanford, Editor. **Description:** On vending-machines businesses. **Nonfiction:** Features and news articles, with photos; pay varies. **Queries:** Preferred. **Payment:** On acceptance.

VIRGINIA BUSINESS
333 E. Franklin St., Suite 105, Richmond, VA 23219. 804-649-6999. E-mail: pgaluszka@va-business.com. Web site: www.virginiabusiness.com. James Bacon, Editor. **Description:** Covers the business scene in Virginia. **Nonfiction:** Articles, 1,000-2,500 words; pay varies. **Queries:** Required. **Payment:** On publication.

WALL STREET JOURNAL SUNDAY
200 Liberty St., New York, NY 10281. 212-416-4370. Weekly. Circ.: 5,000,000. **Description:** Sunday insert to more than 15 major-market newspapers.

WOMEN IN BUSINESS
American Business Women's Assn.
9100 Ward Pkwy., Box 8728, Kansas City, MO 64114-0728. 816-361-6621. E-mail: rwarbing@abwa.org. Web site: www.abwa.org. Bi-monthly. $12/yr (members), $20/yr (others). Rachel Warbingtom, Editor. **Description:** Published by American Business Women's Assn. Focuses on leadership, education, networking support, and national recognition. Helps business women of diverse occupations to grow personally and professionally. **Nonfiction:** How-to business features for working women, ages 35-55 (trends, small-business ownership, self-improvement, retirement issues). Profiles of ABWA members only; 1,000-1,500 words; $.20/word. **E-queries:** Yes. **Unsolicited mss:** Accepts. **Freelance Content:** 2%. **Payment:** On publication.

WORKING WOMAN
135 W. 50th St., 16th Fl., New York, NY 10020-1201. 212-445-6100. E-mail: editors@workingwoman.com. Web site: www.workingwoman.com. **Description:** On business, finance, and technology. Readers are high-level executives and entrepreneurs looking for newsworthy information about the changing marketplace and its effects on their businesses and careers. **Nonfiction:** Articles, 200-1,500 words; pays from $250. **Tips:** No profiles of executives or entrepreneurs. Seeking trend pieces targeting a specific industry, showing how it is affected by new technology, business practices, market situations. **Queries:** Preferred. **Unsolicited mss:** Does not accept. **Payment:** On acceptance.

CAREER & PROFESSIONAL DEVELOPMENT

ADGUIDE'S COLLEGE RECRUITER EMPLOYMENT NEWSLETTER
3722 W. 50th St., Ste. 121, Minneapolis, MN 55410. 800-835-4989 or 952-848-2211. E-mail: StevenR@adguide.com. Web site: www.adguide.com/pages/newsletter.html. Weekly. Steven Rothberg, Publisher. **Description:** For job-seeking college graduates. Seeking employment-related articles. No pay offered; but will include a byline and hypertext link to a website of your choice. **Nonfiction:** Articles, to 500 words.

AMERICAN CAREERS

6701 West 64th St., Overland Park, KS 66202. 913-362-7788.
3x/year. Circ.: 400,000. Mary Pitchford, Editor. **Description:** Classroom career-development program for 9th- and 10th-grade students, with student content in magazine format. Introduces varied careers in different industries that offer realistic opportunities. **Nonfiction:** Stories, interviews, on variety of industries and careers; 300-750 words; pay varies. **Tips:** Send a letter, resumé, and writing samples. Seeking stories that reflect racial and gender equality. **Queries:** Required. **E-queries:** No. **Unsolicited mss:** Accepts. **Response:** Queries 1 month, submissions 1 month, SASE not needed. **Freelance Content:** 50%. **Rights:** All, work for hire. **Payment:** On acceptance.

BLACK COLLEGIAN

140 Carondelet St., New Orleans, LA 70130. 504-523-0154, ext. 234.
E-mail: robert@iminorities.com. Web site: www.black-collegian.com. Biannually (Oct. and Feb.). Circ.: 109,000. Robert G. Miller, Editor. **Description:** Career and self-development for African-American college students (juniors and seniors). Also read by faculty, career counselors, and placement directors. **Nonfiction:** Features on entry-level career opportunities, job search process, how to prepare for entry-level positions, and culture and experiences of African-American collegians; 1,500-2,000 words. **Tips:** Personalize your article; use "you" rather than the impersonal "college students." Most articles are assigned; will consider ideas with a brief, detailed query letter to the editor. **Queries:** Required. **E-queries:** Yes. **Unsolicited mss:** Accepts. **Response:** Queries 1 week. **Freelance Content:** 90%. **Rights:** 1st. **Payment:** On publication.

CAMPUS CANADA

287 MacPherson Ave., Toronto, Ontario, Canada M4V 1A4. 416-928-2909.
Web site: www.campus.ca. Quarterly. **Description:** Articles to inform, entertain, and educate the student community. **Nonfiction:** Pay varies. **Queries:** Preferred.

CAREER DIRECTIONS

21 N. Henry St., Edgerton, WI 53534. 608-884-3367.
Diane Everson, President and Publisher. **Description:** "Current News & Career Opportunities for Students." Career-related articles, 500-1,500 words, especially how-to. **Nonfiction:** Pays $50-$150. **Payment:** On acceptance. *No recent report.*

CAREER WORLD

GLC, 900 Skokie Blvd., Suite 200, Northbrook, IL 60062-4028. 847-205-3000.
E-mail: crubenstein@glcomm.com. Bi-monthly. Carole Rubenstein, Senior Editor. **Description:** Educational magazine for junior and senior high-school students, to help them prepare for college and career choices. **Nonfiction:** Gender-neutral articles about specific occupations, career awareness and development. Topics: evaluating interests, setting goals, career planning, college choices, getting hired, hot jobs. **Tips:** Send query, with resumé and clips. **Queries:** Required. **E-queries:** Yes.

Unsolicited mss: Does not accept. **Response:** Queries 1-6 months. **Freelance Content:** 80%. **Rights:** All. **Payment:** On publication.

CAREERS AND THE COLLEGE GRAD

Brass Ring Diversity, 170 High St., Waltham, MA 02454. 800-299-7494. E-mail: diversity@brassring.com. Web site: www.brassringdiversity.com. Annual. Kathleen Grimes, Publisher. **Description:** Career-related articles, for junior and senior liberal arts students. No payment. Publishes a number of other specialty magazines for the college market. **Nonfiction:** 1,500-2,000 words. **Fillers:** Career-related fillers, 500 words. **Art:** Line art, color prints. **Queries:** Preferred.

CAREERS & COLLEGES

989 Ave. of the Americas, New York, NY 10018. 212-563-4688. E-mail: staff@careersandcolleges.com. Web site: www.careersandcolleges.com. Quarterly. $3.95. Circ.: 500,000. Don Rauf. **Description:** Guides high-school juniors and seniors through college admissions process, financial aid, life skills, and career opportunities. **Nonfiction:** Interesting, new takes on college admission, scholarships, financial aid, work skills, and careers; 800-2,500 words; pay varies. **Queries:** Required. **E-queries:** No. **Unsolicited mss:** Does not accept. **Response:** 1 month, SASE. **Freelance Content:** 80%. **Rights:** 1st NA. **Payment:** On publication. **Contact:** Traci Mosser.

CIRCLE K MAGAZINE

3636 Woodview Trace, Indianapolis, IN 46268-3196. 317-875-8755. E-mail: ckimagazine@kiwanis.org. Web site: www.circlek.org/magazine. 5x/year. $6/year. Circ.: 15,000. Shanna Mooney, Executive Editor. **Description:** Readers are members of Circle K International (world's largest collegiate service organization), college students committed to community service and leadership development. **Nonfiction:** Serious and light nonfiction, on community leadership and service; 1500-2,000; $150-$400. **Tips:** Focus on interviews and research, not personal insights. Use illustrative examples and expert quotes. **Queries:** Preferred. **E-queries:** Yes. **Unsolicited mss:** Accepts. **Response:** up to 30 days, SASE required. **Freelance Content:** 70%. **Rights:** Exclusive for 30 days. **Payment:** On acceptance.

DIRECT AIM

3100 Broadway, 660 Pen Tower, Kansas City, MO 64111-2413. 816-960-1988. Quarterly. Michelle Paige, Editor. **Description:** For African American and Hispanic students in colleges, universities, and junior colleges. **Nonfiction:** Topics include career preparation, college profiles, financial-aid sources, and interviews with college students across the U.S.; pay varies. **Queries:** Required.

FLORIDA LEADER

Oxendine Publishing, P.O. Box 14081, Gainesville, FL 32604-2081. 352-373-6907. Web site: www.floridaleader.com. 3x/year. **Description:** For Florida college students. Focuses on leadership, college success, profiles of growth careers in Florida and the Southeast. **Nonfiction:** Articles, 800-1,000 words; pays $35-$75. **Payment:** On publication.

HISPANIC TIMES
P.O. Box 579, Winchester, CA 92596. 951-926-2119.
Web site: www.hispanictimesmag.com. **Description:** For Hispanic professionals and college students. All about careers, businesses and employment of Hispanics.

JOURNAL OF CAREER PLANNING & EMPLOYMENT
62 Highland Ave., Bethlehem, PA 18017. 610-868-1421.
Web site: www.naceweb.org. Quarterly. Mimi Collins, Editor. **Description:** On topics related to career planning, placement, recruitment, and employment of new college graduates. **Nonfiction:** Articles, 3,000-4,000 words; pays $100-$200. **Tips:** Send clips. **Queries:** Preferred. **Payment:** On acceptance.

LINK MAGAZINE
32 E. 57th St., 11th Fl., New York, NY 10022. 212-980-6600.
E-mail: editor@linkmag.com. Web site: www.linkmag.com. **Description:** News, lifestyle, and entertainment issues, for college students. **Nonfiction:** Well-researched, insightful, authoritative articles, 2,000-3,000 words; pays $.50/word. **Columns, Departments:** Informational how-to and short features, 300-500 words, on education news, finances, academics, employment, lifestyles, trends, entertainment, sports, and culture. **Queries:** Preferred. **Payment:** On publication. **Contact:** Elizabeth Kessler.

MINORITY ENGINEER
1160 E. Jericho Turnpike, Suite 200, Huntington, NY 11743. 631-421-9421.
E-mail: info@eop.com. Web site: www.eop.com. Tri-annual. Circ.: 17,000. James Schneider, Editor. **Description:** For minority engineering students and professionals. **Nonfiction:** For college students, on career opportunities, job-hunting echniques, new technologies, role-model profiles and interviews; 1,000-2,000 words; $.10/word. **Queries:** Preferred. **E-queries:** Yes. **Unsolicited mss:** Does not accept. **Response:** Queries/submissions 2 weeks, SASE. **Freelance Content:** 60%. **Rights:** 1st. **Payment:** On publication.

STUDENT LEADER
Oxendine Publishing Inc.
P.O. Box 14081, Gainesville, FL 32604-2081. 352-373-6907.
Web site: www.studentleader.com. Semiannual. **Description:** "For America's Most Outstanding Students." On leadership issues and career and college success. **Nonfiction:** Articles, 800-1,000 words; pays $50-$100. **Tips:** Include quotes from faculty, corporate recruiters, current students, recent alumni. **Payment:** On publication. **Contact:** Jennifer Lind.

SUCCEED

Ramholtz Publishing Inc.

2071 Clove Rd., Suite 206, Staten Island, NY 10304-1643. 718-273-5700. E-mail: editorial@collegebound.net. Quarterly. $15/yr. Circ.: 155,000. Gina LaGuardia, Editor-in-Chief. **Description:** Lifelong learning, recommitment to education, or career transition, for adults. Includes database of graduate programs and continuing education classes. **Nonfiction:** 700-1,500 words; $125-$175. **Columns, Departments:** On financial advice, career-related profiles, news, book and software reviews, continuing education resources; 400-600; $75-$100. **Tips:** Query with 3 writing clips. Manuscripts must be accompanied by a source list. Use attributable expert advice and real-life scenarios. **Queries:** Preferred. **E-queries:** Yes. **Unsolicited mss:** Accepts. **Response:** Queries 4 weeks, submissions 6 weeks, SASE. **Freelance Content:** 70%. **Rights:** 1st, 2nd. **Payment:** On publication.

TRAINING

50 S. Ninth St., Minneapolis, MN 55402. 612-333-0471. E-mail: edit@trainingmag.com. Web site: www.trainingmag.com. Tammy Galvin, Editor. **Description:** For managers of training and development activities in corporations, government, etc. **Nonfiction:** Articles, 1,000-2,500 words; pay varies. **Queries:** Preferred. **Payment:** On acceptance.

UNIQUE OPPORTUNITIES

455 S. 4th Ave., #1236, Louisville, KY 40202. 502-589-8250. E-mail: tellus@uoworks.com. Web site: www.uoworks.com. Bimonthly. $5/$25. Circ.: 80,000. Mollie V. Hudson, Editor. **Description:** Offers guidance to physicians on career development, with physician perspectives and current information on all aspects of practice search. **Nonfiction:** Geared to helping physicians navigate their careers (securing a position, making decisions, financial/legal matters, practice management); 1,000-3,000 words; $.50/word. **Queries:** Preferred. **E-queries:** Yes. **Unsolicited mss:** Accepts. **Response:** Queries 2 months, SASE. **Freelance Content:** 45%. **Rights:** FNASR. **Payment:** On acceptance.

COMPUTERS

ACCESS INTERNET MAGAZINE

35 Highland Cir, Needham, MA 02494. 781-453-3990. Monthly. Circ.: 5,000,000. **Description:** This insert into newspapers around the U.S. offers a variety of information on World Wide Web sites, activities, and techniques for successful use.

BRILL'S CONTENT

1230 6th Ave., 16th Fl., New York, NY 10020. 212-332-6300. Web site: www.brillscontent.com. Monthly. Michael Kramer. **Description:** "The survival guide to the information age." Articles and features on media and information technology from perspective of the consumer. **Queries:** Preferred.

C/C++ (USERS JOURNAL)
1601 W. 23rd St., Suite 200, Lawrence, KS 66046-4153. 785-841-1631. Web site: www.cuj.com. Marc Briand. **Description:** On C/C++ programming (algorithms, class designs, book reviews, tutorials). **Nonfiction:** Practical, how-to articles, 2,500 words (including up to 250 lines of code); pays $.10-$.12/word. **Tips:** No programming "religion." **Queries:** Preferred. **Payment:** On publication.

CANADA'S HI-TECH CAREER JOURNAL
355 Harry Walker Parkway, Suite 4, Newmarket, ON, L3Y 7B3 Canada. 905-773-7405. E-mail: htc@HiTechCareer.com. Web site: www.BrassRing.com/Canada. 12x/year. Free (Canada); $39.95 (U.S.). Circ.: 80,000. Lynn Lievonen, Editor-in-Chief. **Description:** For Canadian IT and Engineering professionals; covers industry trends and issues affecting work environment and employment opportunities in the industry. **Nonfiction:** Hi-tech employment issues in Canada; 750 words; $200. **Tips:** Welcomes new writers. Send brief outline of proposed article; must be written exclusively for hi-tech with Canadian content, except for annual supplement, "Uncle Sam Wants You" (employment opportunities and issues in U.S.). **Queries:** Required. **E-queries:** Yes. **Unsolicited mss:** Accepts. **Response:** 24 hours by e-mail, SASE (for mailed queries). **Freelance Content:** 50%. **Rights:** 1st. **Payment:** On publication.

CLOSING THE GAP
526 Main St., P.O. Box 68, Henderson, MN 56044. 507-248-3294. Web site: www.closingthegap.com. Megan Turek, Managing Editor. **Description:** Focuses on microcomputer products that affects the education, vocation, recreation, mobility, communication, etc., of persons who are handicapped or disabled. **Nonfiction:** Articles, 700-1,500 words. Non-product related articles also used.

COMPUTER GAZETTE
324 W. Wendover Ave., Suite 200, Greensboro, NC 27408. David Hensley, Managing Editor. **Description:** Covers home, education, and business applications; games; programming. **Tips:** Limited freelance content. **Queries:** Preferred. **Unsolicited mss:** Does not accept.

COMPUTER GRAPHICS WORLD
Penn Well, 98 Spit Brook Rd., Nashua, NH 03062-2801. 847-559-7500. Web site: www.cgw.com. Phil LoPiccolo, Editor. **Description:** On computer graphics technology and its use in science, engineering, architecture, film and broadcast, and interactive entertainment. Computer-generated images. **Nonfiction:** Articles, 1,000-3,000 words; pays $600-$1,000. **Queries:** Preferred. **Payment:** On acceptance.

HOME OFFICE COMPUTING

Scholastic, Inc., 180 Freedom Ave., Murfreesboro, TN 37129. Bernadette Grey, Editor-in-Chief. **Description:** Focuses on microcomputers, software, home office products, and issues affecting small and home businesses. **Nonfiction:** Practical information on how to run a business and use technology effectively (3,000 words). Profiles of small-business owners. Education and entertainment pieces (800-1,500 words) for Family Computing section. **Columns, Departments:** Finance, legal issues, sales and marketing, communications, government; 1,200 words. **Queries:** Preferred. **Unsolicited mss:** Accepts. **Payment:** On acceptance.

MACWORLD COMMUNICATIONS

301 Howard St., Floor 16, San Francisco, CA 94105. 415-243-0505. Web site: www.macworld.com. **Description:** Covers all aspects of Macintosh computers. **Nonfiction:** Reviews, news, consumer, how-to articles, varying lengths, related to Macintosh computers. Query with clips only. Pays $150-$3,500. **Queries:** Preferred. **Unsolicited mss:** Does not accept. **Payment:** On acceptance.

NETWORK WORLD

118 Turnpike Rd., Southborough, MA 01772-9108. 800-622-1108. Web site: www.nwfusion.com. Adam Gaffin, Editor. **Description:** About applications of communications technology for management-level users of data, voice, and video communications systems. **Nonfiction:** Articles, to 2,500 words; pay varies. **Payment:** On acceptance.

PEI (PHOTO ELECTRONIC IMAGING)

229 Peachtree St. NE, Suite 2200, International Tower, Atlanta, GA 30303. 404-522-8600. Web site: www.peimag.com. Terry Murphy, Editor. **Description:** On electronic imaging, computer graphics, desktop publishing, pre-press and commercial printing, multimedia, and web design. **Nonfiction:** Articles on professional imaging trends and techniques, 1,000-3,000 words; pay varies. **Tips:** By assignment only. **Queries:** Required. **Payment:** On publication.

TECHNOLOGY & LEARNING

Miller Freeman, Inc., 600 Harrison St., San Francisco, CA 94107-1370. 415-947-6041. Web site: www.techlearning.com. Susan McLester, Editor-in-Chief. **Description:** For teachers K-12, about uses of computers and related technology in the classroom: human-interest and philosophical articles, how-to pieces, software reviews, and hands-on ideas. **Nonfiction:** Articles, to 3,000 words; pay varies. **Payment:** On acceptance.

TECHNOLOGY REVIEW

One Main St., 7th Floor, Cambridge, MA 02142. 617-475-8000. E-mail: mitaatr@mit.edu. Web site: www.techreview.com. John Benditt, Editor. **Description:** General-interest articles on technology and innovation. **Nonfiction:** Pay varies. **Queries:** Preferred. **Payment:** On acceptance.

WIRED

660 Third St., 1st Floor, San Francisco, CA 94107. 800-769-4733. E-mail: submit@wired.com. Web site: www.wired.com. Monthly. Circ.: 500,000. Katrian Heron, Editor-in-Chief. **Description:** Lifestyle magazine for the "digital generation." Discusses the meaning and context of digital technology in today's world. **Fiction:** Yes. **Nonfiction:** Articles, essays, profiles, etc.; pay varies. **Payment:** On acceptance.

YAHOO! INTERNET LIFE

Ziff Davis Media, 28 E. 28th St., 12th Fl., New York, NY 10016. 212-503-4790. E-mail: first_last@ziffdavis.com. Web site: www.yil.com. Monthly. $3.99/$14.97. Circ.: 1,100,000. Barry Golson, Editor. **Description:** Consumer magazine on Internet, lifestyle, cultural topics. **Queries:** Preferred. **Unsolicited mss:** Accepts. **Freelance Content:** 30%. **Payment:** On publication.

CONSUMER & PERSONAL FINANCE

THE AMERICAN SPECTATOR

2020 N. 14th St., #750, Arlington, VA 22201. 703-243-3733. Web site: www.spectator.org. Monthly. Circ.: 130,000. Richard Vigilante, Editor. **Description:** Technical, political, and cultural guide for the investor in the new economy. **Nonfiction:** Pay varies. **Tips:** Query with article clips. Sample copy, $5.95. **Queries:** Required. **E-queries:** No. **Unsolicited mss:** Does not accept. **Response:** 30 days. **Freelance Content:** 50%. **Rights:** All.

CONSUMER REPORTS

101 Truman Ave., Yonkers, NY 10703. 914-378-2000. Web site: www.ConsumerReports.org. Monthly. $26. Circ.: 4,100,000. Julia Kagan, Editor. **Description:** Award-winning journalistic research on health, personal finance, and matters of public policy. Also, independent product-testing reports. **Tips:** Mostly staff-written, escept for occasional back-of-book column on health or personal finance **Queries:** Required. **E-queries:** Yes. **Unsolicited mss:** Accepts. **Response:** 1-3 weeks, SASE required. **Freelance Content:** 1%. **Rights:** All. **Payment:** On acceptance.

CONSUMERS DIGEST

8001 N. Lincoln Ave., 6th Fl., Skokie, IL 60077. 847-763-9200. Web site: www.consumersdigest.com. Bimonthly. $2.99/issue, $15/year. Circ.: 1,200,000. John Manos, Editor. **Description:** Helps readers make lifestyle, purchasing, investment, and personal financial decisions to benefit their daily lives. Thoroughly and objectively evaluates a wide range of brand-name products and services. **Nonfiction:** Consumer issues. **Tips:** Also covers how to get the best value for key services: doctors, lawyers, hospitals, financial advisers, etc. No "how-to" articles.

Queries: Required. **E-queries:** No. **Unsolicited mss:** Does not accept. **Rights:** All. **Payment:** On publication. **Contact:** Jim A. Gorzelany.

KIPLINGER'S PERSONAL FINANCE

1729 "H" Street NW, Washington, DC 20006. 202-887-6400. Web site: www.kiplinger.com. Monthly. Circ.: 1,300,000. Ted Miller, Editor. **Description:** Covers personal finance issues. **Nonfiction:** Articles on personal finance (i.e., buying insurance, mutual funds). **Queries:** Required. **Payment:** On acceptance.

THE MONEYPAPER

1010 Mamaroneck Ave., Mamaroneck, NY 10543. 914-381-5400; 800-388-9993. Web site: www.moneypaper.com. Vita Nelson, Editor. **Description:** Financial news and money-saving ideas. Brief, well-researched articles on personal finance, money management, saving, earning, investing, taxes, insurance, and related subjects. **Nonfiction:** Pays $75 for articles. **Tips:** Include resumé and writing sample. Seeking information about companies with dividend reinvestment plans. **Queries:** Preferred. **Payment:** On publication.

PRIME TIMES

P.O. Box 391, Madison, WI 53701. 608-231-7272. E-mail: tom.burton@cunamutual.com. **Description:** For retirees associated with credit unions. **Queries:** Preferred. **Contact:** Tom Burton, Managing Editor.

YOUR MONEY

8001 N. Lincoln Ave., 6th Fl., Skokie, IL 60077-2403. 847-763-9200. E-mail: bhessel@consumersdigest.com. Web site: www.consumersdigest.com. Bimonthly. Circ.: 500,000. Dennis Fertig, Editor. **Description:** For the general reader on investment opportunities and personal finance. **Nonfiction:** Informative, jargon-free personal finance articles; to 2,000 words; $.60/word. **Tips:** Send clips for possible assignments. **Queries:** Required. **Payment:** On acceptance. **Contact:** Brooke Hessel, Asst. Ed.

ZILLIONS

101 Truman Ave., Yonkers, NY 10703-1057. 914-378-2553. Web site: www.consumerreports.org. **Description:** An online version of *Consumer Reports* for children, found at Zillions.org. For readers, ages 8-14, with Internet access.

CONTEMPORARY CULTURE

AMERICAN DEMOGRAPHICS

P.O. Box 10580, Riverton, NJ 08076. 800-529-7502. Web site: www.demographics.com. Jill Kirschenbaum, Executive Editor.

Description: Articles, 500-2,000 words, on four key elements of a consumer market (size, needs and wants, ability to pay, and how it can be reached). With specific examples of how companies market to consumers. Readers include marketers, advertisers, and planners. **Queries:** Preferred.

AMERICAN SCHOLAR
1785 Massachusetts Ave. NW, 4th Fl., Washington, DC 20036. 202-265-3808. E-mail: scholar@pbk.org. Web site: www.pbk.org. Quarterly. $6.95/issue. Circ.: 26,000. Anne Fadiman, Editor. **Description:** For intelligent people who love the English language. **Nonfiction:** By experts, for general audience; 3,000-5,000 words; $500. **Poetry:** Highly original; up to 33 lines; $50. **Queries:** Preferred. **E-queries:** Yes. **Unsolicited mss:** Accepts. **Response:** 2-8 weeks, SASE required. **Freelance Content:** 100%. **Rights:** 1st. **Payment:** On acceptance.

AMERICAN VISIONS
1101 Pennsylvania Ave NW, Suite 820, Washington, DC 20004. 202-347-3820. E-mail: editor@avs.americanvisions.com. Web site: www.americanvisions.com. Bimonthly. Circ.: 125,000. Joanne Harris, Editor. **Description:** African-American culture, with focus on the arts. **Nonfiction:** Articles; 1,500-2,500 words; pays $100-$600. **Columns, Departments:** Columns; 1,000 words; pay varies. **Queries:** Required. **Payment:** On publication.

AMERICAS
1889 F St. N.W., Washington, DC 20006. 202-458-3510. E-mail: americas@oas.org. Web site: www.oas.org. James Patrick Kiernan, Director. **Description:** Features, on Latin America and the Caribbean. Wide focus: anthropology, the arts, travel, science, and development. **Nonfiction:** 2,500-4,000 words; pays from $400. **Tips:** Prefers stories that can be well-illustrated. No political material. **Payment:** On publication. **Contact:** Rebecca Read Medrano, Managing Ed.

BET WEEKEND
One BET Plaza, 1900 W. Place NE, Washington, DC 20018-1211. **Description:** On lifestyle, arts, education, and entertainment of the African-American community. **Nonfiction:** Articles, 200-500 words; pays $.50-$1.00/word. **Tips:** Do not send manuscript; query first with SASE. **Payment:** On publication. *No recent report.*

CHRONICLES
The Rockford Institute, 928 N. Main St., Rockford, IL 61103. 815-964-5054. Web site: www.chroniclesmagazine.org. Scott Richard. **Description:** "A Magazine of American Culture." Articles and poetry that display craftsmanship and a sense of form.

COMMONWEAL
475 Riverside Dr., Room 405, New York, NY 10115. 212-662-4200. E-mail: commonweal@msn.com. Web site: commonwealmagazine.org. 22x/year.

$2.50. Circ.: 20,000. Margaret O'Brien Steinfels, Editor. **Description:** Review of public affairs, religion, literature and the arts, published by Catholic lay people. **Nonfiction:** On political, religious, social, and literary subjects; 1,000-3,000 words; $100. **Poetry:** Submit 5 poems maximum (Oct.-May), serious, witty; $.75/line. **Columns, Departments:** Brief newsy facts, behind the headlines, reflective pieces; 750-1,000 words; $75. **Tips:** Focus on religion, politics, culture; how they intertwine. No simultaneous submissions. **Queries:** Not necessary. **E-queries:** Yes. **Unsolicited mss:** Accepts. **Response:** Queries 1 month, submissions 6 weeks, SASE required. **Freelance Content:** 20%. **Rights:** All. **Payment:** On publication.

GEIST

1014 Homer St., #103, Vancouver, BC, Canada V6B 2W9. 604-681-9161. E-mail: geist@geist.com. Web site: www.geist.com. Quarterly. **Description:** "Canadian Magazine of Ideas and Culture." **Nonfiction:** Creative nonfiction, 200-1,000 words; excerpts, 300-1,500 words, from works in progress; long essays and short stories, 2,000-5,000 words. Pay varies. **Queries:** Preferred. **Payment:** On publication.

HISPANIC

999 Ponce de Leon Blvd., Suite 600, Coral Gables, FL 33134. 305-442-2462. Web site: www.hisp.com. Monthly. Carlos Verdecia, Editor. **Description:** General-interest (career, business, politics, and culture). Confronts issues affecting the Hispanic community, emphasis on solutions rather than problems. English-language. **Nonfiction:** Features, 1,400-2,500 words; $450. **Columns, Departments:** Hispanic Journal, Portfolio; $75-$150. **Queries:** Preferred.

JUXTAPOZ

Hi-Speed Production Inc., 1303 Underwood Ave., P.O. Box 884570, San Francisco, CA 94124-3308. 415-822-3083. E-mail: editor@juxtapoz.com. Web site: www.juxtapoz.com. Jamie O'Shea, Editor. **Description:** About modern arts and culture.

NATIVE PEOPLES

5333 N. 7th St., Suite C-224, Phoenix, AZ 85014-2804. 602-265-4855. E-mail: gavey@nativepeoples.com. Web site: www.nativepeoples.com. Bimonthly. $4.95/issue. Circ.: 60,000. Gary Avey, Editor. **Description:** Full-color, offers sensitive portrayal of arts and lifestyle of native peoples of the Americas. **Nonfiction:** Artist profiles (traditional and contemporary); issue-oriented pieces with Native American angle; program/people profiles in education, health, politics; economic development; 1,000-3,000 words; $.25/word. **Columns, Departments:** Pathways (travels with Native site/culture/history focus; Viewpoint (open subject matter); 400-1,200 words; $.25/word. **Art:** Color, b/w. **Tips:** Readership is both Native American and those interested in Native culture. Our stories need to appeal to both, serving as a bridge between cultures. **Queries:** Preferred. **E-queries:** Yes. **Unsolicited mss:** Accepts.

Response: 4 weeks, SASE required. **Freelance Content:** 80%. **Rights:** First-time rights. **Payment:** On publication. **Contact:** Daniel Gibson, Managing Editor.

PARABOLA
Society for Study of Myth & Tradition
656 Broadway, New York, NY 10012-2317. 212-505-9037.
E-mail: parabola@panix.com. Web site: www.parabola.org. Quarterly. Circ.: 40,000.
Natalie Baan, Managing Editor. **Description:** "The magazine of myth and tradition." Thematic issues presents traditional stories, folk and fairy tales. **Fiction:** 500 words. **Nonfiction:** Articles retelling traditional stories, folk and fairy tales; to 4,000 words; pay varies. **Tips:** Contact for upcoming themes. Looking for a balance between scholarly and accessible writing, on the ideas of myth and tradition. **Queries:** Preferred.

ROLLING STONE
1290 Ave. of the Americas, 2nd Fl., New York, NY 10104. 212-484-1616.
Web site: www.rollingstone.com. **Description:** Magazine of American music, culture, and politics. **Tips:** Rarely accepts freelance material. No fiction. **Queries:** Required. **Unsolicited mss:** Does not accept.

SOUTHWEST REVIEW
P.O. Box 750374, Dallas, TX 75275-0374. 214-768-1037.
E-mail: swr@mail.smu.edu. Quarterly. $6/issue. Elizabeth Mills, Editor. **Description:** Varied, wide-ranging content of adult interest: contemporary affairs, history, folklore, fiction, poetry, literary criticism, art, music, and theater. **Fiction:** 3,500-7,000 words; $100-$300. **Nonfiction:** 3,500-7,000 words; $100-$300. **Poetry:** 1 page (generally); $50-$150. **Queries:** Not necessary. **E-queries:** No. **Unsolicited mss:** Accepts. **Response:** Submissions 3 months, SASE required. **Rights:** 1st NA. **Payment:** On publication.

THIRSTY EAR
P.O. Box 29600, Santa Fe, NM 87592. 505-473-5723.
E-mail: thirstyearmag@yahoo.com. Web site: www.thirstyearmagazine.com. 5x/year. $15/$25. Circ.: 80,000. Michael Koster, Editor. **Description:** Covers music, art, and culture. **Fiction:** Short stories with music, arts, or American culture themes; up to 2,500 words; $75-$100. **Nonfiction:** Articles on "non-tuxedo" music; also reviews, 300-500 words. **Columns, Departments:** Opinion; 800-1,000 words; $100. **Queries:** Required. **E-queries:** Yes. **Unsolicited mss:** Does not accept. **Response:** Varies. **Freelance Content:** 80%. **Rights:** 1st NA. **Payment:** On publication.

TROIKAMAGAZINE.COM
P.O. Box 1006, Weston, CT 06883. 203-319-0873.
E-mail: eric@troikamagazine.com. Web site: www.troikamagazine.com. Daily. Circ.: 400,000. Eric and Celia Meadow, Editors. **Description:** Cutting-edge, online contemporary culture forum. Informs, entertains and enlightens; a global voice in a rapidly globalizing world. **Fiction:** All types; varied length; $200 and up. **Nonfiction:**

Features on arts, health, science, human interest, international interests, business, leisure, ethics. For educated, affluent baby-boomers, seeking to balance personal achievements, family commitments, and community involvement; varied length; $200 and up. **Poetry:** All types; varied length. **Queries:** Not necessary. **E-queries:** Preferred. **Unsolicited mss:** Accepts; "Please send—we respond to all!" **Response:** Queries 10 days, submissions to 3 months, SASE. **Freelance Content:** 100%. **Rights:** worldwide, 1st NA. **Payment:** 90 days from publication. **Contact:** submit@troikamagazine.com.

UTNE READER

Lens Publishing Co.
1624 Harmon Pl., Fawkes Bldg., Minneapolis, MN 55403-1906. 612-338-5040. E-mail: editor@utne.com. Web site: www.utne.com. Bimonthly. $4.99/issue $19.97/year. Circ.: 232,000. Jay Waljasper, Editor. **Description:** Offers alternative ideas and culture, reprinting articles selected from over 2,000 alternative media sources. **Nonfiction:** Short pieces and reviews, 300-1,000 words. Provocative perspectives, analysis of art and media, down-to-earth news and resources; compelling people and issues. **Queries:** Preferred. **E-queries:** Yes. **Unsolicited mss:** Accepts. **Response:** 4-6 weeks, SASE. **Freelance Content:** 20%. **Rights:** Nonexclusive worldwide. **Payment:** On publication.

YAHOO! INTERNET LIFE

Ziff Davis Media, 28 E. 28th St., 12th Floor, New York, NY 10016. 212-503-4790. E-mail: first_last@ziffdavis.com. Web site: www.yil.com. Monthly. $3.99/$14.97. Circ.: 1,100,000. Barry Golson, Editor. **Description:** Consumer magazine on Internet, lifestyle, cultural topics. **Queries:** Preferred. **Unsolicited mss:** Accepts. **Freelance Content:** 30%. **Payment:** On publication.

CURRENT EVENTS & POLITICS

AMERICAN EDUCATOR

American Federation of Teachers
555 New Jersey Ave. NW, Washington, DC 20001. 202-879-4400.
Web site: www.aft.org. Quarterly. Liz McPike, Editor. **Description:** On trends in education; also well-researched news features on current problems in education, education law, professional ethics; "think" pieces and essays that explore current social issues relevant to American society. **Nonfiction:** Articles, 500-2,500 words; pays from $300. **Queries:** Preferred. **Payment:** On publication.

AMERICAN LEGION

P.O. Box 1055, Indianapolis, IN 46206-1055. 317-630-1200.
E-mail: tal@legion.org. Web site: www.legion.org. John B. Raughter, Exec. Editor. **Description:** Covers current world affairs, public policy, and subjects of contemporary

interest. **Nonfiction:** 750 to 2,000 words; pay negotiable. **Queries:** Preferred. **Payment:** On acceptance.

AMICUS JOURNAL

Natural Resources Defense Council
40 W. 20th St., New York, NY 10011. 212-727-4412.
E-mail: amicus@nrdc.org. Web site: www.nrdc.org. Quarterly. $2.95/issue. Circ.: 250,000. Kathrin Day Lassila, Editor. **Description:** Journal of thought and opinion for general public on environmental affairs, especially on policies of national and international significance. Strives to be a flagship of environmental thinking, covering critical emerging events and new ideas. **Nonfiction:** Investigative articles, profiles, book reviews, essays; pay varies. **Poetry:** Conveying emotional, spiritual sources of environmental commitment; $50. **Art:** By request only. **Tips:** Submit strong, well-conceived ideas (Who will you interview? Why of great importance?). Must send clips. **Queries:** Required. **E-queries:** No. **Unsolicited mss:** Accepts. **Response:** 6-8 weeks, SASE required. **Freelance Content:** 40%. **Payment:** On publication.

BRIARPATCH

2138 McIntyre St., Regina, Saskatchewan, Canada S4P 2R7. 306-525-2949.
E-mail: briarpatch.mag@sk.sympatico.ca. Web site: www.briarpatchmagazine.com. 10x/year. $3/$24.61. Debra Brin, Editor. **Description:** Progressive Canadian newsmagazine with a left-wing political slant. **Nonfiction:** Articles on politics, women's issues, environment, labor, international affairs for Canadian activists involved in social-change issues. Also, short reviews of recent books, CDs. **Tips:** Use journalistic style, with quotes from involved people. Looking for hard-hitting, thought-provoking stories. **Queries:** Preferred. **E-queries:** Yes. **Unsolicited mss:** Accepts. **Response:** Immediately. **Freelance Content:** 100%. **Rights:** None. **Payment:** In copies.

CALIFORNIA JOURNAL

2101 K St., Sacramento, CA 95816. 916-444-2840.
E-mail: cindic@statenet.com. Web site: www.statenet.com. Monthly. $39.95. Circ.: 11,000. Cynthia H. Craft. **Description:** Nonpartisan, reports on California government and politics. **Nonfiction:** 1,000-2,000 words; $400-$1,200. **Queries:** Required. **E-queries:** Yes. **Unsolicited mss:** Does not accept. **Response:** 1-2 weeks, SASE. **Freelance Content:** 30%. **Rights:** All. **Payment:** On acceptance.

CAMPAIGNS & ELECTIONS

1414 22nd St., Washington, DC 20037. 202-887-8530; 800-888-5767.
Web site: www.campaignline.com. Ron Faucheux. **Description:** On strategies, techniques, trends, and personalities of political campaigning. **Nonfiction:** Features, 700-4,000 words; campaign case-studies, 1,500-3,000 words; how-tos, 700-2,000 words, on aspects of campaigning; in-depth studies, 700-3,000 words, on public opinion, election results, and political trends. **Columns, Departments:** 100-800 words, for Inside Politics. **Payment:** In copies.

CHRISTIAN SOCIAL ACTION

100 Maryland Ave. NE, Washington, DC 20002. 202-488-5600. E-mail: ealsgaard@umc-gbcs.org. Web site: www.umc-gbcs.org. Bi-monthly. Circ.: 3,000. Erik Alsgaard, Editor. **Description:** For United Methodist clergy and lay people interested in the role and involvement of the church in social issues. **Nonfiction:** Stories that educate, inspire, motivate people to Christian social action on justice and advocacy issues; 1,500-2,000 words; $125-$175. **Fillers:** Social satire; 500 words; $100. **Art:** Hard copy, electronic. **Tips:** Less academic, more "folksy" language preferred. **Queries:** Preferred. **E-queries:** Yes. **Unsolicited mss:** Accepts. **Response:** Queries 4-6 weeks, SASE required. **Freelance Content:** 30%. **Rights:** 1st. **Payment:** On publication.

CIVILIZATION

Worth Media, 575 Lexington Ave., 33rd Fl., New York, NY 10022. 212-230-3790. Web site: www.civmag.com. Bimonthly. Circ.: 200,000. Regan Solmo, Managing Sr. Editor. **Description:** Membership publication, for supporters of Library of Congress. **Nonfiction:** Thought-provoking articles and essays; some book reviews; pay varies. **Fillers:** Some puzzles; pay varies. **Queries:** Required.

COLUMBIA JOURNALISM REVIEW

Columbia University, 700 Journalism Bldg., New York, NY 10027. 212-854-1881. Web site: www.cjr.org. Gloria Cooper, Managing Editor. **Description:** Amusing mistakes in news stories, headlines, photos, etc. (original clippings required), for "Lower Case." Pays $25. **Payment:** On publication.

COMMENTARY

165 E. 56th St., New York, NY 10022. 212-751-4000. Web site: www.commentarymagazine.com. Neal Kozodoy, Editor. **Description:** Fiction, of literary quality, on contemporary social or Jewish issues, from 5,000-7,000 words. Articles, 5,000-7,000 words, on contemporary issues, Jewish affairs, social sciences, religious thought, culture. Serious fiction; book reviews. **Payment:** On publication.

THE CRISIS

P.O. Box 26616, Baltimore, MD 21707; or 4805 Mt. Hope Dr. Baltimore, MD 21215. Web site: www.naacp.org. Ida Lewis, Editor-in-Chief. **Description:** On the arts, civil rights, and problems and achievements of blacks and other minorities. **Nonfiction:** Articles, to 1,500 words; pays $75-$500. **Payment:** On acceptance.

FOREIGN SERVICE JOURNAL

2101 "E" Street NW, Washington, DC 20037. 202-338-4045. E-mail: journal@afsa.org. Web site: www.afsa.org/fsj/index.html. Monthly. $3.50/issue. Circ.: 12,000. Bob Guldin, Editor. **Description:** Covers foreign affairs and the U.S. Foreign Service. **Fiction:** Stories with overseas settings, for fiction issue (summer), submit in April; 3,000 words; $250. **Nonfiction:** On foreign policy and international issues, for Foreign Service and diplomatic community. **Columns, Departments:** Short travel pieces about foreign scene, person, place, incident; 600-700 words; $100. **Tips:** Knowledge of foreign service concerns essential. **Queries:** Not necessary. **Unsolicited mss:** Accepts. **Response:** Queries 1 month. **Freelance Content:** 25%. **Payment:** On publication.

FREE INQUIRY

P.O. Box 664, Amherst, NY 14226-0664. 716-636-7571.
E-mail: tflynn@centerforinquiry.com. Web site: www.secularhumanism.com. $5.95/issue. Circ.: 20,000. Thomas Flynn, Editor. **Description:** Edited from the secular humanist viewpoint, which holds that life should be guided by science and reason. **Fiction:** 1,500-3,000 words. **Nonfiction:** 1,500-3,000 words. **Poetry:** ½ to 1 page. **Fillers:** 100-300 words. **Columns, Departments:** 1,500 words. **Art:** PDF; $50-$100. **Tips:** Write for sophisticated, well-educated audience interested in academic research, politics, religion, current events in U.S. and abroad. **Queries:** Not necessary. **E-queries:** Yes. **Unsolicited mss:** Accepts. **Response:** Queries 1 week, submissions 6 weeks, SASE required. **Freelance Content:** 10%. **Rights:** 1st NA.

HARPER'S MAGAZINE

666 Broadway, 11th Floor, New York, NY 10012. 212-614-6500.
Web site: www.harpers.org. Monthly. Circ.: 216,000. Lewis H. Lapham, Editor. **Description:** For women, on politics, literary, cultural, scientific issues. **Fiction:** Will consider unsolicited manuscripts; SASE required. **Nonfiction:** Very limited market; 2,000-5,000 words. **Queries:** Required. **Response:** SASE required.

THE HOMELESS REPORTER NEWS-SHEET

P.O. Box 1053, Dallas, TX 75221-1053.
Bill Mason, Editor. **Description:** An insider's view and dialogue on solving homelessness. Seeks articles and essays on ways to solve the socio-economic problems of homelessness and poverty. Also publishes human-interest love stories set in that context. **Nonfiction:** Articles, essays; 300-1,500 words. **Queries:** Preferred. **E-queries:** Yes. **Unsolicited mss:** Accepts. **Payment:** in copies.

IDEAS ON LIBERTY

Foundation for Economic Education
30 S. Broadway, Irvington-on-Hudson, NY 10533. 914-591-7230.
Web site: www.fee.org. Sheldon Richman, Editor. **Description:** On economic, political, and moral implications of private property, voluntary exchange, and individual choice. **Nonfiction:** Articles, to 3,500 words; pays $.10/word. **Payment:** On publication.

IN THESE TIMES

2040 N. Milwaukee Ave., Chicago, IL 60647. 773-772-0100.
E-mail: itt@inthesetimes.com. Web site: www.inthesetimes.com. Bi-weekly. $2.50/$36.95. Circ.: 20,000. Joel Bleifuss, Editor. **Description:** Seeks to inform and

analyze popular movements for social, environmental and economic justice in the U.S. and abroad; opposes dominance of transnational corporations, tyranny, and marketplace value over human values. **Nonfiction:** News reporting, op-eds, and book reviews on left politics, the environment, human rights, labor, etc.; 500-3,000 words; $.12/word. **Tips:** Avoid excessive editorializing; strong news reporting and writing skills more valued. **Queries:** Preferred. **E-queries:** Yes. **Response:** 6-8 weeks, SASE. **Freelance Content:** 90%. **Rights:** reprint. **Payment:** On publication.

JUNIOR SCHOLASTIC

Scholastic, Inc., 555 Broadway, New York, NY 10012. 212-343-6295. E-mail: junior@scholastic.com. Web site: www.juniorscholastic.com. Lee Baier. **Description:** On-the-spot reports from countries in the news. **Nonfiction:** Pay varies; **Queries:** Required. **Payment:** On acceptance.

LATINO LEADERS

363 N. Sam Houston Pkwy. E., Ste. 1100, Houston, TX 77060-2413. 888-528-4532. Monthly. Circ.: 90,000. **Description:** Covers diverse leaders in the Latino community.

MIDSTREAM

633 Third Ave., 21st Fl., New York, NY 10017. E-mail: info@midstream.org. Web site: www.midstream.org. 8x/year. $3/$21/year. Circ.: 8,000. Joel Carmichael, Editor. **Description:** Zionist publication, content ranges from political U.S. and Israel culture, literature, book reviews, poetry, comments on religion. Varied points of view presented. **Fiction:** Stories on Jewish themes; 1,500-4,000 words; $.05/word. **Nonfiction:** Jewish (Zionist) political, cultural, literary, religious themes; 1,500-6,000 words; $.05/word. **Poetry:** Jewish themes; 20 lines; $25/poem. **Tips:** Readers mostly elderly, scholarly, Israel-oriented. **Queries:** Not necessary. **E-queries:** No. **Unsolicited mss:** Accepts. **Response:** up to 1 month, SASE. **Freelance Content:** 20%. **Rights:** 1st. **Payment:** On publication.

MIDWEST QUARTERLY

Pittsburgh State Univ., Pittsburgh, KS 66762. 316-235-4369. E-mail: midwestq@pittstate.edu. Web site: www.pittstate.edu/engl/midwest.htm. Quarterly. $12. Circ.: 550. James B. M. Schick, Editor. **Description:** Scholarly articles on varied subjects of current interest. **Nonfiction:** Scholarly articles on contemporary academic and public issues; 18-20 pages. **Poetry:** up to 70 lines. **Queries:** Preferred. **E-queries:** Yes. **Unsolicited mss:** Accepts. **Response:** Queries 1 week, submissions 4-6 months, SASE required. **Payment:** None.

MONTHLY REVIEW

122 W. 27th St., New York, NY 10001. 212-691-2555. E-mail: mrmag@monthlyreview.org. Web site: www.monthlyreview.org. 11x/year. $4/issue, $29/year. Circ.: 7,000. John Bellamy Foster, Editor. **Description:** Covers political, economic, international affairs, current events, from an independent socialist perspective. **Nonfiction:** Analytical articles on politics and economics; articles

(3,000-4,000 words), $50; reviews (1,500-2,000 words), $25. **Tips:** Avoid pieces that date quickly, as it takes 6 months to publish. Looking for solid Marxist analysis. **Queries:** Not necessary. **E-queries:** Yes. **Unsolicited mss:** Accepts. **Response:** Submissions, 8 weeks. **Freelance Content:** 95%. **Payment:** On publication.

MOTHER JONES
731 Market St., Suite 600, San Francisco, CA 94103. 415-665-6637. E-mail: query@motherjones.com. Web site: www.motherjones.com. Bimonthly. $4.95/issue $20/year. Circ.: 170,000. Roger Cohn, Editor. **Description:** Independent journalism focusing on issues of social justice. **Nonfiction:** Features, 1,500-4,000 words, $1,500-$4,000. Short pieces, 100-800 words, $100-$500. Book, film, and music reviews. **Art:** Photos, illustrations. **Tips:** Looking for investigative reports exposing government cover-ups, corporate malfeasance, scientific myopia, institutional fraud or hypocrisy. **Queries:** Required. **E-queries:** Yes. **Unsolicited mss:** Does not accept. **Response:** 2-3 months, SASE. **Freelance Content:** 95%. **Rights:** FNASR. **Payment:** On acceptance.

MS.
Liberty Media for Women
20 Exchange Pl., 22nd Fl., New York, NY 10005. 212-509-2092. E-mail: info@msmagazine.com. Web site: www.msmagazine.com. Bimonthly. Circ.: 200,000. Marcia Gillespie, Editor-in-Chief. **Description:** Articles relating to feminism, women's roles, and social change. **Nonfiction:** National and international news reporting, profiles, essays, theory, and analysis. **Tips:** Query with resumé, published clips, and SASE. No fiction or poetry. **Queries:** Required.

THE NATION
33 Irving Place, 8th Fl., New York, NY 10003. 212-209-5400. E-mail: info@thenation.com. Web site: www.thenation.com. Weekly. $2.75/Issue, $35.97/year. Circ.: 100,000. Katrina Vanden Heuvel, Editor. **Description:** Politics and culture from a liberal, left perspective, on national and international affairs. **Nonfiction:** Editorials and full-length pieces; 1,500-2,500 words; $75/printed page ($300 maximum). **Poetry:** Quality poems. **Columns, Departments:** Editorials; 750-1,000 words. **Tips:** Looking for reporting, with fresh analysis and national significance, on U.S. civil liberties, civil rights, labor, economics, environmental, feminist issues, and role and future of Democratic Party. **Queries:** Required. **Unsolicited mss:** Accepts. **Response:** SASE. **Payment:** On publication.

NETWORK
Gray Panthers, 733 15th St. NW, #437, Washington, D.C. 20005-2112. 202-737-6637. Web site: www.graypanthers.org. **Description:** National advocacy magazine for older adults.

NEW JERSEY REPORTER

164 Nassau St., 2nd Floor, Princeton, NJ 08542. 609-924-9750. E-mail: njreporter@rcn.com. Web site: www.njreporter.org. Bimonthly. Circ.: 3,200. Mark Magyar, Editor. **Description:** New Jersey politics and public affairs. **Nonfiction:** In-depth articles; 1,000-4,000 words; $175-$800. **Queries:** Required. **Payment:** On publication.

THE NEW YORKER

4 Times Square, New York, NY 10036. 212-536-5400. E-mail: themail@newyorker.com. Web site: www.newyorker.com. Weekly. $3.50/issue. Circ.: 851,000. **Description:** Covers the vital stories of our time with intelligence, wit, stylish prose, and a keen eye. **Fiction:** Short stories, humor, and satire. **Nonfiction:** Amusing mistakes in newspapers, books, magazines, etc. Factual and biographical articles for Profiles, Reporter at Large, etc. Political/social essays, 1,000 words. **Poetry:** Quality poetry. **Queries:** Not necessary. **E-queries:** No. **Unsolicited mss:** Accepts. **Payment:** On publication. **Contact:** Perri Dorset.

NEWSDAY

235 Pinelawn Rd., Melville, NY 11747-4250. 516-843-2900. E-mail: oped@newsday.com. Web site: www.newsday.com. Daily. Circ.: 555,203. Noel Rubinton, Viewpoints Editor. **Description:** Opinion section of newspaper covering issues of national or local importance, lifestyle, government, current events and trends. **Nonfiction:** Op-ed pieces, on varied topics; 700-800 words; $150. **Queries:** Preferred. **Payment:** On publication.

THE OLDER AMERICAN

Massachusetts Assn. of Older Americans
108 Arlington St., Boston, MA 02116. 617-426-0804. Web site: maoa-inc.org. Quarterly. Circ.: 9,000. **Description:** Local, state, and national advocacy and current affairs magazine for older adults.

POLICY REVIEW

214 Massachusetts Ave. NE, Washington, DC 20002. 202-608-6161. E-mail: polrev@heritage.org. Web site: www.policyreview.com. Bimonthly. $6/issue. Circ.: 14,000. Tod Lindberg, Editor. **Description:** Book reviews, full-length articles on public policy; 1,000-5,000 words. **Tips:** Freelance content limited. **Queries:** Preferred. **E-queries:** Yes. **Unsolicited mss:** Accepts. **Response:** 2-4 weeks, SASE. **Freelance Content:** 5%. **Payment:** On publication. **Contact:** Kelly Sullivan.

THE PROGRESSIVE

409 E. Main St., Madison, WI 53703. 608-257-4626. E-mail: editorial@progressive.org. Web site: www.progressive.org. Monthly. $3.50/issue, $32/yr. Circ.: 30,000. Matthew Rothschild, Editor. **Description:** A leading voice for peace and social justice, with fresh and lively commentary on major issues. **Nonfiction:** Investigative reporting; coverage of elections, social movements,

foreign policy; interviews, activism, book reviews; $50-$1,300. **Poetry:** On political concerns; $150/poem. **Columns, Departments:** On the Line; $50-100. **Queries:** Preferred. **Unsolicited mss:** Accepts. **Freelance Content:** 75%. **Payment:** On publication.

PUBLIC CITIZEN NEWS
1600 20th St. NW, Washington, DC 20009-1001. 202-588-1000. E-mail: pc_mail@citizen.org. Web site: www.citizen.org. Bimonthly. Circ.: 100,000. Bob Mentzinger, Editor. **Description:** Investigative reports and articles of timely political interest, for members of Public Citizen: consumer rights, health and safety, environmental protection, safe energy, tax reform, international trade, and government and corporate accountability. **Art:** Photos, illustrations. **Payment:** Honorarium.

REASON
3415 S. Sepulveda Blvd., Suite 400, Los Angeles, CA 90034. 310-391-2245. Web site: www.reason.com. Rick Henderson. **Description:** "Free Minds and Free Markets." Looks at politics, economics, and culture from libertarian perspective. **Nonfiction:** Articles, 850-5,000 words; pay varies. **Queries:** Preferred. **Payment:** On acceptance.

ROLL CALL
50 "F" Street NW, 700, Washington, DC 20001. 202-824-6800. Web site: www.rollcall.com. Susan Glasser, Editor. **Description:** Covers Capitol Hill. Factual, breezy articles, political or Congressional angle (history, human-interest, political lore, opinion, commentary). **Queries:** Preferred. **Payment:** On publication.

THE SENIOR ADVOCATE
Mar-Len Publications, 131 Lincoln St., Worcester, MA 01605. 508-752-3400. Web site: www.mrln.com/sahome.html. Bi-weekly. Circ.: 75,000. **Description:** Covers local, state, and national issues, for seniors.

SOCIAL JUSTICE REVIEW
3835 Westminster Pl., St. Louis, MO 63108-3409. 314-371-1653. E-mail: centbur@juno.com. Web site: www.socialjusticereview.org. Bi-monthly. $20. Circ.: 5,500. Rev. John H. Miller, C.S.C., Editor. **Description:** Focuses on social justice and related issues. **Nonfiction:** under 3,000 words; $.02/word. **Tips:** Submissions must be faithful to doctrine of the Catholic Church. **Queries:** Preferred. **E-queries:** No. **Unsolicited mss:** Accepts. **Response:** Queries 2 weeks, SASE. **Freelance Content:** 80%. **Rights:** 1st. **Payment:** On publication.

SPY
49 E. 21st St., 11th Fl., New York, NY 10016. 212-260-7210. Adam Lehner. **Description:** High-concept, fact-based articles, 5,000 words, especially satirical or irreverent pieces "that feel as if they were written by an insider."

Shorter pieces used for "Naked City" section. Pays $1/word (less for Naked City). **Queries:** Required. **Payment:** On publication. *No recent report.*

TIKKUN

2107 Van Ness Ave., Ste. 302, San Francisco, CA 94109. 415-575-1200. E-mail: magazine@tikkun.org. Web site: www.tikkun.org. Bimonthly. $5.95/$29. Circ.: 20,000. Michael Lerner, Editor. **Description:** Jewish commentary on politics, culture, and society. Based on Jewish principle of Tikkun Olam (healing the world), encourages writers to join spirituality to politics, for politics infused with compassion and meaning. **Fiction:** 3,000 words. **Nonfiction:** 1,600 words. **Poetry:** 20 lines. **Art:** Electronic (.jpeg, .tiff); $50/photo. **Tips:** Avoid "My trip to Israel (or Eastern Europe/Auschwitz)", "My adult bar mitzvah," "How I became religious." **Queries:** Not necessary. **E-queries:** No. **Unsolicited mss:** Accepts. **Response:** 3-4 months, SASE. **Freelance Content:** 20%. **Rights:** 1st, web reprint. **Payment:** in copies.

UTNE READER

Lens Publishing Co.
1624 Harmon Pl., Fawkes Bldg., Minneapolis, MN 55403-1906. 612-338-5040. E-mail: editor@utne.com. Web site: www.utne.com. Bimonthly. $4.99/issue $19.97/year. Circ.: 232,000. Jay Waljasper, Editor. **Description:** Offers alternative ideas and culture, reprinting articles selected from over 2,000 alternative media sources. **Nonfiction:** Short pieces and reviews, 300-1,000 words. Provocative perspectives, analysis of art and media, down-to-earth news and resources; compelling people and issues. **Queries:** Preferred. **E-queries:** Yes. **Unsolicited mss:** Accepts. **Response:** 4-6 weeks, SASE. **Freelance Content:** 20%. **Rights:** Nonexclusive worldwide. **Payment:** On publication.

VILLAGE VOICE

36 Cooper Sq., New York, NY 10003.
Doug Simmons, Editor. **Description:** On current or controversial topics. **Nonfiction:** Articles, 500-2,000 words; pays $100-$1,500. **Queries:** Preferred. **Response:** SASE required. **Payment:** On publication. *No recent report.*

THE WALL STREET JOURNAL

200 Liberty St., New York, NY 10281. 212-416-2000.
Web site: www.wsj.com. Daily. **Description:** Newspaper. Op-Ed articles, to 1,500 words, on politics, economics, law, education, environment, some humor, and foreign and domestic affairs. Must be timely, heavily reported, and of national interest by writers with expertise. Pays $150-$300. **Payment:** On publication.

THE WASHINGTON MONTHLY

1611 Connecticut Ave. NW, Washington, DC 20009. 202-462-0128.
Web site: www.washingtonmonthly.com. Charles Peters, Editor. **Description:** Helpful, informative articles, 1,000-4,000 words, on DC-related topics, including politics, and government and popular culture. Pays $.10/word, on publication.

WOMEN'S INTERNATIONAL NET (WIN)
301 E. 79th St., Suite 12A, New York, NY 10021. 646-349-2763.
E-mail: editor@winmagazine.com.
Web site: http://welcome.to/winmagazineMonthly. Monthly. Free Online.
Description: E-zine; offers a broad range of opinions on women's issues throughout the world. Seeks to improve status of women everywhere by comparing problems and solutions. Not aligned with any political view. Seeks reports, personal accounts, interviews, and short stories. **Fiction:** Short stories. **Nonfiction:** Personal accounts, interviews, reports. **Tips:** No material that is sexist, racist, homophobic, or otherwise discriminatory. Readers are intellectual, general audience.

YES!
Box 10818, Bainbridge Island, WA 98110. 206-842-0216.
E-mail: editors@futurenet.org. Web site: www.futurenet.org. Quarterly. Circ.: 14,000.
Carol Estes. **Description:** "Journal of Positive Futures." Focuses on ways people are working to create a more just, sustainable, and compassionate world. **Tips:** Don't simply expose problems; highlight a practical solution. **Queries:** Required. **Payment:** On publication.

EDUCATION

AMERICAN EDUCATOR
American Federation of Teachers, 555 New Jersey Ave. NW, Washington, DC 20001.
202-879-4400.
Web site: www.aft.org. Quarterly. Liz McPike, Editor. **Description:** On trends in education; also well-researched news features on current problems in education, education law, professional ethics; "think" pieces and essays that explore current social issues relevant to American society. **Nonfiction:** Articles, 500-2,500 words; pays from $300. **Queries:** Preferred. **Payment:** On publication.

AMERICAN SCHOOL BOARD JOURNAL
1680 Duke Street, Alexandria, VA 22314. 703-838-6722.
Web site: www.asbj.com. **Description:** Publishes informative articles in a practical format regarding educational trends for school board members and administrators.

AMERICAN SCHOOL & UNIVERSITY
155 Village Blvd., Princeton, NJ 08540.
Web site: www.industryclick.com. Joe Agron, Editor. **Description:** Articles and case studies, 1,200-1,500 words, on design, construction, operation, and management of school and university facilities. **Queries:** Preferred.

AMERICAN STRING TEACHER
468 Rebecca Street, Morgantown, WV 26505. 304-598-3249.
Web site: www.astaweb.com. Quarterly. **Description:** Published by American String

Teachers Association and National School Orchestra Association. Seeking research-based articles with national appeal. **Tips:** Avoid opinion or personal-experience stories. **Queries:** Preferred.

BLACK ISSUES IN HIGHER EDUCATION
10520 Warwick Ave., Suite B-8, Fairfax, VA 22030-3136. 703-385-2981. E-mail: hilary@cmcbiccw.com. Web site: www.blackissues.com. Biweekly. $3.50/$26. Circ.: 12,000. Hilary L. Hurd, Editor. **Description:** News and features on blacks in post-secondary education and public policy. **Nonfiction:** On issues affecting minorities in higher education. **Fillers:** On education and public policy. **Columns, Departments:** Opinion pieces. **Queries:** Preferred. **E-queries:** Yes. **Unsolicited mss:** Accepts. **Freelance Content:** 40%. **Payment:** On publication.

CABLE IN THE CLASSROOM
141 Portland St., #8200, Cambridge, MA 02139-1937. 617-254-9481. E-mail: cic@cicrosby.com. Web site: www/ciconline.org. Monthly. $21.95/yr. Circ.: 120,000. Al Race. **Description:** Lists commercial free, educational cable programming, plus online resources. Profiles educators who use programming and resources; offers tips for finding and using resources effectively. **Nonfiction:** Articles by or about K-12 teachers, librarians, and media specialists who use educational cable technology and programming to benefit students. By assignment, no unsolicited manuscripts; 500-1,000 words; $250-$500. **Columns, Departments:** Teacher-authored tips for using Cable in the Classroom resources to meet curriculum requirements. Query first; 100-150 words; $50. **Tips:** By assignment only. Don't pitch a story without identifying educators and the classroom cable connection. **Queries:** Required. **E-queries:** Yes. **Unsolicited mss:** Does not accept. **Response:** Queries 1-3 months, SASE. **Freelance Content:** 50%. **Payment:** On acceptance.

CHRISTIAN EDUCATION LEADERSHIP
1080 Montgomery Ave. NE, PO Box 2250, Cleveland, TN 37320-2250. 800-553-8506. E-mail: ycessse@extremegen.org. Web site: www.pathwaypress.org. Quarterly. $8. Circ.: 10,000. Tony P. Lane, Editor. **Description:** For Christian education workers who teach God's word to kids, teens, and adults. **Nonfiction:** To encourage, inform, and inspire those who teach the Bible in local churches; 500-600 words; $25-$40. **Queries:** Not necessary. **E-queries:** Yes. **Unsolicited mss:** Accepts. **Response:** Submissions 3-6 weeks, SASE. **Payment:** On acceptance.

CHURCH EDUCATOR
Educational Ministries, Inc., 165 Plaza Dr., Prescott, AZ 86303. 800-221-0910. E-mail: edmin2@aol.com. Web site: www.educational ministries.com. Monthly. $28/year. Circ.: 3,000. Robert G. Davidson, Editor. **Description:** Resource for mainline Protestant Christian educators. **Nonfiction:** Programs used in mainline churches; 200-1,500 words; $.03/word. **Queries:** Not necessary. **E-queries:** Yes. **Unsolicited mss:** Accepts. **Response:** Queries 1 week, submissions 3 months,

SASE required. **Freelance Content:** 80%. **Rights:** One Time Rights. **Payment:** On publication. **Contact:** Linda Davidson.

THE CLEARING HOUSE
Heldref Publications, 1319 18th St. NW, Washington, DC 20036. 202-296-6267. E-mail: tch@heldref.org. Web site: www.heldref.org. Bi-monthly. $11.75/$38. Circ.: 2,000. Melody Warnick, Editor. **Description:** Scholarly journal, covers topics for middle-level and high-school teachers and administrators. **Nonfiction:** Scholarly articles on educational trends and philosophy, learning styles, curriculum, effective schools, testing and measurement, instructional leadership; up to 2,500 words. **Columns, Departments:** Short articles, new trends; 100-900 words. **Tips:** Writers are generally university professors in education. **Queries:** Not necessary. **E-queries:** No. **Unsolicited mss:** Accepts. **Response:** Submissions 1-2 months, SASE. **Freelance Content:** 100%. **Payment:** in copies.

COMMUNITY COLLEGE WEEK
10520 Warwick Ave., #B-8, Fairfax, VA 27030. 703-385-2981. E-mail: scottc@cmabiccw.com. Web site: www.ccweek.com. Bi-weekly. $2.75/issue. Circ.: 7,000. Scott Cech, Editor. **Description:** Cover community, technical, and junior-college issues. **Nonfiction:** Articles of interest to 2-year academia; 500-700 words; $.35/word. **Tips:** Use AP style. **Queries:** Required. **E-queries:** Yes. **Unsolicited mss:** Accepts. **Response:** 1-7 days, SASE. **Freelance Content:** 100%. **Rights:** nonexclusive. **Payment:** On publication.

CREATIVE CLASSROOM
149 Fifth Ave., 12th Fl., New York, NY 10010. 212-353-3639. E-mail: ccmedit@inch.com. Web site: www.creativeclassroom.com. **Description:** Hands-on magazine for elementary-school teachers. Articles on all curriculum areas, child developmental issues, technology and the Internet in the classroom, professional development, and issues facing elementary teachers. **Tips:** SASE for guidelines.

CURRENT HEALTH
900 Skokie Blvd., Suite 200, Northbrook, IL 60062-4028. 847-405-3000. E-mail: crubenstein@glcomm.com. 8x/school year. $9.15 (quantities of 15). Carole Rubenstein, Editor. **Description:** For classrooms. Covers physical and pyschological health issues, in two editions (for grades 4-7, and grades 7-12). **Nonfiction:** Articles on drug education, nutrition, diseases, fitness and exercise, first aid and safety, and environmental awareness. By assignment only, no unsolicited manuscripts. Pay varies. **Tips:** Must write well for appropriate age level. Send query with resumé, clips. **Queries:** Required. **E-queries:** No. **Unsolicited mss:** Does not accept. **Response:** Queries 1-6 months. **Freelance Content:** 80%. **Rights:** All. **Payment:** On publication.

EARLY CHILDHOOD NEWS

2 Lower Ragsdale, Suite 125, Monterey, CA 93940. 831-333-2000. E-mail: mshaw.ec@earlychildhood.com. Web site: www.earlychildhood.com. Bimonthly. Circ.: 50,000. Megan Shaw, Editor. **Description:** For teachers and parents of young children, infants to age 8. On developmentally appropriate activities, behavior, health and safety, and more. **Fiction:** Personal-experience stories, written from teacher's perspective; 500 words max. **Nonfiction:** Research-based articles on child development, behavior, curriculum, health and safety, etc.; 500-2,000 words. **Poetry:** Related to young children (birth-age 6), teaching, educating, or family; 100 words. **Columns, Departments:** Ask the Expert, newsletters for child care staff, Problem-Solving Parent; 500-600 woods. **Queries:** Preferred. **E-queries:** Yes. **Unsolicited mss:** Accepts. **Response:** Queries 6 weeks, submissions 2-3 months, SASE not needed. **Freelance Content:** 75%. **Rights:** All. **Payment:** On publication.

EARLY CHILDHOOD TODAY

Scholastic, Inc., 555 Broadway, 5th Fl., New York, NY 10012. 212-343-6100. Web site: www.earlychildhoodtoday.com. **Description:** For teachers. Offers practical information, strategies, and tips on child development and education. Also personal stories and program spotlights. **Nonfiction:** Articles, 500-900 words; pay varies. **Queries:** Preferred. **Payment:** On publication. **Contact:** Article Submissions.

ENGLISH JOURNAL

NCTE, 1111 W. Kenyon Rd., Urbana, IL 61801-1096. 217-328-3870. Web site: www.ncte.org. **Description:** For high-school English and language-arts teachers. Sponsored by a Section of NCTE (National Council of Teachers of English). **Queries:** Preferred.

GIFTED EDUCATION PRESS QUARTERLY

10201 Yuma Ct., P.O. Box 1586, Manassas, VA 20108. 703-369-5017. E-mail: mdfish@cais.com. Web site: www.giftedpress.com. Quarterly. Circ.: 1,000. Maurice Fisher, Editor. **Description:** Covers problems and issues of identifying and educating gifted students. **Nonfiction:** Teaching science and humanities; educating gifted children at home; 3,500-4,000 words. **Tips:** Looking for highly imaginative, knowledgeable writers to write about this field. **Queries:** Required. **E-queries:** Yes. **Unsolicited mss:** Does not accept. **Response:** 1 month, SASE required. **Freelance Content:** 50%.

THE HISPANIC OUTLOOK IN HIGHER EDUCATION

210 Rt. 4 E., Suite 310, Paramus, NJ 07652. 201-587-8800. E-mail: sloutlook@aol.com. Web site: www.Hispanicoutlook.com. Adalyn Hixson, Editor. **Description:** On issues, concerns, and potential models for furthering academic results of Hispanics in higher education. **Nonfiction:** Articles, 1,500-2,000 words; pay varies. **Queries:** Preferred. **Payment:** On publication.

HOME EDUCATION
P.O. Box 1083, Tonasket, WA 98855-1083. 509-486-1351.
E-mail: HEM@home-ed-magazine.com. Web site: www.home-ed-magazine.com.
Bimonthly. $6.50/issue, $32.50/year. Circ.: 12,000. Helen E. Hegener, Managing
Editor. **Description:** For home-schooling families. **Nonfiction:** Articles on educa-
tion and socialization of home-schooled children; 1,000-2,000 words; $50-$150.
Poetry: Poetry by homeschoolers only. **Tips:** Encourages submissions from home-
schooling parents who love to write. Focus on practical experience, not textbook the-
ories. **Queries:** Not necessary. **E-queries:** Yes. **Unsolicited mss:** Accepts.
Response: 1-2 months, SASE required. **Freelance Content:** 60%. **Rights:**
FNASR. **Payment:** On publication.

INSTRUCTOR
Scholastic, Inc., 555 Broadway, New York, NY 10012. 212-343-6100.
Web site: www.scholastic.com/instructor. 8x/year. $19.95/yr. Circ.: 200,000. Jennifer
Prescott, Managing Editor. **Description:** Prominent national magazine for K-8 teachers. **Nonfiction:** Topics for teachers (timely issues, classroom ideas, activities, ways to
improve); 800-2,000 words; $500-$1,200. **Fillers:** E-Classroom (tech-based activities);
also, short, ready-to-use activities by teachers, for teachers; 100 words; $50. **Columns,
Departments:** End of the Day (revelatory or humorous pieces about your experience
as a teacher); 400-500 words; $250. **Tips:** Keep in mind: Can a teacher take these ideas
into the classroom immediately? **Queries:** Not necessary. **E-queries:** Yes.
Unsolicited mss: Accepts. **Response:** Queries 1 month, submissions 2 months,
SASE. **Freelance Content:** 80%. **Rights:** All. **Payment:** On publication.

JOURNAL OF HEALTH EDUCATION
1900 Association Dr., Reston, VA 20191. 703-476-3400.
Web site: www.aahperd.org/aahe.html. **Description:** For health educators, sponsored by American Alliance for Health, Physical Education, Recreation and Dance.
For those who work with students (elementary to college grades), to encourage professional growth. **Queries:** Preferred.

LEARNING
3515 W. Market St., Greensboro, NC 27403. 336-854-0309.
Web site: www.theeducationcenter.com. Quarterly. **Description:** For K-6 teachers,
to help them deal with issues such as stress, motivation, burnout, and other self-
improvement topics; successful teaching strategies to reach today's kids; and ideas to
get parents involved. **Nonfiction:** Articles, 50-1,500 words. **Response:** 3 months,
SASE required. **Payment:** in gift certificates.

MATRIX
Professional Media Group, 488 Main St., Norwalk, CT 06850. 203-847-7200.
Web site: www.matrix-magazine.com. Bonnie Reidinger, Editor. **Description:** For
managers in the field of higher education. Online and print versions.

MEDIA & METHODS

1429 Walnut St., Philadelphia, PA 19102. 215-563-6005.
Web site: www.media-methods.com. Christine Weiser, Editor. **Description:** On media, technologies, and methods used to enhance instruction and learning in K-12th-grade classrooms. **Nonfiction:** Articles, 800-1,000 words; pays $50-$200. **Queries:** Required. **Payment:** On publication.

MOMENTUM

National Catholic Educational Assn.
1077 30th St. N.W., Suite 100, Washington, DC 20007-3852. 202-337-6232.
Web site: www.ncea.org. Margaret Bonilla, Editor. **Description:** On outstanding programs, issues, and research in education. **Nonfiction:** Articles, 500-1,500 words; pays $25-$75. **Columns, Departments:** Book reviews. **Tips:** No simultaneous submissions. **Queries:** Preferred. **Payment:** On publication.

SCHOLASTIC DYNAMATH

555 Broadway, Room 367, New York, NY 10012-3999. 212-343-6100.
E-mail: dynamath@scholastic.com. Web site: www.scholastic.com. 8x/year. $6.75.
Circ.: 200,000. Matt Friedman, Editor. **Description:** Offer an engaging mix of humor, news, popular-culture references, and original activities to help readers enjoy learning, while reinforcing and applying key math curriculum concepts. Content must be acceptable for classroom use. **Nonfiction:** Fun math content, tied to current events, popular culture, cool real-life kids, or national holidays (i.e., Martin Luther King Day, President's Day, Thanksgiving); to 600 words; $350-$450/article. **Fillers:** $25-$50 puzzles, to 75 words. **Art:** $50-$400. **Tips:** Has dual goals of being entertaining and educational. Need to get style and mathematical grade level just right. Request a sample copy to familiarize yourself with unique approach. **Queries:** Preferred. **E-queries:** Yes. **Unsolicited mss:** Accepts. **Response:** 2 months, SASE required. **Freelance Content:** 25%. **Rights:** All. **Payment:** On acceptance.

THE SCHOOL ADMINISTRATOR

American Assn. of School Administrators, 1801 N. Moore St., Arlington, VA 22209
E-mail: magazine@aasa.org. Web site: www.aasa.org. 11x/year. Members only. Circ.: 23,000. Jay P. Goldman, Editor. **Description:** For school administrators (K-12), on school system practices, policies, and programs with wide appeal. **Nonfiction:** 1,500-3,000 words; pay varies. **Fillers:** To 400 words. **Columns, Departments:** To 750 words. **Art:** See guidelines on web. **Queries:** Preferred. **E-queries:** Yes. **Unsolicited mss:** Accepts. **Response:** Queries 2 weeks, submissions 8-10 weeks. **Freelance Content:** 10%. **Rights:** All. **Payment:** On publication.

SCHOOL ARTS

50 Portland St., Worcester, MA 01608. 508-754-7201.
Web site: www.davis-art.com. 9x/year. $4/issue. Circ.: 25,000. Dr. Eldon Katter, Editor. **Description:** Covers the field of art education. **Nonfiction:** Articles, 600-1,400 words, on art education in the classroom: successful, meaningful approaches to

teaching, innovative projects, uncommon applications of techniques or equipment, etc. Pays $30-$150. **Art:** professional-quality photos showing lessons in art; pay varies. **Queries:** Preferred. **E-queries:** Yes. **Unsolicited mss:** Accepts. **Response:** 3 months, SASE. **Freelance Content:** 85%. **Rights:** All. **Payment:** On publication.

SCIENCE AND CHILDREN
1840 Wilson Blvd., Arlington, VA 22201. 703-243-7100.
Web site: www.nsta.org. **Description:** Articles and activities, based on current approaches to instruction and issues in science education. For Pre-K to 8th-grade science teachers. **Queries:** Preferred.

TEACHING ELEMENTARY PHYSICAL EDUCATION
P.O. Box 5076, Champaign, IL 61825-5076. 217-351-5076.
Web site: www.humankinetics.com. Bimonthly. **Description:** Resources and ideas on instructional and fun physical-education programs for K-8 physical education teachers. **Queries:** Preferred.

TEACHING K-8
40 Richards Ave., Norwalk, CT 06854. 203-855-2650.
E-mail: pat@teachingk-8@aol.com. Web site: www.teachingk-8. 8x/year. $23.97/yr. Circ.: 100,000. Patricia Broderick, Editor. **Description:** A classroom service magazine. **Nonfiction:** Articles, 1,000 words, on classroom-tested ideas, techniques, strategies for teaching students (K-8) . **Queries:** Not necessary. **E-queries:** No. **Unsolicited mss:** Accepts. **Response:** Submissions 1 month, SASE. **Freelance Content:** 0%. **Rights:** All. **Payment:** On publication.

TEACHING THEATRE
2343 Auburn Ave., Cincinnati, OH 45219. 513-421-3900.
Web site: www.etassoc.org. Quarterly. **Description:** Newsletter for middle- and high-school drama educators. Offers play suggestions, curriculum ideas, classroom exercises, and technical production. **Queries:** Preferred.

TEACHING TOLERANCE
Southern Poverty Law Center, 400 Washington Ave., Montgomery, AL 36104.
Web site: www.teachingtolerance.org. Bi-annual. Free to educators. Circ.: 600,000. Jim Carnes. **Description:** Helps teachers promote interracial and intercultural understanding in the classroom and beyond. **Nonfiction:** E.g., role of white teachers in multicultural education; teaching respect for dialects; creating safe space for refugee students to tell their stories; how assistive devices allow more inclusion for disabled; gay student comes out at school, etc.; 500-3,500 words; $1/word. **Art:** Rarely uses stock images. Seeking photographer to travel on assignment, work well with school children and teachers/administrators, in varied locations; b/w, color, hand-tinted; $100-$800. **Tips:** Submit clear focused query. No rhetoric, scholarly analysis, articles that reinvent the wheel on multicultural education. **Queries:** Preferred.

E-queries: No. **Unsolicited mss:** Accepts. **Response:** up to 3 months, SASE. **Freelance Content:** 75%. **Rights:** All. **Payment:** On acceptance.

TECH DIRECTIONS

Prakken Publications
3970 Varsity Dr., Ann Arbor, MI 48107-8623. 734-975-2800.
Web site: www.techdirecions.com. Tom Bowden, Editor. **Description:** For teachers in industrial, technology, and vocational educational fields. Seeking classroom projects, computer uses, and legislative issues. **Nonfiction:** Articles, 6-10 double-spaced typed pages; pays $50-$150. **Fillers:** Cartoons (pays $20); puzzles, brainteasers, humorous anecdotes, short classroom activities; (pays $25); humorous anecdotes (pays $5). **Payment:** On publication.

TECHNOLOGY & LEARNING

600 Harrison St., San Francisco, CA 94107. 415-947-6041.
Web site: www.techlearning.com. 10x/year. $29.95 (U.S.), $39.95 (Canada/Mexico). Circ.: 80,000. Susan McLester, Editor-in-Chief. **Description:** For elementary, junior-high and senior-high school teachers, technology coordinators, and administrators, at the building and district levels. **Nonfiction:** Software evaluations and success stories from schools/districts using technology in innovative ways to help students, teachers, and community members; 1,200-1,700 words; $400 and up. **Tips:** Seeking articles that encourage educators to think about new approaches to teaching and new ways to use technology in the classroom. Emphasizes material that uses computers, also peripheral hardware (i.e., videodisc and CD-ROM programs, integrated learning systems,etc.). **Queries:** Preferred. **E-queries:** Yes. **Unsolicited mss:** Accepts. **Response:** 3-4 months, SASE required. **Freelance Content:** 70%. **Rights:** All. **Payment:** On publication.

TODAY'S CATHOLIC TEACHER

330 Progress Rd., Dayton, OH 45449. 937-847-5900.
E-mail: mnoschang@peterli.com. Web site: www.catholic.com. Bi-monthly. $14.95 yr. Circ.: 50,000. Mary Noschang, Editor. **Description:** For K-8 educators concerned with private education in general and Catholic education in particular. **Nonfiction:** Curriculum, classroom management, other articles (religious and non-religious) for classroom teachers in Catholic K-12 schools; 700-3,000 words; $150-$300. **Queries:** Not necessary. **E-queries:** Yes. **Unsolicited mss:** Accepts. **Response:** 2 months, SASE. **Freelance Content:** 80%. **Rights:** 1st NA. **Payment:** On publication.

ENVIRONMENT, CONSERVATION, NATURE

(See also Sports, Recreation, Ourdoors)

ADIRONDACK LIFE

P.O. Box 410, Jay, NY 12941. 518-946-2191.
E-mail: aledit@primelink1.net. 8x/year. Circ.: 50,000. Elizabeth Folwell, Editor.

Description: Outdoor and environmental activities, issues, arts, wilderness, wildlife, profiles, history, and fiction; focuses on the Adirondack Park region of New York State. **Nonfiction:** Features; to 5,000 words; $.25/word. **Queries:** Preferred. **E-queries:** Yes. **Unsolicited mss:** Accepts. **Response:** Responds in 45 days, SASE required. **Rights:** 1st NA. **Payment:** On acceptance.

ALTERNATIVES JOURNAL
Faculty of Environmental Studies
Univ. of Waterloo, Waterloo, Ontario, Canada N2L 3G1. 519-888-4442.
E-mail: altsed@fes.uwaterloo.ca. Web site: www.fes.uwaterloo.ca/alternatives/.
Quarterly. Anicka Quin. **Description:** Environmental thought, policy, and action. Canadian focus. **Nonfiction:** Feature articles, 4,000 words; notes, 200-500 words; and reports, 750-1,000 words; no payment.

AMERICAN FORESTS
910 17th St., Suite 600, Washington, DC 20006. 202-955-4500 X203.
E-mail: mrobbins@amfor.org. Web site: www.americanforests.org. Quarterly. $3/issue, $25/year. Circ.: 25,000. Michelle Robbins, Editor. **Description:** For people, rural and urban, who share a love for trees and forests. **Nonfiction:** Articles on trees, forests, issues (worldwide); inspirational, educational; 150-2,000 words; $100-$1,200. **Poetry:** Yes. **Fillers:** Yes. **Columns, Departments:** Communities (working together on problems); Woodswise (for small-forest owners); Perspectives (current events); Earthkeepers (1-page profiles); Clippings (news briefs). **Art:** 35mm or larger; b/w or color; $75-$400. **Tips:** Write for general audience but on a slightly more informed level. Tell specifics: issues, what's being done, how it has affected forests. Looking for skilled science writers for assignments documenting forest use, enjoyment, and management. **Queries:** Required. **E-queries:** Yes. **Unsolicited mss:** Accepts. **Response:** Queries 2 months, submissions 1 months, SASE required. **Freelance Content:** 10%. **Rights:** one-time. **Payment:** On acceptance.

AMICUS JOURNAL
Natural Resources Defense Council
40 W. 20th St., New York, NY 10011. 212-727-4412.
E-mail: amicus@nrdc.org. Web site: www.nrdc.org. Quarterly. $2.95/issue. Circ.: 250,000. Kathrin Day Lassila, Editor. **Description:** Journal of thought and opinion for general public on environmental affairs, especially on policies of national and international significance. Strives to be a flagship of environmental thinking, covering critical emerging events and new ideas. **Nonfiction:** Investigative articles, profiles, book reviews, essays; pay varies. **Poetry:** Conveying emotional, piritual sources of environmental commitment; $50. **Art:** By request only. **Tips:** Submit strong, well-conceived ideas (Who will you interview? Why of great importance?). Must send clips. **Queries:** Required. **E-queries:** No. **Unsolicited mss:** Accepts. **Response:** 6-8 weeks, SASE required. **Freelance Content:** 40%. **Payment:** On publication.

ANIMALS

350 S. Huntington Ave., Boston, MA 02130. 617-522-7400. Web site: www.animelsmagazine.com. Quarterly. $15/year. Circ.: 50,000. Paula Abend, Editor. **Description:** Full-color publication with timely, reliable, provocative coverage of wildlife issues, pet-care topics, and animal protection concerns. **Nonfiction:** Informative, well-researched articles, to 2,500 words. **Columns, Departments:** Profiles, 800 words, on individuals who work to make life better for animals, wild or domestic, or to save habitat. Reviews, 300-500 words. **Art:** Do not send originals. **Tips:** No personal accounts or favorite pet stories. **Queries:** Required. **E-queries:** No. **Unsolicited mss:** Accepts. **Response:** 6 weeks, SASE required. **Freelance Content:** 90%. **Rights:** NA. **Payment:** On acceptance.

ATLANTIC SALMON JOURNAL

Atlantic Salmon Federation, P.O. Box 807, Calais, ME 04619-0807. E-mail: asfpub@nbnet.nb.ca. Web site: www.asf.ca. Quarterly. Circ.: 10,000. Jim Gourlay, Editor. **Description:** Covers fishing, conservation, ecology, travel, politics, biology, how-tos, and anecdotes. **Nonfiction:** Articles related to Atlantic salmon; 1,500-3,000 words; $100-$400. **Fillers:** Salmon politics, conservation, and nature; 50-100 words; $25. **Queries:** Preferred. **Payment:** On publication.

AUDUBON

National Audubon Society, 700 Broadway, New York, NY 10003-9501. E-mail: editor@audubon.org. Web site: www.audubon.org. Bimonthly. Circ.: 460,000. Lisa Gosselin, Editor in Chief. **Description:** Conservation and environmental issues, natural history, ecology, and related subjects. **Nonfiction:** Articles; 150-4,000 words; pay varies. **Tips:** Submit queries, with clips and SASE, to Editorial Asst. **Queries:** Required. **Payment:** On acceptance.

BIRD WATCHER'S DIGEST

P.O. Box 110, Marietta, OH 45750. 740-373-8443. E-mail: editor@birdwatchersdigest.com. Web site: www.birdwatchersdigest.com. Bimonthly. Circ.: 90,000. William H. Thompson III, Editor. **Description:** Bird-watching experiences and expeditions; interesting backyard topics and how-tos. **Nonfiction:** Articles for bird watchers: first-person accounts; profiles of bird species; 600-2,500 words; from $100. **Queries:** Preferred. **Response:** 8 weeks, SASE required. **Payment:** On publication.

BIRDER'S WORLD

P.O. Box 1612, 21027 Crossroads Circle, Waukesha, WI 53187-1612. 262-796-8776. Web site: www.birdersworld.com. Bi-monthly. $4.50/$22.50. Circ.: 70,000. Diane Jolie, Editor. **Description:** On all aspects of birding, especially on particular species or status of endangered species. Tips on birding, attracting, or photographing birds. **Nonfiction:** Feature articles, 2,200-2,400 words; pays $350-$450. **Columns, Departments:** Book reviews (to 500 words); personal essays (500-1,500 words). **Queries:** Preferred. **E-queries:** No. **Unsolicited mss:** Accepts. **Response:** 3

months, SASE (if visuals are sent). **Freelance Content:** 75%. **Rights:** 1st NA. **Payment:** On publication.

BLUELINE

English Dept., SUNY, Potsdam, NY 13676. 315-267-2043. E-mail: blueline@potsdam.edu. Web site: www.potsdam.edu/engl/blueline. Annual. $10/yr. Circ.: 600. Rick Henry, Editor. **Description:** Poems, stories, and essays on the Adirondack and regions similar in geography and spirit, or on the shaping influence of nature. **Fiction:** Yes; to 3,500 words. **Nonfiction:** On Adirondack region or similar areas; to 3,500 words. **Poetry:** Submit up to 5 poems; to 75 lines. **Queries:** Not necessary. **E-queries:** Yes. **Unsolicited mss:** Accepts. **Response:** Queries, 1 week. **Rights:** FNASR. **Payment:** in copies.

BUGLE, ELK COUNTRY

Rocky Mountain Elk Fdn., 2291 W. Broadway, Missoula, MT 59808. 406-523-4510. E-mail: bugle@rmef.org. Web site: www.rmef.org. Bimonthly. $5.95/30. Circ.: 195,000. Dan Crockett, Editor. **Description:** Journal of the Rocky Mountain Elk Foundation. Original, critical thinking about wildlife conservation, elk ecology, and hunting. **Fiction:** Thoughtful elk-hunting stories; human-interest stories; 1,500-4,500 words; $.20/word. **Nonfiction:** About conservation, elk ecology and natural history, elk hunting; 1,500-4,500 words; $.20/word. **Poetry:** 1 page; $100/poem. **Fillers:** Humor. **Columns, Departments:** Essays on hunting or conservation issues; 1,000-3,000 woods; $.20/word. **Art:** See photo wish-list on website. **Tips:** How-to and where-to stories. **Queries:** Preferred. **E-queries:** Yes. **Unsolicited mss:** Accepts. **Response:** 3 months, SASE. **Freelance Content:** 80%. **Rights:** 1st NA. **Payment:** On acceptance. **Contact:** Lee Cromrich, Asst. Ed.

CALIFORNIA WILD

California Academy of Sciences Golden Gate Park, San Francisco, CA 94118-4599. 415-750-7116. E-mail: calwild@calacademy.org. Web site: www.calacademy.org. Quarterly. $4.00/$12.95. Circ.: 30,000. Gordy Slack, Associate Editor. **Description:** Based at the research facility, natural-history museum, and aquarium in San Francisco's Golden Gate Park. **Nonfiction:** Well-researched articles, 1,500-3,000 words, on natural history and preservation of the environment. Pays $.25/word. **Columns, Departments:** Skywatcher; Trail Less Traveled; At Home in the Natural World. **Art:** Color, transparencies. **Unsolicited mss:** Accepts. **Rights:** 1st NA. **Payment:** On publication.

CANADIAN GEOGRAPHIC

39 McArthur Ave., Ottawa, Ont., Canada K1L 8L7. 613-745-4629. E-mail: editorial@cangeo.ca. Web site: www.canadiangeographic.ca. Bimonthly. $5.95/$29.95. Circ.: 240,000. Rick Boychuk, Editor. **Description:** Covers the Canadian landscape, its nature and peoples. **Nonfiction:** On interesting places, nature, and wildlife in Canada. Pay varies. **Art:** Yes. **Queries:** Required. **E-queries:**

Yes. **Unsolicited mss:** Does not accept. **Response:** 3 months, SASE. **Rights:** 1st. **Payment:** On publication.

CANADIAN WILDLIFE

11450 Albert Hudon, Montreal North, Quebec, Canada H1G 3J9. Martin Silverstone. **Description:** On national and international wildlife issues. **Nonfiction:** On wild areas, nature-related research, endangered species, wildlife management, land-use issues, character profiles, and science and politics of conservation; 1,500-2,500 words; pays $500-$1,600 (Canadian). **Columns, Departments:** Backyard Habitat, Last Call, Species at Risk, Book Reviews; 150-500 words; pays $50-$100. **Queries:** Preferred. **Payment:** On publication. *No recent report.*

THE COUNTRY CONNECTION

Pinecone Publishing, 691 Pine Crest Rd., Boulter, ON, Canada K0L 1G0. 613-332-3651. E-mail: magazine@pinecone.on.ca. Web site: www.pinecone.on.ca. Biannual. $3.95. Circ.: 10,000. Gus Zylstra, Editor. **Description:** Pro-nature, for Ontario. Focuses on nature, heritage, the arts. **Tips:** Canadian material only. **Queries:** Not necessary. **E-queries:** Yes. **Unsolicited mss:** Accepts. **Response:** Queries 1 week, submissions to 6 months, SASE (Canadian postage). **Freelance Content:** 75%. **Rights:** 1st. **Payment:** On publication.

THE DOLPHIN LOG

Cousteau Society, 3612 E. Tremont Ave., Bronx, NY 10465-2022. 718-409-3370. Lisa Rao, Editor. **Description:** On a variety of topics related to our global water system (marine biology, ecology, natural history, and water-related subjects, for 7-13-year-olds). **Nonfiction:** Articles, 400-600 words; pays $50-$200. **Queries:** Preferred. **Payment:** On publication.

E MAGAZINE

Earth Action Network
P.O. Box 5098, 28 Knight Street, Norwalk, CT 06851. 203-854-5559. E-mail: info@emagazine.com. Web site: www.emagazine.com. Semi-annual. $3.95/issue, $20/year. Circ.: 50,000. Jim Motavalli, Editor. **Description:** "The environmental magazine." Focuses on environmental concerns. **Nonfiction:** Features and short pieces, on environmental issues (community gardens, mass transit, global warming, activism, trends, etc.); 400-4,200 words. **Columns, Departments:** Your Health, Money Matters, Eating Right, Going Green, House and Home, Consumer News; 750-1,200 words. **Art:** Color. Send stock list only, or upon request. **Tips:** Must be objective reporting, include quoted sources and end-of-article contact information. Sample copy, $5. **Queries:** Preferred. **E-queries:** Yes. **Unsolicited mss:** Accepts. **Freelance Content:** 60%. **Rights:** 1st. **Payment:** On publication.

ENVIRONMENT

1319 18th St. NW, Washington, DC 20036-1802. 202-296-6267.
E-mail: env@heldref.org. Web site: www.heldref.org. 10x/yr. $4.95/issue. Circ.: 8,000.
Barbara T. Richman, Managing Editor. **Description:** Solid analysis of environmental science and policy issues. **Nonfiction:** On major scientific and policy issues of a significant topic; concise, objective, accurate, jargon-free; use graphics and sidebars for key points; 2,500-4,000 words. **Fillers:** Cartoons; $50. **Columns, Departments:** Education, energy, economics, public opinion; 1,000-1,700 words; $100. **Tips:** Avoid news and feature formats. **Queries:** Required. **E-queries:** Yes. **Unsolicited mss:** Accepts. **Response:** 6-8 weeks, SASE not required. **Freelance Content:** 98%. **Rights:** 1st. **Payment:** On publication.

FLORIDA WILDLIFE

620 S. Meridian St., Tallahassee, FL 32399-1600. 850-488-5563.
Web site: www.floridawildlifemagazine.com. Bimonthly. Dick Sublette, Editor. **Description:** Published by Florida Fish and Wildlife Conservation Commission. **Nonfiction:** Articles, 800-1,200 words, that promote native flora and fauna, hunting, fishing in Florida's waters, outdoor ethics, and conservation of natural resources. Pays $55/page. **Payment:** On publication.

HIGH COUNTRY NEWS

Box 1090, Paonia, CO 81428. 970-527-4898.
E-mail: betsym@hcn.org. Web site: www.hcn.org. Biweekly. $32/year. Circ.: 22,000.
Betsy Marston, Editor. **Description:** Western environmental and public lands issues, management, rural community, and natural resource issues; profiles of innovators; western politics. **Nonfiction:** Articles (2,000 words) and roundups (750 words). **Art:** b/w photos. **Queries:** Preferred. **E-queries:** Yes. **Unsolicited mss:** Accepts. **Freelance Content:** 90%. **Payment:** On publication.

THE ILLINOIS STEWARD

1102 S. Goodwin, W503 Turner Hall, Urbana, IL 61801. 217-333-2778.
Web site: ilsteward.nres.uiuc.edu. Phyllis Picklesimer, Editor. **Description:** On Illinois history and heritage, with natural-resource stewardship theme. No payment. **Nonfiction:** Articles, 1,700-1,800 words. **Queries:** Preferred.

INTERNATIONAL WILDLIFE

National Wildlife Federation, 11100 Wildlife Center Dr.,
Reston, VA 20190-5362. 703-438-6510.
E-mail: pubs@nwf.org. Web site: www.nwf.org. Bimonthly. $26 (members). Circ.: 160,000. Jonathan Fisher, Editor. **Description:** Published by National Wildlife Federation. Covers wildlife, conservation, and environmental issues outside the U.S. **Nonfiction:** Articles on nature, and human use and stewardship of it; buys species profiles and status reports, on-scene issue pieces, personality profiles, science stories; 1,200-2,000 words; $800-$2,200. **Art:** 35mm; $300 up. **Tips:** Visually oriented; consider photo potential of story ideas. **Queries:** Required. **E-queries:** Yes.

Unsolicited mss: Does not accept. **Response:** 4 weeks, SASE required. **Freelance Content:** 85%. **Rights:** Exclusive 1st-time worldwide rights; non-exclusive worldwide thereafter. **Payment:** On acceptance.

MOTHER EARTH NEWS

P.O. Box 56302, Boulder, CO 80322. 800-234-3368. E-mail: letters@motherearthnews.com. Web site: www.motherearthnews.com. Bimonthly. Circ.: 450,000. Matthew Scanlon, Editor. **Description:** Helps readers become more self-sufficient, financially independent, and environmentally aware. For rural and urban readers: home improvements, how-tos, indoor and outdoor gardening, health, food, ecology, energy, and consumerism. **Nonfiction:** Articles on organic gardening, building projects, herbal or home remedies, alternative energy projects, wild foods, and environment and conservation; pay varies. **Art:** Photos, diagrams. **Payment:** On publication.

NATIONAL GEOGRAPHIC

1145 17th St. NW, Washington, DC 20036. 202-857-7868. E-mail: opayne@ngs.org. Web site: nationalgeographic.com. Monthly. $3.95/$29 year. Circ.: 7,800,000. William Allen, Editor-in-Chief. **Description:** On geography, world cultures, and environmental conservation. **Nonfiction:** First-person, general-interest, heavily illustrated articles on science, natural history, exploration, and geographical regions. **Tips:** 40% staff-written; balance by published authors. **Queries:** Required. **E-queries:** No. **Unsolicited mss:** Does not accept. **Response:** 4 weeks, SASE. **Freelance Content:** 70%. **Rights:** One-time worldwide serial, plus secondary NGS rights. **Payment:** On publication. **Contact:** Oliver Payne, Sr. Editor, Manuscripts.

NATIONAL GEOGRAPHIC WORLD

1145 17th St. NW, Washington, DC 20036-4688. 202-857-7729. E-mail: jajnone@ngs.org. Web site: www.national geographic.com/world. Monthly. $17.95/year. Circ.: 770,000. Melina Bellows, Chief Editor. **Description:** For kids, ages 8-14, who dare to explore. Seeks to increase geographic awareness by inspiring young readers' curiosity, with big, bold photos and fun, fact-filled stories. **Nonfiction:** Adventure, outdoors, sports, geography, history, archaeology, paleontology, human interest, natural history, science, technology, "My World" (stories on lives of remarkable kids; "Friends USA" (on groups of kids doing things together); 400-1,200 words; $.80-$1/word. **Fillers:** Just Joking, Fun Stuff (games, laughs, things to do); $.80-$1/word. **Columns, Departments:** World News (short, fun news items with kid appeal), Kids Did It! (achievements), Amazing Animals; 50-150 words; $.80-$1/word. **Art:** Yes. **Tips:** Send relevant clips with cover letter; research magazine first. **Queries:** Required. **E-queries:** No. **Unsolicited mss:** Does not accept. **Response:** 2 months, SASE. **Freelance Content:** 90%. **Rights:** All. **Payment:** On publication. **Contact:** Julie Agnone, Exec. Ed.

NATIONAL PARKS

1300 19th St., NW, Suite 300, Washington, DC 20036. 202-223-6722. E-mail: npmag@npca.org. Web site: www.npca.org. Bimonthly. $2.50. Circ.: 400,000. Linda M. Rancourt, Editor. **Description:** Covers areas within the National Park System. **Nonfiction:** Articles, 1,500-2,000 words, on National Park areas, proposed new areas, threats to parks or wildlife, new trends in use, legislative issues, endangered species. **Tips:** Write for non-scientific but well-educated audience. Be specific, with descriptive details and quotes. No "My Trip to . . ." stories. **Queries:** Required. **E-queries:** Yes. **Unsolicited mss:** Does not accept. **Response:** 2 months, SASE. **Freelance Content:** 60%. **Rights:** FNASR. **Payment:** On acceptance.

NATURE FRIEND

2727 TR 421, Sugarcreek, OH 44681. 330-852-1900. Monthly. Circ.: 9,000. Marvin Wengerd, Owner/Editor. **Description:** Stories, puzzles, activities, experiments about nature for children. **Nonfiction:** Articles for children that teach them to be kind to animals, plants, and nature, increase their awareness of God, and illustrate spiritual lessons; $.05/word. **Fillers:** Fillers and games; $15. **Tips:** Sample issues, $5.

THE NEW YORK STATE CONSERVATIONIST

50 Wolf Rd., Rm. 548, Albany, NY 12233-4502. 518-457-5547. E-mail: dhnleson@gw.dec.state.ny.us. Web site: www.dec.state.ny.us. Bi-monthly. $12. Circ.: 100,000. David H. Nelson, Editor. **Description:** Published by New York State Dept. of Environmental Conservation. **Nonfiction:** Articles on environmental/conservation programs and policies of New York; pays $50-$100. **Columns, Departments:** Books, letters. **Art:** Transparencies, photos, slides; $50. **Queries:** Preferred. **Payment:** On publication.

ORION AFIELD

Orion Society, 195 Main St., Great Barrington, MA 01230. 413-528-4422. E-mail: orion@orionsociety.org. Web site: www.orionsociety.org/afield.html. Quarterly. $4 issue. Circ.: 13,000. Jennifer Sahn. **Description:** Stories and profiles of organizations and individuals exploring new models for effecting change through grassroots and community-building work. **Nonfiction:** Portraits of extraordinary individuals; conservation, restoration, education, and environmental success stories; 750-2,400 words; manuscripts longer than 4,000 words may not be considered; $0.10/word. **Poetry:** Submit up to 8 poems, on issue's theme; $100/poem. **Columns, Departments:** Opinion pieces; book reviews (including manuals, field guides, curriculum); 750 words; $0.10/word. **Tips:** Contact for upcoming themes. **Queries:** Not necessary. **E-queries:** No. **Unsolicited mss:** Accepts. **Response:** 10-12 weeks, SASE. **Freelance Content:** 20%. **Rights:** FNASR. **Payment:** On publication. **Contact:** Dianna Downing.

OUTDOOR AMERICA

Izaak Walton League of America, 707 Conservation Ln., Gaithersburg, MD 20878-2983. 301-548-0150. E-mail: zachh@iwla.org. Web site: www.iwla.org. Quarterly. Circ.: 50,000. Zachary Hoskins, Editor. **Description:** Publication of the Izaak Walton League of America. Covers national conservation issues that are top priorities of the league. **Nonfiction:** On endangered species, public lands management, and the protection of air quality, water quality and water resources. Also, farm-related issues, wildlife and fisheries management controversies of national interest; 1,500-3,000 words; $.30/word. **Tips:** Send clips. **Queries:** Preferred. **Response:** SASE required.

RANGE

106 E. Adams, Suite 201, Carson City, NV 89706. 775-884-2200. E-mail: cj@range.carsoncity.nu.us. Web site: www.rangemagazine.com. Quarterly. $3.95/$19.95. Circ.: 21,000. Caroline Joy Hadley, Editor. **Description:** No stranger to controversy, Range is a forum for viewpoints, seeking solutions to halt the depletion of a national resource: the American cowboy. Devoted to issues that threaten the West, its people, lifestyles, rangelands, and wildlife. **Nonfiction:** Feature articles; 1,500-1,800. **Poetry:** Short; $40-$75. **Columns, Departments:** Red Meat Survivors (500 words, interviews with oldtimers, including historic/current photos); 500 words; $100-$150. **Art:** Original illustrations, slides, high-quality prints; $40-$150. **Tips:** Submit concise, colorful pieces that address issues affecting those who live on and work the land. Avoid academic, overly technical. **Queries:** Preferred. **E-queries:** Yes. **Unsolicited mss:** Accepts. **Response:** Queries 4 weeks, submissions 4-8 weeks, SASE. **Freelance Content:** 90%. **Rights:** 1st NA. **Payment:** On publication.

SIERRA

85 2nd St., 2nd Fl., San Francisco, CA 94105-3441. E-mail: sierra.letters@sierraclub.org. Web site: www.sierraclub.org. Bi-monthly. $2.95/issue. Circ.: 570,000. Joan Hamilton, Editor. **Description:** Environmental publication of the Sierra Club, with outstanding nature photography and outdoor recreation and travel information. **Fiction:** Outdoors stories that also deal with environmental politics/issues. **Nonfiction:** Stories on nature and environmental issues; 100-4,000 words; $1/word. **Columns, Departments:** what you can do in your home to make the environment safer; visiting a wild place; environmental problems, policy, etc.; 750-1,500 words; $1/word. **Queries:** Required. **E-queries:** Accepts. **Unsolicited mss:** Accepts. **Response:** 6 weeks. **Freelance Content:** 70%. **Rights:** FNASR and electronic. **Payment:** On acceptance.

TEXAS PARKS & WILDLIFE

Fountain Park Plaza, 3000 S. Interstate Hwy. 35, Suite 120, Austin, TX 78704. 512-912-7000. E-mail: magazine@tpwd.state.tx.us. Web site: www.tpwmagazine.com. Monthly. Circ.: 150,000. Susan Ebert. **Description:** Promotes conservation and enjoyment of Texas wildlife, parks, waters, and all outdoors. **Nonfiction:** Features on hunting, fishing, birding, camping, and the environment. Photos a plus; 400-1,500 words; $.30-$.50/word. **Payment:** On acceptance.

VIRGINIA WILDLIFE
P.O. Box 11104, Richmond, VA 23230-1104.
E-mail: lwalker@dgif.state.va.us. Web site: www.dgif.state.va.us. **Description:** On fishing, hunting, wildlife management, outdoor safety and ethics; with Virginia tie-in. **Nonfiction:** Articles, 500-1,200 words, may be accompanied by color photos; pays from $.18/word, extra for photos. **Queries:** Preferred. **Payment:** On publication. *No recent report.*

WHOLE EARTH
1408 Mission Ave., San Rafael, CA 94901. 415-256-2800.
E-mail: editor@wholeearthmag.com. Web site: www.wholeearthmag.com. Quarterly. Circ.: 30,000. Peter Warshall, Editor. **Description:** Covers issues related to the environment and conservation. **Nonfiction:** Articles; pay varies. Book reviews, $40. **Tips:** Good article material can be found in passionate personal statements or descriptions of the writer's activities in this area. **Queries:** Preferred. **Payment:** On publication.

WILD OUTDOOR WORLD
Box 1329, Helena, MT 59624. 406-449-1335.
E-mail: wowgirl@uswest.net. Web site: www.wowmag.com. Carolyn Cunningham. **Description:** On North American wildlife, for readers ages 8-12. **Nonfiction:** Articles, 600-800 words; pays $100-$300. **Queries:** Preferred. **Payment:** On acceptance.

WILDLIFE CONSERVATION
2300 Southern Blvd., Bronx, NY 10460. 718-220-5898.
E-mail: jdowns@wcs.org. Web site: www.wcs.org. Bimonthly. $24.95/yr. Circ.: 154,000. Joan Downs, Editor. **Description:** Popular natural history. First-person articles, based on authors' research and experience. **Nonfiction:** Include personal observations; weave in atmosphere, sights, sounds, smells, colors, weather; if pertinent, include your own feelings; 1,500-2,000 words; $1,500-$2,000. **Columns, Departments:** Wild places; 1,200 words; $750-$1,200. **Art:** 35mm color slides. **Tips:** Contribute short news items for Conservation Hotline. **Queries:** Required. **E-queries:** Yes. **Unsolicited mss:** Accepts. **Response:** 1 month, SASE. **Freelance Content:** 75%. **Rights:** 1st NA. **Payment:** On acceptance.

ETHNIC & MULTICULTURAL

AFRICAN VOICES
270 W. 96th St., New York, NY 10025. 212-865-2982.
E-mail: africanvoices@aol.com. Web site: www.africanvoices.com. Quarterly. $3/$12. Circ.: 20,000. Carolyn A. Butts, Editor. **Description:** Literary magazine for fiction,

nonfiction, poetry, and visual arts created by people of color. **Fiction:** Humorous, erotic, and dramatic fiction by ethnic writers. All themes, subjects, and styles, emphasis on style and technique; 500-2,000 words. **Nonfiction:** Investigative articles, artist profiles, essays, book reviews, and first-person narratives; 500-2,500 words. **Poetry:** All styles; avant-garde, free verse, haiku, light verse, traditional. Submit up to 5 poems; max. 3 pages. **Columns, Departments:** Book reviews; 500-1,200 words. **Art:** b/w. **Queries:** Preferred. **E-queries:** Accepts. **Unsolicited mss:** Accepts. **Response:** Queries 3 weeks, submissions 6-8 weeks, SASE. **Freelance Content:** 80%. **Rights:** 1st American. **Payment:** in copies. **Contact:** Kim Horne, fiction; Layding Kalbia, poetry; Debbie Officer, book reviews.

AIM

1704 Alder, Milton, WA 98354. 253-952-3930.
E-mail: ruthone@earthlink.net. Web site: www.aimmagazine.org. Quarterly. $3/issue. Circ.: 7,000. Dr. Myron Apilado, Editor. **Description:** "Our purpose is to fight racism." **Fiction:** Short stories, reflecting that people from different backgrounds are more alike than different. "Do not moralize"; 3,500; $25-$100. **Nonfiction:** 1,000-1,500; $15-$25. **Poetry:** 20 lines; $5. **Fillers:** 30 words; $5. **Columns, Departments:** 1,500 words; $15. **Art:** Images promoting racial equality; $10. **Tips:** Write about your experiences. **Queries:** Not necessary. **E-queries:** No. **Unsolicited mss:** Accepts. **Response:** 1 month, SASE required. **Freelance Content:** 75%. **Rights:** 1st. **Payment:** On publication. **Contact:** Ruth Apilado, P.O. Box 1174, Maywood, IL 60153.

ALBERTA SWEETGRASS

Aboriginal Multi-Media Society of Alberta, 15001 112th Ave., Edmonton, Alberta, Canada T5M 2V6. 800-661-5469.
Web site: www.ammsa.com. **Description:** Covers Native topics, with an Alberta angle. **Nonfiction:** Articles, 100-1,000 words (prefers 500-800 words; briefs, 100-150 words): features, profiles, and community-based topics.

AMERICAN INDIAN ART

7314 E. Osborn Dr., Scottsdale, AZ 85251. 480-994-5445.
Roanne P. Goldfein, Editor. **Description:** Detailed articles, on American Indian arts: painting, carving, beadwork, basketry, textiles, ceramics, jewelry, etc. **Nonfiction:** 10-20 double-spaced pages; pay varies. **Queries:** Preferred. **Payment:** On publication.

AMERICAN LEGACY

60 Fifth Ave., New York, NY 10011. 212-620-2200.
E-mail: amlegacy@americanheritage.com.
Web site: www.americanlegacymagazine.com. Quarterly. $2.95/$9.95. Circ.: 500,000. Audrey Peterson, Editor. **Description:** Covers all aspects of Black history and culture. **Nonfiction:** Articles on people and events that have shaped history for African-Americans; up to 4,000 words; pay negotiable. **Tips:** No lifestyle articles, or features on contemporary figures in the black community, unless they have something to do with history. Keep proposals to 1 page, plus 1-page cover letter. **Queries:** Required.

E-queries: Yes. **Unsolicited mss:** Accepts. **Response:** 2 months, SASE. **Freelance Content:** 95%. **Payment:** On acceptance.

AMERICAN VISIONS
1101 Pennsylvania Ave NW, Suite 820, Washington, DC 20004. 202-347-3820. E-mail: editor@avs.americanvisions.com. Web site: www.americanvisions.com. Bimonthly. Circ.: 125,000. Joanne Harris, Editor. **Description:** African-American culture, with focus on the arts. **Nonfiction:** Articles; 1,500-2,500 words; pays $100-$600. **Columns, Departments:** Columns; 1,000 words; Varies. **Queries:** Required. **Payment:** On publication.

AMERICAS
1889 F St. N.W., Washington, DC 20006. 202-458-3510. E-mail: americas@oas.org. Web site: www.oas.org. James Patrick Kiernan, Director. **Description:** Features, on Latin America and the Caribbean. Wide focus: anthropology, the arts, travel, science, and development. **Nonfiction:** 2,500-4,000 words; pays from $400. **Tips:** Prefers stories that can be well-illustrated. No political material. **Payment:** On publication. **Contact:** Rebecca Read Medrano, Managing Ed.

ASIAN PACIFIC AMERICAN JOURNAL
16 W. 32nd St., Suite 10A, New York, NY 10001. 212-494-0061 E-mail: desk@aaww.org. Web site: www.aaww.org. Hanya Yanagihara. **Description:** Short stories, also excerpts from longer fiction works by emerging or established Asian American writers. **Poetry:** Submit up to 10 poems. **Tips:** Send 4 copies of each piece submitted, in all genres. **Queries:** Preferred. **Payment:** in copies.

AVANCE HISPANO
4230 Mission St., San Francisco, CA 94112-1520. 415-585-1080. Bi-monthly. Circ.: 45,000. **Description:** Spanish-language publication for people in the San Francisco Bay area.

BET WEEKEND
One BET Plaza, 1900 W. Place NE, Washington, DC 20018-1211. Web site: www.msbet.com. **Description:** On lifestyle, arts, education, and entertainment of the African-American community. **Nonfiction:** Articles, 200-500 words; pays $.50-$1.00/word. **Tips:** Do not send manuscript; query first with SASE. **Payment:** On publication.

BLACK COLLEGIAN
140 Carondelet St., New Orleans, LA 70130. 504-523-0154 ext. 234. E-mail: robert@iminorities.com. Web site: www.black-collegian.com. Biannually (Oct. & Feb.). Circ.: 109,000. Robert G. Miller, Editor. **Description:** Career and self-development for African-American college students (juniors and seniors). Also read by faculty, career counselors, and placement directors. **Nonfiction:** Features on entry-level career opportunities, job search process, how to prepare for entry-

level positions, and culture and experiences of African-American collegians; 1,500-2,000 words. **Tips:** Personalize your article; use "you" rather than the impersonal "college students." Most articles are assigned; will consider ideas with a brief, detailed query letter to the editor. **Queries:** Required. **E-queries:** Yes. **Unsolicited mss:** Accepts. **Response:** Queries 1 week. **Freelance Content:** 90%. **Rights:** 1st. **Payment:** On publication.

BLACK ELEGANCE

475 Park Ave. S., 8th Floor, New York, NY 10016. 212-689-2830.
Sonia Alleyne, Editor. **Description:** On fashion, beauty, relationships, home design, careers, personal finance, and personalities, for black women ages 25-45. Also, short interviews. **Nonfiction:** Articles; 1,000-2,000 words; pays $150-$225. **Tips:** Include photos if available. **Queries:** Preferred. **Payment:** On publication.

BLACK ENTERPRISE

130 Fifth Ave., 10th Floor, New York, NY 10011. 212-242-8000.
Web site: www.blackenterprise.com. Alfred Edmond, Editor-in-Chief. **Description:** Articles on money management, careers, political issues, entrepreneurship, high technology, and lifestyles for black professionals. Also, profiles. **Queries:** Preferred. **Payment:** On acceptance.

BLACK ENTERPRISE FOR TEENS

Earl G. Graves Publishing Co., 130 5th Ave., 10th Floor,
New York, NY 10011. 212-242-8000.
6x/year. Circ.: 4,000. **Description:** For African-American teens interested in business.

BLACK ISSUES IN HIGHER EDUCATION

10520 Warwick Ave., Suite B-8, Fairfax, VA 22030-3136. 703-385-2981.
E-mail: hilary@cmcbiccw.com. Web site: www.blackissues.com. Biweekly. $3.50 issue $26/year. Circ.: 12,000. Hilary L. Hurd, Editor. **Description:** News and features on blacks in post-secondary education and public policy. **Nonfiction:** On issues affecting minorities in higher education. **Fillers:** On education and public policy. **Columns, Departments:** Opinion pieces. **Queries:** Preferred. **E-queries:** Yes. **Unsolicited mss:** Accepts. **Freelance Content:** 40%. **Payment:** On publication.

BLACK ROMANCE

233 Park Ave. S., New York, NY 10003. 212-780-3500.
E-mail: jivemagazine@yahoo.com. Bimonthly. $2.50. Circ.: 50,000. Takesha D. Powell, Editor. **Description:** Short romantic fiction for African-American women. **Fiction:** Romance fiction, first-person, featuring African-American women; 19-21 pages; pay varies. **Nonfiction:** On relationships. **Columns, Departments:** On spicing up romance/sex lives for couples; tips on dating, beauty; 3 pages; $125. **Tips:** Avoid cultural stereotypes. Stories should be juicy (mild sex scenes), romantic, but not offensive. **Queries:** Not necessary. **E-queries:** Yes. **Unsolicited mss:** Accepts.

Response: 3-4 weeks, SASE. **Freelance Content:** 100%. **Rights:** All. **Payment:** On publication.

BLACK SECRETS
Sterling MacFadden, 233 Park Ave. South, 6th Fl., New York, NY 10003. 212-780-3500. E-mail: jpestaina@sterlingmacfadden.com. Web site: www.sterlingmacfadden.com. Monthly. Circ.: 65,000. Takesha Powell, Editor. **Description:** Erotic, short, romantic fiction for African-American women. **Queries:** Required. **E-queries:** Yes. **Unsolicited mss:** Accepts. **Freelance Content:** 100%. **Rights:** All. **Payment:** On publication.

BLACKLINES
2011 Newkirk Ave., Suite 7D, Brooklyn, NY 11226. 718-703-8000. E-mail: kathleen@blacklines.net. Web site: www.blacklines.net. Quarterly. Carla Robinson, Managing Editor. **Description:** Features black designers in architecture, interior design, construction, development and the arts. Challenges traditional ideas and perceptions, offers a context for design and a means to exchange ideas and information. **Tips:** Send cover letter and resumé for consideration, with 2-5 clips that show your ability to interview diverse subjects. **Queries:** Preferred. **E-queries:** Yes. **Unsolicited mss:** Accepts.

BLUES ACCESS
1455 Chestnut Place, Boulder, CO 80304-3153. 303-443-7245. Web site: www.bluesaccess.com. Quarterly. Circ.: 25,000. Peter Kuykendall, Editor. **Description:** Resource of Blues music, artists, festivals, and more. For fans and professional musicians.

BRAZZIL
2039 N Ave 52, Los Angeles, CA 90042. 323-255-8062. E-mail: brazzil@brazzil.com. Web site: www.brazzil.com. Monthly. $2/issue. Circ.: 12,000. Rodney Mello, Editor. **Description:** English language, on Brazilian politics, way of life, economy, ecology, tourism, music, literature, and the arts. Some short stories in Portuguese. **Fiction:** 1,000-5,000 words. **Nonfiction:** 1,000-5,000 words. **Tips:** Liberal viewpoint; controversial material preferred. **Queries:** Not necessary. **E-queries:** Yes. **Unsolicited mss:** Accepts. **Response:** Queries 2 days, submission 2 days, SASE. **Freelance Content:** 60%. **Rights:** One-time. **Payment:** On publication.

CALLALOO
Univ. of Virginia, Dept. of English, 322 Bryan Hall, P.O. Box 400121, Charlottesville, VA 22904-4121. 804-924-6637. E-mail: callaloo@virginia.edu. Web site: www.people.virginia.edu. Quarterly. $10/issue, $36/year. Circ.: 2,000. Charles H. Rowell, Editor. **Description:** African-American and Africa diaspora literary journal, with original work and critical studies

of black writers worldwide. **Fiction:** Fiction, drama, critical studies, bibliographies; on African-American, Caribbean, and African Diaspora artists and writers; 2,500-5,000 words. **Nonfiction:** Features on theme content; 5,000-7,500 words. **Poetry:** Up to 300 lines. **Queries:** Not necessary. **E-queries:** Yes. **Unsolicited mss:** Accepts. **Response:** Submissions 6-8 months, SASE required. **Freelance Content:** 50%. **Payment:** in copies.

CATHOLIC NEAR EAST

1011 First Ave., New York, NY 10022-4195. 212-826-1480. Web site: www.cnewa.org. Bimonthly. $2.50 issue $12.00/year. Circ.: 90,000. Michael La Civita, Executive Editor. **Description:** Offers educational profiles of cultures, histories, religions, and social issues of the peoples of Eastern Europe, India, the Middle East and Northeast Africa. **Nonfiction:** 1,500 words; $.20/word. **Art:** Slides, prints; $50 and up. **Tips:** Writers and photographers in each Pontifical Mission city and in other CNEWA countries offer the most objective, accurate, sensitive portraits of their subjects. **Queries:** Preferred. **Unsolicited mss:** Accepts. **Response:** SASE required. **Payment:** On publication.

THE CRISIS

P.O. Box 26616, Baltimore, MD 21707; or 4805 Mt. Hope Dr. Baltimore, MD 21215. Web site: www.naacp.org. Ida Lewis, Editor-in-Chief. **Description:** On the arts, civil rights, and problems and achievements of blacks and other minorities. **Nonfiction:** Articles, to 1,500 words; pays $75-$500. **Payment:** On acceptance.

DIRECT AIM

3100 Broadway, 660 Pen Tower, Kansas City, MO 64111-2413. 816-960-1988. Quarterly. Michelle Paige, Editor. **Description:** For African-American and Hispanic students in colleges, universities, and junior colleges. **Nonfiction:** Topics include career preparation, college profiles, financial-aid sources, and interviews with college students across the U.S.; pay varies. **Queries:** Required.

EMERGE

1900 W. Place NE, 1 BET Plaza, Washington, DC 20018. 202-608-2093. E-mail: emergemag@msbet.com. Web site: www.emergemag.com. Monthly. Circ.: 200,000. Florestine Purnell, Managing Editor. **Description:** Newsmagazine, for successful, well-informed African-Americans. **Nonfiction:** Articles on current issues, ideas, or news personalities; 1,200 to 2,000 words; $.50/word. **Columns, Departments:** Varied subjects; 650-700 words. **Queries:** Required. **Payment:** On publication.

ESSENCE

1500 Broadway, New York, NY 10036. 212-642-0600. E-mail: info@essence.com. Web site: www.essence.com. Monthly. Circ.: 1,000,000. Monique Greenwood, Editor-in-Chief. **Description:** Multicultural publication focusing on black women in America today. **Fiction:** 800-2,500 words. **Nonfiction:**

Provocative articles: self-help, how-to, business/finance, work, parenting, health, celebrity profiles, art, travel, political issues; 800-2,500 words; pay varies. **Queries:** Required.

FACES

Cobblestone Publishing, 30 Grove St., Suite C, Peterborough, NH 03458-1454. 603-924-7209. E-mail: facesmag@yahoo.com. Web site: www.cobblestonepub.com. 9x/year. $29.95/year. Circ.: 11,000. Elizabeth Crooker Carpentiere, Editor. **Description:** Introduces young readers to different world cultures or regions. **Fiction:** Retold folktales, legends, plays; must relate to theme; up to 800 words; $.20-$.25/word. **Nonfiction:** In-depth articles on aspect of featured culture; interviews and personal accounts; 600-800 words; $.20-$.25/word. **Fillers:** Activities (crafts, recipes, word puzzles); 100-600 words. **Art:** 35mm; $25-$100. **Tips:** Avoid judgmental tone; give readers a clear image of life in other cultures. Check website for coming themes. **Queries:** Required. **E-queries:** Yes. **Unsolicited mss:** Accepts. **Response:** Queries, 4 weeks, submissions, 4 months, SASE required. **Freelance Content:** 80%. **Rights:** All. **Payment:** On publication.

FILIPINAS

363 El Camino Real, Suite 100, S. San Francisco, CA 94080. 650-872-8660. E-mail: myuchengco@filipinasmag.com. Web site: www.filipinasmag.com. Monthly. $2.95/issue, $18/year. Circ.: 30,000. Mona Lisa Yuchengco, Editor. **Description:** For and about Filipinas and their communities. **Nonfiction:** Profiles on successful Filipino Americans, human-interest stories, issues affecting the Filipino American community; 750-3,000; $50-$100. **Art:** color photo, $25; b/w, $15. **Queries:** Not necessary. **E-queries:** Yes. **Unsolicited mss:** Accepts. **Response:** SASE. **Freelance Content:** 70%. **Rights:** All. **Payment:** On publication.

FOOTSTEPS

Footsteps, 30 Grove St., Suite C, Petersborough, NH 03458. 603-924-7209. E-mail: cfbaker@meganet.com. Web site: www.footstepsmagazine.com. 5x/year. $23.95/yr. Circ.: 3,000. Charles F. Baker, Editor. **Description:** African-American history and heritage for students in grades 4-8. **Fiction:** Authentic retellings of historical and biographical events, adventure, legends; 200-1,000 words; $.20-$.25/word. **Nonfiction:** On issue's theme; 200-1,000 words; $.20-$.25/word. **Art:** Slides, transparencies, digital, prints; pay varies. **Tips:** Contact for upcoming themes. **Queries:** Required. **Unsolicited mss:** Accepts. **Response:** Queries 2-4 months, submissions 2-6 months, SASE. **Freelance Content:** 90%. **Rights:** All. **Payment:** On publication. **Contact:** Charles F. Baker.

GERMAN LIFE

P.O. Box 3000, Denville, NJ 07834. 800-875-2997. E-mail: editor@GermanLife.com. Web site: www.GermanLife.com. Bimonthly. Circ.: 40,000. Carolyn Cook, Editor. **Description:** German culture, its past and present, and how America has been influenced by its German immigrants: history, travel, people, the arts, and social and political issues. **Fillers:** Short pieces and fillers; 50-200 words; to $80. **Queries:** Preferred. **Payment:** On publication.

GIRL

22 East 49th St., New York, NY 10017. 212-843-4038.
Web site: www.girlzine.com. Bimonthly. Corynne Corbett, Editorial Director. **Description:** Multicultural appeal for girls of all shapes and sizes. Covers specific interests and needs of African-American teens. Emphasis on girls of color.

GLOBAL CITY REVIEW

Rifkind Ctr. for the Humanties, City College of NY,
138th St. & Convenient Ave., New York, NY 10031.
E-mail: globalcityreview@aol.com. Biannual. Linsey Abrams. **Description:** Intellectual literary forum for women, lesbian, and gay, and other culturally diverse writers; writers of color, international writers, activist writers. Thematic issues. Fiction, nonfiction, and poetry on issues of gender, race, and women's experience. **Tips:** No queries; send complete manuscripts for review. **Payment:** in copies.

GOSPEL TODAY

761 Old Hickory Blvd., Suite 205, Brentwood, TN 37027. 615-376-5656.
E-mail: gospel2day@aol.com. Web site: www.gospeltoday.com. 8x/year. $3/issue, $20/year. Circ.: 50,000. Teresa E. Harris, Editor. **Description:** "America's leading gospel lifestyle magazine," aimed at African-American Christians. **Nonfiction:** Human-interest stories on Christian personalities, events, and testimonials. Book reviews welcome; 1,500-2,000 words; $150-$250. **Columns, Departments:** $50-$75. **Tips:** No opinions, testimonials, or poetry. **Queries:** Required. **E-queries:** Yes. **Unsolicited mss:** Does not accept. **Response:** Queries 6 weeks, SASE required. **Freelance Content:** 60%. **Rights:** All. **Payment:** On publication.

HEALTH QUEST

200 Highpoint Dr., Suite 215, Chalfont, PA 18914. 215-822-7935.
E-mail: editor@healthquestmag.com. Web site: www.healthquestmag.com. Bimonthly. Circ.: 500,000. Hilary Beard, Editor. **Description:** Health and wellness (body, mind, and spirit) for African-Americans. Traditional and alternative medicine. **Nonfiction:** Health articles. **Queries:** Preferred. **E-queries:** No. **Unsolicited mss:** Accepts. **Freelance Content:** 20%. **Payment:** On publication.

HEART & SOUL

BET Publications, 1900 W. Place NE, One BET Plaza,
Washington, DC 20018. 202-608-2241.
E-mail: heart&soul@BET.net. Web site: www.BET.com. Bimonthly. Circ.: 300,000. Yanick Rice Lamb, Editorial Director. **Description:** The African-American woman's ultimate guide to total well-being—body, mind, and spirit. **Nonfiction:** Health,

beauty, fitness, nutrition, and relationships for African-American women; 800-1,500 words; pay varies. **Queries:** Preferred. **Payment:** On acceptance.

HIGHLANDER
560 Green Bay Rd., Suite 204, Winnetka, IL 60093. 847-784-9660. E-mail: sray5617@aol.com. 7x/year. $17.50/year. Circ.: 35,000. Sharon Kennedy Ray, Editor. **Description:** Covers Scottish heritage (history, clans, families), related to Scotland in the period 1300-1900 A.D. **Nonfiction:** 1,500-2,000 words; $185-$250. **Art:** Photos must accompany manuscripts; b/w, color transparencies, maps, line drawings. **Tips:** Not concerned with modern Scotland. **Queries:** Preferred. **E-queries:** No. **Unsolicited mss:** Accepts. **Response:** Queries 1-2 weeks, submissions 1-2 months, SASE required. **Payment:** On acceptance.

HISPANIC
999 Ponce de Leon Blvd., Suite 600, Coral Gables, FL 33134. 305-442-2462. Web site: www.hisp.com. Monthly. Carlos Verdecia, Editor. **Description:** General-interest (career, business, politics, and culture). Confronts issues affecting the Hispanic community, emphasis on solutions rather than problems. English-language. **Nonfiction:** Features, 1,400-2,500 words; $450. **Columns, Departments:** Hispanic Journal, Portfolio; $75-$150. **Queries:** Preferred.

HISPANIC BUSINESS
425 Pine Ave., Santa Barbara, CA 93117-3709. E-mail: jim.medina@hbinc.com. Web site: www.hispanicbusiness.com. Jim Medina, Managing Editor. **Description:** Features a variety of personalities, political agendas, and fascinating stories. **Nonfiction:** Articles; especially on technology and finance issues; $350 (negotiable). **Tips:** Has an ongoing need for experienced freelance writers.

HISPANIC MARKET NEWS
13014 N. Dale Mabry Hwy. #663, Tampa, FL 33618-2808. 813-264-0560. Monthly. Circ.: 20,000. **Description:** For people involved with merchandising to the Hispanic markets. In both English and Spanish.

HISPANIC MONTHLY
3006 Garrow St., Houston, TX 77003-2326. 713-236-8475. Web site: www.hispanicmonthly.com. Monthly. Miguel Barrientos. **Description:** Covers state and national issues of interest to Hispanics living in Texas. **Nonfiction:** Topics include business, community, education, law, politics, also lighter topics such as fashion, entertainment, health and fitness. Pay varies. **Queries:** Preferred.

THE HISPANIC OUTLOOK IN HIGHER EDUCATION
210 Rt. 4 E., Suite 310, Paramus, NJ 07652. 201-587-8800. E-mail: sloutlook@aol.com. Web site: www.Hispanicoutlook.com. Adalyn Hixson, Editor. **Description:** On issues, concerns, and potential models for furthering

academic results of Hispanics in higher education. **Nonfiction:** Articles, 1,500-2,000 words; pay varies. **Queries:** Preferred. **Payment:** On publication.

HISPANIC TIMES

P.O. Box 579, Winchester, CA 92596. 951-926-2119. Web site: www.hispanictimesmag.com. **Description:** For Hispanic professionals and college students. All about careers, businesses, and employment of Hispanics.

HURRICANE ALICE

Rhode Island College, Dept. of English, Providence, RI 02908. 401-456-8377. E-mail: mreddy@ric.edu. Quarterly. $2.50/issue, $12/year. Circ.: 1,000. Maureen Reddy, Editor. **Description:** Feminist exploration, from diverse perspectives, of all aspects of culture. Especially committed to work by women of color, lesbians, working-class women, and young women. **Fiction:** Fictional critiques of culture; 3,500 words max. **Nonfiction:** Articles, essays, interviews, and reviews; 3,500 words max. **Poetry:** Yes. **Art:** b/w (5x7 or 8x10). **Queries:** Not necessary. **E-queries:** Yes. **Unsolicited mss:** Accepts. **Response:** Queries 30 days, submissions 6 months, SASE required. **Freelance Content:** 100%. **Rights:** FNASR. **Payment:** in copies.

IMAGEN: REFLECTIONS OF TODAY'S LATINO

P.O. Box 7487, Albuquerque, NM 87194-7487. 505-889-4088. Web site: www.imagenmag.com. Monthly. **Description:** Focus on New Mexico's Latino community.

INDIA CURRENTS

P.O. Box 21285, San Jose, CA 95151. 408-274-6966. E-mail: editor@indiacurrents.com. Web site: www.indiacurrents.com. 11x/year. $19.95/yr. Circ.: 25,800. Vandana Kumar, Editor. **Description:** Explores the heritage and culture of India. **Fiction:** Max. 3,000 words; $50-$150. **Nonfiction:** Articles on India culture, arts, and entertainment in the U.S. and Canada. Also, music/book reviews, commentary on events affecting the lives of Indians. Travel articles (first-person stories of trips to India or the subcontinent); Max. 3,000 words; $50-$150. **Queries:** Preferred. **E-queries:** Yes. **Unsolicited mss:** Accepts. **Response:** 4 weeks, SASE. **Freelance Content:** 99%. **Rights:** One-time. **Payment:** On publication.

INDIAN LIFE

Box 3765, RPO Redwood Centre, Winnipeg, MB, Canada R2W 3R6. 204-661-9333. E-mail: jim.editor@indianlife.org. Web site: www.indianlife.org. Bimonthly. $10. Circ.: 32,000. Jim Uttley, Editor. **Description:** Presents good news from across Native North America. **Fiction:** Stories which accurately portray Native Americans; 2,000 words; $20-$150. **Nonfiction:** News, first-person, special features, interviews; 500-1,200 words; $20-$150. **Poetry:** 100 words max.; $20-$40. **Fillers:** In good taste; 50-200 words; $10-$25. **Art:** E-mail (.jpeg, 200 dpi); $25-$150. **Tips:** Need to know Native Americans (historical and contemporary). No spirituality, politics, land claims.

Queries: Preferred. **E-queries:** Yes. **Unsolicited mss:** Accepts. **Response:** Queries 4 weeks, submissions 8 weeks, SASE required. **Freelance Content:** 20%. **Rights:** 1st, all. **Payment:** On publication.

IRISH AMERICA

432 Park Ave. S., Suite 1503, New York, NY 10016. 212-725-2993. Web site: www.irishamerica.com. Patricia Harty, Editor. **Description:** For Irish-American audience; prefers history, sports, the arts, and politics. **Nonfiction:** Articles, 1,500-2,000 words; pays $.10/word. **Queries:** Preferred. **Payment:** On publication.

IRISH EDITION

903 E. Willow Grove Ave., Wyndmoor, PA 19038-7909. 215-836-4900. Jane M. Duffin, Editor. **Description:** Short fiction, nonfiction, fillers, humor, and puzzles, for Irish-American and Irish-born readers. Pay negotiable. **Queries:** Preferred. **Payment:** On acceptance.

ITALIAN AMERICA

219 "E" Street NE, Washington, DC 20002-4922. 202-547-2900. Web site: www.uri.edu/prov/italian/italian.html. Quarterly. $12/yr. Circ.: 65,000. C. B. Albright, Editor. **Description:** Published by Sons of Italy in America. Covers Italian-American news, history, personalities, culture, etc. **Nonfiction:** Articles on people, institutions, and events of interest to the Italian-American community. Also book reviews; 1,000-2,500 words; $500-$1,000. **Fillers:** 500-750 words. **Columns, Departments:** Postcard from Italy (on one aspect of travel to Italy), Community Notebook (events, personalities with local Italian-American theme); 500-750 words; $150-$350. **Art:** JPG, TIFF, BMP, etc. **Tips:** Avoid "My grandmother used to spend hours making her spaghetti sauce . . ." Focus on unique, interesting cultural facets. **Queries:** Preferred. **E-queries:** Yes. **Unsolicited mss:** Does not accept. **Response:** 2-3 months. **Freelance Content:** 65%. **Rights:** FNASR. **Payment:** On publication.

JAPANOPHILE

PO Box 7977, 415 N Main St., Ann Arbor, MI 48107. 734-930-1553. E-mail: jpnhane@japanophile.com. Web site: www.japanophile.com. Quarterly. $7/issue. Circ.: 3,000. Susan Aitken, Editor. **Description:** Journal of Japanese culture as it relates to Americans and other non-Japanese persons. **Fiction:** Must involve at least one Japanese and one non-Japanese; 5,000 words max.; $20. **Nonfiction:** Articles about Americans or other non-Japanese interested in Japan. **Poetry:** Either poems whose subjects deal with Japanese culture in some way; or haiku, tauka, or other Japanese forms. **Fillers:** Must relate to Japanese culture. **Art:** Yes. **Queries:** Not necessary. **E-queries:** Yes. **Unsolicited mss:** Accepts. **Response:** 2 months, SASE required. **Freelance Content:** 85%. **Rights:** 1st NA. **Payment:** On publication.

JIVE
Sterling MacFadden
233 Park Ave. South, 6th Fl, New York, NY 10003. 212-780-3500.
E-mail: jpestaina@sterlingmacfadden.com. Web site: www.sterlingmacfadden.com.
Monthly. Circ.: 60,000. Takesha Powell, Editor. **Description:** Romantic fiction for
African-American women. **Fiction:** Focus on emotions of main character; pays
$100-$125. **Queries:** Required. **E-queries:** Yes. **Unsolicited mss:** Accepts.
Freelance Content: 100%. **Rights:** All. **Payment:** On publication.

JOURNAL OF ASIAN MARTIAL ARTS
Via Media Publishing, 821 W. 24th St., Erie, PA 16502. 814-455-9517.
Web site: www.ncinter.net/~viamedia. Quarterly. Michael A. DeMarco, Editor.
Description: On martial arts and Asian culture: interviews (with scholars, master
practitioners, etc.) and scholarly articles based on primary research in key disciplines
(cultural anthropology, comparative religion, etc.). **Nonfiction:** Articles, 2,000-
10,000 words; pays $150-$500. **Columns, Departments:** Reviews, 1,000 words, of
books and audiovisual material; pays in copies. **Payment:** On publication.

JUBILEE
3600 Clipper Mill Rd., Ste. 115, Baltimore, MD 21211. 410-366-7512.
Monthly. Circ.: 90,000. **Description:** For African-American families in the
Baltimore metro area.

LA FACTORIA DE SONIDO
Barrera Publishing, 43 West 38th St., Fl. 5, New York, NY 10018. 212-840-0227.
Web site: www.lafactoriadesonido.com. Bimonthly. Circ.: 110,000. Jennifer Barrera,
Executive Editor. **Description:** Hispanic music and art publication. Music events,
reviews, interviews, fashion and clubs focusing on Hispanic music of all kinds.

LATIN STYLE MAGAZINE
P.O. Box 2969, Venice, CA 90294-2969. 323-462-4409.
Web site: www.latinstylemag.com. Monthly. Circ.: 1,000,000. **Description:** Focuses
on the Hispanic community; printed in English.

LATIN TRADE
Freedom Communications, Inc.
95 Merrick Way, Ste 600, Coral Gables, FL 33134-5311. 305-358-8373.
Web site: www.latintrade.com. **Description:** For business persons in Latin America.
Covers a wide variety of topics relating to trade, markets, research, technology and
investments.

LATINA
1500 Broadway, Ste 600, New York, NY 10036-4015. 212-642-0200.
Web site: www.latina.com. Monthly. Circ.: 170,000. **Description:** For Hispanic
women living in the U.S.

LATINGIRL

70 Hudson Street, 5th Floor, Hoboken, NJ 07030. 201-876-9600. E-mail: editor@latingirlmag.com. Web site: www.latingirlmag.com. Bi-monthly. $2.95 issue, $7.95/year. Circ.: 120,000. Lu Herrera, Editor. **Description:** For smart, savvy Hispanic teen girls who care about their families, friends, cultural backgrounds, appearances, education, and being heard. Shares joys, hopes, and aspirations, and celebrates being bicultural. **Nonfiction:** First-person teen stories, celebrity interviews and news, latest fashion/beauty trends, insightful peer stories, resources, advice on dating, health, family life, school and careers; 100-1,200 words; $1/word. **Fillers:** Quizzes with 8-10 questions and answer key; on personalities, relationships, friendships, fashion, fun; 1,000-1,200 words; $700 fee. **Columns, Departments:** Fashion/beauty stories; 100-400 words; $1/word or fee. **Tips:** Readers aged 12-19, focuses editorial content to the 17-year-old. Send query idea for specific department, with outline, and be patient. No phone calls please. No simutaneous queries. **Queries:** Required. **Unsolicited mss:** Accepts. **Response:** 2-6 months, SASE. **Freelance Content:** 80%. **Rights:** 1st NA serial, electronic. **Payment:** On publication.

LATINO LEADERS

363 N. Sam Houston Pkwy. E., Ste 1100, Houston, TX 77060-2413. 888-528-4532. Monthly. Circ.: 90,000. **Description:** Covers diverse leaders in the Latino community.

LILITH

250 W. 57th St., #2432, New York, NY 10107-0172. 212-757-0818. E-mail: lilithmag@aol.com. Web site: www.lilithmag.com. Quarterly. $6/issue, $18/year. Circ.: 25,000. Susan Weidman Schneider, Editor. **Description:** Showcases Jewish women writers, educators, and artists; illuminates Jewish women's lives in their religious, ethnic, sexual, and social-class diversity. **Fiction:** On the lives of Jewish women; 1,000-2,000 words. **Nonfiction:** Autobiographies, interviews, social analysis, sociological research, oral history, new rituals, reviews, investigative reporting, opinion pieces; also news briefs (500 words); Letters to the Editor; lists of resources, projects, events; 1,000-2,000 words. **Poetry:** Yes. **Art:** Yes. **Queries:** Not necessary. **E-queries:** Yes. **Unsolicited mss:** Accepts. **Response:** 12-16 weeks, SASE.

LIVING BLUES

Univ. of Mississippi, Hill Hall, Room 301, University, MS 38677. 662-915-5742. Web site: www.livingbluesonline.com. David Nelson. **Description:** About living African-American blues artists. **Nonfiction:** Interviews, some retrospective, historical articles or investigative pieces; 1,500-10,000 words; pays $75-$200. **Art:** Photos, $25-$50. **Queries:** Preferred. **Payment:** On publication.

LSR

P.O. Box 440195, Miami, FL 33144. 305-447-3780. E-mail: ejc@lspress.net. 2x/yr. Circ.: 3,000. Nilda Cepero, Editor. **Description:** Bilingual (English and Spanish) literary journal, focusing on Latino topics. **Nonfiction:** Book reviews or interviews, to 750 words. **Poetry:** Submit up to 4 poems,

5-45 lines each. Prefers contemporary, with meaning and message. No surrealism, porn, or religious poetry. **Art:** Line artwork; submit up to 5 illustrations on 3.5″ disk (to be printed 6″x6″ on cover, 8″x10″ on full-page inside). **Tips:** Reprints accepted. Do not query. No submissions in November, December, or January. **Queries:** Not necessary. **E-queries:** No. **Unsolicited mss:** Accepts. **Response:** 9 months, SASE required. **Freelance Content:** 100%. **Rights:** 1st. **Payment:** in copies.

MERCADO

1401 W. Flagler St., #206, Miami, FL 33135-2254. 305-649-7711.
Web site: www.mercadousa.com. Monthly. Circ.: 35,000. **Description:** For people interested in learning about and being involved in the Latin American markets.

MEXICO CONNECT

Telephone: 011-523-766-2267.
E-mail: mexwrite@mexconnect.com. Web site: www.mexconnect.com. Monthly. David H. McLaughlin, Publisher. **Description:** On living in Mexico, Mexico travel (the "Un-Guide Book") and Mexico business. Pay is with a by-line and information about you on our website. **Nonfiction:** Short articles (to 750 words) or long articles, to 2,500 words. **Tips:** Query by e-mail. Submit in English or Spanish.

MOMENT

4710 41st St. NW, Washington, DC 20016. 202-364-3300.
E-mail: editor@momentmag.com. Web site: www.momentmag.com. Bimonthly. $4.50/issue. Circ.: 65,000. Hershel Shanks, Editor. **Description:** On Jewish culture, politics, and religion. **Fiction:** 8,000 max. **Nonfiction:** Sophisticated articles on Jewish culture, politics, religion, personalities. Pay negotiated; 100-3,500 words. **Poetry:** 150-300 words. **Columns, Departments:** Notes and News (250 words, on events, people, and living); Olam/The Jewish World (colorful, first-person "letters from" and reports); Book Reviews (to 400 words); to 1,000 words. **Tips:** Seeking fresh angles on Jewish themes. **Queries:** Preferred. **E-queries:** Yes. **Unsolicited mss:** Accepts. **Response:** 1-2 months, SASE. **Freelance Content:** 90%. **Rights:** FNASR. **Payment:** On publication.

NA'AMAT WOMAN

350 Fifth Ave., Suite 4700, New York, NY 10118. 212-563-5222.
E-mail: judith@nanmat.org. Web site: www.nanmat.org. Quarterly. $25 members, $10 non-members. Circ.: 20,000. Judith A. Sokoloff, Editor. **Description:** For Jewish community, covering varied topics: aspects of life in Israel, Jewish women's issues, social issues, Jewish art and literature. **Fiction:** 2,000-3,000 words; $.10/word. **Nonfiction:** 2,000-3,000 words; $.10-$.12/word. **Columns, Departments:** Book reviews (ca. 800 words); Personal essays (ca. 1,200-1,500 words); $.10/word. **Art:** b/w (hard copy or electronic); $25-$100. **Tips:** Avoid trite Jewish humor, maudlin fiction, war stories. **Queries:** Preferred. **Unsolicited mss:** Accepts. **Response:** Queries 1-2 months, submissions 2-3 months, SASE. **Freelance Content:** 75%. **Rights:** 1st NA. **Payment:** On publication.

NATIVE PEOPLES

5333 N. 7th St., Suite C-224, Phoenix, AZ 85014-2804. 602-265-4855. E-mail: gavey@nativepeoples.com. Web site: www.nativepeoples.com. Bimonthly. $4.95/issue. Circ.: 60,000. Gary Avey, Editor. **Description:** Full-color, offers sensitive portrayal of arts and lifestyle of native peoples of the Americas. **Nonfiction:** Artist profiles (traditional and contemporary); issue-oriented pieces with Native American angle; program/people profiles in education, health, politics; economic development; 1,000-3,000 words; $.25/word. **Columns, Departments:** Pathways (travels with Native site/culture/history focus; Viewpoint (open subject matter); 400-1,200 words; $.25/word. **Art:** Color, b/w. **Tips:** Readership is both Native American and those interested in Native culture. Our stories need to appeal to both, serving as a bridge between cultures. **Queries:** Preferred. **E-queries:** Yes. **Unsolicited mss:** Accepts. **Response:** 4 weeks, SASE required. **Freelance Content:** 80%. **Rights:** First Time Rights. **Payment:** On publication. **Contact:** Daniel Gibson, Managing Editor.

NETWORK JOURNAL

139 Fulton St., Suite 407, New York, NY 10038. 212-962-3791. E-mail: tnj@obe1.com. Web site: www.tnj.com. Monthly. Circ.: 11,000. Njeru Waithaka, Editor. **Description:** Small-business, personal finance, and career management for African-American small-business owners and professionals. **Nonfiction:** Profiles of entrepreneurs; how-to pieces; articles on sales and marketing, managing a small business and personal finance; 800 to 1,500 words; $75 to $150. **Payment:** On acceptance.

PAPYRUS

P.O. Box 270797, West Hartford, CT 06127-0797. E-mail: gwhitaker@imagine.com. Ginger Whitaker, Editor. **Description:** "The writer's craftletter featuring the black experience."

PURPOSE

529 E. Engler St., Columbus, OH 43215-5551. 614-224-2113. Web site: www.purposemagazine.com. **Description:** Multicultural magazine with an uplifting Christian focus.

RAISING BLACK AND BIRACIAL CHILDREN

Heritage Publishing Group, P.O. Box 17479, Beverly Hills, CA 90209. 310-403-3914. E-mail: intrace@aol.com. Web site: www.members@aol.com. 4x/year. $12.95/yr. Circ.: 25,000. Billee Mills, Editor. **Description:** For black, interracial, and transracial families who have children with African-American heritage. Readers include professionals and educators. **Nonfiction:** Building character in African-American children; articles on parenting, family values, interracial friendship among children, self esteem, African-American culture and heritage; 500-1,000 words; $.04/word. **Columns, Departments:** 400-600 words. **Art:** Images of African-American or biracial babies, toddlers, and children up to teens; also, black and interracial families. Prints (to 8x10), b/w or color; pay negotiable. **Tips:** Seeking unique, and standard pieces on parenting, with emphasis on African-American perspective. **Queries:** Not necessary. **Unsolicited mss:** Accepts. **Response:** 1-4 weeks, SASE. **Freelance Content:** 50%. **Rights:** One-time. **Payment:** On publication.

RUSSIAN LIFE

P.O. Box 567, Montpelier, VT 05601-0567. 802-223-4955. E-mail: ruslife@rspubs.com. Web site: www.russian-life.com. Bimonthly. $29/yr. Circ.: 15,000. Mikhail Ivanov, Editor. **Description:** Russian culture, travel, history, politics, art, business, and society. Very visual; most stories include professional-quality photos. **Nonfiction:** 1,000-3,000 words; $.07-$.10/word. **Art:** Slides, prints, color, b/w; $20-$50. **Tips:** Submit solid, third-person American journalism (AP stylebook); frank, terse, and incisive. No stories about personal trips to Russia, editorials on developments in Russia, or articles promoting a specific company, organization, or government agency. **Queries:** Required. **E-queries:** Yes. **Unsolicited mss:** Accepts. **Response:** 1 month, SASE. **Freelance Content:** 40%. **Rights:** All. **Payment:** On publication.

SCANDINAVIAN REVIEW

American-Scandinavian Foundation
58 Park Ave., New York, NY 10016. 212-879-9779.
E-mail: agyongy@amscan.org. Web site: www.amscan.org. 3x/year. Circ.: 5,000. A. Gyongy, Editor. **Description:** Arts, sciences, business, politics, and culture of contemporary Denmark, Finland, Iceland, Norway, and Sweden. **Nonfiction:** Prefers illustrated articles, 1,500-2,000 words; pays to $300. **Art:** Photo payment negotiated separately. **Tips:** No original English-language poetry, only Nordic poetry in English translation. **Queries:** Preferred. **Response:** SASE required. **Freelance Content:** 50%. **Rights:** One-time. **Payment:** On publication.

SELECCIONES DEL READER'S DIGEST

1 Reader's Digest Rd., Pleasantville, NY 10570-7000. 914-238-4559. Web site: www.readersdigest.com. Monthly. Circ.: 130,000. **Description:** Spanish-language version of Reader's Digest.

SELECTA

1717 N. Bayshore Dr., Ste 113, Miami, FL 33132-1195. 305-579-0979. Monthly. Circ.: 27,000. **Description:** For upscale Hispanics in the U.S. and Latin America.

SISTERS IN STYLE

233 Park Ave. S., 5th Fl., New York, NY 10003. 212-780-3500. Web site: www.sterlingmacfadden.com. Bimonthly. Cynthia Marie Horner, Editor. **Description:** "For Today's Young Black Woman." Beauty and fashion articles, quizzes, and advice for African-American teens. **Nonfiction:** Pay varies. **Queries:** Preferred. **Payment:** On publication.

SOUTH AMERICAN EXPLORER

126 Indian Creek Rd., Ithaca, NY 14850. 607-277-0488. E-mail: explorer@samesplo.org. Web site: www.samexplo.org. **Description:** Spotlights travel, history, archeology, scientific discovery, people and language in Central and South America. **Nonfiction:** 3,000-5,000 words. **Art:** Photos. **Queries:** Preferred. **E-queries:** Yes. **Unsolicited mss:** Accepts.

TEACHING TOLERANCE

Southern Poverty Law Center, 400 Washington Ave., Montgomery, AL 36104. Web site: www.teachingtolerance.org. Bi-annual. Free to educators. Circ.: 600,000. Jim Carnes. **Description:** Helps teachers promote interracial and intercultural understanding in the classroom and beyond. **Nonfiction:** E.g., role of white teachers in multicultural education; teaching respect for dialects; creating safe space for refugee students to tell their stories; how assistive devices allow more inclusion for disabled; gay student comes out at school, etc.; 500-3,500 words; $1/word. **Art:** Rarely uses stock images. Seeking photographer to travel on assignment, work well with school children and teachers/administrators, in varied locations; b/w, color, hand-tinted; $100-$800. **Tips:** Submit clear focused query. No rhetoric, scholarly analysis, articles that reinvent the wheel on multicultural education. **Queries:** Preferred. **E-queries:** No. **Unsolicited mss:** Accepts. **Response:** up to 3 months, SASE. **Freelance Content:** 75%. **Rights:** All. **Payment:** On acceptance.

TEMAS

300 W. 55th St., Apt 14P, New York, NY 10019-5172. 212-582-4750. Web site: www.cdiusa.com/revistatemas. Monthly. Circ.: 110,000. **Description:** Topics of interest to Spanish-speaking people in the United States.

VISTA

999 Ponce de Leon Blvd., Suite 600, Coral Gables, FL 33134. 305-442-2462. E-mail: jlobaco@aol.com. Web site: www.vistamagazine.com. Monthly. Circ.: 1,000,000. Julia Bencomo Lobaco, Editor. **Description:** For English-speaking Hispanic Americans. **Nonfiction:** On job advancement, bilingualism, immigration, the media, fashion, education, medicine, sports, and food. Profiles (100 words) of Hispanic Americans in unusual jobs; photos welcome; to 1,500 words; $.20/word. **Queries:** Required. **Payment:** On acceptance.

WINK

Doublespace, 601 West 26th St., 14th Fl, New York, NY 10001. 212-366-1919. Web site: www.winkmag.com. Monthly. Circ.: 50,000. Ralph Clermont, CEO. **Description:** Cross-cultural fashion and beauty magazine. Mingles Black, white, Latino, Asian, Caribbean and African, with all the splendor that arises when different cultures come together. Online and in print.

FAMILY & PARENTING

ADOPTIVE FAMILIES
2472 Broadway, Suite 377, New York, NY 10025. 212-877-1839. E-mail: publisher@adoptivefam.com. Web site: www.adoptivefam.org. Bimonthly. Linda Lynch, Editor. **Description:** On parenting adoptive children and other adoption issues. **Nonfiction:** Articles, 1,000-1,500 words; pay negotiable. **Queries:** Preferred.

AMERICAN BABY
Primedia Consumer Magazines
249 W. 17th St., New York, NY 10011-5300. 212-462-3500. Web site: www.americanbaby.com. Monthly. Circ.: 1,650,000. Judith Nolte, Editor in Chief. **Description:** For new or expectant parents on prenatal and infant care. **Fiction:** No fantasy pieces or dreamy musings. **Nonfiction:** Features, 1,000-2,000 words; personal experience pieces (do not submit in diary format), 900-1,200 words; $800-$2,000. **Columns, Departments:** Crib Notes (news and feature topics); 50-350 words; $500. **Payment:** On acceptance.

AT-HOME MOTHER
406 E. Buchanan Ave., Fairfield, IA 52556-3810. E-mail: editor@athomemothers.com. Web site: www.AtHomeMothers.com. Quarterly. Circ.: 8,000. Jeanette Lisefski, Editor. **Description:** Aimed at women who raise active families, run a home business, manage a household budget, etc. **Nonfiction:** Articles should be helpful, educational, and supportive; pay varies. **Queries:** Required.

ATLANTA PARENT
2346 Perimeter Park Dr., Ste. 101, Atlanta, GA 30341. 770-454-7599. E-mail: atlantaparent@atlantaparent.com. Web site: www.atlantaparent.com. Monthly. $15. Circ.: 85,000. Liz White, Editor. **Description:** For parents with children, birth to 18 years. **Nonfiction:** On family, child, and parent topics; 300-3,000 words; $15-$35. **Fillers:** Humor; 800-1,500 words. **Queries:** Preferred. **E-queries:** Yes. **Unsolicited mss:** Accepts. **Response:** 3-6 months, SASE. **Freelance Content:** 50%. **Rights:** One-time. **Payment:** On publication. **Contact:** Peggy Middendorf.

BABY TALK
530 Fifth Ave., 4th Floor, New York, NY 10036. 212-522-8989. Web site: www.parenting.com. 10x/yr. Circ.: 1,725,000. Susan Kane, Editor in Chief. **Description:** Pregnancy, babies, baby care, women's health, child development, work and family. **Nonfiction:** Articles, by professional writers with expertise and experience; 1,000-3,000 words; pay varies. **Queries:** Required. **Response:** SASE required. **Payment:** On acceptance.

BABYCENTER
163 Freelon St., San Francisco, CA 94107. 415-537-0900.
Web site: www.babycenter.com. **Description:** E-zine for new parents.

BAY AREA PARENT
401 Alberto Way, Suite A, Los Gatos, CA 95032-5404. 707-763-2160.
E-mail: jbordow@unitedad.com. Monthly. Free. Joan Bordow, Editor. **Description:**
Parenting issues for California's Santa Clara County and South Bay area. **Nonfiction:**
For parents of children from birth to early teens; 500-1200 words; $.10/word.
Queries: Required. **E-queries:** Yes. **Unsolicited mss:** Accepts. **Response:**
Queries and submissions 2 months, SASE required. **Freelance Content:** 50%.

BEST WISHES
37 Hanna Ave., Unit 1, Toronto, Ontario, Canada M6K 1W9. 416-537-2604.
Semi-annual. Circ.: 140,000. **Description:** For new moms and dads.

BIG APPLE PARENT
9 E. 38th St., 4th Fl., New York, NY 10016. 212-889-6400.
E-mail: edit@parentsknow.com. Web site: www.parentsknow.com. Monthly. Free.
Circ.: 70,000. Helen Freedman, Editor. **Description:** Newspaper for New York City
parents, with separate editions for Queens and Westchester County. **Nonfiction:** For
parents, on parenting, humor features, op-ed; best chances are "newsy" features with
New York slant; 750 words; $50. **Art:** Hard copy, JPEG; $25. **Tips:** Cover more than
your personal experience. Stories should be about New York City or have information
that can be localized. **Queries:** Not necessary. **E-queries:** Yes. **Unsolicited mss:**
Accepts. **Response:** within 1 week, SASE required. **Freelance Content:** 90%.
Rights: 1st. **Payment:** On publication.

BRAIN CHILD
P.O. Box 1161, Harrisonburg, VA 22801-1161. 540-574-2379.
E-mail: editor@brainchildmag.com. Web site: www.brainchildmag.com. Quarterly.
$5/issue $18/year. Circ.: 10,000. Jennifer Niesslein, Editor. **Description:** Explores
the personal transformation that motherhood brings. Spotlights women's own view of
motherhood. **Fiction:** Literary short stories on an aspects of motherhood; e.g., "The
Life Of the Body," by Jane Smiley; 1,500-4,500 words; pay varies. **Nonfiction:**
Personal essays, features, book reviews, parodies, debate essays. **Columns,
Departments:** Nutshell (stories you won't find in the mainstream media; e.g., "Mom
Brain Explained," by Libby Gruner; 200-800 words. **Tips:** Seeking smart, down-to-
earth work that's sometimes funny, sometimes poignant. **Queries:** Preferred.
E-queries: Yes. **Unsolicited mss:** Accepts. **Response:** 1-3 months, SASE.
Freelance Content: 90%. **Rights:** 1st NA, electronic. **Payment:** On publication.
Contact: Stephanie Wilkerson.

CATHOLIC FAITH & FAMILY

33 Rossotto Dr., Hamden, CT 06514. 203-288-5600.
E-mail: duncan@bestweb.net. Biweekly. Circ.: 16,000. Duncan Maxwell Anderson, Editor. **Description:** How-to articles and interviews of interest to Catholic families, with photos. **Nonfiction:** 1,000-2,000 words; pays $75-$300. **Columns, Departments:** Opinion or inspirational columns, 600-800 words, with strict attention to Catholic doctrine. **Queries:** Preferred. **Unsolicited mss:** Accepts. **Freelance Content:** 95%. **Rights:** 1st. **Payment:** On publication.

CATHOLIC PARENT

Our Sunday Visitor, Inc., 200 Noll Plaza, Huntington, IN 46750. 219-356-8400.
E-mail: cparent@osv.com. Web site: www.osv.com. Woodeene Koenig-Bricker, Editor. **Description:** For Catholic parents. Anecdotal and practical, with an emphasis on values and family life. **Nonfiction:** Features, how-tos, and general-interest articles, 800-1,000 words; pay varies. **Tips:** Don't preach. **Payment:** On acceptance.

CENTRAL CALIFORNIA PARENT

7638 N. Ingram Ave., Suite 101, Fresno, CA 93711-6201. 559-435-1406.
Web site: www.ccparent.com. Sally Cook. **Description:** For parents. **Nonfiction:** Articles, 500-1,500 words; pay varies. **Queries:** Preferred. **Payment:** On publication.

CENTRAL PENN PARENT

101 N. Second St., NW, Harrisburg, PA 17101. 717-236-4300.
Web site: www.journalpub.com. Monthly. $16.95. Circ.: 35,000. Lauren Taylor, Editor. **Description:** On family and parenting issues **Nonfiction:** 1,400 words; $125. **Columns, Departments:** 700 words; $50. **Art:** Submit photos with article. **Tips:** Welcomes new writers. **Queries:** Required. **E-queries:** Yes. **Unsolicited mss:** Accepts. **Response:** 3 weeks, SASE required. **Freelance Content:** 50%. **Rights:** 1st. **Payment:** On publication.

CHICAGO PARENT

141 S. Oak Park Ave., Oak Park, IL 60302-2972. 708-386-5555.
Web site: chicagoparent.com. Monthly. Circ.: 125,000. **Description:** For parents in the Chicago metro area.

CHILD

110 Fifth Ave., New York, NY 10011. 212-499-2000.
Web site: www.childmagazine.com. Monthly. Circ.: 930,000. Freddi Greenberg, Editor. **Description:** Smart, surprising insights into parenting in the new millennium, with its dazzling possibilities and endless choices. **Columns, Departments:** Fashion, Home Environment, Baby Best, Travel. Pays from $750. **Tips:** Offer news that parents need to know, options for products/services, and ways to preserve precious parenthood time, in a lively, stylish fashion. **Queries:** Preferred. **E-queries:** Yes. **Unsolicited mss:** Accepts. **Response:** 2 months, SASE required. **Freelance Content:** 95%. **Rights:** 1st NA. **Payment:** On acceptance.

CHILDBIRTH

249 W. 17th St., New York, NY 10011-5300. 212-462-3300.
Semi-annual. Circ.: 2,000,000. **Description:** For expectant parents.

CHRISTIAN PARENTING TODAY

465 Gundersen Dr., Carol Stream, IL 60188-2489. 630-260-6200.
E-mail: cptmag@aol.com. Bimonthly. Circ.: 90,000. Carala Barnhill, Editor.
Description: Serves needs of today's families in positive and practical format.
Nonfiction: Articles on real-life experiences and truths of the Bible. **Queries:**
Preferred.

CITY PARENT

467 Speers Rd., Oakville, Ontario, Canada L6K 3S4. 905-815-0017.
E-mail: cityparent@metroland.com. Web site: www.cityparent.com. Monthly. Circ.:
200,000. Jane Muller, Editor. **Description:** Offers stories, new-product information,
computer news, parenting advice, places to go and things to do with kids.
Nonfiction: Pays $75-$150. **Queries:** Required. **E-queries:** Yes. **Unsolicited mss:**
Accepts. **Freelance Content:** 50%. **Rights:** All.

CLEVELAND/AKRON FAMILY

3050 Prospect Ave., Cleveland, OH 44115. 216-426-8300.
E-mail: jelfvin@adelphia.net. Monthly. Circ.: 45,000. Jackie Elfvin, Editor.
Description: For parents; seeks to encourage positive family interaction. Provides
articles on general topics, area events, trends, and services for area families.
Nonfiction: Pays $30/article or column. **Queries:** Required. **E-queries:** No.
Unsolicited mss: Accepts. **Payment:** On publication.

THE COMPLEAT MOTHER

P.O. Box 209, Minot, ND 58702. 701-852-2822.
Web site: www.compleatmother.com. Quarterly. Circ.: 12,000. **Description:** For
new moms and mom-to-be.

DAD'S

726 Fairview Ave., Glen Ellyn, IL 60137. 630-790-1007.
Web site: www.dadsmagazine.com. **Description:** For kids and dads of all ages.
Offers information to help fathers nurture their children. **Nonfiction:** Features: fun
activities for dads to do with sons and daughters, baseball, basketball, soccer, surfing,
rollerblading, skateboarding, snow boarding, arts and crafts. Also, issues for single
dads, celebrity dads, and travel topics; to 1,800 words; $75-$200.

DALLAS FAMILY

1321 Valwood Pkwy, Ste 530, Carrollton, TX 75006-8412. 972-488-3555.
Web site: www.parenthood.com. Monthly. Circ.: 75,000. **Description:** For parents in
the Dallas metro area.

DOVETAIL INSTITUTE FOR INTERFAITH FAMILY RESOURCES
775 Simon Greenwell Lane, Boston, KY 40107. 502-549-5499.
E-mail: di-ifr@boardstowm.com. Web site: www.dovetailpublishing.com. Bi-monthly.
$25/year. Circ.: 1,000. Mary Heléne Rosenbaum, Editor. **Description:** Resources for
dual-faith couples, and their families, friends, and professionals who serve them, from
a non-denominational perspective. Readers cover the intermarriage spectrum,
including single-faith and dual-faith households. **Nonfiction:** Advice, anecdotes, and
research on aspects of interfaith marriage; e.g., "Challah Baking: Thoughts of a
Christian Cook," or "Intermarriage in Australia"; 800-1,000; $25. **Fillers:** Related
cartoons, humor, and photos also used. **Tips:** Have experience or knowledge in the
field of intermarriage. Avoid broad generalizations, or strongly partisan religious
creeds. **Queries:** Not necessary. **E-queries:** Yes. **Unsolicited mss:** Accepts.
Response: Queries 2-4 weeks, submissions 4-6 weeks, SASE required. **Freelance
Content:** 80%. **Rights:** All. **Payment:** On publication.

EASTSIDE PARENT
Northwest Parent Publishing
1530 Westlake Ave. N., Suite 600, Seattle, WA 98109. 206-441-0191.
Web site: www.parenthoodweb.com. Virginia Smyth, Editor. **Description:** For parents of children under 14. Readers tend to be professional, two-career families. Also
publishes Portland Parent, Seattle's Child, etc. **Nonfiction:** Articles, 300-2,500
words; pays $50-$600. **Queries:** Preferred. **Payment:** On publication.

EP NEWS
P.O. Box 320 722, Fairfield, CT 06432. 203-371-6212.
E-mail: epideas@en-parent.com. Web site: www.en-parent.com. Bimonthly. Lisa
Roberts, Cofounder. **Description:** E-zine for entrepreneurial parents.

EXPECTING
37 Hanna Ave., Unite 1, Toronto, Ontario, Canada M6K 1W9. 416-537-2604.
Semi-annual. Circ.: 280,000. **Description:** For pregnant Canadian women.

FAMILY
51 Atlantic Ave., Suite 200, Floral Park, NY 11001. 516-616-1930.
Web site: www.familymedia.com. Monthly. Stacy P. Brassington. **Description:** For
military families. Covers topics of interest to women with children (military lifestyle,
home decorating, travel, moving, food, personal finances, career, relationships, family, parenting, health and fitness). **Nonfiction:** Articles, 1,000-2,000 words; pays to
$200. **Payment:** On publication.

FAMILY
1122 US Highway 22, Mountainside, NJ 07092-2812. 908-232-2913.
Monthly. Circ.: 100,000. **Description:** New Jersey information for families.

FAMILY FIRST NEWSLETTER
Telephone: 405-348-2800.
E-mail: jcomm@worldvillage.com. Web site: www.familyfirst.com. Weekly. Joel
Comm, Editor. **Description:** E-zine about family-friendly Internet usage.

FAMILY FUN
244 Main St., Northampton, MA 01060. 413-585-0444.
Web site: www.familyfun.com. 10x/year. Circ.: 1,300,000. Johnathan Adolph,
Executive Editor. **Description:** For parents of children ages 3-12. Offers many easy
and inexpensive ideas for cooped-up kids. **Nonfiction:** Articles on great activities
families can do together; to 1,500 words; pay varies. **Columns, Departments:** My
Great Idea; Family Ties (essays on family life); also recipes, crafts and games;
$.50-$1/word. **Tips:** New writers should consider contributing to departments first.
Contact: See website guidelines for names of editors, by department.

FAMILY LIFE
1271 Avenue of the Americas, 41st Fl., New York, NY 10020. 212-522-6240.
E-mail: familylife@timeinc.com. Web site: familylife.com. Monthly. Circ.: 500,000.
Janet Sireto, Editor. **Description:** For parents of children, ages 5-12. Most readers
are women. **Nonfiction:** Essays on parenting issues, short departments, and features;
2,000-3,500 words. **Columns, Departments:** Mom's health, children's health, crafts,
news briefs; 50-400 words. **Queries:** Required. **E-queries:** Yes. **Unsolicited mss:**
Does not accept. **Response:** Queries 6-8 weeks, SASE. **Freelance Content:** 50%.
Rights: All. **Payment:** On acceptance. **Contact:** Jacqueline Ross.

FAMILY TIMES
P.O. Box 932, Eau Claire, WI 54702.
Nancy Walter, Editor. **Description:** For parents in Wisconsin's Chippewa Valley, on
children and parenting issues. **Nonfiction:** Health, education, how-tos, new studies,
programs for parenting; pays $35-$50. **Queries:** Preferred. **Response:** SASE.
Payment: On publication.

FIRST TIME DAD
214 W. 29th St., Floor 7, New York, NY 10001-5203. 212-273-3700.
Web site: www.dadsworld.com. Quarterly. Circ.: 450,000. **Description:** For first-
time dads.

FOCUS ON THE FAMILY
8605 Explorer Dr., Colorado Springs, CO 80920-1051. 719-531-3400.
Web site: www.family.org. Monthly. Circ.: 2,000,000. **Description:** Christian family
information.

HEALTHY KIDS
Cahners Publishing, 249 W. 17th St., New York, NY 10011-5382. 212-462-3300.
Web site: www.healthykids.com. Phyllis Steinberg, Editor. **Description:** Focuses on

raising a healthy, happy child. Two editions: Birth-3 (quarterly) and 4-10 Years (3 times a year). All articles written by experts or based on interviews with pediatricians and health-care professionals. **Nonfiction:** On basic care, analysis of growing mind, behavior patterns, nutrition, emergencies, etc. 1,500-2,000 words, pays $500-$1,000. **Tips:** Freelance content limited. **Queries:** Preferred. **Payment:** On acceptance.

HOME LIFE

127 Ninth Ave. N, Nashville, TN 37234-0001. 615-251-2860. Monthly. Circ.: 475,000. **Description:** Parenting information for Christian families.

HOUSTON FAMILY

2620 Fountain View Dr., Ste 200, Houston, TX 77057-7627. 713-266-1885. Web site: www.parenthoodweb.com. Monthly. Circ.: 75,000. **Description:** For parents in the Houston area.

L.A. PARENT

443 E. Irving Dr., Burbank, CA 91504. 818-846-0400. Web site: www.parenthoodweb.com. Monthly. Circ.: 100,000. Janis Hashe, National Editor. **Description:** On child development, health, nutrition, and education, for parents of children up to age 10. Also publishes San Diego Parent, and Parenting (Orange Co.). **Nonfiction:** Articles, 1,000 words; pays $100-$350. **Queries:** Preferred. **Payment:** On acceptance.

LAMAZE BABY

9 Old Kings Hwy. S., Darien, CT 06820-4505. 203-656-3600. Web site: www.lamaze.com. Quarterly. Circ.: 3,000,000. **Description:** For parents who use Lamaze methods of childbirth.

METROKIDS

1080 N. Delaware Ave., Suite 702, Philadelphia, PA 19125. 215-291-5560 x102. E-mail: editor@metrokids.com. Web site: www.metrokids.com. Monthly. Free. Circ.: 125,000. Nancy Lisagor, Editor. **Description:** For Delaware Valley area, on parenting kids, ages 0-16. **Nonfiction:** Parenting subjects, products reviews, and travel in the Philadelphia metro region; 800-1500 words; $30-$100. **Columns, Departments:** Product reviews, books, music, video, software, health, women's subjects, family finance; 800; $30-$50. **Queries:** Preferred. **E-queries:** Yes. **Unsolicited mss:** Accepts. **Response:** Queries 2 months, submissions 2 months. **Freelance Content:** 60%. **Rights:** one-time only, website. **Payment:** On publication.

NEW BEGINNINGS

P.O. Box 4079, Schaumburg, IL 60168-4079. 847-519-7730. Web site: www.lalecheleague.org. Bi-monthly. Circ.: 25,000. **Description:** For women who breast-feed.

NEW PARENT
10 New King St., White Plains, NY 10604-1205. 914-949-4726.
Semi-annual. Circ.: 1,300,000. **Description:** For new parents and parents-to-be.

NEW YORK FAMILY
141 Halstead Ave., Suite 3D, Mamaroneck, NY 10543. 914-381-7474.
Web site: www.parenthoodweb.com. Heather Hart, Editor. **Description:** Articles
related to family life in New York City and general parenting topics. **Nonfiction:** Pays
$50-$200. **Payment:** On publication.

NICK, JR.
1515 Broadway, 40th Floor, New York, NY 10036. 212-846-5249.
Web site: www.nickjr.com. **Description:** For children ages 2-7 and their parents.
Fun things to do together.

NORTHEAST OHIO PARENT
20325 Center Ridge Rd., Ste 135, Rocky River, OH 44116-3554. 440-895-9723.
Web site: www.neoparent.com. Monthly. Circ.: 55,000. **Description:** For parents in
Northeast Ohio.

NORTHWEST BABY & CHILD
15417 204th Ave. SE, Renton, WA 98059-9021. 425-235-6826.
Web site: www.nwbaby.com. Monthly. Circ.: 45,000. **Description:** For parents in
Northwest Washington.

NORTHWEST FAMILY
2275 Lake Whatcom Blvd., Ste B-1, Bellingham, WA 98226-2777. 360-734-3025.
E-mail: nwfamily@earthlink.net. Web site: www.nwfamily.com. Monthly. Circ.:
45,000. **Description:** Regional parenting and family publication for Western
Washington. **Nonfiction:** Pays $25-$40. **Poetry:** Pays $5-$15. **Fillers:** Humor; pays
$25-$40. **Art:** Photos; pays $5-$20. **Tips:** Send articles in email (no attachments);
include word count. **Queries:** Required. **E-queries:** Yes. **Unsolicited mss:**
Accepts. **Freelance Content:** 65%. **Rights:** One-time (print and electronic).

OFFSPRING
755 Broadway, Frnt 2, New York, NY 10019. 212-830-9200.
Web site: www.offspringmag.com. Quarterly. Steven Swartz, Editor-In-Chief.
Description: On parenting. Features include education, child development, health
care, fashion, social issues, travel, technology and money.

PARENT CONNECTION
P.O. Box 707, Setauket, NY 11733-0769. 631-751-0356.
Web site: www.tbrnewspapers.com. Monthly. Circ.: 110,000. **Description:** For par-
ents in the New York City and surrounding area.

THE PARENT PAPER
1 Garret Dr., West Paterson, NJ 07424-2724. 973-569-7720.
Web site: www.parentpaper.com. Monthly. Circ.: 45,000. **Description:** For parents in New Jersey.

PARENTGUIDE NEWS
419 Park Ave. S., 13th Fl., New York, NY 10016. 212-123-8840.
E-mail: annmarie@parentguidenews.com. Web site: www.parentguidenews.com.
Monthly. Circ.: 210,000. Ann Marie Evola, Editor. **Description:** For parents with children under 12 years old. Columns and features on parenting, health, education, child-rearing, and more. **Fiction:** 1,000 words. **Nonfiction:** Articles, to 1,000 words, on families and parenting: trends, profiles, health, education, travel, fashion, events, seasonal, products, etc. Humor and women's section. **Queries:** Preferred. **E-queries:** Yes. **Unsolicited mss:** Accepts. **Response:** 1-2 weeks, SASE. **Freelance Content:** 80%.

PARENTING
530 Fifth Avenue, 4th Floor, New York, NY 10019. 212-522-8989.
Web site: www.parenting.com. 10x/year. Janet Chan, Editor-in-Chief. **Description:** Seeks to make pregnancy and parenthood smarter, saner, and easier. Offers resources for moms and dads. **Nonfiction:** On education, health, fitness, nutrition, child development, psychology, and social issues for parents of young children; 500-3,000 words. **Tips:** Focuses on the early years, when parents have many questions and concerns. **Queries:** Preferred. **E-queries:** No. **Unsolicited mss:** Accepts. **Response:** 2 months, SASE.

PARENTING TEENS
P.O. Box 363, Bedford, NY 10506.
Web site: www.parentsofteens.com. Monthly (National). **Description:** For parents of teenagers, also educators working with middle- and high-school students. Topics include: education, social issues, family, relationships, health, finances, college and sports. **Nonfiction:** 200-1,500 words; $250-$600. **Tips:** Editors are looking for freelancers with experience writing in the field of parenting. **Payment:** On publication.

PARENTING TODAY'S TEEN
P.O. Box 11864, Olympia, WA 98508.
E-mail: editor@parentingteens.com Web site: www.parentingteens.com. Bimonthly.
Frances Reza, Managing Editor. **Description:** E-zine, written by parents and professionals, about the issues of parenting teenagers, including tough issues like drug/alcohol abuse, sex, AIDS, violence, and running away. **Nonfiction:** Pays $10-$25. **Queries:** Required. **E-queries:** Yes. **Response:** 2-3 weeks. **Rights:** 1st NA, reverts to author after 90 days. **Contact:** Diana Kathrein.

PARENTLIFE

Msn 140 127 Ninth Ave. North, Nashville, TN 37234-0001. 615-251-5721.
Web site: www.lifeway.com/kidtrek/pl. Monthly. Circ.: 100,000. **Description:**
Christian parenting.

PARENTS EXPRESS

290 Commerce Dr., Fort Washington, PA 19034. 215-629-1774.
Web site: www.parentsexpress.net. Laura Winchester. **Description:** For parents in
southeastern Pennsylvania and southern New Jersey. **Nonfiction:** Articles; pays
$35-$150. **Payment:** On publication.

PITTSBURGH PARENT

P.O. Box 374, Bakerstown, PA 15007-0374. 724-443-1891.
Web site: www.pghparent.com. Monthly. Circ.: 55,000. **Description:** For parents in
the Pittsburgh metro area.

PORTLAND PARENT

1530 Westlake Ave. N, Ste 600, Seattle, WA 98109-3096. 206-441-0191.
Web site: www.parenthoodweb.com. Monthly. Circ.: 35,000. **Description:** For parents in the Portland, WA, metro area.

QUEENS PARENT

9 E 38th St., Fl 4, New York, NY 10016-0003. 212-889-6400.
Web site: www.parentsknow.com. **Description:** For parents in the Northeastern U.S.

RAINY DAY CORNER

6022 N. 29th St., Arlington, VA 22207.
E-mail: idupie@rainydaycorner.com. Web site: www.rainydaycorner.com. Monthly.
Description: A website, with a print newsletter, providing information and tips to
help with homework, family, the working parent, and writing contests for kids.
Nonfiction: Needs: Short articles on how to deal with homework dilemmas, how to
get children interested in reading and writing, all aspects of education K-8, on con-
cerns of parents working in or outside the home; 1,000 words max; $5/article. **Tips:**
If your article is writing- or art-related, write so a child will understand, without talking down to them. Keep your articles conversational, but factual. **Queries:** Preferred.
E-queries: Yes. **Unsolicited mss:** Accepts. **Response:** 2-3 weeks, SASE required.
Rights: 1st. **Payment:** On publication.

RAISING BLACK AND BIRACIAL CHILDREN

Heritage Publishing Group, P.O. Box 17479, Beverly Hills, CA 90209. 310-403-3914.
E-mail: intrace@aol.com. Web site: www.members@aol.com. 4x/year. $12.95/yr.
Circ.: 25,000. Billee Mills, Editor. **Description:** For black, interracial, and transra-
cial families who have children with African-American heritage. Readers include professionals and educators. **Nonfiction:** Building character in African American children; articles on parenting, family values, interracial friendship among children, self

esteem, African-American culture and heritage; 500-1,000 words; $.04/word. **Columns, Departments:** 400-600 words. **Art:** Images of African American or biracial babies, toddlers, and children up to teens; also, black and interracial families. Prints (to 8x10), b/w or color; pay negotiable. **Tips:** Seeking unique, and standard pieces on parenting, with emphasis on African American perspective. **Queries:** Not necessary. **Unsolicited mss:** Accepts. **Response:** 1-4 weeks, SASE. **Freelance Content:** 50%. **Rights:** One-time. **Payment:** On publication.

ROSIE'S MCCALL'S
375 Lexington Ave., New York, NY 10017. 212-499-1720.
Web site: www.mccalls.com. **Description:** For young mothers.

SACRAMENTO SIERRA PARENT
457 Grass Valley Hwy, Ste 5, Auburn, CA 95603-3725. 530-888-0573.
Monthly. Circ.: 60,000. **Description:** Information for California parents.

SAN DIEGO FAMILY
P.O. Box 23960, San Diego, CA 92193-3960. 619-685-6970.
Web site: www.sandiegofamily.com. Monthly. Circ.: 65,000. Sharon Bay, Editor. **Description:** Family magazine for San Diego County. **Nonfiction:** Pays $1.25/column inch. **Queries:** Required. **Freelance Content:** 50%. **Rights:** 1st, 2nd.

SEATTLE'S CHILD
Northwest Parent Publishing, 1530 Westlake Ave. N, Suite 600,
Seattle, WA 98109. 206-441-0191.
Web site: www.parenthoodweb.com. Ann Bergman, Editor. **Description:** For parents, educators, and childcare providers in the Puget Sound region, with children 14 and under. Investigative reports and consumer tips on issues affecting families. **Nonfiction:** Articles, 400-2,500 words; pays $75-$600. **Queries:** Preferred. **Payment:** On publication.

SESAME STREET PARENTS
Children's Television Workshop, One Lincoln Plaza, 2nd Floor,
New York, NY 10023-7129. 212-595-3456.
Web site: www.sesamestreet.com. 10x/year. Circ.: 1,000,000. Susan Lapinski, Editor in Chief. **Description:** Covers parenting issues for families with young children (to 8 years old). **Nonfiction:** Send articles on health to Sandra Lee, Sr. Ed.; on family finance to Arleen Love, Assoc. Ed.; on education, computer material to Karin DeStefano, Lifestyle Ed. Personal essays and other articles to any editor; 800-2,500 words; $1/word. **Payment:** On acceptance.

SINGLE PARENT FAMILY
8605 Explorer Dr., Colorado Springs, CO 80920-1049. 719-531-3400.
Web site: singleparentfamily.org. Monthly. Circ.: 30,000. Susan Goodwin Graham, editor. **Description:** Information for the Christian single-parent. Addresses issues of

divorce, grief, finances, and more. **Nonfiction:** Pay varies. **Queries:** Preferred. **E-queries:** No. **Unsolicited mss:** Accepts. **Response:** SASE required. **Rights:** 1st. **Payment:** On acceptance.

SINGLE PARENTS

BenMar Media, 2118 Wilshire Blvd., Ste 318,
Santa Monica, CA 90403. 323-298-3020.
Web site: www.singleparentsmag.com. quarterly. Circ.: 50,000. **Description:** Practical information for single heads of households. Pay varies. **Columns, Departments:** Family News, Tips & Tidbits, Sanity Savers, Never a Dull Moment, Spiritual Abundance, other columns. **Tips:** Check web site for detailed submission information. **Queries:** Required. **E-queries:** Yes. **Response:** 6 weeks. **Rights:** All.

SOUTH FLORIDA PARENTING

5555 Nob Hill Rd., Sunrise, FL 33351-4707. 954-747-3050.
Web site: www.sfparenting.com. Monthly. Circ.: 100,000. **Description:** For parents in south Florida.

TAMPA BAY FAMILY

1840 Glengary St., Sarasota, FL 34231-3604. 941-922-5437.
Web site: www.familymagazines.net. Bimonthly. Circ.: 60,000. **Description:** For families in and around Tampa, Florida.

TODAY'S FAMILY

280 N. Main St., East Longmeadow, MA 01108. 413-525-6661 x123.
E-mail: news@thereminder.com. Web site: www.thereminder.com. Bimonthly. $9.99. Circ.: 20,000. Carla Valentine, Editor. **Description:** Parenting magazine for Western Massachusetts. Focuses on local news, events, activities for families. Columns on family issues, health, day trips, by local writers. **Tips:** Writers must have expertise on subject and be from the region (Western Mass., Pioneer Valley). **Queries:** Required. **E-queries:** Yes. **Unsolicited mss:** Does not accept. **Response:** Queries 2 weeks; SASE required. **Freelance Content:** 10%.

TODAY'S GRANDPARENT

Today's Parent Group, 269 Richmond St. West,
Toronto, Ontario, Canada M5V 1X1. 416-596-8680.
Web site: www.todaysparent.com. Quarterly. Circ.: 190,000. **Description:** For grandparents of all ages.

TOLEDO AREA PARENT NEWS

1120 Adams St., Toledo, OH 43624. 419-244-9859.
Web site: www.toledoparent.com. Monthly. Circ.: 50,000. Meira Zucker, Editor. **Description:** For parents in Northwest Ohio and Southern Michigan. **Nonfiction:** On parenting, child and family health, other family topics. Writers must be from the region; 750-1,200 words; $75-$100. **Queries:** Preferred. **Unsolicited mss:** Accepts.

TWINS

5350 S. Roslyn St., Suite 400, Englewood, CO 80111-2125. 303-290-8500. E-mail: twins.editor@businessword.com. Web site: www.twinsmagazine.com. Bimonthly. Circ.: 55,000. Sharon Withers, Editor. **Description:** Expert advice from professionals and parents, about the needs of multiple-birth parents. **Fiction:** Annual fiction contest: stories about twin children (or animals) ages 5 and under. Deadline, April 30th. Publication of winner's work. **Nonfiction:** Parenting issues specific to multiples; 1,200 words; $200-225. **Fillers:** Practical tips (for specific ages: birth-2, 3-4, 5-6); 125-150 words; $20. **Columns, Departments:** On Being Parents; Special Miracles (personal experiences); 500-600 words; $40. **Art:** Yes. **Queries:** Preferred. **E-queries:** Accepts. **Unsolicited mss:** Accepts. **Response:** 3 months. **Freelance Content:** 60%. **Payment:** On publication.

WASHINGTON FAMILIES

462 Herndon Pkwy #206, Herndon, VA 20170-5235. 703-318-1385. Web site: www.familiesmagazine.com. Monthly. Circ.: 90,000. **Description:** For families in the Washington D.C. area.

WASHINGTON PARENT

4701 Sangamore Rd., #N270, Bethesda, MD 20816-2508. 301-320-2321. Web site: www.washingtonparent.com. Monthly. Circ.: 90,000. **Description:** For parents in and around Washington, D.C.

ZELLERS FAMILY

269 Richmond St. West, Toronto, Ontario, Canada M5V 1X1. 416-596-8675. 3x/year. Circ.: 1,000,000. **Description:** For Zellers store customers.

FILM, TV, ENTERTAINMENT

ATLANTIC CITY
P.O. Box 2100, Pleasantville, NJ 08232-1924. 609-272-7900.
Doug Bergen, Editor. **Description:** On Atlantic City and southern New Jersey shore, for locals and tourists. Entertainment, casinos, business, recreation, personalities, lifestyle, local color. **Nonfiction:** Lively articles; 200-2,000 words; pays $50-$600. **Queries:** Preferred. **Payment:** On publication.

BACK STAGE WEST
5055 Wilshire Blvd., 6th Fl., Los Angeles, CA 90036. 323-525-2356. Web site: www.backstage.com. Weekly. Robert Kendt. **Description:** Actor's trade paper, West Coast. **Nonfiction:** Articles and reviews; pays $.10-$.15/word. **Queries:** Required. **Payment:** On publication.

BOMB
594 Broadway, Suite 905, New York, NY 10012. 212-431-3943. E-mail: betsy@bombsite.com. Web site: www.bombsite.com. Quarterly. $4.96/$18. Circ.: 20,000. Betsy Sussler, Editor. **Description:** Articles, varying lengths, on artists, musicians, writers, actors, and directors. Some fiction and poetry. Fiction: 30 pages max.; $100. **Nonfiction:** Will consider conversational interviews, but query first. **Poetry:** 10 pages; $100. **Queries:** Preferred. **E-queries:** Yes. Unsolicited mss: Accepts. **Response:** Queries 2 months, submissions 4 months, SASE. Freelance Content: 5%. Rights: 1st serial. **Payment:** On publication. **Contact:** Susan Sherman, Assoc. Ed.

CINEASTE
P.O. Box 2242, New York, NY 10009. 212-982-1241. E-mail: cineaste@cineaste.com. Web site: www.cineaste.com. Quarterly. $6/$20. Circ.: 11,000. Gary Crowdus, Editor. **Description:** Covers art and politics of the cinema. Views, analyzes, and interprets films. **Nonfiction:** 1,000-5,000 words; $20-$100. **Tips:** Readers are intelligent general public, sophisticated about art and politics. No matter how complex the ideas or arguments, style must be readable. **Queries:** Preferred. **E-queries:** Yes. Unsolicited mss: Accepts. **Response:** 2-3 months, SASE required. Freelance Content: 50%. Rights: 1st NA. **Payment:** On publication.

EMMY
5220 Lankershim Blvd., N. Hollywood, CA 91601-2800. 818-754-2800. E-mail: polevoi@emmys.org. Web site: www.emmys.org. Bimonthly. $4.95/$28. Circ.: 15,000. Gail Polevoi, Editor. **Description:** Covers people who make television happen, for TV industry professionals. **Nonfiction:** Profiles and trend stories; 1,500-2,000 words; $800-$1,200. **Columns, Departments:** New writers, could break in with Labors of Love or Viewpoint; 500-1,000 words; $350-$750. **Tips:** Should have TV business background. No academic, fan-magazine, or highly technical articles. **Queries:** Required. **E-queries:** Yes. **Unsolicited mss:** Accepts. **Response:** 4-6

weeks, SASE required (unless by e-mail). **Freelance Content:** 80%. **Rights:** 1st NA. **Payment:** On publication.

ENTERTAINMENT DESIGN

32 W. 18th St., New York, NY 10011. 212-229-2965.

Web site: www.etecnyc.net. Jacqueline Tien, Publisher. **Description:** On design, technical, and management aspects of theater, opera, dance, television, and film for those in performing arts and the entertainment trade. **Nonfiction:** Articles, 500-2,500 words. **Queries:** Preferred. **Payment:** On acceptance.

ENTERTAINMENT WEEKLY

1675 Broadway, New York, NY 10019. 212-522-5600.

Web site: pathfinder.com/ew. **Description:** Letters to the editor are published on the "Mail" page. Include name, address, and telephone number. No payment offered.

ENTERTAINMENTEEN

470 Park Ave. S, Fl8, New York, NY 10016. 212-545-3600.

Hedy End. **Description:** Lifestyle monthly for girls, ages 14-17. **Nonfiction:** Articles include interviews and profiles of popular teen celebrities (actors, actresses, singers, and musicians); pay varies. **Fillers:** Fillers, humor, and jokes welcomed. **Payment:** On publication.

FANGORIA

475 Park Ave. S., 8th Fl., New York, NY 10016. 212-689-2830.

Web site: www.fangoria2000.com. 10x/year. $6.99/issue, $39.97/year. Circ.: 260,000. Anthony Timpone, Editor. **Description:** Nonfiction articles and interviews about horror films, TV series, books, and their creators. Emphasizes personalities and behind-the-scenes angles of horror film making. **Nonfiction:** Movie, TV, and book previews; reviews; and interviews connected to upcoming horror films; 2,000-3,000 words; $150-$250. **Tips:** Fangoria is the trade journal for special makeup FX creators, often interviewed here. A strong love of the genre is essential. Readers are experts on horror, who want to read about the latest films and their makers. **Queries:** Required. **E-queries:** No. **Unsolicited mss:** Does not accept. **Response:** 6-8 weeks, SASE. **Freelance Content:** 92%. **Rights:** All. **Payment:** On publication.

FILM COMMENT

70 Lincoln Ctr. Plaza, New York, NY 10023-6595. 212-875-5610.

Web site: www.filmlinc.com. Bimonthly. **Description:** On films (new and old, foreign and domestic), also performers, writers, cinematographers, studios, national cinemas, genres. Opinion and historical pieces also used. **Nonfiction:** Articles, 1,000-5,000 words; pays $.33/word. **Payment:** On publication.

FILM QUARTERLY

Univ. of California Press Journals

2120 Berkeley Way, Berkeley, CA 94720. 510-643-7154.

Web site: www.ucpress.edu/journals/fq. Ann Martin, Editor. **Description:** Historical, analytical, and critical articles, to 6,000 words. Also, film reviews, book reviews. **Queries:** Preferred.

HADLEY MEDIA
19 Farley St., Greenwich, CT 06830-4603.
10x/year. D. Patrick Hadley, Editor. **Description:** Entertainment news, fashion trends, celebrity interviews, reviews of music, movies, and books, for New York City college students. **Queries:** Preferred.

HEROES FROM HACKLAND
1225 Evans, Arkadelphia, AR 71923. 870-246-6223.
3x/year. $5/$20. Circ.: 150. Mike Grogan, Editor. **Description:** Takes a nostalgic, popular-culture approach to the review of B-movies, cartoons, series books, radio, TV, comic books, and newspaper comic strips. **Nonfiction:** Any fresh article casting light on the popular culture of yesterday and its relation to today; 220-1500 words; $5 and copies. **Poetry:** Nostalgic with a bite, coherent imagery, no impenetrable college quarterly stuff; up to 40 lines; $5 and copies. **Fillers:** Vignettes about customs, little-known facts about pop culture icons. **Art:** b/w only; $5/photo. **Queries:** Not necessary. **Unsolicited mss:** Accepts. **Response:** 10 days, SASE. **Freelance Content:** 35%. **Rights:** 1st. **Payment:** On publication.

HOT
2121 Waukegan Rd., Bannockburn, IL 60015. 847-444-4880.
E-mail: hot@hsmedia.com. Monthly. $4.99/$47.95. Circ.: 250,000. Jennifer Tanalee, Editor. **Description:** For "tweens"—girls between ages of 8-14 years. Offers hot news on cool guys, hip groups, and successful Hollywood girls. Covers fashion trends, beauty, female celebrities, film and television stars, and musical groups. **Nonfiction:** Stories on celebrity-related events. Features on teen celebrities. Concert reviews; 500-2,000 words; $.50/word. **Art:** Slides, photographs, electronic (300 dpi). **Tips:** Successful writers have contacts in the celebrity industry, and use a teen "voice" in their articles. **Queries:** Preferred. **E-queries:** Yes. **Unsolicited mss:** Does not accept. **Freelance Content:** 10%-25%. **Contact:** Laurel Smoke, Asst. Ed.

ILLINOIS ENTERTAINER
124 W. Polk, Suite 103, Chicago, IL 60605.
E-mail: ieeditors@aol.com. Web site: www.illinoisentertainer.com. Monthly. Free. Circ.: 70,000. Michael C. Harris, Editor. **Description:** Covers entertainment and media, especially music. Open to non-music/band features, especially of odd, quixotic kind. **Nonfiction:** On local and national entertainment (especially alternative music) in greater Chicago area. Personality profiles; interviews; reviews. 500-1,500 words; $75. **Art:** by assignment; $30-200. **Tips:** Send clips (via snail mail) and be patient. **Queries:** Not necessary. **E-queries:** Yes. **Unsolicited mss:** Accepts. **Response:** Queries 30 days, submissions 30-90 days, SASE not required. **Freelance Content:** 70%. **Rights:** FNASR. **Payment:** On publication.

INDEPENDENT FILM AND VIDEO MONTHLY

304 Hudson St., 6th Floor, New York, NY 10013. 212-807-1400.
E-mail: editor@aivf.org. Web site: www.aivf.org. 10x/year. $4.95/issue. Circ.: 15,000.
Patricia Thomson, Editor. **Description:** For active mediamakers, covers all aspects of independently produced film and video. Scripting, funding, production, technology, editing, film festivals, distribution. **Nonfiction:** 700-1,300 words; production techniques; interviews with directors, producers, writers; book reviews; technology news, legal issues; media advocacy. Pay varies. **Queries:** Required. **E-queries:** Yes. **Unsolicited mss:** Accepts. **Response:** to 4 months, SASE. **Freelance Content:** 80%. **Rights:** 1st NA, web rights for extra fee. **Payment:** On publication.

KIDS TRIBUTE

71 Barber Greene Rd., Don Mills, Ont., Canada M3C 2A2. 416-445-0544.
Web site: www.tribute.ca. Quarterly. Sandra Stewart, Editor-in-Chief. **Description:** Movie- or entertainment-related articles, for young readers, ages 8-13. **Nonfiction:** 350 words; pays $150-$200 (Canadian). **Queries:** Required. **Payment:** On acceptance.

NEW ENGLAND ENTERTAINMENT DIGEST

P.O. Box 88, Burlington, MA 01803. 781-272-2066.
E-mail: jacneed@aol.com. Web site: www.jacneed.com. Monthly. $2/issue, $20/annually. Circ.: 5,000. Julie Ann Charest, Editor. **Description:** Covers theater and entertainment news for New England (and New York). **Nonfiction:** Length varies, pays per column inch. **Art:** b/w or high-rez electronic; $5/print. **Queries:** Preferred. **E-queries:** Yes. **Unsolicited mss:** Accepts. **Freelance Content:** 25%. **Payment:** On acceptance.

PERFORMING ARTS AND ENTERTAINMENT IN CANADA

104 Glenrose Ave., Toronto, ON M4T 1K8 Canada. 416-484-4534.
Quarterly. $8.56/issue. Circ.: 10,000. Sara B. Hood, Editor and Art Director. **Description:** Canadian performing arts and entertainment, including theater, music (especially classical, new, jazz, world, and folk), dance, film, TV, and related fields. Also profiles, opinion, issues, etc. **Nonfiction:** Should be of national interest, but values submissions from smaller, out-of-the-way locations (not just downtown Montreal and Toronto). Especially interested in stories that reflect some aspect of Canadian diversity. Publishes very few reviews; 1,000-2,500 words; $.25/word. **Art:** Prints (b/w or color); no payment. **Tips:** Welcomes new writers. Prefers stories with original ideas and opinions, or addressing issues of some complexity or sophistication—not just simple profiles of people or companies. **Queries:** Preferred. **E-queries:** Yes. **Unsolicited mss:** Accepts. **Response:** Slow to respond, be patient, SASE required. **Rights:** 1st print and electronic. **Payment:** On publication.

PLAYBILL

52 Vanderbilt Ave., New York, NY 10017. 212-557-5757.
Web site: www.playbill.com. Judy Samelson, Editor. **Description:** Increases the understanding and enjoyment of each Broadway production, certain Lincoln Center

and Off-Broadway productions, and regional attractions. Also, features about theatre personalities, fashion, entertainment, dining, etc. **Unsolicited mss:** Does not accept.

REAL PEOPLE
450 7th Ave., Suite 1701, New York, NY 10123-0073. 212-244-2351. E-mail: mrs-2@idt.net. Bimonthly. Circ.: 75,000. Alex Polner, Brad Hamilton, Editors. **Description:** Interviews with movie or TV actors, musicians, other entertainment celebrities. **Nonfiction:** 1,000 to 1,800 words; $150-$350. **Fillers:** Humorous items from small newspapers, etc.; to 75 words; $25-$50. **Columns, Departments:** True stories, about interesting people for "Real Shorts": strange occurrences, everyday weirdness, occupations, etc.; funny, sad, or hair-raising. Send submissions to Brad Hamilton; to 500 words. **Queries:** Preferred. **Response:** SASE. **Payment:** On publication.

16 SUPERSTARS
Primedia Enthusiast Group
470 Park Ave. S., Floor 8, New York, NY 10016. 212-545-3600.
6x/year. Circ.: 70,000. **Description:** Entertainment topics for teens.

SOAP OPERA DIGEST
Primedia Inc., 745 Fifth Avenue, New York, NY 10151. 800-829-9096. Web site: www.soapdigest.com. Jason Bonderoff, Editor. **Description:** Investigative reports and profiles about New York and Los Angeles-based soaps. **Nonfiction:** to 1,500 words; pays from $250. **Payment:** On acceptance.

SOAP OPERA UPDATE
270 Sylvan Ave., Englewood Cliffs, NJ 07632. 201-569-6699.
Bill Leiberman, Editor. **Description:** Soap-opera oriented. **Nonfiction:** Articles, 750-1,250 words; pays $200. **Fillers:** to 500 words. **Queries:** Preferred. **Payment:** On publication.

STAR
5401 NW Broken Sound Blvd., Boca Raton, FL 33487. 561-997-7733. Web site: www.starmagazine.com. **Description:** on show business and celebrities, health, fitness, parenting, and diet and food. **Nonfiction:** Topical articles, 50-800 words; pay varies.

TIGER BEAT
Sterling/MacFadden Partnership
470 Park Ave. South, New York, NY 10016-6868. 212-545-3603.
Louise Barile, Editor. **Description:** On young people in show business and the music industry. **Nonfiction:** Articles, to 4 pages; pays varying rates. **Queries:** Preferred. **Payment:** On acceptance.

TV GUIDE

1211 Avenue of the Americas, 4th Floor, New York, NY 10036-8701. 212-852-7500. Web site: www.tvguideinc.com. Steven Reddicliffe, Editor-in-Chief. **Description:** Short, light, brightly written pieces about humorous or offbeat angles of television and industry trends. Most personality pieces are staff-written. **Queries:** Required. **Payment:** On acceptance.

UNIVERCITY

Hadley Media, 19 Farley St., Greenwich, CT 06830. 914-479-0655. E-mail: screenplays@univercity. Web site: www.univercity.com. Patrick Hadley, Publisher. **Description:** An entertainment magazine for college students. Has east-coast and west-coast editions. **Tips:** To submit, visit UniverCity's website for details. Also interested in screenplays for their production company. **Queries:** Preferred. **E-queries:** Yes. **Unsolicited mss:** Accepts.

VIDEOMAKER

P.O. Box 4591, Chico, CA 95927. 530-891-8410. E-mail: editor@videomaker.com. Web site: www.videomaker.com. Monthly. Circ.: 80,000. Stephen Muratore, Editor. **Description:** Covers consumer video production: camcorders, computers, tools and techniques. For hobbyists and professional users. **Nonfiction:** Authoritative how-to articles, instructionals, editing, desktop video, audio/video production, innovative applications, tools and tips, industry developments, new products; up to 1,500 words; $.10/word. **Queries:** Preferred. **E-queries:** Yes. **Unsolicited mss:** Accepts. **Response:** 6-8 weeks, SASE. **Freelance Content:** 60%. **Rights:** All. **Payment:** On acceptance.

FITNESS
(See also Health)

AMERICAN FITNESS

15250 Ventura Blvd., Suite 200, Sherman Oaks, CA 91403. 818-905-0040. Web site: www.afaa.com. Bimonthly. $48/year. Circ.: 39,000. Peg Jordan, Editor. **Description:** Trade journal for fitness instructors. **Nonfiction:** Articles on exercise, health, trends, research, nutrition, class instruction, alternative paths. No first-person stories; 1,200 words; $200/article. **Art:** Slides; $35/slide. **Tips:** Needs research-oriented articles. **Queries:** Required. **E-queries:** Yes. **Unsolicited mss:** Accepts. **Response:** 2 months, SASE required. **Freelance Content:** 90%. **Rights:** All. **Payment:** On publication.

FIT

419 Park Ave. S., 18th Floor, New York, NY 10016. 212-541-7100. Bimonthly. Circ.: 125,000. Lisa Klugman, Editor. **Description:** Lively, readable service-oriented articles on exercise, nutrition, lifestyle, and health for women ages 18-35. **Nonfiction:** Writers should background in or knowledge of sports, fitness,

and/or health; 800-1,200 words; $300-500. **Columns, Departments:** Finally Fit (500-word essays, by readers who have lost weight and kept it off). **Queries:** Required. **Payment:** On publication.

FITNESS

Gruner & Jahr USA Publishing, 375 Lexington Ave., New York, NY 10017-5514. 212-499-2000. Monthly. Emily Listfield, Editor. **Description:** Health, exercise, sports, nutrition, diet, psychological well-being, alternative therapies, and beauty. For readers, average age 30. **Nonfiction:** 500-2,000 words; $1/word. **Queries:** Required. **Payment:** On acceptance.

FITNESS PLUS

3402 E. Kleindale Rd., Tucson, AZ 85716. Bimonthly. Wendy Graham, Editor. **Description:** On serious health and fitness training for men. **Nonfiction:** Articles, 1,000-3,000 words; pay varies. **Queries:** Preferred. **Payment:** On publication.

IDEA HEALTH & FITNESS SOURCE

6190 Cornerstone Ct. E., Suite 204, San Diego, CA 92121. 858-535-8979. Web site: www.ideafit.com. 10x/year. Circ.: 19,000. Diane Lofshult, Editor. **Description:** Leading publication for all levels of fitness professionals. **Nonfiction:** Practical articles on new exercise programs, business management, nutrition, health, motivation, sports medicine, group exercise, one-to-one training techniques. Length, pay varies. **Tips:** Must be geared toward exercise studio owner or manager, personal trainer, and fitness instructor. No consumer or general health pieces. **Queries:** Preferred. **E-queries:** Yes. **Unsolicited mss:** Accepts. **Response:** Queries 2-3 months. **Freelance Content:** 75%. **Rights:** All NA (print and electronic). **Payment:** On acceptance.

IDEA PERSONAL TRAINER

Suite 204, 6190 Cornerstone Ct. E., San Diego, CA 92121-3773. 858-535-8979. Web site: www.ideafit.com. 10x/year. $5/issue. Circ.: 20,000. Nicholas Drake, Editor. **Description:** For the professional personal trainer. **Nonfiction:** On exercise science; program design; profiles of successful trainers; business, legal, and marketing topics; tips for networking with other trainers and with allied medical professionals; client counseling; and training tips. Pay varies. **Columns, Departments:** What's New (industry news, products, research). **Queries:** Preferred. **E-queries:** Yes. **Unsolicited mss:** Accepts. **Response:** 1 month, SASE for mailed materials. **Payment:** On publication.

MEN'S FITNESS

21100 Erwin St., Woodland Hills, CA 91367. 818-884-6800. Web site: www.mensfitness.com. Jerry Kindela, Editor. **Description:** On sports, fitness, health, nutrition, and men's issues. **Nonfiction:** Authoritative, practical articles,

1,500-1,800 words; pays $500-$1,000. **Columns, Departments:** 1,200-1,500 words. **Tips:** Send clips. **Queries:** Preferred. **Payment:** On acceptance.

MUSCULAR DEVELOPMENT

150 Motor Pkwy., Suite 120, Hauppauge, NY 11788.
Steve Blechman, Editor-in-Chief. **Description:** For serious weight-training athletes, on any aspect of competitive body building, powerlifting, sports, and nutrition. **Nonfiction:** Articles, 1,000-2,500 words, photos; pays $50-$400. **Queries:** Preferred. **Payment:** On publication.

THE PHYSICIAN AND SPORTS MEDICINE MAGAZINE

4530 W. 77th St., Minneapolis, MN 55435. 952-835-3222.
E-mail: susan_hawthorne@mcgraw-hill.com. Web site: www.physsportmed.com. Susan Hawthorne, Editor. **Description:** News articles, with sports-medicine angle. **Nonfiction:** Pays $300-$50. **Queries:** Preferred. **Payment:** On acceptance.

SHAPE

21100 Erwin St., Woodland Hills, CA 91367-3772. 818-595-0593.
Web site: www.shapemag.com. Monthly. $2.99. Circ.: 1,500,000. Barbara Harris, Editor. **Description:** Provides women with tools to create better lives and a deeper understanding of fitness. **Nonfiction:** New and interesting ideas on physical and mental aspects of getting and staying in shape; 1,200-1,500 words; pay varies. **Tips:** Uses only solid, well-respected experts in fields of exercise, health, nutrition, sport, beauty, and psychology. **Queries:** Preferred. **Unsolicited mss:** Accepts. **Payment:** On acceptance. **Contact:** Peg Moline.

SWEAT

5743 E. Thomas #2, Scottsdale, AZ 85251. 480-997-3900.
E-mail: Westwoman@aol.com. Web site: www.sweatmagazine.com. Joan Westlake, Editor. **Description:** On amateur sports, outdoor activities, wellness, or fitness, with an Arizona angle. **Nonfiction:** Articles, 500-1,200 words. No self-indulgent or personal tales. Prefers investigative pieces, must relate to Arizona or Arizonans. Pays $25-$60. **Art:** Photos, $15-$70. **Queries:** Required. **Unsolicited mss:** Does not accept. **Payment:** On publication.

TEACHING ELEMENTARY PHYSICAL EDUCATION

P.O. Box 5076, Champaign, IL 61825-5076. 217-351-5076.
Web site: www.humankinetics.com. Bimonthly. **Description:** Resources and ideas on instructional and fun physical-education programs for K-8 physical education teachers. **Queries:** Preferred.

VIM & VIGOR

1010 E. Missouri Ave., Phoenix, AZ 85014. 602-395-5850.
E-mail: sallyc@mcmurry.com. Web site: vigormagazine.com. Quarterly. $2.95. Circ.: 1,500,000. Sally J. Clasen, Editor. **Description:** A national health and fitness publi-

cation, with 20 large regional editions. **Nonfiction:** Positive articles, with medical facts, healthcare news, medical breakthroughs, exercise/fitness, health trends, wellness, general physical and emotional health, disease updates; written for a general reader; 900-1,500 words; up to $750. **Tips:** No healthcare product promotion, book reviews, personal accounts (unless to illustrate a topic) or unfounded medical claims for disease prevention and treatment. Style is serious, poignant, informative; with a slant that speaks to the reader as "you." Write for an educated reader, but remember to explain scientific terms and complex procedures. **Queries:** Preferred. **E-queries:** Yes. **Unsolicited mss:** Does not accept. **Rights:** 1st NA, international and electronic. **Payment:** On publication.

WALKING MAGAZINE
45 Bromfield St., 8th Fl., Boston, MA 02108. 617-574-0076. Web site: www.walkingmag.com. Seth Bauer, Editor. **Description:** On fitness, health, equipment, nutrition, travel and adventure, and other walking-related topics. **Nonfiction:** Articles, 1,500-2,500 words; pays $750-$1,800. **Columns, Departments:** Shorter pieces, 150-800 words; essays for Ramblings page; pays $100-$500. **Art:** Photos. **Payment:** On acceptance.

WEIGHT WATCHERS
360 Lexington Ave 11th Floor, New York, NY 10017. 212-370-0644. Web site: www.weightwatchers.com. 6x/year. Circ.: 500,000. Nancy Gagliarch, Editor in Chief. **Description:** Health, nutrition, fitness, and weight-loss motivation and success. **Nonfiction:** Articles on fashion, beauty, food, health, nutrition, fitness, and weight-loss motivation and success; from $1/word. **Queries:** Required. **Payment:** On acceptance.

FOOD & WINE

BON APPETIT
Conde Nast Publications, 6300 Wilshire Blvd., 10th Fl., Los Angeles, CA 90048. 323-965-3600. Web site: www.epicurious.com. Monthly. $3.50/issue. Circ.: 5,300,000. Barbara Fairchild, Executive Editor. **Description:** Covers food, entertainment, and travel. **Art:** Photos, illustrations. **Queries:** Preferred. **E-queries:** No. **Unsolicited mss:** Does not accept. **Response:** 4-6 weeks, SASE required. **Rights:** All. **Payment:** On acceptance.

BREW YOUR OWN
Battenkill Communications, 5053 Main St., Suite A, Manchester Center, VT 05255. 802-362-3981. E-mail: edit@byo.com. Web site: www.byo.com. Monthly. Circ.: 42,000. Kathleen James Ring, Editor. **Description:** Practical how-to articles for homebrewers. **Queries:** Required. **Payment:** On publication.

CHEF

Talcott Communications Corp., 20 N. Wacker Dr., Suite 1865, Chicago, IL 60606. 312-849-2220. Web site: www.chefmagazine.com. Brent T. Frei. **Description:** "The Food Magazine for Professionals." Offers professionals in the foodservice business ideas for food marketing, preparation, and presentation. **Nonfiction:** Articles, 800-1,200 words; pays $250 to first-time writers, others $300. **Payment:** On publication.

CHOCOLATIER

45 W. 34th St., #600, New York, NY 10001. Michael Schneider, Editor. **Description:** Articles related to chocolate and desserts, cooking and baking techniques, lifestyle and travel. **Nonfiction:** Pay varies. **Queries:** Required. **Payment:** On acceptance.

COOK'S ILLUSTRATED

17 Station St., Brookline, MA 02445. 617-232-1000. Web site: cooksillustrated.com. Bimonthly. Christopher Kimball, Editor. **Description:** Articles on techniques of home cooking. Master recipes based on careful testing, trial and error. **Nonfiction:** Pay varies. **Queries:** Preferred. **Payment:** On acceptance.

COOKING FOR PROFIT

P.O. Box 267, Fond du Lac, WI 54936-0267. 920-923-3700. Web site: www.cookingforprofit.com. Colleen Phalen, Editor. **Description:** For foodservice professionals. **Nonfiction:** Profiles of successful restaurants, chains, and franchises, schools, hospitals, nursing homes, etc. Also, case studies on energy management in foodservice environment. Business-to-business articles. Pay varies. **Payment:** On publication.

COOKING LIGHT

2100 Lake Shore Dr., Birmingham, AL 35209. 205-877-6000. Web site: www.cookinglight.com. 11x/year. Circ.: 1,600,000. Douglas Crichton, Editor. **Description:** Fitness, exercise, health and healthful cooking, nutrition, and healthful recipes. **Tips:** Query with clips and SASE. **Queries:** Required.

FANCY FOOD & CULINARY PRODUCTS

Talcott Communications Corp., 20 N. Wacker Dr., Suite 1865, Chicago, IL 60606-2905. 312-849-2220, ex.34. E-mail: fancyfood@talcott.com. Web site: www.talcott.com. monthly. $3.95/issue. Circ.: 28,000. Daniel Von Rabenav, Managing Editor. **Description:** Covers the business of specialty foods, coffee and tea, natural foods, confections, and upscale housewares. **Nonfiction:** 1,200-1,500 words; $300. **Art:** prints, transparencies, digital; $50. **Tips:** Readers are retailers, not customers. **Queries:** Required. **E-queries:** Yes. **Unsolicited mss:** Accepts. **Response:** 1 month. **Freelance Content:** 35%. **Rights:** FNASR. **Payment:** On publication. **Contact:** Brent Frei.

GOURMET

Conde Nast, 4 Times Square, New York, NY 10036. 212-286-2860.
Web site: www.epicurious.com. **Description:** "The magazine of good living."
Queries: Preferred. **Unsolicited mss:** Does not accept.

HOMETOWN COOKING

Meredith Corp., 1716 Locust St., Des Moines, IA 50309. 515-284-3000.
Web site: www.hometowncook.com. Monthly. Joy Taylor, Editor. **Description:** Great-tasting, tried-and-true recipes from America's most popular hometown cookbooks.
Nonfiction: Features include dinnertime survival recipes, prizewinning recipes, family-approved recipes, and beautiful full-color photos of recipes. Pay varies.

KITCHEN GARDEN

P.O. Box 5506, Newtown, CT 06470-5506. 203-426-8171.
E-mail: kg@taunton.com. Web site: www.taunton.com. Bimonthly. **Description:** For home gardeners who love to grow their own vegetables, fruits, and herbs and use them in cooking. **Nonfiction:** Nonfiction articles, varying lengths. **Columns, Departments:** Plant Profiles, Garden Profiles, Techniques, Design, Projects, Cooking; pays $150/page. **Queries:** Preferred. **Payment:** On publication.

VEGGIE LIFE

1041 Shary Cir., Concord, CA 94518. 925-671-9852.
Web site: www.veggielife.com. Quarterly. Deerra Shehabi. **Description:** For people interested in lowfat, meatless cuisine, natural health, nutrition, and herbal healing.
Nonfiction: Food features (include 8-10 recipes); 1,500-2,000 words. **Columns, Departments:** 1,000-1,500 words. **Queries:** Preferred. **Payment:** On publication.

WINE SPECTATOR

387 Park Ave. S., New York, NY 10016. 212-684-4224.
Web site: www.winespectator.com. Thomas Matthews, Editor. **Description:** On news and people in the wine world, travel, food, and other lifestyle topics.
Nonfiction: Features, 600-2,000 words, preferably with photos; pays from $400, extra for photos. **Queries:** Required. **Payment:** On publication.

WINE TIDINGS

5165 Sherbrooke St. W., Suite 414, Montreal,
Quebec, Canada H4A 1T6. 514-481-5892.
Web site: www.cmpa.ca. 8x/year. Tony Aspler, Editor. **Description:** Accurate wine information, written for Canadian audience. **Nonfiction:** Articles (1,000-1,500 words, $100-$300), and shorts (400-1,000 words, $30-$150). **Art:** b/w photos, $20-$50; color, $200-$400 (covers). **Queries:** Preferred. **Payment:** On publication.

WINES & VINES

1800 Lincoln Ave., San Rafael, CA 94901. 415-453-9700.
E-mail: winesandvines.com. Web site: www.winesandvines.com. Monthly. Philip E.

Hiaring, Editor. **Description:** On grape and wine industry, emphasizing marketing, management, vineyard techniques, and production. Emphasizes technology with valuable, scientific winemaking articles. **Nonfiction:** Articles, 2,000 words; pays $.15/word. **Queries:** Required. **E-queries:** Yes. **Unsolicited mss:** Accepts. **Payment:** On acceptance.

ZYMURGY
736 Pearl St., Boulder, CO 80302. 303-447-0816.
Web site: www.beertown.org. Ray Daniels, Editor. **Description:** Articles appealing to beer lovers and homebrewers. **Queries:** Preferred. **Payment:** On publication.

GAMES & PASTIMES
(See also Hobbies, Crafts, Collecting)

BINGO BUGLE
Frontier Publications, P.O. Box 527, Vashon, WA 98070. 206-463-5656.
Web site: www.bingobugle.com. Monthly. Circ.: 900,000. **Description:** For bingo players.

CARD PLAYER
3140 S. Polaris, Suite #8, Las Vegas, NV 89102. 702-871-1720.
E-mail: info@cardplayer.com. Web site: www.cardplayer.com. Bi-weekly. $59/year. Circ.: 50,000. Steve Radulovich, Editor. **Description:** For competitive players, on poker events, personalities, legal issues, new casinos, tournaments, and prizes. Also strategies, game psychology to improve poker play. Occasionally humor, cartoons, puzzles, or anecdotal material. **Queries:** Preferred. **E-queries:** No. **Unsolicited mss:** Accepts. **Response:** Submissions 1 month, SASE not required. **Freelance Content:** 1%. **Payment:** On publication.

CASINO PLAYER
Bayport One, Suite 470, 8025 Black Horse Pike,
W. Atlantic City, NJ 08232. 609-484-8866.
Web site: www.casinocenter.com. Adam Fine, Editor. **Description:** For beginning to intermediate gamblers, on slots, video poker, and table games. **Nonfiction:** Articles, 1,000-2,000 words, with photos; pays from $250. **Tips:** No first-person or real-life gambling stories. **Payment:** On publication.

CHANCE
ARC Publishing, Inc., 16 E 41st St, Fl 2, New York, NY. 212-889-3467.
Web site: www.chancemag.com. Bimonthly. Circ.: 160,000. **Description:** "The Best of Gaming." For casino and betting individuals.

CHESS LIFE

3054 NYS Rte. 9W, New Windsor, NY 12553-7698. 845-562-8650. E-mail: magazines@uschess.org. Web site: www.uschess.org. Monthly. $3.75/issue, $30/year. Circ.: 67,000. Peter Kurzdorfer, Editor. **Description:** Published by United States Chess Federation. Covers news of major chess events (U.S. and abroad), with emphasis on the triumphs and exploits of American players. **Fiction:** 500-2,000 words. **Nonfiction:** Articles, 500-3,000 words, on news, profiles, technical aspects. Features on history, humor, puzzles, etc. **Art:** b/w glossies, color slides. Pays $25-$35. **Queries:** Preferred. **Unsolicited mss:** Accepts. **Payment:** On publication.

COMPUTER GAMES MAGAZINE

The Globe.com, 63 Millet St., Richmond, VT 05477. 802-434-3060. Web site: www.cdmag.com. Monthly. Circ.: 200,000. **Description:** Computer gaming information.

COMPUTER GAMING WORLD

Ziff-Davis Publishing Co., 50 Beale St., Ste 12, San Francisco, CA 94105. 415-357-4900. Web site: www.computergaming.com. Monthly. Circ.: 325,000. **Description:** All aspects of computer gaming.

ELECTRONIC GAMING MONTHLY

Ziff-Davis Publishing Co., P.O. Box 3338, Hinsdale, IL 60522. 630-382-9000. Web site: www.videogames.com. Monthly. Circ.: 400,000. **Description:** Reports on home video console games.

FAMILY FUN

Disney Magazine Publishing Inc. 244 Main St., Northampton, MA 01060-3107. 413-585-0444. Web site: www.familyfun.com. 10x/year. Circ.: 1,300,000. **Description:** Thousands of ideas for you and your kids. Offers many easy and inexpensive ideas for cooped-up kids. **Nonfiction:** Articles on great activities families can do together; to 1,500 words; pay varies. **Queries:** Required. **Payment:** On acceptance. **Contact:** Fred Levine, Features Editor.

GAMEPRO

Games Media Group, 501 2nd St., Ste 114, San Francisco, CA 94107. 415-979-9845. Web site: www.gamepro.com. Monthly. Circ.: 500,000. **Description:** For computer and video gamers.

GAMES

7002 W Butler Pike, Suite 210, Ambler, PA 19002; also, P.O. Box 184, Fort Washington, PA 19034. 215-643-6385. E-mail: gamespub@tidalwave.com. 9x/year. Circ.: 175,000. R. Wayne Schmittberger, Editor in Chief. **Description:** "For creative minds at play." **Nonfiction:** Features and short articles on games and playful, offbeat subjects. Visual and verbal puzzles, pop culture quizzes, brainteasers, contests, game reviews. **Tips:** Send SASE for guidelines (specify writer's, crosswords, puzzles, or brainteasers). **Payment:** On publication.

JACKPOT!
Morris Specialty Publications, 6064 Apple Tree Dr., #9, Memphis, TN 38115. 901-360-0777. Web site: www.jackpot.com. Semimonthly. Circ.: 35,000. **Description:** Covers all aspects of casino entertainment, gaming, and food.

ON TRACK
120 W. Morehead St., Ste 320, Charlotte, NC 28202. 704-371-3966. Web site: ontrackonline.com. Jon Gunn, Editor. **Description:** Features and race reports **Nonfiction:** 500-2,500 words; pays $5.25/column inch. **Queries:** Preferred. **Response:** 2 weeks. **Payment:** On publication.

REALMS OF FANTASY
Sovereign Media Co., 11305 Sunset Hills Rd., Reston, VA 20190. 703-471-1556. Bi-monthly. Circ.: 110,000. **Description:** Topics and reviews of interest to readers of science fiction, including role-playing games.

RENAISSANCE
Phantom Press Publications, 13 Appleton Rd., Nantucket, MA 02554. E-mail: renzine@aol.com. Web site: www.renaissancemagazine.com. Quarterly. Circ.: 30,000. Kim Guarnaccia, Managing Editor. **Description:** Renaissance and Medieval history, costuming, heraldry, reenactments, role-playing, and Renaissance faires. **Nonfiction:** Interviews, reviews of books, music, movies, and games; $.06/word. **Queries:** Preferred. **Payment:** On publication.

WINNING!
NatCom, Inc., 5300 City Plex Twr 2448 E 81st St., Tulsa, OK 74137. 918-491-6100. Web site: www.winningnews.com. Monthly. Circ.: 120,000. **Description:** Articles on how to win.

GAY & LESBIAN

EMPIRE
Two Queens, Inc., 230 W. 17th St., 8th Fl, New York, NY 10011. 212-352-3535. E-mail: akrach@hx.com. Web site: www.empiremag.com. Bill Henning, Editor. **Description:** For gay men who want the most out of life.

GENRE
7080 Hollywood Blvd., Suite 818, Hollywood, CA 90028. 323-467-8300. E-mail: gkaan@genre.com. Web site: www.genremagazine.com. Monthly.

$4.95/issue, $24.95/year. Circ.: 45,000. Gil Kaan, Editor. **Description:** Covers fashion, entertainment, travel, fiction, reviews, health, and spirituality for gay men. **Fiction:** Gay themes. Pay varies; 2,000 words. **Nonfiction:** Travel, celebrity interviews, medical updates; 300-1,500 words; $.20/word. **Poetry:** Humorous, spiritual; 100-300 words. **Art:** slides, .jpgs. **Queries:** Preferred. **E-queries:** Accepts. **Unsolicited mss:** Accepts. **Response:** 2-3 weeks, SASE required. **Freelance Content:** 60%. **Rights:** Print, electronic. **Payment:** On publication.

GLOBAL CITY REVIEW
Rifkind Ctr. for the Humanties, City College of NY,
138th St. & Convenient Ave., New York, NY 10031.
E-mail: globalcityreview@aol.com. Biannual. Linsey Abrams. **Description:** Intellectual literary forum for women, lesbian, and gay, and other culturally diverse writers; writers of color, international writers, activist writers. Thematic issues. Fiction, nonfiction, and poetry on issues of gender, race, and women's experience. **Tips:** No queries; send complete manuscripts for review. **Payment:** in copies.

HURRICANE ALICE
Rhode Island College, Dept. of English, Providence, RI 02908. 401-456-8377.
E-mail: mreddy@ric.edu. Quarterly. $2.50/$12. Circ.: 1,000. Maureen Reddy, Editor.
Description: Feminist exploration, from diverse perspectives, of all aspects of culture. Especially committed to work by women of color, lesbians, working-class women, and young women. **Fiction:** Fictional critiques of culture; 3,500 words max. **Nonfiction:** Articles, essays, interviews, and reviews; 3,500 words max. **Poetry:** Yes. **Art:** b/w (5x7 or 8x10). **Queries:** Not necessary. **E-queries:** Yes. **Unsolicited mss:** Accepts. **Response:** Queries 30 days, submissions 6 months, SASE required. **Freelance Content:** 100%. **Rights:** FNASR. **Payment:** in copies.

JAMES WHITE REVIEW
Lambda Literary Foundation, P.O. Box 73910,
Washington, DC 20056-3910. 202-682-0952.
E-mail: LLFGregh@aolcom. Web site: www.lambdalit.org. Quarterly. $4.95/$17.50.
Circ.: 3,000. Patrick Merla, Editor. **Description:** Gay men's literary magazine, with fiction, poetry, photography, art, essays and reviews. **Fiction:** Seeking well-crafted literary fiction with strongly-developed characters; gay themes; to 10,000 words; pay varies. **Poetry:** Submit up to 3 poems at a time. **Tips:** Be patient, small staff with a lot of submissions. **Queries:** Preferred. **E-queries:** No. **Unsolicited mss:** Accepts. **Response:** Queries 3 weeks, submissions 3-6 months, SASE. **Rights:** 1st. **Payment:** On publication. **Contact:** Greg Harren, Asst. Ed.

JOEY
11901 Santa Monica Blvd., Suite 598, Los Angeles, CA 90025.
E-mail: joeymagazinesCG@aol.com. Quarterly. Charles Gage, Associate Editor.
Description: For gay males between ages 15-25. Features personal experience, lifestyle issues, essays, and entertainment. **Tips:** Prefers personal accounts and infor-

mational articles. Seeks submissions from writers familiar with gay lifestyle. **Freelance Content:** 95%. **Rights:** All.

LAMBDA BOOK REPORT
1773 "T" Street NW, Suite One, Washington, DC 20009. 202-462-7924. **Description:** Reviews and features on gay and lesbian books. **Nonfiction:** 250-1,500 words; pays $10-$75. **Queries:** Preferred. **Payment:** On publication.

OUT MAGAZINE
The Soho Bldg., 110 Greene St., Suite 600, New York, NY 10012. 212-334-9119. Web site: www.out.com. Tom Beer, Editor-in-Chief. **Description:** Articles, 50-8,000 words, on arts, politics, fashion, finance and other subjects for gay and lesbian readers. No fiction or poetry. Pay varies. **Queries:** Preferred. **Payment:** On publication.

GENERAL INTEREST

ACCESS INTERNET MAGAZINE
Access Magazine, 35 Highland Cir, Needham, MA 02494. 781-453-3990. Monthly. Circ.: 5,000,000. **Description:** This insert into newspapers around the U.S. offers a variety of information on World Wide Web sites, activities, and techniques for successful use.

AMERICAN HERITAGE
90 Fifth Ave., New York, NY 10011. 212-367-3100. E-mail: mail@americanheritage.com. Web site: www.americanheritage.com. 8x/year. $4.95/issue. Circ.: 310,000. Richard F. Snow, Editor. **Description:** Covers the American experience, from serious concerns to colorful sidelights, from powerful institutions to ordinary men and women, using the past to illuminate the present. **Nonfiction:** On the American experience. Annotate all quotations and factual statements; include brief biographical note about yourself; 6,000 words max; pay varies. **Art:** b/w prints, color slides. **Tips:** Welcome freelancers, but needs detailed queries in advance. Also, consult indexes first. No fiction or poetry. **Queries:** Preferred. **E-queries:** No. **Unsolicited mss:** Accepts. **Response:** 8-10 weeks, SASE required. **Payment:** On acceptance.

ARIZONA REPUBLIC
200 E. Van Buren St., Phoenix, AZ 85004. 602-444-8000. Web site: www.arizonarepublic.com. Daily. Stephanie Robertson. **Description:** Newspaper, with diverse articles, 800-1,000 words, on lifestyles, environment, religion, politics, law, etc. **Queries:** Preferred. **Rights:** Exclusive (AZ).

ATLANTA CONSTITUTION
P.O. Box 4689, Atlanta, GA 30302. 404-526-5151. Web site: www.ajc.com. Daily. **Description:** Articles related to Southeast, Georgia,

or Atlanta metro area. **Nonfiction:** Submit complete manuscript. Varied topics: law, economics, politics, science, environment, performing arts, humor, education; religious, seasonal; 200-600 words; pays $75-$125. **Payment:** On publication.

ATLANTIC MONTHLY
77 N. Washington St., Boston, MA 02114. 617-854-7700. Web site: www.theatlantic.com. Monthly. $3.95/issue. Circ.: 500,000. Michael Kelly, Editor. **Description:** At the leading edge of contemporary issues, plus the best in fiction, travel, food, and humor. **Fiction:** 2,000-6,000 words; pays to $3,000. **Nonfiction:** 1,000-7,500 words; pay varies. **Poetry:** Yes. **Queries:** Preferred. **E-queries:** No. **Unsolicited mss:** Accepts. **Response:** 2-4 weeks, SASE required. **Freelance Content:** 50%. **Rights:** 1st NA. **Payment:** On acceptance.

BALTIMORE SUN
P.O. Box 1377, Baltimore, MD 21278-0001. 410-332-6459. Web site: www.sunspot.com. Daily. **Description:** Covers a wide range of topics (politics, education, foreign affairs, science, travel, lifestyles, humor). **Nonfiction:** Short articles; to 750 words; pays $50-$150. **Rights:** Exclusive for MD and DC area. **Payment:** On publication.

BLACK BOOK
116 Prince St., 2nd Fl., New York, NY 10012-3178. 212-334-1800. Web site: www.blackbookmag.com. Quarterly. Anuj Desai, Editor-in-Chief. **Description:** Entertainment magazine, on trends, beauty and fashion, news, and cutting-edge journalism. Also, some fiction. **Queries:** Preferred.

THE BOSTON GLOBE
135 Morrissey Blvd., P.O. Box 2378, Boston, MA 02107-2378. 617-929-2000. Web site: www.boston.com. Daily. Marjorie Pritchard. **Description:** Newspaper. Articles, to 700 words, on economics, education, environment, foreign affairs, and regional interest. **Tips:** Send complete manuscript. **Rights:** Exclusive (New England).

BOSTON HERALD
One Heerald Square, P.O. Box 2096, Boston, MA 02106-2096. 617-426-3000. Web site: www.bostonherald.com. Daily. Andrew Costello, Executive Editor. **Description:** On economics, foreign affairs, politics, regional interest, seasonal topics. **Nonfiction:** Short articles; 600-700 words; pay varies. **Tips:** Prefers submissions from regional writers. **Rights:** Exclusive for MA, RI, and NH. **Payment:** On publication.

BUTTON
Box 26, Lunenburg, MA 01462. E-mail: buttonsx26@aol.com. Annual. $2/issue. Circ.: 1,500. Sally Cragin, Editor. **Description:** "America's Tiniest Magazine." **Fiction:** Short stories. **Nonfiction:** Wit, brevity, well-conceived essay, recipes, sheet music, how-to, celebrity gossip, book

and album reviews; pay varies. **Poetry:** No sentimental or song lyrics. **Queries:** Not necessary. **E-queries:** No. **Unsolicited mss:** Accepts. **Response:** Submissions 2-3 months, SASE. **Freelance Content:** 60%. **Payment:** On publication.

THE CAPITAL TIMES

P.O. Box 8060, Madison, WI 53708. 608-252-6400.
Web site: www.madison.com. Daily. Jennie Buckner, Editor. **Description:** On education, environment, regional interest, and religion. **Nonfiction:** Short articles; 600-700 words; pays $25. **Payment:** On publication.

CHARLOTTE OBSERVER

P.O. Box 30308, Charlotte, NC 28230-0308. 707-358-5000.
Web site: www.charlotte.com. Daily. **Description:** On local (Carolinas) issues or that use local examples to illustrate larger issues. **Nonfiction:** Well-written, thought-provoking articles; to 700 words; pays $50. **Tips:** No simultaneous submissions in NC or SC. **Payment:** On publication.

CHICAGO READER

11 E. Illinois St., Chicago, IL 60611. 312-828-0350.
Web site: www.chicagoreader.com. **Description:** Free weekly. **Queries:** Preferred.

CHICAGO TRIBUNE

435 N. Michigan Ave., Chicago, IL 60611. 312-222-3232.
Web site: www.chicagotribune.com. Daily. **Description:** On domestic and international affairs, environment, regional interest, and personal essays. **Nonfiction:** Short articles (to 800 words); profiles and features, to 6,000 words, on public, social, and cultural issues in the Midwest/Chicago area; pays $250-$1,500. **Queries:** Preferred. **Response:** SASE required. **Payment:** On publication.

CHICAGO TRIBUNE MAGAZINE

Chicago Tribune, 435 N. Michigan Ave., Chicago, IL 60611. 312-222-3232.
Web site: www.chicagotribune.com. **Description:** Sunday magazine of the *Chicago Tribune.*

CHRISTIAN SCIENCE MONITOR

One Norway St., Boston, MA 02115. 617-450-2372.
E-mail: oped@csps.com. Web site: www.csmonitor.com. Daily. Circ.: 95,000. **Description:** Lifestyle trends, women's rights, family, community, and how-to. **Nonfiction:** Pieces on domestic and foreign affairs, economics, education, environment, law, media, politics, and cultural commentary. Retains all rights for 90 days after publication; 400-900 words; up to $400. **Poetry:** Finely crafted poems that explore and celebrate daily life. Short preferred; submit no more than 5 poems at a time. Seasonal material always needed. (No violence or sensuality; death or disease; helplessness or hopelessness.) **Columns, Departments:** Arts and Leisure, Learning, Ideas, Home Front, National, International, Work & Money; 800 words; pay varies.

THE CLEVELAND PLAIN DEALER

1801 Superior Ave., Cleveland, OH 44114. 216-999-4500 or 216-999-4145. E-mail: forum@plaind.com. Web site: www.cleveland.com. Daily. **Description:** On variety of subjects: domestic affairs, economics, education, environment, foreign affaris, humor, policties, and regional interest. **Nonfiction:** Op-ed pieces, to 750 words; pays $75. **Tips:** No room for historical pieces not tied to a recent event. **E-queries:** Yes. **Response:** 2-3 days. **Freelance Content:** 10-15%. **Rights:** non-exclusive worldwide. **Payment:** On publication.

COLUMBIA

Knights of Columbus, 1 Columbus Plaza, New Haven, CT 06510. 203-772-2130. E-mail: thickey@kofc.supreme.com. Web site: www.kofc.org. Monthly. $6/year. Circ.: 1,600,000. Tim S. Hickey, Editor. **Description:** Published by Knights of Columbus (world largest Catholic family fraternal service organization). Articles on current events, societal trends, family life and parenting, finances, Catholic practice and teachings. **Nonfiction:** Articles, 500-1,500 words, on topics of interest to K. of C. members, their families, and the Catholic layman; current events, religion, education, art, etc. Pays to $600. **Tips:** Write for sample copy (free), with guidelines. **Queries:** Required. **E-queries:** Yes. **Response:** Queries 2 weeks,submissions 2 weeks, SASE required. **Freelance Content:** 80%. **Payment:** On acceptance.

CONVERSELY

PMB #121, 3053 Fillmore St., San Francisco, CA 94123. E-mail: writers@conversely.com. Web site: www.conversely.com. Monthly. **Description:** Online, explores all aspects of relationships between men and women. **Fiction:** Literary stories on female-male relationships; to 3,000 words; $50-$150. **Nonfiction:** Essays and personal stories (memoirs); 750-3,000 words; $50-$150. **Tips:** Value personal opinion highly, witty, intelligent, entertaining. Avoid how-to, didactic material, or over-used romantic themes. **Queries:** Not necessary. **E-queries:** Yes. **Unsolicited mss:** Accepts. **Response:** 2-3 weeks queries, 8-10 weeks submissions, SASE (for submissions via mail). **Freelance Content:** 70%. **Rights:** 90-day exclusive electronic, non-exclusive thereafter. **Payment:** On publication.

DALLAS MORNING NEWS

Communications Ctr., P.O. Box 655237, Dallas, TX 75265. 214-977-8222. Web site: www.dallasnews.com. Daily. **Description:** Op-Ed pieces, 750 words, on politics, education, foreign and domestic affairs, cultural trends, seasonal and regional issues. Pays $75. **Response:** SASE required. **Payment:** On publication.

DENVER POST

P.O. Box 1709, Denver, CO 80201. 303-820-1010. Web site: www.denverpost.com. Daily. **Description:** Newspaper. Articles, 400-700 words, with local or regional angle. No payment for freelance submissions. **Queries:** Preferred.

DES MOINES REGISTER

P.O. Box 957, Des Moines, IA 50304. 515-284-8000.
Web site: www.desmoinesregister.com. Daily. **Description:** National and Iowa focus.

DETROIT FREE PRESS

600 W. Fort St., Detroit, MI 48226. 313-222-6400.
E-mail: oped@freepress.com. Web site: www.freep.com. Daily. **Description:** Wide range of topics. **Tips:** Priority given to local writers. **Queries:** Preferred. **Payment:** On publication.

THE DETROIT NEWS

615 W. Lafayette Blvd., Detroit, MI 48226. 313-222-6400.
Web site: www.detnews.com. Daily. **Description:** Wide variety of subjects. **Queries:** Preferred. **Payment:** On publication.

ELKS

425 W. Diversey Parkway, Chicago, IL 60614-6196. 773-755-4894.
E-mail: annai@elks.org. Web site: www.elks.org/elksmag/. 10x/year. Circ.: 1,200,000. Fred D. Oakes, Editor. **Description:** General interest, published by the Elks fraternal organization. Typical reader is over 40, an above-average income, living in a town of 500,000 or less. **Nonfiction:** Authoritative articles (please include sources) for lay person, varied topics: technology, science, sports, history, seasonal; 1,500-2,500 words; $.20/word. **Art:** Cover art; slides, transparencies; $450. **Tips:** No religion, politics, controversial issues. Avoid queries or clips. **Queries:** Not necessary. **E-queries:** Yes. **Unsolicited mss:** Accepts. **Response:** Queries 1 week, submissions 1-6 weeks, SASE required. **Freelance Content:** 30%. **Rights:** One-time NA serial. **Payment:** On acceptance.

EQUINOX

11450 Albert Hudon Blvd., Montreal North, Quebec, Canada H1G 3J9.
514-327-4464. Martin Silverstone, Editor. **Description:** On popular geography, science, wildlife, natural history, the arts, travel, and adventure. **Nonfiction:** Articles, 2,000-5,000 words; pays $1,500-$3,500. **Columns, Departments:** Nexus (science and medicine), 250-400 words, $150-$350. **Payment:** On acceptance.

FLORIDA

Orlando Sentinel, 633 N. Orange Ave., Orlando, FL 32801. 407-420-5000.
Web site: www.orlandosentinel.com. **Description:** Sunday magazine of the *Orlando Sentinel.*

FREE SPIRIT

107 Sterling Pl., Brooklyn, NY 11217. 718-638-3733.
Bimonthly. Paul English, Editor. **Description:** On environmental issues, holistic health, political issues, culture/art, and general interest for readers in Manhattan.

Interviews welcomed. **Nonfiction:** Articles, 4,000 words; pays $.10/word. **Queries:** Preferred. **Payment:** On acceptance.

FRESNO BEE
1626 E St., Fresno, CA 93786-0001. 559-441-6111. Web site: www.fresnobee.com. Daily. **Description:** Newspaper. Articles, 750 words, by central California writers only.

FRIENDLY EXCHANGE
P.O. Box 2120, Warren, MI 48090-2120. 810-753-8326. Web site: www.friendlyexchange.com. Quarterly. Circ.: 6,200,000. Dan Grantham, Editor. **Description:** For policyholders of Farmers Insurance Group of Companies. **Nonfiction:** Articles with "news you can use," on home, health, personal finance, travel; 700-1,500 words; $400-$1,000. **Art:** Photos. **Queries:** Required.

GENERATIONS PUBLISHING
8647 S. Colfax Ave., Chicago, IL 60617. 773-933-1338. Bimonthly. Allen Rafalson. **Description:** Covers topics of interest to men and women "of the current generation." **Nonfiction:** Insightful first-person opinion pieces; pay varies. **Queries:** Preferred.

GLOBE
5401 NW Broken Sound Blvd., Boca Raton, FL 33487. 561-997-7733. Larry Brown, Editor. **Description:** Exposés, celebrity interviews, consumer and human-interest pieces. **Nonfiction:** Articles, 500-1,000 words, with photos; pays $50-$1,500.

GRIT
Ogden Publications, 1503 S.W. 42nd St., Topeka, KS 66609-1265. 785-274-4300. E-mail: grit@cjnetworks.com. Web site: www.grit.com. Biweekly. $1.95/issue, $27.98/year. Circ.: 180,000. Donna Doyle, Editor in Chief. **Description:** On American life and traditions, stories about ordinary people doing extraordinary things. **Fiction:** Heartwarming stories with a message, upbeat storyline and ending; 1,000-10,000 words; $.10-.15/word. **Nonfiction:** Features on places or events, unsung heroes, nostalgic remembrances of rural communities and small towns; 500-1,800 words. **Poetry:** Romance; relationships; nature; family interaction; up to 30 lines; $2/line. **Fillers:** Sayings, humor, funny sayings from children; up to 25 words; $5-$15. **Art:** Photos must accompany features; $35-$50 ($100-$250 cover). **Queries:** Preferred. **E-queries:** No. **Unsolicited mss:** Accepts. **Freelance Content:** 90%. **Rights:** 1st. **Payment:** On publication.

HAPPY
240 E. 35th St., Suite 11A, New York, NY 10016. E-mail: bayardx@aol.com. Bi-annual. $15/$40 (2 yrs.). Circ.: 350. Bayard, Editor. **Description:** General-interest publication. **Fiction:** Original work only. No racist,

sexist, pornographic; 500-6,000 words; $.01-$.03/word. **Tips:** Avoid being dull, dim witted, boring. **Queries:** Not necessary. **E-queries:** No. **Unsolicited mss:** Accepts. **Response:** 1 week, SASE. **Freelance Content:** 100%. **Rights:** one-time. **Payment:** On publication.

HARPER'S MAGAZINE

666 Broadway, 11th Floor, New York, NY 10012. 212-614-6500. Web site: www.harpers.org. Monthly. Circ.: 216,000. Lewis H. Lapham, Editor. **Description:** For women, on politics, literary, cultural, scientific issues. **Fiction:** Will consider unsolicited manuscripts; SASE required. **Nonfiction:** Very limited market; 2,000-5,000 words. **Queries:** Required. **Response:** SASE required.

HOPE

PO Box 160, Brooklin, ME 04616. 207-359-4651. E-mail: info@hopemag.com. Web site: www.hopemag.com. Quarterly. Circ.: 22,000. Kimberly Ridley, Editor. **Description:** About people making a difference. **Nonfiction:** No nostalgia, sentimental, political, opinion, or religious pieces; 150-5,000 words; $.30/word. **Queries:** Required. **Payment:** On publication.

IDEALS

535 Metroplex Dr., Suite 250, Nashville, TN 37211. 615-333-0478. Web site: www.idealspublications.com. Bimonthly. $5.95 issue, $19.95/year. Circ.: 200,000. Michelle Prater Burke, Editor. **Description:** Thematic poetry and prose, with artwork and photography, in turn on Easter, Mother's Day, country, friendship, Thanksgiving, and Christmas. **Fiction:** Holiday themes; 800-1,000 words; $.10/word. **Nonfiction:** On issue's theme; 800-1,000 words; $.10/word. **Poetry:** Light, nostalgic pieces; $10/poem. **Queries:** Not necessary. **E-queries:** No. **Unsolicited mss:** Accepts. **Response:** Submissions 4-6 weeks, SASE required. **Rights:** One-time. **Payment:** On publication.

INDIANAPOLIS STAR

P.O. Box 145, Indianapolis, IN 46206-0145. 317-444-4000; 800-669-7827. Web site: www.starnews.com. Daily. , Editor. **Description:** Newspaper. **Nonfiction:** Short articles, 700-800 words; pays $40. **Rights:** Exclusive (IN). **Payment:** On publication.

INQUIRER

400 N. Broad St., P.O. Box 8263, Philadelphia, PA 19101. 215-854-4580. E-mail: inquirer.magazine@phillynews.com. Web site: www.phillynews.com. Weekly. Circ.: 800,000. Ms. Avery Rome, Editor. **Description:** Sunday newspaper magazine, with strong journalism and storytelling, focusing on Philadelphia area. **Nonfiction:** Varied topics for family audiences, and local-interest features; 3,000 words; $500-$2,500. **Queries:** Required. **E-queries:** Yes. **Unsolicited mss:** Accepts. **Response:** SASE required. **Freelance Content:** 20%. **Rights:** One-time. **Payment:** On publication.

JOURNAL AMERICA
2019 Greenwood Lake Tpke., P.O. Box 459, Hewitt, NJ 07421-0459. 973-728-8355. E-mail: journal@warick.net. Web site: www.ajournal.com. Monthly. Glen Malmgren. **Description:** Covers varied subjects of interest to the American family. **Nonfiction:** On science, nature, or "true but strange stories." Also, articles on all aspects of today's demanding lifestyle, with a touch of humor; 200-1,000 words; pay varies. **Queries:** Preferred.

KIWANIS
3636 Woodview Trace, Indianapolis, IN 46268-3196. 317-875-8755. E-mail: cjonak@kiwanis.org. Web site: www.kiwanis.org. 10x/year. $2/issue. Circ.: 240,000. Chuck Jonak, Managing Editor. **Description:** For Kiwanians, community leaders involved in volunteer service work through their clubs. **Nonfiction:** On home; family; international issues; career and community concerns, and social, health, and emotional needs of youth (especially under age 6). No travel pieces, interviews, profiles. Also, financial planning for younger families; retirement planning for older people; 1,500-2,500; $400-$1,000. **Queries:** Preferred. **E-queries:** Yes. **Unsolicited mss:** Accepts. **Response:** Queries 1-2 weeks,submissions 2-4 weeks, SASE required. **Freelance Content:** 40%. **Rights:** First. **Payment:** On acceptance.

LATIN STYLE MAGAZINE
P.O. Box 2969, Venice, CA 90294-2969. 323-462-4409. Web site: www.latinstylemag.com. Monthly. Circ.: 1,000,000. **Description:** Focuses on the Hispanic community; printed in English.

LONG BEACH PRESS-TELEGRAM
604 Pine Ave., Long Beach, CA 90844. 562-436-3676. Web site: www.presstelegram.com. Daily. **Description:** Newspaper. **Nonfiction:** Op-Ed articles, 750-900 words, on regional topics. Pays $75. **Rights:** exclusive (regional). **Payment:** On publication.

LOS ANGELES TIMES
202 W. 1st Street, Los Angeles, CA 90012. 213-237-7811. E-mail: latmag@latimes.com. Web site: www.latimes.com. Weekly. Circ.: 1,300,000. Alice Short, Editor. **Description:** Major urban newspaper, with weekly magazine. **Nonfiction:** Articles on issues, general interest, profiles, crime, first persons, photo spreads, narratives on current events; 400-4,000 words; $1/word. **Queries:** Preferred. **E-queries:** Yes. **Unsolicited mss:** Accepts. **Response:** 4 weeks, SASE. **Freelance Content:** 60%. **Payment:** On publication.

LOS ANGELES TIMES MAGAZINE
202 W 1st St., Los Angeles, CA 90012. 213-237-5000. Web site: www.latimes.com. **Description:** Sunday magazine of the LA Times.

LOUISVILLE COURIER-JOURNAL

525 W. Broadway, P.O. Box 740031, Louisville, KY 40202. 502-582-4011. Web site: www.courier-journal.com. Daily. **Description:** Newspaper. Very limited market. **Nonfiction:** Op-Ed pieces, 750 words, on regional topics. Local writers preferred. Pays $25-$50. **Payment:** On publication.

NATIONAL ENQUIRER

600 East Coast Ave., Lantana, FL 33464-0002. David Perei, Executive Editor. **Description:** Short, humorous or philosophical fillers, witticisms, anecdotes, jokes, tart comments. Original items only. Mass audience: topical news, celebrities, how-to, scientific discoveries, human drama, adventure, medical news, personalities. **Poetry:** Short, 8 lines or less, traditional rhyming verse (amusing, philosophical, or inspirational in nature). No obscure or artsy poetry. **Tips:** Submit seasonal/holiday material at least 3 months in advance. **Queries:** Preferred. **Response:** SASE. **Payment:** On publication.

NATIONAL GEOGRAPHIC

1145 17th St. NW, Washington, DC 20036. 202-857-7868. E-mail: opayne@ngs.org. Web site: nationalgeographic.com. Monthly. $3.95/$29 year. Circ.: 7,800,000. William Allen, Editor-in-Chief. **Description:** On geography, world cultures, and environmental conservation. **Nonfiction:** First-person, general-interest, heavily illustrated articles on science, natural history, exploration, and geographical regions. **Tips:** 40% staff-written; balance by published authors. **Queries:** Required. **E-queries:** No. **Unsolicited mss:** Does not accept. **Response:** 4 weeks, SASE. **Freelance Content:** 70%. **Rights:** One-time worldwide serial, plus secondary NGS rights. **Payment:** On publication. **Contact:** Oliver Payne, Sr. Editor, Manuscripts.

THE NEW YORK TIMES

229 W. 43rd St., New York, NY 10036. 212-556-1234. Web site: www.nytimes.com. Daily. **Description:** Newspaper. **Nonfiction:** Travel articles; query with writer's background, description of proposed article. Opinion pieces: 650-800 words, any topic (public policy, science, lifestyles, and ideas). News items, trends, and culture. **Tips:** Send clips. Include your daytime phone number and social security number with submission. "If you haven't heard from us in 2 weeks, assume we are not using your piece." **Response:** SASE required. **Rights:** 1st NA. **Payment:** On publication.

NEWSWEEK

251 W. 57th St., New York, NY 10019-1894. 212-778-4000. Web site: www.newsweek.co. Pam Hamer. **Description:** Covers news throughout the world. Mostly staff-written. **Columns, Departments:** My Turn (original first-person opinion essays, must contain verifiable facts. Submit manuscript with SASE); 850-900 words; $1,000. **Queries:** Preferred. **Response:** 2 months, SASE. **Rights:** Non-exclusive worldwide. **Payment:** On publication. **Contact:** Pam Hamer.

THE ORANGE COUNTY REGISTER
625 N. Grand Ave., Santa Ana, CA 92701. 714-796-7000.
Web site: www.ocregister.com. Daily. **Description:** Newspaper. Op-Ed articles on a wide range of local and national issues and topics. **Nonfiction:** Pays $50-$100. **Payment:** On publication.

PARADE
711 Third Ave., New York, NY 10017. 212-450-7000.
Web site: www.parade.com. Weekly. Circ.: 81,000,000. Walter Anderson, Editor. **Description:** National Sunday newspaper magazine. Subjects of national interest. **Fiction:** No fiction. **Nonfiction:** Factual and authoritative articles on social issues, common health concerns, sports, community problem-solving, and extraordinary achievements of ordinary people; 1,200 to 1,500 words; From $1,000. **Poetry:** No poetry. **Fillers:** No games, nostalgia, quotes, or puzzles. **Art:** No cartoons. **Tips:** "We seek unique angles on all topics." **Queries:** Required. **Contact:** Paula Silverman.

PEOPLE
Time-Life Bldg., Rockefeller Ctr., New York, NY 10020. 212-522-1212.
Web site: www.people.com. Carol Wallace, Editor. **Description:** Mostly staff-written. Will consider article proposals, 3-4 paragraphs, on timely, entertaining, and topical personalities. **Payment:** On acceptance.

PORTLAND PRESS HERALD
P.O. Box 1460, Portland, ME 04104-5009. 207-791-6650.
Web site: www.portland.com. Daily. **Description:** Newspaper. Op-Ed articles, 750 words, on any topic with state tie-in. **Rights:** exclusive (ME). *No recent report.*

READER'S DIGEST
Readers Digest Rd., Pleasantville, NY 10570-7000. 914-238-1000.
Web site: www.readersdigest.com. Monthly. Circ.: 1,300,000. Kenneth Tomlinson, Editor-in-Chief. **Description:** Offers stories of broad interest. **Nonfiction:** Only general-interest articles already in print and well-developed story proposals will be considered. Send reprint or query to any editor on the masthead. **Fillers:** Short humor, check "Wanted: Your Laugh Lines" page in guidelines, or website. **Tips:** Submissions are not acknowledged or returned. **Queries:** Preferred.

THE SACRAMENTO BEE
P.O. Box 15779, Sacramento, CA 95852-0779. 916-321-1000.
Web site: www.sacbee.com. Daily. **Description:** Newspaper. Op-Ed pieces, to 750 words; state and regional topics preferred.

ST. LOUIS POST-DISPATCH
400 S. Fourth St., Suite 1200, St. Louis, MO 63102. 314-552-1555.
E-mail: oped@postnet.com. Web site: www.stltoday.com. Daily. Donna Korando. **Description:** Newspaper. Op-Ed articles, 700 words, on economics, education,

science, politics, foreign and domestic affairs, and the environment. Pays $70. **Tips:** Seeks local writers. **Payment:** On publication.

ST. PAUL PIONEER PRESS
345 Cedar St., St. Paul, MN 55101. 651-222-5011.
Web site: www.pioneerpress.com. Daily. **Description:** Newspaper. Op-Ed articles, to 750 words, on a variety of topics. Pays $75. **Tips:** Strongly prefers authors or topics with a local connection. **Payment:** On publication.

ST. PETERSBURG TIMES
490 First Ave. S., Petersburg, FL 33731. 727-893-8111.
Web site: www.sptimes.com. Daily. **Description:** Newspaper. Authoritative articles, to 2,000 words, on current political, economic, and social issues. Pay varies. **Queries:** Preferred. **Payment:** On publication.

THE SAN FRANCISCO CHRONICLE
901 Mission St., San Francisco, CA 94103. 415-777-1111.
Web site: www.sfgate.com. Daily. **Description:** Newspaper. Articles, 400-650 words, with lively writing, pertinent to public policy debates, moving the debate forward. Pays to $150 ($75-$100 for unsolicited pieces). **Payment:** On publication. **Contact:** Lisa Zaffarese.

SAN FRANCISCO EXAMINER
988 Market St., San Francisco, CA 94102. 415-359-2600.
Web site: www.examiner.com. Daily. **Description:** Newspaper. Well-written articles, 500-650 words; prefers local/state issues and subjects bypassed by other news media. Pay varies. **Tips:** No sports. **Payment:** On publication.

SAN FRANCISCO EXAMINER MAGAZINE
110 5th St., San Francisco, CA 94103. 415-777-2424.
Web site: www.examiner.com. **Description:** Sunday magazine of the San Francisco Examiner.

SATURDAY EVENING POST
1100 Waterway Blvd., Indianapolis, IN 46206. 317-636-8881.
E-mail: satevepst@aol.com. Web site: www.satevepst.org. Bimonthly. Circ.: 400,000. Ted Kreiter, Editor. **Description:** Family-oriented, with humor, preventive medicine, health and fitness, destination-oriented travel pieces (not personal experience), celebrity profiles, arts, and sciences. **Nonfiction:** 1,500-3,000 words; pay varies. **Fillers:** Humor/satire, to 100 words, upbeat and positive. Light verse, cartoons, jokes, humorous, clean limericks, short narratives. No conventional poetry, original material only. Pays $15 for verse; $125 for cartoons. **Queries:** Preferred. **Response:** SASE. **Payment:** On publication.

SEATTLE POST-INTELLIGENCER

P.O. Box 1909, Seattle, WA 98111-1909. 206-448-8000.
Web site: www.seattle-pi.com. Daily. Ken Bunting, Executive Editor. **Description:** Newspaper. Articles, 750-800 words, on foreign and domestic affairs, environment, education, politics, regional interest, religion, science, and seasonal material. Prefer writers who live in the Pacific Northwest. Pays $75-$100. **Response:** SASE required. **Payment:** On publication.

SELECCIONES DEL READER'S DIGEST

1 Reader's Digest Rd., Pleasantville, NY 10570-7000. 914-238-4559.
Web site: www.readersdigest.com. Monthly. Circ.: 130,000. **Description:** Spanish-language version of Reader's Digest.

SELECTA

1717 N. Bayshore Dr., Ste 113, Miami, FL 33132-1195. 305-579-0979.
Monthly. Circ.: 27,000. **Description:** For upscale Hispanics in the U.S. and Latin America.

SMITHSONIAN

900 Jefferson Dr., Washington, DC 20560. 202-786-2900.
E-mail: siarticles@aol.com. Web site: www.simag.si.edu. Monthly. Circ.: 2,100,000. Don Moser, Editor. **Description:** Wide-ranging coverage of history, art, natural history, physical science, profiles, etc. **Nonfiction:** History, art, natural history, physical science, profiles; 2,000-5,000 words; pay varies. **Queries:** Required. **E-queries:** Yes. **Unsolicited mss:** Accepts. **Response:** 6-8 weeks, SASE. **Contact:** Marlan A. Liddell, Articles Editor.

STAR

5401 NW Broken Sound Blvd., Boca Raton, FL 33487. 561-997-7733.
Web site: www.starmagazine.com. **Description:** on show business and celebrities, health, fitness, parenting, and diet and food. **Nonfiction:** Topical articles, 50-800 words; pay varies.

STORYHOUSE.COM

4019 SE Hawthorne Blvd., Portland, OR 97214. 503-233-1144.
E-mail: mrcoffee@storyhouse.com. Web site: www.storyhouse.com. Ongoing. Todd and Esther Cowing, Editors. **Description:** A website exploring the art and philosophy of coffee and storytelling. This is the Web presence of a Portland-based coffee-roasting and coffee home-delivery service. **Nonfiction:** Art, stories, letters, articles. Current need is for nonfiction material. Stories are run over several weeks, so chapter or section breaks should be at 1,000 words. Also, seeking debate and academic pieces; 1,000 words; $25/1,000 words. **Poetry:** Yes; pay varies. **Tips:** See guidelines on website for details on editorial process involved. **Queries:** Preferred. **E-queries:** Yes. **Unsolicited mss:** Accepts. **Response:** SASE required for regular mail. **Rights:** Author retains copyright. **Payment:** On acceptance.

SUITE101.COM

E-mail: jason@suite101.com. Web site: www.suite101.com. Jason Pamer, Editor-in-Chief. **Description:** Online publishing site, with "sections" covering hundreds of topics. Rather than submitting a query or mss., one applies to become an "editor" of a topical section. If accepted, a new editor updates his/her own work periodically using a built-in, easy-to-use "article upload" form. (You may upload previously published material if you own the copyright.) **Nonfiction:** Regular contributors who submit weekly articles receive $25/month (biweekly, $20/month; monthly, $15/month). **Tips:** Seeking regular contributors ("sections editors") to update topical collections of articles (weekly, biweekly, or monthly) with new original articles that they have written. To apply to become a section editor, you must first register (at no cost) with Suite101.com. New and experienced writers accepted; passion-driven dedication to chosen topic is essential. **Queries:** Required. **E-queries:** Yes. **Unsolicited mss:** Accepts. **Rights:** Online (90 days). **Payment:** On publication. **Contact:** Jennie S. Bev, Editor Affiliate.

SUN

Sun Publishing Co., 107 N. Roberson St., Chapel Hill, NC 27516. 919-942-5282. Web site: www.thesunmagazine.org. Monthly. $3.95/issue, $34 yr. Circ.: 50,000. Sy Safransky, Editor. **Description:** Essays, stories, interviews, and poetry, in which people write of their struggles to understand their lives, often with surprising intimacy. Looking for writers willing to take risks, to describe life honestly. **Fiction:** Fiction that feels like lived experience; up to 7,000 words; $300-500. **Nonfiction:** Personal essays, interviews; up to 7,000 words; $300-1,000. **Poetry:** 1-2 pages; $50-200. **Art:** b/w; $50-200. **Tips:** No journalistic, academic, opinion pieces. **Queries:** Not necessary. **E-queries:** No. **Unsolicited mss:** Accepts. **Response:** 3 months, SASE. **Freelance Content:** 80%. **Rights:** One-time. **Payment:** On publication.

TEMAS

300 W. 55th St., Apt 14P, New York, NY 10019-5172. 212-582-4750. Web site: www.cdiusa.com/revistatemas. Monthly. Circ.: 110,000. **Description:** Topics of interest to Spanish-speaking people in the United States.

TEXAS MAGAZINE

801 Texas St., Houston, TX 77002. 713-220-7171. Web site: www.houstonchronicle.com. **Description:** Sunday magazine of the *Houston Chronicle*.

TULSA WORLD

P.O. Box 1770, Tulsa, OK 74102. 918-581-8300. Web site: www.tulsaworld.com. Daily. **Description:** Newspaper. Articles, about 600 words, on subjects of local or regional interest. No payment offered. **Tips:** Prefers local or regional writers. **Rights:** Exclusive (Tulsa area). *No recent report.*

USA TODAY

1000 Wilson Blvd., Arlington, VA 22229. 703-276-3400.
Web site: www.usatoday.com. Daily. **Description:** Newspaper. Op-Ed articles, 700-1,000 words, on American culture, politics, economics and "the real lives people live." No unnamed sources or composite anecdotes. Pays $300. **Payment:** On publication.

USA WEEKEND

1000 Wilson Blvd., Arlington, VA 22209. 703-276-6445.
Web site: www.usaweekend.com. Weekly. Circ.: 20,000,000. **Description:** Sunday supplement to more than 500 newspapers.

VANTAGE

C-E Publishing, 30400 Van Dyke Ave., Warren, MI 48093. 810-753-8355.
Quarterly. Circ.: 225,000. **Description:** For active older adults.

THE WALL STREET JOURNAL

200 Liberty St., New York, NY 10281. 212-416-2000.
Web site: www.wsj.com. Daily. **Description:** Newspaper. Op-Ed articles, to 1,500 words, on politics, economics, law, education, environment, some humor, and foreign and domestic affairs. Must be timely, heavily reported, and of national interest by writers with expertise. Pays $150-$300. **Payment:** On publication.

THE WASHINGTON POST

1150 15th St. NW, Washington, DC 20071. 202-334-7585.
E-mail: 20071@washpost.com. Web site: www.washingtonpost.com. Weekly. Circ.: 1,200,000. John Cotter, Senior Editor. **Description:** Sunday Post edition offers groundbreaking journalism, lifestyle features, and political and popular-culture commentary. **Nonfiction:** Length, pay varies. **Queries:** Preferred. **E-queries:** Prefer hard copy. **Unsolicited mss:** Accepts. **Response:** 3 weeks. **Freelance Content:** 2%.

WASHINGTON TIMES

3600 New York Ave. NE, Washington, DC 20002. 202-636-3000.
Web site: www.washtimes.com. Daily. **Description:** Newspaper. Op-Ed articles, 800-1,000 words, on a variety of subjects. No first-person. Pays $150. **Tips:** Find a topic that is off the beaten path. **Rights:** Exclusive (Washington, DC, and Baltimore). **Payment:** On publication.

THE WORLD & I

3600 New York Ave. NE, Washington, DC 20002. 202-635-4000.
E-mail: theworldandi@mcimail.com. Web site: www.worldandi.com. Monthly. Circ.: 30,000. Michael Marshall, Executive Editor. **Description:** Current issues, arts, natural science, life, and culture. **Nonfiction:** Scholarly articles; 2,500 words; pay varies. **Payment:** On publication.

HEALTH

(See also Fitness)

AMERICAN JOURNAL OF NURSING

345 Hudson St., 16th Floor, New York, NY 10014. 212-886-1200. Web site: www.nursingcenter.com. Santa J. Crisall, Editor. **Description:** Articles, 1,500-2,000 words, with photos or illustrations, on nursing or disease processes. **Queries:** Preferred.

AMERICAN MEDICAL NEWS

515 N. State St., Chicago, IL 60610. 312-464-5000. Web site: www.amednews.com. Greg Borzo, Topic Editor. **Description:** Articles, on socioeconomic developments in health care, of interest to physicians across the country. Guidelines available. **Nonfiction:** Seeks well-researched, innovative pieces about health and science from physician's perspective; 900-1,500 words; pays $500-$1,500. **Queries:** Required. **Payment:** On acceptance.

ARTHRITIS TODAY

Arthritis Foundation, 1330 W. Peachtree St., Atlanta, GA 30309. 404-872-7100. E-mail: writers@arthritis.org. Web site: www.arthritis.org. Bimonthly. $4.95/issue $20/year. Circ.: 650,000. Cindy McDaniel, Editor. **Description:** Comprehensive information about arthritis research, care, and treatment, offering help and hope to over 40 million Americans with an arthritis-related condition. **Nonfiction:** Features on research, care, treatment of arthritis; self-help, how-to, general interest, general health, lifestyle topics (very few inspirational articles); 200-1,000 words; $75-$1,000. **Tips:** Readers are well-informed; desire fresh, in-depth information. Looking for talented writers/reporters to execute staff-generated ideas; send published clips. **Queries:** Preferred. **E-queries:** Yes. **Unsolicited mss:** Accepts. **Response:** 4 weeks. **Freelance Content:** 50%. **Rights:** FNASR. **Payment:** On acceptance. **Contact:** Michele Taylor, Asst. Ed.

ASTHMA

3 Bridge St., Newton, MA 02158. 617-964-4910. E-mail: letters@asthmamagazine.com. Bimonthly. Circ.: 100,000. Rachel Butler, Editor in Chief. **Description:** Focuses on ways to manage asthma. **Nonfiction:** Articles on health and medical news, also human-interest stories about children, adults, and the elderly; to 1,200 words. **Queries:** Required. **Payment:** On acceptance.

BABY TALK

530 Fifth Ave., 4th Floor, New York, NY 10036. 212-522-8989. Web site: www.parenting.com. 10x/yr. Circ.: 1,725,000. Susan Kane, Editor in Chief. **Description:** Pregnancy, babies, baby care, women's health, child development, work and family. **Nonfiction:** Articles, by professional writers with expertise and experience; 1,000-3,000 words; pay varies. **Queries:** Required. **Response:** SASE required. **Payment:** On acceptance.

BETTER HEALTH

1450 Chapel St., New Haven, CT 06511-4440. 203-789-3972.
Web site: www.srhs.org. Bimonthly. Circ.: 500,000. Cynthia Wolfe Boynton, Editor.
Description: Wellness and prevention magazine, published by Hospital of Saint Raphael. **Nonfiction:** Upbeat articles to encourage healthier lifestyle, with quotes and narrative from healthcare professionals at Saint Raphael's and other local services. No first-person or personal-experience articles; 2,000-2,500 words; $500. **Queries:** Required. **Response:** SASE. **Payment:** On acceptance.

CONSCIOUS CHOICE

920 N. Franklin, Ste. 202, Chicago, IL 60610-3179.
E-mail: editor@consciouschoice.com. Web site: www.consciouschoice.com. Monthly. $36/yr. Circ.: 50,000. Sheri Reda, Editor. **Description:** Covers issues and information on natural health, natural foods, and the environment. Encourages people to take personal responsibility for their health, attitudes, growth, and contribution to community life. **Nonfiction:** On environment, science, health, food, spirituality, travel, adventure, and fitness; 1,200-2,200 words; $75-$150. **Tips:** Readers are mostly well-educated women, average age 35, with substantial income level. **Queries:** Preferred. **E-queries:** Yes. **Unsolicited mss:** Accepts. **Response:** 1-8 weeks. **Freelance Content:** 90%. **Rights:** 1st NA (print and web). **Payment:** On publication.

COPING WITH ALLERGIES & ASTHMA

P.O. Box 682268, Franklin, TN 37068-2268. 615-790-2400.
Web site: www.copingmag.com. 5x/year. $13.95/year. **Description:** Provides "knowledge, hope, and inspiration to help readers learn to live with their conditions in the best ways possible." Seeks original manuscripts and photography. No payment. **Queries:** Not necessary.

COPING WITH CANCER

P.O. Box 682268, Franklin, TN 37068. 615-790-2400.
Web site: www.copingmag.com. Bimonthly. $19/year. Kay Thomas. **Description:** Uplifting and practical articles for people living with cancer: medical news, lifestyle issues, and inspiring personal essays. No payment.

CURRENT HEALTH

900 Skokie Blvd., Suite 200, Northbrook, IL 60062-4028. 847-405-3000.
E-mail: crubenstein@glcomm.com. 8x/school year. $9.15 (quantities of 15). Carole Rubenstein, Editor. **Description:** For classrooms. Covers physical and psychological health issues, in two editions (for grades 4-7, and grades 7-12). **Nonfiction:** Articles on drug education, nutrition, diseases, fitness and exercise, first aid and safety, and environmental awareness. By assignment only, no unsolicited manuscripts. Pay varies. **Tips:** Must write well for appropriate age level. Send query with resumé, clips. **Queries:** Required. **E-queries:** No. **Unsolicited mss:** Does not accept. **Response:** Queries 1-6 months. **Freelance Content:** 80%. **Rights:** All. **Payment:** On publication.

DIABETES SELF-MANAGEMENT

150 W. 22nd St., New York, NY 10011. 212-989-0200.
E-mail: editor@diabetes-self-mgmt.com. Web site: www.diabetes-self-mgmt.com. Bimonthly. $18/yr. Circ.: 465,000. James Hazlett, Editor. **Description:** For people with diabetes who want to know more about controlling and managing their diabetes. Authoritative information on nutrition, pharmacology, exercise, medical advances, self-help, and other "how-to" subjects. **Nonfiction:** Nutrition, meal-planning tips, medical updates, coping strategies; 2,000-2,500 words; pay varies. **Tips:** Use plain English; avoid medical jargon, but explain technical terms in simple language. Writing style: upbeat, and leavened with tasteful humor where possible. Information should be accurate, up-to-date, and from reliable sources; references from lay publications not acceptable. No celebrity profiles or personal experiences. **Queries:** Required. **E-queries:** Yes. **Unsolicited mss:** Accepts. **Response:** 3-4 weeks, SASE. **Rights:** All. **Payment:** On publication. **Contact:** Ingrid Strauch, Managing Editor.

FIT PREGNANCY

21100 Erwin St., Woodland Hills, CA 91367-3712. 818-595-0444.
Web site: www.fitpregnancy.com. Amy Goldhammer, Editor. **Description:** For the "whole nine months and beyond." Expert advice for the pregnant or postpartum woman and her newborn: safe workouts, nutrition guidance, meal plans, medical news, baby gear and more. **Nonfiction:** Articles, 500-2,000 words, on women's health (pregnant and postpartum), nutrition, and physical fitness. **Queries:** Preferred. **Unsolicited mss:** Accepts. **Payment:** On publication.

HEALTH PRODUCTS BUSINESS

Cygnus Publishing, 445 Broad Hollow Rd., Suite 21,
Melville, NY 11747. 631-845-2700 x214.
E-mail: susanne.alberto@cygnuspub.com. Web site: www.healthproducts.com. Monthly. Circ.: 16,100. Susan Alberto, Editor. **Description:** Helps retailers and manufacturers navigate challenges of health and nutrition industry. **Nonfiction:** Stories on health products (supplements, skin/body care, organic food and medicine, sports nutrition, etc.); 1,000-2,000 words; pay varies. **Tips:** Seeking writers in the industry with credentials and expert knowledge on health/nutrition products. **Queries:** Required. **E-queries:** Yes. **Unsolicited mss:** Does not accept. **Response:** SASE. **Freelance Content:** 25%. **Rights:** All. **Payment:** On publication.

HEALTH PROGRESS

4455 Woodson Rd., St. Louis, MO 63134-3797. 314-427-2500.
Web site: www.chausa.org. Terry Van Schaik, Editor. **Description:** On hospital/nursing-home management and administration, medical-moral questions, health care, public policy, technological developments and their effects, nursing, financial and human resource management for administrators, and innovative programs in hospitals and long-term care facilities. **Nonfiction:** Features, 2,000-4,000 words; pay negotiable. **Queries:** Preferred.

HEALTH QUEST

200 Highpoint Dr., Suite 215, Chalfont, PA 18914. 215-822-7935. E-mail: editor@healthquestmag.com. Web site: www.healthquestmag.com. Bimonthly. Circ.: 500,000. Hilary Beard, Editor. **Description:** Health and wellness (body, mind, and spirit) for African Americans. Traditional and alternative medicine. **Nonfiction:** Health articles. **Queries:** Preferred. **E-queries:** No. **Unsolicited mss:** Accepts. **Freelance Content:** 20%. **Payment:** On publication.

HEART & SOUL

BET Publications, 1900 W. Place NE, One BET Plaza, Washington, DC 20018. 202-608-2241. E-mail: heart&soul@BET.net. Web site: www.BET.com. Bimonthly. Circ.: 300,000. Yanick Rice Lamb, Editorial Director. **Description:** The African-American woman's ultimate guide to total well-being—body, mind, and spirit. **Nonfiction:** Health, beauty, fitness, nutrition, and relationships for African-American women; 800-1,500 words; pay varies. **Queries:** Preferred. **Payment:** On acceptance.

HERBALGRAM

P.O. Box 144345, Austin, TX 78714-4345. 512-926-4900. E-mail: bj@herbalgram.org. Web site: www.herbalgram.org. Quarterly. Barbara Johnson, Managing Editor. **Description:** On herb and medicinal plant research, regulatory issues, market conditions, native plant conservation, and other aspects of herbal use. **Nonfiction:** Articles, 1,500-3,000 words. **Payment:** in copies.

HERBS FOR HEALTH

Herb Companion, 243 E. Fourth St., Loveland, CO 80537. 970-663-0831. E-mail: herbs for health@hcpress.com. Web site: www.discoverherbs.com. Bimonthly. $4.99/issue. Circ.: 255,000. Susan Clotfelter, Editor. **Description:** Offers sound information for general public on the wide range of benefits of herbs, including their role in various healing arts. **Fiction:** 500-2000 words; pays $.33/word. **Columns, Departments:** 200-500 words. **Art:** 300 dpi (cmyk), slides. **Tips:** List your sources, keep it short, focus on reader benefit. **Queries:** Preferred. **E-queries:** Yes. **Unsolicited mss:** Accepts. **Response:** 1-3 months, SASE required. **Freelance Content:** 90%. **Rights:** 1st NA. **Payment:** On acceptance.

HOMECARE

23815 Stuart Ranch Rd., Malibu, CA 90265. Web site: www.homecaremag.com. Monthly. Marie Blakey, Editor. **Description:** Leading resource for the home health industry. Covers the business of renting and selling home medical-equipment products and services; industry news, trend analysis, product segment features, stories with management and operational ideas. **Nonfiction:** Seeking writers with health industry experience; $.50/word. **Queries:** Required. **E-queries:** Yes. **Unsolicited mss:** Accepts. **Response:** 2-8 weeks, SASE required. **Freelance Content:** 20%. **Payment:** On acceptance.

JOURNAL OF HEALTH EDUCATION

1900 Association Dr., Reston, VA 20191. 703-476-3400. Web site: www.aahperd.org/aahe.html. **Description:** For health educators, sponsored by American Alliance for Health, Physical Education, Recreation and Dance. For those who work with students (elementary to college grades), to encourage professional growth. **Queries:** Preferred.

LET'S LIVE

PO Box 74908, 320 N Larchmont Blvd, Los Angeles, CA 90004-3030. 323-469-3901. E-mail: info@letslivemag.com. Web site: www.letsliveonline.com. Monthly. Circ.: 1,700,000. Beth Salmon, Editor in Chief. **Description:** Preventive medicine and nutrition, alternative medicine, diet, vitamins, herbs, exercise. **Nonfiction:** 1,500-1,800 words; up to $800. **Queries:** Required. **Payment:** On publication. **Contact:** Laura Barnaby, Managing Editor.

LISTEN

55 W. Oak Ridge Dr., Hagerstown, MD 21740. 301-393-4019. E-mail: listen@healthconnection.org. Monthly. $24.95/year. Circ.: 50,000. Larry Becker, Editor. **Description:** Provides teens with vigorous, positive, educational approach to problems arising from use of tobacco, alcohol, and other drugs. **Fiction:** True-to-life stories; 1,000-1,200 words; $.05-$.10/word. **Nonfiction:** For teenagers, on problems of alcohol and drug abuse; personality profiles; self-improvement; drug-free activities; 1,000-1,200 words; $.05-$.10/word. **Poetry:** From high-school students only. **Fillers:** puzzles; $15-$25. **Tips:** Use upbeat approach. **Queries:** Preferred. **E-queries:** Accepts. **Unsolicited mss:** Accepts. **Response:** 2 weeks queries, 3 months submissions; SASE. **Rights:** FNASR. **Payment:** On acceptance. **Contact:** Anita Jacobs.

LIVING IN BALANCE

7860 Peters Rd., Plantation, FL 33324. 954-382-4325. E-mail: publisher@livinginbalancemagazine.com. Web site: www.livinginbalancemagazine.com. **Description:** A "health, wealth and happiness" magazine. Strives to provide straightforward, expert and motivational solutions to pressing issues facing baby boomers. **Nonfiction:** Short articles on self-development and personal growth; 250-500 words. **Tips:** Send submissions in an e-mail attachment. **Queries:** Preferred. **E-queries:** Yes. **Unsolicited mss:** Accepts.

MAMM

349 W. 12th St., New York, NY 10014. 212-242-2163. Web site: www.mamm.com. Monthly. **Description:** On cancer prevention, treatment, and survival, for women. **Nonfiction:** Articles on conventional and alternative treatment and medical news; survivor profiles; investigative features; essays; pay varies. **Queries:** Preferred. **Payment:** On acceptance.

MANAGED CARE

275 Phillips Blvd., Trenton, NJ 08618. 609-671-2100.
E-mail: editors@managedcaremag.com. Web site: www.managedcaremag.com.
Monthly. $84/yr. Circ.: 60,000. John Marcille, Editor. **Description:** Covers issues in managed health care, health-care financing and cost-effectiveness. Also, peer-reviewed scientific studies of the relationship between models of health care delivery and costs associated with them. **Nonfiction:** 1,000-3,000 words; $.60-$.80/word. **Columns, Departments:** News and Commentary, 300 words, $100. **Art:** Provide contact info for prominent people interviewed in your articles; they will assign a photographer to take photos. **Tips:** Current needs: Writers who cover the business side of health care and who have an ear to the ground for trends or interesting case-studies involving cost-effective care. Also, looking for academic-style writers willing to ghostwrite scientific or medical review articles for peer review. **Queries:** Preferred. **E-queries:** Yes. **Unsolicited mss:** Accepts. **Response:** 1 month, SASE required. **Freelance Content:** 60%. **Rights:** All. **Payment:** On publication.

MEDIPHORS

P.O. Box 327, Bloomsburg, PA 17815.
E-mail: mediphor@ptd.net. Web site: www.mediphors.org. Semiannual. $6.95. Circ.: 1,000. Eugene D. Radice, MD, Editor. **Description:** Literary magazine publishing broad range of work in medicine and health. For healthcare professionals, as well as general readers interested in creative writing in medicine. Short stories, essays, and poetry broadly related to medicine and health. **Fiction:** Short stories. **Nonfiction:** Essays; 3,000 words. **Poetry:** 30 lines. **Fillers:** Humor; 3,000 words. **Art:** b/w photos. **Tips:** Topics may be quite broad, from short story or historical fiction to current healthcare criticisms to science fiction. **Queries:** Not necessary. **E-queries:** No. **Unsolicited mss:** Accepts. **Response:** Queries 1 month, submissions 4 months, SASE. **Freelance Content:** 98%. **Rights:** FNASR. **Payment:** in copies.

MEN'S HEALTH

Rodale Press, 33 E. Minor St., Emmaus, PA 18098. 610-967-5171.
Web site: www.menshealth.com. 10x/year. $3.79. Circ.: 1,600,000. David Zinczenko, Senior Editor. **Description:** Covers fitness, health, sex, nutrition, relationships, lifestyle, sports, travel. **Nonfiction:** Useful articles, for men ages 25-55; 1,000-2,000 words; $.50/word. **Queries:** Required. **E-queries:** Yes. **Payment:** On acceptance.

THE NEW PHYSICIAN

American Medical Student Assn.
1902 Association Dr., Reston, VA 20191. 703-620-6600.
E-mail: rebecca@www.amsa.org. Web site: www.amsa.org. 9x/year. $25/yr. Circ.: 30,000. Rebecca Sernett, Editor. **Description:** On medical policy issues, of interest to medical students. **Nonfiction:** On social, ethical, and political issues in medical education. Recent articles: teaching hospitals, dating in med school; learning disabilities in med school, etc.; up to 2,500 words; pay varies. **Tips:** Readers are highly

educated, generally in their 20s. **Queries:** Preferred. **Unsolicited mss:** Accepts. **Freelance Content:** 50%. **Rights:** 1st. **Payment:** On publication.

NURSING 2001

1111 Bethlehem Pike, P.O. Box 908, Springhouse, PA 19477-0908. 215-646-8700. Web site: www.springnet.com. **Description:** For direct caregivers. Also covers legal, ethical, and career aspects of nursing; narratives about personal nursing experiences. **Nonfiction:** Most articles clinically oriented, written by nurses; pays $25-$300. **Queries:** Preferred. **Payment:** On publication.

NUTRITION HEALTH REVIEW

P.O. Box 406, Haverford, PA 19041. 610-896-1853. Quarterly. $3.00/issue, $24/year. Andrew Rifkin, Editor. **Description:** Vegetarian-oriented publication. **Nonfiction:** Articles on medical progress, nutritional therapy, genetics, psychiatry, behavior therapy, surgery, pharmacology, animal health; vignettes on health and nutrition. **Fillers:** Humor, cartoons, illustrations. **Tips:** No material involving subjects that favor animal testing, animal foods, cruelty to animals, recipes with animal products. **Queries:** Required. **Unsolicited mss:** Accepts. **Response:** SASE required. **Payment:** On publication.

PATIENT CARE

5 Paragon Dr., Montvale, NJ 07645. 201-358-7421. Web site: www.pdr.net. Deborah Kaplan, Editor. **Description:** On medical care, for primary-care physicians. **Nonfiction:** Articles; pay varies. **Tips:** All articles by assignment only. **Queries:** Required. **Payment:** On acceptance.

THE PHOENIX

7152 Unity Ave. N., Brooklyn Ctr., MN 55429. 651-291-2691. E-mail: phoenix1@winternet.com. Web site: www.phoenixrecovery.org. Monthly. Free at newsstands; $18 by mail. Circ.: 40,000. Pat Samples, Editor. **Description:** For people working on their physical, mental, emotional and spiritual well-being, seeking peace and serenity. Covers a broad spectrum of recovery, renewal, and growth information. **Nonfiction:** Articles, 800-1,500 words. **Columns, Departments:** Getting a Life; Basic Steps; Bodywise. **Tips:** Contact for upcoming themes. **Queries:** Not necessary. **E-queries:** Yes. **Unsolicited mss:** Accepts. **Response:** Queries 2 months, submission 3 months, SASE. **Freelance Content:** 90%. **Rights:** 1st. **Payment:** On publication.

PREVENTION

33 E. Minor St., Emmaus, PA 18098. 610-967-5171. Web site: www.prevention.com. Anne Alexander, Editor-in-Chief. **Description:** Leading magazine for preventative health research and practices. **Tips:** Freelance content limited. **Queries:** Required.

PSYCHOLOGY TODAY
Sussex Publishing, 49 E. 21st St., 11 Fl., New York, NY 10010. 212-260-7210.
Web site: www.psychologytoday.com. Bimonthly. Michael Seeber, Deputy Editor.
Description: On general-interest psychological research. Timely subjects and news.
Nonfiction: Articles, 800-2,000 words; pays varies. **Tips:** No personal "memoir-style" stories. **Payment:** On publication.

REMEDY
120 Post Rd. W., Westport, CT 06880. 203-341-7000.
Web site: www.remedyonline.com. Bimonthly. Shari Miller Sims, Editor.
Description: On health and medication issues, for readers 50 and over. **Nonfiction:** Articles, 600-2,500 words; pays $1.00-$1.25/word. **Columns, Departments:** Dispensary; Nutrition Prescription. **Queries:** Preferred. **Payment:** On acceptance.

RX.MAGAZINE
Rx.com. 512-652-1244.
E-mail: kyreo@rx.com. Web site: www.rx.com/magazine. **Description:** General interest e-zine focusing on family and senior health issues. **Queries:** Preferred. **Contact:** Kyre Osborn, editorial assistant.

T'AI CHI
P.O. Box 39938, Los Angeles, CA 90039. 323-665-7773.
Web site: www.tai-chi.com. Marvin Smalheiser, Editor. **Description:** For persons interested in T'ai Chi Ch'uan (Taijiquan), Qigong, and other internal martial arts, and in similar Chinese disciplines which contribute to fitness, health, and a balanced sense of well being. **Nonfiction:** Style, self-defense techniques, martial arts principles and philosophy, training methods, weapons, case histories of benefits, new or unusual uses for T'ai Chi Ch'uan, interviews; 100-4,500 words; $75-500. **Art:** 4x6 or 5x7 glossy b/w prints. **Tips:** Readers' abilities range from beginners to serious students and teachers. **Queries:** Required. **E-queries:** Yes. **Unsolicited mss:** Does not accept. **Response:** 2-3 weeks, SASE. **Freelance Content:** 85%. **Rights:** 1st NA, reprint. **Payment:** On publication.

TOTAL HEALTH FOR LONGEVITY
Total Health Communications, Inc., 165 N. 100 E. #2,
St. George, UT 84770. 435-673-1789.
E-mail: thm@infowest.com. Web site: www.totalhealthmagazine.com. Editor/Publisher, Lyle Hurd. **Description:** On preventative health care, fitness, diet, and mental health. **Nonfiction:** Articles, 1,200-1,400 words; pays $50-$75. **Art:** Color or b/w photos. **Queries:** Preferred. **Payment:** On publication.

TURTLE MAGAZINE
1100 Waterway Blvd., P.O. Box 567, Indianapolis, IN 46206-0567. 317-636-8881.
Web site: www.turtlemag.com. Bimonthly. Circ.: 300,000. Ms. Terry Harshman, Editor. **Description:** Emphasis on health and nutrition for 2- to 5-year-olds.

Fiction: Humorous, entertaining fiction; to $.22/word. **Nonfiction:** Heavily illustrated articles with an emphasis on health and nutrition for 2- to 5-year-olds. Also, crafts, recipes, activities, simple science experiments, and read-aloud stories; to 300 words; to $.22/word. **Poetry:** Simple poems, action rhymes; From $25. **Rights:** All. **Payment:** On publication.

VEGETARIAN TIMES
4 High Ridge Park, Stamford, CT 06905. 203-328-7040.
Web site: www.vegetariantimes.com. Donna Sapolin, Anne Russell, Editor. **Description:** Articles, 1,200-2,500 words, on vegetarian cooking, nutrition, health and fitness, and profiles of prominent vegetarians; pays $75-$1,000. **Columns, Departments:** News Items; In Print (book reviews), to 500 words; Herbalist (medicinal uses of herbs) to 1,800 words. **Queries:** Required. **Payment:** On acceptance.

VEGETARIAN VOICE
P.O. Box 72, Dolgeville, NY 13329. 518-568-7970.
E-mail: navs@telenet.net. Web site: www.navs-online.org. Quarterly. Maribeth Abrams-McHenry, Managing Editor. **Description:** Consumer concerns, health, nutrition, animal rights, the environment, world hunger, etc. Total vegetarian philosophy; all recipes are vegan and we do not support the use of leather, wool, silk, etc. **Payment:** in copies.

VIBRANT LIFE
55 W. Oak Ridge Dr., Hagerstown, MD 21740-7390. 301-393-4019.
E-mail: vibrantlife@rhpa.org. Web site: www.vibrantlife.com. Bimonthly. Circ.: 50,000. Larry Becker, Editor. **Description:** Total health: physical, mental, and spiritual. **Nonfiction:** Upbeat articles on the family and how to live happier and healthier lives, emphasizing practical tips; Christian slant; 600-2,000 words; $80-$250. **Payment:** On acceptance. (Open Monday through Thursday only.)

WEIGHT WATCHERS
360 Lexington Ave 11th Floor, New York, NY 10017. 212-370-0644.
Web site: www.weightwatchers.com. 6x/year. Circ.: 500,000. Nancy Gagliarch, Editor in Chief. **Description:** Health, nutrition, fitness, and weight-loss motivation and success. **Nonfiction:** Articles on fashion, beauty, food, health, nutrition, fitness, and weight-loss motivation and success; from $1/word. **Queries:** Required. **Payment:** On acceptance.

YOGA JOURNAL
2054 University Ave., #601, Berkeley, CA 94704-1082. 510-841-9200.
Web site: www.yogajournal.com. Monthly. Circ.: 130,000. Kathryn Arnold, Editor in Chief. **Description:** Serves the hatha yoga community. Holistic health, meditation, conscious living, spirituality, and yoga. **Queries:** Preferred. **E-queries:** Yes. **Unsolicited mss:** Accepts. **Response:** 4 weeks, SASE. **Freelance Content:** 10%.

Rights: non-exclusive worldwide, print and non-print. Payment: On acceptance. Contact: Nora Isaacs.

HISTORY

AIR COMBAT
7950 Deering Ave., Canoga Park, CA 91304-5007. Bimonthly. Michael O'Leary. Description: Articles on latest warplanes and the men who fly them, recent air battles, and America's aerial involvement in Vietnam. Tips: Send for guidelines. Queries: Preferred.

ALABAMA HERITAGE
Univ. of Alabama, Box 870342, Tuscaloosa, AL 35487-0342. 205-348-7467. Web site: bama.va.edu/heritage/. Quarterly. $6/$18.95. Circ.: 6,500. Suzanne Wolfe, Editor. Description: Focuses on the events that have shaped Alabama and the South. Nonfiction: Interested in stories ignored, forgotten, or given short-shrift by historians. Also, Civil War articles if the story has an Alabama connection; 4,000-5,000 words; up to $400. Columns, Departments: Recollections (a specific remembrance of an Alabamian, often sent in by readers), up to 1,000 words; Alabama Album (the story behind an old photograph), up to 250 words; no payment. Queries: Not necessary. E-queries: No. Unsolicited mss: Accepts. Response: Queries 1-2 weeks, submissions 3-4 weeks. Freelance Content: 40%.

AMERICA'S CIVIL WAR
Primedia History Group, 741 Miller Dr. SE, Suite D2, Leesburg, VA 20175-8920. 703-779-8302. Web site: www.historynet.com. Bi-monthly. $3.99/issue. Circ.: 110,000. Roy Morris, Editor. Description: Popular history for general readers and Civil War buffs, on strategy, tactics, history, narrative. Nonfiction: Strategy, tactics, personalities, arms and equipment; 3,500-4,000 words, plus 500-word sidebar; $200-400. Columns, Departments: 2,000 words or less; $100-200. Art: Cite known color or b/w illustrations, and sources (museums, historical societies, private collections, etc.). Tips: Readable style and historical accuracy imperative. Use action and quotes where possible. Attribute quotes, cite major sources. Queries: Preferred. E-queries: No. Unsolicited mss: Accepts. Response: 6 months, SASE. Freelance Content: 98%. Payment: Both on acceptance and on publication; kill fee offered.

AMERICAN HERITAGE
90 Fifth Ave., New York, NY 10011. 212-367-3100. E-mail: mail@americanheritage.com. Web site: www.americanheritage.com. 8x/year. $4.95/issue. Circ.: 310,000. Richard F. Snow, Editor. Description: Covers the American experience, from serious concerns to colorful sidelights, from powerful institutions to ordinary men and women, using the past to illuminate the present. Nonfiction: On the American experience. Annotate all quotations and factual state-

ments; include brief biographical note about yourself; 6,000 words max.; pay varies. **Art:** b/w prints, color slides. **Tips:** Welcome freelancers, but needs detailed queries in advance. Also, consult indexes first. No fiction or poetry. **Queries:** Preferred. **E-queries:** No. **Unsolicited mss:** Accepts. **Response:** 8-10 weeks, SASE required. **Payment:** On acceptance.

AMERICAN HERITAGE OF INVENTION & TECHNOLOGY
60 Fifth Ave., New York, NY 10011.
E-mail: it@americanheritage.com. Web site: www.americanheritage.com/i&t. Quarterly. Circ.: 320,000. Frederick Allen, Editor. **Description:** Lively, authoritative prose and illustrations (archival photos, rare paintings), on the history of technology in America, for the sophisticated general reader. **Nonfiction:** Articles, 2,000-5,000 words, on great men and scoundrels, popular music and high art, our grandest national impulses (and, occasionally, our basest). **Queries:** Not necessary. **E-queries:** Yes. **Payment:** On acceptance.

AMERICAN HISTORY
6405 Flank Dr., Harrisburg, PA 17112. 717-657-9555.
E-mail: christine@cowles.com. Web site: thehistorynet.com. Bimonthly. $3.99/issue, $23.95/year. Circ.: 100,000. Tom Huntington, Editor. **Description:** Accurate, lively narratives with clear insights into the people, places, and events of the American past. **Nonfiction:** 3,000-3,500 words; $500-$600. **Tips:** Seeking tightly focused stories that show an incident or short period of time in history, rather than general biographies or the history of the Revolutionary War. **Queries:** Required. **E-queries:** Yes. **Unsolicited mss:** Does not accept. **Response:** 3-4 weeks, SASE required. **Freelance Content:** 70%. **Rights:** First NA. **Payment:** On acceptance.

AMERICAN LEGACY
60 Fifth Ave., New York, NY 10011. 212-620-2200.
E-mail: amlegacy@americanheritage.com.
Web site: www.americanlegacymagazine.com. Quarterly. $2.95/$9.95. Circ.: 500,000. Audrey Peterson, Editor. **Description:** Covers all aspects of Black history and culture. **Nonfiction:** Articles on people and events that have shaped history for African-Americans; up to 4,000 words; pay negotiable. **Tips:** No lifestyle articles, or features on contemporary figures in the black community, unless they have something to do with history. Keep proposals to 1 page, plus 1-page cover letter. **Queries:** Required. **E-queries:** Yes. **Unsolicited mss:** Accepts. **Response:** 2 months, SASE. **Freelance Content:** 95%. **Payment:** On acceptance.

AMERICAN OUTBACK JOURNAL
21 N. Tejon, Ste. 202, Colorado Springs, CO 80903. 719-475-2469.
E-mail: curt@americanoutback.com. Web site: www.americanoutback.com. Curt Penergraft, Editor. **Description:** Print and e-zine on the American West. Publish articles on lore, history, culture, ecology, politics, humor, and travel to off-beat western destinations. **Queries:** Preferred.

ANCESTRY

360W 4800N, Provo, UT 84604. 801-705-7304.
E-mail: ameditor@ancestry.com. Web site: www.ancestry.com. Bi-monthly. $24.95/yr. Circ.: 53,000. Jennifer Utley, Managing Editor. **Description:** Family history/genealogy magazine for professional family historians and hobbyists interested in getting the most out of their research. **Nonfiction:** Family articles, especially stories where novel approaches are used to find information on the lives of ancestors; 2,000-3,500 words; $500. **Fillers:** Humorous pieces about pursuit of the author's family history; 800 words; $200. **Art:** Interesting old photographs of ancestors. **Tips:** No typical family histories, only interesting angles on family history and specific case studies. **Queries:** Preferred. **E-queries:** Yes. **Unsolicited mss:** Accepts. **Response:** Queries 2 months, submissions 2 months,SASE. **Freelance Content:** 20%. **Rights:** All. **Payment:** On publication. **Contact:** Jennifer Utley.

ANCIENT AMERICAN

P.O. Box 370, Colfax, WI 54730. 715-962-3299.
E-mail: info@ancientamerican.com. Web site: www.ancientamerican.com. Bimonthly. $4.95/$24.95. Circ.: 12,000. Frank Joseph, Editor. **Description:** Describes prehistory of American Continent, regardless of presently fashionable beliefs. A public forum for experts and nonprofessionals alike to freely express their views without fear nor favor. **Nonfiction:** Articles on prehistory in clear, nontechnical language, with original color photographs and artwork; 2,000-3,000 words; $75-$150. **Art:** Adobe PhotoShop, TIFF. **Tips:** Translate complex research into accessible, attractive language with visually appealing format for ordinary readers. **Queries:** Not necessary. **E-queries:** Yes. **Unsolicited mss:** Accepts. **Freelance Content:** 50%. **Payment:** On publication.

ARMOR

4401 Vine Grove Rd., Fort Knox, KY 40121-2103. 502-624-2249.
Bi-monthly. $3/issue. Circ.: 12,500. John Clemons, Managing Editor. **Description:** Professional magazine of the Armor Branch for military units and agencies responsible for direct-fire ground combat. **Nonfiction:** Military history; research and development of armaments; tactical benefits and strategies, logistics, and related topics; up to 13 double-spaced pages. **Art:** Write captions on paper and tape to the back of the photos (don't write on photo backs). Indicate if you want the photos returned. **Response:** Submissions, 2 weeks.

AVIATION HISTORY

Primedia History Group, 741 Miller Dr., Ste. D-2,
Leesburg, VA 20175-8994. 703-779-8302.
Web site: www.thehistorynet.com. Arthur Sanfelici, Editor. **Description:** Covers military and civilian aviation, from man's first attempts at flight to the jet age. **Nonfiction:** Entertaining, informative, unusual stories. Favors carefully researched, third-person articles, or firsthand accounts that give the reader a sense of experiencing historical events. Include 500-word sidebar; 3,500-4,000 words; $200-$400.

Columns, Departments: 2,000 words or less; $100-$200. **Tips:** Include a brief bio, a description of your expertise in the subject matter, and suggestions for further reading. **Queries:** Required. **Unsolicited mss:** Does not accept. **Response:** 6 months. **Payment:** On publication.

THE BEAVER

167 Lombard Ave., #478, Winnipeg, Manitoba, Canada R3B 0T6. 204-988-9300. E-mail: beaver@historysociety.ca. Web site: www.historysociety.ca. Bimonthly. $4.95 issue, $27.50/year. Circ.: 45,000. Annalee Greenberg, Editor. **Description:** Canadian history for a general audience. **Nonfiction:** Canadian history subjects; Max. 3,500 words; $.30/word. **Tips:** Combine impeccable research with good nonfiction story-writing skills. **Queries:** Required. **E-queries:** No. **Unsolicited mss:** Accepts. **Response:** 6 weeks, SASE. **Freelance Content:** 50%. **Rights:** FNASR, electronic. **Payment:** On acceptance.

CALLIOPE

Cobblestone Publishing
30 Grove St., Ste. C, Peterborough, NH 03458. 603-924-7209.
E-mail: custsvc@cobblestone.mu.com. Web site: www.cobblestonepub.com. 9x/year. $29.95/yr. Circ.: 10,000. Rosalie F. Baker , Editor. **Description:** World history for youg people. Issues are thematic, exciting, colorful, with maps, timelines, illustrations, and art from major museums. **Fiction:** Fiction with historical, biographical, adventure themes; retold legends; 400-1,200 words; $.20-$.25/word. **Nonfiction:** Articles, 400-1,200 words, with lively, original approach to world history (through Renaissance). Shorts, 200-750 words, on little-known information related to issue's theme; $.20-$.25/word. **Fillers:** Activities, to 800 words. Puzzles, games. **Art:** any format. **Tips:** Contact for upcoming themes. **Queries:** Preferred. **E-queries:** No. **Unsolicited mss:** Prefer not to accept. **Response:** 2-4 months, SASE. **Freelance Content:** 80%. **Rights:** All. **Payment:** On publication.

CAROLOGUE

South Carolina Historical Society
100 Meeting St., Charleston, SC 29401-2299. 843-723-3225.
Web site: www.schistory.org. Peter A. Rerig, Editor. **Description:** On South Carolina history. **Nonfiction:** General-interest articles, to 10 pages. **Queries:** Preferred. **Payment:** in copies.

CIVIL WAR TIMES ILLUSTRATED

6405 Flank Dr., Harrisburg, PA 17112. 717-6557-9555.
E-mail: cwt@cowles.com. Web site: www.thehistorynet.com. 7x/year. Circ.: 170,000. James Kushlan, Editor. **Description:** Accurate, annotated stories of the Civil War. Relies heavily on primary sources and words of eyewitnesses. **Nonfiction:** Articles; 2,500-3,000 words; $400-$650. **Tips:** Prefers gripping, top-notch accounts of battles in the Eastern Theater of the war, eyewitness accounts (memoirs, diaries, letters), and common soldier photos. **Payment:** On acceptance.

COBBLESTONE

30 Grove St., Suite C, Peterborough, NH 03458-1454. 603-924-7209. Web site: www.cobblestonepub.com. 9x/year. $4.95/issue. Circ.: 33,000. Meg Chorlian, Editor. **Description:** American history for young readers. **Fiction:** Authentic historical or biographical fiction, retold legends, etc., on issue's theme; up to 800 words; $.20-$.25/word. **Nonfiction:** In-depth nonfiction, plays, first-person accounts, biographies; 300-600 words; $.20-$.25/word. **Poetry:** Clear, objective imagery, serious and light verse; up to 100 lines. **Fillers:** Crossword and other word puzzles using vocabulary of issue's theme. **Art:** Photographs, related to theme; color, transparencies, slides. **Queries:** Preferred.

COLUMBIA

Washington State Historical Society
315 N. Stadium Way, Tacoma, WA 98403. 253-798-5918.
E-mail: cdubois@wshs.wa.gov. Web site: www.wshs.org. Quarterly. $6/issue. Circ.: 4,200. Christina Dubois, Editor. **Description:** History publication for the Pacific Northwest. **Nonfiction:** Articles and commentary edited for the general reader. Submissions average 4,000 words. **Queries:** Not necessary. **E-queries:** Yes. **Unsolicited mss:** Accepts. **Response:** 1-2 weeks, SASE. **Freelance Content:** 80%. **Rights:** 1st.

COMMAND

P.O. Box 4017, San Luis Obispo, CA 93403. 805-546-9596.
Web site: www.commandmagazine.com. Bimonthly. Ty Bomba. **Description:** On military history or current military affairs. **Nonfiction:** Articles; popular, not scholarly, analytical military history, 800-10,000 words; pays $.05/word. **Queries:** Preferred. **Payment:** On publication.

COUNTRY FOLK

HC 77, Box 608, Pittsburgh, MO 65724. 417-993-5944.
E-mail: salaki@country folkmag.com. Web site: www.countryfolkmag.com. Bi-monthly. $2.75/issue $15.00/year. Circ.: 6,000. Susan Salaki, Editor. **Description:** True Ozark history stories, old rare recipes, historical photos, and interesting fillers. **Nonfiction:** Ozark history; 1,000-1,200 words; $20-$50. **Poetry:** Standard rhyming; 3 verses max.; 0-$5. **Freelance Content:** 99%.

EARLY AMERICAN LIFE

Box 8200, 6405 Flank Dr., Harrisburg, PA 17105-8200. 717-730-6263.
E-mail: ginnys@celticmooninc.com. Web site: earlyamericanlife.com. 8x/year. $2.99/issue, $19.95/year. Virginia P. Stimmel, Editor. **Description:** On early American past (traditions, antiques, architecture, history, period style). For people who are passionate about tangible aspects of the American past and aspire to incorporate them into their lifestyles and homes. **Nonfiction:** Detailed articles about American domestic past (1600-1850); travel, historic places, preservation, restoration, antiques, houses, textiles, furniture, decorative objects; 1,500-2,000 words; $500-

$600. **Columns, Departments:** Eye on Antiques, Worth Seeing, Life in Early America, Side by Side; 800-1,500 words; $250-$600. **Queries:** Preferred. **E-queries:** Yes. **Unsolicited mss:** Accepts. **Response:** 30 days, SASE required. **Freelance Content:** 10-20%. **Rights:** One-time worldwide. **Payment:** On acceptance.

FAMILY TREE

1507 Diana Ave., Cincinnati, OH 45207. 513-531-2690.
Web site: www.familytreemagazine.com. **Description:** Genealogy publication. **Queries:** Preferred.

FASHION FLASHBACKS

Platform Publishing, P.O. Box 138, San Mateo, CA 94401. 650-344-6977.
E-mail: lanajean@best.com. Web site: www.best.com/~lanajean/flashbacks.html. Lanajean Vecchoine, Editor/Publisher. **Description:** Online and in print. Focuses on fashion design and history from 1960-1979. **Nonfiction:** Articles, photos, and press releases about notable events accepted. **Tips:** Include both your email and mailing addresses. **Payment:** in copies.

FOOTSTEPS

Footsteps, 30 Grove St., Suite C, Petersborough, NH 03458. 603-924-7209.
E-mail: cfbaker@meganet.com. Web site: www.footstepsmagazine.com. 5x/year. $23.95/yr. Circ.: 3,000. Charles F. Baker, Editor. **Description:** African American history and heritage for students in grades 4-8. **Fiction:** Authentic retellings of historical and biographical events, adventure, legends; 200-1,000 words; $.20-$.25/word. **Nonfiction:** On issue's theme; 200-1,000 words; $.20-$.25/word. **Art:** Slides, transparencies, digital, prints; pay varies. **Tips:** Contact for upcoming themes. **Queries:** Required. **Unsolicited mss:** Accepts. **Response:** Queries 2-4 months, submissions 2-6 months, SASE. **Freelance Content:** 90%. **Rights:** All. **Payment:** On publication. **Contact:** Charles F. Baker.

GOLDENSEAL

The Cultural Ctr., 1900 Kanawha Blvd. E.,
Charleston, WV 25305-0300. 304-558-0220.
Web site: www.wvculture.org/goldenseal. John Lilly, Editor. **Description:** On traditional West Virginia culture and history. Oral histories, old and new b/w photos, research articles. **Nonfiction:** Features, 3,000 words, and shorter articles, 1,000 words; pays $.10/word. **Payment:** On publication.

GOOD OLD DAYS

306 E. Parr Rd., Berne, IN 46711. 219-589-4000.
E-mail: editor@goodolddaysonline.com. Web site: www.goodoldday-magazine.com. Monthly. $2.50/issue. Circ.: 200,000. Ken Tate, Editor. **Description:** First-person nostalgia from the "Good Old Days" era (defined as 1900-1955), especially from start of the Great Depression in 1929 to end of World War II. **Nonfiction:** First-person nostalgia within this timeframe. Make sure story is sprinkled with plenty of warmth,

humor, poignance; 500-1,500; $.02-$04/word. **Poetry:** Prefers good meter and distinct rhyme scheme; 8-24 lines; pay varies. **Columns, Departments:** Good Old Days in the Kitchen (cooking, cleaning, about a particular favorite dish; include recipe); Good Old Days on Wheels (planes, trains, automobiles; needs accurate facts); 500-1,500; 2-4 cents/word. **Art:** Good photos helpful. Photocopies okay for submission; submit original or high-quality reproduction upon acceptance; prints; $5/photo. **Tips:** Readers are generally older, rather conservative. Keep a positive, pleasant tone. **Queries:** Not necessary. **E-queries:** Yes. **Unsolicited mss:** Accepts. **Response:** Submissions 2 months, SASE required. **Freelance Content:** 85%. **Rights:** All. **Payment:** On acceptance.

HERITAGE QUEST

Sierra Home, P.O. Box 329, Bountiful, UT 84011. 801-298-5358. E-mail: leland@heritaequest.com. Web site: www.heritagequest.com. Bi-monthly. $6.95 issue, $28/year. Circ.: 21,000. Leland Meitzler, Editor. **Description:** Offers help with genealogical research. **Nonfiction:** Genealogical how-to articles; 1,800-8,000 words; $75/printed page. **Art:** Electronic TIFF; submit with article. **Tips:** Readers range from beginners to professionals. **Queries:** Preferred. **E-queries:** Yes. **Unsolicited mss:** Accepts. **Response:** 60 days,SASE not required. **Freelance Content:** 90%. **Rights:** All. **Payment:** On publication.

HIGHLANDER

560 Green Bay Rd., Suite 204, Winnetka, IL 60093. 847-784-9660. E-mail: sray5617@aol.com. 7x/year. $17.50/year. Circ.: 35,000. Sharon Kennedy Ray, Editor. **Description:** Covers Scottish heritage (history, clans, families), related to Scotland in the period 1300-1900 A.D. **Nonfiction:** 1,500-2,000 words; $185-$250. **Art:** Photos must accompany manuscripts; b/w, color transparencies, maps, line drawings. **Tips:** Not concerned with modern Scotland. **Queries:** Preferred. **E-queries:** No. **Unsolicited mss:** Accepts. **Response:** Queries 1-2 weeks, submissions 1-2 months, SASE required. **Payment:** On acceptance.

THE ILLINOIS STEWARD

1102 S. Goodwin, W503 Turner Hall, Urbana, IL 61801. 217-333-2778. Web site: ilsteward.nres.uiuc.edu. Phyllis Picklesimer, Editor. **Description:** On Illinois history and heritage, with natural-resource stewardship theme. No payment. **Nonfiction:** Articles, 1,700-1,800 words. **Queries:** Preferred.

MHQ: QUARTERLY JOURNAL OF MILITARY HISTORY

Primedia History Group, 741 Miller Dr. S.E., Suite D-2, Leesburg, VA 20175. 703-771-9400. Web site: www.historynet.com. Quarterly. $48/year. Circ.: 45,000. Mike Haskew, Editor. **Description:** Offers an undistorted view of history, encourages understanding of events, personalities, and artifacts of the past. **Nonfiction:** Well-written military history; 3,500-4,000 words, with 500-word sidebar; $200-$400. **Columns, Departments:** 2,500 words. **Art:** Color, b/w illustrations. **Queries:** Preferred.

E-queries: Yes. **Unsolicited mss:** Accepts. **Response:** Queries 2-4 weeks, submissions 6-8 weeks,SASE. **Freelance Content:** 50%. **Payment:** On publication.

MILITARY

2122 28th St., Sacramento, CA 95818. 916-457-8990.
E-mail: military@ns.net. Web site: www.milmag.com. Monthly. $14.79/yr. Circ.: 18,000. Rick McCusker, Editor. **Description:** Military history (WWII, Korea, Viet Nam, and today). Dedicated to all who served in the armed forces. **Nonfiction:** Personal war experiences; 4,000 words or less. **Fillers:** Humor in uniform, military humor; 1,000 words or less. **Art:** 200 dpi or better. **Queries:** Preferred. **E-queries:** Yes. **Unsolicited mss:** Accepts. **Payment:** No payment.

MONTANA

225 N. Roberts St., Box 201201, Helena, MT 59620-1201. 406-444-4741.
Web site: www.montanahistoricalsociety.org. Quarterly. $8.50/$29 yr. Circ.: 10,000. **Description:** For members of state historical society and Western History Assn., covering history of Montana and the American and Canadian west. **Nonfiction:** Authentic articles on history of the region; new interpretative approaches to major developments in western history. Must use footnotes or bibliography; 3,500-5,500 words; N/A. **Queries:** Preferred. **E-queries:** Yes. **Unsolicited mss:** Accepts. **Response:** Queries 3 months, submissions 1 month, SASE. **Freelance Content:** 95%. **Rights:** All. **Payment:** N/A.

NAVAL HISTORY

291 Wood Rd., Annapolis, MD 21402. 410-295-1079.
E-mail: fschultz@usni.org. Web site: www.usni.org/navalhistory/nh.html. Bimonthly. Circ.: 40,000. Fred L. Schultz, Editor-in-Chief. **Description:** On international naval and maritime history, published by U.S. Naval Institute. **Nonfiction:** Essays, book excerpts, interviews, profiles, personal experience, technical, photo feature; 1,000-3,000 words; pays $300-$500 (assigned articles); $75-$400 (unsolicited). **Fillers:** Humor, inspirational; 50-100 words; pays $10-$50. **Tips:** Write a good, concise story; support it with primary sources and good illustrations. Historian David McCullough called this "one of the best magazines in the country." **Queries:** Preferred. **E-queries:** Yes. **Unsolicited mss:** Accepts. **Response:** Queries 1 month, submissions 2 months, SASE required. **Freelance Content:** 90%. **Rights:** FNASR. **Payment:** On acceptance.

NEBRASKA HISTORY

P.O. Box 82554, Lincoln, NE 68501. 402-471-4747.
E-mail: publish@nebraskahistory.org. Web site: www.nebraskahistory.org. Quarterly. $30/yr. Circ.: 3,800. James E. Potter, Editor. **Description:** Well-researched articles, edited documents, and other annotated primary materials on history of Nebraska and the Great Plains. **Nonfiction:** 3,000-7,000 words. **Art:** 8x10 b/w, 600 dpi scans. **Tips:** Rarely publishes family history or reminiscence. **Queries:** Preferred. **E-queries:**

Yes. **Unsolicited mss:** Accepts. **Response:** Queries 1 week, submissions in 2 months, SASE. **Payment:** in copies.

NOW & THEN

CASS/ETSU, P.O. Box 70556, Johnson City, TN 37614-0556. 423-439-5348. E-mail: cass@etsu.edu. Web site: www.cass.etsu.edu/n&t. 3x/year. $20. Circ.: 1,500. Jane Harris Woodside, Editor. **Description:** Each issue focuses on one aspect of life in Appalachian region (from Northern Mississippi to Southern New York). Previous themes: women, religion, blacks, Cherokees, the environment, music. **Fiction:** 1,500-3,000 words: must relate to theme of issue and Appalachian region. **Nonfiction:** Articles, interviews, essays, memoirs, book reviews; 1,000-2,500 words. **Poetry:** up to 5 poems. **Tips:** Topics can be contemporary or historical. **Queries:** Preferred.

OLD CALIFORNIA GAZETTE

2454 Heritage Park Row, San Diego, CA 92110. 619-491-0099. E-mail: gazettes@cts.com. Monthly. Circ.: 1,000,000. Karen Spring, Editor. **Description:** California history, 1800-1920s. **Fiction:** 500-1,000 words; $.10/word. **Nonfiction:** 500-1,000 words; $.10/word. **Tips:** $50/bonus if piece on front cover. **Queries:** Preferred. **E-queries:** Yes. **Unsolicited mss:** Accepts. **Response:** 1 month, SASE not needed. **Freelance Content:** 50%. **Rights:** 1st. **Payment:** On publication.

PENNSYLVANIA HERITAGE

PO Box 11466, Harrisburg, PA 17108-1466. 717-787-7522. E-mail: momalley@phmc.state.pa.us. Web site: www.paheritage.org. Quarterly. Circ.: 13,000. Michael J. O'Malley III, Editor. **Description:** Published by Pennsylvania Historical and Museum Commission and the Pennsylvania Heritage Society, to introduce readers to the state's rich culture and historic legacy. **Nonfiction:** Articles on Pennsylvania fine and decorative arts, architecture, archaeology, history, industry and technology, travel, and folklore, with suggestions for possible illustration; 2,500-3,500 words; to $500. **Art:** Photos, drawings; photo essays; up to $100. **Tips:** Seeks unusual, fresh angle to make history come to life, including pictorial or photo essays, interviews, travel/destination pieces. Submit complete manuscript. **Queries:** Preferred. **Payment:** On acceptance.

PERSIMMON HILL

1700 N.E. 63rd St., Oklahoma City, OK 73111. 405-478-6404. E-mail: editor@nationalcowboymuseum.org. Web site: www/nationalcowboymuseum.org. Quarterly. $30/yr. Circ.: 15,000. M.J. Van Deventer, Editor. **Description:** Historical and contemporary themes related to the American West, from Hollywood to cowboys. Honors those who have made positive contributions to the West, past or present. **Nonfiction:** On Western history and art, cowboys, ranching, rodeo, and nature; 1,000-1,500 words; $150-$350. **Columns, Departments:** Great hotels and lodgings; entrepreneurs; events, interesting places to visit, personalities; 750-1,000 words; $75-$150. **Art:** Slides, transparencies; up to

$50/image. **Tips:** No stories on western outlaws or "bad guys" (Billy the Kid) stories. **Queries:** Required. **E-queries:** Yes. **Unsolicited mss:** Accepts. **Response:** Queries 6 weeks, submissions 2 months, SASE. **Freelance Content:** 95%. **Rights:** One-time NA. **Payment:** On publication.

PRESERVATION
1785 Massachusetts Ave. NW, Washington, DC 20036. 202-588-6388. E-mail: preservation@nthp.org. Web site: www.nthp.org. Bimonthly. $5/issue, $20/year. Circ.: 200,000. Robert Wilson, Editor. **Description:** Encourages a sense of place and passion for historic preservation. **Nonfiction:** Articles on the built environment, place, architecture, preservation issues, and people involved. Mostly freelance; 150-6,000 words; $.50-$1.00/word. **Queries:** Preferred. **E-queries:** Yes. **Unsolicited mss:** Accepts. **Response:** Queries 2-3 weeks, submissions 6-8 weeks, SASE required. **Freelance Content:** 80%. **Rights:** 1st NA, archival. **Payment:** On acceptance.

REMINISCE
Reiman Publications, 5400 S. 60th St., Greendale, WI 53129. 414-423-0100. E-mail: editor@reminisce.com. Web site: www.reminisce.com. Bimonthly. $14.98/yr. Circ.: 1,200,000, Editor. **Description:** "A stroll down memory lane." Vintage photographs and real-life, first-person stories recall the "good old days." **Nonfiction:** Needs an "I remember" element; 750 words; $125 (full-page features). **Art:** Good, candid photos. **Queries:** Not necessary. **Unsolicited mss:** Accepts. **Response:** 2 months. **Freelance Content:** 90%. **Payment:** On acceptance.

RENAISSANCE
Phantom Press Publications, 13 Appleton Rd., Nantucket, MA 02554. E-mail: renzine@aol.com. Web site: www.renaissancemagazine.com. Quarterly. Circ.: 30,000. Kim Guarnaccia, Managing Editor. **Description:** Renaissance and Medieval history, costuming, heraldry, reenactments, role-playing, and Renaissance faires. **Nonfiction:** Interviews, reviews of books, music, movies, and games; $.06/word. **Queries:** Preferred. **Payment:** On publication.

SOUTHERN OREGON HERITAGE TODAY
106 N. Central Ave., Medford, OR 97501-5926. 541-773-6536. Web site: www.sohs.org. Monthly. Marcia W. Somers. **Description:** On history of the southern Oregon region (people, places, buildings, and events). **Nonfiction:** Well-written articles, 800-2,500 words; pays $50-$250. **Tips:** "Make sure there is a storyline, not just a reiteration of facts." **Payment:** On publication.

TIMELINE
1982 Velma Ave., Columbus, OH 43211-2497. 614-297-2360. E-mail: timeline@ohiohistory.org. Bi-monthly. $6/$30. Circ.: 15,000. Christopher S. Duckworth, Editor. **Description:** Covers fields of history, prehistory, and natural sciences, directed towards readers in the Midwest. **Nonfiction:** History, politics, eco-

nomics, social, and natural history for lay readers in Ohio and the Midwest; 1,000-5,000 words. **Tips:** Writing style should be simple and direct; avoid jargon. **Queries:** Preferred. **E-queries:** Yes. **Unsolicited mss:** Accepts. **Response:** 2 weeks, SASE. **Freelance Content:** 90%. **Rights:** 1st NA. **Payment:** On acceptance.

TRUE WEST

P.O. Box 8008, Cave Creek, AZ 85327. 888-587-1881. E-mail: mail@truewestmagazine.com. Web site: www.truewestmagazine.com. Monthly. Circ.: 50,000. Marcus Huff, Editor. **Description:** About the Old West, to 1920. **Nonfiction:** True stories, with photos. Some contemporary stories with historical slant. Must list your sources; 500-4,500 words. **Payment:** On acceptance.

VIETNAM

Primedia History Group, 741 Miller Dr. S.E., Suite D-2, Leesburg, VA 20175-8920. 703-771-9400. E-mail: sbailey@cowles.com. Web site: www.thehistorynet.com. Bi-monthly. $3.99/$19.95. Circ.: 100,000. David T. Zabecki, Editor. **Description:** Popular military-history magazine. Seeks to record and document "the many truths about Vietnam." **Nonfiction:** First-person and third-person accounts of all aspects of Vietnam War; strategy, tactics, personalities, arms and equipment; 3,500-4,000 words; $200. **Columns, Departments:** Arsenal, Fighting Forces, Personality, Perspectives; 1,500-2,000 words; $100-$150. **Tips:** Readers are Vietnam veterans, current military personnel, military historians and enthusiasts. Does not publish "war stories." **Queries:** Preferred. **E-queries:** Accepts. **Unsolicited mss:** Accepts. **Rights:** All worldwide, reprint. **Payment:** On publication.

THE WESTERN HISTORICAL QUARTERLY

Utah State Univ., Logan, UT 84322-0740. 435-797-1301. E-mail: whq@hass.usu.edu. Web site: www.usu.edu/history/whq. Quarterly. Circ.: 2,200. Anne M. Butler, Editor. **Description:** Covers the American West: United States, Canada, and Mexico. Occupation, settlement; political, economic, social, cultural and intellectual history. **Nonfiction:** Original articles about the American West, the Westward movement, 20th-century regional studies, Spanish borderlands, Canada, northern Mexico, Alaska, and Hawaii; to 10,000 words; no payment. **Tips:** Prefers descriptive, interpretive, and analytical essays on broad themes; use of primary sources and monographic literature. **Queries:** Not necessary. **E-queries:** Yes. **Unsolicited mss:** Accepts. **Response:** 1 week, SASE required.

WILD WEST

Primedia History Group, 741 Miller Dr. S.E., Suite D-2, Leesburg, VA 20175-8920. 703-779-8302. Web site: www.thehistorynet.com./wildwest. Bimonthly. Gregory Lalire, Editor. **Description:** History of people, places, battles, and events that led to the taming of the great American frontier. **Nonfiction:** Articles, artwork, and picture essays on life and times of settlers, cowboys, Indians, gunmen, lawmen, all the fascinating characters and aspects of Western lore and culture; 3,500-4,000 words; $200-$400. **Columns, Departments:** up to 2,000 words. **Art:** Put your full name on each photo. **Queries:** Preferred. **E-queries:** Yes. **Unsolicited mss:** Accepts. **Response:** 6 months, SASE. **Payment:** On publication.

WORLD WAR II
Primedia History Group, 741 Miller Dr. S.E., Suite D-2, Leesburg, VA 20175-8920. 703-779-8302. Web site: www.thehistorynet.com. Bimonthly. Michael Haskew, Editor. **Description:** Strategy, tactics, personalities, arms and equipment. **Nonfiction:** Features, 3,500-4,000 words, plus 500-word sidebar; up to $200. **Art:** Cite any color or b/w illustrations, and sources. **Tips:** Readable style and historical accuracy imperative. **Queries:** Preferred. **Unsolicited mss:** Accepts. **Response:** 6 months, SASE. **Rights:** Exclusive worldwide. **Payment:** On publication.

HOBBIES, CRAFTS, COLLECTING
(See also Games & Pastimes)

AIRBRUSH ACTION
P.O. Box 2052, 1985 Swarthmore Ave., Lakewood, NJ 08701. 800-876-2472. E-mail: kpriest@idt.net. Web site: www.airbrushaction.com. Bi-monthly. $5.99/issue, $26.95/year. Circ.: 60,000. Kathryn Priest, Editor. **Description:** Showcases innovative airbrush art. Profiles on notable artists, step-by-step "how-to"; columns on T-shirt painting, automotive airbrushing, fingernail design. Also, regular Buyer's Guides with comparisons of airbrush art supplies. **Nonfiction:** Profiles of artists by request only; 1,000-2,000 words; $.15/word. **Queries:** Required. **E-queries:** Yes. **Unsolicited mss:** Accepts. **Response:** 2 weeks, SASE required. **Freelance Content:** 50%. **Rights:** All. **Payment:** On publication.

ANCESTRY
360W 4800N, Provo, UT 84604. 801-705-7304. E-mail: ameditor@ancestry.com. Web site: www.ancestry.com. Bi-monthly. $24.95/yr. Circ.: 53,000. Jennifer Utley, Managing Editor. **Description:** Family history/genealogy magazine for professional family historians and hobbyists interested in getting the most out of their research. **Nonfiction:** Family articles, especially stories where novel approaches are used to find information on the lives of ancestors; 2,000-3,500 words; $500. **Fillers:** Humorous pieces about pursuit of the author's family history; 800 words; $200. **Art:** Interesting old photographs of ancestors. **Tips:** No typical family histories, only interesting angles on family history and specific case studies. **Queries:** Preferred. **E-queries:** Yes. **Unsolicited mss:** Accepts. **Response:** Queries 2 months, submissions 2 months, SASE. **Freelance Content:** 20%. **Rights:** All. **Payment:** On publication. **Contact:** Jennifer Utley.

ANTIQUE SHOPPE

P.O. Box 2175, Keystone Heights, FL 32656. 352-475-1679.
E-mail: antshoppe@aol.com. Web site: www.antique.com. Monthly. $17. Circ.: 20,000. Bruce G. Causey, Editor. **Description:** Serves antique and collection industry. **Nonfiction:** On antiques, collectibles, communities with antique districts, historical locations, local auctions or shows; 1,000 words; $50/story. **Art:** Prefers stories with photos. **Queries:** Preferred. **E-queries:** Yes. **Unsolicited mss:** Accepts. **Freelance Content:** 60%. **Payment:** On publication.

ANTIQUE TRADER PUBLICATIONS

Box 1050, Dubuque, IA 52004. 319-588-2073.
Web site: www.collect.com. Virginia Hill, Managing Editor. **Description:** Covers all types of antiques and collectors' items. **Nonfiction:** Articles; 1,000-2,000 words; pays $50-$250. **Art:** Photos. **Rights:** non-exclusive. **Payment:** On publication.

ANTIQUES & AUCTION NEWS

P.O. Box 500, Mount Joy, PA 17552. 717-653-1833.
Weekly. Denise Sater, Editor. **Description:** Factual articles, 600-1,500 words, on antiques, collectors, collections, and places of historic interest. **Nonfiction:** Pays $10-$35. **Art:** Photos. **Queries:** Required. **Payment:** On publication.

ANTIQUEWEEK

P.O. Box 90, Knightstown, IN 46148. 800-876-5133.
Web site: www.antiqueweek.com. Tom Hoepf, Connie Swaim, Editors. **Description:** Weekly antique, auction, and collectors' newspaper. Guidelines available. **Nonfiction:** Articles, 500-2,000 words, on antiques, collectibles, genealogy, auction and antique show reports; pays $40-$200 for in-depth articles. **Art:** Photos. **Queries:** Preferred. **Payment:** On publication.

AUCTION EXCHANGE

P.O. Box 57, Plainwell, MI 49080-0057. 888-339-3795.
E-mail: auctionexchange@wmis.net. Web site: www.eauctionexchange.com. Weekly. $23/yr. Circ.: 13,000. Lars Suendsen, Editor. **Description:** Serves Michigan, Indiana, Ohio. For dealers and collectors, on auctions, antiques, and collectibles. **Nonfiction:** 500 words; $1.50/column. **Art:** $3/photo. **Queries:** Not necessary. **E-queries:** Yes. **Unsolicited mss:** Accepts. **Freelance Content:** 70%. **Rights:** One-time. **Payment:** On publication. **Contact:** Lars Suendsen.

AUTOGRAPH COLLECTOR

Odyssey Publications, 510-A S. Corona Mall, Corona, CA 91719-1420. 909-371-7137.
Web site: www.AutographCollector.com. Ev Phillips, Editor. **Description:** Covers all areas of autograph collecting (preservation, framing, and storage, specialty collections, documents and letters, collectors and dealers). **Nonfiction:** Articles; 1,000-2,000 words; pay varies. **Queries:** Preferred.

BEAD & BUTTON

Kalmbach Publishing Co., P.O. Box 1612, 21027 Crossroads Circle, Waukesha, WI 53187. 262-796-8776, ex304. 6x/year. Circ.: 75,000. Alice Korach, Editor. **Description:** Illustrated bead projects for enthusiasts: jewelry, decorative crafts, clothing, and more. **Nonfiction:** Pay varies. **Art:** Photos. **Queries:** Required. **E-queries:** Yes. **Unsolicited mss:** Does not accept. **Response:** 2 months. **Freelance Content:** 60%. **Rights:** All. **Payment:** On acceptance.

BECKETT BASKETBALL CARD MONTHLY

15850 Dallas Pkwy., Dallas, TX 75248. 972-448-4600. E-mail: jkelley@beckett.com. Web site: www.beckett.com. Monthly. $4.99/$27.99. Circ.: 100,000. John Kelley, Editor. **Description:** For hobbyists who collect cards and memorabilia. (Also publishes *Beckett Sports Collectibles & Autographs, Football Card Monthly, Hockey Collector,* and *Racing and Motorsports.*) **Nonfiction:** Sports collectibles stories, with a trading card/basketball angle; 800-2,000 words. **Tips:** Promote the hobby in a positive, fun-loving way. **Queries:** Preferred. **E-queries:** Yes. **Unsolicited mss:** Accepts. **Response:** 10 days, SASE not needed. **Freelance Content:** 30%. **Rights:** All. **Payment:** On publication.

THE BLADE

Krause Publications, P.O. Box 5010, Iola, WI 54945-5010. 715-445-2214. E-mail: blade@krause.com. Web site: www.blademag.com. Monthly. $4.95/issue, $25.98/year. Circ.: 54,000. Steve Shackleford, Editor. **Description:** Information for knife makers, collectors, daily knife users, and enthusiasts. **Nonfiction:** Anything new and unusual about handmade and factory knives, historical pieces, interviews, celebrities, values on collectible knives and accessories, tips on use; 1,000-1,500 words. **Art:** Varied formats. **Queries:** Preferred. **E-queries:** Yes. **Unsolicited mss:** Accepts. **Response:** Queries 1 month, submissions 2 months, SASE required. **Freelance Content:** 5%. **Rights:** All. **Payment:** On publication.

BREW YOUR OWN

Battenkill Communications, 5053 Main St., Suite A, Manchester Center, VT 05255. 802-362-3981. E-mail: edit@byo.com. Web site: www.byo.com. Monthly. Circ.: 42,000. Kathleen James Ring, Editor. **Description:** Practical how-to articles for homebrewers. **Queries:** Required. **Payment:** On publication.

CANADIAN STAMP NEWS

103 Lakeshore Rd., Suite 202, St. Catharines, Ont., Canada L2N 2T6. 905-646-7744. E-mail: stamps@trajan.com. Web site: www.canadianstampnews.com. Biweekly. Virginia St. Denis, Editor. **Description:** On stamp collecting news, rare and unusual stamps, and auction and club reports. Special issues throughout the year. **Nonfiction:** Articles, 1,000-2,000 words; pays from $50-$85. **Art:** Photos. **Payment:** On publication.

CAR TOY COLLECTIBLES

Challenge Publications, 7950 Deering Avenue, Canoga Park, CA 91304-5007. 818-887-0550. E-mail: mail@challengeweb.com. Web site: www.challenge.com. 9x/year. $21.50/yr. Kevin Boales, Editor. **Description:** For car lovers. Covers industry news, events, companies, and artists that produce cars and accessories. **Nonfiction:** Fun and informative articles on model cars; new and old, domestic and imported; also automobilia. **Queries:** Preferred.

CAROUSEL NEWS & TRADER

87 Park Ave. W., Suite 206, Mansfield, OH 44902-1612. 419-529-4999. E-mail: cnsam@aol.com. Web site: www.carousel.net/trader/. 10x/year. $3.95/issue $35/year. Circ.: 3,500. Walter L. Loucks, Editor. **Description:** Covers all aspects of carousels (Merry-Go-Rounds), including complete machines, individual animals, restoration, history, carving, buy-sell-trade. **Nonfiction:** On carousel history, profiles of operators and carvers, collectors, preservationists, restorationists; 500-1,000 words plus photos; $50/printed page. **Art:** Photos. **Queries:** Preferred. **E-queries:** Yes. **Unsolicited mss:** Accepts. **Response:** 4 weeks, SASE. **Payment:** On publication.

CLASSIC TOY TRAINS

21027 Crossroads Cir., Waukesha, WI 53187. 262-796-8776. E-mail: editor@classtrain.com. Web site: www.classtrain.com. 9x/year. $4.95/issue, $36.95/year. Circ.: 70,000. Neil Besougloff, Editor. **Description:** For enthusiasts of old and new toy trains produced by Lionel, American Flyer, and their competitors. **Nonfiction:** Articles, with photos, on toy train layouts and collections. Also toy train manufacturing history and repair/maintenance. Pays $75/printed page. **Queries:** Preferred. **E-queries:** Yes. **Unsolicited mss:** Accepts. **Response:** Queries 15 days,submissions 30 days. **Freelance Content:** 60%. **Rights:** All. **Payment:** On acceptance.

COLLECTOR EDITIONS

1107 Broadway, Suite 1210-N, New York, NY 10010. 212-989-8700. Web site: www.collectoreditions.com. Bimonthly. $4.99/issue, $29.90/year. Circ.: 90,000. James van Maanen, Editor. **Description:** Covers limited and open-edition collectibles, figurines, plates, prints, crystal glass, porcelain, and related items, for individual collectors. **Nonfiction:** 250-1,000 words. Pays $100-$300. **Queries:** Required. **Unsolicited mss:** Does not accept. **Response:** Queries 30 days. **Freelance Content:** 10-15%. **Rights:** 1st NA. **Payment:** six wks after acceptance.

COLLECTOR GLASS NEWS

P.O. Box 308, Slippery Rock, PA 16057. 724-946-2838. E-mail: mark@glassnews.com. Web site: www.glassnews.com. Bimonthly. $3/issue. Circ.: 850. Dr. Mark E. Chase, Managing Editor. **Description:** For collectors of cartoon, promotional, sports, and fast-food glassware produced in past 70 years. **Nonfiction:** Well-researched pieces on specific promotions, glass sets, glass producers, or personalities; 100-500 words; $30-$50. **Tips:** No general articles; readers are advanced collectors looking for information on obscure sets or producers. **Queries:** Preferred. **E-queries:** Yes. **Unsolicited mss:** Accepts. **Response:** 1-2 weeks, SASE required. **Freelance Content:** 30%. **Rights:** 1st NA. **Payment:** On publication.

COLLECTORS NEWS

P.O. Box 306, 502 2nd St, Grundy Ctr., IA 50638. 319-824-6981. E-mail: collectors@collectors-news.com. Web site: www.collectors-news.com. Monthly. $4/issue, $28/year. Circ.: 10,000. Linda Kruger, Editor. **Description:** Antiques and collectibles magazine for casual collector and experienced dealer. Accurate information on wide variety of types, market trends, events, and collector interaction. **Nonfiction:** Background of collectibles; how to identify, care for, value items. 20th-century nostalgia, Americana, glass and china, music, furniture, transportation, timepieces, jewelry, farm-related items, and lamps; 900-1,200 words; $1.10/column inch. **Art:** Quality color or b/w photos. **Queries:** Preferred. **E-queries:** Yes. **Response:** Queries 2 weeks, submissions 6 weeks, SASE required. **Freelance Content:** 30%. **Rights:** 1st serial, one-time. **Payment:** On publication.

CRAFTING TRADITIONS

5400 S. 60th St., Greendale, WI 53129. 414-423-0100. Web site: reimanpub.com. Kathleen Anderson, Editor. **Description:** All types of craft designs (needlepoint, quilting, woodworking, etc.) with complete instructions and full-size patterns. **Nonfiction:** Pays $25-$250. **Rights:** all. **Payment:** On acceptance.

CRAFTS

Primedia Enthusiast Group, P.O. Box 1790, Peoria, IL 61656-1790. 309-682-6626. Web site: www.craftsmag.com. Monthly. Circ.: 250,000. **Description:** In-depth information on a wide variety of crafts.

CRAFTS 'N THINGS

2400 Devon, Suite 375, Des Plaines, IL 60018-4618. 847-635-5800. E-mail: bsunderlage@clapper.com. Web site: www.craftideas.com. 8x/year. $4.99/issue. Circ.: 250,000. Barbara Sunderlage, Editor. **Description:** How-to articles on varied craft projects, with instructions. **Nonfiction:** Instructions, with photo of finished item. Pays $50-$250. **Tips:** Limited freelance content. **Queries:** Required. **Payment:** On acceptance.

THE CRAFTS REPORT

P.O. Box 1992, Wilmington, DE 19899-1992. 302-656-2209. Web site: www.craftsreport.com. Monthly. Circ.: 18,000. **Description:** Focuses on the business side of the crafts industry; marketing, growing your craft business, time management, studio safety, retail relationships, features on other crafts professionals at all levels of the field, industry news and more.

CREATIVE QUILTING

450 Fashion Ave., Suite 1701, New York, NY 10123-1799. 212-244-2351. Bimonthly. Jan Burns. **Description:** For experienced and novice quilters. **Nonfiction:** Articles should contain detailed instructions and diagrams for making quality quilts. Also, book reviews, articles on quilt exhibitions, and profiles of well-known quilters. Pay varies. **Queries:** Preferred.

DECORATIVE ARTIST'S WORKBOOK

1507 Dana Ave., Cincinnati, OH 45207-1005. 513-531-2690. E-mail: dawedit@fwpubs.com. Web site: www.decorativeartist.com. Bimonthly. Circ.: 90,000. Anne Hevener, Editor. **Description:** How-to articles on decorative painting. **Nonfiction:** Painting projects only, not crafts; 1,000-1,500 words; $150-$300. **Columns, Departments:** Artist of the Issue (profiles of up-and-coming painters); 500 words; $100-$150. **Queries:** Required. **Payment:** On acceptance.

DOLL WORLD

306 E. Parr Rd., Berne, IN 46711. 219-724-0499. E-mail: doll_world@whitebirches.com. Web site: dollworld-magazine.com. Bimonthly. $4.95/issue, $19.97/year. Circ.: 65,000. Vicki Steensma, Editor. **Description:** For readers of all ages, about antique, contemporary, and collectible dolls of all kinds. **Nonfiction:** On doll history, preservation, restoration, events, museums, costumes, artists; 1,000-1,200 words; Pay varies. **Fillers:** Nostalgia and humor are welcome touches. **Art:** Prefers that doll makers/collectors send us the doll(s) whenever possible to get photos shot in our studio. If not possible, send high-quality slides and disk images .tiff, high resolution, 250 dpi, CMYK color, Mac format. **Tips:** Be professional, neat, and respectful. Know your subject and be familiar with the magazine you are submitting to. **Queries:** Not necessary. **E-queries:** Yes. **Unsolicited mss:** Accepts. **Response:** 1 month, SASE required. **Freelance Content:** 50%. **Rights:** All. **Payment:** On acceptance.

DOLLHOUSE MINIATURES

21027 Crossroads Cir., P.O. Box 1612, Waukesha, WI 53187. 262-796-8776. E-mail: cstjacques@dhminiatures.com. Web site: www.dhminiatures.com. Monthly. $4.95/$39.95 year. Circ.: 35,000. Candice St. Jacques, Editor. **Description:** America's leading miniatures magazine, for artisans, collectors, and hobbyists. Stories on artisans, exhibits, and collections from around the world to inspire readers to try colorful, creative, and fun projects. **Nonfiction:** How-tos with easy-to-follow instructions, photos, and illustrations; profiles, collections, museums, industry news. **Art:** Color slides, b/w prints essential. Pay varies. **Tips:** Focus on an artisan or collector, with careful, specific story and professional visuals. Don't condescend; this is art form for high-end artisans. **Queries:** Preferred. **E-queries:** Yes. **Unsolicited mss:** Accepts. **Response:** Queries 2-4 months, submissions 3-6 months, SASE. **Freelance Content:** 25%. **Rights:** All. **Payment:** On acceptance.

DOLLS

1107 Broadway, Suite 1210, New York, NY 10010. E-mail: nr@collector-online.com. 10x/year. Circ.: 100,000. Nayda Rondon, Editor. **Description:** For knowledgeable doll collectors. **Nonfiction:** Sharply focused, with strong collecting angle and concrete information (value, identification, restoration, etc.). Include quality slides or transparencies; 500-1,500 words; $100-$350. **Queries:** Required. **Payment:** On acceptance.

EDGES

Krause Publications, 700 E. State St., Iola, WI 54945. 715-445-2214. Web site: www.krause.com. **Description:** On collectible knives: combat, antique, modern, handmade, and commemorative knives, with value charts for each knife mentioned. **Nonfiction:** Articles, 500-1,500 words.

FIBERARTS

50 College St., Asheville, NC 28801. 828-253-0467. E-mail: editor@fiberartsmagazine.com. Web site: www.fiberartsmagazine.com. 5x/year. $4.50/issue, $22/year. Circ.: 24,000. Sunita Patterson, Editor. **Description:** Covers all fiber-arts: weaving, quilting, embroidery, wearable art, 3-D work, basketry, and more. Readers include professional artists, craftspeople, hobbyists, collectors, curators. **Nonfiction:** Articles and interviews (outstanding artists and craftspeople, trends and issues, exhibitions, business concerns, historic and ethnic textiles); 250-2,000 words; $65-$500. **Columns, Departments:** Profile (1 artist); Reviews (exhibits/books). Commentary; Notable Events (conferences, exhibitions); Art & Technology; 250-500 words; $65-$125. **Art:** 35mm slides, transparencies; b/w glossies; electronic images (if 300 dpi or greater resolution. No color prints. **Tips:** Good visuals key to acceptance. Submit with synopsis, outline, writing samples. Use accessible, not scholarly, writing tone. **Queries:** Preferred. **E-queries:** No. **Unsolicited mss:** Accepts. **Response:** 1 month, SASE required. **Freelance Content:** 90%. **Rights:** 1st NA. **Payment:** On publication.

FINE LINES

Box 8928, New Castle, PA 16105. 724-652-6259. E-mail: hngottice@aol.com. Web site: www.historicneedlework.com. Quarterly. $6/issue. Circ.: 3,800. Deborah Novak Crain, Editor. **Description:** All about needlework. **Nonfiction:** Travel to historic places with significant needlework; museums; stitching (samplers, needlework tools, etc.); pay varies; 500-1,500 words. **Queries:** Not necessary. **E-queries:** Yes. **Unsolicited mss:** Accepts. **Response:** SASE. **Freelance Content:** 35%. **Rights:** 1st NA. **Payment:** On publication.

FINE WOODWORKING

63 S. Main St., PO Box 5506, Newtown, CT 06470-5506. 203-426-8171. E-mail: fw@taunton.com. Web site: www.taunton.com. Bimonthly. Circ.: 270,000. Timothy Schreiner, Editor. **Description:** On high-quality worksmanship, thoughtful designs, safe and proper procedures for outstanding results. **Nonfiction:** Articles on

basics of tool use, stock preparation and joinery; specialized techniques and finishing; shop-built tools, jigs and fixtures; or any stage of design, construction, finishing, and installation of cabinetry and furniture; $150/page. **Columns, Departments:** Methods of Work, Q&A, Master Class, Finish Line, Tools & Materials, and Notes & Comment; From $10. **Queries:** Required. **Payment:** On publication.

FINESCALE MODELER

21027 Crossroads Circle, P.O. Box 1612, Waukesha, WI 53187-1612. 262-796-8776. E-mail: editor@finescale.com. Web site: www.finescale.com. 10x/year. $4.50/issue, $37.95/year. Circ.: 60,000. Terry Thompson, Editor. **Description:** Largest-circulation magazine for scale modelers, especially builders of model aircraft, armor, ships, autos, and military figures. **Nonfiction:** How-to articles for people who make non-operating models of aircraft, automobiles, boats, and figures. Photos and drawings should accompany articles. Also, 1-page model-building hints and tips. Length, pay varies. **Art:** Prefers slides or medium-format transparencies. **Tips:** Stories on scale-modeling hobby only. Prefers how-to stories. **Queries:** Preferred. **E-queries:** Yes. **Unsolicited mss:** Accepts. **Response:** Queries 4 weeks, SASE required. **Freelance Content:** 80%. **Rights:** All. **Payment:** On acceptance.

GARDEN RAILWAYS

P.O. Box 460222, Denver, CO 80246. 303-377-7785. E-mail: mhorovitz@gardenrailways.com. Web site: www.gardenrailways.com. Bimonthly. Circ.: 36,000. Marc Horovitz, Editor. **Description:** Covers all aspects of the garden-railroading hobby, including building, operating, and landscaping of garden railway trains. **Nonfiction:** Articles; 500-2,500 words; pays $30/page (including photos). **Queries:** Required. **E-queries:** Yes. **Unsolicited mss:** Accepts. **Response:** 30 days. **Freelance Content:** 75%. **Rights:** All, one-time. **Payment:** On acceptance.

GOOD OLD BOAT

7340 Niagara Lane North, Maple Grove, MN 55311-2655. 763-420-8923. E-mail: karen@goodoldboat.com. Web site: www.goodoldboat.com. Bimonthly. $39.95 in U.S./Canada, $63.95 other. Karen Larson, Editor. **Description:** For sailors with boats 10 years old and older. Provides information on upgrading, maintaining and restoring them. **Nonfiction:** Technical material relevant to most older sailboats: in-depth how-to articles on blister repair, deck delamination repair, tack repair, and so on. Also short refit articles on "quick and easy" tips; 1,500-5,000 words; Varies with type of article. **Art:** Prefers slides, accept b/w photos, sometimes drawings/sketches. Pays in copies, unless on assignment. Covers, $100. Special photo spreads, $200. **Tips:** Sometimes sends freelancers on feature assignments. **E-queries:** Yes. **Response:** 2-6 weeks, SASE required. **Rights:** 1st NA. **Payment:** On publication.

GREAT AMERICAN CRAFTS
Krause Publications, 700 E. State St., Iola, WI 54990-0001. 715-445-2214. Web site: www.krause.com. Monthly. Circ.: 76,000. **Description:** Patterns and projects for sewing, needlework, and crafts.

HERITAGE QUEST
Sierra Home, P.O. Box 329, Bountiful, UT 84011. 801-298-5358. E-mail: leland@heritaequest.com. Web site: www.heritagequest.com. Bi-monthly. $6.95/issue, $28/year. Circ.: 21,000. Leland Meitzler, Editor. **Description:** Offers help with genealogical research. **Nonfiction:** Genealogical how-to articles; 1,800-8,000 words; $75/printed page. **Art:** Electronic TIFF; submit with article. **Tips:** Readers range from beginners to professionals. **Queries:** Preferred. **E-queries:** Yes. **Unsolicited mss:** Accepts. **Response:** 60 days,SASE not required. **Freelance Content:** 90%. **Rights:** All. **Payment:** On publication.

HOBBY MERCHANDISER
225 Gordons Corner Rd., P.O. Box 420, Manalapan, NJ 07726-0420. 800-969-7176. Web site: www.hobbymerchandiser.com. Monthly. Jeff Troy, Editor-in-Chief. **Description:** For the professional hobby business; also general small-business advice. **Nonfiction:** Articles, 800-1,500 words; pays $75-$200. **Payment:** On publication.

INTERWEAVE KNITS
Interweave Press, 201 E. Fourth St., Loveland, CO 80537-5655. 970-669-7672. Web site: www.interweave.com. Quarterly. Melanie Falick. **Description:** For those who love to knit. Presents beautifully finished projects, with clear step-by-step instruction. **Nonfiction:** Related to knitting; profiles of people who knit; pays $100/published page. **Queries:** Preferred. **Payment:** On publication.

KITPLANES
8745 Aero Dr., Suite 105, San Diego, CA 92123. 858-694-0491. E-mail: dave@kitplanes.com. Web site: www.kitplanes.com. Monthly. $3.99/issue, $29.95/year. Circ.: 75,000. Dave Martin, Editor. **Description:** For designers, builders, and pilots of home-built experimental aircraft. **Nonfiction:** On all aspects of design, construction, and performance for aircraft built from kits and plans by home craftsmen; 1,500-2,500 words; $70/page. **Queries:** Preferred. **E-queries:** Yes. **Unsolicited mss:** Accepts. **Response:** Queries 2 days, submissions 2 weeks, SASE not required. **Freelance Content:** 80%. **Payment:** On publication.

LAPIDARY JOURNAL
Primedia Enthusiast Group, 60 Chestnut Ave., Ste 201, Devon, PA 19333-1312. 610-964-6300. Web site: www.lapidaryjournal.com. Monthly. Circ.: 55,000. **Description:** All about amateur and professional jewelry making.

LOST TREASURE

P.O. Box 451589, Grove, OK 74345. 918-786-2182.
E-mail: managingeditor@losttreasure.com. Web site: www.losttreasure.com.
Monthly. $4.50/issue, $27.95/year. Circ.: 50,000. Patsy Beyerl, Managing Editor.
Description: The treasure hunter's "magazine of choice." **Nonfiction:** How-tos,
legends, folklore, stories of lost treasures; 500-1500 words; $.04/word. **Art:** jpg, color,
b&w photos; $5. **Queries:** Not necessary. **E-queries:** Yes. **Unsolicited mss:**
Accepts. **Response:** Queries/submissions 1-2 weeks. **Freelance Content:** 35%.
Rights: All. **Payment:** On publication.

MIDATLANTIC ANTIQUES

P.O. Box 5040, Monroe, NC 28111. 704-289-1541.
E-mail: maeditor@TheEJ.com. Monthly. $18/yr. Jennifer Benson, Editor.
Description: Covers antique auctions, art and collectibles, news from Pennsylvania
to Georgia. **Nonfiction:** Yes. **Fillers:** Unusual items; little-known tidbits. **Tips:**
Color photos with stories helpful. **Queries:** Preferred. **E-queries:** Yes. **Unsolicited
mss:** Accepts. **Response:** Queries 2 months, SASE. **Payment:** On publication.

MINIATURE COLLECTOR

801 W. Norton Ave., Suite 200, Muskegon, MI 49441-4155. 231-733-9382.
Ruth Keessen, Editor. **Description:** On outstanding 1/12-scale (dollhouse) miniatures
and the people who make and collect them. Original, illustrated how-to projects for
making miniatures. **Nonfiction:** Articles, 800-1,200 words, with photos; pay varies.
Tips: Submit photos with queries. **Queries:** Preferred. **Payment:** On acceptance.

MODEL AIRPLANE NEWS

P.O. Box 428, Mt. Morris, IL 61054. 800-827-0323.
Web site: www.airage.com. Monthly. **Description:** For enthusiasts of radio-
controlled model airplanes. **Nonfiction:** Articles include advice from experts in the
radio-controlled aviation field; also pieces on design and construction of model airplanes, reviews of new products. Pay varies. **Queries:** Preferred.

MODEL RAILROADER

21027 Crossroads Cir., P.O. Box 1612, Waukesha, WI 53187. 262-796-8776.
E-mail: mrmag@mrmag.com. Web site: www.modelrailroader.com. Monthly.
$4.50/issue, $39.95/year. Circ.: 190,000. Andy Sperandeo, Editor. **Description:**
Everything related to railroads, big and small. Covers hobby topics, with expanded
reporting. **Nonfiction:** How-to stories on model railroading; any length; $90/printed
page. **Tips:** Authors must be model railroad hobbyists. **Queries:** Preferred.
E-queries: Yes. **Unsolicited mss:** Accepts. **Rights:** All. **Payment:** On acceptance.

MODELER'S RESOURCE

4120 Douglas Blvd., #306-372, Granite Bay, CA 95746-5936. 916-784-9517.
E-mail: modres@quiknet.com. Web site: www.modelersource.com. Bimonthly. $22.
Fred DeRuvo, Executive Publisher. **Description:** Caters to builders of models,

especially sci-fi, fantasy, vehicular, and figures. Each issue includes previews, photos, reviews, and features on the latest genre kits. **Nonfiction:** Quality articles that delve into building and painting models, product reviews, interviews with the names behind the product, show coverage; 2,500 words; pays fee per page. **Art:** Quality glossy color photos, TIFs, slides; no payment. **Tips:** Welcomes new writers. Seeking articles that go beyond the norm. Be clear and concise, yet allow your personal style to flow. "Often, new writers tend to not be instructive enough, or conversely, tend to go off on tangents." **E-queries:** Yes. **Response:** 1-2 weeks, SASE required. **Freelance Content:** 30%. **Rights:** All. **Payment:** On publication. **Contact:** Silvia DeRuvo, Managing Editor.

NEEDLEWORK RETAILER

P.O. Box 2438, Ames, IA 50010. 515-232-6507.
Web site: yarntree.com/nr.htm. Bimonthly. Megan Chriswisser, Editor. **Description:** For owners and managers of independent needlework retail stores. **Nonfiction:** Profiles of shop owners; articles about a successful store event or promotion, 500-1,000 words; pay varies. **Tips:** No generic business articles. **Payment:** On acceptance.

NEW ENGLAND ANTIQUES JOURNAL

4 Church St., Ware, MA 01082. 800-432-3505.
E-mail: neajtpub@aol.comq. Web site: www.antiquesjournal.com. Monthly. $2/$12. Circ.: 25,000. Jamie Mercier, Editor. **Description:** For antiques trade, with informative features for antiques professionals and casual collectors. Includes event calendars, auction coverage, and more. **Nonfiction:** On antiques, fine arts, and collectibles; 2,000 words; $200-$500. **Tips:** Submit well-researched articles with at least 12 high-quality images. **Queries:** Preferred. **E-queries:** Yes. **Unsolicited mss:** Accepts. **Response:** Queries 1 month, submissions 2 months. **Freelance Content:** 20%. **Rights:** 1 year. **Payment:** On publication.

PIECEWORK

Interweave Press, 201 E. 4th St., Loveland, CO 80537. 970-669-7672.
E-mail: pieceworks@interweave.com. Web site: www.interweave.com. Bi-monthly. $5.95/$24. Circ.: 47,000. Jeanne Hutchins, Editor. **Description:** Needlework and textile history. Presents stories and projects based on makers and techniques from needlework's rich past. **Nonfiction:** Well-researched articles on history of needlework techniques, motifs, artists; 1,500-2,000 words; $100-$300. **Tips:** Prefers stories with needlework projects to demonstrate techniques covered in the article. Contact for coming editorial themes. **Queries:** Preferred. **E-queries:** Yes. **Unsolicited mss:** Accepts. **Response:** Queries 1-2 weeks submissions 1-4 months, SASE. **Freelance Content:** 80%. **Rights:** 1st NA. **Payment:** On publication.

POPTRONICS

275-G Marcus Blvd., Hauppauge, NY 11788. 631-592-6720.
E-mail: popeditor@gernsback.com. Web site: www.gernsback.com. Monthly. Circ.:

104,000. Carl Laron, Editor. **Description:** For electronics hobbyists and experimenters. **Nonfiction:** Readers are science and electronics oriented, understand computer theory and operation, and like to build electronics projects; 2,000-3,500 words; $150-$500. **Fillers:** Fillers and cartoons. **Payment:** On acceptance.

POPULAR MECHANICS
810 Seventh Ave., 6th Floor, New York, NY 10019. 212-649-2853.
E-mail: popularmechanics@hearst.com. Web site: www.popularmechanics.com.
Monthly. Circ.: 1,400,000. Joe Oldham, Editor in Chief. **Description:** Latest developments in mechanics, industry, science, telecommunications. **Nonfiction:** Features on hobbies with a mechanical slant; how-tos on home and shop projects; features on outdoor adventures, boating, and electronics. Photos and sketches a plus; 300-1,500 words; to $1,500 (to $500 for short pieces). **Rights:** all. **Payment:** On acceptance. **Contact:** Sarah Deem, Managing Editor.

POPULAR WOODWORKING
1507 Dana Ave., Cincinnati, OH 45207. 513-531-2690.
E-mail: popwood@fwpubs.com. Web site: www.popularwoodworking.com. Circ.: 200,000. Steve Shanesy, Editor. **Description:** Technique articles, tool reviews, and projects for the home woodworker. Emphasis on practical techniques that have stood the test of time. **Nonfiction:** On woodworking (600 words); woodworking tips and tricks; techniques; 1-6 pages; $150/page and up. **Tips:** Tool reviews written in-house. No profiles of woodworkers. Seeking well-written essays on the craft, good techniques, and the occasional project. **Queries:** Preferred. **E-queries:** Yes. **Unsolicited mss:** Accepts. **Response:** 3-4 months, SASE. **Freelance Content:** 30%. **Rights:** 1st worldwide, 2nd. **Payment:** On acceptance.

QUICK & EASY CRAFTS
306 E. Parr Rd., Berne, IN 46711. 219-589-4000.
Web site: www.whitebirches.com. Beth Schwartz, Editor. **Description:** How-to and instructional needlecrafts and other arts and crafts, book reviews, and tips. **Nonfiction:** Pay varies. **Art:** Photos. **Payment:** On acceptance.

QUILTING TODAY
Dhitra Publications, 2 Public Ave., Montrose, PA 18801. 570-278-1984.
E-mail: chritra@epix.net. Web site: www.quilttownusa.com. Bi-monthly. $3.99/issue, $19.95/year. Joyce Libal, Editor. **Description:** Colorful pictures, quilting-world news, and projects for traditional and original designs, from teachers and talented quilters. **Nonfiction:** Features on quilt history, techniques, tools. Quilt patterns (following magazine's established format). Book and product reviews; 750-1,500 words; $75 (800 words). **Columns, Departments:** The Sampler (news column). **Art:** Professional-quality photos of quilts; 35mm glossy; pay varies. **Queries:** Not necessary. **E-queries:** Accepts. **Unsolicited mss:** Accepts. **Response:** 2 weeks, SASE. **Payment:** On publication.

R/C MODELER
P.O. Box 487, Sierra Madre, CA 91025. 626-355-1476.
E-mail: info@rcmmagazine.com. Web site: www.rcmmagazine.com. Monthly.
$3.99/$25 yr. Circ.: 165,000. Patricia E. Crews, Editor. **Description:** For the radio-control model aircraft enthusiast. **Nonfiction:** How-to, related to radio-control model aircraft, helicopters, boats, cars. Pays $50-$350 for features; $50-$250 for other articles. **Fillers:** $25-$75. **Queries:** Not necessary. **E-queries:** Yes. **Response:** Queries 1 week,submissions 1-3 weeks, SASE. **Freelance Content:** 60%. **Rights:** 1st worldwide. **Payment:** On publication.

RAILROAD MODEL CRAFTSMAN
P.O. Box 700, Newton, NJ 07860-0700. 973-383-3355.
E-mail: bills@rrmodelcraftsman.com. Web site: www.rrmodelcraftsman.com.
William C. Schaumburg, Editor. **Description:** How-to articles on scale model railroading; cars, operation, scenery, etc. **Payment:** On publication.

RUG HOOKING
Stackpole Magazines, 1300 Market St., Suite 202,
Lemoyne, PA 17043. 717-234-5091.
E-mail: rughook@paonline.com. Web site: www.rughookingonline.com. 5x/year.
$6.95/issue, $27.95/year. Patrice Crowley, Editor. **Description:** How-to and features on rug hooking for beginners and advanced artists. **Nonfiction:** Instructional articles; also, profiles of fiber artists; 500-3,000 words; pay varies. **Queries:** Preferred. **E-queries:** Yes. **Unsolicited mss:** Accepts. **Response:** 3 months, SASE. **Freelance Content:** 90%. **Payment:** On publication.

SCALE AUTO ENTHUSIAST
Kalmbach Publishing Co., 21027 Crossroads Circle, P.O. Box 1612,
Waukesha, WI 53187. 262-796-8776.
E-mail: editor@scaleautomag.com. Web site: www.scaleautomag.com. Terry Thompson, Editor. **Description:** For the adult model builder. Features "how-to" articles, modeling history, contest coverage and kit and product news. **Nonfiction:** To 3,000 words, with photos; pays $75/page. **Tips:** For "how-to" articles, the key is including many clean, crisp, step-by-step photos. **Queries:** Required. **E-queries:** Yes. **Unsolicited mss:** Accepts. **Response:** 90 days. **Freelance Content:** 50%. **Rights:** All. **Payment:** On acceptance.

SCHOOL MATES
U.S. Chess Federation, 3054 NYS Rt. 9W, New Windsor, NY 12553-7646.
E-mail: publications@uschess.org. Web site: www.uschess.org. Quarterly. $2.50/issue, $12/year. Circ.: 35,000. Pat Kurzdorfer, Editor. **Description:** Published by United States Chess Federation. Covers major chess events, U.S. and abroad, with emphasis on triumphs and exploits of American players. **Fiction:** Chess related. **Nonfiction:** Instructive, and short fillers, for beginning chess players (primarily children, ages 6-15); 800-1,000 words; $50/page. **Fillers:** Puzzles, cartoons, anecdotes. **Art:** b/w, or

color slides (preferred), glossies accepted; $25 1st use, $15 subsequent use. **Queries:** Preferred. **Unsolicited mss:** Accepts. **Payment:** On acceptance.

SEW NEWS

741 Corporate Circle, Suite A, Golden, CO 80401. 800-289-6397. Web site: www.sewnews.com. Linda Turner Griepentrog, Editor. **Description:** Seeks articles that teach a specific technique, inspire a reader to try new sewing projects, or inform about an interesting person, company, or project related to sewing, textiles, or fashion. Emphasis on fashion (not craft) sewing. **Nonfiction:** Articles, to 3,000 words; pays $25-$400. **Queries:** Preferred. **Unsolicited mss:** Does not accept. **Payment:** On acceptance.

SPORTS COLLECTORS DIGEST

Krause Publications, 700 E. State St., Iola, WI 54990. 715-445-2214. E-mail: kpsports@aol.com. Web site: www.krause.com. Weekly. Circ.: 52,000. Tom Mortenson, Editor. **Description:** Sports memorabilia and collectibles. **Nonfiction:** Articles on old baseball card sets and other sports memorabilia; 750-2,000 words; $50-$100. **Columns, Departments:** Query; 600-3,000 words; $90-150. **Art:** Unusual collectibles; b&w photos; $25-150. **Response:** Queries, 5 weeks; submissions 2 months. **Rights:** FNASR. **Payment:** On publication.

TEDDY BEAR AND FRIENDS

Cowles Enthusiast Media, 6405 Flank Dr., Harrisburg, PA 17112. 717-657-9555. Web site: www.teddybearandfriends.com. Mindy Kinsey. **Description:** For adult collectors of teddy bears; profiles of artists and manufacturers. **Nonfiction:** Articles, 1,000-1,500 words; pays $.20-$.25/word. **Tips:** No fiction or personal-experience stories. **Queries:** Preferred. **Payment:** On publication.

TEDDY BEAR REVIEW

Collector Communications Corp., 6405 Plank Drive, Harrisburg, PA 17112. 717-540-6652. Web site: www.teddybearreview.com. Bi-monthly. $4.99/issue, $19.95/year. Circ.: 50,000. Mindy Kinsey, Editor. **Description:** For adult soft-sculpture collectors. **Nonfiction:** On antique and contemporary teddy bears for makers, collectors, enthusiasts.; 800-1,000 words; $300. **Art:** Yes. **Tips:** Looking for articles on artists and manufacturers; prefers specialized topics. Submit photos of bears with queries. Readers treat teddy bears as art. No stories from the bear's point of view. **Queries:** Preferred. **E-queries:** Yes. **Unsolicited mss:** Accepts. **Response:** 8-12 weeks, SASE. **Freelance Content:** 70%. **Rights:** All. **Payment:** On acceptance.

THREADS

Taunton Press, 63 S. Main St., PO Box 5506, Newtown, CT 06470. 203-426-8171. Web site: www.taunton.com. Bimonthly. Circ.: 176,000. Chris Timmons, Editor. **Description:** Garment construction and embellishment. **Nonfiction:** Technical pieces on garment construction and embellishment by writers who are expert sewers, quilters, embellishers, and other needle workers. Also covers sewing soft furnishings for home decor; $150/published page. **Payment:** On publication.

TRADITIONAL QUILTWORKS

Chitra Publications, 2 Public Ave., Montrose, PA 18801. 570-278-1984. E-mail: chitraed@epix.net. Web site: www.quilttownusa.com. Bi-monthly. $3.95/$19.99. Joyce Libal, Senior Editor. **Description:** A pattern magazine, with articles on quilt history, techniques, and tools. **Nonfiction:** Articles with 1-2 pages of text and quilts that illustrate the content; 750 words; pay varies. **Art:** 35mm color slides. **Queries:** Preferred. **E-queries:** Yes. **Unsolicited mss:** Accepts. **Response:** Queries 2 weeks, submissions 4 weeks, SASE. **Rights:** 1st. **Payment:** On publication.

TRAINS

Kalmbach Publishing Co., 21027 Crossroads Cir., P.O. Box 1612, Waukesha, WI 53187. 262-796-8776. E-mail: editor@trainsmag.com. Web site: www.trainsmag.com. Monthly. $4.50. Circ.: 120,000. Mark W. Hemphill, Editor. **Description:** For railroad enthusiasts. **Nonfiction:** History, business analysis, economics, technology, and operations studies of railroads in North America and elsewhere. Occasional first-person recollections; 600-8,000 words; $.10-$.15/word. **Art:** 35mm or medium-format slides; quality 8x10 or larger. Color and b/w prints; $30-$300. **Tips:** Avoid first-person travelogues or trip reports, unless historical. Requires a good knowledge of industry and its technology. **Queries:** Preferred. **E-queries:** Yes. **Unsolicited mss:** Accepts. **Response:** Queries 60 days, submissions 90 days, SASE. **Freelance Content:** 90%. **Rights:** all (manuscripts), one-time (art). **Payment:** On acceptance.

WATERCOLOR

770 Broadway, New York, NY 10003. 646-654-5220. Quarterly. M. Stephen Doherty, Editor-in-chief. **Description:** On watercolor and other water media (gouache, casein, acrylic, etc.). **Nonfiction:** How-to articles, varying lengths; pay varies. **Queries:** Preferred. **Payment:** On publication.

WESTERN & EASTERN TREASURES

P.O. Box 1598, Mercer Island, WA 98040-1598. 206-230-9224. E-mail: westeast@halcyon.com. Web site: www.treasurenet.com. Monthly. $4.50/$27.95. Circ.: 100,000. Rosemary Anderson, Editor. **Description:** For metal detectorists, covers all aspects of the hobby. Field-proven advice and instruction; entertaining presentation. **Nonfiction:** Articles new, true and treasure-oriented, from all fields of responsible recreational metal detecting; 1,500 words; $.02-$.04/word. **Art:** Photo prints/35mm; $5-$7.50, $50-$100 (cover). **Queries:** Not necessary. **E-queries:** No. **Unsolicited mss:** Accepts. **Response:** 1 month, SASE required. **Freelance Content:** 100%. **Rights:** All rights reserved. **Payment:** On publication.

WILDFOWL CARVING
1300 Market St., Suite 202, Lemoyne, PA 17043-1420. 717-234-5091. Web site: wildfowl-carving.com. Cathy Hart, Editor-in-Chief. **Description:** Articles on bird carving; collecting antique and contemporary carvings. **Nonfiction:** How-to and reference articles, of varying lengths; pay varies. **Queries:** Preferred. **Payment:** On acceptance.

WOODWORK
42 Digital Dr., Suite 5, Novato, CA 94949. 415-382-0580. E-mail: woodworkingmag@aol.com. Bimonthly. $4.99/$17.95. John Lavine, Editor. **Description:** Covers all aspects of woodworking. Assumes medium to advanced understanding in technical articles. Also, artist profiles, reviews. **Nonfiction:** Profiles, technical articles, projects, how-to; also shows, exhibition reviews, etc; 1,000-4,000 words; $150-$200/printed page. **Art:** Slides preferred. **Queries:** Preferred. **E-queries:** Yes. **Unsolicited mss:** Accepts. **Freelance Content:** 90%. **Rights:** 1st. **Payment:** On publication.

YELLOWBACK LIBRARY
P.O. Box 36172, Des Moines, IA 50315. 515-287-0404. Monthly. $30/yr. Circ.: 500. Gil O'Gara, Editor. **Description:** For collectors, dealers, enthusiasts and researchers of children's series books such as Hardy Boys, Nancy Drew, Tom Swift. Dime novels and related juvenile literature also included. **Nonfiction:** Especially interested in interviews with, or articles by, past and present writers of juvenile series fiction; 300-3,000 words. **Tips:** No articles that ridicule the literature or try to fit it into a political, sexual, pyschological, or religious context. Nostalgic reflections okay if interesting. **Queries:** Preferred. **E-queries:** No. **Unsolicited mss:** Accepts. **Response:** Queries 2 days, submissions 1 week. **Freelance Content:** 100%. **Payment:** in copies.

YESTERYEAR
P.O. Box 2, Princeton, WI 54968. E-mail: yesteryear@vbe.com. Michael Jacobi, Editor. **Description:** On antiques and collectibles for readers in WI, IL, IA, MN, and surrounding states. **Nonfiction:** Articles; pays from $20. **Art:** Photos. **Tips:** Will consider regular columns on collecting or antiques. **Payment:** On publication. *No recent report.*

ZYMURGY
736 Pearl St., Boulder, CO 80302. 303-447-0816. Web site: www.beertown.org. Ray Daniels, Editor. **Description:** Articles appealing to beer lovers and homebrewers. **Queries:** Preferred. **Payment:** On publication.

HOME & GARDEN

(See also Lifestyles)

AFRICAN VIOLET

2375 North St., Beaumont, TX 77702. 409-839-4725. Web site: www.avsa.org. Ruth Rumsey. **Description:** On growing methods for African violets. No payment. **Nonfiction:** Articles, 700-1,400 words; history and personal experience with African violets.

AMERICAN GARDENER

7931 E. Boulevard Dr., Alexandria, VA 22308-1300. 703-768-5700. Web site: www.ahs.org. Bimonthly. $4.95. Circ.: 20,000. David J. Ellis, Editor. **Description:** Published by American Horticultural Society (AHS), national organization for gardeners. **Nonfiction:** Latest scientific findings; history of gardening and gardens in America. Seeks articles on unusual plants, personalities, and issues that will enrich passionate gardeners. Also, how to construct simple garden features; illustrate gardening techniques; 1,500-2,500 words; $300-$500. **Columns, Departments:** Urban Gardener, Habitat Gardening, Natural Connections, Conservationist's Notebook, Regional Happenings; 250-1,200 words; $50-$200. **Tips: Queries:** describe topic and explain relevance to a national audience of knowledgeable gardeners; outline major points to be covered. First-time authors send relevant writing samples and qualifications. **Queries:** Not necessary. **E-queries:** Yes. **Unsolicited mss:** Accepts. **Response:** 90 days, SASE. **Freelance Content:** 75%. **Rights:** 1st NA. **Payment:** On publication.

AMERICAN HOMESTYLE & GARDENING

Gruner & Jahr USA Publishing, 375 Lexington Ave., 8th Fl., New York, NY 10017-5514. 212-499-2000. E-mail: ahsmail@americanhomestyle.com. Web site: http://www.gjusa.com/homestyle.cfm. 10x/year. Circ.: 1,000,000. Kathleen Madden. **Description:** Provides design solutions at realistic prices, with product and shopping information to help readers work with designer and express their personal style. **Nonfiction:** under 2,000 words. **Tips:** Requires published writers with knowledge of interior design, building/remodeling, or gardening. Query for assignments with scouting photos to indicate visual elements. **Queries:** Preferred. **E-queries:** Accepts. **Unsolicited mss:** Accepts. **Response:** 1 month, SASE. **Freelance Content:** 20%. **Rights:** print. **Payment:** On publication. **Contact:** Articles Editor.

AMERICAN ROSE

P.O. Box 30000, Shreveport, LA 71130-0030. 318-938-5402. Web site: www.ars.org. **Description:** Articles on home rose gardens (varieties, products, helpful advice, rose care, etc.). **Queries:** Preferred.

ATLANTA HOMES AND LIFESTYLES

1100 Johnson Ferry Rd., #595, Atlanta, GA 30342. 404-252-6670. Web site: www.atlantahomesmag.com. Monthly. $3.95/$24. Circ.: 33,000. Oma Blaise Ford, Editor. **Description:** On upscale home and gardens. **Nonfiction:** Original stories with local angle (mostly by assignment), on homes, gardening, food, wine, entertaining, and remodeling; 300-1,200 words; $75-$500. **Columns, Departments:** Remodeling, shopping, profiles (on assignment; 200-700 words. $75-$200). **Queries:** Required. **Unsolicited mss:** Does not accept. **Response:** 3 months, SASE. **Freelance Content:** 50%. **Payment:** On acceptance.

BETTER HOMES AND GARDENS

1716 Locust St., Des Moines, IA 50309-3023. 515-284-3000. Web site: www.bhg.com. Monthly. $2.99/issue, $19/year. Circ.: 7,600,000. Jean LemMon, Editor. **Description:** Home and family magazine. Covers entertainment, building, decorating, food, money management, health, travel, pets, environment, and cars. **Tips:** A freelancer's best chances are in travel, health, parenting, and education. No political subjects, poetry, beauty, or fiction. **Queries:** Preferred. **E-queries:** No. **Unsolicited mss:** Does not accept. **Response:** 2-3 weeks, SASE required. **Freelance Content:** 15%. **Rights:** All. **Payment:** On acceptance.

BIRDS AND BLOOMS

5925 Country Lane, Greendale, WI 53129. 414-453-0100. E-mail: editors@birdsandblooms.com. Web site: www.birdsandblooms.com. Bimonthly. Jeff Nowak, Editor. **Description:** For people who love the beauty of their own backyard. Focuses on background birding and gardening. **Nonfiction:** First-person experiences from your own backyard; 200-900 words; $100-$200. **Fillers:** 50-300 words; $50-$75. **Art:** Slides; $75-$300. **Tips:** Write conversationally, include tips to benefit readers, keep stories short and to the point. Submit photos. No bird rescue stories. **Queries:** Not necessary. **E-queries:** Yes. **Unsolicited mss:** Accepts. **Response:** Queries 1-2 months, submissions 2-3 months, SASE. **Freelance Content:** 25%. **Rights:** 1st NA. **Payment:** On publication. **Contact:** Jeff Nowak.

CANADIAN GARDENING

340 Ferrier St., Suite 210, Markham, Ont., Canada L3R 2Z5. 905-475-8440. E-mail: letters@canadiangardening.com. Web site: www.canadiangardening.com. Aldona Satterthwaite, Editor. **Description:** Helps avid home gardeners in Canada solve problems or inspires them with garden ideas. Canadian angle imperative. **Nonfiction:** How-to pieces (to 1,000 words), on garden projects, include introduction and step-by-step instructions. Profiles of gardens (to 2,000 words). Pays $75-$700. **Columns, Departments:** 200-400 words. **Queries:** Preferred. **Payment:** On acceptance.

CAROLINA GARDENER

P.O. Box 4504, Greensboro, NC 27404. 800-245-0142. Web site: www.carolinagardener.com. Bimonthly. L.A. Jackson, Editor. **Description:** Specific to Southeast gardening (profiles of gardens in the region, new cultivars, "good ol' southern heirlooms"). **Nonfiction:** Articles, 750-1,000 words; slides and illustrations essential to accompany articles; pays $175. **Queries:** Required. **Payment:** On publication.

COUNTRY GARDENS
1716 Locust St., Des Moines, IA 50309-3023. 515-284-3515.
Bimonthly. LuAnn Brandsen. **Description:** Features gardens that are informal, lush, and old-fashioned. Stories emphasize both inspiration and information. **Nonfiction:** Garden-related how-tos and profiles of gardeners, 750-1,500 words; pays $350-$800. **Columns, Departments:** 500-700 words, on garden-related travel, food, projects, decorating, entertaining; pays $450 and up. **Queries:** Required. **Payment:** On acceptance.

COUNTRY KITCHENS
1115 Broadway, 8th Fl., New York, NY 10010-2803. 212-807-7100.
Annual. Barbara Jacksier. **Description:** Articles offering bright, inviting, and afford-able decorating ideas. **Queries:** Preferred.

COUNTRY LIVING
224 W. 57th St., New York, NY 10019. 212-649-3500.
Web site: www.countryliving.com. Monthly. $3.50. Circ.: 1,600,000. Nancy Soriano, Editor in Chief. **Description:** Lifestyle, decorating, antiques, cooking, travel, home building, crafts, and gardens. **Nonfiction:** 500 words and up; pay varies. **Tips:** Avoid grandmother stories. **Queries:** Not necessary. **E-queries:** No. **Unsolicited mss:** Accepts. **Response:** 4 weeks, SASE. **Freelance Content:** 30%. **Rights:** All, 1st serial. **Payment:** On acceptance. **Contact:** Marjorie E. Gage.

COUNTRY LIVING GARDENER
1790 Broadway, Fl 12, New York, NY 10019-1412. 212-649-2000.
E-mail: mgage@hearst.com. Web site: www.countryliving.com. Bimonthly. **Description:** On gardens, crafts, decorating ideas, food, entertaining, and travel. **Nonfiction:** Articles, pay varies. **Queries:** Preferred. **Payment:** On publication.

ELLE DECOR
1633 Broadway, New York, NY 10019. 212-767-5800.
Kendall Coonstrom, Features Editor. **Description:** On designers and craftspeople, and on houses and apartments with notable interior design and/or architecture. **Nonfiction:** Articles, 300-1,000 words; pays $1.25/word. **Tips:** Query with photos of designers and their work. **Queries:** Preferred. **Payment:** On publication.

FINE GARDENING
The Taunton Press, P.O. Box 5506, 63 S Main St,
Newtown, CT 06470-5506. 203-426-8171.
E-mail: fg@taunton.com. Web site: www.finegardening.com. Bimonthly. Circ.: 200,000. Marc Vassallo, Editor. **Description:** For readers with a serious interest in

gardening. Focuses on ornamental gardening and landscaping. **Nonfiction:** How-tos, garden design, as well as pieces on specific plants or garden tools. Picture possibilities are essential; 800-2,000 words; $300-$1,200. **Art:** Photos; $75-$500. **Queries:** Required. **Payment:** On acceptance.

FLOWER & GARDEN
51 Kings Hwy. West, Haddenfield, MO 08033. 856-354-5034.
E-mail: kcpublishing@earthlink.net. Web site: www.flowerandgardenmag.com. Bimonthly. $3.99/issue, $19.95/year. Circ.: 300,000. Jonathan Prebick, Editor. **Description:** Offers ideas for outdoor environments, for home gardens. **Nonfiction:** Practical how-to articles. Historical and background articles, if related to home gardening; 1,000 words max. **Art:** Yes. **Tips:** Provide well-researched material. **Queries:** Not necessary. **E-queries:** Yes. **Unsolicited mss:** Accepts. **Response:** Queries 4-6 weeks, SASE required. **Freelance Content:** 75%. **Rights:** One-time (print and electronic).

GARDEN COMPASS
22310 NE 62nd Place, Redmond, WA 98053. 425-868-4414.
E-mail: siri@overthehedge.net. Web site: www.overthehedge.net. Bimonthly. Circ.: 54,000. Siri Kay Jostad, Editor. **Description:** For California gardening enthusiasts. **Nonfiction:** Features, to 2,000 words. **Fillers:** Crossword puzzles. **Art:** Photos. **E-queries:** Yes. **Response:** several months. **Freelance Content:** 20%.

GARDEN DESIGN
100 Ave. of the Americas, 7th Fl., New York, NY 10013. 212-334-1212.
Web site: www.gardendesignmag.com. Dorothy Kalins, Editor. **Description:** On private, public, and community gardens; articles on art and history as they relate to gardens. **Nonfiction:** Features, 500-1,000 words, pays from $.50/word. **Payment:** On acceptance.

GARDEN GATE
P.O. Box 842, Des Moines, IA 50304. 800-341-4769.
Web site: www.gardengatemagazine.com. Bimonthly. Steven Nordmeyer. **Description:** On planting, nurturing and harvesting, designs for beautiful landscaping and garden designs, and practical how-tos for growing plants and flowers. Also, information on perennials, annuals, vegetables, shrubs, trees, and indoor plants. **Nonfiction:** Articles; pay varies. **Queries:** Preferred.

GARDEN RAILWAYS
P.O. Box 460222, Denver, CO 80246. 303-377-7785.
E-mail: mhorovitz@gardenrailways.com. Web site: www.gardenrailways.com. Bimonthly. Circ.: 36,000. Marc Horovitz, Editor. **Description:** Covers all aspects of the garden-railroading hobby, including building, operating and landscaping of garden railway trains. **Nonfiction:** Articles; 500-2,500 words; pays $30/page (including photos). **Queries:** Required. **E-queries:** Yes. **Unsolicited mss:** Accepts.

Response: 30 days. **Freelance Content:** 75%. **Rights:** All, one-time. **Payment:** On acceptance.

GARDEN SHOWCASE

P.O. Box 23669, Portland, OR 97281-3669. 503-684-0153. E-mail: editor@gardenshowcase.com. Web site: www.gardenshowcase.com. Monthly except Dec. and Jan. $2.95/issue, $19.95/year. Circ.: 30,000. Lynn Lustberg, Editor. **Description:** Distributed in Oregon and Washington. Features regional plants, gardens, and nurseries, with gardening ideas and examples. Also, home decorating and design articles to connect the garden and the home. **Nonfiction:** Articles on outstanding gardens, etc.; 800-1,000 words; $160. **Columns, Departments:** Q&A, Planting by Design, Gardening 101, Through the Grapevine; 380-400; $100. **Queries:** Preferred. **E-queries:** Yes. **Unsolicited mss:** Accepts. **Response:** Queries 1-2 mos. Submissions 2-3 months, SASE required. **Freelance Content:** 100%. **Rights:** 1st. **Payment:** On publication.

THE HERB COMPANION

Herb Companion Press, 243 E. Fourth St., Loveland, CO 80537. 970-663-0831. E-mail: herbcompanion@hcpress.com. Web site: www.discoverherbs.com. Bimonthly. $4.99/issue. Circ.: 186,000. Susan Clotfeller, Editor. **Description:** For herb gardeners, cooks, crafters, and general enthusiasts. **Nonfiction:** Practical horticultural information, original recipes using herbs, well-researched historical insights, step-by-step instructions for herbal craft projects, book reviews.; 500-2,000 words; $.33/word, negotiable. **Columns, Departments:** 200-500 words. **Art:** 300 dpi, slides; pay varies. **Tips:** Technical accuracy essential. Strive for conciseness, clear organization; include subheads where appropriate, lists of similar information in chart form. **Queries:** Preferred. **E-queries:** Yes. **Unsolicited mss:** Accepts. **Response:** 1-3 months, SASE. **Freelance Content:** 90%. **Payment:** On acceptance.

HERB QUARTERLY

P.O. Box 689, San Anselmo, CA 94960-0689. E-mail: herbquarg@aol.com. Web site: www.HerbQuarterly.com. Quarterly. Circ.: 35,000. Jennifer Barrett, Editor. **Description:** Covers practical and professional aspects of herbs. **Nonfiction:** Practical uses, cultivation, gourmet cooking, landscaping, herb tradition, medicinal herbs, crafts ideas, unique garden designs, profiles of experts, and how-tos for the herb businessperson; 2,000-4,000 words. **Tips:** Include garden design when possible. **Payment:** On publication.

HOME POOL & BAR-B-QUE

P.O. Box 272, Cranford, NJ 07016-0272. 908-755-6138. E-mail: jeanette@hawksmedia.com. Annual. $10. Circ.: 2,500. Jeanette Hawks, Editor. **Description:** For upscale owners of pools, hot tubs, and spas. **Nonfiction:** Pool experience, recipes; 1,500; $40. **Art:** b/w, color, disk; pools, spas, barbecue grills (built-in especially); $10. **Queries:** Preferred. **E-queries:** Yes. **Unsolicited mss:**

Accepts. **Response:** 1 month, SASE. **Freelance Content:** 40%. **Rights:** All, may reassign. **Payment:** On publication.

HORTICULTURE
98 N Washington St., Boston, MA 02114. 617-367-6364.
E-mail: tfischer@primediasi.com. Web site: www.hortmag.com. 8x/year. Circ.: 300,000. Thomas Fischer, Exec. Editor. **Description:** Covers all aspects of gardening. **Nonfiction:** Authoritative, well-written articles on gardening; 500-2,500 words; pay varies. **Queries:** Required. **Payment:** On publication.

HOUSE BEAUTIFUL
1700 Broadway, New York, NY 10019. 212-903-5084.
Web site: www.housebeautiful.com. Marian McEvoy, Editor-in-Chief. **Description:** Pieces on design, travel, and gardening. **Nonfiction:** A literary, personal memoir, each month, 3,000 words, "Thoughts of Home." Pays $1/word. **Tips:** Send detailed outline and SASE. **Queries:** Preferred. **Payment:** On acceptance.

KITCHEN GARDEN
P.O. Box 5506, Newtown, CT 06470-5506. 203-426-8171.
E-mail: kg@taunton.com. Web site: www.taunton.com. Bimonthly. **Description:** For home gardeners who love to grow their own vegetables, fruits, and herbs and use them in cooking. **Nonfiction:** Nonfiction articles, varying lengths. **Columns, Departments:** Plant Profiles, Garden Profiles, Techniques, Design, Projects, Cooking; pays $150/page. **Queries:** Preferred. **Payment:** On publication.

LOG HOME DESIGN IDEAS
H&S Media, 1620 Lawe St., Ste. 2, Appleton, WI 54915. 920-830-1701.
E-mail: editor@athenet.net. Web site: www.loghomeideas.com. **Description:** For people interested in log homes. **Queries:** Preferred.

LOG HOME LIVING
4200-T Lafayette Center Dr., Chantilly, VA 20151-1208.
800-826-3893 or 703-222-9411.
E-mail: plobred@homebuyerpubs.com. Web site: www.loghomeliving.com. Monthly. Circ.: 132,000. Peter Lobred, Editor. **Description:** For people who own or are planning to build contemporary log homes. Readers are mostly married couples, 30-45 years old, well-educated, do-it-yourselfers. **Nonfiction:** About people who have built modern log homes from manufactured or handcrafted kits. Conversational; describe home, tell how it came to be. Emphasize special elements: intent, design, solutions to problems, features, furnishings, interior design, landscaping; 1,000-2,000 words; $250-$300 article. **Art:** All stories must include color (professional quality) photos; floor plans, construction costs, schedules a plus. **Tips:** Seeks long-term relationships with contributors who deliver quality work. **Queries:** Preferred. **E-queries:** Yes. **Response:** SASE. **Freelance Content:** 50%. **Rights:** FNASR. **Payment:** On publication.

METROPOLITAN HOME

1633 Broadway, New York, NY 10019. 212-767-6041. Web site: www.hfnm.com. Michael Lassell, Editor. **Description:** Service and informational articles for residents of houses, co-ops, lofts, and condominiums, on real estate, equity, wine and spirits, collecting, trends, etc. Interior design and home furnishing articles with emphasis on lifestyle. **Nonfiction:** Pay varies. **Tips:** Send clips. **Queries:** Preferred.

NATURAL HOME

201 E. 4th St., Loveland, CO 80537. 970-669-7672.
E-mail: claudia@naturalhomemagazine.com.
Web site: www.naturalhomemagazine.com. Claudia Chesneau, Editorial Assistant. **Description:** Promotes earth-inspired living. Features "green," sustainable homes and lifestyles. **Nonfiction:** Pays $.33-$.55/word; 300-2,000 words. **Tips:** Needs fresh, cutting-edge ideas on green living; also small, newsy items for front-of-the-book Journal section. Submit query or complete manuscript. Guidelines available for SASE or by e-mail. **Queries:** Preferred. **E-queries:** Yes. **Unsolicited mss:** Accepts. **Rights:** 1st NA. **Payment:** On publication.

OLD HOUSE INTERIORS

2 Main St., Gloucester, MA 01930. 978-283-3200.
Web site: www.oldhouseinteriors.com.
Regina Cole. **Description:** On architecture, decorative arts, and history. **Nonfiction:** Articles, 300-1,500 words; pays $1/word, or $200 page min. **Tips:** Most important thing is the art; when proposing an article, know how it should be illustrated. Professional photos not necessary. Query, with clips. **Payment:** On acceptance.

ORGANIC GARDENING

33 E. Minor St., Emmaus, PA 18098. 610-967-8282.
E-mail: organicgardening.com. Web site: www.organicgardening.com. 7x/year. $3.99/$19.96. Circ.: 600,000. John Grogan, Editor. **Description:** North America's largest gardening magazine and the only one dedicated wholely to organic practices. **Nonfiction:** Gardening how-to, solid organic advice; profiles of organic gardens and gardeners; profiles of a vegetable, fruit, or flower; 1,000-1,800 words; $.80-$1.00/word. **Fillers:** Gardener-to-Gardener (tips); 100-300 words; $25-$75. **Columns, Departments:** Healing Garden; Healthy Eating; New Products; 500 words; 500. **Queries:** Preferred. **E-queries:** Yes. **Unsolicited mss:** Accepts. **Response:** Queries 4 weeks, submissions 6 weeks, SASE. **Freelance Content:** 40%. **Rights:** All. **Payment:** On acceptance.

SOUTHERN ACCENTS

2100 Lakeshore Dr., Birmingham, AL 35209. 205-877-6000.
Web site: www.southernaccents.com. Bimonthly. $28. Circ.: 350,000. Frances MacDougall, Senior Editor. **Description:** Celebrates southern style in interiors, gardens, art, antiques, and entertaining. Focuses on affluent houses and gardens in

a 16-state region. Also features the homes of southerners living abroad, also travel destinations visited by upscale readership. **Nonfiction:** Query first with appropriate story ideas; 800-1,200 words; pay negotiable. **Queries:** Preferred. **Payment:** On acceptance.

STYLE AT HOME
25 Sheppard Ave W, Suite 100, Toronto, Ont., Canada M2N 6S7. 416-733-7600. E-mail: letters@styleathome.com. 8x/year. Circ.: 205,000. Gail Johnston Habs, Editor. **Description:** Profiles of Canadian homes, renovation, decoration, and gardening. Canadian content and locations only. **Nonfiction:** How-to articles; 800-1,500 words; $400-$900 (Canadian). **Queries:** Preferred. **Payment:** On acceptance.

SUNSET
80 Willow Rd., Menlo Park, CA 94025. 650-321-3600. Web site: www.sunset.com. Monthly. $3.99. Circ.: 1,500,000. Rosalie Muller Wright, Editor. **Description:** Regional magazine for Western America, covering travel and recreation; garden and outdoor living; food and entertaining; building, design, and crafts. **Nonfiction:** Looking for well-written stories and Travel Guide items offering satisfying travel experiences accomplished in a day or weekend, or as part of a vacation, in American West, also parts of Canada and Mexico; 300-1,000 words; $1/word. **Queries:** Preferred. **E-queries:** No. **Unsolicited mss:** Does not accept. **Response:** 1-3 months, SASE. **Freelance Content:** 5%. **Payment:** On acceptance.

TODAY'S HOMEOWNER
2 Park Ave., 9th Floor, New York, NY 10016. 212-779-5000. Web site: www.todayshomeowner.com. Paul Spring, Editor. **Description:** On home improvement and home-related topics (money management, home care, home environment, home security, yard care, design and remodeling, tools, repair and maintenance, electronics, new products and appliances, building materials, lighting and electrical, home decor). **Nonfiction:** Pays from $900 for features. **Freelance Content:** 15%.

VICTORIAN HOMES
265 S. Anita Dr., Suite 120, Orange, CA 92868. 714-939-9991. E-mail: ekotite@hotmail.com. Web site: www.victorianhomesmag.com. Bi-monthly. $3.99/$19.95. Circ.: 80,000. Erika Kotite, Editor. **Description:** Covers the lifestyle of Victorian Revival. Articles explore decoration and architecture of 19th- and early 20th-century homes restored, decorated and lived-in by real people, also period museum houses. **Nonfiction:** On interior design, furnishings, gardens, florals, table settings, and decorative accessories. Also, kitchen or bathroom makeovers, whole-house restorations, renovation tips, paint colors/wall coverings, etc.; 1,000-1,500 words; $400-$500. **Columns, Departments:** Victorian furnishings, antiques, collectibles, lighting, flowers and food, for today's home. **Queries:** Preferred. **E-queries:** Accepts. **Unsolicited mss:** Accepts. **Response:** 6-8 weeks. **Freelance Content:** 80%. **Rights:** All or 1st (1 year). **Payment:** On acceptance.

IN-FLIGHT MAGAZINES

ABOARD PUBLISHING
100 Almeria Ave., Suite 220, Coral Gables, FL 33134. 305-441-9738.
E-mail: aboard@worldnet.att.net. Web site: www.aboardmagazines.com. Monthly.
Sarah Munoz, Editorial Dept. **Description:** Publishes seven bilingual (English and Spanish) in-flight magazines for travelers going to and from Central and South America. **Fiction:** Travel, legends, tourism; 750 words; $.20/word. **Nonfiction:** Travel, tourism; 750 words; $.20/word. **Art:** Submit by request only; transparencies, slides. **Queries:** Not necessary. **E-queries:** Yes. **Unsolicited mss:** Accepts. **Freelance Content:** 50%. **Payment:** On publication. **Contact:** Angel Martinez.

ABOVE & BEYOND
First Air, P.O. Box 13142, Kanata, Ontario, Canada K2K 1X3. 613-599-4190.
Web site: www.above-n-beyond.com. Bimonthly. Circ.: 20,000. **Description:** In-flight magazine for First Air Airlines (in the Canadian arctic).

AIRTRAN ARRIVALS
Rivers/Kerley Communications, 2870 Peachtree Rd. N.E., #161,
Atlanta, GA 30305-2918. 404-239-9939.
Bimonthly. Circ.: 45,000. M.R. Kerley. **Description:** On dining, hotels, entertainment, lifestyle, and general interest; also, some profiles. **Nonfiction:** Articles, varying lengths; pay varies. **Queries:** Preferred.

ALASKA AIRLINES
Paradigm Communications Group, 2701 First Ave., Ste. 250,
Seattle, WA 98121. 206-441-5871.
Paul Frichtl, Editor. **Description:** On business, travel, and profiles of regional personalities for West Coast business travelers. **Nonfiction:** Articles, 250-2,500 words; pay varies. **Queries:** Preferred. **Payment:** On publication.

AMERICA WEST AIRLINES
Skyword Marketing, 4636 E. Elwood St., Suite 5,
Phoenix, AZ 85040-1963. 602-997-7200.
Web site: www.skyword.com. Monthly. Circ.: 135,000. Michael Derr, Editor.
Description: Offers articles on business trends, first-person profiles, destination pieces, fiction, arts and culture, thoughtful essays. **Nonfiction:** Articles; 500-2,000 words; from $250. **Tips:** Send clips with query. **Queries:** Preferred. **Response:** SASE. **Payment:** On publication.

AMERICAN WAY
14770 Trinity Blvd., Mail Drop 1625,
Fort Worth, TX 76155. 817-967-1804.
E-mail: elaine@amercanwaymag.com. Web site: www.AA.com/away/. Biweekly.
Elaine Gray Srnka, Editor. **Description:** Travel, business, food and wine, health, and

technology. **Nonfiction:** Features; 1,500-2,000 words. **Columns, Departments:** Sojourns; Travel Stories. **Queries:** Required. **Response:** SASE.

ATMOSPHERE
Melaine Communications Group, 703 Evans Ave., #106, Toronto, Ontario, Canada M9C 2E9. 416-622-1680. 3x/year. Circ.: 115,000. **Description:** For airline passengers of Canada 3000.

BOSTON AIRPORT JOURNAL
Air Travel Publications, 256 Marginal St., East Boston, MA 02128. 617-561-4000. Bimonthly. Circ.: 15,000. **Description:** Logan International Airport publication.

CONNECTIONS
GSA Publishing Group, 209-1015 Burrard St., Vancouver, BC, Canada V6Z 1Y5. 604-689-2909. Web site: www.gsapublishing.com. Bimonthly. Circ.: 3,000. **Description:** In-flight magazine for travelers to British Columbia and Canadian southwest.

ENROUTE
Spafax Canada, Inc., 355 Sainte Catherine W #400, Montreal, Quebec, Canada H3B 1A5. 514-844-2001. Monthly. Circ.: 180,000. **Description:** Air Canada in-flight magazine.

FRONTIER
Frontier Airlines, 650 S. Orcas St., Ste. 103, Seattle, WA 98108. 206-762-1922. E-mail: swilson@adventuremedia.com. Web site: www.adventuremedia.com. Monthly. Circ.: 20,000. M. Susan Wilson, Managing Editor. **Description:** In-flight magazine for Frontier Air Lines, serving northwest U.S. **Nonfiction:** 50-2000 words; $.25-$.50/word. **Queries:** Required. **E-queries:** Yes. **Unsolicited mss:** Accepts. **Response:** 6 weeks. **Freelance Content:** 70%. **Rights:** 1st NA serial, exclusive web (90 days). **Payment:** On publication.

HEMISPHERES
Pace Publications, 1301 Carolina St., Greensboro, NC 27401. 336-275-7714. Web site: www.hemispheresmagazine.com. Monthly. $50/yr. Circ.: 500,000. Randy Johnson, Editor. **Description:** Offers global perspective in a fresh, artful publication. **Fiction:** 1,500-3,000 words; pay varies. **Nonfiction:** Articles on universal issues; 2,000-3,000 words; $.75/word and up. **Columns, Departments:** See writer guidelines; 1,500-1,800 words; $.50/word. **Tips:** Prefers writers who live in the places whereof they write. **Queries:** Preferred. **E-queries:** No. **Unsolicited mss:** Accepts. **Response:** 2 months, SASE. **Freelance Content:** 95%. **Rights:** 1st worldwide. **Payment:** On acceptance. **Contact:** Sally Bateman, Lisa Fann.

HORIZON AIR

2701 First Ave., #250, Seattle, WA 98121-1123. 206-441-5871.
Monthly. $45/yr. Circ.: 416,000. Michele Andrus Dill, Editor. **Description:** For travelers in the Northwest, Silicon Valley, Northern California, Southern British Columbia and Southern Alberta. **Nonfiction:** Business, travel, lifestyle, sports, and leisure; 500-2,500 words; pay varies. **Columns, Departments:** Personal essay on business, travel, life in Northwest; 500-1,500 words. **Art:** Transparencies, slides. **Tips:** Query with samples (photocopies preferred, not originals). **Queries:** Required. **E-queries:** No. **Unsolicited mss:** Accepts. **Response:** 1-6 months, SASE. **Freelance Content:** 80%. **Rights:** FNASR. **Payment:** On publication.

LATITUDES

World Publications, Inc., P.O. Box 2456,
Winter Park, FL 32790-2456. 407-628-4802.
Web site: www.worldpub.net. Bimonthly. Circ.: 80,000. **Description:** American Eagle in-flight for those traveling to Florida and the Caribbean.

MERIDIAN

650 S. Orcas St., Ste 103, Seattle, WA 98108. 206-762-1922.
Monthly. **Description:** On varied topics (technology, health, adventure, finance, entertainment, and profiles of local celebrities). Editorial features cover a different region in each issue. **Nonfiction:** Articles, varying lengths; pay varies. **Queries:** Preferred.

MIDWEST EXPRESS

Paradigm Communications Group, 2701 First Ave., Ste. 250,
Seattle, WA 98121. 206-441-5871.
E-mail: paradigmcg@aol.com. Bimonthly. Steve Hansen, Managing Editor. **Description:** Inflight magazine for Midwest Express Airlines. **Nonfiction:** Travel stories, business trends, general features; 300-1,600 words. **Tips:** Keep queries concise. **Queries:** Required. **E-queries:** No. **Unsolicited mss:** Accepts. **Response:** 2 months, SASE. **Freelance Content:** 60%. **Rights:** 1st NA. **Payment:** On publication.

NORTHWEST AIRLINES WORLD TRAVELER

Skies America Publishing Co., P.O. Box 4005,
Beaverton, OR 97076-4005. 503-520-1955.
Monthly. Circ.: 340,000. **Description:** For passengers of Northwest Airlines.

ROYAL AIRLINES MAGAZINE

Formula Publications, 447 Speers Rd., #4, Oakville,
Ontario, Canada L6K 3S7. 905-842-6591.
Web site: www.carguideca.com. Quarterly. Circ.: 65,000. **Description:** For passengers of Royal Air Lines.

SKY
1301 Carolina St., Greensboro, NC 27401-1090. 336-378-6065. Web site: www.delta-sky.com. David Bailey, Editor. **Description:** Delta Air Lines inflight magazine. **Nonfiction:** Articles on business, lifestyle, high tech, sports, arts; pay varies. **Art:** Color slides. **Queries:** Preferred. **Response:** SASE required. **Payment:** On acceptance.

SOLEIL
Abarta Media, 11900 Biscayne Blvd., Ste 300, Miami, FL 33181. 305-892-6644. Web site: www.abartamedia.com. **Description:** For travelers on Sun Country Airlines.

SOUTHWEST AIRLINES SPIRIT
American Airlines Publishing, 14770 Trinity Blvd., Fort Worth, TX 76155. 817-967-6212. Web site: www.spiritmag.com. Monthly. Circ.: 280,000. **Description:** For passengers of Southwest Airlines.

SPIRIT OF ALOHA
Honolulu Publishing Co., 36 Main St., Honolulu, HI 96813. 808-524-7400. Web site: www.honolulupublishing.com. Janice Otaguro, Editor. **Description:** Hawaiian Island focus, magazine for Aloha Airlines. **Queries:** Preferred.

TWA AMBASSADOR
Pohly & Partners, 27 Melcher St., Fl 2, Boston, MA 02210. 617-451-1700. Web site: www.twa.com. Monthly. Circ.: 180,000. **Description:** For domestic and international travelers.

US AIRWAYS ATTACHÉ
1301 Carolina St., Greensboro, NC 27401. 336-378-6065. E-mail: attacheair@aol.com. Web site: www.attachemag.com. Monthly. $50/yr. Circ.: 375,000. Lance Elko, Editor. **Description:** General-interest articles. **Nonfiction:** 1,500-2,000 words; $1/word. **Columns, Departments:** Homefront; Sports; Things that Grow; Things that Go; Golf; Insider's Guide to . . . (destination piece). **Tips:** Include clips or list of past clients. **Queries:** Required. **E-queries:** Yes. **Unsolicited mss:** Accepts. **Response:** 1 month, SASE. **Freelance Content:** 75%. **Rights:** exclusive worldwide for 90 days. **Payment:** On acceptance.

JUVENILE

ACORN
8717 Mockingbird Road, Platteville, WI 53818. 608-348-8662. E-mail: buroakpress@yahoo.com. Web site: www.geocities.com/buroakpress. Quarterly. $3.95/$14.95. Circ.: 1,000. Susan Pagnucci. **Description:** Stories, plus the hats, masks, or flannel board patterns needed to tell them. Themed issues, with

awards, bookmarks, name tags, read-alouds, etc. For pre-K to 3rd-grade children. **Fiction:** Folktales for the very young (gingerbread boy, a forgetful farmer, etc.); 400-500 words. **Nonfiction:** Sports, transportation, space, insects, etc. **Tips:** Avoid seasonal, stories for the older child. Seeking short stories with conflict (problem to solve, with solution clever, yet understandable to the young child). Use lots of dialogue; readers tell these stories aloud. **Queries:** Not necessary. **E-queries:** No. **Unsolicited mss:** Accepts. **Response:** 3 months. **Freelance Content:** 3%. **Rights:** 1st. **Payment:** in copies. **Contact:** Susan Pagnucci.

AMERICAN GIRL

8400 Fairway Place, Middleton, WI 53562. 608-836-4848.
E-mail: im_agmag_editor@pleasantco.com. Web site: www.americangirl.com. Bimonthly. $3.95/$9.95. Circ.: 650,000. Kristi Thom, Editor. **Description:** Full-color, for girls ages 8 and up. "Our mission is to celebrate girls, yesterday and today. *American Girl* readers are girls in their formative years, girls who dream big dreams. **Fiction:** Protagonist should be a girl between 8 and 12. No science fiction, fantasy or first romance stories. Good children's literature, with thoughtful plots and characters; 2,500 words; pay negotiable. **Nonfiction:** By assignment only; 150-1,000 words; typically $1/word. **Fillers:** Visual puzzles, mazes, math puzzles, word games, simple crosswords, cartoons. Seasonal ideas welcome; $50/puzzle. **Columns, Departments:** Girls Express (short profiles of girls doing great, interesting things); 150 words; $1/word. **Tips:** The girl must be the story's "star," told from her point of view. "Girls Express" offers best chance to break in. **Queries:** Preferred. **E-queries:** No. **Unsolicited mss:** Accepts. **Response:** 3 months, SASE. **Freelance Content:** 5%. **Payment:** On acceptance. **Contact:** Magazine Dept. Asst.

APPLESEEDS

Cobblestone Publishing Co., 30 Grove St., #C,
Peterborough, NH 03458. 603-924-7209.
E-mail: barbara_burt@post.harvard.edu. Web site: www.cobblestonepub.com. 9x/year. Barbara Burt. **Description:** Multidisciplinary social studies magazine for children 7-10. Curriculum-related. **Fiction:** Short fiction, to 300 words. **Nonfiction:** Feature articles, profiles, and activities; pays $50/page; 400-600 words; $.20-$.25/word. **Fillers:** To 300 words. **Tips:** All material must be theme-related; write for coming themes. **Queries:** Required.

BABYBUG

Carus Publishing Co., P.O. Box 300, 315 Fifth St, Peru, IL 61354. 815-224-6656. Web site: www.cricketmag.com. Monthly. $5/issue, $35.97/year. Circ.: 46,000. Paula Morrow, Editor. **Description:** Simple rhymes and stories that parents will delight in reading to their babies. Each page bursts with bright colors that babies love. Pays $25/piece. **Fiction:** Very simple and concrete; read-aloud and picture stories for infants and toddlers; 4-6 short sentences. **Nonfiction:** Very basic words and concepts; 10 words max. **Poetry:** Rhythmic, rhyming. Humor or ending with mild surprise a plus; 8 lines max. **Art:** Art by assignment only; no photos. Submit samples (tear sheets, photocopies) for consideration. Pays $250/page, $500/spread. **Payment:** On publication.

BOYS' LIFE

1325 W. Walnut Hill Ln., Irving, TX 75038. 972-580-2366. Web site: www.bsa.scouting.org. Monthly. $18/year. Circ.: 1,300,000. W.E. Butterworth IV, Managing Editor. **Description:** Published by Boy Scouts of America, for boys ages 8-14. Covers broad range of interests (sports, hobbies, careers, crafts, and special interests of scouting). **Fiction:** 1-2 short stories per issue; featuring 1 or more boys; humor, mystery, science fiction, adventure; 1,000-1,500 words; $750 and up. **Nonfiction:** From professional sports to American history to how to pack a canoe; 500-1,500 words; $400-$1,500. **Columns, Departments:** Science, nature, earth, health, sports, space and aviation, cars, computers, entertainment, pets, history, music, 300-750 words, $150-$400. Also, last page how-to features ($250-$300). **Art:** Quality photos only; most work by assignment. **Tips:** Write for a boy you know who is 12. Use crisp, punchy writing; short, straightforward sentences. **Queries:** Required for nonfiction. **E-queries:** Prefer mail. **Unsolicited mss:** Accepts fiction only. **Response:** 6-8 weeks, SASE required. **Freelance Content:** 75%. **Rights:** FNASR. **Payment:** On acceptance.

BOYS' QUEST

P.O. Box 227, Bluffton, OH 45817-0227. 419-358-4610. Web site: www.boysquest.com. Bi-monthly. $4.95/$17.95. Circ.: 8,500. Marilyn Edwards, Editor. **Description:** Captures interests of all boys with exciting, unique activities and fascinating articles. Each issue focuses on a theme. **Fiction:** Stories on childhood interests, featuring young boys in wholesome childhood activities and pursuits; 350-600 words; $.05/word min. **Nonfiction:** About boys in activities both unusual and worthwhile. Photos with story essential; 500 words; $.05/word min. **Poetry:** Yes; $10/poem min. **Fillers:** Puzzles, jokes, riddles, games; $10/puzzle min., varies for other fillers. **Art:** b/w photos, color slides, pen-and-ink illustrations; $5-$35. **Tips:** Readers are boys, ages 8-10. Avoid Halloween, horror, etc. Prefers traditional childhood themes. Buys 3 nonfiction articles for each 1 fiction story. **Queries:** Not necessary. **E-queries:** No. **Unsolicited mss:** Accepts. **Response:** 4-6 weeks, SASE. **Rights:** 1st NA. **Payment:** On publication.

CALLIOPE

Cobblestone Publishing, 30 Grove St., Ste. C, Peterborough, NH 03458. 603-924-7209. E-mail: custsvc@cobblestone.mu.com. Web site: www.cobblestonepub.com. 9x/year. $29.95/yr. Circ.: 10,000. Rosalie F. Baker, Editor. **Description:** World history for youg people. Issues are thematic, exciting, colorful, with maps, timelines, illustrations, and art from major museums. **Fiction:** Fiction with historical, biographical, adventure themes; retold legends; 400-1,200 words; $.20-$.25/word. **Nonfiction:** Articles, 400-1,200 words, with lively, original approach to world history (through Renaissance). Shorts, 200-750 words, on little-known information related to issue's theme; $.20-$.25/word. **Fillers:** Activities, to 800 words. Puzzles, games. **Art:** any format. **Tips:** Contact for upcoming themes. **Queries:** Preferred. **E-queries:** No. **Unsolicited mss:** Prefer not to accept. **Response:** 2-4 months, SASE. **Freelance Content:** 80%. **Rights:** All. **Payment:** On publication.

CHICKADEE

179 John St., Suite 500, Toronto, Ont., Canada M5T 3G5. 416-340-2700. E-mail: bayard@owl.on.ca. Web site: www.owlkids.com. 10x/year. $3.50/issue, $24/year. Circ.: 70,000. Hilary Bain, Editor. **Description:** For children, ages 6-9. Well-written animal features, also fiction, games, simple science experiments help children look more closely at their surroundings. **Fiction:** Stories to encourage children to read and learn at the world around them; 600-800 words; $100-$300. **Nonfiction:** Encouraging, inspiring articles for children; $100-$300. **Poetry:** Humorous; $100-$300. **Fillers:** Puzzles, activities, observation games. **Art:** Slide (max. 20); electronic (max. 10); $125-$450. **Tips:** Lively writing and strong visual component are needed in any piece for Chickadee. **Queries:** Not necessary. **E-queries:** No. **Unsolicited mss:** Accepts. **Response:** 12 weeks, SASE required. **Freelance Content:** 1%. **Rights:** Worldwide. **Payment:** On publication. **Contact:** Klara Pachner.

CHILDREN'S DIGEST

1100 Waterway Blvd., P.O. Box 567, Indianapolis, IN 46206. 317-636-8881. Web site: www.childrensplaymatemag.org. 8x/year. **Description:** General interest for young readers. **Nonfiction:** Seeking articles on health, fitness, and nutrition; pay varies. **Queries:** Required.

CHILDREN'S PLAYMATE

1100 Waterway Blvd., PO Box 567, Indianapolis, IN 46206-0567. 317-636-8881 x267. Web site: www.childrensplaymatemag.org. 8x/year. Ms. Terry Harshman, Editor. **Description:** For 6-8 year-olds, emphasizing health, fitness, sports, safety, and nutrition. **Fiction:** Plays. **Nonfiction:** Articles, crafts, recipes, general-interest, and health-related short stories. Easy recipes and how-to crafts pieces with simple instructions; 500-600 words; to $.17/word. **Poetry:** Yes; from $30. **Fillers:** Puzzles, games, mazes. **Queries:** Preferred. **Rights:** all. **Payment:** On publication.

CHIRP

179 John St., Suite 500, Toronto, Ontario M5T 3G5. 416-340-2700. Web site: www.owl.on.ca. 9x/year. **Description:** Offers puzzles, games, rhymes, stories, and songs for children, ages 2-6. Goal is to introduce preschool children to the relationship between words and pictures. **Fiction:** 300-400 words; pay varies. **Nonfiction:** 300-400 words; pay varies. **Queries:** Preferred. **E-queries:** Yes. **Unsolicited mss:** Accepts. **Payment:** On publication.

CLICK

332 S. Michigan Ave., Suite 1100, Chicago, IL 60604. 312-939-1500. Web site: www.caruspub.com. 10x/year. $32.97/yr. Circ.: 42,000. Deborah L. Pool,

Editor. **Description:** For children, ages 3-7. Themes introduce ideas and concepts in natural, physical, or social sciences, the arts, technology, math, and history. **Fiction:** Addressing a question about the world; 600-1,000 words; pay varies. **Nonfiction:** Articles, to 400 words, that explain "how" and "why" of something in engaging, perhaps humorous way. Pay varies. **Fillers:** 1 page. **Tips:** If article or story is accepted, may commission future work. **Queries:** Not necessary. **E-queries:** No. **Unsolicited mss:** Accepts. **Response:** 3-4 months, SASE. **Freelance Content:** 1% unsolicited, 90% commissioned. **Rights:** 1st. **Payment:** On publication.

CLUBHOUSE

Box 15, Berrien Springs, MI 49103. 616-471-3701. E-mail: etrumbo@hotmail.com. Web site: www.yourstoryhour.org. Monthly. $5/year. Circ.: 1,000. Elaine Trumbo, Editor. **Description:** Offers b/w photography, stories, poems, puzzles, recipes, and cartoons (for kids ages 9-12), with Christian background. **Nonfiction:** Action-oriented Christian stories, 800-1,200 words, with children in stories who are wise, brave, funny, kind. Pays $25-$35. **Queries:** Preferred.

CLUBHOUSE JR.

8605 Explorer Dr., Colorado Springs, CO 80920. 719-531-3400. Monthly. $1.50/$15. Circ.: 96,000. Annette Bourland, Editor. **Description:** Inspires, entertains, and teaches Christian values to children ages 4-8. **Fiction:** Fresh, inviting, well-developed characters; fast-paced, interesting story. Stories not explicitly Christian but built on foundations of belief and family values; 250-750 words (for young readers), 700-1,000 (for parents); $125-$200. **Nonfiction:** Articles about real adults or children with interesting experience. Science and nature, from unique perspective. Use short-caption styled format.; 500 max.; $125-$200. **Poetry:** Real-life experience of young children; humorous, descriptive; 250 max.; $50-$100. **Fillers:** Puzzles (no crosswords); fun crafts, parent/child together; repetition of images, concise wording, humorous or insightful ending; 1 page; $25-$45. **Art:** Send samples. **Tips:** No queries. **E-queries:** No. **Unsolicited mss:** Accepts. **Response:** Submissions 4-6 weeks, SASE. **Freelance Content:** 25%. **Rights:** 1st. **Payment:** On acceptance.

COBBLESTONE

30 Grove St., Suite C, Peterborough, NH 03458-1454. 603-924-7209. Web site: www.cobblestonepub.com. 9x/year. $4.95/issue. Circ.: 33,000. Meg Chorlian, Editor. **Description:** American history for young readers. **Fiction:** Authentic historical or biographical fiction, retold legends, etc., on issue's theme; up to 800 words; $.20-$.25/word. **Nonfiction:** In-depth nonfiction, plays, first-person accounts, biographies; 300-600 words; $.20-$.25/word. **Poetry:** Clear, objective imagery, serious and light verse; up to 100 lines. **Fillers:** Crossword and other word puzzles using vocabulary of issue's theme. **Art:** Photographs, related to theme; Color, transparencies, slides. **Queries:** Preferred.

CRACKED

Globe Communications, Inc., 3 E. 54th St., 15th Fl., New York, NY 10022-3108. E-mail: dkulpa@globefl.com. Web site: www.cracked.com. Lou Silverstone / Andy Simmons, Editor. **Description:** Cartoon humor, 1-5 pages, for readers, ages 10-15. No text pieces accepted. Pays from $100 per page. **Queries:** Preferred. **Payment:** On acceptance.

CRICKET

P.O. Box 300, 315 Fifth St, Peru, IL 61354-0300. 815-224-6656. Web site: www.cricketmag.com. $5/issue, $35.97/year. Circ.: 68,000. Alice Letvin, Editorial Director. **Description:** Folk tales, fantasy, science fiction, history, poems, science, sports, and crafts, for young readers. **Fiction:** Any topic of interest to children; up to 2,000 words; $.25/word. **Nonfiction:** Science, biography, history, nature; up to 1,500 words; $.25/word. **Poetry:** Brief lyric poems; up to 25 lines; $3/line. **Fillers:** Word or math puzzles, recipes, crafts, experiments; 150-200 words; $100. **Tips:** Include bibliography with nonfiction. **Queries:** Not necessary. **E-queries:** No. **Unsolicited mss:** Accepts. **Response:** Submissions 8-12 weeks. **Freelance Content:** 90%. **Rights:** One-time serial. **Payment:** On publication.

DISCOVERY TRAILS

1445 Boonville Ave., Springfield, MO 65802-1894. 417-862-2781. E-mail: rl-discoverytrails@gph.org. Web site: www.radiantlife.org. Quarterly. Circ.: 36,000. Sinda Zinn, Editor. **Description:** Take-home paper for children 10-11 years old, with fiction stories, activities, poems, articles, and puzzles to reinforce daily Christian living. **Fiction:** Stories that promote Christian living through application of biblical principles by the characters; 1000 words; $.07-$.10/word. **Nonfiction:** Articles about topics that show God's power, wisdom in creation, or correlation to a relationship with God; 300-500 words; $.07-$.10/word. **Tips:** No Santa, Easter Bunny, Halloween stories. **Queries:** Not necessary. **E-queries:** No. **Unsolicited mss:** Accepts. **Response:** SubmissioN 2-4weeks, SASE required. **Freelance Content:** 90%. **Payment:** On acceptance.

EXPLORE!

Pinatubo Press, P.O. Box 2539, 39 Biltmore Ave., Asheville, NC 28802. 828-254-9400. E-mail: editor@exploremagazine.com. Web site: www.exploremagazine.com. 10x/year. $3.95. Nat Belz, Publisher. **Description:** To foster curiosity, honor vocations, and challenge kids to think critically about how the world works. Articles from ancient history to modern technology. **Tips:** SASE for author guidelines.

FACES

Cobblestone Publishing, 30 Grove St., Suite C, Peterborough, NH 03458-1454. 603-924-7209. E-mail: facesmag@yahoo.com. Web site: www.cobblestonepub.com. 9x/year. $29.95/year. Circ.: 11,000. Elizabeth Crooker Carpentiere, Editor. **Description:** Introduces young readers to different world cultures or regions. **Fiction:** Retold folktales, legends, plays; must relate to theme; up to 800 words; $.20-$.25/word. **Nonfiction:** In-depth articles on aspect of featured culture; interviews and personal accounts; 600-800 words; $.20-$.25/word. **Fillers:** Activities (crafts, recipes, word puzzles); 100-600 words. **Art:** 35mm; $25-$100. **Tips:** Avoid judgmental tone; give readers a clear image of life in other cultures. Check website for coming themes. **Queries:** Required. **E-queries:** Yes. **Unsolicited mss:** Accepts. **Response:** Queries, 4 weeks, submissions, 4 months, SASE required. **Freelance Content:** 80%. **Rights:** All. **Payment:** On publication.

FAMILY FUN
244 Main St., Northampton, MA 01060. 413-585-0444. Web site: www.familyfun.com. Johnathan Adolph, Executive Editor. **Description:** For parents of children ages 3-12. Offers fun ideas and activities. **Columns, Departments:** My Great Idea; Family Ties (essays on family life); also recipes, crafts and games; $.50-$1/word. **Tips:** Nw writers should consider contributing to departments first. **Contact:** Ann Hallock, Editor.

FOOTSTEPS
150 Page St., New Bedford, MA 02740. E-mail: custsvc@cobblestone.mv.com. Web site: www.cobblestonepub.com. Charles F. Baker. **Description:** Fiction and nonfiction on African-American history and culture, for children 8-14. **Fiction:** to 700 words; $.20-$.25/word. **Nonfiction:** Features, 600-750 words; $.20-$.25/word. **Fillers:** Activities, short articles, to 600 words. **Tips:** Cultural sensitivity and historical accuracy required. Contact for upcoming themes. **Queries:** Preferred. **Payment:** On publication.

GIRLS' LIFE
Monarch Avalon, Inc., 4517 Harford Rd., Baltimore, MD 21214. 410-426-9600. E-mail: kellygirl@girlslife.com. Web site: www.girlslife.com. Bimonthly. $2.95/issue, $14.99/year. Circ.: 2,000,000. Kelly White, Senior Editor. **Description:** For girls, ages 9-15. Offers honest advice, fun quizzes, and real-life solutions to growing-up problems. **Nonfiction:** Fun features and quizzes on school, friendships, crushes, pop culture; 750-2,000 words. **Columns, Departments:** Sports, Celebrity Interviews, New Trends; 750-1,000 words. **Art:** Color slides. **Tips:** Use teen language, and don't condescend. **Queries:** Preferred. **E-queries:** No. **Unsolicited mss:** Accepts. **Response:** 1 month, SASE required. **Freelance Content:** 25%. **Rights:** 1st, all. **Payment:** On publication.

GUIDEPOSTS FOR KIDS
P.O. Box 638, Chesterton, IN 46304. 219-929-4429. E-mail: gp4k@guideposts.org. Web site: www.gp4k.com. Bimonthly. $15.95/yr. Circ.: 200,000. Rosanne Tolin, Editor. **Description:** For children, ages 7-12. Offers inspiring stories that focus on traditional values, also fun puzzles, trivia, and true-life comics. **Fiction:** by noted authors; 1,000 words; $250-$500. **Nonfiction:** Profiles of athletes and celebrities (150-500 words); feature (1,000 words) that encourage kids to

think; $150-$500. **Poetry:** 50-150 words; $25-$100. **Fillers:** $25-150. **Columns, Departments:** The Buzz (profiles of kids doing cool things); sidebars; 250-350 words; $150-$350. **Art:** Photos, illustrations. **Tips:** "We do not consider ourselves a religious magazine. No Bible-toting kids or preachy stories, please." **Queries:** Preferred. **E-queries:** Yes. **Unsolicited mss:** Accepts. **Response:** 6 weeks, SASE. **Freelance Content:** 80%. **Rights:** All. **Payment:** On acceptance. **Contact:** Allison Payne, Asst. Ed.

HIGHLIGHTS FOR CHILDREN

803 Church St., Honesdale, PA 18431-1824. 570-253-1080.
E-mail: highlights@ezaccess.net. Web site: www.highlights.com. Monthly. $29.64/year. Circ.: 2,000,000. Kent L. Brown, Managing Editor. **Description:** "Fun with a purpose." The stories, Hidden Pictures, jokes, and activities bring engaging entertainment to children, ages 2-12, while developing learning skills. **Fiction:** Humor, mystery, sports, adventure, folktales, world cultures, urban stories. Engaging plot, strong characterization, lively language; up to 900 words; $150 and up. **Nonfiction:** Biography, autobiography, arts, science, history, sports, world cultures. If for younger readers (ages 3-7 years), 400 words or less; up to 800 words; $150 and up. **Poetry:** 16 lines, $25 and up. **Fillers:** Crafts (3-7 numbered steps), $30 and up; include a sample; use common household items or inexpensive, easy-to-obtain materials. Holiday/religious/world cultures crafts welcome. **Tips:** Prefers stories in which protagonist solves a dilemma through his/her own resources. Avoid stories that preach. **Queries:** Preferred. **E-queries:** No. **Unsolicited mss:** Accepts. **Response:** 6-8 weeks, SASE required. **Rights:** All. **Payment:** On acceptance. **Contact:** Beth Troop, Manuscript Coordinator.

HOPSCOTCH

P.O. Box 164, Bluffton, OH 45817-0164. 419-358-4610.
Web site: www.hopscotchmagazine.com. Bi-monthly. $4.95/issue, $17.95/year. Circ.: 15,000. Marilyn Edwards, Editor. **Description:** Written for girls, without the emphasis on fads and fashion, boyfriends and shopping. Focuses on educational activities and stories. Makes reading an adventure, and problem-solving fun. **Fiction:** Feature girls in wholesome childhood activities and pursuits; 500 words; $.05/word and up. **Nonfiction:** Features girls directly involved in an unusual and worthwhile activity. Nonfiction is 75% of magazine's contents. Photos essential; 500 words; $.05/word and up. **Poetry:** Yes; $10/poem. **Fillers:** Puzzles, games, crafts, cartoons, recipes; $10/puzzle min. **Art:** b/w photos, color slides, illustrations; $5-$35. **Tips:** Contact for upcoming themes. **Queries:** Not necessary. **E-queries:** No. **Unsolicited mss:** Accepts. **Response:** 4-6 weeks, SASE required. **Rights:** 1st NA. **Payment:** On publication.

THE HORN BOOK

56 Roland St., Suite 200, Boston, MA 02129. 617-628-0225.
E-mail: info@hbook.com. Web site: www.hbook.com. Bimonthly. $9.50/issue, $45/year. Circ.: 18,500. Roger Sutton, Editor-in-Chief. **Description:** A critical review of introductory children's and young adult books. Also, editorials, columns, and

articles about children's literature. **Nonfiction:** Critical essays on children's literature and related subjects for librarians, teachers, parents; up to 280 words. **Queries:** Not necessary. **E-queries:** Yes. **Unsolicited mss:** Accepts. **Response:** 4-6 months, SASE required. **Payment:** On publication. **Contact:** Roger Sutton.

HUMPTY DUMPTY'S

1100 Waterway Blvd., P.O. Box 567, Indianapolis, IN 46206. 317-636-8881. Web site: www.humptydumptymag.org. 8x/year. $21.95/year. Circ.: 200,000. Sheila Rogers, Editor. **Description:** Encourages children, ages 4-6, to strive for excellence, with focus on academics, health, personal fitness, medicine, and science. **Fiction:** up to 350 words; to $.22/word. **Nonfiction:** up to 350 words; to $.22/word. **Poetry:** Short verse, narrative; $25 min. **Fillers:** Games, puzzles, crafts, simple science experiments, healthy and "no-cook" recipes (with minimum adult guidance). Clear brief instructions. **Tips:** Should have good "read-aloud" quality. **Unsolicited mss:** Accepts. **Response:** Submissions 3 months, SASE required. **Freelance Content:** 25-30%. **Rights:** All. **Payment:** On publication.

JACK AND JILL

1100 Waterway Blvd., P.O. Box 567, Indianapolis, IN 46206. 317-636-8881. Web site: www.jackandjillmag.org. 8x/year. $21.95/year. Circ.: 200,000. Daniel Lee, Editor. **Description:** For children, ages 7-10, offers health, fitness, science, and general-interest material. Encourages active, challenging lifestyles, and accomplishment and learning with a hearty helping of fun! **Fiction:** 700 words; $.17/word. **Nonfiction:** On history, biography, life in other countries, etc; 500 words; $.17/word. **Poetry:** $15-$50. **Fillers:** Games, puzzles, projects, recipes. **Art:** Photos. **Tips:** Avoid usual topics of divorce, moving, new kid in school, etc. **Queries:** Not necessary. **E-queries:** No. **Unsolicited mss:** Accepts. **Response:** Submissions 12 weeks, SASE required. **Freelance Content:** 50%. **Rights:** All. **Payment:** On publication.

JUNIOR SCHOLASTIC

Scholastic, Inc., 555 Broadway, New York, NY 10012. 212-343-6295. E-mail: junior@scholastic.com. Web site: www.juniorscholastic.com. Lee Baier. **Description:** On-the-spot reports from countries in the news. **Nonfiction:** Pay varies; **Queries:** Required. **Payment:** On acceptance.

KIDS TRIBUTE

71 Barber Greene Rd., Don Mills, Ont., Canada M3C 2A2. 416-445-0544. Web site: www.tribute.ca. Quarterly. Sandra Stewart, Editor-in-Chief. **Description:** Movie- or entertainment-related articles, for young readers, ages 8-13. **Nonfiction:** 350 words; pays $150-$200 (Canadian). **Queries:** Required. **Payment:** On acceptance.

KIDS' WALL STREET NEWS

WORLD, P.O. Box 1207, Rancho Santa Fe, CA 92067. 760-591-7681. E-mail: emailkwsn@aol.com. Bimonthly. Kate Allen, Editor-in-Chief. **Description:** On money matters and other topics. **Columns, Departments:** Adventure, Sports

Arena, Think about This, Money & Banking, to 500 words. **Art:** Photos, graphs, and artwork. **Tips:** Submit material on a Mac format disk, with hard copy. **Payment:** On publication.

LADYBUG

315 Fifth St., Peru, IL 61354. 815-224-6656.
Web site: www.ladybugmag.com. Monthly. $5/issue, $35.97/year. Circ.: 126,000.
Paula Morrow, Editor. **Description:** Stories, poems, songs, games, and adventures for young children, ages 1-2. Each page illustrated to delight parents and children alike. **Fiction:** Picture, read-aloud, and early reader stories with lively characters. Genres: adventure, humor, mild suspense, fairy tales, folktales, contemporary fiction; up to 850 words; $.25/word $25 min. **Nonfiction:** How-to, informational and humorous pieces, on age-appropriate topics; up to 300 words; $.25/word $25 min. **Poetry:** Rhythmic, rhyming, serious, humorous, active; up to 20 lines; up to $3/line $25 min. **Fillers:** Rebus, learning activities, games, crafts, songs, finger games. **Art:** see guidelines. **Tips:** Always looking for more activities. **Queries:** Not necessary. **E-queries:** No. **Unsolicited mss:** Accepts. **Response:** 12 weeks, SASE required. **Freelance Content:** 70%. **Rights:** 1st serial. **Payment:** On publication.

MAD

1700 Broadway, 5th Fl., New York, NY 10019. 212-506-4850.
Web site: www.madmag.com. Monthly. **Description:** Humorous pieces on a wide variety of topics. **Art:** cartoons, 2-8 panels (not necessary to include sketches with submission); pays top rates. **Response:** SASE. **Payment:** On acceptance. **Contact:** Editorial Department.

MUSE

Cricket Magazine Group, 332 S. Michigan Ave., Suite 1100,
Chicago, IL 60604. 312-939-1500.
E-mail: muse@caruspub.com. Web site: www.musemag.com. 10x/year. Diana Lutz, Editor. **Description:** Focuses on problems connected with a discipline or area of practical knowledge, for children, ages 8-14. **Nonfiction:** 1,000-2,500 words; $.50/word. **Tips:** Query with resumé, writing samples, list of possible topics, SASE. **Queries:** Required. **Response:** SASE.

MY FRIEND

Pauline Books & Media, Daughters of St. Paul, 50 St. Pauls Ave.,
Boston, MA 02130-3491. 617-541-8911.
E-mail: myfriend@pauline.org. Web site: www.pauline.org. Monthly. $2. Circ.: 11,500. Sister Kathryn James Hermes, Editor. **Description:** Catholic magazine for boys and girls, ages 6-12, celebrating the Catholic Faith as lived by today's children. **Fiction:** Stories with good dialogue, realistic character development. Can entertain, inspire, or teach; 800-1,100 words; $75-150. **Nonfiction:** Fresh perspectives into a child's world: imaginative,unique, challenging, informative, fun. Prefers visual

articles, with multiple points of entry. **Queries:** Preferred. **Unsolicited mss:** Accepts. **Freelance Content:** 40%. **Rights:** 1st.

NATIONAL GEOGRAPHIC WORLD

1145 17th St. NW, Washington, DC 20036-4688. 202-857-7729. E-mail: jajnone@ngs.org. Web site: www.national geographic.com/world. Monthly. $17.95/year. Circ.: 770,000. Melina Bellows, Chief Editor. **Description:** For kids, ages 8-14, who dare to explore. Seeks to increase geographic awareness by inspiring young readers' curiosity, with big, bold photos and fun, fact-filled stories. **Nonfiction:** Adventure, outdoors, sports, geography, history, archaeology, paleontology, human interest, natural history, science, technology, "My World" (stories on lives of remarkable kids; "Friends USA" (on groups of kids doing things together); 400-1,200 words; $.80-$1/word. **Fillers:** Just Joking, Fun Stuff (games, laughs, things to do); $.80-$1/word. **Columns, Departments:** World News (short, fun news items with kid appeal), Kids Did It! (achievements), Amazing Animals; 50-150 words; $.80-$1/word. **Art:** Yes. **Tips:** Send relevant clips with cover letter; research magazine first. **Queries:** Required. **E-queries:** No. **Unsolicited mss:** Does not accept. **Response:** 2 months, SASE. **Freelance Content:** 90%. **Rights:** All. **Payment:** On publication. **Contact:** Julie Agnone, Exec. Ed.

NATURE FRIEND

2727 TR 421, Sugarcreek, OH 44681. 330-852-1900. Monthly. Circ.: 9,000. Marvin Wengerd, Owner/Editor. **Description:** Stories, puzzles, activities, experiments about nature for children. **Nonfiction:** Articles for children that teach them to be kind to animals, plants, and nature, increase their awareness of God, and illustrate spiritual lessons; $.05/word. **Fillers:** Fillers and games; $15. **Tips:** Sample issues, $5.

NEW MOON

P.O. Box 3620, Duluth, MN 55803-3620. 218-728-5507. E-mail: girl@newmoon.org. Web site: www.newmoon.org. Bi-monthly. $5.50/$29. Circ.: 35,000. Deb Mylin, Editor. **Description:** Celebrates girls—their accomplishments and efforts to hold onto their voices, their strengths, their dreams as they move from being girls to becoming women. **Fiction:** Stories by female authors, with girls as main characters. Fiction should fit theme (contact for upcoming list), for girls ages 8-14; 900 words; $.06-$.10/word. **Nonfiction:** Women's work (profiles a woman and her job, relates to theme); Her Story (profiles a woman from history); Body Language (about puberty, body image, depression, menstruation, etc.); Girls on the Go (by girl or woman adventurers); 600 words; $.06-$.10/word. **Art:** By assignment; send samples; pay varies. **Queries:** Not necessary. **E-queries:** Accepts. **Unsolicited mss:** Accepts. **Response:** 2 months, SASE. **Freelance Content:** 10%. **Rights:** All. **Payment:** On publication.

NICK, JR.
1515 Broadway, 40th Floor, New York, NY 10036. 212-846-5249.
Web site: www.nickjr.com. **Description:** For children ages 2-7 and their parents.
Fun things to do together.

ON THE LINE
616 Walnut, Scottdale, PA 15683-1999. 724-887-8500.
E-mail: otl@mph.org. Web site: www.mph.org. Monthly. $2.20/$26.50. Circ.: 5,500.
Mary Clemens Meyer, Editor. **Description:** For youth, ages 9-14, to reinforce
Christian values. Seeks to help upper elementary and junior high school kids under-
stand God, the created world, themselves, and others. **Fiction:** Solving everyday
problems, humor, holidays, Christian values; 1,000-1,800 words; $.03-$.05/word.
Nonfiction: Nature, history, health, how-to; 300-500 words; $.03-$.05/word. **Poetry:**
Light verse, humor, nature, holidays; 3-24 lines; $10-$25. **Fillers:** Cartoons, cross-
words, word finds, scrambled letters, mazes, codes, jokes, riddles, recipes; $10-$25.
Tips: Let the story give the moral subtly; keep it fun. **Queries:** Not necessary.
Unsolicited mss: Accepts. **Response:** Submissions 1 month, SASE. **Freelance
Content:** 85%. **Rights:** One-time. **Payment:** On acceptance.

OWL
Owl Group, Bayard Press, 179 John St., Suite 500,
Toronto, Ont., Canada M5T3G5. 416-340-2700.
E-mail: owl@owlkids.com. Web site: www.owlkids.com. 9x/year. Circ.: 75,000.
Elizabeth Siegel, Editor. **Description:** For children ages 9-12, about animals, sci-
ence, people, technology, new discoveries, activities. **Nonfiction:** 500-1,000 words;
pay varies. **Tips:** No fiction. **Payment:** On acceptance.

PASSPORT
6401 The Paseo, Kansas City, MO 64131.
E-mail: kneal@nazarene.org.
Quarterly printing, weekly distribution. Circ.: 18,000. Emily Freeburg, Editor.
Description: Full-color newspaper for preteens, with resources for spiritual transformation and holy living. Corresponds with WordAction Sunday School materials
(for 11-12 year olds). **Nonfiction:** 400-600 words, for grades 5-6, hot topics and relevant issues. Pays $.05/word for original work, less for reprints. **Fillers:** Pays $15 for
cartoons and puzzles. **Queries:** Preferred. **E-queries:** Yes. **Unsolicited mss:**
Accepts. **Response:** 6-8 weeks, SASE required. **Freelance Content:** 10%. **Rights:**
Multi-use. **Payment:** On publication. **Contact:** Kathy Neal.

POCKETS
P.O. Box 340004, 1908 Grand Ave, Nashville, TN 37203-0004. 615-340-7333.
E-mail: pockets@upperroom.org. Web site: www.upperroom.org. 11x/year. $16.95.
Circ.: 90,000. Janet Knight, Editor. **Description:** Non-denominational, seeks to pro-
mote the Gospel of Jesus Christ to children and help them grow in their relationship
with God. Readers include children of many ethnic and cultural backgrounds.

Fiction: Stories to help children deal with everyday life. Prefers real-life settings; 600-1400 words; $.14/word. **Nonfiction:** Theme for each issue. Profiles of persons whose lives reflect Christian communities; value articles about children involved in environmental, community, peace/justice issues; 400-1000; $.14/word. **Fillers:** Puzzles, games (on theme); $25 and up. **Columns, Departments:** Pocketful of Love Prayer; $.14/word. **Tips:** Looking for puzzles and activities with colorful illustrations and graphics. **E-queries:** No. **Unsolicited mss:** Accepts. **Response:** SASE. **Freelance Content:** 90%. **Payment:** On acceptance.

RANGER RICK

National Wildlife Federation, 11100 Wildlife Center Dr., Reston, VA 20190. 703-438-6000.
Web site: www.nwf.org. Monthly. $17/year. Circ.: 650,000. Gerald Bishop, Editor. **Description:** Write for photo and art guidelines. No unsolicited queries or manuscripts.

SCHOLASTIC DYNAMATH

555 Broadway, New York, NY 10012-3999. 212-343-6458.
Web site: www.scholastic.com. **Description:** Articles, games, and puzzles for 5th and 6th grade math students. **Tips:** Send 9x12 SASE for free sample issue. **Queries:** Preferred.

SKIPPING STONES

P.O. Box 3939, Eugene, OR 97403. 541-342-4956.
E-mail: skipping@efn.org. Web site: http://www.efn.org/~skipping//. 5x/year. $25/yr. Circ.: 2,500. Arun N. Toké, Executive Editor. **Description:** Encourages cooperation, creativity, celebration of cultural diversity, and nature awareness. **Fiction:** Social awareness, interpersonal relationships; 750 words max. **Nonfiction:** Nature awareness, multicultural education, social responsibility, travelogues, journal entries; up to 750 words. **Poetry:** by authors under age 19 only; on nature, social issues, reflections; up to 30 lines. **Fillers:** Multicultural, nature; 150 words. **Art:** b/w, color. **Queries:** Not necessary. **E-queries:** Accepts. **Unsolicited mss:** Accepts. **Response:** Queries to 1 month, submissions to 3 months,SASE. **Freelance Content:** 80%. **Rights:** 1st serial, nonexclusive reprint. **Payment:** in copies.

SOCCER JR.

27 Unquowa Rd., Fairfield, CT 06430. 800-872-2970.
E-mail: soccerjrol@aol.com. Web site: www.soccerjr.com. Joe Provey, Editor. **Description:** Fiction and fillers about soccer for readers ages 8 and up. Pays $450 for a feature or story; $250 for shorter pieces. **Queries:** Preferred. **Payment:** On acceptance.

SPIDER

P.O. Box 300, Peru, IL 61354. 815-224-6656.
Web site: www.spidermag.com. Monthly. $4.95/issue. Circ.: 87,000. Tracy Schoenle,

Associate Editor. **Description:** Stories, poems, science, fantasy, and activities for children. Original artwork fills each issue. **Fiction:** Easy-to-read realistic stories (fantasy, myths, fairy tales, fables, and science fiction). **Nonfiction:** Interviews, profiles, and how-to articles; on science, animals, nature, technology, and multicultural topics. **Poetry:** Yes. **Fillers:** Yes. **Art:** Art (especially children, animals, action, scenes from a story); photography (photo essays or article illustrations), color preferred, b/w considered. **Tips:** Looking for more nonfiction submissions, also activity ideas, puzzles, jokes. **Queries:** Preferred. **E-queries:** No. **Unsolicited mss:** Accepts. **Response:** 12 weeks, SASE. **Freelance Content:** 95%. **Payment:** On publication.

SPORTS ILLUSTRATED FOR KIDS
Sports Illustrated Bldg., 135 West 50th St., New York, NY 10020-1393. 212-522-1212. E-mail: sikids@timeinc.com. Web site: www.sikids.com. Monthly. $2.99/$29.95. Circ.: 950,000. Neil Cohen, Editor. **Description:** Focuses on the excitement, joy, and challenge of sports, for boys and girls, ages 8-14. Provides action photos, interactive stories, profiles, puzzles, playing tips. Also, drawings and writing by kids. **Nonfiction:** Current, biographical, sports-related artcles for kids age 8-14; 500-700 words; $500-1,250. **Columns, Departments:** 300-500 words. **Art:** Photos, illustrations (submit non-returnable portfolio). **Queries:** Required. **E-queries:** Yes. **Unsolicited mss:** Accepts. **Response:** 4-6 weeks, SASE. **Rights:** Exclusive. **Payment:** 40% on acceptance, 60% on publication. **Contact:** Kim Fusco.

STONE SOUP
Box 83, Santa Cruz, CA 95063-0083. 831-426-5557. E-mail: editor@stonesoup.com. Web site: www.stonesoup.com. Bimonthly. $5.50/$33. Circ.: 20,000. Gerry Mandel, Editor. **Description:** Stories, poems, book reviews, and art work by young writers and artists, ages 8-13. **Fiction:** Personal narratives, arrival stories, family histories, sport stories, science fiction; 2,500 words; $25. **Nonfiction:** Book reviews by children under 14. Prefers writing based on real-life experiences. **Poetry:** Free-verse only; $25. **Art:** For ages 8-13 only; please send 2-3 samples of your work. **Tips:** No adults! **Queries:** Not necessary. **E-queries:** No. **Unsolicited mss:** Accepts. **Response:** Queries 2 weeks, submissions 4 weeks, SASE. **Freelance Content:** 100%. **Rights:** All. **Payment:** On publication.

STORY FRIENDS
Mennonite Publishing House, 616 Walnut Ave, Scottdale, PA 15683. 724-887-8500. Monthly. Circ.: 6,000. Rose Stutzman, Editor. **Description:** For ages 4-9, promoting kindness, teaching children they are loved by God. Published by North American Mennonite Church. **Fiction:** Realistic stories that empower children to face fears; that help them enjoy and care for things in nature; 300-800 words; $.03/word. **Nonfiction:** About animals, unusual nature facts; about a child who has done something to promote kindness; cross-cultural experiences; 100-200 words; $.03/word. **Poetry:** Seasonal poems, or about ordinary events in child's life (i.e., new shoes); 8-20 lines; $10/poem. **Fillers:** Age-appropriate; puzzles, picture-based or with simple words and concepts. **Tips:** Humor and unique treatment of problem helps to break

in to this market. Avoid talking animals and "naughty children" stories. Avoid stories where adults provide all solutions; respect young characters' strength and ingenuity. Also, many parents of these readers have lived in third-world countries; they value cross-cultural understanding. **Queries:** Not necessary. **E-queries:** No. **Unsolicited mss:** Accepts. **Response:** SASE. **Freelance Content:** 70%. **Rights:** 1st, one-time. **Payment:** On acceptance. **Contact:** Susan Reith Swan.

SURPRISES

3000 N. 2nd St., Minneapolis, MN 55411-1608. 612-588-7571. Web site: www.graf-x.net. Bimonthly. Emily Meinke. **Description:** For readers 5-11. **Nonfiction:** Articles, 50-250 words; puzzles, games, artwork; pays $25-$100. **Payment:** On publication.

TOUCH

Box 7259, Grand Rapids, MI 49510. E-mail: sara@gemsgc.org. Web site: www.gospelcom.net/gems. Carol Smith, Managing Editor. **Description:** Upbeat fiction and features, 500-1,000 words, for Christian girls ages 8-14; personal life, nature, crafts. **Nonfiction:** Pays $.025/word, extra for photos. **Fillers:** Puzzles, pays $10-$15. **Tips:** Query with SASE for coming themes. **Payment:** On publication.

TURTLE MAGAZINE

1100 Waterway Blvd., PO Box 567, Indianapolis, IN 46206-0567. 317-636-8881. Web site: www.turtlemag.com. Bimonthly. Circ.: 300,000. Ms. Terry Harshman, Editor. **Description:** Emphasis on health and nutrition for 2- to 5-year-olds. **Fiction:** Humorous, entertaining fiction; to $.22/word. **Nonfiction:** Heavily illustrated articles with an emphasis on health and nutrition for 2- to 5-year-olds. Also, crafts, recipes, activities, simple science experiments, and read-aloud stories. Pay varies; To 300 words; To $.22/word. **Poetry:** Simple poems, action rhymes; From $25. **Rights:** All. **Payment:** On publication.

U.S. KIDS

P.O. Box 567, Indianapolis, IN 46206. 317-636-8881. E-mail: danny885@aol.com. Web site: www.uskids.com. 8x/year. $21.95/yr. Circ.: 250,000. Daniel Lee, Editor. **Description:** For kids, ages 6-10. True-life stories, science/nature features, health/fitness, kids in the news, color photos, and lots of fun games, activities, and contests. **Fiction:** Science fiction, nature, etc; 700 words; $.17/word. **Nonfiction:** Looking for profiles on interesting, regular kids (no celebrities), ages 5-10, involved in unusual pursuits (sports, adventures, science); 500-600 words; Pay varies. **Fillers:** Humor; 75 words; $35-$50. **Tips:** Avoid counter culture, irony/sarcasm, depressing topics. Stay upbeat and wholesome. **Queries:** Preferred. **E-queries:** Yes. **Unsolicited mss:** Accepts. **Response:** 12 weeks, SASE. **Freelance Content:** 20%. **Rights:** All. **Payment:** On publication.

WILD OUTDOOR WORLD
Box 1329, Helena, MT 59624. 406-449-1335.
E-mail: wowgirl@uswest.net. Web site: www.wowmag.com. Carolyn Cunningham.
Description: On North American wildlife, for readers ages 8-12. **Nonfiction:** Articles, 600-800 words; pays $100-$300. **Queries:** Preferred. **Payment:** On acceptance.

YES MAG
3968 Long Gun Place, Victoria, BC, Canada V8N 3A9. 250-477-5543.
E-mail: editor@yesmag.ca. Web site: www.yesmag.ca. Bimonthly. $3.25/$18 (Canadian). Circ.: 18,000. Shannon Hunt, Editor. **Description:** Canadian children's science magazine. Makes science accessible, interesting, and exciting, for children ages 8-14. Covers science and technology news, do-at-home projects, science-related book and software reviews, profiles of Canadian students and scientists. **Nonfiction:** Science, technology, engineering, and math articles for kids, ages 8-14; 250-1,250 words; $.15/word. **Tips:** Seeking imaginative, fun, well-researched pieces. Be specific in query; ideally send an outline of the article, indicating how you will approach the topic. **Queries:** Preferred. **E-queries:** Yes. **Unsolicited mss:** Accepts. **Response:** 2 weeks, SASE. **Freelance Content:** 60%. **Rights:** One-time. **Payment:** On publication.

YOUNG BUCKS OUTDOORS
P.O. Box 244022, Montgomery, AL 36124-4022. 1-800-240-3337.
E-mail: gsmith@buckmasters.com. Web site: www.youngbucks.rivals.com. Quarterly. free. Circ.: 25,000. Gita M. Smith, Editor. **Description:** For readers ages 7-13. Encourages children of all races, gender, and range of abilities to step outside and enjoy themselves. **Fiction:** Stories with child at center of plot. No "I recall when I was a child" stories; up to 800 words; $150-$250. **Nonfiction:** Stories about nature and outdoors pursuits (animals, birds, nature, camping, fishing, hunting, ecology, outdoor pastimes), suitable for a bright 10-year-old. Query first, include photo ideas; 200-1,000 words; $150-$400. **Art:** Prefers slides; $50-$500 (cover). **Tips:** No anti-hunting/fishing sentiments. Appreciates good science content in stories. Stories must be geared to 10-year-old's reading level. **Queries:** Required. **E-queries:** Yes. **Unsolicited mss:** Accepts. **Response:** Queries 1-2 weeks, submissions 3 months, SASE. **Freelance Content:** 90%. **Rights:** 1st print, electronic. **Payment:** On publication.

YOUNG RIDER
Box 8237, Lexington, KY 40533. 859-260-9800.
Web site: www.animalnetwork.com. Bimonthly. Lesley Ward. **Description:** About horses and children. **Nonfiction:** No overly sentimental stories, or stories with "goody two-shoes" characters, 1,200 word stories; pays $120. **Art:** Photos. **Tips:** Query or send manuscript. **Queries:** Not necessary. **Payment:** On publication.

YOUTHLINE USA FUN & FEATURE MAGAZINE

Bartash Printing, 300 Knickerbocker Rd., Cresskill, NJ 07626. 201-568-1333. Web site: www.youthline-usa.com. Monthly. Circ.: 250,000. **Description:** Educational magazine for children and young teens.

ZILLIONS

101 Truman Ave., Yonkers, NY 10703-1057. 914-378-2553. Web site: www.consumerreports.org. **Description:** An online version of Consumer Reports for children, found at Zillions.org. For readers, ages 8-14, with Internet access.

LIFESTYLES

ABLE

P.O. Box 395, Old Bethpage, NY 11804-0395. 516-939-2253. Web site: ablenews.com. Monthly. Angela Miele Melledy. **Description:** "Positively for, by, and about the disabled." **Nonfiction:** to 500 words; pays $25. **Art:** Color and b/w photos. **Payment:** On publication.

ACTIVE LIVING

P.O. Box 237, Grimbsy, Ontario Canada L3M 4G3. 905-957-6016. Bimonthly. **Description:** Health, fitness, and recreation magazine for people with a disability. **Nonfiction:** Articles, 750-1,000 words, on improving fitness and mobility, accessible travel and leisure, and new therapeutic and sporting activities; pays $.18/word. **Tips:** Avoid labeling or condescending language. **Queries:** Preferred. **Payment:** On publication.

AMERICAN SURVIVAL GUIDE

Y-Visionary, L.P., 265 S. Anita Dr., Suite 120, Orange, CA 92868. 714-939-9991,ex.204. Jim Benson. **Description:** On human and natural forces that pose threats to everyday life, all forms of preparedness, food production and storage, self defense and weapons, etc. **Nonfiction:** Articles, 1,500-2,000 words, with photos; pays $80/published page. **Art:** Photos essential for all articles. **Queries:** Preferred. **Payment:** On publication.

BLUE

611 Broadway, Suite 405, New York, NY 10012. 212-777-0024. E-mail: Claire@blueadventure.com. Web site: www.blueadventure.com. Bimonthly. Claire Hochachka, Executive Editor. **Description:** Seeks material that is wonderfully hip, personal, and alive, and also delivers information. Described by one reviewer as "National Geographic with a rock-and-roll soundtrack." **Nonfiction:** Features in 3 categories: Blue Planet, Blue Nation, and Blue Asphalt. Exploration is key, whether a profile of coal miners of Bolivia, or inline skating through Central Park. **Tips:** A well-written query is a good start. Convey your idea in a 500-word pitch;

include any appropriate writing samples. Relies on freelance contributions; is seeking new writers stationed in exotic locales with great stories to tell—who feel that life is, well, an adventure. **Queries:** Preferred. **E-queries:** Yes. **Unsolicited mss:** Accepts.

CAPPER'S

Ogden Publications, 1503 S.W. 42nd St., Topeka, KS 66609-1265. 785-274-4300. E-mail: cappers@cjnetworks.com. Web site: www.cappers.com. Bi-weekly. $27.95/year. Circ.: 250,000. Ann Crahan, Editor. **Description:** Focuses on home and family, for readers in the rural Midwest. **Fiction:** Query first, with brief description; $75-$300. **Nonfiction:** Inspirational, nostalgic, family-oriented, travel, human-interest; 700 words max.; $2.50/inch. **Poetry:** Easy to read, down-to-earth themes; 4-16 lines; $10-$15. **Fillers:** Jokes (limit submissions to batches of 5-6; no jokes returned); $2 gift certificate. **Art:** slides, transparencies, prints; include captions; $5-$40. **Queries:** Preferred. **E-queries:** Yes. **Unsolicited mss:** Accepts. **Response:** Submissions 2-6 months. SASE required. **Freelance Content:** 25%. **Rights:** FNASR. **Payment:** On publication.

CHRISTIAN SINGLE

127 Ninth Ave. N., Nashville, TN 37234-0140. **Description:** For single adults about leisure activities, issues related to single parents, inspiring personal experiences, humor, life from a Christian perspective. **Nonfiction:** Articles, 600-1,200 words; pay varies. **Queries:** Preferred. **Payment:** On acceptance. *No recent report.*

COLORADO HOMES AND LIFESTYLES

7009 S. Potomac St., Englewood, CO 80112. 303-662-5204. E-mail: emcgraw@coloradohomesmag.com. Web site: www.coloradohomesmag.com. 9x/year. $3.95/$16.97. Circ.: 35,000. Evalyn K. McGraw, Editor. **Description:** Affluent, upscale homes and lifestyles. **Nonfiction:** Articles, 1,300-1,500 words, on Colorado homes and interiors. Features on upscale homes, unusual lifestyles. **Columns, Departments:** Architecture, artists, food and wine, design trends, profiles, gardening, and travel; 1,100-1,300 words. **Queries:** Preferred. **Payment:** On acceptance.

DIVERSION

1790 Broadway, New York, NY 10019. 212-969-7517. E-mail: tpassavant@hearst.com. Web site: www.diversionmag.com. Monthly. Circ.: 175,000 physicians. Tom Passavant, Editor-in-Chief. **Description:** Travel and lifestyle magazine for physicians. No health-related subjects; features profiles of doctors who excel at nonmedical pursuits and volunteer medical work. **Nonfiction:** Travel, food, wine, sports, books, electronic gear, gardening, photography, art, music, film, television, finance and humor. 2,200 words, $800. **Columns, Departments:** 1,200 words, $500. **Art:** Do not send originals or slides. **Tips:** Query first with brief proposal, explain story focus; include credentials and clips of published work. **Queries:** Required. **E-queries:** Yes. **Unsolicited mss:** Accepts.

FIFTYPLUS

1510 Willow Lawn Dr., Suite 203, Richmond, VA 23230-3429. 804-673-5203. E-mail: rpmag@aol.com. Web site: www.fiftyplus.com. Monthly. $15/yr. Circ.: 30,000. George Cruger, Editor. **Description:** Reflects and enhances 50-plus lifestyles in Virginia region, with reader dialogue and input. **Queries:** Required. **E-queries:** Yes. **Response:** 2-4 weeks, SASE. **Rights:** 1st (regional). **Payment:** On publication.

HIP

1563 Solano Avenue, Suite 137, Berkeley, CA 94707. 510-848-9650. Web site: www.hipmag.org. **Description:** For children with a hearing loss.

HOME EDUCATION

P.O. Box 1083, Tonasket, WA 98855. 509-486-1351. Web site: www.home-edmagazine.com. Bimonthly. Helen Hegener, Managing Editor. **Description:** Seeking submissions from writers who are familiar with home schooling and can share the humorous side (and not be negative about the alternatives).

INMOTION

Amputee Coalition of America, 900 E. Hill Ave., Ste. 285, Knoxville, TN 37915. 865-524-8772. Web site: www.amputee-coalition.org. Bimonthly. Nancy Carroll. **Description:** On topics of interest to amputees (new technology, camps for children, etc.). **Nonfiction:** Articles, to 3,000 words; pays $.25-$.38/word. **Art:** Photos. **Payment:** On publication.

INSIDE

2100 Arch St., Philadelphia, PA 19102-3392. 215-832-0797. E-mail: mledger@insidemagazine.com. Quarterly. $3.50/issue, $10.95/year. Circ.: 60,000. Jane Biberman, Editor. **Description:** Focuses on Jewish lifestyle. Covers ethnic interest, as well as lifestyle subjects (fashion, home, health, finance, travel, dining). **Fiction:** 2,000 words; $500. **Nonfiction:** On Jewish issues, health, finance, and the arts; 2,000-3,000 words; $600-$1,000. **Art:** $250, illustrations. **Tips:** Write gracefully for upscale readers. Teach something useful. **Queries:** Preferred. **E-queries:** Yes. **Unsolicited mss:** Accepts. **Freelance Content:** 80%. **Rights:** 1st only. **Payment:** On publication.

LIVING ABOARD

P.O. Box 91299, Austin , TX 78709-1299. 512-892-4446. E-mail: editor@livingaboard.com. Web site: www.livingaboard.com. Linda Ridihalgh. **Description:** Lifestyle magazine for those who live or dream of living on their boats. **Nonfiction:** Articles, 1,000-2,000, on personal experience or practical information about living aboard; pays $.05/word. **Art:** Photos welcomed. **Tips:** Send complete manuscript with bio and credits; e-mail or disk submissions preferred. **Payment:** On publication.

LIVING IN BALANCE

7860 Peters Rd., Plantation, FL 33324. 954-382-4325.
E-mail: publisher@livinginbalancemagazine.com.
Web site: www.livinginbalancemagazine.com. **Description:** A "health, wealth and happiness" magazine. Strives to provide straightforward, expert and motivational solutions to pressing issues facing baby boomers. **Nonfiction:** Short articles on self-development and personal growth; 250-500 words. **Tips:** Send submissions in an e-mail attachment. **Queries:** Preferred. **E-queries:** Yes. **Unsolicited mss:** Accepts.

MAGICAL BLEND

133-1/2 Broadway St., Chico, CA 95928-5317. 888-296-2442.
E-mail: mbedit@outrageous.net. Web site: www.magicalblend.com. Bimonthly. Circ.: 60,000. Michael Peter Langevin, Editor. **Description:** Offers entertaining and unique look at modern spiritual lifestyles. **Nonfiction:** Positive, uplifting articles on spiritual exploration, alternative health, social change, self improvement, stimulating creativity, lifestyles, interviews; 2000 words max.; $250. **Art:** Hard or digital copies (233-3000 dpi). **Tips:** No preaching. **Queries:** Not necessary. **E-queries:** Yes. **Unsolicited mss:** Accepts. **Response:** Queries 1-3 months, submissions 1-6 months. **Freelance Content:** 90%. **Payment:** On publication.

MEN'S JOURNAL

1290 Avenue of the Americas, New York, NY 10104-0298. 212-484-1616.
Web site: www.mensjournal.com. 10 x/year. Circ.: 550,000. Mark Bryant, Editor. **Description:** Lifestyle magazine for active men, ages 25-49. **Nonfiction:** Articles and profiles on travel, fitness, health, adventure, and participatory sports; 2,000-7,000 words; good rates. **Columns, Departments:** Equipment, Fitness; 400-1,800 words. **Queries:** Required. **Payment:** On acceptance.

MOTHER EARTH NEWS

P.O. Box 56302, Boulder, CO 80322. 800-234-3368.
E-mail: letters@motherearthnews.com. Web site: www.motherearthnews.com. Bimonthly. Circ.: 450,000. Matthew Scanlon, Editor. **Description:** Helps readers become more self-sufficient, financially independent, and environmentally aware. For rural and urban readers: home improvements, how-tos, indoor and outdoor gardening, health, food, ecology, energy, and consumerism. **Nonfiction:** Articles on organic gardening, building projects, herbal or home remedies, alternative energy projects, wild foods, and environment and conservation; pay varies. **Art:** Photos, diagrams. **Payment:** On publication.

MOTORHOME

2575 Vista Del Mar, Ventura, CA 93001. 805-667-4100.
Web site: www.motorhomemagazine.com. Barbara Leonard, Editor. **Description:** Covers destinations for RV travelers. Also, activities, hobbies, and how-tos. **Nonfiction:** Travel destinations and other articles; 150-2,500 words; $100-500. **Columns, Departments:** Crossroads (varied topics: unique motorhomes to great

cafes, museums to festivals; with 1-2 good color transparencies); Quick Tips (do-it-yourself ideas for motorhomes; no photo, just a sketch if necessary; 150 words; $100). **Art:** 35mm slides, $25-500. **Tips:** Departments are easiest way to break in. Readers are active travelers; most retirees, but more baby boomers entering the RV lifestyle, so some articles directed to novices, families. No diaries or product tests. **Queries:** Preferred. **E-queries:** No. **Unsolicited mss:** Accepts. **Response:** 3-4 weeks, SASE. **Freelance Content:** 65%. **Payment:** On acceptance.

MOUNTAIN LIVING
7009 S. Potomac St., Englewood, CO 80112-4037. 303-397-7600. E-mail: irawlings@mountainliving.com. Web site: www.mountainliving.com. 6x/year. $3.95/issue. Circ.: 38,000. Irene Rawlings, Editor. **Description:** Home, garden, travel, and decorating; for people who live in the mountains or dream of living there. **Nonfiction:** 100-1,200 words; $35-$500. **Columns, Departments:** Destinations, Trail's End. **Tips:** Best way to break in: write for Destinations or back-page essay, Trail's End. **Queries:** Required. **E-queries:** Yes. **Unsolicited mss:** Accepts. **Response:** 4 weeks. **Freelance Content:** 50%. **Payment:** On acceptance.

NATURAL HOME
201 E. 4th St., Loveland, CO 80537. 970-669-7672. E-mail: claudia@naturalhomemagazine.com. Web site: www.naturalhomemagazine.com. Claudia Chesneau, Editorial Assistant. **Description:** Promotes earth-inspired living. Features "green," sustainable homes and lifestyles. **Nonfiction:** Pays $.33-$.55/word; 300-2,000 words. **Tips:** Needs fresh, cutting-edge ideas on green living; also small, newsy items for front-of-the-book Journal section. Submit query or complete manuscript. Guidelines available for SASE or by e-mail. **Queries:** Preferred. **E-queries:** Yes. **Unsolicited mss:** Accepts. **Rights:** 1st NA. **Payment:** On publication.

NATURAL LIVING TODAY
Tyler Publishing, 175 Varick St., 9th Fl., New York, NY 10014. 212-924-1762. Web site: www.naturallivingmag.com. Bimonthly. , Editorial Department. **Description:** On all aspects of a natural lifestyle for women. **Nonfiction:** Articles, 1,000-2,000 words; pays $75-$200. **Queries:** Preferred. **Payment:** On publication.

PENTHOUSE VARIATIONS
11 Penn Plaza, 12th Fl., New York, NY 10001. 212-702-6000. E-mail: variations@generalmedia.com. Web site: www.variations.com. Monthly. $4.99/issue, $30/year. Circ.: 400,000. Victor Kingy, Associate Publisher. **Description:** Offers couples-style erotica for liberated lovers (healthy sexual acts and fantasy). **Nonfiction:** First-person narrative accounts of highly explicit sex scenes; 3,000; $400. **Tips:** Original work only. **Queries:** Not necessary. **E-queries:** No. **Unsolicited mss:** Accepts. **Response:** Queries 1 month, submissions 2 months, SASE required. **Freelance Content:** 100%. **Rights:** All. **Payment:** On acceptance.

PERCEPTIONS

10736 Jefferson Blvd., Suite 502, Culver City, CA 90230.
Judi V. Brewer, Editor. **Description:** For single adults about leisure activities, issues related to single parents, inspiring personal experiences, humor, life from a Christian perspective. **Nonfiction:** Articles, 600-1,200 words; pay varies. **Queries:** Preferred. **Payment:** On acceptance. *No recent report.*

PRESENCE SENSE

P.O. Box 547, Rancocas, NJ 08073.
E-mail: presencesensemag@jersey.net. Web site: www.PresenceSense.com. Bimonthly. Circ.: 5,000. Kimberly Teed, Editor. **Description:** Looks at social customs, etiquette, and lifestyle. **Nonfiction:** Articles on manners, humor, recipes, wedding planning, and life's pleasures and mysteries; length varies. **Queries:** Preferred.

REUNIONS

P.O. Box 11727, Milwaukee, WI 53211-0727. 414-263-4567.
E-mail: reunions@execpc.com. Web site: www.reunionsmag.com. Quarterly. $6/$24. Circ.: 12,000. Edith Wagner, Editor. **Description:** For persons who are organizing a family, class, military, or other reunion. **Fiction:** About reunion tips and techniques (e.g. How to make a memory book sparkle, how to cook for 150); 1,500 words max., prefer shorter; $20-$50. **Fillers:** Brief tips/hints; Clippings (about reunions for us to summarize); funny material; puzzles (appropriate for reunions). Examples: photo preservation, should you invite teachers?, time capsules, hot ideas, etc.; 500 works or less; $5-$10. **Art:** With articles. **Tips:** Avoid class-reunion catharsis. **Queries:** Not necessary. **E-queries:** Yes. **Response:** over 2 years at present, SASE. **Freelance Content:** 70%. **Rights:** One-time. **Payment:** On publication.

ROBB REPORT

1 Acton Pl., Acton, MA 01720. 978-795-3000.
Web site: www.theluxurysource.com. Monthly. Circ.: 100, 000. Larry Bean, Editor. **Description:** Consumer magazine for high-end luxury market. Lifestyles, home interiors, boats, travel, investment opportunities, exotic automobiles, business, technology, etc. **Nonfiction:** Geared to affluent lifestyles (travel, fashion, automobiles, etc.); 500-5,000 words. **Queries:** Required. **E-queries:** No. **Unsolicited mss:** Accepts. **Response:** 1-3 months, SASE. **Freelance Content:** 75%. **Rights:** All. **Payment:** On publication.

SECOND HOME

Wiesner Publishing, 1100 Johnson Ferry Rd., Ste. 595,
Atlanta, GA 30342. 404-252-6670.
Web site: www.secondhomemag.com. Oma Blaise, Editor. **Description:** For second-home owners and buyers. **Queries:** Preferred. **Contact:** Lisa Gaddy.

SIMPLER LIVING

P.O. Box 61605, Santa Barbara, CA 93111.
E-mail: editor@simplerliving.com. Web site: www.simplerliving.com. Monthly. Edel Jarboe, Editor. **Description:** Online publication, focused on women who want to improve their lives. Articles with practical information about work, money, health and nutrition, fitness, parenting, relationships, cooking, time management. **Nonfiction:** 500-2,000 words; $30 (features); $10 (reprints). **Tips:** Looking for self-help articles based on interviews or research. Query with subject of article, title, word count, and 50-word description. **Queries:** Required. **E-queries:** Yes. **Response:** 2-3 days. **Rights:** 1st online (for 1 month).

SMOKE AFFAIR

6685 Via Regina, Boca Raton, FL 33433. 719-635-5200.
E-mail: micky@smokeaffair.com. 3x/year. $11.50. Circ.: 50,000. Micky Handler, Editor. **Description:** Upscale,full-color, glossy publication focusing on the lifestyle of the cigar smoker. **Nonfiction:** Articles featuring travel and leisure, financial, real estate investment, the arts, and cigar personalities; 1,000-4,000 words; negotiable fee. **Art:** Photo/art discussed on assignment. **Tips:** Welcome new writers; seeking writers for assignments. **Queries:** Preferred. **E-queries:** Yes. **Unsolicited mss:** Accepts. **Response:** 30 days, SASE required. **Rights:** negotiable. **Payment:** On publication.

SOUTHERN ACCENTS

2100 Lakeshore Dr., Birmingham, AL 35209. 205-877-6000.
Web site: www.southernaccents.com. Bimonthly. $28. Circ.: 350,000. Frances MacDougall, Senior Editor. **Description:** Celebrates southern style in interiors, gardens, art, antiques, and entertaining. Focuses on affluent houses and gardens in a 16-state region. Also features the homes of southerners living abroad, also travel destinations visited by upscale readership. **Nonfiction:** Query first with appropriate story ideas; 800-1,200 words; pay negotiable. **Queries:** Preferred. **Payment:** On acceptance.

SUNSET

80 Willow Rd., Menlo Park, CA 94025. 650-321-3600.
Web site: www.sunset.com. Monthly. $3.99. Circ.: 1,500,000. Rosalie Muller Wright, Editor. **Description:** Regional magazine for Western America, covering travel and recreation; garden and outdoor living; food and entertaining; building, design, and crafts. **Nonfiction:** Looking for well-written stories and Travel Guide items offering satisfying travel experiences accomplished in a day or weekend, or as part of a vacation, in American West, also parts of Canada and Mexico; 300-1,000 words; $1/word. **Queries:** Preferred. **E-queries:** No. **Unsolicited mss:** Does not accept. **Response:** 1-3 months, SASE. **Freelance Content:** 5%. **Payment:** On acceptance.

TOWN & COUNTRY

1700 Broadway, New York, NY 10019. 212-903-5000.
Web site: www.hearstcorp.com. Monthly. Circ.: 488,000. Pamela Fiori, Editor.

Description: For upscale market, covers travel, beauty, fashion, individuals, and the arts. **Nonfiction:** Considers 1-page proposals; include clips, resumé. **Queries:** Required. **Unsolicited mss:** Does not accept. **Freelance Content:** 40%. **Payment:** On acceptance.

TRAILER LIFE

2575 Vista Del Mar, Ventura, CA 93001. 805-667-4352.
E-mail: bleonard@affinity.com. Web site: www.rv.net. Monthly. $3.99. Circ.: 280,000. Barbara Leonard, Editor. **Description:** New product information and tests, do-it-yourself articles, plus North American travel and lifestyle for RV owners. **Nonfiction:** On trailers, motor homes, truck campers used by active adventurous travelers, visiting interesting destinations and participating in colorful hobbies; 200-2,000 words; pays $100-$700. **Fillers:** 50-1,000 words; $75-$400. **Art:** 35mm, 2¼; $75-$250; $500-$700 (cover). **Tips:** Supply good photos (35 mm slides) and submit a complete package. **Queries:** Required. **E-queries:** Yes. **Response:** 2-3 weeks, SASE. **Freelance Content:** 45%. **Rights:** 1st NA and electronic. **Payment:** On acceptance.

VEGGIE LIFE

1041 Shary Cir., Concord, CA 94518. 925-671-9852.
Web site: www.veggielife.com. Quarterly. Deerra Shehabi. **Description:** For people interested in lowfat, meatless cuisine, natural health, nutrition, and herbal healing. **Nonfiction:** Food features (include 8-10 recipes); 1,500-2,000 words. **Columns, Departments:** 1,000-1,500 words. **Queries:** Preferred. **Payment:** On publication.

WHOLE LIFE TIMES

21225 Pacific Coast Hwy., Suite B, P.O. Box 1187, Malibu, CA 90265. 310-317-4200. E-mail: swholelifex@aol.com. Web site: www.wholelifetimes.com. Monthly. Free. Circ.: 58,000. Abigail Lewis, Editor. **Description:** Covers holistic lifestyle: health, healing, food and nutrition, environment, spirituality, personal growth, travel, science and metaphysics, longevity. **Nonfiction:** Up to 2,000 words; $.05/word. **Tips:** Understand the holistic mindset. Readers are fairly sophisticated; avoid "Yoga 101." Contact for upcoming themes. **Queries:** Not necessary. **E-queries:** Yes. **Unsolicited mss:** Accepts. **Response:** 1 month-1 year, SASE. **Freelance Content:** 75%. **Rights:** 1st NA. **Payment:** On publication. **Contact:** Kerri Hikida, Assoc. Ed.

WIRED

660 Third St., 1st Floor, San Francisco, CA 94107. 800-769-4733.
E-mail: submit@wired.com. Web site: www.wired.com. Monthly. Circ.: 500,000. Katrian Heron, Editor in Chief. **Description:** Lifestyle magazine for the "digital generation." Discusses the meaning and context of digital technology in today's world. **Fiction:** Yes. **Nonfiction:** Articles, essays, profiles, etc.; pay varies. **Payment:** On acceptance.

YOGA JOURNAL
2054 University Ave., #601, Berkeley, CA 94704-1082. 510-841-9200. Web site: www.yogajournal.com. Monthly. Circ.: 130,000. Kathryn Arnold, Editor in Chief. **Description:** Serves the hatha yoga community. Holistic health, meditation, conscious living, spirituality, and yoga. **Queries:** Preferred. **E-queries:** Yes. **Unsolicited mss:** Accepts. **Response:** 4 weeks, SASE. **Freelance Content:** 10%. **Rights:** non-exclusive worldwide, print and non-print. **Payment:** On acceptance. **Contact:** Nora Isaacs.

MEN'S

ADAM
4517 Harford Rd., Baltimore, MD 21214. 410-254-9200. E-mail: adameditor@aol.com. Web site: adam-mag.com. Bimonthly. $14.95/yr. Miguel Vilar, Editor. **Description:** For boys and men, ages 15-35. Offers creative nonfiction, opinion, personal experience, informational and self-help articles, profiles, and interviews. **Fiction:** 2,000 words; $400. **Nonfiction:** Articles on history, video, audio, music, relationships, electronics, computers, sports and entertainment. Example: A boy's view of the U.S. Civil War; 1,500-2,000 words; $350-$400. **Fillers:** Humor, jokes, puzzles; pay varies. **Columns, Departments:** 500-800 words; $300. **Tips:** Avoid first-person, and use quotes from experts. **Queries:** Preferred. **E-queries:** Yes. **Response:** 2-4 weeks, SASE required. **Freelance Content:** 50%. **Rights:** 1st. **Payment:** On publication.

CHIC
8484 Wilshire Blvd., Suite 900, Beverly Hills, CA 90211. 323-651-5400. Web site: www.chic.com. Ellen Thompson, Editor. **Description:** Sex-related articles, interviews, erotic fiction, 2,500 words. Pays $150 for brief interviews, $350 for fiction **Tips:** Need not query for fiction. **Queries:** Preferred. **Payment:** On acceptance.

ESQUIRE
250 W. 55th St., New York, NY 10019. 212-649-2000. E-mail: esquire@hearst.com. Web site: www.esquire.com. Monthly. David Granger, Editor in Chief. **Description:** For intelligent adult male readers. **Fiction:** Short stories; submit only 1 at a time. No pornography, science fiction, poetry, or "true romance"; pay varies. **Nonfiction:** 2,500-6,500 words; pay varies. **Tips:** Query with clips; unpublished writers, send complete manuscripts. **Queries:** Required. **Payment:** On publication.

GALLERY
401 Park Ave. S., New York, NY 10016-8802. 212-779-8900. Web site: www.gallerymagazine.com. C.S. O'Brien, Editor. **Description:** Articles, investigative pieces, interviews, profiles. Also, erotic and general fiction, short humor,

satire, service pieces, to 2,500 words, for men's market. We encourage quality work from unpublished writers. Pay varies, send SASE for guidelines. **Payment:** On publication.

GENESIS
210 E. State Rt. 4, #211, Paramus, NJ 07652. 201-843-4004. Web site: www.genesismagazine.com. Dan Davis, Managing Editor. **Description:** Sexually explicit fiction and nonfiction features, 800-2,000 words. Celebrity interviews, photo-essays, product and film reviews. **Tips:** Send clips. **Queries:** Preferred. **Payment:** On publication.

GENTLEMEN'S QUARTERLY
Conde Nast Publications, Inc., 4 Times Square, New York, NY 10036. Monthly. **Description:** For male readers. Covers politics, personalities, lifestyles, trends, grooming, sports, travel, business. **Nonfiction:** Articles, 1,500-4,000 words. **Columns, Departments:** Private Lives (essays by men on life); All about Adam (nonfiction by women about men); Games (sports); Health; Humor; also on fitness, nutrition, investments, music, wine and food. 1,000-2,500 words. **Tips:** Send clips. **Queries:** Required. **Unsolicited mss:** Does not accept.

MEN'S FITNESS
21100 Erwin St., Woodland Hills, CA 91367. 818-884-6800. Web site: www.mensfitness.com. Jerry Kindela, Editor. **Description:** On sports, fitness, health, nutrition, and men's issues. **Nonfiction:** Authoritative, practical articles, 1,500-1,800 words; pays $500-$1,000. **Columns, Departments:** 1,200-1,500 words. **Tips:** Send clips. **Queries:** Preferred. **Payment:** On acceptance.

MEN'S HEALTH
Rodale Press, 33 E. Minor St., Emmaus, PA 18098. 610-967-5171. Web site: www.menshealth.com. 10x/year. $3.79. Circ.: 1,600,000. David Zinczenko, Senior Editor. **Description:** Covers fitness, health, sex, nutrition, relationships, lifestyle, sports, travel. **Nonfiction:** Useful articles, for men ages 25-55; 1,000-2,000 words; $.50/word. **Queries:** Required. **E-queries:** Yes. **Payment:** On acceptance.

MEN'S JOURNAL
1290 Avenue of the Americas, New York, NY 10104-0298. 212-484-1616. Web site: www.mensjournal.com. 10 x/year. Circ.: 550,000. Mark Bryant, Editor. **Description:** Lifestyle magazine for active men, ages 25-49. **Nonfiction:** Articles and profiles on travel, fitness, health, adventure, and participatory sports; 2,000-7,000 words; good rates. **Columns, Departments:** Equipment, Fitness; 400-1,800 words. **Queries:** Required. **Payment:** On acceptance.

PENTHOUSE
11 Penn Plaza, 12th Floor, New York, NY 10001. 212-702-6000. Web site: www.penthousemag.com. Monthly. Circ.: 1,100,000. Peter Bloch, Editor.

Description: Essays, sociological studies, travel, humor, food and fashion, for the sophisticated male. **Fiction:** No unsolicited fiction. **Nonfiction:** General-interest profiles, interviews (with introduction), and investigative or controversial pieces; to 5,000 words; to $1/word. **Queries:** Preferred.

PLAYBOY
680 North Shore Dr., Chicago, IL 60611. 312-751-8000.
E-mail: articles@playboy.com. Monthly. Circ.: 3,125,000. Stephen Randall, Editor.
Description: For urban men. **Fiction:** Sophisticated fiction, 1,000-10,000 words (5,000 preferred), for urban men. Pays $2,000 for short-shorts. **Nonfiction:** Articles, 3,500-6,000 words, for urban men; pays to $5,000. **Queries:** Required. **E-queries:** No. **Unsolicited mss:** Does not accept. **Response:** 1 month, SASE. **Rights:** FNASR. **Payment:** On acceptance.

SMOKE AFFAIR
6685 Via Regina, Boca Raton, FL 33433. 719-635-5200.
E-mail: micky@smokeaffair.com. 3x/year. $11.50. Circ.: 50,000. Micky Handler, Editor. **Description:** Upscale,full-color, glossy publication focusing on the lifestyle of the cigar smoker. **Nonfiction:** Articles featuring travel and leisure, financial, real estate investment, the arts, and cigar personalities; 1,000-4,000 words; negotiable fee. **Art:** Photo/art discussed on assignment. **Tips:** Welcome new writers; seeking writers for assignments. **Queries:** Preferred. **E-queries:** Yes. **Unsolicited mss:** Accepts. **Response:** 30 days, SASE required. **Rights:** negotiable. **Payment:** On publication.

MILITARY

AIR COMBAT
7950 Deering Ave., Canoga Park, CA 91304-5007.
Bimonthly. Michael O'Leary. **Description:** Articles on latest warplanes and the men who fly them, recent air battles, and America's aerial involvement in Vietnam. **Tips:** Send for guidelines. **Queries:** Preferred.

AMERICA'S CIVIL WAR
Primedia History Group, 741 Miller Dr. SE, Suite D2,
Leesburg, VA 20175-8920. 703-779-8302.
Web site: www.historynet.com. Bi-monthly. $3.99/issue. Circ.: 110,000. Roy Morris, Editor. **Description:** Popular history for general readers and Civil War buffs, on strategy, tactics, history, narrative. **Nonfiction:** Strategy, tactics, personalities, arms and equipment; 3,500-4,000 words, plus 500-word sidebar; $200-400. **Columns, Departments:** 2,000 words or less; $100-200. **Art:** Cite known color or b/w illustrations, and sources (museums, historical societies, private collections, etc.). **Tips:** Readable style and historical accuracy imperative. Use action and quotes where possible. Attribute quotes, cite major sources. **Queries:** Preferred. **E-queries:** No.

Unsolicited mss: Accepts. **Response:** 6 months, SASE. **Freelance Content:** 98%. **Payment:** Both on acceptance and on publication; kill fee offered.

ARMOR

4401 Vine Grove Rd., Fort Knox, KY 40121-2103. 502-624-2249. Bi-monthly. $3/issue. Circ.: 12,500. John Clemons, Managing Editor. **Description:** Professional magazine of the Armor Branch for military units and agencies responsible for direct-fire ground combat. **Nonfiction:** Military history; research and development of armaments; tactical benefits and strategies, logistics, and related topics; up to 13 double-spaced pages. **Art:** Write captions on paper and tape to the back of the photos (don't write on photo backs). Indicate if you want the photos returned. **Response:** Submissions, 2 weeks.

ARMY

2425 Wilson Blvd., Box 1560, Arlington, VA 22201-3385. 703-841-4300. E-mail: armymag@ausa.org. Web site: www.ausa.org. Monthly. Circ.: 1,000. Mary Blake French, Editor-in-Chief. **Description:** Military subjects, essays, humor, history (especially World War II), news reports, first-person anecdotes. **Nonfiction:** 1,500 words; $.12-$.18/word. **Fillers:** Cartoons, strong military slant; $35-$50. **Columns, Departments:** Military news, books, commentary. **Art:** 35mm slides, 8x10 b/w; 8x10 color glossy prints; pay varies. **Queries:** Not necessary. **E-queries:** No. **Unsolicited mss:** Accepts. **Freelance Content:** 70%. **Rights:** All. **Payment:** On publication. **Contact:** Mary Blake French.

ARMY RESERVE

1421 Jefferson, Davis Hwy., Suite 12300, Arlington, VA 22202-3259. 703-601-0854. Vicki Washington, Editor. **Description:** Military training and the history of the Army Reserve, interesting people, military family life, humor, and anecdotes. **Tips:** Submit manuscripts with quality color slides or photos.

COAST GUARD

Commandant (G-IPA-1), 2100 2nd St. SW, Room 3403, Washington, D.C. 20593. E-mail: vcady@comdt.uscg.mil. Web site: www.uscg.mil/hq/g-cp/cb/magazine.html. Monthly. $44/yr. Circ.: 23,000. PAC Veronica Cady, Editor. **Description:** Mainly for active-duty members of the Coast Guard. No payment offered. **Fiction:** Coast Guard or general military-related items only. **Nonfiction:** Same as fiction. **Art:** Photos, illustrations. **Queries:** Preferred. **E-queries:** Yes. **Unsolicited mss:** Does not accept. **Response:** Queries, 5-10 days. **Freelance Content:** 0%. **Rights:** Associated Press only.

COMMAND

P.O. Box 4017, San Luis Obispo, CA 93403. 805-546-9596. Web site: www.commandmagazine.com. Bimonthly. Ty Bomba. **Description:** On military history or current military affairs. **Nonfiction:** Articles; popular, not scholarly, analytical military history, 800-10,000 words; pays $.05/word. **Queries:** Preferred. **Payment:** On publication.

FAMILY

51 Atlantic Ave., Suite 200, Floral Park, NY 11001. 516-616-1930. Web site: www.familymedia.com. Monthly. Stacy P. Brassington. **Description:** For military families. Covers topics of interest to women with children (military lifestyle, home decorating, travel, moving, food, personal finances, career, relationships, family, parenting, health and fitness). **Nonfiction:** Articles, 1,000-2,000 words; pays to $200. **Payment:** On publication.

LEATHERNECK

Box 1775, Quantico, VA 22134-0776. 703-640-6161. Web site: www.mca-marines.org. William V. H. White, Editor. **Description:** On U.S. Marines. **Nonfiction:** Articles, to 3,000 words, with photos; pays $50/printed page. **Queries:** Preferred. **Payment:** On acceptance.

MARINE CORPS GAZETTE

Box 1775, Quantico, VA 22134. 703-640-6161. E-mail: gazette@mca-marines.org. Monthly. $3/$23. Circ.: 29,099. Jack Glascow, Editor. **Description:** Professional journal of U.S. Marines, oriented to officers and senior enlisted. **Nonfiction:** On the U.S. Marine Corps of today, tomorrow, and yesterday; 750-1,500; pay varies. **Tips:** Serves primarily as a forum for active duty officers to exchange views on professional topics. **Queries:** Preferred. **E-queries:** Yes. **Unsolicited mss:** Accepts. **Rights:** All. **Payment:** On publication.

MHQ: QUARTERLY JOURNAL OF MILITARY HISTORY

Primedia History Group, 741 Miller Dr. S.E., Suite D-2, Leesburg, VA 20175. 703-771-9400. Web site: www.historynet.com. Quarterly. $48/year. Circ.: 45,000. Mike Haskew, Editor. **Description:** Offers an undistorted view of history, encourages understanding of events, personalities, and artifacts of the past. **Nonfiction:** Well-written military history; 3,500-4,000 words, with 500-word sidebar; $200-$400. **Columns, Departments:** 2,500 words. **Art:** Color, b/w illustrations. **Queries:** Preferred. **E-queries:** Yes. **Unsolicited mss:** Accepts. **Response:** Queries 2-4 weeks, submissions 6-8 weeks,SASE. **Freelance Content:** 50%. **Payment:** On publication.

MILITARY

2122 28th St., Sacramento, CA 95818. 916-457-8990. E-mail: military@ns.net. Web site: www.milmag.com. Monthly. $14.79/yr. Circ.: 18,000. Rick McCusker, Editor. **Description:** Military history (WWII, Korea, Viet Nam, and today). Dedicated to all who served in the armed forces. **Nonfiction:** Personal war experiences; 4,000 words or less. **Fillers:** Humor in uniform, military humor; 1,000 words or less. **Art:** 200 dpi or better. **Queries:** Preferred. **E-queries:** Yes. **Unsolicited mss:** Accepts. **Payment:** No payment.

NATIONAL GUARD

One Massachusetts Ave. NW, Washington, DC 20001-1431. 202-789-0031. Web site: www.ngaus.org. **Description:** Articles on national defense. **Nonfiction:** Pay varies. **Queries:** Preferred. **Payment:** On publication.

NAVAL AVIATION NEWS

1231 10th St. SE, Suite 1000, Washington, DC 20374-5059. 202-433-4407. E-mail: nanews@nhc.navy.mil. Web site: www.history.navy.mil. Bi-monthly. $16. Circ.: 27,000. Cdr. Jim Carlton. **Description:** For the U.S. Naval Aviation community, with history, technology, and personnel issues. Limited freelance content. **Nonfiction:** Naval Aviation history, operations. **Art:** High-rez JPG or TIF; color, b/w, slide. **Queries:** Preferred. **E-queries:** Yes. **Unsolicited mss:** Accepts. **Response:** 3 weeks, SASE not needed. **Freelance Content:** 2%.

RETIRED MILITARY FAMILY

51 Atlantic Ave., #200, Floral Park, NY 11001-2721. 516-616-1930. Web site: www.familymedia.com. Stacy P. Brassington. **Description:** For military retirees and their families. Covers travel, finance, food, hobbies, second careers, grandparenting, etc. **Nonfiction:** Articles, 1,000-1,500 words; pays to $200. **Payment:** On publication.

RETIRED OFFICER

201 N. Washington St., Alexandria, VA 22314-2539. 703-838-8115. E-mail: editor@troa.org. Web site: www.troa.org/magazine. Monthly. $20/yr. Circ.: 386,000. Warren S. Lacy, Editor. **Description:** For retired and soon-to-be-retired members. Readers (commissioned/warrant officers, families, and surviving spouses) represent one of the youngest, most active groups in the senior market. **Nonfiction:** Current military/political affairs, recent history (especially Vietnam and Korea), retirement topics, and general interest. Original only, no reprints; 1,400-2,500 words; $1,200-$1,700. **Columns, Departments:** Travel; financial planning; health and fitness; military family; retirement lifestyles; and general interest; 750 words; $500. **Art:** Color transparencies preferred. **Tips:** Active voice, nontechnical, with direct quotes. Optimistic, upbeat themes. **Queries:** Required. **E-queries:** Yes. **Unsolicited mss:** Does not accept. **Response:** 90 days. **Rights:** 1st, also Internet and reprint. **Payment:** On acceptance. **Contact:** Heather Lyons.

SIGNAL

4400 Fair Lakes Court, Fairfax, VA 22033-3899. 703-631-6100. E-mail: signal@afcea.org. Web site: www.afcea.org/signal. Monthly. $50. Circ.: 30,000. Maryann Lawlor, Senior Editor. **Description:** Focuses on communications, electronics in the information systems arena. Reader include military, industry and government leadership. **Nonfiction:** Communications/electronics issues within military, industry and government; 1,400-2,500 words; $650 for 1,800 words. **Art:** Must include art with submission. **Tips:** Only works with published writers. **Queries:**

Required. **E-queries:** Yes. **Unsolicited mss:** Accepts. **Response:** 1-4 months, SASE required. **Freelance Content:** 10%. **Rights:** 1st. **Payment:** On publication.

TIMES NEWS SERVICE

Army Times Publishing Co., Springfield, VA 22159. 703-750-7479. E-mail: gwillis@atpco.com. Web site: www.militarycity.com. Weekly. $2.25/$52. Circ.: 300,000. G.E. Willis, Features Editor. **Description:** Publishes *Air Force Times, Army Times, Navy Times* (Gannett weeklies serving the military community, covering breaking developments that affect the careers of readers). **Nonfiction:** Features on contemporary home and family life in the military. Recreation, finances, parenting, etc.; up to 1,500 words; up to $500. **Columns, Departments:** Fitness for young and athletic people; personal finance for moderate incomes; 500 words; $200. **Art:** color slides, electronic (high-rez .jpeg); $75/image. **Tips:** Pitch an original story, interesting and entertaining, with a military connection, preferably with military people in the story. **Queries:** Required. **E-queries:** Yes. **Unsolicited mss:** Does not accept. **Response:** Queries 2-8 weeks, submissions 1-3 weeks, SASE. **Freelance Content:** 75%. **Payment:** On acceptance.

VFW

406 W. 34th St., Kansas City, MO 64111. 816-756-3390. E-mail: pbrown@vfw.org. Web site: www.vfw.org. Monthly. $10/yr. Circ.: 1,800,000. Richard K. Kolb, Editor. **Description:** Focuses on military history, issues relating to veterans and the military. **Nonfiction:** Articles on current foreign policy and defense, along with all veterans' issues; 1,000 words. **Tips:** Write with clarity and simplicity, concrete detail and short paragraphs. Use active voice, and avoid flowery prose and military jargon. **Queries:** Preferred. **Unsolicited mss:** Accepts. **Rights:** FNASR. **Payment:** On publication.

VIETNAM

Primedia History Group, 741 Miller Dr. S.E., Suite D-2, Leesburg, VA 20175-8920. 703-771-9400. E-mail: sbailey@cowles.com. Web site: www.thehistorynet.com. Bi-monthly. $3.99/issue, $19.95/year. Circ.: 100,000. David T. Zabecki, Editor. **Description:** Popular military-history magazine. Seeks to record and document "the many truths about Vietnam." **Nonfiction:** First-person and third-person accounts of all aspects of Vietnam War; strategy, tactics, personalities, arms and equipment; 3,500-4,000 words; $200. **Columns, Departments:** Arsenal, Fighting Forces, Personality, Perspectives; 1,500-2,000 words; $100-$150. **Tips:** Readers are Vietnam veterans, current military personnel, military historians and enthusiasts. Does not publish "war stories." **Queries:** Preferred. **E-queries:** Accepts. **Unsolicited mss:** Accepts. **Rights:** All worldwide, reprint. **Payment:** On publication.

WORLD WAR II

Primedia History Group, 741 Miller Dr. S.E., Suite D-2, Leesburg, VA 20175-8920. 703-779-8302. Web site: www.thehistorynet.com. Bimonthly. Michael Haskew, Editor. **Description:** Strategy, tactics, personalities, arms and equipment. **Nonfiction:** Features, 3,500-4,00 words, plus 500-word sidebar; up to $200. **Art:** Cite any color or b/w illustrations, and sources. **Tips:** Readable style and historical accuracy imperative. **Queries:** Preferred. **Unsolicited mss:** Accepts. **Response:** 6 months, SASE. **Rights:** Exclusive worldwide. **Payment:** On publication.

NEW AGE & SPIRITUAL

ALIVE NOW!

P.O. Box 340004, Nashville, TN 37203-0004. 615-340-7218. E-mail: mtidwell@upperroom.org. Web site: www.upperroom.org/alivenow/. Bimonthly. $3/issue, $11.95/year. Circ.: 65,000. Melissa Tidwell, Editor. **Description:** Encourages those looking for a sacred way of living in the world. Each issue focuses on contemporary topic, explored through prayers, personal experiences, poetry, photographs, and art. **Nonfiction:** Personal experiences of how contemporary issues affect spiritual life, meditations on scripture, prayers, and litanies; 350-600 words; $40-$150. **Poetry:** On the issue's theme; 40 lines or less; $25-$100. **Tips:** See website for coming themes. Use inclusive language, and personal approach. "Don't tell us what we should believe; tell us why you believe what you do!" Readership is clergy and lay, across denominations and theological spectrum. **Queries:** Not necessary. **E-queries:** Yes. **Unsolicited mss:** Accepts. **Response:** Queries 30 days, submissions 60 days, SASE required. **Freelance Content:** 30%. **Rights:** serial (print and electronic). **Payment:** On acceptance.

AQUARIUS

1035 Green St., Roswell, GA 30075. 770-641-9055. E-mail: aquarius-editor@mindspring.com. Web site: www.aquarius-atlanta.com. Monthly. free at newsstands; $30/yr. by mail. Circ.: 50,000. Kathryn Sargent, Editor. **Description:** A newspaper for expanding awareness and supporting all those seeking spiritual growth. No payment offered. **Nonfiction:** E.g., on genetically engineered foods, intentional communities, meditation, yoga, herbs, aromatherapy, healing, health, Reihi, Roltun, crystals, divination, etc.; 850 words. **Poetry:** to 850 words. **Art:** Cover art (full color, light tones); JPEGs, transparencies. **Tips:** Avoid spaceships, aliens, channeled communications, lots of biblical quotations. **Queries:** Preferred. **E-queries:** Yes. **Unsolicited mss:** Accepts. **Response:** Queries 1 month, submissions vary, SASE. **Freelance Content:** 90%.

FATE

P.O. Box 64383, St. Paul, MN 55164-0383. 651-291-1970. E-mail: fate@llewellyn.com. Web site: www.fatemag.com. Monthly. $4.95/issue,

$24.95/year. Circ.: 35,000. Phyllis Galde, Editor. **Description:** Covers the strange and unknown, for people willing to believe that unexplainable things happen. **Nonfiction:** True reports of the strange and unknown; 1,500-5,000 words; $.10/word. **Poetry:** Briefs on unusual events, odd folklore; up to 1,500 words; $.10/word. **Columns, Departments:** My Proof of Survival (true personal accounts of survival after death); True Mystic Experiences (personal accounts of unexplained happenings); up to 1,000 words; $25. **Tips:** Much of the content contributed by readers. **Queries:** Preferred. **E-queries:** Yes. **Response:** Queries 6 weekssubmissions 3 months, SASE required. **Freelance Content:** 80%. **Rights:** All. **Payment:** On publication.

JOYFUL TIMES
P.O. Box 3808, Sedona, AZ 86340.
E-mail: joyful@sedona.net. Web site: www.joy4u.org/index.htm. Bimonthly. Peggy Jenkins, Editor. **Description:** Articles, 500-800 words, exploring how society can nurture children and adults to express their potential and release their inner joy. Uplifting and inspirational.

NEW AGE
42 Pleasant St., Watertown, MA 02472. 617-926-0200.
E-mail: forum@newage.com. Web site: www.newage.com. Bimonthly. $4.95/$14.95. Circ.: 225,000. Jennifer Cook, Editor. **Description:** A guide for holistic living. Covers alternative medicine, natural foods, self-help psychology, spirituality, mind/body connection, right livelihood, and green politics. **Nonfiction:** For readers with active interest in social change, personal growth, health, and contemporary issues; 2,000-4,000 words; pay varies. **Columns, Departments:** Holistic Health, Food, Nutrition, Spirit, Home, Community, Travel, Life Lessons; book and music reviews (200-750 words); short news items (50-250 words); 600-1,300 words. **Tips:** Include recent clips and resumé. **Queries:** Required. **E-queries:** No. **Response:** Queries/submissions 8 weeks, SASE. **Freelance Content:** 90%. **Rights:** 1st NA and electronic. **Contact:** Christine Richmond, Ed. Asst.

PANGAIA
PO Box 641, Point Arena, CA 95468-0641. 707-882-2052.
E-mail: editor@pangaia.com. Web site: www.pangaia.com. Quarterly. Circ.: 5,000. Diane Conn Darling, Editor. **Description:** Exploring the Pagan World. **Nonfiction:** 1,500-3,000 words; $.01/word. **Tips:** Query for guidelines.

PARABOLA
Society for Study of Myth & Tradition, 656 Broadway,
New York, NY 10012-2317. 212-505-9037.
E-mail: parabola@panix.com. Web site: www.parabola.org. Quarterly. Circ.: 40,000. Natalie Baan, Managing Editor. **Description:** "The magazine of myth and tradition." Thematic issues presents traditional stories, folk and fairy tales. **Fiction:** 500 words. **Nonfiction:** Articles retelling traditional stories, folk and fairy tales; to 4,000 words;

pay varies. **Tips:** Contact for upcoming themes. Looking for a balance between scholarly and accessible writing, on the ideas of myth and tradition. **Queries:** Preferred.

SAGEWOMAN

P.O. Box 641, Point Arena, CA 95468-0641. 707-882-2052. E-mail: editor@sagewoman.com. Web site: www.sagewoman.com. Quarterly. $6.59/issue, $21/year. Circ.: 25,000. Anne Newkirk Niven. **Description:** Helps women explore spiritual, emotional, and mundane lives, respecting all persons, creatures, and the Earth. Focuses on material which expresses an Earth-centered spirituality. **Nonfiction:** On women's spiritual experience; focuses on issues of concern to pagan and other spiritually-minded women; 1,000-5,000 words; $.01-$.25/word. **Poetry:** Limited amount only; 10-50 lines; $10. **Art:** Original work only; signed releases from people depicted required; send portfolio of b/w prints, color negatives or slides; $15-$200. **Tips:** Write in the first person. **Queries:** Not necessary. **E-queries:** Yes. **Unsolicited mss:** Accepts. **Response:** Queries 1 month, submissions 3 months, SASE. **Freelance Content:** 80%. **Rights:** 1st worldwide serial. **Payment:** On publication.

SCIENCE OF MIND

PO Box 75127, 3251 W Sixth St, Los Angeles, CA 90075-0127. 213-388-2181. E-mail: sdelgado@scienceofmind.com. Web site: www.scienceofmind.com. Monthly. Keneth Lind, Editor in Chief. **Description:** Thoughtful perspective on how to experience greater self-acceptance, empowerment, and a meaningful life. **Nonfiction:** Inspiring first-person pieces, 1,000-2,000 words. Interviews with notable spiritual leaders, 3,500 words; $25/page.

VENTURE INWARD

215 67th Ave., Virginia Beach, VA 23451. 757-428-3588. E-mail: are@edgarcayce.org. Web site: www.edgarcayce.org. Bimonthly. Circ.: 25,000. A. Robert Smith, Editor. **Description:** Membership magazine for Edgar Cayce organizations (A.R.E., Edgar Cayce Fdn., Atlantic Univ.), on holistic health, spiritual development, mystical experiences, and Cayce philosophy (reincarnation, etc.). **Nonfiction:** Personal mystical or holistic health experiences; up to 3,000 words; $300-$400. **Columns, Departments:** Guest Column (opinion, to 800 words); Turning Point (a personal turning-point experience, to 800 words); The Mystical Way (a personal paranormal experience, to 1,500 words); Holistic Health (brief accounts of success using Edgar Cayce remedies); book reviews, to 500 words. Pays $50-$400. **Queries:** Required. **E-queries:** Yes. **Unsolicited mss:** Does not accept. **Response:** Queries 2 weeks, submissions 1 month, SASE. **Freelance Content:** 75%. **Payment:** On publication.

WHOLE LIFE TIMES

21225 Pacific Coast Hwy., Suite B, P.O. Box 1187, Malibu, CA 90265. 310-317-4200. E-mail: swholelifex@aol.com. Web site: www.wholelifetimes.com. Monthly. Free. Circ.: 58,000. Abigail Lewis, Editor. **Description:** Covers holistic lifestyle: health, healing, food and nutrition, environment, spirituality, personal growth, travel, science and metaphysics, longevity. **Nonfiction:** Up to 2,000 words; $.05/word. **Tips:** Understand the holistic mindset. Readers are fairly sophisticated; avoid "Yoga 101." Contact for upcoming themes. **Queries:** Not necessary. **E-queries:** Yes. **Unsolicited mss:** Accepts. **Response:** 1 month-1 year, SASE. **Freelance Content:** 75%. **Rights:** 1st NA. **Payment:** On publication. **Contact:** Kerri Hikida, Assoc. Ed.

PERFORMING ARTS

ACOUSTIC GUITAR
PO Box 767, San Anselmo, CA 94979. 415-485-6946. Web site: www.acousticguitar.com. Jeffrey Pepper Rodgers, Editor. **Description:** For players of acoustical guitars. **Queries:** Preferred.

AMERICAN SQUAREDANCE
P.O. Box 777, North Scituate, RI 02857. 401-647-9688. Web site: www.squaredance.ws. Ed and Pat Juaire, Editors. **Description:** Articles and fiction, 1,000-1,500 words, related to square dancing. Pays $1.50/column inch. **Poetry:** Yes. **Fillers:** to 100 words.

AMERICAN STRING TEACHER
468 Rebecca Street, Morgantown, WV 26505. 304-598-3249. Web site: www.astaweb.com. Quarterly. **Description:** Published by American String Teachers Association and National School Orchestra Association. Seeking research-based articles with national appeal. **Tips:** Avoid opinion or personal-experience stories. **Queries:** Preferred.

AMERICAN THEATRE
355 Lexington Ave., New York, NY 10017. 212-697-5230. Web site: www.tcg.org. Jim O'Quinn, Editor. **Description:** Features, 250-2,500 words, on the theater and theater-related subjects. **Nonfiction:** Pay varies. **Columns, Departments:** Profiles, Books, Commentary, Media. **Queries:** Preferred. **Payment:** On publication.

BACK STAGE
770 Broadway, New York, NY 10003. 646-654-5702. E-mail: seaker@backstage.com. Web site: www.backstage.com. Weekly. $2.95/issue. Circ.: 99,000. Sherry Eaker, Editor. **Description:** Main focus is theater, cabaret, and dance. Some coverage of films, also performing unions. Most features are how-to service pieces, to inform readers how to deal with the business behind show business. **Nonfiction:** Must be relevant to pursing a career in the performing arts; 150-2,500 words; pay varies. **Tips:** Must have considerable knowledge about the performing-arts industry. No fan-magazine style celebrity interviews. **Queries:** Required. **E-queries:** Yes. **Unsolicited mss:** Does

not accept. **Response:** Queries 3 weeks. **Freelance Content:** 85%. **Rights:** All. **Payment:** On publication.

BLUEGRASS UNLIMITED

P.O. Box 771, Warrenton, VA 20186. 540-349-8181.
E-mail: editor@bulegrassmusic.com. Web site: www.bluegrassmusic.com. Monthly. Circ.: 27,000. Peter V. Kuykendall, Editor. **Description:** Bluegrass and traditional country music. **Nonfiction:** Articles; to 3,000 words; pays $.08-$.10/word. **Art:** Photos. **Queries:** Preferred.

BLUES ACCESS

1455 Chestnut Place, Boulder, CO 80304-3153. 303-443-7245.
Web site: www.bluesaccess.com. Quarterly. Circ.: 25,000. Peter Kuykendall, Editor. **Description:** Resource of Blues music, artists, festivals, and more. For fans and professional musicians.

CHART

41 Britain St., Suite 200, Toronto, Ontario, Canada M5A 1R7. 416-363-3101.
E-mail: chart@chartattack.com. Web site: www.chartattack.com. 10x/year. $3.95/issue, $19.95/year. Circ.: 40,000. Nada Laskovski, Editor. **Description:** Covers Canada's music and pop culture, with slant to the cutting edge. **Queries:** Preferred.

CHURCH MUSICIAN TODAY

127 Ninth Ave. N., Nashville, TN 37234-0160. 615-251-2913.
E-mail: churchmusician@lifeway.com. Monthly. $3/issue. Circ.: 6,000. Jere Adams, Editor. **Description:** For music leaders, worship leaders, pastors, organists, pianists, and members of church music council or worship committees. **Nonfiction:** Choral techniques, instrumental groups, worship planning, directing choirs (all ages), music equipment, drama/pageants, hymn studies, book reviews. **Fillers:** 50 words, $10. **Queries:** Not necessary. **E-queries:** Yes. **Unsolicited mss:** Accepts. **Response:** Queries 1 week, submissions 4 weeks, SASE required. **Freelance Content:** 30%. **Rights:** All. **Payment:** On publication.

CLAVIER

200 Northfield Rd., Northfield, IL 60093. 847-446-5000.
10x/year. Circ.: 16,000. Judy Nelson, Editor. **Description:** Professional journal for piano teachers at all levels. **Nonfiction:** Interview/profiles on artists, teachers, composers; teaching articles, music discussion, master classes, and humor pieces for performers and teachers; 7-8 page mss; $40-$80/printed page. **Art:** Color prints, $100/full page. **Tips:** Writers should have music degrees. **Queries:** Preferred. **E-queries:** No. **Unsolicited mss:** Accepts. **Response:** 4-6 weeks, SASE required. **Freelance Content:** 75%. **Rights:** All. **Payment:** On publication.

DANCE
33 W. 60th St., New York, NY 10023. 510-839-6060. Web site: www.dancemagazine.com. Richard Philip, Editor-in-Chief. **Description:** Covers all aspects of the world of dance. **Nonfiction:** On dancers, companies, history, professional concerns, health, news events. **Tips:** Freelance content limited. **Queries:** Preferred.

DANCE SPIRIT
250 W. 57th St., Ste. 420, New York, NY 10107. 212-265-8890. E-mail: editor@lifestyleventures.com. Web site: www.dancespirit.com. Monthly. Circ.: 150,000. Julie Davis, Editorial Director. **Description:** For dancers of all disciplines **Nonfiction:** Articles on training, instruction and technique, choreography, dance styles, and profiles of dancers; pay varies. **Art:** Photos. **Payment:** On publication. **Contact:** Sheila Noone.

DANCE TEACHER
Lifestyle Ventures, 250 W. 57th St., Suite 420, New York, NY 10107. 212-265-8890. E-mail: csims@lifestyleventures.com. Web site: www.dance_teacher.com. Monthly. Circ.: 20,000. Caitlin Sims, Editor. **Description:** For dance professionals. **Nonfiction:** For educators, students, and professionals; practical information on economic/business issues. Profiles of schools, methods, and people. 500-1,500 words. Pays $100-$300. Photos helpful. **Tips:** Must be thoroughly researched. **Queries:** Preferred. **E-queries:** Yes. **Unsolicited mss:** Accepts. **Freelance Content:** 70%.

ELECTRONIC MUSICIAN
P.O. Box 1929, Marion, OH 43306. E-mail: emeditorial@intertec.com. Web site: www.emusician.com. Monthly. Steve Oppenheimer,Editor. **Description:** On audio recording, live sound engineering, technical applications, and product reviews. **Nonfiction:** Articles, 1,500-3,500 words; pays $350-$750. **Payment:** On acceptance.

ENTERTAINMENT DESIGN
32 W. 18th St., New York, NY 10011. 212-229-2965. Web site: www.etecnyc.net. Jacqueline Tien, Publisher. **Description:** On design, technical, and management aspects of theater, opera, dance, television, and film for those in performing arts and the entertainment trade. **Nonfiction:** Articles, 500-2,500 words. **Queries:** Preferred. **Payment:** On acceptance.

FLUTE TALK
Instrumentalist Publishing Co., 200 Northfield Rd., Northfield, IL 60093. 847-446-5000. Monthly. $2. Circ.: 13,000. Kim Diehnelt, Editor. **Description:** For flute teachers or performers. **Nonfiction:** Interviews with players, teachers, composers; other articles on flute playing; 3-5 pages; $90-$100/printed page. **Art:** Slides, color prints. **Queries:**

Preferred. **E-queries:** No. **Unsolicited mss:** Accepts. **Response:** Queries 1 week, submissions 1 month, SASE required. **Payment:** On publication.

GLORY SONGS
127 Ninth Ave. N., Nashville, TN 37234. 800-458-2772. E-mail: don.schlosser@lifeway.com. Don Schlosser, Editor. **Description:** Choral music, for volunteer and part-time music directors and members of church choirs. Very easy music and accompaniments designed specifically for the small church (4-6 songs per issue). **Queries:** Preferred. **Payment:** On acceptance.

GUITAR ONE
Cherry Lane Music, 6 E. 32nd St., Fl. 11, New York, NY 10016. E-mail: editors@guitarmag.com. Web site: www.guitaronemag.com. **Description:** For serious guitarists. **Queries:** Preferred.

GUITAR PLAYER
2800 Campus Dr., San Mateo, CA 94403. 650-513-4300. Web site: www.guitarplayer.com. Lonni Gause, Executive Editor. **Description:** On guitars and related subjects. **Nonfiction:** Articles, from 200 words; pays $100-$600. **Rights:** All. **Payment:** On acceptance.

INTERNATIONAL MUSICIAN
Paramount Bldg., 1501 Broadway, Suite 600, New York, NY 10036. 212-869-1330. Web site: www.afm.org. Antoinette Follette, Managing Editor. **Description:** For professional musicians. **Nonfiction:** Articles, 1,500-2,000 words; pay varies. **Queries:** Preferred. **Payment:** On acceptance.

JAZZIZ
2650 N. Military Trail, Suite 140, Boca Raton, FL 33431. 561-893-6868. E-mail: mail@jazziz.com. Web site: www.jazziz.com. Monthly. $3.99. Circ.: International. David Pulizzi, Editor. **Description:** Jazz musician publication. **Nonfiction:** On all aspects of adult contemporary music: interviews, profiles, concept pieces. Pay varies. **Columns, Departments:** Reviews of varied music genres, radio, and video; mostly new releases. Pay varies. **Tips:** Send resumé with manuscript. **E-queries:** Yes. **Freelance Content:** 80%. **Payment:** On acceptance.

KEYBOARD
2800 Campus Dr., San Mateo, CA 94403. 650-513-4300. Web site: www.keyboardonline.com. Marvin Sanders, Editor. **Description:** On keyboard instruments, MIDI and computer technology, and players. **Nonfiction:** Articles, 300-5,000 words, photos; pays $200-$600. **Queries:** Preferred. **Payment:** On acceptance.

LA FACTORIA DE SONIDO
Barrera Publishing, 43 West 38th St., Fl 5, New York, NY 10018. 212-840-0227.

Web site: www.lafactoriadesonido.com. Bimonthly. Circ.: 110,000. Jennifer Barrera, Executive Editor. **Description:** Hispanic music and art publication. Music events, reviews, interviews, fashion and clubs focusing on Hispanic music of all kinds.

LIVING BLUES
Univ. of Mississippi, Hill Hall, Room 301, University, MS 38677. 662-915-5742. Web site: www.livingbluesonline.com. David Nelson. **Description:** About living African-American blues artists. **Nonfiction:** Interviews, some retrospective, historical articles or investigative pieces; 1,500-10,000 words; pays $75-$200. **Art:** Photos, $25-$50. **Queries:** Preferred. **Payment:** On publication.

LOLLIPOP
P.O. Box 441493, Boston, MA 02144. 617-623-5319. Web site: www.lollipop.com. Quarterly. Scott Hefflon. **Description:** On music and youth culture. Fiction, essays, and "edgy" commentary. Reviews and interviews related to underground culture. **Nonfiction:** To 2,000 words; pays $25 (for anything over 1,000 words). **Art:** Photos, drawings; $25. **Queries:** Preferred.

MIX MAGAZINE
6400 Hollis St., Suite 12, Emeryville, CA 94608. Web site: www.mixmag.com. George Peterson, Editor. **Description:** For professionals, on audio, audio post-production, sound production, live sound, and music entertainment technology. **Nonfiction:** Articles, varying lengths; pay varies. **Queries:** Preferred. **Payment:** On publication.

MODERN DRUMMER
12 Old Bridge Rd., Cedar Grove, NJ 07009. 209-239-4140. E-mail: mdinfo@moderndrummer.com. Web site: www.moderndrummer.com. Monthly. Circ.: 102,000. Ronald L. Spagnardi, Editor in Chief. **Description:** Drumming how-tos, interviews. **Nonfiction:** 500-2,000 words; $50-$500. **Payment:** On publication.

OPERA NEWS
Metropolitan Opera Guild, 70 Lincoln Ctr. Plaza, New York, NY 10023-6593. 212-769-7080. Web site: www.operanews.com. Rudolph S. Rauch, Editor. **Description:** On all aspects of opera. **Nonfiction:** Articles, 600-2,500 words; pay varies. **Queries:** Preferred. **Payment:** On publication.

PERFORMING ARTS AND ENTERTAINMENT IN CANADA
104 Glenrose Ave., Toronto, ON M4T 1K8 Canada. 416-484-4534. Quarterly. $8.56/issue. Circ.: 10,000. Sara B. Hood, Editor & Art Director. **Description:** Canadian performing arts and entertainment, including theater, music (especially classical, new, jazz, world, and folk), dance, film, TV and related fields. Also profiles, opinion, issues, etc. **Nonfiction:** Should be of national interest, but

values submissions from smaller, out-of-the-way locations (not just downtown Montreal and Toronto). Especially interested in stories that reflect some aspect of Canadian diversity. Publishes very few reviews; 1,000-2,500 words; $.25/word. **Art:** Prints (b/w or color); No payment. **Tips:** Welcomes new writers. Prefers stories with original ideas and opinions, or addressing issues of some complexity or sophistication—not just simple profiles of people or companies. **Queries:** Preferred. **E-queries:** Yes. **Unsolicited mss:** Accepts. **Response:** Slow to respond, be patient, SASE required. **Rights:** 1st print and electronic. **Payment:** On publication.

ROLLING STONE

1290 Ave. of the Americas, 2nd Fl., New York, NY 10104. 212-484-1616. Web site: www.rollingstone.com. **Description:** Magazine of American music, culture, and politics. **Tips:** Rarely accepts freelance material. No fiction. **Queries:** Required. **Unsolicited mss:** Does not accept.

SHEET MUSIC MAGAZINE

333 Adams St., Bedford Hills, NY 10507. 914-244-8500. E-mail: sheetmusic@yestermusic.com. Web site: www.sheetmusicmagazine.com. Bimonthly. $3.95/issue, $18.97/year. Circ.: 50,000. Kirk Miller, Editor. **Description:** For amateur and professional musicians. Most content is the actual reproduction of popular songs (words and music). **Fiction:** On golden era of popular music, 1900-1950; 2,000 words; pay varies. **Nonfiction:** Pieces for pianists, organists, and singers; on musicians, composers, music education, pedagogy; also reviews (to 500 words); no hard rock or heavy metal; 2,000 words; pay varies. **Fillers:** Cartoons on golden era, 1900-1950; $10-$50. **Columns, Departments:** On golden era; keyboard and guitar; how-to; 1,000 words max. **Art:** hard copy, digital. **Queries:** Preferred. **E-queries:** Yes. **Unsolicited mss:** Accepts. **Response:** 2 months, SASE. **Freelance Content:** 50%. **Rights:** Reprint.

STAGE DIRECTIONS

SMW Communications, Inc., 250 W. 57th St., Suite 420, New York, NY 10107. 212-265-8890. E-mail: idorbian@lifestyleventures.com. Web site: www.stage-directions.com. Iris Dorbian. **Description:** On acting, directing, costuming, makeup, lighting, set design and decoration, props, special effects, fundraising, and audience development, for readers active in all aspects of community, regional, academic, or youth theater. **Nonfiction:** How-to articles, to 2,000 words; pays $.10/word. **Tips:** Short pieces, 400-500 words, "are a good way to approach us first." **Payment:** On publication.

STORYTELLING

101 Courthouse Sq., Jonesborough, TN 37659. 423-913-8201. E-mail: nsn@naxs.net. Web site: www.storynet.org. Bimonthly. $4.95, member benefit. Circ.: 5,000. Mary Whited, Editor. **Description:** For the professional storyteller; focuses on the oral tradition. **Nonfiction:** On the oral tradition; 1,000-2,000 words. **Columns, Departments:** Unusual events or applications; 200-400 words. **Queries:**

Required. **E-queries:** Yes. **Unsolicited mss:** Accepts. **Response:** 2 weeks. **Payment:** in copies.

SYMPHONY
33 W. 60th St., Fifth Floor, New York, NY 10023. 212-262-5161. E-mail: editor@symphony.org. Web site: www.symphony.org. Bimonthly. $35. Circ.: 20,000. Melinda Whiting, Editor-in-Chief. **Description:** Discusses issues critical to the orchestra community. Communicates to the public the value and importance of orchestras and their music. **Columns, Departments:** Book and CD reviews; profiles of musicians, orchestras, and conductors; 1,000-3,000 words; $250-$500. **Art:** Photos. **Tips:** Welcomes new writers. Prefers queries with ideas that can be shaped to match readers' interests. Serves the orchestral industry; while general-interest classical-music subjects may be of interest, look first for specific orchestral connection before querying. **Queries:** Preferred. **E-queries:** Yes. **Unsolicited mss:** Accepts. **Response:** 1 day to 3 months, SASE required. **Freelance Content:** 30-50%. **Rights:** 1st. **Payment:** On acceptance. **Contact:** Rebecca Winzenried, Managing Editor.

TDR
721 Broadway, 6th Fl., New York, NY 10003. 212-998-1626. E-mail: tdr@nyu.edu. Quarterly. $10/issue, $38/year, $22 (students). Circ.: 3,000. Richard Schechner, Editor. **Description:** "The drama review." A journal of performance studies; with intercultural, intergeneric, interdisciplinary focus. About performance in its broadest sense: dance, music, media; sports, rituals, daily life; anthropology, psychology, and politics. **Nonfiction:** Eclectic articles on experimental performance and performance theory; cross-cultural, examining social, political, historical, and theatrical contexts in which performance happens; to 30 pages (mss.). **Queries:** Required. **E-queries:** No. **Unsolicited mss:** Accepts. **Response:** 3 monoths, SASE. **Freelance Content:** 50%. **Payment:** On publication.

TEACHING THEATRE
2343 Auburn Ave., Cincinnati, OH 45219. 513-421-3900. Web site: www.etassoc.org. Quarterly. **Description:** Newsletter for middle- and high-school drama educators. Offers play suggestions, curriculum ideas, classroom exercises, and technical production. **Queries:** Preferred.

THIRSTY EAR
P.O. Box 29600, Santa Fe, NM 87592. 505-473-5723. E-mail: thirstyearmag@yahoo.com. Web site: www.thirstyearmagazine.com. 5x/year. $15/$25. Circ.: 80,000. Michael Koster, Editor. **Description:** Covers music, art and culture. **Fiction:** Short stories with music, arts, or American culture themes; up to 2,500 words; $75-$100. **Nonfiction:** Articles on "non-tuxedo" music; also reviews, 300-500 words. **Columns, Departments:** Opinion; 800-1,000 words; $100. **Queries:** Required. **E-queries:** Yes. **Unsolicited mss:** Does not accept. **Response:** Varies. **Freelance Content:** 80%. **Rights:** 1st NA. **Payment:** On publication.

URB

1680 N. Vine St., Suite 1012, Los Angeles, CA 90028-8836. 323-993-0291. E-mail: wordsurb@urb.com. Web site: www.urb.com. 10x/year. $3.95/issue, $12/year. Circ.: 75,000. Stacy Osbaum, Editor. **Description:** Focuses on future music culture: electronic dance music, independent hip-hop and DJ culture. **Nonfiction:** Features, on dance and underground hip-hop music (profiles of emerging musicians, singers, and groups); pays $.10/word. **Tips:** Send published clips. **Queries:** Required. **E-queries:** Yes. **Response:** Queries 1 month. **Freelance Content:** 80%. **Payment:** On publication.

VELOCITY

346 N. Justine #300, Chicago, IL 60607. 312-397-9388. Web site: www.velocitymag.com. Bryan A. Bushemi, Copy Editor. **Description:** Covers Chicago's music scene. **Queries:** Preferred. *No recent report.*

REGIONAL & CITY

ALABAMA HERITAGE

Univ. of Alabama, Box 870342, Tuscaloosa, AL 35487-0342. 205-348-7467. Web site: bama.va.edu/heritage/. Quarterly. $6/$18.95. Circ.: 6,500. Suzanne Wolfe, Editor. **Description:** Focuses on the events that have shaped Alabama and the South. **Nonfiction:** Interested in stories ignored, forgotten, or given short-shrift by historians. Also, Civil War articles if the story has an Alabama connection; 4,000-5,000 words; up to $400. **Columns, Departments:** Recollections (a specific remembrance of an Alabamian, often sent in by readers), up to 1,000 words; Alabama Album (the story behind an old photograph), up to 250 words; no payment. **Queries:** Not necessary. **E-queries:** No. **Unsolicited mss:** Accepts. **Response:** Queries 1-2 weeks, submissions 3-4 weeks. **Freelance Content:** 40%.

ALASKA

619 E Ship Creek Ave, Suite 329, Anchorage, AK 99501. 907-272-6070. E-mail: bwwoods@alaskamagazine.com. Monthly. Circ.: 205,000. Bruce Woods, Editor. **Description:** Covers all aspects of life in Alaska. **Nonfiction:** Articles; 1,500 words; pay varies. **Tips:** Send SASE for guidelines. **Queries:** Preferred. **Payment:** On publication.

ALASKA BUSINESS MONTHLY

501 Northern Lights Blvd., Ste. 100, Anchorage, AK 99503. 907-276-4373. E-mail: info@akbizmag.com. Web site: www.akbizmag.com. Monthly. $3.95/$21.95. Circ.: 10,000. Debbie Cutler, Editor. **Description:** For Alaskans and other audiences interested in the business affairs of the 49th State. Thorough, objective analysis of issues and trends affecting Alaskan businesses. **Art:** 35mm photos; pay varies. **Tips:** Query first, Alaska business topics only. Avoid generalities, need to be specific for this market. **Queries:** Preferred. **E-queries:** Yes. **Unsolicited mss:** Accepts. **Response:** 1 month. **Freelance Content:** 80%. **Rights:** All. **Payment:** On publication.

ALBEMARLE

1224 W. Main St., #220, Charlottesville, VA 22903-2858. 804-817-2000. E-mail: kvalenzi@cjp.com. Web site: www.cjp.com. Bimonthly. Circ.: 10,000. Kathleen D. Valenzi, Editor. **Description:** Lifestyle magazine highlighting the news and events of Virginia. **Nonfiction:** Topics include health and medicine, the arts, home architecture, interior design, and gardening; pay varies.

ALBERTA SWEETGRASS

Aboriginal Multi-Media Society of Alberta, 15001 112th Ave., Edmonton, Alberta, Canada T5M 2V6. 800-661-5469. Web site: www.ammsa.com. **Description:** Covers Native topics, with an Alberta angle. **Nonfiction:** Articles, 100-1,000 words (prefers 500-800 words; briefs, 100-150 words): features, profiles, and community-based topics.

AMERICAN OUTBACK JOURNAL

21 N. Tejon, Ste. 202, Colorado Springs, CO 80903. 719-475-2469. E-mail: curt@americanoutback.com. Web site: www.americanoutback.com. Curt Penergraft, Editor. **Description:** Print and e-zine on the American West. Publish articles on lore, history, culture, ecology, politics, humor, and travel to off-beat western destinations. **Queries:** Preferred.

ANNAPOLIS CYBER REVIEW

E-mail: acr@avmcyber.com. Web site: avmcyber.com/acr. Joseph Patrick Bulko, Editor. **Description:** E-zine with "all the news that bytes!"

ARIZONA HIGHWAYS

2039 W. Lewis Ave., Phoenix, AZ 85009. 602-271-5900. E-mail: arizonahighways.com. Web site: www.arizonahighways.com. Monthly. $3.50/issue, $19/year. Circ.: 365,000. Robert J. Early, Editor. **Description:** Covers travel in Arizona; pieces on adventure, humor, lifestyles, nostalgia, history, archaeology, nature, etc. Some Arizona-based fiction on occasion. **Fiction:** Preferably frontier-oriented, must be upbeat and wholesome (for December and April issues); 1,800-2,500 words; $.55-$1.00/word. **Nonfiction:** Travel adventure, history, destinations; personal-experience pieces; 800-1,800 words; $.55-$1.00/word. **Fillers:** Jokes (humor page); 200 words or less; $75. **Columns, Departments:** Mileposts, Focus on Nature, Along the Way, Back Road Adventures, Hiking, Great Weekends, Arizona Humor. Insightful or nostalgic viewpoint; 650 words; $440. **Art:** 4x5 preferred; landscapes, also images to illustrate a story; pay varies. **Tips:** To break in, submit short items to Off Ramp department. Use active verbs. No stories on religion, government, or politics. **E-queries:** Yes. **Unsolicited mss:** Accepts. **Response:** 30 days or less, SASE required. **Freelance Content:** 100%. **Rights:** print (online for extra fee). **Payment:** On acceptance. **Contact:** Rebecca Mong.

ARIZONA TRENDS OF THE SOUTHWEST

P.O. Box 8508, Scottsdale, AZ 85252-8508. 480-948-1799. 10x/year. Randy Barocas, Editor. **Description:** Features on fashion, health and beauty, special events, dining, the performing arts, and book reviews. **Queries:** Preferred.

ARKANSAS TIMES

Box 34010, Little Rock, AR 72203. 501-375-2985. Web site: www.arktimes.com. John Brummett, Editor. **Description:** On Arkansas history, people, travel, politics. **Nonfiction:** Articles, strong Arkansas orientation; to 6,000 words; pays to $500. **Payment:** On acceptance.

ASPEN

720 E. Durant Ave., #E-8, Aspen, CO 81611-2071. 970-920-4040 ext.22. E-mail: staff@aspenmagazine.com. Web site: aspenmagazine.com. Bimonthly. $4.95. Circ.: 20,000. Janet O'Grady, Editor. **Description:** City and regional news about Aspen, Colorado. **Nonfiction:** Lifestyle articles on Aspen and Snowmass area; out-

Get writing tips and inspiration every month!

The Writer Magazine has something to offer both novice and experienced writers of all genres! Each issue includes:

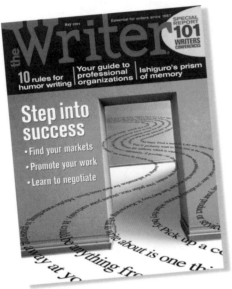

- **Writer's Wanted** Up-to-date market news, special markets, and market listings
- **Bottom Line** A look at the business of writing
- **Ethics** The issues that face writers today
- **Poet to Poet** Strictly poetry
- **@ Deadline** Industry and people news of interest to writers
- **WriteStuff** Current book, tape and products reviews
- **Dear Writer** Answers to readers' questions

For over 100 years, *The Writer* has guided writers at every level. It has helped launch careers, inspire masterpieces, and encourage new writers.

The Writer covers every genre of writing including fiction, poetry, freelance articles, scripts, children's books, profiles, memoirs and more!

[**Save 52%**]

door sports, arts, profiles, environment, news, photo essays. **Queries:** Required. **E-queries:** Yes. **Unsolicited mss:** Does not accept. **Response:** 4 weeks, SASE. **Freelance Content:** 50%. **Payment:** On publication.

ATLANTA

1330 W. Peachtree St., Suite 450, Atlanta, GA 30309-3214. 404-872-3100. Web site: www.atlantamagazine.com. Monthly. Circ.: 65,000. Lee Walburn, Editor-in-Chief. **Description:** Atlanta subjects or personalities. **Nonfiction:** Articles; 1,500-5,000 words; pays $300-$2,000. **Queries:** Required. **Payment:** On publication.

ATLANTA CONSTITUTION

P.O. Box 4689, Atlanta, GA 30302. 404-526-5151. Web site: www.ajc.com. Daily. **Description:** Articles related to Southeast, Georgia, or Atlanta metro area. **Nonfiction:** Submit complete manuscript. Varied topics: law, economics, politics, science, environment, performing arts, humor, education; religious, seasonal; 200-600 words; pays $75-$125. **Payment:** On publication.

ATLANTA HOMES AND LIFESTYLES

1100 Johnson Ferry Rd., #595, Atlanta, GA 30342. 404-252-6670. Web site: www.atlantahomesmag.com. Monthly. $3.95/issue, $24/year. Circ.: 33,000. Oma Blaise Ford, Editor. **Description:** On upscale home and gardens. **Nonfiction:** Original stories with local angle (mostly by assignment), on homes, gardening, food, wine, entertaining, and remodeling; 300-1,200 words; $75-$500. **Columns, Departments:** Remodeling, shopping, profiles (on assignment; 200-700 words. $75-$200). **Queries:** Required. **Unsolicited mss:** Does not accept. **Response:** 3 months, SASE. **Freelance Content:** 50%. **Payment:** On acceptance.

ATLANTIC CITY

P.O. Box 2100, Pleasantville, NJ 08232-1924. 609-272-7900. Doug Bergen, Editor. **Description:** On Atlantic City and southern New Jersey shore, for locals and tourists. Entertainment, casinos, business, recreation, personalities, lifestyle, local color. **Nonfiction:** Lively articles; 200-2,000 words; pays $50-$600. **Queries:** Preferred. **Payment:** On publication.

AVANCE HISPANO

4230 Mission St., San Francisco, CA 94112-1520. 415-585-1080. Bi-monthly. Circ.: 45,000. **Description:** Spanish-language publication for people in the San Francisco Bay area.

BACK HOME IN KENTUCKY

Back Home in Kentucky, 295 Old Forge Mill Rd., P.O. Box 710, Clay City, KY 40312-0710. 606-663-1011. Bi-monthly. $2/issue, $15/year. Circ.: 8,000. Jerlene Rose, Editor/Publisher. **Description:** Focuses on Kentucky destinations, profiles, personal memories, county spotlights, natural history, and nostalgia. **Nonfiction:** 400-1000 words; $25 and up. **Columns, Departments:** Chronicles (Kentucky history, 400-1,000 words); $25- $100. **Art:** Slides, photos; $25 and up. **Queries:** Not necessary. **E-queries:** Yes. **Unsolicited mss:** Accepts. **Response:** 30 days. **Freelance Content:** 75%. **Payment:** On publication.

BALTIMORE
1000 Lancaster St., Suite 400, Baltimore, MD 21202. 410-752-4200. E-mail: smarge@baltimoremag.com. Web site: www.baltimoremag.com. Monthly. $3.50/issue, $15/year. Circ.: 56,000. Margaret Guroff, Managing Editor. **Description:** Covers Baltimore metro area: local people, events, trends, and ideas. **Nonfiction:** Consumer advice, investigative, lifestyle, profiles, humor, personal experience; 250-4,000 words; $125 and up. **Columns, Departments:** News You Can Use (business round-ups, etc.); Hot Shot; Health; 900-1,500 words; $200 up. **Tips:** Consider short articles for departments; send query letter and clips. **Queries:** Required. **E-queries:** Yes. **Response:** Queries 1 month, submissions 2 months, SASE required. **Freelance Content:** 60%. **Rights:** 1st serial, reprint. **Payment:** On publication.

BAY AREA PARENT
401 Alberto Way, Suite A, Los Gatos, CA 95032-5404. 707-763-2160. E-mail: jbordow@unitedad.com. Monthly. Free. Joan Bordow, Editor. **Description:** Parenting issues for California's Santa Clara County and South Bay area. **Nonfiction:** For parents of children from birth to early teens; 500-1200 words; $.10/word. **Queries:** Required. **E-queries:** Yes. **Unsolicited mss:** Accepts. **Response:** Queries and submissions 2 months, SASE required. **Freelance Content:** 50%.

BIG APPLE PARENT
9 E. 38th St., 4th Fl., New York, NY 10016. 212-889-6400. E-mail: edit@parentsknow.com. Web site: www.parentsknow.com. Monthly. Free. Circ.: 70,000. Helen Freedman, Editor. **Description:** Newspaper for New York City parents, with separate editions for Queens and Westchester County. **Nonfiction:** For parents, on parenting, humor features, op-ed; best chances are "newsy" features with New York slant; 750 words; $50. **Art:** Hard copy, JPEG; $25. **Tips:** Cover more than your personal experience. Stories should be about New York City or have information that can be localized. **Queries:** Not necessary. **E-queries:** Yes. **Unsolicited mss:** Accepts. **Response:** within 1 week, SASE required. **Freelance Content:** 90%. **Rights:** 1st. **Payment:** On publication.

BIG SKY JOURNAL
P.O. Box 1069, Bozeman, MT 59771. 406-586-2712. Web site: www.boisemag.com. 5x/year. Michelle A. Steven-Orton. **Description:** On Montana art and architecture, hunting and fishing, ranching and recreation. **Fiction:** to 4,000 words. **Nonfiction:** Articles, to 2,500 words; pay varies. **Queries:** Preferred. **Payment:** On publication.

BIRMINGHAM

2027 First Ave. N., Birmingham, AL 35203. 205-250-7653.
Web site: www.bhammag.com. Monthly. Joe O'Donnell, Editor. **Description:**
Spotlights events, people, and activities in and around Birmingham. **Nonfiction:**
Profiles, business articles, and nostalgia pieces, with local focus. Also, business features, dining, fashion, and general-interest. To 2,500 words; pays $50-$175.
Response: SASE. **Payment:** On publication.

BLUE RIDGE COUNTRY

P.O. Box 21535, Roanoke, VA 24018. 540-989-6138.
E-mail: krheinheimen@leisurepublishers.com. Web site: www.blueridgecounty.com.
Bi-monthly. $3.50/$16.95. Circ.: 80,000. Kurt Rheinheimer, Editor. **Description:**
Regional magazine. **Nonfiction:** Articles that explore and extol the beauty, history,
and travel opportunities in the mountain regions of VA, NC, WV, TN, KY, MD, SC,
and GA; 250-1,800 words; $25-$250. **Art:** Color slides, b/w prints considered; pays
$200 for photo features. **Queries:** Preferred. **Response:** 1-2 months, SASE.
Freelance Content: 70%. **Payment:** On publication.

BOCA RATON

JES Publishing, Amtec Ctr., Suite 100, 6413 Congress Ave.,
Boca Raton, FL 33487. 561-997-8683.
E-mail: bocamag@aol.com. Web site: www.bocamag.com. Bimonthly. Circ.: 20,000.
Marie Speed, Editor. **Description:** Focuses on southern Florida. Fashion, cuisine,
travel, finance, health, and profiles of local residents and celebrities. **Nonfiction:**
Articles on Florida topics, personalities, and travel; 800-3,000 words; $50-$500. **Tips:**
Query first, clips required. **Queries:** Required. **Payment:** On acceptance.

BOISE

4619 Emerald, Suite D-1, Boise, ID 83701. 208-338-5454.
E-mail: colleen@boisemag.com. Quarterly. Circ.: 12,000. Colleen Birch Maile,
Managing Editor. **Description:** Lifestyle magazine for Boise area. Dining, cooking,
decorating, local personalities, sports, and fashion. **Fiction:** Regional or Idaho
themes; no genre fiction (sf, romance, western, adventure, religious); 1,000-2,500
words; $200. **Nonfiction:** Essays, general interest, travel, humor, book excerpts.
Indicate availability of photos with submission; 500-3,500 words; $500. **Columns,
Departments:** Life in Boise; About Idaho; Book Reviews; 500-1,200 words; $150-
$200. **Tips:** Prefers regional writers, requires Idaho or northwest/intermountain
theme. To break in, try About Idaho and Book Reviews. **Queries:** Preferred. **E-
queries:** Yes. **Unsolicited mss:** Accepts. **Response:** Queries 6 weeks, submissions
3 months, SASE. **Freelance Content:** 90%. **Rights:** 1st. **Payment:** On publication.

THE BOSTON GLOBE

P.O. Box 2378, Boston, MA 02107-2378. 617-929-2155.
Web site: www.boston.com/globe/magazine. Weekly. Nick King, Editor.
Description: Covers arts, entertainment, shopping, and news in the Boston area.

Nonfiction: 2,500-5,000 words. **Tips:** Send query first. **Queries:** Preferred. **Unsolicited mss:** Accepts. **Response:** 3 weeks, SASE required. **Freelance Content:** Varies. **Rights:** 1st NA. **Payment:** On publication.

BOSTON MAGAZINE

300 Massachusetts Ave., Boston, MA 02115. 617-262-9700. Web site: www.bostonmagazine.com. Monthly. Circ.: 125,000. Jon Marcus, Executive Editor. **Description:** Boston-area personalities, institutions, and phenomena. **Nonfiction:** Informative, entertaining features; 1,000-3,000 words; pays to $2,000. **Queries:** Required. **Payment:** On publication.

BOSTONIA

10 Lenox St., Brookline, MA 02146. 617-353-3081. Web site: www.bu.edu/alumni/bostonia/index.html. **Description:** "The magazine of culture and ideas." Covers politics, literature, music, art, science, and education, especially from a Boston angle. **Nonfiction:** Articles; to 3,000 words; pays $150-$2,500. **Queries:** Required.

BROOKLYN BRIDGE

388 Atlantic Ave., Brooklyn, NY 11217-1703. 718-596-7400. Bimonthly. Circ.: 40,000. Joe Fodor, Sr. Editor. **Description:** Topics of regional and national interest, including arts and cultural activities, investigative reports, and the "politics" of Brooklyn. *No recent report.*

BUFFALO SPREE

5678 Main St., Williamsville, NY 14221. 716-634-0820. E-mail: elicata@buffalospree.com. Web site: www.buffalospree.com. Quarterly. Circ.: 25,000. Elizabeth Licata, Editor. **Description:** For thoughtful readers in the western New York region. **Nonfiction:** Articles of local interest; to 1,800 words; $125-$150. **Payment:** On publication. Not accepting unsolicited manuscripts at this time (5/01).

CAPE COD LIFE

P.O. Box 1385, Pocasset, MA 02559-1385. 508-564-4466. E-mail: apetrucelli@capecodlife.com. Web site: www.capecodlife.com. 7x/year. Circ.: 40,000. Alan W. Petrucelli, Editor. **Description:** About life on Cape Cod, Martha's Vineyard, and Nantucket (past, present and future). **Nonfiction:** On events, business, art, history, gardening, nautical lifestyle of region; 800-2,500 words; $.15-.25/word. **Art:** Transparencies. **Queries:** Preferred. **E-queries:** Yes. **Unsolicited mss:** Accepts. **Response:** 1-2 months, SASE required. **Freelance Content:** 90%. **Rights:** All. **Payment:** On acceptance.

CAROLINA GARDENER

P.O. Box 4504, Greensboro, NC 27404. 800-245-0142. Web site: www.carolinagardener.com. Bimonthly. L.A. Jackson, Editor. **Description:** Specific to Southeast gardening (profiles of gardens in the region, new cultivars, "good ol' southern heirlooms"). **Nonfiction:** Articles, 750-1,000 words; slides and illustrations essential to accompany articles; pays $175. **Queries:** Required. **Payment:** On publication.

CAROLOGUE
South Carolina Historical Society, 100 Meeting St., Charleston, SC 29401-2299. 843-723-3225. Web site: www.schistory.org. Peter A. Rerig, Editor. **Description:** On South Carolina history. **Nonfiction:** General-interest articles, to 10 pages. **Queries:** Preferred. **Payment:** In copies.

CASCADES EAST
716 N. E. 4th St., PO Box 5784, Bend, OR 97708-5784. 541-382-0127. E-mail: sunpub@sun-pub.com. Web site: www.sun-pub.com. Quarterly. Circ.: 10,000. Geoff Hill, Editor. **Description:** Outdoor activities (fishing, hunting, golfing, backpacking, rafting, skiing, snowmobiling, etc.), history, special events, and scenic tours in central Oregon Cascades. **Nonfiction:** 1,000-2,000 words; $.05-$.15/word. **Fillers:** Travel, history, and recreation in central Oregon; $.05-.$15/word. **Art:** Photos; pays extra. **Queries:** Preferred. **Payment:** On publication.

CENTRAL CALIFORNIA PARENT
7638 N. Ingram Ave., Suite 101, Fresno, CA 93711-6201. 559-435-1406. E-mail: ccparent@gnis.com. Web site: www.ccparent.com. Sally Cook. **Description:** For parents. **Nonfiction:** Articles, 500-1,500 words; pay varies. **Queries:** Preferred. **Payment:** On publication.

CENTRAL PA
P.O. Box 2954, 1982 Locust Ln., Harrisburg, PA 17105. 717-221-2800. Web site: www.centralpa.org. Steve Kennedy, Editor. **Description:** Topics of interest to central Pennsylvania, including profiles of notable central Pennsylvanians, and broadly based articles of social interest that "enlighten and inform." **Nonfiction:** Articles, 1,500-3,500 words; pays $.10/word. **Payment:** On publication.

CENTRAL PENN PARENT
101 N. Second St., NW, Harrisburg, PA 17101. 717-236-4300. Web site: www.journalpub.com. Monthly. $16.95. Circ.: 35,000. Lauren Taylor, Editor. **Description:** On family and parenting issues **Nonfiction:** 1,400 words; $125. **Columns, Departments:** 700 words; $50. **Art:** Submit photos with article. **Tips:** Welcomes new writers. **Queries:** Required. **E-queries:** Yes. **Unsolicited mss:** Accepts. **Response:** 3 weeks, SASE required. **Freelance Content:** 50%. **Rights:** 1st. **Payment:** On publication.

CHARLESTON
P.O. Box 1794, Mt. Pleasant, SC 29465-1794. 843-971-9811. E-mail: dshankland@charlestonmag.com. Web site: www.charlestonmag.com.

Bimonthly. Circ.: 20,000. Darcy Shankland, Editor. **Description:** Nonfiction articles on local topics. **Nonfiction:** Past articles have ranged from winter getaways and holiday gift ideas to social issues like homeless shelters. **Columns, Departments:** In Good Taste, Top of the Shelf, Midday Recipes, Cityscape. **Tips:** Send SASE for guidelines. **Queries:** Preferred. **Payment:** On publication.

CHARLOTTE

127 W. Worthington Ave., Ste. 208, Charlotte, NC 28203. 704-335-7181. Web site: www.charlottemag.com. Richard Thurmond, Editor. **Description:** Covers social, economic, and cultural life of Charlotte and surrounding area. **Nonfiction:** Politics, business, art and entertainment, education, sports, travel, society; pay varies.

CHESAPEAKE BAY

1819 Bay Ridge Ave., Annapolis, MD 21403. 410-263-2662. E-mail: cbmeditor@cbmmag.net. Monthly. $3.95/issue. Circ.: 46,000. Tim Sayles, Editor. **Description:** For recreational boaters who enjoy boating, fishing, destinations, people, history, and traditions of the Chesapeake Bay. **Nonfiction:** to 4,000 words; $75-$1,200. **Art:** Photos. Pays $100-$700. **Tips:** Need to be familiar with Chesapeake Bay region and boating. Readers are well educated, well traveled. **Queries:** Preferred. **E-queries:** Yes. **Unsolicited mss:** Accepts. **Response:** Queries 1 week, submissions 1 month, SASE required. **Freelance Content:** 30%. **Rights:** FNASR. **Payment:** On acceptance.

CHICAGO MAGAZINE

500 N. Dearborn, Suite 1200, Chicago, IL 60610-4901. E-mail: chimagst@aol.com. Web site: www.chicagomag.com. Monthly. Circ.: 175,000. Shane Tritsch, Managing Editor. **Description:** Topics related to Chicago. **Nonfiction:** 1,000-5,000 words; pay varies. **Queries:** Required. **Payment:** On acceptance.

CHICAGO READER

11 E. Illinois St., Chicago, IL 60611. 312-828-0350. Web site: www.chicagoreader.com. **Description:** Free weekly. **Queries:** Preferred.

CINCINNATI MAGAZINE

One Centennial Plaza, 705 Central Ave., Suite 370, Cincinnati, OH 45202. 513-421-4300. Monthly. Circ.: 25,000. Kitty Morgan, Editor. **Description:** Cincinnati people and issues. **Nonfiction:** 500-3,500 words; $50-$500. **Tips:** Query with writing sample.

CITY AZ

2525 E. Camelback Rd., #120, Phoenix, AZ 85016-4223. 602-667-9798. E-mail: cityaz@aol.com. Web site: www.cityaz.com. Bimonthly. Circ.: 40,000. Michelle Savoy, Exec. Editor. **Description:** For Phoenix area professionals. Covers fashion, beauty, and fitness; local and national profiles; as well as architecture and design. **Queries:** Required.

COLORADO HOMES AND LIFESTYLES

7009 S. Potomac St., Englewood, CO 80112. 303-662-5204. E-mail: emcgraw@coloradohomesmag.com. Web site: www.coloradohomesmag.com. 9x/year. $3.95/issue, $16.97/year. Circ.: 35,000. Evalyn K. McGraw, Editor. **Description:** Affluent, upscale homes and lifestyles. **Nonfiction:** Articles, 1,300-1,500 words, on Colorado homes and interiors. Features on upscale homes, unusual lifestyles. **Columns, Departments:** Architecture, artists, food and wine, design trends, profiles, gardening, and travel; 1,100-1,300 words. **Queries:** Preferred. **Payment:** On acceptance.

COMMON GROUND

P.O. Box 99, 6 W. John St., McVeytown, PA 17051-0099. 717-899-6133. E-mail: commonground@acsworld.net. Quarterly. $3.50/issue, $12.95/year. Circ.: 9,000. Ruth Dunmire, Pam Brumbaugh. **Description:** Focuses on Pennsylvania's Juniata River Valley. **Nonfiction:** Hiking destinations, local history, personality profiles; $40/printed page. **Poetry:** Short; $5-$25. **Art:** Prints; $15-$25. **Tips:** Write for upcoming themes. **Queries:** Not necessary. **E-queries:** Yes. **Unsolicited mss:** Accepts. **Response:** 1 month, SASE. **Freelance Content:** 90%. **Rights:** 1st. **Payment:** On publication.

COMMONWEALTH

18 Tremont Street, Suite 1120, Boston, MA 02111. 617-742-6800. E-mail: rkeough@massinc.org. Web site: www.massinc.org. Quarterly. $5. Circ.: 8,000. Robert Keough, Editor. **Description:** Politics, ideas, and civic life in Massachusetts. Pays $.35-$.50/word **Nonfiction:** On politics, public policy; 3,000 words and up. **Columns, Departments:** Reflective essays on civic life; 800-1,500 words. **Queries:** Preferred. **E-queries:** Yes. **Unsolicited mss:** Accepts. **Response:** Varies, SASE. **Rights:** FNASR. **Payment:** On acceptance.

CONNECTICUT MAGAZINE

35 Nutmeg Dr., Trumbull, CT 06611. 203-380-6600. E-mail: cmonagan@connecticutmag.com. Web site: www.connecticutmag.com. Monthly. Circ.: 86,820. Charles Monagan, Editor. **Description:** Connecticut topics, issues, people, and lifestyles. **Nonfiction:** 1,500-3,500 words; $500-$1,200. **Payment:** On acceptance.

THE COUNTRY CONNECTION

Pinecone Publishing, 691 Pine Crest Rd., Boulter, ON, Canada K0L 1G0. 613-332-3651. E-mail: magazine@pinecone.on.ca. Web site: www.pinecone.on.ca. Biannual. $3.95. Circ.: 10,000. Gus Zylstra, Editor. **Description:** Pro-nature, for Ontario. Focuses on nature, heritage, the arts. **Tips:** Canadian material only. **Queries:** Not necessary.

E-queries: Yes. **Unsolicited mss:** Accepts. **Response:** Queries 1 week, submissions to 6 months, SASE (Canadian postage). **Freelance Content:** 75%. **Rights:** 1st. **Payment:** On publication.

CRAIN'S CHICAGO BUSINESS
740 Rush St., Chicago, IL 60611. 312-649-5411.
Web site: www.chicagobusiness.com. **Description:** Business articles about Chicago metro area.

CRAIN'S DETROIT BUSINESS
1400 Woodbridge Ave., Detroit, MI 48207. 313-446-0419.
E-mail: jmelton@crain.com. Web site: www.crainsdetroit.com. Weekly. $1.50/issue. Circ.: 38,000. Mary Kramer, Managing Editor. **Description:** Local business publication. **Columns, Departments:** Business articles about Detroit; 800 words; $10/column inch. **Queries:** Required. **E-queries:** Yes. **Payment:** On publication. **Contact:** James Melton, Asst. Ed.

DELAWARE TODAY
P.O. Box 2800, Wilmington, DE 19805. 302-656-1809.
Web site: www.delawaretoday.com. Marsha Mah, Editor. **Description:** On topics of local interest. **Nonfiction:** Service articles, profiles, news, etc. Pays $150 for department pieces, $200-$500 for features. **Tips:** Queries with clips required. **Payment:** On publication.

DOWN EAST
P.O. Box 679, Camden, ME 04843. 207-594-9544.
Web site: www.downeast.com. **Description:** Articles, 1,500-2,500 words, on all aspects of life in Maine. **Art:** Photos. **Queries:** Preferred. **Payment:** On acceptance.

EASTSIDE PARENT
Northwest Parent Publishing, 1530 Westlake Ave. N., Suite 600,
Seattle, WA 98109. 206-441-0191.
Web site: www.parenthoodweb.com. Virginia Smyth, Editor. **Description:** For parents of children under 14. Readers tend to be professional, two-career families. Also publishes *Portland Parent, Seattle's Child,* etc. **Nonfiction:** Articles, 300-2,500 words; pays $50-$600. **Queries:** Preferred. **Payment:** On publication.

FAMILY TIMES
P.O. Box 932, Eau Claire, WI 54702.
Nancy Walter, Editor. **Description:** For parents in Wisconsin's Chippewa Valley, on children and parenting issues. **Nonfiction:** Health, education, how-tos, new studies, programs for parenting; pays $35-$50. **Queries:** Preferred. **Response:** SASE. **Payment:** On publication.

FIFTY-PLUS
Alliance Media, Meadow Mill at Woodbury, 3600 Clipper Mill Rd., Ste. 115, Baltimore, MD 21211. 410-366-7512. Melinda Greenberg. **Description:** For Baltimore area seniors. **Queries:** Preferred.

FLORIDA
Orlando Sentinel, 633 N. Orange Ave., Orlando, FL 32801. 407-420-5000. Web site: www.orlandosentinel.com. **Description:** Sunday magazine of the *Orlando Sentinel.*

FLORIDA LIVING
102 Drennen Road, Suite C-5, Orlando, FL 32806. 407-816-9596. E-mail: editor@flaliving.com. Web site: www.floridamagazine.com. Monthly. $2.99/issue, $21.95/year. Circ.: 201,189. Jacqui Langton, Editor. **Description:** Statewide lifestyle. **Nonfiction:** Articles and columns; 700-2,000 words; pays $.25/word. **Art:** Transparencies; $50 and up. **Queries:** Preferred. **E-queries:** Yes. **Unsolicited mss:** Accepts. **Response:** 1 week, SASE. **Freelance Content:** 50%. **Rights:** 1st. **Payment:** On publication.

FLORIDA WILDLIFE
620 S. Meridian St., Tallahassee, FL 32399-1600. 850-488-5563. Web site: www.floridawildlifemagazine.com. Bimonthly. Dick Sublette, Editor. **Description:** Published by Florida Fish and Wildlife Conservation Commission. **Nonfiction:** Articles, 800-1,200 words, that promote native flora and fauna, hunting, fishing in Florida's waters, outdoor ethics, and conservation of natural resources. Pays $55/page. **Payment:** On publication.

FRANCE
4101 Reservoir Rd. NW, Washington, DC 20007-2186. 202-944-6069. Quarterly. Karen Taylor. **Description:** On business, culture, and society, for well-educated Francophiles throughout the U.S. Also, sightseeing information and tips on good restaurants and accomodations. **Nonfiction:** Articles, varying lengths. **Queries:** Preferred.

FREDERICK
6 East St., #301, Frederick, MD 21701-5680. 301-662-8171. E-mail: dpatrell@fredmag.com. Monthly. $2.95/$19.95. Circ.: 18,000. Dan Patrell, Editor. **Description:** Covers lifestyle and issues in mid-Maryland, in and around Frederick County. Each month includes a photo essay. **Nonfiction:** With a direct link to Maryland, especially Frederick Co.; 800-3,000 words; $100-$300. **Art:** Electronic, transparancies, slides; $25-$300. **Queries:** Required. **E-queries:** Yes. **Unsolicited mss:** Does not accept. **Response:** Queries 1-3 months, submissions 1 month. **Freelance Content:** 100%. **Rights:** 1st NA. **Payment:** On publication.

FREE SPIRIT

107 Sterling Pl., Brooklyn, NY 11217. 718-638-3733. Bimonthly. Paul English, Editor. **Description:** On environmental issues, holistic health, political issues, culture/art, and general interest for readers in Manhattan. Interviews welcomed. **Nonfiction:** Articles, 4,000 words; pays $.10/word. **Queries:** Preferred. **Payment:** On acceptance.

GARDEN SHOWCASE

P.O. Box 23669, Portland, OR 97281-3669. 503-684-0153. E-mail: editor@gardenshowcase.com. Web site: www.gardenshowcase.com. Monthly except Dec. and Jan. $2.95/issue, $19.95/year. Circ.: 30,000. Lynn Lustberg, Editor. **Description:** Distributed in Oregon and Washington. Features regional plants, gardens, and nurseries, with gardening ideas and examples. Also, home decorating and design articles to connect the garden and the home. **Nonfiction:** Articles on outstanding gardens, etc.; 800-1,000 words; $160. **Columns, Departments:** Q&A, Planting by Design, Gardening 101, Through the Grapevine; 380-400; $100. **Queries:** Preferred. **E-queries:** Yes. **Unsolicited mss:** Accepts. **Response:** Queries 1-2 mos. Submissions 2-3 months, SASE required. **Freelance Content:** 100%. **Rights:** 1st. **Payment:** On publication.

GO

6600 AAA Dr., Charlotte, NC 28212-8250. 704-569-7733. E-mail: trcrosby@aaaga.com. Web site: aaacarolinas.com. 7x/year. for members. Circ.: 750,000. Tom Crosby. **Description:** For AAA members in North and South Carolina. Features on automotive, finance, insurance, and travel. **Columns, Departments:** Travel, auto safety; 750-1,000 words; $.15 /word. **Queries:** Preferred. **E-queries:** No. **Unsolicited mss:** Accepts. **Response:** 1-3 weeks, SASE. **Freelance Content:** 15%. **Payment:** On publication. **Contact:** Jacquie Hughett, Asst. Ed.

GOLDENSEAL

The Cultural Ctr., 1900 Kanawha Blvd. E., Charleston, WV 25305-0300. 304-558-0220. Web site: www.wvculture.org/goldenseal. John Lilly, Editor. **Description:** On traditional West Virginia culture and history. Oral histories, old and new b/w photos, research articles. **Nonfiction:** Features, 3,000 words, and shorter articles, 1,000 words; pays $.10/word. **Payment:** On publication.

GRAND RAPIDS

549 Ottawa N.W., Grand Rapids, MI 49503. 616-459-4545. Web site: www.geminipub.com. Monthly. Circ.: 20,000. Carole R. Valade, Editor. **Description:** Covers local area. **Nonfiction:** Service articles (dining guide, travel, personal finance, humor) and issue-oriented pieces. Pays $35-$200. **Queries:** Preferred. **Unsolicited mss:** Accepts. **Payment:** On publication.

GULFSHORE LIFE
2975 S. Horseshoe Dr., Suite 100, Naples, FL 34104-6189. 941-643-3933.
Monthly. Circ.: 24,000., Nancy Theoret, Editor. **Description:** On southwest Florida
personalities, travel, sports, business, interior design, arts, history, and nature.
Nonfiction: Articles, 800-3,000 words; pays from $200. **Queries:** Preferred.

HAWAII
3 Burroughs, Irvine, CA 92618.
Bimonthly. June Kikuchi, Editor. **Description:** On topics related to Hawaii.
Nonfiction: Articles, 1,000-2,500 words; pays $.10/word. **Queries:** Preferred.
Payment: On publication.

HISPANIC MONTHLY
3006 Garrow St., Houston, TX 77003-2326. 713-236-8475.
Web site: www.hispanicmonthly.com. Monthly. Miguel Barrientos. **Description:**
Covers state and national issues of interest to Hispanics living in Texas. **Nonfiction:**
Topics include business, community, education, law, politics, also lighter topics such
as fashion, entertainment, health and fitness. Pay varies. **Queries:** Preferred.

HONOLULU
Honolulu Publishing Co., Ltd., 36 Merchant St., Honolulu, HI 96813. 808-524-7400.
Web site: www.honpub.com. John Heckathorn, Editor. **Description:** Features highlighting contemporary life in the Hawaiian islands: politics, sports, history, people, arts,
events. **Nonfiction:** Pays $300-$700. **Queries:** Required. **Payment:** On acceptance.

ILLINOIS ENTERTAINER
124 W. Polk, Suite 103, Chicago, IL 60605.
E-mail: ieeditors@aol.com. Web site: www.illinoisentertainer.com. Monthly. Free.
Circ.: 70,000. Michael C. Harris, Editor. **Description:** Covers entertainment and
media, especially music. Open to non-music/band features, especially of odd, quixotic
kind. **Nonfiction:** On local and national entertainment (especially alternative music)
in greater Chicago area. Personality profiles; interviews; reviews. 500-1,500 words;
$75. **Art:** by assignment; $30-200. **Tips:** Send clips (via snail mail) and be patient.
Queries: Not necessary. **E-queries:** Yes. **Unsolicited mss:** Accepts. **Response:**
Queries 30 days, submissions 30-90 days, SASE not required. **Freelance Content:**
70%. **Rights:** FNASR. **Payment:** On publication.

IMAGEN: REFLECTIONS OF TODAY'S LATINO
P.O. Box 7487, Albuquerque, NM 87194-7487. 505-889-4088.
Web site: www.imagenmag.com. Monthly. **Description:** Focus on New Mexico's
Latino community.

INDIANAPOLIS MONTHLY
1 Emmis Plaza, 40 Monument Circle, Suite 100, Indianapolis, IN 46204. 317-237-9288.
Web site: www.indianapolismonthly.com. Sam Stall, Editor. **Description:** All material

must have an Indianapolis/Indiana focus. **Nonfiction:** Profiles, sports, business, travel, crime, controversy, service, first-person essays, book excerpts; 2,500-4,000 words, $400-$500. **Columns, Departments:** IndyScene (trendy "quick hits"), to 200 words, $50; departments,1,500 -2,500 words, $250-$350. **Payment:** On publication.

INSIDE CHICAGO
4710 N. Lincoln Ave., Chicago, IL 60625. 773-878-7333.
E-mail: inside@suba.com. Web site: www.insideonline.com. Weekly. Free. Circ.: 49,500. Pier Petersen, Editor. **Description:** Community newspaper for Chicago's North side. **Nonfiction:** News/features on Chicagoans, nightlife, arts, and lifestyle. Short reports (150-300 words); 400-900 words; $25/story. **Art:** $25/photo. **Queries:** Preferred. **E-queries:** Yes. **Unsolicited mss:** Accepts. **Response:** 1 week, SASE required. **Freelance Content:** 40%. **Rights:** One-time (print and electronic). **Payment:** On publication.

THE IOWAN
504 E. Locust, Des Moines, IA 50309. 515-282-8220.
E-mail: kroberson@iowan.com. Web site: iowan@iowan.com. Bi-monthly. $24.50 year. Circ.: 25,000. Jay P. Wagner, Editor. **Description:** Covers history, culture, people, places, and events of Iowa. **Fiction:** short stories; up to 5,000 words; $.30/word. **Nonfiction:** life in Iowa; up to 5,000 words; $.30/word. **Poetry:** $100/poem. **Art:** All formats. **Queries:** Not necessary. **E-queries:** Yes. **Unsolicited mss:** Accepts. **Response:** 12 weeks, SASE required. **Freelance Content:** 80%. **Rights:** One-time NA. **Payment:** On acceptance.

JACKSONVILLE
White Publishing Co., 1032 Hendricks Ave., Jacksonville, FL 32207. 904-396-8666. Monthly. Circ.: 25,000. Joseph White, Managing Editor. **Description:** Issues and personalities of interest to readers in the greater Jacksonville area. **Nonfiction:** Service pieces and articles. Home and garden articles on local homeowners, interior designers, remodelers, gardeners, craftsmen, etc., 1,000-2,000 words; 1,500-2,500 words; $200-$500. **Columns, Departments:** Business, health, travel, personal finance, real estate, arts and entertainment, sports, dining out, food; 1,200-1,500 words. **Queries:** Required. **Payment:** On publication.

KANSAS!
Kansas Dept. of Commerce, 700 S.W. Harrison, Suite 1300, Topeka, KS 66603-3712. 785-296-3479.
E-mail: ksmagazine@kdoch.state.ks.us. Web site: www.travelks.com. Quarterly. $4/issue, $15/year. Circ.: 48,000. **Description:** To encourage travel in Kansas, with its rich history, scenic landscape, exciting attractions, and Midwestern hospitality. **Nonfiction:** Length, pay varies. **Tips:** Avoid topics not travel related, as well as politics, religion, sex, other state's activities. **Queries:** Preferred. **E-queries:** Yes. **Unsolicited mss:** Accepts. **Response:** SASE required. **Freelance Content:** 100%. **Payment:** On acceptance. **Contact:** Carole Frederick.

KANSAS CITY

118 Southwest Blvd., Kansas City, MO 64108. 816-421-4111.
E-mail: zloy@abartapub.com. Web site: www.kcmag.com. 10x/year. $3.50/issue,
$9.98/year. Circ.: 27,000. Zim Loy, Editor. **Description:** Celebrates life in Kansas City.
Nonfiction: Serious piece on local issues; personality profiles; fun features (Weekend
Getaways, etc.); 1,000-3,000 words; $700-$1,000/features. **Columns, Departments:**
Excursions (regional travel); Arts (local scene); 1,200 words; $200-$400. **Art:** prints,
transparancies, b/w, jpg. **Tips:** Avoid generic "fit any market" features. **Queries:**
Preferred. **E-queries:** Yes. **Unsolicited mss:** Accepts. **Response:** queries 2 wks, sub-
missions 4 wks. **Freelance Content:** 90%. **Rights:** 1st. **Payment:** On acceptance.

KENTUCKY LIVING

P.O. Box 32170, Louisville, KY 40232. 502-451-2430.
E-mail: email@kentuckyliving.com. Web site: www.kentuckyliving.com. Monthly.
$15/year. Circ.: 480,000. Paul Wesslund, Editor. **Description:** On the character and
culture of Kentucky. **Nonfiction:** On personalities, history, biography, recreation,
travel, and leisure; 1,000 words; $450. **Queries:** Preferred. **E-queries:** Yes.
Unsolicited mss: Accepts. **Response:** Queries and submissions 4-6 weeks, SASE
required. **Freelance Content:** 75%. **Payment:** On acceptance.

L.A. PARENT

443 E. Irving Dr., Burbank, CA 91504. 818-846-0400.
Web site: www.parenthoodweb.com. Monthly. Circ.: 100,000. Janis Hashe, National
Editor. **Description:** On child development, health, nutrition, and education, for
parents of children up to age 10. Also publishes San Diego Parent, and Parenting
(Orange Co.). **Nonfiction:** Articles, 1,000 words; pays $100-$350. **Queries:**
Preferred. **Payment:** On acceptance.

LAKE SUPERIOR

P.O. Box 16417, Duluth, MN 55816-0417. 218-727-2765.
E-mail: edit@lakesuprior.com. Web site: www.lakesuperior.com. Bimonthly. Paul
Hayden, Editor. **Description:** Focuses on Lake Superior region (U.S. and Canada)
and its peoples. **Nonfiction:** People, events, and places; 1,000-2,000 words; $100-
$600. **Fillers:** Short pieces on Lake life; 600 words or less; $50-$125. **Columns,
Departments:** Science, history, humor, reminiscences; 600-1,500 words; $50-$225.
Art: Varied formats; $25 b/w, $40 color, $125 cover. **Tips:** Lake Superior regional
topics only. **Queries:** Preferred. **E-queries:** No. **Unsolicited mss:** Accepts.
Response: 3-6 months, SASE required. **Freelance Content:** 80%. **Rights:**
FNASR. **Payment:** On publication. **Contact:** Konnie LeMay, Managing Editor.

LAS VEGAS FAMILY

6320 McLeod Dr., Suite 3, Las Vegas, NV 89120. 702-740-2260.
Web site: www.ocfamily.com. Monthly. Craig Reem, Executive Editor. **Description:**
Covers topics such as families, fitness, health care, education, computers, camps,
entertainment and travel. **Contact:** Greg Blake, Managing Editor.

LONG ISLAND WOMAN

P.O. Box 309, Island Park, NY 11558. 516-897-8900.
E-mail: editor@liwomanonline.com. Web site: www.liwomanonline.com. monthly.
Circ.: 32,000. Pat Simms-Elias, Editor. **Description:** For educated, active women of Long Island, NY, region. **Nonfiction:** Pays $10-$150. **Queries:** Required. **E-queries:** Yes. **Unsolicited mss:** Accepts. **Freelance Content:** 80%. **Rights:** 1st. **Payment:** On publication.

THE LOOK

P.O. Box 272, Cranford, NJ 07016-0272. 908-755-6138.
E-mail: jrhawks@thelookmag.com. Web site: www.thelookmag.com. Monthly. Free. Circ.: 3,500. John R. Hawks, Editor. **Description:** New Jersey entertainment magazine. **Nonfiction:** 1,500-3,000 words, on fashion, student life, employment, relationships, and profiles for readers ages 16-26. Also, beach stories about New Jersey shore. Pays $30-$200. **Fillers:** Puzzles, trivia quizzes, about area people, places, events. **Queries:** Preferred. **E-queries:** Yes. **Unsolicited mss:** Accepts. **Response:** Queries 30-60 days. **Freelance Content:** 50%. **Rights:** All, may reassign. **Payment:** On publication.

LOS ANGELES

5900 Wilshire Blvd., 10th Floor, Los Angeles, CA 90025. 323-801-0100.
Web site: www.lamag.com. Monthly. $3.50. Circ.: 184,000. Kit Rachlis, Editor. **Description:** The diary of a great city for those enthralled by what the city has to offer and those overwhelmed by it. An essential guide. **Nonfiction:** Articles, to 3,000 words, for sophisticated, affluent southern Californians, with local focus on a lifestyle topic. Pay varies. **Tips:** Try a well-written first-person account of moving to L.A. **Queries:** Required. **E-queries:** Yes. **Unsolicited mss:** Accepts. **Response:** 2-4 weeks, SASE. **Freelance Content:** 50%. **Rights:** 1st NA. **Payment:** On acceptance.

LOUISVILLE

137 W. Muhammad Ali Blvd., Suite 101, Louisville, KY 40202. 502-625-0100.
Web site: www.louisville.com/loumag.html. Monthly. $3.75. Circ.: 20,000. Bruce Allar, Editor. **Description:** City magazine. **Nonfiction:** On community issues, personalities, and entertainment in the Louisville area. 500-2,500 words. $150-$600. **Queries:** Required. **E-queries:** Yes. **Unsolicited mss:** Accepts. **Response:** 60 days, SASE. **Freelance Content:** 60%. **Rights:** FNASR. **Payment:** On acceptance.

MATURE LIFESTYLES

220 W. Brandon Blvd., Ste 210, Brandon, FL 33511. 813-653-1988.
Web site: www.srconnect.com. Kathy J. Beck. **Description:** For readers over 50, in Florida. **Nonfiction:** Articles, 500-700 words; pays $50. **Tips:** No fiction or poetry. Florida angle required. **Payment:** On publication.

MATURE LIVING
Senior Publishers Media Group, 255 N. El Cielo Rd., #452, Palm Springs, CA 92262. 760-320-2221. **Description:** For older adults in and around Palm Springs, CA.

MEMPHIS
Contemporary Media, Box 1738, 460 Tennessee St., Memphis, TN 38103. 901-521-9000. E-mail: memmag@mem.net. Web site: www.memphismagazine.com. Monthly. Circ.: 24,000. Richard Banks, Editor. **Description:** Topics related to Memphis and the Mid-South region: politics, education, sports, business, history, etc. **Nonfiction:** Articles on a variety of subjects. Profiles; investigative pieces; 1,500-4,000 words; $50-$500. **Queries:** Required. **Payment:** On publication.

METROKIDS
1080 N. Delaware Ave., Suite 702, Philadelphia, PA 19125. 215-291-5560 x102. E-mail: editor@metrokids.com. Web site: www.metrokids.com. Monthly. Free. Circ.: 125,000. Nancy Lisagor, Editor. **Description:** For Delaware Valley area, on parenting kids, ages 0-16. **Nonfiction:** Parenting subjects, products reviews, and travel in the Philadelphia metro region; 800-1500 words; $30-$100. **Columns, Departments:** Product reviews, books, music, video, software, health, women's subjects, family finance; 800; $30-$50. **Queries:** Preferred. **E-queries:** Yes. **Unsolicited mss:** Accepts. **Response:** Queries 2 months, submissions 2 months. **Freelance Content:** 60%. **Rights:** one-time only, website. **Payment:** On publication.

MIAMI METRO
2800 Biscayne Blvd., Suite 1100, Miami, FL 33137. 305-755-9920. Web site: www.miamimetro.com. Nancy Moore, Publisher. **Description:** News and hot topics on South Florida. **Nonfiction:** Features; 1,100-2,000 words. **Columns, Departments:** 200-1,300 words, on news, profiles, and hot topics related to south Florida. Short, bright items, 200-400 words. **Queries:** Preferred. **Payment:** On acceptance. **Contact:** Felicia Levine, Exec. Ed.

MICHIGAN LIVING
Auto Club of Michigan, 1 Auto Club Dr., Dearborn, MI 48126-9982. 248-816-9265. Web site: www.aaamich.com. Ron Garbinski, Editor. **Description:** Michigan topics, also area and Canadian tourist attractions and recreational opportunities **Nonfiction:** Informative travel articles, 300-2,000 words; pays $55-$500. **Art:** Photos; pay varies. **Queries:** Preferred. **Payment:** On publication.

MIDWEST LIVING
1912 Grand Ave., Des Moines, IA 50309. 515-284-2662. Web site: www.midwestliving.com. Bimonthly. Barbara Humeston, Editor. **Description:** Lifestyle articles relating to any or all of the 12 midwest states.

Nonfiction: Town, neighborhood, and personality profiles. Humorous essays occasionally used. Pay varies. **Rights:** All. **Payment:** On acceptance.

MILESTONES
Milestones Publishing, 246 S. 22nd, Philadelphia, PA 19103. 215-732-9029. Monthly. Circ.: 26,000. **Description:** For seniors in the greater Philadelphia area.

MILWAUKEE MAGAZINE
417 E. Chicago, Milwaukee, WI 53202. 414-273-1101. E-mail: jfennell@q6.com. Web site: www.milwaukeemagazine.com. Monthly. $3.00/issue, $18.00/year. Circ.: 40,000. John Fennell, Editor. **Description:** Offers in-depth reporting and analysis of issues, with service features, stories, essays. **Nonfiction:** Must be specific to Milwaukee area, solid research and reporting; 2,000-5,000 words; $500-$1,000. **Columns, Departments:** Issue-oriented commentary, some humor; 900-1200 words; $300-$600. **Queries:** Required. **E-queries:** Yes. **Unsolicited mss:** Accepts. **Response:** Queries 6 weeks, submission 6 weeks if unsolicited, SASE. **Freelance Content:** 50%. **Rights:** 1st. **Payment:** On publication.

MINNESOTA MONTHLY
10 S. Fifth St., Suite 1000, Minneapolis, MN 55402. 612-371-5800 E-mail: phnettleton@mnmo.com. Web site: www.mnmo.com. Monthly. Circ.: 80,000. Pamela Hill Nettleton, Editor. **Description:** People, places, events, and issues in or about Minnesota. **Nonfiction:** To 2,000 words; $150-$2,000. **Queries:** Required. **Payment:** On acceptance.

MISSOURI LIFE
P.O. Box 421, Fayette, MO 65248. 660-248-3489. E-mail: info@missourilife.com. Web site: www.MissouriLife.com. Bi-monthly. $4.50/issue, $19.99/year. Circ.: 50,000. Danita Allen, Editor. **Description:** Explores Missouri and its diverse people and places, past and present. History, weekend getaways and day-trips, interesting people and events. **Nonfiction:** Regular features: Our Town, History, Roundups, People; 1,000-2,000 words; $.30/word. **Fillers:** Best of Missouri; to 300 words; $50. **Columns, Departments:** Missouri Artist, Made in Missouri, Historic Homes, Missouri Memory; 500 words. **Art:** Color slides, photos; $50-$150. **Queries:** Required. **E-queries:** No. **Unsolicited mss:** Accepts. **Response:** 1 week queries, 6 months submissions, SASE. **Freelance Content:** 40%. **Payment:** On acceptance. **Contact:** Carol Moczygemba, Exec. Ed.

MONTANA
P.O. Box 5630, Helena, MT 59604. 406-443-2842. Web site: www.montanamagazine.com. Bimonthly. $4.95. Circ.: 40,000. Beverly R. Magley, Editor. **Description:** Full-color photography and articles reflecting the grandeur and personality of Montana. **Nonfiction:** Montana's culture, history, outdoor recreation, communities, and people. Contemporary issues; places and events, ecology and conservation, unique businesses; 1,500-2,000 words; $.15/word. **Art:**

Slides, transparencies, no digital. **Queries:** Required. **E-queries:** Yes. **Unsolicited mss:** Accepts. **Response:** 4 months, SASE. **Freelance Content:** 100%. **Rights:** one-time. **Payment:** On publication.

MPLS / ST. PAUL

220 S. 6th St., Suite 500, Minneapolis, MN 55402-4507. 612-339-7571. E-mail: edit@mspcommunications.com. Web site: www.mspmag.com. Monthly. $3.50. Circ.: 67,000. Brian E. Anderson, Editor. **Description:** Covers what is new, exciting, newsworthy in the Twin Cities. **Nonfiction:** Timely local issues; dining, arts, and entertainment; home decorating; profiles. **Columns, Departments:** City Limits (news/gossip); About Town (arts and entertainment sidebars). **Tips:** Break in with small features in City Limits and About Town departments. **Queries:** Preferred. **E-queries:** Yes. **Unsolicited mss:** Accepts. **Response:** 6-8 weeks, SASE. **Payment:** On acceptance.

NEBRASKA HISTORY

P.O. Box 82554, Lincoln, NE 68501. 402-471-4747. E-mail: publish@nebraskahistory.org. Web site: www.nebraskahistory.org. Quarterly. $30/yr. Circ.: 3,800. James E. Potter, Editor. **Description:** Well-researched articles, edited documents, and other annotated primary materials on history of Nebraska and the Great Plains. **Nonfiction:** 3,000-7,000 words. **Art:** 8x10 b/w, 600 dpi scans. **Tips:** Rarely publishes family history or reminiscence. **Queries:** Preferred. **E-queries:** Yes. **Unsolicited mss:** Accepts. **Response:** Queries 1 week, submissions in 2 months, SASE. **Payment:** In copies.

NEVADA

401 N. Carson St., Suite 100, Carson City, NV 89701-4291. 775-687-5416. E-mail: editor@nevadamagazine.com. Web site: www.nevadamagazine.com. Bimonthly. Circ.: 90,000. David Moore, Editor. **Description:** Topics related to Nevada: travel, history, recreation, profiles, humor, and attractions. **Nonfiction:** 500-1,800 words; pay varies. **Art:** Photos. **Payment:** On publication.

NEW HAMPSHIRE EDITIONS

100 Main St., Nashua, NH 03060. 603-883-3150. E-mail: editor@nh.com. Web site: www.nhmagazine.com. Monthly. $2/$20. Circ.: 21,000. Rick Broussard, Editor. **Description:** Covers issues and lifestyles of New Hampshire as revealed by the state's best writers, photographers, tourists. **Nonfiction:** Lifestyle, business, and history articles with New Hampshire angle, sources from all regions of the state; 400-2,000 words; $50-$200. **Art:** Prints, slides, negatives, or digital. $25-$300. **Queries:** Preferred. **E-queries:** Yes. **Unsolicited mss:** Accepts. **Response:** 1 month, SASE. **Freelance Content:** 30%. **Rights:** 1st serial and online reprint. **Payment:** On publication.

NEW JERSEY MONTHLY

P.O. Box 920, Morristown, NJ 07963-0920. 973-539-8230. Web site: www.njmonthly.com. **Description:** With New Jersey tie-in. **Nonfiction:** Articles, profiles, and service pieces, 1,500-3,000 words; $600-$1,750. **Columns, Departments:** Health, business, education, travel, sports, local politics, arts; pays $400-$700. **Tips:** Send clips. **Queries:** Preferred. **Payment:** On acceptance.

NEW JERSEY REPORTER

164 Nassau St., 2nd Floor, Princeton, NJ 08542. 609-924-9750. E-mail: njreporter@rcn.com. Web site: www.njreporter.org. Bimonthly. Circ.: 3,200. Mark Magyar, Editor. **Description:** New Jersey politics and public affairs. **Nonfiction:** In-depth articles; 1,000-4,000 words; $175-$800. **Queries:** Required. **Payment:** On publication.

NEW MEXICO

Lew Wallace Bldg., 495 Old Santa Fe Trail, Santa Fe, NM 87501. 505-827-7447. E-mail: enchantment@newmexico.org. Web site: www.newmexico.org. Monthly. $3.95/issue, $23.95/year. Circ.: 102,000. Emily Drabanski, Editor. **Description:** About everything New Mexican (products, places, style, history, books, fashion, food, sports, recreation, photos). **Nonfiction:** Regional interest only; 2,000 words max.; $.30/word. **Fillers:** On museum exhibits, outdoor activities, humor. **Art:** Slides, transparencies; pay varies. **Tips:** Avoid fiction, first-person accounts, political statements, cemeteries, subjects outside region. **Queries:** Required. **E-queries:** Yes. **Unsolicited mss:** Accepts. **Response:** Queries 1-3 months submissions 3-6 months, SASE. **Freelance Content:** 20%. **Rights:** 1st NA, all NA. **Payment:** On acceptance.

NEW MEXICO JOURNEY

3333 Fairview Rd., A-327, Costa Mesa, CA 92626. 714-885-2380. Web site: www.aaa-newmexico.com. Bi-monthly. Circ.: 80,000. Annette Winter, Editor. **Description:** For AAA members. Covers travel and people of New Mexico and surrounding states. **Nonfiction:** 1,000-2,000 words; $1/word. **Columns, Departments:** WeekEnder, DayTripping, RoadszRoam, AutoNews, TravelNews; 100-250 words; $1/word. **Art:** 35mm. **Tips:** Seeks stories and people behind typical destinations and venues **Queries:** Required. **Unsolicited mss:** Does not accept. **Response:** 6 weeks. **Freelance Content:** 80%. **Rights:** 1st NA. **Payment:** On acceptance.

NEW ORLEANS MAGAZINE

111 Veterans Blvd., Metairie, LA 70005. 504-834-9292. Web site: www.neworleansmagazine.com. Errol Laborde, Editor. **Description:** On New Orleans area people and issues. **Nonfiction:** Articles, 3-15 triple-spaced pages; pays $15-$500, extra for photos. **Art:** Photos. **Queries:** Preferred. **Payment:** On publication.

NEW YORK FAMILY
141 Halstead Ave., Suite 3D, Mamaroneck, NY 10543. 914-381-7474. Web site: www.parenthoodweb.com. Heather Hart, Editor. **Description:** Articles related to family life in New York City and general parenting topics. **Nonfiction:** Pays $50-$200. **Payment:** On publication.

NEWPORT LIFE
55 Memorial Blvd., Newport, RI 02840. Web site: www.newportlifemagazine.com. Bimonthly. Lynne Tungett. **Description:** On people, places, attractions of Newport County. **Nonfiction:** Articles, 500-2,500 words, general-interest, historical, profiles, international celebrities, and social and political issues. **Columns, Departments:** 200-750 words; sailing, dining, food and wine, home and garden, arts, in Newport County. **Art:** Photos needed for all articles. **Queries:** Preferred. **Response:** SASE required.

NORTH DAKOTA HORIZONS
PO Box 2639, Bismarck, ND 58502. 701-222-0929. E-mail: lyle-halvorsonegnda.com. Web site: www.ndhorizons.com. Quarterly. $5/issue, $15/year. Circ.: 12,000. Janine Webb, Editor. **Description:** Showcases North Dakota people, places, and events. **Nonfiction:** 1,000-3,000 words; $100-$300. **Art:** All formats; $10-$150/image. **Queries:** Preferred. **E-queries:** Yes. **Unsolicited mss:** Accepts. **Response:** Queries/submissions up to 1 month, SASE. **Freelance Content:** 90%. **Rights:** One-time. **Payment:** On publication.

NORTH GEORGIA JOURNAL
P.O. Box 127, Roswell, GA 30077. 770-642-5569. E-mail: north.ga.travel@mindspring.com. Quarterly. $4.50/$24. Circ.: 18,000. Olin Jackson, Editor. **Description:** For travelers in northern region of the state, offers travel destinations, leisure lifestyles, history. **Nonfiction:** Travel; lifestyles, history, and historic real estate; 1,500-3,000 words; $.08-$.12/word. **Art:** 35 mm. slides; $10, $150 (cover). **Queries:** Required. **E-queries:** Yes. **Unsolicited mss:** Accepts. **Response:** Queries 2 weeks, submissions 3-4 weeks, SASE. **Freelance Content:** 65%. **Rights:** All. **Payment:** On publication.

NORTHEAST
Hartford Courant, 285 Broad St., Hartford, CT 06115. 860-241-3700. E-mail: northeast@courant.com. Web site: ctnow.com. Click on Northeast Weekly (Sunday only). Circ.: 316,000. Larry Bloom, Editor. **Description:** Sunday magazine for the major daily newspaper for Connecticut. **Nonfiction:** Articles spun off the news and compelling personal stories, 750-3,000 words, for Connecticut residents. Pays $250-$1,000. **Queries:** Preferred. **E-queries:** No. **Unsolicited mss:** Accepts. **Response:** Queries/submissions 2-3 months, SASE. **Freelance Content:** 2%. **Rights:** One-time. **Payment:** On acceptance. **Contact:** Jane Bronfonan, Ed. Asst.

NORTHEAST OUTDOORS

2575 Vista Del Mar, Ventura, CA 93001. 800-323-9078. Web site: www.woodalls.com. Melinda Baccanai, Editor. **Description:** On camping and recreational vehicle (RV) touring in northeast U.S. **Nonfiction:** Prefers how-to, where-to (camp cookery, recreational vehicle hints). Articles, 1,000-2,000 words, preferably with b/w photos; pay varies. **Fillers:** Cartoons.

NOT BORN YESTERDAY

Osmon Publications, Inc., 4805 Alta Canyada Rd., La Canada Flintridge, CA 91011. 818-790-0651. Monthly. Circ.: 95,000. **Description:** For Southern California seniors.

NOW & THEN

CASS/ETSU, P.O. Box 70556, Johnson City, TN 37614-0556. 423-439-5348. E-mail: cass@etsu.edu. Web site: www.cass.etsu.edu/n&t. 3x/year. $20. Circ.: 1,500. Jane Harris Woodside, Editor. **Description:** Each issue focuses on one aspect of life in Appalachian region (from Northern Mississippi to Southern New York). Previous themes: women, religion, blacks, Cherokees, the environment, music. **Fiction:** 1,500-3,000 words: must relate to theme of issue and Appalachian region. **Nonfiction:** Articles, interviews, essays, memoirs, book reviews; 1,000-2,500 words. **Poetry:** up to 5 poems. **Tips:** Topics can be contemporary or historical. **Queries:** Preferred.

OHIO

62 E. Broad St., Columbus, OH 43215. 800-426-4624. E-mail: editorial@ohiomagazine.com. Web site: Ohiomagazine.com. Monthly. Circ.: 90,000. Alyson Borgerding, Editor. **Description:** On everything in Ohio, from people and places to food and entertainment. **Nonfiction:** On travel around Ohio, with profiles of people, cities, towns; historic sites, tourist attractions, little-known spots; 1,000-1,200 words. **Tips:** Seeking fresh stories with a decisively different Ohio angle. **Queries:** Preferred. **E-queries:** Yes. **Unsolicited mss:** Accepts. **Response:** 6 weeks, SASE. **Freelance Content:** 25%. **Payment:** On acceptance.

OKLAHOMA TODAY

15 N. Robinson, Suite 100, Oklahoma City, OK 73102. 405-521-2496. E-mail: editorial@oklahomatoday.com. Web site: www.oklahomatoday.com. 7x/year. $3.95/issue, $16.95/year. Circ.: 45,000. Louisa McCune, Editor. **Description:** Covers travel, profiles, history, nature, outdoor recreation, and arts, all with a regional tie-in to Oklahoma. **Nonfiction:** Anecdotes, quotes, and experiences of past and present people. Information on "hot spots" to visit, off the beaten track; 250-3,000 words; $25-$750. **Art:** Seeks contact with photographers in Oklahoma or who have shot there. Send samples and price range. Captions and model releases required; 35mm color transparencies, slides; b/w; $50-$100, b/w; $50-$750 color. **Tips:** Include biography, previous clips. **Queries:** Preferred. **E-queries:** Yes. **Unsolicited mss:**

Accepts. **Response:** 4-6 months, SASE. **Freelance Content:** 80%. **Rights:** 1st serial worldwide. **Payment:** On publication.

ORANGE COAST
3701 Birch St., #100, Newport Beach, CA 92660-2618. 949-862-1133. E-mail: ocmag@aol.com. Web site: www.orangecoastmagazine.com. Monthly. $2.95/$9.98. Circ.: 50,000. Nancy Cheerer, Chief Editor. **Description:** Covers Orange County, California, for educated, sophisticated readers. **Nonfiction:** Local trends, people, and news stories; workplace and family issues; 1,500-3,000 words; $350-$700. **Columns, Departments:** Escape (weekend travel); Close-Up (profiles), 650 words. Short Cuts (local items, 200 words); pay varies. **Tips:** Prefers writers with journalism experience and interesting ideas. **Queries:** Required. **E-queries:** No. **Unsolicited mss:** Accepts. **Response:** 1-2 months. **Freelance Content:** 85%. **Rights:** FNASR; non-exclusive web. **Payment:** On publication. **Contact:** Anastacia Grenda, Managing Ed.

OREGON COAST
4969 Highway 101, #2, P.O. Box 18000, Florence, OR 97439. 541-997-8401. E-mail: judy@ohwy.com, jm@ohwy.com. Web site: www.ohwy.com. Circ.: 65,000. Judy Fleagle, Jim Forst, Editors. **Description:** Covers communities, businesses, people, events, activities, and the natural wonders that make up the Oregon coast. **Nonfiction:** First-person experiences, 500-1,500 words, with details in sidebars, with slides preferred. On travel, history, town/city profiles, outdoor activities, events, and nature. News releases, 200-500 words; $65-$350/features. **Art:** Some stand-alone photos (verticals); also 2 calendars/yr; slides and transparencies; $25-75, $325 (cover). **Queries:** Preferred. **E-queries:** Yes. **Unsolicited mss:** Accepts. **Response:** Queries 3 months, submissions 2-3 months, SASE. **Freelance Content:** 60%. **Rights:** 1st NA, one-time photos. **Payment:** On publication.

OREGON OUTSIDE
Northwest Regional Magazines, 4969 Hwy 101 N, Suite 2, Box 18000, Florence, OR 97439-0130. 800-348-8401. E-mail: judy@ohwy.com. Web site: www.ohwy.com. Quarterly. $3.50/year, $12.95/year. Circ.: 25,000. Jim Forst, Steve Beckner, Editors. **Description:** Covers outdoor activities in Oregon: recreation areas, trails and campgrounds; also events, outfitters, and organizations. **Nonfiction:** First-person, all kinds of adventure, from walks for families to extreme skiing; 500-1,500 words; $75-250. **Columns, Departments:** Focal Points (photography tips, how-to and where); 800 words; $125-$150. **Art:** Slides, transparencies; some stand-alone full-page photos (vertical or horizontal); $325/cover, $25-$75/full page. **Tips:** Compelling lead, solid body, satisfying ending, details in sidebars. **Queries:** Preferred. **E-queries:** Yes. **Unsolicited mss:** Accepts. **Response:** Queries 3 months, submissions 2-3 months, SASE required. **Freelance Content:** 50-60%. **Rights:** 1st NA. **Payment:** On publication.

THE OREGONIAN
1320 S.W. Broadway, Portland, OR 97201.
E-mail: oped@news.oregonian.com. Web site: www.oregonlive.com. Daily. Circ.: 360,000. **Description:** Newspaper, with diverse articles, also op-ed pieces, to 650 words, on regional topics; pays $75-$100. **Queries:** Not necessary. **Unsolicited mss:** Accepts. **Rights:** All. **Payment:** On publication.

ORLANDO
225 South Westmonte D., #1100, Altamonte Springs, FL 32714. 407-767-8338. Web site: members.aol.com/orlandomag/private/omag. Jim Clarke, Editor. **Description:** Locally based articles for residents of Central Florida. **Tips:** Send clips. **Queries:** Preferred.

OUR STATE: DOWN HOME IN NORTH CAROLINA
P.O. Box 4552, Greensboro, NC 27404. 336-286-0600. E-mail: editorial@ourstate.com. Monthly. $3.95/$21.95. Circ.: 70,000. Mary Ellis, Editor. **Description:** About North Carolina culture, travel, folklore. **Fiction:** About North Carolina; 1,500 words; $125-$300. **Nonfiction:** Features on people, events, food, history, travel in North Carolina; 1,500 words; $125-$300. **Columns, Departments:** North Carolina memories (holidays, summer, family). **Art:** 35mm slides; call for editorial calendar; $75-$300. **Tips:** Most readers are over 50. **Queries:** Preferred. **E-queries:** Yes. **Unsolicited mss:** Accepts. **Response:** Queries 4 weeks, submissions 12 weeks, SASE. **Freelance Content:** 30%. **Rights:** 1st NA. **Payment:** On publication.

PALM SPRINGS LIFE
Desert Publications, 303 N. Indian Canyon Dr., Palm Springs, CA 92262. 760-325-2333. E-mail: stewart@palmspringlife.com. Web site: www.palmspring.com. Monthly. $3.95/$38. Circ.: 19,000. Stewart Weiner, Editor. **Description:** Looks at upscale lifestyle of desert residents: celebrity profiles, architecture, fashion, desert ecology, art, interior design, and history. **Nonfiction:** 1,500-2,500 words; $250-$500. **Columns, Departments:** On ecology, people, humor, desert sports, politics; 750; $250-$300. **Queries:** Required. **E-queries:** Yes. **Unsolicited mss:** Accepts. **Response:** Queries 1 month, submissions 2 months, SASE. **Freelance Content:** 60%. **Rights:** 1st NA, all. **Payment:** On publication.

PARENTS EXPRESS
290 Commerce Dr., Fort Washington, PA 19034. 215-629-1774. Web site: www.parentsexpress.net. Laura Winchester. **Description:** For parents in southeastern Pennsylvania and southern New Jersey. **Nonfiction:** Articles; pays $35-$150. **Payment:** On publication.

PENNSYLVANIA MAGAZINE

P O Box 755, Camp Hill, PA 17001-0755. 717-697-4660.
Bi-monthly. $3.50/$19.97. Circ.: 30,000. Matthew K. Holliday, Editor. **Description:** Profiles, events, people, and history of Pennsylvania. **Nonfiction:** General-interest features; 1,000-2,500 words; $.10-$.12/word. **Art:** Essential; send photos or photocopies; $20-$25/photo. **Tips:** No sports, poetry, hunting, or political. **Queries:** Preferred. **E-queries:** Yes. **Unsolicited mss:** Accepts. **Response:** 4-6 weeks, SASE. **Freelance Content:** 95%. **Rights:** 1st, one-time. **Payment:** On acceptance.

PHILADELPHIA

1818 Market St., 36th Floor, Philadelphia, PA 19103. 215-564-7700.
E-mail: mail@phillymag.com. Web site: www.phillymag.com. Monthly. $3.50/issue. Circ.: 143,000. Loren Feldman, Editor. **Description:** Regional general-interest publication. **Nonfiction:** Must be related to the greater Philadelphia area; 100-4,000 words; pay varies. **Queries:** Required. **E-queries:** Yes. **Unsolicited mss:** Accepts. **Response:** Queries, submissions 2 weeks; SASE required. **Freelance Content:** 30%. **Rights:** 1st NA.

PHOENIX

4041 N. Central Ave., Suite 530, Phoenix, AZ 85012. 602-234-0840.
E-mail: phxmag@citieswestpub.com. Monthly. $3.50. Circ.: 60,000. Robert Stieve, Editor. **Description:** Covers Phoenix metro area. **Nonfiction:** Issues relating to Phoenix and surrounding metro area. Service pieces (where to go, what to do) in the city; 50-2,000 words; pay varies. **Tips:** Think small; short, timely pieces are always needed. **Queries:** Required. **E-queries:** Yes. **Unsolicited mss:** Does not accept. **Response:** Queries 6 weeks, submissions 2 weeks, SASE. **Freelance Content:** 80%. **Rights:** 1st NA. **Payment:** On publication. **Contact:** Kathy Khoury, Managing Editor.

PITTSBURGH MAGAZINE

4802 Fifth Ave., Pittsburgh, PA 15213-2957.
Web site: www.wqed.org. Monthly. $3.50/issue, #17.95/yr. Circ.: 68,000. Chris Fletcher, Publisher. **Description:** Covers Pittsburgh and surrounding region. Examines issues and strives to encourage a better understanding of the community. **Nonfiction:** News, features, service pieces, local celebrity profiles, regional lifestyles; must have a Pittsburgh region focus. 500-4,000 words. Pay negotiable. **Art:** Yes. **Tips:** News, business, service pieces needed. **Queries:** Required. **E-queries:** No. **Unsolicited mss:** Does not accept. **Response:** 2 months, SASE. **Freelance Content:** 60%. **Rights:** FNASR. **Payment:** On publication. **Contact:** Michelle Pilecki, Exec. Ed.

PITTSBURGH SENIOR NEWS

Pittsburgh Senior News, Inc., 3345 Evergreen Rd.,
Pittsburgh, PA 15237. 412-367-2522.
Monthly. Circ.: 35,000. **Description:** Topics of interest to older adults in the Pittsburgh area.

PORTLAND
578 Congress St., Portland, ME 04101. 207-775-4339. E-mail: staff@portlandmagazine.com. Web site: www.portlandmagazine.com. Monthly. Circ.: 100,000. Colin Sargent, Editor. **Description:** Celebrates the region, with columns on the waterfront; profiles of business and people; and features on arts, getaways, maritime history, geography, and cuisine. **Fiction:** Fiction, to 750 words. **Nonfiction:** Articles on local people, legends, culture, trends. **Queries:** Required. **E-queries:** Yes. **Unsolicited mss:** Accepts.

PRIME
Shearin Publishing, P.O. Box 40, Scotland Neck, NC 27874. 252-826-2111. Quarterly. Circ.: 10,000. **Description:** Senior citizens magazine.

THE PRIME TIMES
Life Printing & Publishing, 709 Enterprise Drive, Oak Brook, IL 60523. 630-368-1100. Monthly. Circ.: 60,000. **Description:** Chicago city and suburban publication for older adults.

PRIME TIMES
Times-Beacon-Record Newspapers, P.O. Box 707, East Setauket, NY 11733. 631-751-0356. Monthly. Circ.: 45,000. **Description:** For older adults on Long Island, NY.

PROVINCETOWN ARTS
650 Commercial St., Provincetown, MA 02657. 508-487-3167. E-mail: cbusa@mediaone.net. Annual. $10. Circ.: 8,000. Christopher Busa, Editor. **Description:** On Cape Cod's artists, performers, and writers. Covers the cultural life of the nation's oldest continuous art colony, a century-long tradition of art, theater, and writing. **Fiction:** Mainstream fiction and novel excerpts; 500-5,000 words; $50-$150. **Nonfiction:** Essays, interviews, journals, performance pieces, profiles, reviews; showing the vitality of this community of artists; 500-5,000 words; $50-$150. **Poetry:** Submit up to 3 at a time; $25-$100. **Queries:** Not necessary. **E-queries:** No. **Unsolicited mss:** Accepts. **Response:** Queries 3 weeks, submissions 4 months, SASE. **Freelance Content:** 90%. **Payment:** On publication.

RANCH & COVE
P.O. Box 676130, Rancho Santa Fe, CA 92121-2766. 760-942-2330. E-mail: edit@ranchlove.com. Monthly. Circ.: 18,000. Collette Murphy, Editor. **Description:** For affluent residents of Rancho Santa Fe, La Jolla, and San Diego's coastal North country, on regional lifestyle. **Nonfiction:** Upscale fashion, travel, golf, shopping, wine and dining, autos, antiques, entertainment, spas, gala events, etc.; 500-1,500 words; $.10/word. **Columns, Departments:** 300-500 words. **Art:** Digital (Mac) .eps or .tiff; $25-$75. **Queries:** Preferred. **E-queries:** Yes. **Response:** 2-4 weeks, SASE. **Freelance Content:** 75%. **Rights:** one-time. **Payment:** On publication.

RANGE

106 E. Adams, Suite 201, Carson City, NV 89706. 775-884-2200.
E-mail: cj@range.carsoncity.nu.us. Web site: www.rangemagazine.com. Quarterly.
$3.95/issue, $19.95/year. Circ.: 21,000. Caroline Joy Hadley, Editor. **Description:** No
stranger to controversy, *Range* is a forum for viewpoints, seeking solutions to halt the
depletion of a national resource: the American cowboy. Devoted to issues that
threaten the West, its people, lifestyles, rangelands, and wildlife. **Nonfiction:**
Feature articles; 1,500-1,800. **Poetry:** Short; $40-$75. **Columns, Departments:**
Red Meat Survivors (500 words, interviews with oldtimers, including historic/current
photos); 500 words; $100-$150. **Art:** Original illustrations, slides, high-quality prints;
$40-$150. **Tips:** Submit concise, colorful pieces that address issues affecting those
who live on and work the land. Avoid academic, overly technical. **Queries:** Preferred.
E-queries: Yes. **Unsolicited mss:** Accepts. **Response:** Queries 4 weeks,submis-
sions 4-8 weeks, SASE. **Freelance Content:** 90%. **Rights:** 1st NA. **Payment:** On
publication.

RECREATION NEWS

P.O. Box 32335, Washington, DC 20007-0635. 301-474-4600.
E-mail: editor@recreationnews.com. Web site: www.recreationnews.com. Monthly.
$12/yr. Circ.: 100,000. Christy Law, Editor. **Description:** Regional recreational activ-
ities, historical sites, fishing, parks, video reviews, weekend getaways, day-off trips,
etc. **Nonfiction:** On recreation and travel around the mid-Atlantic region for government and private sector workers in the Washington, DC, area. Conversational
tone, lean and brisk; 900-2,200 words; $50 reprints, $300 cover features. **Queries:**
Preferred. **Unsolicited mss:** Accepts. **Payment:** On publication.

RHODE ISLAND MONTHLY

280 Kinsley Ave., Providence, RI 02903. 401-421-2552.
E-mail: rimonthly.com. Web site: www.rimonthly.com. Monthly. Circ.: 41,000. Paula
M. Bodah, Editor. **Description:** Rhode Island and southeastern Massachusetts:
places, customs, people, and events. **Nonfiction:** Features, from investigative reporting and in-depth profiles to service pieces and visual stories, seasonal material; 1,000-
2,000 words; $250-$1,000. **Fillers:** On Rhode Island places, customs, people, events,
products and services, restaurants and food; 150-500 words; $50-$150. **Queries:**
Required. **Payment:** On acceptance.

THE RHODE ISLANDER

Providence Sunday Journal, 75 Fountain St., Providence, RI 02902. 401-277-7000.
Web site: www.projo.com. Elliot Krieger, Editor. **Description:** Material with a New
England focus. **Nonfiction:** Articles, 500-3,000 words; pays $75-$500. **Payment:** On
publication.

RUNNER TRIATHLETE NEWS

P.O. Box 19909, 14201 Memorial Dr, Houston, TX 77224. 281-759-0555.
E-mail: rtnews@ixnetcom.com. Web site: www.runnertriathletenews.com. Monthly.

Circ.: 12,000. Lance Phegley, Editor. **Description:** Covers running, cycling, triathlons, and duathlons in a 5-state area: Texas, Louisiana, Arkansas, Oklahoma, New Mexico. **Nonfiction:** On running for road racing, and multi-sport enthusiasts. Pay varies. **Queries:** Preferred. **E-queries:** Yes. **Unsolicited mss:** Accepts. **Response:** Queries 3-7 days, submissions 1-3 days. **Freelance Content:** 40%. **Payment:** On publication.

RV WEST
Vernon Publications, 3000 Northup Way, Suite 200, Bellevue, WA 98009-9643. Michelle Arab. **Description:** For RV owners; where to go and what to do in 13 western states. **Nonfiction:** Travel and destination articles, 750-1,750 words. Pays $1.50/column inch. **Art:** Color slides, b/w prints must accompany articles. **Queries:** Preferred. **Unsolicited mss:** Accepts. **Payment:** On publication.

SACRAMENTO MAGAZINE
4471 D St., Sacramento, CA 95819. 916-452-6200. Web site: www.sacmag.com. Monthly. Circ.: 29,000. Krista Minard, Editor. **Description:** Interesting and unusual people, places, and behind-the-scenes news items. **Nonfiction:** Articles, 1,000-1,500 words, on destinations within a 6-hour drive of Sacramento. Features, 2,500 words, on broad range of topics related to the region; pay varies. **Columns, Departments:** City Lights, 400 words; $50-$300. **Queries:** Required. **Payment:** On publication.

SAN FRANCISCO MAGAZINE
243 Vallejo, San Francisco, CA 94111. 415-398-2800. E-mail: letters@sanfran.com. Web site: www.sanfran.com. Monthly. $3.95. Circ.: 132,000. Bruce Kelley, Editor. **Description:** Exploring and celebrating San Francisco and bay area. Insightful analysis, investigative reporting, and eye-catching coverage of local food, culture, design, travel, and politics. **Nonfiction:** Service features, profiles, investigative pieces, 2,500-3,000 words. News items, 250-800 words, from business to arts to politics. Pay varies. **Queries:** Preferred. **Unsolicited mss:** Accepts. **Payment:** On acceptance. **Contact:** Lisa Trottier.

SAVANNAH
P.O. Box 1088, Savannah, GA 31402. 912-652-0293. E-mail: lindaw@savannahnow.com. Web site: www.savannahmagazine.com. Bi-monthly. $3.95/$15.95. Circ.: 11,000. Linda Wittish, Editor. **Description:** On lifestyles of coastal Georgia and South Carolina low country. **Nonfiction:** On local people, travel destinations (in a day's drive), local history, restaurants, business; 500-2,500 words; $100-$350. **Columns, Departments:** Travel Business; 1,000-1,500; $200-$300. **Queries:** Preferred. **E-queries:** Yes. **Unsolicited mss:** Accepts. **Response:** Queries 2-3 weeks, submissions 3-4 weeks, SASE. **Freelance Content:** 100%. **Rights:** 1st NA. **Payment:** On acceptance.

SCOTTSDALE LIFE
4041 N. Central #A-100, Phoenix, AZ 85012. 602-234-0840.
E-mail: kmccarthy@citieswestpub.com. Monthly. Free. Circ.: 30,000. Karlin McCarthy, Editor. **Description:** On people, places, and things in Scottsdale. **Nonfiction:** 400-2,000 words; $.15/word. **E-queries:** Yes. **Response:** Queries to 6 months, submissions 2 months, SASE. **Freelance Content:** 30-40%. **Payment:** On publication.

SEATTLE MAGAZINE
423 Third Ave. West, Seattle, WA 98119. 206-284-1750.
E-mail: editor@seattlemag.com. Web site: www.seattlemag.com. 10x/year. $3.50/issue. Circ.: 40,000. Rachel Hart, Editor. **Description:** To help people live better in Seattle. **Nonfiction:** City, local issues, home, lifestyle articles on greater Seattle area; 50-3,000 words; $50-$1,200. **Art:** film, slides; $50-$1,200. **Queries:** Required. **E-queries:** No. **Unsolicited mss:** Accepts. **Response:** 3 months, SASE. **Freelance Content:** 70%. **Rights:** Exclusive 60 days. **Payment:** On publication.

SEATTLE WEEKLY
1008 Western, Suite 300, Seattle, WA 98104. 206-623-0500.
Knute Berger, Editor. **Description:** Focuses on a Northwest perspective. **Nonfiction:** Articles, 250-4,000 words; pays $25-$800. **Queries:** Preferred. **Payment:** On publication.

SEATTLE'S CHILD
Northwest Parent Publishing, 1530 Westlake Ave. N, Suite 600, Seattle, WA 98109. 206-441-0191.
Web site: www.parenthoodweb.com. Ann Bergman, Editor. **Description:** For parents, educators, and childcare providers in the Puget Sound region, with children 14 and under. Investigative reports and consumer tips on issues affecting families. **Nonfiction:** Articles, 400-2,500 words; pays $75-$600. **Queries:** Preferred. **Payment:** On publication.

SENIOR CONNECTION
News Connection USA, 220 W. Brandon Blvd., Ste 210, Brandon, FL 33511. 813-653-1988.
Web site: www.srconnect.com. Monthly. Circ.: 130,000. **Description:** General-interest articles, for senior citizens in the west central and Tampa areas of Florida.

SENIOR CONNECTION
Churchhill Publications, P.O. Box 38, Dundee, IL 60118. 847-428-0205.
Description: For Catholics, ages 50-plus, with connections to northern Illinois parishes.

SENIOR NEWS
Senior News, P.O. Box 23307, Waco, TX 76702. 254-399-9811.
Monthly. Circ.: 250,000. **Description:** For senior citizens in Texas.

SENIOR TIMES
Senior Publishing Co., P. O. Box 30965, Columbus, OH 43230. 614-337-2055. Monthly. Circ.: 55,000. **Description:** For older adults in Ohio.

SENIOR TIMES
Journal News Publishing, P.O. Box 142020, Spokane, WA 99214-2020. 509-924-2440. Monthly. Circ.: 50,000. **Description:** For senior citizens in Washington State.

SILENT SPORTS
717 10th St., P.O. Box 152, Waupaca, WI 54981-9990. 715-258-5546. E-mail: info@silentsports.net. Web site: www.silentsports.net. **Description:** On bicycling, cross country skiing, running, canoeing, hiking, backpacking, and other "silent" sports. Must have regional (upper Midwest) focus. **Nonfiction:** Articles, 1,000-2,000 words; pays $50-$100 for features; $20-$50 for fillers. **Queries:** Preferred. **Payment:** On publication.

SOUTH CAROLINA WILDLIFE
P. O. Box 167, Columbia, SC 29202-0167. 803-734-3972. Web site: www.scwildlife.com. Bi-monthly. $10/yr. Circ.: 60,000. John E. Davis, Editor. **Description:** Published by Dept. of Natural Resources, for readers interested in the outdoors. **Nonfiction:** South Carolina focus, on outdoor interests; 1,500 words; $.15-$.20/word. **Art:** 35mm or large transparencies; pay varies. **Tips:** Avoid first-person accounts. **Queries:** Preferred. **E-queries:** Yes. **Unsolicited mss:** Accepts. **Response:** 3-6 weeks, SASE. **Freelance Content:** 75%. **Rights:** FNASR. **Payment:** On acceptance. **Contact:** Linda Renshaw, Managing Editor.

SOUTHERN EXPOSURE
P.O. Box 531, Durham, NC 27702. 919-419-8311. Web site: www.i4south.org. Quarterly. Chris Kromm, Editor. **Description:** Forum on "Southern politics and culture." **Fiction:** Short stories, to 3,600 words; pays $25-$250. **Nonfiction:** Essays, investigative journalism, and oral histories, 500-3,600 words; pays $25-$250. **Queries:** Preferred. **Payment:** On publication.

SOUTHERN HUMANITIES REVIEW
9088 Haley Ctr., Auburn Univ., AL 36849. E-mail: shrengl@auburn.edu. Quarterly. $5/$15. Circ.: 700. Dan R. Latimer, Virginia M. Kouidis, Co-editors. **Description:** Scholarly, literary magazine. **Fiction:** Short stories; 3,500-15,000 words. **Nonfiction:** Essays, criticism; 3,500-15,000 words. **Poetry:** 2 pages. **Queries:** Not necessary. **E-queries:** Yes. **Unsolicited mss:** Accepts. **Response:** Queries 1-2 weeks, submissions 1-3 months, SASE. **Freelance Content:** 70%. **Rights:** 1st, reverts to author. **Payment:** In copies.

SOUTHERN OREGON HERITAGE TODAY

106 N. Central Ave., Medford, OR 97501-5926. 541-773-6536.
Web site: www.sohs.org. Monthly. Marcia W. Somers. **Description:** On history of the
southern Oregon region (people, places, buildings, and events). **Nonfiction:** Well-
written articles, 800-2,500 words; pays $50-$250. **Tips:** "Make sure there is a storyline, not just a reiteration of facts." **Payment:** On publication.

SPIRIT PLUS

1830 Rt. 9, Toms River, NJ 08755. 732-505-9700.
E-mail: spiritmag50@aol.com. Biannual. Circ.: 250,000. Pat Jasin, editor.
Description: For active adults aged 45-65, in states of New Jersey, New York, and
Pennsylvania. Upbeat articles on travel, sex, computers, dating, heatlh and fitness.
Nonfiction: Travel, etc. **Queries:** Required. **E-queries:** No. **Unsolicited mss:**
Does not accept. **Response:** 2 months. **Freelance Content:** 10%. **Rights:** 1st NA.
Payment: In copies.

SPRINGFIELD

P.O. Box 4749, Springfield, MO 65808. 417-882-3966.
Monthly. $16.99/yr. **Description:** About local people, places, events, and issues.
Nonfiction: Articles must have a clear link to Springfield, Missouri. Historical/
nostalgic pieces and book reviews. **Queries:** Preferred. **E-queries:** Yes. **Unsolicited
mss:** Accepts. **Response:** 1-2 weeks. **Freelance Content:** 85%. **Rights:** 1st serial.
Payment: On acceptance.

SUNSHINE

The Sun-Sentinel, 200 E. Las Olas Blvd.,
Ft. Lauderdale, FL 33301-2293. 954-356-4000.
Web site: www.sun-sentinel.com. weekly. Mark Gauert, Editor. **Description:** Sunday
Magazine of the *Sun-Sentinel*. **Nonfiction:** Articles, 1,000-3,000 words, on topics of
interest to south Floridians; pays $300-$1,200. **Queries:** Preferred. **Payment:** On
acceptance.

SWEAT

5743 E. Thomas #2, Scottsdale, AZ 85251. 480-997-3900.
E-mail: Westwoman@aol.com. Web site: www.sweatmagazine.com. Joan Westlake,
Editor. **Description:** On amateur sports, outdoor activities, wellness, or fitness, with
an Arizona angle. **Nonfiction:** Articles, 500-1,200 words. No self-indulgent or personal tales. Prefers investigative pieces, must relate to Arizona or Arizonans. Pays
$25-$60. **Art:** Photos, $15-$70. **Queries:** Required. **Unsolicited mss:** Does not
accept. **Payment:** On publication.

TALLAHASSEE

P.O. Box 1837, Tallahassee, FL 32302-1837. 850-878-0554.
E-mail: snollArowlandinc.com. Bi-monthly. $2.95/$16.95. Circ.: 17,000. Susan Noll,
Editor. **Description:** Lifestyle of "Emerald Coast" and Tallahassee. **Nonfiction:** On

local history, people, organizations; 1,500-3,000 words; pay varies. **Columns, Departments:** Humor; 850 words; $200. **Queries:** Not necessary. **E-queries:** Yes. **Unsolicited mss:** Accepts. **Response:** 1 week, SASE. **Freelance Content:** 15%. **Payment:** On publication.

TEXAS GOLFER
10301 Northwest Freeway, Suite 418, Houston, TX 77092. 713-680-1680. Web site: www.texasgolfermagazine.com. Monthly. $22. Circ.: 50,000. Bob Gray, Managing Editor. **Description:** For Texas golfers, with golf-course and tournament information, golf tips, and news. **Nonfiction:** Articles, 800-1,500 words, for north Texas golfers. **Tips:** Most freelance by assignment. **Queries:** Required. **E-queries:** Yes. **Unsolicited mss:** Accepts. **Response:** 2-4 Weeks, SASE. **Freelance Content:** 20%. **Rights:** All. **Payment:** On publication.

TEXAS HIGHWAYS
PO Box 141009, Austin, TX 78714-1009. 512-486-5858. E-mail: editors@texashighways,com. Web site: www.texashighways.com. Monthly. Circ.: 300,000. Jack Lowry, Editor. **Description:** Texas travel, history, and scenic features. **Nonfiction:** Travel, historical, cultural, scenic features on Texas; 200-1,800 words; $.40-$.50/word. **Art:** Photos, $80-$550. **Queries:** Required.

TEXAS JOURNEY
AAA Texas, Inc., 3333 S Fairview Road, Costa Mesa, CA 92626. 714-885-2380. Web site: www.aaa-texas.com. Bi-monthly. Circ.: 580,000. Annette Winter, Editor. **Description:** Travel and people in Texas and surrounding states. **Nonfiction:** 200-2,000 words; $1/word. **Columns, Departments:** 200 words. **Art:** 35mm. **Tips:** Prefers published writers. Submit articles that help readers meet people, not just places, behind the scenes at established destinations/venues. **Queries:** Required. **E-queries:** No. **Unsolicited mss:** Does not accept. **Response:** 6 weeks, SASE. **Freelance Content:** 80%. **Rights:** 1st NA. **Payment:** On acceptance.

TEXAS MONTHLY
P.O. Box 1569, Austin, TX 78767-1569. 512-320-6900. Web site: www.texasmonthly.com. Evan Smith, Editor. **Description:** Covers issues of public concern in Texas. **Nonfiction:** Features, 2,500-5,000 words, on art, architecture, food, education, business, politics, etc.; pay varies. Articles must appeal to an educated Texas audience; solidly researched reporting on issues (offbeat and previously unreported topics, or with novel approach to familiar topics). **Queries:** Preferred. **E-queries:** No. **Unsolicited mss:** Accepts. **Response:** 6 to 8 weeks. **Payment:** On acceptance.

TEXAS PARKS & WILDLIFE
Fountain Park Plaza, 3000 S. Interstate Hwy. 35, Suite 120, Austin, TX 78704. 512-912-7000. E-mail: magazine@tpwd.state.tx.us. Web site: www.tpwmagazine.com. Monthly.

Circ.: 150,000. Susan Ebert. **Description:** Promotes conservation and enjoyment of Texas wildlife, parks, waters, and all outdoors. **Nonfiction:** Features on hunting, fishing, birding, camping, and the environment. Photos a plus; 400-1,500 words; $.30-$.50/word. **Payment:** On acceptance.

TODAY'S FAMILY
280 N. Main St., E. Longmeadow, MA 01028. 413-525-6661. E-mail: news@thereminder.com. **Description:** For families in western Massachusetts. **Nonfiction:** Articles, 300-700 words; on family issues, with advice, new recipes, and daytrip suggestions.

TOLEDO AREA PARENT NEWS
1120 Adams St., Toledo, OH 43624. 419-244-9859. Web site: www.toledoparent.com. Monthly. Circ.: 50,000. Meira Zucker, Editor. **Description:** For parents in Northwest Ohio and Southern Michigan. **Nonfiction:** On parenting, child and family health, other family topics. Writers must be from the region; 750-1,200 words; $75-$100. **Queries:** Preferred. **Unsolicited mss:** Accepts.

TORONTO LIFE
59 Front St. E., Toronto, Ont., Canada M5E 1B3. 416-364-3333. E-mail: editorial@torontolife.com. Web site: www.torontolife.com. Monthly. Circ.: 92,438. John Macfarlane, Editor. **Description:** Covers the urban scene. **Nonfiction:** Articles on Toronto; 1,500-4,500 words; 1,500-$3,500. **Queries:** Required. **Payment:** On acceptance.

TUCSON LIFESTYLE
Old Pueblo Press, 7000 E. Tanque Verde, Tucson, AZ 85715. 520-721-2929. E-mail: tucsonlife@aol.com. Monthly. $2.95. Circ.: 33,000. Sue Giles, Editor-In-Chief. **Description:** Covers subjects around Southern Arizona. **Nonfiction:** On businesses, lifestyles, the arts, homes, fashion, and travel; 1,000-4,000 words; $125-$500. **Tips:** Base your article on interviews and research. No travel pieces or anecdotes as articles. **Queries:** Required. **E-queries:** Yes. **Unsolicited mss:** Accepts. **Response:** 2 weeks, SASE. **Freelance Content:** 80%. **Rights:** 1st NA. **Payment:** On acceptance. **Contact:** Scott Barker, Exec. Ed.

VANCOUVER
Ste. 300 East Tower, 555 W. 12th Ave., Vancouver, BC, Canada V5Z 4L4. 604-877-7732. E-mail: mail@vanmag.com. Web site: vancouvermagazine.com. 10x/year. $3.50. Circ.: 65,000. Nick Rockel, Editor. **Description:** City magazine with a focus on urban life (restaurants, fashion, shopping, and nightlife). **Nonfiction:** Seeking articles, varying lengths, including front-of-book pieces; 400-4,000 words; $.50/word. **Columns, Departments:** Sports, civics, social affairs, business, politics, media; 1,500-2,000 words; $.50/word. **Art:** Slides, prints; negotiable. **Queries:** Preferred. **E-queries:**

Yes. **Unsolicited mss:** Accepts. **Response:** 2 weeks minimum. **Freelance Content:** 70%. **Rights:** FNASR. **Payment:** On acceptance.

VELOCITY
346 N. Justine #300, Chicago, IL 60607. 312-397-9388.
Web site: www.velocitymag.com. Bryan A. Bushemi, Copy Editor. **Description:** Covers Chicago's music scene. **Queries:** Preferred. *No recent report.*

VERMONT LIFE
6 Baldwin St., Montpelier, VT 05602. 802-828-3241.
Web site: www.vtlife.com. Quarterly. $3.95/$14.95. Circ.: 85,000. Tom Slayton, Editor. **Description:** Explores and celebrates Vermont today, with quality photographs and articles. **Nonfiction:** Articles about people, places, history, issues; 200-2,000 words; $100-$700. **Art:** Slides, transparencies; no prints; $75-$500. **Tips:** No "my recent trip to Vermont" or old jokes, rural homilies. Submit articles that shed light on and accurately reflect Vermont experience today. **Queries:** Preferred. **E-queries:** Yes. **Unsolicited mss:** Accepts. **Response:** 2-4 weeks,SASE. **Freelance Content:** 90%. **Rights:** 1st NA. **Payment:** On acceptance.

VERMONT MAGAZINE
228 Maple St., PO Box 800, Middlebury, VT 05753. 802-388-8480.
Web site: www.vermontmagazine.com. Julie Kirgo. **Description:** On all aspects of contemporary Vermont (its people, culture, politics, and special places). **Nonfiction:** Articles; pays $200-$1,000. **Queries:** Preferred. **Payment:** On publication.

VIRGINIA BUSINESS
333 E. Franklin St., Suite 105, Richmond, VA 23219. 804-649-6999.
E-mail: pgaluszka@va-business.com. Web site: www.virginiabusiness.com. James Bacon, Editor. **Description:** Covers the business scene in Virginia. **Nonfiction:** Articles, 1,000-2,500 words; pay varies. **Queries:** Required. **Payment:** On publication.

VIRGINIA WILDLIFE
P.O. Box 11104, Richmond, VA 23230-1104.
E-mail: lwalker@dgif.state.va.us. Web site: www.dgif.state.va.us. **Description:** On fishing, hunting, wildlife management, outdoor safety and ethics; with Virginia tie-in. **Nonfiction:** Articles, 500-1,200 words, may be accompanied by color photos; pays from $.18/word, extra for photos. **Queries:** Preferred. **Payment:** On publication. *No recent report.*

WASHINGTON FLYER
1707 "L" Street NW, Suite 700, Washington, DC 20036. 202-331-9393.
Web site: www.washingtonflyermag.com. Bimonthly. Michael McCarthy, Editor-in-Chief. **Description:** For upscale Washington residents and visitors. Dining, entertainment, events in the D.C. area. **Nonfiction:** Briefs and features, 350-1,500 words; pays $150-$800. **Art:** Color photos. **Queries:** Preferred. **Payment:** On publication.

THE WASHINGTONIAN

1828 "L" St. NW, Suite 200, Washington, DC 20036. 202-296-3600. E-mail: editorial@washingtonian.com. Web site: www.washingtonian.com. Monthly. $2.95/$18. Circ.: 160,000. John Limpert, Editor. **Description:** Covers Washington, D.C., topics. **Queries:** Preferred. **E-queries:** Yes. **Unsolicited mss:** Accepts. **Response:** 2-8 weeks, SASE. **Freelance Content:** 50%. **Rights:** FNASR. **Payment:** On publication.

THE WESTERN HISTORICAL QUARTERLY

Utah State Univ., Logan, UT 84322-0740. 435-797-1301. E-mail: whq@hass.usu.edu. Web site: www.usu.edu/history/whq. Quarterly. Circ.: 2,200. Anne M. Butler, Editor. **Description:** Covers the American West: United States, Canada, and Mexico. Occupation, settlement; political, economic, social, cultural and intellectual history. **Nonfiction:** Original articles about the American West, the Westward movement, 20th-century regional studies, Spanish borderlands, Canada, northern Mexico, Alaska, and Hawaii; to 10,000 words; no payment. **Tips:** Prefers descriptive, interpretive, and analytical essays on broad themes; use of primary sources and monographic literature. **Queries:** Not necessary. **E-queries:** Yes. **Unsolicited mss:** Accepts. **Response:** 1 week, SASE required.

WESTERN SPORTSMAN

780 Beatty Street, #300, Vancouver, BC V6B 2MI CA. 604-606-4644. Web site: www.oppub.com. George Gruenefeld, Editor. **Description:** On hunting and fishing in British Columbia, Alberta, Saskatchewan, and Manitoba. **Nonfiction:** Informative, how-tos, to 2,500 words; pays $75-$300. **Art:** Photos. **Payment:** On publication.

WINDY CITY SPORTS

1450 W. Randolph, Chicago, IL 60607. 312-421-1551. E-mail: jason@windycitysportsmag.com. Web site: www.windycitysports.com. Monthly. Free. Circ.: 110,000. Jason Effmann, Editor. **Description:** Covers amateur sports in Chicago and surrounding area. **Nonfiction:** up to 1,200 words. **Art:** Hard copies, electronic (300 dpi or more). **Tips:** Need to be knowledgeable in sport covered. **Queries:** Preferred. **E-queries:** Yes. **Unsolicited mss:** Accepts. **Response:** 2 weeks, SASE. **Freelance Content:** 25%. **Rights:** 1st. **Payment:** On publication.

WISCONSIN TRAILS

P.O. Box 317, 1131 Mills Street, Black Earth, WI 53515. 608-767-8000. E-mail: kbast@wistrails.com. Web site: www.wistrails.com. Bimonthly. $4.95/issue, $24.95/year. Circ.: 50,000. Kate Bast, Editor. **Description:** On Wisconsin people, history, nature, adventure, lifestyle, arts, theater, crafts, sports, recreation and business. **Fiction:** Occasionally, 1,000 words; $.25/word. **Nonfiction:** 800-3,000 words, $.25/word. About the joys and experiences of living in the Badger state (history, wildlife, natural history, environment, travel, profiles, culture). **Fillers:** Tasteful Wisconsin-oriented humor, crossword puzzles, cartoons, 50-300 words, $.25/word.

Columns, Departments: My WI (essays); Discover (events); State Talk (short, quirky news); Profile (noteworthy people); Gone for the Weekend (travel destination), 50-1,000 words, $.25/word. **Art:** Color transparencies, slides, illustrations (8x11 largest); pay varies. **Tips:** Readers mostly in their 40s and 50s, active, well educated, with children and grandchildren. **Queries:** Required. **E-queries:** Yes. **Unsolicited mss:** Accepts. **Response:** 3-5 months, SASE. **Freelance Content:** 40%. **Rights:** 1st NA, one-time. **Payment:** On publication.

WISCONSIN WEST
2905 Seymour Rd., Eau Claire, WI 54701. 715-835-3800.
E-mail: mei@charter.net. Bimonthly. $2.50. Circ.: 5,000. **Description:** Covers Western Wisconsin. **Nonfiction:** Restaurants, weekend leisure activities and getaways, famous people of western Wisconsin, history, short humor; up to 3,000 words; $75-$150. **Art:** Slides, photos; $100-$150. **Queries:** Preferred. **E-queries:** Yes. **Unsolicited mss:** Accepts. **Freelance Content:** 100%. **Rights:** 1st, 2nd. **Payment:** On publication.

YANKEE
Yankee Publishing Co., P.O. Box 502, Dublin, NH 03444. 603-563-8111.
E-mail: queries@yankeepub.com. Web site: www.newengland.com. 10x/year. $2.99/$18.99. Circ.: 600,000. Jim Collins, Editor. **Description:** On travel and life in New England. **Fiction:** Short stories, true to life, contemporary, rooted in New England; up to 4,000 words; up to $2,500. **Nonfiction:** Narrative journalism, personal essay, travel, food; 150-5,000 words; $50-$5,000. **Poetry:** up to 36 lines; $50. **Queries:** Preferred. **E-queries:** Yes. **Unsolicited mss:** Accepts. **Response:** 8 weeks, SASE. **Freelance Content:** 80%. **Rights:** FNASR. **Payment:** On acceptance.

YANKEE MAGAZINE'S TRAVEL GUIDE TO NEW ENGLAND
Main Street, Dublin, NH 03444.
E-mail: travel@yankeepub.com. Annual. $4.99. Circ.: 100,000. Jim Collins, Editor. **Description:** Covers New England travel, with features and travel information. **Nonfiction:** 500-1,500 words; $1/word. **Art:** Photos. **Tips:** Looking for fresh ideas. **Queries:** Required. **E-queries:** Yes. **Freelance Content:** 70%. **Payment:** On acceptance.

YESTERYEAR
P.O. Box 2, Princeton, WI 54968.
E-mail: yesteryear@vbe.com. Michael Jacobi, Editor. **Description:** On antiques and collectibles for readers in WI, IL, IA, MN, and surrounding states. **Nonfiction:** Articles; pays from $20. **Art:** Photos. **Tips:** Will consider regular columns on collecting or antiques. **Payment:** On publication.

RELIGION

AMERICA

106 W. 56th St., New York, NY 10019-3893. 262-581-4640. E-mail: articles@americapress.org. Web site: www.americapress.org. Weekly. $2.25/issue. Circ.: 400. Thomas J. Reese, Editor. **Description:** For thinking Catholics and those interested in what Catholics are thinking. Emphasis on social justice and religious and ethical perspective on current issues facing the church and the world. **Nonfiction:** Features on contemporary issues from a religious and ethical perspective; 1,500-2,000 words. **Poetry:** Serious poetry in contemporary prose idiom, free or formal verse, 20-35 lines. Submit 2-3 poems with SASE. Pays $2-$3/line. **Art:** Send portfolio. **Tips:** No sermons or speeches. Address educated audience who are not experts in your topic. **Queries:** Not necessary. **Unsolicited mss:** Accepts. **Response:** Queries 1 week, submission 3 weeks, SASE required. **Freelance Content:** 50%. **Rights:** All. **Payment:** On acceptance.

AMIT

817 Broadway, New York, NY 10003-4761. 212-477-4720. E-mail: amitmag@aol.com. Web site: www.amitchildren.org. Quarterly. $35/year (with membership). Circ.: 37,000. Debra Stahl, Editor. **Description:** Published by a nonprofit, orthodox Jewish organization which sponsors network of schools helping 15,000 underprivileged Israeli youths. **Nonfiction:** Articles of interest to Jewish women: Middle East, Israel, history, holidays, travel, culture, food, and education; 2,500 words; $250-$500. **Columns, Departments:** Mind/Body Connection (sports in education); Beit Hayeled (interviews with Amit students in Israel); Interviews (innovators in education, art, music); Book Reviews; Parenting (on Jewish parenting and education); 700 words; $100. **Tips:** Avoid politics and religion. Focus on innovations in education, and on Amit students in Israel. **Queries:** Preferred. **E-queries:** Yes. **Unsolicited mss:** Accepts. **Response:** 2 weeks, SASE required. **Freelance Content:** 50%. **Payment:** On acceptance.

ANGLICAN JOURNAL

600 Jarvis St., Toronto, Ont., Canada M4Y 2J6. 416-924-9192. E-mail: editor@national.anglican.com. Web site: www.anglicanjournal.com. 10x/year. $10/year. Circ.: 245,000. Vianney (Sam) Carriere, Editor. **Description:** Newspaper of Anglican Church of Canada. News and features of the Anglican Church, including social and ethical issues, and human-interest. **Nonfiction:** up to 1,000 words; $.23/word. **Queries:** Required. **E-queries:** Yes. **Unsolicited mss:** Does not accept. **Response:** Varies. **Freelance Content:** 15%. **Rights:** 1st. **Payment:** On publication.

ANNALS OF ST. ANNE DE BEAUPRÉ

P.O. Box 1000, St. Anne de Beaupré, Quebec, Canada G0A 3C0. 418-827-4538. Roch Achard, C.Ss.R., Editor. **Description:** Articles, 500-1,500 words, that promote devotion to St. Anne and Christian family values. Pays $.03-$.04/word. **Tips:** Prefers work that is inspirational, educational, objective, and uplifting. No poetry. **Payment:** On acceptance.

THE BANNER
2850 Kalamazoo Ave. SE, Grand Rapids, MI 49560. 616-224-0732. Web site: www.thebanner.org. John D. Suk. **Description:** For members of Christian Reformed Church in North America. **Fiction:** to 2,500 words. **Nonfiction:** to 1,800 words; pays $125-$200. **Poetry:** to 50 lines; $40. **Queries:** Preferred. **Payment:** On acceptance.

BIBLE ADVOCATE
P.O. Box 33677, Denver, CO 80233. 303-452-7973. E-mail: bibleadvocate@cog7.org. Web site: www.cog7.org/ba. 10x/year. Circ.: 13,000. Calvin Burrell, Editor. **Description:** Helps Christians understand and obey the Bible. **Nonfiction:** On Bible doctrine, current social and religious issues, everyday-living Bible topics, textual or Biblical book studies, prophecy and personal experience; 1500 words; $25-$55. **Poetry:** Free verse, blank verse, religious themes; 5-20 lines; $20. **Fillers:** Facts, inspirational pieces, anecdotes; 100-400 words; $20. **Columns, Departments:** Opinions; 650 words. **Tips:** No articles on Christmas or Easter. Theme list available. **Queries:** Not necessary. **E-queries:** Yes. **Unsolicited mss:** Accepts. **Response:** Queries 4 weeks, submissions 4-8 weeks, SASE. **Freelance Content:** 10-20%. **Rights:** 1st, reprints, electronic. **Payment:** On publication.

BOOKS & CULTURE: A CHRISTIAN REVIEW
Christianity Today International, 465 Gundersen Dr., Carol Stream, IL 60188. 630-260-6200. Web site: www.christianity.net. Bimonthly. Circ.: 18,000. **Description:** Looks at Christian books, culture, and religion.

BREAD FOR GOD'S CHILDREN
P.O. Box 1017, Arcadia, FL 34265-1017. Semi-annual. Circ.: 10,000. Judith M. Gibbs, Editor. **Description:** Christian family magazine with Bible study, stories, teen pages, parent news, ideas, and more. **Nonfiction:** Articles or craft ideas based on Christian principles or activities; how to implement Christian ways into daily living; 600-800 words; $20-$30. **Tips:** Stories must be from a child's point of view, with story itself getting message across; no preaching or moralizing, no tag endings. No stories with speaking animals, occult, fantasy, or romance. **Queries:** Not necessary. **Unsolicited mss:** Accepts. **Response:** Submissions 1-6 months, SASE. **Freelance Content:** 20%. **Rights:** 1st. **Payment:** On publication.

BRIGADE LEADER
Box 150, Wheaton, IL 60189. 630-582-0630. E-mail: dchristensen@csbministries.org. Web site: csbministries.org. Quarterly. $10. Circ.: 6,000. Deborah Christensen, Managing Editor. **Description:** An evangelical

Christian publication, for adult youth leaders in Christian Service Brigade Ministries (Christian Service Brigade, Girls Alive, and Brigade Air). **Nonfiction:** Leadership and inspirational articles for program leaders; 500-1,000 words; $.05-$.10/word. **Tips:** Most articles assigned; limited freelance content. Query with clips. **Queries:** Required. **E-queries:** No. **Unsolicited mss:** Does not accept. **Response:** SASE required. **Payment:** On publication.

CAMPUS LIFE

465 Gundersen Dr., Carol Stream, IL 60188. 630-260-6200.
E-mail: clmag@campuslife.net. Web site: www.campuslife.net. 9x/year. $19.95/year. Circ.: 100,000. Chris Lutes, Editor. **Description:** Advice on love, sex, self-image, popularity, and loneliness, with dramatic stories about teens radically changed by God, plus in-depth profiles about favorites in Christian music. **Fiction:** A "life lesson" with a Christian worldview, by experienced writers; 2,000 words max.; $.15-.20/word. **Nonfiction:** First-person stories presenting the lives of teenagers, ordinary or dramatic; 2,000 words max.; $.15-.20/word. **Tips:** Avoid religious clichés, misuse of religious language, lack of respect or empathy for teenagers. **Queries:** Required. **E-queries:** Accepts. **Unsolicited mss:** Does not accept. **Response:** 4-6 weeks, SASE required. **Freelance Content:** 10%. **Rights:** 1st. **Payment:** On acceptance; kill fee offered. **Contact:** Amber Penney.

CATECHIST

330 Progress Rd., Dayton, OH 45449. 937-847-5900.
Web site: www.catechist.com. Patricia Fischer, Editor. **Description:** For Catholic teachers, coordinators, and administrators in religious education programs. **Nonfiction:** Informational and how-to articles; 1,200-1,500 words; pays $25-$100. **Payment:** On publication.

CATHOLIC DIGEST

2115 Summit Ave., St. Paul, MN 55105-1081. 651-962-6739.
E-mail: cdigest@stthomas.edu. Web site: www.catholicdigest.org. Monthly. $2.25/issue, $19.95/year. Circ.: 400,000. Richard J. Reece, Editor. **Description:** For adult Roman Catholic readers, with general-interest topics on family life, religion, science, health, good works, and relationships. **Nonfiction:** Humor, profiles, how-to, personal experiences. Topics: saints, prayer, relationships, family issues, health, history, nostalgia, science; 1,000-3,000 words; $100-$400. **Columns, Departments:** True incidents about good works, parish life, conversion to Catholicism; 100-500 words; $2/line. **Tips:** Interested in articles about the family and career concerns of baby boomers who have a stake in being Catholic. Illustrate topic with a series of true-life, interconnected vignettes. **Queries:** Not necessary. **E-queries:** No. **Unsolicited mss:** Accepts. **Response:** Submissions 6-8 weeks, SASE required. **Freelance Content:** 20%. **Rights:** one-time. **Payment:** On publication.

CATHOLIC FAITH & FAMILY

33 Rossotto Dr., Hamden, CT 06514. 203-288-5600. E-mail: duncan@bestweb.net. Biweekly. Circ.: 16,000. Duncan Maxwell Anderson, Editor. **Description:** How-to articles and interviews of interest to Catholic families, with photos. **Nonfiction:** 1,000-2,000 words; pays $75-$300. **Columns, Departments:** Opinion or inspirational columns, 600-800 words, with strict attention to Catholic doctrine. **Queries:** Preferred. **Unsolicited mss:** Accepts. **Freelance Content:** 95%. **Rights:** 1st. **Payment:** On publication.

CATHOLIC NEAR EAST

1011 First Ave., New York, NY 10022-4195. 212-826-1480. Web site: www.cnewa.org. Bimonthly. $2.50/$12.00. Circ.: 90,000. Michael La Civita, Executive Editor. **Description:** Offers educational profiles of cultures, histories, religions, and social issues of the peoples of Eastern Europe, India, the Middle East, and Northeast Africa. **Nonfiction:** 1,500 words; $.20/word. **Art:** Slides, prints; $50 and up. **Tips:** Writers and photographers in each Pontifical Mission city and in other CNEWA countries offer the most objective, accurate, sensitive portraits of their subjects. **Queries:** Preferred. **Unsolicited mss:** Accepts. **Response:** SASE required. **Payment:** On publication.

CATHOLIC PARENT

Our Sunday Visitor, Inc., 200 Noll Plaza, Huntington, IN 46750. 219-356-8400. E-mail: cparent@osv.com. Web site: www.osv.com. Woodeene Koenig-Bricker, Editor. **Description:** For Catholic parents. Anecdotal and practical, with an emphasis on values and family life. **Nonfiction:** Features, how-tos, and general-interest articles, 800-1,000 words; pay varies. **Tips:** Don't preach. **Payment:** On acceptance.

THE CHRISTIAN CENTURY

104 S. Michigan Ave., Chicago, IL 60603. 312-263-7510. E-mail: main@christiancentury.org. Web site: www.christiancentury.org. Weekly. Circ.: 30,000. John M. Buchanan, Editor. **Description:** Shows how Christian faith calls people to a profound engagement with the world, how faith is revealed in areas of poverty, international relations, popular culture. **Nonfiction:** Religious angle on political/social issues, international affairs, culture, the arts, and challenges in everyday lives; 1,500-3,000 words; $75-200. **Poetry:** Free verse, traditional, haiku. No sentimental or didactic poems; 20 lines; $50. **Art:** Photos, $25-$100. **Tips:** Many readers are ministers or teachers of religion. **Queries:** Preferred. **E-queries:** Yes. **Response:** Queries 1 week, submissions 2 months, SASE required. **Freelance Content:** 90%. **Rights:** one-time. **Payment:** On publication.

CHRISTIAN EDUCATION COUNSELOR

General Council of the Assemblies of God, 1445 Boonville Ave., Springfield, MO 65802-1894. 417-862-2781. E-mail: cecounselor@ag.org. Web site: www.ag.org/counselor. Sylvia Lee, Editor. **Description:** On teaching and administrating Christian education in the local church, for local Sunday school and Christian school personnel. **Nonfiction:** Articles, 600-800 words; pays $.05-$.10/word. **Payment:** On acceptance.

CHRISTIAN EDUCATION LEADERSHIP

1080 Montgomery Ave. NE, PO Box 2250, Cleveland, TN 37320-2250. 800-553-8506. E-mail: ycessse@extremegen.org. Web site: www.pathwaypress.org. Quarterly. $8. Circ.: 10,000. Tony P. Lane, Editor. **Description:** For Christian education workers who teach God's word to kids, teens, and adults. **Nonfiction:** To encourage, inform, and inspire those who teach the Bible in local churches; 500-600 words; $25-$40. **Queries:** Not necessary. **E-queries:** Yes. **Unsolicited mss:** Accepts. **Response:** Submissions 3-6 weeks, SASE. **Payment:** On acceptance.

CHRISTIAN HOME & SCHOOL

3350 E. Paris Ave. SE, Grand Rapids, MI 49512. 616-957-1070 x239. E-mail: rogers@csionline.org. Web site: www.csi.org/csi/chs. Bimonthly. Circ.: 65,000. Gordon L. Bordewyk, Exec. Editor. **Description:** For parents in Canada and U.S. who send their children to Christian schools and are concerned about challenges facing families today. Articles pay from $125-$200. **Queries:** Preferred. **Payment:** On publication.

CHRISTIAN PARENTING TODAY

465 Gundersen Dr., Carol Stream, IL 60188-2489. 630-260-6200. E-mail: cptmag@aol.com. Bimonthly. Circ.: 90,000. Carala Barnhill, Editor. **Description:** Serves needs of today's families in positive and practical format. **Nonfiction:** Articles on real-life experiences and truths of the Bible. **Queries:** Preferred.

CHRISTIAN SINGLE

127 Ninth Ave. N., Nashville, TN 37234-0140. **Description:** For single adults about leisure activities, issues related to single parents, inspiring personal experiences, humor, life from a Christian perspective. **Nonfiction:** Articles, 600-1,200 words; pay varies. **Queries:** Preferred. **Payment:** On acceptance. *No recent report.*

CHRISTIAN SOCIAL ACTION

100 Maryland Ave. NE, Washington, DC 20002. 202-488-5600. E-mail: ealsgaard@umc-gbcs.org. Web site: www.umc-gbcs.org. Bi-monthly. Circ.: 3,000. Erik Alsgaard, Editor. **Description:** For United Methodist clergy and lay people interested in the role and involvement of the church in social issues. **Nonfiction:** Stories that educate, inspire, motivate people to Christian social action on justice and advocacy issues; 1,500-2,000 words; $125-$175. **Fillers:** Social satire; 500 words; $100. **Art:** Hard copy, electronic. **Tips:** Less academic, more "folksy" language preferred. **Queries:** Preferred. **E-queries:** Yes. **Unsolicited mss:** Accepts. **Response:**

Queries 4-6 weeks, SASE required. **Freelance Content:** 30%. **Rights:** 1st. **Payment:** On publication.

CHRISTIANITY TODAY

465 Gundersen Dr., Carol Stream, IL 60188. 630-260-6200. E-mail: cteditor@christianitytoday.com. Web site: www.christianitytoday.com. 14x/year. $3.95/issue. Circ.: 150,000. David Neff, Editor. **Description:** Evangelical Christian publication covering Christian doctrines, current events, news, trends, and issues. **Nonfiction:** Doctrinal social issues and interpretive essays, 1,500-3,000 words, from evangelical Protestant perspective. Pays $200-$500. **Tips:** Seeking internet-related stories with human interest. **Queries:** Preferred. **E-queries:** Yes. **Unsolicited mss:** Accepts. **Response:** 3 months, SASE required. **Freelance Content:** 80%. **Rights:** One-time. **Payment:** On acceptance. **Contact:** Mark Salli.

CHURCH EDUCATOR

Educational Ministries, Inc., 165 Plaza Dr., Prescott, AZ 86303. 800-221-0910. E-mail: edmin2@aol.com. Web site: www.educational ministries.com. Monthly. $28/year. Circ.: 3,000. Robert G. Davidson, Editor. **Description:** Resource for mainline Protestant Christian educators. **Nonfiction:** Programs used in mainline churches; 200-1,500 words; $.03/word. **Queries:** Not necessary. **E-queries:** Yes. **Unsolicited mss:** Accepts. **Response:** Queries 1 week, submissions 3 months, SASE required. **Freelance Content:** 80%. **Rights:** One Time Rights. **Payment:** On publication. **Contact:** Linda Davidson.

CHURCH MUSICIAN TODAY

127 Ninth Ave. N., Nashville, TN 37234-0160. 615-251-2913. E-mail: churchmusician@lifeway.com. Monthly. $3/issue. Circ.: 6,000. Jere Adams, Editor. **Description:** For music leaders, worship leaders, pastors, organists, pianists, and members of church music council or worship committees. **Nonfiction:** Choral techniques, instrumental groups, worship planning, directing choirs (all ages), music equipment, drama/pageants, hymn studies, book reviews. **Fillers:** 50 words, $10. **Queries:** Not necessary. **E-queries:** Yes. **Unsolicited mss:** Accepts. **Response:** Queries 1 week, submissions 4 weeks, SASE required. **Freelance Content:** 30%. **Rights:** All. **Payment:** On publication.

CIRCUIT RIDER

201 8th Ave. S, P.O. Box 801, Nashville, TN 37202-0801. E-mail: jredding@umpublishing.org. Web site: www.umph.org. Bimonthly. $20/year. Circ.: 42,000. Jill Redding, Editor. **Description:** For United Methodist pastors. Offers curriculum, books, and program resources to help adults come to know God through Jesus Christ, and choose to serve God and neighbor. **Nonfiction:** 800-1,600 words. Pays $50-$200. **Queries:** Preferred. **Payment:** On acceptance.

CLUB CONNECTION

1445 Boonville Ave., Springfield, MO 65802. 417-862-2781 ext. 4067. E-mail: clubconnection@ag.org. Web site: www.missionettes.ag.org. Quarterly. $6.50/yr. Circ.: 15,000. Debby Seler, Editor. **Description:** Full-color, for Missionettes ages 7-14. Brings girls together with common interests. The message of salvation is presented in each issue. **Fiction:** Fictional short stories; up to 850 words; $25-$40. **Nonfiction:** Articles on subjects of friends, school, God, family, music, fun activities; up to 850 words; $25-$40. **Poetry:** Pertaining to leadership/devotional; up to 850 words; $25-$40. **Fillers:** Crafts, games, puzzles, snack recipes, etc.; pays $10. **Columns, Departments:** Book, video and music reviews; missions facts and trivia. **Tips:** For leaders of Missionettes clubs; Leader's Connection provides ideas and resources, discipleship materials, etc. **Queries:** Preferred. **E-queries:** Yes. **Unsolicited mss:** Accepts. **Freelance Content:** 35%. **Rights:** 1st. **Payment:** On acceptance. **Contact:** Diana Black.

CLUBHOUSE JR.

8605 Explorer Dr., Colorado Springs, CO 80920. 719-531-3400. Monthly. $1.50/$15. Circ.: 96,000. Annette Bourland, Editor. **Description:** Inspires, entertains, and teaches Christian values to children ages 4-8. **Fiction:** Fresh, inviting, well-developed characters; fast-paced, interesting story. Stories not explicitly Christian but built on foundations of belief and family values; 250-750 words (for young readers), 700-1,000 (for parents); $125-$200. **Nonfiction:** Articles about real adults or children with interesting experience. Science and nature, from unique perspective. Use short-caption styled format; 500 max.; $125-$200. **Poetry:** Real-life experience of young children; humorous, descriptive; 250 max.; $50-$100. **Fillers:** Puzzles (no crosswords); fun crafts, parent/child together; repetition of images, concise wording, humorous or insightful ending; 1 page; $25-$45. **Art:** Send samples. **Tips:** No queries. **E-queries:** No. **Unsolicited mss:** Accepts. **Response:** Submissions 4-6 weeks, SASE. **Freelance Content:** 25%. **Rights:** 1st. **Payment:** On acceptance.

COLUMBIA

Knights of Columbus, 1 Columbus Plaza, New Haven, CT 06510. 203-772-2130. E-mail: thickey@kofc.supreme.com. Web site: www.kofc.org. Monthly. $6/year. Circ.: 1,600,000. Tim S. Hickey, Editor. **Description:** Published by Knights of Columbus (world largest Catholic family fraternal service organization). Articles on current events, societal trends, family life and parenting, finances, Catholic practice and teachings. **Nonfiction:** Articles, 500-1,500 words, on topics of interest to K. of C. members, their families, and the Catholic layman; current events, religion, education, art, etc. Pays to $600. **Tips:** Write for sample copy (free), with guidelines. **Queries:** Required. **E-queries:** Yes. **Response:** Queries 2 weeks, submissions 2 weeks, SASE required. **Freelance Content:** 80%. **Payment:** On acceptance.

COMMENTARY

165 E. 56th St., New York, NY 10022. 212-751-4000. Web site: www.commentarymagazine.com. Neal Kozodoy, Editor. **Description:**

Fiction, of literary quality, on contemporary social or Jewish issues, from 5,000-7,000 words. Articles, 5,000-7,000 words, on contemporary issues, Jewish affairs, social sciences, religious thought, culture. Serious fiction; book reviews. **Payment:** On publication.

COMMONWEAL

475 Riverside Dr., Room 405, New York, NY 10115. 212-662-4200. E-mail: commonweal@msn.com. Web site: commonwealmagazine.org. 22x/year. $2.50. Circ.: 20,000. Margaret O'Brien Steinfels, Editor. **Description:** Review of public affairs, religion, literature and the arts, published by Catholic lay people. **Nonfiction:** On political, religious, social, and literary subjects; 1,000-3,000 words; $100. **Poetry:** Submit 5 poems max. (Oct.-May), serious, witty; $.75/line. **Columns, Departments:** Brief newsy facts, behind the headlines, reflective pieces; 750-1,000 words; $75. **Tips:** Focus on religion, politics, culture; how they intertwine. No simultaneous submissions. **Queries:** Not necessary. **E-queries:** Yes. **Unsolicited mss:** Accepts. **Response:** Queries 1 month, submissions 6 weeks, SASE required. **Freelance Content:** 20%. **Rights:** All. **Payment:** On publication.

THE COVENANT COMPANION

5101 N. Francisco Ave., Chicago, IL 60625-3611. 773-784-3000. E-mail: companion@covoffice.org. Web site: www.covchurch.org. Monthly. $19.95. Circ.: 18,000. Donald L. Meyer, Editor. **Description:** Publication of Evangelical Covenant Church. Discusses issues of faith, spirituality, social justice, local ministry, and the life of the church. **Nonfiction:** Biographical profiles, local church ministries, interviews with authors; 1,200-1,800 words; $35-$100. **Tips:** No "rants" about the culture or political agendas. Prefers human-interest or articles on practical spirituality. **Queries:** Not necessary. **E-queries:** Yes. **Unsolicited mss:** Accepts. **Response:** Queries 4 weeks, submissions 6 weeks, SASE required. **Freelance Content:** 40%. **Rights:** 1st NA. **Payment:** On publication.

CRUSADER

P.O. Box 7259, Grand Rapids, MI 49510. 616-241-5616. Web site: www.gospelcom.net/cadets. 7x/year. Circ.: 12,000. G. Richard Broene, Editor. **Description:** Christian-oriented magazine for boys, ages 9-14, especially to members of Calvinist Cadet Corps. Purpose is to show how God is at work in the lives of the cadets and in the world around them. **Fiction:** Fast-moving stories that appeal to a boy's sense of adventure and humor; 1,000-3,000 words; pay varies. **Tips:** Request list of themes and free sample copy. **Queries:** Preferred. **Unsolicited mss:** Accepts. **Payment:** On acceptance.

DAILY MEDITATION

Box 2710, San Antonio, TX 78299. 210-735-5247. Semi-annual. $16/year. Circ.: 761. Emilia Devno, Editor. **Description:** Inspirational, self-improvement, nonsectarian religious articles, showing the way to greater spiritual growth. **Nonfiction:** 300-1,600 words. Pays $.02/word. **Poetry:** up to 350 words;

$.14/line. **Tips:** No fiction, handwritten material, meditations, photographs, dated material. **Queries:** Not necessary. **E-queries:** No. **Unsolicited mss:** Accepts. **Response:** SASE required. **Rights:** FNASR. **Payment:** On acceptance.

DECISION
Billy Graham Evangelistic Assn., 1300 Harmon Pl.,
P.O. Box 779, Minneapolis, MN 55440-0779.
E-mail: submissions@bgea.org. Web site: www.billygraham.org/decision. 11x/year.
$9/yr. Circ.: 1,400,000. Kersten Beckstrom, Editor. **Description:** Offers religious inspirational, personal experience, and how-to articles. **Nonfiction:** Personal conversion testimonies, personal experience articles on how God has intervened in a person's daily life; how scripture was applied to solve a problem; 400-1,500 words; $30-260. **Poetry:** Free verse and rhymed; 4-16 lines; $.60/word. **Fillers:** Anecdotes; 300-500 words; $25-$75. **Columns, Departments:** Where are they now? (Stories of people who have become Christians through Bill Graham ministries); 500-600 words; $85. **Tips:** Submit articles "with strong take-away message for readers." **Queries:** Not necessary. **E-queries:** Yes. **Unsolicited mss:** Accepts. **Response:** Queries, 3 months; submissions, 10 months, SASE required. **Freelance Content:** 40%. **Rights:** 1st. **Payment:** On publication. **Contact:** Bob Paulson.

DISCIPLESHIP JOURNAL
Box 35004, Colorado Springs, CO 80935. 719-531-3514.
E-mail: sue.kline@navpress.com. Web site: www.disciplejournal.com. Bi-monthly.
$3.95/issue, $21.97/year. Circ.: 130,000. Sue Kline, Editor. **Description:** Christian growth, practical application of scripture. **Nonfiction:** Teaching based on Scripture (e.g., what Bible says on forgiveness); how-tos (to deepen devotional life; to reach out in community); 1,000-3,000; $.25/word. **Columns, Departments:** On the Home Front (Q&A on family issues); Getting into God's word (devotional or Bible study); DJ+ (up to 500 words, on practical ministry, leading small groups, evangelism, etc.); 750-950 words; $.25/word. **Tips:** First-time writers encouraged to write non-theme articles, on any aspect of living as a disciple of Christ. Seeking articles encouraging involvement in world's mission, personal evangelism, and Christian leadership. No testimonies, devotionals, book reviews, or news. **Queries:** Required. **E-queries:** Yes. **Unsolicited mss:** Does not accept. **Response:** 6 weeks, SASE. **Freelance Content:** 80%. **Rights:** 1st, electronic, anthology. **Payment:** On acceptance.

DISCOVERIES
WordAction Publishing Co., 6401 The Paseo, Kansas City, MO 64131.
E-mail: kneal@nazarene.org. weekly. Circ.: 22,000. Virginia Folsom, Editor. **Description:** Full-color story paper for 3rd and 4th graders, connecting Evangelical Sunday School learning with daily growth of a middle-grade child. **Fiction:** Contemporary, true-to-life portrayals of 8-10 year olds; 500 words; $.05/word. **Fillers:** Bible trivia and puzzles. **Tips:** Illustrate character building and scriptural application. Send for guidelines and coming themes. **Queries:** Preferred. **E-queries:** Yes.

Unsolicited mss: Accepts. **Response:** 6-8 weeks, SASE required. **Freelance Content:** 80%. **Rights:** Multi-use. **Payment:** On publication. **Contact:** Kathy Neal.

DISCOVERY TRAILS

1445 Boonville Ave., Springfield, MO 65802-1894. 417-862-2781. E-mail: rl-discoverytrails@gph.org. Web site: www.radiantlife.org. Quarterly. Circ.: 36,000. Sinda Zinn, Editor. **Description:** Take-home paper for children 10-11 years old, with fiction stories, activities, poems, articles, and puzzles to reinforce daily Christian living. **Fiction:** Stories that promote Christian living through application of biblical principles by the characters; 1000 words; 7-10 cents/word. **Nonfiction:** Articles about topics that show God's power, wisdom in creation, or correlation to a relationship with God; 300-500 words; 7-10 cents/word. **Tips:** No Santa, Easter Bunny, Halloween stories. **Queries:** Not necessary. **E-queries:** No. **Unsolicited mss:** Accepts. **Response:** SubmissioN 2-4weeks, SASE required. **Freelance Content:** 90%. **Payment:** On acceptance.

DOVETAIL INSTITUTE FOR INTERFAITH FAMILY RESOURCES

775 Simon Greenwell Lane, Boston, KY 40107. 502-549-5499. E-mail: di-ifr@boardstowm.com. Web site: www.dovetailpublishing.com. Bi-monthly. $25/year. Circ.: 1,000. Mary Heléne Rosenbaum, Editor. **Description:** Resources for dual-faith couples, and their families, friends, and professionals who serve them, from a non-denominational perspective. Readers cover the intermarriage spectrum, including single-faith and dual-faith households. **Nonfiction:** Advice, anecdotes, and research on aspects of interfaith marriage; e.g., "Challah Baking: Thoughts of a Christian Cook," or "Intermarriage in Australia"; 800-1,000; $25. **Fillers:** Related cartoons, humor, and photos also used. **Tips:** Have experience or knowledge in the field of intermarriage. Avoid broad generalizations, or strongly partisan religious creeds. **Queries:** Not necessary. **E-queries:** Yes. **Unsolicited mss:** Accepts. **Response:** Queries 2-4 weeks, submissions 4-6 weeks, SASE required. **Freelance Content:** 80%. **Rights:** All. **Payment:** On publication.

ENRICHMENT

1445 Boonville Ave., Springfield, MO 65802-1894. 417-862-2781. E-mail: enrichment@ag.org. Quarterly. $22/yr. Circ.: 33,000. Gary Allen, Editor. **Description:** Resources to assist Pentecostal ministers in effective ministry. **Nonfiction:** Articles and features on wide range of ministry-related topics; 1,200-2,100; to $.10/word. **Queries:** Not necessary. **E-queries:** Yes. **Unsolicited mss:** Accepts. **Response:** 1 week, SASE required. **Freelance Content:** less than 10%. **Rights:** 1st NA. **Payment:** On publication. **Contact:** Rich Knoth.

EVANGEL

Light and Life Communications, Box 535002, Indianapolis, IN 46253-5002. 317-244-3660. Quarterly. $1.85/issue. Circ.: 12,000. Julie Innes, Editor. **Description:** Devotional in nature, seeks to increase reader's understanding of the nature and character of God and life lived under lordship of Christ. **Fiction:** Solving problems through faith; max. 1,200 words; $.04/word. **Nonfiction:** Free Methodist. Personal experience articles; short devotional items, 300-500 words (1,200 max.); $.04/word. **Poetry:** Devotional or nature; 8-16 lines. **Fillers:** Crypto puzzles, cartoons; $.10-.20/word. **Queries:** Not necessary. **E-queries:** No. **Unsolicited mss:** Accepts. **Response:** Queries 2 weeks, submissions 6-8 weeks, SASE required. **Freelance Content:** 100%. **Rights:** One-time. **Payment:** On publication.

EVANGELICAL BEACON
901 E. 78th St., Minneapolis, MN 55420. 952-854-1300. Web site: www.efc.org/beacon.html. Carol Madison, Editor. **Description:** Published by Evangelical Free Church. **Nonfiction:** Articles, 500-2,000 words, that fit editorial themes; pays $.03-$.07/word. **Poetry:** Some, related to Christian faith. **Payment:** On publication.

FAITH TODAY
M.I.P. Box 3745, Markham, Ontario, Canada L3R OY4. 905-479-6071 X245. E-mail: ft@efc-canada.com. Web site: www.efc-canada.com/subs.htm. Bimonthly. $18. Circ.: 17,000. Gail Reid, Managing Editor. **Description:** Thoughts, trends, issues, and events from a Canadian evangelical Christian perspective. **Nonfiction:** News stories and features on social trends and church trends in Canada. Also, short, quirky items, with photo, on Christianity in Canada; 400-3,000 words; $.20-$.30/word. **Tips:** No devotionals or generic Christian-living material. **Queries:** Required. **E-queries:** Yes. **Unsolicited mss:** Does not accept. **Response:** 3 weeks, SASE required. **Freelance Content:** 75%. **Rights:** FNASR. **Payment:** On publication.

THE FAMILY DIGEST
PO Box 40137, Fort Wayne, IN 46804. Bi-monthly. Circ.: 150,000. Corine B. Erlandson, Editor. **Description:** Dedicated to the joy and fulfillment of Catholic family and parish life. We especially look for upbeat articles which affirm the simple ways in which the Catholic faith is expressed in daily life. **Nonfiction:** Seeking articles on family life, parish life, spiritual life, Saint's lives, prayer, how-to, and seasonal (seasonal should be submitted 7 months prior to issue date); 650-1,250 words; $40-$60. **Fillers:** Funny and unusual stories drawn from personal, real-life experience; 10-100 words; $25. **Tips:** Writing must have a Catholic theme. Prefers original articles; will consider reprints of pieces which appeared in noncompeting markets. **Queries:** Not necessary. **E-queries:** No. **Unsolicited mss:** Accepts. **Response:** 4-8 wks, SASE required. **Freelance Content:** 90%. **Rights:** 1st NA. **Payment:** On acceptance.

FELLOWSHIP
Box 271, Nyack, NY 10960-0271. 845-358-4601. E-mail: fellowship@forusa.org. Web site: www.forusa.org. Bimonthly. $4.50/issue. Circ.: 9,000. Richard Deats, Editor. **Description:** Magazine of peace, justice, and nonviolence. Published by Fellowship of Reconciliation, an interfaith, pacifist organ-

ization. **Nonfiction:** Articles for a just and peaceful world community; 750-2,500 words. **Art:** b/w photo-essays on active nonviolence, peace and justice, opposition to war. **Queries:** Not necessary. **Unsolicited mss:** Accepts. **Freelance Content:** 25%. **Payment:** In copies.

FIRST THINGS

Institute on Religion & Public Life, 156 Fifth Ave., #400, New York, NY 10010-7002. 212-627-1985. E-mail: ft@firstthing.com. Web site: www.firstthings.com. 10x/year. Circ.: 32,000. James Nuechterlein, Editor. **Description:** General social commentary for academics, clergy, and general educated readership, on the role of religion in public life. **Nonfiction:** Essays and features; 1,500 words-6,000 words; $300-$800. **Poetry:** 4-40 lines. **Queries:** Preferred. **Payment:** On publication.

FOURSQUARE WORLD ADVANCE

1910 W. Sunset Blvd., Suite 200, P.O. Box 26902, Los Angeles, CA 90026. E-mail: comm@foursquare.org. Web site: www.foursquare.org. Ronald D. Williams, Editor. **Description:** Published by International Church of the Foursquare Gospel. Religious fiction and nonfiction, 1,000-1,200 words, and religious poetry. Pays $75. Guidelines available. **Payment:** On publication.

THE FRIEND

50 E North Temple, 24th Floor, Salt Lake City, UT 84150-3226. 801-240-2210. Monthly. $8/year. Circ.: 275,000. Vivian Paulsen, Managing Editor. **Description:** Literary journal with fiction and nonfiction. **Queries:** Preferred. **E-queries:** No. **Unsolicited mss:** Does not accept. **Response:** Submissions 8-12 weeks. **Rights:** All. **Payment:** On acceptance.

FRIENDS JOURNAL

1216 Arch St., 2A, Philadelphia, PA 19107. 215-563-5629. E-mail: info@friendsjournal.org. Web site: www.friendsjournal.org. Monthly. $29/yr. Circ.: 8,000. Susan Corson-Finnerty, Editor. **Description:** Reflects Quaker life today: commentary on social issues, spiritual reflection, experiential articles, Quaker history, world affairs. **Nonfiction:** With awareness of Friend's concerns and ways; fresh, nonacademic style; use language that clearly includes both sexes; up to 2,500 words. **Poetry:** up to 25 lines. **Fillers:** Quaker-related humor, games, puzzles. **Tips:** Articles with positive approach to problems and spiritual seeking preferred. **Queries:** Not necessary. **E-queries:** Yes. **Unsolicited mss:** Accepts. **Response:** Queries 3 week, submissions 4 months, SASE. **Freelance Content:** 70%. **Payment:** None.

THE GEM

Box 926, Findlay, OH 45839-0926. Mac Cordell, Editor. **Description:** True experiences of God's help, of healed relationships, and maturing in faith; for adolescents to senior citizens. **Fiction:** 1,000-1,600 words; $15. **Nonfiction:** 300-1,600 words, $15. **Fillers:** $5-$10.

GOSPEL TODAY

761 Old Hickory Blvd., Suite 205, Brentwood, TN 37027. 615-376-5656. E-mail: gospel2day@aol.com. Web site: www.gospeltoday.com. 8x/year. $3/issue, $20/year. Circ.: 50,000. Teresa E. Harris, Editor. **Description:** "America's leading gospel lifestyle magazine," aimed at African-American Christians. **Nonfiction:** Human-interest stories on Christian personalities, events, and testimonials. Book reviews welcome; 1,500-2,000 words; $150-$250. **Columns, Departments:** $50-$75. **Tips:** No opinions, testimonials, or poetry. **Queries:** Required. **E-queries:** Yes. **Unsolicited mss:** Does not accept. **Response:** Queries 6 weeks, SASE required. **Freelance Content:** 60%. **Rights:** All. **Payment:** On publication.

GROUP

Box 481, Loveland, CO 80539. 970-669-3836. E-mail: greditor@grouppublishing.com. Web site: www.groupmag.com www.youth-ministry.com. $29.95. Circ.: 55,000. Rick Lawrence, Editor. **Description:** Inter-denominational Youth Ministry magazine, for leaders of Christian youth. Supplies ideas, practical help, inspiration, and training. **Nonfiction:** 500-2,000 words, $125-$225. **Columns, Departments:** Try This One (short ideas for groups: games, fundraisers, Bible study); Hands on Help (tips for leaders); Strange but True (a funny or remarkable youth ministry experience); $40. **Tips:** Use real-life examples, personal experience. Include practical tips, self-quizzes, checklists. Use Scripture. **Queries:** Not necessary. **Unsolicited mss:** Accepts. **Response:** 6-8 weeks, SASE required. **Freelance Content:** 70%. **Rights:** All. **Payment:** On publication.

GUIDE

Review & Herald Publishing Assn., 55 W. Oak Ridge Dr., Hagerstown, MD 21740. 301-393-4038. E-mail: guide@rpha.org. Web site: www.guidemagazine.org. Weekly (52/year). $41.95/year. Circ.: 33,000. Randy Fishell, Editor. **Description:** Christian publication for young people, ages 10-14. **Nonfiction:** Adventure, personal growth, Christian humor, inspiration, biography, nature; with spiritual emphasis; 800-1,200 words. **Tips:** Set forth a clearly evident Christian principle without being preachy. **Queries:** Not necessary. **Unsolicited mss:** Accepts. **Response:** 4-6 weeks, SASE required. **Freelance Content:** 95%. **Rights:** 1st, or one-time reprint. **Payment:** On acceptance.

GUIDEPOSTS

16 E. 34th St., New York, NY 10016. 212-251-8100. E-mail: gp4k@guideposts.org. Web site: www.gp4k.com. Monthly. $12.97/year. Circ.: 3,500,000. Edward Grinnan, Editor. **Description:** First-person inspirational magazine about people overcoming challenges through faith. **Nonfiction:** First-person true stories of people who face challenges, fears, illnesses through faith; 500 words and up; $100-$400. **Fillers:** Spiritual quotes; $25. **Columns, Departments:** What Prayer Can Do (power of prayer); Pass it on (people helping people) His Mysterious Ways (more than coincidence); 50-500 words; $25-$100. **Tips:** Don't tell an entire life story; pick your specific "take-away" message. **E-queries:** No. **Unsolicited mss:**

Accepts. **Response:** Queries and submissions 3 months. SASE required. **Freelance Content:** 75%. **Rights:** All. **Payment:** On publication.

GUIDEPOSTS FOR TEENS

P.O. Box 638, Chesterton, IN 46304. 219-929-4429.
E-mail: gp4t@guideposts.org. Web site: www.gp4teens.com. Bimonthly. Circ.: 180,000. Betsy Kohn, Editor. **Description:** Interfaith, offering teens (ages 12-18) true stories filled with adventure and inspiration. Quizzes, how-to, advice, music reviews, Q&As, profiles of role models (celebrity and "real" teens). **Nonfiction:** True first-person dangerous, miraculous, inspirational stories; ghostwritten for (or written by) teens. Protagonist must change in course of the story; must deliver clear inspirational takeaway. **Fillers:** Quizzes (Are you a winner or a whiner? Are you dating a dud?); How-tos (how to find a good job, how to get along with your parents); Celebrity Q&As, interviews. **Art:** Send samples. **Tips:** No preachy, overtly religious stories. **Queries:** Preferred. **E-queries:** Yes. **Unsolicited mss:** Accepts. **Response:** Queries 4 weeks, submissions 6 weeks, SASE. **Freelance Content:** 80%. **Rights:** All. **Payment:** On acceptance. **Contact:** Allison Payne, Asst. Ed.

HADASSAH

50 W. 58th St., New York, NY 10019. 212-355-7900.
Web site: www.hadassah.org. **Description:** For Jewish Americans. **Queries:** Preferred.

JEWISH CURRENTS

22 E. 17th St., #601, New York, NY 10003. 212-924-5740.
11x/year. $30. Circ.: 2,100. Morris U. Schappes, Editor. **Description:** Articles, review, fiction, and poetry on Jewish subjects or presenting Jewish point of view on an issue. **Fiction:** Jewish angle, humor sought; 2,500. **Nonfiction:** Jewish history, politics, culture, Yiddish language and literature (in English); 2,500. **Poetry:** Jewish focus. **Tips:** Reader are secular, politically liberal. **Queries:** Not necessary. **E-queries:** No. **Unsolicited mss:** Accepts. **Response:** Queries/submissions 1 month, SASE. **Payment:** In copies.

THE JEWISH HOMEMAKER

391 Troy Ave., Brooklyn, NY 11213. 718-756-7500.
Web site: www.ok.org. Quarterly. Avraham M. Goldstein, Editor. **Description:** For a traditional/Orthodox Jewish audience. **Nonfiction:** Articles, 1,200-2,000 words; pay varies. **Queries:** Preferred. **Payment:** On publication.

THE JEWISH MONTHLY

B'nai B'rith International, 1640 Rhode Island Ave. NW,
Washington, DC 20036. 202-857-6646.
E-mail: ijm@binaibrith.org. Web site: www.bnaibrith.org. 5x/year. Circ.: 200,000. Eric Rozenman, Executive Editor. **Description:** Published by B'nai B'rith, with general-interest stories. **Nonfiction:** Profiles, stories of interest to Jewish communities in

U.S. and abroad, politics, arts, Middle East; 1,500-2,000 words; $450-$700. **Queries:** Preferred.

JOURNAL OF CHRISTIAN NURSING

P.O. Box 1650, Downers Grove, IL 60515-1650. 630-734-4030. E-mail: jcn@ivpress.com. Web site: www.ncf-jcn.org. Quarterly. $22.95. Circ.: 9,000. Judy Shelly, Editor. **Description:** Practical, biblically based articles to help nurses meet patient's spiritual needs and face ethical dilemmas, and to grow spiritually themselves. **Nonfiction:** to help view nursing practice through the eyes of faith: spiritual care, ethics, values, healing and wholeness, psychology and religion, personal and professional ethics, etc. Priority to nurse authors; work by others considered. Pays $25-$80; 8-12 pages. **Poetry:** 1 page or less; $25. **Tips:** Avoid academic style. **Queries:** Not necessary. **E-queries:** Yes. **Unsolicited mss:** Accepts. **Response:** Queries 2-3 weeks, submissions 1-2 month, SASE. **Rights:** 1st time, some reprint. **Payment:** On acceptance.

JOYFUL WOMAN

P.O. Box 90028, Chattanooga, TN 37412. 706-866-5522. E-mail: info@joyfulwoman.org. Web site: www.joyfulwoman.org. Bi-monthly. $4/$19.95. Circ.: 6,000. Joy Rice Martin, Editor. **Description:** Encourages Christian women, of all ages, in every aspect of their lives. **Fiction:** Thoughtful stories about Christian women; 500-1,000 words; $20-$25. **Nonfiction:** Profiles of Christian women, first-person inspirational true stories, practical and Bible-oriented how-to articles; 500-1,000 words; $20-$25. **Poetry:** on occasion. **Fillers:** occasional. **Queries:** Preferred. **E-queries:** Yes. **Unsolicited mss:** Does not accept. **Response:** 4-6 weeks, SASE. **Freelance Content:** 45%. **Payment:** On publication.

LEADERSHIP

465 Gundersen Dr., Carol Stream, IL 60188. 630-260-6200. E-mail: ljeditor@leadershipjournal.net. Web site: www.leadershipjournal.net. Quarterly. $24.95/year. Circ.: 65,000. Marshall Shelley, Editor. **Description:** For church leaders, first-person accounts of real-life experiences in the ministry. **Nonfiction:** First-person stories of life in ministry; situation faced, solutions found. Articles must offer practical help (how-to format) for problems church leaders face; 2,000 words; $.15/word. **Tips:** Avoid essays expounding, editorials arguing, or homilies explaining. **Queries:** Preferred. **E-queries:** Yes. **Unsolicited mss:** Accepts. **Response:** Queries 3 weeks, submissions 6 weeks, SASE. **Freelance Content:** 30%. **Payment:** On acceptance.

LIBERTY

12501 Old Columbia Pike, Silver Spring, MD 20904-1608. 301-680-6690. E-mail: steed@nad.adventist.org. Web site: www.liberty magazine.org. Bimonthly. $6.95/issue. Circ.: 200,000. Lincoln Steed, Editor. **Description:** Focuses on religious freedom and church-state relations. Readers are legislators at every level, judges, lawyers, and other leaders. **Nonfiction:** On religious freedom and 1st amendment rights; 1,000-2,500 words; $250 and up. **Tips:** Submit resumé and clips. **Queries:** Preferred. **E-queries:** Yes. **Unsolicited mss:** Does not accept. **Response:** Queries 1-3 months, submissions 30 days, SASE. **Freelance Content:** 95%. **Rights:** 1st NA. **Payment:** On acceptance.

LIFEWISE

Focus on the Family, 8655 Explorer Drive, Colorado Springs, CO 80920-1049. 719-531-3400. Web site: www.family.org. Monthly. Circ.: 45,000. **Description:** Christian publication for older adults.

LIGHT AND LIFE

P.O. Box 535002, Indianapolis, IN 46253-5002. 317-2443660. E-mail: llmaauthors@fmcna.org. Bimonthly. $16/year. Circ.: 18,000. Doug Newton, Editor. **Description:** Social and cultural analysis from evangelical perspective. **Fiction:** 800-2,000; 800-2,000. **Nonfiction:** Thoughtful articles about practical Christian living; 800-2,000; 800-2,000. **Queries:** Not necessary. **E-queries:** Yes. **Unsolicited mss:** Accepts. **Response:** Queries/submissions 6-8 weeks, SASE. **Rights:** 1st. **Payment:** On publication.

LIGUORIAN

One Liguori Dr, Liguori, MO 63057. 636-464-2500. E-mail: aweinert@liguorian.org. Web site: www.liguori.org. 10x/year. Circ.: 242,000. Fr.Allan Weinert, Editor. **Description:** Faithful to the charisma of St. Alphonsus, seeks to help readers develop a personal call to holiness. **Fiction:** Short stories with Catholic content; 1700-1900 words; $.12/word. **Nonfiction:** On Catholic Christian values in modern life; 1700-1900 words; $.12/word. **Queries:** Preferred. **E-queries:** Yes. **Unsolicited mss:** Accepts. **Response:** Queries, 1 week, submissions 8 weeks; SASE. **Freelance Content:** 20-30%. **Payment:** On acceptance.

LILITH

250 W. 57th St., #2432, New York, NY 10107-0172. 212-757-0818. E-mail: lilithmag@aol.com. Web site: www.lilithmag.com. Quarterly. $6/issue, $18/year. Circ.: 25,000. Susan Weidman Schneider, Editor. **Description:** Showcases Jewish women writers, educators, and artists; illuminates Jewish women's lives in their religious, ethnic, sexual, and social-class diversity. **Fiction:** On the lives of Jewish women; 1,000-2,000 words. **Nonfiction:** Autobiographies, interviews, social analysis, sociological research, oral history, new rituals, reviews, investigative reporting, opinion pieces; also news briefs (500 words); Letters to the Editor; lists of resources, projects, events; 1,000-2,000 words. **Poetry:** Yes. **Art:** Yes. **Queries:** Not necessary. **E-queries:** Yes. **Unsolicited mss:** Accepts. **Response:** 12-16 weeks, SASE.

THE LIVING LIGHT

U.S. Catholic Conference, Dept. of Ed., Caldwell 345, Catholic Univ. of America, Washington, DC 20064. 202-319-6660. E-mail: bridoyle@aol.com. Quarterly. $39.95. Circ.: 5,000. Berard Marthaler, Editor. **Description:** Catechetical educational journal sponsored by U.S. Catholic Conference. **Nonfiction:** Theoretical and practical articles, 1,500-4,000 words, on religious education, catechesis, and pastoral ministry. **Queries:** Preferred. **E-queries:** No. **Unsolicited mss:** Does not accept. **Payment:** On publication.

THE LOOKOUT

8121 Hamilton Ave., Cincinnati, OH 45231. 513-931-4050. Web site: www.standardpub.com. David Faust, Editor. **Description:** Focuses on spiritual growth, family issues, people overcoming problems and applying Christian faith to current issues. **Nonfiction:** Articles, 500-1,800 words. Inspirational or humorous shorts, 500-800 words. Pays $.05-$.15/word. **Queries:** Preferred. **Payment:** On acceptance.

THE LUTHERAN

8765 W. Higgins Rd., Chicago, IL 60631-4183. 773-380-2540. E-mail: lutheran@elca.org. Web site: www.TheLutheran.org. Monthly. Circ.: 620,000. David L. Miller, Editor. **Description:** Christian ideology, personal religious experiences, social and ethical issues, family life, church, and community of Evangelical Lutheran Church in America. **Nonfiction:** To 1,200 words; pays $100-$500. **Queries:** Required. **Payment:** On acceptance.

MARRIAGE PARTNERSHIP

Christianity Today, 465 Gundersen Dr., Carol Stream, IL 60188. 630-260-6200. E-mail: mp@marriagepartnership.com. Web site: www.marriagepartnership.com. Quarterly. $19.95/year. Circ.: 50,000. Caryn Rivadeneira, Managing Editor. **Description:** Offers realistic help and ideas for Christian married couples. **Nonfiction:** Related to marriage for men and women who wish to fortify their relationships; 1,000-2,000; $.15/word. **Fillers:** humor welcomed; 1200 words. **Queries:** Required. **E-queries:** Yes. **Unsolicited mss:** Does not accept. **Response:** Queries 8 weeks, SASE. **Freelance Content:** 25%. **Rights:** 1st. **Payment:** On acceptance.

MARYKNOLL MAGAZINE

Maryknoll, NY 10545. 914-941-7590. E-mail: mklmag@maryknoll.org. Web site: www.maryknoll.org. 11x/year. $10/year. Circ.: 600,000. Frank Maurovich, Editor. **Description:** Christian-oriented, focusing on articles concerning the work of our missioners overseas. **Nonfiction:** Articles relating to missions or missioners overseas; 1,500-2,000 words; $150. **Art:** Prints or slides; $50. **Queries:** Not necessary. **E-queries:** Yes. **Unsolicited mss:** Accepts. **Response:** SASE. **Freelance Content:** 25%. **Payment:** On publication.

MATURE LIVING

127 Ninth Ave. N., Nashville, TN 37234-0140. 615-251-2274. E-mail: matureliving@lifeway.com. Monthly. N/A. Circ.: 350,000. Judy Pregel, Editor. **Description:** A leisure reading magazine for Christian seniors, 50 years and older. **Fiction:** Quality fiction for seniors, with strong story line underscoring a biblical truth; 1,200 words; $75. **Nonfiction:** Nostalgia about "good old days" (personal memories or historical). Travel articles with general appeal, descriptive information; 600-1,200 words; $.05/word, min. $75. **Poetry:** Yes. **Fillers:** Cartoons. **Tips:** Looking for pieces with human interest, Christian warmth, and humor. **Queries:** Not necessary. **Unsolicited mss:** Accepts. **Response:** 6-8 weeks, SASE. **Freelance Content:** 75%. **Rights:** All. **Payment:** On acceptance.

MATURE YEARS

United Methodist Publishing House, 201 Eighth Ave. South, Nashville, TN 37202. E-mail: matureyears@umpublishing.org. Quarterly. $18. Circ.: 50,000. Marvin W. Cropsey, Editor. **Description:** Helps persons in and near retirement years to understand the appropriate resources of the Christian faith to deal with specific problems and opportunities of aging. **Nonfiction:** Religious and inspirational articles; also, older adults in active lifestyles; 2,000 words; $.05/word. **Columns, Departments:** Health and fitness, personal finance, travel, poetry, fiction. **Art:** Photos. **Tips:** Welcomes new writers. **Queries:** Preferred. **E-queries:** Yes. **Unsolicited mss:** Accepts. **Response:** 4-8 weeks, SASE required. **Rights:** One-time NA. **Payment:** On acceptance.

THE MENNONITE

1700 S. Main St., Newton, KS 67114. 219-535-6051. E-mail: ejthomas@mph.org. Web site: www.themennonite.org. Weekly. $1.50. Circ.: 16,000. Everett Thomas, Editor. **Description:** For members of the Mennonite church. **Nonfiction:** Stories, faith perspectives emphasizing Christian theme; 1,400 words; $.07/word. **Poetry:** 2 pages or less; $50-$75/poem. **Art:** electronic preferred; $35-$50. **Queries:** Not necessary. **E-queries:** Yes. **Unsolicited mss:** Accepts. **Response:** 1 week, SASE. **Freelance Content:** 20%. **Rights:** One-time. **Payment:** On publication. **Contact:** Gordon Honser.

MESSENGER OF THE SACRED HEART

661 Greenwood Ave., Toronto, Ont., Canada M4J 4B3. 416-466-1195. Monthly. Circ.: 15,000. F. J. Power, S. J., Editor. **Description:** For American and Canadian Catholics. **Fiction:** Short stories; about 1,500 words; $.06/word and up. **Nonfiction:** Articles; about 1,500 words; $.06/word and up. **Payment:** On acceptance.

MIDSTREAM

633 Third Ave., 21st Fl., New York, NY 10017. E-mail: info@midstream.org. Web site: www.midstream.org. 8x/year. $3/issue, $21/year. Circ.: 8,000. Joel Carmichael, Editor. **Description:** Zionist publication, content ranges from political U.S. and Israel culture, literature, book reviews, poetry, com-

ments on religion. Varied points of view presented. **Fiction:** Stories on Jewish themes; 1,500-4,000 words; $.05/word. **Nonfiction:** Jewish (Zionist) political, cultural, literary, religious themes; 1,500-6,000 words; $.05/word. **Poetry:** Jewish themes; 20 lines; $25/poem. **Tips:** Readers mostly elderly, scholarly, Israel-oriented. **Queries:** Not necessary. **E-queries:** No. **Unsolicited mss:** Accepts. **Response:** up to 1 month, SASE. **Freelance Content:** 20%. **Rights:** 1st. **Payment:** On publication.

MINISTRY & LITURGY

160 E. Virginia St., #290, San Jose, CA 95112. 408-286-8505. Web site: www.rpinet.com/ml. Nick Wagner, Editor. **Description:** Practical, imaginative how-to help for Roman Catholic liturgy planners. **Queries:** Required. **Payment:** In copies.

THE MIRACULOUS MEDAL

475 E. Chelten Ave., Philadelphia, PA 19144-5785. 215-848-1010. Quarterly. William J. O'Brien, C.M., Editor. **Description:** Religious literary journal focusing on the Catholic Church. **Fiction:** Any subject matter which does not not contradict teachings of Roman Catholic Church; 1,000-2,400; $.02/word. **Poetry:** Religious, preferably about Blessed Virgin Mary; 20 lines; $.50/line. **Tips:** Original material only. **Queries:** Preferred. **E-queries:** No. **Response:** queries/ submissions 6 months, SASE. **Freelance Content:** 25%. **Rights:** 1st NA. **Payment:** On acceptance.

MOMENT

4710 41st St NW, Washington, DC 20016. 202-364-3300. E-mail: editor@momentmag.com. Web site: www.momentmag.com. Bimonthly. $4.50/issue. Circ.: 65,000. Hershel Shanks, Editor. **Description:** On Jewish culture, politics, and religion. **Fiction:** 8,000 max. **Nonfiction:** Sophisticated articles on Jewish culture, politics, religion, personalities. Pay negotiated; 100-3,500 words. **Poetry:** 150-300 words. **Columns, Departments:** Notes and News (250 words, on events, people, and living); Olam/The Jewish World (colorful, first-person "letters from" and reports); Book Reviews (to 400 words); to 1,000 words. **Tips:** Seeking fresh angles on Jewish themes. **Queries:** Preferred. **E-queries:** Yes. **Unsolicited mss:** Accepts. **Response:** 1-2 months, SASE. **Freelance Content:** 90%. **Rights:** FNASR. **Payment:** On publication.

MOODY

Moody Bible Institute, 820 N. LaSalle Blvd., Chicago, IL 60610. 312-329-2164. E-mail: moodyedit@moody.edu. Web site: www.moody.edu. Bimonthly. Circ.: 112,000. Andrew Scheer, Managing Editor. **Description:** Evangelical Christian experience in the home, the community, and the workplace. **Nonfiction:** Anecdotal articles; 1,200-2,000 word; $.15-$.20/word. **Queries:** Required. **Unsolicited mss:** Does not accept. **Payment:** On acceptance.

MY FRIEND
Pauline Books & Media, Daughters of St. Paul, 50 St. Pauls Ave., Boston, MA 02130-3491. 617-541-8911. E-mail: myfriend@pauline.org. Web site: www.pauline.org. Monthly. $2. Circ.: 11,500. Sister Kathryn James Hermes, Editor. **Description:** Catholic magazine for boys and girls, ages 6-12, celebrating the Catholic Faith as lived by today's children. **Fiction:** Stories with good dialogue, realistic character development. Can entertain, inspire, or teach; 800-1,100 words; $75-150. **Nonfiction:** Fresh perspectives into a child's world: imaginative, unique, challenging, informative, fun. Prefers visual articles, with multiple points of entry. **Queries:** Preferred. **Unsolicited mss:** Accepts. **Freelance Content:** 40%. **Rights:** 1st.

NEW COVENANT
200 Noll Plaza, Huntington, IN 46750. 219-356-8400. Web site: www.osv.com. Jim Manney, Editor. **Description:** Seeks to foster renewal in the Catholic Church, especially the charismatic, ecumenical, and evangelical dimensions of that renewal. **Nonfiction:** Articles and testimonials, 1,000-4,000 words; pays from $.15/word. **Queries:** Preferred. **Payment:** On acceptance.

NEW WORLD OUTLOOK
475 Riverside Dr., Rm. 1476, New York, NY 10115. 212-870-3765. Web site: gbgm-umc.org/nwo. Alma Graham, Editor. **Description:** On United Methodist missions and Methodist-related programs and ministries. Focus on national, global, and women's and children's issues, and on men and youth in missions. **Nonfiction:** Articles, 500-2,000 words, illustrated with color photos. **Queries:** Preferred. **Payment:** On publication.

OBLATES
9480 N. De Mazenod Dr., Belleville, IL 62223-1160. 618-398-4848. Web site: www.snows.org. Bimonthly. Membership in Missionary Association. Circ.: 450,000. Christine Portell, Editor. **Description:** Published by Missionary Assn. of Mary Immaculate. **Nonfiction:** Articles, to 500 words, that inspire, uplift, and motivate through positive Christian values in everyday life; $150. **Poetry:** Perceptive, inspirational verse. Avoid obscure imagery, allusions, irreverent humor. Make rhyme and rhythm flow; 12 lines max.; $50. **Tips:** Try first-person approach. No preachy, psychological, theological, or spiritual journey pieces. Christian slant or Gospel message should be apparent, but subtle. **Queries:** Not necessary. **E-queries:** No. **Unsolicited mss:** Accepts. **Response:** 4-6 weeks, SASE required. **Freelance Content:** 15%. **Rights:** FNASR. **Payment:** On acceptance. **Contact:** Mary Morhman.

ON THE LINE
616 Walnut, Scottdale, PA 15683-1999. 724-887-8500. E-mail: otl@mph.org. Web site: www.mph.org. Monthly. $2.20/$26.50. Circ.: 5,500. Mary Clemens Meyer, Editor. **Description:** For youth, ages 9-14, to reinforce Christian values. Seeks to help upper elementary and junior high school kids under-

stand God, the created world, themselves, and others. **Fiction:** Solving everyday problems, humor, holidays, Christian values; 1,000-1,800 words; $.03-$.05/word. **Nonfiction:** Nature, history, health, how-to; 300-500 words; $.03-$.05/word. **Poetry:** Light verse, humor, nature, holidays; 3-24 lines; $10-$25. **Fillers:** Cartoons, crosswords, word finds, scrambled letters, mazes, codes, jokes, riddles, recipes; $10-$25. **Tips:** Let the story give the moral subtly; keep it fun. **Queries:** Not necessary. **Unsolicited mss:** Accepts. **Response:** Submissions 1 month, SASE. **Freelance Content:** 85%. **Rights:** One-time. **Payment:** On acceptance.

OTHER SIDE

2221 N.E. 164 St., Suite 1112, North Miami Beach, FL 33160. Web site: www.theotherside.com. Bimonthly. Circ.: 14,000. Dee Dee Risher, Doug Davidson, Coeditors. **Description:** Independent, ecumenical, progressive Christian magazine devoted to issues of social justice, Christian spirituality, and the creative arts. **Fiction:** That deepens readers' encounter with mystery of God and the mystery of ourselves; 500-5,000 words; $75-$250. **Nonfiction:** On contemporary social, political, economic, or racial issues in U.S. or abroad; 500-4,000 words (most under 2,000 words); $20-$350. **Poetry:** Submit up to 3 poems; to 50 lines; $15. **Payment:** On acceptance.

OUR FAMILY

Box 249, Battleford, Sask., Canada S0M 0E0. 306-937-7771. E-mail: editor@ourfamilymagazine.com. Web site: www.ourfamilymagazine.com. 10x/year. $2/Canadian. Circ.: 7,000. Marie-Louise Ternier-Gommers, Editor. **Description:** Addresses Catholic faith issues pertinent to family life. **Nonfiction:** Articles with an experiential, reflective, descriptive style (on marriage and family life, blended families, youth and the church, etc.). Faith dimension essential; 1,200-2,000 words; $.05/word. **Poetry:** Religious/inspirational insight; $.45/line. **Fillers:** Humor, cartoons. **Art:** b/w, color prints; $24. **Tips:** Especially encourages Canadian authors. **Queries:** Not necessary. **E-queries:** Yes. **Unsolicited mss:** Accepts. **Response:** 2 months, SASE. **Freelance Content:** 75%. **Rights:** one-time, 1st. **Payment:** On acceptance.

OUR SUNDAY VISITOR

200 Noll Plaza, Huntington, IN 46750. 800-348-2440. E-mail: oursunvis$osv.com. Web site: www.osv.com. Weekly. $1.58/$58 yearly. Circ.: 70,000. Gerald Korson, Editor. **Description:** Reports on national and international news for Catholics, from Orthodox Catholic perspective. **Columns, Departments:** On the Catholic church in America today; 800 words; $200. **Art:** Any. Pay negotiable. **Queries:** Preferred. **E-queries:** Yes. **Unsolicited mss:** Accepts. **Response:** 3 weeks, SASE. **Freelance Content:** 10%. **Rights:** 1st. **Payment:** On acceptance. **Contact:** Michael DuBrueil, Beth McNamara.

PASSPORT

6401 The Paseo, Kansas City, MO 64131.

E-mail: kneal@nazarene.org. Quarterly printing, weekly distribution. Circ.: 18,000. Emily Freeburg, Editor. **Description:** Full-color newspaper for preteens, with resources for spiritual transformation and holy living. Corresponds with WordAction Sunday School materials (for 11-12 year olds). **Nonfiction:** 400-600 words, for grades 5-6, hot topics and relevant issues. Pays $.05/word for original work, less for reprints. **Fillers:** Pays $15 for cartoons and puzzles. **Queries:** Preferred. **E-queries:** Yes. **Unsolicited mss:** Accepts. **Response:** 6-8 weeks, SASE required. **Freelance Content:** 10%. **Rights:** Multi-use. **Payment:** On publication. **Contact:** Kathy Neal.

PASTORAL LIFE

Box 595, Canfield, OH 44406-0595. 330-533-5503.

E-mail: paultheapostle@msn.com. Web site: www.albahouse.org. Monthly. $17/yr. Circ.: 1,200. Rev. Matthew Roehrig. SSP, Editor. **Description:** Articles, 2,000-2,500 words, addressing the issues of Catholic pastoral ministry. Pays $.04/word. **Nonfiction:** On religious, pastoral ministry; 1,000-2,500 words; $.04/word. **Queries:** Not necessary. **E-queries:** Yes. **Unsolicited mss:** Accepts. **Payment:** On publication.

PENTECOSTAL EVANGEL

1445 Boonville Ave., Springfield, MO 65802. 417-862-2781.

E-mail: pe@ag.org. Web site: www.pe@ag.org. Weekly. $24.99/year. Circ.: 265,000. Hal Donaldson, Editor. **Description:** For Assemblies of God members and potential members. Provides biblical and practical articles to inspire believers. **Nonfiction:** Religious, personal experience, devotional; 800-1000 words; $.08/word. **Queries:** Preferred. **E-queries:** Yes. **Unsolicited mss:** Accepts. **Response:** Queries 2 weeks, submissions 6 weeks, SASE. **Freelance Content:** 5%. **Rights:** 1st and electronic. **Payment:** On acceptance.

THE PENTECOSTAL MESSENGER

PO Box 850, Joplin, MO 64802. 417-624-7050.

Web site: www.pcg.org. **Description:** On issues of Christian commitment (human interest, inspiration, social and religious issues, Bible topics, and seasonal material). **Nonfiction:** Articles, 500-2,000 words; pays $.015/word. **Payment:** On publication.

PERCEPTIONS

10736 Jefferson Blvd., Suite 502, Culver City, CA 90230.

Judi V. Brewer, Editor. **Description:** For single adults about leisure activities, issues related to single parents, inspiring personal experiences, humor, life from a Christian perspective. **Nonfiction:** Articles, 600-1,200 words; pay varies. **Queries:** Preferred. **Payment:** On acceptance. *No recent report.*

POCKETS

P.O. Box 340004, 1908 Grand Ave, Nashville, TN 37203-0004. 615-340-7333.

E-mail: pockets@upperroom.org. Web site: www.upperroom.org. 11x/year. $16.95.

Circ.: 90,000. Janet Knight, Editor. **Description:** Non-denominational, seeks to promote the Gospel of Jesus Christ to children and help them grow in their relationship with God. Readers include children of many ethnic and cultural backgrounds. **Fiction:** Stories to help children deal with everyday life. Prefers real-life settings; 600-1400 words; $.14/word. **Nonfiction:** Theme for each issue. Profiles of persons whose lives reflect Christian communities; value articles about children involved in environmental, community, peace/justice issues; 400-1000; $.14/word. **Fillers:** Puzzles, games (on theme); $25 and up. **Columns, Departments:** Pocketful of Love Prayer; $.14/word. **Tips:** Looking for puzzles and activities with colorful illustrations and graphics. **E-queries:** No. **Unsolicited mss:** Accepts. **Response:** SASE. **Freelance Content:** 90%. **Payment:** On acceptance.

PRESBYTERIAN RECORD
50 Wynford Dr., Toronto, Ont., Canada M3C 1J7. 416-441-1111. E-mail: jcongram@presbyterian.ca. Web site: www.presbyterian.ca/record. 11x/year. $20/yr. (U.S. & Foreign). Circ.: 50,000. John Congram, Editor. **Description:** Published by Presbyterian Church in Canada. **Fiction:** Stories of faith in action, contemporary, often controversial in nature; 1,500 words; $60. **Nonfiction:** On children and youth ministries, lay ministries, etc.; 1,500 words; $60. **Poetry:** Length, pay varies. **Columns, Departments:** Opinion, Church in Action, Meditation; 800 words; $40. **Art:** Prints preferred. **Queries:** Preferred. **E-queries:** Yes. **Unsolicited mss:** Accepts. **Response:** 1-2 weeks, SASE. **Freelance Content:** 30%. **Rights:** one-time. **Payment:** On publication.

PRESBYTERIANS TODAY
100 Witherspoon, Louisville, KY 40202-1396. 502-569-5637. E-mail: today@pcusa.org. Web site: www.pcusa.org/today. 10x/year. $12.95. Circ.: 60,000. Eva Stimson, Editor. **Description:** General-interest magazine for members of the Presbyterian church (U.S.). **Nonfiction:** About Presbyterian people and churches; guidance for daily living; current issues; 1,200-1,500 words; $200. **Fillers:** Humorous anecdotes; 100 words or less; no payment. **Queries:** Preferred. **E-queries:** Yes. **Unsolicited mss:** Accepts. **Response:** Queries 2-4 weeks, submissions 4-6 weeks, SASE. **Freelance Content:** 30%. **Rights:** 1st. **Payment:** On acceptance.

THE PRIEST
200 Noll Plaza, Huntington, IN 46750-4304. 219-356-8400. E-mail: tpriest@osv.com. Web site: www.dsv.com. Monthly. $5/$39.95. Circ.: 6,500. Msgr. Owen F. Campion, Editor. **Description:** Assists priests, deacons, and seminarians in day-to-day ministry. Items on spirituality, counseling, administration, theology, personalities, the saints, etc. **Nonfiction:** Historical/nostalgic, humor, inspirational, interview/profile, opinion, personal experience, religious; relating to priests and church; 1,500-5,000; $175-$250. **Columns, Departments:** Viewpoints; 1,000 or less; $75. **Tips:** Freelancers most often published in "Viewpoints." **Queries:** Preferred. **E-queries:** Yes. **Unsolicited mss:** Accepts. **Response:** Queries 5 weeks,

submissions 3 months, SASE. **Freelance Content:** 25%. **Rights:** FNASR. **Payment:** On acceptance. **Contact:** Murray Hubley, Assoc. Ed.

PURPOSE

616 Walnut Ave., Scottdale, PA 15683-1999. 724-887-8500. E-mail: horsch@mph.org. Web site: www.mph.org. Monthly. $18.95/yr. Circ.: 11,000. James E. Horsch, Editor. **Description:** For committed Christians who want to apply their faith in daily life. Suggests ways to resolve life's issues consistent with biblical principles. **Fiction:** Christian themes to nurture desire for world peace and provide tools for peaceful living. Introducing children to many cultures; 750 words; up to $.05/word. **Nonfiction:** To help others to grow toward commitment to Christ and the church; 750 words; up to $.05/word. **Poetry:** Positive expression of love and caring; up to 16 lines; up to $20. **Queries:** Not necessary. **E-queries:** Yes. **Unsolicited mss:** Accepts. **Response:** Up to 3 months, SASE. **Freelance Content:** 90%. **Rights:** One-time. **Payment:** On acceptance.

PURPOSE

529 E. Engler St., Columbus, OH 43215-5551. 614-224-2113. Web site: www.purposemagazine.com. **Description:** Multicultural magazine with an uplifting Christian focus.

QUAKER LIFE

Friends United Meeting, 101 Quaker Hill Dr., Richmond, IN 47374-1980. 265-962-7573. E-mail: quakerlife@fum.org. Web site: www.fum.org/ql. 10x/year. $24/yr. Circ.: 7,000. Trish Edwards-Konic, Editor. **Description:** For members of Friends United Meeting, other Friends (Quakers), evangelical Christians, religious pacifists. **Nonfiction:** Inspirational, first-person, articles on Bible applied to daily living. News and analysis, devotional and study articles, personal testimonies; 750-1,500 words. **Poetry:** Evangelical in nature. **Queries:** Not necessary. **E-queries:** Yes. **Unsolicited mss:** Accepts. **Response:** Queries 2 weeks, submissions 2 months, SASE. **Freelance Content:** 80%. **Rights:** 1st and multimedia. **Payment:** In copies.

QUEEN OF ALL HEARTS

26 S. Saxon Ave., Bay Shore, NY 11706-8993. 631-665-0726. Bi-monthly. Father Roger Charest, S.S.M., Managing Editor. **Description:** Covers Marian doctrine and devotion, with focus on St. Louis de Montfort's Trinitarian and Christoecentric approach to Mary in spiritual lives. **Fiction:** 1,500-2,000 words; $40-$60. **Nonfiction:** Essays, inspirational, personal experience; 750-2,000 words; $40-$60. **Poetry:** Free verse; 2 poems max. **Queries:** Preferred. **Unsolicited mss:** Accepts. **Rights:** One-time. **Payment:** On publication.

THE QUIET HOUR

4050 Lee Vance View, Colorado Springs, CO 80919. 719-536-0100. Gary Wilde, Editor. **Description:** Short devotionals. **Nonfiction:** Pays $15. **Tips:** By assignment only. **Queries:** Preferred. **Payment:** On acceptance.

RECONSTRUCTIONISM TODAY

30 Old Whitfield Rd., Accord, NY 12404. 845-626-2427. E-mail: Babush@ulster.net. Web site: www.jrf.org. Lawrence Bush, Editor. **Description:** Reconstructionist synagogue movement, with emphasis on creative Jewish living. **Nonfiction:** On contemporary Judaism and Jewish culture; 1,000-2,000 words. **Queries:** Preferred. **E-queries:** Yes. **Unsolicited mss:** Accepts. **Response:** Queries 1 month, submissions 2 months, SASE. **Freelance Content:** 25%. **Rights:** 1st NA. **Payment:** In copies.

REFORM JUDAISM

Union of American Hebrew Congregations, 633 3rd Ave., 6th Fl., New York, NY 10017. 212-650-4240. Web site: http://uahc.org/rjmag. Quarterly. $3.50/issue. Circ.: 310,000. Aron Hirt-Manheimer. **Description:** Published by Union of American Hebrew Congregations, to convey creativity, diversity, and dynamism of Reform Judaism. **Fiction:** Thought-provoking, contemporary Jewish fiction; 1,200-2,000 words; $0.30/word. **Nonfiction:** 1,200-3,500 words; $0.30/word. **Columns, Departments:** 1,200-1,500 words; e.g., "Travel to Jewish India"; $0.30/word. **Art:** Slides, prints; pay varies. **Queries:** Not necessary. **E-queries:** No. **Unsolicited mss:** Accepts. **Response:** 6-8 weeks; SASE or postage-paid postcard. **Freelance Content:** 25%. **Rights:** FNASR. **Payment:** On publication. **Contact:** Joy Weinberg, Managing Ed.

REVIEW FOR RELIGIOUS

3601 Lindell Blvd., St. Louis, MO 63108. 314-977-7363. E-mail: foppema@slu.edu. Bimonthly. David L. Fleming, S.J., Editor. **Description:** Catholic spirituality tradition stemming from Catholic religious communities. **Nonfiction:** Informative, practical, or inspirational articles; 1,500-5,000 words; $6/page. **Queries:** Preferred. **Payment:** On publication.

SACRED JOURNEY

291 Witherspoon St., Princeton, NJ 08542. 609-924-6863. E-mail: editorial@sacredjourney.org. Web site: www.sacredjourney.org. Bimonthly. $18. Circ.: 5,000. Rebecca Laird, Editor. **Description:** Journal of fellowship in prayer. Focuses on spiritual practice, prayer, meditation, and service issues. **Nonfiction:** Articles, to 1,500 words, about spiritual life, practiced by men and women of all faith traditions. **Art:** b/w prints; $40. **Tips:** Use inclusive language where possible. **Queries:** Not necessary. **E-queries:** Yes. **Unsolicited mss:** Accepts. **Response:** Submissions 2 months, SASE. **Freelance Content:** 75%. **Rights:** One-time. **Payment:** In copies.

ST. ANTHONY MESSENGER

1615 Republic St., Cincinnati, OH 45210-1298. 513-241-5615. E-mail: stanthony@americancatholics.org. Web site: www.americancatholics.org. Lisa Biedenbach, Managing Editor. **Description:** Seeks to evangelize, inspire, and inform those who search for God and a richer Catholic Christian, human life, in the style of Saints Francis and Anthony. **Tips:** Readers are priests and directors of religious education, catechists, teachers, people involved in parish life; small-group leaders; people seeking inspiration or help with special problems; parents. **Contact:** Ericka Snyder, Ed. Asst.

SEEK

8121 Hamilton Ave., Cincinnati, OH 45220. 513-931-4050. E-mail: ewilmoth@standardpub.com. Web site: www.standardpub.com. Weekly. Circ.: 34,000. Eileen H. Wilmoth, Editor. **Description:** Relates faith in action or Christian living, through inspirational or controversial topics, timely religious issues, testimonials. **Fiction:** 400-1,200 words; pays $.05/word. **Nonfiction:** Articles, 400-1,200 words; pays $.05/word. **Queries:** Not necessary. **E-queries:** No. **Unsolicited mss:** Accepts. **Response:** Queries 3 months, submission 3-6 months, SASE. **Freelance Content:** 95%. **Rights:** 1st. **Payment:** On acceptance.

SENIOR CONNECTION

Churchhill Publications, P.O. Box 38, Dundee, IL 60118. 847-428-0205. **Description:** For Catholics, ages 50-plus, with connections to northern Illinois parishes.

SHARING THE VICTORY

Fellowship of Christian Athletes, 8701 Leeds Rd., Kansas City, MO 64129. 816-921-0909. Web site: www.fca.org. 9x/year. $2.50/issue. Circ.: 90,000. Allen Palmeri, Editor. **Description:** Offers spiritual advice to coaches and athletes, and those whom they influence. **Nonfiction:** 1,200-1,500 words; $100-$250. **Poetry:** Short; $25. **Tips:** All materials (profiles on Christian athletes, poem, etc.) must present Christian inspiration. **Unsolicited mss:** Does not accept. **Freelance Content:** 50%. **Payment:** On publication.

SIGNS OF THE TIMES

P. O. Box 5353, Nampa, ID 83653-5353. 208-465-2577. Web site: www.pacificpress.com/signs. Monthly. $18.95. Circ.: 200,000. Marvin Moore, Editor. **Description:** For the public, showing the way to Jesus, based on the beliefs of the Seventh-day Adventist church. **Nonfiction:** Articles, 600-1,500 words, on Christians who have performed community services; first-person experiences, to 1,000 words; health, home, marriage, human-interest pieces; inspirational articles; $.10-$.20/word. **Queries:** Not necessary. **E-queries:** Yes. **Unsolicited mss:** Accepts. **Response:** Queries 2 weeks, submission 6 weeks, SASE required. **Freelance Content:** 20%. **Rights:** First. **Payment:** On acceptance.

SPIRITUAL LIFE

2131 Lincoln Rd. NE, Washington, DC 20002-1151. 202-832-8489. E-mail: editor@spiritual-life.org. Web site: www.spiritual-life.org. Quarterly. $4.50/issue, $16/year. Circ.: 11,000. Edward O'Donnell, O.C.D., Editor. **Description:** A professional religious journal, with essays on Christian spirituality with a pastoral application to everyday life. **Nonfiction:** 5,000-8,000 words; $50/page. **Art:** b/w cover; $100-$200. **Queries:** Not necessary. **E-queries:** Yes. **Unsolicited mss:** Accepts. **Response:** Submissions 8-10 weeks, SASE. **Freelance Content:** 90%. **Rights:** FNASR. **Payment:** On acceptance.

STANDARD

6401 The Paseo, Kansas City, MO 64131. 816-333-7000. E-mail: evlead@nazarene.org. Web site: www.nazarene.org. Weekly. $9.95. Circ.: 150,000. Everett Leadingham, Editor. **Description:** Denominational Sunday School take-home paper, with leisure reading for adults (generally older adults with conservative Holiness church background). **Fiction:** Inspirational stories, Christianity in action; 1200 words; $.035/word (1st); $.02/ word (reprint). **Nonfiction:** helpful articles; 1200 words. **Poetry:** Christian themes; 25 lines; $.25/line (min. $5). **Fillers:** Inspirational; 300-500 words. **Art:** b/w preferred; pay varies. **Tips:** New writers welcome. Prefers short fiction; avoid fictionalized Bible stories. **Queries:** Not necessary. **E-queries:** No. **Unsolicited mss:** Accepts. **Response:** 3 months. **Freelance Content:** 100%. **Rights:** One-time. **Payment:** On acceptance.

STORY FRIENDS

Mennonite Publishing House, 616 Walnut Ave, Scottdale, PA 15683. 724-887-8500. Monthly. Circ.: 6,000. Rose Stutzman, Editor. **Description:** For ages 4-9, promoting kindness, teaching children they are loved by God. Published by North American Mennonite Church. **Fiction:** Realistic stories that empower children to face fears; that help them enjoy and care for things in nature; 300-800 words; $.03/word. **Nonfiction:** About animals, unusual nature facts; about a child who has done something to promote kindness; cross-cultural experiences; 100-200 words; $.03/word. **Poetry:** Seasonal poems, or about ordinary events in child's life (i.e., new shoes); 8-20 lines; $10/poem. **Fillers:** Age-appropriate; puzzles, picture-based or with simple words and concepts. **Tips:** Humor and unique treatment of problem helps to break in to this market. Avoid talking animals and "naughty children" stories. Avoid stories where adults provide all solutions; respect young characters' strength and ingenuity. Also, many parents of these readers have lived in third-world countries; they value cross-cultural understanding. **Queries:** Not necessary. **E-queries:** No. **Unsolicited mss:** Accepts. **Response:** SASE. **Freelance Content:** 70%. **Rights:** 1st, one-time. **Payment:** On acceptance. **Contact:** Susan Reith Swan.

TEACHERS INTERACTION

3558 S. Jefferson Ave., St. Louis, MO 63118. 314-268-1083. E-mail: tom@nummela@cph.org. Quarterly. $3.95/$12.95. Circ.: 14,000. Tom Nummela, Editor. **Description:** Builds up volunteer teachers of the faith, and church professionals who support them, in ministry of sharing ideas, inspirational stories, and education. **Nonfiction:** Practical assistance for volunteer Christian teachers, especially Sunday school. Each issue on a central theme; inquire about upcoming themes; 1,000-1,200 words; $110. **Fillers:** Teachers Interchange (short activities, ideas for Sunday school classes, creative and practical); 150-200 words; $20-$40. **Columns, Departments:** 9 regular columns; 400-500 words; $55. **Art:** Color photos of children, all ages, in Christian education settings other than day school; seeks to include children with disabilities and children of various ethnic backgrounds; $50-$100. **Queries:** Preferred. **E-queries:** Yes. **Unsolicited mss:** Accepts. **Response:** 10-30 days, SASE. **Freelance Content:** 30%. **Rights:** All. **Payment:** On acceptance.

TEAM NYI
NYI Ministries, 6401 The Paseo, Kansas City, MO 64131. 816-333-7000. E-mail: teamnyi@nazarene.com. Quarterly. Circ.: 10,000. Jeff Edmondson, Editor. **Description:** Focuses on the business and philosophy of youth ministry. **Nonfiction:** On youth ministry for both professional and volunteers. Must have solid Christian, biblical foundation and conform to Nazarene theology; 500-1,000 words; $50-$100. **Tips:** Avoid ideas from the '70s and '80s; 21st-century teens are different. Need a good handle on postmodern mindset and millennial generation. Send e-mail query, or cover letter with attached article. **Queries:** Preferred. **E-queries:** Yes. **Unsolicited mss:** Accepts. **Response:** 4 weeks, SASE. **Freelance Content:** 60%. **Rights:** 1st NA, reprints, some work-for-hire assignments. **Payment:** On acceptance.

TIKKUN
2107 Van Ness Ave., Ste. 302, San Francisco, CA 94109. 415-575-1200. E-mail: magazine@tikkun.org. Web site: www.tikkun.org. Bimonthly. $5.95/$29. Circ.: 20,000. Michael Lerner, Editor. **Description:** Jewish commentary on politics, culture, and society. Based on Jewish principle of Tikkun Olam (healing the world), encourages writers to join spirituality to politics, for politics infused with compassion and meaning. **Fiction:** 3,000 words. **Nonfiction:** 1,600 words. **Poetry:** 20 lines. **Art:** Electronic (.jpeg, .tiff); $50/photo. **Tips:** Avoid "My trip to Israel (or Eastern Europe/Auschwitz)", "My adult bar mitzvah," "How I became religious." **Queries:** Not necessary. **E-queries:** No. **Unsolicited mss:** Accepts. **Response:** 3-4 months, SASE. **Freelance Content:** 20%. **Rights:** 1st, web reprint. **Payment:** In copies.

TODAY'S CATHOLIC TEACHER
330 Progress Rd., Dayton, OH 45449. 937-847-5900. E-mail: mnoschang@peterli.com. Web site: www.catholic.com. Bi-monthly. $14.95 yr. Circ.: 50,000. Mary Noschang, Editor. **Description:** For K-8 educators concerned with private education in general and Catholic education in particular. **Nonfiction:** Curriculum, classroom management, other articles (religious and non-religious) for classroom teachers in Catholic K-12 schools; 700-3,000 words; $150-$300. **Queries:** Not necessary. **E-queries:** Yes. **Unsolicited mss:** Accepts. **Response:** 2 months, SASE. **Freelance Content:** 80%. **Rights:** 1st NA. **Payment:** On publication.

TODAY'S CHRISTIAN WOMAN

465 Gundersen Dr., Carol Stream, IL 60188. 630-260-6200. E-mail: tcwedit@christianitytoday.com. Bi-monthly. Circ.: 300,000., Managing Editor. **Description:** For women, ages 20-40, on contemporary issues and hot topics that impact their lives, providing depth, balance, and biblical perspective to their daily relationships. **Nonfiction:** Articles to help women grow in their relationship to God, and to provide practical help on family/parenting, friendship, marriage, health, single life, finances, and work; 1,000-1,800 words. **Tips:** No poetry, fiction or Bible studies. Looking for humor; issues/hot topics; "my story" articles. **Queries:** Required. **E-queries:** Yes. **Unsolicited mss:** Accepts. **Response:** 8 weeks, SASE. **Rights:** 1st. **Payment:** On acceptance.

TRICYCLE

92 Vandam St., New York, NY 10013. 212-645-1143. E-mail: editorial@tricycle.com. Web site: www.tricycle.com. Quarterly. **Description:** "The Buddhist Review." Brings historical, philosophical, and artistic content to an upscale audience, appealing to all interested in social change, philosophy, psychology, and the human-potential movement. **Tips:** Prefers short pieces (less than 3,000 words), typed, double-spaced; include word count. First, send a 1-page query outlining your idea, with any relevant information about yourself, your familiarity with subject matter, any clips or writing samples. **Queries:** Preferred. **E-queries:** Yes. **Unsolicited mss:** Accepts.

TURNING WHEEL

P.O. Box 4650, Berkeley, CA 94704. 510-655-6169. E-mail: turningwheel@bpf.org. Web site: www.bpf.org/bpf. Quarterly. $5/$35. Circ.: 8,000. Susan Moon, Editor. **Description:** Journal of socially-engaged Buddhism, covers issues of social justice and environment from a Buddhist perspective. **Nonfiction:** On social-justice work from a Buddhist perspective, experimental and theoretical; themes for each issue (e.g., aging; death penalty; class divide); 1,800-3,500 words. **Poetry:** Related to theme. **Columns, Departments:** Reviews of books and films on social/spiritual issues; 450-850 words. **Art:** prints, TIF or EPS files. **Tips:** Avoid academic prose and new-age mushiness. Submit compelling personal experience, with analytical commentary. Contact for upcoming themes. **Queries:** Preferred. **E-queries:** Yes. **Unsolicited mss:** Accepts. **Response:** Queries 1 month, submissions 2 months, SASE. **Freelance Content:** 40%. **Rights:** One-time. **Payment:** In copies.

U.S. CATHOLIC

Claretian Publications, 205 W. Monroe St., Chicago, IL 60606. 312-236-7782. E-mail: editors@uscatholic.org. Monthly. $22/yr. Circ.: 50,000. Rev. Mark J. Brummel, C.M.F., Editor. **Description:** Celebrates vibrancy, diversity of contemporary Catholicism; promotes a positive vision of Catholic faith today. Combines tradition with sense of humor and a firm belief. **Fiction:** With strong characters that cause readers to stop and consider their relationships with others, the world, and/or God.

Overtly religious themes not required; 2,000 words; $300. **Poetry:** All forms and themes; no light verse; submit 3-5 original poems; up to 50 lines; $75/poem. **Queries:** Not necessary. **E-queries:** Yes. **Unsolicited mss:** Accepts. **Response:** 8-10 weeks, SASE not required. **Freelance Content:** 10%. **Rights:** First North American. **Payment:** On acceptance. **Contact:** Fran Hurst.

THE UNITED CHURCH OBSERVER

478 Huron St., Toronto, Ont., Canada M5R 2R3. 416-960-8500. 11x/year. Web site: www.ucobserver.org. **Description:** On religious trends, human problems, social issues. **Nonfiction:** Factual articles, 1,500-2,500 words. **Tips:** No poetry. **Queries:** Preferred. **Payment:** On publication.

UNITED SYNAGOGUE REVIEW

155 Fifth Ave., New York, NY 10010. 212-533-7800. E-mail: info@uscj.org. Web site: www.uscj.org. 2x/year. Circ.: 250,000. Ms. Lois Goldrich, Editor. **Description:** Publication of the Conservative Movement, with features related to synagogues, Jewish law, and that organization. **Nonfiction:** Stories about congregational programs or developments in Conservative Judaism; 1,500 words. **Art:** Photographic prints; $200 (cover photo). **Tips:** No payment, but wide exposure to 1 million readers. Writing should be crisp but not edgy or overly familiar. **Queries:** Not necessary. **E-queries:** Yes. **Unsolicited mss:** Accepts. **Response:** Queries immediate, submissions 1-3 months. **Freelance Content:** 25%.

THE WAR CRY

Salvation Army, 615 Slaters Lane, Alexandria, VA 22314. 703-684-5500, ext. 518. E-mail: salvationarmyusa.org. Web site: www.warcry@usn.salvationarmy.org. Bi-weekly. Lt. Col. Marlene Chase, Editor. **Description:** Evangelist periodical used to spread the Word of God. **Nonfiction:** Must relate to modern life, and offer inspiration, information, or evangelization; essays with insightful perspective on living the Christian life; 800-1,500 words; $.10-$.20/word. **Art:** 5x7 or 8x10 color prints, transparencies; $50, $250 (cover). **Queries:** Not necessary. **Response:** Queries 2 weeks, SASE. **Payment:** On acceptance.

WITH

722 Main St., Box 347, Newton, KS 67114. 316-283-5100. Web site: www.withonline.org. Bi-monthly. $23.50 yr. Circ.: 5,000. Carol Duerksen, Editor. **Description:** "The Magazine for Radical Christian Youth." For teens, empowers them to be radically committed to Jesus Christ, to peace and justice, and to sharing God's good news through words and action. **Fiction:** First-person stories; 1,500 words; $100. **Nonfiction:** Creative, "inside the life of a teen," first-person preferred. Avoid preaching. Themes: sex and dating, Holy Spirit, integrity, service and mission; 1,500 words; pay varies. **Poetry:** Yes. **Fillers:** Wholesome humor. **Art:** b/w 8x10s. **Queries:** Not necessary. **E-queries:** Yes. **Unsolicited mss:** Accepts. **Response:** 1 month, SASE. **Freelance Content:** 20%. **Rights:** One-time and website. **Payment:** On acceptance.

WOMAN'S TOUCH

1445 Boonville, Springfield, MO 65802-1894.
E-mail: womanstouch@ag.org. Web site: www.ag.org/womanstouch. 6x/year.
$8.50/issue. Circ.: 18,000. Darla Knoth, Managing Editor. **Description:** Not-for-profit ministry magazine, for Christian women. **Nonfiction:** About triumph in times of trouble, celebrity interviews with women leaders, cooking, reaching the unchurched, testimonies, unique activities for women's groups or mature singles; 800 words; $20-$40. **Fillers:** Humor only; 500-800 words; $20-$40. **Columns, Departments:** Parenting, singlehood; 500-600 words; $20-$40. **Tips:** Seeking humor pieces, articles with fresh themes; send 3 suggested headlines with article. Publishes some book excerpts. Most readers over 35. Query or submit via email. **Queries:** Not necessary. **E-queries:** Yes. **Unsolicited mss:** Accepts. **Response:** 12 weeks. **Freelance Content:** 20%. **Rights:** One-time. **Payment:** On publication.

WONDER TIME

6401 The Paseo, Kansas City, MO 64131. 816-333-7000 Ext. 2244.
Weekly. Circ.: 14,000. Pamela Smits, Editor. **Description:** For children, ages 5-7. Emphasis on the religious instruction of children and parents. Issues are thematic. **Fiction:** A Christian emphasis to correlate with Sunday school curriculum. **Poetry:** Free verse or rhyming; 6-12 lines; $.25/word. **Columns, Departments:** Parent or family fun; 25-50 words; $15/activity. **Queries:** Preferred. **E-queries:** No. **Unsolicited mss:** Does not accept. **Response:** 1-2 months, SASE. **Freelance Content:** 50%. **Rights:** All. **Payment:** On publication.

YOU!

29963 Mulholland Hwy., Agoura Hills, CA 91301. 818-991-1813.
E-mail: youmag@earthlink.net. Web site: www.youmagazine.com. **Description:** For teenagers, especially on moral issues, faith, and contemporary pop culture, viewed from the Catholic/Christian perspective. No payment. **Nonfiction:** Articles, 200-1,000 words.

YOUNG SALVATIONIST

The Salvation Army, P.O. Box 269,
Alexandria, VA 22313. 703-684-5500.
E-mail: ys@usn.salvationarmy.org. Tim Clark, Editor. **Description:** Seeks to teach Christian view of everyday living, for teenagers. **Nonfiction:** Articles (to 600-1,200 words); short-shorts, first-person testimonies (600-800 words). Pays $.15/word ($.10/word for reprints). **Response:** SASE required. **Payment:** On acceptance.

YOUR CHURCH

465 Gundersen Dr., Carol Stream, IL 60188. 630-260-6200.
E-mail: yceditor@yourchurch.net. Web site: www.yourchurch.net. Bi-monthly. Circ.: 150,000. Phyllis Ten Elshof, Editor. **Description:** Trade publication to help church leaders with the business side of ministry. **Nonfiction:** Articles on hiring from within

a church, how to avoid affinity fraud schemes, etc.; 1,250-1,500 words. **Queries:** Preferred. **Unsolicited mss:** Accepts. **Response:** Queries 1-2 months. **Freelance Content:** 10%. **Rights:** 1st. **Payment:** On acceptance.

YOUTHWALK
6401 The Paseo, Kansas City, MO 64131. 816-333-7000.
E-mail: youthwalk@wordaction.com. Web site: www.waction.com. Bimonthly. $1.95. Circ.: 24,000. Matt Price, Editor. **Description:** About theology, devotional classics, spiritual disciplines, and the Christian calendar, in language that speaks to today's students. **Nonfiction:** Articles about teens demonstrating Christian principles in real-life situations; 300-600 words; $30. **Columns, Departments:** Christian themes; 300-600 words; $30. **Tips:** Articles should come from working with teenagers. **Queries:** Required. **E-queries:** Yes. **Unsolicited mss:** Does not accept. **Response:** Queries 30 days, submissions 2 months, SASE. **Freelance Content:** 20%. **Rights:** All. **Payment:** On publication.

SCIENCE

AD ASTRA
National Space Society, 600 Pennsylvania Ave. S.E., #201, Washington, DC 20003-4316. 202-543-1900.
Web site: www.nss.org/adastra. Frank Sietzen, Jr., Editor-in-Chief. **Description:** Lively, semi-technical features, on all aspects of international space exploration. **Nonfiction:** Interested in "Living in Space" articles; commercial and human space flight technology; to 2,000 words; pays $150-$250. **Queries:** Preferred. **Payment:** On publication.

AIR & SPACE/SMITHSONIAN
750 9th Street NW, 7th Floor, Washington, DC 20001. 202-275-1230.
E-mail: editors@airspacemag.com. Web site: www.airspacemag.com. Bimonthly. $3.95. Circ.: 250,000. George C. Larson, Editor. **Description:** Original articles on aerospace topics for a lay audience. **Nonfiction:** Feature stories with original reporting, research, and quotes. General-interest articles on aerospace experience, past, present, and future; 2,000-5,000 words; $2,000-$3,500. **Columns, Departments:** Book reviews, soft news pieces, first-person recollections, and essays; 500-1,500 words; $350-$1,500. **Art:** Yes. **Tips:** Avoid sentimentalities (the majesty of flight, etc.). Don't rehash; original research only. Send 1-2 page proposal detailing sources and interview list, with published clips. Emphasize fresh angle. **Queries:** Required. **E-queries:** Yes. **Unsolicited mss:** Accepts. **Response:** 4-8 weeks, SASE required. **Freelance Content:** 90%. **Rights:** FNASR. **Payment:** On acceptance.

AMERICAN HERITAGE OF INVENTION & TECHNOLOGY
60 Fifth Ave., New York, NY 10011.
E-mail: it@americanheritage.com. Web site: www.americanheritage.com/i&t.

Quarterly. Circ.: 320,000. Frederick Allen, Editor. **Description:** Lively, authoritative prose and illustrations (archival photos, rare paintings), on the history of technology in America, for the sophisticated general reader. **Nonfiction:** Articles, 2,000-5,000 words, on great men and scoundrels, popular music and high art, our grandest national impulses (and, occasionally, our basest). **Queries:** Not necessary. **E-queries:** Yes. **Payment:** On acceptance.

ANNALS OF IMPROBABLE RESEARCH

AIR, PO Box 380853, Cambridge, MA 02238. 617-491-4437. E-mail: air@improbable.com. Bi-monthly. $23/year. Marc Abrahams, Editor. **Description:** This is the place to find the mischievous, funny, iconoclastic side of science. Editorial board consists of 50 eminent scientists and doctors from around the world, including 8 Nobel Prize-winners and a convicted felon. **Nonfiction:** Science reports and analysis; humor; 1-4 pages. **Poetry:** Brief science-related poetry. **Art:** b/w. **Queries:** Preferred. **E-queries:** Yes. **Unsolicited mss:** Accepts. **Response:** SASE required.

ARCHAEOLOGY

135 William St., New York, NY 10038. 212-732-5154. E-mail: peter@archaeology.org. Web site: www.archaeology.org. Bimonthly. $4.95/issue, $20/year. Circ.: 210,000. Peter A. Young, Editor-in-Chief. **Description:** News magazine about archaeology worldwide, written for lay people by professionals or writers with a solid knowledge of the field. **Nonfiction:** Profiles, excavation reports, discoveries, photo essays; 500-2,500 words; $500-$1,500. **Columns, Departments:** Multimedia, museum news, book reviews; 1,500 words; $500-$1,000. **Art:** Electronic or slides; pay varies. **Queries:** Required. **E-queries:** Yes. **Unsolicited mss:** Accepts. **Response:** 1 month, SASE required. **Freelance Content:** 5%. **Payment:** On acceptance.

ASTRONOMY

Kalmbach Publishing Co., P.O. Box 1612, 21027 Crossroads Circle, Waukesha, WI 53187. Web site: www.astronomy.com. Monthly. $4.50/issue, $35.95/year. Circ.: 175,000. Bonnie Gordon, Editor. **Description:** Astronomical science and hobby activities, covering our solar system, Milky Way galaxy, black holes, deep-space observing, personality profiles, astronomical travel, etc. **Nonfiction:** Articles on astronomy, astrophysics, space programs, recent discoveries. Hobby pieces on equipment and celestial events; short news items; 2,000 words; $200-$1,000. **Art:** Photos of astronomical phenomena and other affiliated subjects relating to stories; digital, slides, print; $25/use. **Queries:** Preferred. **E-queries:** Yes. **Unsolicited mss:** Accepts. **Rights:** 1st serial, all. **Payment:** On acceptance.

ENVIRONMENT

1319 18th St. NW, Washington, DC 20036-1802. 202-296-6267. E-mail: env@heldref.org. Web site: www.heldref.org. 10x/yr. $4.95/issue. Circ.: 8,000.

Barbara T. Richman, Managing Editor. **Description:** Solid analysis of environmental science and policy issues. **Nonfiction:** On major scientific and policy issues of a significant topic; concise, objective, accurate, jargon-free; use graphics and sidebars for key points; 2,500-4,000 words. **Fillers:** Cartoons; $50. **Columns, Departments:** Education, energy, economics, public opinion; 1,000-1,700 words; $100. **Tips:** Avoid news and feature formats. **Queries:** Required. **E-queries:** Yes. **Unsolicited mss:** Accepts. **Response:** 6-8 weeks, SASE not required. **Freelance Content:** 98%. **Rights:** 1st. **Payment:** On publication.

NATURAL HISTORY
American Museum of Natural History, Central Park W. at 79th St., New York, NY 10024. 212-769-5500.
E-mail: nhmag@amnh.org. Web site: www.naturalhistory.com. 10x/year. $30/year. Circ.: 300,000. Ellen Goldensohn, Editor. **Description:** Published by American Museum of National History. Articles mostly by scientists, on biological sciences, cultural and physical anthropology, archaeology, earth sciences, astronomy, vertebrates and invertebrates. **Nonfiction:** Informative articles; 800-2,500 words; $500-$2,500. **Art:** $350 (full page), $500 (Natural Moment section photo). **Tips:** Read magazine first, and research recent articles before sending query. **Queries:** Preferred. **E-queries:** No. **Unsolicited mss:** Accepts. **Response:** Queries 4-6 months. **Freelance Content:** 30%. **Rights:** 1st. **Payment:** On publication.

ODYSSEY
Cobblestone Publishing, 30 Grove St., Suite C, Peterborough, NH 03458. 603-924-7209.
Web site: odysseymagazine.com. 9x/year. Circ.: 21,000. Elizabeth Lindstrom, Editor. **Description:** Features, 750-1,000 words, on science and technology, for readers, ages 10-16. Science-related fiction, myths, legends, and science-fiction stories. Activities. Pays $.20-$.25/word. **Fiction:** Science-related stories, poems, science fiction, retold legends, etc., relating to theme; up to 1,000 words; $.20-$.25/word. **Nonfiction:** Subjects directly and indirectly related to theme; with little-known information (but don't overlook the obvious); 720-950 words; $.20-$.25/word. **Fillers:** Critical-thinking activities, experiments, models, science fair projects, etc., for children alone, with adult supervision, or in classroom setting. **Columns, Departments:** Far Out; Places, Media, People to Discover; Fantastic Journeys; 400-650 words. **Art:** Transparencies, slides, color prints; $15-$100 (b/w); $25-$100 (color). **Tips:** Material must relate to specific theme; contact for upcoming list. Scientific accuracy, lively approach, and inclusion of primary research are crucial to being accepted. **Rights:** All. **Payment:** On publication.

POPULAR SCIENCE
2 Park Ave., New York, NY 10016. 212-779-5000.
Web site: www.popsci.com. Cecilia Wessner, Editor. **Description:** On developments in science and technology. **Nonfiction:** Short illustrated articles on new inventions

and products; photo-essays, book excerpt; with photos and/or illustrations; pay varies. **Payment:** On acceptance.

SCIENCE AND CHILDREN
1840 Wilson Blvd., Arlington, VA 22201. 703-243-7100. Web site: www.nsta.org. **Description:** Articles and activities, based on current approaches to instruction and issues in science education. For Pre-K to 8th-grade science teachers. **Queries:** Preferred.

SCIENCE WORLD
Scholastic, Inc., 555 Broadway, New York, NY 10012-3999. 212-343-6100. Web site: scholastic.com. Mark Bregman. **Description:** On life science, earth science, physical science, environmental science, or health science, for 7th-10th graders, ages 12-15. **Nonfiction:** Science articles, 750 words; $200-$650. **Columns, Departments:** Science news, 200 words; pays $100-$125. **Tips:** Submit well-researched proposal, with anticipated sources, 2-3 clips of your work, and SASE. Writing should be lively, with an understanding of teens' perspectives and interests.

THE SCIENCES
655 Madison Ave., 16th Fl., New York, NY 10021. 212-838-6727. Web site: www.nyas.org. Peter G. Brown, Editor. **Description:** On all scientific disciplines. **Nonfiction:** Essays and features (2,000-4,000 words). **Columns, Departments:** Book reviews. **Queries:** Preferred. **Payment:** honorarium, on publication.

SCIENTIFIC AMERICAN
415 Madison Ave., New York, NY 10017. 212-754-0550. E-mail: editors@sciam.com. Web site: www.sciam.com. Philip Yam, News Editor. **Description:** Addresses all aspects of American scientific endeavor. **Queries:** Preferred.

SKY & TELESCOPE
Sky Publishing Corp., 49 Bay State Rd., Cambridge, MA 02138. 617-864-7360. Web site: www.skypub.com. Bud Sadler. **Description:** For amateur and professional astronomers worldwide. **Nonfiction:** Articles, mention availability of diagrams and other illustrations; pays $.10-$25/word. **Columns, Departments:** Amateur Astronomers, Astronomical Computing, Astro Imaging, Telescope Plus, Observer's Log, Gallery. Also, 800-word opinion pieces, for Focal Point. **Queries:** Required. **Payment:** On publication.

SPACE ILLUSTRATED
212-703-5854. E-mail: thoughts@space.com. Web site: www.space.com. **Description:** The companion in-print magazine to Space.com website. Articles on space. **Tips:** Also publishes Space News, an industry publication.

TECHNOLOGY REVIEW

One Main St., 7th Floor, Cambridge, MA 02142. 617-475-8000. E-mail: mitaatr@mit.edu. Web site: www.techreview.com. John Benditt, Editor. **Description:** General-interest articles on technology and innovation. **Nonfiction:** Pay varies. **Queries:** Preferred. **Payment:** On acceptance.

TIMELINE

1982 Velma Ave., Columbus, OH 43211-2497. 614-297-2360. E-mail: timeline@ohiohistory.org. Bi-monthly. $6/$30. Circ.: 15,000. Christopher S. Duckworth, Editor. **Description:** Covers fields of history, prehistory, and natural sciences, directed towards readers in the Midwest. **Nonfiction:** History, politics, economics, social, and natural history for lay readers in Ohio and the Midwest; 1,000-5,000 words. **Tips:** Writing style should be simple and direct; avoid jargon. **Queries:** Preferred. **E-queries:** Yes. **Unsolicited mss:** Accepts. **Response:** 2 weeks, SASE. **Freelance Content:** 90%. **Rights:** 1st NA. **Payment:** On acceptance.

21ST CENTURY: SCIENCE AND TECHNOLOGY

P.O. Box 16285, Washington, DC 20041. 703-777-7473. E-mail: tcs@mediasoft.net. Web site: www.21stcenturysciencetech.com. Quarterly. $3.50/issue. Circ.: 23,000. Laurence Hecht, Editor. **Description:** Promotes unending scientific progress which serves the proper common aims of mankind. **Queries:** Required. **E-queries:** No. **Unsolicited mss:** Does not accept. **Response:** Varies, SASE. **Rights:** One-time. **Payment:** On publication. **Contact:** Marjorie Mazel Hecht, Managing Ed.

WEATHERWISE

Heldref Publications, 1319 18th St. NW, Washington, DC 20036. 202-296-6267. E-mail: ww@heldref.org. Web site: www.weatherwise.org. 6x/yr. Circ.: 11,000. Doyle Rice, Managing Editor. **Description:** All about weather. **Nonfiction:** 1,500-2,000 words; pays $200-$500. **Columns, Departments:** 300-1,000 words; pays to $200. **Queries:** Required. **E-queries:** Yes. **Unsolicited mss:** Accepts. **Response:** 2 months. **Freelance Content:** 50%. **Rights:** FNASR.

YES MAG

3968 Long Gun Place, Victoria, BC, Canada V8N 3A9. 250-477-5543. E-mail: editor@yesmag.ca. Web site: www.yesmag.ca. Bimonthly. $3.25/$18 (Canadian). Circ.: 18,000. Shannon Hunt, Editor. **Description:** Canadian children's science magazine. Makes science accessible, interesting, and exciting, for children ages 8-14. Covers science and technology news, do-at-home projects, science-related book and software reviews, profiles of Canadian students and scientists. **Nonfiction:** Science, technology, engineering, and math articles for kids, ages 8-14; 250-1,250 words; $.15/word. **Tips:** Seeking imaginative, fun, well-researched pieces. Be specific in query; ideally send an outline of the article, indicating how you will approach the topic. **Queries:** Preferred. **E-queries:** Yes. **Unsolicited mss:**

Accepts. **Response:** 2 weeks, SASE. **Freelance Content:** 60%. **Rights:** One-time. **Payment:** On publication.

SENIORS

AARP BULLETIN
601 "E" Street NW, Washington, DC 20049. 800-424-3410. Web site: www.aarp.org. Elliot Carlson, Editor. **Description:** Publication of American Association of Retired Persons. **Nonfiction:** Pay varies. **Queries:** Required. **Payment:** On acceptance.

FIFTY-PLUS
Alliance Media, Meadow Mill at Woodbury, 3600 Clipper Mill Rd., Ste. 115, Baltimore, MD 21211. 410-366-7512. Melinda Greenberg. **Description:** For Baltimore area seniors. **Queries:** Preferred.

FOREVER YOUNG
467 Speers Rd, Oakville, Ontario, Canada L6K 3S4. 905-815-0017. Web site: www.starcitysearch.com/todaysseniors. Don Wall. **Description:** Multiprovince Canadian publication, for senior citizens. **Queries:** Preferred.

GOOD TIMES
Senior Publications, 25 Sheppard Ave., Suite 100, Toronto, Ontario. 416-733-7600. E-mail: goodtimes@transcontinental.ca. 11x/year. $21.95/yr. Judy Brandow, Editor. **Description:** Canadian magazine for successful retirement, lifestyles for mature market. **Nonfiction:** Celebrity profiles, also practical articles on health, beauty, cuisine, hobbies, fashion, leisure activities, travel, taxes, legal rights, consumer protection; 1,300-1,500 words; $.40/word. **Poetry:** Yes; no payment. **Columns, Departments:** health, relationship, travel stories for mature market; 1,500-2,000 words; $.40/word. **Art:** To accompany articles. **Tips:** Canadian content only. **Queries:** Required. **E-queries:** Yes. **Freelance Content:** 100%. **Rights:** 1st Canadian. **Payment:** On acceptance.

LIFE LINES
129 N. 10th St., Rm. 408, Lincoln, NE 68508-3627. 402-441-7022. Dena Rust Zimmer. **Description:** For seniors. **Fiction:** Short stories. **Poetry:** To 50 lines. **Fillers:** Short humor. **Columns, Departments:** Sports and Hobbies, Remember When . . ., Travels With . . ., Perspectives on Aging; to 450 words. **Payment:** No payment.

LIFEWISE

Focus on the Family, 8655 Explorer Drive, Colorado Springs, CO 80920-1049. 719-531-3400. Web site: www.family.org. Monthly. Circ.: 45,000. **Description:** Christian publication for older adults.

MATURE LIFESTYLES

P.O. Box 44327, Madison, WI 53744. 608-274-5200. E-mail: anitaj@execpc.com. Anita J. Martin. **Description:** Newspaper for active 50-plus population, for South Central Wisconsin.

MATURE LIFESTYLES

220 W. Brandon Blvd., Ste 210, Brandon, FL 33511. 813-653-1988. Web site: www.srconnect.com. Kathy J. Beck. **Description:** For readers over 50, in Florida. **Nonfiction:** Articles, 500-700 words; pays $50. **Tips:** No fiction or poetry. Florida angle required. **Payment:** On publication.

MATURE LIVING

127 Ninth Ave. N., Nashville, TN 37234-0140. 615-251-2274. E-mail: matureliving@lifeway.com. Monthly. N/A. Circ.: 350,000. Judy Pregel, Editor. **Description:** A leisure reading magazine for Christian seniors, 50 years and older. **Fiction:** Quality fiction for seniors, with strong story line underscoring a biblical truth; 1,200 words; $75. **Nonfiction:** Nostalgia about "good old days" (personal memories or historical). Travel articles with general appeal, descriptive information; 600-1,200 words; $.05/word, min. $75. **Poetry:** Yes. **Fillers:** Cartoons. **Tips:** Looking for pieces with human interest, Christian warmth, and humor. **Queries:** Not necessary. **Unsolicited mss:** Accepts. **Response:** 6-8 weeks, SASE. **Freelance Content:** 75%. **Rights:** All. **Payment:** On acceptance.

MATURE LIVING

Senior Publishers Media Group, 255 N. El Cielo Rd., #452, Palm Springs, CA 92262. 760-320-2221. **Description:** For older adults in and around Palm Springs, CA.

MATURE YEARS

United Methodist Publishing House, 201 Eighth Ave. South, Nashville, TN 37202. 615-749-6292. E-mail: matureyears@umpublishing.org. Quarterly. $18. Circ.: 50,000. Marvin W. Cropsey, Editor. **Description:** Helps persons in and near retirement years to understand the appropriate resources of the Christian faith to deal with specific problems and opportunities of aging. **Fiction:** Older adult characters in older adult situations; up to 2,000 words. **Nonfiction:** Religious and inspirational articles; also, older adults in active lifestyles; 2,000 words; $.05/word. **Fillers:** Bible puzzles. **Columns, Departments:** Health and fitness, personal finance, travel, poetry, fiction. **Art:** Photos. **Tips:** Welcomes new writers. **Queries:** Preferred. **E-queries:** Yes.

Unsolicited mss: Accepts. **Response:** 4-8 weeks, SASE required. **Rights:** One-time NA. **Payment:** On acceptance.

MILESTONES
Milestones Publishing, 246 S. 22nd, Philadelphia, PA 19103. 215-732-9029. Monthly. Circ.: 26,000. **Description:** For seniors in the greater Philadelphia area.

MODERN MATURITY
601 "E" Street NW, Washington, DC 20049. 202-434-6880. Web site: www.aarp.org/mmaturity. Bimonthly. $10/yr. Circ.: 22,000,000. Amelia Jones. **Description:** General-interest membership magazine for members of AARP. **Nonfiction:** Articles of interest for people 55 and older. Health, money, travel, consumer topics most needed; 1,500-5,000; $1/word and up. **Columns, Departments:** See nonfiction topics; 300-1,500 words; $1/word and up. **Tips:** No queries by phone. Call only to ask which editor handles the subject matter you are proposing, then send material to that editor only. Welcomes new writers. **Queries:** Required. **E-queries:** Yes. **Unsolicited mss:** Does not accept. **Response:** 3 weeks to 3 months, SASE required. **Freelance Content:** 80%. **Rights:** 1st worldwide. **Payment:** On acceptance.

NETWORK
Gray Panthers, 733 15th St. NW, #437, Washington, DC 20005-2112. 202-737-6637. Web site: www.graypanthers.org. **Description:** National advocacy magazine for older adults.

NEW CHOICES
Reader's Digest Publications, Reader's Digest Rd., Pleasantville, NY 10570. 914-238-1000. E-mail: newchoices@readersdigest.com. Web site: www.newchoices.com. 10x/year. $2.95/issue, $15/year. Circ.: 600,000. Greg Daugherty, Editor-in-Chief. **Description:** Practical information for living better after 50. Covers health, personal finance, travel, and the Internet, in an upbeat and inspiring manner. **Nonfiction:** On retirement planning, financial strategies, housing options, health and fitness, travel, leisure pursuits, etc.; 100-3,500 words; $1/word and up. **Tips:** Prefers writers with established credentials in subject area. **Queries:** Required. **E-queries:** No. **Unsolicited mss:** Does not accept. **Response:** 2-4 weeks, SASE required. **Freelance Content:** 95%. **Rights:** 1st NA. **Payment:** On acceptance.

NOT BORN YESTERDAY
Osmon Publications, Inc., 4805 Alta Canyada Rd., La Canada Flintridge, CA 91011. 818-790-0651. Monthly. Circ.: 95,000. **Description:** For Southern California seniors.

THE OLDER AMERICAN
Massachusetts Assn. of Older Americans, 108 Arlington St.,
Boston, MA 02116. 617-426-0804.
Web site: maoa-inc.org. Quarterly. Circ.: 9,000. **Description:** Local, state, and national advocacy and current affairs magazine for older adults.

PITTSBURGH SENIOR NEWS
Pittsburgh Senior News, Inc., 3345 Evergreen Rd.,
Pittsburgh, PA 15237. 412-367-2522.
Monthly. Circ.: 35,000. **Description:** Topics of interest to older adults in the Pittsburgh area.

PLUS
3565 S. Higuera St., San Luis Obispo, CA 93401. 805-544-8711.
Web site: www.seniormagazine.com. Monthly. Circ.: 60,000. George Brand, Editor. **Description:** Entertainment and information, for readers aged 50 and over. **Nonfiction:** Articles, 600-1200 words: profiles, travel, business, sports, movies, television, and health; book reviews of interest to seniors. **Fillers:** Humor. **Queries:** Preferred. **E-queries:** No. **Unsolicited mss:** Accepts. **Response:** Queries 1 week, submission 2 weeks, SASE. **Freelance Content:** 60%. **Rights:** 1st. **Payment:** On publication.

PRIME
Shearin Publishing, P.O. Box 40, Scotland Neck, NC 27874. 252-826-2111.
Quarterly. Circ.: 10,000. **Description:** Senior citizens magazine.

PRIME TIMES
CUNA MUTUAL Group/Publications, 5910 Mineral Point Rd.,
Madison, WI 53705. 608-231-7188.
E-mail: tom.burton@cunamutual.com. **Description:** For retirees associated with credit unions. **Queries:** Preferred. **Contact:** Tom Burton, managing editor.

THE PRIME TIMES
Life Printing & Publishing, 709 Enterprise Drive,
Oak Brook, IL 60523. 630-368-1100.
Monthly. Circ.: 60,000. **Description:** Chicago city and suburban publication for older adults.

PRIME TIMES
Times-Beacon-Record Newspapers, P.O. Box 707,
East Setauket, NY 11733. 631-751-0356.
Monthly. Circ.: 45,000. **Description:** For older adults on Long Island, NY.

REMEDY

120 Post Rd. W., Westport, CT 06880. 203-341-7000.
Web site: www.remedyonline.com. Bimonthly. Shari Miller Sims, Editor.
Description: On health and medication issues, for readers 50 and over. **Nonfiction:**
Articles, 600-2,500 words; pays $1.00-$1.25/word. **Columns, Departments:**
Dispensary; Nutrition Prescription. **Queries:** Preferred. **Payment:** On acceptance.

RETIRED MILITARY FAMILY

51 Atlantic Ave., #200, Floral Park, NY 11001-2721. 516-616-1930.
Web site: www.familymedia.com. Stacy P. Brassington. **Description:** For military
retirees and their families. Covers travel, finance, food, hobbies, second careers,
grandparenting, etc. **Nonfiction:** Articles, 1,000-1,500 words; pays to $200.
Payment: On publication.

RETIRED OFFICER

201 N. Washington St., Alexandria, VA 22314-2539. 703-838-8115.
E-mail: editor@troa.org. Web site: www.troa.org/magazine. Monthly. $20/yr. Circ.:
386,000. Warren S. Lacy, Editor. **Description:** For retired and soon-to-be-retired
members. Readers (commissioned/warrant officers, families, and surviving spouses)
represent one of the youngest, most active groups in the senior market. **Nonfiction:**
Current military/political affairs, recent history (especially Vietnam and Korea),
retirement topics, and general interest. Original only, no reprints; 1,400-2,500 words;
$1,200-$1,700. **Columns, Departments:** Travel; financial planning; health and fitness; military family; retirement lifestyles; and general interest; 750 words; $500. **Art:**
Color transparencies preferred. **Tips:** Active voice, nontechnical, with direct quotes.
Optimistic, upbeat themes. **Queries:** Required. **E-queries:** Yes. **Unsolicited mss:**
Does not accept. **Response:** 90 days. **Rights:** 1st, also Internet and reprint.
Payment: On acceptance. **Contact:** Heather Lyons.

RETIREMENT LIFE

National Assn. of Retired Federal Employees, 606 N. Washington St.,
Alexandria, VA 22314. 703-838-7760.
Web site: www.narfe.org. Monthly. Circ.: 350,000. **Description:** Focuses on issues of
interest to retired federal employees.

SECURE RETIREMENT

National Committee to Preserve Social Security and Medicare,
10 "G" St. NE, Suite 600, Washington, DC 20002-4215. 703-914-9200.
E-mail: bsmith@strattonpub.com. Web site: www.ncpssm.org. Bi-monthly. for members. Circ.: 1,900,000. Angela Angerosa, Editor. **Description:** Advocates health and
retirement issues. Readers are mainly seniors. Covers policy, also lifestyle features and
departments. **Nonfiction:** Articles on age-related and retirement issues; 500-1,500
words; pay varies. **Queries:** Preferred. **E-queries:** Yes. **Unsolicited mss:** Accepts.
Response: 2-6 weeks. **Freelance Content:** 70%. **Payment:** On publication.

THE SENIOR ADVOCATE
Mar-Len Publications, 131 Lincoln St., Worcester, MA 01605. 508-752-3400. Web site: www.mrln.com/sahome.html. Bi-weekly. Circ.: 75,000. **Description:** Covers local, state and national issues, for seniors.

SENIOR CONNECTION
News Connection USA, 220 W. Brandon Blvd., Ste 210, Brandon, FL 33511. 813-653-1988. Web site: www.srconnect.com. Monthly. Circ.: 130,000. **Description:** General-interest articles, for senior citizens in the west central and Tampa areas of Florida.

SENIOR NEWS
Senior News, P.O. Box 23307, Waco, TX 76702. 254-399-9811. Monthly. Circ.: 250,000. **Description:** For senior citizens in Texas.

THE SENIOR TIMES
Senior Times Publishing Co., 435 King St., Littleton, MA 01460. 978-745-9171. E-mail: theseniortimes@aol.com. Monthly. Free newstand/$18 subscription. Circ.: 25,000. Theresa Murphy, Editor. **Description:** For the active adult, over age 50. Arts and entertainment, also a poetry page. **Nonfiction:** Articles on travel, entertainment, health, finance, senior advocacy issues, opinion, advice columns, local interviews. **Poetry:** Yes. **Art:** Photos; 8x10 b/w; subjects from the greater Boston area (people, places, art); pay negotiable. **Queries:** Not necessary. **E-queries:** Yes. **Unsolicited mss:** Does not accept. **Response:** SASE. **Payment:** On publication.

SENIOR TIMES
Senior Publishing Co., P. O. Box 30965, Columbus, OH 43230. 614-337-2055. Monthly. Circ.: 55,000. **Description:** For older adults in Ohio.

SENIOR TIMES
Journal News Publishing, P.O. Box 142020, Spokane, WA 99214-2020. 509-924-2440. Monthly. Circ.: 50,000. **Description:** For senior citizens in Washington State.

SPIRIT PLUS
1830 Rt. 9, Toms River, NJ 08755. 732-505-9700. E-mail: spiritmag50@aol.com. Biannual. Circ.: 250,000. Pat Jasin, editor. **Description:** For active adults aged 45-65, in states of New Jersey, New York, and Pennsylvania. Upbeat articles on travel, sex, computers, dating, heatlh and fitness. **Nonfiction:** Travel, etc. **Queries:** Required. **E-queries:** No. **Unsolicited mss:** Does not accept. **Response:** 2 months. **Freelance Content:** 10%. **Rights:** 1st NA. **Payment:** In copies.

TODAY'S GRANDPARENT
Today's Parent Group, 269 Richmond St. West, Toronto, Ontario, Canada M5V 1X1. 416-596-8680. Web site: www.todaysparent.com. Quarterly. Circ.: 190,000. **Description:** For grandparents of all ages.

VANTAGE
C-E Publishing, 30400 Van Dyke Ave., Warren, MI 48093. 810-753-8355. Quarterly. Circ.: 225,000. **Description:** For active older adults.

WHERE TO RETIRE
Vacation Publications, 1502 Augusta Dr., Ste 415, Houston, TX 77057. 713-974-6903. **Description:** For anyone seeking retirement locale advice.

SPORTS, RECREATION, OUTDOORS

ADVENTURE CYCLIST
Adventure Cycling Assn., P.O. Box 8308, Missoula, MT 59807. 406-721-1776. E-mail: ddambrosio@adventurecycling.org. Web site: www.adventurecycling.org. 9x/year. Circ.: 25,000. Daniel D'Ambrosio, Editor. **Description:** Covers the bicycling world. **Nonfiction:** Bike travel; 1,500-3,000 words; $450-$1,200. **Columns, Departments:** In Bicycle Circles (news shorts). **Queries:** Not necessary. **E-queries:** Yes. **Unsolicited mss:** Accepts. **Response:** 3 weeks, SASE required. **Freelance Content:** 80%. **Rights:** 1st. **Payment:** On publication.

ALL-STATER SPORTS
1373 Grandview Ave., Suite 206, Columbus, OH 43212. 614-487-1280. Web site: www.allstater.com. Stephanie Strong, Managing Editor. **Description:** Sports magazine for high-school athletes. **Queries:** Preferred.

AMERICAN FIELD
542 S. Dearborn St., Suite 1350, Chicago, IL 60605. 312-663-9797. Web site: www.americanfield.com. B.J. Matthys, Managing Editor. **Description:** Short items and anecdotes on hunting dogs and field trials for bird dogs. Yarns on hunting trips, bird-shooting; articles, to 1,500 words, on dogs and field trials, emphasizing conservation of game resources. Pay varies. **Payment:** On acceptance.

AMERICAN HANDGUNNER
591 Camino de la Reina, Suite 200, San Diego, CA 92108. 619-819-4535. Web site: www.americanhandgunner.com. Cameron Hopkins, Editor. **Description:** Semi-technical articles on shooting sports, gun repair and alteration, handgun matches and tournaments, for lay readers. **Nonfiction:** Pays $100-$500. **Queries:** Preferred. **Payment:** On publication.

AMERICAN HUNTER

NRA Publications, 11250 Waples Mill Rd., Fairfax, VA 22030. 703-267-1332. E-mail: publications@nrahq.org. Web site: nra.org. Monthly. Membership. Circ.: 1,070,000. John Zent, Editor. **Description:** On all aspects of hunting and related activities. Includes techniques, equipment, top places to hunt, legislation and current issues, and role of hunting in wildlife management. Safety and sportsmanship emphasized. **Nonfiction:** Features on deer, upland birds, waterfowl, big game and varmints/small game. Varied styles, including expository how-to, where-to; general-interest pieces; humor; personal narratives and semi-technical articles on firearms, wildlife management or hunting; 1,800-2,000 words; up to $800. **Columns, Departments:** Hunting Guns, Public Hunting Grounds; 1,000-1,200 words; $300-$450. **Art:** Color slides; pays on publication; pay varies, $450-$600 (cover). **Tips:** Submissions judged on 3 criteria: story angle, quality of writing, quality and quantity of photos. **Queries:** Preferred. **E-queries:** Yes. **Unsolicited mss:** Accepts. **Response:** 2 months or more, SASE required. **Freelance Content:** 50%. **Rights:** FNASR, reprint in NRA publication. **Payment:** On acceptance.

AMERICAN RIFLEMAN

11250 Waples Mill Rd., Fairfax, VA 22030. 703-267-1336. Mark Keefe, Managing Editor. **Description:** Articles on use and enjoyment of sporting firearms. **Payment:** On acceptance.

AQUA-FIELD

66 West Gilbert St., Shrewsbury, NJ 07702. 17x/year. **Description:** Recreation and outdoors publication, interested in new approaches to activities or improvements on tried-and-true methods. **Nonfiction:** How-to features, 2,000-3,000 words, on hunting, fishing, fly-fishing, gardening, outdoor adventure, woodworking, deck building. **Art:** color slides, b/w prints. **Queries:** Preferred.

BACKPACKER

Rodale Press, 33 E. Minor St., Emmaus, PA 18098. 610-967-8296. E-mail: editor@backpacker.com. Web site: www.backpacker.com. Thom Hogan, Executive Editor. **Description:** On self-propelled backcountry travel (backpacking, kayaking/canoeing, mountaineering; technique, nordic skiing, health, natural science). **Nonfiction:** Articles; 250-3,000 words; pay varies. **Art:** Photos. **Tips:** Send queries to Tom Shealey, editor. **Queries:** Preferred.

BACKWOODSMAN

P.O. Box 627, Westcliffe, CO 81252. 719-783-9028. E-mail: bwmmag@ris.net. Web site: www.backwoodsmanmag@.com. Bimonthly. $3.95. Circ.: 35,000. Charlie Richie, Editor. **Description:** On muzzleloaders, 19th-century woods lore, early cartridge guns, primitive survival, craft items, American history, gardening, leather crafting, homesteading, log cabin construction, mountain men, Indians, building primitive weapons. **Nonfiction:** Historical and how-to articles for the 21st-century frontiersman; no payment. **Queries:** Preferred. **E-queries:** Yes. **Unsolicited mss:** Accepts. **Response:** 3 days, SASE. **Freelance Content:** 50%.

BASSIN'

5300 CityPlex Tower, 2448 E. 81st St., Tulsa, OK 74137-4207. 918-491-6100. Web site: www.ebassin.com. Mark Chesnut, Executive Editor. **Description:** How and where to bass fish, for the amateur fisherman. **Nonfiction:** Articles; 1,200-1,400 words; pays $350-$500. **Queries:** Preferred. **Payment:** On acceptance.

BASSMASTER

B.A.S.S. Publications, 5845 Carmichael Rd., Montgomery, AL 36117. 334-272-9530. E-mail: editorial@bassmaster.com. Web site: www.bassmaster.com. Monthly. $3.95. Circ.: 600,000. Dave Precht, Editor. **Description:** For members of the Bass Anglers Sportsman Society (B.A.S.S.), on fishing for freshwater bass: largemouth, small-mouth, spotted, redeye, and shoal. (White, striped, and hybrid bass covered on a limited basis.) **Nonfiction:** Features (1,200-1,800 words); shorts (250-750 words); include photos; $.30/word. **Art:** 35mm slides; pays $700 for cover. **Tips:** Promote catch-and-release, conservation, where-to-go stories about good bass fishing in North America and abroad. No first-person accounts ("How I caught my bass"). **Queries:** Preferred. **E-queries:** Yes. **Unsolicited mss:** Accepts. **Response:** Queries 1-2 weeks, submissions 2-4 weeks, SASE required. **Freelance Content:** 80%. **Rights:** 1st, electronic. **Payment:** On acceptance.

BAY & DELTA YACHTSMAN

4090 S. McCarran, Suite E, Reno, NV 89502. 775-353-5100. E-mail: donabbott@yachtsforsale.com. Monthly. $2.95. Don Abbott, Publisher. **Description:** Cruising stories and features, how-tos, with northern California focus. **Nonfiction:** Boating experiences, anecdotes, around San Francisco Bay and Delta; 2,000 words; pay varies. **Columns, Departments:** Boating stories, boat maintenance; 4,000 words. **Art:** .tif or .jpeg (300 dpi). **Queries:** Preferred. **E-queries:** Yes. **Unsolicited mss:** Accepts. **Response:** 1 week, SASE required. **Freelance Content:** 0%. **Payment:** On publication.

BICYCLING

Rodale Press, Inc., 400 S. Tenth St., Emmaus, PA 18098. 610-967-5171. Web site: www.bicycling.com. Stan Zukowski, Managing Editor. **Description:** For cyclists, on recreational riding, fitness training, nutrition, bike maintenance, equipment, racing and touring. Covers all aspects of sport (road, mountain biking, leisure, etc.). **Nonfiction:** Articles; 500-2,500 words; pays $50-$2,000. **Fillers:** Bike Shorts (anecdotes, helpful cycling tips, etc.); 150-250 words. **Art:** Photos, illustrations. **Payment:** On acceptance.

BIRD WATCHER'S DIGEST

PO Box 110, Marietta, OH 45750. 740-373-8443. E-mail: editor@birdwatchersdigest.com. Web site: www.birdwatchersdigest.com.

Bimonthly. Circ.: 90,000. William H. Thompson III, Editor. **Description:** Bird-watching experiences and expeditions; interesting backyard topics and how-tos. **Nonfiction:** Articles for bird watchers: first-person accounts; profiles of bird species; 600-2,500 words; from $100. **Queries:** Preferred. **Response:** 8 weeks, SASE required. **Payment:** On publication.

BIRDER'S WORLD
P.O. Box 1612, 21027 Crossroads Circle, Waukesha, WI 53187-1612. 262-796-8776. Web site: www.birdersworld.com. Bi-monthly. $4.50/$22.50. Circ.: 70,000. Diane Jolie, Editor. **Description:** On all aspects of birding, especially on particular species or status of endangered species. Tips on birding, attracting or photographing birds. **Nonfiction:** Feature articles, 2,200-2,400 words; pays $350-$450. **Columns, Departments:** Book reviews (to 500 words); personal essays (500-1,500 words). **Queries:** Preferred. **E-queries:** No. **Unsolicited mss:** Accepts. **Response:** 3 months, SASE (if visuals are sent). **Freelance Content:** 75%. **Rights:** 1st NA. **Payment:** On publication.

BLACK BELT
Black Belt Communications, Inc., P.O. Box 918, 24715 Ave. Rockefeller, Valencia, CA 91380. 661-257-4066 (for Canadians); 800-423-2874 (in U.S.). Web site: www.blackbeltmag.com. WM: Bob Young, Editor. **Description:** Articles related to self-defense (how-tos on fitness and technique; historical, travel, philosophy). **Nonfiction:** Pays $100-$300. **Payment:** On publication.

BOUNDARY WATERS JOURNAL
9396 Rocky Ledge Rd., Ely, MN 55731. 218-365-6184. Web site: www.boundarywatersjournal.com. Quarterly. $4.95/issue, $18/year. Circ.: 3,200. Stuart Osthoff, Editor. **Description:** Covers Boundary Waters Canoe Area Wilderness, Quetico Provincial Park, and surrounding Superior National Forest. Includes canoe-route journals, fishing, camping, hiking, cross-country skiing, wildlife and nature, regional lifestyles, history, and events. **Fiction:** Must relate to this area; canoe routes, nature essays; 1-5 typed pages; $100-$400. **Nonfiction:** Articles, 2,000-3,000 words, on regional wilderness, recreation, nature, conservation; $100-$400. **Poetry:** under 1 page; $50-$100. **Art:** Slides, film. Pays $50-$100, $150 (cover). **Tips:** Needs winter stories especially, but open to all stories dealing with this area. **Queries:** Not necessary. **E-queries:** Yes. **Unsolicited mss:** Accepts. **Response:** Queries 1-2 weeks submissions 1-3 months, SASE required. **Freelance Content:** 50%+. **Rights:** 1st NA. **Payment:** On publication.

BOW & ARROW HUNTING
265 S. Anita, Suite 120, Orange, CA 92868. 714-939-9991. Web site: www.bowandarrowhunting.com. Joe Bell, Editor. **Description:** On bowhunting (profiles and technical pieces), primarily on deer hunting. **Nonfiction:** Articles; 1,200-2,500 words; with color slides, b/w or color photos; pays $250-$500. **Payment:** On acceptance.

BOWHUNTER

6405 Flank Dr., Harrisburg, PA 17112. 717-657-9555.
E-mail: bowhunter@cowless.com. Web site: www.bowhunter.com. 9x/year.
$3.50/issue, $23.94/year. Circ.: 180,250. Dwight Schuh, Editor-in-Chief.
Description: Information for bowhunters, on all aspects of the sport, to entertain
and inform readers, making them better bowhunters. **Nonfiction:** General interest,
how-to, interview/profile, opinion, personal experience, photo features; 250-2,000
words; $100-$400. **Art:** 35mm slides, 5x7 or 8x10 prints; $75-$250. **Tips:** Anticipate
all questions, then answer them in article or sidebar. Must know bowhunting.
Queries: Preferred. **E-queries:** Yes. **Unsolicited mss:** Accepts. **Response:**
Queries 1 month, submissions 5 weeks, SASE required. **Freelance Content:** 100%.
Rights: FNASR, one-time. **Payment:** On acceptance. **Contact:**.

BOWHUNTING WORLD

601 Lakeshore Pkwy., Suite 600, Minnetonka, MN 55305. 612-476-2200.
E-mail: mike-s@mail.epgine.com. Bimonthly. Circ.: 130,000. Mike Strandlund,
Editor. **Description:** Covers all aspects of bowhunting and competitive archery
equipment, with photos. **Nonfiction:** Seeking how-to articles on bowhunting techniques, feature articles on hunting and the mechanics of archery gear (traditional to
high-tech); 1,800-3,000 words. **Columns, Departments:** Mini-features; 1,000-1,600
words. **Tips:** Outline no more than 6 article ideas per query. **Queries:** Preferred.
E-queries: Yes. **Unsolicited mss:** Accepts. **Response:** Queries 3 week, submission
6 weeks, SASE required. **Freelance Content:** 50%. **Rights:** 1st. **Payment:** On
acceptance.

BOWLERS JOURNAL INTERNATIONAL

122 S. Michigan Ave., #1506, Chicago, IL 60603-6107. 312-341-1110.
Web site: www.bowlersjournal.com. Jim Dressel, Editor. **Description:** On bowling.
Nonfiction: Trade and consumer articles; 1,200-2,200 words, with photos; pays
$75-$200. **Payment:** On acceptance.

BOWLING

675 N Brookfield Rd., Brookfield, WI 53045. 262-641-2003.
Bi-monthly. $2.50/issue. Circ.: 90,000. Bill Vint, Editor. **Description:** Covers the
world of ten-pin bowling. **Nonfiction:** Seeking unique, unusual stories about bowling people and places. Human-interest features, with quality photos; 500-1,500
words; $100-$250. **Art:** Prints preferred. **Queries:** Preferred. **E-queries:** No.
Response: Queries 1-2 weeks, submissions 1-2 weeks, SASE required. **Freelance
Content:** 20-30%. **Rights:** All. **Payment:** On acceptance.

BOYS' LIFE

1325 W. Walnut Hill Ln., Irving, TX 75038. 972-580-2366.
Web site: www.bsa.scouting.org. Monthly. $18/year. Circ.: 1,300,000. W. E.
Butterworth IV, Managing Editor. **Description:** Published by Boy Scouts of
America, for boys ages 8-14. Covers broad range of interests (sports, hobbies, careers,

crafts, and special interests of scouting). **Fiction:** 1-2 short stories per issue; featuring 1 or more boys; humor, mystery, science fiction, adventure; 1,000-1,500 words; $750 and up. **Nonfiction:** From professional sports to American history to how to pack a canoe; 500-1,500 words; $400-$1,500. **Columns, Departments:** Science, nature, earth, health, sports, space and aviation, cars, computers, entertainment, pets, history, music, 300-750 words, $150-$400. Also, last page how-to features ($250-$300). **Art:** Quality photos only; most work by assignment. **Tips:** Write for a boy you know who is 12. Use crisp, punchy writing; short, straightforward sentences. **Queries:** Required for nonfiction. **E-queries:** Prefer mail. **Unsolicited mss:** Accepts fiction only. **Response:** 6-8 weeks, SASE required. **Freelance Content:** 75%. **Rights:** FNASR. **Payment:** On acceptance.

BUCKMASTERS WHITETAIL

P.O. Box 244022, Montgomery, AL 36124-4022. 334-215-3337. Web site: www.buckmasters.com. Russell Thornberry. **Description:** For serious sportsmen. **Nonfiction:** Articles, to 2,500 words. "Big Buck Adventures" capture details and adventure of the hunt of a newly discovered trophy. Fresh, new whitetail hunting how-tos; new useful biological information about whitetail deer. Pays $250-$400. **Columns, Departments:** Entertaining deer stories. **Art:** Photos helpful. **Queries:** Preferred.

CANOE & KAYAK

Canoe America Associates, P.O. Box 3146, Kirkland, WA 98083. 425-827-6363. E-mail: editor@canoekayak.com. Web site: www.canoekayak.com. Jan Nesset, Editor-in-Chief. **Description:** Canoeing or kayaking adventures, destinations, boat and equipment reviews, techniques and how-tos, short essays, camping, environment, safety, humor, health, history. **Nonfiction:** Features (2,000-2,500 words); department pieces (500-1,200 words); pays $.13/word. **Queries:** Preferred. **Payment:** On publication.

CASCADES EAST

716 N. E. 4th St., P.O. Box 5784, Bend, OR 97708-5784. 541-382-0127. E-mail: sunpub@sun-pub.com. Web site: www.sun-pub.com. Quarterly. Circ.: 10,000. Geoff Hill, Editor. **Description:** Outdoor activities (fishing, hunting, golfing, backpacking, rafting, skiing, snowmobiling, etc.), history, special events, and scenic tours in central Oregon Cascades. **Nonfiction:** 1,000-2,000 words; $.05-$.15/word. **Fillers:** Travel, history, and recreation in central Oregon; $.05-.$15/word. **Art:** Photos; pays extra. **Queries:** Preferred. **Payment:** On publication.

CHESAPEAKE BAY

1819 Bay Ridge Ave., Annapolis, MD 21403. 410-263-2662. E-mail: cbmeditor@cbmmag.net. Monthly. $3.95/issue. Circ.: 46,000. Tim Sayles, Editor. **Description:** For recreational boaters who enjoy boating, fishing, destinations, people, history, and traditions of the Chesapeake Bay. **Nonfiction:** to 4,000 words; $75-$1,200. **Art:** Photos. Pays $100-$700. **Tips:** Need to be familiar with

Chesapeake Bay region and boating. Readers are well educated, well traveled. **Queries:** Preferred. **E-queries:** Yes. **Unsolicited mss:** Accepts. **Response:** Queries 1 week, submissions 1 month, SASE required. **Freelance Content:** 30%. **Rights:** FNASR. **Payment:** On acceptance.

CROSS COUNTRY SKIER
MD 60 1107 Hazelfine, Chaska, MN 55318. 952-361-6760.
Web site: www.crosscountryskier.com. Aaron Kellogg, Editor. **Description:** On all aspects of cross-country skiing. **Nonfiction:** Articles, to 2,000 words; pays $300-$700. **Columns, Departments:** 1,000-1,500 words, on ski maintenance, ski techniques, health and fitness; pays $100-$350. **Tips:** Published October through February. **Queries:** Preferred. **Payment:** On publication.

CURRENTS
212 W. Cheyenne Mountain Blvd., Colorado Springs, CO 80906. 719-579-8759.
Web site: www.nors.org. Quarterly. **Description:** "Voice of the National Organization for Rivers." For kayakers, rafters, and river canoeists, pertaining to whitewater rivers and/or river running. **Nonfiction:** Articles, 500-2,000 words; pays from $40. **Art:** b/w action photos ($30- $50). **Queries:** Preferred.

DAKOTA OUTDOORS
Hipple Publishing Co., P.O. Box 669, 333 W. Dakota Ave.,
Pierre, SD 57501. 605-224-7301.
Web site: www.capjournal.com\dakotaoutdoors. Monthly. $2.25/issue, $10/year. Circ.: 8,000. Kevin Hipple, Editor. **Description:** Hunting and fishing, for outdoorsman in the Dakotas. **Fiction:** 1,000-1,500 words; $5-$50. **Nonfiction:** 1,000-1,500 words; $5-$50. **Art:** b/w, color. **Queries:** Not necessary. **E-queries:** No. **Unsolicited mss:** Accepts. **Response:** Queries 2 weeks, SASE. **Freelance Content:** 75%. **Rights:** One-time. **Payment:** On publication.

THE DIVER
P.O. Box 28, St. Petersburg, FL 33731-0028. 813-866-9856.
Bob Taylor, Editor. **Description:** Articles on divers, coaches, officials, springboard and platform techniques, training tips, etc. Pays $15-$50, $5-$10 for cartoons, extra for photos. **Payment:** On publication.

DIVER
Seagraphics Publications Ltd., P.O. Box 1312,
Delta, B.C., Canada V4M 3Y8. 604-948-9937.
E-mail: divermag@axion.net. Web site: www.divermag@axion.net. 9x/year. $18/year (U.S.), $25 (Canada). Circ.: 10,000. Stephanie Bold, Editor. **Description:** On scuba diving, ocean science, and technology for well-educated, outdoor enthusiasts. **Nonfiction:** Illustrated articles, 500-1,000 words, on dive destinations, interviews, personal experiences. Shorter pieces welcome. Travel features, keep brief, include slides or prints, and map. Unsolicited articles reviewed only from Aug.-Oct. Pay

varies. **Columns, Departments:** Book reviews (200 words max.), no payment. **Art:** Prints, slides, .jpeg. **Tips:** Canadian and U.S. stories preferred. **Queries:** Not necessary. **E-queries:** Yes. **Unsolicited mss:** Accepts. **Response:** SASE required. **Freelance Content:** 50%. **Rights:** FNASR. **Payment:** On publication.

ELYSIAN FIELDS QUARTERLY

P.O. Box 14385, St. Paul, MN 55114-0385. 651-644-8558. E-mail: info@efqreview.com. Web site: www.efqreview.com. Quarterly. $5.95/issue, $22.50/year. Circ.: 2,000-2,500. Tom Goldstein, Editor. **Description:** The literary review for baseball, with essays, poetry, commentary, drama, and humor. Length: 400-2,000 words. **Tips:** Must have a passion and appreciation for baseball, and be able to write well. This is not a hero-worship, nostalgia journal. Sentimental, ill-conceived, formulaic writing from would-be writers or those looking to publish a "baseball" story get tossed quickly. **Queries:** Not necessary. **E-queries:** Yes. **Unsolicited mss:** Accepts. **Response:** 6 months (fiction/poetry), 3 months (other), SASE. **Freelance Content:** 75%. **Rights:** One-time, anthology. **Payment:** In copies.

FIELD & STREAM

2 Park Ave., New York, NY 10016. 212-779-5285. E-mail: fsinfo@aol.com. Web site: www.fieldandstream.com. Monthly. $3.97/issue, $12/year. Circ.: 1,750,000. Slaton White, Editor. **Description:** The nation's largest hunting and fishing magazine. **Nonfiction:** On aspects of hunting and fishing: how-to, nostalgia, conversation essays, profiles, humor. Pay, length varies. **Fillers:** Cartoons, small fillers (how-to); $100-$250. **Art:** Pay varies. **Queries:** Preferred. **E-queries:** No. **Unsolicited mss:** Accepts. **Response:** 2-4 weeks, SASE required. **Freelance Content:** 85%. **Rights:** 1st NA. **Payment:** On acceptance.

FISHING FACTS

111 Shore Dr., Burr Ridge, IL 60521. 630-887-7722. E-mail: info@midwestoutdoors.com. Web site: www.fishingfacts.com. Bimonthly. $23.95. Gene Laulunen, Publisher/Editor. **Description:** For the angler who wants to improve skills and maximize success. In-depth articles on fish behavior, techniques for taking fish from all kinds of structure, the latest in fishing products and technology, and simple tips from experts. **Nonfiction:** Seeking cutting-edge information on latest fishing techniques and tips; 750-1,500 words; $30 fee. **Art:** Submit quality, full-color prints with each article. **Tips:** No elementary fishing techniques or everyday fishing stories. **Queries:** Required. **E-queries:** Yes. **Unsolicited mss:** Accepts. **Response:** 10 days, SASE required. **Rights:** 1st. **Payment:** On publication. **Contact:** Dena Kollman, Asst. Ed.

FLIGHT JOURNAL

Air Age Publishing, 100 E. Ridge, Ridgefield, CT 06877-4606. 203-431-9000. Web site: www.flightjournal.com. Tom Atwood. **Description:** Covers "the history, the hardware, and the human heart of aviation." **Nonfiction:** Articles, 2,500-3,000 words; pays $600. **Tips:** Submit 1-page outline. **Contact:** Dana Donia, Ed. Asst.

FLY ROD & REEL

P.O. Box 370, Camden, ME 04843. 207-594-9544.
E-mail: jbutler@flyrodreel.com. Web site: www.flyrodreel.com. James E. Butler,
Editor. **Description:** On fly-fishing **Fiction:** Occasionally. **Nonfiction:** Articles on
fly-fishing, on culture and history of areas being fished, 2,000-2,500 words; pay varies.
Queries: Preferred. **Payment:** On acceptance.

FLYER

P.O. Box 39099, Lakewood, Wa 98439-0099. 253-471-9888.
E-mail: kirk.gomerly@flyer-online.com. Web site: www.flyer-online.com. Biweekly.
Circ.: 35,000. Kirk Gormley, Editor. **Description:** Of interest to "general aviation"
pilots. **Nonfiction:** 500-2,500 words; to $3/column inch (about 40 words). **Art:** $10
for b/w photos; $50 for color photos. **Payment:** Within one month of publication.

FOOTBALL DIGEST

Century Publishing Co., 990 Grove St., Evanston, IL 60201. 847-491-6440.
Web site: www.centurysports.net. Jim O'Connor, Editor-in-Chief. **Description:** For
the hard-core football fan. Profiles of pro and college stars, nostalgia, trends in the
sport. **Nonfiction:** Articles, 1,500-2,500 words. **Queries:** Preferred. **Payment:** On
publication.

FUR-FISH-GAME

2878 E. Main St., Columbus, OH 43209. 614-231-9585.
Monthly. $3.99/issue. Circ.: 107,000. Mitch Cox, Editor. **Description:** For serious
outdoorsmen of all ages. Covers hunting, trapping, freshwater fishing, predator call-
ing, camping, boating, woodcrafting, conservation, related topics. **Nonfiction:** Short
how-to, humor, and human-interest articles needed; 2,000 -3,000 words; $100-150.
Art: Varied photos (close-ups, overall scenes); Color slides, b/w, color prints; $25.
Queries: Required. **E-queries:** Yes. **Unsolicited mss:** Accepts. **Freelance
Content:** 75%. **Rights:** 1st NA. **Payment:** On acceptance.

GAME AND FISH PUBLICATIONS

P.O. Box 741, Marietta, GA 30061. 770-953-9222.
Ken Dunwoody, Editorial Department. **Description:** Publishes 30 monthly outdoor
magazines for 48 states. **Nonfiction:** Articles, 1,500-2,500 words, on hunting and
fishing (how-tos, where-tos, and adventure). Profiles of successful hunters and fishermen. No hiking, canoeing, camping, or backpacking pieces. Pays $125-$175 for
state-specific articles, $200-$250 for multi-state articles. **Art:** Photos; pays $25-$75
(interior), $250 (covers). **Payment:** On acceptance.

GOLF

2 Park Ave., New York, NY 10016. 212-779-5000.
Web site: www.golfonline.com. Jim Frank, Editor. **Description:** Articles, 1,000
words with photos, on golf history and travel (places to play around the world); pro

files of professional tour players. Shorts, to 500 words. Pays $.75 a word, on acceptance. Queries preferred.

GOLF COURSE NEWS
United Publications, Inc., 106 Lafayette St., P.O. Box 997, Yarmouth, ME 04096. 207-846-0600. E-mail: mleslie@golfcoursenews.com. Web site: www.golfcoursenews.com. Mark Leslie, Editor. **Description:** Features and news analyses, 500-1,000 words, on all aspects of golf course maintenance, design, building, and management. Pays $200, on acceptance.

GOLF DIGEST
5520 Park Ave., Trumbull, CT 06611. 203-373-7000. E-mail: editor@golfdigest.com. Web site: www.golfdigest.com. Monthly. $3.99. Circ.: 1,550,000. Jerry Tarde, Editor. **Description:** Covers golf instruction, equipment, and travel. Freelance content limited. **Queries:** Required.

GOLF DIGEST WOMAN
1120 Avenue of the Americas, New York, NY 10018. 212-789-3000. Web site: www.gdwoman.com. Rona Cherry. **Description:** Seeking published authors (in national magazines) who have in-depth knowledge of golf and golf-related subjects. **Nonfiction:** Pay varies. **Payment:** On publication.

GOLF FOR WOMEN
125 Park Ave., 15th Fl., New York, NY 10017. 212-551-6958. E-mail: gfwmag@mdp.com. Leslie Day Craige, Editor-in-Chief. **Description:** Golf lifestyle magazine for avid women golfers. Includes travel, instruction, fashion, equipment, news. Query with clips.

GOLF JOURNAL
Golf House, 1 Libery Connor Road, Far Hills, NJ 07931-0708. 908-234-2300. E-mail: golfjournal@usga.org. Web site: www.golfjournal.org. 9x/year. Membership publication. Circ.: 800,000. Brett Avery, Editor. **Description:** Published by United States Golf Assn., general interest, on contemporary issues and history as seen in the game, people, and values. **Fiction:** On humor, values; 500 words and up; $1/word. **Nonfiction:** On golf history, lore, rules, equipment, general information. Focus is on amateur golf. No jokes, instruction, or travel pieces. Accepts poignant, humorous stories and essays; 500 words and up; $1/word. **Queries:** Not necessary. **E-queries:** Yes. **Unsolicited mss:** Accepts. **Response:** Queries and submissions, 4 weeks, SASE required. **Freelance Content:** 35-40%. **Payment:** On publication.

GOLF TIPS
P.O. Box 56381, Boulder, CO 80322. 800-537-4619. Web site: www.golftipsmag.com. John Ledesma. **Description:** For serious golfers.

Nonfiction: Articles, 500-1,500 words, unique golf instruction, golf products, interviews with pro players; pays $200-$600. **Fillers:** Short "shotmaking" instruction tips. **Queries:** Preferred. **Payment:** On publication.

GUN DIGEST
Krause Publications, 700 E. State St., Iola, WI 54990. 888-457-2873. E-mail: ramayek@krause.com. Web site: www.krause.com. Ken Ramage, Editor. **Description:** On guns and shooting, equipment, etc. **Nonfiction:** Well-researched articles, to 5,000 words; pays from $.10 a word. **Art:** Photos. **Queries:** Preferred. **Payment:** On acceptance.

GUN DOG
P.O. Box 35098, Des Moines, IA 50315. 515-243-2472. Web site: www.emapusa.com. **Description:** On bird hunting (how-tos, where-tos, dog training, canine medicine, breeding strategy). Some fiction, humor. **Nonfiction:** Features, 1,000-2,500 words, with photos; $150-$450. **Fillers:** $150-$450 for features,. **Payment:** On acceptance.

GUNGAMES MAGAZINE
421 Coeur d'Alene Ave., Coeur d'Alene, Idaho 83814. 800-771-3020. Web site: www.gungames.com. Bimonthly. Michael Bane. **Description:** Articles and fiction, 1,200-1,500 words, about "the fun side of guns and shooting. No self-defense articles." Pays $150-$250. **Payment:** On publication.

GUNS & AMMO
6420 Wilshire Blvd., Los Angeles, CA 90048. 323-782-2160. Web site: www.emapusa.com. Lee Hoots, Editor. **Description:** On guns, ammunition, and target shooting. **Nonfiction:** Technical and general articles, 800-2,500 words; pays from $150. **Art:** Photos. **Payment:** On acceptance.

HANG GLIDING
U.S. Hang Gliding Assn., 31441 Santa Margarita Pkwy., A-256, Rancho Santa Margarita, CA 92688-1836. 949-888-7363. Web site: www.ushga.org. Gilbert Dodgen, Editor. **Description:** On hang gliding. **Nonfiction:** Articles, 2-3 pages; pays to $50. **Queries:** Preferred. **Payment:** On publication.

HIGHWIRED SPORTS
1373 Grandview Ave., Ste. 206, Columbus, OH 43212. E-mail: contact@highwired-inc.com. Web site: www.HighWiredSports.com. Bimonthly. $2.95/$14.95. Circ.: 100,000. Nancy Petro, Editor. **Description:** Covers high-school sports. Offers information, recognition, and inspiration for today's student-athlete. **Nonfiction:** Profiles of top teams and athletes; articles on recruiting and scholarships, health, nutrition, training, sports camps; 300-500 words; pay varies. **Tips:** Articles on successful athlete or team needs strong distinguishing factor; what

makes their story unique? **Queries:** Preferred. **E-queries:** Accepts. **Unsolicited mss:** Accepts. **Rights:** All. **Payment:** On publication. **Contact:** Stephanie Strong.

HORSE & RIDER

PO Box 4101, 741 Corporate Circle, Suite A, Golden, CO 80401. 720-836-1257. E-mail: hrsenrider@cowles.com. Web site: www.equisearch.com. Monthly. $3.50/issue, $19.95/year. Circ.: 165,000. René E. Riley, Executive Editor. **Description:** For competitive and recreational Western riders. Training articles, stable management, health care tips, safe trail-riding practices, consumer advice, and behind-the-scenes coverage of major equine events. **Nonfiction:** How-tos (training, horse care/horsekeeping). Consumer buying advice. Profiles of Western horse show people; 150-2,000 words; $150-$1,000. **Fillers:** Humorous experiences; 150-1,000 words; $150-$1,000. **Columns, Departments:** Real-life horse stories. Trail-riding tips. Training tips. Horsekeeping tips; 150-1,000 words; $0-$1,000. **Queries:** Preferred. **E-queries:** No. **Unsolicited mss:** Accepts. **Response:** 3 months, SASE required. **Freelance Content:** 5-10%. **Rights:** 1st NA. **Payment:** On acceptance.

HOT BOAT

Sport Publications, 8484 Wilshire Blvd., #900, Beverly Hills, CA 90211. 323-651-5400. E-mail: H2oEdits@aol.com. Web site: www.hotboat.net. Brett Bayne, Editor. **Description:** On motorized water sport events and personalities: general-interest, how-to, and technical features. **Nonfiction:** Family-oriented articles, 600-1,000 words; pays $85-$300. **Queries:** Preferred. **Payment:** On publication.

IN-FISHERMAN

Two In-Fisherman Dr., Brainerd, MN 56425-8098. 218-829-1648. Web site: www.in-fisherman.com. 7x/year. Doug Stange, Editor. **Description:** On all aspects of freshwater fishing. **Nonfiction:** How-to articles, 1,500-4,500 words; pays $250-$1,000. **Columns, Departments:** Reflections (humorous or nostalgic looks at fishing), 1,000-1,500 words. **Payment:** On acceptance.

INSIDE TEXAS RUNNING

9514 Bristlebrook Dr., Houston, TX 77083. 281-498-3208. E-mail: insidetx@aol.com. Web site: www.insidetexasrunning.com. 10x/year. $12. Circ.: 8,000. Joanne Schmidt, Editor. **Description:** Tabloid newspaper, for runners in Texas. **Nonfiction:** Travel pieces for runners attending out-of-town races; unusual runners (not just fast runners); race write-ups; 300-1,500 words; $300-$1,500. **Columns, Departments:** Short news items for Texas Roundup (2-5 paragraphs max.). **Art:** $10-$25. **Tips:** Avoid "How I ran the marathon" articles or subject matter on other sports. Use quotes. Welcomes new writers with appropriate expertise. **Queries:** Required. **E-queries:** Yes. **Unsolicited mss:** Accepts. **Response:** 4 weeks, SASE required. **Freelance Content:** 30%. **Rights:** One-time. **Payment:** On publication.

JOURNAL OF ASIAN MARTIAL ARTS

Via Media Publishing, 821 W. 24th St., Erie, PA 16502. 814-455-9517. Web site: www.ncinter.net/~viamedia. Quarterly. Michael A. DeMarco, Editor. **Description:** On martial arts and Asian culture: interviews (with scholars, master practitioners, etc.) and scholarly articles based on primary research in key disciplines (cultural anthropology, comparative religion, etc.). **Nonfiction:** Articles, 2,000-10,000 words; pays $150-$500. **Columns, Departments:** Reviews, 1,000 words, of books and audiovisual material; pays in copies. **Payment:** On publication.

JUMP

21100 Erwin St., Woodland Hills, CA 91367-3712. 10x/year. Lori Berger, Editor-in-Chief. **Description:** For girls who are into sports, strong minds, and living with a healthy lifestyle. **Nonfiction:** Articles include the latest news in beauty, style, sports, music, body and soul, etc.; pay varies. **Queries:** Preferred.

KITPLANES

8745 Aero Dr., Suite 105, San Diego, CA 92123. 858-694-0491. E-mail: dave@kitplanes.com. Web site: www.kitplanes.com. Monthly. $3.99/issue, $29.95/year. Circ.: 75,000. Dave Martin, Editor. **Description:** For designers, builders, and pilots of home-built experimental aircraft. **Nonfiction:** On all aspects of design, construction, and performance for aircraft built from kits and plans by home craftsmen; 1,500-2,500 words; $70/page. **Queries:** Preferred. **E-queries:** Yes. **Unsolicited mss:** Accepts. **Response:** Queries 2 days, submissions 2 weeks, SASE not required. **Freelance Content:** 80%. **Payment:** On publication.

LAKELAND BOATING

500 Davis St., Suite 1000, Evanston, IL 60201-5047. 847-869-5400. E-mail: lb@omeara-brown.com. Web site: www.lakelandboating.com. 11x/year. Mathew Wright, Editor. **Description:** On boating in the Great Lakes and surrounding areas. **Nonfiction:** Cruising features, boating and Great Lakes information. also, newsy bits, maintenance tips (100 words up); 800-2,500 words; $50-$600. **Columns, Departments:** Cruising, Port O' Call, Weekender, Historical Subjects, Environment, Bosun's Locker, Antique and Classic Boats, Profiles; 800-2,500 words; $50-$600. **Tips:** Looking for freelance writers who are also skilled photographers. **Queries:** Required. **E-queries:** Yes. **Unsolicited mss:** Accepts. **Response:** 2-4 weeks, SASE. **Rights:** FNASR and electronic. **Payment:** On publication.

MICHIGAN OUT-OF-DOORS

P.O. Box 30235, Lansing, MI 48909. 517-371-1041. E-mail: magazine@mucc.org. Web site: www.mucc.org. Monthly. $3.50/issue, $25/year. Circ.: 100,000. Dennis Knickerbocker, Editor. **Description:** On Michigan's natural environment and outdoor recreation, emphasis on hunting, fishing, and nature study. **Nonfiction:** Informative, entertaining features for sportsmen/women, and all who enjoy the out-of-doors; 1,000-5,000 words; $90-$200. **Art:** 35mm color slides, prints; $40, $175 cover. **Queries:** Preferred. **E-queries:** No. **Unsolicited mss:** Accepts. **Response:** Queries 1 month, submissions 3-4 months, SASE. **Freelance Content:** 75%. **Payment:** On acceptance.

MID-WEST OUTDOORS

111 Shore Dr., Hinsdale, IL 60521-5885. 638-887-7722.
E-mail: glaulenen@midwestoutdoors.com. Web site: www.midwestoutdoors.com. Annual. $2.99/issue, $14.95/year. Circ.: 45,000. Gene Laulunen, Editor. **Description:** Seeks to help people enjoy the outdoors, with positive stories about outdoor experiences. **Nonfiction:** Where, when, why, how-to articles about the Midwest; 1500 words; $30. **Tips:** Avoid first-time experience stories. **Queries:** Not necessary. **E-queries:** No. **Unsolicited mss:** Accepts. **Response:** varies. **Freelance Content:** 95%. **Rights:** One-time and web. **Payment:** On publication.

MOUNTAIN BIKE

135 N. Sixth St., Emmaus, PA 18049. 610-967-5171.
Web site: www.mountainbike.com. Zapata Espinoza, Executive Editor. **Description:** On mountain-bike touring; major off-road cycling events; political, sport, or land-access issues; riding techniques; fitness and training tips. **Nonfiction:** Articles, 500-2,000 words; pays $100-$650. **Columns, Departments:** Descriptions, detailing routes of off-road rides, to 500 words; pays $75. **Queries:** Preferred. **Payment:** On publication.

MUSHING

P.O. Box 149, Ester, AK 99725-0149. 907-479-0454.
E-mail: editor@mushing.com. Web site: www.mushing.com. Todd Hoener, Editor. **Description:** Dog-driving how-tos, innovations, history, profiles, interviews, and features related to sled dogs. International audience. **Nonfiction:** 1,200-2,000 words. **Columns, Departments:** Competitive and recreational dog drivers; weight pullers, dog packers, and skijorers; 500-1,000 words. **Art:** Photos; $20-$250. **Queries:** Preferred.

MUZZLE BLASTS

P.O. Box 67, Friendship, IN 47021-0067. 812-667-5131.
E-mail: mblastdop@seidata.com. Web site: www.nm/ra/org. Monthly. $35/yr for members. Circ.: 22,000. Eric A. Bye, Editor. **Description:** Published by National Muzzleloading Rifle Assn. **Nonfiction:** Articles on antique muzzleloading guns, gunmakers, events in America's past; how-tos on crafts related to muzzleloaders (gunbuilding, making powder horns, engraving, etc.), safehandling, loading, etc.; 1,500-2,000 words; $150-$250. **Art:** Photos, illustrations; must reflect highest standard of safety. **Tips:** Must know muzzleloaders (preferably traditional) and safety; generally, avoid modern topics. **Queries:** Preferred. **E-queries:** Yes. **Unsolicited mss:** Accepts. **Response:** Queries 2-3 weeks, submissions 4-6 weeks. **Freelance Content:** 70%. **Rights:** 1st NA. **Payment:** On publication.

NEW HAMPSHIRE WILDLIFE
54 Portsmouth St., Concord, NH 63301. 603-224-5953.
E-mail: nhwf@aol.com. Web site: www.nhwf.org. Bimonthly. Circ.: 7,000. Margaret
Lane, Editor. **Description:** Hunting, fishing, trapping and other active outdoor pursuits in New Hampshire. No payment offered. **Nonfiction:** First-person experiences;
400-1,500 words. **Fillers:** Wildlife, outdoors; Short. **Queries:** Not necessary.
Unsolicited mss: Accepts.

NORTHEAST OUTDOORS
2575 Vista Del Mar, Ventura, CA 93001. 800-323-9078.
Web site: www.woodalls.com. Melinda Baccanai, Editor. **Description:** On camping
and recreational vehicle (RV) touring in northeast U.S. **Nonfiction:** Prefers how-to,
where-to (camp cookery, recreational vehicle hints). Articles, 1,000-2,000 words,
preferably with b/w photos; pay varies. **Fillers:** Cartoons.

OFFSHORE
220 Reservoir St., Suite 9, Needham, MA 02494-3133. 781-449-6204.
E-mail: editors@offshoremag.net. Web site: www.offshoremag.net. Monthly.
$3.50/issue, $19.95/year. Circ.: 32,000. Betsy Frawley Haggerty, Editor.
Description: Northeast power boaters and sailboaters (East Coast from Maine to
New Jersey). **Nonfiction:** Destinations (seaports in New England, New York, New
Jersey); things to do, places to see, navigation guidelines. First-hand accounts of boating adventures and mishaps. Also, fishing pieces; 1,500-3,000 words; $350-$700.
Columns, Departments: Marina profiles (detail on Northeast marinas); Boater's
workshop (tips and techniques on boat care); 200-1500 words; $100-$350. **Art:** 35mm
color slides; $45-$300/image. **Queries:** Required. **E-queries:** Yes. **Unsolicited
mss:** Accepts. **Response:** Queries 2 weeks, submissions 4 weeks, SASE. **Freelance
Content:** 80%. **Rights:** 1st NA. **Payment:** On acceptance.

OREGON OUTSIDE
Northwest Regional Magazines, 4969 Hwy 101 N, Suite 2, Box 18000,
Florence, OR 97439-0130. 800-348-8401.
E-mail: judy@ohwy.com. Web site: www.ohwy.com. Quarterly. $3.50/year,
$12.95/year. Circ.: 25,000. Jim Forst, Steve Beckner, Editors. **Description:** Covers
outdoor activities in Oregon: recreation areas, trails and campgrounds; also events,
outfitters, and organizations. **Nonfiction:** First-person, all kinds of adventure, from
walks for families to extreme skiing; 500-1,500 words; $75-250. **Columns,
Departments:** Focal Points (photography tips, how-to and where); 800 words; $125-
$150. **Art:** Slides, transparencies; some stand-alone full-page photos (vertical or horizontal); $325/cover, $25-$75/full page. **Tips:** Compelling lead, solid body, satisfying
ending, details in sidebars. **Queries:** Preferred. **E-queries:** Yes. **Unsolicited mss:**
Accepts. **Response:** Queries 3 months, submissions 2-3 months, SASE required.
Freelance Content: 50-60%. **Rights:** 1st NA. **Payment:** On publication.

OUTDOOR CANADA

340 Ferrier St., Suite 210, Markham, Ont., Canada L3R 2Z5. 905-475-8440. E-mail: jameslittle@outdoorcanadamagazine.com. 8x/year. Circ.: 95,000. James Little, Editor in Chief. **Description:** Articles on fishing, hunting, and conservation. **Nonfiction:** 1,500-4,000 words; $500 and up. **Payment:** On acceptance.

OUTDOOR EXPLORER

2 Park Avenue, 10th Floor, New York, NY 10016. 212-779-5000. Web site: www.outdoorexplorer.com. Bimonthly. Steve Madden, Editor-in-Chief. **Description:** Seeks to present real adventures for real people. Sophisticated, cutting-edge, unique content for active adults who enjoy sharing outdoor experiences with family and friends. **Nonfiction:** Well-crafted articles (ranging from a literary feature on backpacking in North Cascades National Park by novelist Peter Landesman to a do-it-yourself bike tour). **Tips:** Most staff members are veterans of Sports Illustrated, with ties to established writers. Query with outstanding ideas only. **Queries:** Preferred. **E-queries:** Yes. **Unsolicited mss:** Accepts.

OUTSIDE

Outside Plaza, 400 Market St., Santa Fe, NM 87501. 505-989-7100. E-mail: letters@outsidemag.com. Web site: www.outsidemag.com. Monthly. $4.95/$18. Circ.: 600,000. Hal Epsen, Editor. **Description:** Active lifestyle; outdoor sports, adventure travel; environment; outdoor equipment. **Nonfiction:** On the environment, outdoor sports, how-to, personal experience, reviews of equipment, etc. 1,500-4,000 words. **Columns, Departments:** Dispatches (news events); Destinations (places to explore). **Tips:** Departments are best areas for new writers to break in. **Queries:** Preferred. **Unsolicited mss:** Does not accept. **Response:** 2 months, SASE. **Freelance Content:** 90%. **Rights:** FNASR.

PADDLER

P.O. Box 775450, Steamboat Springs, CO 80477. 970-879-1450. Web site: www.paddlermagazine.com. Eugene Buchanan, Editor. **Description:** On canoeing, kayaking, rafting, sea kayaking. **Nonfiction:** Articles; pays $.15-$.25/word. **Columns, Departments:** Hotlines; Paddle People. **Tips:** Best way to break in is to target a specific department. **Queries:** Preferred. **Payment:** On publication. **Contact:** Tom Bie.

PARAGLIDING

U.S. Hang Gliding Assn., P.O. Box 1330, Colorado Springs, CO 80901. 719-632-8300. Web site: www.ushga.org. Gil Dodgen. **Description:** On paragliding. **Nonfiction:** 2-3 pages; pays $50. **Queries:** Preferred. **Payment:** On publication.

PENNSYLVANIA ANGLER AND BOATER

Pennsylvania Fish and Boat Commission, P.O. Box 67000, Harrisburg, PA 17106-7000. 717-657-4520. Web site: www.fish.state.pa.us. Art Michaels, Editor. **Description:** On freshwater fishing and boating in Pennsylvania. **Nonfiction:** Articles, 500-3,000 words, with photos; pays $50-$300. **Queries:** Preferred. **Response:** SASE required. **Payment:** On acceptance.

PENNSYLVANIA GAME NEWS

Game Commission, 2001 Elmerton Ave., Harrisburg, PA 17110-9797. 717-787-3745. Monthly. $1.50/issue. Circ.: 120,000. Bob Mitchell, Editor. **Description:** Published by the state Game Commission, to promote wildlife programs, hunting, and trapping in the state. **Nonfiction:** On hunting or wildlife, with Pennsylvania interest; 2,000 words; $.08/word. **Tips:** No controversial issues, or technical subjects by freelancers. Avoid "first deer" stories. **Queries:** Not necessary. **E-queries:** No. **Unsolicited mss:** Accepts. **Response:** 4-6 weeks, SASE. **Freelance Content:** 40%. **Rights:** 1st. **Payment:** On acceptance.

PETERSEN'S BOWHUNTING

6420 Wilshire Blvd., Los Angeles, CA 90048-5515. 323-782-2721. E-mail: strangisj@emapusa.com. Web site: www.emapusa.com. Monthly (9/year). $3.99/issue, $11.97/year. Circ.: 194,000. Jay Michael Strangis, Editor. **Description:** How-to help for bowhunter enthusiasts. Also, interesting stories about bowhunting. **Nonfiction:** Bowhunting adventure stories. How-to and technical (equipment, products) articles; 2,000 words; $150-$400. **Art:** Photos must accompany all manuscripts; color, b/w; $100-$600. **Queries:** Preferred. **E-queries:** Yes. **Unsolicited mss:** Accepts. **Response:** Queries 3-4 days, submissions 6-7 days, SASE. **Freelance Content:** 40%. **Rights:** All, 1st (photos). **Payment:** On acceptance.

PETERSEN'S HUNTING

6420 Wilshire Blvd., 14th Fl., Los Angeles, CA 90048-5515. 323-782-2000. Web site: www.huntingmag.com. Monthly. $3.99/issue, $17.94/year. Circ.: 350,000. J. Scott Rupp, Editor. **Description:** In-depth coverage of varied hunting disciplines, and destination articles on the continent's hunting "hot spots." **Nonfiction:** Strategies for hunting game animals in North America, also destination pieces describing hunting opportunities in a given region; 2,100-2,400 words; $500-600. **Tips:** Submit only articles that inform readers how and where. No "me and Joe" hunting tales. **Queries:** Required. **E-queries:** No. **Unsolicited mss:** Does not accept. **Response:** 30-45 days, SASE. **Freelance Content:** 20%. **Rights:** All, 1st (photos). **Payment:** On acceptance.

PGA

33469 W 14 Mile Rd., Ste 100, Farmington Hills, MI 48331-1589. 248-661-0800. Matt Marsom, Managing Editor: **Description:** On golf-related subjects. **Nonfiction:** Articles, 1,500-2,500 words; pays $300-$500. **Queries:** Preferred. **Payment:** On acceptance.

PLANE & PILOT

12121 Wilshire Blvd., #1200, Los Angeles, CA 90025-1175. 310-820-1500. Web site: www.planeandpilotmag.com. Steve Werner. **Description:** Aviation-related articles, for pilots of single-engine, piston-powered recreational airplanes. **Nonfiction:** Training, maintenance, travel, equipment, pilot reports. Occasional features on antique, classic, and kit- or home-built aircraft. 1,500-2,500 word; pay varies. **Queries:** Preferred. **Payment:** On publication.

POWER AND MOTORYACHT

260 Madison Ave., 8th Fl., New York, NY 10016. 917-256-2267. E-mail: rthiel@primediasi.com. Monthly. Circ.: 157,400. Richard Thiel, Editor. **Description:** For affluent, experienced owners of powerboats 24 feet and larger. Reaches almost every U.S. owner of a large powerboat, with advice on how to choose, operate, and maintain their boats. **Nonfiction:** Clear, concise, authoritative articles. Include personal experience and information from marine industry experts where appropriate; 800-1,400 words; $500-$1,200. **Tips:** No stories on powerboats smaller than 24', or sailboats of any length. **Queries:** Required. **E-queries:** Yes. **Unsolicited mss:** Does not accept. **Response:** Queries 1 month, SASE required. **Freelance Content:** 20-25%. **Rights:** All, print, electronic. **Payment:** On acceptance.

POWERBOAT

1691 Spinnaker Dr., Suite 206, Ventura, CA 93001. 805-639-2222. E-mail: edit-dept@powerboatmag.com. Web site: www.powerboatmag.com. 11x/year. $3.95/issue, $27/year. Circ.: 41,000. Jo Stich, Editor. **Description:** Covers all types of powerboats, from tournament inboards to offshore boats. **Nonfiction:** For high-performance powerboat owners, on achievements, water-skiing, competitions; technical articles on hull and engine developments; how-to; 500-3,000 words; pay negotiable. **Art:** 35mm or larger formats; $50-$400. **Queries:** Required. **E-queries:** Yes. **Unsolicited mss:** Accepts. **Response:** 3 weeks, SASE. **Freelance Content:** 35%. **Payment:** On publication. **Contact:** Brett Becker.

PRACTICAL HORSEMAN

Box 589, Unionville, PA 19375. 610-380-8977. E-mail: Prachorse@aol.com. Mandy Lorraine, Editor. **Description:** How-to articles conveying leading experts' advice on English riding, training, and horse care. **Tips:** Send clips. **Queries:** Preferred. **Payment:** On acceptance.

PRIVATE PILOT

265 S. Anita Dr., Suite 120, Orange, CA 92868-3310. 714-939-9991. E-mail: bfedork@aol.com. Web site: www.privatepilotmag.com. Monthly. $3.99/issue $21.95/year. Circ.: 60,000. Bill Fedorko, Editor. **Description:** General aviation, for pilots and owners of single and multi-engine aircraft, who want to read about places to go, aircraft, and ways to save money. **Nonfiction:** Fly-in destinations, hands-on, how-to, informative articles for pilots, aircraft owners, and aviation enthusiasts; 1,500-3,000 words; $400-$700. **Art:** $300 fee for photography assignments. **Queries:**

Preferred. **E-queries:** No. **Unsolicited mss:** Accepts. **Response:** 2-4 weeks, SASE. **Freelance Content:** 80%. **Rights:** 1st NA. **Payment:** On publication. **Contact:** Linda Hice, Deputy Editor.

REAL SPORTS

P.O. Box 8204, San Jose, CA 95155-8204. 831-661-4848. E-mail: freelance@real-sports.com. Web site: www.real-sports.com. Bimonthly. $3.95/issue, $16.83/year. Circ.: 150,000. Amy Love, Editor. **Description:** Authoritative coverage of women's sports. Girls' and women's sports, team sports; professional, collegiate and amateur. Uses action-oriented photographs to show drama of competition. **Nonfiction:** Women's sports coverage; 500-2,000 words; $.50/word. **Art:** Slides; pay varies. **Tips:** Submit original, insightful, realistic portraits of women's sports. **Queries:** Required. **E-queries:** Yes. **Unsolicited mss:** Does not accept. **Response:** 2 weeks, SASE. **Freelance Content:** 70%. **Rights:** 1st. **Payment:** On publication.

ROCK & ICE

5455 Sprine Rd., Mezzanine A, Boulder, CO 80301. 303-499-8410. Web site: www.rockandice.com. Bimonthly. Dougald MacDonald. **Description:** For technical rock and ice climbers (sport climbers, mountaineers, alpinists, and other adventurers). **Nonfiction:** Articles, 500-4,000 words; pays $300/published page. **Art:** Slides, b/w photos considered. **Queries:** Preferred.

RUNNER TRIATHLETE NEWS

P.O. Box 19909, 14201 Memorial Dr, Houston, TX 77224. 281-759-0555. E-mail: rtnews@ixnetcom.com. Web site: www.runnertriathletenews.com. Monthly. Circ.: 12,000. Lance Phegley, Editor. **Description:** Covers running, cycling, triathlons, and duathlons in a 5-state area: Texas, Louisiana, Arkansas, Oklahoma, New Mexico. **Nonfiction:** On running for road racing, and multi-sport enthusiasts. Pay varies. **Queries:** Preferred. **E-queries:** Yes. **Unsolicited mss:** Accepts. **Response:** Queries 3-7 days, submissions 1-3 days. **Freelance Content:** 40%. **Payment:** On publication.

RUNNER'S WORLD

Rodale Press, 33 E. Minor St., Emmaus, PA 18098. 610-967-5171. E-mail: rwedit@rodak.com. Web site: www.runnersworld.com. Monthly. Circ.: 550,000. Bob Wischnia, Editor. **Description:** For recreational runners who train for and race in long-distance events. **Nonfiction:** to 3,000 words. **Tips:** No first-time marathon stories. **Queries:** Required. **E-queries:** Yes. **Unsolicited mss:** Accepts. **Response:** 2 weeks, SASE. **Freelance Content:** 25%. **Rights:** worldwide. **Payment:** On acceptance.

RUNNING TIMES

213 Danbury Rd., Wilson, CT 06897-4006. 203-761-1113. E-mail: editor@runningtimes.com. Web site: www.runningtimes.com. 10x/year. $3.99/issue, $24.97/year. Circ.: 70,000. Jonathan Beverly, Editor. **Description:** For

the experienced running participant and fan. **Fiction:** Running related, any genre; 1,500-3,000 words; $100-$500. **Nonfiction:** Book excerpts, essays, historical/ nostalgic, how-to, humor, inspirational, interview/profile, new product, opinion, personal experience, photo feature, travel, news, reports; 1,500-3,000 words; $100-$500. **Columns, Departments:** Training (short topics on enhancing performance, 1,000 words); Sports-Med (applying medical knowledge, 1,000 words); Nutrition, 1,000 words); Cool Down (lighter essay on aspect of the running life), 400 words; 400-1,000 words; $50-$200. **Tips:** Get to know runners and running culture, at participant and professional, elite level. No basic, beginner's how-to, generic fitness/nutrition or generic first-person stories. **Queries:** Preferred. **E-queries:** Yes. **Unsolicited mss:** Accepts. **Response:** Queries 2-4 weeks, submissions 4-6 weeks, SASE. **Freelance Content:** 50%. **Rights:** 1st NA, electronic. **Payment:** On publication.

SAFARI

4800 W. Gates Pass Rd., Tucson, AZ 85745. 520-620-1220. Web site: www.safariclub.org. William Quimby, Editor. **Description:** On worldwide big game hunting and/or conservation projects of Safari Club International's local chapters. **Nonfiction:** Articles, 2,000 words; pays $200, extra for photos. **Payment:** On publication.

SAIL

98 N. Washington St., 2nd Floor, Boston, MA 02114. 617-720-8600. Web site: www.sailing.com. Patience Wales, Editor. **Description:** On sailboats, equipment, racing, and cruising. How-tos on navigation, sail trim, etc. **Nonfiction:** Articles, 1,000-2,500 words, with photos; pays $75-$1,000. **Payment:** On publication. **Contact:** Amy Ullrich.

SAILING

125 E. Main St., P.O. Box 249, Port Washington, WI 53074-1915. 262-284-7760. E-mail: sailing@execpc.com. Web site: sailingonline.com. Monthly. $3.99/issue. Circ.: 40,000. Gregory O. Jones, Editor. **Description:** Illustrated, for the experienced sailor. Covers cruises, races, boat tests, gear and book reviews, personality profiles; also regular columns. **Nonfiction:** No cruising stories that are just logbooks. No "my first sail" stories. Writers must be familiar with sailing, provide good photos, and write for readers who are also genuine sailors; 200-4,000 words; $125-$600. **Art:** 35 mm transparencies; $50-$600. **Tips:** Suggest a story not done in the past four years, include good photographs, and you're in! **Queries:** Preferred. **E-queries:** Yes. **Unsolicited mss:** Accepts. **Response:** 2-4 weeks. **Freelance Content:** 60%. **Payment:** On publication.

SALT WATER SPORTSMAN

263 Summer St., Boston, MA 02210. 617-303-3660. E-mail: barry@saltwatersportsman.com. Web site: www.saltwatersportsman.com. Monthly. $4.99/issue, $22.95/year. Circ.: 161,000. Barry Gibson, Editor. **Description:** Covers salt-water sport fishing in U.S., Canada, Bahamas, Central and

South America. **Fiction:** Fishing stories, humor, mood, nostalgia for back-page "Backcasts"; 1,500-2,000; $1,000. **Nonfiction:** How-to, where-to, for salt-water fishing; 150-1,500; $500-$750. **Columns, Departments:** Short how-to (tackle, rigs, boat equipment); up to 250 words; $150. **Art:** No photos of big piles of dead fish. Stress quality, not quantity; color slides; $100-$500, $1,500 (covers). **Tips:** No blood and thunder, no overly romantic "remember when." **Queries:** Preferred. **E-queries:** Yes. **Unsolicited mss:** Accepts. **Response:** Queries 2 weeks, submissions 2 weeks, SASE. **Freelance Content:** 50%. **Rights:** 1st NA. **Payment:** On acceptance.

SCORE, CANADA'S GOLF MAGAZINE

287 MacPherson Ave., Toronto, Ont., Canada M4V 1A7. 416-928-2909. Web site: www.scoregolf.com. Bob Weeks, Editor. **Description:** On travel, golf equipment, golf history, personalities, and prominent professionals. Canadian content only. **Nonfiction:** Articles, 800-2,000 words (by assignment); pays $125-$600. **Fillers:** 50-100 words, on Canadian golf scene. Rarely uses humor or poems. Pays $10-$25. **Tips:** Query with SASE (IRC); send published clips. **Queries:** Required. **Payment:** On publication.

SEA

Duncan McIntosh Co., 17782 Cowan, Suite C, Irvine, CA 92614. 949-660-6150. E-mail: editorial@goboatingamerica.com. Web site: www.goboatingamerica.com. Monthly. $3.50/issue, $16.97/yr. Circ.: 50,000. Eston Ellis, Managing Editor. **Description:** Four-color, for active West Coast boat owners. Readers are power boaters and sportfishing enthusiasts, Alaska to Mexico, across the Pacific to Hawaii. **Nonfiction:** West Coast boating destination stories, new trends in power boat design, late-season maintenance secrets, how to finance a new boat; 1,200-1,600 words; $250-$400. **Columns, Departments:** Hands-On Boater (do-it-yourself boat maintenance tips); 500-1,200 words; $100-$200. **Art:** 35mm color transparencies; $50, $250 (cover). **Tips:** No articles on sailboats, cruise ships, commercial sportfishing party boats, accidents, historic vessels, or chartering. **Queries:** Not necessary. **E-queries:** Yes. **Unsolicited mss:** Accepts. **Response:** 6 weeks. **Freelance Content:** 60%. **Rights:** 1st NA, reprint (print and electronic). **Payment:** On publication.

SEA KAYAKER

P.O. Box 17170, Seattle, WA 98107. 206-789-9536. E-mail: editorial@seakayakermag.com. Web site: www.seakayakermag.com. Bimonthly. Circ.: 25,000. Christopher Cunningham, Editor. **Description:** For serious paddlers. Guides sea kayakers through salty waters and gives readers both entertainment and information. **Fiction:** Short stories on ocean kayaking; 1,000-3,000 words; pays $.12/word. **Nonfiction:** Articles, 1,500-4,000 words, on ocean kayaking (technical, personal experience, profile, new product). Pays $.12-$.15/word; $.18-$.20/word (by assignment). **Art:** Send photos with submission. **Tips:** Combine personal narrative with a sense of place. **Queries:** Preferred. **E-queries:** Yes. **Unsolicited mss:** Accepts. **Response:** 2 months, SASE. **Freelance Content:** 95%. **Rights:** FNASR or second serial. **Payment:** On publication. **Contact:** Leslie Forsberg, Exec. Editor.

SHARING THE VICTORY

Fellowship of Christian Athletes, 8701 Leeds Rd., Kansas City, MO 64129. 816-921-0909. Web site: www.fca.org. 9x/year. $2.50/issue. Circ.: 90,000. Allen Palmeri, Editor. **Description:** Offers spiritual advice to coaches and athletes, and those whom they influence. **Nonfiction:** 1,200-1,500 words; $100-$250. **Poetry:** Short; $25. **Tips:** All materials (profiles on Christian athletes, poem, etc.) must present Christian inspiration. **Unsolicited mss:** Does not accept. **Freelance Content:** 50%. **Payment:** On publication.

SHOTGUN SPORTS

P.O. Box 6810, Auburn, CA 95604. 530-889-2220; 800-676-8920. Web site: www.shotgunsportsmagazine.com. Frank Kodl, Editor. **Description:** On trap and skeet shooting, sporting clays, hunting with shotguns, reloading, gun tests, and instructional shooting. **Nonfiction:** Articles with photos; pays $25-$200. **Payment:** On publication.

SILENT SPORTS

717 10th St., P.O. Box 152, Waupaca, WI 54981-9990. 715-258-5546. E-mail: info@silentsports.net. Web site: www.silentsports.net. **Description:** On bicycling, cross country skiing, running, canoeing, hiking, backpacking, and other "silent" sports. Must have regional (upper Midwest) focus. **Nonfiction:** Articles, 1,000-2,000 words; pays $50-$100 for features; $20-$50 for fillers. **Queries:** Preferred. **Payment:** On publication.

SKATING

20 First Street, Colorado Springs, CO 80906. 719-635-5200. E-mail: lfawcett@usfsa.org. Web site: www.usfsa.org. 10x/year. $25 (U.S.), $35 (Canada). Circ.: 48,000. Laura Fawcett, Director of Publications/Editor. **Description:** Official publication of the U.S. Figure Skating Association. Communicates information about the sport to USFSA membership and figure-skating fans. Promotes USFSA programs, personalities, and trends that affect the sport. **Nonfiction:** Feature articles profiling interesting USFSA members: athletes, coaches, judges, etc. Looking for what makes these people unique besides their skating; 1,500 words and up; $75-$150. **Art:** Photos, discussed when story is assigned, usually must be included. Pay negotiable. **E-queries:** Yes. **Unsolicited mss:** Accepts. **Response:** 1-3 months, SASE required. **Freelance Content:** 75%. **Rights:** 1st serial. **Payment:** On publication.

SKI

Times Mirror Magazines, 929 Pearl St., Suite 200, Boulder, Co 80302. 303-448-7600. Web site: www.skinet.com. Andrew Bigford, Editor. **Description:** For experienced skiers: profiles, and destination articles. **Nonfiction:** Articles, 1,300-2,500 words; pays from $50. **Columns, Departments:** Ski Life (news items, 100-300 words). **Tips:** Send clips. **Queries:** Preferred. **Payment:** On acceptance.

SKI RACING INTERNATIONAL

6971 Main St., Suite No. 1, Waitsfield, VT 05673. 802-496-7700. Web site: www.skiracing.com. Tim Etchells, Editor. **Description:** On race techniques and conditioning secrets. Coverage of World Cup, pro, collegiate, and junior ski and snowboard competition. **Nonfiction:** Articles by experts, with photos; pay varies.

SKIING

929 Pearl St., #200, Boulder, CO 80302-5108. 303-448-7600. E-mail: backtalk@skiingmag.com. Web site: www.skiingmag.com. 7x/year. $13.94. Circ.: 413,000. Rick Kahl, Editor-in-Chief. **Description:** For the active skier, with destination ideas and instructional tips. Departments include health, fitness, latest trends in skiing industry. Also, profiles of regional runs and their users. **Nonfiction:** Personal adventures on skis, from 2,500 words (no "first time on skis" stories); profiles and interviews, 50-300 words. Pays $150-$300/printed page. **Fillers:** Humorous vignettes, skiing oddities. Pays from $.15/word. **Tips:** Look for a ski adventure new, undiscovered, close to home for a lot of people. Write in first-person. **Queries:** Preferred. **E-queries:** Yes. **Unsolicited mss:** Accepts. **Freelance Content:** 10%. **Contact:** Helen Olsson, Exec. Ed.

SKIN DIVER

6420 Wilshire Blvd., Los Angeles, CA 90048-5515. 323-782-2960. E-mail: skindiver@petersenpub.com. Web site: www.skin-diver.com. Al Hornsby, Editor. **Description:** On scuba diving activities, equipment, and dive sites. **Nonfiction:** Illustrated articles, 500-1,000 words; pays $50/published page. **Payment:** On publication.

SKYDIVING

1725 N. Lexington Ave., DeLand, FL 32724. 904-763-4793. E-mail: sue@skydivingmagazine.com. Web site: www.skydivingmagazine.com. Annual. $4/issue. Circ.: 14,000. Sue Clifton, Editor. **Description:** Techniques, equipment, places, people and events of sport parachuting, written by jumpers for jumpers. **Nonfiction:** Timely news articles on sport and military parachuting; pay varies. **Queries:** Preferred. **E-queries:** Yes. **Unsolicited mss:** Accepts. **Response:** 2 wks. **Freelance Content:** 40%. **Rights:** All.

SNOWBOARDER

P.O. Box 1028, Dana Point, CA 92629. 949-496-5922. Web site: www.snowboardermag.com. Bimonthly. Mark Sullivan, Editor. **Description:** On snowboarding personalities, techniques, and adventure. **Nonfiction:** Articles, with color transparencies or b/w prints; 1,000-1,500 words; pays $150-$800. **Payment:** On publication.

SNOWEST

520 Park Ave., Idaho Falls, ID 83402. 208-524-7000. E-mail: lindstrm@snowest.com. Web site: www.snowest.com. Monthly. $2.95. Circ.:

160,000. Lane Lindstrom, Editor. **Description:** SnoWest is a family-oriented, snow-mobile publication for winter recreationists across U.S. and parts of Canada. **Nonfiction:** Manufacturer reviews, test reports, travel destinations, new product reviews, land use issues, events, technical information, anything related to winter motorized recreation. Also, fillers (500-1,500 words). Query first; 2,000 word max.; $100-$300 (with photos). **Art:** color transparencies (Kodachrome or FujiChrome). **Tips:** Submit 10-15 photos to illustrate a feature, with people involved in every photo; show action; use dawn/dusk for dramatic lighting. **Queries:** Preferred. **Unsolicited mss:** Accepts. **Rights:** FNASR. **Payment:** On publication.

SOCCER AMERICA
P O Box 23704, Oakland, CA 94623. 510-528-5000. Web site: www.socceramerica.com. Paul Kennedy, Editor. **Description:** On soccer news; profiles. **Nonfiction:** Articles, to 500 words; pays $50. **Payment:** On publication.

SOCCER JR.
27 Unquowa Rd., Fairfield, CT 06430. 800-872-2970. E-mail: soccerjrol@aol.com. Web site: www.soccerjr.com. Joe Provey, Editor. **Description:** Fiction and fillers about soccer for readers ages 8 and up. Pays $450 for a feature or story; $250 for shorter pieces. **Queries:** Preferred. **Payment:** On acceptance.

SOUTH CAROLINA WILDLIFE
P. O. Box 167, Columbia, SC 29202-0167. 803-734-3972. Web site: www.scwildlife.com. Bi-monthly. $10/yr. Circ.: 60,000. John E. Davis, Editor. **Description:** Published by Dept. of Natural Resources, for readers interested in the outdoors. **Nonfiction:** South Carolina focus, on outdoor interests; 1,500 words; $.15-$.20/word. **Art:** 35mm or large transparencies; pay varies. **Tips:** Avoid first-person accounts. **Queries:** Preferred. **E-queries:** Yes. **Unsolicited mss:** Accepts. **Response:** 3-6 weeks, SASE. **Freelance Content:** 75%. **Rights:** FNASR. **Payment:** On acceptance. **Contact:** Linda Renshaw, Managing Editor.

SPORT
EMAP USA, 110 Fifth Ave., 3rd Floor, New York, NY 10011. 212-886-3600. E-mail: sport@emapusa.com. Web site: www.emapusa.com. Monthly. Circ.: 1,000,000. Norb Garrett, Editor. **Description:** For the active adult sports fan. Reports on different sports, features on sports figures, as well as reviews and predictions for present and future seasons. **Nonfiction:** Book excerpts, expose, historic/nostalgic, humor, interview/profile, photo feature, travel. Pays $1/word. **Columns, Departments:** Business (800 words), Media (1,200 words), Raw Sport (400 words). **E-queries:** No. **Unsolicited mss:** Does not accept. **Response:** 2 months. **Freelance Content:** 10%. **Rights:** FNASR & electronic. **Payment:** On publication. **Contact:** Steve Gordon.

THE SPORTING NEWS
10176 Corporate Square Dr., #200, St. Louis, MO 63132. 314-997-7111. Web site: www.sportingnews.com. John D. Rawlings, Editor. **Description:** Covers timely topics in baseball, football, basketball, hockey, and other sports. **Tips:** Accepts some guest columns; read back issues carefully before submitting. **Queries:** Preferred.

SPORTS AFIELD
11650 Riverside Dr., North Hollywood, CA 91602. 818-763-9221. E-mail: sportsafield@sportsafield.com. Web site: www.sportsafield.com. Jack Larson, Editor. **Description:** Hunting, fishing, outdoorsmanship, hiking, camping, natural history. **Nonfiction:** Unusual, useful tips, information,. **Fillers:** Jokes, anecdotes, etc. **Columns, Departments:** Almanac, 100-300 words. **Payment:** On publication.

SPORTS ILLUSTRATED
Time-Life Magazine Co., Time & Life Bldg., Rockefeller Center, New York, NY 10020. 212-522-1212. Web site: www.cnnsi.com. Weekly. Circ.: 3,339,000. Bill Colson, Managing Editor. **Description:** Sports news magazine. **Nonfiction:** 800-1,200 words; pay varies. **Queries:** Required. **E-queries:** No. **Unsolicited mss:** Accepts. **Response:** 4 weeks, SASE required. **Freelance Content:** less than 5%. **Rights:** all. **Payment:** On acceptance. **Contact:** Myra Gelband.

SPORTS ILLUSTRATED FOR KIDS
Sports Illustrated Bldg., 135 West 50th St., New York, NY 10020-1393. 212-522-1212. E-mail: sikids@timeinc.com. Web site: www.sikids.com. Monthly. $2.99/$29.95. Circ.: 950,000. Neil Cohen, Editor. **Description:** Focuses on the excitement, joy, and challenge of sports, for boys and girls, ages 8-14. Provides action photos, interactive stories, profiles, puzzles, playing tips. Also, drawings and writing by kids. **Nonfiction:** Current, biographical, sports-related artcles for kids age 8-14; 500-700 words; $500-1,250. **Columns, Departments:** 300-500 words. **Art:** Photos, illustrations (submit non-returnable portfolio). **Queries:** Required. **E-queries:** Yes. **Unsolicited mss:** Accepts. **Response:** 4-6 weeks, SASE. **Rights:** Exclusive. **Payment:** 40% on acceptance, 60% on publication. **Contact:** Kim Fusco.

SPORTS ILLUSTRATED FOR WOMEN
135 W. 50th St., New York, NY 10020-1393. 212-522-2248. Web site: www.siforwomen.com. Bimonthly. $3.50. Circ.: 400,000. Sandy Bailey, Editor. **Description:** For women interested in and/or participating in sports. **Nonfiction:** Service items, short profiles, product reviews, or Q&A series. 300-1,000 words, Pays $1.25/word. **Queries:** Preferred. **E-queries:** Yes. **Unsolicited mss:** Accepts. **Payment:** On publication.

SURFER

PO Box 1028, Dana Point, CA 92629. 949-496-5922.
Web site: www.surfermag.com. Sam George, Editor. **Description:** On surfing and surfers. **Nonfiction:** Articles, 500-5,000 words, photos; pays $.20-$.30/word, $10-$600 for photos. **Payment:** On publication.

SURFING

P.O. Box 3010, San Clemente, CA 92674. 949-492-7873.
E-mail: surfing@mcmullenargus.com. Web site: www.surfingthemag.com. Pete Rocky, Executive Editor. **Description:** Short newsy and humorous articles, 200-500 words. Pay varies. **Tips:** No first-person travel articles. **Payment:** On publication.

T'AI CHI

P.O. Box 39938, Los Angeles, CA 90039. 323-665-7773.
Web site: www.tai-chi.com. Marvin Smalheiser, Editor. **Description:** For persons interested in T'ai Chi Ch'uan (Taijiquan), Qigong, and other internal martial arts, and in similar Chinese disciplines which contribute to fitness, health, and a balanced sense of well being. **Nonfiction:** Style, self-defense techniques, martial arts principles and philosophy, training methods, weapons, case histories of benefits, new or unusual uses for T'ai Chi Ch'uan, interviews; 100-4,500 words; $75-500. **Art:** 4x6 or 5x7 glossy b/w prints. **Tips:** Readers' abilitiesrange from beginners to serious students and teachers. **Queries:** Required. **E-queries:** Yes. **Unsolicited mss:** Does not accept. **Response:** 2-3 weeks, SASE. **Freelance Content:** 85%. **Rights:** 1st NA, reprint. **Payment:** On publication.

TENNIS

810 Seventh Ave., 4th Fl., New York, NY 10019. 212-636-2723.
Web site: www.tennis.com. Mark Woodruff, Editor. **Description:** Instructional articles, features, profiles of tennis stars, grassroots articles, humor. **Nonfiction:** 800-2,500 words, with photos; pay varies. **Tips:** No phone queries. **Queries:** Preferred. **Payment:** On publication.

TENNIS WEEK

341 Madison Ave., #600, New York, NY 10017-3705. 212-808-4750.
E-mail: tennisweek@tennisweek.com. Web site: www.tennisweek.com. 16x/year. $4/issue, $50/year. Circ.: 94,000. Eugene L. Scott, Editor. **Description:** Covers ATP and WTA (men's and women's professional tours), tennis industry, major tournaments, new products, retail stores, schedules, scores, rankings, earnings. **Nonfiction:** In-depth, researched articles on current issues and personalities; 1,500-2,000 words; pay varies. **Queries:** Required. **E-queries:** No. **Unsolicited mss:** Does not accept. **Response:** SASE. **Rights:** 1st NA. **Payment:** On publication.

TEXAS GOLFER

10301 Northwest Freeway, Suite 418, Houston, TX 77092. 713-680-1680.
Web site: www.texasgolfermagazine.com. Monthly. $22. Circ.: 50,000. Bob Gray,

Managing Editor. **Description:** For Texas golfers, with golf-course and tournament information, golf tips, and news. **Nonfiction:** Articles, 800-1,500 words, for north Texas golfers. **Tips:** Most freelance by assignment. **Queries:** Required. **E-queries:** Yes. **Unsolicited mss:** Accepts. **Response:** 2-4 Weeks, SASE. **Freelance Content:** 20%. **Rights:** All. **Payment:** On publication.

TRAILER BOATS

20700 Belshaw Ave., Carson, CA 90746-3510. 310-537-6322. Web site: www.trailerboats.com. Monthly. $3.99/$16.97. Circ.: 98,000. Jim Hendricks, Editor. **Description:** Covers trailer boating: lifestyle, technical and how-to articles. **Nonfiction:** On boat, trailer, or tow-vehicle maintenance and operation; skiing, fishing, and cruising. Also, fillers, humor. 500-2,000 words, pays $100-$700. **Art:** Photos, slides, transparencies. **Queries:** Preferred. **Unsolicited mss:** Accepts. **Response:** Queries 6 weeks, SASE. **Freelance Content:** 51%. **Payment:** On acceptance.

TRIATHLETE

2037 San Elijo, Cardiff, CA 92007. 760-634-4100. Web site: www.triathletemag.com. 12x/year. Christina Gandolfo, Editor. **Description:** Covers the sport of triathlon. **Nonfiction:** Articles, varying lengths, with color slides; pays $.20/word. **Tips:** No "my first triathlon" stories. **Payment:** On publication.

USA CYCLING

One Olympic Plaza, Colorado Springs, CO 80909. 179-578-4581. E-mail: media@usacycling.org. Web site: www.usacycling.org. Bimonthly. $25/yr (nonmembers). Circ.: 65,000., Communications Director. **Description:** On bicycle racing; contains U.S. cycling news, race coverage and results, features, race information, information on training and coaching. **Nonfiction:** Articles on bicycle racing and racers. **Queries:** Preferred.

USA GYMNASTICS

Pan American Plaza, 201 S. Capitol Ave., Suite 300, Indianapolis, IN 46225. 317-237-5050. E-mail: publications@usa-gymnastics.org. Web site: www.usa-gymnastics.org. Bimonthly. $15. Circ.: 95,000. Luan Peszek, Editor. **Description:** Covers gymnastics, including men's artistic and women's artistic, rhythmic, trampoline, and tumbling. Coverage of national and international competitions leading up to Olympic Games. In-depth features on athletes and coaches, provides coaching tips. **Nonfiction:** Gymnastics-related articles; fee negotiable. **Tips:** Query or call first to discuss article and interest level. Welcomes new writers. **Queries:** Preferred. **E-queries:** Yes. **Unsolicited mss:** Accepts. **Response:** 4-6 weeks, SASE required. **Freelance Content:** 10%. **Rights:** 1st. **Payment:** On publication.

VELONEWS

1830 N. 55th St., Boulder, CO 80301. 303-440-0601.
E-mail: vnedit@7dogs.com. Web site: www.velonews.com. 20x/year. Circ.: 48,000.
Kip Mikler, Editor. **Description:** Journal of record for North American bicycle racing, and the world's largest competitive cycling publication. **Nonfiction:** On competitive cycling, training, nutrition; profiles, interviews. No how-to or touring articles; 500-1,500 words; pay varies. **Tips:** Focus on elite, competitive aspect of the sport. **Queries:** Required. **E-queries:** Yes. **Response:** Queries 1 month, SASE. **Freelance Content:** 20%. **Payment:** On publication.

WALKING MAGAZINE

45 Bromfield St., 8th Fl., Boston, MA 02108. 617-574-0076.
Web site: www.walkingmag.com. Seth Bauer, Editor. **Description:** On fitness, health, equipment, nutrition, travel and adventure, and other walking-related topics. **Nonfiction:** Articles, 1,500-2,500 words; pays $750-$1,800. **Columns, Departments:** Shorter pieces, 150-800 words; essays for Ramblings page; pays $100-$500. **Art:** Photos. **Payment:** On acceptance.

THE WATER SKIER

1251 Holy Cow Rd., Polk City, FL 33868-8200. 863-324-4341.
E-mail: satkinson@usawaterski.org. Web site: www.usawaterski.org. 9x/year.
$3.50/issue. Circ.: 35,000. Scott Atkinson, Editor. **Description:** Published by USA Water Ski, national governing body for competitive water skiing in the U.S. **Nonfiction:** On water skiing (interviews, profiles must be assigned), new products, equipment for boating and water skiing; 1,500-3,000 words; pays $100-$150 (for assigned features). **Art:** Color slides. **Tips:** Submit articles about people involved in the competitive sport. **Queries:** Preferred. **E-queries:** No. **Unsolicited mss:** Does not accept. **Response:** Queries 24 hours, submissions 1 week, SASE. **Freelance Content:** 10%. **Rights:** All. **Payment:** On publication.

WATERSKI

World Publications, Inc., 460 N. Orland Ave., Winter Park, FL 32789. 407-628-5662.
Web site: www.worldpub.net. Rob May. **Description:** On boating and water skiing.
Nonfiction: Instructional features, 1,350 words, including sidebars; $125-$500.
Fillers: Quick tips, 350 words; $35. **Tips:** Travel pieces and profiles by assignment only. **Queries:** Preferred. **Payment:** On acceptance.

WESTERN OUTDOORS

3197-E Airport Loop, Costa Mesa, CA 92626. 714-546-4370 x 50.
E-mail: lew@wonews.com. 9x/year. $3.50/$14.95. Circ.: 100,000. Lew Carpenter, Editor. **Description:** On Western saltwater and freshwater fishing techniques, tackle, and destinations. Includes the far west states of California, Oregon, and Washington, also Alaska, Baja California, and British Columbia. **Nonfiction:** On saltwater or freshwater fishing in the West; facts and comments must be attributed to recognized authorities in their fields; 1,500 words; $450-$600. **Art:** Quality photos

and artwork to illustrate articles; 35mm; $50-$300. **Tips:** Present seasonal materials 6 months in advance. Best time to query is June. **Queries:** Required. **E-queries:** Yes. **Unsolicited mss:** Accepts. **Response:** 4-6 weeks, SASE. **Freelance Content:** 75%. **Rights:** FNASR. **Payment:** On acceptance.

WESTERN SPORTSMAN
780 Beatty Street, #300, Vancouver, BC V6B 2MI CA. 604-606-4644. Web site: www.oppub.com. George Gruenefeld, Editor. **Description:** On hunting and fishing in British Columbia, Alberta, Saskatchewan, and Manitoba. **Nonfiction:** Informative, how-tos, to 2,500 words; pays $75-$300. **Art:** Photos. **Payment:** On publication.

WILDFOWL
321 E. Walnut St., Suite 130, Des Moines, IA 50315. 515-243-2472. Web site: www.emapusa.com. R. Sparks, Editor. **Description:** Occasional fiction, humor, related to duck hunters and wildfowl. Pays $400. **Payment:** On acceptance.

WINDSURFING
P.O. Box 2456, Winter Park, FL 32790. 407-628-4802. Web site: www.windsuringmag.com. Jason Upwright, Editor. **Description:** For experienced boardsailors. **Nonfiction:** Features and instructional pieces ($250-$300), tips ($50-$75), extra for photos. **Art:** Fast action photos. **Response:** SASE required.

WINDY CITY SPORTS
1450 W. Randolph, Chicago, IL 60607. 312-421-1551. E-mail: jason@windycitysportsmag.com. Web site: www.windycitysports.com. Monthly. Free. Circ.: 110,000. Jason Effmann, Editor. **Description:** Covers amateur sports in Chicago and surrounding area. **Nonfiction:** up to 1,200 words. **Art:** Hard copies, electronic (300 dpi or more). **Tips:** Need to be knowledgeable in sport covered. **Queries:** Preferred. **E-queries:** Yes. **Unsolicited mss:** Accepts. **Response:** 2 weeks, SASE. **Freelance Content:** 25%. **Rights:** 1st. **Payment:** On publication.

WOODENBOAT
P.O. Box 78, Brooklin, ME 04616. 207-359-4651. Web site: www.woodenboat.com. Bi-monthly. $5.50/$29. Circ.: 110,000. Matthew Murphy, Editor. **Description:** For wooden boat owners, builders, and designers. Covers design, construction, and maintenance. **Nonfiction:** How-to and technical articles on construction, repair, and maintenance; design, history, and use; profiles of outstanding builders, designers; wooden boat lore; 1,000-5,000 words; $.25/word. **Queries:** Required. **Unsolicited mss:** Accepts. **Response:** 3 months, SASE. **Freelance Content:** 70%. **Rights:** 1st worldwide serial. **Payment:** On publication.

YACHTING
20 E. Elm St., Greenwich, CT 06830. 203-625-4480. Web site: www.yachtingnet.com. Annual. $5/issue. Circ.: 132,000. Kenny Wooton,

Executive Editor. **Description:** For the seasoned, upscale boating enthusiast. Covers news and trends, for power, sail, and charter. **Nonfiction:** Articles, 1,500 words, on upscale recreational power- and sail-boating. **Art:** Photos; pays $350-$1,000. **Tips:** No "how-to" articles. **Queries:** Preferred. **Unsolicited mss:** Accepts. **Response:** 1-3 months. **Freelance Content:** 15-25%. **Rights:** All. **Payment:** On publication. **Contact:** Kim Kavin.

YOUNG BUCKS OUTDOORS

P.O. Box 244022, Montgomery, AL 36124-4022. 1-800-240-3337. E-mail: gsmith@buckmasters.com. Web site: www.youngbucks.rivals.com. Quarterly. free. Circ.: 25,000. Gita M. Smith, Editor. **Description:** For readers ages 7-13. Encourages children of all races, gender, and range of abilities to step outside and enjoy themselves. **Fiction:** Stories with child at center of plot. No "I recall when I was a child" stories; up to 800 words; $150-$250. **Nonfiction:** Stories about nature and outdoors pursuits (animals, birds, nature, camping, fishing, hunting, ecology, outdoor pastimes), suitable for a bright 10-year-old. Query first, include photo ideas; 200-1,000 words; $150-$400. **Art:** Prefers slides; $50-$500 (cover). **Tips:** No anti-hunting/fishing sentiments. Appreciates good science content in stories. Stories must be geared to 10-year-old's reading level. **Queries:** Required. **E-queries:** Yes. **Unsolicited mss:** Accepts. **Response:** Queries 1-2 weeks, submissions 3 months, SASE. **Freelance Content:** 90%. **Rights:** 1st print, electronic. **Payment:** On publication.

TEENS

ALL ABOUT YOU

EMAP USA, 6420 Wilshire Blvd., Los Angeles, CA 90048. 323-782-2950. Web site: www.emapusa.com. 3x/year. Circ.: 400,000. **Description:** Teen magazine for younger teens.

BREAKAWAY

8605 Explorer Dr., Colorado Springs, CO 80920. 719-531-3400. Web site: www.family.org. Michael Ross. **Description:** Readers are Christian boys, ages 12-16. **Fiction:** Fiction, to 1,800 words; must have a male slant. **Nonfiction:** Real-life adventure articles, to 1,500 words; pays $.12-$.15/word. **Fillers:** Humor and interesting facts, 500-800 words. **Payment:** On acceptance.

BRIO

Focus on the Family, 8605 Explorer Dr., Colorado Springs, CO 80920. 719-531-3400. E-mail: brio@macmail.fotf.org. Web site: www.briomag.com. Susie Shellenberger. **Description:** For Christian teen girls (profiles, how-to pieces, adventures that show the fun Christian teens can have together). **Fiction:** Fiction, to 2,000 words, with realistic character development, good dialogue, and a plot that teen girls will be drawn to. May contain a spiritual slant but should not be preachy. **Nonfiction:** Articles; pays $.08-$.12/word. **Fillers:** Short humorous pieces. **Payment:** On acceptance.

CAMPUS LIFE

465 Gundersen Dr., Carol Stream, IL 60188. 630-260-6200.
E-mail: clmag@campuslife.net. Web site: www.campuslife.net. 9x/year. $19.95/year.
Circ.: 100,000. Chris Lutes, Editor. **Description:** Advice on love, sex, self-image, popularity, and loneliness, with dramatic stories about teens radically changed by God, plus in-depth profiles about favorites in Christian music. **Fiction:** A "life lesson" with a Christian worldview, by experienced writers; 2,000 words max.; $.15-.20/word. **Nonfiction:** First-person stories presenting the lives of teenagers, ordinary or dramatic; 2,000 words max.; $.15-.20/word. **Tips:** Avoid religious clichés, misuse of religious language, lack of respect or empathy for teenagers. **Queries:** Required. **E-queries:** Accepts. **Unsolicited mss:** Does not accept. **Response:** 4-6 weeks, SASE required. **Freelance Content:** 10%. **Rights:** 1st. **Payment:** On acceptance; kill fee offered. **Contact:** Amber Penney.

COLLEGE BOUND

Ramholtz Publishing, Inc., 2071 Clove Rd., Suite 206,
Staten Island, NY 10304. 718-273-5700.
E-mail: editorial@collegebound.net. Web site: www.collegeboundmag.com.
13x/year. $15/yr. Circ.: 755,000. Gina LaGuardia, Editor. **Description:** For high school students, offers insider's look at all aspects of college life. **Nonfiction:** Real-life student experiences and expert voices. Stories and survival tips on dealing with dorm life, choosing right college, joining a fraternity/sorority. College dating, campus events, scholarship strategies, etc.; 600-1000 words; $75-$100. **Columns, Departments:** Straight Up Strategies (fun service pieces: campus survival tips, admissions advice, etc.); Cash Crunch (money-related tips, scholarship news); Personal Statement (first-person account of a college-related experience); Debate Team (op-ed style views on college controversies); 300-1000 words; $50-$75. **Tips:** Send 2-3 clips or samples of your work (from college newspaper, journalism class, etc.). **Queries:** Preferred. **E-queries:** Yes. **Unsolicited mss:** Accepts. **Response:** Queries 4-5 weeks, submissions 6 weeks. SASE. **Freelance Content:** 75%. **Rights:** FNASR. **Payment:** On publication.

COSMOGIRL!

1790 Broadway, 20th Fl., New York, NY 10019. 212-492-8473.
E-mail: amadrano@hearst.com. Web site: www.cosmogirl.com. Autumn Madrano.
Description: Teen version of *Cosmopolitan*, for girls 12-17. Snappy, teen-friendly style. **Nonfiction:** Articles, 900 words, about outstanding young women; first-person narratives of interesting or unusual happenings in the lives of young women; pay varies. **Fillers:** Fillers, 150 words, on ways readers can get involved in social issues. **Queries:** Preferred. **Payment:** On publication.

ENCOUNTER

8121 Hamilton Ave., Cincinnati, OH 45231. 513-931-4050.
E-mail: kcarr@standardpub.com. Web site: www.standardpub.com. Quarterly. $13.
Circ.: 32,000. Kelly Carr, Editor. **Description:** For Christian teens whose focus is to

encourage other teens in their daily walk with God. Nonfiction, fiction, and daily devotion. **Fiction:** Contemporary teens, with dialogue, uplifting and character-building, conflicts resolved realistically, with moral message; 500-1,100 words; $.08/word (1st), $.06/word (reprint). **Nonfiction:** Current issues from Christian perspective. Also, teen profiles. Topics: school, family, recreation, friends, part-time jobs, dating, music; 500-1,100; pays same as fiction. **Poetry:** from teens only; $15/poem. **Queries:** Not necessary. **E-queries:** Yes. **Unsolicited mss:** Accepts. **Response:** Queries 1-3 weeks, submissions 8-12 weeks, SASE. **Freelance Content:** 40%. **Rights:** 1st, one-time. **Payment:** On acceptance.

ENTERTAINMENTEEN

470 Park Ave. S, Fl8, New York, NY 10016. 212-545-3600.
Hedy End. **Description:** Lifestyle monthly for girls, ages 14-17. **Nonfiction:** Articles include interviews and profiles of popular teen celebrities (actors, actresses, singers, and musicians); pay varies. **Fillers:** Fillers, humor, and jokes welcomed. **Payment:** On publication.

GIRL

22 East 49th St., New York, NY 10017. 212-843-4038.
Web site: www.girlzine.com. Bimonthly. Corynne Corbett, Editorial Director. **Description:** Multicultural appeal for girls of all shapes and sizes. Covers specific interests and needs of African-American teens. Emphasis on girls of color.

GIRL'S LIFE

Girl's Life, 4517 Harford Rd., Baltimore, MD 21214. 410-426-9600.
E-mail: editorial@girlslife.com. Web site: www.girlslife.com. Kelly White, Editor. **Description:** For girls, ages 10-15, on friends, parents, school, siblings, beauty, and fashion. Pays $75-$800. **Tips:** Include resumé and samples, SASE. **Queries:** Required. **E-queries:** No. **Unsolicited mss:** Accepts. **Response:** in 90 days. **Freelance Content:** 25%. **Rights:** 1st NA. **Payment:** On publication.

GO-GIRL.COM

Ramholtz Publishing, Inc., 2071 Clove Rd., Suite 206,
Staten Island, NY 10304. 718-273-5700.
E-mail: editorial@collegebound.net. Web site: www.go-girl.com. Monthly. Gina La Guardia, Editor. **Description:** Addresses social and academic needs of adolescent females. Provides cutting-edge information not only in beauty, fitness, fashion, entertainment, and more, but also in scholastic savviness. **Nonfiction:** Seeking articles with real-life experiences girls will relate to; lessons to learn from others like them; on entertainment personalities they adore and admire; savvy scoops on outstanding high-GPA divas; etc.; 200-600 words; $50-$125. **Columns, Departments:** Go Beauty, Go Fashion, Go Serious, Go Fitness, Go Dottie, Go Play, Go Study. **Queries:** Preferred. **E-queries:** Accepts. **Unsolicited mss:** Does not accept. **Response:** Queries to 2 months, assigned submissions 2 weeks, SASE. **Freelance Content:** 50%. **Rights:** 1st, online. **Payment:** On publication.

GUIDEPOSTS FOR TEENS

P.O. Box 638, Chesterton, IN 46304. 219-929-4429.
E-mail: gp4t@guideposts.org. Web site: www.gp4teens.com. Bimonthly. Circ.: 180,000. Betsy Kohn, Editor. **Description:** Interfaith, offering teens (ages 12-18) true stories filled with adventure and inspiration. Quizzes, how-to, advice, music reviews, Q&As, profiles of role models (celebrity and "real" teens). **Nonfiction:** True first-person dangerous, miraculous, inspirational stories; ghostwritten for (or written by) teens. Protagonist must change in course of the story; must deliver clear inspirational takeaway. **Fillers:** Quizzes (Are you a winner or a Whiner? Are you dating a dud?); How-tos (how to find a good job, how to get along with your parents); Celebrity Q&As, interviews. **Art:** Send samples. **Tips:** No preachy, overtly religious stories. **Queries:** Preferred. **E-queries:** Yes. **Unsolicited mss:** Accepts. **Response:** Queries 4 weeks, submissions 6 weeks, SASE. **Freelance Content:** 80%. **Rights:** All. **Payment:** On acceptance. **Contact:** Allison Payne, Asst. Ed.

HOT

2121 Waukegan Rd., Bannockburn, IL 60015. 847-444-4880.
E-mail: hot@hsmedia.com. Monthly. $4.99/$47.95. Circ.: 250,000. Jennifer Tanalee, Editor. **Description:** For "tweens"—girls between ages of 8-14 years. Offers hot news on cool guys, hip groups, and successful Hollywood girls. Covers fashion trends, beauty, female celebrities, film and television stars, and musical groups. **Nonfiction:** Stories on celebrity-related events. Features on teen celebrities. Concert reviews; 500-2,000 words; $.50/word. **Art:** Slides, photographs, electronic (300 dpi). **Tips:** Successful writers have contacts in the celebrity industry, and use a teen "voice" in their articles. **Queries:** Preferred. **E-queries:** Yes. **Unsolicited mss:** Does not accept. **Freelance Content:** 10%-25%. **Contact:** Laurel Smoke, Asst. Ed.

JUMP

Weider Publications, 21100 Erwin St., Woodland Hills, CA 91367. 818-884-6800.
Web site: www.jumponline.com. 10x/year. **Description:** On topics of interest to teen girls (new products, food and nutrition, sports, health, outrageous trends, and personal experience). **Nonfiction:** Feature articles, 1,500-2,500 words; columns, 600-800 words. **Queries:** Preferred.

KEYNOTER

3636 Woodview Trace, Indianapolis, IN 46268. 317-875-8755.
E-mail: keynoter@kiwanis.org. Web site: www.keyclub.org. 7x/year. $4/year. Circ.: 200,000. Amy L. Wiser, Executive Editor. **Description:** For teens, ages 13-18, offering informative, entertaining articles on self-help, school, and community issues. **Nonfiction:** For service-minded high-school students; well-researched, with expert references, interviews with respected sources; 1,200 words; $200-$400. **Tips:** No first-person accounts, fiction, or articles for younger readers. **Queries:** Preferred. **E-queries:** Yes. **Unsolicited mss:** Accepts. **Response:** Queries 1-4 months, submissions 1 week, SASE required. **Freelance Content:** 65%. **Rights:** FNASR. **Payment:** On acceptance.

LATINGIRL

70 Hudson Street, 5th Floor, Hoboken, NJ 07030. 201-876-9600. E-mail: editor@latingirlmag.com. Web site: www.latingirlmag.com. Bi-monthly. $2.95/$7.95. Circ.: 120,000. Lu Herrera, Editor. **Description:** For smart, savvy Hispanic teen girls who care about their families, friends, cultural backgrounds, appearances, education and being heard. Shares joys, hopes, and aspirations, and celebrates being bicultural. **Nonfiction:** First-person teen stories, celebrity interviews and news, latest fashion/beauty trends, insightful peer stories, resources, advice on dating, health, family life, school and careers; 100-1,200 words; $1/word. **Fillers:** Quizzes with 8-10 questions and answer key; on personalities, relationships, friendships, fashion, fun; 1,000-1,200 words; $700 fee. **Columns, Departments:** Fashion/beauty stories; 100-400 words; $1/word or fee. **Tips:** Readers aged 12-19, focuses editorial content to the 17-year-old. Send query idea for specific department, with outline, and be patient. No phone calls please. No simutaneous queries. **Queries:** Required. **Unsolicited mss:** Accepts. **Response:** 2-6 months, SASE. **Freelance Content:** 80%. **Rights:** 1st NA serial, electronic. **Payment:** On publication.

LISTEN

55 W. Oak Ridge Dr., Hagerstown, MD 21740. 301-393-4019. E-mail: listen@healthconnection.org. Monthly. $24.95/year. Circ.: 50,000. Larry Becker, Editor. **Description:** Provides teens with vigorous, positive, educational approach to problems arising from use of tobacco, alcohol, and other drugs. **Fiction:** True-to-life stories; 1,000-1,200 words; $.05-$.10/word. **Nonfiction:** For teenagers, on problems of alcohol and drug abuse; personality profiles; self-improvement; drug-free activities; 1,000-1,200 words; $.05-$.10/word. **Poetry:** From high-school students only. **Fillers:** puzzles; $15-$25. **Tips:** Use upbeat approach. **Queries:** Preferred. **E-queries:** Accepts. **Unsolicited mss:** Accepts. **Response:** 2 weeks queries, 3 months submissions; SASE. **Rights:** FNASR. **Payment:** On acceptance. **Contact:** Anita Jacobs.

MERLYN'S PEN

P.O. Box 910, East Greenwich, RI 02818. 401-885-5175. E-mail: merlynspen@aol.com. Web site: www.merlynspen.com. Annual. $29.95. Circ.: 5,000. R. James Stahl, Editor. **Description:** Fiction, essays, and poems by America's teens. All work written by students. Looking for new voices, teen writers who have something to say and say it with eloquence, honesty, and distinctiveness. **Fiction:** Realistic fiction about contemporary teen life; also science fiction, fantasy, adventure, historical fiction; to 8,500 words; $20-$200. **Nonfiction:** Personal essays, memoirs, autobiographies, humorous or descriptive essays; 500-5,000 words. **Poetry:** Free verse, metric verse; $20-$50. **Art:** b/w illustrations; by assignment, submit samples. **Tips:** No adult authors. **Queries:** Required. **E-queries:** No. **Unsolicited mss:** Accepts. **Response:** 10-12 weeks, SASE. **Freelance Content:** 100%. **Rights:** All. **Payment:** On publication.

THE NEW YORK TIMES UPFRONT
555 Broadway, New York, NY 10012-3999. 212-343-6100.
Web site: www.nytimes.com/upfront. Biweekly. Herbert Buchsbaum, Editor.
Description: For teenagers. **Nonfiction:** News articles, 500-1,500 words; pays $150 and up. **Queries:** Preferred. **Payment:** On acceptance.

ODYSSEY
Cobblestone Publishing, 30 Grove St., Suite C,
Peterborough, NH 03458. 603-924-7209.
Web site: odysseymagazine.com. 9x/year. Circ.: 21,000. Elizabeth Lindstrom, Editor.
Description: Features, 750-1,000 words, on science and technology, for readers, ages 10-16. Science-related fiction, myths, legends, and science-fiction stories. Activities. Pays $.20-$.25/word. **Fiction:** Science-related stories, poems, science fiction, retold legends, etc., relating to theme; up to 1,000 words; $.20-$.25/word. **Nonfiction:** Subjects directly and indirectly related to theme; with little-known information (but don't overlook the obvious); 720-950 words; $.20-$.25/word. **Fillers:** Critical-thinking activities, experiments, models, science fair projects, etc., for children alone, with adult supervision, or in classroom setting. **Columns, Departments:** Far Out; Places, Media, People to Discover; Fantastic Journeys; 400-650 words. **Art:** Transparencies, slides, color prints; $15-$100 (b/w); $25-$100 (color). **Tips:** Material must relate to specific theme; contact for upcoming list. Scientific accuracy, lively approach, and inclusion of primary research are crucial to being accepted. **Payment:** On publication.

SCHOLASTIC SCOPE
Scholastic, Inc., 555 Broadway, New York, NY 10012. 212-343-6100.
Web site: www.scholastic.com. **Description:** Fiction for 15-18-year-olds, with 4th-6th grade reading ability. Short stories, 400-1,200 words, on teenage interests and relationships; family, job, and school situations. Plays to 5,000 words. Pays good rates. **Payment:** On acceptance.

SCIENCE WORLD
Scholastic, Inc., 555 Broadway, New York, NY 10012-3999. 212-343-6100.
Web site: scholastic.com. Mark Bregman. **Description:** On life science, earth science, physical science, environmental science, or health science, for 7th-10th graders, ages 12-15. **Nonfiction:** Science articles, 750 words; $200-$650. **Columns, Departments:** Science news, 200 words; pays $100-$125. **Tips:** Submit well-researched proposal, with anticipated sources, 2-3 clips of your work, and SASE. Writing should be lively, with an understanding of teens' perspectives and interests.

SEVENTEEN
850 Third Ave., 9th Fl., New York, NY 10022. 212-407-9700.
Web site: www.seventeen.com. Monthly. $2.99/issue, $11.96/10-issue subscription. Circ.: 2,340,000. Patrice Adcroft, **Description:** Popular beauty/fashion magazine, written for young women, ages 13-21. **Fiction:** Stories with issues important and

familiar to our readers, that also challenge them and make them think; 1,000-3,500 words. **Nonfiction:** Feature stories unique and relevant to teenage girls; up to 2,500 words; $1-$1.25/word. **Columns, Departments:** Features, Guys, Voice, Eat, Bodyline, College, Quizzes; 500-1,200 words; pay varies. **Tips:** Ideas should spring from teenage viewpoint and sensibility, not that of parent, teacher, other adult. **Queries:** Preferred; query with clips or complete manuscript. **E-queries:** Accepts. **Unsolicited mss:** Accepts. **Response:** 1-4 weeks, SASE. **Freelance Content:** 30%. **Rights:** 1st NA. **Payment:** On publication.

SISTERS IN STYLE

233 Park Ave. S., 5th Fl., New York, NY 10003. 212-780-3500.
Web site: www.sterlingmacfadden.com. Bimonthly. Cynthia Marie Horner, Editor. **Description:** "For Today's Young Black Woman." Beauty and fashion articles, quizzes, and advice for African-American teens. **Nonfiction:** Pay varies. **Queries:** Preferred. **Payment:** On publication.

16 SUPERSTARS

Primedia Enthusiast Group, 470 Park Ave. S., Fl 8,
New York, NY 10016. 212-545-3600.
6x/year. Circ.: 70,000. **Description:** Entertainment topics for teens.

SPANK!

Laughing Dog Publishing, 11, 2206a 4th Street SW,
Calgary, Alberta, Canada T2S 1W9. 403-571-0170.
E-mail: cassady@spankmag.com. Web site: www.spankmag.com. Robin Thompson, diva@spankmag.com. **Description:** E-zine written by youth for youth, "for ages 13 and up."

STUDY BREAKS

3809 Cherrywood Rd., Austin, TX 78722-1217. 512-477-3411.
Web site: www.studybreaks. 7x/year. Circ.: 10,000. Steve Viner. **Description:** For students. **Nonfiction:** Spring-break travel, European travel. **Poetry:** Drinking/smoking poems. **Fillers:** Puzzles. **Columns, Departments:** Music, videogames. **Tips:** We look for humor. **Queries:** Not necessary. **E-queries:** Yes. **Unsolicited mss:** Accepts. **Payment:** On publication.

TEEN

6420 Wilshire Blvd., Los Angeles, CA 90046. 323-782-2950.
Web site: www.teenmag.com. Tommi Lewis, Editor-in-Chief. **Description:** On issues of interest to middle-school girls. **Fiction:** Short stories (mystery, teen situations, adventure, romance, humor), for teens; 2,500-4,000 words; pays from $250-$450. **Nonfiction:** Articles, 1,000-1,500 words; pay varies. **Rights:** All. **Queries:** Preferred. **Payment:** On acceptance.

TEEN VOICES

515 Washington St., Boston, MA 02111. 617-426-5505.
E-mail: womenexp@teenvoices.com. Web site: www.teenvoices.com. Quarterly.
$2.95/$19.95. Circ.: 25,000. Alison Amoroso, Editor. **Description:** Written by, for,
and about teenaged and young-adult women. Offers a place to share thoughts with
others the same age. **Fiction:** Short stories, any subject and length. **Nonfiction:**
About any issue that is important to you, or an important experience you've had.
Poetry: Your feelings, thoughts, etc. **Columns, Departments:** Opinions/editorial
pieces. **Art:** Digital file (.tif or .eps), or hardcopy. **Tips:** Be honest, candid and true to
yourself. Appreciates material that promotes feminism, equality, self-esteem, "You're
more than just a pretty face." **Queries:** Not necessary. **E-queries:** Yes. **Unsolicited
mss:** Accepts. **Response:** Submissions, a few days, SASE not required. **Rights:** 1st.
Payment: In copies.

TIGER BEAT

Sterling/MacFadden Partnership, 470 Park Ave. South,
New York, NY 10016-6868. 212-545-3603.
Louise Barile, Editor. **Description:** On young people in show business and the music
industry. **Nonfiction:** Articles, to 4 pages; pays varying rates. **Queries:** Preferred.
Payment: On acceptance.

TWIST

270 Sylvan Ave., Englewood Cliffs, NJ 07632. 201-569-6699.
Web site: www.twistmagazine.com. Monthly. Jeannie Kim. **Description:** On relationships, entertainment, fitness, fashion, and other topics, for today's young women. **Nonfiction:** Articles, 1,500 words. **Tips:** Mostly staff-written; queries with clips required.

WHAT

108-93 Lombard Ave., Winnipeg, Manitoba, Canada R3B 3B1. 204-985-8160.
E-mail: l.malkin@2ci.mb.ca. Web site: www.whatmagnet.com. Bimonthly. $14. Circ.:
250,000. Leslie Malkin, Editor. **Description:** Canadian teen pop-culture magazine
(including music, movie and TV interviews, typical issues and themes affecting readers, ages 13-19). **Nonfiction:** Charged, edgy, unconventional, from pop culture to
social issues; 450 words and up; pay negotiable. **Tips:** Query with working story title,
1-sentence explanation of angle, justification and proposed treatment, potential contacts, proposed length. Welcomes new writers. **Queries:** Required. **E-queries:** Yes.
Unsolicited mss: Does not accept. **Response:** 1-2 months, SASE. **Freelance
Content:** 60%. **Rights:** 1st Canadian. **Payment:** On publication.

WITH

722 Main St., Box 347, Newton, KS 67114. 316-283-5100.
Web site: www.withonline.org. Bi-monthly. $23.50 yr. Circ.: 5,000. Carol Duerksen,
Editor. **Description:** "The Magazine for Radical Christian Youth." For teens,
empowers them to be radically committed to Jesus Christ, to peace and justice, and
to sharing God's good news through words and action. **Fiction:** First-person stories;

1,500 words; $100. **Nonfiction:** Creative, "inside the life of a teen," first-person preferred. Avoid preaching. Themes: sex and dating, Holy Spirit, integrity, service and mission; 1,500 words; pay varies. **Poetry:** Yes. **Fillers:** Wholesome humor. **Art:** b/w 8x10s. **Queries:** Not necessary. **E-queries:** Yes. **Unsolicited mss:** Accepts. **Response:** 1 month, SASE. **Freelance Content:** 20%. **Rights:** One-time and website. **Payment:** On acceptance.

YM

375 Lexington Ave., 8th Floor, New York, NY 10017-5514. E-mail: sglassman@ym.com. Web site: www.ym.com. 10x/year. $2.99/issue. Circ.: 12,000,000. Annemarie Iverson, Editor. **Description:** Sourcebook for fashion, beauty, boys, advice, and features for girls, ages 12-24. **Queries:** Required. **Unsolicited mss:** Accepts. **Response:** Queries 1-2 months. **Freelance Content:** 40%. **Payment:** On publication.

YOU!

29963 Mulholland Hwy., Agoura Hills, CA 91301. 818-991-1813. E-mail: youmag@earthlink.net. Web site: www.youmagazine.com. **Description:** For teenagers, especially on moral issues, faith, and contemporary pop culture, viewed from the Catholic/Christian perspective. No payment. **Nonfiction:** Articles, 200-1,000 words.

YOUNG AND ALIVE

P.O. Box 6097, Lincoln, NE 68506. E-mail: crsnet.compuserve.net. Quarterly. Free to blind youth. Circ.: 25,000. Gaylena Gibson, Editor. **Description:** For blind and visually impaired young adults, from a non-denominational Christian viewpoint, on adventure, biography, camping, careers, health, history, hobbies, holidays, marriage, nature, practical Christianity, sports, and travel. **Nonfiction:** Features, 800-1,400 words, pay varies. **Art:** slides, prints; $10/photo. **Queries:** Not necessary. **E-queries:** No. **Unsolicited mss:** Accepts. **Response:** Queries 6 months, submissions 9 months, SASE. **Freelance Content:** 90%. **Rights:** One-time. **Payment:** On acceptance.

YOUNG SALVATIONIST

The Salvation Army, P.O. Box 269, Alexandria, VA 22313. 703-684-5500. E-mail: ys@usn.salvationarmy.org. Tim Clark, Editor. **Description:** Seeks to teach Christian view of everyday living, for teenagers. **Nonfiction:** Articles (to 600-1,200 words); short-shorts, first-person testimonies (600-800 words). Pays $.15/word ($.10/word for reprints). **Response:** SASE required. **Payment:** On acceptance.

YOUTH UPDATE

St. Anthony Messenger Press, 1615 Republic St., Cincinnati, OH 45210. 513-241-5615. Web site: www.americancatholic.org. Monthly. Circ.: 23,000. Carol Ann Morrow, Editor. **Description:** Newsletter, to support the growth of Catholic teens, of high school age, in a life of faith. **Nonfiction:** Biblical books; personal growth; doctrinal truths; issues of peace and justice; 2,300 words; $.16/word. **Queries:** Required. **E-queries:** Yes. **Unsolicited mss:** Accepts. **Response:** 6-8 weeks. **Freelance Content:** 50%. **Payment:** On acceptance.

YOUTHLINE USA FUN & FEATURE MAGAZINE

Bartash Printing, 300 Knickerbocker Rd., Cresskill, NJ 07626. 201-568-1333. Web site: www.youthline-usa.com. Monthly. Circ.: 250,000. **Description:** Educational magazine for children and young teens.

TRADE & TECHNICAL

AMERICAN CITY & COUNTY

155 Village Blvd., Princeton, NJ 08540. E-mail: anet@intertec.com. Web site: www.industryclick.com. Janet Ward. **Description:** On local government issues (wastewater, water, solid waste, financial management, information technology, etc.). **Nonfiction:** Articles, 600-2,500 words. **Tips:** Readers are elected and appointed local government officials.

AMERICAN COIN-OP

500 N. Dearborn St., Ste 1000, Chicago, IL 60610-9988. 312-337-7700. Paul Partika, Editor. **Description:** Articles, on successful coin-operated laundries (management, promotion, decor, maintenance). SASE for guidelines. **Nonfiction:** To 2,500 words; pays from $.08/word. **Art:** b/w photos; pays $8/each. **Queries:** Preferred.

AMERICAN DEMOGRAPHICS

P.O. Box 10580, Riverton, NJ 08076. 800-529-7502. Web site: www.demographics.com. Jill Kirschenbaum, Executive Editor. **Description:** Articles, 500-2,000 words, on four key elements of a consumer market (size, needs and wants, ability to pay, and how it can be reached). With specific examples of how companies market to consumers. Readers include marketers, advertisers, and planners. **Queries:** Preferred.

AMERICAN FARRIERS JOURNAL

P.O. Box 624, Brookfield, WI 53008-0624. 262-782-4480. Web site: www.americanfarriers.com. Frank Lessiter, Editor. **Description:** Articles, 800-2,000 words, on farriery issues, hoof care, tool selection, equine lameness, and horse handling. **Nonfiction:** Pays $.50/published line. **Art:** Pays $13/illustration or photo. **Queries:** Preferred. **Payment:** On publication.

AMUSEMENT TODAY
P.O. Box 5427, Arlington, TX 76005. 817-460-7220.
Web site: www.amusementtoday.com. Monthly. Circ.: 4,500. **Description:** Amusement industry publication.

AREA DEVELOPMENT
400 Post Ave., Westbury, NY 11590-2289. 516-338-0900.
E-mail: gerri@area-development.com. Web site: www.areadevelopment.com. Monthly. Circ.: 45,500. Geraldine Gambale, Editor. **Description:** Covers site-selection and facility-planning issues for executives at industrial companies. **Nonfiction:** Stories on location issues for industrial companies (site selection, real estate, taxes, labor, energy, environment, government regulations, etc.); 2,000 words; $.30/word. **Queries:** Preferred. **E-queries:** Yes. **Unsolicited mss:** Accepts. **Freelance Content:** 90%. **Payment:** On publication.

AUTOMATED BUILDER
1445 Donlon St., Suite 16, Ventura, CA 93003. 805-642-9733.
E-mail: info@automatedbuilder.com. Web site: www.automatedbuilder.com. Annual. Circ.: 25,000. Don Carlson, Editor. **Description:** Focuses on home manufacturers and dealers. **Nonfiction:** Technical articles on methods, materials and technologies for in-plant building industry; 750-1,000 words; $300. **Queries:** Required. **Unsolicited mss:** Accepts. **Response:** Queries 10 days, SASE required. **Freelance Content:** 10%. **Payment:** On acceptance. **Contact:** Don Carlson.

BEBIDAS
P.O. Box 16116, Cleveland, OH 44116-0116. 440-331-9100.
E-mail: bebidas@aol.com. Bimonthly. Circ.: 8,000. **Description:** Trade magazine for the Spanish-language beverage industry.

BUILDER
Hanley-Wood, One Thomas Cir. NW, Suite 600, Washington, DC 20005.
202-452-0800.
Web site: www.hbrnet.com. Boyce Thompson, Editor. **Description:** On trends and news in home building (design, marketing, new products, etc.). **Nonfiction:** Articles; to 1,500 words; pay negotiable. **Queries:** Preferred. **Payment:** On acceptance.

BUSINESS AND COMMERCIAL AVIATION
4 International Dr., Suite 260, Rye Brook, NY 10573. 914-933-7600.
E-mail: p02cs@mcgraw-hill.com. Web site: www.aviationnow.com. **Description:** For pilots, on use of private aircraft for business transportation. **Nonfiction:** Articles; 2,500 words, with photos; pays $100-$500. **Queries:** Preferred. **Payment:** On acceptance.

CALIFORNIA LAWYER

1145 Market St., 8th Fl., San Francisco, CA 94103.
E-mail: tema_goodwin@dailyjournal.com. Web site: dailyjournal.com. Monthly.
$5/issue, $45/year. Circ.: 140,000. Peter Allen, Senior Editor. **Description:** For lawyers (distributed to active bar members). Offers news, commentary, features, essays, technology, some legal advice. **Nonfiction:** For California attorneys on legal subjects (or legal aspects of political or social issues); how-tos, law-office technology; 300 words and up; $300-$2,500. **Tips:** Start with something small in news section. **Queries:** Preferred. **E-queries:** No. **Unsolicited mss:** Accepts. **Response:** 1-6 weeks. **Freelance Content:** 80%. **Payment:** On acceptance. **Contact:** Tema Goodwin, Managing Editor.

CLEANING AND MAINTENANCE MANAGEMENT

13 Century Hill Dr., Latham, NY 12110-2197. 518-783-1281.
Web site: www.cmmonline.com. Chris Sanford, Managing Editor. **Description:** On managing efficient cleaning and custodial/maintenance operations; also technical/mechanical how-tos. **Nonfiction:** Articles, 500-1,200 words; pays to $300 for commissioned features. **Art:** Photos. **Queries:** Preferred. **Payment:** On publication.

COLLEGE STORE EXECUTIVE

825 Old Country Rd., P.O. Box 1500, Westbury, NY 11590. 516-334-3030.
Web site: www.ebmpubs.com. Janice A. Costa, Editor. **Description:** For college store industry only; news, profiles. **Nonfiction:** Articles, 1,000 words; pays $4-$5/column inch (extra for photos). **Tips:** No general business or how-to articles. **Queries:** Preferred. **Payment:** On publication.

COMMERCIAL CARRIER JOURNAL

Cahner Business Information, Valley Forge Park Place, 1018 W. Ninth Ave., 3rd Floor, King of Prussia, PA 19406-1223. 610-205-1061.
E-mail: prichards@cahners.com. Web site: www.ccjmagazine.com. Paul Richards, Executive Editor. **Description:** Thoroughly researched articles on private fleets and for-hire trucking operations. Pays from $50. **Queries:** Required. **Payment:** On acceptance.

THE CONSTRUCTION SPECIFIER

Construction Specifications Institute, 99 Canal Center Plaza, Suite 300, Alexandria, VA 22314. 800-689-2900.
E-mail: csimail@csinet.org. Web site: www.csinet.org. Katie Sears, Acting Editor.
Description: Articles, 2,000-3,000 words, on the "nuts and bolts" of nonresidential construction, for owners/facility managers, architects, engineers, specifiers, contractors, and manufacturers.

COOKING FOR PROFIT

P.O. Box 267, Fond du Lac, WI 54936-0267. 920-923-3700.
Web site: www.cookingforprofit.com. Colleen Phalen, Editor. **Description:** For

foodservice professionals. **Nonfiction:** Profiles of successful restaurants, chains, and franchises, schools, hospitals, nursing homes, etc. Also, case studies on energy management in foodservice environment. Business-to-business articles. Pay varies. **Payment:** On publication.

DAIRY FOODS

Cahners Publishing Co., 2000 Clearwater Dr., Oak Brook, IL 60523-8809. 630-320-7485. Web site: www.dairyfoods.com. Dave Fusaro, Editor. **Description:** On innovative dairies, processing operations, marketing, new products for milk handlers and makers of dairy products. **Nonfiction:** Articles, to 2,500 words; pay varies.

DEALERSCOPE

North American Publishing Co., 401 N. Broad St., 5th Floor Philadelphia, PA 19108. 215-238-5300. Web site: www.dealerscope.com. Janet Pinkerton, Editor. **Description:** On new consumer electronics, computer and electronics products, and new technologies. **Nonfiction:** Articles, to 1,000 words, pay varies. **Tips:** Query with clips and resumé. **Payment:** On publication.

DENTAL ECONOMICS

P.O. Box 3408, Tulsa, OK 74101. 918-835-3161. Web site: www.dentaleconomics.com. Joseph Blaes, Editor. **Description:** On business side of dental practice, patient and staff communication, personal investments. **Nonfiction:** Articles, 1,200-3,500 words; pays $100-$400. **Payment:** On acceptance.

DRUG TOPICS

5 Paragon Dr., Montvale, NJ 07645-1742. 201-358-7951. Web site: www.drugtopics.com. Harold E. Cohen, R.P., Editor. **Description:** News items, 500 words, on pharmacists and associations; pays $100-$150. Merchandising features, 1,000-1,500 words; pays $200-$400. **Queries:** Preferred. **Payment:** On acceptance.

ELECTRONIC INFORMATION REPORT

Simba Information, P.O. Box 4234, Stamford, CT 06907. 203-358-4100. Web site: www.simbanet.com. Weekly. **Description:** Covers all aspects of the marketing of electronic information.

ELECTRONIC MUSICIAN

P.O. Box 1929, Marion, OH 43306. E-mail: emeditorial@intertec.com. Web site: www.emusician.com. Monthly. Steve Oppenheimer, Editor. **Description:** On audio recording, live sound engineering, technical applications, and product reviews. **Nonfiction:** Articles, 1,500-3,500 words; pays $350-$750. **Payment:** On acceptance.

ENGINEERED SYSTEMS

7314 Hart St., Mentor, OH 44060. 248-362-3700.
Web site: www.esmagazine.com. Robert L. Beverly, Editor. **Description:** Articles, case histories, and product information related to engineered HVAC systems in commercial, industrial, or institutional buildings. **Nonfiction:** Pays $4.75/column inch, $12/illustration. **Queries:** Preferred. **Payment:** On publication.

THE ENGRAVERS JOURNAL

26 Summit St., P. O. Box 318, Brighton, MI 48116.
E-mail: info@engraversjournal.com. Web site: www.engraversjournal.com. Monthly. Rosemary Farrell, Editor. **Description:** Trade magazine for engravers. **Nonfiction:** Articles on small business operations. Pays $75-$300. **Queries:** Preferred. **E-queries:** No. **Unsolicited mss:** Accepts. **Rights:** Varies. **Payment:** On acceptance.

FIRE CHIEF

35 E. Wacker Dr., Suite 700, Chicago, IL 60601-2198. 312-726-7277.
E-mail: www.firechief.com. Web site: www.firechief.com. Monthly. Scott Baltic. **Description:** For fire officers. **Nonfiction:** Articles, 1,000-5,000 words; pays to $.30/word. **Columns, Departments:** Training Perspectives, EMS Viewpoint, Sound Off; 1,000-1,800 words. **Queries:** Preferred. **Response:** SASE. **Payment:** On publication.

FIREHOUSE

Cygnus Publishing Co., 445 Broad Hollow Rd., Suite 21,
Melville, NY 11747. 631-845-2700.
Web site: www.firehouse.com. Harvey Eisner, Editor-in-Chief. **Description:** On-the-scene accounts of fires, trends in firefighting equipment, fire-service issues, lifestyles. **Nonfiction:** Articles, 500-2,000 words. **Queries:** Preferred. **Response:** SASE required.

FISHING TACKLE RETAILER

P.O. Box 17900, Montgomery, AL 36141; 5845 Carmichael Rd., Montgomery, AL 36117. 334-272-9530.
Dave Ellison, Editor. **Description:** For merchants who carry angling equipment. Business focus; provides practical information for improving management and merchandising. **Nonfiction:** Articles, 300-1,250 words. **Payment:** On acceptance.

FOOD MANAGEMENT

The Penton Media Building, 1300 E. Ninth St., Cleveland, OH 44114. 216-696-7000.
Web site: www.penton.com. John Lawn, Editor. **Description:** On food service in hospitals, nursing homes, schools, colleges, prisons, businesses, and industrial sites. **Nonfiction:** Trends, legislative issues, how-tos, management, and retail-oriented food service pieces. **Queries:** Required.

FOUNDATION NEWS & COMMENTARY

1828 "L" Street NW, Washington, DC 20036. 202-467-0467. E-mail: curtj@cof.org. Web site: www.foundationnews.org. Bimonthly. $48/year. Circ.: 10,000. Jody Curtis, Editor. **Description:** Covers the world of grant making, for professional grant makers, volunteer trustees, and grant seekers. **Nonfiction:** 1,200-3,000 words; pay varies. **Tips:** Avoid fundraising topics. **Queries:** Required. **E-queries:** Yes. **Unsolicited mss:** Accepts. **Response:** Varies. **Freelance Content:** 25%. **Rights:** All. **Payment:** On acceptance.

GLASS DIGEST

Ashlee Publishing, 18 E. 41st St., New York, NY 10017-6222. 212-376-7722. Web site: www.ashlee.com. Julian Phillips, Editor. **Description:** On building projects and glass/metal dealers, distributors, storefront and glazing contractors. **Nonfiction:** Articles, 1,200-1,500 words. **Payment:** On publication.

GOVERNMENT EXECUTIVE

1501 "M" St. N.W., #300, Washington, DC 20005. 202-739-8501. E-mail: govexec@govexec.com. Web site: govexec.com. Timothy Clark, Editor. **Description:** Articles, 1,500-3,000 words, for civilian and military government workers at the management level.

HEATING/PIPING/AIR CONDITIONING/ENGINEERING

1300 E. Ninth St., Cleveland, OH 44114. 216-696-7000. Web site: www.hpac.com. Michael G. Ivanovich, Editor. **Description:** On heating, piping, and air conditioning systems and related issues (indoor air quality, energy efficiency), for industrial plants and large buildings only. **Nonfiction:** Articles, to 3,500 words; pays $70/printed page. **Queries:** Preferred. **Payment:** On publication.

HOME SHOP MACHINIST

2779 Aero Park Dr., Box 1810, Traverse City, MI 49686. 231-946-3712. E-mail: jrice@villagepress.com. Web site: www.homeshopmachinist.com. Bimonthly. $5.95. Circ.: 36,000. Joe D. Rice, Editor. **Description:** For machinists, how-to articles. Readers are machinists, some as a hobby, but all very serious about machining. **Nonfiction:** Machine how-to projects. Photos, drawings and text required. No people profiles; $40/page. **Art:** $9/photo. **Tips:** Write in first-person only; accuracy and detail essential. **Queries:** Preferred. **E-queries:** Yes. **Unsolicited mss:** Accepts. **Response:** Queries 1 week, submissions 1 month, SASE required. **Freelance Content:** 95%. **Rights:** FNASR. **Payment:** On publication.

HOSPITALS & HEALTH NETWORKS

One N. Franklin St., 29th Fl., Chicago, IL 60606. 312-893-6800. Web site: www.hhnmag.com. Bill Santamour, Managing Editor. **Description:** For health-care executives, hospital administrators, on financing, staffing, coordinating, and providing facilities for health-care services. **Nonfiction:** Articles, 250-1,800 words. **Payment:** On publication.

INDUSTRIA ALIMENTICIA

Stagnito Communications, 1935 Shermer Rd., Ste 100, Northbrook, IL 60062. 847-205-5660. Web site: www.stagnito.com. Monthly. Circ.: 45,000. **Description:** Spanish-language publication. Covers the food-processing industry in Latin America.

INTERNAL MEDICINE WORLD REPORT

241 Forsgate Drive, Jamesburg, NJ 08831. 732-656-1140. E-mail: jcharnow@mwc.com. Web site: www.imwronline.com. Monthly. Circ.: 104,000. Jody A Charnow, Editor. **Description:** Provides practicing internists with relevant clinical news. **Nonfiction:** Articles based on scientific presentations at medical conferences or reports in major medical journals; 150-250 words; $.50/word. **Tips:** No articles animal or test-tube studies. No articles of a promotional nature, such as those reporting on talks given at events sponsored by drug companies. Welcomes new writers. **Queries:** Preferred. **E-queries:** Yes. **Unsolicited mss:** Accepts. **Response:** 1 week, SASE required. **Freelance Content:** 90%. **Rights:** All (print and electronic). **Payment:** On publication.

JD JUNGLE

Jungle Interactive Media, 10 E. 18th Street, 8th Fl, New York, NY 10003. 212-352-0840. E-mail: editors@jdjungle.com. Web site: www.jdjungle.com. John Gluck, Editor. **Description:** For law students. Seeks to provide professionals with the tools they need to be succesful. Online and print versions. **Queries:** Preferred. **Unsolicited mss:** Accepts. **Response:** SASE required.

JOURNAL OF EMERGENCY MEDICAL SERVICES

P.O. Box 2789, Carlsbad, CA 92018. 800-266-5367. Web site: www.jems.com. Monthly. $27.97. Circ.: 40,000. A.J. Heightman, Editor-in-Chief. **Description:** A leading voice in emergency medicine and prehospital care. Readers include EMTs, paramedics, nurses, physicians, EMS managers, administrators, and educators. **Nonfiction:** On provider health and professional development; innovative applications of EMS; interviews/profiles, new equipment and technology; industry news and commentary; $200-$400. **Columns, Departments:** Yes; $150-$200/depts., $25/new items. **Art:** Only real-life EMS action shots; completed model release form must accompany photos when appropriate; varied formats; $150-$400 (cover). **Queries:** Preferred. **E-queries:** Yes. **Unsolicited mss:** Accepts. **Response:** Submissions 3 months. **Freelance Content:** 70%. **Payment:** On publication.

LP-GAS

131 W. First St., Duluth, MN 55802. 440-243-8100. Web site: www.lpgasmagazine.com. Zane Chastain, Editor. **Description:** On LP-gas dealer operations: marketing, management, etc. **Nonfiction:** Articles, 1,500-2,500 words, with photos; pays to $.15/word, extra for photos. **Queries:** Preferred. **Payment:** On acceptance.

MACHINE DESIGN

Penton Publishing Co., 1100 Superior Ave., Cleveland, OH 44114. 216-696-7000. Web site: www.machinedesign.com. Ronald Khol, Editor. **Description:** On mechanical and electromechanical design topics for engineers. **Nonfiction:** Articles, to 10 typed pages; pay varies. **Queries:** Preferred. **Payment:** On publication.

MAINTENANCE TECHNOLOGY

1300 S. Grove Ave., Barrington, IL 60010. 847-382-8100. Web site: www.mt-online.com. Robert C. Baldwin, Editor. **Description:** Technical articles with how-to information to increase reliability and maintainability of electrical and mechanical systems and equipment. Readers are managers, supervisors, and engineers in all industries and facilities. **Nonfiction:** Pay varies. **Queries:** Preferred. **Payment:** On acceptance.

NATIONAL FISHERMAN

P.O. Box 2038, Marion, OH 43306. 800-959-5073. Web site: www.nationalfisherman.com. Jerry Fraser, Editor. **Description:** For commercial fishermen and boat builders. **Nonfiction:** Articles, 200-2,000 words; pays $4-$6/inch, extra for photos. **Queries:** Preferred. **Payment:** On publication.

THE NORTHERN LOGGER AND TIMBER PROCESSOR

Northeastern Logger's Assn., P.O. Box 69, Old Forge, NY 13420. 315-369-3078. Eric A. Johnson, Editor. **Description:** Covers the forest-product industry. **Nonfiction:** Features, 1,000-2,000 words; pays $.15/word. **Art:** Photos. **Queries:** Preferred. **Payment:** On publication. *No recent report.*

P.I. MAGAZINE

755 Bronx Ave., Toledo, OH 43609. 419-382-0967. E-mail: pimag1@aol.com. Web site: www.PIMAG.com. Circ.: 5,200. Bob Mackowiak, Editor. **Description:** "America's Private Investigation Journal." Profiles of professional investigators, with true accounts of their most difficult cases. **Nonfiction:** Pays $75-$100. **Tips:** No fiction. **Payment:** On publication.

PIZZA TODAY

P.O. Box 1347, New Albany, IN 47151. 812-949-0909. Web site: www.pizzatoday.com. Becky Kavka, Editor. **Description:** On pizza business management for pizza entrepreneurs. **Nonfiction:** Articles, pizza business profiles, to 2,500 words; pays $75-$150/published page. **Queries:** Preferred. **Payment:** On publication.

PRACTICE STRATEGIES

Amer. Optometric Assn., 243 N. Lindbergh Blvd, St. Louis, MO 63141. 314-991-4100 ext. 267. E-mail: rfpieper@theaoa.org. Web site: www.aoanet.org. Monthly. Members. Circ.: 33,000. Bob Pieper, Editor. **Description:** Published by a section of the Journal of

American Optometric Assn., on practice management issues. **Nonfiction:** On business aspects (insurance issues, motivating staff, government health programs). **Queries:** Preferred. **E-queries:** Yes. **Unsolicited mss:** Accepts. **Response:** 1 month. **Freelance Content:** 25%. **Rights:** All. **Payment:** On publication.

PRECISION

3300 Bass Lake Rd., Suite 120, Minneapolis, MN 55429.
8x/year. Circ.: 7,000. Jaime Hunt, Editor in Chief. **Description:** For manufacturing job shops in the state of Minnesota and neighboring counties. Focuses on trends, personalities, and successes in the manufacturing industry. **Nonfiction:** Seeking skilled writers for profile pieces; length varies; to $100 page. **Art:** Uses some freelance photographers. Send samples of work. **Tips:** Welcomes new writers. **Queries:** Required. **E-queries:** Yes. **Unsolicited mss:** Accepts. **Response:** 2-4 weeks, SASE required. **Freelance Content:** 50%. **Rights:** One-time and reprint. **Payment:** On publication.

PUBLISH

Publish Media, LLC., 462 Boston St., Topsfield, MA 01983. 978-887-7900.
Web site: www.publish.com. Jennifer Carton, Editor. **Description:** On all aspects of enterprise communication and publishing technology. **Nonfiction:** Features (1,500-2,000 words); reviews (400-800 words); Pay varies. **Payment:** On acceptance.

REMODELING

Hanley-Wood, Inc., One Thomas Cir. NW, Suite 600,
Washington, DC 20005. 202-452-0390.
E-mail: pdeffenb@harley-wood.com. Web site: www.harley-wood.com. Monthly. Free. Circ.: 80,000. Paul Deffenbaugh, Editor. **Description:** For remodeling contractors. **Nonfiction:** By assignment only, 250-1,700 words, on industry news for residential and light commercial remodelers. **Queries:** Required. **E-queries:** Yes. **Unsolicited mss:** Does not accept. **Response:** Queries 1 month. **Freelance Content:** 10%. **Rights:** All NA. **Payment:** On acceptance.

REVISTA AREA

310 E. 44th St., #1601, New York, NY 10017-4420. 212-370-1740.
Web site: www.revistaaerea.com. 8x/yr. Circ.: 10,000. **Description:** Covers both military and commercial aviation industries in Latin America, and other countries where Spanish is the primary language.

RV BUSINESS

2575 Vista Del Mar Dr., Ventura, CA 93001. 800-765-1912.
E-mail: rub@tl.com. Web site: www.rvbusiness.com. Sherman Goldenberg, Editor. **Description:** On RV industry news and product-related features; legislative matters affecting the industry. **Nonfiction:** Articles, to 1,500 words; pays varies. **Tips:** No generic business features.

SOFTWARE
40 Speen St., Suite 403, Framingham, MA 01701. 508-875-9555. Web site: www.softwaremag.com. Monthly. Circ.: 110,000. Colleen Trye, Managing Editor. **Description:** For corporate systems managers and MIS personnel. **Nonfiction:** Features and information on latest software.

SOUTHERN LUMBERMAN
P.O. Box 681629, Franklin, TN 37068-1629. 615-791-1961. E-mail: ngregg@southernlumber.com. Web site: southernlumberman.com. Monthly. $23/yr. Circ.: 15,500. Nanci P. Gregg, Editor. **Description:** For owners and operators of small- to medium-sized sawmills. **Nonfiction:** Ideal: a feature on a sawmill with description of equipment and tips from owner/manager on how to work efficiently, save and make money; 500-2,500 words; $100-$300. **Queries:** Preferred. **E-queries:** No. **Unsolicited mss:** Accepts. **Response:** 4-6 weeks, SASE. **Freelance Content:** 45%. **Rights:** FNASR. **Payment:** On publication.

STITCHES
16787 Warden Ave., RR #3, Newmarket, Ont., Canada L3Y 4W1. 905-853-1884. E-mail: stitches@attglobal.com. Monthly. $40/yr (Canada), $45 (U.S.). Circ.: 39,000. Simon Hally, Editor. **Description:** "The Journal of Medical Humor." Humor and lifestyle pieces, 250-2,000 words, for physicians. **Fiction:** Up to 2,000 words; $.35/word (Canada), $.25/word (U.S.). **Nonfiction:** Up to 2,000 words. **Poetry:** Shorter; $.50/word (Canada), $.40/word (U.S.). **Columns, Departments:** Humor. **Art:** Cartoons only. $50 (Canada), $40 (U.S.). **Queries:** Not necessary. **E-queries:** Yes. **Unsolicited mss:** Accepts. **Freelance Content:** 95%. **Rights:** FNASR. **Payment:** On publication.

STONE WORLD
299 Market St., Suite 320, Saddle Brook, NJ 07663. 201-291-9001. Web site: www.stoneworld.com. Michael Reis, Editor. **Description:** On new trends in installing and designing with stone. For architects, interior designers, design professionals, and stone fabricators and dealers. **Nonfiction:** Articles, 750-1,500 words; pays $6/column inch. **Queries:** Preferred. **Payment:** On publication.

TECHNICAL COMMUNICATION
Society for Technical Communication, 901 N. Stuart St., Ste 904, Arlington, VA 22203. 703-522-4114. Web site: www.stc-va.org. Quarterly. Circ.: 18,000. **Description:** Industry information for technical writers, publishers, and editors.

TODAY'S FACILITY MANAGER
121 Monmouth St., Red Bank, NJ 07701. 732-842-7433. Web site: www.tfmgr.com. Monthly. $30 (nonprofessionals) Free to trade professionals. Circ.: 40,000. Jill Aronson, Editor. **Description:** News and new-product information for in-house, on-site facility professionals. **Nonfiction:** 1,000-2,500 words;

pays flat fee. **Tips:** Welcomes new writers. Requires solid research and reporting skills. **Queries:** Preferred. **E-queries:** Yes. **Unsolicited mss:** Accepts. **Response:** Varies, SASE required. **Freelance Content:** 30%. **Rights:** flexible. **Payment:** On acceptance.

WASTE AGE
6151 Powers Ferry Rd. NW, Ste. 200, Atlanta, GA 30339. 770-618-0112. E-mail: bill.wolpin@intertec.com. Web site: www.wasteage.com. Monthly. Circ.: 43,000. Bill Wolpin, Editorial Director. **Description:** Covers collection, transfer, processing, and disposal of waste. Analysis of relevant news, trends, products, people, and events. **Nonfiction:** Case studies, market analysis, how-to articles, 2,000-3,000 words, with solutions to problems in the field. **Queries:** Required. **E-queries:** Yes. **Unsolicited mss:** Accepts. **Response:** 2 months, SASE. **Rights:** worldwide. **Payment:** On publication.

WOODSHOP NEWS
35 Pratt St., Essex, CT 06426-1185. 860-767-8227. E-mail: woodshopnews@att.net. Web site: www.woodshopnews.com. $3.95/$21.95. A.J. Hamler, Editor. **Description:** For people who work with wood: business stories, profiles, news. **Nonfiction:** Business advice for professional woodworkers; profiles of shops with unique businesses, furniture lines, or stories; up to 1,400 words; $150-$500. **Tips:** Need profiles of woodworkers outside the Northeast region. **Queries:** Preferred. **Response:** up to several weeks, SASE. **Payment:** On publication.

WORKBOAT
P.O. Box 1348, Mandeville, LA 70470. 504-626-0298. Web site: workboat.com. David Krapf, Editor. **Description:** Current, lively information for workboat owners, operators, crew, suppliers, and regulators. **Nonfiction:** Features, to 2,000 words, and shorts, 500-1,000 words. Topics: construction and conversion; diesel engines and electronics; politics and industry; unusual vessels; new products; profiles. Pay varies. **Queries:** Preferred. **Payment:** On publication.

TRAVEL

AAA GOING PLACES TODAY
1515 N. Westshore Blvd., Tampa, FL 33607. 813-289-1391. E-mail: sklim@aaasouth.com. Web site: aaagoingplaces.com. Bi-monthly. Circ.: 4,000,000. Sandy Klim, Editor. **Description:** On domestic travel and lifestyle, for AAA Members. **Nonfiction:** Well-researched domestic and international travel, automotive, lifestyle. 3rd-person preferred; 800-1,200 words; $200-$400. **Art:** Color photos. **Tips:** Prefers general, rather than niche, travel stories to a destination, with an angle; e.g., Washington D.C., "The Monuments," rather than the annual art exhibit at Lincoln Memorial. Weekend or weeklong vacation ideas for seniors and families. Fun vacation stops, a little unusual but with lots to offer ("Hersey, PA: something for

everyone"). **Queries:** Not necessary. **E-queries:** Yes. **Unsolicited mss:** Accepts. **Response:** Queries 6 months, submissions 3 months, SASE. **Freelance Content:** 50%. **Rights:** 1st, web, and reprint rights, some reprints from local markets. **Payment:** On acceptance.

ARIZONA HIGHWAYS

2039 W. Lewis Ave., Phoenix, AZ 85009. 602-271-5900. E-mail: arizonahighways.com. Web site: www.arizonahighways.com. Monthly. $3.50/issue, $19/year. Circ.: 365,000. Robert J. Early, Editor. **Description:** Covers travel in Arizona; pieces on adventure, humor, lifestyles, nostalgia, history, archaeology, nature, etc. Some Arizona-based fiction on occasion. **Fiction:** Preferably frontier-oriented, must be upbeat and wholesome (for December and April issues); 1,800-2,500 words; $.55-$1.00/word. **Nonfiction:** Travel adventure, history, destinations; personal-experience pieces; 800-1,800 words; $.55-$1.00/word. **Fillers:** Jokes (humor page); 200 words or less; $75. **Columns, Departments:** Mileposts, Focus on Nature, Along the Way, Back Road Adventures, Hiking, Great Weekends, Arizona Humor. Insightful or nostalgic viewpoint; 650 words; $440. **Art:** 4x5 preferred; landscapes, also images to illustrate a story; pay varies. **Tips:** To break in, submit short items to Off Ramp department. Use active verbs. No stories on religion, government, or politics. **E-queries:** Yes. **Unsolicited mss:** Accepts. **Response:** 30 days or less, SASE required. **Freelance Content:** 100%. **Rights:** print (online for extra fee). **Payment:** On acceptance. **Contact:** Rebecca Mong.

BIG WORLD

P.O. Box 8743-A, Lancaster, PA 17604. 717-569-0217. E-mail: karen@bigworld.com. Web site: www.bigworld.com. Quarterly. $3.50/issue, $12/year. Circ.: 15,000. Karen Stone, Editor. **Description:** For budget and independent travelers. Most readers are younger, down-to-earth world travelers. **Nonfiction:** Useful how-to stories or thoughtful retellings of travels. Advice on work and study abroad, humorous anecdotes, first-person experiences, or other travel information. For readers who wish to responsibly discover, explore, and learn, in touch with locals and traditions, in harmony with environment; 500-2,500 words; up to $50. **Tips:** Stories should reflect earthy, on-the-cheap travel. **Queries:** Not necessary. **E-queries:** Yes. **Unsolicited mss:** Accepts. **Response:** Queries 2 months, submissions 2 months, SASE. **Freelance Content:** 80%. **Rights:** 1st. **Payment:** On publication.

BRITISH HERITAGE

6405 Flank Dr., Harrisburg, PA 17112-2750. 717-657-9555. Web site: www.thehistorynet.com/britishheritage. **Description:** Travel articles on places to visit in the British Isles. **Nonfiction:** Articles; 800-1,500 words; include detailed historical information in a "For the Visitor" sidebar. Pays $100-$200. **Payment:** On acceptance. Not accepting unsolicited manuscripts at this time (5/01).

CARIBBEAN TRAVEL AND LIFE

460 N. Orlando, Suite 200, Winter Park, FL 32789. 407-628-4802. Web site: www.caribbeantravelmag.com. Steve Blount. **Description:** For the upscale traveler, on travel, recreation, leisure, and culture in the Caribbean, the Bahamas, and Bermuda. **Nonfiction:** Topics include shopping, dining, arts and entertainment, and sightseeing suggestions, 500-3,000 words; pays $75-$750. **Tips:** Send published clips. **Queries:** Preferred. **Payment:** On publication.

COAST TO COAST

2575 Vista del Mar Dr., Ventura, CA 93001. 805-667-4100. Web site: www.rv.net. 8/year. $4/$28. Circ.: 200,000. Valerie Law, Editor. **Description:** Membership magazine for a network of private RV resorts across North America. Focuses on travel and outdoor recreation. **Nonfiction:** Essays on travel, recreation, and good times. Destination features on a North American city or region, going beyond typical tourist stops to interview locals. Activity/recreation features introduce a sport, hobby, or other diversion. Also, features on RV lifestyle; 1,200-3,500 words; $300-$600. **Art:** Slides, digital images, prints; $75-$600. **Queries:** Not necessary. **E-queries:** No. **Unsolicited mss:** Accepts. **Response:** SASE. **Freelance Content:** 75%. **Rights:** 1st NA, sometimes electronic. **Payment:** On acceptance.

CRUISE TRAVEL

990 Grove St., Evanston, IL 60201. 847-491-6440. Web site: www.travel.org/cruisetravel. Robert Meyers, Editor. **Description:** Ship-, port-, and cruise-of-the-month features, 800-2,000 words; cruise guides; cruise roundups; cruise company profiles; travel suggestions for one-day port stops. **Nonfiction:** Photo-features strongly recommended; pay varies. **Tips:** Query by mail only, with sample color photos. **Queries:** Preferred. **Payment:** On acceptance.

ENDLESS VACATION

9998 N. Michigan Rd., Carmel, IN 46032-9640. 317-805-8120. E-mail: julie.woodward@rci.com. Web site: www.rci.com. Bimonthly. $84/yr. Circ.: 1,100,000. Geri Bain, Editor. **Description:** Describes where to go and what to do on vacation, and why. Addresses issues of timeshare ownership and exchanges. **Nonfiction:** Focus is primarily on domestic vacation travel, with some mainstream international vacation articles. Features should cover new and interesting vacation options, with a solid angle; 1,000-2,000 words; $500-$1,200. **Columns, Departments:** Weekend travel destinations, health and safety on the road, short travel news-oriented and service pieces, hot news tips and travel trends; 800-1,200; $300-$800. **Art:** Travel-oriented photos (landscapes, scenics, people, activities, etc.); slides, originals. **Tips:** Write for doers, not dreamers. Describe activities in which readers can participate. **Queries:** Preferred. **E-queries:** No. **Response:** 4-8 weeks. **Freelance Content:** 90%. **Rights:** 1st NA. **Payment:** On acceptance. **Contact:** Julie Woodward.

FAMILY MOTOR COACHING

8291 Clough Pike, Cincinnati, OH 45244-2796. 513-474-3622. E-mail: magazine@fmca.com. Web site: www.fmca.com. Monthly. $3.99/$27. Circ.: 126,000. Robbin Gould, Editor. **Description:** Published by Family Motor Coach Assn., international organization for motorhome owners. **Nonfiction:** Travel articles, keyed to noteworthy national events. Describe scenic amenities, accommodations, geography, or history; pays $50-$500; 1,500-2,000 words. **Art:** Articles with photos preferred. Transparencies preferred; digital if resolution 400 dpi or higher. Drawings, sketches, or photos should accompany technical articles. **Tips:** Articles must be geared to Family Assn. members. **Queries:** Preferred. **E-queries:** Yes. **Unsolicited mss:** Accepts. **Response:** 4-6 weeks, SASE. **Rights:** FNASR and electronic. **Payment:** On acceptance.

FRANCE

4101 Reservoir Rd. NW, Washington, DC 20007-2186. 202-944-6069. Quarterly. Karen Taylor. **Description:** On business, culture, and society, for well-educated Francophiles throughout the U.S. Also, sightseeing information and tips on good restaurants and accomodations. **Nonfiction:** Articles, varying lengths. **Queries:** Preferred.

HIGHWAYS

2575 Vista Del Mar Dr., P O Box 8545, Ventura, CA 93001. 805-667-4100. E-mail: kwinters@tl.com. Web site: www.goodsamclub.com. 11x/year. $25 yr (includes membership). Circ.: 985,000. Kimberly Winters, Managing Editor. **Description:** Published for Good Sam Club, world's largest recreation vehicle owner's organization. Industry news, also travel and technical features. **Fillers:** Humorous vignettes on an aspect of RV lifestyle; 800-1,400 words; $200 and up. **Columns, Departments:** Highway (columns assigned; submit ideas for consideration). **Art:** Travel features should include at leat 15 color transparencies (originals). **Queries:** Required. **E-queries:** Yes. **Unsolicited mss:** Does not accept. **Response:** Queries 4 weeks submissions 8 weeks, SASE. **Freelance Content:** 40%. **Rights:** 1st NA, electronic. **Payment:** On acceptance.

HOME & AWAY INDIANA

3750 Guion Rd., Indianapolis, IN 46222-7602. 317-923-1500. Bimonthly. Kathy Neff, Editor. **Description:** On travel topics. **Nonfiction:** Articles, of varying lengths. **Art:** Photos, slides.

INTERLINE ADVENTURES

211 E. 7th St., #1100, Austin, TX 78701. E-mail: ckosta@perx.com. Bimonthly. Circ.: 150,000. Christina Kosta, Editor. **Description:** Airline-employee news and travel information. **Nonfiction:** Articles on worldwide destinations, to 2,500 words; $300-$700. **Columns, Departments:** Golf, resorts, cruise ships, traveling with grandchildren; 800-1,000 words; $200-$400. **Queries:** Not necessary. **E-queries:** Yes. **Unsolicited mss:** Accepts.

Response: 2-6 months, SASE. **Freelance Content:** 70%. **Rights:** One-time. **Payment:** On publication.

THE INTERNATIONAL RAILWAY TRAVELER

Editorial Office, P.O. Box 3747, San Diego, CA 92163. 619-260-1332. E-mail: irteditor@aol.com. Web site: www.irtsociety.com. Monthly. $65/U.S. $70/Canada. Circ.: 5,000. Gena Holle, Editor. **Description:** Train-travel stories from around the world, written with veve and wit, that show writer's love of train travel as the most environmentally friendly, adventurous, and exciting mode of travel. **Nonfiction:** Anything involving trains, from luxury to seat-of-the-pants trips. Hotels with a rail history, sightseeing by tram or metro. Articles must be factually sound, with ample logistical detail so readers can easily replicate the author's trip; 300-1,400 words; $.03/word. **Art:** We always need good photos of trains to go with stories; b&w glossies, transparencies, or color prints; $10 inside stories, $20 for cover. **Tips:** Your travel stories need not be written chronologically. Try building your story around a few key points or impressions from your trip. **Queries:** Preferred. **E-queries:** Yes. **Unsolicited mss:** Accepts. **Response:** 2 months, SASE required. **Freelance Content:** 80%. **Rights:** FNASR, electronic. **Payment:** On publication.

INTERVAL

6262 Sunset Dr., Miami, FL 33143. 305-668-3414; 888-784-3447. Web site: www.intervalworld.com. **Description:** For time-share vacationers. **Contact:** Elizabeth Willard, Asst. V.P.

ISLANDS

6309 Carpinteria Ave., Carpinteria, CA 93013. 805-745-7100. E-mail: islands@islands.com. Web site: www.islands.com. 8x/year. $4.95/issue, $24.95/year. Circ.: 280,000. Joan Tapper, Editor-in-Chief. **Description:** About islands around the world, the crossroads of romance and adventure. Writing and photos take readers to Bora-Bora, Bali, and remote island outposts known only to a few. **Nonfiction:** Illuminate what makes a place tick. Profiles of unforgettable people; 1,500-4,000 words; $.50/word and up. **Columns, Departments:** Horizons (short, quickie island-related items); 50-1,500 words. **Art:** 35mm. **Tips:** Find out what characterizes the place and you'll find an Islands article. **Queries:** Preferred. **E-queries:** Yes. **Unsolicited mss:** Accepts. **Response:** 3 months, SASE required. **Freelance Content:** 90%. **Rights:** All. **Payment:** On acceptance.

MEXICO CONNECT

Telephone: 011-523-766-2267. E-mail: mexwrite@mexconnect.com. Web site: www.mexconnect.com. Monthly. David H. McLaughlin, Publisher. **Description:** On living in Mexico, Mexico travel (the "Un-Guide Book") and Mexico business. Pay is with a by-line and information about you on our website. **Nonfiction:** Short articles (to 750 words) or long articles, to 2,500 words. **Tips:** Query by e-mail. Submit in English or Spanish.

MICHIGAN LIVING

Auto Club of Michigan, 1 Auto Club Dr., Dearborn, MI 48126-9982. 248-816-9265. Web site: www.aaamich.com. Ron Garbinski, Editor. **Description:** Michigan topics, also area and Canadian tourist attractions and recreational opportunities **Nonfiction:** Informative travel articles, 300-2,000 words; pays $55-$500. **Art:** Photos; pay varies. **Queries:** Preferred. **Payment:** On publication.

THE MIDWEST TRAVELER

12901 N. Forty Dr., St. Louis, MO 63141. 314-523-7350. E-mail: aaapub@ibm.net. Web site: www.aaa.missouri.com. Bimonthly. $3/year. Circ.: 435,000. Michael J. Right, Editor. **Description:** For AAA members in Missouri and parts of Illinois, Indiana and Kansas. **Nonfiction:** Lively writing to encourage readers to take the trip they've just read about. Include useful information (travel tips). AAA properties preferred; 1,200-1,500 words; $150-$350. **Art:** Slides (color), prints, or digital; $75-$150. **Tips:** Request editorial calendar. **Queries:** Preferred. **E-queries:** No. **Unsolicited mss:** Accepts. **Response:** 4-6 weeks, SASE. **Freelance Content:** 80%. **Rights:** 1st NA, reprint, electronic. **Payment:** On acceptance.

MOTORHOME

2575 Vista Del Mar, Ventura, CA 93001. 805-667-4100. Web site: www.motorhomemagazine.com. Barbara Leonard, Editor. **Description:** Covers destinations for RV travelers. Also, activities, hobbies, and how-tos. **Nonfiction:** Travel destinations and other articles; 150-2,500 words; $100-500. **Columns, Departments:** Crossroads (varied topics: unique motorhomes to great cafes, museums to festivals; with 1-2 good color transparencies); Quick Tips (do-it-yourself ideas for motorhomes; no photo, just a sketch if necessary; 150 words; $100). **Art:** 35mm slides, $25-500. **Tips:** Departments are easiest way to break in. Readers are active travelers; most retirees, but more baby boomers entering the RV lifestyle, so some articles directed to novices, families. No diaries or product tests. **Queries:** Preferred. **E-queries:** No. **Unsolicited mss:** Accepts. **Response:** 3-4 weeks, SASE. **Freelance Content:** 65%. **Payment:** On acceptance.

NATIONAL GEOGRAPHIC ADVENTURE

104 W. 40th St., 17th Fl., New York, NY 10018. 212-790-9020. E-mail: adventure@ngs.org. Web site: www.nationalgeographic.com/adventure. Bimonthly. Mark Jannot. **Description:** Covers adventure and general travel (adventure as travel designed to push the envelope on experience and to some degree, comfort. Destinations are divided evenly between U.S. and international. **Nonfiction:** Features, 4,000-8,000 words, on well-known adventures, expeditions, and scientific exploration; unknown historical tales. E.g., diving near Australia's Ningaloo Reef; paddling on New England's Merrimack River. **Columns, Departments:** Profiles, opinions, commentaries (2,000-3,000 words); Compass (500-2,000 words, how readers can bring adventure into their own lives). **Tips:** Helps to have written for other travel magazines. Carefully target query and make it compelling. Readers aged 20-55. **Queries:** Preferred. **Unsolicited mss:** Accepts. **Freelance Content:** 90%.

NATIONAL GEOGRAPHIC TRAVELER

1145 17th St. N.W., Washington, DC 20036. 202-857-7000. Web site: nationalgeographic.com/traveler. Keith Bellows, Editor. **Description:** Most articles by assignment only; query first with 1-2-page proposal, resumé, and published clips required. **Nonfiction:** Articles 1,500-4,000 words; pays $1/word. **Payment:** On acceptance.

NATIONAL MOTORIST

National Automobile Club, 1151 E. Hillsdale Blvd., Foster City, CA 94404. 650-294-7000. Web site: www.nationalautoclub.com. Quarterly. Jane Offers, Editor. **Description:** For California motorists, on motoring in the West, domestic and international travel, car care, roads, news, transportation, personalities, places, etc. **Nonfiction:** Illustrated articles, 500-1,100 words; pays from $.20/word, extra for photos. **Art:** Color slides. **Queries:** Preferred. **Response:** SASE required. **Payment:** On publication.

NAVIGATOR

Pace Communications, 1301 Carolina St., Greensboro, NC 27401. 336-378-6065. Bimonthly. Susanna Rodell. **Description:** General-interest magazine distributed at Holiday Inn Express Hotels. Articles on sports, entertainment, and food. Photo essays, news on traveling trends, gear, and information. **Tips:** SASE for guidelines.

NORTHWEST TRAVEL

4969 Highway 101, #2, P.O. Box 18000, Florence, OR 97439. 800-348-8401. E-mail: judy@ohwy.com or jm@ohwy.com. Web site: www.ohwy.com. Bi-monthly 6x/year. Circ.: 50,000. Judy Fleagle, Jim Forst, Editors. **Description:** Where to go and what to see in Oregon, Washington, Idaho, British Columbia, Western Montana, sometimes Alaska. Every article has a travel connection; each issue has detailed drive guide to one area. **Nonfiction:** First-person experience. Put details in sidebars; 500-1,500 words; $65-$350/features,. **Fillers:** Worth a Stop; $50. **Art:** Seeking terrific slides of wildlife, artsy or dramatic scenery shots. Also does 2 annual calendars; slides, transparencies; $25-75 ($325 cover). **Queries:** Preferred. **Unsolicited mss:** Accepts. **Response:** Queries 3 months, submissions 2-3 months, SASE. **Freelance Content:** 60%. **Rights:** one-time, 1st NA (photos). **Payment:** On publication.

OUTDOOR EXPLORER

2 Park Avenue, 10th Floor, New York, NY 10016. 212-779-5000. Web site: www.outdoorexplorer.com. Bimonthly. Steve Madden, Editor-in-Chief. **Description:** Seeks to present real adventures for real people. Sophisticated, cutting-edge, unique content for active adults who enjoy sharing outdoor experiences with family and friends. **Nonfiction:** Well-crafted articles (ranging from a literary feature on backpacking in North Cascades National Park by novelist Peter Landesman to a do-it-yourself bike tour). **Tips:** Most staff members are veterans of Sports Illustrated, with ties to established writers. Query with outstanding ideas only. **Queries:** Preferred. **E-queries:** Yes. **Unsolicited mss:** Accepts.

RIDER

2575 Vista Del Mar Dr., Ventura, CA 93001. 805-667-4100. E-mail: editor@ridermagazine.com. **Monthly. Circ.:** 140,000. Mark Tuttle Jr., Editor. **Description:** Covers travel, touring, commuting, and camping motorcyclists. **Nonfiction:** to 2,000 words; $100-$750. **Art:** Color slides. **Queries:** Required. **Response:** SASE. **Payment:** On publication.

ROUTE 66

326 W. Route 66, Williams, AZ 86046-2427. 520-635-4322. E-mail: info@route66magazine.com. Web site: www.route66magazine.com. Paul Taylor. **Description:** On travel and life along Route 66 between Chicago and Los Angeles. **Nonfiction:** Articles, 1,500-2,000 words; pays $20/column. **Fillers:** Fillers, jokes, puzzles (for Children's Page). **Art:** b/w, color photos. **Queries:** Preferred. **Payment:** On publication.

RV WEST

Vernon Publications, 3000 Northup Way, Suite 200, Bellevue, WA 98009-9643. Michelle Arab. **Description:** For RV owners; where to go and what to do in 13 western states. **Nonfiction:** Travel and destination articles, 750-1,750 words. Pays $1.50/column inch. **Art:** Color slides, b/w prints must accompany articles. **Queries:** Preferred. **Unsolicited mss:** Accepts. **Payment:** On publication.

SOUTH AMERICAN EXPLORER

126 Indian Creek Rd., Ithaca, NY 14850. 607-277-0488. E-mail: explorer@samesplo.org. Web site: www.samexplo.org. **Description:** Spotlights travel, history, archeology, scientific discovery, people and language in Central and South America. **Nonfiction:** 3,000-5,000 words. **Art:** Photos. **Queries:** Preferred. **E-queries:** Yes. **Unsolicited mss:** Accepts.

SPECIALTY TRAVEL INDEX

305 San Anselmo Ave., #313, San Anselmo, CA 94960. 800-442-4922. E-mail: info@specialtytravel.com. Web site: www.specialty travel.com. **Biannual.** $6/issue. **Circ.:** 45,000. Risa Weinreb, Editor. **Description:** Travel directory listing of 500 worldwide operators, with travel articles, for consumers and travel agents. **Nonfiction:** Stories on special interest, adventure-type travel, from soft adventures (e.g., cycling through French wine country) to daring exploits (an exploratory river-rafting run in Pakistan). Varied styles okay (first-person, descriptive); in general, not written in the present tense, but with a lively immediacy; 1,250 words; $300. **Art:** Slides, EPS digital, pay varies. **Tips:** Seeking off-the-beaten-path perspectives. Send published clips. **Queries:** Preferred. **E-queries:** Yes. **Unsolicited mss:** Accepts. **Response:** 3-6 months, SASE. **Freelance Content:** 80%. **Payment:** On acceptance. **Contact:** Susan Kostrzewa, Managing Editor.

TRAILER LIFE

2575 Vista Del Mar, Ventura, CA 93001. 805-667-4352. E-mail: bleonard@affinity.com. Web site: www.rv.net. Monthly. $3.99. Circ.: 280,000. Barbara Leonard, Editor. **Description:** New product information and tests, do-it-yourself articles, plus North American travel and lifestyle for RV owners. **Nonfiction:** On trailers, motor homes, truck campers used by active adventurous travelers, visiting interesting destinations and participating in colorful hobbies; 200-2,000 words; pays $100-$700. **Fillers:** 50-1,000 words; $75-$400. **Art:** 35mm, 2¼; $75-$250; $500-$700 (cover). **Tips:** Supply good photos (35 mm slides) and submit a complete package. **Queries:** Required. **E-queries:** Yes. **Response:** 2-3 weeks, SASE. **Freelance Content:** 45%. **Rights:** 1st NA and electronic. **Payment:** On acceptance.

TRANSITIONS ABROAD

P.O. Box 1300, Amherst, MA 01004-1300. 413-256-3414. Web site: www.transitionsabroad.com. Bimonthly. $4.95/$28. Circ.: 15,000. Max Hartshorne, Editor. **Description:** International travel and life, for overseas travelers of all ages who seek enriching, in-depth experience of the culture: work, study, travel, budget tips. **Nonfiction:** Practical how-to travel articles; 800-1,000 words; $2/word. **Columns, Departments:** Info exchange (200-300 words, free subscription); Itineraries (up to 500 words, $25-$50). **Art:** b/w, jpeg; $25-$50; $150 (cover). **Tips:** Eager for new writers with information not usually found in guidebooks. Also seeking special expertise on cultural travel opportunities for specific groups: seniors, students, families, etc. No journal writing; no U.S. travel. **Queries:** Required. **E-queries:** Yes. **Unsolicited mss:** Accepts. **Response:** SASE. **Freelance Content:** 95%. **Rights:** 1st NA. **Payment:** On publication.

TRAVEL AMERICA

World Publishing Co., 990 Grove St., Evanston, IL 60201-4370. 847-491-6440. E-mail: rmink@centurysports.net. Web site: www.travelamerica.com. Bimonthly. $5.99/$23.94 yr. Circ.: 300,000. Robert Meyers, Editor. **Description:** Consumer travel magazine, exclusively U.S. destinations. **Nonfiction:** General destination stories; 1,000 words; $300. **Columns, Departments:** If You Only Have a Day (in any city); 500-600 words; $150-$175. **Art:** Slides, usually with text package; individual photos $25-$35. Uses p.r. photos most often. **Tips:** Submit short 1-page stories on narrow topics. **Queries:** Not necessary. **E-queries:** No. **Unsolicited mss:** Accepts. **Response:** 2-6 weeks, SASE. **Freelance Content:** 80%. **Rights:** 1st. **Payment:** On publication.

TRAVEL & LEISURE

1120 Ave. of the Americas, New York, NY 10036. 212-382-5600. E-mail: tlquery@amexpub.com. Web site: www.traveland leisure.com. Monthly. $4.50/$39. Circ.: 1,000,000. Nancy Novogrod, Editor. **Description:** International travel destinations, luxury lodgings, travel-related fashion and products, with practical advice for leisure travelers. **Nonfiction:** Travel-related stories on shopping, trends, new hotels, products, nightlife, art, architecture; 1,000-4,000 words; $1,000-$5,000.

Columns, Departments: T&L Reports; Smart Going. **Tips:** Departments are best chances for new writers. Writers should have same sophistication and travel experience as readers. **Queries:** Required. **E-queries:** Yes. **Unsolicited mss:** Does not accept. **Response:** Queries 4 weeks, submissions 2 weeks, SASE. **Freelance Content:** 80%. **Rights:** 1st. **Payment:** On acceptance.

TRAVEL SMART
40 Beechdale Rd., Dobbs Ferry, NY 10522-3098. 914-693-8300.
Web site: travelsmartnews.com. **Description:** Covers interesting, unusual, or economical places. Offers useful travel-related tips; practical information for vacation or business travel. **Nonfiction:** Short pieces, 250-1,000 words; pays $5-$150. **Tips:** Give specific details on hotels, restaurants, transportation, and costs. Query for longer pieces. **Payment:** On publication.

TRAVEL TRADE PUBLICATIONS
Travel Publication, Inc., 15 W. 44th St., Floor 16, NewYork, NY 10036. 212-730-6600. Web site: www.traveltrade.com. Elizabeth Hettich, Editor. **Description:** Informative, lively features, 1,400-3,000 words, on foreign and domestic travel. Query with clips.

TRAVELOCITY
P.O. Box 619640, Dallas-Ft. Worth Airport, TX 75261. 817-785-8000.
Web site: www.travelocitymagazine.com. Bimonthly. Circ.: 250,000. Chuck Thompson, Executive Editor. **Description:** Ranges from business travel to adventure, for readers who rely on the Web. Offers listings of websites, stories on booking online, ways to help people travel more effectively. **Nonfiction:** Wide-ranging travel-adventure themes (e.g., pros and cons of animal attractions—swimming with dolphins, looking for bears, etc.). **Columns, Departments:** "Loaded" (front-section pieces, 50-500 words, tips on destinations, cool restaurants, personalities, funny observations, etc.). **Tips:** All queries must include writing samples. **Queries:** Preferred. **E-queries:** No. **Unsolicited mss:** Accepts. **Response:** SASE required.

TRIPS
Suite 245, 155 Filbert St., Oakland, CA 94607. 510-834-3433.
E-mail: edit@tripsmag.com. Web site: www.tripsmag.com. Bi-monthly. $3.50/issue, $11.95/year. Circ.: 100,000. Tony Stucker, Editor-in-Chief. **Description:** Contemporary adventurous travel journal that lives by the credo, "People don't take trips—trips take people." **Nonfiction:** Features, essays; seeks eclectic/irreverent mix; 2,000-5,000; $500-$1,500. **Fillers:** 100-500; $50-$200. **Columns, Departments:** Trips (articles with a strong voice; should evoke emotion and leave impression); 600-2,000; $150-$600. **Art:** Photographs, slides. **Tips:** Target market mostly young singles or couples in 20s to mid-40s; no family travel. Avoid formulaic stories. **Queries:** Preferred. **E-queries:** Yes. **Unsolicited mss:** Accepts. **Response:** 1 month, SASE. **Freelance Content:** 100%. **Rights:** 1st NA. **Payment:** On publication.

WESTWAYS

P.O. Box 25001, Santa Ana, CA 92799-5001. 714-885-2376.
Web site: www.aaa-calif.com. **Description:** Travel articles, on southern California, the West, greater U.S., and foreign destinations. **Nonfiction:** 1,000-2,500 words; pays $1/word. **Queries:** Preferred. **Payment:** On acceptance.

YANKEE MAGAZINE'S TRAVEL GUIDE TO NEW ENGLAND

Main Street, Dublin, NH 03444.
E-mail: travel@yankeepub.com. Annual. $4.99. Circ.: 100,000. Jim Collins, Editor.
Description: Covers New England travel, with features and travel information.
Nonfiction: 500-1,500 words; $1/word. **Art:** Photos. **Tips:** Looking for fresh ideas.
Queries: Required. **E-queries:** Yes. **Freelance Content:** 70%. **Payment:** On acceptance.

WOMEN

ALL THAT WOMEN WANT

E-mail: editor@allthatwomenwant.com. Web site: www.allthatwomenwant.com.
Monthly. Colleen Moulding, Editor. **Description:** E-zine of general topics of interest to women.

BBW: BIG BEAUTIFUL WOMAN

P.O. Box 1297, Elk Grove, CA 95759.
E-mail: sesmith@bbwmagazine.com. Web site: www.bbwmagazine.com. Sally E. Smith, Editor-in-Chief. **Description:** For women ages 25-45, especially plus-size women, including interviews with successful plus-size women. **Nonfiction:** Articles; 800-3000 words; pay varies. **Queries:** Preferred. **Payment:** On publication.

BLACK ELEGANCE

475 Park Ave. S., 8th Floor, New York, NY 10016. 212-689-2830.
Sonia Alleyne, Editor. **Description:** On fashion, beauty, relationships, home design, careers, personal finance, and personalities, for black women ages 25-45. Also, short interviews. **Nonfiction:** Articles; 1,000-2,000 words; pays $150-$225. **Tips:** Include photos if available. **Queries:** Preferred. **Payment:** On publication.

BRAIN CHILD

P.O. Box 1161, Harrisonburg, VA 22801-1161. 540-574-2379.
E-mail: editor@brainchildmag.com. Web site: www.brainchildmag.com. Quarterly.
$5/$18. Circ.: 10,000. Jennifer Niesslein, Editor. **Description:** Explores the personal transformation that motherhood brings. Spotlights women's own view of motherhood.
Fiction: Literary short stories on an aspects of motherhood; e.g., "The Life Of the Body," by Jane Smiley; 1,500-4,500 words; pay varies. **Nonfiction:** Personal essays, features, book reviews, parodies, debate essays. **Columns, Departments:** Nutshell (stories you won't find in the mainstream media; e.g., "Mom Brain Explained," by

Libby Gruner; 200-800 words. **Tips:** Seeking smart, down-to-earth work that's sometimes funny, sometimes poignant. **Queries:** Preferred. **E-queries:** Yes. **Unsolicited mss:** Accepts. **Response:** 1-3 months, SASE. **Freelance Content:** 90%. **Rights:** 1st NA, electronic. **Payment:** On publication. **Contact:** Stephanie Wilkerson.

BRIDAL GUIDE
Globe Communications Corp., 3 E. 54th St., 15th Fl,
New York, NY 10022. 212-838-7733; 800-472-7744.
Web site: www. bridalguide.com. Bimonthly. Diane Forden, Editor-in-Chief. **Description:** On wedding planning, relationships, sexuality, health and nutrition, psychology, travel, and finance. **Nonfiction:** Articles, 1,500-3,000 words. **Tips:** No beauty, fashion articles; no fiction, essays, poetry. **Queries:** Preferred. **Response:** SASE. **Payment:** On acceptance. **Contact:** Denise Schipani, Exec. Ed.

BRIDE AGAIN
1240 N. Jefferson Ave., Suite G, Anaheim, CA 92807. 714-632-7000.
Web site: www.brideagain.com. Quarterly. $3.99/issue. Circ.: 145,000. Beth Reed Ramirez, Editor. **Description:** For "encore" brides (women who are planning to remarry). **Nonfiction:** Helpful, positive, upbeat articles; no first-person. Topics: remarriage, blending families/religions, etiquette, finances, legal issues, honeymoon locations, book reviews; 1,000 words; $.35/word. **Tips:** Articles should be specific to second-time brides. **Queries:** Not necessary. **E-queries:** No. **Unsolicited mss:** Does not accept. **Response:** Submissions 2 months, SASE. **Freelance Content:** 70%. **Rights:** 1st NA. **Payment:** On publication.

BRIDE'S
Conde Nast Publications, 4 Times Square, 6th Fl,
New York, NY 10036. 212-286-7528.
Sally Kilbridge, Managing Editor. **Description:** For engaged couples or newlyweds, on wedding planning, relationships, communication, sex, decorating, finances, careers, health, birth control, religion, in-laws. **Nonfiction:** Articles, 800-3,000 words, for newlyweds; pays $.50/word. **Queries:** Preferred. **Unsolicited mss:** Accepts. **Payment:** On acceptance.

CHATELAINE
777 Bay St., Toronto, Ont., Canada M5W 1A7. 416-596-5425.
Web site: WWW.chatelaine.com. Monthly. $3.50/issue (Canadian). Circ.: 800,000. Rona Maynard, Editor. **Description:** Empowers Canada's busiest women to create the lives they want. Speaks to the strength of the inner woman—her passion, purpose, and sense of possibility. **Nonfiction:** Articles of interest to Canadian women, on all aspects of Canadian life. A written proposal is essential; 500-3,000 words; $500 and up. **Columns, Departments:** Upfront (relationships, health, parents/kids). **Queries:** Required. **E-queries:** Yes. **Unsolicited mss:** Accepts. **Response:** 6 weeks, SASE required. **Freelance Content:** 75%. **Rights:** 1st. **Payment:** On acceptance.

COMPLETE WOMAN

875 N. Michigan Ave., Suite 3434, Chicago, IL 60611. 312-266-8680. Bi-monthly. $3.50/issue. Circ.: 350,000. Bonnie L. Krueger, Editor. **Description:** Practical advice for women on love, sex, careers, health, and personal relationships. **Nonfiction:** Article with how-to sidebars, with practical advice for women; 1,000-2,000 words. **Art:** Single-frame comics. **Queries:** Not necessary. **E-queries:** No. **Unsolicited mss:** Accepts. **Response:** 90 days. **Freelance Content:** 90%. **Rights:** One-time, all rights. **Payment:** On acceptance. **Contact:** Lora Wintz, Exec. Ed.

COSMOPOLITAN

224 W. 57th St., New York, NY 10018. 212-649-3570. Web site: www.cosmo.women.com. Kate White, Editor. **Description:** On issues affecting young career women, with emphasis on relationships, jobs and personal life. **Fiction:** On male-female relationships (only publishes fiction excerpted from a forthcoming novel). **Nonfiction:** Articles, to 3,000 words; features, 500-2,000 words. **Tips:** Submissions must be sent by a publisher or agent.

COUNTRY WOMAN

Reiman Publications, 5925 Country Lane, Greendale, WI 53129. 414-423-0100. E-mail: editors@countrywomanmagazine.com. Web site: www.countrywomanmagazine.com. Bimonthly. $3.50/issue. Circ.: 1,700,000. Kathy Pohl, Executive Editor. **Description:** For women living in the country or interested in country life. Recipes, craft projects, fiction and nostalgia stories, decorating and fashion, profiles of country woman, and poetry. **Fiction:** Wholesome fiction with country perspective or rural theme; 1,000 words; $90-$125. **Nonfiction:** Nostalgia pieces, essays on farm/country life, humorous stories, decorating features, inspirational articles; 750-1,000 words; $50-$75. **Poetry:** Good rhythm and rhyme, seasonal in nature; 12-24 lines; $10-$25. **Art:** Good candid color photos. **Queries:** Not necessary. **Unsolicited mss:** Accepts. **Response:** 2-3 months, SASE required. **Freelance Content:** 90%. **Payment:** On acceptance. **Contact:** Kathleen Anderson, Managing Editor.

ESSENCE

1500 Broadway, New York, NY 10036. 212-642-0600. E-mail: info@essence.com. Web site: www.essence.com. Monthly. Circ.: 1,000,000. Monique Greenwood, Editor-in-Chief. **Description:** Multicultural publication focusing on black women in America today. **Fiction:** 800-2,500 words. **Nonfiction:** Provocative articles: self-help, how-to, business/finance, work, parenting, health, celebrity profiles, art, travel, political issues; 800-2,500 words; Pay varies. **Queries:** Required.

FAMILY CIRCLE

375 Lexington Ave., New York, NY 10017-5514. 212-499-2000. E-mail: nclark@familycircle.com. Web site: www.family circle.com. 17x/year. $1.69/issue. Circ.: 5,000,000. Susan Ungaro, Senior Editor. **Description:** Covers

women who have made a difference. Also marriage, family, and childcare/eldercare issues; consumer affairs; psychology; humor. **Nonfiction:** Useful articles for all phases of a woman's life; true life, dramatic narratives; pays $1/word; 1,000-2,000 words. **Fillers:** Humor about family life; 70 words. **Columns, Departments:** Full Circle (current issues affecting families); 750 words. **Tips:** Often uses new writers in "Women Who Make a Difference" column. **Queries:** Required. **E-queries:** No. **Unsolicited mss:** Accepts. **Response:** 4 weeks, SASE not required. **Freelance Content:** 80%. **Rights:** One-time, electronic. **Payment:** On acceptance.

FIRST FOR WOMEN

270 Sylvan Ave., Englewood Cliffs, NJ 07632. 201-569-6699.
Web site: www.ffwmarket.com. Jane Traulsen, Editor. **Description:** Reflecting concerns of contemporary women. **Nonfiction:** Articles,1,500-2,500 words; pay varies. **Queries:** Preferred. **Response:** 2 months. **Payment:** On acceptance.

FIT PREGNANCY

21100 Erwin St., Woodland Hills, CA 91367-3712. 818-595-0444.
Web site: www.fitpregnancy.com. Amy Goldhammer, Editor. **Description:** For the "whole nine months and beyond." Expert advice for the pregnant or postpartum woman and her newborn: safe workouts, nutrition guidance, meal plans, medical news, baby gear, and more. **Nonfiction:** Articles, 500-2,000 words, on women's health (pregnant and postpartum), nutrition, and physical fitness. **Queries:** Preferred. **Unsolicited mss:** Accepts. **Payment:** On publication.

GLAMOUR

4 Times Square, New York, NY 10036. 212-286-2860.
E-mail: letters@glamour.com. Web site: www.glamour.com. Bonnie Fuller, Editor-in-Chief. **Description:** On careers, health, psychology, politics, current events, interpersonal relationships, for women, ages 18-35. **Nonfiction:** Articles, from 1,000 words; pays from $500. **Columns, Departments:** Hear Me Out (opinion page), 1,000 words. **Tips:** Fashion, entertainment, travel, food, and beauty pieces are staff-written. **Queries:** Required. **Payment:** On acceptance.

GOLF DIGEST WOMAN

1120 Avenue of the Americas, New York, NY 10018. 212-789-3000.
Web site: www.gdwoman.com. Rona Cherry. **Description:** Seeking published authors (in national magazines) who have in-depth knowledge of golf and golf-related subjects. **Nonfiction:** Pay varies. **Payment:** On publication.

GOLF FOR WOMEN

125 Park Ave., 15th Fl., New York, NY 10017. 212-551-6958.
E-mail: gfwmag@mdp.com. Leslie Day Craige, Editor-in-Chief. **Description:** Golf lifestyle magazine for avid women golfers. Includes travel, instruction, fashion, equipment, news. Query with clips.

GOOD HOUSEKEEPING

959 Eighth Ave., New York, NY 10019. 212-649-2200.
Web site: www.goodhousekeeping.com. Monthly. $1.95/issue. Circ.: 2,400,000. Ellen
Levine, Editor-in-Chief. **Description:** Expert advice on marriage and family,
finances, health issues, and more. **Nonfiction:** Better Way (consumer pieces),
300-500 words. Profiles (on people involved in inspiring, heroic, fascinating pursuits),
400-600 words. My Story (first-person or as-told-to, in which a woman (using her real
name) tells how she overcame a difficult problem. **Queries:** Required. **E-queries:**
No. **Unsolicited mss:** Accepts. **Response:** 2-3 months, SASE required.

HARPER'S BAZAAR

1700 Broadway, 37th Fl., New York, NY 10019. 212-903-5000.
Web site: www.bazaar411.com. Monthly. Circ.: 711,000. Katherine Betts, Editor-in-
Chief. **Description:** For active, sophisticated women. **Nonfiction:** Arts, world
affairs, travel, families, education, careers, health, sexuality; 1,500-2,500 words; pay
varies. **Tips:** Send query with proposal of 1-2 paragraphs; include clips. **Queries:**
Required. **Unsolicited mss:** Does not accept. **Response:** SASE required.
Payment: On acceptance.

THE JEWISH HOMEMAKER

391 Troy Ave., Brooklyn, NY 11213. 718-756-7500.
Web site: www.ok.org. Quarterly. Avraham M. Goldstein, Editor. **Description:** For a
traditional/Orthodox Jewish audience. **Nonfiction:** Articles, 1,200-2,000 words; pay
varies. **Queries:** Preferred. **Payment:** On publication.

JOYFUL WOMAN

P.O. Box 90028, Chattanooga, TN 37412. 706-866-5522.
E-mail: info@joyfulwoman.org. Web site: www.joyfulwoman.org. Bi-monthly.
$4/$19.95. Circ.: 6,000. Joy Rice Martin, Editor. **Description:** Encourages Christian
women, of all ages, in every aspect of their lives. **Fiction:** Thoughtful stories about
Christian women; 500-1,000 words; $20-$25. **Nonfiction:** Profiles of Christian
women, first-person inspirational true stories, practical and Bible-oriented how-to
articles; 500-1,000 words; $20-$25. **Poetry:** on occasion. **Fillers:** occasional.
Queries: Preferred. **E-queries:** Yes. **Unsolicited mss:** Does not accept.
Response: 4-6 weeks, SASE. **Freelance Content:** 45%. **Payment:** On publication.

LADIES' HOME JOURNAL

125 Park Ave., 20th Floor, New York, NY 10017-5516. 212-557-6600.
E-mail: lhj@mdp.com. Web site: www.lhj.com. Monthly. $2.49/issue. Circ.: 4,100,000.
Sarah Mahoney, Editor-in-Chief. **Description:** Information on topics of interest to
today's woman. Most readers in their 30s, married, working at least part-time.
Fiction: Fiction, only through agents. **Nonfiction:** From health reports to psychol-
ogy to human-interest stories, etc.; 1,000-3,000 words; pay varies. **Columns,
Departments:** Parenting, health, and first-person drama; 150-1,500 words. **Tips:**
Starting with human-interest pieces, shorter items, new twists on established themes.

Queries: Preferred. **E-queries:** No. **Unsolicited mss:** Accepts. **Response:** Queries 8 weeks, submissions 4 weeks, SASE required. **Freelance Content:** 70%. **Rights:** All. **Payment:** On acceptance.

LATINA
1500 Broadway, Ste 600, New York, NY 10036-4015. 212-642-0200. Web site: www.latina.com. Monthly. Circ.: 170,000. **Description:** For Hispanic women living in the U.S.

MADEMOISELLE
350 Madison Ave., New York, NY 10017. 212-880-8800. Web site: www.mademoiselle.com. Monthly. Circ.: 1,200,000. Faye Haun, Managing Editor. **Description:** Subjects of interest to single, working women in their 20s. **Nonfiction:** Reports, essays, first-person accounts, and humor; how-tos on personal relationships, work, and fitness; 750-2,500 words. **Tips:** Send clips. **Queries:** Required. **Payment:** On acceptance.

MAMM
349 W. 12th St., New York, NY 10014. 212-242-2163. Web site: www.mamm.com. Monthly. **Description:** On cancer prevention, treatment, and survival, for women. **Nonfiction:** Articles on conventional and alternative treatment and medical news; survivor profiles; investigative features; essays; pay varies. **Queries:** Preferred. **Payment:** On acceptance.

MCCALL'S
375 Lexington Ave., New York, NY 10017-5514. 212-499-2000. Web site: www.mccalls.com. Monthly. Circ.: 4,200,000. Sally Koslow, Editor. **Description:** Covers issues of personal importance to women. **Nonfiction:** Human-interest, current issues, self-help, social issues, family relationships, popular psychology; 1,200-2,000 words; Pay varies. **Columns, Departments:** Couples (first-person essays, 1,400 words); Families (how-tos, 1,400 words); Health Sense (short, newsy items) and Medical Report (1,200 words); Varies, on acceptance. **Queries:** Required. **Contact:** Emily Listfield.

MODERN BRIDE
249 W. 17th St., New York, NY 10011. 212-462-3400. Web site: www.modernbride.com. Alyssa Bellaby, Assistant Editor. **Description:** For bride and groom, on wedding planning, financial planning, juggling career and home, etc. **Nonfiction:** Articles, 1,500-2,000 words, Pays $600-$1,200. **Fillers:** Humorous pieces, 500-1,000 words, for brides. **Payment:** On acceptance.

MORE
Meredith Corp., 125 Park Ave., New York, NY 10017. E-mail: more@mdp.com. Web site: www.moremag.com. 10x/year. Circ.: 600,000. Susan Crandell, Editor. **Description:** For women of baby-boomer generation;

sophisticated and upscale; little service/how-to pieces. **Nonfiction:** Essays, interviews, etc. **Queries:** Preferred. **E-queries:** No. **Unsolicited mss:** Accepts. **Response:** to 3 months, SASE. **Rights:** 1st NA, all. **Payment:** On acceptance.

MOTHERING

P.O. Box 1690, Santa Fe, NM 87504. 505-984-8116.
E-mail: ashisha@mothering.com. Web site: www.mothering.com. Bimonthly.
Ashisha. **Description:** On natural family living, covering topics such as pregnancy, birthing, parenting, etc. **Nonfiction:** Articles, to 2,000 words; pays $200-$500. **Poetry:** 3-20 lines. **Queries:** Preferred. **Payment:** On publication.

MOXIE

1230 Glen Ave., Berkeley, CA 94708. 510-540-5510.
Web site: www.moxiemag.com. **Description:** For confident, assertive women.

MS.

Liberty Media for Women, 20 Exchange Pl., 22nd Fl.,
New York, NY 10005. 212-509-2092.
E-mail: info@msmagazine.com. Web site: www.msmagazine.com. Bimonthly. Circ.: 200,000. Marcia Gillespie, Editor in Chief. **Description:** Articles relating to feminism, women's roles, and social change. **Nonfiction:** National and international news reporting, profiles, essays, theory, and analysis. **Tips:** Query with resumé, published clips, and SASE. No fiction or poetry. **Queries:** Required.

NA'AMAT WOMAN

350 Fifth Ave., Suite 4700, New York, NY 10118. 212-563-5222.
E-mail: judith@nanmat.org. Web site: www.nanmat.org. Quarterly. $25 members, $10 non-members. Circ.: 20,000. Judith A. Sokoloff, Editor. **Description:** For Jewish community, covering varied topics: aspects of life in Israel, Jewish women's issues, social issues, Jewish art and literature. **Fiction:** 2,000-3,000 words; $.10/word. **Nonfiction:** 2,000-3,000 words; $.10-$.12/word. **Columns, Departments:** Book reviews (ca. 800 words); Personal essays (ca. 1,200-1,500 words); $.10/word. **Art:** b/w (hard copy or electronic); $25-$100. **Tips:** Avoid trite Jewish humor, maudlin fiction, war stories. **Queries:** Preferred. **Unsolicited mss:** Accepts. **Response:** Queries 1-2 months, submissions 2-3 months, SASE. **Freelance Content:** 75%. **Rights:** 1st NA. **Payment:** On publication.

NATURAL LIVING TODAY

Tyler Publishing, 175 Varick St., 9th Fl., New York, NY 10014. 212-924-1762.
Web site: www.naturallivingmag.com. Bimonthly., Editorial Department.
Description: On all aspects of a natural lifestyle for women. **Nonfiction:** Articles, 1,000-2,000 words; pays $75-$200. **Queries:** Preferred. **Payment:** On publication.

NEW WOMAN

733 3rd Ave., 12th Fl., New York, NY 10017. 212-697-2040.
E-mail: newwomandm@aol.com. Web site: www.newwoman.com. Monthly.
$16.97/year. Circ.: 1,175,000. Sharlene Breaky, Chief Editor. **Description:** For modern women. Looks at how women relate to and express themselves in areas of beauty, fashion, fitness, sex, health, money, and family. **Nonfiction:** For women, ages 25-49, on self-discovery, self-development, and self-esteem. Features: relationships, careers, health and fitness, money, fashion, beauty, food and nutrition, travel with self-growth angle, essays by and about women. Articles, 500-2,500 words, on relationships/sex and psychology, health news; book excerpts, essays, personal experience, some travel. Pay varies. **Queries:** Preferred. **Unsolicited mss:** Accepts.

PLAYGIRL

801 Second Ave., 9th Floor, New York, NY 10017. 212-661-7878.
Web site: www.playgirl.com. Monthly. $4.99. Circ.: 500,000. Ronnie Koenig, Managing Editor. **Description:** Women's magazine focusing on sex, relationships, and women's health. **Fiction:** Erotic first-person fiction. Female perspective for Fantasy Forum section; 1,700-2,100 words. **Nonfiction:** Articles, 750-3,000 words, on women's issues, sexuality, relationships, and celebrities, for women, ages 18 and up. Erotic fantasies, 1,300-2,000 words. **Fillers:** Quizzes. **Tips:** Easiest way to break in is to write for Fantasy Forum. **Queries:** Preferred. **E-queries:** No. **Unsolicited mss:** Accepts. **Response:** 1 month. **Freelance Content:** 20%. **Payment:** On publication.

PRIMAVERA

Box 37-7547, Chicago, IL 60637.
Annual. $10. Circ.: 1,000. **Description:** Original fiction and poetry, that reflects the experience of women of different ages, races, sexual orientations, social classes. **Fiction:** 25 page max. **Poetry:** On the experiences of women. **Tips:** Encourages new writers. No confessional, formulaic, scholarly. **Queries:** Not necessary. **E-queries:** No. **Unsolicited mss:** Accepts. **Response:** Queries 2 weeks, submissions 1-6 months, SASE required. **Freelance Content:** 100%. **Rights:** 1st. **Payment:** In copies.

QUARANTE

2300 N Street, NW, Washington, D.C. 20037. 202-663-9099.
Michele Linden, Editor. **Description:** "Style and Substance for the Woman Who Has Arrived." **Fiction:** Fiction (to 3,000 words). **Nonfiction:** Features (800-1,500 words), on fashion, politics, health, cuisine, and finance for women over 35. Pays to $150. **Poetry:** Poetry (3-18 lines). **Columns, Departments:** Women of Substance (short profiles). **Tips:** Freelance content limited. **Queries:** Preferred. **Payment:** On publication.

REDBOOK

224 W. 57th St., New York, NY 10019. 212-649-3450.
Web site: www.redbookmag.com. **Description:** On subjects related to relationships, marriage, sex, current social issues, crime, human interest, health, psychology, and

parenting. **Fiction:** Fresh, distinctive short stories, of interest to women. No unsolicited poetry, novellas, or novels; query first. Pays from $1,500 for short stories (to 25 pages). **Nonfiction:** Articles, 1,000-2,500 words; dramatic inspirational narratives, 1,000-2,000 words; pay varies. **Tips:** Send published clips, writing samples. **Queries:** Preferred. **Response:** Allow 12 weeks, SASE required. **Payment:** On acceptance.

ROOM OF ONE'S OWN

PO Box 46160, Sta. D, Vancouver, BC, Canada V6J 5G5.
E-mail: contactroom@hotmail.com.
Web site: http://www.islandnet.com/Room/enter/. Quarterly. $22/yr (Can.), $25 (U.S.)., Editorial Collective. **Description:** Short stories, poems, art, and reviews; by, for, and about women. One of Canada's oldest literary magazines, offers a forum for women to sharing their unique perspectives. **Fiction:** To 5,000 words. **Nonfiction:** Creative nonfiction and essays; to 5,000 words. **Poetry:** Prefers groups of poems, rather than single poems. **Columns, Departments:** Book reviews; to 700 words. **Art:** Seeking original art and photography by women, on the female experience; Slides, photos, photocopies. **E-queries:** No. **Unsolicited mss:** Accepts. **Response:** SASE (Canadian postage). **Rights:** FNASR. **Payment:** In copies. **Contact:** Editorial Collective.

ROSIE'S MCCALL'S

375 Lexington Ave., New York, NY 10017. 212-499-1720.
Web site: www.mccalls.com. **Description:** For young mothers.

SAGEWOMAN

P.O. Box 641, Point Arena, CA 95468-0641. 707-882-2052.
E-mail: editor@sagewoman.com. Web site: www.sagewoman.com. Quarterly. $6.59/issue, $21/year. Circ.: 25,000. Anne Newkirk Niven. **Description:** Helps women explore spiritual, emotional, and mundane lives, respecting all persons, creatures, and the Earth. Focuses on material which expresses an Earth-centered spirituality. **Nonfiction:** On women's spiritual experience; focuses on issues of concern to pagan and other spiritually-minded women; 1,000-5,000 words; $.01-$.25/word. **Poetry:** Limited amount only; 10-50 lines; $10. **Art:** Original work only; signed releases from people depicted required; send portfolio of b/w prints, color negatives or slides; $15-$200. **Tips:** Write in the first person. **Queries:** Not necessary. **E-queries:** Yes. **Unsolicited mss:** Accepts. **Response:** Queries 1 month, submissions 3 months, SASE. **Freelance Content:** 80%. **Rights:** 1st worldwide serial. **Payment:** On publication.

SELF

4 Times Square, 5th Fl., New York, NY 10036. 212-286-2860.
Web site: www.self.com. Monthly. $2.99/issue, $12/yr. Circ.: 1,300,000. Cynthia Leive, Editor-in-Chief. **Description:** Covers all aspects of healthy lifestyle, with latest information on health, fitness, nutrition, mental wellness, beauty and style. **Nonfiction:** Reports, features, stories, personal essays; on topics related to women's

health and well-being; Up to 4,000 words. **Columns, Departments:** health, nutrition, fitness, beauty, style, psychology. **Tips:** Pitch stories with a news hook. **Queries:** Preferred. **E-queries:** Yes. **Unsolicited mss:** Accepts. **Response:** 1 month, SASE. **Freelance Content:** 75%. **Rights:** 1st NA. **Payment:** On acceptance. **Contact:** Dana Points, Exec. Ed.

SIMPLER LIVING

PO Box 61605, Santa Barbara, CA 93111.
E-mail: editor@simplerliving.com. Web site: www.simplerliving.com. Monthly. Edel Jarboe, Editor. **Description:** Online publication, focused on women who want to improve their lives. Articles with practical information about work, money, health and nutrition, fitness, parenting, relationships, cooking, time management. **Nonfiction:** 500-2,000 words; $30 (features); $10 (reprints). **Tips:** Looking for self-help articles based on interviews or research. Query with subject of article, title, word count, and 50-word description. **Queries:** Required. **E-queries:** Yes. **Response:** 2-3 days. **Rights:** 1st online (for 1 month).

SO TO SPEAK

George Mason Univ., 4400 University Dr., MS2D6,
Fairfax, VA 22030-4444. 703-993-3625.
E-mail: sts@gmu.edu. Web site: www.gmu.edu/org/sts. Bi-annual. $6/issue, $11/year. Circ.: 1,300. Kaia Sand, Editor. **Description:** Feminist journal of language and arts, concerned with the history of women, of feminists, and looking to see the future through art. Includes fiction, poetry, nonfiction, reviews, visual arts (b/w). **Fiction:** Literary, feminist; to 5,000 words. **Nonfiction:** Literary, lyrical, critical; reviews (feminist books and hypertext); to 4,000 words. **Poetry:** Literary, feminist; experimental, lyrical, narrative. **Art:** b/w art, seeking color cover art. **Queries:** Not necessary. **E-queries:** No. **Unsolicited mss:** Accepts. **Response:** Submissions 3-4 months, SASE. **Payment:** In copies.

SPORTS ILLUSTRATED FOR WOMEN

135 W. 50th St., New York, NY 10020-1393. 212-522-2248.
Web site: www.siforwomen.com. Bimonthly. $3.50. Circ.: 400,000. Sandy Bailey, Editor. **Description:** Sports with a female interest focus. **Queries:** Preferred.

TODAY'S CHRISTIAN WOMAN

465 Gundersen Dr., Carol Stream, IL 60188. 630-260-6200.
E-mail: tcwedit@christianitytoday.com. Bi-monthly. Circ.: 300,000., Managing Editor. **Description:** For women, ages 20-40, on contemporary issues and hot topics that impact their lives, providing depth, balance, and biblical perspective to their daily relationships. **Nonfiction:** Articles to help women grow in their relationship to God, and to provide practical help on family/parenting, friendship, marriage, health, single life, finances, and work; 1,000-1,800 words. **Tips:** No poetry, fiction or Bible studies. Looking for humor; issues/hot topics; "my story" articles. **Queries:** Required.

E-queries: Yes. **Unsolicited mss:** Accepts. **Response:** 8 weeks, SASE. **Rights:** 1st. **Payment:** On acceptance.

TRUE CONFESSIONS

233 Park Ave. S, 5th Floor, New York, NY 10003. 212-979-4800. E-mail: trueconfessionsmail@yahoo.com. Monthly. Circ.: 200,000. Pat Byrdsong, Editor. **Description:** Timely, emotional, first-person stories on romance, family life, and problems of today's young working-class women. **Nonfiction:** Prefers stories from 5,000-8,000 words; 1,000-9,000 words; $.05/word. **Fillers:** Woman to Woman; My Moment with God; My Man; Incredible but True (warm, inspirational first-person fillers about love, marriage, family life, prayer, to 300 words). Also, short stories, 1,000-2,000 words; $.05/word. **Tips:** Very interested in stories highlighting experiences of Asian, African, and Latina Americans. **Rights:** All. **Payment:** On publication.

TRUE LOVE

233 Park Ave. S., 6th Floor, New York, NY 10003. 212-979-4800. Web site: www.truestorymail.com. Alison Way, Editor. **Description:** Fresh, young, true-to-life stories, on love and topics of current interest. **Nonfiction:** Pays $.03/word. **Tips:** Must use past tense and first-person style. **Payment:** On publication.

VOGUE

Conde Nast, 4 Times Square, New York, NY 10036. 212-286-7351. Web site: www.vogue.com. **Description:** General features. **Nonfiction:** Articles, to 1,500 words, on women, entertainment and arts, travel, medicine, and health. **Queries:** Preferred.

WAHM.COM

Maricle Communications, P.O. Box 366, Folsom, CA 95763. 916-985-2078. E-mail: chdemas@aol.com. Web site: www.wahm.com. Weekly. Cheryl Demas, Publisher. **Description:** E-zine for work-at-home moms.

WINK

Doublespace, 601 West 26th St., 14th Fl, New York, NY 10001. 212-366-1919. Web site: www.winkmag.com. Monthly. Circ.: 50,000. Ralph Clermont, CEO. **Description:** Cross-cultural fashion and beauty magazine. Mingles Black, white, Latino, Asian, Caribbean, and African, with all the splendor that arises when different cultures come together. Online and in print.

WOMAN TODAY

501 S. Spring St., Penthouse, CA 90013. E-mail: celia@mail.ishark.com. Web site: www.womantoday.com. Monthly. Celia A. Esguerra, Editor-in-Chief. **Description:** E-zine for women.

WOMAN'S DAY

1633 Broadway, New York, NY 10019. 212-767-6418. Web site: www.womansday.com. Sara Glines, Editor. **Description:** Covers marriage, child-rearing, health, careers, relationships, money management. **Nonfiction:** Human-interest or service-oriented articles, 750-1,200 words. Dramatic first-person narratives of medical miracles, rescues, women's experiences, etc. Pays standard rates.

WOMAN'S OWN

1115 Broadway, New York, NY 10010. 212-807-7100. Web site: womansown.com. Rachael Butler, Editor. **Description:** Inspirational, practical advice on relationships, career, and lifestyle choices for women, ages 25-35. Topics: staying together, second marriages, working women, asserting yourself, meeting new men, sex, etc. **Nonfiction:** Articles, 1,500-2,000 words; pays $50-$500. **Fillers:** Woman in the News (profiles, 250-500 words, women who have overcome great odds); fun, in-depth quizzes; Let's Put Our Heads Together (short pieces on trends and breakthroughs). **Columns, Departments:** Suddenly Single, Moving Up, Round-Up, Mindpower, Dieter's Notes, Fashion Advisor, Financial Advisor; 800 words. **Queries:** Preferred. **Payment:** On acceptance.

WOMAN'S TOUCH

1445 Boonville, Springfield, MO 65802-1894. 417-862-2781. E-mail: womanstouch@ag.org. Web site: www.ag.org/womanstouch. 6x/year. $8.50/issue. Circ.: 18,000. Darla Knoth, Managing Editor. **Description:** Not-for-profit ministry magazine, for Christian women. **Nonfiction:** About triumph in times of trouble, celebrity interviews with women leaders, cooking, reaching the unchurched, testimonies, unique activities for women's groups or mature singles; 800 words; $20-$40. **Fillers:** Humor only; 500-800 words; $20-$40. **Columns, Departments:** Parenting, singlehood; 500-600 words; $20-$40. **Tips:** Seeking humor pieces, articles with fresh themes; send 3 suggested headlines with article. Publishes some book excerpts. Most readers over 35. Query or submit via email. **Queries:** Not necessary. **E-queries:** Yes. **Unsolicited mss:** Accepts. **Response:** 12 weeks. **Freelance Content:** 20%. **Rights:** One-time. **Payment:** On publication.

WOMAN'S WORLD

270 Sylvan Ave., Englewood Cliffs, NJ 07632. E-mail: dearww@aol.com. Stephanie Saible, Editor-in-Chief. **Description:** For middle-income women, ages 18-60, on love, romance, careers, medicine, health, psychology, family life, travel; dramatic stories of adventure or crisis, investigative reports. **Fiction:** Fast-moving short stories, 1,000 words, with light romantic theme; prefers dialogue-driven to propel the story. (Specify "short story" on outside of envelope.) Mini-mysteries, 1,200 words, with "whodunit" or "howdunit" theme. No science fiction, fantasy, horror, ghost stories, or gratuitous violence. Pays $1,000 for short stories; $500 for mini-mysteries. **Nonfiction:** Articles (query first), 600-1,800 words; pays $300-$900. **Payment:** On acceptance.

WOMEN IN BUSINESS

American Business Women's Assn., 9100 Ward Pkwy., Box 8728, Kansas City, MO 64114-0728. 816-361-6621. E-mail: rwarbing@abwa.org. Web site: www.abwa.org. Bi-monthly. $12/yr (members), $20/yr (others). Rachel Warbingtom, Editor. **Description:** Published by American Business Women's Assn. Focuses on leadership, education, networking support and national recognition. Helps business women of diverse occupations to grow personally and professionally. **Nonfiction:** How-to business features for working women, ages 35-55 (trends, small-business ownership, self-improvement, retirement issues). Profiles of ABWA members only; 1,000-1,500 words; $.20/word. **E-queries:** Yes. **Unsolicited mss:** Accepts. **Freelance Content:** 2%. **Payment:** On publication.

WOMEN TODAY

P.O. Box 300, Vancouver, British Columbia, Canada V6C 2X3. 604-514-2000, x283. E-mail: editor@womentodaymagazine.com. Web site: www.womentodaymagazine.com. Monthly. **Description:** E-zine for women. International focus. **Nonfiction:** Pays with byline and hyperlink. **Queries:** Required. **E-queries:** Yes. **Response:** 4 weeks. **Rights:** one-time.

WOMEN'S INTERNATIONAL NET (WIN)

301 E. 79th St., Suite 12A, New York, NY 10021. 646-349-2763. E-mail: editor@winmagazine.com. Web site: http://welcome.to/winmagazineMonthly. Monthly. Free Online. **Description:** E-zine; offers a broad range of opinions on women's issues throughout the world. Seeks to improve status of women everywhere by comparing problems and solutions. Not aligned with any political view. Seeks reports, personal accounts, interviews, and short stories. **Fiction:** Short stories. **Nonfiction:** Personal accounts, interviews, reports. **Tips:** No material that is sexist, racist, homophobic, or otherwise discriminatory. Readers are intellectual, general audience.

WORKING MOTHER

MacDonald Communications, 135 W. 50th St., 16th Fl., New York, NY 10020-1201. 212-445-6100. E-mail: editors@workingmothers.com. Monthly. $2.99/month, $9.97/year. Circ.: 990,000. Lisa Benenson, Editor. **Description:** Articles to help women in their task of juggling job, home, and family. Everything a working mother needs. **Nonfiction:** Solving or illuminating a problem for working mothers; 1,500-2,000 words; pay varies. **Queries:** Required. **E-queries:** Yes. **Freelance Content:** 40%. **Rights:** All. **Payment:** On publication.

WORKING WOMAN

135 W. 50th St., 16th Fl., New York, NY 10020-1201. 212-445-6100. E-mail: editors@workingwoman.com. Web site: www.workingwoman.com. **Description:** On business, finance, and technology. Readers are high-level executives and entrepreneurs looking for newsworthy information about the changing

marketplace and its effects on their businesses and careers. **Nonfiction:** Articles, 200-1,500 words; pays from $250. **Tips:** No profiles of executives or entrepreneurs. Seeking trend pieces targeting a specific industry, showing how it is affected by new technology, business practices, market situations. **Queries:** Preferred. **Unsolicited mss:** Does not accept. **Payment:** On acceptance.

YM

375 Lexington Ave., 8th Floor, New York, NY 10017-5514. E-mail: sglassman@ym.com. Web site: www.ym.com. 10x/year. $2.99/issue. Circ.: 12,000,000. Annemarie Iverson, Editor. **Description:** Sourcebook for fashion, beauty, boys, advice, and features for girls, ages 12-24. **Queries:** Required. **Unsolicited mss:** Accepts. **Response:** Queries 1-2 months. **Freelance Content:** 40%. **Payment:** On publication.

WRITING & PUBLISHING

AKKADIAN

KBST Publishing, P.O. Box 601, Hastings-on-Hudson, NY 10706. 914-478-5754. E-mail: editor@akkadian.com. Web site: www.akkadian.com. Kate Foss, Managing Editor. **Description:** E-zine for younger, unpublished writers. **Tips:** Guidelines, policies, and payment information on website. **Queries:** Preferred. **E-queries:** Yes. **Unsolicited mss:** Accepts.

AMERICAN JOURNALISM REVIEW

Univ. of Maryland, 1117 Journalism Bldg. #2116, College Park, MD 20742-7111. 301-405-8803. E-mail: editor@ajr.umd.edu. Web site: www.ajr.org. Monthly. Circ.: 25,000. Rem Rieder, Editor. **Description:** Covers print, broadcast, and online journalism. Articles, 500-5,000 words, on trends, political issues, ethics, and coverage that falls short. Pay varies. **Queries:** Required. **E-queries:** Yes. **Unsolicited mss:** Accepts. **Freelance Content:** 70%. **Rights:** print and electronic. **Payment:** On publication.

BLOOMSBURY REVIEW

1553 Platte St., Suite 206, P.O. Box 8928, Denver, CO 80201. 303-455-3123. E-mail: bloomsb@aol.com. Bimonthly. $3. Circ.: 50,000. Tom Auer, Editor. **Description:** Book reviews, also literary features, interviews, essays, poetry. **Nonfiction:** Essays, features, and interviews; 600 words or more; $10-$40. **Poetry:** Yes; $5-$15/poem. **Queries:** Preferred. **E-queries:** Yes. **Unsolicited mss:** Accepts. **Response:** Queries 2 weeks, submissions 2 months, SASE required. **Freelance Content:** 25%. **Rights:** 1st. **Payment:** On publication.

BOOKPAGE

ProMotion, Inc., 2143 Belcourt Ave., Nashville, TN 37212. 615-292-8926. E-mail: katherine_wyrick@bookpage.com. Web site: www.bookpage.com. Monthly. Circ.: 650,000. Lynn Green, Editor. **Description:** Book reviews, for a consumer-oriented tabloid used by booksellers and libraries to promote new titles and authors. **Nonfiction:** 500 words; $20/review. **Tips:** Query with writing samples and areas of interest; Editor will make assignments for reviews. **Queries:** Required.

BOOKS & CULTURE: A CHRISTIAN REVIEW

Christianity Today International, 465 Gundersen Dr., Carol Stream, IL 60188. 630-260-6200. Web site: www.christianity.net. Bimonthly. Circ.: 18,000. **Description:** Looks at Christian books, culture, and religion.

BUSINESS READER REVIEW

The Business Reader, 409 Yorkshire Dr., Williamsburg, VA 23185. 757-258-4746. E-mail: bizbooks@gte.net. Web site: home1.gte.net/bizbooks. monthly. Theodore Kinni, Editor. **Description:** Reviews of business management books published in the last 30 days. **E-queries:** Yes. **Unsolicited mss:** Accepts.

BYLINE

Box 130596, Edmond, OK 73013. 405-348-5591. E-mail: mpreston@bylinemag.com. Web site: www.ByLineMag.com. Monthly. $22/year. Marcia Preston, Editor. **Description:** Publication for writers. **Fiction:** Genre, mainstream or literary. No graphic sex or violence; no sci-fi; 2,000-4,000 words; $100. **Nonfiction:** On the craft and business of writing; 1,500-1,800 words; $75. **Poetry:** About writing or the creative process; 30 lines max.; $10. **Fillers:** Humor; 100-500 words; $15-$25. **Columns, Departments:** End Piece (700 words, $35); First Sale (250-300 words, $20); Great American Bookstores (500-600 words, $35-$40). **Tips:** Include practical information that can help writers succeed. **Queries:** Preferred. **E-queries:** Accepts. **Unsolicited mss:** Accepts. **Response:** Queries 1-3 weeks, 1 month for submissions, SASE required. **Freelance Content:** 80%. **Rights:** FNASR. **Payment:** On acceptance.

CANADIAN WRITER'S JOURNAL

Box 5180, New Liskeard, Ontario P0J 1P0. 705-647-5424. E-mail: cwj@ntl.sympatico.ca. Web site: www.nt.net/~cwj/index.htm. Bimonthly. Circ.: 350. Carole Manseau, Managing Editor. **Description:** For writers. Emphasizes short "how-to" articles which convey easily understood information useful to both apprentice and professional writers. **Fiction:** Bi-annual short fiction contests (deadlines: Sept. 30th and March 31st). **Nonfiction:** Any subject related to writing, from generating ideas to marketing and publishing. Verify sources or quotes. Book reviews, 250-500 words, on books about writing or books published in Canada; 400-2,000 words; $5/page (450 words). **Poetry:** Original, unpublished only; pays $2-$5/poem. **Fillers:** Humorous or seasonal items related to inspiration or the writing experience. **Columns, Departments:** Opinion pieces on issues affecting writers/publishers. **Tips:** Prefers electronic submissions. Be specific, precise. Use your personal experience and achievements. Avoid overworked subjects (overcoming writer's block, handling rejection, finding time to write, etc.). **Queries:** Preferred. **E-queries:** Yes. **Unsolicited mss:** Accepts. **Response:** 2 months, SASE required (use IRCs). **Freelance Content:** 75%. **Payment:** On publication.

CATHOLIC LIBRARY WORLD
Catholic Library Assn., 100 North St., Suite 224, Pittsfield, MA 01201-5109. 413-443-2CLA. E-mail: cla@vgernet.net. Web site: http://www.cathla.org. Quarterly. $60/yr. Mary E. Gallagher, SSJ, Editor. **Description:** Published by Catholic Library Assn. Articles, reviews, and association news, for librarians. No payment offered. **Nonfiction:** For school, academic, and institutional archivists. **Queries:** Not necessary. **E-queries:** Yes. **Unsolicited mss:** Accepts.

CHILDREN'S BOOK INSIDER
901 Columbia Rd., Ft. Collins, CO 80525-1838. 800-807-1916. E-mail: cbi@sendfree.com. Web site: www.write4kids.com. Monthly. **Description:** The "inside scoop" on publishing books for children.

CHILDREN'S WRITER
93 Long Ridge Rd., West Redding, CT 06896-1124. 800-443-6078. Web site: www.childrenswriter.com. Monthly. $24.95/year. **Description:** A newsletter reporting on the marketplace for children's writing. **Nonfiction:** Pays $150-$250 for very tightly written articles; 850-2,000 words; $200-$250. **Queries:** Preferred. **Response:** within one month, SASE. **Rights:** First time rights.

CYBER OASIS
E-mail: eide491@earthlink.net. Web site: people.delphi.com/eide491/oasis.html. Monthly. David Eide, Editor. **Description:** Original material on issues and concerns for writers. Also, some literary material. **Nonfiction:** 700-3,000 words, pays $10-20. **Tips:** Query by email. **Queries:** Preferred. **E-queries:** Yes. **Unsolicited mss:** Accepts.

EDITOR & PUBLISHER
770 Broadway 7th Fl, New York, NY 10003. 646-654-5270. Web site: www.editorandpublisher.com. Weekly. **Description:** On the newspaper industry. Newspaper websites, features, how-tos, opinion pieces, etc. **Nonfiction:** News articles, 900 words; pay varies. **Tips:** Send complete manuscripts. **Payment:** On publication.

THE EDITORIAL EYE
66 Canal Center Plz, Ste 200, Alexandria, VA 22314-5507. 703-683-0683. Web site: www.eeicommunications.com. **Description:** Resource for editors, writers, managers, journalists and educators. All about the written word.

FOLIO

Simba Information, 11 River Bend Dr. S, Stamford, CT 06907-0949. 203-358-9900. Web site: www.foliomag.com. 17x/year. Circ.: 16,000. **Description:** For the magazine publishing executive.

FOREWORD

129 East Front St., Traverse City, MI 49684-2508. 231-933-3699. E-mail: mlink@forewordmagazine.com. Web site: www.forewordmagazine.com. 8x/year. Circ.: 15,000. Mardi Link, Editor. **Description:** Trade journal for independent publishers and booksellers. **Columns, Departments:** "Afterword" essay, 700 words; pays $100. **Tips:** Sample copy, $5. **Queries:** Required. **E-queries:** Yes. **Unsolicited mss:** Accepts. **Freelance Content:** 10%.

THE HORN BOOK MAGAZINE

56 Roland St., Suite 200, Boston, MA 02129. 617-628-0225. E-mail: info@hbook.com. Web site: www.hbook.com. Bimonthly. $9.50/issue, $45/year. Circ.: 18,500. Roger Sutton, Editor-in-Chief. **Description:** A critical review of introductory children's and young adult books. Also, editorials, columns, and articles about children's literature. **Nonfiction:** Critical essays on children's literature and related subjects for librarians, teachers, parents; up to 280 words. **Queries:** Not necessary. **E-queries:** Yes. **Unsolicited mss:** Accepts. **Response:** 4-6 months, SASE required. **Payment:** On publication. **Contact:** Roger Sutton.

THE INTERNET WRITING JOURNAL

Writer's Write, Inc. E-mail: journal@writerswrite.com. Web site: www.writerswrite.com. Claire E. White, Editor-in-Chief. **Description:** Articles on all aspects of writing, in all genres. No payment, offers byline and links to websites of the author's choosing. **Nonfiction:** To 1,750 words. **Tips:** E-Query only, in body of email or as text file.

IPI GLOBAL JOURNALIST

132 A Neff Annex, Columbia, MO 65211. 573-884-1599. E-mail: ipi_report@jmail.jour.missouri.edu. Web site: www.freemedia.at; go to IPI Report. Quarterly. $19.95/yr. Circ.: 4,500. Prof. Stuart H. Loory, Editor. **Description:** International journalism for academics, working journalists, and the general public. Encourages submissions from journalism students. **Nonfiction:** Articles on current events in international news; interviews with journalists in the field; survey articles on international press freedom concerns; 300-1,200 words; $350 fee. **Queries:** Preferred. **E-queries:** Yes. **Unsolicited mss:** Accepts. **Response:** 1-2 weeks, SASE required. **Freelance Content:** 70%. **Rights:** 1st. **Payment:** On publication.

IPI REPORT

University of Missouri, 132A Neff Annex, School of Journalism, Columbia, MO 65211. 573-884-7542. E-mail: stuart_loory@jmail.jour.missouri.edu. Quarterly. Prof. Stuart Loory.

Description: Short articles on international journalism, press coverage, and free-press issues around the world. **Nonfiction:** Pay varies. **Tips:** SASE for guidelines; prefers e-mail submissions. **Queries:** Required. **Payment:** On publication.

LAMBDA BOOK REPORT
1773 "T" Street NW, Suite One, Washington, DC 20009. 202-462-7924.
Description: Reviews and features on gay and lesbian books. **Nonfiction:** 250-1,500 words; pays $10-$75. **Queries:** Preferred. **Payment:** On publication.

LITERARY TRAVELER
Somerville, MA 02144. 617-628-3504.
E-mail: francis@literarytraveler.com. Web site: www.literarytraveler.com. Linda McGovern, Editor. **Description:** E-zine, for articles about writers or places that have literary significance. **Nonfiction:** Pays $5-25. **Queries:** Preferred. **E-queries:** Yes. **Unsolicited mss:** Accepts.

LITTERA LAPIS
E-mail: mike@bookstones.com. Web site: www.bookstones.com/zine. Monthly. Mike Decker, Publisher. **Description:** E-zine for people who love books.

LOCUS
P.O. Box 13305, Oakland, CA 94661. 510-339-9196.
Web site: www.locusmag.com. Monthly. Circ.: 7,500. **Description:** For professional writers and publishers of science-fiction, covers industry news.

NEWSLETTER ON NEWSLETTERS
P.O. Box 348, Rhinebeck, NY 12572. 845-876-5222.
Semi-monthly. **Description:** For professionals involved in publishing newsletters.

OHIO WRITER
P.O. Box 91801, Cleveland, OH 44101. 216-421-0403.
E-mail: poetsleague@yahoo.com. 6x/year. Circ.: 1,000. Gail and Stephen Bellamy, Editors. **Description:** Features, interviews, how-tos, and articles relevant to writing in Ohio. Annual contest for fiction, poetry, columns, and literary nonfiction categories. **Tips:** Sample copy, $3. **Queries:** Required. **Response:** 3 months. **Freelance Content:** 5%. **Rights:** revert to author after publication. **Payment:** On publication.

ONCE UPON A TIME
553 Winston Ct., St. Paul, MN 55118. 651-457-6223.
E-mail: audreyouat@aol.com. Web site: www.members@aol.com. Quarterly. $25. Circ.: 1,000. Audrey B. Baird, Editor. **Description:** Wisdom and advice for those who write and illustrate for children. **Nonfiction:** Writing and/or illustrating how-tos (plotting, character development, revising, dialogue, illustrating techniques and materials, etc.), how you work, handle rejections, the story behind your book, etc.;

100-900 words. **Poetry:** On related topics; 30 lines. **Art:** Illustrations, black ink on white paper only. **Tips:** Use friendly style, with tips and information that really work. **E-queries:** No. **Unsolicited mss:** Accepts. **Response:** Submissions 1 month, SASE. **Freelance Content:** 50%. **Rights:** one-time. **Payment:** In copies.

PAPYRUS

P.O. Box 270797, West Hartford, CT 06127-0797.
E-mail: gwhitaker@imagine.com. Ginger Whitaker, Editor. **Description:** "The writer's craftletter featuring the black experience."

PRESSTIME

Newspaper Assn. of America, 1921 Gallows Rd., Ste 600,
Vienna, VA 22182. 703-902-1600.
Web site: www.naa.org/ptime. Monthly. Circ.: 15,000. **Description:** Published by the Newspaper Association of America.

PUBLISHERS WEEKLY

245 W. 17th St., New York, NY 10011. 212-463-6758.
Web site: wwwpublishersweekly.com. Daisy Maryles, Editor. **Description:** Seeking essays, 900 words, on current issue or problem facing publishing and book-selling for "My Say" column. Articles for "Booksellers' Forum" may be somewhat longer. Pay varies.

QUILL

2900 Warden Ave., P.O. Box 92207, Toronto,
Ontario, Canada M1W 3Y9. 416-410-0277.
E-mail: austin@quill.com. Web site: www.thequill.com. Quarterly. Charlotte Austine, Editor. **Description:** E-zine for beginning writers. **Nonfiction:** Seeking quality articles, 800-1,200 words, on the craft of writing; pays $50-60. **Queries:** Required. **E-queries:** Yes. **Unsolicited mss:** Accepts. **Payment:** On acceptance.

RAINY DAY CORNER

6022 N. 29th St., Arlington, VA 22207.
E-mail: idupie@rainydaycorner.com. Web site: www.rainydaycorner.com. Monthly. **Description:** A website, with a print newsletter, providing information and tips to help with homework, family, the working parent, and writing contests for kids. **Nonfiction:** Needs: Short articles on how to deal with homework dilemmas, how to get children interested in reading and writing, all aspects of education K-8, on concerns of parents working in or outside the home; 1,000 words max.; $5/article. **Tips:** If your article is writing- or art-related, write so a child will understand, without talking down to them. Keep your articles conversational, but factual. **Queries:** Preferred. **E-queries:** Yes. **Unsolicited mss:** Accepts. **Response:** 2-3 weeks, SASE required. **Rights:** 1st. **Payment:** On publication.

READERS AND WRITERS MAGAZINE

P.O. Box 231023, Encinitas, CA 92023-1023. 760-632-9268.
E-mail: chas@artichokepublishing.com. Charles McStravick, Managing Editor.
Description: For writers. Offers author interviews and profiles, book reviews, and creative nonfiction articles about the writing and publishing world, about literary arts culture. **Nonfiction:** Feature-length articles (1,200-3,300 words), $20-$75; smaller articles and reviews (600-800 words), $20.

ROMANTIC TIMES MAGAZINE

55 Bergen St., Brooklyn, NY 11201. 718-237-1097.
Web site: romantictimes.com. **Description:** Topics on the romance-fiction publishing industry.

SCAVENGER'S NEWSLETTER

833 Main, Osage City, KS 66523-1241. 785-528-3538.
E-mail: foxscar1@jc.net. Web site: www.jlgiftsshop.com/scav/index.html. Monthly. $22/yr. Circ.: 600. Janet Fox, Editor. **Description:** Market newsletter for science fiction, fantasy, horror, and mystery writers and artists, focusing on small presses. **Fiction:** Flash genre fiction; up to 1,200 words; $5. **Nonfiction:** Articles for genre writers/artists; up to 1,500 words; $5. **Poetry:** Avoid rhymed; up to 10 lines; $3. **Fillers:** Short writer/artist humor; 500-700 words; $3. **Art:** Black-and-white illustrations, 7" x 8½" covers and small fillers; $5 per cover and $3 per filler. **Tips:** Do not ignore word-length guidelines; space is limited. **Queries:** Not necessary. **E-queries:** Accepts. **Unsolicited mss:** Accepts. **Response:** Queries 2-7 days, submissions 1-4 weeks. **Freelance Content:** 10%. **Payment:** On acceptance.

SMALL PRESS REVIEW

Dustbooks, P.O. Box 100, Paradise, CA 95967. 530-877-6110.
E-mail: dustbooks@desi.net. Web site: www.dustbooks.com. Bimonthly. $25/yr. Circ.: 2,500. Len Fulton, Editor. **Description:** Reviews and news about small presses and magazines. **Nonfiction:** Reviews, 200 words, of small-press literary books and magazines; essays on small publishers, small-circulation magazines. **Queries:** Preferred.

SOCIETY OF CHILDREN'S BOOK WRITERS & ILLUSTRATORS

8271 Beverly Blvd., Los Angeles, CA 90048. 323-782-1010.
E-mail: scbwi@scbwi.org. Web site: scbwi.org. Monthly. **Description:** Articles pertinent to writers and/or illustrators of children's books. **Nonfiction:** Pays $50 for articles. **Art:** Pays $10 for line drawings; $25 for b/w cover photo. **Queries:** Required. **Rights:** 1st time.

THE STRAND

P.O. Box 1418, Birmingham, MI, 48012. 248-788-5948.
Quarterly. Circ.: 14,000. **Description:** About books and people involved in publishing fiction in genres of mystery, detective stories, and horror.

TECHNICAL COMMUNICATION

Society for Technical Communication, 901 N. Stuart St., Ste 904, Arlington, VA 22203. 703-522-4114. Web site: www.stc-va.org. Quarterly. Circ.: 18,000. **Description:** Industry information for technical writers, publishers, and editors.

THE WRITE MOVES

E-mail: kal_1@msn.com. Web site: www.allthewritemoves.com. Bimonthly. Circ.: 3,500. Kyle Looby, Publisher. **Description:** Articles on writing and publishing. Success stories, book reviews, how-to topics. **Nonfiction:** 800-1,000 words; $20/original article ($10/reprints). **Tips:** Will also include a picture, bio, and link to your web site. **Queries:** Required. **E-queries:** Yes. **Unsolicited mss:** Accepts. **Response:** 1-2 weeks. **Rights:** One-time electronic, plus display on website for one month. **Payment:** In copies.

THE WRITER

Kalmbach Publishing Co., P.O. Box 1612, 21027 Crossroads Circle, Waukesha, WI 53187-1612. 262-796-8776. E-mail: editor@writermag.com. Web site: www.writermag.com. Monthly. Circ.: 18,000. Elfrieda Abbe, Editor. **Description:** Articles about writing, for writers, since 1887. **Nonfiction:** Articles, to 3,000 words. How-to, marketing ideas, publishing trends, profiles, and book reviews. Pays $300-$800. **Poetry:** About writing; pays $20-$35. **Fillers:** Cartoons; pays $25. **Columns, Departments:** Book reviews; pays $50. **Art:** Photos; pays $50-$100. **Tips:** Prefers electronic submission; query with sample clips. Sample copies $2.75, plus tax, S/H.

WRITER ONLINE

40 Royal Oak Dr., Rochester, NY 14624. E-mail: email@novalearn.com. Web site: www.novalearn.com/wol. Biweekly. Circ.: 35,000. T.M. Wright, Editor. **Description:** Free newsletter (e-zine) for all writers. Many have been previously published; most are motivated by the desire to sell their writing. Fiction and nonfiction. Pays $.05-$.10/word. **Nonfiction:** Articles addressing the craft of writing. Prefers articles that offer examples and use direct quotes from credible sources. Articles connected to recognizable names are of premier value; up to 1,800 words.

THE WRITER'S CHRONICLE

Associated Writing Programs, MSN 1E3, George Mason University, Fairfax, VA 22030. E-mail: awpchron@mason.gmu.edu. 6x/yr. Circ.: 20,000. **Description:** "For serious writers." **Nonfiction:** Information on grants, awards, fellowships, articles, news, and reviews. Pays $7 per 100 words, or as negotiated. **Tips:** Email query preferred.

WRITER'S DIGEST

Citicorp Venture Capital, 1507 Dana Ave.,
Cincinnati, OH 45207-1005. 513-531-2690.
Web site: www.writersdigest.com. Monthly. Circ.: 170,000. **Description:** Covers all aspects of the American writing market.

WRITERS' JOURNAL

P.O. Box 394, Perham, MN 56573-0394. 218-346-7921.
E-mail: writersjournal@wadena.net. Web site: www.writersjournal.com. Bimonthly.
Circ.: 26,000. **Description:** For writers, including professional communicators, independent/self-publishers, part- or full-time freelancers, screenwriters, desktop publishers, authors, editors, teachers, and poets. **Nonfiction:** Practical advice on business side of writing (tips, techniques, record keeping, how to increase production, taxes, financial aspects); 1,000-1,500 words, pays $20. **Poetry:** Light verse, preferably about writing. Also buys a few serious pieces, any subject, any style, with strong imagery and impact; 25 lines max.; pays $10. **Columns, Departments:** Book reviews on recent books on writing, of use to writers; 200-250 words. **Tips:** Submit articles with positive, practical advice. **Queries:** Required. **E-queries:** Yes. **Unsolicited mss:** Accepts. **Response:** Queries 6 weeks, submissions 6 months, SASE required. **Rights:** One-time. **Payment:** On publication.

WRITER'S LIFELINE

P.O. Box 1641, Cornwall, Ontario, Canada ON K6H 5V6. 613-932-2135.
Quarterly. Circ.: 1,000. **Description:** Book reviews, poetry; how-tos (on the art and business of writing).

FICTION & POETRY
MAGAZINES

FICTION & POETRY MAGAZINES

The following section presents a list of magazines whose primary focus in most cases is publishing fiction and poetry. The fiction usually appears in the form of short stories; however, some magazines also publish excerpts from novels and longer works.

The list is divided into markets for specific genres of fiction. These include: Fiction for Children, Fiction for Teens, Literary Magazines, Mystery and Detective, Romance and Confession, and Science Fiction and Fantasy.

The largest number of magazines are found in the Literary Magazine portion. These independent and college journals often publish not only fiction and poetry but also a potent range of creative nonfiction essays on varied cultural topics, as well as book reviews and interviews with authors and artists.

Although payment from these relatively small magazines, which range in circulation from 300 to 10,000, is modest (often in copies only), publication can begin to establish a writer's serious literary credentials and often will help bring the work of a beginning writer to the attention of editors at larger magazines. Notably, some of America's leading authors still contribute work to the smaller literary magazines. Together with emerging new voices, they form a community of writers whose only criteria are excellence and the elevation of stimulating thought in literary discourse.

These literary journals, little magazines, and college quarterlies welcome work from novices and pros alike; editors are always interested in seeing traditional and experimental fiction, poetry, essays, reviews, short articles, criticism, and satire. As long as the material is well-written, the fact that a writer has not yet been widely published doesn't adversely affect his or her chances for acceptance.

Most of these literary publications have small budgets and staffs, so they may be slow in their reporting time; several months is not unusual. In addition, some (particularly the college-based magazines) do not read manuscripts during the summer.

Publication may also lead to having one's work chosen for reprinting in one of the prestigious annual collections of work from the little magazines.

For a complete list of the thousands of literary publications and little magazines in existence, writers may wish to consult such comprehensive reference works as *The International Directory of Little Magazines and Small Presses*, published annually by Dustbooks (P.O. Box 100, Paradise, CA 95967) and available at many public libraries.

FICTION FOR CHILDREN

AMERICAN GIRL

8400 Fairway Place, Middleton, WI 53562. 608-836-4848. E-mail: im_agmag_editor@pleasantco.com. Web site: www.americangirl.com. Bimonthly. $3.95/issue, $9.95/year. Circ.: 650,000. Kristi Thom, Editor. **Description:** Full-color, for girls ages 8 and up. "Our mission is to celebrate girls, yesterday and today. American Girl readers are girls in their formative years, girls who dream big dreams. **Fiction:** Protagonist should be a girl between 8 and 12. No science fiction, fantasy or first romance stories. Good children's literature, with thoughtful plots and characters; 2,500 words; pay negotiable. **Nonfiction:** By assignment only; 150-1,000 words; typically $1/word. **Fillers:** Visual puzzles, mazes, math puzzles, word games, simple crosswords, cartoons. Seasonal ideas welcome. $50/puzzle. **Columns, Departments:** Girls Express (short profiles of girls doing great, interesting things); 150 words; $1/word. **Tips:** The girl must be the story's "star," told from her point of view. "Girls Express" offers best chance to break in. **Queries:** Preferred. **E-Queries:** No. **Unsolicited mss:** Accepts. **Response:** 3 months, SASE. **Freelance Content:** 5%. **Payment:** On acceptance. **Contact:** Magazine Dept. Asst.

BABYBUG

Carus Publishing Co., P.O. Box 300, 315 Fifth St, Peru, IL 61354. 815-224-6656. Web site: www.cricketmag.com. Monthly. $5/issue, $35.97/year. Circ.: 46,000. Paula Morrow, Editor. **Description:** Simple rhymes and stories that parents will delight in reading to their babies. Each page bursts with bright colors that babies love. Pays $25/piece. **Fiction:** Very simple and concrete; read-aloud and picture stories for infants and toddlers; 4-6 short sentences. **Nonfiction:** Very basic words and concepts; 10 words max. **Poetry:** Rhythmic, rhyming. Humor or ending with mild surprise a plus; 8 lines max. **Art:** By assignment only; no photos. Submit samples (tear sheets, photocopies) for consideration. Pays $250/page, $500/spread. **Payment:** On publication.

BOYS' LIFE

1325 W. Walnut Hill Lane, Irving, TX 75038. 972-580-2366. Web site: www.bsa.scouting.org. Monthly. $18/year. Circ.: 1,300,000. W. E. Butterworth IV, Managing Editor. **Description:** Published by Boy Scouts of America, for boys ages 8-14. Covers broad range of interests (sports, hobbies, careers, crafts, and special interests of scouting). **Fiction:** 1-2 short stories per issue; featuring 1 or more boys; humor, mystery, science fiction, adventure; 1,000-1,500 words; $750 and up. **Nonfiction:** From professional sports to American history to how to pack a canoe; 500-1,500 words; $400-$1,500. **Columns, Departments:** Science, nature, earth, health, sports, space and aviation, cars, computers, entertainment, pets, history, music, 300-750 words, $150-$400. Also, last-page how-to features ($250-$300). **Art:** Quality photos only; most work by assignment. **Tips:** Write for a boy you know who is 12. Use crisp, punchy writing; short, straightforward sentences. **Queries:** Required for nonfiction. **E-Queries:** Prefer mail. **Unsolicited mss:** Accepts fiction only. **Response:** 6-8 weeks, SASE required. **Freelance Content:** 75%. **Rights:** FNASR. **Payment:** On acceptance.

CHIRP

179 John St., Suite 500, Toronto, Ontario M5T 3G5. 416-340-2700. Web site: www.owl.on.ca. 9x/year. **Description:** Offers puzzles, games, rhymes, stories, and songs for children, ages 2-6. Goal is to introduce preschool children to the

relationship between words and pictures. **Fiction:** 300-400 words; pay varies. **Nonfiction:** 300-400 words; pay varies. **Queries:** Preferred. **E-Queries:** Yes. **Unsolicited mss:** Accepts. **Payment:** On publication.

CRICKET

P.O. Box 300, 315 Fifth St, Peru, IL 61354-0300. 815-224-6656. Web site: www.cricketmag.com. $5/issue, $35.97/year. Circ.: 68,000. Alice Letvin, Editorial Director. **Description:** Folk tales, fantasy, science fiction, history, poems, science, sports, and crafts, for young readers. **Fiction:** Any topic of interest to children; up to 2,000 words; $.25/word. **Nonfiction:** Science, biography, history, nature; up to 1,500 words; $.25/word. **Poetry:** Brief lyric poems; up to 25 lines; $3/line. **Fillers:** Word or math puzzles, recipes, crafts, experiments; 150-200 words; $100. **Tips:** Include bibliography with nonfiction. **Queries:** Not necessary. **E-Queries:** No. **Unsolicited mss:** Accepts. **Response:** Submissions 8-12 weeks. **Freelance Content:** 90%. **Rights:** One-time serial. **Payment:** On publication.

CRUSADER

P.O. Box 7259, Grand Rapids, MI 49510. 616-241-5616. Web site: www.gospelcom.net/cadets. 7x/year. Circ.: 12,000. G. Richard Broene, Editor. **Description:** Christian-oriented magazine for boys, ages 9-14, especially members of Calvinist Cadet Corps. Purpose is to show how God is at work in the lives of the cadets and in the world around them. **Fiction:** Fast-moving stories that appeal to a boy's sense of adventure and humor; 1,000-3,000 words; pay varies. **Tips:** Request list of themes and free sample copy. **Queries:** Preferred. **Unsolicited mss:** Accepts. **Payment:** On acceptance.

DISCOVERIES

WordAction Publishing Co., 6401 The Paseo, Kansas City, MO 64131. E-mail: kneal@nazarene.org. Weekly. Circ.: 22,000. Virginia Folsom, Editor. **Description:** Full-color story paper for 3rd and 4th graders, connecting Evangelical Sunday School learning with daily growth of a middle-grade child. **Fiction:** Contemporary, true-to-life portrayals of 8-10 year olds; 500 words; $.05/word. **Fillers:** Bible trivia and puzzles. **Tips:** Illustrate character building and scriptural application. Send for guidelines and coming themes. **Queries:** Preferred. **E-Queries:** Yes. **Unsolicited mss:** Accepts. **Response:** 6-8 weeks, SASE required. **Freelance Content:** 80%. **Rights:** Multi-use. **Payment:** On publication. **Contact:** Kathy Neal.

DISCOVERY TRAILS

1445 Boonville Ave., Springfield, MO 65802-1894. 417-862-2781. E-mail: rl-discoverytrails@gph.org. Web site: www.radiantlife.org. Quarterly. Circ.: 36,000. Sinda Zinn, Editor. **Description:** Take-home paper for children 10-11 years old, with fiction stories, activities, poems, articles, and puzzles to reinforce daily Christian living. **Fiction:** Stories that promote Christian living through application of biblical principles by the characters; 1000 words; $.07-$.10/word. **Nonfiction:**

Articles about topics that show God's power, wisdom in creation, or correlation to a relationship with God; 300-500 words; 7-10 cents/word. **Tips:** No Santa, Easter Bunny, Halloween stories. **Queries:** Not necessary. **E-Queries:** No. **Unsolicited mss:** Accepts. **Response:** Submissions 2-4 weeks, SASE required. **Freelance Content:** 90%. **Payment:** On acceptance.

HIGHLIGHTS FOR CHILDREN

803 Church St., Honesdale, PA 18431-1824. 570-253-1080. E-mail: highlights@ezaccess.net. Web site: www.highlights.com. Monthly. $29.64/year. Circ.: 2,000,000. Kent L. Brown, Managing Editor. **Description:** "Fun with a purpose." Stories, Hidden Pictures, jokes and activities bring engaging entertainment to children, ages 2-12, while developing learning skills. **Fiction:** Humor, mystery, sports, adventure, folktales, world cultures, urban stories. Engaging plot, strong characterization, lively language; up to 900 words; $150 and up. **Nonfiction:** Biography, autobiography, arts, science, history, sports, world cultures; to 800 words; $150 and up. (For younger readers, ages 3-7 years, 400 words or less.) **Poetry:** 16 lines, $25 and up. **Fillers:** Crafts (3-7 numbered steps), $30 and up; include a sample; use common household items or inexpensive, easy-to-obtain materials. Holiday/religious/world cultures crafts welcome. **Tips:** Prefers stories in which protagonist solves a dilemma through his/her own resources. Avoid stories that preach. **Queries:** Preferred. **E-Queries:** No. **Unsolicited mss:** Accepts. **Response:** 6-8 weeks, SASE required. **Rights:** All. **Payment:** On acceptance. **Contact:** Beth Troop, Manuscript Coordinator.

HOPSCOTCH

P.O. Box 164, Bluffton, OH 45817-0164. 419-358-4610. Web site: www.hopscotchmagazine.com. Bi-monthly. $4.95/issue, $17.95/year. Circ.: 15,000. Marilyn Edwards, Editor. **Description:** Written for girls, without the emphasis on fads and fashion, boyfriends and shopping. Focuses on educational activities and stories. Makes reading an adventure, and problem-solving fun. **Fiction:** Feature girls in wholesome childhood activities and pursuits; 500 words; $.05/word and up. **Nonfiction:** Features girls directly involved in an unusual and worthwhile activity. Nonfiction is 75% of magazine's contents. Photos essential. 500 words; $.05/word and up. **Poetry:** Yes; $10/poem. **Fillers:** Puzzles, games, crafts, cartoons, recipes; $10/puzzle min. **Art:** b/w photos, color slides, illustrations; $5-$35. **Tips:** Contact for upcoming themes. **Queries:** Not necessary. **E-Queries:** No. **Unsolicited mss:** Accepts. **Response:** 4-6 weeks, SASE required. **Rights:** 1st NA. **Payment:** On publication.

LADYBUG

315 Fifth St., Peru, IL 61354. 815-224-6656. Web site: www.ladybugmag.com. Monthly. $5/issue, $35.97/year. Circ.: 126,000. Paula Morrow, Editor. **Description:** Stories, poems, songs, games, and adventures for young children, ages 1-2. Each page illustrated to delight parents and children alike. **Fiction:** Picture, read-aloud, and early reader stories with lively characters.

Genres: adventure, humor, mild suspense, fairy tales, folktales, contemporary fiction; up to 850 words; $.25/word; $25 min. **Nonfiction:** How-to, informational, and humorous pieces, on age-appropriate topics; up to 300 words; $.25/word; $25 min. **Poetry:** Rhythmic, rhyming, serious, humorous, active; up to 20 lines; up to $3/line; $25 min. **Fillers:** Rebus, learning activities, games, crafts, songs, finger games. **Art:** see guidelines. **Tips:** Always looking for more activities. **Queries:** Not necessary. **E-Queries:** No. **Unsolicited mss:** Accepts. **Response:** 12 weeks, SASE required. **Freelance Content:** 70%. **Rights:** 1st serial. **Payment:** On publication.

STONE SOUP

Box 83, Santa Cruz, CA 95063-0083. 831-426-5557.
E-mail: editor@stonesoup.com. Web site: www.stonesoup.com. Bimonthly. $5.50/$33. Circ.: 20,000. Gerry Mandel, Editor. **Description:** Stories, poems, book reviews, and art work by young writers and artists, ages 8-13. **Fiction:** Personal narratives, arrival stories, family histories, sport stories, science fiction; 2,500 words; $25. **Nonfiction:** Book reviews by children under 14. Prefers writing based on real-life experiences. **Poetry:** Free-verse only; $25. **Art:** For ages 8-13 only; please send 2-3 samples of your work. **Tips:** No adults! **Queries:** Not necessary. **E-Queries:** No. **Unsolicited mss:** Accepts. **Response:** Queries 2 weeks, submissions 4 weeks, SASE. **Freelance Content:** 100%. **Rights:** All. **Payment:** On publication.

WONDER TIME

6401 The Paseo, Kansas City, MO 64131. 816-333-7000 (Ext. 2244).
Weekly. None. Circ.: 14,000. Pamela Smits, Editor. **Description:** For children, ages 5-7. Emphasis on the religious instruction of children and parents. Issues are thematic. **Fiction:** A Christian emphasis to correlate with Sunday school curriculum. **Poetry:** Free verse or rhyming; 6-12 lines; $.25/word. **Columns, Departments:** Parent or family fun; 25-50 words; $15/activity. **Queries:** Preferred. **E-Queries:** No. **Unsolicited mss:** Does not accept. **Response:** 1-2 months, SASE. **Freelance Content:** 50%. **Rights:** All. **Payment:** On publication.

FICTION FOR TEENS

BREAKAWAY

8605 Explorer Dr., Colorado Springs, CO 80920. 719-531-3400.
Web site: www.family.org. Michael Ross, Editor. **Description:** Readers are Christian boys, ages 12-16. **Fiction:** Fiction, to 1,800 words; must have a male slant. **Nonfiction:** Real-life adventure articles, to 1,500 words; pays $.12-$.15/word. **Fillers:** Humor and interesting facts, 500-800 words. **Payment:** On acceptance.

BRIO

Focus on the Family, 8605 Explorer Dr., Colorado Springs, CO 80920. 719-531-3400.
E-mail: brio@macmail.fotf.org. Web site: www.briomag.com. Susie Shellenberger. **Description:** For Christian teen girls (profiles, how-to pieces, adventures that show

the fun Christian teens can have together). **Fiction:** Fiction, to 2,000 words, with realistic character development, good dialogue, and a plot that teen girls will be drawn to. May contain a spiritual slant but should not be preachy. **Nonfiction:** Articles; pays $.08-$.12/word. **Fillers:** Short humorous pieces. **Payment:** On acceptance.

CICADA
P.O. Box 300, 315 Fifth St., Peru, IL 61354. 812-224-6656.
Bi-monthly. $8.50/issue, $35.97/year. Circ.: 13,000. John Allen, Editor. **Description:** For teens, fiction and poetry that is thought-provoking, yet entertaining, often humorous. Also publishes stories by teens reflecting their own unique perspective. **Fiction:** Literary and genre fiction (realistic, humorous, science fiction and fantasy; up to 10,000 words; $.25/word. **Nonfiction:** Essays on personal experience, especially from teen authors; up to 2,000; $.25/word. **Poetry:** up to 25 lines; $3/line. **Queries:** Not necessary. **E-Queries:** No. **Unsolicited mss:** Accepts. **Response:** Submissions 8-12 weeks, SASE. **Freelance Content:** 90%. **Rights:** one-time. **Payment:** On publication. **Contact:** Debbie Vetter.

CLAREMONT REVIEW
4980 Wesley Rd., Victoria, BC, Canada V84 1Y9. 250-658-5221.
E-mail: aurora.home.com. Web site: www.members.home.net/. Semi-annual. $6/issue, $12/year. Circ.: 500. Susan Field, Business Editor. **Description:** Fiction and poetry by young writers in the English-speaking world, ages 13-19. **Fiction:** Fiction, with strong voice, 500-3,000 words. **Poetry:** Poetry that stirs the heart; 1 page. **Tips:** Fantasy, science fiction not accepted. **Queries:** Not necessary. **Unsolicited mss:** Accepts. **Response:** 6 weeks, SASE. **Freelance Content:** 100%.

ENCOUNTER
8121 Hamilton Ave., Cincinnati, OH 45231. 513-931-4050.
E-mail: kcarr@standardpub.com. Web site: www.standardpub.com. Quarterly. $13. Circ.: 32,000. Kelly Carr, Editor. **Description:** For Christian teens whose focus is to encourage other teens in their daily walk with God. Nonfiction, fiction, and daily devotion. **Fiction:** Contemporary teens, with dialogue, uplifting and character-building, conflicts resolved realistically, with moral message; 500-1,100 words; $.08/word (1st), $.06/word (reprint). **Nonfiction:** Current issues from Christian perspective. Also, teen profiles. Topics: school, family, recreation, friends, part-time jobs, dating, music; 500-1,100; pays same as fiction. **Poetry:** from teens only; $15/poem. **Queries:** Not necessary. **E-Queries:** Yes. **Unsolicited mss:** Accepts. **Response:** Queries 1-3 weeks, submissions 8-12 weeks, SASE. **Freelance Content:** 40%. **Rights:** 1st, one-time. **Payment:** On acceptance.

MERLYN'S PEN
P.O. Box 910, East Greenwich, RI 02818. 401-885-5175.
E-mail: merlynspen@aol.com. Web site: www.merlynspen.com. Annual. $29.95. Circ.: 5,000. R. James Stahl, Editor. **Description:** Fiction, essays, and poems by America's teens. All work written by students. Looking for new voices, teen writers

who have something to say and say it with eloquence, honesty, and distinctiveness. **Fiction:** Realistic fiction about contemporary teen life; also science fiction, fantasy, adventure, historical fiction; to 8,500 words; $20-$200. **Nonfiction:** Personal essays, memoirs, autobiographies, humorous or descriptive essays; 500-5,000 words. **Poetry:** Free verse, metric verse; $20-$50. **Art:** b/w illustrations (by assignment), submit samples. **Tips:** No adult authors. **Queries:** Required. **E-Queries:** No. **Unsolicited mss:** Accepts. **Response:** 10-12 weeks, SASE. **Freelance Content:** 100%. **Rights:** All. **Payment:** On publication.

NEW MOON

P.O. Box 3620, Duluth, MN 55803-3620. 218-728-5507. E-mail: girl@newmoon.org. Web site: www.newmoon.org. Bi-monthly. $5.50/issue, $29/year. Circ.: 35,000. Deb Mylin, Editor. **Description:** Celebrates girls—their accomplishments and efforts to hold onto their voices, their strengths, their dreams as they move from being girls to becoming women. **Fiction:** Stories by female authors, with girls as main characters. Fiction should fit theme (contact for upcoming list), for girls ages 8-14; 900 words; $.06-$.10/word. **Nonfiction:** Women's work (profiles a woman and her job, relates to theme); Her Story (profiles a woman from history); Body Language (about puberty, body image, depression, menstruation, etc.); Girls on the Go (by girl or woman adventurers); 600 words; $.06-$.10/word. **Art:** By assignment; send samples; pay varies. **Queries:** Not necessary. **E-Queries:** Accepts. **Unsolicited mss:** Accepts. **Response:** 2 months, SASE. **Freelance Content:** 10%. **Rights:** All. **Payment:** On publication.

SCHOLASTIC SCOPE

Scholastic, Inc., 555 Broadway, New York, NY 10012. 212-343-6100. Web site: www.scholastic.com. **Description:** Fiction for 15- to 18-year-olds, with 4th- to 6th-grade reading ability. Short stories, 400-1,200 words, on teenage interests and relationships; family, job, and school situations. Plays, to 5,000 words. Pays good rates. **Payment:** On acceptance.

TEEN

6420 Wilshire Blvd., Los Angeles, CA 90046. 323-782-2950. Web site: www.teenmag.com. Tommi Lewis, Editor-in-Chief. **Description:** Short stories (mystery, teen situations, adventure, romance, humor), for teens; 2,500-4,000 words; pays from $250-$450. **Rights:** All. **Payment:** On acceptance.

TEEN VOICES

515 Washington St., Boston, MA 02111. 617-426-5505. E-mail: womenexp@teenvoices.com. Web site: www.teenvoices.com. Quarterly. $2.95/issue, $19.95/year. Circ.: 25,000. Alison Amoroso, Editor. **Description:** Written by, for, and about teenaged and young-adult women. Offers a place to share thoughts with others the same age. **Fiction:** Short stories, any subject and length. **Nonfiction:** "About any issue that is important to you, or an important experience you've had." **Poetry:** "Your feelings, thoughts, etc." **Columns, Departments:**

Opinions/editorial pieces. **Art:** Digital file (.tif or .eps), or hardcopy. **Tips:** "Be honest, candid and true to yourself." Appreciates material that promotes feminism, equality, self-esteem ("You're more than just a pretty face"). **Queries:** Not necessary. **E-Queries:** Yes. **Unsolicited mss:** Accepts. **Response:** Submissions, a few days, SASE not required. **Rights:** 1st. **Payment:** In copies.

LITERARY MAGAZINES

AFRICAN VOICES
270 W. 96th St., New York, NY 10025. 212-865-2982.
E-mail: africanvoices@aol.com. Web site: www.africanvoices.com. Quarterly. $3/issue, $12/year. Circ.: 20,000. Carolyn A. Butts, Editor. **Description:** Literary magazine for fiction, nonfiction, poetry and visual arts created by people of color. **Fiction:** Humorous, erotic, and dramatic fiction by ethnic writers. All themes, subjects, and styles, emphasis on style and technique; 500-2,000 words. **Nonfiction:** Investigative articles, artist profiles, essays, book reviews, and first-person narratives; 500-2,500 words. **Poetry:** All styles; avant-garde, free verse, haiku, light verse, traditional. Submit up to 5 poems; max. 3 pages. **Columns, Departments:** Book reviews; 500-1,200 words. **Art:** b/w. **Queries:** Preferred. **E-Queries:** Accepts. **Unsolicited mss:** Accepts. **Response:** Queries 3 weeks, submissions 6-8 weeks, SASE. **Freelance Content:** 80%. **Rights:** 1st American. **Payment:** In copies. **Contact:** Kim Horne, fiction; Layding Kalbia, poetry; Debbie Officer, book reviews.

AFTERIMAGES
E-mail: justgus@access.digex.net. Web site: www.access.digex.net/~justgus/afterimages/. Mike Stoddard, Editor. **Description:** Literary e-zine, with "a compendium of oddities." No pay; but offers hyperlink to a site of author's choosing. **Fiction:** Prefers fantasy and science fiction; other material also accepted; 2,000-6,000 words. **Queries:** Not necessary. **E-Queries:** Yes. **Unsolicited mss:** Accepts. **Rights:** One-time.

AGNI
Boston University, Creative Writing Program, 236 Bay State Rd., Boston, MA 02215. 617-353-7135.
E-mail: agni@bu.edu. Web site: www.bu.edu/agni. Semi-annual. $8.95/issue, $15/year. Circ.: 1,800. Askold Melnyczuk, Editor. **Description:** Contemporary literature by established and new writers, on literary and political subjects, to engage readers in a broad cultural conversation. Length varies. Pays $20-150 ($10/page). **Fiction:** Criterion is excellence. **Nonfiction:** Thoughtful pieces on a group of books (not reviews of single books) or broader cultural or literary issues. **Poetry:** Yes. **Art:** Paintings, photos. **Queries:** Not necessary. **E-Queries:** No. **Unsolicited mss:** Accepts. **Response:** 2-4 months, SASE required. **Freelance Content:** 15%. **Rights:** 1st serial. **Payment:** On publication.

AGNIESZKA'S DOWRY
Small Garlic Press, 5455 Sheridan, #3003, Chicago, IL 60460.
E-mail: marek@enteract.com. Web site: www.enteract.com/~asgp/agnieszka.html.
Marek Lugowski, Editor. **Description:** On-line and in-print; a literary (primarily poetry) community. **Tips:** Policies and guidelines at website.

AKKADIAN
KBST Publishing, P.O. Box 601, Hastings-on-Hudson, NY 10706. 914-478-5754.
E-mail: editor@akkadian.com. Web site: www.akkadian.com. Kate Foss, Managing Editor. **Description:** E-zine for younger, unpublished writers. **Tips:** Guidelines, policies, and payment information on website. **Queries:** Preferred. **E-Queries:** Yes. **Unsolicited mss:** Accepts.

ALASKA QUARTERLY REVIEW
Univ. of Alaska-Anchorage, 3211 Providence Dr.,
Anchorage, AK 99508. 907-786-6916.
E-mail: ayaqr@uaa.alaska.edu. Web site: www.uaa.alaska.edu/aqr. Quarterly.
$6.95/issue. Circ.: 2,200. Ronald Spatz, Editorial Dept. **Description:** "One of the nation's best literary magazines" (Washington Post Book World). **Fiction:** Experimental and traditional literary forms. No romance, children's, or inspirational/religious; up to 20,000 words. **Nonfiction:** Literary nonfiction, essays, and memoirs; 20,000 words. **Poetry:** Avant-garde, free verse, traditional. No light verse; 10 poems max. **Queries:** Not necessary. **E-Queries:** No. **Unsolicited mss:** Accepts. **Response:** SASE required. **Freelance Content:** 95%. **Rights:** 1st NA. **Payment:** In copies.

AMELIA
329 E St., Bakersfield, CA 93304. 661-323-4064.
E-mail: amelia@lightspeed.net. Web site: www.ameliamagazine.net. Quarterly.
$10.95/issue, $30/year. Circ.: 1,800. Frederick A. Raborg, Jr., Editor. **Description:** All forms of fiction and poetry, including gay and ethnic themes. Eclectic readership, 70% college-educated. **Fiction:** All genres; 300-5,000 words; $10-$50. **Nonfiction:** 500-2,500 words; $15-$50. **Poetry:** 2-500 lines; $2-$25. **Fillers:** Funny or philosophical; 1 line-500 words; $2-$10. **Art:** b/w inside, color cover; $10-$25, $50-$100 (cover). **Queries:** Not necessary. **E-Queries:** Yes. **Unsolicited mss:** Accepts. **Response:** Queries 1-2 weeks, submissions 1 week to 3 months, SASE required. **Freelance Content:** 95%. **Rights:** 1st NA. **Payment:** On acceptance.

AMERICA
106 W. 56th St., New York, NY 10019-3893. 262-581-4640.
E-mail: articles@americapress.org. Web site: www.americapress.org. Weekly.
$2.25/issue. Circ.: 400. Thomas J. Reese, Editor. **Description:** For thinking Catholics and those interested in what Catholics are thinking. Emphasis on social justice, and religious and ethical perspectives on current issues facing the church and the world. **Nonfiction:** Features on contemporary issues from a religious and ethical

perspective; 1,500-2,000 words. **Poetry:** Serious poetry in contemporary prose idiom, free or formal verse, 20-35 lines. Submit 2-3 poems with SASE; pays $2-$3/line. **Art:** Send portfolio. **Tips:** No sermons or speeches. Address educated readers who are not experts in your topic. **Queries:** Not necessary. **Unsolicited mss:** Accepts. **Response:** Queries 1 week, submission 3 weeks, SASE required. **Freelance Content:** 50%. **Rights:** All. **Payment:** On acceptance.

AMERICAN BOOK REVIEW
Illinois State Univ., Unit for Contemporary Literature, Campus Box 4241, Normal, IL 61790-4241. Web site: www.litline.org/abr/abr. Bimonthly. $4/issue. Circ.: 6,000. Ron Sukenick, Editor. **Description:** Literary book reviews. **Fiction:** Essays on literature; 750-1,250 words; $50. **Columns, Departments:** Reviews of literary books; 750-1,250 words; $50. **Queries:** Preferred. **E-Queries:** Yes. **Response:** Queries 1 week to 1 month, submissions 1 month, SASE required. **Freelance Content:** 20%. **Payment:** On publication. **Contact:** Rebecca Kaiser.

AMERICAN LITERARY REVIEW
Univ. of North Texas, P.O. Box 311307, English Dept., Denton, TX 76203-1307. 940-565-2755. E-mail: americanliteraryreview@yahoo.com. Web site: www.engl.univ.edu/alr. Bi-annual. $5.00 newstand/$10/year. Circ.: 500. Lee Martin, Editor. **Description:** Literary journal with fiction, creative nonfiction, and poetry. In print and online. **Fiction:** Character-driven literary short stories. **Nonfiction:** Creative nonfiction. **Poetry:** Length varies. **Queries:** Not necessary. **E-Queries:** No. **Unsolicited mss:** Accepts. **Response:** Submissions 3 months, SASE. **Freelance Content:** 90%. **Rights:** 1st American serial. **Payment:** In copies.

AMERICAN POETRY REVIEW
1721 Walnut St., Philadelphia, PA 19103. 215-496-0439. Web site: www.aprweb.org. Bi-monthly. $3.95. Circ.: 20,000. Stephen Berg, David Bonanno, Editors. **Description:** Premier forum for contemporary poetry, since 1912. **Poetry:** Submit up to 4 poems, any length; $2/line. **Queries:** Not necessary. **E-Queries:** No. **Unsolicited mss:** Accepts. **Response:** Submissions 6-8 weeks, SASE required. **Payment:** On publication.

AMERICAN SCHOLAR
1785 Massachusetts Ave. NW, 4th Floor, Washington, DC 20036. 202-265-3808. E-mail: scholar@pbk.org. Web site: www.pbk.org. Quarterly. $6.95/issue. Circ.: 26,000. Anne Fadiman, Editor. **Description:** For intelligent people who love the English language. **Nonfiction:** By experts, for general audience; 3,000-5,000 words; $500. **Poetry:** Highly original; up to 33 lines; $50. **Queries:** Preferred. **E-Queries:** Yes. **Unsolicited mss:** Accepts. **Response:** 2-8 weeks, SASE required. **Freelance Content:** 100%. **Rights:** 1st. **Payment:** On acceptance.

AMERICAN WRITING

4343 Manayunk Ave., Philadelphia, PA 19128. 215-483-7051. E-mail: AMWR@concentric.net. Semiannual. $6/$10. Circ.: 2,500. Alexandra Grilikhes, Editor. **Description:** Offers bold experiments in poetry and prose. **Fiction:** The voice of the loner, in whatever situation it finds itself; up to 3,500 words. **Nonfiction:** Personal essays on art, memoir, anything the writer is obsessed by; 3,500 words. **Poetry:** Nonacademic, serious material, nothing that rhymes; up to 10 pages. **Fillers:** States of being. first-person, not necessarily narrative. **Tips:** Do not query. No pieces about sports. **Queries:** Not necessary. **E-Queries:** No. **Unsolicited mss:** Accepts. **Response:** 2 weeks to 6 months, SASE. **Freelance Content:** 98%. **Rights:** 1st serial. **Payment:** In copies.

ANCIENT PATHS

PMB 223, 2000 Benson Rd. S. #115, Renton, WA 98055. E-mail: skylar.burris@gte.net. Web site: www.geocities.com/journalancient. Semi-annual. $6/yr. Circ.: 200. Skylar Hamilton Burris, editor. **Description:** Digest featuring poetry, stories, reflection, and reviews. **Fiction:** Short stories, novel excerpts; prefers third-person; to 2,500 word. **Nonfiction:** Personal narratives, book reviews, few articles, reviews of Judeo-Christian literature; to 2,500 words. **Poetry:** Free verse or formal (ballads, sonnets, quatrains, etc.); to 70 lines. **Art:** b/w art. **Tips:** Open to subtle Judeo-Christian themes; no preaching, but say something meaningful. Avoid obscure academic, singsong rhymes, avant garde, stream of consciousness. **Queries:** Not necessary. **E-Queries:** Yes. **Unsolicited mss:** Accepts. **Response:** Submissions 3-4 weeks, SASE. **Freelance Content:** 99%. **Rights:** One-time. **Payment:** In copies.

ANOTHER CHICAGO MAGAZINE

3709 N. Kenmore, Chicago, IL 60613-2905. E-mail: editors@anotherchicagomag.com. Web site: www.anotherchicagomag.com. Semiannual. $14.95. Circ.: 2000. Barry Silesky, Editor. **Description:** Literary publication with fresh poetry, fiction, and commentary. Also, each issue features an interview with a noted writer, also translations, reviews of current literature, and an 8-page center art folio. **Fiction:** Quality, literary. **Fiction:** urgent, new, worldly; 30 pages or less. **Poetry:** Yes. **Columns, Departments:** Reviews of current fiction and poetry; 500 words. **Art:** Interesting b/w photography; 8 photos (from a single artist) in each issue. **Tips:** Seeks unusual, engaged work of highest quality only. **Queries:** Not necessary. **E-Queries:** No. **Unsolicited mss:** Accepts. **Response:** Submissions 10 weeks or longer, SASE required. **Freelance Content:** 10%. **Rights:** FNASR. **Payment:** On publication. **Contact:** Barry Silesky.

ANTHOLOGY

P.O. Box 4411, Mesa, AZ 85211-4411. 480-461-8200. E-mail: sharon@inkwellpress.com. Web site: www.anthologymagazine.com. Bi-monthly. $3.95/issue, $20/year. Circ.: 1,500. Sharon Skinner, Executive Editor. **Description:** Poetry, prose, and art from new and upcoming writers and artists from around the world. E-zine and print. **Fiction:** Any genre. Also accepts stories based in the fictional city of Haven, where people make their own heroes; 5,000 words. **Nonfiction:** Any genre; 5,000 words. **Poetry:** Any style, to 100 lines. **Art:** b/w only; pays in ad space offered. **Queries:** Not necessary. **E-Queries:** No. **Unsolicited mss:** Accepts. **Response:** Queries to 60 days, submissions to 90 days, SASE. **Freelance Content:** 90%. **Rights:** 1st NA. **Payment:** In copies.

❦ ANTIETAM REVIEW

41 S. Potomac St., Hagerstown, MD 21740. 301-791-3132. Annual. $6.30/issue. Ethan Fischer, Editors-in-Chief. **Description:** Quality fiction, poetry, and photography. **Fiction:** Well-crafted, any subject; 5,000 words. **Poetry:** Accomplished (not haiku); 1 page. **Art:** b/w photo. **Queries:** Not necessary. **E-Queries:** No. **Unsolicited mss:** Accepts. **Response:** 3-6 months, SASE required. **Freelance Content:** 80%. **Rights:** 1st. **Payment:** On publication.

ANTIGONISH REVIEW

St. Francis Xavier Univ., P.O. Box 5000, Antigonish, NS, Canada B2G 2W5. 902-867-3962. E-mail: tar@stfx.ca. Web site: www.antigonish.com/review/. Quarterly. $24/year. Circ.: 800. George Sanderson, Editor. **Description:** Poetry, short stories, essays, book reviews. **Fiction:** 2,000-5,000 words; $50-$80. **Nonfiction:** 2,000-5,000 words; $50-$200. **Poetry:** Any subject, any point of view. **Tips:** Considers stories from anywhere, original or translations, but encourages Atlantic Canadians and Canadian writers, and new and young writers. **Queries:** Preferred. **E-Queries:** No. **Unsolicited mss:** Accepts. **Response:** Queries 3-6 months, SASE required. **Freelance Content:** 100%. **Payment:** On publication.

❦ ANTIOCH REVIEW

P.O. Box 148, Yellow Springs, OH 45387-0148. 937-754-6808. Web site: www.antioch.edu/review. Quarterly. $35/year. Circ.: 5,100. Robert S. Fogarty, Editor. **Description:** Fiction, essays, and poetry from emerging and established authors. Pays $10/published page. **Fiction:** Intelligent, compelling stories, written with distinction; up to 8,000 words. **Nonfiction:** Social sciences, humanities, literary journalism; up to 8,000 words. **Poetry:** Submit 3-6 poems. **Tips:** Read an issue for better idea of subjects, treatment, lengths. **Queries:** Not necessary. **E-Queries:** No. **Unsolicited mss:** Accepts. **Response:** 8-10 weeks, SASE required. **Freelance Content:** 100%. **Payment:** On publication.

ARACHNE

2363 Page Rd., Kennedy, NY 14747-9717.
E-mail: litteacher199@yahoo.com. Semiannual. $10/year. Circ.: 500. Susan L. Leach, Editor. **Description:** Rural themes, focusing on America's grassroots authors. **Fiction:** 1,500 words. **Poetry:** Submit up to 7 poems. **Tips:** No simultaneous submissions. **Queries:** Preferred. **E-Queries:** No. **Unsolicited mss:** Accepts. **Response:** Queries 1-2 weeks, submissions up to 5 months, SASE required. **Freelance Content:** 100%. **Rights:** 1st. **Payment:** In copies.

ART TIMES

P.O. Box 730, Mt. Marion, NY 12456. 845-246-6944.
E-mail: info@arttimesjournal.com. Web site: www.arttimesjournal.com. 11x/year. Circ.: 23,000. Raymond J. Steiner, Editor. **Description:** Commentary and resource on fine and performing arts. **Fiction:** No excessive sex, violence, racist themes; 1,500 words; $25 and subscription. **Nonfiction:** Feature essays are staff-written. **Poetry:** All forms; 20 lines; pays in copies. **Queries:** Not necessary. **E-Queries:** No. **Unsolicited mss:** Accepts. **Response:** Submission 6 months, SASE. **Freelance Content:** 100%. **Rights:** 1st NA. **Payment:** On publication.

ASCENT

Dept. of English, Concordia College, 901 8th St. S., Moorhead, MN 56562. 218-299-4000.
E-mail: ascent@cord.edu. Web site: www.cord.edu/dept/english/ascent. 3x/year. W. Scott Olsen, Editor. **Description:** Fiction, nonfiction, and poetry. No reviews or editorial articles. Submit complete manuscripts with SASE. **Payment:** In copies.

ASIAN PACIFIC AMERICAN JOURNAL

16 W. 32nd St., Suite 10A, New York, NY 10001. 212-494-0061
E-mail: desk@aaww.org. Web site: www.aaww.org. Hanya Yanagihara. **Description:** Short stories, also excerpts from longer fiction works by emerging or established Asian American writers. **Poetry:** Submit up to 10 poems. **Tips:** Send 4 copies of each piece submitted, in all genres. **Queries:** Preferred. **Payment:** In copies.

ATLANTIC MONTHLY

77 N. Washington St., Boston, MA 02114. 617-854-7700.
Web site: www.theatlantic.com. Monthly. $3.95/issue. Circ.: 500,000. Michael Kelly, Editor. **Description:** At the leading edge of contemporary issues, plus the best in fiction, travel, food, and humor. **Fiction:** 2,000-6,000 words; pays to $3,000. **Nonfiction:** 1,000-7,500 words; pay varies. **Poetry:** Yes. **Queries:** Preferred. **E-Queries:** No. **Unsolicited mss:** Accepts. **Response:** 2-4 weeks, SASE required. **Freelance Content:** 50%. **Rights:** 1st NA. **Payment:** On acceptance.

AURA LITERARY/ARTS REVIEW

HUC 135, 1530 3rd Ave., South, Birmingham, AL 35294. 205-934-3216.
E-mail: aura@larry.huc.edu. Biannual. $6/issue. Russell Helms, Editor. **Description:**

Student-produced magazine for written and visual art. Accepts original, non-published fiction, poetry, art, and b/w photography. **Fiction:** Up to 5,000 words. **Poetry:** Up to 10 pages. **Art:** Slides (originals preferred). **Queries:** Not necessary. **Unsolicited mss:** Accepts. **Response:** SASE required.

BEACON STREET REVIEW

100 Beacon St., Boston, MA 02116. 617-824-8750.
E-mail: beaconstreetreview@hotmail.com. Semiannual. $4/issue. Circ.: 1,000. Joy Fisher Williams, Editor-in-Chief. **Description:** New fiction, nonfiction and poetry. **Poetry:** 5 poems, up to 25 pages total. **Tips:** Seeks more postmodern work in coming months. Blind reading policy; writer should send 4 copies of each manuscript. Annual awards of $100. **Queries:** Not necessary. **E-Queries:** No. **Unsolicited mss:** Accepts. **Response:** Queries 1-2 weeks, submissions (responds in March and Nov.), SASE. **Rights:** 1st. **Payment:** On publication.

BEAR DELUXE

P.O. Box 10342, Portland, OR 97296. 503-242-2330.
E-mail: bear@teleport.com. Web site: www.or10.org/beardeluxe. Tri-annual. $16 (4 issues). Circ.: 17,000. Tom Webb, Editor. **Description:** Environmental arts. Poetry to journalism, fiction, essays, artist profiles, reviews and opinions, also visual art, photography, illustration and cartooning. Pays $.05/word, plus subscription and copies. **Fiction:** Stories with environmental themes; new, unique, well-crafted; 4,000 words. **Nonfiction:** Short news, reports. Seeking cultural connections to environmental issues, i.e., relationships between hunters and conservationists; 200-400 words. **Poetry:** Less narrative; 50 line max. **Fillers:** First-person opinion (no rants); 500-1,500 words. **Columns, Departments:** Artist profiles, interviews, hands-on pieces; 750 words. **Art:** b/w only; send prints with SASE, or good photocopies; $30/image. **Queries:** Preferred. **Unsolicited mss:** Accepts. **Response:** Queries 1-2 months, submissions 3-6 months, SASE. **Freelance Content:** 50%. **Rights:** 1st. **Payment:** On publication.

✦ BELLINGHAM REVIEW

Western Washington Univ., Signpost Press, MS-9053,
Bellingham, WA 98225. 360-650-4863.
E-mail: bhreview@cc.wwu.edu. Web site: www.wwu.edu/bhreview. Semiannual. Brenda Miller, Editor-In-Chief. **Description:** Journal for fiction, poetry, and essays "of palpable quality." Up to 9,000 words, pays $15/printed page. **Tips:** Annual contests for creative nonfiction, fiction, and poetry; $1,000 prizes; see website for guidelines. **Queries:** Not necessary. **E-Queries:** No. **Unsolicited mss:** Accepts. **Response:** No queries, submission 2 months, SASE required. **Freelance Content:** 100%. **Rights:** one-time. **Payment:** On publication.

BELLOWING ARK

P.O. Box 55564, Shoreline, WA 98155. 260-440-0791.
Bimonthly. $3/issue, $15/year. Circ.: 700. Robert R. Ward, Editor. **Description:**

Follows romantic tradition, but very eclectic contents, showing that life is meaningful and worth living. **Fiction:** Short fiction, portraying life as positive and meaningful; length varies. **Poetry:** Yes. **Tips:** Double-space prose, single-space poetry (1 poem/page). **Queries:** Not necessary. **E-Queries:** No. **Unsolicited mss:** Accepts. **Response:** Submissions 2-4 months, SASE required. **Freelance Content:** 95%. **Rights:** 1st, reprint. **Payment:** In copies.

BELOIT FICTION JOURNAL
Box 11, Beloit College, 700 College St, Beloit, WI 53511. 608-363-2577. Annual. $14.00. Clint McCown, Editor. **Description:** Literary fiction. Interested in new and established writers. **Fiction:** Literary fiction, any theme (no genre fiction). Stories from 1-40 pages long, ave. 15 pages. **Tips:** Submit with a great opening line, original language, strong forward movement. No pornography, political propaganda, religious dogma. Reading period: Aug. 1- Dec. 1. **Queries:** Not necessary. **E-Queries:** No. **Unsolicited mss:** Does not accept. **Response:** 2-4 weeks, SASE required. **Payment:** In copies only. **Contact:** Heather Skyler, Managing Editor.

BELOIT POETRY JOURNAL
24 Berry Cove Rd., Lamoine, ME 04605. 207-667-5598. Web site: www.bpj.org. Quarterly. $5/$18. Circ.: 1,200. Marion Stocking, Editor. **Description:** Publishes the best poems received, without bias for length, form, subject or tradition. Looking to discover new voices. **Poetry:** Contemporary poetry, any length or mode. **Tips:** Avoid lineated journal entries, clichés, self-absorbed "how I feel" verse. A strong poem needs fresh insight and a distinctive music. Book reviews are by editor. **Queries:** Not necessary. **E-Queries:** No. **Unsolicited mss:** Accepts. **Response:** Submissions up to 4 months, SASE required. **Payment:** In copies.

BIBLIOPHILOS
Bibliophile Publishing, 200 Security Bldg., Fairmont, WV 26554. 304-366-8107. Quarterly. $5/issue, $18/year. Circ.: 225. Dr. Gerald J. Bobango, Editor. **Description:** Scholastically oriented. Seeks to promote worldview of the pre-1960s, to show importance of books and scholarly endeavor (and to encourage people to relegate their PCs and laptops to the dustbin). **Fiction:** Stories about growing up in rural West Virginia in the 1930s and WWII; people with nontraditional values; stories of love and kindness; 3,000 word max.; $5-$25. **Nonfiction:** Reviews of history, literature, and literary criticism needed (e.g., "Mona-Lisa's Landscape," a study of the painting's background; "Cruising With the Cruisers," on Caribbean cruises, sociology of passenger and crew); 3,000 words; $5-$25. **Poetry:** No poetry that Ann Landers or Erma Bombeck would use or praise; 30-35 lines; $5-$25. **Fillers:** "Hemingway and Faulkner Reminisce About the Prom," in their respective style; 25-300 words; $5-$10. **Columns, Departments:** Book reviews. **Art:** b/w; $5-$25. **Queries:** Required. **E-Queries:** No. **Unsolicited mss:** Does not accept. **Response:** Queries 2 weeks, submissions 2 weeks, SASE. **Freelance Content:** 50%. **Rights:** FNASR. **Payment:** On publication.

BITTER OLEANDER

4983 Tall Oaks Dr., Fayetteville, NY 13066-9776. 315-637-3047. E-mail: bones44@ixnetcom.com. Web site: www.bitteroleander.com. Bi-annual. $8/$15. Circ.: 1,200. Paul B. Roth, Editor. **Description:** Imaginative poetry, fiction, interviews with known and new writers whose work is featured. **Fiction:** Original, imaginative, aware of language as possibility instead of slave; 2,500 words. **Poetry:** Imaginative, concentration on "deep image," the concrete particular; 2 pages. **Tips:** Seeking more contemporary poetry in translation. No confessional storytelling, overly abstract poetry. **Queries:** Not necessary. **E-Queries:** Yes. **Unsolicited mss:** Accepts. **Response:** Queries 1 week, submissions 1 month, SASE. **Freelance Content:** 80%. **Rights:** All, revert back to author. **Payment:** In copies.

BLACK BEAR REVIEW

Black Bear Publications, 1916 Lincoln St., Croydon, PA 19021-8026. E-mail: bbreview@earthlink.net. Web site: www.home.earthlink.net/~bbreview. Biannual. $12. Circ.: 750. Ave Jeanne, Editor. **Description:** International literary magazine for the concerned poet and artist. **Tips:** Prefers poems on social and environmental concerns. Avoid traditional forms. **Queries:** Not necessary. **E-Queries:** Yes. **Unsolicited mss:** Does not accept. **Response:** Queries 1 week, submissions 1 week, SASE not required. **Freelance Content:** 100%. **Rights:** FNASR. **Payment:** In copies.

BLACK WARRIOR REVIEW

P.O. Box 862936, Tuscaloosa, AL 35486-0027. 205-348-4518. Web site: www.sa.ua.edu/osm/bwr. Bi-annual. $14/yr. Circ.: 2,000. T.J. Beitelman, Editor. **Description:** The best in contemporary fiction, poetry, nonfiction, art, interviews, reviews, and photography. **Tips:** Seeking emerging writers and experimental work; writing that is fresh, that sings. **Queries:** Not necessary. **Unsolicited mss:** Accepts. **Response:** 1-4 months.

BLOOMSBURY REVIEW

1553 Platte St., Suite 206, P.O. Box 8928, Denver, CO 80201. 303-455-3123. E-mail: bloomsb@aol.com. Bimonthly. $3. Circ.: 50,000. Tom Auer, Editor. **Description:** Book reviews, also literary features, interviews, essays, poetry. **Nonfiction:** Essays, features, and interviews; 600 words or more; $10-$40. **Poetry:** Yes; $5-$15/poem. **Queries:** Preferred. **E-Queries:** Yes. **Unsolicited mss:** Accepts. **Response:** Queries 2 weeks, submissions 2 months, SASE required. **Freelance Content:** 25%. **Rights:** 1st. **Payment:** On publication.

BLUE UNICORN

22 Avon Rd., Kensington, CA 94707. 516-526-8439. 3x/year. $5/issue, $12/year. Circ.: 500. Ruth G. Iodice, Editor. **Description:** Has published many of the nation's best poets over the years. **Poetry:** Well-crafted poems, in form or free verse, also expert translations. Shorter is better. **Tips:** Study great poets, but develop your own voice; avoid copying whatever is popular. The sound of a poem

helps make it memorable. **Queries:** Preferred. **E-Queries:** No. **Unsolicited mss:** Accepts. **Response:** Queries as possible, submissions 4-6 months, SASE required. **Freelance Content:** 100%. **Rights:** 1st. **Payment:** In copies.

BLUELINE
English Dept., SUNY, Potsdam, NY 13676. 315-267-2043. E-mail: blueline@potsdam.edu. Web site: www.potsdam.edu/engl/blueline. Annual. $10/yr. Circ.: 600. Rick Henry, Editor. **Description:** Poems, stories, and essays on the Adirondack and regions similar in geography and spirit, or on the shaping influence of nature. **Fiction:** Yes; to 3,500 words. **Nonfiction:** On Adirondack region or similar areas; to 3,500 words. **Poetry:** Submit up to 5 poems; to 75 lines. **Queries:** Not necessary. **E-Queries:** Yes. **Unsolicited mss:** Accepts. **Response:** Queries, 1 week. **Rights:** FNASR. **Payment:** In copies.

BOSTON REVIEW
MIT, 30 Wadsworth St., E53, Room 407, Cambridge, MA 02139. 617-253-3642. E-mail: bostonreview@mit.edu. Web site: www.bostonreview.mit.edu. Bimonthly. Circ.: 20,000. Josh Cohen, Editor. **Description:** Politics, literature, art, music, film, photography, poetry. **Fiction:** 1,000-5,000 words; $40-$100. **Queries:** Preferred. **Contact:** Jefferson Decker, Managing Editor.

BOTTOMFISH
De Anza College, 21250 Stevens Creek Blvd., Cupertino, CA 95014. 408-864-8600. E-mail: rns@2107@mercury.fhda.edu. Annual. $5/year. Circ.: 500. Randolph Splitter, Editor. **Description:** Fiction, poetry, creative nonfiction, photography, comics, and drawings. **Fiction:** Short stories; to 4,000 words. **Nonfiction:** Creative nonfiction; to 4,000 words. **Poetry:** 5 poems max. **Fillers:** Drawings, comics, other visual art forms. **Art:** b/w. **Tips:** Accepts work in September-December only. Diverse voices welcome. **Queries:** Not necessary. **E-Queries:** No. **Unsolicited mss:** Accepts. **Response:** Submissions 1-6 months, SASE required. **Freelance Content:** 95%.

BOULEVARD
4579 Laclede Ave., #332, St. Louis, MO 63108-2103. 314-361-2986. Web site: www.boulevardmagazine.com/. 3x/year. $8/issue, $15/year. Circ.: 3,500. Richard Burgin, Editor. **Description:** Publishes the finest established writers, and new writers with exceptional promise. Recent authors: Joyce Carol Oates, Stephen Dixon, Alice Hoffman, Alice Adams. **Fiction:** Well-constructed, moving stories, in an original voice; up to 30 typed pages; $150-$300. **Nonfiction:** Literary, film, music, criticism, travel pieces, memoirs, philosophical or social issues. **Poetry:** No light verse. Submit up to 5 poems of up to 200 lines. Pays $25-$300/poem. **Tips:** No science fiction, erotica, westerns, horror, romance, or children's stories. **Queries:** Not necessary. **E-Queries:** No. **Unsolicited mss:** Accepts. **Response:** Queries 1 week, submissions 1-2 months, SASE required. **Freelance Content:** 85%. **Rights:** 1st. **Payment:** On publication.

BRIAR CLIFF REVIEW
Briar Cliff College, 3303 Rebecca St., Sioux City, IA 51104.
E-mail: currans@briar-cliff.edu. Web site: www.briar-cliff.edu/bcreview. Tricia Currans-Sheehan. **Description:** An eclectic literary and cultural magazine focusing on regional writers and subjects. **Fiction:** Yes. **Nonfiction:** To 5,000 words: humor/satire, Siouxland history, thoughtful essays. **Poetry:** Yes. **Columns, Departments:** Book reviews. **Tips:** Manuscripts read August-October. **Payment:** In copies.

BRIDGE/STORIES & IDEAS
1357 N. Ashland Ave., #3A, Chicago, IL 60622.
E-mail: submissions@bridgemagazine.org. Web site: www.bridgemagazine.org. **Description:** A magazine based on "the simple belief that separate fields of inquiry can and should be thought of as having shared horizons." **Fiction:** Realistic fiction; 2,000-5,000 words. **Nonfiction:** Critical nonfiction; 2,000-5,000 words. **Queries:** Preferred. **Response:** SASE required.

BYLINE
Box 130596, Edmond, OK 73013. 405-348-5591.
E-mail: mpreston@bylinemag.com. Web site: www.ByLineMag.com. Monthly. $22/year. Marcia Preston, Editor. **Description:** Publication for writers. **Fiction:** Genre, mainstream or literary. No graphic sex or violence; no sci-fi; 2,000-4,000 words; $100. **Nonfiction:** On the craft and business of writing; 1,500-1,800 words; $75. **Poetry:** About writing or the creative process; 30 lines max.; $10. **Fillers:** Humor; 100-500 words; $15-$25. **Columns, Departments:** End Piece (700 words, $35); First Sale (250-300 words, $20); Great American Bookstores (500-600 words, $35-$40). **Tips:** Include practical information that can help writers succeed. **Queries:** Preferred. **E-Queries:** Accepts. **Unsolicited mss:** Accepts. **Response:** Queries 1-3 weeks, 1 month for submissions, SASE required. **Freelance Content:** 80%. **Rights:** FNASR. **Payment:** On acceptance.

CALLALOO
Univ. of Virginia, Dept. of English, 322 Bryan Hall, P.O. Box 400121, Charlottesville, VA 22904-4121. 804-924-6637.
E-mail: callaloo@virginia.edu. Web site: www.people.virginia.edu. Quarterly. $10/issue, $36/year. Circ.: 2,000. Charles H. Rowell, Editor. **Description:** African American and Africa diaspora literary journal, with original work and critical studies of black writers worldwide. **Fiction:** Fiction, drama, critical studies, bibliographies; on African-American, Caribbean, and African Diaspora artists and writers; 2,500-5,000 words. **Nonfiction:** Features on theme content; 5,000-7,500 words. **Poetry:** Up to 300 lines. **Queries:** Not necessary. **E-Queries:** Yes. **Unsolicited mss:** Accepts. **Response:** Submissions 6-8 months, SASE required. **Freelance Content:** 50%. **Payment:** In copies.

CALYX

P.O. Box B, Corvallis, OR 97339. 541-753-9384.
E-mail: calyx@proaxis.com. Web site: www.calyxpress.com. Biannual. $9.50/issue.
Circ.: 5,000. Beverly McFarland, Managing Editor. **Description:** Journal of art and literature by women, with poetry, prose, art, and book reviews. Presents wide spectrum of women's experience, especially work by unheard voices (new writers, women of color, working-class, older women). **Fiction:** 5,000 words. **Nonfiction:** 5,000 words. **Poetry:** 6 poems max. **Art:** Color cover, plus 16 pp. of b/w art. See guidelines. **Tips:** Submit prose and poetry only from Oct. 1 to Dec. 15 (postmark date). Art submissions accepted anytime. Query regarding book reviews. **Queries:** Not necessary. **E-Queries:** No. **Unsolicited mss:** Accepts. **Response:** Submissions 6-8 months, SASE required. **Payment:** In copies.

CAPE ROCK

Southeast Missouri State Univ., Dept. of English,
Cape Girardeau, MO 63701. 573-651-2500.
E-mail: hhecht@sermovn.semo.edu. Bi-annual. $5/issue, $7 year. Circ.: 500. Harvey E. Hecht, Editor. **Description:** Poetry journal, with photography. **Poetry:** to 70 lines; pays $200 for "Best in issue." **Art:** A series of 12-15 b/w photos, featuring a sense of place; $100. **Tips:** Manuscripts read August-April. **Queries:** Not necessary. **E-Queries:** Yes. **Unsolicited mss:** Accepts. **Response:** Queries 1-2 weeks submissions 2-4 months, SASE required. **Rights:** all; will release. **Payment:** In copies.

THE CAPILANO REVIEW

2055 Purcell Way, N. Vancouver, B.C., Canada V7J 3H5. 604-984-1712.
E-mail: tcr@capcollege.bc.ca. Web site: www.capcollege.bc.ca/dept/tcr. 3x/year. $25/year. Circ.: 900. Ryan Knighton, Editor. **Description:** Innovative poetry, fiction, drama, and word in the visual media, in a cross-disciplinary format. **Fiction:** To 6,000 words (drama, to 10,000 words); $50-$200 (Canadian). **Poetry:** 5-6 poems; $50-$200 (Canadian). **Tips:** Looks for work pushing beyond the boundaries of traditional art and writing. **Queries:** Preferred. **E-Queries:** No. **Unsolicited mss:** Accepts. **Response:** 4 months, SASE required. **Rights:** FNASR. **Payment:** On publication. **Contact:** Carol L. Hamshaw, Managing Editor.

CARIBBEAN WRITER

University of the Virgin Islands, RR 02, Box 10,000,
Kingshill, St. Croix, USVI 850. 340-692-4152.
E-mail: qmars@uvi.edu. Web site: www.uvi.edu/caribbeanwriter/. Annual. $12/issue. Circ.: 1,000. Dr. Erika J. Waters, Editor. **Description:** Literary anthology with Caribbean focus. **Fiction:** Personal essays, also one-act plays (max. 3,500 words or 10 pages), or up to 2 short stories (15 pages or less); Caribbean experience or heritage central. **Poetry:** Caribbean focus; submit up to 5 poems. **Tips:** Original, unpublished work only (if self-published, give details). Blind submissions policy: print only the title on your manuscript; give your name, address, and title on a separate sheet. **Queries:** Not necessary. **E-Queries:** Yes. **Unsolicited mss:** Accepts. **Response:** SASE

required. **Freelance Content:** 80%. **Rights:** one-time. **Payment:** In copies. **Contact:** Ms. Quilin Mars.

CAROLINA QUARTERLY

Univ. of North Carolina, Greenlaw Hall CB#3520, Chapel Hill, NC 27599-3520. Brian Carpenter, Editor. **Description:** Features new and established writers. **Fiction:** To 5,000 words. **Nonfiction:** Some nonfiction articles accepted. **Poetry:** To 300 lines. **Tips:** Manuscripts read year-round. *No recent report.*

CHARITON REVIEW

Truman State Univ., Kirksville, MO 63501-9915. 660-785-4499. Semiannual. Circ.: 1,800. Jim Barnes, Editor. **Description:** Quality poetry and fiction; modern and contemporary translations. **Fiction:** to 6,000 words; $5/printed page. **Poetry:** to 6,000 words; $5/printed page.

CHATTAHOOCHEE REVIEW

Georgia Perimeter College, 2101 Womack Rd., Dunwoody, GA 30338-4497. Quarterly. $6/issue. Lawrence Hetrick, Editor. **Description:** Promotes fresh writing by emerging and established voices. **Fiction:** up to 5,000 words; $20/page. **Nonfiction:** $15/page; reviews $50. **Poetry:** $50/poem. **Tips:** No simultaneous submissions. Annual Lamar York Prize for Nonfiction. **Queries:** Not necessary. **E-Queries:** No. **Response:** Queries 1 week, submissions 3-4 months, SASE. **Freelance Content:** 80%. **Rights:** 1st. **Payment:** On publication.

CHELSEA

P.O. Box 773, Cooper Station, New York, NY 10276. Semiannual. $8/issue, $13/year. Circ.: 1,800. Richard Foerster, Editor. **Description:** New and established voices in literature. Eclectic, lively, sophisticated, with accent on translations, art, and cross-cultural exchange. Pays $15/page, plus copies. **Fiction:** Mainstream, literary; up to 25 pages. **Nonfiction:** Essays; up to 25 pages. **Poetry:** Traditional, avant-garde; 3-6 poems. **Columns, Departments:** Book reviews, by assignment. **Art:** Submit slides; color (cover), b/w inside. **Tips:** Interested in avant-garde: original ideas and use of language. **Queries:** Not necessary. **E-Queries:** No. **Unsolicited mss:** Accepts. **Response:** 3-6 months, SASE. **Rights:** 1st. **Payment:** On publication.

❧ CHICAGO REVIEW

5801 S. Kenwood Ave., Chicago, IL 60637. E-mail: chicago-review@uchicago.edu. Web site: www.humanities.uchicago.edu/review. Andrew Rathmann, Editor. **Description:** Essays, interviews, reviews, fiction, translations, poetry. **Tips:** Manuscripts read year-round. **Response:** 2-3 months. **Payment:** In copies. *No recent report.*

CHIRON REVIEW
702 No. Prairie, St. John, KS 67576-1516.
Web site: www.geocities.com/soho/nook/1748/. Quarterly. $4/issue, $12/year. Circ.: 1,000. Michael Hathaway, Editor. **Description:** Wide range of contemporary creative writing (fiction and nonfiction, traditional and off-beat), with artwork. **Fiction:** Contemporary fiction; 700-3,000 words. **Nonfiction:** 500-1,000 words. **Poetry:** length varies. **Queries:** Not necessary. **E-Queries:** No. **Unsolicited mss:** Accepts. **Response:** Queries 2-4 weeks, Submissions 2-6 weeks, SASE required. **Freelance Content:** 100%. **Rights:** one-time. **Payment:** In copies.

CICADA
329 E St., Bakersfield, CA 93304. 661-323-4064.
E-mail: amelia@lightspeed.net. Web site: www.cricketmag.com. Quarterly. Circ.: 800. Frederick A. Raborg, Jr., Editor. **Description:** Literary publication for teenagers. Offers literature that is thought-provoking, entertaining, often humorous. Pieces written by outstanding adult authors, and by teens themselves. **Fiction:** Fantasy, horror, mainstream, mystery, romance, suspense, science fiction. 500-2,500 words. Pays $10-$20. **Nonfiction:** Essays, historical/nostalgic, humor, profile/interview, personal experience, travel. 500-2,500 words. Pays $10. **Poetry:** Submit 12 poems max., 1-50 lines. Pays $10. **Fillers:** Short humor. 25-500 words. No payment. **Queries:** Preferred. **E-Queries:** Yes. **Unsolicited mss:** Accepts. **Response:** 2 weeks queries, 3 months submissions, SASE required. **Freelance Content:** 100%. **Rights:** 1st NA. **Payment:** On publication.

CIMARRON REVIEW
Oklahoma State Univ., 205 Morrill Hall, Stillwater, OK 74078-0135.
E-mail: cimarronreview@hotmail.com. Web site: http://cimarronreview.okstate.edu. Quarterly. Circ.: 800. E. P. Walkiewicz, Editor. **Description:** Poetry, fiction, and essays. Seeks work with individual, innovative style, contemporary themes. **Fiction:** 300-800 words, pays $50 and copies. **Tips:** Anything fresh, exciting, savvy. **Queries:** Not necessary. **E-Queries:** No. **Unsolicited mss:** Accepts. **Response:** 1-2 months, SASE required. **Rights:** FNASR. **Payment:** On acceptance.

CLOCKWATCH REVIEW
Illinois Wesleyan Univ., Dept. of English,
Bloomington, IL 61702-2900. 309-556-3352.
E-mail: jplath@titan.iwu.edu. Web site: http://titan.iwu.edu/~jplath/clockwatch.html. James Plath, Zarina Mullan Plath, Editors. **Description:** Literary e-zine. Accepts poetry (to 32 lines), fiction (to 4,000 words), essays, criticism, and reviews. SASE. Email query okay; but no electronic submissions. **Fiction:** upbeat, engaging, distinctive voice; to 4,000 words; $25. **Poetry:** strong, mature, natural voice with fresh images; to 32 lines; $5/poem. **Queries:** Required. **E-Queries:** Yes. **Rights:** 1st NA and electronic; re-assigned to author on request.

COLLAGES & BRICOLAGES

P.O. Box 360, Shippenville, PA 16254.
E-mail: cb@penn.com. Web site: www.angelrive.com/on2/collagesbricolages. Annual.
$10. Marie-José Fortis, Editor. **Description:** Innovative literary journal, with poetry, short stories and plays, essays, interviews, book reviews, editorials. **Fiction:** Stories, one-act avant-garde comedies/dramas, poetry (max. 25 pages). **Nonfiction:** Innovative nonfiction, interviews, book reviews (max. 25 pages). **Art:** b/w photos; photo-collages. Surrealistic, feminist, expressionistic drawings in ink. **Tips:** Often focuses on one subject; query for themes. Manuscripts read Aug.-Nov. **Queries:** Preferred. **Unsolicited mss:** Accepts. **Response:** 1-3 months. **Payment:** In copies.

COLORADO REVIEW

Colorado State Univ., English Dept., Fort Collins, CO 80523. 970-491-5449.
E-mail: creview@vines.colostate.edu. Web site: www.colostate.edu/depts/
english/english-ns4.html. Tri-annual. $9.50/issue, $24/year. Circ.: 1,300. David Milofsky, Editor. **Description:** Fiction, poetry, and personal essays by new and established writers. Seeking work that is vital, imaginative, highly realized, and avoids mere mannerism to embody human concern. Pays $5/page. **Fiction:** Short fiction, contemporary themes; up to 20 pages. **Nonfiction:** Up to 20 pages. **Poetry:** Length varies. **Art:** slides, $100 (cover). **Tips:** No simultaneous submissions. No e-mail. Reading period, Sept.-April only; submissions sent outside this period are returned unread. **Queries:** Not necessary. **E-Queries:** No. **Unsolicited mss:** Accepts. **Response:** Queries 2-4 weeks, submissions 4-6 weeks, SASE required. **Rights:** 1st NA. **Payment:** On publication.

COLUMBIA

Columbia University, 415 Dodge Hall, New York, NY 10027. 212-854-4216.
E-mail: arts-litjournal@columbia.edu. Web site: www.columbia.edu/cu/arts/writing/
columbiajournal/index.html. Annual. $15. Circ.: 2,200. **Description:** Literary journal, with contemporary poetry, fiction, and creative nonfiction from established and emerging voices. **Fiction:** No restrictions (avoid children's stories or genre pieces). Open to experimental writing, mainstream narratives, work that takes risk; 25 pages or less. **Nonfiction:** Same as fiction (no reviews or academic criticism); 25 pages or less. **Poetry:** Wide range of forms and styles; 7 poems max. **Art:** Slides. **Queries:** Not necessary. **E-Queries:** No. **Unsolicited mss:** Accepts. **Response:** Queries 2 weeks, 3 months submissions, SASE required. **Freelance Content:** 65%. **Rights:** 1st U.S. **Payment:** In copies.

CONCHO RIVER REVIEW

Angelo State Univ., English Dept., San Angelo, TX 76909.
Web site: www.angelo.edu/dept/eng. Bi-annual. $8/$14. Circ.: 300. James A. Moore, Editor. **Description:** Literary journal with fiction, essays, poetry, and book reviews.
Fiction: Primarily Texas and Southwest writers. Traditional stories, with strong sense of conflict, finely-drawn characters, crisp dialogue; 1,500-5,000 words. **Nonfiction:** Critical papers, personal essays, and reviews. Topics on Texas and/or Southwest;

1,500-5,000 words. **Poetry:** Send 3-5 poems at a time; 1 page or less. **Queries:** Not necessary. **E-Queries:** Yes. **Unsolicited mss:** Accepts. **Response:** Queries 2-4 weeks, submissions 3-6 months, SASE. **Freelance Content:** 100%. **Rights:** 1st. **Payment:** In copies.

CONFLUENCE

P.O. Box 336, Belpre, OH 45714-0336.
Web site: www.artswindow.org. Annual. $5. Circ.: 1,000. Wilma Acree, Editor. **Description:** Presents the work of emerging and established authors. **Fiction:** Literary fiction; to 5,000 words. **Nonfiction:** Interviews, essays; to 5,000 words. **Poetry:** Lyric, narrative poetry with fresh images. No rhymed poetry unless of exceptional quality; up to 60 lines. **Tips:** No previously published work, simultaneous submissions. Cover letter with short bio required. **Queries:** Not necessary. **E-Queries:** Yes. **Unsolicited mss:** Accepts. **Response:** Queries 1 month, submissions 1-5 months, SASE. **Freelance Content:** 80%. **Rights:** 1st. **Payment:** On publication.

CONFRONTATION

C.W. Post of L.I.U., Dept. of English, Brookville, NY 11548. 516-299-2720.
E-mail: mtucker@liu.edu. Semiannual. $10. Circ.: 2,000. Martin Tucker, Editor. **Description:** Literary magazine, with poetry, fiction, essays, and memoir material; original work by famous and emerging writers. **Fiction:** Up to 30 pages; $25-$150. **Nonfiction:** Mostly memoirs. Other nonfiction, including reviews, are assigned; $25-$150. **Poetry:** Pays $15-$100. **Tips:** Manuscripts read Sept. through May. **Queries:** Preferred. **E-Queries:** No. **Unsolicited mss:** Accepts. **Response:** Queries 2-4 weeks, submissions 6-8 weeks, SASE required. **Freelance Content:** 75%. **Rights:** FNASR. **Payment:** On publication.

CONNECTICUT RIVER REVIEW

P.O. Box 4053, Waterbury, CT 06704-0053. 203-753-7815.
E-mail: ctriverreview@aol.com. Web site: www.hometown.aol.com/ctpoetrysociety/. Biannual. $11/year. Circ.: 500. Kevin Carey, Editor. **Description:** Poetry only; well-crafted, original, unpublished poems from new and well-established poets. Published by Connecticut Poetry Society, but poets need not be Connecticut residents. **Poetry:** Any subject, form, length. **Queries:** Preferred. **E-Queries:** No. **Unsolicited mss:** Accepts. **Response:** Queries 6-8 weeks, submission 8-12 weeks, SASE required. **Rights:** 1st, and reprint in CRR. **Payment:** In copies. **Contact:** Claire Warner, Co-Editor.

COTTONWOOD

Cottonwood Magazine, Box J, 400 Kansas Union,
University of Kansas, Lawrence, KS 66045.
3x/year. **Description:** Publishes new and well-known writers. No rhymed poetry. Kansas and midwestern focus. Photos, graphics, and book reviews from midwest presses also accepted. **Fiction:** Work from experience; no contrived or slick fiction. Submit only 1 story at a time; 1,500-8,000 words. **Poetry:** Submit up to 5 poems;

10-80 lines. **Art:** Photos, other graphic arts. **Tips:** Published work eligible for annual awards. **E-Queries:** No. **Response:** 3-6 months, SASE required. **Rights:** 1st NA. **Payment:** In copies.

CQ
California State Poetry Society, 21 Whitman Ct., Irvine, CA 92612. 949-854-8024. E-mail: jipalley@aol.com. Quarterly. $5/issue, $20/year. Circ.: 250. Julian Palley, Editorial Board. **Description:** "California State Poetry Quarterly." **Poetry:** Brief, any subject or style. Submit up to 6 poems; up to 40 lines. **Queries:** Not necessary. **E-Queries:** Yes. **Unsolicited mss:** Accepts. **Response:** 5-6 months, SASE. **Freelance Content:** 100%. **Rights:** revert to poet. **Payment:** In copies.

CRAB CREEK REVIEW
P.O. Box 840, Vashon, WA 98070.
Semiannual. Linda Clifton, Editor. **Description:** Poetry, fiction, and creative nonfiction. **Fiction:** Clear, dynamic fiction, to 4,000 words. **Nonfiction:** to 4,000 words. **Poetry:** to 80 lines. **Queries:** Preferred. **Payment:** In copies.

THE CREAM CITY REVIEW
Univ. of Wisc.-Milwaukee, English Dept., P.O. Box 413,
Milwaukee, WI 53201. 414-229-4708.
E-mail: creamcity@uwm.edu. Web site: www.earthjam.com/sites/creamcity/main.htm. Semi-annual. $7/issue; $12/year. Circ.: 700. Peter Whalen, Editor. **Description:** Literary journal with fiction, poetry, nonfiction. **Queries:** Not necessary. **E-Queries:** No. **Unsolicited mss:** Accepts. **Response:** Queries 2 weeks, 3 months for submissions, SASE required. **Freelance Content:** 100%. **Rights:** 1st NA. **Payment:** 1-year subscription.

CREATIVE NONFICTION
5501 Walnut, Suite 202, Pittsburgh, PA 15232. 412-688-0304.
E-mail: info@creativenonfiction.org. Web site: www.creativenonfiction.org. 3x/year. $10/issue, $29.95 (4 issues). Circ.: 4,000. Lee Gutkind, Editor-In-Chief. **Description:** Literary journal, devoted exclusively to non-fiction. Personal essays, memoirs literary journalism, profiles of creative nonfiction authors, book reviews. **Nonfiction:** Prose, rich with detail and distinctive voice on any subject; seeking essays based on research; $10/page. **Tips:** Can be personal but must reach out universally in some way. **Queries:** Not necessary. **E-Queries:** Yes. **Unsolicited mss:** Accepts. **Response:** Submissions 1 month, SASE. **Freelance Content:** 95%. **Rights:** 1st serial and reprint. **Payment:** On publication.

CUMBERLAND POETRY REVIEW
Acklen Sta., P.O. Box 120128, Nashville, TN 37212.
2x/year. $9/issue. Circ.: 300. Eva Touster, Editors. **Description:** Devoted to poetry and poetry criticism. No restrictions on form, style, or subject matter. **Queries:** Not

necessary. **E-Queries:** No. **Unsolicited mss:** Accepts. **Response:** 6 months, SASE. **Payment:** In copies.

CUTBANK
Univ. of Montana, English Dept., Missoula, MT 59812. 406-243-6156. E-mail: cutbank@selway.umt.edu. Web site: www.umt.edu/cutbank. Biannual. $6.95/issue, $12/year. Circ.: 500. **Description:** Fiction and poetry, also reviews, interviews, and artwork. **Fiction:** Yes. **Poetry:** Yes. **Tips:** All work considered for Richard Hugo Poetry Award and A.B. Guthrie, Jr. Short Fiction Award. **Queries:** Not necessary. **E-Queries:** No. **Unsolicited mss:** Accepts. **Response:** 3-4 months, SASE. **Freelance Content:** 90%. **Payment:** In copies.

DESCANT
T.C.U. Box 297270, Fort Worth, TX 76129. 817-257-6537. E-mail: d.kuhne@tcu.edu. Web site: www.eng.tcu.edu/usefulsites/descant.htm. $12. Circ.: 1,000. Dave Kuhne, Editor. **Description:** Seeks quality work in traditional or innovative form. **Fiction:** No restrictions; 5,000 words. **Poetry:** 60 lines. **Tips:** Annual O'Connor Award ($500) for best short story; Colquitt Award ($500) for best poetry. Submit Sept. through May only. **Queries:** Not necessary. **E-Queries:** No. **Unsolicited mss:** Accepts. **Response:** 6 weeks, SASE required. **Freelance Content:** 100%. **Rights:** 1st. **Payment:** In copies.

THE DISTILLERY
Motlow State Community College, P.O. Box 8500, Lynchburg, TN 37352-8500. 931-393-1700. Web site: www.mscc.cc.tn.vs/distillery/. Semiannual. $9/$15. Circ.: 750. Inman Majors, Editor. **Description:** Literary journal of poetry, fiction, nonfiction, art, and photography. **Fiction:** Literary, emphasis on style, character, voice; 4,000 words. **Nonfiction:** Creative nonfiction, with a sense of style. Critical and personal essays; 4,000 words. **Poetry:** Voice, style, and image; any length. **Art:** Slides. **Tips:** Avoid warmed-over exercises in K-mart realism. **Queries:** Not necessary. **E-Queries:** No. **Unsolicited mss:** Accepts. **Response:** Submissions 2-4 months, SASE. **Rights:** 1st NA. **Payment:** In copies.

DOUBLE DEALER REDUX
624 Pirate's Alley, New Orleans, LA 70116. 504-586-1612. E-mail: faulkhouse@aol.com. Web site: www.wordsandmusic.org. Annual. $10. Circ.: 5,000. Rosemary James, Editor. **Description:** Poems, short stories, and essays, also portions of novels and novellas. **Tips:** Has published entire novellas. **Queries:** Preferred.

DOUBLETAKE
55 Davis Square, Somerville, MA 02144. 617-591-9389. E-mail: dtmag@doubletakemagazine.org. Web site: www.doubletakemagazine.org. Quarterly. $10/issue, $24/year. Circ.: 40,000. Robert Coles, Editor. **Description:**

Fiction, poetry, and photo-essays that reveal extraordinary events and qualities found in everyday lives of Americans and others. **Fiction:** Stories, narrative realism that observes life, quietly but with understanding and compassion. **Nonfiction:** Narrative, with documentary, literary, esthetic, or reportorial excellence. **Poetry:** Yes. **Art:** Photos. **Queries:** Not necessary. **E-Queries:** No. **Unsolicited mss:** Accepts. **Response:** 3 months, SASE. **Freelance Content:** 90%. **Rights:** 1st worldwide English-language serial. **Payment:** On acceptance.

DREAMS & VISIONS

Skysong Press, 35 Peter St. S., Orillia, Ontario, Canada L3V 5A8. E-mail: skysong@bconnex.net. Web site: www.bconnex.net/~skysong. Annual. $4.95/issue. Circ.: 200. Steve Stanton, Editor. **Description:** Short literary fiction from a Christian perspective (science fiction, humor, fantasy, magic realism, contemporary, inspirational). No genre excluded. **Fiction:** Based on Biblical norms or traditions, but portraying spiritual truths in new, innovative ways; 2,000-6,000 words; $.005/word. **Queries:** Not necessary. **Unsolicited mss:** Accepts. **Response:** SASE w/Canadian postage. **Freelance Content:** 100%.

EARTH'S DAUGHTERS

Central Park Station, P.O. Box 41, Buffalo, NY 14215. 838-2410. Web site: www.earthsdaughter.org. 3x/year. $18/year. Circ.: 2,000. Pat Covland, Joyce Kessel, Editors. **Description:** Feminist literary small press (mostly poetry). **Fiction:** Finely crafted work, feminist theme; 1,000-1,200 words. **Poetry:** Yes. **Queries:** Preferred. **E-Queries:** Yes. **Unsolicited mss:** Does not accept. **Response:** Queries 2 weeks, submissions 2 months plus, SASE required. **Freelance Content:** 85%. **Rights:** 1st. **Payment:** In copies.

ELYSIAN FIELDS QUARTERLY

P.O. Box 14385, St. Paul, MN 55114-0385. 651-644-8558. E-mail: info@efqreview.com. Web site: www.efqreview.com. Quarterly. $5.95/issue, $22.50/year. Circ.: 2,000-2,500. Tom Goldstein, Editor. **Description:** The literary review for baseball, with essays, poetry, commentary, drama, and humor. Length: 400-2,000 words. **Tips:** Must have a passion and appreciation for baseball, and be able to write well. This is not a hero-worship, nostalgia journal. Sentimental, ill-conceived, formulaic writing from would-be writers or those looking to publish a "baseball" story get tossed quickly. **Queries:** Not necessary. **E-Queries:** Yes. **Unsolicited mss:** Accepts. **Response:** 6 months (fiction/poetry), 3 months (other), SASE. **Freelance Content:** 75%. **Rights:** One-time, anthology. **Payment:** In copies.

EPOCH

Cornell Univ., 251 Goldwin Smith Hall, Ithaca, NY 14853-3201. 607-255-3385. Tri-annual. $5/issue, $11/year. Circ.: 1,000. Michael Koch, Editor. **Description:** Literary magazine of serious fiction and poetry. Pays $5/page and up. **Fiction:** Literary fiction. **Nonfiction:** Personal essays. **Poetry:** All types. **Queries:** Not necessary. **E-Queries:** No. **Unsolicited mss:** Accepts. **Response:** Queries 2 weeks, submissions 4-6 weeks, SASE required. **Freelance Content:** 100%. **Rights:** 1st NA. **Payment:** On publication.

EUREKA LITERARY
Eureka College, 300 E. College Ave., Eureka, IL 61530-1500. 309-467-6336. E-mail: llogsdon@eureka.com. Biannual. $7.50/issue. Circ.: 500. Loren Logsdon, Editor. **Description:** Stories and poems. **Fiction:** Well-made stories; prefers traditional but will use experimental if appealing; 2-28 pages. **Poetry:** Length varies. **Queries:** Not necessary. **E-Queries:** Yes. **Unsolicited mss:** Accepts. **Response:** Queries 2-3 weeks, submissions 4-5 months, SASE. **Freelance Content:** 100%. **Rights:** one-time. **Payment:** In copies.

EVENT
Douglas College, Box 2503, New Westminster, BC, Canada V3L 5B2. 604-527-5293. E-mail: event@douglas.bc.ca. Web site: event.douglas.bc.ca. 3x/year. $8/issue, $22/year. Circ.: 1,250. Calvin Wharton, Editor. **Description:** Mostly fiction, poetry, and creative nonfiction. Pays $22/page, up to $500. **Fiction:** Readable, well-handled characters, strong point of view; 5,000 words max. **Nonfiction:** 5,000 words max. **Poetry:** Appreciate strong narrative, sometimes confessional modes. Eclectic, always open to content that invites involvement. Submit 3-8 poems. **Art:** For cover only; $150. **Tips:** Mostly Canadian writers, but open to anyone writing in English. **Queries:** Not necessary. **E-Queries:** No. **Unsolicited mss:** Accepts. **Response:** Submissions 1-4 weeks, SASE required. **Freelance Content:** 85%. **Rights:** FNASR. **Payment:** On publication.

FICTION
English Dept., The City College of New York, Convent Ave. at 138th St., New York, NY 10031. 212-650-6319. E-mail: fictionmagazine@yahoo.com. Web site: www.fictioninc.com. 2-3x/year. $8/issue. Circ.: 800. Mark Jay Mirsky, Editor. **Description:** Experimental and new fiction, supporting new and published authors. **Fiction:** Yes. **Nonfiction:** Yes. **Poetry:** Yes. **Queries:** Not necessary. **E-Queries:** No. **Unsolicited mss:** Accepts. **Response:** Queries to 1 month, submissions 4-6 months, SASE. **Freelance Content:** 100%. **Rights:** All, revert to author.

FIELD
Rice Hall, Oberlin College, 10 N. Professor St., Oberlin, OH 44074. 440-775-8408. E-mail: oc.press@oberlin.edu. Web site: www.oberlin.edu/~ocpress. Bi-annual. $14/year. Circ.: 1,000. 440-775-8124, David Young. **Description:** Lively, established American poets and new voices, also international poetry in fresh translations. Fall issue features symposium on a famous writer. **Poetry:** Varied formats, length. Pays $15/page, plus copies. **Tips:** Submit 3-5 poems at one time. **E-Queries:** Yes. **Unsolicited mss:** Does not accept. **Response:** Queries 1 week, Submissions 6 weeks, SASE required. **Payment:** On publication. **Contact:** David Walker.

FINE MADNESS

P.O. Box 31138, Seattle, WA 98103-1138.
E-mail: beastly@oz.net. Web site: www.scn.org/arts/finemadness. Semiannual. $5/issue, $9/year. Circ.: 1,000. Bentley Malek-Pitkin, Editor. **Description:** International poetry by writers, well-known and new, highly original in language and content. **Poetry:** Form open, strong sense of language, original imagery. **Tips:** Avoid concrete poetry, light verse, topical poetry, over-dependence on form. Prefers lyrical poems that use language in thoughtful and thought-provoking way. **Queries:** Preferred. **E-Queries:** Yes. **Unsolicited mss:** Accepts. **Response:** Queries 1-2 months, submissions 3-4 months, SASE required. **Freelance Content:** 100%.

FIRST INTENSITY

P.O. Box 665, Lawrence, KS 66044-0665. 785-479-1501.
E-mail: leechapman@aol.com. Lee Chapman, Editor. **Description:** Literary journal with poetry, short fiction, prose poetry, book reviews, interviews. Essays on poetics, writing, writers, visual artists. **Fiction:** 10 pages max. **Poetry:** 10 pages max. **Tips:** Seeking fresh, experimental work, nothing "mainstream." **Queries:** Not necessary. **E-Queries:** Yes. **Unsolicited mss:** Accepts. **Response:** Queries 2 weeks, submissions 8-10 weeks, SASE required. **Freelance Content:** 50%. **Payment:** On publication.

THE FIRST LINE

K Street Ink, P.O. Box 0382, Plano, TX 75025-0382.
E-mail: info@the firstline.com. Bi-monthly. $2/$10. Circ.: 200. David LaBounty. **Description:** Celebrates the first line. A forum for discussing favorite lines, also seeks different short stories stemming from a common first line. **Fiction:** All stories must stem from the same first line; 300-700 words. **Nonfiction:** My Favorite First Line series (essays about a first line from book or story); 300-700 words. **Tips:** Also sponsors several contests with cash prizes. **Queries:** Not necessary. **E-Queries:** Yes. **Unsolicited mss:** Accepts. **Response:** Queries 2 weeks, submissions 2-6 weeks, SASE. **Freelance Content:** 90%. **Rights:** 1st NA, electronic, anthology. **Payment:** On publication.

FIVE POINTS

Georgia State Univ., University Plaza, Atlanta, GA 30303-3083.
Web site: www.webdelsol.com/five_points. 3x/year. $7/$20. Circ.: 2,000. David Bottoms, Pam Durban, Editors. **Description:** Quality fiction, poetry, essays, and interviews; with original voice, substance and significance. **Fiction:** 7,500 words; $15/page, $250 max. **Nonfiction:** Personal essays, literary essays, and creative non-fiction; 7,500 words; $15/page, $250 max. **Poetry:** 100 lines max. per poem; $50/poem. **Art:** Art photography only. Paintings, illustrations sometimes considered; slides, prints; pay varies. **Queries:** Not necessary. **E-Queries:** No. **Unsolicited mss:** Accepts. **Response:** Queries 2 months, submission 3 months, SASE. **Freelance Content:** 10%. **Rights:** 1st NA. **Payment:** On publication.

FLINT HILLS REVIEW

Bluestem Press, Dept. of English, Box 4019,
Emporia State University, Emporia, KS 66801-5087. 316-341-5216.
E-mail: webbamy@emporia.edu. Web site: http://emporia.edu.fhr/index.htm.
Annual. $5.50/issue. Circ.: 500. Amy Sage Webb, Philip Heldrich, Editors.
Description: Writing from and about Kansas and the Great Plains region, conveying a strong sense of place. **Fiction:** Place-focused writing about or set in the region. **Nonfiction:** Interviews, esays; offers annual prize of $200. **Poetry:** Strong imagery, fidelity to place. **Art:** Place-based b/w photos, ideally which redefine the region. **Tips:** Do not send genre fiction, religious writing, or unsolicited critical essays or interviews (query first for these). **Queries:** Not necessary. **E-Queries:** Yes. **Unsolicited mss:** Accepts. **Response:** 2 months queries, 6 months submissions, SASE. **Freelance Content:** 5%. **Rights:** 1st. **Payment:** In copies.

THE FLORIDA REVIEW

Univ. of Central Florida, English Dept.,
PO Box 622950, Orlando, FL 32816. 407-823-2038.
Web site: www.pegasus.cc.ucf.edu. Bi-annual. $6/$10. Circ.: 1,000. Pat Rushin, Editor. **Description:** Mainstream and experimental fiction, nonfiction, and poetry, to 10,000 words. **Queries:** Not necessary. **E-Queries:** Yes. **Unsolicited mss:** Accepts. **Response:** 2 weeks queries, 1-2 months submissions; SASE required. **Rights:** 1st. **Payment:** In copies. **Contact:** Terry Hess.

FLYWAY LITERARY REVIEW

206 Ross Hall, Iowa State Univ., Ames, IA 50011.
E-mail: flyway@iastate.edu. Web site: www.engl.iastate.edu/main/resources/flyway/flyway.html. Tri-annual. $18/year. Circ.: 500. Stephen Pett, Editor. **Description:** Quality poetry, nonfiction, and fiction by new and established writers. **Fiction:** Literary fiction; up to 20 pages. **Nonfiction:** Personal essays; up to 20 pages. **Poetry:** Ambitious; "open to all poetry that takes its experience seriously, including humorous poems." **Art:** Seeking cover art; send slides or photos. **Queries:** Not necessary. **E-Queries:** No. **Unsolicited mss:** Accepts. **Response:** 2 weeks, SASE. **Freelance Content:** 90%. **Rights:** one-time. **Payment:** In copies.

FOLIO

American Univ., Dept. of Literature, Washington, DC 20016.
Bi-annual. $6/year. Circ.: 500. Eve Rosenbaum, Editor. **Description:** Quality fiction and poetry. **Fiction:** Up to 4,000 words. **Nonfiction:** Creative nonfiction and memoirs; up to 4,000 words. **Poetry:** Up to 5 poems. **Art:** b/w photos, slides. **Tips:** Submissions read Sept.-March 15. **Queries:** Not necessary. **E-Queries:** No. **Unsolicited mss:** Accepts. **Response:** Submissions 2-6 months, SASE required. **Freelance Content:** 90%. **Payment:** In copies.

THE FORMALIST

320 Hunter Dr., Evansville, IN 47711.

$12 (2 issues). Mona Baer, Director. **Description:** Poetry in contemporary idiom, using meter and traditional poetic conventions in vigorous, interesting ways. Especially interested in sonnets, couplets, tercets, ballads, etc. (no haikus). **Tips:** Offers Howard Nemerov Sonnet Award, $1,000. **Queries:** Required. **Response:** Queries in 8 weeks, SASE. **Payment:** In copies.

FOURTEEN HILLS

San Francisco State Univ., Creative Writing Dept.,

1600 Holloway Ave., San Francisco, CA 94132-1722. 415-338-3083.

E-mail: hills@sfsu.edu. Web site: www.fourteenhills.com. Biannual. $7/issue, $12/year. Circ.: 600. **Description:** Innovative fiction, poetry, drama, and interviews. Seeking matter or styles overlooked by traditional journals. **Fiction:** Up to 5,000 words. **Poetry:** Submit up to 5 poems. **Queries:** Not necessary. **E-Queries:** No. **Unsolicited mss:** Accepts. **Response:** Queries 2 weeks, submissions up to 10 months. **Rights:** 1st NA. **Payment:** In copies.

FROGPOND

P.O. Box 2461, Winchester, VA 22604-1661. 540-722-2156.

E-mail: redmoon@shentel.net. Web site: www.octet.com. 3x/year. $28/yr. Circ.: 1,000. Jim Kacian, Editor. **Description:** Published by Haiku Society of America. **Nonfiction:** Articles, essays, and reviews. **Poetry:** The finest haikus, and related forms; $1/poem. **Tips:** Know what is current in contemporary haiku. **E-Queries:** Yes. **Unsolicited mss:** Accepts. **Response:** 2-3 weeks, SASE. **Freelance Content:** 95%. **Rights:** 1st NA. **Payment:** On acceptance.

FUGUE

Univ. of Idaho, English Dept., Brink Hall, Room 200, Moscow, ID 83844-1102.

E-mail: ronmcf@uidaho.edu. Web site: www.uidaho.edu/ls/eng/fugue. Semiannual. $6/issue, $10/year. Circ.: 300. Andrea Mason, Editor. **Description:** Dedicated to new voices and quality writing. **Fiction:** Well written, traditional as well as experimental; up to 6,000 words; $20. **Nonfiction:** Seeking creative nonfiction; up to 6,000 words; $20. **Poetry:** Any length and topic; submit up to 4 poems at a time; $10. **Art:** Seeking cover art; $50. **Tips:** Don't send more than one genre together. Avoid cliché or worn-out language. Looking for new, innovative, edgy pieces. **Queries:** Not necessary. **E-Queries:** No. **Unsolicited mss:** Accepts. **Response:** Queries 2 weeks, submissions 2-4 months, SASE required. **Freelance Content:** 20%. **Rights:** one-time, reverts with credit. **Payment:** On publication.

FUTURES

3039 38th Ave. South, Minneapolis, MN 55406-2140. 612-724-4023.

E-mail: barbl@telacom. Web site: www.firetowrite.com. Monthly. Barbara Lakey, Editor. **Description:** "Everything under the sun" (short fiction, essays, and inspiration for writers and readers). Seeking writers with verve and imagination. **Fiction:** No query needed; short fiction, 500 - 3,500 words. **Nonfiction:** Essays; to 3,500 words. **Queries:** Preferred.

THE GEORGIA REVIEW

Univ. of Georgia, Athens, GA 30602-9009. 706-542-3481. E-mail: bkeen@arches.uga.edu. Web site: www.uga.edu/garev. Quarterly. $9/issue. Circ.: 5,500. Stephen Corey, Editor. **Description:** An eclectic blend of essays, fiction, poetry, graphics, and book reviews. **Fiction:** Short stories, no novel excerpts. Pays $40/printed page. **Nonfiction:** Essays, no book chapters; $40/page. **Poetry:** $3/line. **Art:** Cover, plus 8-page interior portfolio in each issue; $450 for the 9 images. **Queries:** Preferred. **E-Queries:** No. **Unsolicited mss:** Does not accept. **Response:** Queries 1-2 weeks, submissions 1-3 months, SASE required. **Freelance Content:** 80%. **Payment:** On publication.

GETTYSBURG REVIEW

Gettysburg College, Gettysburg, PA 17325. 717-337-6770. E-mail: mdrew@gettysburg.edu. Web site: www.gettysburgreview.com. Quarterly. $6/issue. Circ.: 3,500. Peter Stitt, Editor. **Description:** Quality poetry, fiction, essays, essay reviews, and graphics by beginning and established writers and artists. **Fiction:** Literary fiction, fresh and surprising, including novel excerpts; 1,000-20,000 words; $25/printed page. **Nonfiction:** Varied (memoir, literary criticism, creative nonfiction, other); 3,000-7,000 words; $25/printed page. **Poetry:** All styles and forms; $2/line. **Queries:** Not necessary. **E-Queries:** No. **Unsolicited mss:** Accepts. **Response:** Queries 2-3 weeks, submissions 3-6 months, SASE required. **Freelance Content:** 100%. **Rights:** 1st NA serial. **Payment:** On publication.

GLIMMER TRAIN STORIES

710 SW Madison St., #504, Portland, OR 97205. 503-221-0836. Web site: www.glimmertrain.com. Quarterly. $32/yr. Circ.: 18,000. Linda Burmeister Davies, Editor. **Description:** Short stories by established and emerging writers. A feast of fiction for the mind and heart, beautifully written and emotionally affecting. **Fiction:** Literary short stories; 800-1,200 words; $500/story. **Queries:** Not necessary. **E-Queries:** No. **Unsolicited mss:** Accepts. **Response:** 3 months, SASE required. **Freelance Content:** 100%. **Rights:** First publication. **Payment:** On acceptance.

GLOBAL CITY REVIEW

Rifkind Ctr. for the Humanities, City College of NY, 138th St. & Convenient Ave., New York, NY 10031. E-mail: globalcityreview@aol.com. Biannual. Linsey Abrams. **Description:** Intellectual literary forum for women, lesbian, and gay, and other culturally diverse writers; writers of color, international writers, activist writers. Thematic issues. Fiction, nonfiction, and poetry on issues of gender, race, and women's experience. **Tips:** No queries; send complete manuscripts for review. **Payment:** In copies.

GRAIN

Saskatchewan Writers Guild, PO Box 1154, Regina, Saskatchewan, Canada S4P3B4. 306-244-2828. E-mail: grain.mag@sk.simpatico.ca. Web site: www.skwriter.com. Quarterly. $7.95/issue, $26.95/year. Circ.: 1,300. Elizabeth Philips, Editor. **Description:** Literary magazine; fresh, startling, imaginative, and accessible. Often publishes new emerging writers, and established writers from Canada and around the world. Pays $40-$175. **Fiction:** Literary fiction in any style, well-crafted stories. No mainstream romance or historical fiction; up to 30 pages. **Nonfiction:** Creative nonfiction; up to 30 pages. **Poetry:** Up to 8 poems. Avoid avant garde; does publish work that pushes boundaries. Favors thoughtful work that takes risks. **Tips:** Pay attention to a story's subtext. Prefers imaginative fiction, even quirky. Original work only, no reprints. **Queries:** Not necessary. **E-Queries:** No. **Unsolicited mss:** Accepts. **Response:** 1-3 months, SASE (or give e-mail address). **Freelance Content:** 100%. **Rights:** 1st Canadian serial. **Payment:** On publication.

GRAND STREET

214 Sullivan St., 6C, New York, NY 10012. 212-533-2944. E-mail: info@grandstreet.com. Web site: www.grandstreet.com. Quarterly. Jean Stein, Editor. **Description:** Art, fiction, nonfiction and poetry. **Poetry:** Any length; $3/line. **Queries:** Not necessary. **E-Queries:** No. **Unsolicited mss:** Does not accept. **Response:** Queries 7 days, submissions 12-16 weeks, SASE. **Payment:** On publication.

GRASSLANDS REVIEW

P.O. Box 626, Berea, OH 44017. E-mail: glreview@aol.com. Web site: www.hometown.aol.com/g/review/prof/index.htm. Semiannual. $10/yr. Laura Kennelly, Editor. **Description:** Encourages new writers. Seeks "imagination without sloppiness, ideas without lectures, and delight in language." Accepts manuscripts postmarked March or October only. **Fiction:** Short stories, 1,000-3,500 words. **Poetry:** Any length. **Queries:** Not necessary. **Response:** SASE. **Payment:** In copies.

GREEN MOUNTAINS REVIEW

Johnson State College, Johnson, VT 05656. 802-635-1350. E-mail: gmr@badger.jsc.vsc.edu. Biannual. $7/issue. Circ.: 1,700. Neil Shepard, General Editor; Tony Whedon, Poetry Editor. **Description:** Poems, stories, and creative nonfiction by well-known and promising new authors. Also, interviews, literary criticism, and book reviews. **Fiction:** Wide range of styles and subjects; up to 30 pages. **Nonfiction:** Interviews with writers, also literary essays; up to 30 pages. **Poetry:** Any type. **Art:** b/w photos. **Tips:** Publishes only 2% of submissions. Occasional special-theme issues, **Queries:** Not necessary. **E-Queries:** No. **Unsolicited mss:** Accepts. **Response:** 1 week-1 month, SASE. **Freelance Content:** 80%. **Rights:** FNASR. **Payment:** In copies.

THE GREENSBORO REVIEW
MFA Program, Dept. of English, 134 McIver Bldg.,
UNCG, PO Box 26170, Greensboro, NC 27402-6170.
E-mail: jlclark@uncg.edu. Web site: www.uncg.edu/eng/mfa/review/review.htm.
Semi-annual. $5/issue. Circ.: 800. Jim Clark, Editor. **Description:** Quality poetry and
fiction. **Fiction:** Any theme, subject, or style; up to 7,500 words. **Poetry:** Varied.
Tips: Original work only, no multiple submissions. **Queries:** Not necessary. **E-Queries:** No. **Unsolicited mss:** Accepts. **Rights:** FNASR. **Payment:** In copies.

GULF COAST
English Dept., Univ. of Houston, Houston, TX 77204. 713-743-3223.
E-mail: ppeschi@bayou.nh.edu. Web site: www.gulfcoast.uh.edu. Semiannual. $7.
Circ.: 1,000. Pablo Peschiera, Editor. **Description:** A journal of literary fiction, non-fiction, poetry and fine art. **Queries:** Not necessary. **E-Queries:** No. **Unsolicited
mss:** Accepts. **Response:** 3-6 months, SASE.

HARP-STRINGS
P.O. Box 640387, Beverly Hills, FL 34464.
E-mail: verdure@digitalusa.net. Web site: www.verdurapubs.com. Quarterly.
$3.50/issue, $12/year. Circ.: 105. Madelyn Eastlund, Editor. **Description:** Seeks
poetry: narrative, lyrics, ballads, sestinas, rondeau redoubles, blank verse, villanelles,
sonnets, prose poems, haiku sequences, etc. **Poetry:** Memorable, haunting; 14-80
lines. **Tips:** No trite, broken prose masquerading as poetry; no confessions or raw-guts poems. **Queries:** Not necessary. **E-Queries:** Yes. **Unsolicited mss:** Accepts.
Freelance Content: 100%. **Rights:** one-time. **Payment:** In copies.

HAWAII REVIEW
Univ. of Hawaii, Dept. of English,
1733 Donaggho Rd., Honolulu, HI 96822. 808-956-3030.
E-mail: hi-review@hawaii.edu. Bi-annual. $10/issue. Circ.: 1,000. Michael Pulelua,
Editor. **Description:** Literary poetry, fiction, nonfiction, and reviews. **Fiction:** up to
20 pages. **Nonfiction:** up to 20 pages. **Tips:** Submissions accepted year-round.
Queries: Not necessary. **E-Queries:** Yes. **Unsolicited mss:** Accepts. **Response:**
Queries 2-3 weeks submissions 3-6 months, SASE required. **Rights:** 1st NA.

HAYDEN'S FERRY REVIEW
Arizona State University, Box 871502, Tempe, AZ 85287-1502. 480-965-1243.
E-mail: hfr@asu.edu. Web site: www.haydensferryreview.com. Biannual. $5/issue,
$10/year. Circ.: 1,300. Salima Keegan, Editor. **Description:** Literary and art maga-zine, with art, poetry, fiction, and creative nonfiction by new and established artists
and writers. Pays $25/page ($100 max.). **Fiction:** Yes. **Nonfiction:** Yes. **Poetry:** Up
to 6 poems. **Tips:** Include brief bio. **Queries:** Not necessary. **Unsolicited mss:**
Accepts. **Response:** Queries 1 week, submissions 8-12 weeks, SASE required.
Freelance Content: 80%. **Rights:** NA serial. **Payment:** On publication. **Contact:**
Poetry or Fiction Editor.

HEAVEN BONE

P.O. Box 486, Chester, NY 10918. 845-469-9018.
Annual. $10. Circ.: 2,500. Steve Hirsch, Editor. **Description:** Poetry, fiction, reviews, and artwork with emphasis on surreal, neo-beat, experimental, and Buddhist concerns. **Fiction:** 2,500-10,000 words. **Nonfiction:** Essays on creativity, philosophy, and conciousness studies, relating to writing; 7,500 words. **Poetry:** Surreal, experimental, visual, neo-beat, Buddhist. **Art:** digital, traditional formats. **Tips:** Despite "Heaven" in title, this is not a religious publication. **Queries:** Preferred. **E-Queries:** Yes. **Unsolicited mss:** Accepts. **Response:** Queries 3 weeks, submissions up to 1 year, SASE. **Rights:** 1st NA. **Payment:** In copies.

HIGH PLAINS LITERARY REVIEW

180 Adams St., Suite 250, Denver, CO 80206. 303-320-6828.
Tri-annual. $7/issue. Circ.: 2,500. Robert O. Greer, Editor. **Description:** Publishes fiction, poetry, essays, reviews and interviews, to bridge the gap between academic quarterlies and commercial reviews. **Fiction:** Yes; 3,000-6,500 words; $5/printed page. **Nonfiction:** Yes; $5/page. **Poetry:** Yes; $10/page. **Queries:** Preferred. **E-Queries:** No. **Unsolicited mss:** Accepts. **Response:** Submissions 6-12 weeks, SASE required. **Payment:** On publication.

THE HOLLINS CRITIC

Hollins University, P.O. Box 9538, Roanoke, VA 24020. 540-362-6275.
E-mail: acockrell@hollins.edu. Web site: www.hollins.edu. 5x/year. $6/issue. Circ.: 500. R.H.W. Dillard, Editor. **Description:** Features an essay on a contemporary fiction writer, poet, or dramatist (cover sketch, brief biography, and book list). **Nonfiction:** Book reviews, essays; $25. **Queries:** Not necessary. **E-Queries:** No. **Unsolicited mss:** Accepts. **Response:** Submission 2 months, SASE required. **Freelance Content:** 100%. **Rights:** 1st, reverts following publication. **Payment:** On publication.

HUDSON REVIEW

684 Park Ave., New York, NY 10021. 212-650-0020.
E-mail: emontjoy@erols.com. Web site: www.litline.org. Quarterly. $8/issue, $28/year. Circ.: 5,000. Paula Deitz, Editor. **Description:** Fiction, poetry, essays, book reviews; criticism of literature, art, theatre, dance, film and music; and articles on contemporary culture. **Fiction:** Yes. **Nonfiction:** Yes. **Poetry:** Yes. **Queries:** Preferred. **E-Queries:** No. **Unsolicited mss:** Accepts. **Response:** 4-8 weeks, SASE. **Payment:** On publication.

HURRICANE ALICE

Rhode Island College, Dept. of English, Providence, RI 02908. 401-456-8377.
E-mail: mreddy@ric.edu. Quarterly. $2.50/issue. Circ.: 1,000. Maureen Reddy, Editor. **Description:** Feminist exploration, from diverse perspectives, of all aspects of culture. Especially committed to work by women of color, lesbians, working-class women, and young women. **Fiction:** Fictional critiques of culture; 3,500 words max.

Nonfiction: Articles, essays, interviews, and reviews; 3,500 words max. **Poetry:** Yes. **Art:** b/w (5x7 or 8x10). **Queries:** Not necessary. **E-Queries:** Yes. **Unsolicited mss:** Accepts. **Response:** Queries 30 days, submissions 6 months, SASE required. **Freelance Content:** 100%. **Rights:** FNASR. **Payment:** In copies.

THE ICONOCLAST

1675 Amazon Rd., Mohegan Lake, NY 10547. 914-528-2553. 6x/year. $2.50/issue. Circ.: 600. Phil Wagner, Editor. **Description:** For readers and writers of original work bypassed by corporate and institutional publications. **Fiction:** Literary stories, plots, and ideas with active characters engaged with the world; 100-3,500 words; $.01/word. **Nonfiction:** Nothing topical, fashionable, political, or academic; 100-3,500 words; $.01/word. **Poetry:** Well-crafted, with something to say; send 2-5 poems; up to 2 pages. **Fillers:** Humor (nothing silly, self-consciously zany); 20-2,000 words; $.01/word. **Art:** Line drawings; pay varies. **Queries:** Preferred. **Unsolicited mss:** Accepts. **Response:** Queries 1 week, submissions 1 month, SASE. **Freelance Content:** 90%. **Rights:** 1st, some one-time. **Payment:** On acceptance.

ILLYA'S HONEY

Dallas Poets Community, P.O. Box 225435, Dallas, TX 75222-5435. E-mail: dpcmail@dallaspoets.org. Web site: www.dallaspoets.org. Quarterly. $6/issue, $18/year. Circ.: 150. Ann Howels, Meghan Robert, Editors. **Description:** Mostly poetry, some micro-fiction. **Fiction:** Flash fiction, sharp, well-crafted; 200 words. **Poetry:** Any form, any subject; prefers free verse. **Queries:** Not necessary. **E-Queries:** Yes. **Unsolicited mss:** Accepts. **Response:** Submissions 3-4 months, SASE. **Freelance Content:** 98%. **Rights:** 1st NA. **Payment:** In copies.

INDIANA REVIEW

Indiana University, Ballantine Hall 465, 1020 E. Kirkwood Ave., Bloomington, IN 47408. 812-855-3439. Web site: www.indiana.edu/~interview/ir.html. Semi-annual. $8/issue, $14/year. Circ.: 2,000. Simeon Berry, Editor. **Description:** For emerging and established writers, quality writing within a wide aesthetic. Pays $5/page ($10 min.) and in copies. **Fiction:** Daring stories which integrate theme, language, character, and form, with consequence beyond the world of its narrator; up to 40 pages. **Nonfiction:** Lively essays on engaging topics. Interviews with established writers, book reviews; up to 30 pages. **Poetry:** Intelligent form and language, with risk, ambition, and scope. **Queries:** Not necessary. **E-Queries:** Yes. **Unsolicited mss:** Accepts. **Response:** 1 week queries, submissions 2-3 months, SASE required. **Freelance Content:** 90%. **Rights:** FNASR. **Payment:** On publication. **Contact:** Poetry or Fiction Editor.

INDIGENOUS FICTION

P.O. Box 2078, Redmond, WA 98073-2078. E-mail: decker@earthlink.net. Web site: www.home.earthlink.net. Tri-annual. $6/issue, $15/year. Circ.: 300. Sherry Decker, Editor. **Description:** Short fiction. Wondrously weird and offbeat genre; odd literary. **Fiction:** Bizarre, unusual, quirky, surprising; genre and odd literary; 1-8,000; $5-$20. **Poetry:** Moody, tell a bit of story. Submit up to 5 poems at a time; 30 lines max./poem; $5/poem. **Art:** Send samples (copies, not originals). **Tips:** Avoid adverbs. Stay in one character's point of view. **Queries:** Not necessary. **E-Queries:** Yes. **Unsolicited mss:** Accepts. **Response:** Queries 1-2 days, submission 2 weeks, SASE. **Freelance Content:** 98%. **Rights:** 1st NA. **Payment:** On publication.

INTERNATIONAL POETRY REVIEW
Univ. of North Carolina, Dept. of Romance Languages, P.O. Box 26170, Greensboro, NC 27402-6170. Quarterly. $15. Circ.: 200. Kathleen Koestler, Editor. **Description:** Features work that crosses language barriers to present the voices of poets in different countries. **Nonfiction:** Book reviews, interviews, and short essays, to 1,500 words. **Poetry:** Up to 6 pages at a time; original English poems and contemporary translations from other languages. **Tips:** Prefers material with cross-cultural or international dimension. **Queries:** Preferred. **Unsolicited mss:** Accepts. **Payment:** In copies.

IOWA REVIEW
Univ. of Iowa, 308 EPB, Iowa City, IA 52242. 319-335-0462. E-mail: iowa-review@uiowa.edu. Web site: www.uiowa.edu/~iareview. Tri-annual. $6.95/issue, $18/year. Circ.: 3,000. David Hamilton, Editor. **Description:** Essays, poems, stories, reviews. Strives to discover new writers; to be local but not provincial; experimental, but not without elegance. **Fiction:** Short stories; any length; $10/printed page. **Nonfiction:** Essays, reviews; any length; $10/printed page. **Poetry:** any length; $20/printed page. **Queries:** Not necessary. **E-Queries:** Accepts. **Unsolicited mss:** Accepts. **Response:** 1-3 months, SASE required. **Freelance Content:** 98%. **Rights:** FNASR. **Payment:** On publication.

JAMES WHITE REVIEW
Lambda Literary Foundation, P.O. Box 73910, Washington, DC 20056-3910. 202-682-0952. E-mail: LLFGregh@aolcom. Web site: www.lambdalit.org. Quarterly. $4.95/issue, $17.50/year. Circ.: 3,000. Patrick Merla, Editor. **Description:** Gay men's literary magazine, with fiction, poetry, photography, art, essays and reviews. **Fiction:** Seeking well-crafted literary fiction with strongly-developed characters; gay themes; to 10,000 words; pay varies. **Poetry:** Submit up to 3 poems at a time. **Tips:** Be patient, small staff receives many submissions. **Queries:** Preferred. **E-Queries:** No. **Unsolicited mss:** Accepts. **Response:** Queries 3 weeks, submissions 3-6 months, SASE. **Rights:** 1st. **Payment:** On publication. **Contact:** Greg Harren, Asst. Ed.

JOURNAL OF NEW JERSEY POETS
County College of Morris, 214 Center Grove Rd., Randolph, NJ 07869-2086. 973-328-5471. E-mail: szulauf@ccm.edu. Web site: www.ccm.edu/humanities/humanities/journal/html. Bi-annual. $5/issue. Circ.: 600. Sander Zulauf, Editor. **Description:**

New poetry by poets who live or have lived in New Jersey. **Nonfiction:** Essays on poetry, book reviews on new work by New Jersey poets; up to 1,500 words. **Poetry:** Send up to 3 poems at a time (no epics). **Tips:** New Jersey not required as subject matter; seeks work universal in scope. **Queries:** Not necessary. **E-Queries:** No. **Unsolicited mss:** Accepts. **Response:** Queries 2 weeks, submissions 6 months to 1 year, SASE. **Freelance Content:** 100%. **Rights:** FNASR. **Payment:** In copies.

KALEIDOSCOPE

United Disability Services, 701 S. Main St., Akron, OH 44311-1019. 330-762-9755. E-mail: mshiplett@udsakron.org. Web site: www.udsakron.org. Semi-annual. $5/issue, $9/year. Circ.: 1,000. Darshan Perusek, Ph.D., Editor-in-Chief. **Description:** Explores the experience of disability through literature and fine arts, from perspectives of individuals, families, health-care professionals, and society. Seeks to challenge and overcome stereotypical, patronizing, sentimental attitudes about disability. Pay $25 and 2 copies. **Fiction:** Character-centered stories, not action pieces. No romance. 5,000 words max. **Nonfiction:** Narratives and articles on experiences and issues of disability; 5,000 words max. **Poetry:** Free verse on disability or written by someone with a disability. Also, short nature poems and light humor; 1-5 poems. **Art:** 35mm color, b/w 8x10 glossy; up to $100. **Tips:** Photos a plus. **Queries:** Not necessary. **E-Queries:** Yes. **Unsolicited mss:** Accepts. **Response:** Queries 2 weeks, submissions 6 months, SASE required. **Freelance Content:** 60%. **Rights:** 1st serial. **Payment:** On publication.

KALLIOPE

Florida Comm. College at Jacksonville, 3939 Roosevelt Blvd., Jacksonville, FL 32205. 904-381-3511. Web site: www.fccj.org/kalliope. Semiannual. $14.95/yr. Circ.: 1,600. Mary Sue Koeppel, Editor. **Description:** Journal of women's literature and art, with poetry, short fiction, interviews, reviews, and visual art by women. **Fiction:** Well-constructed literary work; 2,000 words. **Nonfiction:** Interviews with writers and/or artists; 200-2,000 words. **Poetry:** 3-4 pages. **Art:** Fine art, slides or glossies. **Queries:** Not necessary. **E-Queries:** No. **Unsolicited mss:** Accepts. **Response:** Queries 1-3 weeks, submissions 3-6 months, SASE. **Freelance Content:** 100%. **Rights:** 1st. **Payment:** In copies.

KARAMU

Dept. of English, Eastern Illinois Univ., Charleston, IL 61920. 217-581-6297. Annual. $7.50. Circ.: 500. Olga Abella, Editor. **Description:** Publishes poetry, fiction, and essays. **Fiction:** Stories that capture something essential about life, beyond the superficial, and develop genuine voices; 3,500 words. **Nonfiction:** Any subject, not religious or political; 3,500 words. **Poetry:** Yes. **Tips:** Avoid rhyming poetry or didactic prose. **Queries:** Preferred. **E-Queries:** No. **Unsolicited mss:** Accepts. **Response:** Queries 2-3 days, submissions 4-6 months, SASE required. **Freelance Content:** 100%. **Rights:** One-time. **Payment:** In copies.

KARITOS REVIEW

35689 N. Helendale Rd., Ingleside, IL 60041. 847-587-9111.
E-mail: robuserid@prodigy.net. Web site: www.karitos.com. Annual. $3. Circ.: 150.
Gina Merritt (fiction), Karen Beattie (poetry), Editors. **Description:** Literary magazine, published in conjunction with Karitos Christian Arts Festival in Chicago. **Fiction:** Considers anything (except straight romance); 2,500 words. **Poetry:** Any style (except greeting-card verse); 2 pages, limit 2 poems. **Tips:** Send all work in duplicate. Work must have literary merit; does not have to be religious, but should reflect Christian worldview. Especailly seeking work from minority authors reflecting their cultural background. Romance okay as element in story, but no genre romance fiction. **Queries:** Not necessary. **E-Queries:** Yes. **Unsolicited mss:** Accepts. **Response:** Queries 2 weeks, submissions 4 months, SASE required. **Freelance Content:** 50%. **Rights:** First or reprint. **Payment:** In copies.

KELSEY REVIEW

Mercer County Community College, P.O. Box B,
Trenton, NJ 08690. 609-586-4800 (ext. 3326).
E-mail: kelsey.review@mccc.edu. Web site: www.mccc.edu. Annual. Free. Circ.: 1,750. Robin Schore, Editor. **Description:** Literary journal exclusively for writers living or working in Mercer Country, NJ. Fiction, essays, poetry, line art. **Fiction:** 2,000 words. **Nonfiction:** 2,000 words. **Poetry:** Up to 6 poems. **Art:** b/w line art. **Queries:** Not necessary. **Unsolicited mss:** Accepts. **Response:** Deadline May 1st. Responds by June 30th. **Freelance Content:** 100%. **Rights:** None. **Payment:** In copies.

THE KENYON REVIEW

Kenyon College, 102 College Drive, Gambier, OH 43022. 740-427-5208.
E-mail: kenyonreview@kenyon.edu. Web site: www.kenyonreview.org. Tri-annual. $8/issue. Circ.: 5,000. David H. Lynn, Editor. **Description:** Features new writing from emerging and established writers. Poetry, fiction, creative nonfiction, interviews, reviews, and more. **Fiction:** To 7,500 words; $10/printed page. **Nonfiction:** To 7,500 words; $10/page. **Poetry:** To 10 pages; $15/page. **Art:** b/w; $100. **Queries:** Not necessary. **E-Queries:** No. **Unsolicited mss:** Accepts. **Response:** Queries 1-2 months, submissions 3-4 months, SASE required. **Freelance Content:** 90%. **Rights:** 1st NA. **Payment:** On publication.

KIMERA

N 1316 Hollis St., Spokane, WA 99201. 509-326-6641.
E-mail: editor@js.spokane.wa.us. Web site: http://js.spokane.wa.us/kimera. Annual. $10/yr. Circ.: 300. Jan Strever, Editor. **Description:** For fine writing, in print and online. Uses John Locke's premise,"Where is the head with no chimeras?" **Fiction:** Work that plays with language, has a strong sense of itself; no erotica. **Poetry:** No "message" poems. **Queries:** Not necessary. **E-Queries:** Accepts. **Unsolicited mss:** Accepts. **Response:** 3 months, SASE. **Freelance Content:** 100%. **Rights:** 1st, electronic. **Payment:** In copies.

THE KIT-CAT REVIEW

244 Halstead Ave., Harrison, NY 10528. 914-835-4833. Quarterly. $7/issue, $25/year. Circ.: 300. Claudia Fletcher. **Description:** Seeks excellence and originality. **Fiction:** Example: "The Heisenberg Approach," a fictional excerpt from Werner Heisenberg's diary. Up to 5,000 words, prefers shorter. **Nonfiction:** Example: "Wishing for Miracles: Tijuana Interviews," about life in modern-day Tijuana. Up to 6,000 words, prefer shorter. **Poetry:** All types and lengths, except greeting card or deliberately obscure. **Tips:** Avoid O. Henry-type endings. No excessive vulgarity or profanity. **Queries:** Not necessary. **E-Queries:** No. **Unsolicited mss:** Accepts. **Response:** Queries 2 weeks, submissions 1 month, SASE. **Freelance Content:** 100%. **Rights:** 1st, one-time. **Payment:** On acceptance.

THE LARCOM REVIEW

P.O. Box 161, Prides Crossing, MA 01965. 978-927-8707. E-mail: amp@larcompress.com. Web site: www.larcompress.com. Semi-annual. $12/issue, $20/year. Circ.: 300. Susan Oleksiw, Editor. **Description:** Contemporary short fiction, poetry, and essays about New England life, written by New Englanders. **Fiction:** Stories from quiet pieces on family life to suspense mystery fiction, from short-short with sharp impact to longer, thoughtful tales to be savored over an evening; 3,000 words; $25. **Nonfiction:** Entertaining, accessible essays and articles; 3,000 words; $25. **Art:** Prints, slides, illustrations; $25. **Tips:** Seeking stories on all aspects of life in 6 states in region, including stories by New Englanders living elsewhere. Don't submit fiction and nonfiction together. No gratuitous sex, violence, foul language as a substitute for thinking and feeling. **Queries:** Not necessary. **E-Queries:** No. **Unsolicited mss:** Accepts. **Response:** Submission 3-4 months, SASE. **Rights:** 1st NA. **Payment:** On publication.

THE LEDGE

78-44 80th St., Glendale, NY 11385. Annual. $7/issue. Circ.: 1,000. Timothy Monaghan, Editor. **Description:** Poetry journal; seeks exceptional contemporary work, powerful poems with purpose. No restrictions on style or form. **Poetry:** up to 80 lines. **Queries:** Not necessary. **E-Queries:** No. **Unsolicited mss:** Accepts. **Response:** Queries 2-3 weeks, submissions 3 months, SASE. **Freelance Content:** 100%. **Rights:** FNASR. **Payment:** In copies.

LIGHT

Box 7500, Chicago, IL 60680. 847-853-1028. Web site: www.litline.org/light. Quarterly. $5/issue, $18/year. Circ.: 1,000. John Mella, Editor. **Description:** Devoted exclusively to light verse. **Nonfiction:** Reviews, essays. **Poetry:** Yes. **Tips:** Think James Thurber, E.B.White, Odgen Nash; if it has wit, point, edge, or barb, it has a home here. **Queries:** Preferred. **E-Queries:** No. **Unsolicited mss:** Accepts. **Response:** Queries 1-4 months. **Payment:** On publication.

LIMESTONE CIRCLE

P.O. Box 453, Ashburn, VA 20146-0453.
E-mail: renjef@earthlink.net. Biannual. $8/yr. Circ.: 75. Renee Carter Hall, Editor. **Description:** Journal of poetry. **Poetry:** Well-crafted, accessible poetry from new and established poets. Prefers free verse, traditional, and oriental forms; avoid rhyming or slam poetry; 1-2 pages. **Art:** b/w artwork, photos; all styles/subjects considered (nature, urban, still life, abstract, etc.). **Tips:** Seeking poems using ordinary experiences to subtly reflect extraordinary concepts; poems that use vivid images, not abstract generalizations; accessible works, subtle and deep without being obscure and difficult. **Queries:** Not necessary. **E-Queries:** No. **Unsolicited mss:** Accepts. **Response:** E-mail submissions 2 weeks, submissions by mail to 8 weeks, SASE required. **Freelance Content:** 100%. **Rights:** 1st. **Payment:** On publication.

LITERAL LATTE

61 E. 8th St., Suite 240, New York, NY 10003.
E-mail: LitLatte@aol.com. Web site: www.literal-latte.com. Bimonthly. $3/issue. Circ.: 25,000. Jenine Gordon Bockman, Editor. **Description:** Stimulating literary journal, brimming with stories, poetry, essays, and art. **Fiction:** Varied styles; the word is as important as the tale; 6,000 words. **Nonfiction:** Personal essays, all topics; thematic book reviews done as personal essays; 6,000 words. **Poetry:** All styles; 2,000 word max. **Fillers:** Intelligent literary cartoons. **Art:** Photocopies or slides (of photos, drawings, paintings, b/w or color). Open to all styles, abstraction to photorealism. **Tips:** Looking for new talent. Annual Fiction Awards ($1,500 in prizes). **Queries:** Not necessary. **E-Queries:** Accepts. **Unsolicited mss:** Accepts. **Rights:** FNASR. **Payment:** On publication.

LITERARY MAGAZINE REVIEW

Univ. of Northern Iowa, Dept. of English Language and Lit.,
117 Baker Hall, Cedar Falls, IA 50614-0502. 319-273-2821.
E-mail: grant.tracey@uni.edu. Quarterly. Circ.: 500. Grant Tracey, Editor. **Description:** For writers and readers of contemporary literature. **Nonfiction:** Reviews and articles concerning literary magazines; 1,000-1,500 words. **Queries:** Required. **Payment:** In copies.

♥ THE LITERARY REVIEW

Fairleigh Dickinson Univ., 285 Madison Ave., Madison, NJ 07940. 973-443-8564.
E-mail: tlr@fdu.edu. Web site: www.webdelsol.com. Quarterly. $5/issue. Circ.: 2,000. Walter Cummins, Editor. **Description:** International journal of poetry, fiction, essays, and contemporary review essays. **Fiction:** Open format. **Nonfiction:** Yes. **Poetry:** Yes. **Tips:** Encourages new writers, new ideas, new themes. **Queries:** Not necessary. **E-Queries:** Yes. **Unsolicited mss:** Accepts. **Response:** Queries, 1 week, submissions 8-12 weeks, SASE. **Rights:** 1st NA. **Payment:** In copies.

LOLLIPOP

P.O. Box 441493, Boston, MA 02144. 617-623-5319.
Web site: www.lollipop.com. Quarterly. Scott Hefflon, Editor. **Description:** On music and youth culture. Fiction, essays, and "edgy" commentary. Reviews and interviews related to underground culture. **Nonfiction:** To 2,000 words; pays $25 (for anything over 1,000 words). **Art:** Photos, drawings; $25. **Queries:** Preferred.

LONG SHOT

P.O. Box 6238, Hoboken, NJ 07030.
Web site: www.longshot.org. Semiannual. $8/year. Circ.: 1,500. Editorial Board. **Description:** Features raw, graphic, exuberant poetry (within reason), devoid of pretense. **Fiction:** to 10 pages. **Nonfiction:** to 10 pages. **Poetry:** to 8 pages. **Art:** b/w photos, drawings. **Queries:** Preferred. **E-Queries:** Yes. **Unsolicited mss:** Accepts. **Response:** 8-12 weeks, SASE. **Freelance Content:** 20%. **Payment:** In copies.

THE LONG STORY

18 Eaton St., Lawrence, MA 01843. 978-686-7638.
E-mail: RPBTLS@aol. Web site: www.litline. Annual. $6/issue. Circ.: 1,000. R.P. Burnham, Editor. **Description:** Stories about common folk. **Fiction:** Stories with a moral/thematic core, particularly about poor and working-class people. 8,000-12,000 words (occasionally to 20,000). **Queries:** Not necessary. **E-Queries:** No. **Unsolicited mss:** Accepts. **Response:** 2 months, SASE. **Freelance Content:** 95%. **Rights:** 1st NA. **Payment:** In copies.

LONZIE'S FRIED CHICKEN LITERARY

P.O. Box 189, Lynn, NC 28750.
E-mail: lonziesfriedchicken@teleplex.net. Web site: www.lonziesfriedchicken.com. Semi-annual. $8.95/$14.95. E.H. Goree, Editor. **Description:** Accessible southern fiction and poetry. **Fiction:** Accessible, with "a feel for the South"; 10 pages or less. **Poetry:** Accessible, southern; 40 lines. **Tips:** Contributors include "those who have always lived in the south," "those trying to come 'home' to the south," and "those who have driven through it." **Queries:** Not necessary. **E-Queries:** No. **Unsolicited mss:** Accepts. **Response:** Queries 1 week, submissions 3-6 months, SASE. **Freelance Content:** 100%. **Rights:** 1st, one-time anthology. **Payment:** In copies.

LSR

P.O. Box 440195, Miami, FL 33144. 305-447-3780.
E-mail: ejc@lspress.net. 2x/yr. Circ.: 3,000. Nilda Cepero, Editor. **Description:** Bilingual (English and Spanish) literary journal, focusing on Latino topics. **Nonfiction:** Book reviews or interviews, to 750 words. **Poetry:** Submit up to 4 poems, 5-45 lines each. Prefers contemporary, with meaning and message. **Art:** Line artwork; submit up to 5 illustrations on 3.5" disk (to be printed 6"x6" on cover, 8"x10" as full-page inside). **Tips:** Reprints accepted. Do not query. No submissions in November, December, or January. **Queries:** Not necessary. **E-Queries:** No.

Unsolicited mss: Accepts. **Response:** 9 months, SASE required. **Freelance Content:** 100%. **Rights:** 1st. **Payment:** In copies.

LUCID STONE

P.O. Box 940, Scottsdale, AZ 85252-0940. 480-947-0371. Quarterly. $6/issue, $16/year. Circ.: 200. Pauline Mounsey, Editor. **Description:** Literary journal that seeks to place quality poetry in every nook and cranny of sentient life. **Poetry:** Any length. **Art:** b/w or color photos; photos of paintings; pen-and-ink drawings. **Tips:** Appreciates a good sonnet as much as a free-verse poem. **Queries:** Not necessary. **Unsolicited mss:** Accepts. **Response:** 3-4 months, SASE. **Freelance Content:** 100%. **Rights:** 1st. **Payment:** In copies.

LYNX EYE

Scribblefest Literary Group, 1880 Hill Dr., Los Angeles, CA 90041. 323-550-8522. E-mail: pamccully@aol.com. Quarterly. $7.95/issue, $25/year. Circ.: 500. Pam McCully , Editor. **Description:** Stories, poetry, essays, and b/w artwork, in formats familiar and experimental. Pays $10, plus copies. **Fiction:** Short stories, vignettes, novel excerpts, one-act plays, belle letters, satires; 500-1,500 words; $10/piece, plus copies. **Nonfiction:** Essays only; 500-5,000 words. **Poetry:** 30 lines. **Art:** b/w drawings only. **Tips:** Avoid memoirs, autobiographical pieces. **Queries:** Not necessary. **E-Queries:** No. **Unsolicited mss:** Accepts. **Response:** 12 weeks, SASE. **Freelance Content:** 100%. **Rights:** FNASR. **Payment:** On acceptance.

MALAHAT REVIEW

Univ. of Victoria, P.O. Box 1700, Stn CSC,
University of Victoria, Victoria, BC, Canada V8W 2Y2. 250-721-8524. E-mail: malahat@uvic.ca. Web site: http://wes.uvic.ca/malahat. Quarterly. $10/issue, $30/year (Canadian). Circ.: 1,000. Marlene Cookshaw, Editor. **Description:** Short fiction, poetry, and reviews of Canadian fiction or poetry books. Seeks balance of views and styles, by established and new writers. Pays $30/page. **Fiction:** Yes. **Nonfiction:** Yes. **Poetry:** Yes. **Queries:** Not necessary. **E-Queries:** Yes. **Unsolicited mss:** Accepts. **Response:** Up to 3 months, SASE. **Freelance Content:** 100%. **Rights:** 1st worldwide. **Payment:** On acceptance.

MANOA

Univ. of Hawaii Press, English Dept., 1733 Donaghho Rd,
Honolulu, HI 96822. 808-956-3070.
E-mail: fstewart@hawaii.edu. Web site: www2.hawaii.edu/mjournal. Semiannual. Circ.: 2,500. Frank Stewart, Editor. **Description:** A Pacific journal of international fiction and poetry. **Fiction:** to 30 pages; $20-$25/page. **Nonfiction:** Essays, to 25 pages; book reviews (4-5 pages, $50). **Poetry:** Submit 4-6 poems; $50. **Queries:** Preferred. **Payment:** On publication.

MANY MOUNTAINS MOVING

420 22nd St., Boulder, CO 80302. 303-545-9942.
E-mail: mmm@mmminc.org. Web site: www.mmminc.org. 2x/year. $9/issue, $16/year. Circ.: 3,000. Naomi Horii, Editor. **Description:** Literary journal of contemporary voices from diverse cultural backgrounds. No payment. **Fiction:** Excellent quality; under 20,000 words. **Nonfiction:** under 20,000 words. **Poetry:** Submit 3-10 poems at a time; any length. **Tips:** Contact for upcoming themes. **Queries:** Not necessary. **E-Queries:** No. **Unsolicited mss:** Accepts. **Response:** Submissions 1 week, SASE. **Freelance Content:** 100%. **Rights:** 1st NA.

THE MARLBORO REVIEW

PO Box 243, Marlboro, VT 05344.
Web site: www.marlbororeview.com. Biannual. Ellen Dudley, Editor. **Description:** Literary journal of poetry, fiction, essays, translations, reviews, interviews. **Fiction:** up to 30 pages. **Nonfiction:** Literary/personal essays only; up to 30 pages. **Poetry:** Any length. **Art:** For cover; film or camera-ready. **Tips:** Interested in cultural, philosophical, scientific issues, seen from a writer's sensibility. **Queries:** Not necessary. **E-Queries:** Yes. **Unsolicited mss:** Accepts. **Response:** Queries 1 month, submissions to 3 months, SASE. **Freelance Content:** 80%. **Rights:** 1st. **Payment:** On publication, in copies only.

MASSACHUSETTS REVIEW

Univ. of Massachusetts, South College, Amherst, MA 01003-9934. 413-545-2689.
E-mail: massrev@external.umass.edu. Web site: www.litline.org/html/massreview.
Quarterly. Editorial Board. **Description:** Literary publication for fiction, poetry and nonfiction. **Fiction:** Short fiction; 15-25 pages; $50. **Nonfiction:** Essays, translations, interviews; $50. **Poetry:** $.35/line ($10 min.). **Art:** Photos, art. **Tips:** Reads submissions from Oct. 1-June 1. **Response:** SASE. **Payment:** On publication.

MEDIPHORS

P.O. Box 327, Bloomsburg, PA 17815.
E-mail: mediphor@ptd.net. Web site: www.mediphors.org. Semiannual. $6.95/issue. Circ.: 1,000. Eugene D. Radice, MD, Editor. **Description:** Literary magazine publishing broad range of work in medicine and health. For healthcare professionals, as well as general readers interested in creative writing in medicine. Short stories, essays, and poetry broadly related to medicine and health. **Fiction:** Short stories. **Nonfiction:** Essays; 3,000 words. **Poetry:** 30 lines. **Fillers:** Humor; 3,000 words. **Art:** b/w photos. **Tips:** Topics may be quite broad, from short story or historical fiction to current healthcare criticisms to science fiction. **Queries:** Not necessary. **E-Queries:** No. **Unsolicited mss:** Accepts. **Response:** Queries 1 month, submissions 4 months, SASE. **Freelance Content:** 98%. **Rights:** FNASR. **Payment:** In copies.

MID-AMERICA POETRY REVIEW

P.O. Box 575, Warrensburg, MO 64093-0575. 660-747-3481.
E-mail: rnjones@iland.net. 3x/year. $6/issue, $15/year. Robert C. Jones, Editor.

Description: Annual award for best poet. **Poetry:** to 36 lines. **Queries:** Not necessary. **E-Queries:** Yes. **Unsolicited mss:** Accepts. **Response:** 2-4 weeks, SASE required. **Freelance Content:** 100%. **Rights:** 1st NA (reverts to author after 6 months). **Payment:** In copies.

MINDPRINTS
Allan Hancock College, Disabled Student Programs & Services,
800 South College Dr., Santa Maria, CA 93454-6399. 805-922-6696 (ext. 3274).
E-mail: htcdsps@sbceo.org. Annual. Free. Circ.: 500. Paul Fahey, Editor.
Description: Literary journal of short fiction, memoir, poetry, and art for writers with disabilities and writers with an interest in this field. Showcases a variety of talent from this diverse population. **Fiction:** Short-short fiction, flash fiction; 250-750 words. **Nonfiction:** Short memoir, creative nonfiction (often disability-related); 250-750 words. **Poetry:** Rhymed and prose; up to 25 lines. **Art:** b/w photos and artwork. **Queries:** Not necessary. **E-Queries:** Yes. **Unsolicited mss:** Accepts; cover letter with bio required. **Response:** 1 week queries, 2-3 months submissions, SASE. **Rights:** One-time. **Payment:** In copies.

THE MINNESOTA REVIEW
University of Missouri, Dept. of English,
110 Tate Hall, Columbia, MO 65211. 573-882-3059.
E-mail: williamsjeff@missouri.edu. Semiannual. $12.50/year. Circ.: 1,300. Jeffrey Williams, Editor. **Description:** A journal of committed writing, progressive in nature, committed to socialist and feminist writing. (Note: does not have a Minnesota focus; was founded there, but later moved and kept name.) **Fiction:** Political, experimental; up to 5,000 words. **Nonfiction:** Essays, reviews. **Poetry:** Political; 1-10 pages. **Tips:** Issues are often organized around a special topic. **Queries:** Not necessary. **E-Queries:** No. **Unsolicited mss:** Accepts. **Response:** Queries 2-4 weeks, submissions 4-6 weeks, SASE required. **Freelance Content:** 100%. **Rights:** FNASR. **Payment:** In copies.

THE MIRACULOUS MEDAL
475 E. Chelten Ave., Philadelphia, PA 19144-5785. 215-848-1010.
Quarterly. William J. O'Brien, C.M., Editor. **Description:** Religious literary journal focusing on the Catholic Church. **Fiction:** Any subject matter which does not not contradict teachings of Roman Catholic Church; 1,000-2,400; $.02/word. **Poetry:** Religious, preferably about Blessed Virgin Mary; 20 lines; $.50/line. **Tips:** Original material only. **Queries:** Preferred. **E-Queries:** No. **Response:** 6 months, SASE. **Freelance Content:** 25%. **Rights:** 1st NA. **Payment:** On acceptance.

MISSISSIPPI REVIEW
Ctr. for Writers, Univ. of Southern Mississippi,
Southern Sta., Box 5144, Hattiesburg, MS 39406-5144. 601-266-4321.
E-mail: rief@netdoor.com. Web site: sushi.st.usm.edu/mrw. Frederick Barthelme,

Editor. **Description:** Literary journal, poetry and fiction. **Tips:** Annual fiction/poetry competition; deadline, May 31. **Payment:** In copies.

THE MISSOURI REVIEW

Univ. of Missouri-Columbia, 1507 Hillcrest Hall, Columbia, MO 65211. 573-882-4474. Tri-annual. $7.95/$25. Circ.: 6,500. Speer Morgan, Editor. **Description:** Literary magazine with contemporary fiction, poetry, interviews, and personal essays. **Fiction:** Yes. **Nonfiction:** Book reviews, interviews. **Poetry:** 6-14 pages of poetry by 3-5 poets each issue; pays $125-$300. **Queries:** Not necessary. **E-Queries:** No. **Response:** Submissions 6 weeks, SASE. **Freelance Content:** 90%. **Rights:** All; revert to author. **Payment:** On acceptance.

MODERN HAIKU

P.O. Box 1752, Madison, WI 53701-1752. 608-233-2738. Tri-annual. $20. Circ.: 780. Robert Spiess, Editor. **Description:** A journal of English-language haiku and translations, book reviews, articles, and essays on haiku. International circulation (20 foreign countries), carried in many university/public libraries. **Nonfiction:** Haiku and articles about haiku; pays $5/page for articles. **Poetry:** $1/haiku and senryu, $5 haiku and prose; $200 in awards each issue. **Tips:** No sentimental, pretty-pretty, or psuedo-Japanese work. Write about what you actually experience, not about an exotic, imaginary place. Juxtaposition of disparate perceptions that form a harmony is desirable. **Queries:** Not necessary. **E-Queries:** No. **Unsolicited mss:** Accepts. **Response:** Queries 2 days, submissions 2 weeks, SASE. **Freelance Content:** 90%. **Rights:** 1st NA.

NATURAL BRIDGE

Dept. of English, Univ. of Missouri-St.Louis, 8001 Natural Bridge Rd., St. Louis, MO 63121-4499. E-mail: natural@jinx.umsl.edu. Web site: www.umsl.edu/~natural/index.htm. Biannual. Steven Schreiner. **Description:** Short fiction, essays, and poetry. **Tips:** Submission periods are July 1 to August 31, and November 1 to December 31. Simultaneous submissions accepted. **Payment:** In copies.

NEBO

Arkansas Tech. Univ., Dept. of English, Russellville, AR 72801-2222. E-mail: michael.ritchie@mail.atu.edu. Biannual. $10/annual. Circ.: 100. Michael Ritchie, Editor. **Description:** Publishes fiction and poetry. Prefers new writers. **Fiction:** Experimental short fiction, realistic fiction; up to 2,000 words. **Poetry:** Formal, metered verse; experimental free verse. **Queries:** Not necessary. **E-Queries:** No. **Unsolicited mss:** Accepts. **Response:** up to 3 months, SASE. **Rights:** 1st. **Payment:** In copies.

NEBRASKA REVIEW

Univ. of Nebraska at Omaha, Writer's Workshop, FAB 212, Omaha, NE 68182-0324. 402-554-3159. E-mail: jreed@unomaha.edu. Bi-annual. $8/$15. Circ.: 1,000. James Reed, Editor. **Description:** Contemporary fiction, poetry, and creative nonfiction. **Fiction:** Literary mainstream; 7,500 words. **Nonfiction:** Creative non-fiction and personal essays; 7,500 words. **Poetry:** Contemporary, literary; 5-6 pages max. **Tips:** Eclectic tastes, professional, non-dogmatic; in fiction, seeking strong voices. **Queries:** Not necessary. **E-Queries:** No. **Unsolicited mss:** Accepts. **Response:** Submissions 3-6 months, SASE. **Freelance Content:** 100%. **Rights:** 1st NA. **Payment:** In copies.

NEW AUTHOR'S JOURNAL

1542 Tibbits Ave., Troy, NY 12180. 518-274-2648. Quarterly. $3.75/issue. Mario V. Farina, Editor. **Description:** Literary journal of short stories and poetry, for new authors previously unpublished. **Fiction:** Short stories, up to 2,000 words. **Nonfiction:** Topical nonfiction, up to 2,000 words. **Tips:** Manuscripts read year-round. **Queries:** Not necessary. **Unsolicited mss:** Accepts. **Response:** SASE. **Rights:** Author retains all rights. **Payment:** In copies.

NEW DELTA REVIEW

Louisiana State Univ., 15 Allen Hall, Dept. of English, Baton Rouge, LA 70803. 225-388-4079. Web site: http://english.lsu.edu/journals/ndr. Semiannual. $7/$12. Circ.: 500. Sean Cavanaugh, Editor. **Description:** Literary journal, focusing especially on work of new writers. **Fiction:** Quality stories that compel readers to continue reading; 6,000 words. **Nonfiction:** Creative nonfiction, interviews, reviews, no academic essays; 5,000 words. **Poetry:** Submit up to 4 poems, any length. **Art:** Color slides; cover art and images (8) of artwork; mostly of paintings, but will consider all visual media. **Queries:** Not necessary. **E-Queries:** No. **Unsolicited mss:** Accepts. **Response:** Queries 1 week, submissions 3 months, SASE required. **Freelance Content:** 95%. **Rights:** 1st NA. **Payment:** In copies.

NEW ENGLAND REVIEW

Middlebury College, Middlebury, VT 05753. 802-443-5075. E-mail: nereview@middlebury.edu. Web site: www.middlebury.edu. Quarterly. $7/issue. Circ.: 2,000. Stephen Donadio, Editor. **Description:** Short stories, short-shorts, novellas, and excerpts from novels. Also, long and short poems, interpretive and personal essays, book reviews, critical reassessments, and letters from abroad. **Fiction:** 10,000 words; $10/page. **Nonfiction:** Exploration of all forms of contemporary cultural expression; 10,000 words; $10/page. **Poetry:** submit up to 6 poems; any length; $10/page, $20 min. **Queries:** Not necessary. **E-Queries:** No. **Unsolicited mss:** Accepts. **Response:** Queries 2 weeks, submissions 12 weeks, SASE. **Payment:** On publication.

NEW ENGLAND WRITERS NETWORK

P.O. Box 483, Hudson, MA 01749-0483.
E-mail: newnmag@aol.com. $20/yr. Glenda Baker, Editor. **Description:** Literary journal with fiction, nonfiction and poetry. **Fiction:** Short stories, novel excerpts, to 2,000 words. All genres; no pornography or excessive violence; pays $10. **Nonfiction:** Personal, humorous essays, to 1,000 words; pays $5. **Poetry:** Upbeat, positive, to 32 lines. Pays $3. **Tips:** June-August reading period. **Queries:** Not necessary. **E-Queries:** No. **Unsolicited mss:** Accepts. **Payment:** On publication.

NEW LAUREL REVIEW

828 Lesseps St., New Orleans, LA 70117. 504-947-6001.
Annual. $10. Lee Meitzen Grue, Fiction Editor. **Description:** Literary journal of poetry, essays, short fiction, poetry translations. **Fiction:** 10 pages or less. **Poetry:** Yes. **Tips:** No clichés, slick fiction, or inspirational verse. **Queries:** Not necessary. **E-Queries:** No. **Unsolicited mss:** Accepts. **Response:** Submissions 1-3 months, SASE. **Freelance Content:** 98%. **Rights:** 1st. **Payment:** In copies. **Contact:** Lenny Emmanuel, Poetry Editor.

NEW LETTERS

Univ. House, Univ. of Missouri-Kansas City,
5101 Rockhill Rd., Kansas City, MO 64110-2499. 816-235-1168.
Quarterly. $5/issue, $17/year. Circ.: 6,000. James McKinley, Editor. **Description:** Poetry, fiction, art, essays, of fresh, sophisticated writing, clearly written by people who have lived interesting lives and read widely. **Fiction:** Any style, subject, or genre; 5,000 words max. **Nonfiction:** Essays, profiles; 5,000 words max. **Poetry:** Submit 3-6 poems. **Art:** Prints. **Queries:** Not necessary. **E-Queries:** No. **Unsolicited mss:** Accepts. **Response:** 3 months, SASE. **Freelance Content:** 50%. **Rights:** 1st. **Payment:** On publication.

THE NEW YORKER

4 Times Square, New York, NY 10036. 212-536-5400.
E-mail: themail@newyorker.com. Web site: www.newyorker.com. Weekly. $3.50/issue. Circ.: 851,000. **Description:** Covers the vital stories of our time with intelligence, wit, stylish prose, and a keen eye. **Fiction:** Short stories, humor, and satire. **Nonfiction:** Amusing mistakes in newspapers, books, magazines, etc. Factual and biographical articles for Profiles, Reporter at Large, etc. Political/social essays, 1,000 words. **Poetry:** Quality poetry. **Queries:** Not necessary. **E-Queries:** No. **Unsolicited mss:** Accepts. **Payment:** On publication. **Contact:** Perri Dorset.

NEXUS

Wright State Univ., W016A Student Union, Dayton, OH 45435. 937-775-5533.
E-mail: nexus_magazine@hotmail.com. 3x/year. $7/year. Mindy Cooper, Editor. **Description:** Journal of poetry, fiction, and artwork for Wright State community, also poetry, artwork and photography from around the world. **Fiction:** Strong, innovative fiction on human condition (short, flash fiction). **Poetry:** Essays, interviews; 1-2

pages. **Art:** b/w. **Tips:** Include brief cover letter with submissions, describing sub-mission, previous publication, and a brief bio. **Queries:** Preferred. **E-Queries:** Yes. **Unsolicited mss:** Accepts. **Response:** 2 weeks, SASE. **Freelance Content:** 50%. **Payment:** In copies.

NIMROD INTERNATIONAL JOURNAL
Univ. of Tulsa, 600 S. College Ave., Tulsa, OK 74104-3189. 918-631-3080. E-mail: nimrod@utulsa.edu. Web site: www.utulsa.edu/nimrod. Semi-annual. $17.50/yr. Circ.: 3,000. Dr. Francine Ringold, Editor. **Description:** Quality prose and fiction by emerging writers of contemporary literature. **Fiction:** Quality fiction (no genre fiction), vigorous writing with believable characters and dialogue; 7,500 words max. **Nonfiction:** Vivid essays related to annual theme; 7,500 words max. **Poetry:** 1,900 words max. **Queries:** Not necessary. **E-Queries:** Yes. **Unsolicited mss:** Accepts. **Response:** Submissions 6-8 weeks, SASE. **Freelance Content:** 100%. **Rights:** 1st. **Payment:** In copies.

96 INC.
P.O. Box 15559, Boston, MA 02215. 617-267-0543. E-mail: 96inc@ici.net. Annual. $5/issue. Circ.: 3,000. Anderson, Gold, Mehegon, Editors. **Description:** Dedicated to new voices, and integration of the established and beginner. **Fiction:** All types. No restrictions on style or subject; up to 3,000 words. **Nonfiction:** Stories with useful information for other writers (new publishers, etc.); 2,500 words. **Queries:** Preferred. **E-Queries:** No. **Unsolicited mss:** Accepts. **Response:** 6 months to 1 year, SASE. **Rights:** One-time. **Payment:** In copies. **Contact:** Vera Gold.

NO EXPERIENCE REQUIRED
P.O. Box 131032, The Woodlands, TX 77393-1032. E-mail: nerzine@excite.com. 3x/year. $5/issue. Circ.: 300. **Description:** Small literary magazine for new and undiscovered writers. **Fiction:** All genres; 2,500 words. **Poetry:** All forms; 60 lines. **Art:** Publishes in b/w. **Tips:** Make sure submissions are free of major spelling/grammer errors. No pornography. **Queries:** Not necessary. **E-Queries:** No. **Response:** 6 months, SASE. **Freelance Content:** 100%. **Rights:** 1st, one-time. **Payment:** In copies.

THE NORTH AMERICAN REVIEW
Univ. of Northern Iowa, 1222 W. 27th St., Cedar Falls, IA 50614-0516. 319-273-6455. E-mail: nar@uni.edu. Web site: webdelsol.com/NorthAmReview/NAR/. Bimonthly. $22/year. Circ.: 5,000. Vince Gotera, Editor. **Description:** Poetry, fiction, and non-fiction on contemporary North American concerns and issues, especially environment, gender, race, ethnicity, and class. **Fiction:** Literary realism, multicultural; up to 12,000 words; $20-$100. **Nonfiction:** Creative nonfiction, journals and diaries, letters, memoirs, profiles; nature, travel, and science writing; also literary journalism and essays; up to 12,000 words; $20-$100. **Poetry:** Traditional or experimental, formal or free verse (closed or open form); length varies; $20-$100. **Tips:** Likes stories with

strong narrative arc and sense of humor, where characters act on the world, are responsible for their decisions, make mistakes. **Queries:** Not necessary. **E-Queries:** No. **Unsolicited mss:** Accepts. **Response:** 3 months submissions, SASE. **Freelance Content:** 80%. **Rights:** FNASR. **Payment:** On publication.

NORTH CAROLINA LITERARY REVIEW

East Carolina University, Bate Building, English Dept., Greenville, NC 27858-4353. 252-328-1537. E-mail: bauerm@mail.edu.edu. Web site: www.edu.edu/english/journals/NCLR. Annual. Circ.: 600. **Description:** By and about North Carolina writers. Covers history, culture and literature. Mostly nonfiction, accepts some poetry. Pays $50/story or illustration. **Tips:** Sample copies, $15. **Queries:** Required. **Response:** 1 month. **Rights:** 1st. **Payment:** On publication.

NORTH DAKOTA QUARTERLY

Univ. of North Dakota, Grand Forks, ND 58202-7209. 701-777-3322. E-mail: ndq@sage.und.nodak.edu. Web site: www.und.nodak.edu/org/ndq/. Quarterly. $8/sample, $12/special issue. Circ.: 500-700. Robert W. Lewis, Editor. **Description:** Fiction, nonfiction, poetry, and criticism, often from the unique perspective of the Northern Plains. **Fiction:** Yes. **Nonfiction:** Yes. **Poetry:** Yes. **Queries:** Not necessary. **E-Queries:** Yes. **Unsolicited mss:** Accepts. **Response:** Queries 2-4 weeks, submissions 2-4 months, SASE. **Freelance Content:** 90%. **Rights:** 1st serial. **Payment:** In copies.

NORTHWEST REVIEW

369 PLC, Univ. of Oregon, Eugene, OR 97403. 541-346-3957. E-mail: jwitte@oregon.uoregon.edu. Web site: www.darkwing.uoregon.edu. 3x/year. $7/issue, $20/year. Circ.: 1,000. John Witte, Editor. **Description:** Oldest literary journal west of the Mississippi, offers a forum for talented emerging young writers. **Fiction:** All lengths. **Nonfiction:** Eclectic commentary, essays. **Poetry:** All lengths. **Queries:** Not necessary. **E-Queries:** No. **Unsolicited mss:** Accepts. **Response:** Queries immediately, submissions 8-10 weeks, SASE. **Freelance Content:** 100%. **Rights:** 1st NA serial. **Payment:** In copies.

NORTHWOODS JOURNAL

P.O. Box 298, Thomaston, ME 04861. 207-354-0998. E-mail: cal@americanletters.com. Web site: www.americanletters.org. Quarterly. $5.50/issue. Circ.: 300. Robert W. Olmsted. **Description:** For writers working "the press scene." **Fiction:** Any length. **Nonfiction:** Any length. **Poetry:** Any length. **Tips:** Charges small reading fee "to keep submissions down so an editor can actually read your manuscripts." **Queries:** Not necessary. **E-Queries:** No. **Unsolicited mss:** Accepts. **Response:** 3-4 months. **Freelance Content:** 85%. **Rights:** 1st American serial. **Payment:** On acceptance.

NOTRE DAME REVIEW

Univ. of Notre Dame, English Dept.,
Creative Writing Program, Notre Dame, IN 46556.
E-mail: englishndreview1@nd.edi. Web site: www.nd.edu. Bi-annual. $8/issue,
$15/year. Circ.: 2,000. Steve Tomasula, Senior Editor. **Description:** Literary maga-
zine. **Fiction:** Any length. **Nonfiction:** Long and short reviews by assignment; query
first. **Poetry:** Any length. **Queries:** Not necessary. **E-Queries:** Yes. **Unsolicited
mss:** Accepts. **Response:** Queries 1 month, submissions 3-5 months, SASE.
Freelance Content: 60%. **Rights:** 1st Serial. **Payment:** On publication.

OASIS

P.O. Box 626, Largo, FL 33779-0626. 727-449-2186.
E-mail: oasislit@aol.com. Web site: www.litline.org. Quarterly. $20/year. Circ.: 300.
Neal Storrs, Editor. **Description:** Literary magazine of stories and poetry, some nonfiction. **Fiction:** Style paramount, powerfully original; "the style should seem to be
the subject"; any length; $15/story. **Nonfiction:** Avoid reviews, profiles, interviews;
$15. **Poetry:** Prefers free verse with a distinct, subtle music. No old-fashioned
rhymes or rhythms; $15. **Queries:** Not necessary. **E-Queries:** Yes. **Unsolicited
mss:** Accepts. **Response:** Submissions same day, SASE required. **Freelance
Content:** 95%. **Rights:** 1st. **Payment:** On publication.

OFFERINGS

P.O. Box 1667, Lebanon, MO 65536.
Quarterly. $5/issue, $16/year. Circ.: 75. Velvet Fackeldey, Editor. **Description:**
Quality poetry, all forms. **Poetry:** 30 lines max. **Tips:** Overstocked with nature poetry.
Queries: Not necessary. **E-Queries:** Yes. **Unsolicited mss:** Accepts. **Response:** 2-
4 weeks, SASE. **Freelance Content:** 100%. **Rights:** 1st. **Payment:** On publication.

THE OLD RED KIMONO

Humanities Div., Floyd College, P.O. Box 1864, Rome, GA 30162.
E-mail: napplega@mail.fc.peachnet.edu. Annual. $3. Circ.: 1,400. Adam Stanley,
Editor. **Description:** Poems and short stories of all types. **Tips:** Local writers consti-
tute 50% of journal. Sponsors annual Paris Lake Poetry Contest. **Queries:** Not nec-
essary. **E-Queries:** Yes. **Unsolicited mss:** Accepts. **Response:** 8 weeks, SASE.
Freelance Content: 100%. **Rights:** 1st. **Payment:** On publication.

OREGON EAST

Hoke College Center, EOSC, La Grande, OR 97850.
Annual. $5. Circ.: 1,000. Annie White, Editor. **Description:** Literary journal with
short fiction, nonfiction, one-act plays, poetry, and high-contrast graphics. **Fiction:**
any subject; 3,000 words. **Poetry:** Any form (no "greeting card" verse); 60 lines. **Art:**
Photos of original graphics should be b/w glossies, 4x5 or 5x7, high-contrast. Include
titles or captions. **Queries:** Not necessary. **E-Queries:** No. **Unsolicited mss:**
Accepts. **Response:** 2-3 months, SASE. **Freelance Content:** 100%. **Rights:** 1st.
Payment: In copies.

OSIRIS

P.O. Box 297, Deerfield, MA 01342. 413-774-4027. E-mail: moorhead@k12s.phast.umass.edu. Semiannual. $7.50/issue. Circ.: 500. Andrea Moorhead, Editor. **Description:** A multilingual international poetry journal. Features contemporary foreign poetry in original language (English and French are principle languages of this journal). Other works appear in original language, with facing-page English translation. **Poetry:** Length varies. **Tips:** Seeking poetry that is well-crafted, non-narrative, rooted in experience, lyrical. Translators need to secure permission of both poet and publisher. **Queries:** Not necessary. **E-Queries:** Yes. **Unsolicited mss:** Accepts. **Response:** Submissions 4 weeks, SASE required. **Freelance Content:** 30%. **Payment:** In copies.

OTHER VOICES

Univ. of Illinois at Chicago, Dept. of English (M/C 162), 601 S. Morgan St., Chicago, IL 60607-7120. 312-413-2209. E-mail: othervioces@listser.uic.edu. Web site: www.othervoicesmagazine.org. Semiannual. $7/issue. Circ.: 1,500. Editorial Board. **Description:** Short stories, novels excerpts, one-act plays, book reviews, and interviews with esteemed fiction writers. **Fiction:** Literary, traditional, or experimental (no genre fiction); to 7,500 words. **Tips:** No queries, send manuscripts. **Queries:** No. **E-Queries:** Yes. **Unsolicited mss:** Accepts. **Response:** Submissions up to 3 months, SASE. **Freelance Content:** 100%. **Rights:** 1st serial, reverts to author. **Payment:** In copies.

THE OXFORD AMERICAN

P.O. Box 1156, Oxford, MS 38655. 662-236-1836. Web site: www.oxfordamericanmag.com. $19.95. Circ.: 45,000. Marc Smirnoff, Editor. **Description:** "The Southern Magazine of Good Writing." Literary magazine studying and exploring the American South. **Fiction:** Length, pay varies. **Nonfiction:** Varies. **Poetry:** $125/poem. **Fillers:** Cartoons. **Tips:** "Writers should try to learn a little bit about the homes where their writing ends up!" **Queries:** Not necessary. **E-Queries:** No. **Unsolicited mss:** Accepts. **Response:** Queries varies, submissions up to 3 months, SASE. **Freelance Content:** 50%. **Rights:** FNASR. **Payment:** On publication.

OYSTER BOY REVIEW

PO Box 77842, San Francisco, CA 94107-0842. Web site: www.oysterboyreview.com. Quarterly. Damon Sauve, Editor. **Description:** Literary magazine, in print and online, features the underrated, ignored, misunderstood, and varietal. **Fiction:** General, not genre, any length. **Queries:** Not necessary. **E-Queries:** Yes. **Unsolicited mss:** Accepts. **Response:** 1-2 months. **Rights:** 1st serial. **Payment:** In copies.

PAINTBRUSH

Truman State Univ., Language & Literature Div.,
Kirksville, MO 63501. 660-785-4185.
Web site: www.paintbrush.org. Annual. Circ.: 500. Ben Bennani, Editor.
Description: International journal of poetry and translation. **Nonfiction:**
Translations, interviews, book reviews; some special issues on individual writers.
Poetry: Send cover letter, 3-5 poems. **Tips:** Serious, original, highly imaginative work
only. Sponsors $2,000 Ezra Pound Poetry Award. **Queries:** Preferred. **E-Queries:**
Yes. **Unsolicited mss:** Accepts. **Response:** Queries ASAP, submissions 8-10 weeks,
SASE. **Freelance Content:** 60%. **Rights:** 1st NA. **Payment:** On publication.

PAINTED BRIDE QUARTERLY

Rutgers University, English Dept., ATG Hall, Camden, NJ 08102. 856-225-6129.
E-mail: pbquarterly@hotmail.com. Web site: www.webdelsol.com/pbq
or www.pbq.rutgers.edu. Quarterly. $15/yr. Circ.: 1,500. Marion Wrenn, Editor.
Description: Literary journal of fiction and poetry, in print and online. **Fiction:** Yes.
Nonfiction: Yes. **Poetry:** Length varies. **Queries:** Not necessary. **Unsolicited mss:**
Accepts. **Response:** Submissions to 3 months, SASE. **Freelance Content:** 100%.
Rights: 1st. **Payment:** On publication.

PALO ALTO REVIEW

Palo Alto College, 1400 W. Villaret, San Antonio, TX 78224-2499. 210-921-5017.
E-mail: emshull@aol.com. Semi-annual. $5.00. Circ.: 500. Ellen Shull, Editor.
Description: Fiction and articles, 5,000 words; on varied historical, geographical,
scientific, mathematical, artistic, political, and social topics. **Fiction:** No experimental or excessively avant-garde fiction. **Nonfiction:** Original,unpublished articles; also
interviews; photos okay. **Poetry:** Submit 3-5 poems; to 50 lines. **Columns,**
Departments: Food for Thought (200-word think pieces); reviews, to 500 words, of
books, films, videos, or software. **Art:** Photo essays welcome. **Tips:** A "journal of
ideas." Send SASE for upcoming themes **Payment:** In copies.

❧ PANGOLIN PAPERS

P.O. Box 241, Nordland, WA 98358. 360-385-3626.
E-mail: trtlbluf@olympus.net. Tri-annual. $5.95/issue, $15/year. Circ.: 350. Pat Britt,
Editor. **Description:** Literary short stories. **Fiction:** Up to 8,000 words. **Tips:** No
poetry, genre fiction, essays. **Queries:** Not necessary. **E-Queries:** No. **Unsolicited**
mss: Accepts. **Response:** Submissions 3 months, SASE required. **Rights:** 1st
American. **Payment:** In copies.

❧ THE PARIS REVIEW

541 E. 72nd St., New York, NY 10021. 212-861-0016.
E-mail: tpr@the parisreview.com. Web site: www.parisreview.com. Quarterly.
$12/$40. Circ.: 12,000. George Plimpton, Editor. **Description:** International literary
quarterly, with fiction, poetry, interviews, essays, and features from established and
emerging writers and artists. **Fiction:** High literary quality. **Poetry:** Varied formats.

Fillers: Humor. **Art:** Slides, drawings, copies. **Tips:** Annual prizes, in several categories, up to $1,000. **Queries:** Not necessary. **E-Queries:** Yes. **Unsolicited mss:** Accepts. **Response:** Queries 2-3 weeks, submissions 3-4 months, SASE. **Freelance Content:** 75%. **Rights:** 1st NA. **Payment:** On publication.

PARNASSUS
205 W. 89th St., Apt. 8F, New York, NY 10024-1835. 212-362-3492. E-mail: parnew@aol.com. Semi-annual. $12-$15. Circ.: 2,500. Herbert Leibowitz, Editor. **Description:** In-depth analysis of contemporary books of poetry. **Nonfiction:** Critical essays and reviews on contemporary poetry. No academic or theoretical work, looks for criticism that is colorful, idiosyncratic, well-written; $150, 20 pages. **Poetry:** Mostly by request; $25/page. **Queries:** Not necessary. **E-Queries:** Yes. **Unsolicited mss:** Accepts. **Response:** Submissions, usually in 2 mos., SASE. **Freelance Content:** 100%. **Rights:** All, reverts to author. **Payment:** On publication.

PARTING GIFTS
3413 Wilshire, Greensboro, NC 27408. Web site: http://users.aol.com/marchst. Semi-annual. $6. Robert Bixby, Editor. **Description:** Literary journal. **Fiction:** 500-1,000 words. **Poetry:** Up to 50 lines. **Tips:** Manuscripts read January-June. **Queries:** Not necessary. **E-Queries:** Yes. **Unsolicited mss:** Accepts. **Response:** Queries same day, submissions in 1 week, SASE. **Freelance Content:** 100%. **Rights:** 1st NA. **Payment:** In copies.

PARTISAN REVIEW
Boston Univ., 236 Bay State Rd., Boston, MA 02215. 617-353-4260. E-mail: partisan@bu.edu. Web site: www.partisanreview.org. Quarterly. $6/issue, $22/year. Circ.: 8,000. William Phillips, Editor in Chief. **Description:** Influential American literary and cultural journal, home to many fine writers. **Fiction:** Yes. **Poetry:** Yes. **Queries:** Preferred. **E-Queries:** No. **Unsolicited mss:** Accepts. **Response:** 4-8 weeks, SASE. **Payment:** On publication.

PASSAGES NORTH
Northern Michigan Univ., Dept. of English, 1401 Presque Isle Ave., Marquette, MI 49855. 906-227-1203. E-mail: passages@nmu.edu. Web site: hppt://vm.nmu.edu/passages:http//bme.html. Annual. $13. Circ.: 1,000. Kate Myers Hanson, Editor. **Description:** Literary fiction, poetry, and nonfiction, for established and emerging writers. **Fiction:** Short stories (no genre fiction); under 5,000 words. **Nonfiction:** Interviews, essays, literary nonfiction; under 5,000 words. **Poetry:** up to 6 poems. **Tips:** Looks for work that expresses culltural diversity and a keen knowledge of craft. **Queries:** Not necessary. **E-Queries:** Yes. **Unsolicited mss:** Accepts. **Response:** 6-8 weeks, SASE. **Freelance Content:** 95%. **Rights:** 1st NA. **Payment:** On publication.

❶ PATERSON LITERARY REVIEW

Passaic Co. Comm. College, College Blvd., Paterson, NJ 07505-1179. 973-684-6555. E-mail: mgillian@pccc.cc.nj.us. Web site: www.pccc.cc.nj.us/poetry. Annual. $10. Circ.: 1,000. Maria Mazziotti Gillan, Editor. **Description:** Literary publication of fiction, poetry, book reviews, articles, and artwork. **Fiction:** 1,500 words. **Nonfiction:** 1,000 words. **Poetry:** 100-line limit. **Queries:** Not necessary. **E-Queries:** No. **Unsolicited mss:** Accepts. **Response:** Submissions 6 months, SASE required. **Freelance Content:** 100%. **Rights:** 1st. **Payment:** In copies.

❷ PEARL

3030 E. Second St., Long Beach, CA 90803. 562-434-4523. E-mail: mjohn5150@aol.com. Web site: www.pearlmag.com. Bi-annual. $8/$18. Circ.: 700. Marilyn Johnson, Joan Jobe Smith, Editors. **Description:** Contemporary poetry and short fiction. **Fiction:** Accessible humanistic fiction, related to real life. Ironic, serious, and intense humor and wit welcome; 1,200 words. **Poetry:** Humanistic; 40 lines or less. **Art:** Camera-ready b/w. **Queries:** Not necessary. **E-Queries:** Yes. **Unsolicited mss:** Accepts. **Response:** Queries 1 week, submissions 6-8 weeks, SASE. **Freelance Content:** 100%. **Rights:** 1st NA. **Payment:** In copies.

PEREGRINE

P.O. Box 1076, Amherst, MA 01004. 413-253-3307. E-mail: awapress@aol.com. Web site: www.amherstwriters.com. Annual. $12. Circ.: 1,000. Pat Schneider, Editor. **Description:** Features poetry, fiction, and personal essays. **Fiction:** All styles, forms, and subjects; 3,000 words. **Nonfiction:** Short personal essays; to 1,500 words. **Poetry:** No greeting-card verse; 70 lines (3-5 poems). **Queries:** Not necessary. **E-Queries:** No. **Unsolicited mss:** Accepts. **Response:** Submissions 2-3 months, SASE. **Payment:** On publication. **Contact:** Nancy Rose, Managing Editor.

PERMAFROST

Univ. of Alaska–Fairbanks, English Dept., P.O. Box 75720, Fairbanks, AK 99775-0640. 907-474-5398. E-mail: fbprfst@vaf.edu. Web site: www.uaf.edu/english/permafrost. Annual. $8/issue. Christian Lybrook, Editor. **Description:** International literary journal for the arts. Fiction, non-fiction, poetry, and artwork of emerging and established writers and artists. **Fiction:** to 30 pages; avoid genre fiction (horror, sci-fi, fantasy). **Nonfiction:** to 30 pages. **Poetry:** up to 5 poems. **Art:** Yes. **Tips:** Alaskan themes not essential. Reading period is Sept.-March 15. **Queries:** Not necessary. **E-Queries:** No. **Unsolicited mss:** Accepts. **Response:** 3 months, SASE. **Rights:** 1st. **Payment:** In copies.

THE PIKEVILLE REVIEW

Humanities Div., Pikeville College, 214 Sycamore St., Pikeville, KY 41501. 606-432-9612. E-mail: eward@pc.edu. Web site: www.pc.edu. Annual. $4. Circ.: 500. Elgin M.

Ward, Editor. **Description:** Contemporary fiction, poetry, creative essays, and book reviews, for Kentucky writers and others. **Nonfiction:** Creative essays, book reviews. **Poetry:** Contemporary. **Tips:** Open to new and unpublished writers. **Queries:** Not necessary. **E-Queries:** Yes. **Unsolicited mss:** Accepts. **Response:** Queries 2 weeks, submissions 30-60 days, SASE. **Payment:** On publication.

PLASTIC TOWER
Box 702, Bowie, MD 20718.
E-mail: rscottk@aol.com. Quarterly. $2.50/issue, $8/year. Circ.: 250. Roger Kyle-Keith, Carol Dyer, Editors. **Description:** Fun, irreverent, but serious about bringing enjoyable poetry to the public. **Nonfiction:** Reviews of literary and poetry magazines; 100 words. **Poetry:** Eclectic, all types of poetry, from sonnets to free verse to limericks; 40 lines max. **Art:** 10-15 small b/w illustrations per issue. **Tips:** Develop a fresh and unique voice, and you will eventually prevail. **Queries:** Not necessary. **E-Queries:** No. **Unsolicited mss:** Does not accept. **Response:** Queries 1 month, submissions to 6 months, SASE. **Freelance Content:** 80%. **Rights:** 1st NA. **Payment:** In copies. **Contact:** Roger Kyle-Keith.

PLEIADES
Central Missouri State Univ., Dept. of English,
Warrensburg, MO 64093. 660-543-8106.
E-mail: kdp8106@cmsu2.cmsu.edu.
Web site: www.cmsu.edu/englphil/pleiades.html. 2x/year. $6/issue. Circ.: 3,000. R.M. Kinder, Kevin Prufer, Editors. **Description:** Traditional and experimental poetry, fiction, criticism, translations, and reviews. Cross-genre especially welcome. **Fiction:** up to 10,000 words. **Nonfiction:** Up to 10,000 words; $10. **Poetry:** Any length; pays $3 or copies. **Tips:** Considers simultaneous submissions. **E-Queries:** No. **Unsolicited mss:** Accepts. **Response:** queries 1 month, submissions 2 months, SASE. **Freelance Content:** 85%. **Rights:** 1st serial, reprint online and in anthology. **Payment:** On publication.

PLOUGHSHARES
Emerson College, 120 Boylston St., Boston, MA 02116-4624. 617-824-8753.
E-mail: pshares@emerson.edu. Web site: www.emerson.edu/ploughshares. 3x/year. $9.95/issue. Circ.: 6,500. Don Lee, Editor. **Description:** Compelling fiction and poetry. Each issue guest-edited by a prominent writer. **Fiction:** Up to 30 pages; $25/printed page ($50 min., $250 max.). **Poetry:** send 1-3 poems; $25/printed page. **Tips:** No genre work, or unsolicited book reviews or criticism. Reading period: Aug. 1-March 31 (postmark); all other submissions April returned unread. **Queries:** Preferred. **E-Queries:** No. **Unsolicited mss:** Accepts. **Response:** 3-5 months, SASE required. **Rights:** 1st serial. **Payment:** On publication.

POEM
English Dept., U.A.H., Huntsville, AL 35899. 824-2379.
Semi-annual. $15. Circ.: 400. Nancy Frey Dillard, Editor. **Description:** Serious lyric

poetry. **Poetry:** Well-crafted, free verse. No light verse; "prose" poems; shaped, "visual" or "conceptual" poetry; or other avant-garde verse; 3-5 poems. **Tips:** Submit brief lyric poems only, with verbal and dramatic tension, that transpire from the particular to the universal. **Queries:** Preferred. **E-Queries:** No. **Unsolicited mss:** Accepts. **Response:** Queries 1 week, submissions 1 month, SASE. **Rights:** 1st. **Payment:** In copies.

POETRY

60 W. Walton St., Chicago, IL 60610. 303-255-3703.
E-mail: poetry@poetrymagazine.org. Web site: www.poetrymagazine.org. Monthly. $3.50/issue. Circ.: 10,000. Joseph Parisi, Editor. **Description:** Literary journal for poetry, by poets famous and new. **Poetry:** Any length; $2/line. **Queries:** Not necessary. **E-Queries:** No. **Unsolicited mss:** Accepts. **Response:** 4 months, SASE. **Freelance Content:** 100%. **Payment:** On publication.

PORTLAND REVIEW

Portland State Univ., P.O. Box 751, Portland, OR 97207.
Web site: www.portlandreview.org. Semiannual. $6/issue. Misty Sturgeon, Editor. **Description:** Short fiction, poetry, and art, by contributors from the celebrated to the unknown. **Fiction:** Short fiction, essays. **Nonfiction:** Reviews. **Poetry:** Yes. **Queries:** Preferred.

POTOMAC REVIEW

P.O. Box 354, Port Tobacco, MD 20677. 301-934-1412.
E-mail: elilujuno.com. Web site: www.meral.com. Quarterly. $5/issue, $18/year. Circ.: 1,500. Eli Flam, Editor. **Description:** Regionally rooted, with a conscience, a lurking sense of humor, and a strong environmental/nature bent. **Fiction:** Vivid, with ethical depth and in Flannery O'Connor's words "the vision to go with it"; 3,000 words. **Nonfiction:** 3,000 words. **Poetry:** That educates, challenges, or diverts in fresh ways; up to 3 poems, 5 pages. **Art:** b/w photos, drawings, and prints. Query first. **Tips:** Contact for upcoming themes. **Queries:** Not necessary. **E-Queries:** No. **Unsolicited mss:** Accepts. **Response:** Submissions 2-3 months, SASE. **Freelance Content:** 75%. **Rights:** 1st NA. **Payment:** In copies.

POTPOURRI

P.O. Box 8278, Prairie Village, KS 66208. 913-642-1503.
E-mail: editor@potpourri.org. Web site: www.potpourri.org. Quarterly. $6.95/issue, $16/year. Circ.: 3,000. Polly W. Swafford, Editor. **Description:** A modern literary journal, falls between serious academic journals and glitzy commercial publications. **Fiction:** Broad genres; no racist, sexist material; 3,500 words. **Nonfiction:** Essays with literary theme. Travel with a cultural theme; 2,500 words. **Poetry:** 75 lines. **Fillers:** Light, humorous stories with fully developed plots. **Art:** b/w line drawings. **Tips:** Seeks to promote work reflecting a culturally diverse society. **Queries:** Not necessary. **E-Queries:** Yes. **Unsolicited mss:** Accepts. **Response:** Queries 3

weeks, submissions 3 months, SASE. **Freelance Content:** 80%. **Rights:** 1st NA. **Payment:** In copies.

THE PRAIRIE JOURNAL OF CANADIAN LITERATURE

PO Box 61203, Brentwood Post Office, Calgary, AB, T2L 2K6 Canada. E-mail: prairiejournal@iname.com. Web site: www.geocities.com/prairiejournal/. Semiannual. $4/issue. Circ.: 600. A. Burke, Editor. **Description:** Devoted to new, previously unpublished writing. **Fiction:** Literary; any length, pay varies. **Nonfiction:** Essays, reviews, interviews, on Canadian subjects. **Poetry:** Any length. **Art:** b/w photos. **Tips:** No simultaneous submissions. **Queries:** Not necessary. **E-Queries:** No. **Unsolicited mss:** Accepts. **Response:** 2-3 months, SASE (no U.S. stamps). **Freelance Content:** 100%. **Payment:** On publication.

PRAIRIE SCHOONER

Univ. of Nebraska, 201 Andrews Hall, Lincoln, NE 68588-0334. 402-472-0911. E-mail: eflanagan2@unl.edu. Web site: www.unl.edu/schooner/psmain.htm. Quarterly. $9/issue, $26/year. Circ.: 5,500. Hilda Raz, Editor. **Description:** Contemporary poetry, fiction, essay, and review. **Fiction:** Short stories; 18-25 pages. **Nonfiction:** Essays, book reviews, translations; 15-25 pages. **Poetry:** Submit 5-7 poems at a time. **Tips:** Annual prizes for work in the magazine, $200-$1,000. **Queries:** Not necessary. **E-Queries:** No. **Unsolicited mss:** Accepts. **Response:** Queries 3 weeks, submissions 3-4 months, SASE. **Rights:** All, electronic, can revert to author. **Payment:** In copies.

PRIMAVERA

Box 37-7547, Chicago, IL 60637. Annual. $10. Circ.: 1,000. **Description:** Original fiction and poetry, that reflects the experience of women of different ages, races, sexual orientations, social classes. **Fiction:** 25 page max. **Poetry:** On the experiences of women. **Tips:** Encourages new writers. No confessional, formulaic, scholarly. **Queries:** Not necessary. **E-Queries:** No. **Unsolicited mss:** Accepts. **Response:** Queries 2 weeks, submissions 1-6 months, SASE required. **Freelance Content:** 100%. **Rights:** 1st. **Payment:** In copies.

PUCKERBRUSH REVIEW

76 Main St., Orono, ME 04473-1430. 207-866-4868. Semiannual. $4. Circ.: 300. Constance Hunting, Editor. **Description:** Literary poetry, fiction, interviews, reviews, and translations; also, work from Europe. **Fiction:** Yes. **Nonfiction:** Essays, personal or literary. Literary news from specific regions and countries. **Poetry:** Yes. **Queries:** Preferred. **E-Queries:** No. **Unsolicited mss:** Accepts. **Response:** 1 month, SASE. **Freelance Content:** 90%. **Payment:** In copies.

PUDDING MAGAZINE

Pudding House Writers Resource Ctr., Bed & Breakfast for Writers, 60 N. Main St., Johnstown, OH 43031. 740-967-6060. E-mail: pudding@johnstown.net. Web site: www.puddinghouse.com. Semi-annual. $7.95 or 3/$18.95. Circ.: 2,000. Jennifer Bosveld, Editor. **Description:** International journal, with poetry, short-short stories, and essays on applied writing/poetry, writing exercises, reviews, and more. **Fiction:** Short-short stories. **Nonfiction:** Articles/essays on poetry in the schools and in human services; 500-2,500 words. **Poetry:** On popular culture, social concerns, personal struggle. **Columns, Departments:** Reviews of poetry books. **Unsolicited mss:** Accepts. **Response:** Submissions, 1 day, SASE. **Freelance Content:** 98%. **Payment:** In copies.

PUERTO DEL SOL
New Mexico State Univ., Dept. of English, MSC 3E,
P.O. Box 30001, Las Cruces, NM 88003-8001.
Web site: www.nmsu.edu/~english/puerto/puerto.html. K. West, Kevin McIlvoy, Editors. **Description:** Short stories and personal essays, to 30 pages; novel excerpts, to 65 pages; articles, to 45 pages, and reviews, to 15 pages. Poetry, photos. **Tips:** Manuscripts read September through February. **Payment:** In copies.

THE QUANDARY
4499 Glencoe Ave., Marina del Rey, CA 90292.
Web site: http://www.geocities.com/~quandary. Frank Backman, Editor. **Description:** Journal of fiction and poetry.

QUARTER AFTER EIGHT
Ohio Univ., 102 Ellis Hall, Athens, OH 45701. 740-593-2827.
E-mail: quarteraftereight@excite.com.
Web site: www.geocities.com/quarteraftereight. Annual. $10. Circ.: 1,000. Christina Veladota, Thom Conroy, Editors. **Description:** Literary publication. **Fiction:** Experimental fiction, sudden fiction; 10,000 words max. **Nonfiction:** Commentary, but not scholarly work; novel excerpts, essays, criticism, investigations, interviews; 10,000 words max. **Poetry:** Submit 3-5 pieces; no traditional lined poetry. **Art:** b/w only. **Queries:** Not necessary. **E-Queries:** No. **Unsolicited mss:** Accepts. **Response:** Submissions 6-8 weeks, SASE. **Rights:** 1st NA. **Payment:** On publication.

QUARTERLY WEST
Univ. of Utah, 200 S. Central Campus Dr., Rm. 317,
Salt Lake City, UT 84112-9109. 801-581-3938.
Web site: www.utah.edu/quarterlywest. Semi-annual. $7.50/issue, $12/yr. Circ.: 1,600. Margot Schilpp, Lynn Kilpatrick. **Description:** Literary journal, for new writers and established authors. **Fiction:** Shorts and longer fiction, that play with form and language, not bound by convention; 500-6,000 words; pay varies. **Nonfiction:** Memoir, books reviews, essays; 500-6,000 words. **Poetry:** Up to 5 pages, 5 poems. **Tips:** No "Western" themes or religious verse. **Queries:** Not necessary. **E-Queries:** No. **Unsolicited mss:** Accepts. **Response:** 2-6 months, SASE. **Freelance Content:** 75%. **Payment:** On publication.

QUEEN'S QUARTERLY
Queens Univ., Kingston, Ont., Canada K7L 3N6. 613-533-2667. E-mail: qquarter@post.queensu.ca. Web site: http://info.queensu.ca/quarterly. Boris Castel, Editor. **Description:** Covers a wide range of topics and fiction. **Fiction:** In English and French; to 5,000 words; to $300. **Nonfiction:** To 5,000 words; to $400. **Poetry:** Send up to 6 poems; to $400. **Art:** b/w art; to $400. **Payment:** On publication.

RAIN CROW
Rain Crow Publishing, 2127 W. Pierce Ave., Apt. 2B, Chicago, IL 60622-1824. 773-562-5786. E-mail: msm@manley.org. Web site: www.rain-crow.com. 3x/year. Circ.: 300. Michael S. Manley, Editor. **Description:** Short fiction, many styles and genres. **Fiction:** 250-8,000 words; $5/page. **Queries:** Not necessary. **Unsolicited mss:** Accepts. **Freelance Content:** 100%. **Rights:** One-time, non-exclusive electronic. **Payment:** On publication.

RAMBUNCTIOUS REVIEW
1221 W. Pratt Blvd., Chicago, IL 60626. 773-338-2439. Annual. $4/issue. Circ.: 500. Editorial Board. **Description:** New and established writers of poetry and fiction. **Fiction:** 12 pages. **Poetry:** 100 typed lines. **Art:** b/w glossies. **Queries:** Not necessary. **E-Queries:** No. **Unsolicited mss:** Accepts. **Freelance Content:** 100%. **Rights:** FNASR. **Payment:** In copies.

REAL
Stephen F. Austin State Univ., P.O. Box 13007, SFA Sta., Nacogdoches, TX 75962. 936-468-2059. E-mail: real@sfasu.edu. Semi-annual. $15. Circ.: 400. W. Dale Hearell, Editor. **Description:** Short fiction, poetry, and criticism. **Fiction:** Realistic portrayal of human situations; to 5,000 words. **Nonfiction:** Well-written, scholarly; to 5,000 words. **Poetry:** Imagistic verse; not just reformatted prose; to 100 lines. **Art:** b/w line drawings. **Queries:** Not necessary. **E-Queries:** No. **Unsolicited mss:** Accepts. **Response:** Queries 1 week, submissions 3-6 weeks, SASE. **Freelance Content:** 100%. **Payment:** In copies.

RED CEDAR REVIEW
Michigan State Univ., Dept. of English, 17-C Morrill Hall, E. Lansing, MI 48824-1036. 517-355-9656. E-mail: rcreview@msu.edu. Web site: www.msu.edu. Biannual. $5/$6. Douglas Dowland, Editor. **Description:** Poetry, fiction, and creative nonfiction, all genres, by published and unpublished authors. **Fiction:** 5,000 words max. **Nonfiction:** Creative nonfiction; 5,000 words max. **Poetry:** Submit up to 5 poems. **Queries:** Preferred. **E-Queries:** Yes. **Unsolicited mss:** Accepts. **Response:** Queries 3 weeks, submissions 3 months, SASE. **Payment:** In copies.

RED ROCK REVIEW

Community College of Southern Nevada, Dept. of English, 3090 El Camino Road, N. Las Vegas, NV 89030. 702-876-1912. E-mail: logsdon@earthlmlc.net. Semiannual. $5.50/$10. Circ.: 1,000. Dr. Richard Logsdon, Editor. **Description:** Featuring work by new and well-established writers. **Fiction:** Mainstream fiction; 5,000 words. **Nonfiction:** Book reviews, recent poetry and fiction; interviews with literary artists; 2,000 words. **Poetry:** up to 60 lines. **Queries:** Not necessary. **E-Queries:** Yes. **Unsolicited mss:** Accepts. **Response:** Queries 2 weeks, (email responses sooner), submissions 2 months, SASE. **Freelance Content:** 60%. **Rights:** 1st NA. **Payment:** On publication.

RIVER CITY

Univ. of Memphis, Dept. of English, Memphis, TN 38152. 901-678-4591. E-mail: rivercity@memphis.edu. Web site: www.people.memphis.edu. Semi-annual. $7/issue, $12/year. Circ.: 1,200. Thomas Russell, Editor. **Description:** Literary journal of the University of Memphis. **Fiction:** Original short stories, no novel excerpts. **Art:** b/w, color photos, b/w illustrations. **Tips:** Avoid sentimental, singsong verse. For theme issues, see web site. **Queries:** Not necessary. **E-Queries:** Yes. **Unsolicited mss:** Accepts. **Response:** Queries, by return mail, submissions 2-6 weeks, SASE. **Freelance Content:** 50%. **Rights:** One-time.

RIVER STYX

634 N. Grand Blvd., 12th Fl., St. Louis, MO 63103. 314-533-4541. Web site: www.riverstyx.org. Tri-annual. $7/issue, $20/year. Circ.: 1,500. Richard Newman, Editor. **Description:** International, multicultural literary journal. Fiction, poetry, essays, and art by emerging and established writers and artists. **Fiction:** Less than 30 pages. **Nonfiction:** Personal essays, literary interviews, etc.; less than 30 pages. **Poetry:** Format open. **Art:** by request only. **Queries:** Not necessary. **E-Queries:** No. **Unsolicited mss:** Accepts. **Response:** Submissions 4-5 weeks, SASE. **Rights:** 1st NA. **Payment:** On publication.

ROANOKE REVIEW

Roanoke College, Salem, VA 24153. 504-334-1458. E-mail: walter@roanoke.edu. Semi-annual. $5. Circ.: 300. Robert R. Walter, Editor. **Description:** Literary magazine featuring fiction and poetry. **Fiction:** to 5,000 words; **Poetry:** to 100 lines. **Queries:** Preferred. **Unsolicited mss:** Accepts. **Payment:** In copies.

ROCKFORD REVIEW

P.O. Box 858, Rockford, IL 61105. 3x/year. $18/yr. Circ.: 250-300. David Ross, Editor. **Description:** Published by Rockford Writer's Guild. **Fiction:** 1,300 words. **Nonfiction:** Essays, short plays; 1,300 words. **Poetry:** Experimental or traditional, to 50 lines (shorter preferred); submit up to 3. **Queries:** Not necessary. **E-Queries:** No. **Unsolicited mss:** Accepts.

Response: Queries 2 weeks, submissions 2 months, SASE. **Rights:** 1st NA. **Payment:** In copies. **Contact:** Max Dodson, Prose; Cindy Gundererman, Poetry.

ROOM OF ONE'S OWN

PO Box 46160, Sta. D, Vancouver, BC, Canada V6J 5G5.
E-mail: contactroom@hotmail.com.
Web site: http://www.islandnet.com/Room/enter/. Quarterly. $22/yr (Can.), $25 (U.S.).
Editorial Collective. **Description:** Short stories, poems, art, and reviews; by, for, and about women. One of Canada's oldest literary magazines, offers a forum for women to sharing their unique perspectives. **Fiction:** To 5,000 words. **Nonfiction:** Creative nonfiction and essays; to 5,000 words. **Poetry:** Prefers groups of poems, rather than single poems. **Columns, Departments:** Book reviews; to 700 words. **Art:** Seeking original art and photography by women, on the female experience; Slides, photos, photocopies. **E-Queries:** No. **Unsolicited mss:** Accepts. **Response:** SASE (Canadian postage). **Rights:** FNASR. **Payment:** In copies. **Contact:** Editorial Collective.

ROSEBUD

P.O. Box 459, Cambridge, WI 53523. 608-423-4750.
Web site: www.rsb.net. 3x/year. $7/issue. Circ.: 9,000. Rod Clark, Editor.
Description: Independent, publishes traditional and non-traditional stories, essays, art, and poems. **Fiction:** Under 2,000 words; $25. **Nonfiction:** Articles, profiles; under 2,000 words; $25. **Poetry:** On love, alienation, travel, humor, nostalgia, and unexpected revelation; 1 page. **Tips:** Avoid pieces too generic, nostalgic, sentimental, straight crime or romance, or purely plot-driven. **Queries:** Not necessary. **E-Queries:** Yes. **Unsolicited mss:** Accepts. **Response:** 30 days (with $1/fee). **Freelance Content:** 60%. **Rights:** 1st serial, one-time. **Payment:** In copies.

SANSKRIT LITERARY-ARTS

Univ. of North Carolina-Charlotte, Cone University Ctr., Charlotte, NC 28223. 704-687-2326.
E-mail: sanskrit@email.uncc.edu. Web site: www.uncc.edu/life/sanskrit. Annual. $10.
Circ.: 3,500. Jennifer Bonacci, Editor. **Description:** Literary journal, all types of poetry. **Fiction:** Short fiction and short-shorts; 3,500 words. **Poetry:** All forms, prefers free form, concrete imagery. **Art:** Slides. **Tips:** Annual deadline, first Friday in November. **Queries:** Not necessary. **E-Queries:** Yes. **Unsolicited mss:** Accepts. **Response:** SASE. **Freelance Content:** 100%. **Rights:** 1st NA, electronic.

THE SEATTLE REVIEW

Univ. of Washington, Padelford Hall, Box 354330, Seattle, WA 98195.
E-mail: seaview@english.washington.edu.
Web site: http://depts.washington.edu/engl/seaview1.html. Colleen J. McElroy, Editor. **Description:** Stories, to 20 pages; poetry; essays on the craft of writing; art; and interviews with Northwest writers. **Tips:** Manuscripts read October 1 through May 31. **Payment:** In copies.

SENECA REVIEW

Hobart & William Smith Colleges, Geneva, NY 14456. 315-781-3392. E-mail: senecareview@hws.edu. Web site: www.hws/senecareview. Bi-annual. $7/issue, $11/year. Circ.: 1,000. Deborah Tall, Editor. **Description:** A journal of poetry and lyric essays, special interest in translations. **Nonfiction:** Format open. **Poetry:** Format open. **Queries:** Not necessary. **E-Queries:** No. **Unsolicited mss:** Accepts. **Response:** Submissions 2-3 months, SASE. **Freelance Content:** 100%. **Rights:** 1st NA. **Payment:** In copies.

THE SEWANEE REVIEW

University of the South, 735 University Ave., Sewanee, TN 37383-1000. **Description:** Tennessee literary reveiw. Only unpublished work considered. Query for essays (7,500 words or less) and reviews; submit fiction (3,500-7,500 words) and poetry (6 poems, 40 lines or less) without query. **Tips:** Do not submit between June 1st and August 31st. No simultaneous submissions. 3 prizes awarded annually, one in each category.

SHENANDOAH

Washington and Lee Univ., Troubadour Theatre, 2nd Fl., Lexington, VA 24450-0303. 540-463-8765. Web site: www.wlu.edu/~shenandoah. Quarterly. $32/yr. Circ.: 1,800. R.T. Smith, Editor. **Description:** A literary arts journal. **Fiction:** $25/page. **Nonfiction:** criticism, essays, interviews; $25/page. **Poetry:** $25/page. **Queries:** Not necessary. **E-Queries:** No. **Unsolicited mss:** Accepts. **Response:** Submissions 8 weeks, SASE. **Freelance Content:** 80%. **Rights:** FNASR. **Payment:** On publication.

SKYLARK

2200 169th St., Hammond, IN 46323. 219-989-2273. Annual. $8. Circ.: 1,000. Pamela Hunter, Editor. **Description:** Publishes work (literary and visual) by children and and more mature adult artists, side-by-side. Interested in new and emerging artists and writers (of any age). **Fiction:** Well-plotted, well-characterized stories, realistic dialogue and action. Central character must be three-dimensional; 4,000 words. **Nonfiction:** Essays that reflect what life in Northwest Indiana; interview with artists, writers, poets; 3,000 words. **Poetry:** Concise wording, rich imagery, honest emotional impact; up to 30 lines. **Art:** Accepts work by either adults or children; original in design, unpublished, and the original artwork (for four-color processing); b/w, color. **Queries:** Not necessary. **E-Queries:** No. **Unsolicited mss:** Accepts. **Response:** 3 months. **Freelance Content:** 80%. **Rights:** 1st. **Payment:** In copies.

SLIPSTREAM

Box 2071, Niagara Falls, NY 14301. 716-282-2616. E-mail: Editors@slipstreampress.org. Web site: www.slipstreampress.org. Annual. $6/issue. Circ.: 750-1,500. Robert Borgatti, Editor. **Description:** Poetry, short fiction, and graphics not normally found in mainstream publications. **Fiction:**

Contemporary urban themes encouraged; up to 15 pages. **Poetry:** Contemporary poetry; 1-6 pages. **Art:** send photocopies first. **Tips:** No rhyming, religious or trite verse. **Queries:** Not necessary. **E-Queries:** Yes. **Unsolicited mss:** Accepts. **Response:** Queries 1 week, submissions 2-6 weeks, SASE. **Freelance Content:** 100%. **Rights:** 1st NA. **Payment:** In copies. **Contact:** Dan Sicoli, Livio Furallo.

THE SMALL POND
P.O. Box 664, Stratford, CT 06615. 203-379-4066.
3x/year. $4/issue, $10/year. Circ.: 300. Napoleon St. Cyr, Editor. **Description:** Literary journal with interesting, quirky fiction and poetry. **Fiction:** 2,500 words max. **Nonfiction:** Anything interesting; 2,500 words. **Poetry:** Any style, subject; 100 lines. **Tips:** Avoid bleeding hearts. **Queries:** Not necessary. **E-Queries:** No. **Unsolicited mss:** Accepts. **Response:** Queries 2-5 days, submissions 2-5 weeks, SASE. **Freelance Content:** 100%. **Rights:** All. **Payment:** On publication.

SNAKE NATION REVIEW
Snake Nation Press, 110 #2 W. Force, Valdosta, GA 31601. 229-244-0752.
E-mail: jean@snakenationpress.org. Web site: www.snakenationpress.org. 3x/year. $6/issue. Circ.: 2,000. Jean Arambula, Editor. **Description:** Well-written fiction and poetry, any topic. **Fiction:** Readable short stories, novel chapters; 5,000 word limit; $5/story. **Nonfiction:** Essays; 5,000 limit; $5. **Poetry:** up to 60 lines; $1. **Queries:** Not necessary. **E-Queries:** Yes. **Unsolicited mss:** Accepts. **Response:** Submissions 1-6 months, SASE. **Freelance Content:** 100%. **Rights:** one-time.

SNOWY EGRET
P.O. Box 9, Bowling Green, IN 47833. 812-829-1910. Bi-annual. $12/issue, $20/year (sample copy $8). Circ.: 400. Philip Repp, Editor. **Description:** Oldest independent journal of nature writing. Emphasis on natural history and human beings in relation to nature from literary, artistic, philosophical and historical perspectives. Pays $2/printed page. **Fiction:** Characters who relate strongly to nature and grow in understanding of themselves and the world; 500-10,000 words. **Nonfiction:** Essays on natural world and relationship of human beings to it, with detailed observations from author's own experience; 500-10,000 words. **Poetry:** Theme oriented. **Columns, Departments:** First-hand experiences with landscape or wildlife encounters; 250-2,000 words. **Tips:** Submit freshly observed material, with plenty of description and/or dialogue. **Queries:** Not necessary. **E-Queries:** No. **Response:** Queries 2 weeks, submissions 2 months, SASE. **Freelance Content:** 95%. **Rights:** 1st NA, one-time. **Payment:** On publication.

SO TO SPEAK
George Mason Univ., 4400 University Dr., MS2D6,
Fairfax, VA 22030-4444. 703-993-3625.
E-mail: sts@gmu.edu. Web site: www.gmu.edu/org/sts. Bi-annual. $6/issue, $11/year. Circ.: 1,300. Kaia Sand, Editor. **Description:** Feminist journal of language and arts, concerned with the history of women, of feminists, and looking to see the future

through art. Includes fiction, poetry, nonfiction, reviews, visual arts (b/w). **Fiction:** Literary, feminist; to 5,000 words. **Nonfiction:** Literary, lyrical, critical; reviews (feminist books and hypertext); to 4,000 words. **Poetry:** Literary, feminist; experimental, lyrical, narrative. **Art:** b/w art, seeking color cover art. **Queries:** Not necessary. **E-Queries:** No. **Unsolicited mss:** Accepts. **Response:** Submissions 3-4 months, SASE. **Payment:** In copies.

SONORA REVIEW

Univ. of Arizona, Dept. of English, Tucson, AZ 85721.
E-mail: sonora@u.Arizona.edu. **Description:** Literary journal. **Tips:** Annual contests; send for guidelines. Manuscripts read year-round.

SOU'WESTER

Southern Illinois Univ. at Edwardsville, Edwardsville, IL 62026-1438. 618-650-3190. Bi-annual. Circ.: 300. Fred W. Robbins, Editor. **Description:** Small literary magazine. **Fiction:** Yes. **Poetry:** Yes. **Queries:** Not necessary. **E-Queries:** Yes. **Response:** Submissions 4-6 months. **Rights:** All. **Payment:** In copies.

SOUTH CAROLINA REVIEW

Clemson Univ., Dept. of English, Clemson, SC 29634-0523.
864-656-5399. E-mail: cwayne@clemson.edu.
Web site: www.hubcap.clemson.edu/aah/engl/screview.htm. Semiannual. Circ.: 450. Wayne Chapman, Editor. **Description:** Fiction, essays, reviews, interviews, and poems. **Fiction:** 1,000-6,000 words. **Queries:** Preferred. **E-Queries:** No. **Response:** Queries 1-2 weeks, 1-2 months, SASE required. **Freelance Content:** 90%. **Rights:** World. **Payment:** In copies.

SOUTHERN EXPOSURE

P.O. Box 531, Durham, NC 27702. 919-419-8311.
Web site: www.i4south.org. Quarterly. Chris Kromm, Editor. **Description:** Forum on "Southern politics and culture." **Fiction:** Short stories, to 3,600 words; pays $25-$250. **Nonfiction:** Essays, investigative journalism, and oral histories, 500-3,600 words; pays $25-$250. **Queries:** Preferred. **Payment:** On publication.

SOUTHERN HUMANITIES REVIEW

9088 Haley Ctr., Auburn Univ., AL 36849.
E-mail: shrengl@auburn.edu. Quarterly. $5/$15. Circ.: 700. Dan R. Latimer, Virginia M. Kouidis, Co-editors. **Description:** Scholarly, literary magazine. **Fiction:** Short stories; 3,500-15,000 words. **Nonfiction:** Essays, criticism; 3,500-15,000 words. **Poetry:** 2 pages. **Queries:** Not necessary. **E-Queries:** Yes. **Unsolicited mss:** Accepts. **Response:** Queries 1-2 weeks, submissions 1-3 months, SASE. **Freelance Content:** 70%. **Rights:** 1st, reverts to author. **Payment:** In copies.

SOUTHERN POETRY REVIEW

Central Piedmont Community College, Advancement Studies, Charlotte, NC 28235. 704-330-6275. Semi-annual. $10. Circ.: 1,000. Ken McLaurin, Editor. **Description:** Literary journal, mostly poetry. **Poetry:** Any style, length, content. **Tips:** Use strong, clear imagery. Avoid sentimental or "proselytizing" content. **Queries:** Not necessary. **E-Queries:** Yes. **Unsolicited mss:** Accepts. **Freelance Content:** 100%. **Rights:** 1st, reverts to writer. **Payment:** On publication.

THE SOUTHERN REVIEW

43 Allen Hall, Louisiana State Univ., Baton Rouge, LA 70803. 225-388-5108. Web site: www.LSU.edu/guests/wwwtsm. Quarterly. Circ.: 3,100. Michael Griffith, Associate Editor. **Description:** Literary publication of contemporary literature, with special interest in Southern culture and history. **Poetry:** up to 4 pages; $20/page. **Tips:** Seeking craftsmanship, technique, and seriousness of subject matter. **Queries:** Preferred. **Response:** 2 months, SASE required. **Rights:** 1st serial. **Payment:** On publication.

SOUTHWEST REVIEW

P.O. Box 750374, Dallas, TX 75275-0374. 214-768-1037. E-mail: swr@mail.smu.edu. Quarterly. $6/issue. Elizabeth Mills, Editor. **Description:** Varied, wide-ranging content of adult interest: contemporary affairs, history, folklore, fiction, poetry, literary criticism, art, music and theater. **Fiction:** 3,500-7,000 words; $100-$300. **Nonfiction:** 3,500-7,000 words; $100-$300. **Poetry:** 1 page (generally); $50-$150. **Queries:** Not necessary. **E-Queries:** No. **Unsolicited mss:** Accepts. **Response:** Submissions 3 months, SASE required. **Rights:** 1st NA. **Payment:** On publication.

SOW'S EAR POETRY REVIEW

19535 Pleasant View Dr., Abingdon, VA 24211-6827. 540-628-2651. E-mail: richman@preferred.com. Quarterly. $5/$10. Circ.: 600. James Owens, Editor. **Description:** Poetry, artwork, and nonfiction. **Nonfiction:** Essay or review. **Poetry:** Contemporary poetry in English; length varies. **Art:** b/w prints, good photocopies of drawings; to complement rather than illustrate poems. **Tips:** Seeking poems that make the strange familiar or the familiar strange, that connect the little story of the text and the big story of the human situation. **Queries:** Not necessary. **E-Queries:** Yes. **Unsolicited mss:** Accepts. **Response:** Queries 1 week, submissions 3-6 months, SASE. **Freelance Content:** 100%. **Rights:** 1st NA. **Payment:** In copies.

SPECTACLE

Pachanga Press, 101 Middlesex Turnpike, Suite 6, PMB 155, Burlington, MA 01803-4914. E-mail: spectaclejournal@hotmail.com. Semi-annual. $7. Circ.: 1,500. Richard Aguilar, Editor. **Description:** Essays, articles, reportage, and fiction on broad spectrum of lively, unconventional themes. **Fiction:** Relevant to issue's theme; up to

5,000 words; $30, and 2 copies. **Nonfiction:** Essays, memoirs, articles, reportage, interviews, and satire; 2,000-5,000 words; $30, and 2 copies. **Tips:** Contact for coming themes. **Queries:** Not necessary. **E-Queries:** Yes. **Unsolicited mss:** Accepts. **Response:** Queries 2 weeks, submissions 6-8 weeks, SASE. **Freelance Content:** 90%. **Rights:** FNASR. **Payment:** On publication.

SPSM&H

329 E St., Bakersfield, CA 93304. 661-323-4064. E-mail: amelia@lightspeed.net. Web site: www.ameliamagazine.net. Quarterly. $10.95/issue, $30/year. Circ.: 1,800. Frederick A. Raborg, Jr., Editor. **Description:** Open to all forms of fiction and poetry, etc., including gay and ethnic themes. Eclectic readership, 70% college educated. **Fiction:** all genres; 300-5,000 words; $15-$50. **Nonfiction:** 500-2,500 words; $15-$50. **Poetry:** 2-500 lines; $2-$25. **Fillers:** funny or philosophical; 1 line-500 words; $2-$10. **Art:** b/w, color cover; $10-25, $50-$100 (cover). **Tips:** Looking for strong themes, thoughtful pieces. Read magazine first. **Queries:** Not necessary. **E-Queries:** Yes. **Unsolicited mss:** Accepts. **Response:** queries 1-2 weeks, submissions 1 week-3 months, SASE. **Freelance Content:** 95%. **Rights:** FNASR. **Payment:** On acceptance.

STAND

Dept. of English, Box 2005, VCU, Richmond, VA 23284-2005. 804-828-1331. Web site: saturn.vcu.edu/~dlatane/stand.html. Quarterly. $12/$49.50. Circ.: 7,500. Michael Huse, John Kinsella, Editors. **Description:** Literary magazine. Pays "modest" amount. **Fiction:** 10,000 words. **Poetry:** up to 250 lines. **Tips:** Probably not the right market for new writers. **Queries:** Not necessary. **E-Queries:** Yes. **Unsolicited mss:** Accepts. **Response:** Submissions 1-3 months, SASE. **Freelance Content:** 60%. **Payment:** On publication.

STORY QUARTERLY

431 Sheridan Road, Kenilworth, IL 60043-1220. 847-256-6998. E-mail: storyquarterly@hotmail.com. Web site: www.storyquarterly.com. Annual. $5. Circ.: 4,500. Marie Hayes, Editors. **Description:** Contemporary American and foreign literature, full range of styles and forms. **Fiction:** Short stories; 250-10,000 words. **Nonfiction:** Interviews; 250-10,000 words. **Art:** b/w. **Tips:** Needs stories with great humor, serious and literary stories of any type or style, short-shorts, also novel excerpts, memoirs. **E-Queries:** Yes. **Response:** Submissions 1-2 months, SASE required. **Freelance Content:** 0-3%. **Payment:** In copies.

STORYWORKS

555 Broadway, New York, NY 10012. 212-343-6100. Bimonthly. Circ.: 250,000. Lauren Tarshis, Editor. **Description:** Literature magazine for 8-12 year olds. **Queries:** Required. **Unsolicited mss:** Does not accept.

SUB-TERRAIN

204-A, 175 E. Broadway, Vancouver, BC, Canada V5T 1W2. 604-876-8710. E-mail: subter@pinc.com. Web site: www.anvilpress.com. 3x/year. $3.95 (U.S.) $4.95 (Canada). Circ.: 5,000. Brian Kaufman, Editor. **Description:** A stimulating fusion of fiction, poetry, photography and graphics from uprising Canadian, U.S., and international writers and artists. **Fiction:** 3,000 words max. **Poetry:** 3-4 pages max. **Art:** 5x7 b/w. **Tips:** Seeking work with a point of view and some passion, on issues of pressing importance (especially with urban slant). No bland, flowery, universal poetry that says nothing in style or content. **Queries:** Preferred. **E-Queries:** Yes. **Unsolicited mss:** Accepts. **Response:** Queries 1-2 weeks, submissions 2-4 months, SASE. **Freelance Content:** 85%. **Rights:** 1st NA. **Payment:** On publication. **Contact:** Tammy Armstrong.

SUN

Sun Publishing Co., 107 N. Roberson St., Chapel Hill, NC 27516. 919-942-5282. Web site: www.thesunmagazine.org. Monthly. $3.95/issue, $34 yr. Circ.: 50,000. Sy Safransky, Editor. **Description:** Essays, stories, interviews, and poetry, in which people write of their struggles to understand their lives, often with surprising intimacy. Looking for writers willing to take risks, to describe life honestly. **Fiction:** Fiction that feels like lived experience; up to 7,000 words; $300-500. **Nonfiction:** Personal essays, interviews; up to 7,000 words; $300-1,000. **Poetry:** 1-2 pages; $50-200. **Art:** b/w; $50-200. **Tips:** No journalistic, academic, opinion pieces. **Queries:** Not necessary. **E-Queries:** No. **Unsolicited mss:** Accepts. **Response:** 3 months, SASE. **Freelance Content:** 80%. **Rights:** One-time. **Payment:** On publication.

SYCAMORE REVIEW

Purdue Univ., Dept. of English, West Lafayette, IN 47907. 765-494-3783. E-mail: sycamore@expert.cc.purdue.edu. Web site: www.sla.purdue.edu. Bi-annual. $7.00/issue, $12.00/year. Circ.: 700. Numsiri Kunakemakorn, Editor. **Description:** Literary journal. **Fiction:** yes. **Nonfiction:** Essays, interviews, translations. **Poetry:** yes. **Queries:** Not necessary. **Unsolicited mss:** Does not accept. **Response:** Queries 1-2 weeks, submissions 3-4 months, SASE.

TALKING RIVER REVIEW

Lewis-Clark State College, 500 8th Ave., Lewiston, ID 83501. 208-799-2307. Biannual. $7/issue, $14/year. Circ.: 350. Carman C. Curton, Editor. **Description:** Publishes the best work from first-time writers. **Fiction:** Short stories; up to 20 pages. **Nonfiction:** Literary essays; up to 20 pages. **Poetry:** Any style; 1-5 pages. **Tips:** Encourages submissions from those who have never published before. **Queries:** Not necessary. **E-Queries:** Yes. **Unsolicited mss:** Accepts. **Response:** No queries, submissions 3-4 months, SASE. **Freelance Content:** 100%. **Rights:** 1st. **Payment:** In copies.

TAR RIVER POETRY
East Carolina Univ., Dept. of English, Greenville, NC 27858-4353. 252-328-6046. Bi-annual. $5/issue. Circ.: 650. Peter Makuck, Editor. **Description:** Formal and open form poetry, reviews, some interviews. **Poetry:** Strong imagery, figurative language; 6 pages max. **Tips:** No sentimental, flat poetry. Emphasize the visual. **Queries:** Not necessary. **E-Queries:** No. **Unsolicited mss:** Accepts. **Response:** Queries 1 week, submissions 4-6 weeks, SASE. **Freelance Content:** 100%. **Payment:** In copies.

THE TEXAS REVIEW
English Dept., Sam Houston State Univ., P.O. Box 2146, Huntsville, TX 77341. 936-294-1992. E-mail: eng_pdrashsu.edu. Web site: www.shsu.edu. Semi-annual. $12/yr. Circ.: 500. Paul Ruffin, Editor. **Description:** Showcases fiction, poetry, nonfiction. **Fiction:** Yes. **Nonfiction:** Yes. **Poetry:** Yes. **Queries:** Not necessary. **E-Queries:** Yes. **Unsolicited mss:** Does not accept. **Response:** Queries 1 week, submissions 6-8 weeks, SASE. **Rights:** 1st.

THEMA
Box 8747, Metairie, LA 70011-8747. 504-887-1263. E-mail: thema@home.com. Web site: www.litline.org/thema. 3x/year. $8/issue, $16/year. Circ.: 300. Virginia Howard, Editor. **Description:** Each issue is a stand-alone, thematic anthology. Provides a forum for writers, and source material for teachers of creative writing. **Fiction:** Less than 6,000 words (20 pages); $10-$25. **Nonfiction:** Less than 6,000 words. **Poetry:** 3-page max.; $10. **Tips:** Request upcoming themes. **Queries:** Not necessary. **E-Queries:** Yes. **Unsolicited mss:** Accepts. **Response:** Queries 2 weeks, submissions 4 months after deadline, SASE. **Freelance Content:** 99%. **Rights:** One-time. **Payment:** On acceptance.

THIRD COAST
Western Michigan Univ., Dept. of English, Kalamazoo, MI 49008-5092. Biannually. $6/issue, $11/year. Circ.: 500. Shanda Hansma Blue, Editor. **Description:** Literary review for contemporary writers and readers. **Fiction:** Yes. **Nonfiction:** Creative nonfiction. **Poetry:** Yes. **Queries:** Not necessary. **E-Queries:** No. **Unsolicited mss:** Accepts. **Response:** SASE. **Freelance Content:** 80%. **Rights:** 1st American serial. **Payment:** On publication.

13TH MOON
Dept. of English, University of Albany, Albany, NY 12222. 518-442-4181. E-mail: moon13@csc.albany.edu. Web site: www.albany.edu/wwwres/13thmoon/main.html. Annual. $10. Circ.: 500. Judith Emlyn Johnson, Editor. **Description:** Feminist literary magazine, with literature and graphic arts by contemporary women. Seeks to draw attention to neglected categories of women artists. **Fiction:** Feminist short fiction, emphasis on work of minority women and lesbians; no length limit. **Poetry:** Feminist, emphasis same as fiction; drama also welcome. **Art:** Welcomes art-

work. **Queries:** Preferred. **E-Queries:** No. **Unsolicited mss:** Accepts. **Response:** Varies, SASE. **Freelance Content:** 100%. **Rights:** One-time. **Payment:** In copies.

THOUGHTS FOR ALL SEASONS
478 NE 56th St., Miami, FL 33137. $6. Circ.: 1,000. Prof. Michel P. Richard, Editor. **Description:** Primarily poetry. Celebrates the epigram, of 2-4 lines, as a literary form. Humor and satire. **Poetry:** Rhyming, quatrains, limericks, nonsense verse with good imagery; up to 1 page. **Columns, Departments:** Thematic by issue; up to 10 pages. **Queries:** Not necessary. **E-Queries:** No. **Response:** Submissions 21 days, SASE. **Freelance Content:** 60%. **Payment:** On publication.

THE THREEPENNY REVIEW
PO Box 9131, Berkeley, CA 94709. 510-849-4545. Web site: www.threepennyreview.com. Quarterly. Circ.: 9,000. Wendy Lesser, Editor. **Description:** "Literary and immensely readable." *(Publishers Weekly)*. **Fiction:** To 5,000 words; to $200. **Nonfiction:** Essays on books, theater, film, dance, music, art, television, politics; 1,500-3,000 words; To $200. **Poetry:** to 100 lines; $100/poem. **Tips:** Manuscripts read Sept. through May. **Queries:** Preferred. **Response:** 2 months, SASE. **Payment:** On publication.

TIGHTROPE
Swamp Press, 15 Warwick Ave., Northfield, MA 01360. Annual. $6/issue. Circ.: 300. Ed Rayher, Editor. **Description:** Letterpress magazine, poetry with original graphics. **Poetry:** Any length. **Queries:** Preferred. **E-Queries:** No. **Unsolicited mss:** Does not accept. **Response:** 1-2 months, SASE. **Rights:** 1st. **Payment:** In copies.

TIMBER CREEK REVIEW
8969 UNCG Station, Greensboro, NC 27413. 336-334-2952. E-mail: jmfreier@uncg.edu. Quarterly. $4.25/issue. Circ.: 150-180. J.M. Freiermuth, Editor. **Description:** Short stories, poetry, and occasional literary nonfiction; well-written, readable stories. **Fiction:** 2,500-7,500 words; $10-$35. **Nonfiction:** 2,500-7,500 words; $10-$35. **Poetry:** 30 lines; pays in copy. **Queries:** Not necessary. **E-Queries:** No. **Unsolicited mss:** Accepts. **Response:** 3-6 months, SASE. **Freelance Content:** 100%. **Rights:** FNASR.

TIN HOUSE
McCormack Communications, 2601 NE Thurman St., Portland, OR 97210. E-mail: tinhouse@aol.com. Web site: www.tinhouse.com. Quarterly. **Description:** General-interest literary quarterly. **Poetry:** Up to 5 poems; $50-$150. **Tips:** Buys 40-80 poems/year. **Queries:** Preferred. **Response:** 3 months, SASE. **Rights:** FNASR, anthology. **Payment:** On publication.

TRIQUARTERLY

Northwestern Univ., 2020 Ridge Ave., Evanston, IL 60208-4302. 847-491-3490. Web site: triquarterly.nwu.edu. 3x/year. $11.95. Circ.: 4,000. Susan Firestone Hahn, Editor. **Description:** Fiction, poetry, and critical commentary, from authors of diverse heritage, backgrounds, and styles. **Fiction:** Literary fiction (not genre); $5/page. **Nonfiction:** Query first; $5/page. **Poetry:** Serious, aesthetically informed, inventive; $.50/line. **Queries:** Not necessary. **E-Queries:** No. **Unsolicited mss:** Accepts. **Response:** Queries 2 months, submissions 3 months, SASE. **Freelance Content:** 50%. **Rights:** FNASR. **Payment:** On publication.

TWO RIVERS REVIEW

215 McCartney St., Easton, PA 18042.
E-mail: tworiversreview@juno.com.
Web site: http://pages.prodigy.net/memmer/trr.html. Bi-annual. $6/$12. Circ.: 400. Philip Memmer, Editor. **Description:** Poetry that displays strong craft and clear language. **Poetry:** Original work only; all varieties with a keen sense of craft. Submit up to 4 poems at a time (no more than 3 times/calendar year); Any. **Queries:** Not necessary. **E-Queries:** Yes. **Unsolicited mss:** Accepts. **Response:** Queries 2 weeks, submissions 4-8 weeks, SASE. **Freelance Content:** 90%. **Rights:** 1st, author may republish with credit given. **Payment:** In copies.

VERMONT INK

P.O. Box 3297, Burlington, VT 05401-3297.
E-mail: vermontink@aol.com. Web site: www.vermontink.com. Quarterly. Donna Leach, Editor. **Description:** Entertaining, well-written short stories and poetry. **Fiction:** Short stories, entertaining, "basically G-rated": adventure, historical, humor, mainstream, mystery and suspense, regional interest, romance, science fiction, westerns; 2,000-3,000 words; $25/story. **Poetry:** Upbeat and humorous; to 25 lines; $10. **Queries:** Preferred.

VERSE

Plymouth State College, English Dept., Plymouth, NH 03264.
3x/year. $8/issue, $18/year. Circ.: 1,000. Brian Henry, Andrew Zawacki, Editors. **Description:** Poetry, criticism, and interviews with poets. Focus is international and eclectic, favors the innovative over the staid. **Nonfiction:** Essays on poetry, interviews, reviews. **Poetry:** Up to 5 poems. **Queries:** Not necessary. **Unsolicited mss:** Accepts. **Response:** Queries 2 months, submissions 1-4 months, SASE. **Freelance Content:** 75%. **Rights:** 1st NA. **Payment:** On publication.

VESTAL REVIEW

2609 Dartmouth Dr., Vestal, NY 13850.
E-mail: editor@stny.rr.com. Web site: www.vestalreview.net. Quarterly. Free. Circ.: 2,000. Mark Budman, Sue O'Neill, Editors. **Description:** Features flash fiction. **Fiction:** Flash fiction, any genre; under 500 words; $.03-$.10/word. **Tips:** Seeking literary stories; no children's stories or syrupy romance. **Queries:** Not necessary.

E-Queries: No. **Unsolicited mss:** Accepts. **Response:** 2 weeks. **Freelance Content:** 100%. **Rights:** 1st electronic. **Payment:** On publication.

THE VIEW

325 N. Clippert St., Suite B, Lansing, MI 48912. Carole Eberly, Ed. **Description:** Literary fiction, with stories related only to Michigan area. Only accepts work from local writers. **Fiction:** Upbeat, 1,500-2,500 words, for Michigan area readers. **Queries:** Preferred. **Payment:** On publication.

THE VILLAGER

135 Midland Ave., Bronxville, NY 10708. 914-337-3252. Monthly. $2/$10. Circ.: 750. Lorraine Lange, Editor. **Description:** Published by a women's club, offers upbeat articles, fiction, and poetry. **Fiction:** Love stories, humorous, poignant; to 2,000 words. **Nonfiction:** On volunteerism, organizations, local celebrities; up to 1,000 words. **Poetry:** Seasonal poems. **Art:** Color (submit with articles). **Queries:** Not necessary. **E-Queries:** No. **Unsolicited mss:** Accepts. **Response:** 1 month, SASE. **Payment:** In copies.

VIRGINIA QUARTERLY REVIEW

One W. Range, Charlottesville, VA 22903. 804-924-3124. E-mail: jc07e@virginia@edu. Web site: www.virginia.edu. Quarterly. $5/$18. Circ.: 4,500. Staige D. Blackford, Editor. **Description:** A journal of literature and discussion. **Fiction:** Quality fiction ; $10/page. **Nonfiction:** Serious essays, articles, 3,000-6,000 words, on literature, science, politics, economics, etc.; $10/page. **Poetry:** $1/line. **Queries:** Preferred. **Unsolicited mss:** Accepts. **Payment:** On publication.

VISIONS INTERNATIONAL

Black Buzzard Press, 1007 Ficklen Rd., Fredericksburg, VA 22405. 540-310-0730. Web site: www.members.tripod.com/VisionsInternational/. 3x/year. $5.50/issue, $15/year. Circ.: 750. Bradley R. Strahan, Editor. **Description:** Promotes world poetry and the arts, offering wide variety of original work and modern translations. **Poetry:** All styles and subjects, well-crafted, no amateur work; up to 3 pages. **Art:** b/w illustrations; send samples only. **Tips:** No racism, sexism, "greeting card"-ism. **Queries:** Not necessary. **E-Queries:** No. **Unsolicited mss:** Accepts. **Response:** SASE. **Freelance Content:** 95%. **Payment:** In copies.

WASCANA REVIEW

Dept. of English, Univ. of Regina, Regina, Sask., Canada S4S 0A2. 306-585-4302. E-mail: kathleenwall@uregina.ca. Web site: www.uregina.ca./english/wrhome.htm. Biannual. $5/issue. Circ.: 250. Dr. Kathleen Wall, Editor. **Description:** Seeks poetry and short fiction that combines craft with risk, pressure with grace. Wide variety of themes. **Fiction:** Meaningful grasp of human experience; 5,000 words; $3/printed page. **Nonfiction:** Cutting-edge literary criticism; articles on contemporary short fiction and poetry; 7,500 words; $3/printed page. **Poetry:** Artistic merit, integrity, originality, craftsmanship; 2 printed pages; $10/printed page.

Queries: Not necessary. E-Queries: Yes. Unsolicited mss: Accepts. Response: Queries 1 week, submission 2 months, SASE. Freelance Content: 100%. Rights: 1st NA. Payment: On publication.

WASHINGTON REVIEW

P.O. Box 50132, Washington, DC 20091-0132. 202-333-6248. Web site: www.washingtonreview.com. Clarissa Wittenberg, Editor. Description: Poetry; articles on literary, performing and fine arts in the Washington, D.C., area. Fiction, 1,000-2,500 words. Tips: Prefers regional writers. Response: 3 months. Payment: In copies.

WEBER STUDIES

Weber State Univ., 1214 University Cir., Ogden, UT 84408-1214. 626-6616. E-mail: weberstudies@weber.edu. Web site: www.weberstudies.edu. Quarterly. Circ.: 1,000. Sherwin W. Howard, Editor. Description: Narrative, critical commentary and opinion, fiction and poetry, dealing with environment and culture of the contemporary American west. Fiction: 5,000; $100-$150. Nonfiction: 5,000; $100-$150. Poetry: Submit multiple poems, up to 6 poems or 200 lines; $25-$50. Queries: Not necessary. Unsolicited mss: Accepts. Response: Queries 1 week,submissions 3-4 months, SASE. Freelance Content: 80%. Rights: 1st and web archive. Payment: On publication.

WEST BRANCH

Bucknell Hall, Bucknell Univ., Lewisburg, PA 17837. 570-577-1853. E-mail: westbranch@bucknell.edu. Web site: www.departments.bucknell.edu. Semi-annual. $6/issue, $10/year. Circ.: 700. Joshua Harmon, Paula Closson Buck, Editors. Description: Quality poetry, fiction, nonfiction, and reviews. Fiction: Realistic and avant garde. Nonfiction: Format open. Poetry: No confessional verse. Queries: Not necessary. E-Queries: Yes. Response: 1 month, SASE. Freelance Content: 90%. Rights: 1st NA. Payment: In copies.

❦ WESTERN HUMANITIES REVIEW

Univ. of Utah, 255 S. Central Campus Dr., Room 3500, Salt Lake City, UT 84112. 801-581-6070. E-mail: whr@mail.hum.utah.edu. Web site: www.hum.utah.edu/whr. Biannually. $14/yr. Barry Weller, Editor. Description: For educated readers. Pays $5/page. Fiction: Literary fiction, exciting and original (no genre fiction). Nonfiction: On humanities issues. Poetry: Yes. Tips: Reads submissions Sept.-May; all other submissions returned unread. Queries: Not necessary. E-Queries: No. Unsolicited mss: Accepts. Response: Queries 2 weeks, submissions 8-10 weeks, SASE. Freelance Content: 0%. Rights: 1st NA. Payment: On publication.

❦ WHETSTONE

P.O. Box 1266, Barrington, IL 60011. 847-382-5626. E-mail: baacouncil@aol.com. Annual. $7. Circ.: 850. Dale Griffith, Editor.

Description: Poetry, short fiction, novel excerpts, and creative fiction, from established and emerging artists across the country. **Fiction:** Character-driven prose that tells truth in detail; 6,500 words; pay varies. **Poetry:** Concrete rather than abstract; submit up to 7 poems. **E-Queries:** Yes. **Unsolicited mss:** Accepts. **Response:** Queries 1-3 days, submissions, 3-5 months, SASE. **Freelance Content:** 100%.

WILLOW SPRINGS

MS-1, Eastern Washington University, 705 W. First, Spokane, WA 99204. 509-623-4349. Biannual. $6/$11.50. Circ.: 1,200. Christopher Howell, Editor. **Description:** Poetry, short fiction, and nonfiction, of literary merit. **Tips:** No multiple submissions. Submit prose and poetry in separate envelopes. Manuscripts read September 15-May 15. **Queries:** Not necessary. **E-Queries:** No. **Unsolicited mss:** Accepts. **Response:** 4-8 weeks, SASE. **Freelance Content:** 100%. **Rights:** 1st. **Payment:** In copies.

WINDSOR REVIEW

Univ. of Windsor, Dept. of English, Windsor, Ont., Canada N9B 3P4. 519-253-3000. E-mail: urevu@uwindsor.ca. Biannual. $12 issue. Circ.: 500. Marty Gervais, Editor. **Description:** Literary fiction and poetry. **Fiction:** Literary fiction; under 5,000 words; $50/story. **Nonfiction:** Interviews with well-known writers; 3,000-7,000 words; $50. **Poetry:** All types; experimental, concrete or traditional; $15/poem. **Art:** Prefer b&w. $100-$200. **Queries:** Not necessary. **E-Queries:** Yes. **Unsolicited mss:** Accepts. **Response:** Submissions 1-3 months, SASE. **Freelance Content:** 90%. **Rights:** 1st. **Payment:** On publication.

WITNESS

Oakland Community College, 27055 Orchard Lake Rd., Farmington Hills, MI 48334. E-mail: stinepj@umich.edu. Peter Stine, Editor. **Description:** Literary journal. **Fiction:** Fiction, 5-20 page; pays $6/page. **Nonfiction:** Essays, 5-20 pages; pays $6/page. **Poetry:** Submit up to 3 at a time; pays $10/page. **Payment:** On publication. *No recent report.*

THE WORCESTER REVIEW

6 Chatham St., Worcester, MA 01609. Web site: www.geocities.com/paris/leftbank. Annual. $10/issue. John Lavine, Editor. **Description:** Literary journal. **Fiction:** 4,000 words. **Nonfiction:** Critical articles about poetry with New England connection. **Poetry:** Submit up to 5 poems at a time. **Queries:** Not necessary. **E-Queries:** No. **Unsolicited mss:** Accepts. **Response:** Submissions 6 months, SASE. **Rights:** 1st. **Payment:** In copies.

WRITER ONLINE

40 Royal Oak Dr., Rochester, NY 14624. E-mail: email@novalearn.com. Web site: www.novalearn.com/wol. Biweekly. Circ.: 35,000. T. M. Wright, Editor. **Description:** Free newsletter (e-zine) for all writers. Many have been previously published; most are motivated by the desire to sell their

writing. Fiction and non-fiction. Pays $.05-$.10/word. **Nonfiction:** Articles addressing the craft of writing. Prefers articles that offer examples and use direct quotes from credible sources. Articles connected to recognizable names are of premier value; up to 1,800 words.

WRITERS ON THE RIVER

P.O. Box 40828, Memphis, TN 38174-0828.
E-mail: mrdcolonel@aol.com. Semi-annual. $4/issue. Circ.: 1,000. Mick Denington, Editor. **Description:** Literary, family-oriented. **Fiction:** To 2,500 words. **Nonfiction:** Adventure, fantasy, historical and regional, mainstream, humor, mystery/suspense; to 2,500 words. **Poetry:** 1 page. **Queries:** Not necessary. **E-Queries:** Yes. **Response:** Submissions 1-2 months, SASE. **Freelance Content:** 100%. **Rights:** 1st, one-time.

YALE REVIEW

Yale Univ., P.O. Box 208243, New Haven, CT 06520-8243. 203-432-0499.
Quarterly. $28/yr. Circ.: 6,000. J.D. McClatchy, Editor. **Description:** Literary magazine with fiction, nonfiction, and poetry. **Fiction:** $400/story. **Nonfiction:** $500. **Poetry:** Serious poetry; pay varies. **Queries:** Not necessary. **E-Queries:** No. **Unsolicited mss:** Accepts. **Response:** Queries 1 month, submissions 2 months, SASE. **Freelance Content:** 30%. **Rights:** 1st serial. **Payment:** On publication.

YEMASSEE

Univ. of South Carolina, Dept. of English, Columbia, SC 29208. 803-777-2085.
Web site: www.cla.sc.edu/ENGL/index.html. Biannual. $15 ($7 student). Circ.: 400. Lisa Kerr, Editor. **Description:** Literary journal of poetry, short fiction, one-act plays, brief essays, and interviews. **Fiction:** Short, smart, accessible, character-driven; to 5,000 words. **Nonfiction:** Literary reviews, interviews with literary figures; to 3,000 words. **Poetry:** No fixed length; prefers poems under 3 pages. **Tips:** Offers $200 award for fiction and poetry in each issue. **Queries:** Not necessary. **E-Queries:** No. **Unsolicited mss:** Accepts. **Response:** 2 months after each deadline, SASE required. **Freelance Content:** 100%. **Rights:** 1st.

ZOETROPE: ALL STORY

1350 Avenue of the Americas, 24th Fl., New York, NY 10019-4801. 212-708-0400.
E-mail: info@all-story.com. Web site: www.zoetrope-stories.com. Quarterly. Circ.: 40,000. Adrienne Brodeur, Editor-in-Chief. **Description:** Literary publication of stories and one-act plays. **Fiction:** Stories and one-act plays; under 7,000 words; good rates. **Tips:** No submissions accepted from June 1 through August 31. **Queries:** Preferred. **Response:** 4 months, SASE. **Payment:** On acceptance.

ZYZZYVA

P.O. Box 590069, San Francisco, CA 94159-0069. 800-462-1985.
E-mail: editor@zyzzyva.org. Web site: www.zyzzyva.org. 3x/year. $11/issue, $24/year. Circ.: 4,000. Howard Junker, Editor. **Description:** A journal of West coast writers

and artists. Pays $50/piece. **Fiction:** Freestanding (i.e., no book excerpts). **Non-fiction:** Essays. **Poetry:** Yes. **Tips:** Accepts material only from current West Coast (CA, OR, WA, HI, AK) residents. **Queries:** Not necessary. **E-Queries:** No. **Unsolicited mss:** Accepts. **Response:** Submissions 1 month, SASE. **Freelance Content:** 85%. **Rights:** 1st serial. **Payment:** On publication.

MYSTERY & DETECTIVE

ALFRED HITCHCOCK'S MYSTERY MAGAZINE
475 Park Ave. S., New York, NY 10016. 212-686-7188.
Web site: www.mysterypages.com. 11x/year. $2.95/issue. Cathleen Jordan, Editor.
Description: Original mystery short stories. **Fiction:** Well-plotted, plausible mystery, suspense, detection, and crime stories. Ghost stories, humor, futuristic, or atmospheric tales considered if they include a crime (or the suggestion of one); up to 14,000 words; $.08/word. **Tips:** Submissions by new writers strongly encouraged. No reprints. **Queries:** Not necessary. **E-Queries:** No. **Unsolicited mss:** Accepts. **Response:** Submissions to 3 months, SASE required. **Freelance Content:** 100%. **Rights:** anthology, foreign serial. **Payment:** On acceptance.

COZY DETECTIVE MYSTERY
686 Jake Ct., McMinnville, OR 97128.
E-mail: papercapers@yahoo.com. 3-5x/year. $4.95/issue. Tom Youngblood, Editor.
Description: Mystery fiction by new authors breaking into the genre. **Fiction:** Mystery and suspense; to 15,000 words; $5-$10/story. **Nonfiction:** to 15,000 words; $5-$10. **Poetry:** With mystery content only; $3. **Tips:** Mystery element may be slight, but should be present. **Queries:** Not necessary. **E-Queries:** Yes. **Unsolicited mss:** Accepts. **Response:** 10-15 weeks, SASE. **Rights:** FNASR. **Payment:** On publication.

ELLERY QUEEN'S MYSTERY MAGAZINE
475 Park Ave. S., New York, NY 12572.
Web site: www.mysterypages.com. 11x/year. $2.95/issue, $33.97/year. Circ.: 300,000. Janet Hutchings, Editor. **Description:** A leading mystery magazine. Features quality writing, original plots, and professional craftsmanship. **Fiction:** All mystery and crime **Fiction:** police procedurals, private-eye stories, tales of suspense, traditional whodunits; 250-20,000 words (usually 2,500-10,000; 20,000 novellas from established authors); $.05-.08/word. **Poetry:** Humorous mystery verses; up to 1-2 pages. **Fillers:** Cartoons, mystery theme. **Tips:** Interested in new authors. Seeking private-eye stories (avoid sex, sadism, sensationalism for its own sake). "We are always in the market for the best detective, crime, and mystery stories being written today." **Queries:** Not necessary. **E-Queries:** No. **Unsolicited mss:** Accepts. **Response:** 3 months, SASE required. **Freelance Content:** 95%. **Rights:** 1st serial. **Payment:** On acceptance.

HARDBOILED

Gryphon Publications, P.O. Box 209, Brooklyn, NY 11228-0209.
Web site: www.gryphonbooks.com. Gary Lovisi, Editor. **Description:** Hard-hitting fiction by new masters. Mind-blasting non-fiction, riveting private eye and crime stories. **Fiction:** Cutting-edge crime fiction, with impact; under 3,000 words. **Queries:** Preferred. **E-Queries:** No. **Unsolicited mss:** Accepts. **Response:** Queries 2 weeks, submissions 6 weeks, SASE. **Freelance Content:** 35%. **Rights:** 1st NA.

THE MYSTERY REVIEW

P.O. Box 233, Colborne, Ontario, Canada K0K 1S0. 613-475-4440.
E-mail: mystery@reach.net. Web site: www.TheMysteryReview.com. Quarterly. Barbara Davey, Editor. **Description:** Reviews, interviews, word games, and puzzles related to mystery titles and authors. No fiction. Pays honorarium. **Queries:** Required. **E-Queries:** Yes. **Unsolicited mss:** Does not accept. **Freelance Content:** 90%. **Rights:** 1st. **Payment:** On publication.

MYSTERY TIME

P.O. Box 2907, Decatur, IL 62524.
Semiannual. $10/yr. Circ.: 100. Linda Hutton, Editor. **Description:** Encourages beginning writers who can produce a clever plot. Female characters preferred. **Fiction:** Suspense; a touch of humor is always welcome; 1,500 words; ¼ cent/word. **Poetry:** Must relate to mysteries or famous authors; 20 lines; $5/poem. **Tips:** Rely on plot twists, rather than blood 'n' gore. Short stories only, do not submit novels. **Queries:** Not necessary. **E-Queries:** No. **Unsolicited mss:** Accepts. **Response:** Submission 1 month, SASE. **Freelance Content:** 90%. **Rights:** One-time. **Payment:** On acceptance.

NEW MYSTERY MAGAZINE

101 W. 23rd St., PMB 7, New York, NY 10011. 212-353-1582.
Web site: www.newmystery.com. Quarterly. Charles Raisch, Editor. **Description:** Mystery, crime, detection, and suspense short stories, **Fiction:** Prefers sympathetic characters in trouble, visual scenes; 2,000-6,000 words; pays to $500. **Columns, Departments:** Book reviews, 250-2,000 words, of upcoming or recent novels. **Tips:** No true-crime stories accepted. **Payment:** On publication.

OVER MY DEAD BODY!

P.O. Box 1778, Auburn, WA 98071-1778.
E-mail: omdb@Worldnet.att.net. Web site: www.overmydeadbody.com. Quarterly. $5.95/issue, $20/year. Circ.: 1,000. Cherie Jung, Editor. **Description:** Mystery, suspense, and crime fiction and nonfiction. **Fiction:** Mystery or crime-related fiction, from cozy to hardboiled, including suspense, and cross-over mysteries; to 4,000 words; $.01/word. **Nonfiction:** Author profiles/interviews, crime and mystery-related topics; to 2,500 words; $10-$35. **Queries:** Required. **E-Queries:** Yes. **Unsolicited mss:** Accepts. **Response:** 2-6 weeks, SASE. **Freelance Content:** 100%. **Rights:** FNASR. **Payment:** On acceptance. **Contact:** Bill Wemple.

THE STRAND

PO Box 1418, Birmingham, MI 48012-1418. 248-788-5948. E-mail: strandmag@worldnet.att.net. Quarterly. Andrew Gulli, Editor. **Description:** Featured pieces are modeled after the writing styles of Sir Arthur Conan Doyle, Daphne de Maurier, and Robert Louis Stevenson. **Fiction:** 3,000-5,000 words; $50-$150. **Payment:** On publication.

ROMANCE & CONFESSION

BLACK ROMANCE

233 Park Ave. S., New York, NY 10003. 212-780-3500. E-mail: jivemagazine@yahoo.com. Bimonthly. $2.50. Circ.: 50,000. Takesha D. Powell, Editor. **Description:** Short romantic fiction for African-American women. **Fiction:** Romance fiction, first-person, featuring African-American women; 19-21 pages; pay varies. **Tips:** Avoid cultural stereotypes. Stories should be juicy (mild sex scenes), romantic, but not offensive. **Queries:** Not necessary. **E-Queries:** Yes. **Unsolicited mss:** Accepts. **Response:** 3-4 weeks, SASE. **Freelance Content:** 100%. **Rights:** All. **Payment:** On publication.

BLACK SECRETS

Sterling MacFadden, 233 Park Ave. South, 6th Fl, New York, NY 10003. 212-780-3500. E-mail: jpestaina@sterlingmacfadden.com. Web site: www.sterlingmacfadden.com. Monthly. Circ.: 65,000. Takesha Powell, Editor. **Description:** Erotic, short, romantic fiction for African-American women. **Queries:** Required. **E-Queries:** Yes. **Unsolicited mss:** Accepts. **Freelance Content:** 100%. **Rights:** All. **Payment:** On publication.

INTIMACY

233 Park Ave. S., 7th Fl., New York, NY 10003. 212-780-3500. E-mail: takpow@aol.com. Web site: www.sterlingmacfadden.com. Bimonthly. $2.50/issue. Circ.: 50,000. Takesha D. Powell, Editor. **Description:** Short first-person romantic fiction, for African-American women. **Fiction:** For black women, ages 18-45; must have contemporary plot with 2 romantic and intimate love scenes; 19-21 pages. **Tips:** Avoid clichés, profanity, stereotypes. **Queries:** Not necessary. **E-Queries:** Yes. **Unsolicited mss:** Accepts. **Response:** 3-4 weeks, SASE required. **Freelance Content:** 100%. **Rights:** All. **Payment:** On publication.

JIVE

Sterling MacFadden, 233 Park Ave. South, 6th Fl, New York, NY 10003. 212-780-3500. E-mail: jpestaina@sterlingmacfadden.com. Web site: www.sterlingmacfadden.com. monthly. Circ.: 60,000. Takesha Powell, Editor. **Description:** Romantic fiction for African-American women. **Fiction:** Focus on emotions of main character; pays

$100-$125. **Queries:** Required. **E-Queries:** Yes. **Unsolicited mss:** Accepts. **Freelance Content:** 100%. **Rights:** All. **Payment:** On publication.

ROMANCE AND BEYOND
3527 Ambassador Caffery Pkwy., PMB 9, Lafayette, LA 70503-5130. 337-991-9095. E-mail: rbeyond@aol.com. Web site: www.romanceandbeyond.com. Quarterly. $20. Mary Tarver, Editor. **Description:** Speculative romantic short stories and poetry, combining elements of romance with science fiction, fantasy, and the paranormal. **Fiction:** Up to 10,000 words; $.005/word. **Poetry:** Length varies; pays in copies. **Tips:** Internal conflict created by attraction between hero and heroine. Tone can be dark to humorous, but story must be a romance with happy ending. Sources of external conflict left to your imagination, the more original the better. **Queries:** Not necessary. **E-Queries:** No. **Unsolicited mss:** Accepts. **Response:** Submission 4 months, SASE. **Freelance Content:** 100%. **Rights:** One-time. **Payment:** On acceptance.

ROMANTIC TIMES MAGAZINE
55 Bergen St., Brooklyn, NY 11201. 718-237-1097.
Web site: romantictimes.com. **Description:** Topics on the romance-fiction publishing industry.

TRUE ROMANCE
233 Park Ave. S., New York, NY 10003. 212-979-4800.
E-mail: trueromance@sterlingmacfadden.com. Web site: www.truestorymail.com. Monthly. $2.50/issue. Circ.: 225,000. Pat Vitucci, Editor. **Description:** From tender passion to broken hearts, offers wonderful stories of romantic love. **Fiction:** Topical stories based on news events; intriguing subjects; 1,000-10,000 words; $.03/word. **Poetry:** Up to 24 lines; $10-30. **Columns, Departments:** That's My Child; Loving Pets (photo and 50 words); Cupid's Corner (photo and 750 words); That Precious Moment (1,000 words); $50-100. **Tips:** Readers must sympathize with the narrator. **Queries:** Preferred. **E-Queries:** No. **Unsolicited mss:** Accepts. **Response:** 8-12 months, SASE. **Freelance Content:** 100%. **Payment:** On publication.

WOMAN'S WORLD
270 Sylvan Ave., Englewood Cliffs, NJ 07632.
E-mail: dearww@aol.com. Kathy Fitzpatrick, Managing Editor. **Description:** For middle-income women, ages 18-60, on love, romance, careers, medicine, health, psychology, family life, travel; dramatic stories of adventure or crisis, investigative reports. **Fiction:** Fast-moving short stories, 1,000 words, with light romantic theme; prefers dialogue-driven to propel the story. (Specify "short story" on outside of envelope.) Mini-mysteries, 1,200 words, with "whodunit" or "howdunit" theme. No science fiction, fantasy, horror, ghost stories, or gratuitous violence. Pays $1,000 for short stories; $500 for mini-mysteries. **Nonfiction:** Articles (query first), 600-1,800 words; pays $300-$900. **Payment:** On acceptance.

SCIENCE FICTION & FANTASY

ABORIGINAL SF
12 Emeline St., Woburn, MA 01801.
Web site: www.AboriginalSF.com. Charles C. Ryan, Editor. **Description:** Short stories (2,500-6,500 words), and poetry (1-2 typed pages), with strong science content; lively, unique characters; well-designed plots. No sword-and-sorcery, horror, or fantasy. SASE for guidelines. **Fiction:** Pays $200. **Poetry:** Pays $15. **Fillers:** Science-fiction jokes, $10; cartoons, $20. **Payment:** On publication.

ABSOLUTE MAGNITUDE
P.O. Box 2988, Radford, VA 24143.
Web site: www.sfsite/dnaweb/home.htm. Quarterly. Warren Lapine. **Description:** Character-driven technical science fiction. **Fiction:** 1,000-25,000 words (no fantasy, horror, satire, or funny science fiction); pays $.01-$.05/word. **Payment:** On publication.

ANALOG SCIENCE FICTION AND FACT
475 Park Ave. S., New York, NY 10016. 212-686-7188.
E-mail: analog@dellmagazines.com. Web site: www.analogsf.com. 11x/year. $3.50/issue, $39.97/year. Circ.: 50,000. Stanley Schmidt, Editor. **Description:** Science fiction, with strong characters in believable future or alien settings. Home to many of science fiction's foremost writers, with long tradition of discovering and cultivating new talent. **Fiction:** Short stories, 2,000-7,500 words; novelettes, 10,000-20,000 words; serials, to 80,000 words; $.04-$.08/word. **Nonfiction:** Future-related articles; up to 4,000 words; $.06/word. **Poetry:** Yes; $1/line. **Queries:** Preferred. **E-Queries:** No. **Unsolicited mss:** Accepts. **Response:** 1 month, SASE required. **Freelance Content:** 100%. **Rights:** FNASR, nonexclusive foreign serial. **Payment:** On acceptance.

ASIMOV'S SCIENCE FICTION MAGAZINE
475 Park Ave. S., 11th Fl., New York, NY 10016. 212-686-7188.
E-mail: asimovs@dellmagazines.com. Web site: www.asimovs.com. 11x/year. Circ.: 40,000. Gardner Dozois, Editor. **Description:** Short, character-oriented science fiction and fantasy. **Fiction:** Stories in which characters, rather than science, provide main focus for reader's interest. Mostly serious, thoughtful fiction, some humorous; up to 30,000 words; $.06-$.08/word. **Poetry:** Up to 40 lines; $1/line. **Tips:** Borderline fantasy fine, but no Sword & Sorcery. No explicit sex or violence. **Queries:** Not necessary. **E-Queries:** No. **Unsolicited mss:** Accepts. **Response:** No queries please, submission 2-3 months, SASE required. **Freelance Content:** 90%. **Rights:** First English Rights, nonexclusive reprint rights. **Payment:** On acceptance.

CENTURY MAGAZINE
Century Publishing, Inc., P.O. Box 150510, Brooklyn, NY 11215-0510.
Web site: www.centurymag.com. Robert K.J. Killheffer. **Description:** Literary

science fiction, fantasy, and magic realism. **Fiction:** 1,000-20,000 words; pays $.04-$.06/word. **Payment:** On acceptance.

DRAGON
1801 Lind Ave. SW, Renton, WA 98055. 425-204-8000.
Web site: www.wizards.com. Dave Gross, Editor. **Description:** On fantasy and science fiction role-playing games. **Fiction:** Fantasy, 1,500-8,000 words; pays $.05-$.08/word. **Nonfiction:** Articles, 1,500-7,500 words; pays $.04/word. **Tips:** All submissions must include a disclosure form. **Payment:** On publication.

FLESH AND BLOOD
121 Joseph St., Bayville, NJ 08712.
E-mail: horrorjack@aol.com. Web site: www.geocities.com. 3x/year. Circ.: 500. Jack Fisher, Editor. **Description:** Features dark fantasy, bizarre, and supernatural stories. Despite name, prefers work that is subtle, magic realism, bizarre eccentric, avant-garde, or any mix thereof. **Fiction:** Currently seeking horror/dark fantasy work. Should have one or more of the following elements: darkly fantastic, surreal, supernatural, bizarre, offbeat; 4,000 words max; $.005-$.02/word. **Tips:** Do not exceed maximum word count. Stories should be unique, entertaining, and imaginative. The more descriptive and dark, the better. Avoid stories with insane main characters; about obese people who eat others or who are evil; stories not set in the modern day; over-used vampire, werewolf stories; tales about evil gods and their followers; based solely on monsters; excessive gore, blood, sex, etc. **Queries:** Preferred. **E-Queries:** Yes. **Unsolicited mss:** Accepts. **Response:** 1-3 weeks, SASE required. **Rights:** FNASR. **Payment:** On publication.

HADROSAUR TALES
Hadrosaur Productions, P.O. Box 8468, Las Cruces, NM 88006.
Semi-annual. $5.95/issue, $10.00/year. Circ.: 100. David Summers, Editors. **Description:** Short stories and poetry. **Fiction:** Literary science fiction and fantasy. Contemporary or historical fiction welcome if a mythic or science-fictional element. Psychological or character-oriented horror considered if no graphic violence; 6,000 words max.; $6/story. **Poetry:** Science fiction and fantasy imagery, themes; 50 lines max.; $2. **Art:** Pen-and-ink line drawings (cover); pay negotiable. **Tips:** Avoid cliche-fantasy (e.g., lone knight goes off to slay the evil dragon). **Queries:** Not necessary. **E-Queries:** Yes. **Unsolicited mss:** Accepts. **Response:** Queries 1 week, submissions 1-6 weeks, SASE. **Freelance Content:** 100%. **Rights:** one-time. **Payment:** On acceptance.

THE LEADING EDGE
3163 JKHB, Provo, UT 84604.
E-mail: tle@byu.edu. Web site: http://tle:clubs.byu.edu. Semiannual. $11.85 (3 issues). Circ.: 500. Brandon Sanderson, Editor. **Description:** Science fiction and fantasy. Publishes many new writers. **Fiction:** 18,000 words max.; $.01/word ($10-$100 max.). **Nonfiction:** On science fiction, fantasy, or author interviews; 10,000 words

max.; pays in copies. **Poetry:** Length varies; $4/page. **Columns, Departments:** Book reviews; pays in copies. **Tips:** Avoid rehashed plots, poor mechanics, poor plot resolution. No sex, graphic violence, strong language. **Queries:** Not necessary. **E-Queries:** No. **Unsolicited mss:** Accepts. **Response:** Submissions 4-6 months, SASE. **Freelance Content:** 100%. **Rights:** FNASR. **Payment:** On publication.

LOCUS
P.O. Box 13305, Oakland, CA 94661. 510-339-9196.
Web site: www.locusmag.com. Monthly. Circ.: 7,500. **Description:** For professional writers and publishers of science-fiction, covers industry news.

MAGAZINE OF FANTASY & SCIENCE FICTION
P.O. Box 3447, Hoboken, NJ 07030.
E-mail: GordonFSF@aol.com. Web site: www.fsfmag.com. Monthly. $3.50/issue (U.S.), $3.95 (Canada). Circ.: 40,000. Gordon Van Gelder, Editor. **Description:** Digest-sized, devoted to speculative fiction. **Fiction:** Prefers character-oriented stories. Science fiction element may be slight, but present; up to 25,000 words; $.05-$.08/word. **Tips:** Receives much fantasy, needs science fiction or humor. **Queries:** Preferred. **E-Queries:** No. **Unsolicited mss:** Accepts. **Response:** 8 weeks, SASE. **Rights:** worldwide serial, and option on anthology. **Payment:** On acceptance.

NIGHT TERRORS
1202 W. Market St., Orrville, OH 44667-1710. 330-683-0338.
E-mail: dedavidson@night-terrors-publications.com.
Web site: www.night-terrors-publications.com. Annual. $6/issue. Circ.: 1,000. Mr. D.E. Davidson, Editor. **Description:** Short stories of psychological horror, the supernatural, or occult. Emphasis on "continuing terror"; stories should have beginning, middle, and end, but in the end, the terror/threat should not be resolved. **Fiction:** 2,000-5,000 words; pay in copies or by arrangement. **Tips:** Prefers stories which make the reader think and grow edgy, not those which make them flinch or grow nauseous. No horror in which women or children are abused; no stories with child as point-of-view character. **Queries:** Not necessary. **E-Queries:** Yes. **Unsolicited mss:** Accepts. **Response:** Queries 1 week, submissions 12 weeks, SASE. **Freelance Content:** 95%. **Rights:** FNASR. **Payment:** On publication.

OF UNICORNS AND SPACE STATIONS
P.O. Box 200, Bountiful, UT 84011-0200.
E-mail: mailroom@genedavis.com. Web site: www.genedavis.com. Semiannual. $4/issues. Circ.: 500. Gene Davis, Editor. **Description:** Science fiction and fantasy magazine, for adults, but family friendly. **Fiction:** Science fiction or fantasy, sometimes a little horror; 250-5,000 words; $.05/word. **Poetry:** Prefers fixed form poetry; any reasonable length; $.05/word, $5 max. **Art:** b/w line art. **Queries:** Not necessary. **E-Queries:** Yes. **Unsolicited mss:** Accepts. **Response:** 3 months, SASE. **Freelance Content:** 100%. **Payment:** On publication.

ON SPEC

P.O. Box 4727, Edmonton, Alberta, Canada T6E 5G6. 780-413-0215. E-mail: onspec@earthling.net. Web site: www.icomm.ca/onspec/. Quarterly. $5.95. Circ.: 1,500. Diane Walton, General Editor. **Description:** Science fiction, horror, fantasy, and speculative fiction; fiction and poetry. **Fiction:** Original unpublished science fiction, fantasy, horror, ghost stories, fairy stories, magic realism, speculative fiction, etc.; up to 6,000 words; to $180 Canadian. **Poetry:** Science fiction, fantasy themes; up to 100 lines; to $20 Canadian. **Queries:** Not necessary. **E-Queries:** Yes. **Unsolicited mss:** Accepts. **Response:** 1-2 weeks, SASE. **Rights:** FNASR. **Payment:** On acceptance.

OUTER DARKNESS

1312 N. Delaware Pl., Tulsa, OK 74110. 918-832-1246. Quarterly. $2.95 (by mail, $3.95). Circ.: 500. Dennis Kirk. **Description:** "Where Nightmares Roam Unleashed," horror and science fiction. Illustrated, also poetry, cartoons, and interviews. **Fiction:** Traditional horror and science fiction; 1,500 words. **Nonfiction:** Interviews with authors, artists, editors; up to 1,500 words. **Poetry:** Some free verse, prefers traditional rhyming; up to 30 lines. **Fillers:** Cartoons. **Art:** All stories illustrated; submit sample work. **Queries:** Not necessary. **E-Queries:** No. **Response:** Queries 2 weeks, submissions 6-8 weeks, SASE. **Freelance Content:** 25%. **Rights:** 1st. **Payment:** In copies.

PEGASUS ONLINE

E-mail: editors@pegasusonline.com. Web site: www.pegasusonline.com. Quarterly. Scott Marlowe, Editor. **Description:** E-zine for fantasy and science-fiction writers and readers. Fiction up to 7,500 words in either genre. No payment.

REALMS OF FANTASY

Sovereign Media Co., 11305 Sunset Hills Rd., Reston, VA 20190. 703-471-1556. Bi-monthly. Circ.: 110,000. **Description:** Topics and reviews of interest to readers of science fiction.

RIVERSIDE QUARTERLY

1101 Washington St., Marion, AL 36756-3213. **Description:** Science fiction and fantasy, reviews, critiques, poetry. **Fiction:** Science fiction and fantasy, to 3,500 words. **Nonfiction:** Reviews, criticism, any length. **Poetry:** Poetry and letters, any length. **Queries:** Preferred. **Unsolicited mss:** Accepts. **Payment:** In copies.

SCAVENGER'S NEWSLETTER

833 Main, Osage City, KS 66523-1241. 785-528-3538. E-mail: foxscar1@jc.net. Web site: www.jlgiftsshop.com/scav/index.html. Monthly. $22/yr. Circ.: 600. Janet Fox, Editor. **Description:** Market newsletter for science fiction, fantasy, horror, and mystery writers and artists, focusing on small presses. **Fiction:** Flash genre fiction; up to 1,200 words; $5. **Nonfiction:** Articles for genre

writers/artists; up to 1,500 words; $5. **Poetry:** Avoid rhymed; up to 10 lines; $3. **Fillers:** Short writer/artist humor; 500-700 words; $3. **Art:** Black-and-white illustrations, 7″ x 8½″ covers and small fillers; $5 per cover and $3 per filler. **Tips:** Do not ignore word-length guidelines; space is limited. **Queries:** Not necessary. **E-Queries:** Accepts. **Unsolicited mss:** Accepts. **Response:** Queries 2-7 days, submissions 1-4 weeks. **Freelance Content:** 10%. **Payment:** On acceptance.

SPACE AND TIME

138 W. 70 St. 4B, New York, NY 10023-4468.
Web site: www.cith.org/space&time.html. Biannual. $5/issue. Circ.: 2,000. Gordon Linzner, Editor. **Description:** Science fiction, fantasy, horror, and things that fall between the cracks. Also, a healthy selection of poetry (same genre), along with the occasion short feature. **Fiction:** Science-fiction, fantasy, horror; 10,000 words max.; $.01/word. **Poetry:** All styles and forms (rhymed, unrhymed, etc.). **Art:** b/w artwork assigned, to illustrate specific stories. Send photocopied samples; $10. **Tips:** Avoid clichés. No media fiction. Appreciates material that deserves to be in print, but which other magazines don't quite know what to do with. **Queries:** Not necessary. **E-Queries:** No. **Unsolicited mss:** Accepts. **Response:** Submissions 1-4 months. **Freelance Content:** 99%. **Rights:** FNASR. **Payment:** on publication.

STRANGE HORIZONS

Web site: www.strangehorizons.com. **Description:** E-zine of speculative and science fiction. **Fiction:** To 5,000 words; pays $.04/word. **Nonfiction:** Articles, 1,000-5,000 words; pay varies. **Poetry:** To 100 lines. **Columns, Departments:** Art and book reviews, 750-1,000 words. **Tips:** No simultaneous submissions. Submit via email: fiction@strangehorizons.com (or: poetry@, gallery@, or articles@). **Queries:** Required. **E-Queries:** Yes. **Rights:** 1st, worldwide (exclusive for 2 months, then reverts to author).

TALEBONES

Fairwood Press, 5203 Quincy Ave. SE, Auburn, WA 98092.
E-mail: talebones@nventure.com. Web site: www.fairwoodpress.com. Quarterly. $5/issue, $18/year. Circ.: 650. Patrick and Honna Swenson, Editors. **Description:** Science fiction and dark fantasy. **Fiction:** Sci-fi and dark fantasy stories with punch, often slanted toward darker fiction. 6,000 words; $.01-$.02/word. **Poetry:** All suitable forms and themes; $7. **Fillers:** Cartoons; $10. **Art:** Most formats; $15-50. **Tips:** Send cover letter, but keep it to the point. **Queries:** Not necessary. **E-Queries:** Yes. **Unsolicited mss:** Accepts. **Response:** 1-8 weeks, SASE. **Rights:** FNASR. **Payment:** On acceptance.

THE URBANITE

Box 4737, Davenport, IA 52808.
Web site: members.tripod.com/theurbanite/. 3x/year. Mark McLaughlin. **Description:** Dark fantasy, horror (no gore), surrealism, reviews, and social commentary **Fiction:**

To 3,000 words; pays $.02-$.03/word. **Poetry:** Free-verse, to 2 pages, $10. **Tips:** Query for coming themes. **Payment:** On acceptance.

WEIRD TALES

DNA Publications, 123 Crooked Ln., King of Prussia, PA 19406-2570. 610-275-4463. E-mail: owlswick@netax.com. Quarterly. $4.95. Circ.: 10,000. George Scithers, Darrell Schweitzer, Editors. **Description:** Horror and fantasy fiction. **Fiction:** Short stories, supernatural content, fantasy and horror (no science fiction); 10,000 words; $.02-$.06/word. **Queries:** Not necessary. **E-Queries:** Yes. **Unsolicited mss:** Accepts. **Response:** Queries 1 week, submissions 1-2 months, SASE. **Freelance Content:** 90%. **Rights:** FNASR. **Payment:** On acceptance.

BOOK PUBLISHERS

GENERAL ADULT BOOKS

This and the two following sections feature publishers, in turn, of general adult books, juvenile books, and religious books. These lists include a wide range of options, from some of the largest trade publishers to a selected list of many smaller presses and university presses.

Many publishers are willing to consider either unsolicited queries or manuscripts, but an increasing number have a policy of only reading submissions sent to them via literary agents. Since finding an agent willing to take on a new writer's work is not always an easy task, many writers still choose to present their manuscripts directly to publishers on their own.

Before even considering submitting a complete manuscript to an editor, it is always advisable to send a brief query letter describing the proposed book, and an SASE. The letter should also include information about the author's special qualifications for dealing with the particular topic covered, as well as any previous publication credits. An outline of the book (or a synopsis for fiction) and a sample chapter may also be included.

While it is common courtesy to submit a book manuscript to only one publisher at a time, it is often acceptable to submit the same query or proposal in advance to more than one editor simultaneously, as it takes an editor less time to review a query and respond with some indication of further interest. When sending multiple queries, however, always state clearly in your letter that you are doing this.

With any submission of manuscript materials to a publisher, be sure to enclose sufficient postage for the manuscript's return.

Royalty rates for hardcover books usually start at 10% of the retail price of the book and increase after a certain number of copies have been sold. Paperbacks generally have a somewhat lower rate, about 5% to 8%. Smaller presses and university presses sometimes base their royalty on net receipts (i.e., what they get after discounts), rather than the retail price (the "list price" printed on the book). It is customary for the publishing company to pay the author a cash advance against royalties when the book contract is signed or when the finished manuscript is received. Some publishers pay on a flat-fee basis.

Writers seeking publication of book-length poetry manuscripts are encouraged to consider contests that offer publication as the prize (see Prizes, in Other Resources).

ABINGDON PRESS
P.O. Box 801, Nashville, TN 37202. 615-749-6290.
Web site: www.abingdon.org.
Joseph A. Crowe, Editor.
Description: General-interest books: mainline, social issues, marriage/family, self-help, exceptional people. **Proposal Process:** Query with outline and 1-2 sample chapters. Guidelines available.

ACADEMIC PRESS

Division of Harcourt, Inc., 525 B St., Ste. 1900, San Diego, CA 92101. 619-231-0926.
Web site: www.academicpress.com.
Description: Scientific and technical books and journals for research scientists, students, and professionals; upper-level undergraduate and graduate science texts.
Contact: Editorial Dept.

ACADEMY CHICAGO PUBLISHERS

363 W. Erie St., Chicago, IL 60610. 312-751-7300.
E-mail: academy363@aol.com. Web site: www.academychicago.com.
Anita Miller, Editor.
Description: General-adult quality fiction and nonfiction. Classic mysteries; history; biographies; travel; books by and about women. No how-to, explicit sex, grotesque violence, sci-fi, horror. **Proposal Process:** Query with 4 sample chapters. SASE required. **Contact:** Jordan Miller.

ACTIVITY RESOURCES

20655 Hathaway Ave., Hayward, CA 94541. 510-782-1300.
E-mail: info@activity_resources.com. Web site: www.activityresources.com.
Mary Laycock, Editor.
Description: Math educational material only. Main focus is grades K-8. **Proposal Process:** Submit complete manuscript. **Payment:** Royalty.

ADAMS MEDIA CORPORATION

260 Center St., Holbrook, MA 02343. 781-767-8100.
E-mail: editors@adamsmedia.com. Web site: www.adamsmedia.com.
Edward Walters, Editor-in-chief.
Description: Nonfiction trade paperbacks with strong backlist potential. Subject categories include: self-help, how-to, lifestyles, relationships, parenting, inspiration, popular reference, business, small business, careers, and personal finance, among others.
Number of Books/Yr.: 60 titles/year. **Proposal Process:** Query with outline and sample chapters, and SASE. Response time: 1 month. Multiple queries accepted. No electronic queries. Hard copy. **Payment:** Royalty.

ADAMS-BLAKE PUBLISHING

8041 Sierra St., Fair Oaks, CA 95628. 916-962-9296.
E-mail: acanton@adams-blake.com. Web site: www.adams-blake.com.
Monica Blane, Senior Editor.
Description: Technical subjects for the corporate market. Books on business, careers, and technology. **Number of Books/Yr.:** 5 titles/year (100 submissions), 90% first-time authors, 100% unagented. **Proposal Process:** Query with outline. Response time: 4 weeks. Considers multiple queries. No electronic queries. Hard copy format preferred. **Payment:** Royalty, 10-15% net.

ADAMS-HALL PUBLISHING

P.O. Box 491002, Los Angeles, CA 90049. 800-888-4452.
Description: Business and personal finance books with wide market appeal.
Proposal Process: Query with proposed book idea, a listing of current competitive books, author qualifications, why the book is unique, and SASE. **Payment:** Royalty.
Contact: Sue Ann Bacon.

ADDISON-WESLEY LONGMAN INC.

One Jacob Way, Reading, MA 01867-3999. 781-944-3700.
Web site: www.awl.com.
Description: Several separate publishing groups. Adult nonfiction on current topics including science, health, psychology, business, biography, child care, etc. Educational focus. Royalty. **Contact:** Editorial Dept.

AFRICAN AMERICAN IMAGES

1909 W. 95th St., Chicago, IL 60643. 773-445-0322.
E-mail: aaf@africanamericanimages.com. Web site: africanamericanimages.com.
Description: Publishes adult and children's nonfiction Africentric books. **Number of Books/Yr.:** 6 title/year (100 submissions), 50% first-time authors, 80% unagented. Writers subsidize 10% of the cost of book production. **Proposal Process:** Query with complete manuscript. Considers multiple queries. Hard copy format. **Payment:** Royalty (10% net). **Tips:** Write to promote self-esteem, collective values, liberation, and skill development. See guidelines. **Contact:** Editorial Department.

ALASKA NORTHWEST BOOKS

Graphic Arts Center Publishing Co., P.O. Box 10306, Portland, OR 97296-0306.
503-226-2402.
E-mail: tricia@gacpc.com. Web site: www.gacpc.com.
Tricia Brown, Acquisitions Editor.
Description: Alaska Northwest Books and Westwinds Press imprints are regional and publish Alaskan subjects: history, natural history, memoir, cookbooks, reference guides, children's books, humor, travel. **Number of Books/Yr.:** 6-8 titles/year (250 Alaskan Northwest submissions and 100 Westwinds Press submissions), 10% by first-time authors, 90% unagented. **Proposal Process:** For nonfiction, query with outline and sample chapters. For children's books, send complete manuscript. Considers electronic queries. Prefers hard-copy format. **Payment:** Pays royalty (10-12% net). **Sample Titles:** Alaska Northwest Books: *Through Yup'ik Eyes* (memoir); *Alone Across the Arctic* (nonfiction adventure); *Quilt of Dreams* (ages 5+). Westwinds Press Books: *San Francisco's Golden Gate Park* (travel); *Heaven on the Half Shell*, (history/cooking); *A Child's California* (ages 7+). **Tips:** Avoid poetry, adult fiction, native "legend" written by non-Native Americans. Children's book authors, avoid partnering with an illustrator before submission has been accepted.

ALGONQUIN BOOKS OF CHAPEL HILL
Workman Publishing, Box 2225, Chapel Hill, NC 27515-2225. 919-967-0108.
Web site: www.algonquin.com.
Description: Trade books, literary fiction and nonfiction, for adults. **Contact:** Shannon Ravenel.

ALLWORTH PRESS
10 E. 23rd St., Suite 210, New York, NY 10010-4402.
Web site: www.allworth.com.
Description: Helpful books for professional artists, designers, writers, and photographers. **Proposal Process:** Query with outline and sample chapters. **Payment:** Royalty. **Contact:** Nicole Potter, Editor.

ALPINE PUBLICATIONS
225 S. Madison Ave., Loveland, CO 80537. 970-667-9317.
Web site: www.alpinepub.com.
B.J. McKinney, Publisher.
Description: Books about dogs and horses; breed books, care, training, health, management, etc. No stories, true or fiction. **Number of Books/Yr.:** 4 titles/year (50 submissions), 50% by first-time authors, 100% unagented. **Proposal Process:** Submit outline and sample chapters or complete manuscript, and SASE. Response time: 8-10 weeks. Electronic and multiple queries accepted. Hard copy preferred. **Payment:** Royalty.

ALYSON PUBLICATIONS
6922 Hollywood Blvd., Ste 1000, P.O. Box 4371, Los Angeles, CA 90078.
323-860-6065.
Web site: www.alyson.com.
Description: Gay and lesbian adult fiction and nonfiction books, from 65,000 words. "Alyson Wonderland" imprint: Children and young adult with gay and lesbian themes. **Proposal Process:** Query with outline only. **Payment:** Royalty. **Tips:** See web site for guidelines.

ANCHOR BOOKS
Knopf Publishing Group, a subsidiary of Random House, Inc., 201 E. 50th St., New York, NY 10022.
Description: Adult trade paperbacks and hardcovers. Original fiction, nonfiction, multicultural, sociology, psychology, philosophy, women's interest, etc. **Proposal Process:** No unsolicited manuscripts. Query first. **Contact:** Editor.

AND BOOKS
702 S. Michigan, South Bend, IN 46601. 219-232-3134.
Description: Adult nonfiction. Topics include computers, fine arts, health, philosophy, regional subjects (midwest), and social justice. **Contact:** Janos Szebedinsky.

ANDREWS MCMEEL

4520 Main Street, Kansas City, MO 64112-7701. 800-255-6734.
Web site: www.uexpress.com.
Description: Humor, how-to, reference, and general adult trade books. **Proposal Process:** Send query letter or proposal with up to 3 sample chapters. Hard copy format preferred. **Payment:** Royalty. **Contact:** Matt Lombardi.

ANHINGA PRESS

P.O. Box 10595, Tallahassee, FL 32302-0595. 850-521-9920.
E-mail: info@anhinga.org. Web site: www.anhinga.org.
Rick Campbell, Editorial Director.
Description: Publishes books of contemporary poetry. **Number of Books/Yr.:** 4 titles/year (ave. 750 submissions), 50% by first-time authors, 99% unagented. **Proposal Process:** Query or send complete manuscripts with SASE. Response time: 6 weeks. Multiple queries accepted. No electronic queries. **Payment:** Royalty or flat fee.

ANVIL PRESS

204A-175 East Broadway St., Vancouver, BC, Canada V5T IW2. 604-876-8710.
Web site: www.anvilpress.com.
Brian Kaufman, Editorial Director.
Description: Fiction, poetry, creative nonfiction, some nonfiction contemporary, progressive literature. **Number of Books/Yr.:** 6 titles/year, (200 submissions), 80% first-time authors, 100% unagented. **Proposal Process:** Query with outline and sample chapters. Considers multiple queries. Electronic queries accepted (letter only). Response time: 4-6 months. Hard copy format preferred. **Payment:** Royalty 10-15% Net. Flat fee advance $200-$500. **Sample Titles:** Adult nonfiction anthology: *Exact Fare Only, Good Bad Ugly Tales of Urban Transit.* Poetry: *Full Magpie Dodge.* **Tips:** Canadian authors only. Avoid sending formulaic writing. Looking for originality in style and voice, contemporary modern.

APPALACHIAN MOUNTAIN CLUB BOOKS

5 Joy St., Boston, MA 02108. 617-523-0636.
Web site: www.outdoors.org.
Beth Krusi, Publisher/editor.
Description: Regional (New England) and national nonfiction titles, 250-400 pages, for adults, juveniles, and young adults. Topics include guidebooks on non-motorized backcountry recreation, nature, outdoor recreation skills (how-to books), mountain history/biography, search and rescue, conservation, and environmental management. **Proposal Process:** Query with outline and sample chapters. Multiple queries considered. **Payment:** Royalty. **Contact:** Editorial Department.

ARCADE PUBLISHING
141 Fifth Ave., New York, NY 10010. 212-475-2633.
E-mail: arcadepub@aol.com.
Richard Seaver, Publisher.
Description: Fiction and nonfiction. **Proposal Process:** No unsolicited manuscripts. Query first. **Contact:** Cal Barksdale, Webb Younce.

ARTE PUBLICO PRESS
University of Houston, 4800 Calhoun, Houston, TX 77204-2174. 713-743-2601.
E-mail: gbaeza@bayou.uh.edu. Web site: www.arte.uh.edu.
Nicola's Kanellos, Editorial Director.
Description: Contemporary and historical literature by U.S. Hispanics, in both Spanish and English, with a focus on women's literature. "Pinata Books." Novels, short stories, poetry, drama, and autobiographies. **Number of Books/Yr.:** 30 titles/year (200 submissions), 80% first-time authors, 20% unagented. **Proposal Process:** Query with outline and sample chapters, and SASE. Accept multiple and electronic queries. Response time: 1 month. Hard copy format preferred. **Payment:** Royalty. **Sample Titles:** Adult Fiction: *Home Killings*. Adult Nonfiction: *Conflicts of Interest: The Collected Letters of Maria Amparo Ruiz de Burton*. Children's: (3-8) *Pepita Takes Time*. (8-13) *Trino's Time/Ankiza*. **Tips:** Looking for work by and about Hispanics in the U.S.

AVALON BOOKS
160 Madison Ave., New York, NY 10016. 212-598-0222.
E-mail: avalon_books@att.net. Web site: www.avalonbooks.com.
Erin Cartwright, Editor.
Description: We publish hardcover secular romances, mysteries, and westerns for the library market. Our books are wholesome, adult fiction, suitable for family reading. **Proposal Process:** Query with first 3 chapters and outline. SASE for guidelines. **Tips:** No old-fashioned, predictable, formulaic books. Avoid graphic or premarital sex or sexual tension in your writing.

AVALON TRAVEL PUBLISHING
Moon Publications, Inc., 5855 Beaudry Street, Emeryville, CA 94608. 530-345-5473.
Web site: www.moon.com.
Karen Bleske, Editor.
Description: Travel guides, 400-500 pages. **Proposal Process:** Will consider multiple submissions. Query. **Payment:** Royalty.

AVERY PUBLISHING GROUP
375 Hudson Street, 4th Fl, New York, NY 10014. 516-741-2155.
E-mail: info@averypublishing.com. Web site: www.averypublishing.com.
Dara Stewart, Managing Editor.
Description: Professional and trade books in health, fitness, nutrition, self-help. **Proposal Process:** Query with outline or sample chapters.

BAEN BOOKS

Baen Publishing Enterprises, P.O. Box 1403, Riverdale, NY 10471-0671.
718-548-3100.
Web site: www.baen.com.
Jim Baen, Editor-in-Chief.
Description: Strongly plotted science-fiction; innovative fantasy. **Proposal Process:** Query with synopsis and manuscript. **Payment:** Advance and royalty. **Tips:** Guidelines available for letter-sized SASE.

BALLANTINE BOOKS

Random House, Inc., 1540 Broadway, New York, NY 10036. 212-782-9000.
Web site: www.randomhouse.com/BB.
Leona Nevler, Editor.
Description: General fiction and nonfiction. **Proposal Process:** Accepts material only through agents.

BALSAM PRESS

36 E. 22nd St., 9th Fl., New York, NY 10010. 212-475-6895.
Barbara Krohn, Executive Editor.
Description: General and illustrated adult nonfiction. **Proposal Process:** Query first. **Payment:** Royalty.

BANKS CHANNEL BOOKS

P.O. Box 4446, Wilmington, NC 28406. 910-762-4677.
Description: Books of regional interest by North Carolina writers only. **Proposal Process:** Query for nonfiction of special interest to southeastern part of state. Fiction through biennial contest only. SASE for guidelines.

BARBOUR PUBLISHING: HEARTSONG PRESENTS

Barbour Publishing, Inc., P.O. Box 719, Uhrichsville, OH 44683. 740-922-6045.
E-mail: info@heartsongpresents.com. Web sites: www.barbourbooks.com or www.heartsongpresents.com.
Rebecca Germany, Acquisitions Editor.
Description: Adult mass-market inspirational romance (contemporary and historical). **Number of Books/Yr.:** 52 titles/year (300 submissions), 15% first-time authors, 90% unagented. **Proposal Process:** Query with outline (1-2 pages), 2-3 sample chapters. No electronic queries. Multiple queries okay. Response time: 3-4 months. Prefer hard-copy format. **Payment:** Royalty (8% net). **Tips:** SASE for guidelines.

BARRON'S EDUCATIONAL SERIES, INC.

250 Wireless Blvd., Hauppauge, NY 11788. 631-434-3311.
E-mail: info@barronseduc.com. Web site: barronseduc.com.
Wayne Barr, Director of Acquisitions.
Description: Nonfiction. Juvenile nonfiction (science, nature, history, hobbies, and how-to) and picture books for ages 3-6. Adult nonfiction (business, pet care,

childcare, sports, test preparation, cookbooks, foreign language instruction). **Proposal Process:** Query with SASE. See guidelines.

WILLIAM L. BAUHAN, PUBLISHER
Box 443, Dublin, NH 03444.
E-mail: wlbinc@aol.com. Web site: www.bauhanpublishing.com.
William L. Bauhan, Editor.
Description: Biographies, fine arts, gardening, architecture, and history books, with an emphasis on New England. **Proposal Process:** Submit query with outline and sample chapter.

BAYLOR UNIVERSITY PRESS
P.O. Box 97363, Baylor Univ., Waco, TX 76798-7363. 254-710-3164.
E-mail: David_Holcomb@baylor.edu. Web site: www.baylor.edu/~BUPress.
J. David Holcomb, editor.
Description: Scholarly nonfiction, especially oral history and church-state issues. **Proposal Process:** Query with outline. **Payment:** Royalty.

BEACON PRESS
25 Beacon St., Boston, MA 02108-2892. 617-742-2110.
Web site: www.beacon.org/Beacon.
Deborah Chasman, Editorial Director.
Description: General nonfiction: world affairs, women's studies, anthropology, history, philosophy, religion, gay and lesbian studies, nature writing, African-American studies, Latino studies, Asian-American studies, Native-American studies. **Proposal Process:** Agented manuscripts only. **Sample Titles:** Series: *Concord Library* (nature writing); *Barnard New Women Poets.*

BEAR & COMPANY, INC.
P.O. Box 2860, Santa Fe, NM 87504. 505-983-5968.
E-mail: bearco@bearco.com.
Gerald Cudahy Clow, Managing Editor.
Description: Nonfiction "that will help transform our culture philosophically, environmentally, and spiritually." **Proposal Process:** Query with outline, sample chapters, and SASE. **Payment:** Royalty.

BEHRMAN HOUSE INC.
11 Edison Place, Springfield, NJ 07081. 973-379-7200.
Web site: www.behrmanhouse.com.
David Behrman, Acquisitions.
Description: Hebrew language and Judaica textbooks for children. Adult Jewish nonfiction. **Proposal Process:** Query with outline and sample chapters. **Payment:** Flat fee or royalty.

BELLWETHER-CROSS PUBLISHING

18319 Highway 20 W., E. Dubuque, IL 61025. 815-747-6255.
E-mail: jcrow@shepherd.clrs.com.
Janet White, Senior Developmental Editor.
Description: College textbooks and lab manuals related to Environmental Science, Biology, Botany, Astronomy, Oceanography, etc. Also computer software related to publishing industry. **Number of Books/Yr.:** 55 titles/year (600 submissions), 100% by first-time authors, 100% unagented. **Proposal Process:** For educational materials, query with proposed book idea, list of current competitive books, and bio. For trade nonfiction, query with outline and sample chapters. SASE. Prefers electronic format. Multiple queries accepted. Response time: 2 weeks. **Payment:** Royalty.

BERKLEY PUBLISHING GROUP

A Division of Penguin Putnam, Inc., 375 Hudson St., New York, NY 10014.
726-282-5074.
E-mail: online@penguinputnam.com. Web site: www.penguinputnam.com.
Jacqueline Sach, Sr. Managing Editor.
Description: General-interest fiction and nonfiction; science fiction, suspense, mystery and romance. Publishes both reprints and originals. Paperback books, except for some hardcover mysteries and science fiction. Imprints include Ace Books, Diamond, Jam, Jove, Perige, and Riverhead Books. **Proposal Process:** Submit through agent only.

BERKSHIRE HOUSE PUBLISHERS

480 Pleasant St., Suite 5, Lee, MA 02138. 413-243-0303.
E-mail: info@berkshirehouse.com. Web site: www.berkshirehouse.com.
Philip Rich, Editorial Director.
Description: A series of regional travel guides and books about specific destinations of unusual charm and cultural importance, e.g., the Berkshires in Western Massachusetts. Occasionally publishes New England cookbooks or on country inns/country living. **Number of Books/Yr.:** 8-10 titles/year (ave. 300 submissions), 10% by first-time authors, 97% unagented. **Proposal Process:** Query letter, outline, prospectus, sample chapter if desired. Considers multiple and electronic queries. Response time: 4 weeks; varies. We do not consider children's manuscripts. **Payment:** Pays royalty. **Sample Titles:** *The Finger Lakes Book* (in *Great Destinations* Series); *The New Red Lion Inn Cookbook*; *The Hamptons Book*, 4th edition; *The Nantucket Book*, 2nd edition; *The NAPA and Sonoma Book*, 6th edition (spring 2002). Children's: We publish no children's books with the exception of *Willie Was Different*, a story by Norman Rockwell. **Tips:** Avoid submitting: general cookbooks (not related to inn, etc.); memoirs, history that is not related to New England; autobiography; biography (unless of relevance to our region). No how-to books. No self-help titles, health, religious, etc. No poetry or fiction (with possible exception of a novel related to our region).

THE BESS PRESS

3565 Harding Ave., Honolulu, HI 96816. (808) 734-7159.
E-mail: editor@besspress.com. Web site: www.besspress.com.
Revé Shapard, Editor.
Description: Nonfiction books about Hawaii and the Pacific for adults, children, and young adults. **Proposal Process:** Send query with outline. Hard copy. **Payment:** Royalty.

BEYOND WORDS PUBLISHING

20827 N.W. Cornell Rd., Suite 500, Hillsboro, OR 97124. 503-531-8700.
E-mail: info@beyondword.com. Web site: www.beyondword.com.
Laura Carlsmith, Adult Acquisitions Editor.
Description: Photography, personal growth, women's, spirituality, and children. **Number of Books/Yr.:** 25 titles/year (4,000 submissions), 90% first-time authors, 75% unagented. **Proposal Process:** Submit outline and sample chapters for adult titles; complete manuscript for juvenile titles. SASE. Multiple queries accepted. No electronic queries. Prefers hard copy format. Response time: 3 months. **Payment:** Royalty. **Tips:** No adult fiction, poetry, or fiction stories by children. Looking for original and creative children's stories. **Contact:** Barbara Mann, Children's Managing Editor.

BICK PUBLISHING HOUSE

307 Neck Rd., Madison, CT 06443. 203-245-0073.
E-mail: bickpubhse@aol.com. Web site: www.bickpubhouse.com.
Dale Carlson, President.
Description: Books, 64-250 pages, on wildlife rehabilitation, special needs/disabilities, psychology. **Proposal Process:** Submit outline and sample chapters. **Payment:** Royalty.

BINFORD & MORT PUBLISHING

5245 NE Elam Young Pkwy., Suite C, Hillsboro, OR 97124. 503-844-4960.
E-mail: polly@binfordandmort.com. Web site: www.binfordandmort.com.
Pam Henningsen, Publisher.
Description: Nonfiction books about the Pacific Northwest. **Number of Books/Yr.:** 10 titles/year (average 200 submissions), 5% by first-time authors, 90% unagented. **Proposal Process:** Send query. Accepts multiple queries. No electronic queries. Response time: 3 months. Prefers electronic or hard-copy format. **Payment:** Pays royalty, typically 5-10% range. **Tips:** No children's stories.

BLACK BELT PRESS

Black Belt Publishing, P.O. Box 551, Montgomery, AL 36101. 334-265-6753.
E-mail: jdavis@blackbelt.com. Web site: www.black-belt.com.
Jim Davis, Editor.
Description: Publishes books about life in the South of yesterday and today

Although specializes in books about Alabama, will consider other Southern subject matter. In some cases, will publish a book not inherently about life in the South (usually under their Starrhill Press imprint), if by a Southern author and very well written. **Number of Books/Yr.:** 10 titles/year (300 submissions), 20% first-time authors, 80% unagented. **Proposal Process:** Send query with sample chapters and SASE. Multiple and electronic queries accepted. Prefer hard copy. Subsidizes. **Payment:** Royalty. **Sample Titles:** Adult Fiction: *Thanh Ho Delivers,* tells the story of a Vietnamese refugee's difficulties starting a new life in Birmingham, Alabama, after the fall of Saigon in the 1970's. Adult Nonfiction: *Turnaround,* tells the inside story of Coach Bear Byrant's first year as head football coach at the University of Alabama. Recent book: *The Map That Lies Between Us,* was written by the popular mystery writer Anne George. **Tips:** Due to the volume of submissions received, we publish almost exclusively experienced and well known authors. We are not a good market for writers with no track record. No children's books, Civil War books, extremely religious books, or textbooks.

BLACK BUZZARD PRESS

Vias, Visions-International, 1007 Ficklen Rd., Fredericksburg, VA 22405. 540-310-0730.
Bradley R. Strahan, Acquisitions Editor.
Description: Serious, carefully crafted poetry. No light verse and no religious or polemic poetry. **Number of Books/Yr.:** 2 titles/year (ave. 100 submissions), 50% by first-time authors, 100% unagented. **Proposal Process:** Query with SASE. Hard copy. No electronic or multiple queries. **Payment:** Royalty. **Tips:** Read a sample Chapbooks $5.00 or full length book $11.00 to see what we do.

BLACKBIRCH PRESS, INC.

260 Amity Rd., P.O. Box 3573, Woodbridge, CT 06525. 203-387-7525.
E-mail: staff@blackbirch.com. Web site: www.blackbirch.com.
Beverly Larson, Editorial Director.
Description: Publishes books in a series, for 6-16-year olds. Series include *The Library of Famous Women* and *Building America.* **Proposal Process:** E-mail queries acceptable.

JOHN F. BLAIR, PUBLISHER

1406 Plaza Dr., Winston-Salem, NC 27103-1470. 336-768-1374.
E-mail: blairpub@blairpub.com. Web site: www.blairpub.com.
Carolyn Sakowski, Editor.
Description: Books, 70,000-100,000 words: biography, history, folklore, and guidebooks, with southeastern tie-in. **Proposal Process:** Query. No electronic submissions. **Payment:** Royalty.

BLOOMBERG PRESS

Bloomberg LP, 100 Business Park Dr., P.O. Box 888, Princeton, NJ 08542-0888. 609-279-4670.

Web site: www.bloomberg.com/books.

Jared Kieling, Editorial Director.

Description: Nonfiction, varying lengths, on topics such as investing, finance, e-commerce, and small business. **Proposal Process:** Query with outline and sample chapter or send complete manuscript. SASE. **Payment:** Royalty.

BLUE HERON PUBLISHING

1234 S.W. Stark St., Portland, OR 97205. 503-221-6841.

E-mail: guidelines@blueheronpublishing.com.

Web site: www.blueheronpublishing.com.

Daniel Urban, Acquisitions Editor.

Description: Books on writing and teaching writing for adults and young adults. Northwestern and Western fiction for adults, universities and high schools (especially multicultural themes), political mysteries. Original cookbooks, guides and how-to books that address such issues as health, wellness, finance, travel, career, and lifestyle. **Number of Books/Yr.:** 10-12 titles, (400-500 submissions). **Proposal Process:** Query with outline and SASE. Hard copy. Multiple queries and electronic queries OK. Response time: 2-4 months. **Payment:** Royalty. **Tips:** Publishes for general readers, writers, teachers, and young readers. No short fiction or nonfiction. Guidelines, including current needs, are posted on website. **Contact:** Dennis Stovall, Publisher.

BONUS BOOKS

160 E. Illinois St., Chicago, IL 60611. 312-467-0580.

E-mail: bb@bonus-books.com. Web site: www.bonus-books.com.

Erin Kahl, Acquisitions Editor.

Description: Publishes primarily nonfiction trade books, both paperback and hardcover. **Number of Books/Yr.:** 20-30 titles/year (avg. 600-800 submissions), 20% by first-time authors, 97% unagented. **Proposal Process:** Query with complete manuscript, include SASE. Multiple and electronic queries accepted. Prefers hard copy format. **Payment:** Royalty. **Sample Titles:** *Get the Edge at Blackjack*, (Games and gambling); *Stock Car Champions* (Sports); *The Coin Collector's Survival Manual* (Collectibles); *The Continuing Journey: Pinpointing Affluence in the 21st Century.* (Fundraising.) **Tips:** No fiction or poetry.

BOTTOM DOG PRESS, INC.

c/o Firelands College of BGSU, Huron, OH 44839. 419-433-5560.

E-mail: lsmithdog@aol.com.

Larry Smith, Director.

Description: Collections of personal essays, fiction, 50-160 pages, and poetry for book publication (50 poems). Subjects should be midwestern or working class in focus. **Proposal Process:** Query first. Do not send manuscripts. **Payment:** Royalty.

BRANDEN PUBLISHING COMPANY

17 Station St., Box 843, Brookline Village, MA 02447. 721-235-3634.
E-mail: branden@branden.com. Web site: www.branden.com.
Adolfo Caso, Editorial Department.
Description: General trade, mostly nonfiction, 250-300 pages. African-American, military, and Italian-American issues, health-related themes and biographies with emphasis on women.

BRASSEY'S, INC.

22841 Quicksilver Dr., Dulles, VA 20166. 202-333-2500.
E-mail: don@booksintl.com. Web site: www.brasseysinc.com.
Don McKeon, Publisher.
Description: Established publisher of military-related nonfiction that has recently expanded to include sports titles. Nonfiction books, 75,000-130,000 words. National and international affairs, history, foreign policy, defense, military biography, sports, and transportation. No fiction. **Number of Books/Yr.:** 60 titles/year (900 submissions), 10% first-time authors, 60% unagented. **Proposal Process:** Send query with synopsis, author bio, outline, sample chapters, and SASE. Response time: 1-2 months. Accepts electronic queries. Prefers hard-copy format. **Payment:** Royalty.

GEORGE BRAZILLER PUBLISHERS

171 Madison Ave., Suite 1103, New York, NY 10016. 212-889-0909.
George Braziller, Publisher.
Description: Fiction and nonfiction. Art history, collections of essays and short stories, anthologies. **Proposal Process:** Send art history manuscripts to Art Ed.; others to Fiction Ed. Send outline with sample chapters.

BREAKAWAY BOOKS

Box 24, Halcottsville, NY 12438. 212-898-0408.
E-mail: garth@breakawaybooks.com. Web site: www.breakawaybooks.com.
Garth Battista, Editor.
Description: Fiction and essays on sports, specifically on the experience of being an athlete. **Number of Books/Yr.:** 8 titles/year (hundreds of submissions), 80% first-time authors, 80% unagented. **Proposal Process:** Query with outline, sample chapters and SASE. Response time is slow. Accepts multiple queries. Prefers electronic queries. **Payment:** Royalty. **Tips:** Literary writing of the highest quality. No genre stories, how-tos, or celebrity bios.

BRIDGE WORKS

Box 1798, Bridgehampton, NY 11932. 631-537-3418.
Web site: bap@hamptons.com.
Barbara Phillips, Editorial Director.
Description: Small press specializing in quality fiction and nonfiction. No family memoirs, cookbooks, sci-fi, supernatural, romances. Biography, public policy, essays

on a single subjects welcome. **Number of Books/Yr.:** 8 titles/year (2,000 submissions), 50% first-time authors, 50% unagented. **Proposal Process:** Query with outline and sample chapters, include SASE. Prefer hard copy but electronic queries accepted. No multiple queries. Response time: 1 month. **Payment:** Royalty. **Tips:** Receives many admissions from agents; any unagented mss. must be very fresh and original in content, character, and setting.

BRIDGEWATER BOOKS
Imprint of Troll Communications, 100 Corporate Dr., Mahwah, NJ 07430.
201-529-4000.
Web site: www.troll.com.
Description: Hardcover picture books and anthologies.

BRISTOL PUBLISHING ENTERPRISES
P.O. Box 1737, San Leandro, CA 94577. 510-895-4461.
Web site: bristolcookbooks.com.
Patricia Hall, Editor.
Description: Cookbooks, craftbooks, health and pet care. **Number of Books/Yr.:** 12-20 titles/year (300 submissions), 18% first-time authors, 100% unagented. **Proposal Process:** Query with outline and sample chapters. Multiple queries accepted, no electronic queries. Prefers hard copy format. SASE required. **Payment:** Royalty. **Tips:** See website.

BROADWAY BOOKS
Doubleday Broadway Publising Group, Random House, Inc., 1540 Broadway, New York, NY 10036. 800-223-6834.
E-mail: (first initiallast name)@randomhouse.com.
Web site: www.broadwaybooks.com.
Lauren Marino, Editor.
Description: Adult nonfiction; small and very selective fiction list. **Proposal Process:** No unsolicited submissions. Query first.

BUCKNELL UNIVERSITY PRESS
Bucknell University, Lewisburg, PA 17837. 570-577-3674.
Web site: www.departments.bucknell.edu/univ_press.
Greg Clingham, Editorial Director.
Description: Scholarship and criticism in English, American, and comparative literature, cultural studies, history, philosophy, modern languages (especially Hispanic and Latin American studies), anthropology, political science, classics, cultural geography, or any combination of the above. **Number of Books/Yr.:** 38 titles/year (500 submissions) 50% by first-time authors, 100% unagented. **Proposal Process:** Query with outline and sample chapters. No multiple or electronic queries. Response time: Proposals 1 month, manuscripts 3-4 months. Hard copy format preferred. **Payment:** Royalty, 10% net. **Tips:** Excellent scholarship in the humanities and related social sciences; no "popular" material.

BULFINCH PRESS
3 Center Plaza, Boston, MA 02108. 617-263-2797.
Web site: www.bulfinchpress.com.
Michael Sand, Managing Editor.
Description: Illustrated fine art and photography books, painting, design (interior, exterior, architecture), coffee-table books, photojournalism. **Number of Books/Yr.:** 50 titles/year. **Proposal Process:** Query with outline or proposal, sample artwork and text (no originals), author/artist bio, and SASE. Accepts multiple queries. No electronic queries. Response time: 1 week-1 month. Hard copy format preferred. **Tips:** Visual material is crucial. **Contact:** Emily Martin, Dept. Asst.

BURFORD BOOKS
32 Morris Ave., Springfield, NJ 07081. 973-258-0960.
Web site: www.burfordbooks.com.
Peter Burford, Acquisition's Editor.
Description: Books on sports, the outdoors, military history, food and wine. **Number of Books/Yr.:** 25 titles/year (250 submissions), 50% first-time authors, 50% unagented. **Proposal Process:** Query with outline. Considers multiple and electronic queries. Prefers hard-copy format. Response time: 3 weeks. **Payment:** Royalty. **Tips:** Seeking well-written books on practically anything that can be done outside, from golf to gardening.

BUTTE PUBLICATIONS
P.O. Box 1328, Hillsboro, OR 97123-1328. 503-648-9791.
Web site: www.buttepublications.com.
Description: Books related to deafness and education, especially texts for pre-K to 12th grade. Also, college texts, parental and professional resources. Texts also used with autistic children, slow readers. Concentration is on the reading and writing aspects of teaching deaf children.

C&T PUBLISHING
1651 Challenge Dr., Concord, CA 94520.
E-mail: ctinfo@ctpub.com. Web site: www.ctpub.com.
Liz Aneloski, Editor.
Description: Quilting books, 64-200 finished pages. Focus is how-to, although will consider picture, inspirational, or history books on quilting. **Proposal Process:** Send query, outline, or sample chapters. Multiple queries considered. **Payment:** Royalty.

CALENDAR ISLANDS PUBLISHERS
477 Congress St., Suite 404-406, Portland, ME 04101. 207-828-0251.
Web site: www.calendarislands.com.
Peter Stillman, Publisher.
Description: Nonfiction, on teaching English from junior high level through college. **Proposal Process:** Query with outline and sample chapter; multiple queries considered. **Payment:** Royalty.

CAMBRIDGE UNIVERSITY PRESS

40 W. 20th St., New York, NY 10011-4211. 212-924-3900.

Web site: www.cup.org.

Richard Ziemacki, Director.

Description: Scholarly books and college textbooks: behavioral, biological, physical, social sciences, computer science, literature, music, and religion.

CAREER PRESS

3 Tice Rd., P.O. 687, Franklin Lakes, NJ 07417-0687. 201-848-0310.

Web site: www.careerpress.com. Also: www.newpagebooks.com.

Karen Wolf, Acquisitions.

Description: Publishes trade books in all business, reference, personal finance, and career categories. Also publishes New Page Books imprint, with general nonfiction in New Age, health, and self-help categories. **Proposal Process:** Query with outline. **Payment:** Royalty.

CAROUSEL PRESS

P.O. Box 6038, Berkeley, CA 94706-0038. 510-527-5849.

E-mail: traveluv@carousel-press.com. Web site: www.carousel-press.com.

Carole T. Meyers, Publisher.

Description: U.S. and Europe round-up travel guides. **Number of Books/Yr.:** 1 title/year (25 submissions), 50% by first-time authors, 75% unagented. **Proposal Process:** Send letter, table of contents, and sample chapter with SASE. Multiple and electronic queries accepted. Hard copy. **Payment:** Modest advance and royalty. **Tips:** We publish one or 2 new books each year and will consider out-of-print books that the author wants to update.

CARROLL AND GRAF PUBLISHERS, INC.

Avalon Publishing Group, 19 W. 21st St., Suite 601, New York, NY 10001. 212-627-8590.

Kent E. Carroll, Executive Editor.

Description: General fiction and nonfiction. **Proposal Process:** No unagented submissions.

CASABLANCA PRESS

Sourcebooks, Inc., 1935 Brookdale Road, #139, Naperville, IL 60563. 603-961-3900.

Web site: www.sourcebooks.com.

Todd Stocke, Editor.

Description: The relationships/love imprint of Sourcebooks, Inc. **Proposal Process:** Query with outline and sample chapters. **Payment:** Royalty.

CASSANDRA PRESS

P.O. Box 150868, San Rafael, CA 94915. 415-382-8507.

Contact Editorial Department.

Description: New age, holistic health, metaphysical, and psychological books.

Number of Books/Yr.: 2 titles/year. **Proposal Process:** Query with outline and sample chapters, or complete manuscript. Include SASE. Accepts multiple queries, no electronic queries. Prefers hard copy format. **Payment:** Royalty.

CATBIRD PRESS

16 Windsor Rd., North Haven, CT 06473-3015. 202-230-2391.
E-mail: catbird@pipline.com. Web site: www.catbirdpress.com.
Robert Wechsler, Acquisitions Editor.
Description: Fiction, literature and translations, creative nonfiction. **Number of Books/Yr.:** 4 titles/year, 10% first-time authors, 75% unagented. **Proposal Process:** Send outline with sample chapters and SASE. Response time: 1 month. Accepts multiple queries, but please notify. No electronic queries. Prefers hard copy format. **Payment:** Royalty, typically 7½%-12½%. **Sample Titles:** Fiction: *All His Sons*, by Frederic Raphael. **Tips:** Interested in high-quality writing, fiction that is not realistic, but instead takes one of the many alternative approaches to reality, with an interest in form and structure—more than plot and character.

CHECKMARK BOOKS

Facts on File, Inc., 11 Penn Plaza, New York, NY 10001-2006. 212-967-8800.
Web site: www.factsonfile.com.
Description: Focuses on careers, education, health, popular history and culture, fashion, and fitness. Looking for materials that fit a particular market niche that are high-quality, with a strong reference component. No memoirs, autobiographies, or fiction. **Proposal Process:** Query, with sample chapters or outline. **Payment:** Avance against royalty. **Contact:** Laurie Likoff.

CHELSEA GREEN PUBLISHING CO.

P.O. Box 428, White River Junction, VT 05001. 802-295-6300.
E-mail: aberolz@chelseagreen.com. Web site: www.chelseagreen.com.
Alan Berolzheimer, Editor.
Description: Publisher of books for sustainable living, based on the principle that human consumption needs to come in harmony with the natural world. Books with a strong practical orientation, on organic gardening, whole-foods cookbooks, alternative building, renewable energy, and nature and environmental titles. **Proposal Process:** Query with outline.

CHICAGO REVIEW PRESS

814 N. Franklin St., Chicago, IL 60610. 312-337-0747.
E-mail: publish@ipgbook.com. Web site: www.ipgbook.com.
Cynthia Sherry, Editor.
Description: Nonfiction: activity books for children, general nonfiction, architecture, parenting, how-to, and regional gardening and other regional topics. **Proposal Process:** Query with outline and sample chapters.

CHINA BOOKS

2929 24th St., San Francisco, CA 94110. 415-282-2994.
E-mail: info@chinabooks.com. Web site: www.chinabooks.com.
Greg Jones, Senior Editor.
Description: We publish books on all subjects relating to China, Chinese culture, and Chinese-American history. Adult nonfiction of varying lengths, also juvenile picture books, fiction, nonfiction, and young adult books. **Tips:** No novels or poetry. No "My trip to China" proposals.

CHRONICLE BOOKS

Chronicle Publishing Co., 85 Second St., 6th Fl, San Francisco, CA 94105. 415-537-3730.
E-mail: frontdesk@chronbooks.com. Web site: www.chronbooks.com.
Amy Novesky, Managing Editor.
Description: Fiction, art, photography, architecture, design, nature, food, giftbooks. Children's books. **Proposal Process:** Send proposal or complete manuscript for fiction with SASE. **Contact:** Editorial Dept..

CLARKSON POTTER PUBLISHERS

A Division of Random House, Inc., 201 E. 50th St., New York, NY 10022. 212-751-2600.
Web site: www.randomhouse.com.
Lauren Shakely, Editorial Director.
Description: Illustrated trade books about such topics as cooking, gardening, and decorating. **Proposal Process:** Submissions accepted through agents only.

CLEAR LIGHT PUBLISHERS

823 Don Diego, Santa Fe, NM 87501-4224. 505-989-9590.
E-mail: clpublish@aol.com. Web site: www.clearlightbooks.com.
Harmon Houghton, Publisher.
Description: Focuses on Southwestern themes, especially Native American cultures. Publishes nonfiction, fiction, picture books, and young adult books. Fiction includes: multicultural, historical, inspirational and regional. Seeking nonfiction mss on history, multicultural, ethnic issues, nature, religion, biographies of Native Americans.

CLEIS PRESS

P.O. Box 14684, San Francisco, CA 94114-0684. 415-575-4700.
Web site: www.cleispress.com.
Frédérique Delacoste, Acquisitions Editor.
Description: Lesbian and gay studies, literature by women; sexuality; travel. Fiction and nonfiction, 200 pages. No poetry. **Proposal Process:** Send SASE with 2 first-class stamps for catalog before querying. **Payment:** Royalty.

CLOVER PARK PRESS

P.O. Box 5067-T, Santa Monica, CA 90409-5067. 310-452-7657.
E-mail: cloverparkpr@loop.com. Web site: www.loop.com/~cloverparkpr.
Martha Grant, Editor.
Description: Nonfiction adult books on California (history, natural history, travel, culture, or the arts), biography of extraordinary women, nature, travel, exploration, scientific/medical discovery, travel, adventure. **Proposal Process:** Query with outline, sample chapter, author bio, and SASE.

COFFEE HOUSE PRESS

27 N. 4th St., Suite 400, Minneapolis, MN 55401. 612-338-0125.
Web site: www.coffeehousepress.org.
Allan Kornblum, Publisher.
Description: Publishes literary novels, full-length short story collections, poetry, essays, memoir, and anthologies. **Number of Books/Yr.:** 14 titles/year (5,000 submissions), 15% by first-time authors, 10% unagented. **Proposal Process:** Query with sample chapters. Considers multiple queries. No electronic queries. Response time: Sample 4-6 weeks, manuscript 2-6 months. Hard copy format preferred. **Payment:** Royalty. **Sample Titles:** *Ex Utero*, by Laurie Foos (Fiction). *Our Sometime Sister,* by Norah Labiner (fiction). *Glory Goes and Gets Some*, by Emily Carter (fiction). **Tips:** No genre fiction (mysteries, gothic romances, westerns, science fiction, or books for children).

CONARI PRESS

2550 Ninth St., Suite 101, Berkeley, CA 94710. 510-649-7192.
Web site: www.conari.com.
Julie Kessler, Editorial Director.
Description: Personal growth, spirituality, women's issues, relationships. **Number of Books/Yr.:** 35 titles/year (600 submissions). **Proposal Process:** Submit outline, sample chapters, and 6½" x 9½" SASE. Hard copy. Multiple queries OK. No electronic queries. Response time: 3-6 months. **Payment:** Royalty. **Contact:** Heather McArthur, Leslie Berriman.

CONFLUENCE PRESS

Lewis-Clark State College, 500 8th Ave., Lewiston, ID 83501-2698. 208-799-2336.
E-mail: conpress@lcsc.edu. Web site: www.confluencepress.com.
James R. Hepworth, Editor.
Description: Trade poetry, fiction, novels, essays, literary criticism, photography, art, science, and folklore. Special interest in the literature of the contemporary and American west. **Number of Books/Yr.:** 2 titles/year (1,000 submissions), 50% first-time authors, 75% unagented. **Proposal Process:** SASE. Include a formal cover letter. Multiple and electronic queries accepted. Hard copy. Response time: 6 weeks. **Payment:** Royalty. **Sample Titles:** Adult Non-Fiction: *Runaway,* by Mary Clearman Blew. Adult Poetry: *Out of the Ruins,* by William Johnson. **Tips:** Seeking writing about the contemporary American Northwest.

COPPER CANYON PRESS

P.O. Box 271, Port Townsend, WA 98368. 360-385-4925.
E-mail: poetry@coppercanyonpress.org. Web site: www.coppercanyonpress.org.
Sam Hamill, Editor.
Description: Poetry publisher. **Number of Books/Yr.:** 18 titles per year; (out of 1,000 submissions) 10% first time authors; 95% unagented. **Proposal Process:** No unsolicited manuscripts. **Payment:** Royalty. **Sample Titles:** *Cool, Calm & Collected,* by Carolyn Kizer. Spring Essence: *The Poetry of Ho Xuan Huong,* translated by John Balaban. **Tips:** Currently not accepting unsolicited manuscripts. Check website for updates. Annual Hayden Carruth Award for first, second, and third books. **Contact:** Michael Wiegers.

CORNELL UNIVERSITY PRESS

Box 250, Sage House, 512 E. State St., Ithaca, NY 14850. 607-277-2338.
Web site: www.cornellpress.cornell.edu.
Frances Benson, Editor-in-Chief.
Description: Scholarly nonfiction with particular strengths in anthropology, Asian studies, biological sciences, classics, history, industrial and labor relations, literary criticism and theory, natural history, philosophy, politics and international relations, psychology, Slavic studies, veterinary science, and women's studies. **Number of Books/Yr.:** 150 titles/year, 30% first-time authors, 90% unagented. **Proposal Process:** Query with outline, sample chapters, and SASE. Response time: 6-8 weeks. Hard copy format preferred but electronic query accepted. No multiple queries. **Payment:** Royalty. **Sample Titles:** *Breaking the Watch: The Meanings of Retirement in America,* by Joel Savishinsky; *Field Guide to the Birds of Cuba,* by Orlanda Garrido and Arturo Kirkconnel; *The Evidence of Things Not Said,* by James Baldwin, and The *Promise of American Democracy,* by Lawrie Balfour. **Tips:** Looking for academically sound books that contribute to scholarship and appeal to the educated general reader.

COUNCIL OAK BOOKS

1290 Chestnut St., Suite 2, San Francisco, CA 94109.
E-mail: kevincob@pacbell.net. Web site: www.counciloakbooks.net.
Kevin Bentley, Editor.
Description: Publisher of distinguished nonfiction books based in personal, intimate history (letters, diaries, memoir, and first-person adventure/travel); Native American history and spiritual teachings; small inspirational gift books; unique vintage photo books and Americana. **Number of Books/Yr.:** 10 titles/year (300 submissions), 25% by first-time authors, 75% unagented. **Proposal Process:** Send query and outline with SASE. Do not send complete manuscript. Multiple and electronic queries accepted. Hard copy format preferred. **Payment:** Royalty. **Tips:** Looking for unique, elegant voices whose history, teachings and experiences illuminate our lives. No fiction, poetry or children's books.

COUNTERPOINT

717 "D" Street NW, #203, Washington, DC 20004. 202-393-8088.
Description: Adult literary nonfiction, including art, religion, history, biography, science, and current affairs; literary fiction. **Proposal Process:** All submissions through agent only. **Payment:** Royalty. **Contact:** Acquisitions Editor.

THE COUNTRYMAN PRESS, INC.

W.W. Norton, P.O. Box 748, Woodstock, VT 05091. 802-457-4826.
Web site: www.countrymanpress.com.
Laura Jorstad, Managing Editor.
Description: Nonfiction: Country living; gardening; nature/environment; how-to; travel guidebooks; regional guidebooks on hiking, walking, canoeing, bicycling, mountain biking, cross-country skiing, and flyfishing for all parts of the country. Fiction: mystery. **Proposal Process:** Submit query or outline and 3 sample chapters, along with SASE. **Payment:** Pays royalty.

COWARD, MCCANN

Putnam & Bentley Publishing Group, 375 Hudson St., New York, NY 10014.
212-366-2000.
Description: Fiction and nonfiction. **Proposal Process:** Through agents only. No freelance submissions.

CRAFTSMAN BOOK COMPANY

6058 Corte del Cedro, P.O. Box 6500, Carlsbad, CA 92018. 760-438-7828.
E-mail: jacobs@costbook.com. Web site: www.craftsman-book.com
Laurence D. Jacobs, Editor.
Description: Construction manuals for the professional builder and contractor. **Number of Books/Yr.:** 12 titles/year (30 submissions), 90% by first-time authors, 100% unagented. **Proposal Process:** Query with outline and SASE. Multiple and Electronic queries accepted. Prefers hardy copy format. **Payment:** Royalty. **Tips:**

Looking for simple, practical hands-on text written in the second person. Only material for the professional builder. No handyman or do-it-yourself stuff.

CRANE HILL PUBLISHERS

3608 Clairmont Ave., Birmingham, AL 35222. 205-714-3007.
Web site: www.cranehill.com.
Shelley Duluca, Managing Editor.
Description: History, biography, memoirs, folklore, cookbooks, art, photography, and humor. Quality books that reflect the history, perceptions, experience, and customs of people in regional locales around the U.S. **Payment:** Royalty.

THE CREATIVE COMPANY

123 S. Broad St., Mankato, MN 56001. 507-388-1364.
E-mail: creativeco@aol.com.
Description: Nonfiction, mainly nature, adventure, memoir, and travel experiences, under 10,000 words; some adult fiction; juvenile fiction, non-fiction, and picture books, under 3,000 words. Royalty or flat fee. Imprints include Creative Education, Creative Editions, and Smart Apple Media. **Proposal Process:** Multiple queries considered. Send complete manuscript. **Contact:** Editorial Department.

CREATIVE HOMEOWNER PRESS

24 Park Way, Box 38, Upper Saddle River, NJ 07458. 201-934-7100.
E-mail: info@creativehomeowner.com. Web site: www.creativehomeowner.com.
Timothy O. Bakke, Editorial Director.
Description: Books on lifestyle for home and garden, including interior design/decorating, gardening/landscaping, and home improvement/repair. **Number of Books/Yr.:** 12-16 titles/year (20-30 submissions), 70% by first-time authors, 98% unagented. **Proposal Process:** Query. Accepts multiple and electronic queries. Response time: 2-4 months. Hard-copy format preferred. **Payment:** Flat fee, typical range is $20,000-$40,000. **Sample Titles:** *Wiring: Basic & Advanced Projects* (home improvement); *Lyn Peterson's Real-Life Decorating* (home decorating); *Advanced Home Gardening* (gardening). **Tips:** Avoid passive voice. Prefers straightforward, expository, instructional text in clear language.

CROSS CULTURAL PUBLICATIONS, INC.

P.O. Box 506, Notre Dame, IN 46556. 219-273-6526.
E-mail: crosscult@aol.com. Web site: crossculturalpub.com.
Cyriac K. Pullapilly, General Editor.
Description: All academic disciplines, also general-interest books. Special interest in intercultural and interfaith issues. Prefers books that push the boundaries of knowledge and existing systems of religion, philosophy, politics, economics, ethics, justice, and arts (whether through fiction, nonfiction, or poetry). **Number of Books/Yr.:** 30 titles/year (5,000 submissions), 30% by first-time authors, 90% unagented. **Proposal Process:** Send proposal with table of contents, resumé, and SASE. Multiple and electronic queries considered. Hard copy format preferred. **Payment:** Royalty. **Tips:** Primary concern is subject matter, then organization, clarity of argument, literary style. No superficially argued books.

THE CROSSING PRESS

97 Hangar Way, Watsonville, CA 95019. 408-722-0711.
E-mail: elaine@crossingpress.com. Web site: www.crossingpress.com.
Elaine Goldman Gill, Publisher.
Description: Natural and alternative health, spirituality, personal growth, self-help, empowerment, and cookbooks. **Payment:** Royalty.

CUMBERLAND HOUSE PUBLISHING

431 Harding Industrial Dr., Nashville, TN 37211. 615-832-1171.
E-mail: info@cumberlandhouse.com. Web site: www.cumberlandhouse.com.
Tilly Katz, Editorial Director.
Description: Historical nonfiction books, cooking, Christian titles. **Number of Books/Yr.:** 60 titles/year (1,300 submissions), 50% by first-time authors, 75% unagented. **Proposal Process:** Query with outline. No multiple or electronic queries accepted. Prefers hard copy format. Response time: 3-6 months. **Payment:** Royalty.
Sample Titles: Adult: *I Remember Joe DiMaggio* (Sports), *At Home in the Kitchen* (Cooking), *The Journey of Prayer* (Christian), and *Return Again to the Scene of the Crime* (History). **Tips:** No poetry or westerns. Accepts fiction, but more interested in nonfiction works.

CURBSTONE PRESS

321 Jackson St., Willimantic, CT 06226. 800-423-5110.
Web site: www.curbstone.org.
Judith Doyle, Alexander Taylor, Directors.
Description: Fiction, nonfiction, poetry books, and picture books that reflect a commitment to social change, with an emphasis on contemporary writing from Latin America and Latino communities in the U.S. **Proposal Process:** Agented material only. **Payment:** Royalty.

DA CAPO PRESS

10 East 53rd St., 19th Fl., New York, NY 10022.
Web site: www.dacapopress.com.
Andrea Schulz, Editorial Director/Acquisitions.
Description: General nonfiction with concentration in music, history, military history, narrative nonfiction, film. **Number of Books/Yr.:** 60 titles/year (250 submissions). **Proposal Process:** Query with outline and sample chapters. Multiple queries accepted. No electronic queries. Prefers hard copy format. Response time: 3-6 months. **Payment:** Royalty. **Tips:** We do fairly serious nonfiction with backlist potential; we're not right for very commercial front list-only titles.

DALKEY ARCHIVE PRESS

Illinois State Univ., Campus Box 4241, Normal, IL 61790-4241. 309-438-7555.
Web site: www.dalkeyarchive.com.
John O'Brien, Publisher.
Description: Avant-garde, experimental fiction, publishes only reprints of the highest literary quality. **Proposal Process:** No unsolicited manuscripts.

JOHN DANIEL AND COMPANY

P.O. Box 21922, Santa Barbara, CA 93121. 805-962-1780.
E-mail: dandd@danielpublishing.com. Web site: www.danielpublishing.com.
John Daniel, Publisher.
Description: Publishes books, to 200 pages, in the field of belles lettres and literary

memoirs; stylish and elegant writing; essays and short fiction dealing with social issues; one poetry title per year. Fiction and nonfiction under 70,000 words. **Number of Books/Yr.:** 4 titles/year (3,000 submissions), 25% by first-time authors, 100% unagented. **Proposal Process:** Send synopsis or outline with no more than 50 sample pages and SASE. Allow 4 weeks for response. Hard copy format preferred. Accepts multiple queries, no electronic queries. **Payment:** Royalty. **Sample Titles:** Adult Fiction: *The Yellow Ribbon Snake*, by J.R. Dailey. Adult Nonfiction: *Hollywood's Revolutionary Decade*, by Charles Champlin. Poetry: *The Privacy of Wind*, by Perie Longo. **Tips:** Looking for good writing that works, poetry that sings, memoirs and essays that make us think.

JONATHAN DAVID PUBLISHERS, INC.

68-22 Eliot Ave., Middle Village, NY 11379. 718-456-8611.
E-mail: info@jdbooks.com. Web site: www.jdbooks.com.
Alfred J. Kolatch, Editorial Director.
Description: Publishes hard cover and trade paperback originals and reports. Nonfiction only. Subject areas include sports, reference, and biography. Area of specialization is popular Judaica. **Number of Books/Yr.:** 25 titles/year (hundreds of submissions), 25% by first-time authors, 90% unagented. **Proposal Process:** Query with outline, sample chapter, resumé, and SASE. No multiple queries. Accepts electronic queries, but prefers hard copy format. **Payment:** Royalty or outright purchase. **Sample Titles:** *Drawing a Crowd Bill Gallo's Greatest Sport Moments,* (Gallo/Cornell). *The President of the United Stated and the Jews,* (Dalin/Kolatch). *The Baseball Catalog: Millennium Edition,* (Schlossberg). *From Central Park to Sinai,* (Newberger). *Reel Jewish,* (Samberg).

DAVIES-BLACK PUBLISHING

Division of Consulting Psychologists Press, Inc., 3803 E. Bayshore Rd., Palo Alto, CA 94303. 650-969-8901.
E-mail: www.cpp-db.com. Web site: www.cpp-db.com.
Melinda Adams, Acquisitions Editor.
Description: Books, 250-400 manuscript pages. Professional and trade titles in business and careers.

DAVIS PUBLICATIONS, INC.

50 Portland St., Worcester, MA 01608. 508-754-7201.
Web site: www.davis-art.com.
Helen Ronan, Editorial Director.
Description: Books, 100-300 manuscript pages, for the art education market; mainly for teachers of art, grades K-12. Must have an educational component. **Proposal Process:** Grades K-8, address Claire M. Golding; grades 9-12, address Helen Ronan. Query with outline and sample chapters. **Payment:** Royalty.

DAW BOOKS, INC.

Affiliate of Penguin Putnam, Inc., 375 Hudson St., 3rd Fl.,
New York, NY 10014-3658. 212-366-2096.
E-mail: daw@penguinputnam.com. Web site: www.dawbooks.com.
Elizabeth R. Wollheim, Publisher.
Description: Specializes in science fiction, fantasy, thrillers. Mostly for adults (but
some are appropriate for young adults). **Contact:** Submissions Editor.

DAYBREAK BOOKS

Imprint of Rodale Books, Inc., 400 S. 10th St., Emmaus, PA 18098. 610-967-5171.
Web site: www.rodalepress.com.
Description: Four main categories: motivation, inspiration, self-help, and spiritual.
Thematic interests include grief/loss, loneliness, and relationships. **Proposal
Process:** Send proposal, bio, table of contents, and 2-3 sample chapters. **Payment:**
Flat fee. **Contact:** Neil Wertheimer.

DEARBORN FINANCIAL PUBLISHING, INC.

155 N. Wacker Dr., Chicago, IL 60606-1719. 312-836-4400.
E-mail: zigmund@dearborn.com. Web site: www.dearborntrade.com.
Cynthia Zigmund, Associate Publisher.
Description: Professional and consumer books and courses on financial services,
real estate, banking, small business, investing, etc. **Proposal Process:** Query with
outline and sample chapters. **Payment:** Royalty and flat fee.

IVAN R. DEE PUBLISHER, INC.

1332 N. Halsted St., Chicago, IL 60622-2637. 312-787-6262.
E-mail: elephant@ivandee.com. Web site: www.ivandee.com.
Ivan R. Dee, Editor.
Description: Serious nonfiction. History, politics, biography, literature, and theatre,
in hardcover and paperback. **Number of Books/Yr.:** 50 titles/year (1,000 submis-
sions). **Proposal Process:** Query with outline and sample chapters, and SASE.
Multiple and electronic queries accepted. Hard copy. **Payment:** Royalty.

DEL REY BOOKS

Ballantine Publishing Group, Random House, Inc., 1540 Broadway, 11th Fl.-J, New
York, NY 10036. 212-782-8393.
E-mail: delrey@randomhouse.com. Web site: www.randomhouse.com/delrey/.
Shelly Shapiro, Editorial Director.
Description: Science fiction and fantasy, 60,000-120,000 words; first novelists
welcome. **Proposal Process:** No unsolicited submissions. **Payment:** Royalty.
Contact: Steve Saffel and Chris Schluep, Editors.

DELACORTE PRESS

Bantam Dell Publishing, 1540 Broadway, New York, NY 10036. 212-782-9000.
Web site: www.randomhouse.com.
Jackie Cantor, Tom Spain, Editors.
Description: General adult fiction and nonfiction. **Proposal Process:** Accepts material from agents only.

DELL BOOKS

Subsidiary of Bantam Dell Publishing Group, A Division of Random House, Inc., 1540 Broadway, New York, NY 10036. 212-782-9000.
Web site: www.randomhouse.com.
Description: Commercial fiction (including romance, mystery, and westerns) and nonfiction (including health, war, and spirituality). **Proposal Process:** Agented submissions only.

DELTA BOOKS

Imprint of Bantam Dell Publishing Group, a Division of Random House, Inc., 1540 Broadway, New York, NY 10036. 212-354-6500.
Web site: www.randomhouse.com.
Description: General-interest, nonfiction and fiction. **Proposal Process:** Nonfiction, submit detailed chapter outline with sample chapters. For fiction, submit full manuscript with narrative synopsis (to 10 pages). Allow 3 months for reply. SASE. **Tips:** No poetry. **Contact:** Editorial Dept., Book Proposal.

DEVIN-ADAIR PUBLISHERS, INC.

P.O. Box A, Old Greenwich, CT 06870. 203-531-7755.
J. Andrassi, Editor.
Description: Books on conservative affairs, Irish topics, photography, Americana, self-help, health, gardening, cooking, and ecology. **Proposal Process:** Send outline, sample chapters, and SASE. **Payment:** Royalty.

DIAL PRESS

Bantam Dell Publishing Group, Random House, Inc., 1540 Broadway, New York, NY 10036. 212-354-6500.
Web site: www.randomhouse.com/bantamdell/.
Susan Kamil, V.P., Editorial Director.
Description: Quality fiction and nonfiction. **Proposal Process:** Query with SASE. No unsolicited material.

DIMI PRESS

3820 Oak Hollow Ln. SE, Salem, OR 97302-4774. 503-364-7698.
E-mail: dickbook@earthlink.net.
Web site: www.members.aol.com/dickbook/dimi_press.html.
Dick Lutz, President.
Description: Nonfiction on unusual things in nature, e.g., unique animals, different

cultures, astonishing natural events or disasters. Also, books on travel (no travel guides). **Proposal Process:** Query. **Payment:** Royalty. **Tips:** Queries without SASE will not be answered. Please read guidelines.

DK PUBLISHING, INC.
Subsidiary of Dorling Kindersley, Ltd., 95 Madison Ave., New York, NY 10016.
212-213-4800.
Web site: www.dk.com.
Neal Porter, Children's Publisher.
Description: Picture books and fiction for middle-grade and older readers. Also, illustrated reference books for both adults and children. **Proposal Process:** Send outline and sample chapter. **Payment:** Royalty or flat fee.

THE DONNING COMPANY
184 Business Park, Suite 206, Virginia Beach, VA 23462. 757-497-1789.
E-mail: dcpr3@pilot.infi.net. Web site: www.donning.com.
Tony Lillis, Editor.
Description: Publishes historical and contemporary profiles of colleges, businesses and associations, multicultural topics, for sponsors. **Proposal Process:** Send credentials and work samples for consideration for comissions. **Payment:** Flat fee.

DOUBLEDAY
Doubleday Broadway Publishing Group, Random House, Inc., 1540 Broadway, New York, NY 10036. 212-782-8911.
Web site: www.randomhouse.com.
William Thomas, V.P./Editor-in-Chief.
Description: Publishes high-quality fiction and nonfiction. Publishes hardcover and trade paperback originals and reprints.

DOWN HOME PRESS
P.O. Box 4126, 1421 Randolf Tabernacle Rd., Asheboro, NC 27204. 336-672-6889.
Jerry Bledsoe, Publisher.
Description: Nonfiction books related to the Carolinas and the South. **Proposal Process:** Query or send complete manuscript. **Payment:** Royalty.

THOMAS DUNNE BOOKS
St. Martin's Press, 175 Fifth Ave., New York, NY 10010. 212-674-5151.
Thomas L. Dunne, Publisher.
Description: Adult fiction (mysteries, trade, etc.) and nonfiction (history, biographies, science, politics, humor, etc.). **Proposal Process:** Query with outline, sample chapters, and SASE. **Payment:** Royalty.

DUQUESNE UNIVERSITY PRESS

600 Forbes Ave., Pittsburgh, PA 15282-0101. 412-396-6610.
Web site: www.dug.edu/dupress.
Susan Wadsworth-Booth, Director.
Description: Scholarly publications in the humanities and social sciences; creative nonfiction (book-length only) by emerging writers.

EAKIN PRESS

P.O. Drawer 90159, Austin, TX 78709-0159. 512-288-1771.
Web site: eakinpress.com.
Melissa Roberts, Editor.
Description: Regional trade books—children and adults. Nonfiction length: 50,000-150,000 words; Fiction 20,000-30,000 words. **Number of Books/Yr.:** 65 titles/year (ave. 1,200 submissions), 40% by first-time authors, 1% unagented. **Proposal Process:** Query with outline. Subsidizes. Multiple queries accepted. No electronic queries. Prefers hard copy format. **Payment:** Pays royalty. **Tips:** Focuses on history, culture, geography, etc. of Texas and the Southwest. Remember: an active and enthusiastic author can sell more books than an expensive advertising campaign bought by a publisher.

EASTERN WASHINGTON UNIVERSITY PRESS

Mail Stop 1, Eastern Washington Univ., 705 W. 1st Ave., Spokane, WA 99201. 509-623-4286.
Scott Poole, Editor.
Description: Poetry, poetry translations, nonfiction, and science fiction. **Number of Books/Yr.:** 6 titles/year (75 submissions). **Proposal Process:** Send complete manuscript, query with outline, or Mac-compatible diskette. Response time: 3-6 months. Prefers hard copy format. Accepts multiple queries. **Payment:** Royalty. **Contact:** Chris Howell.

ELEMENT BOOKS

160 North Washington St., 4th Floor, Boston, MA 02114. 617-915-9400.
E-mail: element2@ix.netcom.com.
Darren Kelly, Editorial Director.
Description: Books on world religions, ancient wisdom, astrology, meditation, women's studies, and alternative health and healing. **Proposal Process:** Study recent catalogue. Query with outline and sample chapters. No phone calls, please. **Payment:** Royalty.

EMC/PARADIGM PUBLISHING INC.

875 Montreal Way, St. Paul, MN 55102. 651-290-2800.
E-mail: educate@empc.com. Web site: www.emcp.com.
George Provol, Publisher.
Description: Vocational, career, and consumer education textbooks. **Proposal Process:** No unsolicited manuscripts. **Payment:** Royalty.

ENTREPRENEUR BOOKS

2445 McCabe Way, Irvine, CA 92614. 949-261-2325.
E-mail: jcalmes@entrepreneur.com. Web site: www.entrepreneur.com.
Jere L. Calmes, Editorial Director.
Description: Nonfiction general and small business trade books. Areas include: business skills, motivational as well as how-to and general business including leadership, marketing, accounting, finance, new economy and business growth and start-ups, customer relations, innovation, stock market and online trading. **Number of Books/Yr.:** 15-20 titles/year (600 submissions), 30% first-time authors. **Proposal Process:** Query with outline, sample chapters, and SASE. Response time: 2 weeks. Multiple and electronic queries accepted. Prefers electronic or hard copy format. **Payment:** Royalty, range is 5-15%. **Sample Titles:** Nonfiction business: *At Work with Thomas Edison: 10 Business Lessons from America's Greatest Innovator.*

EPICENTER PRESS, INC.

P.O. Box 82368, Kenmore, WA 98028. 425-485-6822.
E-mail: epipress@aol.com. Web site: www.epicenterpress.com.
Kent Sturgis, Publisher.
Description: Quality nonfiction trade books, contemporary western art and photography titles, emphasizing Alaska. Regional press whose interests include but are not limited to the arts, history, environment, and diverse cultures and lifestyles of the North Pacific and high latitudes.

PAUL S. ERIKSSON, PUBLISHER

P.O. Box 125, Forest Dale, VT 05745. 802-247-4210.
Description: General nonfiction and some fiction. **Proposal Process:** Send outline and cover letter and 3 chapters, SASE required. **Payment:** Royalty. **Contact:** Editorial Department.

M. EVANS & CO., INC.

216 E. 49th St., New York, NY 10017. 212-688-2810.
E-mail: gdek@mevans.com. Web site: www.mevans.com.
George C. DeKay, Editorial Dept.
Description: Small commercial publisher of books of all sorts. No poetry or belles lettres. General nonfiction with an emphasis on health, cooking, history, relationships, current affairs, how-to, crime; small list of adult commercial fiction. **Number of Books/Yr.:** 30 titles/year, (500 submissions), 10-20% by first-time authors, 10% unagented. **Proposal Process:** Query with outline, sample chapters, and SASE. Multiple and electronic queries okay. Hard-copy format preferred. **Payment:** Royalty. **Sample Titles:** *The Third Consequence,* by Chris Stewart. *Bragging Rights,* by Richard Ernsberger. **Tips:** Open to adult books for which we can identify a market. **Contact:** P.J. Dempsey, Marc Beller.

EXCALIBUR PUBLICATIONS

P.O. Box 35369, Tucson, AZ 85740-5369. 520-575-9057.
E-mail: apetrillo@excaliburpubs.com.
Alan M. Petrillo, Editor.
Description: Publishes work on military history, strategy and tactics, firearms, arms and armor. **Number of Books/Yr.:** 4-6 titles/year, 90% first-time authors, 95% unagented. **Proposal Process:** Query with an outline or synopsis of the work, along with the first or any other consecutive chapters, and SASE. Do not include notes on any photographs, illustrations or maps. Multiple and electronic queries accepted. Hard copy. **Payment:** Royalty/flat fee. **Tips:** Seeking well-researched and documented work. The writer should have a mastery of the subject matter. Unpublished writers are welcome and strongly encouraged.

FACTS ON FILE, INC.

11 Penn Plaza, New York, NY 10001. 212-967-8800.
E-mail: llikoff@factsonfile.com. Web site: www.factsonfile.com.
Laurie Likoff, Editor.
Description: Reference and trade books on science, health, literature, language, history, the performing arts, ethnic studies, popular culture, sports, etc. **Number of Books/Yr.:** 100-150 titles/year (200-250 submissions), 10% by first-time authors, 30% unagented. **Proposal Process:** Query with outline, sample chapter, and SASE. Unsolicited synopses welcome. Multiple queries okay. No electronic queries. Response time: 4-6 weeks. Prefers hard copy format. **Payment:** Royalty. **Tips:** Strictly a reference and information publisher. (No fiction, poetry, computer books, technical books, or cookbooks.)

FAIRVIEW PRESS

2450 Riverside Ave. S., Minneapolis, MN 55454. 800-544-8207.
E-mail: press@fairview.org. Web site: www.fairviewpress.org.
Lane Stiles, Director.
Description: Grief and bereavement, aging and seniors; caregiving; palliative and end of life care; health and medicine (including complementary medicine). Also topics of interest to families, including childcare and parenting; psychology and self help; inspiration and spirituality. **Number of Books/Yr.:** 6-12 titles/year (2,500 submissions), 50% by first-time authors, 70% unagented. **Proposal Process:** Send query with sample chapters and complete manuscript, include SASE. Multiple queries accepted. No electronic queries. Hard copy. **Payment:** Varies. **Tips:** No fiction; no longer acquiring children's picture books or adult memoirs.

FANFARE

Random House, Inc., 201 E. 50th St., New York, NY 10022. 212-751-2600.
Web site: www.randomhouse.com.
Description: Historical and contemporary women's fiction, about 90,000-150,000 words. Study field before submitting. Paperback and hardcover. **Proposal Process:** Query. **Contact:** Editorial Dept.

FARRAR, STRAUS & GIROUX, INC.

19 Union Sq. W., New York, NY 10003. 212-741-6900.
Elisabeth Dyssegaard, Executive Editor.
Description: Adult and juvenile literary fiction and nonfiction.

FAWCETT/IVY BOOKS

A Division of Random House, Inc., 201 E. 50th St., 9th Fl, New York, NY 10022.
Description: Adult mysteries, regencies, and historical romances, 75,000-120,000 words. **Proposal Process:** Acquisitions through agents. Query with outline and sample chapters. Average response time is 3-6 months. **Payment:** Royalty. **Contact:** Editorial Dept.

FREDERICK FELL PUBLISHERS, INC.

2131 Hollywood Blvd., Suite 305, Hollywood, FL 33020. 954-925-5242.
E-mail: info@fellpub.com. Web site: www.fellpub.com.
Barbara Newman, Acquisition Editor.
Description: New Age, self-help, how-to, business, hobbies, and inspirational.
Number of Books/Yr.: 30 titles/year (2,000 submissions), 50% by first-time authors, 90% unagented. **Proposal Process:** Query with sample chapters and SASE. Response time: 2 months. Multiple queries okay. No electronic queries. Hard copy format preferred. **Payment:** Royalty. **Sample Titles:** Since 1942, we have been publishing titles such as *The Greatest Salesman in the World,* by best-selling author Og Mandino. Recent launch, *Fell's Official Know-It-All Guides.* **Tips:** Seeking experts in all genres to help to make *Fell's Official Know-It-All Guides* series grow. **Contact:** Lori Horton, Asstant Editor.

THE FEMINIST PRESS AT THE CITY UNIVERSITY OF NEW YORK

The Graduate School and University Center, 365 Fifth Ave, New York, NY 10016.
212-817-7926.
Web site: www.feministpress.org.
Jean Casella, Publisher.
Description: Educational press publishing books by and about multicultural women. Strive to resurrect the voices of women that have been repressed and silent. Reprints of significant "lost" fiction, original memoirs, autobiographies, biographies; multicultural anthologies; handbooks; bibliographies. **Number of Books/Yr.:** 15 titles/year (200 submissions), 10% by first-time authors, 90% unagented. **Proposal Process:** Send query with sample chapters and SASE. Response time: 6 months, No electronic or multiple queries. Hard copy format preferred. **Payment:** Flat fee. **Tips:** Accepts only fiction by multicultural women; must also be from a feminist slant. Especially interested in international literature, women and peace, women and music, and women of color. **Contact:** Amanda Hamlin.

FERGUSON PUBLISHING COMPANY
200 West Jackson Blvd., 7th Floor, Chicago, IL 60606. 312-580-5480.
Web site: www.fergpubco.com.
Andrew Morkes, Managing Editor.
Description: Nonfiction for the juvenile, young adult, and college markets relating to career preparation and reference.

FIREBRAND BOOKS
LPC Group, 141 The Commons, Ithaca, NY 14850. 607-272-0000.
Web site: www.firebrandbooks.com.
Nancy K. Bereano, Publisher.
Description: Feminist and lesbian fiction and nonfiction. Paperback and library edition cloth. **Payment:** Royalty.

FIRESIDE
Simon & Schuster Trade Division, 1230 Ave. of the Americas, New York, NY 10020. 212-698-7000.
Web site: www.SimonSays.com.
Description: Imprint of Simon & Schuster. Other imprints include Libros en Espanol; Touchstone; Free Press paperbacks and Scribner Poetry. **Proposal Process:** No unsolicited manuscripts.

FODOR'S TRAVEL GUIDES
An imprint of Random House, Inc., 280 Park Ave., New York, NY 10017. 212-572-8702.
E-mail: kcure@fodors.com. Web site: www.fodors.com.
Karen Cure, Editorial Director.
Description: Publishes fact-packed travel guidebook series, covering destinations around the world. Every book is highly detailed. Both foreign and U.S. destinations. **Number of Books/Yr.:** 20/titles/year (100 submissions), 100% unagented. **Proposal Process:** Query first, then send an outline and sample. Response time: 2-10 weeks. Multiple queries accepted. No electronic queries. Hard copy format preferred. **Payment:** Flat fee, depending on the work performed. **Sample Titles:** *Escape to Morocco, Cuba, Brazil, Escape to Ireland, Pocket Aspen.* All travel guides. **Tips:** Avoid pitching general-interest guidebooks to destinations we already cover. Avoid travel literature and other personal narratives.

FONT & CENTER PRESS
P.O. Box 95, Weston, MA 02493. 781-647-9756.
Web site: www.fontandcenter.com.
Description: Cookbooks. How-to books. Alternative history for adults and young adults. **Proposal Process:** Send proposal, outline, and sample chapter(s). Responds in 3 months. SASE. **Payment:** Royalty. **Contact:** Ilene Horowitz.

FOOTSTEPS

Traveler's Tales, Inc., 330 Townshed St., #208, San Francisco, CA 94107.
415-227-8600.
E-mail: submit@travelerstales.com. Web site: www.travelerstales.com.
James O'Reilly, Publisher.
Description: "The Soul of Travel." Personal nonfiction travel narratives. **Number of Books/Yr.:** 16 titles/year (150 submissions). **Proposal Process:** Send outline, sample chapters, and SASE. Multiple and electronic queries accepted. Response time: 3-6 months. **Payment:** Royalty, range is 8-12% net. **Sample Titles:** *Last Trout in Venice*, by Doug Lansley (Humor/Travel). *Kite Strings of the Southern Cross*, by Laurie Gough (Travel/Memoir). **Tips:** Looking for well-crafted travel stories. Avoid: guidebooks, journal entries. **Contact:** Larry Habegger, Executive Director.

FOOTSTEPS PRESS

P.O. Box 75, Round Top, NY 12473.
E-mail: krause5@francomm.com. Web site: www.brasseyinc.com.
Bill Munster, Editor.
Description: Saddle-stitched chapbooks, done on quality paper, with photographs to accent the poems. Usually about 300-500 copies printed. **Number of Books/Yr.:** 2 or more titles/year (200+ submissions), 100% by first-time authors, 100% unagented. **Proposal Process:** Query with complete manuscript and SASE. Hard copy. Accepts multiple queries, no electronic queries. **Payment:** Flat fee. **Tips:** Material submitted may be on any topic. Please include a $10 reading fee. Also looking for anything related to poems about movies, or prose poems.

FORDHAM UNIVERSITY PRESS

University Box L, Bronx, NY 10458-5172. 718-817-4780.
Saverio Procario, Director.
Description: Scholarly books and journals, computer diskettes, videos.

SCOTT FORESMAN

1900 E. Lake Ave., Glenview, IL 60025.
Web site: www.scottforesman.com.
Paul McFall, President.
Description: Elementary textbooks. **Proposal Process:** Must have proper educational credentials in order to submit. **Payment:** Royalty or flat fee.

FORGE

Tom Doherty Associates, 175 Fifth Ave., 14th Fl., New York, NY 10010.
212-388-0100.
E-mail: inquiries@tor.com. Web site: www.tor.com.
Patrick Nielsen Hayden, Senior Editor.
Description: General fiction; limited nonfiction, from 80,000 words. **Proposal Process:** Query with synopsis and first 3 chapters. **Payment:** Advance and royalty.

FORUM

Prima Publishing, 3000 Lava Ridge Ct., Roseville, CA 95661. 916-787-7000. Web site: www.primapublishing.com.

Steven Martin, Publisher.

Description: Serious nonfiction books on current affairs, business, public policy, libertarian/conservative thought, high level management, individual empowerment, and historical biography. Other imprints of Prima Publishing are Prima-tech, Primahealth and Primalifestyle. **Proposal Process:** Submit outline and sample chapters/market research, include SASE. Multiple queries accepted. Hard copy format preferred. **Payment:** Royalty and flat fee, standard range. **Sample Titles:** *Cisco: Unauthorized* (Business/Current affairs); *The Secret History of the CIA* (History); *Theodore Roosevelt on Leadership* (Business Management).

FOUR WALLS EIGHT WINDOWS

39 W. 14th, #503, New York, NY 10011. 212-206-8965.

E-mail: edit@4w8w.com. Web site: www.4w8w.com.

JillEllyn Riley, Acquisitions Editor.

Description: Popular science, history, biography, politics. **Number of Books/Yr.:** 30 titles/year (5,000 submissions), 15% first-time authors, 10% unagented. **Proposal Process:** Query with outline, include SASE. Response time: 2 months. Multiple and electronic queries accepted. Hard-copy format preferred. E-mail queries are accepted; e-mail submissions are not. Unsolicited manuscripts not accepted. **Payment:** Royalty. **Tips:** Write for free catalog or visit our website; send e-mail for a complete set of submission guidelines. Note: No poetry, commercial fiction (i.e., conventional romances, mysteries, thrillers, etc.).

OLIN FREDERICK, INC.

P.O. Box 547, Dunkirk, NY 14048. 716-672-6172.

E-mail: magwynne@olinfrederick.com. Web site: www.olinfrederick.com.

Description: Political nonfiction including works of critique, assessment, and debate of current issues, as well as biography; history; economics; health and medicine; business; and other subjects; political fiction; and poetry all focused on "revealing the truth about issues in the government." **Proposal Process:** Query with outline, synopsis, author bio, and SASE. Please no sample chapters. **Payment:** Royalty.

FULCRUM PUBLISHING

350 Indiana St., Suite 350, Golden, CO 80401. 303-277-1623/800-992-2908. Web site: www.fulcrum-books.com.

Marlene Blessing, Editor-in-Chief.

Description: Adult trade nonfiction: gardening, travel, nature, history, education, and Native American culture; focus on western regional topics. No fiction. **Proposal Process:** Send cover letter, sample chapters, table of contents, author credentials, and market analysis. **Payment:** Royalty.

GLENBRIDGE PUBLISHING LTD.
19923 E. Long Ave., Aurora, CO 80016. 720-870-8381.
E-mail: glenbr@eazy.net.
James A. Keene, Editor.
Description: Nonfiction self-help, business, education, cooking. etc. **Number of Books/Yr.:** 4-6 titles/year, (15,000 submissions), 85% first-time authors, 98% unagented. **Proposal Process:** Query with sample chapter and SASE. Multiple queries okay. No electronic queries. Hard copy format. Response time: 1 month. **Payment:** Royalty. **Sample Titles:** Adult Nonfiction: (3 Book Club Selections) *Three Minute Therapy: Change Your Thinking, Change Your Life* by Michael Edelstein with David R. Steele; *Living Thin: An Attitude, Not a Diet; Living Young: An Attitude, Not an Age* by Sylvia Goldman. **Tips:** Please send double-spaced material. **Contact:** Mary B. Keene, President.

THE GLOBE PEQUOT PRESS
246 Goose Lane, Guilford, CT 06437. 203-458-4500.
Web site: www.globe-pequot.com.
Elizabeth Taylor, Submissions Editor.
Description: Nonfiction with national and regional focus; travel; outdoor recreation; home-based business. **Proposal Process:** Query with sample chapter, contents, and one-page synopsis. SASE required. **Payment:** Royalty or flat fee.

DAVID R. GODINE PUBLISHER
9 Hamilton Place, Boston, MA 02108. 617-451-9600.
E-mail: info@godine.com. Web site: www.godine.com.
Carl W. Scarbrough, Editorial Director.
Description: Fiction, nonfiction, poetry, photography, children's, cooking, translation. **Number of Books/Yr.:** 20 titles/year (800-1,000 submissions). **Proposal Process:** Query with SASE. Response time: 2-4 weeks. No multiple queries. Do not accept multiple manuscripts and prefer agented authors.

GOLDEN WEST PUBLISHERS
4113 N. Longview, Phoenix, AZ 85014. 602-265-4392.
E-mail: goldwest@goodnet.com. Web site: www.goldenwestpublishers.com.
Hal Mitchell, Editor.
Description: Cookbooks and nonfiction Western history and travel books. Currently seeking writers for state and regional cookbooks. **Proposal Process:** Query. **Payment:** Royalty or flat fee.

GRAYWOLF PRESS
2402 University Ave., Suite 203, St. Paul, MN 55114. 651-641-0077.
Web site: www.graywolfpress.org.
Fiona McCrae, Executive Editor.
Description: Literary fiction (short story collections and novels), poetry, and essays.

GREAT QUOTATIONS

2800 Centre Circle, Downers Grove, IL 60515. 630-268-9900.
Ringo Suek, Editor.
Description: Gift book with humorous, inspiration, and business categories. 100-150 pages with short sentences. **Number of Books/Yr.:** 50 titles/year (250 manuscripts) 50% by first-time authors, 70% unagented **Proposal Process:** Query with outline and sample chapters or send complete manuscript, and SASE. Multiple and electronic queries preferred. **Payment:** Royalty and flat fee. **Sample Titles:** (Humorous) e.g., *Secret Language of Women*, short sayings about relationship of men vs. women.

GROVE/ATLANTIC, INC.

841 Broadway, 4th Fl., New York, NY 10003-4793. 212-614-7850.
Joan Bingham, Executive Editor.
Description: Distinguished fiction and nonfiction. **Proposal Process:** Query. No unsolicited manuscripts. **Payment:** Royalty.

HANCOCK HOUSE PUBLISHERS

1431 Harrison Ave., Blaine, WA 98230-5005. 604-538-1114.
E-mail: david@hancockwildlife.org. Web site: www.hancockwildlife.org.
Nancy Miller, Managing Director/Editor.
Description: Adult nonfiction: guidebooks, biographies, natural history, popular science, conservation, animal husbandry, and falconry. Some juvenile nonfiction. **Proposal Process:** Query with outline and sample chapters or send complete manuscript. Multiple queries considered. **Payment:** Royalty.

HARCOURT BRACE PROFESSIONAL PUBLISHING

525 B St., Suite 1900, San Diego, CA 92101-4495. 619-699-6716.
E-mail: propub@harcourt.com. Web site: www.hbpp.com.
Sidney Bernstein, Publisher.
Description: Professional books for practitioners in accounting, auditing, tax and financial planning, law, business management. **Proposal Process:** Query. **Payment:** Royalty and work-for-hire.

HARLEQUIN/SILHOUETE BOOKS

300 E. 42nd St., 6th Fl., New York, NY 10017. 212-682-6080.
Denise O'Sullivan, Associate Senior Editor.
Description: This is the U.S. office of Harlequin, publishing a number of Harlequin series, including: Harlequin American Romances (bold, exciting romantic adventures, "where anything is possible and dreams come true"), Harlequin Intrigue (set against a backdrop of mystery and suspense, worldwide locales), Harlequin Historicals (set in periods from medieval times to the American West), and Silhouette Books (romances in a contemporary setting). Paperback. **Proposal Process:** Query. **Tips:** Send for tip sheets, SASE.

HARLEQUIN ENTERPRISES, LTD.

225 Duncan Mill Rd., Don Mills, Ont., Canada M3B 3K9. 416-445-5860.
Web site: www.romance.net. Also: www.harlequin.ca.
Randall Toye, Editorial Director.
Description: The Canadian home office of Harlequin publishes Mira Books (contemporary women's fiction, to 100,000 words). Harlequin Superromance (contemporary romance, to 85,000 words, with a mainstream edge). Harlequin Temptation (sensuous, humorous contemporary romances, to 60,000 words), and Duets (the lighter side of love, to 55,000 words). **Proposal Process:** Query.

HARPERCOLLINS PUBLISHERS

10 E. 53rd St., New York, NY 10022-5299. 212-207-7000.
Web site: www.harpercollins.com.
Description: General book publisher. **Proposal Process:** Adult trade books, send to Managing Editor for Fiction, Nonfiction (biography, history, etc.). For reference books: submissions from agents only. For college texts: address queries to College Dept. (no unsolicited manuscripts; query first).

HARPER SAN FRANCISCO

HarperCollins Publishers, 353 Sacramento St., Ste 500, San Francisco, CA 94111-3653. 415-477-4400.
Description: Publishes a variety of books on religion and spirituality, drawing from the world's diverse traditions. **Proposal Process:** No unsolicited manuscripts. Submissions accepted from agents only.

HARVARD COMMON PRESS

535 Albany St., Boston, MA 02118-2500. 617-423-5803.
Web site: www.harvardcommonpress.com.
Bruce Shaw, Publisher.
Description: Adult nonfiction: cookbooks, travel guides, books on childcare and parenting, health, small business, etc. **Proposal Process:** Send outline, analysis of competing books, and sample chapters or complete manuscript. SASE. **Payment:** Royalty.

HARVARD UNIVERSITY PRESS

79 Garden St., Cambridge, MA 02138-1499. 617-495-2600.
Web site: www.hup.harvard.edu.
Mary Ann Lane, Managing Editor.
Description: General scholarly books.

HATHERLEIGH PRESS

5-22 46 Ave., Suite 200, Long Island, NY 11101. 212-832-1584.
E-mail: liz@hatherleighpress.com. Web site: www.hatherleighpress.com.
Liz Martinez DeFranco, Editor.
Description: Health, fitness, and self-help. *Living With* series of chronic illness books. Losing weight and keeping fit with a unique twist, e.g., our *Complete Guide*

to Navy Seal Fitness. **Number of Books/Yr.:** 25 titles/year (100 submissions), 20% first-time authors, 90% unagented. **Proposal Process:** Query with sample chapter and SASE. Multiple and electronic queries considered. Response time: 3-6 months. Hard copy format preferred. **Payment:** Royalty or flat fee. **Tips:** No first-person accounts, e.g., "How I survived this illness." It helps if you can bring a celebrity draw to the project. Experts in the fields of health and fitness who can write are very desirable.

HAWORTH PRESS, INC.
10 Alice St., Binghamton, NY 13904-1580. 607-722-5857.
Web site: www.haworthpressinc.com.
Bill Palmer, Managing Editor.
Description: Scholarly press interested in research-based adult nonfiction: psychology, social work, gay and lesbian studies, women's studies, family and marriage; some recreation and entertainment. **Proposal Process:** Send outline with sample chapters or complete manuscript. **Payment:** Royalty.

HAY HOUSE
P.O. Box 5100, Carlsbad, CA 92018-5100. 760-431-7645.
E-mail: jkramer@hayhouse.com. Web site: www.hayhouse.com.
Jill Kramer, Editor.
Description: Self-help, New Age, transformational, alternative health. **Number of Books/Yr.:** 45 titles/year (2,000 submissions), 2% first-time authors, 10% unagented. **Proposal Process:** Query with outline, a few sample chapters, and SASE. Multiple queries accepted. No electronic queries. Hard copy. Response time: 3 weeks. **Payment:** Royalty. **Tips:** Audience is concerned with the planet, the healing properties of love, and self-help principles. Readers are interested in taking more control of their lives. Research the market thoroughly to make sure that there aren't too many books already on the subject that you're interested in writing about. Make sure to have a unique slant on ideas. No poetry, children's books, or books of quotations.

HAZELDEN EDUCATIONAL MATERIALS
Box 176, Center City, MN 55012. 651-213-4017.
Web site: www.hazelden.org.
Joe Riley, Trade Sales and Marketing.
Description: Self-help books, curricula, videos, audios, and pamphlets relating to addiction, recovery, spirituality, mental health, chronic illness, family issues, and wholeness. **Proposal Process:** Query with outline and sample chapters. Multiple queries considered. **Payment:** Royalty.

HEALTH COMMUNICATIONS, INC.
3201 S.W. 15th St., Deerfield Beach, FL 33442. 954-360-0909.
E-mail: editorial@hcibooks.com. Web site: www.hci-online.com.
Christine Belleris, Editor.
Description: Books, 250 pages, on self-help, recovery, inspiration, and personal

growth for adults. **Proposal Process:** Query with outline and 2 sample chapters and SASE. **Payment:** Royalty.

HEALTH INFORMATION PRESS

4727 Wilshire Blvd., #300, Los Angeles, CA 90010. 323-954-0224.
Web site: medicalbookstore.com.
Kathryn Swanson, Acquisitions Editor.
Description: Simplify complicated health and medical issues so that consumers can make informed decisions about their health and medical care. Books average 250 pages. **Proposal Process:** Query with outline and sample chapters. **Payment:** Royalty.

HEALTH PRESS

P.O. Box 1388, Santa Fe, NM 87504. 505-474-0303.
E-mail: goodbooks@healthpress.com. Web site: www.healthpress.com.
K. Schwartz, Editor.
Description: Health-related adult and children's books, 100-300 pages. "We're seeking cutting-edge, original manuscripts that will excite, educate, and help readers." Author must have credentials, or preface/intro must be written by M.D., Ph.D., etc. Controversial topics are desired; must be well researched and documented. **Proposal Process:** Submit outline, table of contents, and first chapter with SASE. **Payment:** Royalty.

HEBREW UNION COLLEGE PRESS

3101 Clifton Ave., Cincinnati, OH 45220. 513-221-1875 ext. 293.
E-mail: hucpressphuc.edu.
Barbara Selya, Acquisitions Editor.
Description: Scholarly Jewish Publisher on very specific topics in Judaic studies. Target audience is mainly rabbis and professors. **Number of Books/Yr.:** 4 titles/year (15 submissions), 100% unagented authors. **Proposal Process:** Query with outline and sample chapters, hardy copy preferred. Response time: 1 week. **Tips:** No Holocaust memoirs or fiction.

HEINEMANN

361 Hanover St., Portsmouth, NH 03801. 603-431-7894.
E-mail: www.heinemann.com. Web site: www.heinemanndrama.com.
Leigh Peake, Executive Editor.
Description: Practical theatre, drama education, professional education, K-12, and literacy education. **Proposal Process:** Query.

HEMINGWAY WESTERN STUDIES SERIES

Boise State University, 1910 University Dr., Boise, ID 83725. 208-426-1999.
Web site: www.boisestate.edu/hemingway/series.htm.
Tom Trusky, Editor.
Description: Books on Idaho and Rocky Mountain culture and environment. **Proposal Process:** Query with letter.

HIGGINSON BOOK COMPANY

148 Washington St., Salem, MA 01970. 978-745-7170.
E-mail: higginson@cove.com. Web site: www.higginsson.books.
Laurie Bjorklund, Editor.
Description: Nonfiction genealogy and local history only, 20-1,000 pages.
Specializes in reprints. **Number of Books/Yr.:** 500 submissions/year, 99% unagented. **Proposal Process:** Query with outline and sample chapters, and SASE.
Multiple queries accepted. Electronic queries preferred. Response time: 1 month.
Payment: Royalty. **Tips:** Specialty press—genealogies and local history only.

HIGHSMITH PRESS

P.O. Box 800, W5527 Hwy. 106, Fort Atkinson, WI 53538-0800. 920-563-9571.
E-mail: hpress@highsmith.com. Web site: www.hpress.highsmith.com.
Matt Mulder, Editor.
Description: Adult books, 80-200 pages, on professional library science and education. Teacher activity and curriculum resource books, 48-240 pages, for pre-K-12.
Focuses on reading activity, Internet skills, library skills, storytelling activity books for
librarians and educators. **Number of Books/Yr.:** 15 titles/year (250 submissions),
30% by first-time authors, 90% unagented. **Proposal Process:** Query with outline
and sample chapters. Multiple and electronic queries accepted. Hard copy. Response
time: 1 month. **Payment:** Royalty. **Tips:** No books for children.

HIPPOCRENE BOOKS

171 Madison Ave., New York, NY 10016. 212-685-4371.
E-mail: hippocre@ix.netcom.com. Web site: www.hippocrenebooks.com.
George Blagowidow, Editorial Director.
Description: Foreign language dictionaries and learning guides; trade nonfiction,
including bilingual anthologies of classic poetry, proverbs, and short stories; international cookbooks, travel; history, military history, WWII, and Holocaust studies; Polish-interest titles, and Judaic interest titles. **Number of Books/Yr.:** 50 titles/year (200-300
submissions), 80% by first-time authors, 90% unagented. **Proposal Process:** Send
query letter describing project and its marketability, with projected table of contents.
Multiple queries accepted. Response time: 1-2 months. Hard copy format preferred.
Payment: Royalty, typically 6-10%. Flat Fee $500-$1,500. **Sample Titles:** *Imperial
Mongolian Cooking* (Cookbook); *Swahili Practical Dictionary* (foreign language reference); *Spain: An Illustrated History, Children's Illustrated Chinese Dictionary* (nonfiction, ages 5-10), **Contact:** Carol Chitnis-Gress (cooking, travel, biography, history);
Caroline Gates (foreign lang./dictionaries); Paul Simpson (illustrated histories).

HENRY HOLT AND CO.

115 W. 18th St., New York, NY 10011. 212-886-9200.
Sara Bershtel, Acquisitions.
Description: Distinguished works of biography, history, fiction, and natural history;
humor; child activity books; parenting books; books for the entrepreneurial business
person; and health books. **Proposal Process:** Prefers submissions from literary agents.

HOME BUILDER PRESS
National Assoc. of Home Builders, 1201 15th St. NW, Washington, DC 20005-2800. 202-822-0394.
E-mail: dtennyson@nahb.com. Web site: www.builderbooks.com.
Doris M. Tennyson, Senior Editor.
Description: How-to and business management books, 150-200 pages, for the building industry professional and consumers. Writers must be experts. **Number of Books/Yr.:** 15 titles (60% unagented authors). **Proposal Process:** Query with outline and sample chapter. Response time 1-2 months. **Payment:** Royalty.

HOMESTEAD PUBLISHING
P.O. Box 193, Moose, WY 83012. 307-733-6248.
Carl Schreier, Publisher.
Description: Fiction, guidebooks, art, history, natural history, and biography. **Payment:** Royalty. *No recent report.*

HOUGHTON MIFFLIN COMPANY
222 Berkeley St., Boston, MA 02116-3764. 617-351-5000.
Janet Silver, Editor-In-Chief.
Description: Trade literary fiction, nonfiction, biography, history, gardening, nature books, cookbooks. Adult fiction/nonfiction to 100,000 words. **Number of Books/Yr.:** 120 titles/year. **Proposal Process:** Query with outline and SASE. Hard-copy format preferred. Response time: 6 months. Multiple or electronic queries not accepted. **Tips:** Unsolicited manuscripts are generally rejected.

HOWARD UNIVERSITY PRESS
2225 Georgia Ave. N.W., Ste. 720, Washington, DC 20059. 202-238-2570.
E-mail: danderson@howard.edu.
D. Kamili Anderson, Director.
Description: Discerning nonfiction scholarly research addressing the concerns, conditions, and contributions of African Americans and other people of African descent in a broad range of disciplines. **Number of Books/Yr.:** 3-6 titles/year (100+ submissions), 20% first-time authors, 90% unagented. **Proposal Process:** Query with outline and sample chapters. Response time: 3-6 months. No multiple or electronic queries. Hard copy. **Payment:** Royalty, 7.5% range. Advance flat fee, range $1,500-$2,500. **Tips:** No fiction, poetry or autobiography. Writers are sometimes asked to subsidize the cost of book production.

HOWELL PRESS
1713-2D Allied Ln., Charlottesville, VA 22903. 804-977-4006.
E-mail: howellpress@aol.com. Web site: www.howellpress.com.
Ross A. Howell, Jr., Editorial Director.
Description: Publish and distribute illustrated and gift books on history, transportation, cooking, wine appreciation, quilts and crafts, and topics of regional interest. **Number of Books/Yr.:** 10-12 titles/year (300 submissions), 60% first-time authors,

95% unagented. **Proposal Process:** Query with outline and sample chapters; multiple queries and electronic queries considered. Hard copy format preferred. **Payment:** Royalty. **Tips:** We seek "quirky" gift books. We do not publish personal memoirs. **Contact:** Meghan Mitchell, Editor.

HP BOOKS
Penguin Putnam, 375 Hudson St., New York, NY 10014.
E-mail: online@penguinputnam.com. Web site: www.penguinputnam.com.
Description: How-tos on cooking, automotive topics. **Proposal Process:** Query with SASE. **Contact:** Editorial Department.

HUNTER HOUSE PUBLISHERS
P.O. Box 2914, 1515½ Park Street, Alameda, CA 94501-0914. 510-865-5282.
E-mail: acquisitions@hunterhouse.com. Web site: www.hunterhouse.com.
Jeanne Brondind, Acquisitions Editor.
Description: Nonfiction for health, family, and community. Topics include health, women's health, personal growth, sexuality and relationships, violence intervention and prevention,and counseling resources. **Number of Books/Yr.:** 21 titles/year (300 submissions), 5% first time authors, 80% unagented. **Proposal Process:** Query for guidelines, then submit complete proposal. Response time: 2 months for query, 3 months for proposal. Hard copy format preferred. Multiple and electronic queries accepted. **Payment:** Royalty, 12% of net. **Sample Titles:** *Chinese Herbal Medicine Made Easy,* by Thomas Richard Joiner; *Men's Cancers,* by Pamela J. Haylock, R.N. **Tips:** No autobiographies, memoirs, personal stories. No fiction.

HUNTER PUBLISHING, INC.
239 S. Beach Route, Hobe Sound, FL 33455. 561-546-7986.
E-mail: hunterp@bellsouth.net. Web site: www.hunterpublishing.com.
Michael Hunter, Acquisitions Department.
Description: Travel guides to the U.S., South America, and the Caribbean. **Number of Books/Yr.:** 70 titles/year (300 submissions), 40% by first-time authors, 90% unagented. **Proposal Process:** Send query and outline and SASE. Response time: 2 weeks. Accepts electronic and multiple queries. **Payment:** Royalty. **Tips:** No travelogs; just practical guide books to various destinations, ave. 100 pages.

HYSTERIA PUBLICATIONS
Sourcebooks, Inc., P.O. Box 4410, Naperville, IL 60567-4410.
Web site: www.sourcebooks.com.
Deborah Werksman, Editor.
Description: Humorous books that are "progressive, provocative, liberating, funny, and insightful," 96-112 finished pages. Also acquires gift, self-help, parenting, business, and media books for Sourcebooks imprint. **Proposal Process:** Query with sample chapters. SASE for guidelines. **Payment:** Royalty.

IDEALS CHILDREN'S BOOKS

Hambleton-Hill Publishing, 1501 County Hospital Rd., Nashville, TN 37218. 615-254-2451.

E-mail: publishicd@aol.com.

Bethany Snyder, Editor.

Description: Seeks only submissions from members of the Society of Children's Book Writers and Illustrators, agented authors, and previously published writers submitting with a list of writing credits.

IMPACT PUBLISHERS, INC.

P.O. Box 6016, Atascadero, CA 93423-6016. 805-466-5917.

E-mail: editor@impactpublishers.com. Web site: www.impactpublishers.com.

Melissa Froehner, Assistant Publisher.

Description: Popular and professional psychology books, from 200 pages. Personal growth, relationships, families, communities, and health for adults. Children's books for *Little Imp* series on issues of self-esteem. **Proposal Process:** Query with outline and sample chapters. **Payment:** Royalty. **Tips:** "Writers must have advanced degrees and professional experience in human-service fields."

INDIANA UNIVERSITY PRESS

601 N. Morton St., Bloomington, IN 47404-3797. 812-855-8817.

Web site: www.indiana.edu/~iupress.

Janet Rabinovitch, Managing Editor.

Description: Scholarly nonfiction, especially cultural studies, literary criticism, music, history, women's studies, African-American studies, science, philosophy, African studies, Middle East studies, Russian studies, anthropology, regional, etc. **Proposal Process:** Query with outline and sample chapters. **Payment:** Royalty.

INNER TRADITIONS INTERNATIONAL, INC.

One Park St., Rochester, VT 05767. 802-767-3174.

E-mail: info@innertraditions.com. Web site: www.innerstraditions.com.

Jon Graham, Acquisitions.

Description: Books on philosophy, spirituality, alternative health, shamanism, and divination. Indigenous studies, sexuality, bodywork, and massage. **Number of Books/Yr.:** 60 titles/year (1,000 submissions), 30% first-time authors, 65% unagented. **Proposal Process:** Query with outline and sample chapters, and SASE. Multiple and electronic queries accepted but hard copy preferred. Response time: 6-12 weeks. **Payment:** Royalty. **Sample Titles:** Adult Nonfiction: *Star Ancestors; Yoga for the Three Stages of Life; Asthma: The Complete Guide to Integrative Therapies.* Picture Books: *Birth of the Ganga; Ancient Celtic Festivals and How We Celebrate Them Today.* **Contact:** Jeanie Levitan.

INNISFREE PRESS, INC.
136 Roumfort Rd., Philadelphia, PA 19119-1632. 215-247-4085.
E-mail: innisfreep@aol.com. Web site: www.innisfreepress.com.
Marcia Broucek, Publisher.
Description: Adult nonfiction, 40,000-60,000 words, on spiritual issues, especially relating to everyday living and spiritual action. **Proposal Process:** Accepts multiple queries. Query with outline and sample chapters. **Payment:** Royalty.

INTERLINK PUBLISHING
Interlink Publishing, 46 Crosby St., Northampton, MA 01060. 413-582-7054.
E-mail: info@interlinkbooks.com. Web site: www.interlinkbooks.com.
Michel Moushabeck, Acquisitions Editor.
Description: Independent, specializes in world travel, history, translated fiction, and illustrated children's books from around the world. Uses 3 imprints: Crocodile Books, Interlink Books, Olive Branch Press. **Number of Books/Yr.:** 50 titles/year (500 submissions), 25% first-time authors, 50% unagented. **Proposal Process:** Submit query with outline and 2 sample chapters, include SASE. Response time: 4-6 weeks. Considers multiple queries. No electronic queries. Hard copy. **Payment:** Royalty, range is 5%-10%. **Sample Titles:** Adult: *A Traveller's History of China*, by Stephen G. Haw. *Pancho Villa & The Mexican Revolution*, by Manuel Plana. Children's: *The Fish Prince & Other Stories*, by Jane Yolen and Shulamith Oppenheim. *How Much Land Does a Man Need?* by Leo Tolstoy, illustrated by Elana Abesinona. **Tips:** Study their list carefully before sending your submission.

INTERNATIONAL MARINE
The McGraw-Hill Companies, Box 220, Camden, ME 04843-0220. 207-236-4838.
Jonathan Eaton, Editorial Director.
Description: Books on boating (sailing and power). Imprint: Seven Seas Press.

IRON CROWN ENTERPRISES
P.O. Box 1605, Charlottesville, VA 22902.
Web site: www.ironcrown.com.
John Curtis III, Editor.
Description: Supplemental texts, 80,000-230,000 words, to accompany fantasy role-playing games. **Proposal Process:** Extremely limited market. Study one of our existing products before querying. **Payment:** Royalty or flat fee. *No recent report.*

IRONWEED PRESS
P.O. Box 754209, Parkside Station, Forest Hills, NY 11375. 718-268-2394.
Description: Multicultural fiction, especially Asian fiction, to 50,000 words. Nonfiction biographies and scholarly works, same length. **Proposal Process:** Query with outline, sample chapters, or complete manuscript. Accepts multiple queries. **Payment:** Royalty. **Contact:** Jin Soo Kang.

ISLAND PRESS

1718 Connecticut Ave. NW, Suite 300, Washington, DC 20009. 202-232-7933.
E-mail: info@islandpress.org. Web site: www.islandpress.org.
Barbara Dean, Executive Editor.
Description: Nonfiction focusing on natural history, literary science, the environment, and natural resource management. Solution-oriented material to solve environmental problems. For our imprint, Shearwater Books, we want books that express new insights about nature and the environment. **Proposal Process:** Query or send manuscript, SASE.

JAI PRESS, INC.

Elsevier Science, 655 Avenue of the Americas, New York, NY 10010-5107.
212-989-5800.
E-mail: jai@jaipress.com. Web site: www.jaipress.com.
Roger A. Dunn, Managing Director.
Description: Research and technical reference books on business, economics, management, sociology, political science, computer science, life sciences, and chemistry. **Proposal Process:** Query or send complete manuscript. **Payment:** Royalty.

JALMAR PRESS

15079 Oak Chase Court, Wellington, FL 33414. 561-753-5587.
E-mail: blwjalmar@att.net. Web site: www.jalmarpress.com.
Susanna Palomones, Editor.
Description: Activity-driven books that develop the social, emotional, ethical, and moral skills that lead to academic achievement and lifelong learning. **Number of Books/Yr.:** 10 titles/year (200 submissions), 1-2% first-time authors, 100% unagented. **Proposal Process:** Query with complete manuscript, include SASE. Multiple and electronic queries accepted. Hard copy. Response time: 4-6 weeks. **Payment:** Royalty.

ALICE JAMES BOOKS

University of Maine at Farmington, 98 Main St., Farmington, ME 04938.
E-mail: ajb@umf.maine.edu. Web site: www.umf.maine.edu/~ajb.
April Ossmann, Editor.
Description: Adult poetry, no light verse. **Number of Books/Yr.:** 5 titles/year (1,000 submissions), 60% first-time authors, 90% unagented. **Proposal Process:** Query with complete manuscript and SASE. Multiple and electronic queries accepted. Prefers hard copy format. Response time: 4 months. **Payment:** Flat fee. **Tips:** Serious poetry. See our website for requirements on poetry competitions.

THE JOHNS HOPKINS UNIVERSITY PRESS

2715 N. Charles St., Baltimore, MD 21218. 410-516-6900.
Trevor Lipscombe, Editor-In-Chief.
Description: Subject areas include ancient studies; history of science, medicine, and technology; history; literary criticism; political science; religious studies; and science.

Proposal Process: Unsolicited queries and proposals are accepted, but nounsolicited poetry or fiction. No email submissions. Hard copy only. Include resumé, description of the project, sample text, and descriptive table of contents.

JOHNSON BOOKS

Johnson Publishing Co., 1880 S. 57th Ct., Boulder, CO 80301. 303-443-9766.
E-mail: books@jpcolorado.com.
Steve Topping, Editorial Director.
Description: Nonfiction: environmental subjects, archaeology, geology, natural history, astronomy, travel guides, outdoor guidebooks, fly fishing, regional. **Proposal Process:** Send proposal. **Payment:** Royalty.

JONA BOOKS

P.O. Box 336, Bedford, IN 47421. 812-278-8370.
E-mail: jonabooks@kiva.net. Web site: www.kiva.net.
Marina Guba, Editor.
Description: Humor, true crime, law enforcement, old west and military history. 50,000 word minimum. **Number of Books/Yr.:** 5 titles/year (200 submissions), 50% first-time authors, 80% unagented. **Proposal Process:** Query with outline and sample chapters, and SASE. Multiple and electronic queries accepted. Hard-copy format preferred. **Payment:** Royalty. **Tips:** Looking for more true crime, stories of individual soldiers, and true stories from the old West. Fiction should be based on a true story.

JOVE BOOKS

375 Hudson St., New York, NY 10014.
E-mail: online@penguinputnam.com. Web site: www.penguinputnam.com.
Description: Imprint of Berkley Publishing, a subsidiary of Penguin Putnam. Fiction and nonfiction. **Proposal Process:** No unsolicited manuscripts. Query first.

KALMBACH PUBLISHING CO.

21027 Crossroads Circle, Waukesha, WI 53187. 262-796-8776.
E-mail: book@kalmbach.com. Web site: www.kalmbachbooks.com.
Dick Christianson, Editor-in-Chief.
Description: Publishes reference materials and how-to publications for serious hobbyists in the rail fan, model railroading, plastic modeling, toy train collecting/operating hobbies, as well as the writing field. **Number of Books/Yr.:** 20 titles/year (100 submissions), 85% by first-time authors, 90% unagented. **Proposal Process:** Query first with detailed outline and complete a sample chapter with photos, drawings and how-to text. Reviews artwork/photos as part of mss package. Include SASE. Accepts multiple and electronic queries. Prefers hard copy format. Response time: 2 months to queries. **Payment:** Royalty, 10% on net price. **Sample Titles:** *The Writer's Handbook 2001, The Basics of Ship Modeling,* Mike Ashey. **Tips:** The hobby books are about half text and half illustrations. Authors must be able to furnish good photographs and rough drawings. Telephone inquiries welcomed to save time, misconceptions, and wasted

work. **Contact:** Kent Johnson, Senior Acquisition Editor; Philip Martin, Acquisitions Editor (*Writer's Handbook,* writing books).

KAR-BEN COPIES
6800 Tildenwood Ln., Rockville, MD 20852. 800-452-7236.
E-mail: karben@aol.com. Web site: www.karben.com.
Judyth Groner, Executive Editor.
Description: Books on Jewish themes for preschool and elementary children (to age 9): picture books, fiction, and nonfiction. **Proposal Process:** Complete manuscript preferred. SASE. **Payment:** Royalty.

KEATS PUBLISHING, INC.
2020 Ave. of the Stars, Suite 300, Los Angeles, CA 90067. 310-552-7555.
E-mail: publish@keats.com. Web site: www.keats.com.
Peter Hoffman, Senior Editor.
Description: Health, nutrition, alternative and complementary medicine, preventive health care, New Age, and spirituality.

KENSINGTON PUBLISHING CORP.
850 Third Ave., 16th Fl., New York, NY 10022. 212-407-1500.
Web site: www.kensingtonbooks.com.
Paul Dinas, Editor-in-Chief.
Description: Alternative health, women's fiction and romance (contemporary and historical), mysteries, true crime, general fiction, westerns; imprints and divisions include Zebra, Pinnacle, Encanto (Hispanic romance), Bet/Arabesque and other Bet titles (African American fiction and nonfiction), Dafina (African American), Brava (erotic romance), Twin Streams (alternative health). **Proposal Process:** Contact editors for guidelines. Unsolicited submissions only for the following lines: Arabesque, Encanto, Zebra Ballad Romance (serial fiction). All other kinds of submissions, agented-only. **Payment:** On a book-by-book basis. **Sample Titles:** Fiction Authors: Fern Michaels, Stella Caneson, Shanon Drake, Janelle Taylor. Alternative Health Authors: Gary Nulli. Mystery Authors: Jonie Jacobs, Troy Soos, Mary Roberts Rinehart

KENT PRESS
P.O. Box 1169, Stamford, CT 06904-1169.
Description: Books on legal issues (intellectual property and licensing). **Proposal Process:** Query. **Payment:** Royalty. **Contact:** Katie DeVito. *No recent report.*

KENT STATE UNIVERSITY PRESS
Kent State Univ., Box 5190, Kent, OH 44242-0001. 330-672-7913.
Web site: www.bookmasters.com/ksu-press.
Joanna Hildebrand Craig, Editor-in-Chief.
Description: Interested in scholarly works in history and literary criticism of high quality, any titles of regional interest for Ohio, scholarly biographies, archaeological research, the arts, and general nonfiction.

KIVAKI PRESS
21 Loop Road, Arden, NC 28704. 828-684-1988.
Greg Cumberford, Editor.
Description: Nonfiction books for the academic, holistic health, and environmental markets covering such topics as person/place narratives, ecological restoration, deep ecology, and indigenous epistemologies. **Proposal Process:** Complete manuscript may be submitted on disk with hard copy of synopsis. If not submitting on disk, send synopsis only for manuscripts over 200 pages. Reports in 6-8 weeks. **Payment:** Royalty.

KLUNER ACADEMIC/PLENUM PUBLISHING CORP.
233 Spring St., New York, NY 10013-1570. 212-620-8000.
E-mail: info@plenum.com.
Linda Greenspan Regan, Acquisitions Editor.
Description: Trade nonfiction, approximately 300 pages, on popular science, criminology, psychology, social science, anthropology, and health. **Proposal Process:** Query with outline, SASE. Hard copy format. **Payment:** Royalty.

ALFRED A. KNOPF, INC.
Subsidiary of Random House, Inc., 201 E. 50th St., New York, NY 10022.
212-782-5623.
Web site: www.randomhouse.com/knopf.
Tracy Gates, Acquisitions.
Description: Distinguished adult fiction and general nonfiction. **Proposal Process:** Query for nonfiction.

KRAUSE PUBLICATIONS, INC.
700 E. State St., Iola, WI 54990-0001. 715-445-2214.
E-mail: krauseb@krause.com. Web site: www.krause.com.
Description: Antiques and collectibles, sewing and crafts, automotive topics, numismatics, sports, philatelics, outdoors, guns and knives, toys, records and comics. **Contact:** Bill Krause, Acquisitions Editor.

LANDMARK SPECIALTY BOOKS
150 W. Brambleton Ave., Norfolk, VA 23510.
Allan W. Miller, Managing Editor.
Description: Collector guides and reference books, on antiques and collectibles. Imprints: Antique Trader Books and Tuff Stuff Books. **Proposal Process:** Query with outline. **Payment:** Royalty. *No recent report.*

LARK BOOKS
Sterling Publishing, 50 College St., Asheville, NC 28801. 828-253-0467.
E-mail: carol.taylor@larkbooks.com. Web site: www.larkbooks.com.
Carol Taylor, Publisher/Acquisitions.
Description: Distinctive books for creative people in crafts, how-to, leisure

activities, and "coffee table" categories. **Proposal Process:** Query with outline. **Payment:** Royalty.

HAL LEONARD BOOKS
151 West 46th Street, 8th Floor, New York, NY 10036. 646-562-5892.
E-mail: bschaefer@halleonard.com. Web site: www.halleonard.com.
Ben Schafer, Editor.
Description: Music books: Nonfiction, biographies, reference, and technical. **Proposal Process:** Query with sample chapters and outline. **Payment:** Royalty or flat fee. **Tips:** Only music-themed books (technical, reference, genre, histories, biographies, etc.).

LIBRA PUBLISHERS, INC.
3089 C Street #383, San Diego, CA 92102. 858-571-1414.
William Kroll, Editorial Director.
Description: Behavior and social sciences, medical and general nonfiction, some fiction and poetry, professional journals.

LINCOLN-HERNDON PRESS, INC.
818 S. Dirksen Pkwy., Springfield, IL 62703. 217-522-2732.
E-mail: lhp@cityscape.net. Web site: www.lincolnherndon.com.
James E. Myers, Editor.
Description: Humor—jokes and stories on various fields. **Number of Books/Yr.:** 3 titles/year, 1% first-time authors, 3% unagented. **Proposal Process:** Send query with complete manuscript, and SASE. No multiple or electronic queries. Hard copy. **Payment:** Royalty. **Contact:** Jean Saul, Assistant Publisher.

LINDEN PUBLISHERS
1750 N. Sycamore, Suite 305, Hollywood, CA 90028.
Description: Poetry, plays. **Proposal Process:** Query. **Payment:** Royalty and flat fees.

LINTEL
24 Blake Lane, Middletown, NY 10940. 914-344-1690.
Description: Nonfiction textbooks and experimental fiction. *No recent report.*

LION BOOKS
Sayre Ross Co., 210 Nelson Road, Scarsdale, NY 10583. 914-725-2280.
Harriet Ross, Editor.
Description: Nonfiction; young adult, sports instruction, craft activity books, politics, black studies.

LITTLE, BROWN & CO.
3 Center Plaza, Boston, MA 02108-2084. 617-227-0730.
Web site: www.littlebrown.com.
Maria Modugno, Editor-in-Chief.

Description: Fiction, biography, history, travel, drama, art and photography, juvenile, health and fitness, paperback, cookbooks, mysteries, reference, science, sports, poetry, inspirational. **Proposal Process:** No unsolicited manuscripts.

LLEWELLYN PUBLICATIONS
P.O. Box 64383, St. Paul, MN 55164-0383. 612-291-1970.
Web site: www.llewellyn.com.
Nancy J. Mostad, Acquisitions Editor.
Description: New Age, occult metaphysical of how-to, self-help nature for adult/young adult audience. **Number of Books/Yr.:** 100 titles/year (2,500 submissions), 100% by first-time authors, 99% unagented. **Proposal Process:** Query. Multiple and electronic queries accepted. Response time: 2 weeks. Hard copy format. **Payment:** Royalty. **Sample Titles:** *True Mystic Experiences, A Witch's Book of Dreams, Wild Girls,* (all New Age trade paperback). **Tips:** Interested in any story as long as the theme is authentic occultism, and the work is entertaining and educational.

LONGSTREET PRESS, INC.
2140 Newmarket Pkwy., Suite 122, Marietta, GA 30067. 770-980-1488.
Web site: www.longstreetpress.net.
Scott Bard, President/Editor.
Description: Nonfiction, varying lengths, appealing to a general audience. **Proposal Process:** Query with outline and sample chapters. Accepts very little fiction, and only through an agent. SASE. Allow 5 months for response. **Payment:** Royalty.

LOUISIANA STATE UNIVERSITY PRESS
P.O. Box 25053, Baton Rouge, LA 70894-5053. 225-388-6294.
E-mail: lsupress@lsu.edu. Web site: www.lsupress.edu.
L.E. Phillabaum, Acquisitions.
Description: Scholarly adult nonfiction, dealing with the U.S. South, its history and its culture. **Proposal Process:** Query with outline and sample chapters. **Payment:** Royalty.

LYONS PRESS
123 W. 18th St., New York, NY 10011. 212-620-9580.
E-mail: richardtlp@aol.com. Web site: www.lyonspress.com.
Richard Rothschild, Editor.
Description: Literary nonfiction, travel, fishing, hunting, outdoor sports, science, cookbooks, horses, gardening, history. **Number of Books/Yr.:** 50 titles/year (200 submissions), 10% by first-time writers, 30% unagented. **Proposal Process:** Send query with outline, sample chapters, or complete manuscript. Multiple queries okay. No electronic queries. Response time: 6 weeks. Query with outline. **Payment:** Royalty.

MACADAM/CAGE PUBLISHING

MacAdam/Cage Publishing, 155 Sansome Street, #620, San Francisco, CA 94104. 415-986-7502.

E-mail: info@macadamcage.com. Web site: www.macadamcage.com.

Pat Walsh, Editor.

Description: Historical, mainstream, contemporary fiction, and narrative nonfiction such as memoirs. **Number of Books/Yr.:** Publishes 10-20 titles per year, 75% first-time authors. **Proposal Process:** Query with author's bio., outline and/or sample chapters. Responds in 3-4 months. **Payment:** Royalty.

MACMILLAN REFERENCE USA

IDG Books/Hungry Minds, 919 E. Hillsdale Blvd., Foster City, CA.

Web site: w3.mgr.com/mgr. Also: www.hungryminds.com.

Description: Titles dealing with technology, business, consumer, and how-to, many in series. **Proposal Process:** Accepts queries and proposals from agents only.

MADISON BOOKS

4720 Boston Way, Lanham, MD 20706. 301-459-3366.

Michael Dorr, Editorial Director/Acquisitions.

Description: Adult trade nonfiction. History, literature, women's studies, philosophy, religion, history of science and technology, history of human development. **Number of Books/Yr.:** 20 titles/year (200 submissions), 5% by first-time authors, 50% unagented. **Proposal Process:** Query with outline and sample chapters, SASE. Response time: 2-4 months. Hard copy format preferred. Accepts multiple queries. No electronic queries. **Payment:** Royalty. **Tips:** A blend of scholarly and journalistic styles. **Contact:** Alyssa Theodore, Assistant Editor.

MCFARLAND & COMPANY, INC.

Box 611, Jefferson, NC 28640. 336-246-4460.

E-mail: info@mcfarlandpub.com. Web site: www.mcfarlandpub.com.

Robert Franklin, President.

Description: Nonfiction, primarily scholarly and reference. Very strong lists in general-reference performing arts, baseball, history (U.S., world, Civil War), women's studies. **Tips:** Seeking thorough, authoritative coverage of subjects not already exhausted by existing books. Sells mostly to libraries and individuals interested in specialized topics. See "Book Proposals" section on web site for submission guidelines. **Contact:** Steve WIlson (Sr. Ed.), Virginia Tobiassen (Ed.).

MCGREGOR PUBLISHING

4532 W. Kennedy Blvd., Suite 233, Tampa, FL 33609. 813-805-2665.

E-mail: mcgregpub@aol.com.

Dave Rosenbaum, Acquisitions.

Description: Publishes only nonfiction, with an emphasis on sports and true crime. **Number of Books/Yr.:** 12 titles/year (300 submissions), 50% first-time authors, 50% unagented. **Proposal Process:** Query with outline and sample chapters, and SASE.

Prefer hard copy but multiple and electronic queries accepted. Response time: 2 months. **Payment:** Royalty.

MENASHA RIDGE PRESS
2000 1st Avenue N., Suite 1400, Birmingham, AL 35203. 205-322-0439.
E-mail: info@menasharidge.com. Web site: www.menashsridge.com.
Bud Zehmer, Editorial Director.
Description: How-to and where-to guidebooks to all outdoor, high adventure sports and activities; limited nonfiction about adventure sports; general travel books. **Number of Books/Yr.:** 20 titles/year (60 submissions), 15% first-time authors, 90% unagented. **Proposal Process:** Query with outline. Considers multiple and electronic queries. Response time: 1-3 months. **Payment:** Royalty, 10% range. **Sample Titles:** *60 Hikes within 60 Miles: Raleigh* (sports); *Ethnic Food Lover's Companion* (dining); *Inn-to-Inn Walking Guide: VA & WV* (sports). **Tips:** Examine market to truly evaluate whether your book is unique.

MENTOR BOOKS
Subsidiary of Penguin Putnam, Inc., 375 Hudson St., New York, NY 10014.
212-366-2000.
Web site: www.penguinputnam.com.
Description: Nonfiction for the college and high-school market. **Proposal Process:** Query required. **Payment:** Royalty. *No recent report.*

MEREDITH CORP. BOOK PUBLISHING
1716 Locust St., Des Moines, IA 50309-3023.
James D. Blume, Editor-in-Chief.
Description: Books on gardening, crafts, decorating, do-it-yourself, cooking, health; mostly staff-written. "Interested in freelance writers with expertise in these areas." **Proposal Process:** Query with SASE.

MICHIGAN STATE UNIVERSITY PRESS
1405 S. Harrison Rd., Suite 25, E. Lansing, MI 48823-5202. 517-355-9543.
Web site: www.msupress.msu.edu.
Martha Bates, Acquisitions Editor.
Description: Scholarly nonfiction, with concentrations in history, regional history, women's studies, African-American history, contemporary culture. Also, series about Native Americans, rhetoric, and poetry. **Number of Books/Yr.:** 35 titles/year (average (2,600 submissions), 30% by first-time authors, 99% unagented. **Proposal Process:** Query with complete manuscript. Multiple queries accepted. Response time: 2 months. Hard copy format preferred. **Payment:** Pays royalty, range is negotiable. **Sample Titles:** *This is the World* (Fiction), *Sixties Sandstorm* (Environmental), *Flow of Life in the Atmosphere* (Science), *Sorrow's Kitchen* (Poetry) and *Peninsula* (Creative Nonfiction.) **Tips:** Lucid writing, original perspective, original scholarship.

MID-LIST PRESS

4324 12th Ave. S., Minneapolis, MN 55407-3218. 612-822-3733.
Web site: www.midlinst.org.
Lane Stiles, Editor.
Description: Literary fiction (novels and short fiction collections), poetry, and creative nonfiction; we do not publish anthologies, so do not send individual short stories or poems. **Number of Books/Yr.:** 5 titles/year (3,000 submissions), 90% first-time authors, 99% unagented. **Proposal Process:** Query with outline, sample chapters, and SASE. Response time: varies. Hard copy format preferred. Will accept multiple and electronic queries. **Payment:** Royalty. **Sample Titles:** Adult Fiction: Recent titles/novels—*The Hand Before the Eye*, by Donald Friedman; *Quick Bright Things*, by Ron Wallace. Adult Nonfiction: *One Degree West* by Julene Boir. Adult Poetry: *Jonah's Promise*, by Adam Sol. **Tips:** Interested in submissions of the highest literary quality. Read some of the books we've published in the past to get a sense of our standards.

MIDDLE PASSAGE PRESS

5517 Secrest Dr., Los Angeles, CA 90043-2029. 213-298-0266
E-mail: bramwell@bmf.usc.edu.
Description: Small press. Nonfiction that focuses on African-American experience in the historical, social, and political context of American life. **Proposal Process:** Query with sample chapters. **Payment:** Royalty. **Contact:** Barbara Bramwell.

MIDNIGHT MYSTERY

Gem Printing, 600 Reisterstown Road, Suite 200 G, Baltimore, MD 21208.
410-764-1075.
E-mail: gemprinting@aol.com.
Joseph Haimowitz, Sheryl Lerner, Acquisitions Editors.
Description: Anthologies (hardcover), magazines (short-story compilations). **Number of Books/Yr.:** 12-15 titles/year (1,200 submissions), 15% first-time authors, 100% unagented. **Proposal Process:** Send complete manuscript, and SASE. Response time: 3-4 months. Multiple queries accepted. No electronic queries. **Payment:** Flat fee, range is $.05-$.10/word. **Sample Titles:** *A Listening People, Marine Corps Detectives, Samson's Lion*. **Tips:** Seeking short mystery and suspense stories. Traditional whodunits also accepted. Most stories range 2,000-10,000 words.

THE MIT PRESS

5 Cambridge Center, Cambridge, MA 02142. 617-253-5646.
Web site: http://mitpress.mit.edu.
Larry Cohen, Editor-in-Chief.
Description: Books on computer science/artificial intelligence; cognitive sciences; economics; finance; architecture; aesthetic and social theory; linguistics; technology studies; environmental studies; and neuroscience.

MONTANA HISTORICAL SOCIETY

P.O. Box 201201, Helena, MT 59620.
Web site: mkohlmhs@aol.com.
Martha Kohl, Editor.
Description: Books on Montana history. **Number of Books/Yr.:** 5 titles/year, (20 submissions), 20% first-time authors, 100% unagented. **Proposal Process:** Query with outline and sample chapters, and SASE. Prefer hard copy format. Electronic query OK. No multiple queries. **Payment:** Royalty. **Sample Titles:** *Journeys to the Land of Gold: Emigrant Diaries from the Bozeman Trail, 1863-1866*, a two-volume, edited compendium of all known firsthand accounts of Bozeman Trails Travels; *Anaconda Copper, Montana Air Pollution, and the Courts, 1890-1920*, a landmark environmental history, and *A Guide to Historical Hamilton, Montana*, an architectural and history guidebook to this Montana town. **Tips:** Looking for well-researched, well-written regional history. Writers should avoid overexposed topics like western gunfighters.

WILLIAM MORROW AND CO., INC.

Harper Collins Publishers, 10 E. 53rd St., New York, NY 10022. 212-207-7000.
Web site: www.harpercollins.com.
Michael Morrison, Editorial Director.
Description: Adult fiction and nonfiction. **Proposal Process:** Query.

MOUNTAIN PRESS PUBLISHING

1301 S. 3rd W., P.O. Box 2399, Missoula, MT 59806. 406-728-1900.
E-mail: mtnpress@montana.com. Web site: www.mountainpresspublish.com.
Kathleen Ort, Science Editor.
Description: Nonfiction trade books for general audiences, primarily adults. Considers proposals for projects in natural history (including field guides for plants, wildlife, birds, etc.); western or frontier history. No technical earth science and ecology. **Number of Books/Yr.:** 12 titles/year (150 submissions), 20% first-time authors, 90% unagented. **Proposal Process:** Query with outline and sample chapters, SASE. Multiple and electronic queries accepted. Response time: 1 week-3 months. **Payment:** Royalty. **Sample Titles:** Mountain Press is best known for its state-by-state series on Roadside Geology and Roadside History. Western history and natural history. Recent titles include: *Stories of Young Pioneers in Their Own Words"*; *Sacagawea's Son: The Life of Jean Baptiste Charbonneau; A Field Guide to Nearby Nature*. **Contact:** Gwen McKenna (history), Jennifer Carey (natural history).

THE MOUNTAINEERS BOOKS

1001 S.W. Klickitat Way, Suite 201, Seattle, WA 98134. 206-223-6303.
E-mail: acquisitions@mountaineers.org. Web site: www.mountaineerbooks.org.
David Emblidge, Editor-in-Chief.
Description: Nonfiction only on the outdoors involving noncompetitive, non-motorized, self-propelled activities such as mountain climbing, hiking, walking, skiing, canoeing, kayaking, snow shoeing and adventure travel. Also publish environmental

and conservation subjects, narratives of expeditions and adventure travel. **Number of Books/Yr.:** 50-60 titles/year (400-500 submissions), 50% by first-time authors, 90% unagented. **Proposal Process:** Query with outline and sample chapters, include SASE. Response time: 2-4 months. Accepts multiple and electronic queries. Hard copy format preferred. **Payment:** Royalty, typical range is $2,400-$4,500. **Sample Titles:** Adult: Outdoor recreation, *Florida State Parks, Best Hikes w/Children Utah, 75 Year-Round Hikes in Northern California.* Adventure Narrative: *The Wildest Dream, Stone Palaces.* **Contact:** Cassandra Conyers, Acquisitions Editor, Margaret Sullivan, Assistant Acquisitions Editor.

MOYER BELL
Kymbolde Way, Wakefield, RI 02879. 401-789-0074.
Web site: www.moyerbell.com.
Jennifer Moyer, Publisher.
Description: Adult fiction, nonfiction, and poetry. Query with sample chapter or send complete manuscript. **Payment:** Royalty.

MUSTANG PUBLISHING CO., INC.
Box 770426, Memphis, TN 38177. 901-684-1200.
E-mail: mustangpub@aol.com. Web site: www.mustangpublishing.com.
Rollin A. Riggs, Acquisitions Editor.
Description: General nonfiction for an 18-50 year-old readership. **Number of Books/Yr.:** 4 titles/year (1,000 submissions), 75% by first-time authors, 100% unagented. **Proposal Process:** Query with outline and sample chapters and SASE. No electronic queries. Multiple queries okay. Response time: 1 month, prefers hard copy format. **Payment:** Royalty. (6-8% net). **Sample Titles:** *The Complete Book of Golf Games, 101 Classic Jewish Jokes, Medical School Admissions: The Insider's Guide.* **Tips:** No travel, memoirs. No phone calls.

THE MYSTERIOUS PRESS
Warner Books, 1271 Ave. of the Americas, New York, NY 10020. 212-522-7200.
Web site: www.twbookmark.
William Malloy, Executive Editor.
Description: Mystery/suspense novels. **Proposal Process:** Agented manuscripts only.

THE NAIAD PRESS, INC.
P.O. Box 10543, Tallahassee, FL 32302. 850-539-5965.
Web site: www.naiadpress.com.
Barbara Grier, Editorial Director.
Description: Adult fiction, 48,000-50,000 words, with lesbian themes and characters: mysteries, romances, gothics, ghost stories, westerns, regencies, spy novels, etc. **Proposal Process:** Query with letter and one-page précis only. **Payment:** Royalty.

NATUREGRAPH PUBLISHERS

P.O. Box 1047, Happy Camp, CA 96039. 530-493-5353.
E-mail: nature@sisqtel.net. Web site: www.naturegraph.com.
Barbara Brown, Editor.
Description: Publish adult nonfiction books in two different niches: Natural history and nature; and Native American culture, outdoor living, land, Indian lore, and how-to. **Number of Books/Yr.:** 2-3 titles/year (400 submissions), almost 100% by first-time authors, 100% unagented. **Proposal Process:** Query with outline and SASE. Response time: 1 month. Hard copy format preferred. Multiple queries okay. No electronic queries. **Payment:** Royalty. **Tips:** No children's books.

THE NAVAL INSTITUTE PRESS

US Naval Institute, 291 Wood Rd., Annapolis, MD 21402-5035. 410-268-6110.
E-mail: esecunda@usni.org. Web site: www.usni.org.
Paul Wilderson, Executive Editor.
Description: Nonfiction, 60,000-100,000 words: military histories; biographies; ship guides. Occasional military fiction, 75,000-110,000 words. **Proposal Process:** Query with outline and sample chapters. **Payment:** Royalty.

NEW DIRECTIONS

80 Eighth Ave., New York, NY 10011. 212-255-0230.
Web site: www.ndpublishing.com.
Barbara Epler, Editor-in-Chief.
Description: Stylistically experimental fiction and poetry. **Proposal Process:** Submit sample chapters or complete manuscript. **Payment:** Royalty.

NEW HARBINGER PUBLICATIONS

New Harbinger Publications, 5674 Shattuck Ave., Oakland, CA 94609-1662.
510-652-0215.
E-mail: tesilya@newharbinger.com. Web site: www.newharbinger.com.
Catharine Sutker, Editor.
Description: Self-help psychology books, workbooks on life issues, women's topics, and balanced living. Read by lay people and used by mental health professionals. **Number of Books/Yr.:** 45 titles, (600+ submissions), 75% first time authors, 90% unagented. **Proposal Process:** Query with an outline and sample chapters. Response time one month. Accept electronic, hard copy submissions. Electronic queries OK. **Payment:** Royalty in 10% range. **Sample Titles:** *The Anxiety & Phobia Workbook* and *The Woman's Guide to Total Self-Esteem.* **Contact:** Tesilya Hanauer.

NEW HORIZON PRESS

P.O. Box 669, Far Hills, NJ 07931. 908-604-6311.
E-mail: nhp@newhorizonpressbooks.com.
Web site: www.newhorizonpressbooks.com.
Dr. Joan Dunphy, Editor-in-Chief.
Description: Nonfiction stories of courageous individuals. Incredible tales of real

people with an intense human interest appeal. Also publishes investigative journalism that probes important public issues. **Number of Books/Yr.:** 12 titles/year, 80% first-time authors, 50% unagented. **Proposal Process:** Send query with outline and sample chapters. Include SASE. Multiple and electronic queries okay. Response time: 4 weeks. Hard copy format preferred. **Payment:** Royalty. **Sample Titles:** Hard cover: *The Other Side, Deadly Deception.* Trade paper: *Older Women, Younger Men.* Children's: *I Am So Angry I Could Scream, A Special Raccoon.* **Tips:** First-time authors welcome. For adult nonfiction, seeking the unsung hero; someone who has taken it upon themselves to correct a social injustice. Also, adult true crimes. **Contact:** Lynda Hatch.

THE NEW PRESS
450 W. 41st St., 6th Floor, New York, NY 10036. 212-629-8802.
Web site: www.thenewpress.com.
Andre Schiffrin, Director.
Description: Serious nonfiction in the fields of history, politics, African American studies, economics, labor, multicultural education, media, and Latin-American studies, among others. Does not publish U.S. fiction or poetry, but has a program in international fiction. **Number of Books/Yr.:** 50 titles/year (from several hundred submissions), 20% by first-time authors, 50% unagented. **Proposal Process:** Query. Response time: 2 months. Multiple queries considered. No electronic queries. Hard copy format preferred. **Payment:** Royalty.

NEW READERS PRESS
1320 Jamesville Ave., Box 131, Syracuse, NY 13210. 315-422-9121.
E-mail: jgehring@laubach.org. Web site: www.newreaderspress.com.
Julie Gehring, Editor.
Description: Fiction, 5,000-9,000 words, for adults who read at low levels for use in basic and ESL programs, volunteer literacy programs, and job training programs. **Proposal Process:** Guidelines. Query; no unsolicited manuscripts. **Payment:** Royalty.

NEW VICTORIA PUBLISHERS
P.O. Box 27, Norwich, VT 05055. 802-649-5297.
E-mail: newvic@aol.com. Web site: www.newvictoria.com.
Rebecca Béguin, Acquisitions Editor.
Description: Publishes mostly mysteries and lesbian novels. **Number of Books/Yr.:** 6 titles/year (150-200 submissions), 2-3% first-time authors, 100% unagented. **Proposal Process:** Query with outline and sample chapters; SASE. No electronic queries. Multiple queries okay. Prefer hard copy format. Response time: 2-3 weeks. **Payment:** Royalty, 10%. **Sample Titles:** *Day Stripper,* mystery; *Mommy Deadest,* mystery; *Circles of Power,* feminist history. **Tips:** Occasionally, we ask writers to subsidize the cost of production.

NEW WORLD LIBRARY
14 Pamaron Way, Novato, CA 94949. 415-884-2100.
Web site: www.nwlib.com.
Georgia Hughes, Editor.
Description: Publishes books that inspire and challenge us to improve the quality of our lives and our world. **Number of Books/Yr.:** 30 titles/year (2,000 submissions), 10% by first-time authors, 50% unagented. **Proposal Process:** Send query with sample chapters or complete manuscript. Multiple queries okay. No electronic queries. Response time: 90 days. Hard copy format preferred. **Payment:** Royalty. **Tips:** Seeks books that inspire and instruct. No personal memoirs or fiction. Books must combine clear writing with a strong voice and unique message.

NEW YORK UNIVERSITY PRESS
838 Broadway, 3rd Floor, New York, NY 10003-4812. 212-998-2575.
Web site: www.nyupress.nyu.edu.
Nikko Pfund, Editor-in-Chief.
Description: Scholarly nonfiction. **Proposal Process:** Submit proposal with sample chapters and curriculum vitae.

NEWCASTLE PUBLISHING
13419 Saticoy St., North Hollywood, CA 91605. 818-787-4378.
Description: Nonfiction manuscripts, 200-250 pages, for older adults on personal health, health care issues, psychology, and relationships. No fads or trends. We want books with a long shelf life. **Proposal Process:** Multiple queries considered. **Payment:** Royalty. **Contact:** Daryl Jacoby.

NEWMARKET PRESS
18 E. 48th St., New York, NY 10017. 212-832-3575.
Web site: www.newmarketpress.com.
Description: Nonfiction on health, psychology, self-help, child care, parenting, music, film, and personal finance. **Proposal Process:** Query. **Payment:** Royalty. **Contact:** Esther Margolis, Publisher.

NORTH COUNTRY PRESS
RR 1, Box 1358, Unity, ME 04988. 207-948-2208.
E-mail: ncp@unisets.net.
Patricia Newell / Mary Kenney, Publishers.
Description: Nonfiction with a Maine and/or New England tie-in with emphasis on the outdoors; also limited fiction (Maine-based mysteries). **Proposal Process:** Query with SASE, outline, and sample chapters. No unsolicited manuscripts. **Payment:** Royalty. *No recent report.*

NORTHEASTERN UNIVERSITY PRESS
360 Huntington Ave., 416 CP, Boston, MA 02115. 617-373-5480.
E-mail: univpress@lynx.neu.edu. Web site: www.neu.edu/nupress.

Description: Nonfiction, 50,000-200,000 words: trade and scholarly titles in music, criminal justice, women's studies, ethnic studies, law, society, and American history. **Proposal Process:** Submit query with outline and sample chapter. **Payment:** Royalty. **Contact:** William Frohlich, Elizabeth Swayze, or John Weingartner.

NORTHERN ILLINOIS UNIVERSITY PRESS

310 N. 5th St., DeKalb, IL 60115. 815-753-1826.
Web site: www.niu.edu/univ_press.
Mary L. Lincoln, Editorial Director.
Description: Nonfiction: History, politics, anthropology, archeology, literary and cultural studies. **Number of Books/Yr.:** 18 titles/year (500 submissions), 50% first-time authors, 1% unagented. **Proposal Process:** Query with outline and sample chapters. Multiple and electronic queries accepted. Response time varies. Prefers hard-copy format. **Payment:** Varies. **Sample Titles:** Adult: *Possessed: Women, Witches, and Demons in Imperial Russia*, by Christine D. Worobec.

NORTHWORD PRESS

5900 Green Oak Dr., Minnetonka, MN 55343.
E-mail: bharold@creativepub.com. Web site: www.howtobookstore.com.
Description: Adult and children's nature and wildlife topics. **Number of Books/Yr.:** 15-20 titles/year. (250 submissions), 25% by first-time authors, 75% unagented. **Proposal Process:** Send query, outline, sample chapters and complete manuscript (for children's only). Accepts multiple and electronic queries. Response time: 60 days. **Payment:** Royalty on ⅓ of projects. Typical royalty range is 10-12% net. Flat fee on ⅔ of projects. Typical fee range $3,000-$10,000. **Sample Titles:** Adult: *Nature Photography, Daybreak 2000, Penguin Planet, Greenland Expedition.* Children ages 6-11 years: *Ferocious Fangs, Lions.* Children ages 0-6 years: *That's What Friends Are For,* storybooks. **Tips:** No poetry or personal memoirs/essays on nature. Also, no "green" or animal rehabilitation stories. **Contact:** Acquisitions Editor.

W.W. NORTON AND CO., INC.

500 Fifth Ave., New York, NY 10110.
Web site: www.wwnorton.com.
Starling Lawrence, Editor-in-Chief.
Description: High-quality literary fiction and nonfiction. **Proposal Process:** Send outline, 3 sample chapters, and SASE to Editorial Dept. **Tips:** No occult, paranormal, religious, genre fiction (formula romance, science fiction, westerns), arts and crafts, young adult, or children's books.

NTC/CONTEMPORARY PUBLISHING GROUP

4255 W. Touhy Ave., Lincolnwood, IL 60712-1975. 847-679-5500.
John T. Nolan, Vice President and Publisher.
Description: Nonfiction trade books with a strong focus on sports and fitness, parenting, self-help, general reference, health, careers, business, foreign language and dictionaries. **Number of Books/Yr.:** 400 titles/year (600 submissions), 10% first-

time authors, 20% unagented. **Proposal Process:** Send query, outline. Considers electronic and multiple queries. Response time: 3 weeks. Hard copy format preferred. **Payment:** Royalty 7.5% list paper, 10-15% list cloth or flat fee—typical range is $1,000-$4,000. **Sample Titles:** Adult: *Mindgames: The Autobiography of Phil Jackson.* Sports, *Grand Slam!, Finding Our Fathers,* self help. *Instant Recall French Vocabulary,* foreign language. *Successful Direct Marketing Methods* (7th edition), business. *Guide to Internet Job Searching,* careers.

OHIO UNIVERSITY PRESS/SWALLOW PRESS
Scott Quadrangle, Athens, OH 45701. 740-593-1155.
Web site: www.ohiou.edu/oupress/.
David Sanders, Director.
Description: Scholarly nonfiction, 300-400 manuscript pages, especially Victorian studies, contemporary history, regional studies, African studies. Swallow Press: general interest and frontier Americana. **Proposal Process:** Query with outline and sample chapters. **Payment:** Royalty. **Tips:** Annual Hollis Summers Poetry Award Competition. Contest guidelines available at web site.

ONJINJINKTA PUBLISHING
P.O. Box 25490, Seattle, WA 98125. 425-290-7809.
Web site: www.rippleon.com.
Peter Orullian, Editor.
Description: Publishes books with inspiration or spiritual content, must contain redeeming themes. Publishes nonfiction aimed at strengthening virtues, also books whose topics extol family values. **Number of Books/Yr.:** 8 titles/year (2,000 submissions), 80% first-time authors, 70% unagented. **Proposal Process:** Accepts multiple queries. Query with outline and sample chapters. Hard-copy format preferred. Multiple queries accepted. No electronic queries. **Payment:** Advance and royalty. **Sample Titles:** Adult Fiction: *Until Forever,* grief and redemption. Adult Nonfiction: *Ripple Effect,* how choice affects many people. Children's Fiction: *Caterpillar Jones* (7-14), teaches kids to be courageous. **Tips:** No New Age books or category fiction. Seeking books with clearly defined subject matter, authoritative writing, and original approaches to classic themes of spirituality.

OPEN COURT PUBLISHING CO.
332 S. Michigan Ave., Suite 1100, Chicago, IL 60604. 312-939-1500.
Web site: www.opencourtbooks.com.
David Ramsay Steele, Editor.
Description: Scholarly books on philosophy, eastern thought, and related areas. Trade books of a thoughtful nature on social issues, Jungian thought, psychology, public policy, education, social issues, and contemporary culture. **Number of Books/Yr.:** 13 titles/year (1,200 submissions), 20% by first-time authors, 70% unagented. **Proposal Process:** Send sample chapters with outline, SASE, and resumé. Response time: varies. Hard copy format preferred. No multiple or electronic queries. **Payment:** Royalty.

OPEN HAND PUBLISHING

P.O. Box 20207, Greensboro, NC 27420. 336-292-8585. **Description:** Books that reflect the diverse cultures within the United States, with emphasis on the African American. Publish books which promote positive social change as well as better understanding between all people. **Proposal Process:** Query. **Payment:** Royalty. **Contact:** Pat Andrus.

ORCHISES PRESS

P.O. Box 20602, Alexandria, VA 22320-1602. 703-683-1243. E-mail: lathbury@gmu.edu. Web site: www.mason.gmu.edu. Roger Lathbury, Editor. **Description:** Original poetry, essays, some humor, textbooks, reprints. No fiction, children's books, or cookbooks. **Number of Books/Yr.:** 5 titles/year (500 submissions), 20-40% first-time authors, 90% unagented. **Proposal Process:** Query with sample chapters and complete manuscript, include SASE. Multiple queries accepted. No electronic queries. Hard copy format preferred. **Payment:** Royalty. **Tips:** For poetry, Orchises is a hard market—that is to say, unless some work has appeared in serious magazines of national stature (*The Atlantic Monthly, Poetry, The New Yorker*) chances are slim. Poetry must be technically adroit, intellectually precise and sophisticated.

OREGON STATE UNIVERSITY PRESS

101 Waldo Hall, Corvallis, OR 97331-6407. 541-737-3166. E-mail: osupress@orst.edu. Web site: http://osu.orst.edu/dept/press. Mary Braun, Aquiring Editor. **Description:** Scholarly books in a limited range of disciplines and books of importance to the Pacific Northwest, especially dealing with the history, natural history, culture, and literature of the region or with natural resource issues. **Proposal Process:** Query with summary of manuscript.

OSBORNE/MCGRAW HILL

2600 Tenth St., Berkeley, CA 94710. 510-549-6600. Web site: www.osborne.com. Roger Stewart, Acquisitions Editor. **Description:** General computer books, from beginner to technical levels. Subject areas: networking, programming, databases, certification, applications, internet, e-business. **Number of Books/Yr.:** 200 titles/year (1,000 submissions), 15% by first-time authors, 30% unagented. **Proposal Process:** Query. Multiple queries okay. Response time: 1-2 weeks. Electronic format preferred. **Payment:** Royalty (10-15% of net). **Tips:** Avoid topics that are already over-published. Knowledge of audience and technical proficiency are crucial. First-time authors should be prepared to submit sample chapters. **Contact:** Roger Stewart (Consumer), Wendy Rinaldi (Programming), Tracy Dunkelberger (Networking).

THE OVERLOOK PRESS

Distributed by Penguin Putnam, 386 W. Broadway, 4th Floor, New York, NY 10012. 212-965-8400.

Web site: www.overlookny.com.

Tracy Carns, Editor.

Description: Literary fiction, fantasy/science fiction, foreign literature in translation. General nonfiction, including art, architecture, design, film, history, biography, crafts/lifestyle, martial arts, Hudson Valley regional interest, and children's books. **Proposal Process:** Query with outline, sample chapters and SASE. **Payment:** Royalty.

OXFORD UNIVERSITY PRESS

198 Madison Ave., New York, NY 10016. 212-726-6000.

Web site: www.oup-usa.org.

Description: Authoritative books on literature, history, philosophy, etc.; college textbooks, medical, scientific, technical and reference books. **Proposal Process:** Query. **Payment:** Royalty.

PANTHEON BOOKS

Knopf Publishing Group, Random House, Inc., 201 E. 50th St., 25th Floor, New York, NY 10022. 212-751-2600.

Daniel Frank, Editorial Director.

Description: Quality fiction and nonfiction. **Proposal Process:** Query. **Payment:** Royalty.

PARA PUBLISHING

P.O. Box 8206-240, Santa Barbara, CA 93118-8206. 805-968-7277.

E-mail: info@parapublishing.com. Web site: www.parapublishing.com.

Dan Poynter, Publisher.

Description: Adult nonfiction books on parachutes and skydiving only. Author must present evidence of having made at least 1,000 jumps. **Proposal Process:** Query. **Payment:** Royalty.

PARAGON HOUSE

2700 University Ave. W., Suite 200, St. Paul, MN 55114-1016. 651-644-3087.

E-mail: paragon@paragonhouse.com. Web site: www.paragonhouse.com.

Laureen Enright, Editorial Director.

Description: Publishes reference and scholarly titles, in the areas of biography, history, philosophy, psychology, religion, spiritual health, political science, and international relations. **Number of Books/Yr.:** 12-15 titles/year (4,500-5,000 submissions), 80% by first-time authors, 90% unagented. **Proposal Process:** Query with an abstract of your project; must include a summary of your premise, main arguments, and conclusion (see guidelines). Electronic or hard copy format preferred. Response time: 3 months. Electronic queries accepted. **Payment:** Royalty, typically 10% net. **Sample Titles:** *Philosophy of Human Rights, Doing Right By Children.* **Tips:** No fiction, poetry, new age. Seeking scholarly, nonfiction books of cultural and intellectual appeal, international and interdisciplinary character.

PARENTING PRESS

P.O. Box 75267, Seattle, WA 98125. 206-364-290.

E-mail: office@parentingpress.com. Web site: www.parentingpress.com.

Carolyn J. Threadgill, Editor.

Description: Publish books offering practical life (social) skills to children and parents, as well as all who care for them. Concrete skills modeling problem-solving processes, provide needed information, and acknowledge the importance of feelings and teaching responsibility. **Number of Books/Yr.:** 6 titles/year (500+ submissions), 80% by first-time authors, 100% unagented. **Proposal Process:** Query with outline, sample chapters and SASE. Multiple queries and electronic queries accepted. Hard copy format. Response time: 6 weeks. **Payment:** Royalty. **Tips:** Niche is social skill-building, dealing with feelings, and abuse prevention. Seeking authors with expertise derived from working with children.

PASSPORT BOOKS

4255 W. Touhy Ave., Lincolnwood, IL 60712. 847-679-5500.

E-mail: ntcpubz@aol.com.

John Nolan, Editorial Director.

Description: Adult nonfiction, 200-400 pages, picture books up to 120 pages, and juvenile nonfiction. **Proposal Process:** Send outline and sample chapters for books on foreign language to Christofer Brown; for travel and culture to Adam Miller. Multiple queries considered. **Payment:** Royalty and flat fee.

PEACHPIT PRESS

Addison Wesley Longman, Inc., 1249 Eighth St., Berkeley, CA 94710. 510-548-4393.

Web site: http://www.peachpit.com.

Cheryl Applewood, Managing Editor.

Description: Books on computer and graphic-design topics. **Proposal Process:** Query with outline and sample chapters for manuscripts, 100-1,100 words, or see proposal template on web site.

PELICAN PUBLISHING CO., INC.

P.O. Box 3110, Gretna, LA 70054. 504-368-1175.

Web site: www.pelicanpub.com.

Nina Kooij, Acquisitions Editor.

Description: General trade. Travel guides (destination specific, no travelogues); children's (holiday, ethnic or regional); popular history (not scholarly); cookbooks (cuisine specific). **Number of Books/Yr.:** 90 titles/year (5,000 submissions) 10% by first-time authors, 90% unagented. **Proposal Process:** Query with outline and sample chapters. SASE required. No multiple or electronic queries. Hard copy format required. **Payment:** Royalty. **Tips:** No autobiographical material. See complete guidelines at web site.

PENGUIN PUTNAM INC.

375 Hudson St., New York, NY 10014. 212-366-2000.
Web site: www.penguinputnam.com.
Phyllis Gran, President.
Description: Adult fiction and nonfiction paperbacks. **Payment:** Royalty.

PENNSYLVANIA STATE UNIVERSITY PRESS

University Support Bldg. 1, Suite C, 820 N. University Dr., University Park, PA 16801. 814-865-1327.
Web site: www.psu.edu/psupress.
Peter Potter, Editor-in-Chief.
Description: Scholarly nonfiction, including anthropology, art history, classical thought, East European studies, economics, environmental studies, gender studies, history, Latin American studies, law, literary criticism, philosophy, photography, political science, religion, and sociology. **Proposal Process:** Query with outline and SASE. Multiple queries considered. **Payment:** Royalty.

THE PERMANENT PRESS

4170 Noyac Rd., Sag Harbor, NY 11963. 631-725-1101.
Web site: www.thepermanentpress.com.
Judith Shepard, Editor.
Description: Literary fiction. Original and arresting adult novels. **Number of Books/Yr.:** 12 titles/year (6,000-7,000 submissions), 30-40% by first-time authors, 70% unagented. **Proposal Process:** Send query with outline and sample chapters. SASE. Multiple queries OK. No electronic queries. Hard copy format preferred. **Payment:** Royalty. **Tips:** Seeks distinctive writing style and original voice in adult fiction.

PERSEUS PUBLISHING

11 Cambridge Center, Cambridge, MA 02142.
Web site: www.perseuspublishing.com.
Chris Coffin, Managing Editor.
Description: Publishes books in business, science, health, parenting, psychology, and general nonfiction. **Number of Books/Yr.:** 130 titles/year (800-1,000 submissions), 40% first-time authors, 40% unagented. **Proposal Process:** Query with outline and sample chapters. Response time: 2 months. Multiple and electronic queries accepted. Hard-copy format preferred. **Payment:** Royalty. **Tips:** Looking for serious professionals, with in-depth knowledge of the subject matter they are tackling.

PERSPECTIVES PRESS

P.O. Box 90318, Indianapolis, IN 46290-0318. 317-872-3055.
E-mail: ppress@iquest.net. Web site: www.perspectivespress.com.
Pat Johnston, Publisher.
Description: Nonfiction on infertility, adoption, closely related reproductive health and child welfare issues (foster care, etc.). **Proposal Process:** Query. **Payment:** Royalty. **Tips:** "Writers must read our guidelines before submitting."

PETERSON'S

202 Carnegie Center, Princeton, NJ 08540. 609-243-9111.
Web site: www.peterson.com.
Rodney Yancey, Marketing Director.
Description: Books that bring a new point of view to perennial business topics or identify new issues and developments in the business world. Books that bring something new to businesspeople's lives, and show the human side of the business world. **Proposal Process:** Submit proposal with one sample chapter. **Payment:** Royalty.

PHILOMEL BOOKS

Penguin Putnam Inc., 345 Hudson St., New York, NY 10014. 212-414-3610.
Patricia Lee Gauch, Editorial Director.
Description: Juvenile picture books and young adult fiction, particularly fantasy and historical. Fresh, original work with compelling characters and sense of the dramatic. **Proposal Process:** Query. **Contact:** Michael Green, Senior Editor.

PINEAPPLE PRESS

P.O. Box 3899, Sarasota, FL 34230. 941-359-0886.
E-mail: info@pineapplepress.com. Web site: www.pineapplepress.com.
June Cussen, Editor.
Description: Trade fiction and nonfiction about Florida. **Number of Books/Yr.:** 20 titles/year (1,500 submissions), 95% by first-time authors, 99% unagented. **Proposal Process:** Query with outline, sample chapters, and SASE. Hard copy format. Multiple queries OK. No electronic queries. **Payment:** Royalty. **Tips:** Looking for excellent books on Florida.

PINNACLE BOOKS

Kensington Publishing Corp., 850 Third Ave., New York, NY 10022.
212-407-1500, 800-221-2647.
Web site: www.kensingtonbooks.com.
Paul Dinas, Editor-in-Chief.
Description: Commercial fiction, including thrillers and true crime, also bilingual (Spanish/English) romances under Encanto imprint. **Proposal Process:** Unsolicited material not accepted. Query first with synopsis.

PLAYERS PRESS, INC.

P.O. Box 1132, Studio City, CA 91614. 818-789-4980.
Robert Gordon, Editor.
Description: Plays and musical books on the performing arts, theatre, film, television, costumes, makeup, technical theatre, technical film, etc. **Number of Books/Yr.:** 30 titles/year (1,000 submissions), 60% first-time authors, 80% unagented. **Proposal Process:** Query with manuscript-size SASE and 2 #10 SASEs for correspondence. Include resumé and/or biography. Responds in 3-12 months. No multiple or electronic queries. Hard copy. **Payment:** Royalty.

PLINTH BOOKS

P.O. Box 271118, W. Hartford, CT 06127-1118.

James Finnegan.

Description: Poetry and chapbooks, 25-100 pages. **Proposal Process:** Query with sample poems. **Payment:** Royalty. *No recent report.*

POCKET BOOKS

Simon & Schuster, 1230 Ave. of the Americas, New York, NY 10020. 212-698-7000.

Emily Bestler, V.P./Editorial Director.

Description: Adult and young adult fiction and nonfiction. Mystery line: police procedurals, private eye, and amateur sleuth novels, 60,000-70,000 words. **Payment:** Royalty.

POISONED PEN PRESS

6962 E. 1st Ave., #103, Scottsdale, AZ 85251.

E-mail: editor@poisonedpenpress.com. Web site: www.poisonedpenpress.com.

Description: Well-written adult mysteries only. **Proposal Process:** Query with outline, sample chapters, and SASE. **Payment:** Royalty. **Contact:** Louis Silverstein.

POPULAR PRESS

Bowling Green State University, Bowling Green, OH 43403. 419-372-7867.

Ms. Pat Browne, Editor.

Description: Books of criticism on popular culture subjects, i.e., film, television, popular literature, women's studies, etc. (200-450 pages). **Number of Books/Yr.:** 15 titles/year (350 submissions), 50% by first-time authors, 100% unagented. **Proposal Process:** Query with outline. SASE. Response time: 3-6 months. No multiple or electronic queries. Hard copy. **Payment:** Flat fee or royalty.

POSSIBILITY PRESS

One Oakglade Cir., Hummelstown, PA 17036. 717-566-0468.

E-mail: PossPress@aol.com. Web site: www.possibilitypress.com.

Marjorie L. Markowski, Editor.

Description: Trade paperback originals. How-to, self help. Subjects include business,current significant events, pop-psychology, success/motivations, inspirations, entrepreneurship, sales and marketing, home-based business topics and human interest success stories. "Our mission is to help the people of the world grow and become the best they can be, through the written and spoken word." **Proposal Process:** SASE for guidelines. Query with outline and 3 sample chapters. **Tips:** Focuses on creating and publishing bestsellers by authors who speak and consult. Seeking authors serious about making a difference in the world.

POWER PUBLICATIONS

56 McArthur Ave., Staten Island, NY 10312.

Elizabeth Wallace, Editor.

Description: Adult nonfiction books on women's issues, nursing, the health field, and gender issues. **Payment:** Royalty. *No recent report.*

PRAEGER PUBLISHERS
Greenwood Publishing Group, Inc.
88 Post Rd. W., P.O. Box 5007, Westport, CT 06881-5007. 203-226-3571.
Web site: www.praeger.com.
Description: General nonfiction; scholarly and textbooks in the social sciences.
Proposal Process: Query with outline. **Payment:** Royalty. **Contact:** Acquisitions.

BYRON PREISS VISUAL PUBLICATIONS
24 W. 25th St., 11th Fl., New York, NY 10010. 212-645-9870.
Description: Book packager. Want samples from established authors who work to specifications on firm deadlines. Genres: science fiction, fantasy, horror, juvenile, young adult, nonfiction. **Payment:** Pays advance against royalties for commissioned work. **Contact:** Editorial Dept..

PRESIDIO PRESS
505-B San Marin Dr., Suite 300, Novato, CA 94945-1340. 415-898-1081.
E-mail: mail@presidiopress.com. Web site: www.presidiopress.com.
E. J. McCarthy, Editor.
Description: Publish nonfiction and nonfiction military-related books. Military memoirs, biographies, unit histories, and battle and campaign books are our specialty.
Number of Books/Yr.: 42 titles/year (1,500 submissions), 75% by first-time authors, 80% unagented. **Proposal Process:** Send query, outline. SASE. Multiple and electronic queries accepted. Hard copy. **Payment:** Royalty. **Sample Titles:** *The Greatest War: Americans in Combat 1941-1945, Black Sheep One: The Life of Gregory "Pappy" Boyington, America's Secret Air War Against the Soviet Union: A Cold War History.* **Tips:** Look for well-written American military history that will make a contribution to the historiography of the subject.

PRICE STERN SLOAN, INC.
Penguin Putnam Inc., 345 Hudson St., New York, NY 10014. 212-414-3610.
Web site: www.penguinputnam.com.
Jon Anderson, Publisher.
Description: Witty or edgy middle-grade fiction and nonfiction, calendars, and novelty juvenile titles. Imprints include Troubador Press, Wee Sing, MadLibs. **Proposal Process:** No unsolicited manuscripts accepted. Query first. **Payment:** Royalty.

PRIMA PUBLISHING
3000 Lava Ridge Ct., Roseville, CA 95661. 916-787-7000.
Web site: www.primapublishing.com.
Alice Feinstein, Editorial Director.
Description: Nonfiction books in diverse areas including health, parenting and education, business, and current affairs. **Proposal Process:** Query with outline and 1

sample chapter and market research. Response time: 6-8 weeks. Hard copy format preferred. **Payment:** Royalty and flat fee, standard range. **Sample Titles:** Adult: *Helping your ADD Child* (Parenting); *How to Plan an Elegant Wedding in 6 Months or Less*, (Home); *Internal Cleansing* (Health) **Contact:** David Richardson, Denise Sternad, Jamie Miller.

PRINCETON UNIVERSITY PRESS
41 William St., Princeton, NJ 08540. 609-258-4900.
Web site: www.pup.princton.edu.
Ann Wald, Editor-in-Chief.
Description: Scholarly and scientific books on all subjects.

PROMPT PUBLICATIONS
5436 W. 78th Street, Indianapolis, IN 46268. 317-334-1256 x219.
E-mail: ajtripp@samswebsite.com. Web site: www.hwsams.com.
Alice Tripp, Editorial Director.
Description: Nonfiction softcover technical books on electronics, how-to, trouble-shooting and repair, electrical engineering, video and sound equipment, etc., for all levels of technical experience. **Number of Books/Yr.:** 25 title/year (40 submissions), 40% first-time authors. **Proposal Process:** Query with outline, sample chapters, author bio, and SASE. Multiple and electronic queries accepted. Prefers electronic format. **Payment:** Royalty, 10-13% range. **Sample Titles:** *Guide to Digital Cameras, Administators Guide to Servers, Computer Networking for the Small Business, Servicing TV/VCR Combo Units, Exploring Microsoft Office XP.* **Tips:** Electronics or computer application topics applied in a style which helps the user solve problems. Contact us for current list of needed topics.

PRUETT PUBLISHING COMPANY
7464 Arapahoe Rd., Suite A-9, Boulder, CO 80303. 303-449-4919.
E-mail: pruettbks@aol.com. Web site: www.pruettpublishing.com.
Jim Pruett, Acquisitions Editor.
Description: Publishes books dealing with outdoor recreation travel and history. **Number of Books/Yr.:** 10 titles/year (300 submissions), 50% first-time authors, 90% unagented. **Proposal Process:** Send outline and sample chapters. Multiple queries considered. Accepts electronic queries. Preferred format: electronic and hard copy. **Payment:** Royalty. (net 10-12%). **Sample Titles:** *Fly Fishing the Coast of Texas.*

QED PRESS
155 Cypress St., Fort Bragg, CA 95437. 707-964-9520.
E-mail: publishing@cypresshouse.com. Web site: www.cypresshouse.com.
John Fremont, Sr. Editor.
Description: Health and healing, self-help, and how to fold paper airplanes. **Proposal Process:** Query with outline and sample chapters. **Payment:** Royalty.

QUARRY PRESS

P.O. Box 1061, Kingston, Ontario, Canada K7L 4Y5. 613-548-8429.
Description: Adult fiction and nonfiction. New and innovative Canadian writing.
Proposal Process: Query with outline, synopsis, and sample chapters. **Payment:**
Royalty.

QUIXOTE PRESS

1856 Hwy. 61, Wever, IA 52658. 319-372-7480.
E-mail: maddmack@interl.com.
Bruce Carlson, President.
Description: Adult fiction and nonfiction including humor, folklore, and regional
cookbooks; some juvenile fiction. **Proposal Process:** Query with sample chapters
and outline. **Payment:** Royalty.

RAINBOW BOOKS, INC.

Box 430, Highland City, FL 33846. 863-648-4420.
E-mail: rbibooks@aol.com.
Betsy Lampe, Editor.
Description: Publishes nonfiction books. Also, recently began a small list of mystery
fiction. **Number of Books/Yr.:** 15-20 titles/year (600 submissions), 85% first-time
authors, 99% unagented. **Proposal Process:** Query with outline and sample chapters, include SASE. Multiple queries accepted. No electronic queries. Hard-copy format preferred. **Payment:** Royalty. **Tips:** Looking for nonfiction books with answers
to questions of importance to our readers. In mystery fiction, primarily seeking
"cozies." **Contact:** Betty Wright.

RED CRANE BOOKS

2008 Rosina St., Suite B, Santa Fe, NM 87505. 505-988-7070.
E-mail: marianne@redcrane.com. Web site: www.redcrane.com.
Marianne O'Shaughnessy, Publisher.
Description: Art and folk art, bilingual material with Spanish and English, cookbooks, gardening, herbal guides, natural history, novels, social and political issues, and
social history. No children's books. **Proposal Process:** Send a short synopsis, 2 sample chapters, resumé, and SASE. **Tips:** Topics vary year to year. Write for guidelines.

RED SAGE PUBLISHING, INC.

P.O. Box 4844, Seminole, FL 33775. 727-391-3847.
E-mail: alekendall@aol.com. Web site: www.redsagepub.com.
Alexandria Kendall, Editor.
Description: Romance-historical, vampire, contemporary, fantasy, etc. Novellas.
Number of Books/Yr.: 1 title/year (300 submissions), ¼% first time authors, ½%
unagented. **Proposal Process:** Query with outline and sample chapters, and SASE.
Hard copy format preferred. Response time: 3 months. No multiple or electronic
queries. **Sample Titles:** Red Sage's *Secret Collections* has won awards and reviews
rave. Check *Secrets* Vol. #6 at www.amazon.com. **Tips:** Story should focus on main

character's relationship, with great character development. Fast pacing, high-interest characters and plot, high-sensuality romance.

THE RED SEA PRESS
Africa World Press, 11-D Princess Rd., Lawrenceville, NJ 08648. 609-844-9583. E-mail: awprsp@africanworld.com. Web site: www.africanworld.com. Kassahun Checole, Publisher. **Description:** Adult nonfiction, 360 double-spaced manuscript pages. Focus on people of African descent, with a specialty on the Horn of Africa. **Proposal Process:** Query. **Payment:** Royalty.

REGNERY PUBLISHING, INC.
One Massachusetts Ave., NW, Washington, DC 20001. 202-216-0600. Web site: www.regnery.com. Harry Crockes, Executive Editor. **Description:** Nonfiction titles on current affairs, politics, history, biography, and other subjects. The Lifeline Press imprint publishes health titles, and the Capital Press imprint releases business titles. **Number of Books/Yr.:** 35 titles/year. **Proposal Process:** Send query with outline and SASE. Hard copy. No multiple or electronic queries. **Payment:** Royalty.

RENAISSANCE HOUSE
5738 N. Central Ave., Phoenix, AZ 85012. 602-234-1574. E-mail: bfessler@earthlink.net. Bill Fessler, Acquisitions. **Description:** Travel and regional subjects, especially about the Southwest U.S. Also publishes history (20th century, World War II, and Middle East conflicts), and "Living the Simple Life" philosophical writings. No fiction. General adult audience. **Number of Books/Yr.:** 5-10 titles/year (20 submissions), 50% by first-time authors, 99% unagented. **Proposal Process:** Send query, outline, and sample chapters if available. Prefer hard copy format. No multiple queries. Response time: 1 month. **Payment:** Royalty (8% net) or flat fee. **Sample Titles:** *Railroads of Colorado, Gems & Minerals of California, Arizona Cactus, The Denver Mint.*

RISING TIDE PRESS
P.O. Box 30457, Tucson, AZ 85751. 520-888-1140. E-mail: milestonepress@gateway.net. Web site: www.risingtidepress.com. Brenda Kazen, Editorial Director. **Description:** Lesbian/feminist fiction and nonfiction. Books for, by, and about women. Fiction, romance, mystery, and young adult and adventure, science fiction/fantasy. **Number of Books/Yr.:** 6-10 titles/year (300 submissions), 75% first-time authors, 95% unagented. **Proposal Process:** Query with sample chapters, include SASE. Response time: 2-3 months. Hard copy. Accepts multiple and electronic queries. **Payment:** Royalty.

RIZZOLI INTERNATIONAL PUBLICATIONS, INC.
300 Park Ave. S., New York, NY 10010.
Marta Hallett, Publisher.
Description: Illustrated books: art, architecture, and lifestyle. **Proposal Process:** Query with SASE or response card. Response time: varies. Hard copy preferred, electronic queries accepted. Considers multiple queries. **Tips:** We do not publish fiction or children's books. Our books are highly illustrated in the categories of art, architecture, and lifestyle. **Contact:** David Morton, Senior Editor, Architecture; Liz Sullivan, Senior Editor, Lifestyle; Isabel Venero, Editor, Art.

ROBINS LANE PRESS
P.O. Box 207, Beltsville, MD 20705. 301-595-9500.
E-mail: info@robinslane.com. Web site: http://www.robinslane.com.
Description: Timely, unique books on subjects of interest to today's parents. **Number of Books/Yr.:** 8 titles/year (100 submissions), 75% first-time authors, 90% unagented. **Proposal Process:** Query with outline and sample chapters if available. Multiple queries considered. Response time: 6-8 weeks. Prefers hard copy format. Electronic queries accepted. **Contact:** Acquisitions Editor.

ROC
375 Hudson St., New York, NY 10014. 212-366-2000.
Web site: www.penguinputnam.com.
Laura Anne Gilman.
Description: Science fiction, fantasy.

ROCKBRIDGE PUBLISHING CO.
Howell Press, Inc., P.O. Box 351, Berryville, VA 22611-0351. 540-955-3980.
E-mail: cwpub@visuallink.com. Web site: www.rockbpubl.com.
Katherine Tennery, Publisher.
Description: Book-length nonfiction on the Civil War, Virginia history, and travel guides to Virginia. **Proposal Process:** Query. **Payment:** Royalty.

RODALE
33 E. Minor Street, Emmaus, PA 18098. 610-967-5171.
Web site: www.rodalepress.com.
Pat Corpora, President, Books Division.
Description: Books on health (men's, women's, alternative, senior), gardening, cookbooks, spirituality, fitness, and pets. **Proposal Process:** Query with resumé, table of contents/outline, and two sample chapters. "The majority of our books are conceived and developed in-house; but we're always looking for truly competent freelancers to write chapters for books." **Payment:** Payment on a work-for-hire basis.

ROYAL FIREWORKS PRESS
Box 399, First Ave., Unionville, NY 10988. 845-726-4444.
Charles Morgan, Editor.

Description: Publish books for gifted children, their parents and teachers. Also publish novels for all children and young adults. **Number of Books/Yr.:** 100 titles/year (2,000 submissions), 40% first-time authors, 95% unagented. **Proposal Process:** Submit complete manuscripts with a brief plot overview. No multiple or electronic queries. Allow a three-week response time. Hard copy. **Payment:** Royalty. **Tips:** Looking for historical fiction; books on growing up; books about kids solving problems, science fiction, mystery-adventure.

RUMINATOR BOOKS
1648 Grand Ave., St. Paul, MN 55105. 651-699-7038.
E-mail: books@ruminator.com. Web site: www.ruminator.com.
Pearl Kilbride, Editor.
Description: Fiction; memoirs; contemporary affairs; cultural criticism; travel essays; nonfiction. No genre fiction, self-help, or poetry. Books that examine the human experience or comments on social and cultural mores. **Proposal Process:** Query with outline and sample chapters. **Payment:** Royalty.

RUNESTONE PRESS
Lerner Publishing Group, 241 First Ave. N., Minneapolis, MN 55401. 612-332-3344.
Web site: www.lernerbooks.com.
Mary M. Rodgers, Editor-in-Chief.
Description: Specializes in reprints of out-of-print nonfiction for grades 5 and up, especially world culture, archaeology, and history topics. **Proposal Process:** Submissions accepted during March and October only. Considers multiple queries. SASE required. **Payment:** Negotiated, usually flat fees.

RUNNING PRESS
125 S. 22nd St., Philadelphia, PA 19103. 215-567-5080.
E-mail: comments@runningpress.com. Web site: www.runningpress.com.
Description: Specialize in publishing illustrated nonfiction for adults and children.
Proposal Process: Query with outline or table of contents and 2-3 page writing sample. Multiple queries accepted. No electronic queries. Hard copy. Response time: 4 weeks. **Payment:** Royalty for some projects; flat fee for others. **Tips:** No fiction or poetry. **Contact:** Susan Phillips.

RUSSIAN HILL PRESS
6410 Geary Blvd., San Francisco, CA 94121. 415-387-0846.
Description: Books, 50,000-120,000 words. Literary and mainstream fiction, including thrillers and suspense. Nonfiction in the areas of politics, sociology, and literary biography. **Payment:** Royalty. **Contact:** Jeff Love.

RUTGERS UNIVERSITY PRESS
100 Joyce Kilmer Ave., Piscataway, NJ 08854-8099. 732-445-7762.
Web site: www.rutgerspress.edu.
Leslie Mitchner, Editor-in-Chief.

Description: Scholarly publisher of religion, history of medicine, biological sciences, media studies, art, literature, history, gender studies, and multicultural studies. Also interested in general studies that have a strong scholarly basis. **Number of Books/Yr.:** 20 titles/year (1,200 submissions), 35% by first-time authors, 85% unagented. **Proposal Process:** Query with outline and sample chapters. Send Humanities proposals to Theresa Liu; Science and Social Sciences proposals to Suzanne Kellam. Hard copy format preferred. No electronic queries. Multiple queries okay. **Payment:** Royalty. **Sample Titles:** Titles: *Hard Road to Freedom, The Story of African America, Biological Theories of Race at the Millennium, Bohemians, The Glamorous Outcasts.* **Tips:** Avoid anything too jargon-laden. Most interested in projects with a strong scholarly foundation. **Contact:** Theresa Liu, Editorial Asst.

RUTLEDGE HILL PRESS
P.O. Box 141000, Nashville, TN 37214-1000. 615-902-2333.
E-mail: tmengesrhp@aol.com. Web site: www.rutledgehill.com.
Lawrence M. Stone, Editor.
Description: General nonfiction. Cookbooks, regional history and topics (Tennessee), philosophy, biography. **Number of Books/Yr.:** 40 titles/year (1,000 submissions), 35% first-time authors, 70% unagented. **Proposal Process:** Query with outline and sample chapters. SASE required. Multiple and electronic queries accepted. Hard copy format preferred. **Payment:** Flat fee. **Tips:** Interested in adult nonfiction.

ST. MARTIN'S PRESS
175 Fifth Ave., New York, NY 10010. 212-674-5151.
Web site: www.stmartins.com.
Description: General adult fiction and nonfiction. **Proposal Process:** Query first. **Payment:** Royalty.

SANDLAPPER PUBLISHING CO, INC.
920 Amelia St., Orangeburg, SC 29115. 803-531-1658.
E-mail: agallman@theisp.net.
Amanda Gallman, Managing Editor.
Description: Nonfiction books on South Carolina history, culture, cuisine. **Proposal Process:** Query with outline, sample chapters, and SASE.

SASQUATCH BOOKS
615 2nd Ave., Suite 260, Seattle, WA 98104. 206-467-4300.
E-mail: books@sasquatchbooks.com. Web site: www.sasquatchbooks.com.
Gary Luke, Editor.
Description: Regional books covering the west coast of the U. S. only. Food, travel, gardening, pop culture, literary nonfiction. **Number of Books/Yr.:** 40 titles/year, 30% by first-time authors, 30% unagented. **Proposal Process:** Query with SASE. Response time: 3 months. No multiple or electronic queries. Hard copy. **Payment:** Royalty. **Tips:** Regional only (Pacific Northwest, Alaska, and California).

SCARECROW PRESS

4720 Boston Way, Lanham, MD 20706. 301-459-3366 Ext. 5306.
E-mail: smoeckel@scarecrowpress.com. Web site: www.scarecrowpress.com.
Shirley Lambert, Editorial Director.
Description: Scholarly bibliographies, historical dictionaries (of countries, religious, organizations, wars, movements, cities, and ancient civilizations). Lists includes textbooks in library and information science. **Number of Books/Yr.:** 150 titles/year (250 submissions), 20% by first-time authors, 95% unagented. **Proposal Process:** Query with subject matter, scope, and intended purpose of your mss. Multiple queries considered. Electronic queries accepted. Hard copy format preferred. Response time: 2-4 months. **Payment:** Royalty, 10% on first 1,000 copies, 15% thereafter. If camera-ready copy is submitted, 15% on all copies. **Tips:** See guidelines. **Contact:** Sydney Moeckel (reference/religion), Rebecca Massa (music and film), Nichole Coviello (young adult literature and library science).

SEAL PRESS

3131 Western Ave., Suite 410, Seattle, WA 98121-1041. 206-283-7844.
E-mail: sealpress@sealpress.com. Web site: www.sealpress.com.
Leslie Miller, Senior Editor.
Description: Publishes titles ranging from literary fiction to health, popular culture, women's studies, parenting and travel/outdoor adventure. Currently focusing our acquisitions in two popular series: *Adventura* (focuses on women's travel/adventure writing) and *Live Girls* (showcases the voices of modern feminism). **Number of Books/Yr.:** 15 titles/year (1,500 submissions), 20% first-time authors, 20% unagented. **Proposal Process:** Query. No electronic or multiple queries. Hard copy format preferred. Response time: 2-4 months. **Payment:** Royalty, 7% net. **Tips:** Read our submission guidelines before submitting.

SEVEN STORIES PRESS

140 Watts St., New York, NY 10013. 212-226-8760.
E-mail: info@sevenstories.com. Web site: www.sevenstories.com.
Daniel Simon, Acquistions.
Description: Small press. Fiction and nonfiction. **Proposal Process:** Query with SASE. **Payment:** Royalty. **Contact:** Editor.

SHAMBHALA PUBLICATIONS, INC.

P.O. Box 308, Boston, MA 02117. 617-424-0030.
E-mail: editors@shambhala.com. Web site: www.shambhala.com.
Peter Turner, Executive Editor.
Description: Eastern religion, especially Buddhism and Taoism, as well as psychology, self-help, and philosophy. **Proposal Process:** Query Laura Stone with outline and sample chapters. **Payment:** Flat fee and royalty.

SIERRA CLUB BOOKS

85 Second St., San Francisco, CA 94105. 415-977-5733.
E-mail: danny.moses@sierraclub.org. Web site: www.sierraclub.org/books.
Danny Moses, Editorial Director.
Description: Publishes books about nature, ecology, and environmental issues.
Number of Books/Yr.: 20 titles/year (1,000 submissions), 10-20% by first-time authors, 40-50% unagented. **Proposal Process:** Query with outline. Considers multiple and electronic queries. Response time: 1 month. Prefers electronic format.
Payment: Royalty, typical range is 10% net. **Sample Titles:** *Seasons of the Arctic, The Mountain World,* and *The Spirit of the Valley.*

SILHOUETTE BOOKS

300 E. 42nd St., New York, NY 10017. 212-682-6080.
Web site: www.eharlequin.com.
Tara Gavin, Editorial Director.
Description: Contemporary and historical romance. Mills & Boon, Harlequin, Silhouette, MIRA, and Steeple Hills books. **Number of Books/Yr.:** 300-350 titles/year. **Proposal Process:** Query with outline and sample chapters. SASE required. Prefers hard copy format. No multiple or electronic queries. **Payment:** Royalty. **Tips:** We encourage you to read many books from each series. The series that emerges as your favorite is probably where you should submit your manuscript.

SILK LABEL BOOKS

1 First Ave., P.O. Box 700, Unionville, NY 10988-0700. 845-726-3434.
William F.V. Neumann, Editorial Director.
Description: Adult fiction; mystery, humor, science fiction, historical fiction.
Number of Books/Yr.: 50 titles/year (500 submissions), 50% first-time authors, 80% unagented. **Proposal Process:** Query with complete manuscript, and SASE. Hard copy format preferred. Subsidizes. **Payment:** Royalty.

SILVERCAT PUBLICATIONS

4070 Goldfinch St., Suite C, San Diego, CA 92103-1865. 619-299-6774.
Description: Nonfiction trade books, 100,000-120,000 words, that deal with consumer and quality-of-life issues. **Proposal Process:** Query. **Payment:** Royalty.
Contact: Robert Outlaw.

SMITH AND KRAUS, INC.

P.O. Box 127, Main St., Lyme, NH 03768. 603-643-6431.
E-mail: sandk@sovernet. Web site: www.smithkraus.com.
Marisa Smith, Editor Director.
Description: Publishes monologue and scene anthologies, biographies of playwrights, translations, books on career development (in theater) and the art of theater, and teaching texts for young actors (K-12). **Number of Books/Yr.:** 30 titles/year (500+ submissions), 20% by first-time authors, 50% unagented. **Proposal Process:** Query with SASE. Response time is 1-2 months. No multiple queries. Electronic

queries accepted as well as hard copy. **Payment:** Royalty and flat fee. **Tips:** Material of interest to the theatre community.

GIBBS SMITH, PUBLISHER
P.O. Box 667, Layton, UT 84041. 801-544-9800.
E-mail: info@gibbs-smith.com. Web site: www.gibbs-smith.com.
Madge Baird, Editor.
Description: Home and hearth, gift, architecture guides and monographs, cookbooks, western culture and lifestyle, children's pictures and activity, primitive skills. **Tips:** We're looking for fresh insights into home decorating. Inspirational stories that can be illustrated for adult gift books, suitable for any occasion. **Contact:** Suzanne Taylor.

SMITH RESEARCH ASSOCIATES
Signature Books, 564 W. 400 North, Salt Lake City, UT 84116-3411.
Web site: www.signaturebooks.com.
Description: Utah history and Mormon studies, from 250 pages. **Contact:** George D. Smith.

SOHO PRESS
853 Broadway, New York, NY 10003. 212-260-1900.
Web site: www.sohopress.com.
Juris Jurjevics, Acquisitions Editor.
Description: Adult literary fiction, mysteries, nonfiction in the areas of memoir, travel, social and cultural history. **Number of Books/Yr.:** 40 titles/year (2,000 submissions), 10% by first-time authors, 10% unagented. **Proposal Process:** Query with the first three sample chapters. Response time: 2 months. Considers multiple queries. No electronic queries. Hard copy. **Payment:** Royalty (net 10%, 12.5%, 15%). **Sample Titles:** Adult: *Gloria,* by Keith Maillard; *Death of a Red Heroine,* Qui Xaolung; *The Gravity of Sunlight,* by Rosa Shand. **Tips:** No mass-market or religious books. **Contact:** Melanie Fleishman.

SOUNDPRINTS
353 Main Ave., Norwalk, CT 06851. 203-840-2274.
E-mail: soundprints@ix.netcom.com. Web site: www.soundprints.com.
Chelsea Shrive, Acquisitions.
Description: Publishes books about wildlife and history created to educate and entertain. Need an exciting storyline. At the same time, each book is based on fact and all aspects must be supported by careful research. **Number of Books/Yr.:** 12 titles/year (100 submissions), 12% unagented. **Proposal Process:** Query. Multiple and electronic queries accepted. Hard copy. Response time: 1 month. **Payment:** Flat fee. **Sample Titles:** Currently publishes 6 series: *Smithsonian Oceanic Collection, Smithsonian's Backyard, Smithsonian Odyssey Collection, Smithsonian Let's Go to the Zoo!, Soundprints Multicultural/Make Friends Around the World,* and *Soundprints Wild Habitats.* **Tips:** Verify in advance that Soundprints has not already

published, or is not currently working on, a book on your chosen topic. A catalog is available on request. **Contact:** Ashley Andersen, Associate Publisher.

SOURCEBOOKS

P.O. Box 4410, Naperville, IL 60567-4410. 630-961-3900.
E-mail: todd.stocke@sourcebooks.com. Web site: www.sourcebooks.com.
Todd Stocke, Editor.
Description: Most nonfiction categories, (entertainment, history, sports, general self-help/psychology, small business, marketing and management, parenting, health and beauty, reference, biography, gift books, and women's issues). Fiction imprint, Sourcebooks Landmark, launched in 2001. **Number of Books/Yr.:** 100 titles/year (3,000+ submissions), 10% first-time authors, 20% unagented. **Proposal Process:** Query with outline and sample chapters, include SASE. Multiple queries OK. No electronic queries. Prefer hard-copy format. **Payment:** Royalty. **Sample Titles:** Adult Fiction: *Man and Boy*, by Tony Parsons; *The Other Adonis*, by Frank Deford. Adult Nonfiction: *What Flavor Is Your Personality*, by Alan Hirsch, MD; *Bathroom Stuff*, by Holman Wang; and *Seduced by Hitler*, by Adam LeBor and Roger Boyes. **Tips:** Know your competition, make your book stand apart.

SOUTH END PRESS

7 Brookline St., Suite One, Cambridge, MA 02139-4146. 617-547-4002.
Web site: www.lbbs.org/sep.htm.
Anthony Arnove, Editor.
Description: Nonprofit, collectively run book publisher with more than 200 titles in print. Committed to the politics of radical social change. Encourage critical thinking and consecutive action on the key political, cultural, social, economic, and ecological issues shaping life in the United States and in the world. **Number of Books/Yr.:** 10 titles/year (1,000 submissions), 5% first-time authors, 95% unagented. **Proposal Process:** Query with sample chapters; multiple queries are accepted. Response time: 6-8 weeks. Hard copy format preferred. **Payment:** Royalty.

SOUTHERN ILLINOIS UNIVERSITY PRESS

P.O. Box 3697, Carbondale, IL 62902-3697. 618-453-6626.
E-mail: jdsin@siu.edu832. Web site: www.siu.edu/~siupress.
James Simmons, Editorial Director.
Description: Nonfiction on the humanities and social studies, 200-300 pages. **Proposal Process:** Query with outline and sample chapters. **Payment:** Royalty.

SOUTHERN METHODIST UNIVERSITY PRESS

Box 415, Dallas, TX 75275-0415. 214-768-1433.
E-mail: klang@mail.smu.edu.
Kathryn Lang, Acquisitions Editor.
Description: Publishes: literary fiction, medical humanities/ethics/death and dying (nonfiction), Southwest life and letters (both fiction and nonfiction), books on film, theatre and performing arts. **Number of Books/Yr.:** 12 titles/year (2,500 submis-

sions), 80% by first-time authors, 90% unagented. **Proposal Process:** Query with outline and sample chapters. Response time: 1 month. Prefers hard copy format. Accepts multiple queries. No electronic queries. **Payment:** Royalty (net 10%). **Sample Titles:** *The Price You Pay*, fiction. *Biography of Wright Payman. La Scala West*, (history of Dallas Opera).

SPECTACLE LANE PRESS

Box 1237, 2165 Country Manor Drive, Mt. Pleasant, SC 29465-1237. 843-971-9165. E-mail: jaskar44@aol.com.

James A. Skardon, Editor.

Description: Humor, text, and cartoons. Lifestyle texts. Subject matter varies, including satire, self-help, business, sports, television topics. Mostly trade paperback and occasional cloth. **Number of Books/Yr.:** 1-3 titles/year (300 submissions), 90% by first-time writers, 90% unagented. **Proposal Process:** Query with outline and sample chapters, and SASE. No multiple queries, electronic queries accepted. Response time: 2-4 weeks. **Payment:** Advance against royalty. **Sample Titles:** *The Difference Between Cats and Dogs*, by Bob Zahn (Cartoons). **Tips:** Humor should be current and sophisticated, nothing scatological. Writing should be clear, straight-forward, well-organized, with base of solid expertise.

SPHINX PRESS

Sourcebooks, Inc., P.O. Box 4410, Naperville, IL 60567-4410. 630-961-3900. E-mail: info@sourcebooks.com. Web site: www.sourcebooks.com.

Hillel Black, Editor.

Description: Nonfiction; legal self-help. **Proposal Process:** Query with outline and sample chapters. **Payment:** Royalty.

SPINSTERS INK

P.O. Box 22005, Denver, CO 80222. 303-761-5552. E-mail: spinster@spinstersink.com. Web site: www.spinsters-ink.com.

Description: Adult fiction and nonfiction books, 200-plus pages that deal with sig-nificant issues in women's lives from a feminist perspective and encourage change and growth. Main characters and/or narrators must be women. **Number of Books/Yr.:** 6/year. 50% first time authors; 80% unagented. **Proposal Process:** Query with out-line; multiple queries considered. Response time 90 days. E-query OK. SASE. **Payment:** Royalty. **Contact:** Sharon Silvas.

STA-KRIS, INC.

107 N. Center St., Marshalltown, IA 50158. 641-753-4139. E-mail: stakris@mcleodusa.net. Web site: www.stakris.com.

Kathy Wagoner, President.

Description: Nonfiction adult-level gift books that portray universal feelings, truths, and values; or have a special-occasion theme. **Proposal Process:** Query with bio, list of credits, complete manuscript, and SASE.

STACKPOLE BOOKS

5067 Ritter Rd., Mechanicsburg, PA 17055. 717-796-0412.
E-mail: jschnell@stackpolebooks.com. Web site: www.stackpolebooks.com.
Judith Schnell, Editorial Director.
Description: Looking for good, well-researched work on interesting topics such as: the outdoors, nature, fishing, fly fishing, climbing, paddling, sports, sporting literature, history, and military reference. **Number of Books/Yr.:** 80 titles/year (150 submissions), 20% first-time authors, 70% unagented. **Proposal Process:** Submit queries with sample chapters to acquisitions editor for the line: Marl Allison (nature), Judith Schnell (fishing/sports), Leigh Ann Berry (History), Kyle Weaver (Pennsylvania). No electronic or multiple queries. Hard copy. **Payment:** Royalty; advance or flat fee. **Tips:** No poetry, cookbooks, fiction, or books on crafts. History books must have some original research involved. **Contact:** Acquisitions Editor.

STANFORD UNIVERSITY PRESS

Stanford University, Stanford, CA 94305-2235. 650-723-9434.
Web site: www.sup.org.
Norris Pope, Editor.
Description: Furthers the University's research and teaching mission through books of significant scholarship. **Number of Books/Yr.:** 120 titles/year (2,000 submissions), 35% by first-time authors, 95% unagented. **Proposal Process:** Query with outline and sample chapters. Response time: varies. Multiple queries accepted. No electronic queries. Hard copy. **Payment:** Royalty. **Tips:** No original fiction or poetry.

STARBURST PUBLISHERS

Box 4123, Lancaster, PA 17604. 717-293-0939.
E-mail: editorial@starburstpublishers.com. Web site: www.starburstpublishers.com.
David A. Robie, Editorial Director.
Description: Self-help, health, and inspiration. Sell to both ABA and CBA markets. No fiction. **Number of Books/Yr.:** 15-20 titles per year (1,000 submissions). **Proposal Process:** Query with outline for nonfiction book, synopsis for fiction book, and 3 sample chapters. Considers multiple queries. Hard copy. **Payment:** Royalty, range 6-16% net. **Sample Titles:** *What's in the Bible for ... Teens?* (Religion). *Cheap Talk with the Frugal Friends,* (Self-help/finance). **Tips:** No fiction, poetry, young adult, or children. Books that will work in both the ABA and CBA (evangelical Christian) markets.

STARRHILL PRESS

Black Belt Publishing, LLC, P.O. Box 551, Montgomery, AL 36101.
E-mail: jdavis@blackbelt.com. Web site: www.black-belt.com.
Jim Davis, Editor.
Description: Publishes high-quality books about a variety of topics including art, gardening, health, history, literature, music, and travel. **Number of Books/Yr.:** 10 titles/year (300 submissions), 10% first-time authors, 80% unagented. **Proposal Process:** Query with cover letter, outline, author bio, and SASE for reply. Response

time: 6 weeks to 6 months. Prefer hard copy format. Multiple and electronic queries accepted. **Payment:** Royalty. **Sample Titles:** Recent title includes: *Beyond Viagra,* written by a distinguished Alabama physician, which discusses alternatives to the popular new medication. Starhill is an imprint of Black Belt Publishing, LLC. **Tips:** A Starhill book is usually a short, somewhat cerebral softcover volume that is modern, topical, and enlightening and makes a great gift. Most of our authors, but not all, are from Alabama or the South.

STATE UNIVERSITY OF NEW YORK PRESS

State Univ. Plaza, Albany, NY 12246-0001. 518-472-5000.
Web site: www.sunypress.edu.
James H. Peltz, Editorial Director.
Description: Scholarly and trade books in the humanities and social science. **Number of Books/Yr.:** 200 titles/year (1,200 submissions), 99% unagented authors. **Proposal Process:** Query with outline and sample chapters. No electronic queries. Multiple queries accepted. Response time: 4-6 weeks. Hard copy format preferred. **Payment:** Royalty (typically 5-10%).

STEERFORTH PRESS

105-106 Chelsea St., Box 70, South Royalton, VT 05068. 802-763-2808.
E-mail: info@steerforth.com. Web site: www.steerforth.com.
Michael Moore, Editor.
Description: Adult nonfiction and some literary fiction. Novels, serious works of history, biography, politics, current affairs. **Proposal Process:** Query with SASE. **Payment:** Royalty.

STEMMER HOUSE PUBLISHERS, INC.

2627 Caves Rd., Owings Mills, MD 21117. 410-363-3690.
E-mail: stemmerhouse@home.com. Web site: www.stemmer.com.
Barbara Holdridge, Editorial Director.
Description: Nonfiction for adults, including the International Design Library, and books/audiocassettes for children. **Number of Books/Yr.:** 4 titles/year (2,000 submissions), 50% by first-time authors, 95% unagented. **Proposal Process:** Query with sample chapters, SASE. Considers multiple and electronic queries. Response time: 2 weeks. Prefer hard copy format. **Payment:** Royalty, 5%-10% net. **Sample Titles:** Adult: *Japanese Garden Journey* (garden appreciation). Children's: *North Atlantic on the Great Ship Normandie,* by Peter Mandel (ages 8-12).

STERLING PUBLISHING

387 Park Ave. S., New York, NY 10016. 212-532-7160.
Web site: www.sterlingpub.com.
Sheila Anne Barry, Acquistions Manager.
Description: How-to, hobby, woodworking, alternative health and healing, fiber arts, crafts, dolls and puppets, ghosts, wine, nature, oddities, new consciousness, puzzles, juvenile humor and activities, juvenile nature and science, medieval history,

Celtic topics, gardening, alternative lifestyle, business, pets, recreation, sports and games books, reference, and home decorating. **Proposal Process:** Query with outline, sample chapter, and sample illustrations. **Payment:** Royalty. **Contact:** Frances Gilbert, Juvenile Ed.

STODDART PUBLISHING COMPANY

General Publishing, 895 Don Mills Rd., Toronto, ON, Canada M8C 1W5. 416-445-3333.

E-mail: gdsinc@genpub.com. Web site: www.genpub.com.

Description: Literary fiction and nonfiction, including business, politics, humor, and sports. **Proposal Process:** Query with an outline and sample chapters; multiple queries are accepted. **Payment:** Royalty.

STONEYDALE PRESS

523 Main St., P.O. Box 188, Stevensville, MT 59870. 406-777-2729.

E-mail: daleburk@montana.com.

Dale A. Burk, Publisher.

Description: Adult nonfiction, primarily how-to, on outdoor recreation with emphasis on big game hunting; some regional history of Northern Rockies. Specialized market. **Proposal Process:** Query with outline and sample chapters essential. **Payment:** Royalty.

STOREY COMMUNICATIONS

Schoolhouse Rd., Pownal, VT 05261. 413-346-2100.

Web site: www.storeybooks.com.

Maggie Lydie, Editorial Director.

Description: Nonfiction how-to in areas of gardening, crafts, natural health, building, pets/animals, nature. Also tips and gift books on lifestyle and juvenile nature books. **Number of Books/Yr.:** 40 titles/year, 50% first-time authors, 80% unagented. **Proposal Process:** Send query with outline and sample chapters, and SASE. Multiple queries accepted. No electronic queries. Hard copy. Response time: 2-3 months. **Payment:** Royalty or flat fee. **Tips:** Well-researched competitive analysis and clearly defined "hook" to make proposed book stand out from competition. Clear, hard-working content, with imaginative presentation.

STORMLINE PRESS

P.O. Box 593, Urbana, IL 61801.

E-mail: rbial@alexia.lis.uiuc.edu.

Raymond Bial, Editor.

Description: Distinctive works of literary and artistic value, with emphasis on rural and small town. **Number of Books/Yr.:** 1 title/year, 10% first-time authors, 10% unagented. **Proposal Process:** Query with outline and sample chapters, SASE. Multiple queries accepted. No electronic queries. Hard copy. **Payment:** Flat fee. **Sample Titles:** *Nonfiction: Living with Lincoln* and *When the Waters Recede,* by Dan Guillory. Fiction: *Silent Friends,* by Margaret Lacey. **Tips:** Please review the kinds of books published by our press to gain a sense of the types of books we publish. We are a very small publisher and do not have the staff to respond to inquiries or submissions. We do not accept unsolicited manuscripts.

STRAWBERRY HILL PRESS
21 Isis Street #102, San Francisco, CA 94103. 415-431-4425.
Daniel F. Vojir, Editor.
Description: Nonfiction: biography, autobiography, history, cooking, health, how-to, philosophy, performance arts, and the Third World. **Proposal Process:** Query with sample chapters, outline, and SASE. **Payment:** Royalty.

SUMMIT UNIVERSITY PRESS
P.O. Box 5000, Corwin Springs, MT 59030-5000. 800-245-5445.
E-mail: info@summituniversitypress.com.
Web site: www.summituniversitypress.com.
Description: Books on spirituality and personal growth, focusing on the practical side of spirituality. **Proposal Process:** Query first. **Payment:** Royalty.

SUNDANCE PUBLISHING
P.O. Box 1326, 234 Taylor St., Littleton, MA 01460. 800-343-8204.
Web site: www.sundancepub.com.
M. Elizabeth Strauss, Director Publishing.
Description: Curriculum materials to accompany quality children's, young adult, and adult literature. **Payment:** Flat fee only.

SYRACUSE UNIVERSITY PRESS
621 Skytop Rd., Ste. 110, Syracuse, NY 13244-5290. 315-443-5534.
E-mail: msevans@syr.edu. Web site: http://sumweb.syr.edu/su_press.
Mary Selden Evans, Acquisitions.
Description: Scholarly general and regional nonfiction.

TAYLOR PUBLISHING CO.
1550 W. Mockingbird Ln., Dallas, TX 75235. 214-819-8334.
Web site: www.taylorpub.com.
Craig Von Pelt, President.
Description: Adult nonfiction: gardening, sports, health, popular culture, celebrity biographies, parenting, and history. **Proposal Process:** Query with outline, sample chapter, author bio, and SASE. **Payment:** Royalty. *No recent report.*

TEMPLE UNIVERSITY PRESS
1601 N. Broad St., USB 305, Philadelphia, PA 19122-6099. 215-204-8787.
E-mail: tempress@astro.ocis.temple.edu. Web site: www.temple.edu/tempress.
Janet Francendese, Editor-in-Chief.
Description: Adult nonfiction. **Proposal Process:** Query with outline and sample chapters. **Payment:** Royalty.

TEN SPEED PRESS

P.O. Box 7123, Berkeley, CA 94707. 510-559-1600.

Web site: www.tenspeed.com.

Kirsty Melville, Editorial Department.

Description: Career and business books. **Number of Books/Yr.:** 150 titles/year (5,000 submissions), 30% first-time authors, 30% unagented. **Proposal Process:** Query with outline and sample chapters, include SASE. Electronic queries okay. Hard copy. No electronic queries. Response time: 6 weeks. **Payment:** Royalty. **Sample Titles:** *What Color Is Your Parachute?*, *Damn Good Resumé* and *Hiring Smart.* **Tips:** Familiarize yourself with our house and our list before submitting mss. Provide a rationale for why we are the best publishing house for your work. **Contact:** Carrie Rodrigues.

THIRD WORLD PRESS

P.O. Box 19730, Chicago, IL 60619. 773-651-0700.

E-mail: twpress3@aol.com. Web site: www.thirdworldpress.com.

Haki R. Madhubuti, Publisher.

Description: Progressive Black Publishing. Adult fiction, nonfiction, and poetry, as well juvenile fiction and young adult books. **Proposal Process:** Query with outline. Send SASE or e-mail for guidelines. **Payment:** Royalty.

THUNDER'S MOUTH PRESS

Avalon Publishing Group, 841 Broadway, 4th Fl., New York, NY 10003. 212-614-7880.

Mary Francis, Editor.

Description: Publishes adult trade books in a variety of subject areas. Concentrates heavily on pop culture, current events, contemporary culture, fantasy and role-playing games, and biography. **Number of Books/Yr.:** 50 titles/year (thousands of submissions), 10% by first-time authors, 0% unagented. **Proposal Process:** Send query with complete manuscript. Response time: varies. No multiple or electronic queries.

TIA CHUCHA PRESS

P.O. Box 476969, Chicago, IL 60647. 773-377-2496.

E-mail: guildcomplex@earthlink.net. Web site: www.nupress.nwu.edu/guild.

Luis Rodriguez.

Description: Poetry, 60-100 pages. Annual deadline: June 30. **Payment:** Royalty.

TIARE PUBLICATIONS

P.O. Box 493, Lake Geneva, WI 53147. 262-248-4845.

E-mail: info@tiare.com. Web site: www.tiare.com.

Gerry L. Dexter, Editor.

Description: Adult nonfiction. Practical how-to guides. **Number of Books/Yr.:** 6 titles/year (40 submissions), 90% unagented. **Proposal Process:** Query with outline and sample chapters, and SASE. Electronic queries accepted. No multiple queries. Hard copy Response time: 2 weeks. **Payment:** Royalty.

TILBURY HOUSE

2 Mechanic St., #3, Gardiner, ME 04345. 207-582-1899.
Web site: www.tilburyhouse.com.
Jennifer Elliott, Publisher.
Description: Small, independent publisher of children's books that deal with cultural diversity or the environment, appeal to children and parents as well as the educational market, and offer possibilities for developing a separate teacher's guide. Adult books: nonfiction books about Maine or the Northeast. **Proposal Process:** Query with outline and sample chapters. Prefers electronic or hard copy format. Accepts unsolicited manuscripts. **Payment:** Pays on publication. **Sample Titles:** Children's: *Talking Walls,* by first-time author Margy Burns Knight.

TOR BOOKS

Tom Doherty Associates, 175 Fifth Ave., New York, NY 10010. 212-388-0100.
E-mail: inquiries@ror.com. Web site: www.tor.com.
Patrick Nielsen Hayden, Senior Editor.
Description: Science fiction and fantasy, from 80,000 words. **Proposal Process:** Query with complete synopsis and first 3 chapters. **Payment:** Advance and royalty.

TRANS NATIONAL GROUP

133 Federal St., Boston, MA 02110. 617-369-1000.
Debra Lance, Editor.
Description: Books for members of the Golf Society of the United States and the Adventure Club of North America. Subjects include golfing, backpacking, bicycling, camping, canoeing, fishing, hiking, mountain biking, outdoor photography, and skiing. **Proposal Process:** Submit proposal with brief description of audience, resumé, and published clips, include SASE. Responds in 2 months. **Payment:** Flat fee.

TRAVELERS' TALES, INC.

330 Townsend St., #208, San Francisco, CA 94107.
E-mail: submit@travelerstales.com. Web site: www.travelerstales.com.
Lisa Bach, Editor.
Description: Travel writing by world-famous authors and new voices. Also travel advice books and imprint, Footsteps, with full-length travel narratives. Sample Titles: *Take Me With You,* by Brad Newsham; *Storm,* by Allen Noren; *Travelers' Tales Greece, Women's Best Spiritual Travel Writing, Not So Funny When It Happened, The Best Travel Humor & Misadventure,* edited by Tim Cahill. Tips: Seeking travel books that inspire, educate, and better prepare travelers with tips and wisdom, original essays; not typical journalistic travel books.

TREADMARK PUBLICATIONS

1731 Howe Ave., #492, Sacramento, CA 95825.
Anton Surivach.
Description: Short-short pieces, 1-5 pages, for anthologies; horror, comedy, bizarre; fast-paced with unusual twists. **Payment:** Royalty and flat fee. *No recent report.*

TRIQUARTERLY BOOKS

2020 Ridge Ave., Evanston, IL 60208-4302. 847-491-3490.
Web site: www.triquarterly.nwu.edu.
Susan Firestone Hahn, Editor.
Description: Short fiction, novels, poetry in translation. **Number of Books/Yr.:** 5
titles/year (200 submissions), 20% first-time authors, 60% unagented. **Proposal
Process:** Query with sample chapters. Response time: 2-6 months. Hard copy format
preferred. Multiple queries accepted. No electronic queries. **Payment:** Royalty
and/or flat fee. **Tips:** Style of writing, subject matter, etc. Writers should avoid literary fiction and poetry.Study our list before submitting material.

TURTLE POINT PRESS

103 Hog Hill Rd., Chappaqua, NY 10514. 914-244-3840, 800-453-2992 (voice & fax).
E-mail: countomega@aol.com. Web site: www.turtlepoint.com.
Jonathan D. Rabinowitz, President.
Description: Forgotten literary fiction, historical and biographical; some contempo-
rary fiction, 200-400 typed pages. Also publishes imprint "Books & Co." **Proposal
Process:** Query with sample chapters. Multiple queries considered. **Payment:**
Royalty.

TURTLE PRESS

P.O. Box 290206, Wethersfield, CT 06129-0206. 860-529-7770.
E-mail: editorial@turtlepress.com. Web site: www.turtlepress.com.
Cynthia Kim, Editor.
Description: Publishes books on mind-body, Eastern philosophy, holistic fitness,
and martial arts. **Number of Books/Yr.:** 4-8 titles/year (350 submissions), 40%
first-time authors, 90% unagented. **Proposal Process:** Query with outline and sample chapters, and SASE. Response time: 2-4 weeks. Multiple and electronic queries
accepted but prefers hard copy format. **Payment:** Royalty.

UNIVERSE PUBLISHING

300 Park Ave. S., New York, NY 10010.
Charles Miers, Publisher.
Description: Publish art and illustrated books typically geared to the adult market
(18-older). Genre includes; fashion, gay subjects, art history, pop culture, design,
architecture, and lifestyle books. Also publishes a few popup books, geared to both
young adults and adults. **Number of Books/Yr.:** 40 titles/year (200 submissions),
30% by first-time authors, 40% unagented. **Proposal Process:** Query with outline
and sample chapters. Include SASE. Response time: 1 month. Hard-copy format preferred. **Payment:** Royalty and flat fee. **Tips:** No children's books.

THE UNIVERSITY OF AKRON PRESS

374-B Bierce Library, Akron, OH 44325-1703. 330-972-5342.
E-mail: uapress@uakron.edu. Web site: www.uakron.edu/uapress.
Michael J. Carley, Editor.

Description: Publish 5 series: *Poetry; Ohio History and Culture; Technology and the Environment; Law, Politics, and Society; International, Political, and Economic History.* **Number of Books/Yr.:** 12 titles/year (100 submissions), 40% first-time authors, 100% unagented. **Proposal Process:** Query with outline and chapters. Multiple and electronic queries accepted. Prefer hard-copy format. Response time: 1-2 months. **Payment:** Royalty. **Tips:** See website for submission guidelines.

UNIVERSITY OF ALABAMA PRESS

P.O. Box 870380, 520 19th Avenue, Tuscaloosa, AL 35487-0380. 205-348-5180. Web site: www.uapress.ua.edu.
Curtis Clark, Editor-in-Chief.
Description: Scholarly and general regional nonfiction. Submit to appropriate editor: Nicole Mitchell, Ed. (history, Latin American history, art, regional southern studies); Curtis Clark, Ed. (African-American, native American, women's and Jewish studies, public adminstration, theater, English, rhetoric and communication); Judith Knight, Ed. (archaeology, anthropology). **Number of Books/Yr.:** 55 titles; 90% unagented and 50% first-time authors. **Proposal Process:** Send cover letter, curriculum vitae, outline, sample chapter(s), and a prospectus outlining the proposed length, illustrations, etc. **Payment:** Royalty, 5-10%.

UNIVERSITY OF ARIZONA PRESS

1230 N. Park Ave., Suite 102, Tucson, AZ 85719-4140. 520-621-1441.
E-mail: uapress@uapress.arizona.edu. Web site: www.uapress.arizona.edu.
Christine Szuter, Editor-in-Chief.
Description: Scholarly and popular nonfiction: Arizona, American West, anthropology, archaeology, behavioral sciences, environmental science, geography, Latin America, Native Americans, natural history, space sciences, women's studies. **Proposal Process:** Query with outline, sample chapters, and current curriculum vitae or resumé. **Payment:** Royalty. **Contact:** Patti Hartmann, Acquiring Ed.

UNIVERSITY OF CALIFORNIA PRESS

2120 Berkeley Way, Berkeley, CA 94720. 510-642-4247.
E-mail: ucpress.comments@ucop.edu. Web site: www.ucpress.edu.
James Clark, Director.
Description: Scholarly nonfiction. **Proposal Process:** Query with cover letter, outline, sample chapters, curriculum vitae, and SASE.

UNIVERSITY OF CHICAGO PRESS

5801 Ellis Ave., 4th Fl., Chicago, IL 60637-1496. 773-702-7700.
Web site: www.pressuchicago.edu.
Anita Samen, Managing Editor.
Description: Scholarly, nonfiction, advanced texts, monographs, clothbound and paperback, reference books.

UNIVERSITY OF GEORGIA PRESS

330 Research Dr., Athens, GA 30602-4901. 706-369-6130.
E-mail: mnunnell@ugapress.uga.edu. Web site: www.uga.edu/ugapress.
Barbara Ras, Director.
Description: Short story collections and poetry, scholarly nonfiction and literary criticism, Southern and American history, regional studies, biography and autobiography. For nonfiction, query with outline and sample chapters. Poetry collections considered in September and January only; short fiction in April and May only. A $15 fee is required for all poetry and fiction submissions. Royalty. SASE for competition guidelines.

UNIVERSITY OF HAWAII PRESS

2840 Kolowalu St., Honolulu, HI 96822. 808-956-8255.
Web site: www.hawaii.edu/uhpress.
Patricia Crosby / Pam Kelley / Sharon Yamamoto, Editors.
Description: Scholarly books on Asian, Asian American, and Pacific studies from disciplines as diverse as the arts, history, language, literature, natural science, philosophy, religion, and the social sciences. **Proposal Process:** Query with outline and sample chapters. **Payment:** Royalty.

UNIVERSITY OF ILLINOIS PRESS

1325 S. Oak St., Champaign, IL 61820-6903. 217-333-0950.
E-mail: uipress@uiuc.edu. Web site: www.press.uillinois.edu.
Willis Regier, Director/Editor-in-Chief.
Description: Scholarly and regional nonfiction. **Proposal Process:** Rarely considers multiple submissions. Query. **Payment:** Royalty.

UNIVERSITY OF IOWA PRESS

119 W. Park Rd., Iowa City, IA 52242-1000. 319-335-2000.
E-mail: holly-carver@uiowa.edu. Web site: www.uiowa.edu/~uipress.
Holly Carver, Director.
Description: Nonfiction. Short fiction and poetry published only through annual competitions. **Proposal Process:** Query with SASE. **Payment:** Pay varies.

UNIVERSITY OF MASSACHUSETTS PRESS

Box 429, Amherst, MA 01004-0429. 413-545-2217.
E-mail: wilcox@umpress.umass.edu. Web site: www.umass.edu/umpress.
Bruce Wilcox, Director.
Description: Scholarly books and books of general interest, African American studies, American studies, architecture, and environmental design. **Proposal Process:** Query with SASE.

UNIVERSITY OF MINNESOTA PRESS

111 Third Ave. S., Suite 290, Minneapolis, MN 55401-2520. 612-627-1970.
Web site: www.upress.umn.edu.
Doug Armato, Editorial Director.
Description: Not-for-profit publisher of academic books for scholars and selected general interest titles. No original fiction or poetry. Areas of emphasis include: American studies, anthropology, art and aesthetics, cultural theory, film and media studies, gay and lesbian studies, geography, literary theory, political and social theory, race and ethnic studies, sociology and urban studies. **Number of Books/Yr.:** 110 titles/year, 50% by first-time authors, 99% unagented. **Proposal Process:** Query with outline, detailed prospectus or introduction, table of contents, sample chapter, and resumé. Multiple queries considered. No electronic queries. Response time: 4-6 weeks. Hard copy. **Payment:** Royalty, 6-10% net. **Sample Titles:** *Postmodern Fables,* by Jean-Francois Lyotard, *The Capture of Speech and Other Writings,* by Michel de Certeau.

UNIVERSITY OF MISSOURI PRESS

2910 LeMone Blvd., Columbia, MO 65201-8227. 573-882-7641.
E-mail: upress@umsystem.edu. Web site: www.system.missouri.edu/upress.
Beverly Jarrett, Acquisitions.
Description: Scholarly books on American and European history; American, British, and Latin American literary criticism; political philosophy; intellectual history; regional studies; and short fiction.

UNIVERSITY OF NEBRASKA PRESS

233 N. 8th St., Lincoln, NE 68588-0255.
E-mail: gdunham@eunl.edu. Web site: www.nebraskapress.unl.edu.
Gary Dunham, Editor-in-Chief.
Description: Scholarly and nonfiction books in Native American Studies, Western history, military history, environmental history, sports history, American Literature. General audience books on American sports.

UNIVERSITY OF NEVADA PRESS

MS 166, Reno, NV 89557. 775-784-6573.
E-mail: dalrympl@scs.unr.edu.
Description: Fiction, nonfiction, and poetry. Nonfiction areas include history, biography, political science, natural history, regional (Nevada), mining, gaming, and Basque studies. **Proposal Process:** Query first, with outline or table of contents, synopsis, estimated length, completion date of manuscript, and resumé. **Payment:** Royalty. **Contact:** Margaret Dalrymple.

UNIVERSITY OF NEW MEXICO PRESS

University of New Mexico, 1720 Lomas Blvd. NE, Albuquerque, NM 87131.
505-277-2346.
E-mail: unmpress@unm.edu. Web site: www.unmpress.com.
Elizabeth C. Hadas, Director.

Description: Scholarly nonfiction on social and cultural anthropology, archaeology, Western history, art, and photography. **Proposal Process:** Query. **Payment:** Royalty. **Contact:** Dana Asbury, or Barbara Guth, Eds.

UNIVERSITY OF NORTH CAROLINA PRESS

P.O. Box 2288, Chapel Hill, NC 27515-2288. 919-966-3561. E-mail: uncpress@unc.edu. Web site: www.uncpress.unc.edu. David Perry, Editor-in-Chief. **Description:** General-interest books (75,000-125,000 words) on the lore, crafts, cooking, gardening, travel, and natural history of the Southeast. No fiction or poetry. **Proposal Process:** Query. **Payment:** Royalty.

UNIVERSITY OF NORTH TEXAS PRESS

P.O. Box 311336, Denton, TX 76203-1336. 940-565-2142. Web site: www.unt.edu/untpress. Karen DeVinney, Acquisitions Editor. **Description:** Military history, Texas history, multicultural, women's history. **Number of Books/Yr.:** 16 titles/year (250 submissions), 95% unagented. **Proposal Process:** Send manuscript or query with sample chapters; no multiple queries. Electronic queries accepted. Hard copy preferred. Response time: Queries 2 weeks, submissions 3 months. **Payment:** Royalty. **Sample Titles:** Series include: *War and the Southwest* (perspectives, histories, and memories of war from authors living in the Southwest); *Western Life Series*; and *Texas Writers* (critical biographies of Texas writers). **Tips:** Prefers writing with scholarly rigor while still appealing to general audience. Avoid personal narrative, unless needed to make an analytical point. No memoirs. Prefers subjects of regional (Southwest) interest. **Contact:** Ronald Chapman, Editor.

UNIVERSITY OF OKLAHOMA PRESS

1005 Asp Ave., Norman, OK 73019-0445. 405-325-5111/877-894-3798. E-mail: cerankin@ou.edu. Web site: www.ou.edu/oupress. Charles E. Rankin, Assistant Director/Editor-In-Chief. **Description:** Books, to 300 pages, on the history of the American West, Indians of the Americas, congressional studies, classical studies, literary criticism, natural history, and women's studies. **Proposal Process:** Query. **Payment:** Royalty.

UNIVERSITY OF PENNSYLVANIA PRESS

4200 Pine St., Philadelphia, PA 19104-4011. 215-898-6261. E-mail: custserv@pobox.upenn.edu. Web site: www.upenn.edu/pennpress. **Description:** Scholarly nonfiction. **Proposal Process:** Query. **Contact:** Eric Halpern.

UNIVERSITY OF PITTSBURGH PRESS

3347 Forbes Ave., Pittsburgh, PA 15213. 412-383-2456. Web site: www.pitts.edu/~edu. Cynthia Miller, Director. **Description:** Scholarly nonfiction (philosophy of science, Latin American studies, political science, urban environmental history, culture, composition, and literacy). For poetry send SASE for rules and reading periods.

UNIVERSITY OF TENNESSEE PRESS

Conference Center Bldg., Suite 110, Knoxville, TN 37996-4108. 865-974-3321. E-mail: harrisj@utk.edu. Web site: www.sunsite.utk.edu/utpress. Joyce Harrison, Editorial Director. **Description:** Publish scholarly and general-interest titles in American studies, in the following subject areas: African American studies, archaeology, architecture, Civil War studies, folklore, history, literary studies, material culture, and religious studies. **Number of Books/Yr.:** 30-35 titles/year, 99% unagented. **Proposal Process:** Query and include SASE. Multiple and electronic queries accepted. Hard copy. **Payment:** Royalty. **Tips:** Scholarly treatment, unique contributions to scholarship. Readable style. Authors should avoid formatting their manuscripts (making them look like books). Sample material should be double-spaced on 8½ x 11 paper.

UNIVERSITY OF TEXAS PRESS

University of Texas, Box 7819, Austin, TX 78713-7819. 512-471-4278. E-mail: utpress@uts.cc.utexas.edu. Web site: www.utexas.edu/utpress. Theresa May, Editorial Director. **Description:** Scholarly works: Latin American studies, Native American studies, anthropology, Texana, natural science and history, environmental studies, Classics, Middle Eastern studies, film and media studies, gender studies, Texas architecture, photography/art. **Number of Books/Yr.:** 90-100 titles/year (800 submissions), 5% first-time authors, 98% unagented. **Proposal Process:** Query with proposal only and SASE. Multiple and electronic queries accepted. Response time: Up to 3 months. **Payment:** Royalty. **Sample Titles:** Recent publications: *How Cities Work, Galveston and the 1900 Storm, Intercultural Communication, Class Struggle in Hollywood, Guide to Offshore Wildlife,* and *Cuba and the Politics of Passion.* **Tips:** No fiction, except occasional translation of literature (Latin American or Middle Eastern). No poetry. Please, no phone calls. **Contact:** Rachell Chance, Assoc. Ed.

UNIVERSITY OF UTAH PRESS

1795 South Campus Dr., Rm. 101, Salt Lake City, UT 84112. 801-581-6771. Web site: www.upress.utah.edu. Dawn Marano, Acquisitions Editor. **Description:** Nonfiction from 200 pages and poetry from 60 pages. (Submit poetry during March only.) **Proposal Process:** Query. **Payment:** Royalty.

UNIVERSITY OF WISCONSIN PRESS

2537 Daniels St., Madison, WI 53718-6772. 608-224-3898. E-mail: uniscpress@uwpress.wisc.edu. Web site: www.wisc.edu/wisconsinpress. Raphael Kadushin, Acquisitions Editor. **Description:** Trade nonfiction, scholarly books and regional titles on the Midwest. Offers Brittingham Prize in Poetry and Pollak Prize in Poetry; query for details.

UNIVERSITY PRESS OF COLORADO

5589 Arapahoe Avenue, 206C, Niwot, CO 80544. 720-406-8849.
E-mail: archer@spot.colorado.edu. Web site: www.upcolorado.com.
Darrin Pratt, Editorial Director.
Description: Scholarly nonfiction in archaeology, environmental studies, local interest titles, history of the American West, and mining history. **Number of Books/Yr.:** 16 titles/year. **Proposal Process:** Query with outline and sample chapters. Hard copy. Multiple and electronic queries accepted. Response time: quick turnaround. **Sample Titles:** *In the Realm of Nachan Kan* (archaeology), *Environmental Conflict in Alaska* (environmental studies), *Cutthroat & Campfire Tales* (American West). **Tips:** Currently not taking submissions for fiction, biographies, and memoirs. **Contact:** David Archer, Editor.

UNIVERSITY PRESS OF FLORIDA

15 N.W. 15th St., Gainesville, FL 32611-2079. 352-392-1351.
Web site: www.upf.com.
M. Babb, Editorial Director.
Description: Scholarly and general audience books in archeology, anthropology, history, women's studies, and Floridians. No fiction. **Number of Books/Yr.:** 80 titles/year (800 submissions), 15% first-time authors, 95% unagented. **Proposal Process:** Query with outline and sample chapters, SASE. Multiple and electronic queries accepted. Hard copy. **Payment:** Royalty. **Tips:** Nonfiction only.

THE UNIVERSITY PRESS OF KENTUCKY

663 S. Limestone St., Lexington, KY 40508-4008. 606-257-8150.
Web site: www.kentuckypress.com.
Kenneth Cherry, Director/Editor.
Description: Scholarly books in the major fields. Serious nonfiction of general interest. Books related to Kentucky and the Ohio Valley, the Appalachians, and the South. No fiction, drama, or poetry. **Proposal Process:** Query. **Contact:** Editor-in-Chief.

UNIVERSITY PRESS OF MISSISSIPPI

3825 Ridgewood Rd., Jackson, MS 39211-6492. 601-432-6205.
E-mail: press@inl.state.ms.us. Web site: www.upress.state.ms.us.
Seetha Srinivasan.
Description: Scholarly and trade titles in American literature, history, and culture; Southern studies; African-American, women's and American studies; popular culture; folklife; art and architecture; natural sciences; health; and other liberal arts.

UNIVERSITY PRESS OF NEW ENGLAND

23 S. Main St., Hanover, NH 03755-2048. 603-643-7100.
E-mail: university.press@dartmouth.edu. Web site: www.upne.com.
Phyllis Deutsch, Editor.
Description: Native and environment, fiction of New England, Jewish studies, women's studies, American studies, maritime studies. **Number of Books/Yr.:** 80

titles/year (3,000 submissions) 30% by first-time authors, 80% unagented. **Proposal Process:** Query. Prefer not to receive multiple queries. No electronic queries. Prefer hard copy format. Response time: 3-6 months **Payment:** Royalty, 0-10% net. **Sample Titles:** Adult: *Hardscrabble Fiction of New England, Pipers at the Gates of Dawn,* by Lynn Stegner. Environmental: *The Return of the Wolf,* edited by John Elder. Decorative Arts: *American Furniture,* by Luke Beckerdite. Women's and Jewish Studies: *Balancing Work and Love,* by Elaine Grudin Denholz. **Contact:** Ellen Wicklum, Assistant Editor Ext. 225.

VANDAMERE PRESS
P.O. Box 17446, Clearwater, FL 33762. 727-556-0950.
Jerry Frank, Editor.
Description: History, biography, disability studies, health care issues, military, the nation's capital for a national audience. **Number of Books/Yr.:** 10 titles/year (2,500 submissions), 10% first-time authors, 75% unagented. **Proposal Process:** Query with outline, sample chapters and manuscript, SASE. Multiple queries accepted. No electronic queries. Response time: 1-6 months. **Payment:** Royalty. **Contact:** Art Browa.

VIKING
375 Hudson St., New York, NY 10014. 212-366-2000.
Web site: www.penguinputnam.com.
Paul Slovak / Ivan Held, Acquistions.
Description: Fiction and nonfiction, including psychology, sociology, child-rearing and development, cookbooks, sports, and popular culture. **Proposal Process:** Query. **Payment:** Royalty.

VINTAGE BOOKS
1540 Broadway, New York, NY 10036. 212-782-9000.
Web site: www.vintagebooks.com.
Martin Asher, Editor-in-Chief.
Description: Quality fiction and serious nonfiction. **Proposal Process:** Submissions accepted from agents only.

VOYAGEUR PRESS
123 N. Second St., Stillwater, MN 55082. 651-430-2210.
E-mail: books@voyageurpress.com. Web site: www.voyageurpress.com.
Michael Dregni, Editorial Director.
Description: Books, 15,000-100,000 words, on wildlife, travel, Americana, collectibles, natural history, and regional topics. "Photography is very important for most of our books." **Proposal Process:** See guidelines. Query with outline and sample chapters. **Payment:** Royalty.

WALKER AND COMPANY

435 Hudson St., New York, NY 10014. 212-727-8300.
George Gibson (Adult Nonfiction).
Description: Adult nonfiction, focusing on history, science, math, technology, health. Crime fiction. Books for young readers, including picture books, young adult novels. **Number of Books/Yr.:** 60 titles/year, 5% by first-time authors. **Proposal Process:** Query with synopsis and SASE. Multiple queries accepted. No electronic queries. Hard copy. **Payment:** Royalty. **Sample Titles:** Adult Nonfiction: *Galileo's Daughter*, by David Sobel; *E=MC²*, by David Bodanis; *Brunelleshi's Dome*, by Ross King. **Tips:** No adult fiction, poetry, travel, biography, photo books, New Age, or memoirs. **Contact:** Michael Seidman (Mysteries), Emily Easton (Juvenile).

WARNER BOOKS

Time and Life Bldg., 1271 Ave. of the Americas, New York, NY 10020. 212-522-7200.
Web site: www.twbookmark.com.
Maureen Egen, President.
Description: Hardcover, trade paperback, and mass market paperback, reprint and original, fiction and nonfiction, audio books, and gift books. **Proposal Process:** No unsolicited manuscripts or proposals. Submissions accepted from agents only.

WASHINGTON STATE UNIVERSITY PRESS

P.O. Box 645910, Pullman, WA 99164-5910. 509-335-3518.
E-mail: wsupress@wsu.edu. Web site: www.wsu.edu/wsupress.
Glen Lindeman, Acquisitions Editor.
Description: Books on northwest history, prehistory, natural history, culture and politics, 200-350 pages. **Proposal Process:** Query. **Payment:** Royalty.

WASHINGTON WRITERS PUBLISHING HOUSE

P.O. Box 15271, Washington, DC 20003.
Web site: www.wwph.org.
Description: Poetry books, 50-60 pages, by writers in the greater Washington, DC and Baltimore area only. SASE for guidelines.

WAYNE STATE UNIVERSITY PRESS

4809 Woodward Ave., Detroit, MI 48201. 313-577-6131.
Web site: www.wsupress.wayne.edu.
Arthur B. Evans, Director/Acquistions.
Description: Scholarly books only, with rare exceptions in the *Great Lakes Books Series.* **Number of Books/Yr.:** 50 titles/year (150 submissions). **Proposal Process:** Send query with complete manuscript, include SASE. Hard copy. No multiple queries. Electronic queries accepted. **Sample Titles:** Series: *African American Life, American Jewish Civilization, Contemporary Film & Television, Humor in Life and Letters, Jewish Folklore and Anthropology,* and the *William Beaumont* Series. *Urban Studies and Labor* is a developing series. **Tips:** No works of fiction. View web site for details. **Contact:** Jane Hoehner, Acquisitions Editor.

SAMUEL WEISER, INC.

P. O. Box 612, York Beach, ME 03910-0612. 207-363-4393.
E-mail: email@weiserbooks.com. Web site: www.weiserbooks.com.
Eliot Stearnes, Editor.
Description: Nonfiction: psychology, Eastern philosophy, esoteric studies, and alternative health. New Red Wheel trade imprint. **Proposal Process:** Query with sample chapters or complete manuscipt. Multiple queries accepted. **Payment:** Royalty.

WESLEYAN UNIVERSITY PRESS

110 Mt. Vernon St., Middletown, CT 06459-0433. 860-685-2980.
E-mail: tradko@wesleyan.edu. Web site: www.wesleyan.edu/wespress.
Tom Radko, Director.
Description: Scholarly Press focusing on poetry, music, dance and performance topics, science fiction studies, gay and lesbian issues, gender, cultural, regional, and American studies. **Number of Books/Yr.:** 30 titles/year (1,500 submissions), 1% first-time authors, 97% unagented. **Proposal Process:** Query with outline and sample chapters, SASE. Multiple and electronic queries accepted. Hard copy. Response time: 2-4 weeks. **Payment:** Royalty. **Sample Titles:** Wesleyan Poetry series: 64-136 pages. **Tips:** Write for a complete catalog and submission guidelines. **Contact:** Suzanna Tamminen, editor-in-chief.

WHITECAP BOOKS

351 Lynn Ave., N. Vancouver, BC, Canada V7J 2C4. 604-980-9852.
E-mail: whitecap@whitecap.ca. Web site: www.whitecap.ca.
Description: Juvenile books, 32-84 pages, and adult books, varying lengths, on such topics as natural history, gardening, cookery, and regional subjects. **Proposal Process:** Query with table of contents, synopsis, and 1 sample chapter. **Payment:** Royalty and flat fee. **Contact:** Robert McCullough.

WHITSTON PUBLISHING COMPANY

1717 Central Avenue, Suite 201, Albany, NY 12205. 518-452-1900.
E-mail: whitston@capital.net. Web site: www.whitston.com.
Michael Laddin, Editor.
Description: Nonfiction, scholarly, reference, literary criticism, anthologies. **Number of Books/Yr.:** 6-12 titles/year (65 submissions), 100% unagented. **Proposal Process:** Send queries, outlines, sample chapters or manuscripts, and SASE. Multiple or electronic queries accepted. Response time: 2-6 months. Hard copy format preferred. **Payment:** Royalty. **Sample Titles:** Adult Nonfiction: *The Major Essays of Henry David Thoreau; Hugh Kenner: A Bibliography; The Collected Plays of Theodore Dreiser.*

WILDERNESS PRESS

1200 5th St., Berkeley, CA 94710. 510-558-1666.
E-mail: mail@wildernesspress.com. Web site: www.wildernesspress.com.
Jannie Dresser, Acquisitions Editor.
Description: Nonfiction books about outdoor activities and travel. **Number of Books/Yr.:** 12 titles/year (250 submissions), 25% by first-time authors, 90% unagented. **Proposal Process:** Query with outline and SASE. Considers multiple or electronic queries. Prefers either electronic, hard copy format. **Payment:** Royalty, typical is 10-12% of net. No flat fee.

JOHN WILEY & SONS, INC.

605 Third Ave., New York, NY 10158-0012. 212-850-6000.
Web site: www.wiley.com.
Gerard Helferich, Publisher, General Interest Books.
Description: History, biography, memoir, popular science, health, self-improvement, reference, African American, narrative fiction, business, computers, cooking, architecture and graphic design, children's. **Number of Books/Yr.:** 1,500 titles/year. **Proposal Process:** Query with outline. Response time: 2 weeks-1 month. Multiple queries accepted. Prefer electronic format. **Payment:** Royalty, range varies. **Sample Titles:** Adult: *The Inextinguishable Symphony: A True Story of Love and Music in Nazi Germany*, by Martin Goldsmith. *The Power of Gold: The History of an Obsession*, by Peter L. Bernstein. *Splendid Soups*, by James Peterson. *The Scientific American Science Desk Reference*. Children's: *New York Public Library Amazing Explorers*, by Brendon January. *Revolutionary War Days*, by David C. King. **Contact:** See appropriate editor for writing category.

WILEY/HALSTED

John Wiley & Sons, 605 Third Ave., New York, NY 10158-6000. 212-850-6000.
Description: Textbooks, educational materials and reference books. **Proposal Process:** Query. **Payment:** Royalty.

WILLOW CREEK PRESS

P.O. Box 147, Minocqua, WI 54548. 715-358-7010.
E-mail: books@willowcreekpress.com. Web site: www.willowcreekpress.com.
Andrea Donner, Editor.
Description: Nonfiction publisher whose books are most generally related to the outdoors, wildlife, pets, hunting, fishing, and cooking. Books, 25,000-50,000 words. **Number of Books/Yr.:** 20 titles/year, 30% first-time authors, 80% unagented. **Proposal Process:** Send an outline and sample of the actual work—not just a query letter, and SASE. Multiple queries accepted. No electronic queries. Hard copy. Response time: 4-6 weeks. **Payment:** Royalty. **Sample Titles:** Gift books: *What Dogs Teach Us, 101 Uses for a Lab*. Outdoor books: *Fishing the National Parks, Bear vs. Man*. Pets: *The 10-Minute Retriever, Urban Dog*. **Tips:** Avoid personal accounts of your pet. No long letters explaining your work and what will be done; let the writing speak for itself.

WILSHIRE BOOK COMPANY

12015 Sherman Rd., N. Hollywood, CA 91605-3781. 818-765-8579.
E-mail: mpowers@mpowers.com. Web site: www.mpowers.com.
Marcia Grad, Editorial Director.
Description: Self-help, motivational, psychology, recovery, adult fables, how-to.
Looking for adult fables that teach principles of psychological/spiritual growth,
30,000-60,000 words. **Number of Books/Yr.:** 25 titles/year (2,500 submissions), 80%
by first-time authors, 90% unagented. **Proposal Process:** Query with complete
manuscript. Multiple and electronic queries accepted. Hard copy. Response time: 2
months. **Payment:** Royalty. **Sample Titles:** Two bestsellers: *The Knight in Rusty
Armor,* by Robert Fisher and *The Princess Who Believed in Fairy Tales,* by Marcia
Grad. **Tips:** Welcomes phone calls to discuss a manuscript.

WINDSWEPT HOUSE PUBLISHERS

P.O. Box 159, Mount Desert, ME 04660. 207-244-5027.
E-mail: windswt@acadia.net. Web site: www.booknotes.com/windswept/.
Mavis Weinberger, Acquisitions Editor.
Description: Adult and children's books (all ages), mostly relating to Maine/New
England area: novels, poetry, nature, history. **Number of Books/Yr.:** 4 titles/year.
Proposal Process: No unsolicited manuscripts. Send SASE for a copy of our guide-
lines. **Payment:** Royalty, to 10%. No flat fee. **Tips:** Children's books needing pictures
should come complete with illustrations.

WIZARDS OF THE COAST

P.O. Box 707, Renton, WA 98057-0707. 425-226-6500.
Web site: www.wizards.com.
Contact Submissions Editor.
Description: We are looking for sword and sorcery, role-playing game-related, fantasy. Very limited science fiction. **Number of Books/Yr.:** 50 titles/year (ave 200 submissions), 10% by first-time authors, 70% unagented. **Proposal Process:** Query with
sample chapters, include SASE. No multiple or electronic queries. Hard copy format
preferred. **Tips:** Read guidelines available at our website; or SASE.

WOODBINE HOUSE

6510 Bells Mill Rd., Bethesda, MD 20817. 301-897-3570.
E-mail: info@woodbinehouse.com. Web site: www.woodbinehouse.com.
Susan Stokes, Editor.
Description: Books for or about people with disabilities only. Current needs include
parenting, reference, special ed., picture books, and novels or nonfiction chapter
books for young readers. **Proposal Process:** Query or submit complete manuscript
with SASE. Guidelines. **Payment:** Royalty.

WORDWARE PUBLISHING
2320 Los Rio Blvd., Suite 200, Plano, TX 75074. 972-423-0090.
E-mail: gbivona@wordware.com. Web site: www.republicoftexaspress.com.
Ginnie Bivona, Editor.
Description: Publish books related to Texas, history, ghost stories, humor, travel guides, general interest books. No fiction or poetry. **Number of Books/Yr.:** 30 titles/year (100+ submissions), 50% by first-time authors, 90% unagented. **Proposal Process:** Query with outline and include SASE. Multiple and electronic queries accepted. Hard copy format preferred. **Payment:** Royalty. **Sample Titles:** *Wordware Computer Books.* **Tips:** Looking for interesting, entertaining books for the mainstream reader. We do not publish family memoirs unless they are famous, or better yet, infamous.

WORKMAN PUBLISHING CO., INC.
708 Broadway, New York, NY 10003-9555. 212-254-5900.
Web site: www.workman.com.
Susan Bolotin, Editorial Director.
Description: Nonfiction (adult and juvenile). Calendars. **Number of Books/Yr.:** 40 titles/year. **Proposal Process:** Query with outline and sample chapters, include SASE. Considers multiple queries. No electronic queries. Response time: varies. Prefers hard-copy format. **Payment:** Royalty or flat fee, range varies. **Tips:** See seb site for details.

WORLDWIDE LIBRARY
225 Duncan Mill Rd., Don Mills, Ont., Canada M3B 3K9. 416-445-5860.
E-mail: feroze_mohammed@harlequin.ca.
Randall Toye, Editorial Director.
Description: Action adventure, paramilitary adventure, science fiction, post-nuclear holocaust fiction. **Number of Books/Yr.:** 36 titles/year, 1% by first-time authors, 99% unagented. **Proposal Process:** Query with outline and sample chapters. Response time: 3 months. Multiple queries accepted. No electronic queries. Hard copy. **Payment:** Flat fee. Typical range: $3,000-$6,000.

WYRICK & COMPANY
1-A Pinckney St., Charleston, SC 29401. 843-722-0881.
E-mail: bookguys@mindspring.com.
Charles L. Wyrick, Jr..
Description: Publishes fiction (particularly set in the South, and nonfiction, including illustrated books on gardening, fine arts, and antiques; food and cooking; history and memoirs; photography; travel and guide books. **Proposal Process:** Queries, proposals, and manuscripts are accepted. Send SASE. Allow 4-6 weeks for response. **Payment:** Royalty.

YALE UNIVERSITY PRESS

P.O. Box 209040, New Haven, CT 06520-9040. 203-432-0960.
Web site: www.yale.edu/yup.
Jonathon Brent, Editorial Director.
Description: Adult nonfiction, 400 manuscript pages. **Proposal Process:** Query.
Payment: Royalty.

YANKEE BOOKS

33 E. Minor St., Emmaus, PA 18098. 610-967-5171.
Web site: www.rodalepress.com.
Sarah Dunn, Editor.
Description: Books relating specifically to New England: travel in the Northeast;
New England cooking and recipes, nature, and lore. Accurate, informative, and
practical books that can be used by visitors and would-be visitors to New England,
as well as residents of the Northeast. **Proposal Process:** Send proposals only.
Payment: Royalty.

ZOLAND BOOKS

384 Huron Ave., Cambridge, MA 02138. 617-864-6252.
E-mail: info@zolandbooks.com. Web site: www.zolandbooks.com.
Roland Pease, Publisher/Editor.
Description: Fiction; nonfiction of literary interest, including art and photography;
and poetry. **Proposal Process:** Queries preferred. **Payment:** Royalty.

JUVENILE BOOKS

Children's book publishing is big business, and getting bigger. With the blockbuster sales of the *Harry Potter* series by author J.K. Rowling, writing children's books has once again been shown to be a legitimate avenue to literary fame and, on occasion, fortune. In fact, curiously, some studies suggest that many children's books are sold to adults who intend to keep the books for themselves, making the question of what makes a children's book hit the bestseller lists an interesting one. For instance, the Dr. Suess book, *Oh, The Places You'll Go!*, is a perennial favorite as a college graduation gift, although the sales show up in the children's book category.

The market for juvenile books is very diverse. Children's books range from colorful board books for toddlers to social-realism novels for young adults on subjects that just a few decades ago were taboo. Many books are issued in series, while others are released as stand-alone titles.

However, as in all areas of publishing, while there is tremendous diversity across the field, there is also increasing specialization by individual publishers. Each seeks to find its own profitable niche within that broad expanse of interest.

Before sending off materials, it is important to study each publisher under consideration very carefully. Start by getting a copy of their guidelines for author queries and submissions; often these can be found on their web site. Also, request a catalog.

The publisher's catalog is one of the best vehicles to understand precisely the kind of books a publisher is acquiring. A marketing tool, a publisher's catalog reveals the special appeal that each book holds for the publisher and—it hopes—for bookstore buyers, librarians, and many eventual readers. A publisher's catalog tells how each book is different from (or similar to) others in the field. Reading a catalog carefully can help you understand clearly the kind of books a publisher is seeking.

As always, before you send a query letter or other materials, you may wish to get the name of the current editor at the publishing house who is in charge of the particular line or type of book that you are proposing. If this information is not available on the web site, make a very brief phone call. Explain your project in just one or two sentences, ask whom to send the query (or manuscript) to, confirm the address, and then thank the receptionist and hang up. Do not try to harangue an editor or pitch your proposal on the phone; a busy editor seldom has time to listen to your idea, and you will not be as convincing as you can be by presenting a professional, well-written query that can be studied in leisure. Trying to pitch an idea on the phone is usually just the best way to annoy an editor.

Be polite, be professional, and remember to target your writing, making sure the language, style, and content are appropriate to your target readers.

ABDO PUBLISHING
4940 Viking Drive., Suite 622, Edina, MN 55435. 612-831-1317.
Web site: www.abdopub.com.
Description: Children's nonfiction books from ages 0-12.

ARCHWAY/MINSTREL BOOKS

Pocket Books, 1230 Ave. of the Americas, New York, NY 10020. 212-698-7268.
Web site: www.simonsays.com.
Patricia MacDonald, Editorial Director.
Description: The young adult division of Pocket Books. Fiction for middle grades, teens, and young adults. **Tips:** No unsolicited manuscripts (except in some cases, from published authors).

ATHENEUM BOOKS FOR YOUNG READERS

Atheneum Publishers, A Division of Simon & Schuster, 1230 Ave. of the Americas, New York, NY 10020. 212-698-7200.
Web site: www.simonsays.com.
Description: Picture books, juvenile fiction, and nonfiction as well as illustrated collections. Query. No unsolicited manuscripts.

AVISSON PRESS, INC.

3007 Taliaferro Rd., Greensboro, NC 27408. 336-288-6989.
Martin L. Hester, Editor.
Description: Young adult biography only. Some literary topics and books by assignment only. **Number of Books/Yr.:** 6-8 titles/year (750 submissions), 25% first-time authors, 80% unagented. **Proposal Process:** Query with outline or sample chapter, bio and SASE. Hard copy format preferred. Multiple queries accepted. No electronic queries. Response time: 2 weeks. **Payment:** Royalty. **Sample Titles:** *Eight Who Made a Difference: Pioneer Women in the Arts, Prince of the Fairway: The Tiger Woods Story.* **Tips:** Young adult biography, collective biography. Women/minorities especially, but any good subject matter.

BENCHMARK BOOKS

99 White Plains Rd., Tarrytown, NY 10591-9001.
Web site: www.marshallcarendish.com.
Kate Nunn, Editorial Director.
Description: Nonfiction school and library books for children K-8. **Number of Books/Yr.:** 120 titles/year, 5% first-time authors, 75% unagented. **Proposal Process:** Send query, outline, and sample chapters. Multiple queries okay. No electronic queries. Hard-copy format preferred. SASE required. **Payment:** Royalty. **Tips:** Quality treatment of curriculum-related topics. Series only; no single titles. **Contact:** Joyce Stanton, Angela Cabalano, Doug Sanders.

BLACK BUTTERFLY CHILDREN'S BOOKS

Writers and Readers Publishing, P.O. Box 461, Village Station, New York, NY 10014. 212-941-0202.
Deborah Dyson, Editor.
Description: Titles featuring black children and other children of color, ages 9-13, for Young Beginners series. Picture books for children to age 11; board books for toddlers. Query. Royalty.

BLUE SKY PRESS

Scholastic Inc., 555 Broadway, New York, NY 10012. 212-343-6100.
Web site: www.scholastic.com.
Bonnie Verburg, Editorial Director.
Description: Fantasy, fairy tales, folklore, adventure.

BOYDS MILLS PRESS

815 Church St., Honesdale, PA 18431. 570-253-1164.
Web site: www.boydsmillspress.com.
Beth Troop, Editor.
Description: Children's books of literary merit, from picture books to novels.
Number of Books/Yr.: 50 titles/year (8,500 submissions), 10% first-time authors,
90% unagented. **Proposal Process:** Send outline and sample chapters for young
adult novels and nonfiction, complete manuscripts for all other categories. Response
time: 30 days. Hard-copy preferred, electronic format okay. No multiple queries.
Payment: Varies. **Tips:** Varied literary fiction. Avoid well-worn themes; no series or
romances.

CANDLEWICK PRESS

2067 Massachusetts Ave., Cambridge, MA 02140. 617-661-3330.
E-mail: bigbear@candlewick.com. Web site: www.candlewick.com.
Elizabeth Bicknell, Editor.
Description: Publisher of high-quality children's books for all ages (middle grade to
young adult fiction). **Tips:** Humorous and/or non-rhyming picture-book texts about
universal childhood experiences; innovative nonfiction and novelty books. High-
quality literary fiction for older readers.

CAPSTONE PRESS, INC.

P.O. Box 669, Mankato, MN 56001. 952-352-0024.
E-mail: freelance.writing@capstone-press.com. Web site: www.capstone-press.com.
Helen Moore, Acquisitions Editor.
Description: Nonfiction children's books for schools and libraries; content includes
curriculum-oriented topics, sports, and pleasure reading materials. **Number of
Books/Yr.:** 250 title/year, 5-10% first-time authors, 99% unagented. **Proposal
Process:** Query only, does not accept submissions or proposals. No multiple queries.
Response time: 4-6 weeks. Electronic queries okay for potential assignments. Either
electronic or hard-copy format. **Payment:** Flat fee. **Sample Titles:** Grades 3-9,
Stealth Bombers: The B-2 Spirits, by Bill Sweetman; Grades 2-6, *The Boyhood Diary
of Charles Lindbergh*, by Megan O'Hara; Grades 1-5, *Greece*, by Janet Rienecky;
Grades K-3, *Frogs: Leaping Amphibians*, by Adele Richardson. **Tips:** No fiction or
poetry. We do hire freelance authors to write titles on assignment.

CAROLRHODA BOOKS, INC.

Lerner Publishing Group, 241 First Ave. N., Minneapolis, MN 55401. 612-332-3344. Web site: www.lernerbooks.com.

Rebecca Poole, Submissions Editor.

Description: Complete manuscripts for ages 4-12: biography, science, nature, history, photo-essays; historical fiction. Guidelines. Hardcover. Accepts submissions from March 1-31 and from October 1-31.

CARTWHEEL BOOKS

Scholastic, Inc., 555 Broadway, New York, NY 10012. 212-343-6100. Web site: www.scholastic.com.

Bernette Ford, Editorial Director.

Description: Picture, novelty, and easy-to-read books, to about 1,000 words, for children, preschool to third grade. No novels or chapter books. Royalty or flat fee. Query. No unsolicited manuscripts.

CHARLESBRIDGE PUBLISHING

85 Main St., Watertown, MA 02472. 617-926-0329. E-mail: tradeeditorial@charlesbridge.com. Web site: www.charlesbridge.com. Submissions Editor.

Description: Nonfiction and fiction children's picture books. Children's nonfiction picture books under Charlesbridge imprint, fiction picture books under Talewinds or Whispering Coyote imprint. **Number of Books/Yr.:** 25 titles/year (2,500-3,000 submissions), 10% first-time authors, 20% unagented. **Proposal Process:** Send complete manuscript. Exclusive submissions only: must indicate on envelope and cover letter. Include SASE. Hard copy. **Payment:** Royalty or flat fee. **Tips:** Not acquiring board books, folk tales, alphabet books, or nursery rhymes at this time.

CHELSEA HOUSE PUBLISHERS

1974 Sproul Rd., Suite 400, Broomall, PA 19008. 610-353-5166. E-mail: chelseahouse@att.net. Web site: www.chelseahouse.com. Sally Cheney, Editorial Director.

Description: Leading publisher of quality nonfiction books for children and young adults, featuring biographies, sports, multicultural studies, science, and high school/college level literary criticism. Age range is 8-15 years old, with literary criticism up to adult ages. **Number of Books/Yr.:** 350 titles/year (500+ submissions), 25% first-time authors, 98% unagented. **Proposal Process:** No unsolicited manuscripts. Query with outline and 2 sample chapters. Only send complete manuscript if asked to. Include SASE. Accepts multiple and electronic queries. Electronic format preferred. **Payment:** Pays flat fee ($1,500-$3,500). **Sample Titles:** Award-winning series include: *Your Government: How it Works, 21st Century Health & Wellness, Crime, Justice & Punishment, Galaxy of Superstars, Black Americans of Achievement.* **Tips:** No autobiographical or fictionalized biography. Writing should be clear and direct, but lively. **Contact:** Sarah Bloom.

CHILD AND FAMILY PRESS

Child Welfare League of America, 440 First St. N.W., Third Fl., Washington, DC 20001-2085. 202-942-0263.
E-mail: ptierney@cwla.org. Web site: www.cwla.org.
Peggy Porter Tierney, Editor.
Description: Positive, upbeat picture books for children. **Number of Books/Yr.:** 20 titles/year (100 submissions), 50% first-time authors, 100% unagented. **Proposal Process:** Send complete manuscript. Multiple and electronic queries are considered. Response time: 3 months. Hard-copy format preferred. **Payment:** Royalty. **Tips:** Avoid anything too cutesy, moralistic, or patronizing.

CHILDREN'S BOOK PRESS

246 First St., Suite 101, San Francisco, CA 94105. 415-995-2200.
E-mail: cbookpress@cbookpress.org.
Harriet Rohmer, Publisher.
Description: Bilingual and multicultural picture books, 750-1,500 words, for children in grades K-6. We publish folktales and contemporary stories reflecting the traditions and culture of minorities and new immigrants in the U.S. Ultimately, we want to help encourage a more international, multicultural perspective on the part of all young people. Query. **Payment:** Advance on royalty.

CHILDREN'S PRESS ·

Grolier Publishing Co., 90 Sherman Turnpike, P.O. Box 1795, Danbury, CT 06816. 203-797-6802.
Web site: www.grolier.com.
Description: Science, social studies, and biography, to 25,000 words, for supplementary use in libraries and classrooms. Royalty or outright purchase. Currently overstocked; not accepting unsolicited manuscripts. No phone inquiries.

CLARION BOOKS

A Division of Houghton Mifflin Co., 215 Park Ave. S., New York, NY 10003. 212-420-5889.
Dinah Stevenson, Acquisitions Editor.
Description: Publishes picture books, nonfiction and fiction for infants-grade 12. Imprint issues about 50 new hardcover titles each year. **Number of Books/Yr.:** 50-60 titles/year (1,000+ submissions), 5% first-time authors, 50-75% unagented. **Proposal Process:** Send query with complete manuscript. No unsolicited material. Multiple queries okay. No electronic queries. Hard-copy format preferred. **Payment:** Royalty. **Contact:** Michele Coppola, Editor; Julie Strauss-Gabel, Associate Editor.

COUNCIL FOR INDIAN EDUCATION

2032 Woody Dr., Billings, MT 59102. 406-652-7398.
E-mail: hapcie@aol.com. Web site: www.mcn.net.
Hap Gilliland, Editor.
Description: Books dealing with Native-American life and culture, for children ages

5-18. Picture books, 30-60 pages; fiction, nonfiction, and young adult books, 30-300 pages. **Number of Books/Yr.:** 6 titles/year (100 submissions), 75% by first-time authors, 100% unagented. **Proposal Process:** Query with complete manuscript. Hard copy format preferred. Response time: 3 months. Multiple queries okay. No electronic queries. **Payment:** Flat fee for short stories in anthologies; royalty for books. **Tips:** Authentic Native American life (past or present) with good plot. No profanity, no condescending material for any culture. Books evaluated for authentic lifestyle by 20-member Intertribal Indian board.

CRICKET BOOKS

Carus Publishing, 332 S. Michigan Ave., Suite 1100, Chicago, IL 60604. 312-939-1500.

Web site: www.cricketbooks.net.

Marc Aronson, Acquisitions Editor.

Description: Publishes picture books, chapter books, and middle-grade novels for children ages 7-14. Marc Aronson, Acquisitions Editor, will be handling fiction and nonfiction for teenagers. **Number of Books/Yr.:** 25 titles/year (1,500 submissions), some first-time and unagented authors. **Proposal Process:** Nonfiction: send query with outline and sample chapters, include SASE. Fiction: send query with outline and complete manuscript, include SASE. Response time: 2 months for proposals/3 months for manuscripts. Considers multiple queries. No electronic queries. Prefers hard-copy format. **Payment:** Royalty, typical range 10%. **Sample Titles:** Juvenile Fiction: picture books, chapter books, middle-grade. Nonfiction and fiction for teens. e.g., *John Riley's Daughter*, by Kezi Mathews; *Two Suns in the Sky*, by Miriane Bat-Ami. **Tips:** Check recent titles. Avoid talking animals who are learning to accept that they are "different." No religious messages. **Contact:** Carol Saller, Editor.

CROWN BOOKS FOR YOUNG READERS

Imprint of Random House Children's Media Group, 1540 Broadway, 19th Fl., New York, NY 10036. 212-782-9000.

Web site: www.randomhouse.com.

Description: Children's nonfiction (science, sports, nature, music, and history) and picture books for ages 3 and up. Send complete manuscript and SASE for picture books. **Contact:** Editorial Dept..

DAWN PUBLICATIONS

P.O. Box 2010, Nevada City, CA 95959. 800-545-7475.

E-mail: glenn@dawnpub.com. Web site: www.dawnpub.com.

Glenn J. Hovemann, Editor.

Description: Nature-awareness/natural science illustrated picture-books for children. No talking animals, fantasies, or legends. **Number of Books/Yr.:** 6 (60% first-time authors). **Proposal Process:** Submit complete manuscript. Response 2-3 months. Hard-copy only. **Payment:** Royalty. **Sample Titles:** *Salmon Stream, Earth and You.*

DELACORTE PRESS BOOKS FOR YOUNG READERS

Subsidiary of Bantam Dell Publishing Group, Division of Random House Inc., 1540 Broadway, New York, NY 10036. 212-782-9000.

Web site: www.randomhouse.com/kids.

Description: General interest fiction and nonfiction for young readers. Also has annual "New Young Adult Novel" contest.

DIAL BOOKS FOR YOUNG READERS

Penguin Putnam Inc., 345 Hudson St., 3rd Floor, New York, NY 10014.

E-mail: online@penguinputnam.com. Web site: www.penguinputnam.com.

Nancy Paulsen, President/Publisher.

Description: Lively, unique picture books for children ages 2-4, and some middle grade novels. Send complete manuscript for picture books; outline and two sample chapters for novels.

DUTTON CHILDREN'S BOOKS

345 Hudson St., New York, NY 10014. 212-414-3700.

Web site: www.penguinputnam.com.

Stephanie Lurie, Publisher.

Description: Trade children's books, sold to bookstores, schools, and libraries for ages 0-18. Our list includes board books, picture books, early readers, chapter books, novels, and nonfiction. **Tips:** Seeking clever wordsmiths who can tell a compelling story, with distinctive style and memorable characters that learn or change in the course of the story. **Contact:** Lucia Monfried, Associate Publisher; Donna Brooks, Editorial Director.

THE EDUCATION CENTER, INC.

3511 W. Market St., Ste. 200, Greensboro, NC 27403.

Description: A resource publisher for K-6 teachers. Seeking writers for a series of high-interest short stories for reading aloud to third through sixth graders. Needs humor, adventure, contemporary realism, suspense, folktales and historical fiction, animal stories, and creative nonfiction.

ELEMENT CHILDREN'S BOOKS

160 N. Washington St., 4th Fl., Boston, MA 02114. 617-915-9400.

Description: Publishes picture books (ages 4-8) and nonfiction books for ages 8 and up. Send SASE and queries to editor. **Payment:** Royalty. **Contact:** Barry Cunningham.

ENSLOW PUBLISHERS, INC.

40 Industrial Rd., P.O. Box 398, Berkeley Heights, NJ 07922-0398. 908-771-9400.

E-mail: braine@enslow.com. Web site: www.enslow.com.

Brian D. Enslow, Editor.

Description: Focuses on books for young adults for schools and public libraries. Nonfiction books: primarily biography, social issue or science related, and back to school curriculum. No fiction or picture books. **Number of Books/Yr.:** 175 titles/year, 50% first-time writers, 99% unagented. **Proposal Process:** Send query with outline and sample chapters. No electronic or multiple queries. Prefers hardcopy format. **Payment:** Royalty or flat fee. **Tips:** Always seeking new or established authors who can write nonfiction in interesting and exciting manner. Propose a new title for an existing series, or possibly a new series idea.

FRANKLIN WATTS

Affiliate or Grolier Company, Sherman Turnpike, Danbury, CT 06813. 203-797-6802.

Web site: www.publishing.grolier.com.

Description: Curriculum-oriented nonfiction for grades K-12, including science, history, social studies, and biography. No unsolicited submissions.

FREE SPIRIT PUBLISHING

400 First Ave. N., Suite 616, Minneapolis, MN 55401-1724. 612-338-2068. E-mail: help4kids@freespirit.com. Web site: www.freespirit.com.

Katrina Wentzel, Editor.

Description: A specialist in self-help for children and teens. Dedicated to publishing high-quality nonfiction materials that empower young people and adults who care deeply about young people. Our commitment has led us to develop a very specialized publishing focus. **Number of Books/Yr.:** 25 titles/year (thousands of submissions), 50% first-time authors, 70% unagented. **Proposal Process:** Query with outline and sample chapters. Multiple and electronic queries accepted. Hard copy. Response time: 3-4 months. **Payment:** Advance and royalty. **Tips:** Prefers a natural, friendly style; avoid education/psychology jargon. Prefers titles written by specialists (educators, counselors, and other professionals who work with children and teens).

FRONT STREET BOOKS, INC.

20 Battery Park Ave., #403, Asheville, NC 28801. 828-236-3097. E-mail: contactus@frontstreetbooks.com. Web site: www.frontstreetbooks.com.

Stephen Roxburgh, Editor.

Description: An independent publisher of books for children and young adults. **Number of Books/Yr.:** 10-15 titles/year, 30% by first-time authors, 90% unagented. **Proposal Process:** Query with sample chapters. Multiple and electronic queries accepted. Hard-copy. **Payment:** Royalty. **Tips:** Currently not accepting picture-book manuscripts that are not accompanied by illustrations.

GIRL PRESS

P.O. Box 480389, Los Angeles, CA 90048.

Web site: www.girlpress.com.

Description: Dedicated to making strong books for teenage girls. Nonfiction, biography, instructional titles. **Tips:** Seeking new ideas and new writers, in fiction.

GOLDEN BOOKS PUBLISHING

888 Seventh Ave., New York, NY 10106-4100. 212-547-6700.
E-mail: info@goldenbooks.com. Web site: www.goldenbooks.com.
Description: Children's fiction and nonfiction: picture books, storybooks, concept books, novelty books. No unsolicited manuscripts. Royalty or flat fee.

GREENWILLOW BOOKS

HarperCollins Publishers, 1350 Ave. of the Americas, New York, NY 10019. 212-261-6500.
Web site: www.harperchildrens.com.
Description: Children's books for all ages. Picture books. Fiction and nonfiction. Simultaneous submissions OK. SASE. Responds within 10 weeks. **Number of Books/Yr.:** 50 titles per year, with 90% unagented authors; 2% first-time authors. **Proposal Process:** For novels: query with a synopsis and sample chapters. Submit complete manuscript for picture books. Submit in hard-copy only. **Payment:** Royalty.

GROSSET AND DUNLAP PUBLISHERS

Penguin Putnam, Inc., 345 Hudson St., New York, NY 10014.
Web site: www.penguinputnam.com.
Jane O'Connor, President.
Description: Mass-market children's books. Not accepting unsolicited manuscripts. Royalty.

HARCOURT INC./CHILDREN'S BOOK DIV.

525 B St., Suite 1900, San Diego, CA 92101-4495. 619-261-6616.
Web site: www.harcourtbooks.com
Description: Juvenile fiction and nonfiction for beginning readers through young adults. Imprints include Gulliver Books, Red Wagon Books, Odyssey Classics, Silver Whistle, Magic Carpet Books, Harcourt Children's Books, Harcourt Young Classics, Green Light Readers, Harcourt Paperbacks, Voyager Books/Libros Viajeros. No unsolicited submissions or queries; submissions via agents only.

HARPERCOLLINS CHILDREN'S BOOKS

HarperCollins Publishers, 1350 Ave. of the Americas, New York, NY 10019. 212-261-6500.
Web site: www.harpercollins.com.
Kate Morgan Jackson, Editor-in-Chief.
Description: Picture books, chapter books, and fiction and nonfiction for middle-grade and young adult readers. Imprints (Avon, HarperFestival, HarperTempest, HarperTrophy, Joanna Cotler Books, Laura Geringer Books, and Greenwillow Books) are committed to producing imaginative and responsible children's books. From pre-school to young adult titles. Guidelines available. Royalty.

HOLIDAY HOUSE, INC.
425 Madison Ave., New York, NY 10017. 212-688-0085.
Suzanne Reinoehl, Acquisitions.
Description: General juvenile fiction and nonfiction. Query with SASE. Royalty.
Hardcover only.

HUMANICS PUBLISHING GROUP
P.O. Box 7400, Atlanta, GA 30357. 404-874-1930.
E-mail: humanics@mindspring.com. Web site: www.humanicspub.com.
Description: Self-help, philosophy, spirituality. Teacher resource (pre-K-3).
Number of Books/Yr.: 24 titles/year (600 submissions), 80% first-time authors, 90%
unagented. **Proposal Process:** Query with outline, sample chapters and SASE.
Electronic queries accepted. No multiple queries. Hard copy. **Payment:** Royalty.
Tips: Interested in books that provide help, guidance, and inspiration. **Contact:** W.
Arthur Bligh.

HYPERION
77 W. 66th, 11th Floor, New York, NY 10023. 212-456-0100.
E-mail: georganne.barry@disney.com. Web site: http://hyperionbooks.go.com.
Description: A division of Walt Disney Co. Material accepted from agents only. No
unsolicited manuscripts or queries considered. "Michael di Capua Books," imaginative and responsible children's books.

JOY STREET BOOKS
Little, Brown & Co., 3 Center Plaza, Floor 3, Boston, MA 02108. 617-227-0730.
Web site: www.littlebrown.com.
Description: Juvenile picture books; fiction and nonfiction for middle readers and
young adults. Especially interested in fiction for 8-12-year-olds and innovative nonfiction. **Proposal Process:** Query with outline and sample chapters for nonfiction;
send complete manuscript for fiction. **Payment:** Royalty.

JUST US BOOKS
356 Glenwood Ave., East Orange, NJ 07017. 973-672-7701.
E-mail: justusbooks@aol.com. Web site: www.justusbooks.com.
Cheryl Willis Hudson, Editorial Director.
Description: Specialize in children's books and learning materials that focus on the
Black experience. No unsolicited material.

KIDS CAN PRESS
29 Birch Avenue, Toronto, ON, Canada M4V 1E2. 416-925-5437.
E-mail: rcranley@kidscan.com.
Rivka Cranley, Editor-in-Chief.
Description: Picture books, 24 pages; juvenile nonfiction, 24-144 pages; and young
adult novels, to 256 pages. Query with outline and sample chapters or complete manuscript with SASE (IRC coupon or postal order). Multiple queries considered.

ALFRED A. KNOPF BOOKS FOR YOUNG READERS

Imprint of Random House Children's Media Group, 201 E. 50th St., New York, NY 10022. 212-752-2600.
Web site: www.randomhouse.com/kids.
Description: Distinguished juvenile fiction and nonfiction. Query; no unsolicited manuscripts. Royalty. Guidelines. Imprint of Random House Children's Media Group.

LADYBIRD BOOKS, INC.

Imprint of Penguin USA, 375 Hudson St., New York, NY 10014-3657.
Description: Books for toddlers, preschoolers, and older children. Fairy tales, classics, science and nature, and novelty items. No unsolicited manuscripts; query required. *No recent report.*

LANDOLL, INC./AMERICAN EDUCATION PUBLISHING

Imprint of McGraw-Hill, 8787 Orion Place, Columbus, OH 43240. 614-430-6322.
Description: McGraw-Hill Children's books. Submit writing samples and resumé for consideration as a freelance writer.

LEE & LOW BOOKS

95 Madison Ave., New York, NY 10016. 212-779-4400 x24.
E-mail: lmay@leeandlow.com. Web site: www.leeandlow.com.
Louise May, Senior Editor.
Description: Quality children's book publisher specializing in multicultural themes. **Number of Books/Yr.:** 12-15 titles/year (1,500 submissions), 35% first-time authors, 80% unagented. **Proposal Process:** We consider manuscripts from writers at all levels of experience. Prefers hard-copy. Include SASE. **Payment:** Advance/royalty. **Tips:** No folk tales or animal stories. Seeking character-driven realistic fiction about children of color, with special interest in stories set in contemporary U.S. Visit web site for details.

LERNER PUBLISHING GROUP

241 First Ave. N, Minneapolis, MN 55401. 612-332-3344.
Web site: www.lernerbooks.com.
Rebecca Poole/Jennifer Zimian, Editors.
Description: Primarily, we publish books for children ages 7-18. Our nonfiction books cover a variety of subjects: social issues, history, biography, science and technology, geography, the environment, sports, entertainment, the arts and crafts, and activities. We also publish some fiction. **Number of Books/Yr.:** 120-175 titles/year (2,200 submissions), 15% first-time authors, 75% unagented. **Proposal Process:** Query with outline and sample chapters, include SASE. Multiple queries are considered. No electronic queries. Prefers hard-copy format. Please allow 2-6 months for response. **Payment:** Mostly flat fee, but negotiated per contract. **Tips:** Seeking manuscripts that are well-researched, well-organized, written clearly and simply with fresh engaging language. No textbooks, workbooks, songbooks, puzzles, plays, or religious materials.

ARTHUR A. LEVINE BOOKS

Imprint of Scholastic, Inc., 555 Broadway, New York, NY 10012. 212-343-4436.
Web site: www.scholastic.com.
Description: Beautiful picture books and literary fiction for children of all ages.
Contact: Arthur A. Levine.

LITTLE SIMON

Simon & Schuster Children's Publishing Division, Simon & Schuster, 1230 Ave. of the
Americas, New York, NY 10020. 212-698-7200.
Web site: www.simonsayskids.com.
Robin Corey, Vice President/Publisher.
Description: Novelty books, board books, pop-up books, lift-the-flap, touch-and-
feel, bath books, and sticker books. No picture or chapter books. Audience is children
6 months to 8 years old.

LUCENT BOOKS

P.O. Box 289011, San Diego, CA 92198-9011. 619-485-7424.
Web site: www.lucentbooks.com.
Lori Shein, Managing Editor.
Description: Books for junior high/middle school students, 18,000-25,000 words.
"Overview" series: current issues (political, social, historical, environmental topics).
Other series include *World History, The Way People Live* (exploring daily life and cul-
ture of communities worldwide, past and present), *Modern Nations.* No unsolicited
material; work is by assignment only. Flat fee. Query for guidelines and catalogue.

MAGINATION PRESS

750 First St., N.E., Washington, DC 20002. 202-218-3982.
Web site: www.maginationpress.com.
Darcie Conner Johnston, Managing Editor.
Description: Publishes illustrated story books of a clearly psychological nature for
children. Picture books for children 4-11; nonfiction for children 8-18. **Number of
Books/Yr.:** 8-12 titles/year, (500 submissions), 50% first-time authors, 80% un-
agented. **Proposal Process:** Submit query with complete mss., and SASE. No electronic submissions. Multiple queries accepted. Hard copy. Response time: 3-5
months. **Payment:** Royalty. **Sample Titles:** Children's Nonfiction: Ages 4-8; 8-13;
teens to college age. *I Don't Want to Talk About It* (about divorce, for ages 4-8).
*Putting on the Brakes: Young People's Guide to Understanding Attention Deficit
Hyperactivity Disorder.* **Tips:** See submission guidelines. Looking for strong psychological content in stories that focus on an issue that affects children, plus engaging
writing. No young-adult fiction or chapter books. Many of these books are written by
medical or mental-health professionals.

MARGARET K. MCELDERRY BOOKS

1230 6th Ave., New York, NY 10020. 212-698-2761.

Web site: www.simonsayskids.com.

Emma D. Dryden, Executive Editor.

Description: Books for all ages: infant through young adult; literary hardcover trade; fiction; some poetry and nonfiction. Guidelines available. **Number of Books/Yr.:** 25-30 titles/year (4,000 submissions), 35% by first-time authors, 50% unagented. **Proposal Process:** Query with outline and sample chapters. Response time: 3 months. Accepts both multiple and electronic queries. Prefers hard-copy format. **Payment:** Royalty. **Tips:** Looking for unique perspectives on unique topics of interest to children. No science fiction, does publish some fantasy. **Contact:** Kristen McCurry, Asst. Ed.

ME & MI PUBLISHING

128 South County Farm Rd., Wheaton, IL 60187

E-mail: m3@memima.com. Web site: www.memima.com

Description: Bilingual (English/Spanish) books for parents who want their preschool children to learn basic concepts in English and Spanish. Query first; no unsolicited manuscripts accepted. **Payment:** Flat fee.

MEADOWBROOK PRESS

5451 Smetana Dr., Minnetonka, MN 55343. 952-930-1100.

Web site: www.meadowbrookpress.com.

Bruce Lansky, Editorial Director.

Description: Adult: Parenting, pregnancy and childbirth, party planning, relationships. Children: Children's poetry and fiction. Guidelines available. **Number of Books/Yr.:** 20 titles/year (600 submissions), 80% first-time authors, 90% unagented. **Proposal Process:** Send query with SASE. Hard-copy format preferred. Multiple queries accepted. **Payment:** Royalty or flat fee. **Sample Titles:** *Pregnancy, Childbirth and the Newborn, The Toddler's Busy Book.*

MEGA-BOOKS, INC.

240 E. 60th St., New York, NY 10022.

Description: Book packager. Young adult books, 150 pages, children's books. Query for guidelines. Flat fee. **Contact:** John Craddock. *No recent report.*

MILKWEED EDITIONS

1011 Washington Ave., S., Suite 300, Minneapolis, MN 55415. 612-332-3192.

Web site: www.milkweed.org.

Emilie Buchwald, Editorial Director.

Description: Literary fiction for middle graders (ages 8-13). Guidelines available. **Number of Books/Yr.:** 15 titles/year (3,000 submissions), 60% by first-time authors, 75% unagented. **Proposal Process:** Query with SASE. Hard-copy format. Response time: 2-6 months. Multiple queries okay. No electronic queries. **Payment:** Royalty. **Sample Titles:** V.M. Caldwell, *Tides.* David Haynes, *Business as Usual: The West 7th*

Wildcats. John Armistead, *The $66 Summer.* **Tips:** Looking for a fresh, distinctive voice. No genre fiction, picture books, etc. The natural world is a central concern. Seeks to give new writers a forum; publishing history isn't as important as excellence and originality. **Contact:** Elisabeth Fitz, First Reader.

THE MILLBROOK PRESS
2 Old New Milford Rd., P.O. Box 335, Brookfield, CT 06804. 203-740-2220. Web site: www.millbrookpress.com.
Description: Children's book publisher, with 3 imprints: Copper Beech, Twenty-First Century, and Roaring Brook. Quality nonfiction for the school and library market. Main market is middle-school children, but titles range from infant picture books to historical fictions. **Number of Books/Yr.:** 150 titles/year (5,000 submissions), 50% by first-time authors, 75% unagented. **Proposal Process:** Query with outline and sample chapters, include SASE. Response time: 1 month. Hard-copy. Multiple queries okay. No electronic queries. **Payment:** Royalty or flat fee. **Tips:** SASE for guidelines or get from web site.

MONDO PUBLISHING
980 Avenue of the Americas, 2nd Fl., New York, NY 10018. 212-268-3560. Don L. Curry, Executive Editor.
Description: Children's trade and educational. Picture books, nonfiction, and early chapter books for readers ages 4-10. Beautiful books that children can read on their own and enjoy over and over. **Number of Books/Yr.:** 50 titles/year (1,000 submissions), 30% by first-time authors. **Proposal Process:** Query with complete manuscript. No multiple or electronic queries. Hard-copy. **Payment:** Varies.

NATIONAL GEOGRAPHIC SOCIETY
1145 17th St. N.W., Washington, DC 20036-4688. 202-857-7000. E-mail: jtunstal@ngs.org.
Nancy Feresten, Editorial Director.
Description: Mainly nonfiction books in the areas of history, adventure, biography, multicultural themes, science, nature, reference for children ages 4-14. **Number of Books/Yr.:** 25 titles/year (1,000 submissions), 5% first-time authors, 50% unagented. **Proposal Process:** Query with complete manuscript, and SASE. Response time: several months. Multiple queries accepted. Hard-copy format preferred. **Payment:** Royalty or flat fee. **Tips:** We like a strong writer's voice telling an interesting story, on a subject of interest to young people.

THE OLIVER PRESS
Charlotte Square, 5707 W. 36th St., Minneapolis, MN 55416. 952-926-8981. E-mail: queries@oliverpress.com. Web site: www.oliverpress.com.
Denise Sterling, Editor.
Description: Publish collective biographies for middle and senior high school students. Currently offering six different curriculum-based series such as *Profiles, Business Builders,* and *Innovators* (history of technology). Ages 10-young adult.

Proposal Process: Submit proposals for books, 20,000-25,000 words, on people who have made an impact in such areas as history, politics, crime, science, and business. SASE. Multiple and electronic queries accepted. Hard copy. Payment: Royalty or flat fee. Tips: Book proposals should fit one of our existing series; provide brief summaries of 8-12 people who could be included. Looking for authors who thoroughly research their subject and are accurate and good storytellers. No fiction, picture books, or single-person biographies. **Contact:** Jenna Anderson, Associate Editor.

RICHARD C. OWEN PUBLISHERS, INC.

Children's Book Dept., P.O. Box 585, Katonah, NY 10536. 914-232-3903. Web site: www.rcowen.com.
Janice Boland, Editor.
Description: Brief, original, well-structured children's books that youngsters (in K-2 grades) can read by themselves. Also short, snappy bright articles, stories for children, ages 7-8. **Number of Books/Yr.:** 15 titles/year (1,000 submissions), 95% first-time authors, 100% unagented. **Proposal Process:** Send SASE for guidelines. Query with complete manuscript. Multiple queries okay. No electronic queries. Prefers hard-copy format. **Payment:** Royalty for writers. Flat fee for illustrators. **Sample Titles:** Fiction and nonfiction. *Young Learners* collection. *Fluent Readers* collection. **Tips:** Fresh, bright, energetic, crisp, clear style. Subjects that appeal to today's children.

PACIFIC VIEW PRESS

P.O. BOX 2657, Berkley, CA 94702.
Pam Zumwalt, Acquisitions Editor.
Description: Small publishing house specializing in nonfiction for 8-12 year-olds. Focus on the culture and history of countries of the Pacific Rim. Also, for middle-grade readers: Asian and Chinese cooking books and books on innovative aspects of Chinese history.

PEACHTREE PUBLISHERS, LTD.

494 Armour Cir. N.E., Atlanta, GA 30324. 404-876-8761.
Web site: www.peachtree-online.com.
Lyn Deardorff, Editor.
Description: Children's, middle readers, young adults, nonfiction: regional, health, regional travel (Southeast only), southern fiction, historical fiction for young adults. **Number of Books/Yr.:** 20 titles/year (20,000 submissions), % of first-time authors and unagented authors: varies. **Proposal Process:** Send outline and sample chapters. SASE required. Multiple queries okay. No fax or electronic queries. Response time: 4 months. Hard-copy format preferred. **Payment:** Royalty. **Tips:** Strong writing with unique subject matter or approach. No adult fiction, fantasy, sci-fi, romance, anthologies, or short stories.

PINATA BOOKS

Arte Publico Press, University of Houston, 4800 Calhoun, Houston, TX 77204-2174. 713-743-2841.

Web site: www.arte.uh.edu.

Nicolas Kanellos, President.

Description: Picture books, fiction, and autobiographies for children and young adults. Query with outline and sample chapters, or send complete manuscript. **Payment:** Royalty.

PIPPIN PRESS

229 E. 85th St., Gracie Sta., Box 1347, New York, NY 10028. 212-288-4920.

Barbara Francis, Editor.

Description: Publish picture books, early chapter books, middle group fiction, and unusual nonfiction for children ages 4-14, and humor for all ages. **Number of Books/Yr.:** 6 titles/year (3,000 submissions), 10% by first-time authors, 90% ungented. **Proposal Process:** Query with SASE. No unsolicited manuscripts. Hardcopy format. No multiple or electronic queries. **Payment:** Royalty. **Tips:** Looking for small chapter books (64-pages), on historical events in which young people are the heroes. Also looking for childhood memoirs and humor for all ages. **Contact:** Joyce Segal, Senior Ed.

PLEASANT COMPANY PUBLICATIONS

8400 Fairway Pl., Middleton, WI 58562-0998. 608-836-4848.

Web site: www.americangirl.com.

Erin Falligant, Submissions Editor.

Description: Books, 40,000-60,000 words, for 10-13-year-old girls: historical mystery/suspense, contemporary fiction, and contemporary advice and activity. Query with outline and sample chapters or send complete manuscript. Royalty or flat fee. **Tips:** Small "concept-driven" list; requires experienced writers.

PUFFIN BOOKS

Penguin Putnam Inc., 345 Hudson St., New York, NY 10014-3647. 212-414-2000.

Web site: www.penguinputnam.com/childrens.

Tracy Tang, President/Publisher.

Description: Children's fiction and nonfiction for all ages.

G.P. PUTNAM'S SONS BOOKS FOR YOUNG READERS

345 Hudson St., 14th Floor, New York, NY 10014. 212-366-2000.

Web site: www.penguinputnam.com.

Nancy Paulsen, Editorial Director.

Description: General trade nonfiction and fiction for ages 2-18. Mostly picture books and middle-grade novels. **Number of Books/Yr.:** 45 titles/year (avg. 12,000 submissions), 5% by first-time authors, 50% unagented. **Proposal Process:** Children's novels: query with 3 sample chapters. Picture books: send complete manuscript (if less than 10 pages). Considers multiple queries. No electronic queries.

Hard-copy format preferred. Response time: 1-3 months. **Payment:** Pays royalty. **Sample Titles:** *Saving Sweetness*, by Diane Stanley, illustrated by Brian Karas (ages 4-8); and *Amber Brown Sees Red*, by Paula Danziger (ages 7-10). **Tips:** Multicultural books should reflect different cultures accurately, but unobtrusively. Stories about physically or mentally challenged children should portray them accurately, without condescension. Avoid series, romances. Very little fantasy.

RAINTREE STECK-VAUGHN PUBLISHERS

15 East 26th Street, New York, NY 10010. 646-935-3702.
Walter Kossmann, Editorial Director.
Description: Children's nonfiction in series only. No single titles. All published books are curriculum-oriented. **Number of Books/Yr.:** 200 titles/year (500 submissions), a few first-time authors, almost all are unagented. **Proposal Process:** Query with outline and sample chapters, include SASE. Response time: 2-4 months. Multiple queries accepted with advance notice. No electronic queries. **Payment:** Flat fee (varies). **Sample Titles:** Children: *America into a New Millennium*, (Ages 11-14); *Phosphorus*, (ages 11-14); *The Secret World of Snakes*, (Ages 8-10); *Pollution and Conservation*, (Ages 8-10).

RANDOM HOUSE BOOKS FOR YOUNG READERS

Random House Inc., 201 E. 50th St., New York, NY 10022. 212-751-2600.
Web site: www.randomhouse.com/kids.
Kate Klimo, Vice President/Publishing Director.
Description: Fiction and nonfiction for beginning readers; paperback fiction line for 7-9 year-olds. No unsolicited manuscripts. Agented material only.

RED WAGON BOOKS

Harcourt Trade Publishers/Children's Book Div.
525 B St., Suite 1900, San Diego, CA 92101-4495. 619-231-6616.
Description: Fiction and nonfiction for children. Query with SASE.

MORGAN REYNOLDS, INC.

620 S. Elm St., Suite 384, Greensboro, NC 27406. 336-275-1311.
E-mail: editors@morganreynolds.com. Web site: www.morganreynolds.com.
John Riley, Editorial Director.
Description: Lively, well written biographies and histories for young adults. Suitable subjects include important historical events and important historical and contemporary figures. **Number of Books/Yr.:** 20 titles/year (300 submissions), 50% first-time authors, 90% unagented. **Proposal Process:** Send query with outline and sample chapters, SASE. Multiple and electronic queries considered. Prefers hard-copy format. Response time: 1 month. **Payment:** Royalty. **Sample Titles:** Children's Nonfiction: *Edgar Rice Burroughs, Creator of Tarzan*; *The Firing on Fort Sumter, A Splintered Nation Goes to War*. **Tips:** Only nonfiction, for young adults. Avoid eccentric topics, autobiographies, and "cute" writing styles. Market includes middle- and high-school libraries and public libraries. **Contact:** Laura Shoemaker.

RISING MOON
Northland Publishing, P.O. Box 1389, Flagstaff, AZ 86002-1389. 520-774-5251.
E-mail: aj@northlandpub.com. Web site: www.northlandpub.com.
Aimee Jackson, Editor.
Description: Picture books for children ages 5-8. Fiction and nonfiction, ages 8-12; no longer accepts unsolicited manuscripts. Interested in material on contemporary subjects. **Number of Books/Yr.:** 10-12 titles/year (3,000 submissions), 25% unagented. **Proposal Process:** No unsolicited manuscripts. Considers multiple queries. Electronic queries not accepted. Prefers hard-copy format. Response time: 3 months. **Payment:** Royalty or flat fee. **Tips:** Please submit through your agent, and review guidelines carefully first. **Contact:** Brad Melton/Northland Publishing.

ROSEN PUBLISHING GROUP, INC.
29 E. 21st St., New York, NY 10010. 646-205-7434.
Kathy Kuhtz Campbell, Managing Editor.
Description: All nonfiction: sports, history, guidance and safety, social studies, cultural diversity, science and health, animals, biographies. Pre-K to 2 and Grades 2-4. Also books for emergent and beginning readers. (Most are 24 pages). **Number of Books/Yr.:** 200 titles/year. **Proposal Process:** Query. Hard-copy. No electronic queries. **Payment:** Royalty and/or flat fee. **Tips:** Nonfiction work-for-hire series format (6 books to a series).

SANDCASTLE PUBLISHING
1723 Hill Drive, P.O. Box 3070, South Pasadena, CA 91031-6070.
Description: A 10-year-old company specializing in books introducing children to the performing arts. Fiction and nonfiction ranges from easy readers to young adult titles.

SCHOLASTIC PROFESSIONAL BOOKS
555 Broadway, New York, NY 10012-3999. 212-343-6511.
Web site: www.scholastic.com.
Adriane Rozier, Editor.
Description: Books by and for teachers of kindergarten through eighth grade. Instructor Books: practical, activity/resource books on teaching reading and writing, science, math, etc. Teaching Strategies Books: 64-96 pages on new ideas, practices, and approaches to teaching. Query with outline, sample chapters or activities, contents page, and resumé. Flat fee or royalty. Multiple queries considered. 8½" x 11" SASE for guidelines.

SEASTAR BOOKS
1123 Broadway, Suite 800, New York, NY 10010.
Andrea Schneeman, Editor-in-Chief.
Description: Literary children's hardcover books. Picture books and middle-grade fiction and nonfiction. Only accepts submissions from SCBWI members.

17TH STREET PRODUCTIONS

33 W. 17th St., New York, NY 10011.
Ann Brashares, Les Morgenstein, Co-Presidents.
Description: Book packager. Young adult books, 36,000 words; middle grade books, 29,000 words; elementary books, 10,000-12,000 words. **Payment:** Royalty and flat fee.

SILVER MOON PRESS

160 Fifth Ave., Suite 622, New York, NY 10010. 212-242-6499.
E-mail: mail@silvermoonpress.com. Web site: www.silvermoonpress.com.
Carmen McCain, Editor.
Description: American historical fiction for children, ages 8-12. Educational test prep material/English language arts and social studies. **Number of Books/Yr.:** 5 titles/year (75-100 submissions), 80% first-time authors, 80% unagented. **Proposal Process:** Query with outline and sample chapters. Multiple and electronic queries accepted. Response time: 1-3 months. Hard-copy. **Payment:** Royalty. **Tips:** American historical fiction. Young protagonists. Biographical fiction. **Contact:** Karen Lillebo.

SIMON & SCHUSTER BOOKS FOR YOUNG READERS

Simon & Schuster Children's Publishing Div., 1230 Ave. of the Americas, New York, NY 10020. 212-698-2851.
Web site: www.simonsays.com.
Stephanie Owens Lurie, Associate Publisher / V.P. / Editorial Director.
Description: Books for ages preschool through high school: picture books to young adult; nonfiction for all age levels. Hardcover only. Request guidelines before querying. SASE required for reply.

SPORTS PUBLISHING INC.

804 N. Neil, Champaign, IL 61820. 217-359-5940.
E-mail: mpearson@sagamorepub.com. Web site: www.sportspublishing.com.
Description: Leading publisher of regional sports covering a wide range of sports. A series for readers in grades 3-5 is entitled *Kids Superstars.* **Contact:** Mike Pearson

GARETH STEVENS

330 West Olive St., Suite 100, Milwaukee, WI 53212. 414-332-3520.
E-mail: info@gsinc.com. Web site: www.garethstevens.com.
Description: Children's books, often issued in series; multicultural themes, world cultures, science and natural history. Much of the catalog focuses on reprints for libraries of popular mass-marketed titles. Send query first.

STODDART KIDS BOOKS

34 Lesmill Road, Toronto, Ontario, M3B 2T6 Canada. 416-445-3333.
Web site: www.genpub.com.
Kathryn Cole, Publisher.
Description: Books for children of all ages, this Canadian publisher has traditionally focused on fiction. In 1999, however, it introduced its first nonfiction series, the

Discovery series. Stoddart plans to continue to expand its nonfiction list. It is looking for titles with hands-on activities using a fresh approach, for ages 8-11 years.

TIME-LIFE FOR CHILDREN
2000 Duke St., Alexandria, VA 22314. 703-838-7000.
Mary J. Wright, Managing Editor.
Description: Juvenile books. Publishes series of 12-36 volumes (no single titles). Author must have a series concept. Publisher has discontinued accepting unsolicited work.

TRICYCLE PRESS
Ten Speed Press, P.O. Box 7123, Berkeley, CA 94707. 510-559-1600.
Web site: www.tenspeed.com.
Nicole Geiger, Publisher.
Description: Children's books: Picture books, board books, "tween" books, photographic nonfiction. Submit complete manuscripts. Activity books, submit about 20 pages and complete outline. "Real life" books that help children cope with issues. **Number of Books/Yr.:** 20 titles/year (8,000-10,000 submissions), 15-20% by first-time authors, 50% unagented. **Proposal Process:** No queries. Send outline and sample chapters for novels and activity books, complete mss. for picture books. No electronic queries or faxed submissions. Prefer hard-copy format. **Payment:** Royalty; typical range is 15-20% net. **Sample Titles:** Children's: *G is for Googol*, by David Schwartz, illustrations by Marissa Moss (8 and up). *Storm Boy*, by Paul Owen Lewis, *Ancient Fire*, by Mark London Williams.

TROLL COMMUNICATIONS
100 Corporate Dr., Mahwah, NJ 07430. 201-529-4000.
Web site: www.troll.com.
Description: Juvenile fiction and nonfiction. Query preferred. Royalty or flat fee.
Contact: M. Francis.

TSR INC.
Wizards of the Coast, P.O. Box 707, 1801 Lind Avenue, SW, Renton, WA 98055. 425-226-6500.
Web site: www.wizards.com.
Description: Fantasy and science fiction, for juvenile, young-adult markets.

TURTLE BOOKS
866 United Nations Plaza, Suite 525, New York, NY 10017. 212-644-2020.
Web site: www.turtlebooks.com.
John Whitman, Publisher.
Description: Children's picture books only. Submit complete manuscript with SASE. **Payment:** Royalty.

TWENTY-FIRST CENTURY BOOKS

The Millbrook Press, P.O. Box 335, 2 Old New Milford Rd., Brookfield, CT 06804. 203-740-2220.

Kristen Vibbert, Editorial Director.

Description: Curriculum-oriented titles for the school and library market, focusing on current issues, U.S. history, biography and social studies, etc. **Number of Books/Yr.:** 135 titles/year (2,000 submissions). **Proposal Process:** Query with outline. Considers multiple queries. Response 2-3 months. Hard copy. No electronic queries. **Payment:** Royalty. **Sample Titles:** Children's: *Breast Cancer,* (age 12-up); *Heroes of the Holocaust,* (Age 12-up); *Steve Jobs: Think Different,* (age 10-up). **Tips:** Accepts submissions through agents only. Requires proposals with strong tie to an upper-elementary or middle-school curriculum. Picture books, activity books, parent's guides, etc. will not be considered. Send for guidelines or catalog.

VIKING CHILDREN'S BOOKS

Penguin Putnam Inc., 375 Hudson St., New York, NY 10014. 212-366-2000.

Web site: www.penguinputnam.com.

Elizabeth Law, Editor-in-Chief.

Description: Fiction and nonfiction, including biography, history, and sports, for ages 7-14. Humor and picture books for ages 3-8. Query Children's Book Dept. with outline and sample chapter. For picture books, please send entire manuscript. SASE. Advance and royalty.

ALBERT WHITMAN & CO.

6340 Oakton, Morton Grove, IL 60053. 847-581-0033.

Web site: www.awhitmanco.com.

Kathleen Tucker, Editor.

Description: Children's books. Picture books for ages 2-8; novels, biographies, mysteries, and nonfiction for middle-grade readers. Send SASE for guidelines. Send complete manuscript for picture books, 3 chapters and outline for longer fiction; query for nonfiction. Royalty.

WILEY CHILDREN'S BOOKS

605 Third Ave., New York, NY 10158-0012. 212-850-6000.

Web site: www.wiley.com.

Description: Nonfiction books, 96-128 pages, for 8-12-year-old children. Query. Royalty.

WILLIAMSON PUBLISHING CO.

P.O. Box 185, Charlotte, VT 05445. 802-425-2102.

Web site: www.williamsonbooks.com.

Susan Williamson, Editorial Director.

Description: How-to-do-it learning books based on a philosophy that says "learning is exciting, mistakes are fine, and involvement and curiosity are wonderful." **Number of Books/Yr.:** 15 titles/year (800-1,000 submissions), 50% by first-time authors, 90%

unagented. **Proposal Process:** Send query with outline and sample chapters. Response time: 2-3 months. No multiple or electronic queries. Hard copy. **Payment:** Royalty or flat fee. **Sample Titles:** *Bridges; Little Hands Art Book; Hands on Math for Real World Fun; The Kids Book of Natural History.* **Tips:** Looking for very well-executed writing, filled with information and how-to activities that make learning a positive and memorable experience. All of our books are written directly to kids.

THE WRIGHT GROUP

19201 120th Avenue, NE, Bothel, WA 98011. 425-486-8011.
Web site: www.wrightgroup.com.
Description: Books for the elementary-school market.

YEARLING BOOKS

Random House, 1540 Broadway, New York, NY 10036.
Description: Children's titles. Not accepting unsolicited material. Imprints include Skylark Books.

ZINO PRESS CHILDREN'S BOOKS

P.O. Box 52, Madison, WI 53701. 608-836-6660.
Web site: www.zinopress.com.
Judith Laitman, Editor-in-Chief.
Description: Fun, humorous, offbeat educational picture books and nonfiction books for children, some with multicultural themes, on music, literature, culture, nature, and social skills. **Proposal Process:** Send query first. **Payment:** Royalty or flat fee.

RELIGIOUS BOOKS

Religious book publishing is growing in leaps and bounds. In the 21st century, it ranges from books on Jewish traditions to Christian devotionals, from picture books for children to religious romances, from scholarly works on theology to the popular prophesy of the fictional *Left Behind* series (published by Tyndale House), found high on *The New York Times* bestseller lists.

Clearly, each publisher of religious books has a distinctive mission, often with a specialized sense of ideal approach and language to be used. Publishers expect their authors to be knowledgeable about readers' needs, to be familiar with the appropriate methods and concerns required for any book in this field to succeed.

Perhaps even more so than for other markets, before sending off materials, research each publisher under consideration carefully. Request a catalog, and get a copy of their guidelines for queries and submissions (often found on publisher websites). Be sure to send an SASE with your query, as well as sufficient return postage for any subsequent materials or illustrations sent.

ACCENT PUBLICATIONS
Cook Communications Ministries, P.O. Box 36640, 4050 Lee Vance View, Colorado Springs, CO 80936. 719-536-0100.
Jim Eyet, Managing Editor.
Description: Nonfiction church resources for Christian education curriculum programs for the local church; evangelical Christian perspective; no trade books. Guidelines available. Royalty. Paperback only.

JASON ARONSON, INC.
230 Livingston St., Northvale, NJ 07647-1726. 201-767-4093.
Web site: www.aronson.com.
Arthur Kurzweil, Editor-in-Chief.
Description: Nonfiction on all aspects of Jewish life, including such topics as anti-semitism, the Bible, Hasidic thought, genealogy, medicine, folklore and storytelling, interfaith relations, the Holocaust, the Talmud, women's studies, and travel. **Proposal Process:** Send complete manuscript or query with outline and sample chapters. **Payment:** Royalty.

BAKER BOOK HOUSE
P. O. Box 6287, Grand Rapids, MI 49516-6287. 616-676-9185.
E-mail: submissions@bakerbooks.com. Web site: www.bakerbooks.com.
Rebecca Cooper, Editor.
Description: Evangelical publisher offering more than 2000 releases per year in its five separate divisions. Publish hardcover and trade paperbacks in both fiction and nonfiction categories: trade books for the general public, professional books for church and parachurch leaders; texts for college and seminary classrooms. Topics include contemporary issues, women's concerns, parenting, singleness, children's

books, Bible study, Christian doctrine, reference books, books for pastors and church leaders, textbooks for Christian colleges and seminaries, and literary novels focusing on women's concerns. **Tips:** Begin with a formal proposal. Visit website for details.

BETHANY HOUSE PUBLISHERS
11400 Hampshire Ave. S., Minneapolis, MN 55438. 952-829-2500.
E-mail: info@bethanyhouse.com. Web site: www.bethanyhouse.com.
Steve Laube, Senior Editor.
Description: Religious fiction and nonfiction. Adults: personal growth books; divorce; euthanasia; women's issues; spirituality; abortion; and cults. Children and teens: first chapter books, 6,000-7,500 words, of biblical lessons and Christian faith for ages 7-10; imaginative stories and believable characters, 20,000-40,000 words, for middle grade readers; and at least 40,000-word stories with strong plots and realistic characters for teens of ages 12-17. Send synopsis, three sample chapters, bio, and SASE to Sharon Madison.

BLUE DOLPHIN PUBLISHING, INC.
P.O. Box 8, Nevada City, CA 95959. 800-643-0765.
E-mail: bdolphin@nutshel.net. Web site: www.bluedolphinpublishing.com.
Paul M. Clemens, President.
Description: Books, 200-300 pages, on comparative spiritual traditions, lay and transpersonal psychology, self-help, health, healing, and whatever helps people grow in their social awareness and conscious evolution. **Proposal Process:** Query with outline, sample chapters, and SASE. **Payment:** Royalty.

BRAZOS PRESS
Division of Baker Book House, P.O. Box 6287, Grand Rapids, MI 49516-6287. 616-676-9185.
E-mail: rclapp@brazospress.com.
Rodney Clapp, Acquisitions Editor.
Description: Publisher of books in Christian theology, spirituality, biblical studies and culture. No fiction or children's books. **Number of Books/Yr.:** 25 titles/year (300 submissions), 5% first-time authors, 50% unagented. **Proposal Process:** Query. Hard-copy preferred. No electronic queries. Multiple queries okay. Response time: 6 weeks. **Payment:** Royalty.

BROADMAN AND HOLMAN PUBLISHERS
127 Ninth Ave. N., Nashville, TN 37234-0115.
E-mail: brosenb@lifeway.com.
Bucky Rosenbaum, V.P. Trade.
Description: Trade, academic, religious and inspirational nonfiction. Query with SASE. Royalty. Guidelines.

THE CATHOLIC UNIVERSITY OF AMERICA PRESS
620 Michigan Ave. N.E., Washington, DC 20064. 202-319-5052.
E-mail: cua-press@cua.edu. Web site: http://cuapress.cua.edu.
David J. McGonagle, Director.
Description: Scholarly books (humanities, social studies, theology). Query first.

CHARIOT/VICTOR PUBLISHING
Cook Communications Ministries, 4050 Lee Vance View, Colorado Springs, CO
80918. 719-536-3271.
Web site: www.chariot.victor.com.
Description: Chariot Children's Books: fiction that "helps children better understand
themselves and their relationship with God"; nonfiction that illuminates the Bible; picture books for ages 1-7; fiction for ages 8-10, 10-12, and 12-14. Life Journey General
Titles: fiction with underlying spiritual theme; books on parenting from a Christian
perspective. Lengths and payment vary. Query required. Guidelines available.

CHRISTIAN PUBLICATIONS
Imprint of Horizon Books, 3825 Hartzdale Dr., Camp Hill, PA 17011. 717-761-7044.
E-mail: editors@cp-horizon.com. Web site: www.christianpublications.com.
David Fessenden, Editorial Director.
Description: Evangelical Christian nonfiction for adults. **Number of Books/Yr.:**
30-35 titles/year (1,000 submissions), 20% first-time authors, 90% unagented.
Proposal Process: Query with outline, proposal and sample chapters, include
SASE. Multiple and electronic queries accepted. Response time: 2-3 months. Hard-
copy format preferred. **Payment:** Royalty, 10% net. Flat fee paid on booklets only,
range is $100-$200. **Sample Titles:** *Thirsting After God* (Devotional). *As You Walk
Along the Way* (Parenting). **Tips:** Looking for good writers with a passion for their
topic, a respect for scripture and a desire to communicate well.

CONCORDIA PUBLISHING HOUSE
3558 S. Jefferson Ave., St. Louis, MO 63118-3968. 314-268-1187.
E-mail: boverton@cphnet.org. Web site: www.cph.org.
Dawn Weinstock, Managing Editor.
Description: Practical family books and devotionals. Must have explicit Christian
content. No poetry. Query. Royalty.

EERDMANS BOOKS FOR YOUNG READERS
William B. Eerdmans Publishing Co., 255 Jefferson Avenue, S.E., Grand Rapids, MI
99503. 616-459-4591.
Web site: www.eerdmans.com/youngreaders/.
Judy Zylstra, Editor-in-Chief.
Description: Scholarly religious reference, social concerns, and children's books.
Number of Books/Yr.: 12-15/yr; 3,000 submissions. **Proposal Process:** Typed,
double-spaced. Send complete mss. for picture books and those under 200 pages. For
longer books, send query letter and 3-4 sample chapters. Responds in 2-3 months.

WM. B. EERDMANS PUBLISHING COMPANY, INC.

255 Jefferson Ave. S.E., Grand Rapids, MI 49503. 616-459-4591.
Web site: www.eerdmans.com.
Jon Pott, Editor-in-Chief.
Description: Christian theological nonfiction; religious history and biography; ethics; philosophy; literary studies; spiritual growth. For children's religious books, query Judy Zylstra, Editor. Royalty.

EVERGREEN PUBLICATIONS

1444 104th Lane, N.W., Loon Rapids, MN 55433.
Description: Evangelical Christian books. Adult fiction and nonfiction, 200 pages, and children's and young adult fiction, 200 pages. **Proposal Process:** Query with outline and sample chapters. **Payment:** Royalty.

FORTRESS PRESS

P.O. Box 1209, Minneapolis, MN 55440. 612-330-3300.
E-mail: booksub@augsburgfortess.org. Web site: www.augsburgfortress.org.
Dana Dreibelbis, V.P. Publications.
Description: Publishing house of Evangelical Lutheran Church in America. Books of biblical studies, theology, ethics, professional ministry, and church history for academic and professional markets, including libraries. Query.

GENESIS PUBLISHING CO., INC.

1547 Great Pond Rd., N. Andover, MA 01845-1216. 978-688-6688.
Web site: ourworld.compuserve.com/homepages/genesisbooks.
Gerard M. Verschuuren, President.
Description: Adult fiction and nonfiction, especially religion and philosophy books. Query. **Payment:** Royalty.

GROUP PUBLISHING

P.O. Box 481, Loveland, CO 80539. 970-669-3836.
Web site: www.grouppublishing.com.
Description: Christian publications for children-young adults. Sunday School and other ministries.

HACHAI PUBLISHING

156 Chester Ave., Brooklyn, NY 11218. 718-633-0100.
E-mail: info@hachai.com. Web site: www.hachai.com.
Dina Rosenfeld, Editor.
Description: Judaica children's picture books for readers ages 2-8. Interested in biographies of spiritually great men and women in Jewish history, historical fiction. **Number of Books/Yr.:** 4 titles/year (300 submission), 60% first-time authors, 90% unagented. **Proposal Process:** Query or send complete manuscript, and SASE. Multiple queries accepted. No electronic queries. Hard copy. Response time: 6 weeks. **Payment:** Flat fee. **Tips:** Looking for stories that convey traditional Jewish

experience in modern times; traditional Jewish observance such as holidays and year-round mitzvahs; positive character traits.

HARPER SAN FRANCISCO

HarperCollins Publishers, 353 Sacramento St., Ste 500, San Francisco, CA 94111-3653. 415-477-4400.

Web site: www.harpercollins.com.

Description: Books on spirituality and religion. No unsolicited manuscripts; query required. **Contact:** Acquisitions Editor.

HARVEST HOUSE PUBLISHERS

1075 Arrowsmith, Eugene, OR 97402. 541-343-0123.

Carolyn McCready, Editorial Director.

Description: Providing high-quality books and products that glorify God, affirm biblical values, help people grow spiritually strong, and proclaim Jesus Christ as the answer to every human need. Query. **Sample Titles:** Adult Fiction: *City Girl*, by Lori Wick. (Yellow Rose Trilogy). Picture Books: *My Very First Book of Manners* (10 pages) Children's Fiction: *Amazing Mazes for Kids,* by Steve & Becky Miller. Adult Nonfiction: *Awesome God,* by Neil T. Anderson and Rich Miller. **Tips:** Harvest House no longer accepts unsolicited submissions; writers must query first before sending any manuscript materials. **Contact:** Pat Mathis.

HORIZON BOOKS

Christian Publications, 3825 Hartzdale Dr., Camp Hill, PA 17011.

E-mail: editors@cpi-horizon.com.

George McPeek, Editor.

Description: Adult nonfiction from an evangelical Christian viewpoint, centering on personal spiritual growth, usually with a "deeper life" theme. **Number of Books/Yr.:** 35 titles/year (1,000 submissions), 30% first-time authors, 90% unagented. **Proposal Process:** Query with outline/sample chapters. Multiple and electronic queries considered. Hard-copy format preferred. **Payment:** Royalty. **Sample Titles:** Adult Nonfiction: Recent freelance purchases include *Harry Potter and the Bible* (popular apologetics), *Reality Check: A Survival Manual for Christians in the Workplace* (devotional) and *Song of the Fiddle: The Challenge of Followership* (Christian living/discipleship). **Tips:** Seeking writing that grows out of author's personal relationship with Christ and experience in Christian service, whether lay or ordained. Especially interested in books on spiritual growth with practical application ("sanctification with running shoes on"). Not interested in "new believer" material or "everything about the Bible in 150 pages." May consider Bible study books, but no Bible commentaries.

JOURNEY BOOKS

Bob Jones University Press, 1700 Wade Hampton Blvd., Greenville, SC 29614. 864-370-1800 x 4350.

E-mail: syoung@bju.edu. Web site: www.home.bju.com.

Susan Young, Managing Editor-Children's, Nancy Lohr, Manuscript Editor, Suzette Jordan, Adult Manuscript Editor.

Description: Books for young readers, ages 6-12, that reflect "the highest Christian standards of thought, feeling, and action." **Number of Books/Yr.:** 16 titles/year (500 submissions). **Proposal Process:** Query with outline and sample chapters or complete manuscript. Accepts both multiple and electronic queries. Hard-copy format preferred. **Payment:** Royalty; first-time authors, flat fee (both are negotiable). **Sample Titles:** Adults: *Proverbs Commentary, Ribbing Him Rightly, God's Prophetic Blueprint.* Children: *Little Bear and the Cruncheroo Cookies,* (ages 2-6), *Arby Jenkins Meets His Match,* (ages 9-12), *The Way of Escape,* (ages 12 and up). **Tips:** For line of fiction, secular conflicts are considered, but only within a Christian worldview. Avoid modern humanistics philosophy in stories; instead, emphasize a biblically conservative lifestyle that best serves the individual and society. The writing must be excellent and the story engaging. For our adult nonfiction line, we prefer KJV and adherence to our statement of faith. **Contact:** Nancy Bopp, Asst. Ed., Children.

JUDSON PRESS

American Baptist Churches, P.O. Box 851, Valley Forge, PA 19482-0851. 610-768-2109.

E-mail: randy.frame@abc-usa.org. Web site: www.judsonpress.com.

Randy Frame, Editor.

Description: Publishes resources to enhance individual Christian living and the life of the church. **Number of Books/Yr.:** 30 title/year (700 submissions), 20% first-time authors, 90% unagented. **Proposal Process:** Query with proposal, table of contents, estimated length of book, sample chapters, target audience, expected completion date, and bio. Multiple queries accepted. Electronic queries okay, but not for proposals. Hard-copy format preferred. **Payment:** Royalty. **Tips:** Avoid life stories or poetry. Looking for unusually good writing and original ideas.

KREGEL PUBLICATIONS

Kregel, Inc., P.O. Box 2607, Grand Rapids, MI 49501-2607. 616-451-4775.

E-mail: kregelbooks@kregel.com. Web site: www.kregel.com.

Dennis Hillman, Publisher.

Description: Evangelical Christian publisher interested in pastoral ministry, Christian education, family and marriage, devotional books, and biblical studies. No poetry, general fiction, or cartoons. **Proposal Process:** Query with summary, target audience, brief bio, an outline or table of contents, 2 sample chapters, and an SASE. Allow 6-8 weeks for a response. **Payment:** Royalty.

LOYOLA PRESS

3441 N. Ashland Ave., Chicago, IL 60657-1397. 773-281-1818.
E-mail: editorial@loyolapress.com. Web site: www.loyolapress.org.
Jim Manney, Editorial Director.
Description: Religious and ethics-related material for college-educated Christian readers. *Loyola Press Series:* art, literature, and religion; contemporary Christian concerns. **Number of Books/Yr.:** 30 titles/year (200 submissions) 25% by first-time authors, 75% unagented. **Proposal Process:** Send query with outline. Multiple and electronic queries accepted. Hard-copy format preferred. Response time: 4-6 weeks. **Payment:** Royalty, typically 15% net. **Sample Titles:** *Spirituality at Work, Book of Catholic Prayer, Raising Faith-Filled Kids.*

MOODY PRESS

820 N. LaSalle Blvd., Chicago, IL 60610-3284. 800-678-8001.
E-mail: acquisitions@moody.edu. Web site: www.moodypress.org.
James Bell, Editorial Director.
Description: Christian material including personal experiences, new Bible translations, and Bible study material, and some juvenile books; no picture books. **Number of Books/Yr.:** 60 titles/year (3,000 submissions), 1% first-time authors, 1% unagented. **Proposal Process:** Agented queries only. Send complete manuscript or 3 sample chapters, outline, table of contents, introduction, and target audience of proposed book. Multiple queries accepted. Response time: 2 months. Hard-copy format preferred. **Payment:** Royalty. **Sample Titles:** Adult: *Lies Women Believe,* by Nancy Leigh DeMoss (Women's nonfiction); *Free at Last,* by Tony Evans (Christian Living); *The Five Love Languages of Teenagers,* by Gary Chapman (Parenting). Children's: *Saved Race,* by Stephanie Perry Moore (fiction, ages 12-18), *New Sugar Creek Gang,* series (fiction, ages 7-13).

MOREHOUSE PUBLISHING

4775 Linglestown Rd., Harrisburg, PA 17112. 717-541-8130.
E-mail: mfretz@morehousegroup.com. Web site: www.morehousepublishing.com..
Mark Fretz, Publisher and Editorial Director.
Description: Theology, pastoral care, church administration, spirituality, Anglican studies, history of religion, books for children. **Number of Books/Yr.:** 30-35 titles/year (500-750 submissions), 60% by first-time authors, 90% unagented. **Proposal Process:** Query with cover letter, brief proposal, resumé, short book description, outline, market analysis, sample chapters (20 pages). Multiple queries okay. No electronic queries. Response time: 4-6 weeks. Hard-copy format preferred. **Tips:** Children's books should contain rich theological concepts framed in terms children can understand. Must be clearly Christian, or Judeo-Christian; should approach subject matter in fresh, exciting ways. No fiction, poetry.

MULTNOMAH PUBLISHERS, INC.

P.O. Box 1720, Sisters, OR 97759. 541-549-1144.
Web site: www.multnomahbooks.com.
Rod Morris, Editor.
Description: Evangelical, Christian publishing house with 2 imprints. Multnomah Books are message-driven, clean, moral, uplifting fiction, and nonfiction. Alabaster Books are contemporary women's fiction that upholds strong Christian values. **Proposal Process:** Submit 2-3 sample chapters with outline, cover letter, and SASE. **Payment:** Royalty.

THOMAS NELSON PUBLISHERS

Nelson Word Publishing Group, P.O. Box 141000, Nashville, TN 37214-1000.
Description: Nonfiction: adult inspirational, motivational, devotional, self-help, Christian living, prayer, and evangelism. Fiction from a Christian perspective. Query with resumé, sample chapter, synopsis, and SASE. Allow 12 weeks for response.

NEW CANAAN PUBLISHING COMPANY

P.O. Box 752, New Canaan, CT 06840.
E-mail: djm@newcanaanpublishing.com. Web site: www.newcanaanpublishing.com.
Kathy Mittelstadt, Editor.
Description: Publisher of children's for readers ages 5-16 and young adult fiction and nonfiction and Christian works. **Number of Books/Yr.:** 3-4 titles/year, (120 submissions), 50% first-time authors, 100% unagented. **Proposal Process:** Submit complete manuscript, and SASE. Accepts multiple queries, no electronic queries. Response time: 6 months. Hard copy. **Payment:** Royalty. **Tips:** Seeking strong educational and moral content.

NEW LEAF PRESS, INC.

P.O. Box 726, Green Forest, AR 72638. 870-438-5288.
E-mail: nlp@newleafpress.net. Web site: www.newleafpress.net.
Roger Howerton, Editorial Director.
Description: Nonfiction, 100-400 pages, for Christian readers: how to live the Christian life, devotionals, gift books. No poetry. fiction, or personal stories. Master Books is looking for projects related to creationism, including children's books, scholarly works and books for the layman. **Number of Books/Yr.:** 15-20 titles/year (1,200 submissions), 15% first-time authors. **Proposal Process:** Query with outline and sample chapters. Multiple and electronic queries accepted. Response time: 3 months. **Payment:** Royalty, 10% of net. **Sample Titles:** Adult Fiction: *The Answers Book; Special Wonders of the Wild Kingdom; Buried Alive; When He Appears; The Wonder of It All.* Adult Nonfiction: *365 Fascinating Facts about Jesus; The Silent War; Living For Christ in the Endtimes.* Young Adult: *The Childrens Illustrated Bible.* **Tips:** Tell us why this book is marketable and to which market(s) it is directed. How will it fulfill the needs of Christians?

OUR SUNDAY VISITOR PUBLISHING

200 Noll Plaza, Huntington, IN 46750. 219-356-8400.
E-mail: booksed@osv.com. Web site: www.osv.com.
Jacquelyn M. Lindsey / Mike Dubruiel, Acquisitions Editors.
Description: Catholic-oriented books of various lengths. No fiction. **Number of Books/Yr.:** 20-30 titles/year (500+ submissions), 10% first-time authors, 90% unagented. **Proposal Process:** Query with proposal with outline/define market. Include SASE. Response time: 3 months. **Payment:** Royalty. **Sample Titles:** *Our Sunday Visitor's Treasury of Catholic Stories,* by Gerald Costello. **Tips:** Seek well-researched Church histories.

PARACLETE PRESS

P.O. Box 1568, Orleans, MA 02653. 508-255-4685.
E-mail: mail@paracletepress.com. Web site: www.paracletepress.com.
Editorial Review Committee.
Description: An ecumenical publisher. Specializes in full-length, nonfiction works for the adult Christian market. **Number of Books/Yr.:** 16 titles/year, (150-250 submissions). **Proposal Process:** Query with summary of proposed book and its target audience, estimated length of book, table of contents, and 1-2 sample chapters. Multiple queries accepted. Response time: 8 weeks. **Payment:** Royalty.

PAULINE BOOKS & MEDIA

Daughters of St. Paul's Ave., 50 St. Paul's Avenue, Jamaica Plain, MA 02130-3491. 617-522-8911.
Web site: www.pauline.org.
Description: Roman Catholic publications for both adults and children.

PAULIST PRESS

997 MacArthur Blvd., Mahwah, NJ 07430. 201-825-7300.
Web site: www.paulistpress.com.
Lawrence Boadt, Publisher.
Description: Adult nonfiction, 120-250 pages, on ecumenical theology, Roman Catholic studies, liturgy, spirituality, church history, ethics, education, and philosophy. They also publish a limited number of story books for children. **Proposal Process:** For adult books, query with SASE. For juvenile books, submit complete manuscript, with one sample illustration. No multiple submissions. **Payment:** Flat fee or royalty.

QUEST BOOKS

Theosophical Publishing House, 306 W. Geneva Rd., P. O. Box 270, Wheaton, IL 60189-0270. 630-665-0130.
E-mail: questbooks@aol.com. Web site: www.theosophical.org.
Brenda Rosen, Acquisitions Editor.
Description: Nonfiction books on Eastern and Western religion and philosophy, holistic health, healing, transpersonal psychology, men's and women's spirituality,

creativity, meditation, yoga, ancient wisdom. Query with outline and sample chapters. Royalty or flat fee. **Contact:** Vija Bremanis.

ST. ANTHONY MESSENGER PRESS

1615 Republic St., Cincinnati, OH 45210-1298. 513-241-5615.
E-mail: stanthony@americancatholic.org. Web site: www.americancatholic.org.
Lisa Biedenbach, Acquisitions Editor.
Description: Inspirational nonfiction for Catholics, supporting a Christian lifestyle in our culture; prayer aids, scripture, church history, education, practical spirituality, parish ministry, liturgy resources, Franciscan resources, family-based religious education program, and children's books. **Proposal Process:** Query with 500-word summary. **Payment:** Royalty.

SAINT MARY'S PRESS

702 Terrace Heights, Winona, MN 55987-1320. 800-533-8095.
Web site: www.smp.org.
Steve Nagel, Editor.
Description: Progressive Catholic publisher. Fiction, to 40,000 words, for young adults ages 11-17, that gives insight into the struggle of teens to become healthy, hopeful adults and also sheds light on Catholic experience, history, or cultures.

SCHOCKEN BOOKS

299 Park Ave., New York, NY 10171. 212-572-2559.
Web site: www.schocken.com.
Susan Ralston, Editorial Director.
Description: Fiction and nonfiction books of Jewish interest. **Number of Books/Yr.:** 6 titles published/year (200 submissions). **Proposal Process:** Query with outline and sample chapters. No electronic queries. Multiple queries okay. Response time: 1 month. Hard copy. **Payment:** Royalty. **Tips:** Looking for well-written fiction, history, biography, current affairs for general readers. No non-Jewish religious treatises, nor for any kind of spirituality, New Age, humor, academic, or Holocaust memoirs.

STANDARD PUBLISHING

8121 Hamilton Ave., Cincinnati, OH 45231. 513-931-4050.
Web site: www.standardpub.com.
Diane Stortz, Ruth Frederick, Editorial Directors.
Description: Christian children's books-board books, picture books, coloring books, Christian church curriculum/teacher resources. **Number of Books/Yr.:** 100 titles/year (2,000 submissions), 15% by first-time authors, 80% unagented. **Proposal Process:** Query with outline. Multiple queries accepted. No electronic queries. Hard-copy format. Response time: 3 months. **Payment:** Royalty (typically 5-10%) and flat fee (varies). **Sample Titles:** *My Good Night Devotions*, (Children's devotions, ages 3-6); *Noah, Noah!* (board book, ages 3-6). **Tips:** Currently seeking picture books, early readers, and board books. Call or write for up-to-date guidelines before submitting.

STEEPLE HILL

300 E. 42nd St., 6th Fl., New York, NY 10017. 212-682-6080.
Web site: www.eharlequin.com.
Tara Gavin, Editor.
Description: Mills & Boon, Harlequin, Silhouette, MIRA, and Steeple Hill books. Romance with an element of Christian faith, 70,000-75,000 words, that promote strong family values and high moral standards. **Number of Books/Yr.:** 36 titles/year. **Proposal Process:** Query with two- to five-page double-spaced synopsis of the story and SASE with sufficient postage. No multiple or electronic queries. Prefer hard-copy format. Response time: 3 months. **Payment:** Royalty. **Tips:** Write from the heart. Physical interaction should emphasize emotional tenderness rather than sexual desire. Avoid situations with sexual intercourse between characters unless they are married. **Contact:** Tracy Farell, Senior Editor.

TRINITY PRESS INTERNATIONAL

Morehouse Group, P.O. Box 1321, Harrisburg, PA 17105. 717-541-8130.
Web site: www.trinitypressintl.com.
Henry L. Carrigan, Jr., Editorial Director.
Description: Serious studies and research in Bible and theology/religion, interfaith studies, African-American religious life and thought, biblical interpretation, and methodology. **Number of Books/Yr.:** 30 titles/year. **Proposal Process:** Query the editor with outline and sample chapters or send complete manuscript. Multiple and electronic queries are considered. Response time: 4-6 weeks. Hard-copy format preferred. **Payment:** Royalty.

TYNDALE HOUSE

351 Executive Dr., Carol Stream, IL 60188. 630-668-8300.
Web site: www.tyndale.com.
Ron Beers, Editorial Director.
Description: Adult fiction and nonfiction on subjects of concern to Christians. **Number of Books/Yr.:** 160 titles/year, 10% first-time authors, 15% unagented. **Proposal Process:** No unsolicited mss. Agented only. Response time: 3 months. Hard copy. No electronic queries. **Payment:** Royalty. **Sample Titles:** Fiction: *The Mark, The Indwelling.* Nonfiction: *How Now Shall We Live? The Control Freak.* Children's: *Mars Diaries Little Blessings Series.* **Tips:** No unsolicited manuscripts. SASE for guidelines.

UAHC PRESS

633 Third Ave., New York, NY 10017. 212-650-4120.
E-mail: uahcpress@uahc.org. Web site: www.uahcpress.com.
Rabbi Hara Person, Editor.
Description: Publishes trade books and textbooks of Jewish interest for preschool through adult readers. **Number of Books/Yr.:** 18 titles/year (300 submissions), 17% by first-time authors, 100% unagented. **Proposal Process:** Query with outline and sample chapters. Response time: 4-8 weeks. Multiple queries considered. Hard-copy

format preferred. **Payment:** Royalty. **Sample Titles:** Adult: *The Reform Judaism Reader: North American Documents*, by Michael A. Meyer and W. Gunther Plaut (reference); *Jewish Living: A Guide to Contemporary Reform Practice*, by Mark Washofsky (Jewish sourcebook). Children's: *The God Around Us, Volume II, The Valley of Blessings*, by Mira Pollak Brichto (ages 2-5); *Solomon and the Trees*, by Matt Biers-Ariel (ages 5-8). **Tips:** Seeking books dealing with Jewish topics in areas of textbooks for religious school classrooms, children's trade books, and adult nonfiction.

THE UPPER ROOM MINISTRIES

1908 Grand Ave., Nashville, TN 37202. 615-340-7000.
Web site: www.upperroom.org.
Joanne Miller, Editorial Director.
Description: Focuses on Christian spiritual formation (families, churches, small groups, congregational leaders, and individuals). **Number of Books/Yr.:** 25 titles/year (300 submissions), 2% by first-time authors, 100% unagented. **Proposal Process:** Query with outline, sample chapters, and SASE. Multiple queries considered. Hard-copy format preferred. **Payment:** Royalty. **Tips:** Keep these categories in mind: Opening Our Hearts and Minds to God, Walking Together with Christ, Preparing the Spiritual Way for Emerging Generations, Maturing as Spiritual Leaders, and Realizing Our Oneness in Christ. No fiction or poetry.

ZONDERKIDZ

5300 Patterson Avenue SE, Grand Rapids, MI 49530. .
Web site: www.zondervan.com.
Julie Marchese, Editorial Assistant.
Description: A division of Zondervan Publishing—publishes books based on Christian values, for children to age 12. **Tips:** Prospective writers must follow guidelines closely, or submissions will go unread.

ZONDERVAN PUBLISHING HOUSE

5300 Patterson S.E., Grand Rapids, MI 49530. 616-698-6900.
E-mail: zpub@zph.com. Web site: www.zondervan.com.
Diane Gloem, Manuscript Editor.
Description: Christian titles. General fiction and nonfiction; for children and adults. SASE. Guidelines. No manuscripts or queries via e-mail. No poetry, drama, sermons, cookbooks or dissertations. Payment varies. **Number of Books/Yr.:** 150 titles per year. **Proposal Process:** Query with outline and sample chapters. Will consider multiple queries. Hard-copy submission only: typed, double space, 12 pt. Times New Roman font. **Payment:** Varies. **Sample Titles:** *When Bad Things Happen to Good Marriages; Hustling God; The Life Promises Bible.*

OTHER MARKETS

DRAMA & THEATER

Community, regional, and civic theaters and college dramatic groups offer the best opportunities today for playwrights to see their work produced, whether on the stage or in dramatic readings.

Indeed, aspiring playwrights will be encouraged to hear that many well-known playwrights received their first recognition in the regional theaters. Payment is generally nominal, but regional and university theaters usually buy only the right to produce a play, and all further rights revert to the author. Since most directors like to work closely with authors on any revisions necessary, theaters will often pay the playwright's expenses while in residence during rehearsals.

The thrill of seeing your play come to life on the stage is one of the pleasures of being on hand for rehearsals and performances. In addition to producing plays and giving dramatic readings, many theaters also sponsor competitions or new-play festivals. Aspiring playwrights should query college and community theaters in their region to find out which ones are interested in seeing original scripts.

Dramatic associations of interest to playwrights include the Dramatists Guild (1501 Broadway, Suite 701, New York, NY 10036), and Theatre Communications Group, Inc. (355 Lexington Ave., New York, NY 10017), which publishes the annual *Dramatists Sourcebook: The Playwright's Companion*, published by Feedback Theatrebooks (305 Madison Ave., Suite 1146, New York, NY 10165), is an annual directory of theaters, play publishers, and prize contests seeking scripts. See Organizations for Writers listings (in Other Resources section of this book) for details on dramatists' associations.

Some of the theaters on this list require that playwrights submit all or some of the following with scripts—cast list, synopsis, resumé, recommendations, and return postcard—and with scripts and queries, SASEs must always be enclosed.

Also, writers who want to try their hand at writing screenplays for television or film may find it helpful to gain experience in playwriting and further their knowledge of dramatic structure by working in amateur, community, or professional theaters.

The following list also includes a number of publishers of full-length or one-act plays for use by juvenile and adult drama programs.

A. D. PLAYERS
2710 W. Alabama, Houston, TX 77098.
E-mail: adplayers@itern.org. Web site: www.adplayers.org.
Jeannette Clift George, Artistic Director.
Description: Full-length or one-act comedies, dramas, musicals, children's plays, and adaptations with Christian worldview. SASE.

ACADEMY THEATRE
501 Means St., Atlanta, GA 30318.
Elliott J. Berman, Artistic Director.
Description: Comedies and dramas that "stretch the boundaries of imagination with poetic language and imagery." Prefers Southeast regional playwrights or subjects. SAS postcard.

ACTORS' PLAYHOUSE AT THE MIRACLE THEATRE
280 Miracle Mile, Coral Gables, FL 33134. 305-444-9293.
E-mail: apmiracle@aol.com. Web site: www.actorsplayhouse.org.
David Arisco, Artistic Director.
Description: Seeking new readings for comedy, drama and musicals. Smaller casts preferred. Minimal set restrictions for readings/workshop productions. Looking to expand Reading Series, 6-10 readings/ season. A new black box space allows workshop performances of already read material, and small performance pieces.

ACTORS THEATRE OF LOUISVILLE
316 W. Main St., Louisville, KY 40202. 502-584-1265.
Web site: www.actorstheatre.org.
Tanya Palmer, Literary Manager.
Description: Literary Prize/Award offers: National Ten-Minute Play Contest: for plays to 10 pages which have not had an equity production. U.S. citizens or residents. Limit: 1 script per person. Prize: $1,000 Heideman Award, possible production. Write for guidelines, SASE. Deadline December 1. No fees.

ALABAMA SHAKESPEARE FESTIVAL
The State Theatre, 1 Festival Dr., Montgomery, AL 36117-4605. 334-271-5300.
E-mail: asfmail@mindspring.com. Web site: www.asf.net.
Kent Thompson, Artistic Director.
Description: Southern and African-American themes/writers. Seeking new full-length plays for production. Sponsors local young playwrights' contest (new). Offers workshops/readings; 1-2 will see full production. SASE. Tips: Be familiar with Southern writing. Avoid cliché, plays that recall the movies.

ALLEY THEATRE
615 Texas Ave., Houston, TX 77002.
Travis Mader, Artistic Director.
Description: Full-length plays, including translations and adaptations. SASE.

ALLIANCE THEATRE COMPANY
1280 Peachtree St. N.E., Atlanta, GA 30309. 404-733-4650.
E-mail: Freddie.Ashley@woodruffcenter.org. Web site: www.alliancetheatre.org.
Kenny Leon, Artistic Director.
Description: New full-length children's plays, comedy or drama. Plays for a

culturally diverse community, told in stylish or adventurous ways. SASE. Contact: Literary Department.

AMERICAN LITERATURE THEATRE PROJECT
Fountain Theatre, 5060 Fountain Ave., Los Angeles, CA 90029.
Simon Levy.
Description: One-act and full-length stage adaptations of classic and contemporary American literature. Sets and cast size unrestricted. Send synopsis and SAS postcard. Standard pay, set by Dramatists Guild.

AMERICAN LIVING HISTORY THEATER
P.O. Box 752, Greybull, WY 82426.
Dorene Ludwig, Artistic Director.
Description: One-act dramas, ideally, 1 or 2 characters, historically accurate, about American historical and literary characters and events. SAS postcard.

AMERICAN PLACE THEATRE
111 W. 46th St., New York, NY 10036.
Martin Blank, Artistic Director.
Description: Agent submission only. Seek challenging, innovative works, not obviously commercial. SAS postcard. Unsolicited mss: Do not accept.

AMERICAN REPERTORY THEATRE
64 Brattle St., Cambridge, MA 02138.
Description: No unsolicited material. Contact: Office of New Play Development.

AMERICAN STAGE
P.O. Box 1560, St. Petersburg, FL 33731.
Victoria Holloway, Artistic Director.
Description: Full-length comedies and dramas. Send synopsis with short description of cast and production requirements. SAS postcard. Pays negotiable rates. Submit September-January.

AMERICAN STAGE COMPANY
FDU, Box 336, Teaneck, NJ 07666.
James Vagias, Executive Producer.
Description: Full-length comedies, dramas, and musicals for cast of 5-6, single set. No unsolicited scripts.

AMERICAN THEATRE OF ACTORS
314 W. 54th St., New York, NY 10019.
James Jennings, Artistic Director.
Description: Full-length dramas for a cast of 2-6. Submit complete play. Responds in 1-2 months. SASE.

ANCHORAGE PRESS

Box 8067, New Orleans, LA 70182.

Description: Publishes plays, proven in multiple production, for children (grades K-12); 8-10 new playbooks, 1-3 new hardcover books each year. Royalty.

MAXWELL ANDERSON PLAYWRIGHTS SERIES

Box 671, W. Redding, CT 06896.

Bruce Post, Artistic Director.

Description: Produces 6 professional staged readings of new plays each year. Send complete script with SASE.

ARENA STAGE

1101 Sixth St. S.W., Washington, DC 20024. 202-554-9066.

E-mail: cmaidson@arenastage.org.

Cathy Madison, Literary Manager.

Description: D.C. metro-area writers only; send synopsis, 10 pages of dialogue, bio, and reviews if available. Currently looking for American settings and themes. SASE.

ARKANSAS ARTS CENTER CHILDREN'S THEATRE

Box 2137, Little Rock, AR 72203.

Bradley Anderson, Artistic Director.

Description: Seeks solid, professional full-length or one-act scripts, especially work adapted from contemporary and classic literature. Some original work. SASE.

ARKANSAS REPERTORY THEATRE COMPANY

601 S. Main, P.O. Box 110, Little Rock, AR 72203-0110. 501-378-0445.

E-mail: therep@alltel.net. Web site: www.therep.org.

Brady Moody, Literary Manager.

Description: Full-length comedies, dramas, and musicals; prefer up to 8 characters. Send synopsis, cast list, resumé, and SASE; do not send complete manuscript. Responds in 3 months.

BAKER'S PLAYS

P.O. Box 69922, Quincy, MA 02269-9222. 617-745-0805.

E-mail: info@bakersplays.com. Web site: www.bakersplays.com.

Ray Pape, Associate Editor.

Description: Publishes full-length or one-act plays for young audiences, musicals, chancel dramas. Prefers produced plays; for high school, community and regional theaters. "Plays from Young Authors" features work by high school playwrights. Send resumé; include press clippings if available. SASE. Responds in 2-6 months.

BARTER THEATER

P.O. Box 867, Abingdon, VA 24212-0867.
E-mail: barter@naxs.com.
Richard Rose, Artistic Director.
Description: Full-length dramas, comedies, adaptations, and children's plays. Submit synopsis and dialogue sample. SASE. Responds in 6-8 months. Standard royalty.

BERKELEY REPERTORY THEATRE

2025 Addison St., Berkeley, CA 94704. 510-647-2900.
Web site: www.berkeleyrep.org.
Tony Taccone, Artistic Director.
Description: Seeking new full-length plays for production, 5 mainstage/2 parallel season productions, mid-level career and above. Some work commissioned. No restrictions on cast or set. SASE. Contact: Luan Schooler, Literary Manager.

BERKSHIRE THEATRE FESTIVAL

Box 797, Stockbridge, MA 01262.
Web site: www.berkshiretheatre.org.
Kate Maguire, Producing Director.
Description: Full-length comedies, musicals, and dramas; cast to 8. Submit through agent only.

BLIZZARD PUBLISHING

73 Furby St., Winnipeg, Manitoba, Canada R3C 2A2.
Peter Atwood, Artistic Director.
Description: Publishes one-act and full-length dramas, children's plays, and adaptations. Queries preferred. Responds in 3-4 months. Royalty.

BOARSHEAD THEATER

425 S. Grand Ave., Lansing, MI 48917. 517-484-7800.
E-mail: boarshead@voyager.net. Web site: www.boarshead.org.
John Peakes, Artistic Director.
Description: Seeking new full-length plays, comedy and drama, cast of 4-10. Single or unit set preferred. SASE.

BRISTOL RIVERSIDE THEATRE

Box 1250, Bristol, PA 19007.
Susan D. Atkinson.
Description: Full-length plays,up to 15 actors, and simple set. SASE.

CALIFORNIA UNIVERSITY THEATRE

California, PA 15419.
Dr. Richard J. Helldobler, Chairman.
Description: Unusual, avant-garde, and experimental one-act and full-length

comedies and dramas, children's plays, and adaptations. Cast size varies. Submit synopsis with short, sample scene(s). SASE. Payment available.

CENTER STAGE
700 N. Calvert St., Baltimore, MD 21202. 410-685-3200.
James Magruder, Resident Dramaturg.
Description: Full-length comedies, dramas, translations, adaptations. No unsolicited manuscripts. Send synopsis, a few sample pages, resumé, cast list, and production history. SASE. Responds in 8-10 weeks.

CHILDSPLAY INC.
Box 517, Tempe, AZ 85280-0517. 480-350-8101.
E-mail: childsplayaz@juno.com. Web site: www.tempe.gov/childsplay.
David Saar, Artistic Director.
Description: Seeking new full-length and one-act children's plays, multi-generational, 45-120 minutes: dramas, musicals, and adaptations for family audiences. Cast up to 12. Set: no restrictions. Productions may need to travel. Prefer visual, theatrical pieces rather than didactic message plays. SASE. Contact: Graham Whitehead.

CIRCLE IN THE SQUARE THEATRE SCHOOL
1633 Broadway, New York, NY 10019-6795.
E-mail: circleinthesquare@worldnet.att.net. Web site: www.circlesquare.org.
Dr. Rhonda R. Dodd, Associate Director.
Description: Accepts scripts, tapes, and sheet music for children's theatre using 4-6 adult actors. Prefer multi-cultural or American historical themes, 35-45 minutes long, may include music. SASE.

CITY THEATRE COMPANY
57 S. 13th St., Pittsburgh, PA 15203.
Web site: www. citytheatre-phg.org.
Carlyn Ann Aquiline, Literary Manager.
Description: Full-length comedies, musicals, and dramas; innovative contemporary plays of substance. No unsolicited or e-mail submissions. Agent submissions, or query with resumé, detailed synopsis, character breakdown, dialogue sample (15-20 pages), development/production history. Royalty.

I. E. CLARK PUBLICATIONS
P.O. Box 246, Schulenburg, TX 78956.
E-mail: ieclark@cvtv.net. Web site: www.ieclark.com.
Donna Cozzaglio, Artistic Director.
Description: Publishes one-act and full-length plays and musicals, for children, young adults, and adults, that have been produced. Serious drama, comedies, classics, fairytales, melodramas, and holiday plays. Responds in 2-6 months. Royalty.

CLASSIC STAGE COMPANY

136 E. 13th St., New York, NY 10003. 212-677-4210.
E-mail: classicliterary@classicstage.org. Web site: www.classicstage.org.
Barry Edelstein, Artistic Director.
Description: Not currently seeking new productions. Produces classical plays, often in new full-length translations or adaptations. Smaller cast is better, as appropriate; same for set. SASE.

COLUMBIA COLLEGE

Theatre-Music Center, 72 E. 11th St., Chicago, IL 60605.
Sheldon Patinkin.
Description: New Musicals Project supports playwrights, lyricists, and composers in writing process. Submit original bound script, idea treatment, or outline of idea with narrative synopsis and project history. Include resumé and tape of music. SASE. Workshop participation May-September. Offers weekly salary, directorial and dramaturge assistance, staged readings or workshops with cast, and studio recording of score. Responds in 3 months.

THE CONSERVATORY THEATRE ENSEMBLE

Tamalpais High School, 700 Miller Ave., Mill Valley, CA 94941.
E-mail: suebrash@earthlink.net.
Susan Brashear, Artistic Director.
Description: Comedies, dramas, children's plays, adaptations, and scripts on high school issues, for casts of 8-20. Plays with flexible casting, adaptable to "ensemble" style. One-act, 30-minute plays are especially needed; produce 50 short plays each season using teenage actors. Send synopsis and resumé.

CONTEMPORARY DRAMA SERVICE

Meriwether Publishing Co., 885 Elkton Dr., Colorado Springs, CO 80907.
E-mail: merpcds@aol.com. Web site: meriwetherpublishing.com.
Arthur Zapel, Editor/Artistic Director.
Description: Publishes plays, and books on theatrical subjects, for middle grade, high school and college use. New full-length and one-act plays, comedy or musicals. Prefers large-cast scripts, with limited staging requirements. No obscene language, unsuitable subject matter, or violence. Prefers comedic material, but publishes some serious work appropriate to this market. SASE. Contact: Ted Zapel.

CREATIVE THEATRE

102 Witherspoon St., Princeton, NJ 08540.
Pamela Hoffman, Artistic Director.
Description: Participatory plays for children, grades K-6; cast of 4-6; arena or thrust stage. Submit manuscript with synopsis and cast list. SASE. Pay varies.

CROSSROADS THEATRE CO.

7 Livingston Ave., New Brunswick, NJ 08901. 908-249-5581.
E-mail: crossroads@10p.com. Web site: www.crossroadstheatre.org.
Ricardo Khan, Artistic Director.
Description: Full-length and one-act dramas, comedies, musicals, and adaptations; issue-oriented experimental plays with honest, imaginative, and insightful examinations of the African-American experience. Also interested in African and Caribbean plays and plays exploring cross-cultural issues. No unsolicited scripts; query first with synopsis, cast list, and resumé. SASE.

DELAWARE THEATRE COMPANY

200 Water St., Wilmington, DE 19801-5030.
Web site: www.delawaretheatre.org.
Cleveland Morris, Artistic Director.
Description: Full-length comedies, dramas, and musicals. Cast up to 10. Responds in 6 months. Unsolicited manuscripts from local authors only. Agent submissions considered. SASE.

DENVER CENTER THEATRE COMPANY

1050 13th St., Denver, CO 80204.
Web site: www.denvercenter.org.
Donovan Marley, Artistic Director.
Description: Seeking new full-length plays. No restrictions on cast or set. Sponsors contests; write for guidelines. SASE. Offers workshops/readings. Contact: Bruce K. Sevy, Associate Artistic Dir./New Play Development.

DETROIT REPERTORY THEATRE

13103 Woodrow Wilson Ave., Detroit, MI 48238.
Barbara Busby.
Description: Full-length comedies and dramas. Scripts accepted October-April. Pays royalty. SASE.

DORSET THEATRE FESTIVAL

Box 510, Dorset, VT 05251. 802-867-2223.
E-mail: theatre@sover.net. Web site: www.theatredirectories.com.
Jill Charles, Artistic Director.
Description: Seeking new full-length scripts with general audience appeal, comedy and drama. Cast: Prefer less than 8. Prefer unit set. Also operates a writers' colony, Dorset Colony for Writers. SASE. Tips: Most new plays come from professional contacts or through our writers' colony.

DRAMATIC PUBLISHING COMPANY
311 Washington St., Woodstock, IL 60098. 815-338-7170.
E-mail: plays@dramaticpublishing.com. Web site: www.dramaticpublishing.com.
Linda Habjan, Editor.
Description: Publishes full-length and one-act plays and musicals for professional, stock, amateur, and children's theater market. Send SASE. Royalty. Responds in 4-6 months.

DRAMATICS
Educational Theatre Assoc., 2343 Auburn Ave., Cincinnati, OH 45219-2815. 513-421-3900.
E-mail: dcorathers@etassoc.org. Web site: www.etassoc.org.
Don Corathers, Editor.
Description: Publishes scripts for high-school students of the performing arts with emphasis on theater: acting, directing, playwriting, technical subjects. Nonfiction: Articles, interviews, how-tos. Also publishes one-act and full-length plays for high school production. Pays $25 to $400 honorarium or one-time, non-exclusive publication rights. Complete manuscripts preferred.; $100-$400. Art: Graphics and photos accepted. Tips: Before submitting any script, have a reading, collect feedback, and make revisions to help bring your characters to life. Be aware of the script's production demands. Queries: Preferred. Unsolicited mss: Accepts. Payment: On acceptance. Contact: Don Corathers.

DRIFTWOOD SHOWBOAT
Box 1032, Kingston, NY 12401.
Fred Hall.
Description: Full-length family comedies for cast of 2-6, single setting. No profanity. Submit cast list and synopsis. September-June.

EAST WEST PLAYERS
244 S. San Pedro St., #301, Los Angeles, CA 90012. 213-625-7000.
E-mail: info@eastwestplayers.org. Web site: www.eastwestplayers.org.
Tim Dang, Artistic Director.
Description: Seeking new full-length plays in comedy, drama, musicals and special material dealing with Asian/Asian Pacific/Asian American issues. Offers periodic contests and workshops/readings. Tips: Avoid Asian stereotypes.

ELDRIDGE PUBLISHING CO.
P. O. Box 1595, Venice, FL 34284. 941-496-4679.
E-mail: info@histage.com. Web site: http.//www.histage.com.
Susan Shore, Editorial Department.
Description: Publishes one-act and full-length plays and musicals for schools, churches, and community theatre groups. Comedies, tragedies, dramas, skits, spoofs, and religious plays (all holidays). Submit complete manuscript with cover letter, and

biography. Responds in 2 months. Flat fee for religious plays, royalty for full-length or one-act plays.

ENSEMBLE STUDIO THEATRE
549 W. 52nd St., New York, NY 10019. 212-247-4982.
Web site: www.ensemblestudiotheatre.org.
Curt Dempster, Artistic Director.
Description: Seeking new full-length and one-act plays: comedy, drama, and science/technology, plays by African-American women writers. New one-act plays, 15-45 minutes (annual spring one-act play marathon; deadline, December 1). New full-length plays by African-American women ("Going to the River Series"; deadline, January 15). New readings of plays in development. Contact: Tom Rowan, Literary Manager.

FLORIDA STUDIO THEATRE
1241 N. Palm Ave., Sarasota, FL 34236. 941-366-9017.
E-mail: james@fst2000.org. Web site: www.fst2000.org.
Richard Hopkins, Artistic Director.
Description: Seeking new full-length plays in comedy, drama, musicals, children's and adaptations; highly theatrical, innovative plays with universal themes. Cast: Less than 10. Single set. Offers contests, workshops, readings. All submissions considered for our new play festivals. Contact: James Ashford, Casting & Literary Coordinator.

WILL GEER THEATRICUM BOTANICUM
Box 1222, Topanga, CA 90290.
E-mail: theatricum@mindspring.com. Web site: www.theatricum.com.
Ellen Geer, Artistic Director.
Description: Seeking new full-length plays: comedy, drama, and musicals, for large outdoor rustic stage. All types of scripts for outdoor theater. Playreading performances.

THE GOODMAN THEATRE
170 N. Dearborn Street., Chicago, IL 60601. 312-443-3811.
E-mail: staff@goodman-theatre.org. Web site: www.goodman-theatre.org.
Susan V. Booth, Director of New Play Development.
Description: No unsolicited scripts; queries from recognized literary agents or producing organizations required for full-length comedies or dramas. Send synopsis, professional recommendation, and letter of inquiry.

THE GUTHRIE THEATER
725 Vineland Pl., Minneapolis, MN 55403.
E-mail: joh@guthrietheater.org.
Description: Full-length dramas and adaptations of world literature, classic masterworks, oral traditions, and folktales. No unsolicited scripts; send query with synopsis, resumé, and professional recommendation. Responds in 3-4 months.

HARRISBURG COMMUNITY THEATRE
513 Hurlock St., Harrisburg, PA 17110.
Thomas G. Hostetter, Artistic Director.
Description: Full-length comedies, dramas, musicals, and adaptations; cast to 20; prefers simple set. Query first, then submit script with cast list, resumé, synopsis, and SAS postcard. Best time to submit: June-August. Responds in 6 months. Negotiable rates.

HARTFORD STAGE COMPANY
50 Church St., Hartford, CT 06103.
Nadia Zonis.
Description: Full-length plays, all types, for cast up to 12. No unsolicited manuscripts; submit through agent or send synopsis. Pays varying rates.

HEDGEROW THEATRE
146 Rose Valley Rd., Moylan, PA 19086.
David Zum Brunnen.
Description: Full-length comedies, dramas, musicals, children's plays, and adaptation for 15-person cast. Small theater seats 150. Send script in spring or summer with resumé, return postcard, cast list, and SASE. Responds in 2 months.

HEUER PUBLISHING COMPANY
P.O. Box 248, Cedar Rapids, IA 52406. 319-364-6311.
E-mail: editor@hitplays.com. Web site: www.hitplays.com.
C. Emmett McMullen, Artistic Director/Editor.
Description: Publishes new full-length and one-act plays in comedy, drama, musicals, and adaptations. Prefers large cast, mostly female, and simple sets. Tips: No violence or derogatory, racist, or sexist language or situations.

HIPPODROME STATE THEATRE
25 S.E. Second Pl., Gainesville, FL 32601.
Tamerin Dygert.
Description: Full-length plays with unit sets and casts up to 6. No unsolicited material. Agent submissions and professional recommendations only, accepted May-August. Send synopsis only, with reviews and recommendations.

HOLLYWOOD THESPIAN COMPANY
12838 Kling St., Studio City, CA 91604-1127.
Rai Tasco, Artistic Director.
Description: Full-length comedies and dramas for integrated cast. Include cast list and SAS postcard with submission.

HONOLULU THEATRE FOR YOUTH
2846 Ualena St., Honolulu, HI 96819.
Peter C. Brosius, Artistic Director.
Description: Plays, 60-90 minutes, for young people and family audiences. Adult casts. Contemporary issues, Pacific themes, etc. Unit sets, small cast. Query or send cover letter with synopsis, cast list, and SASE. Royalties negotiable.

HORIZON THEATRE COMPANY
P. O. Box 5376, Station E, Atlanta, GA 31107. 404-523-1477.
Lisa Adler, Artistic Directors.
Description: Full-length comedies, dramas, and satires. Encourages submissions by women writers. Cast up to 10. Submit synopsis with cast list, resumé, and recommendations. Pays percentage. Readings. Responds in 6 months.

HUNTINGTON THEATRE COMPANY
264 Huntington Ave., Boston, MA 02115-4606.
Nicholas Martin, Artistic Director.
Description: Agent submissions only.

ILLINOIS THEATRE CENTER
371 Artists' Walk, P.O. Box 397, Park Forest, IL 60466.
Description: Full-length comedies, dramas, musicals, and adaptations, for unit/fragmentary sets, up to 8 cast members. Send summary and SAS postcard. No unsolicited manuscripts. Negotiable rates. Workshops and readings offered.

INSTITUTE FOR CONTEMPORARY EASTERN EUROPEAN DRAMA AND THEATRE
Graduate Ctr., 33 W. 42nd St., Rm. 801, New York, NY 10036.
Daniel C. Gerould, Artistic Director.
Description: Full-length and one-act translations of contemporary Eastern European plays. Query. Payment varies.

INVISIBLE THEATRE
1400 N. First Ave., Tucson, AZ 85719.
Deborah Dickey, Artistic Director.
Description: Letter of introduction from theatre professional must accompany submissions for full-length comedies, dramas, musicals, and adaptations. Submit after October. Cast up to 10; simple set. Also one-act plays. Pays royalty.

JEWISH REPERTORY THEATRE
1395 Lexington Ave., New York, NY 10128. 212-415-5550.
Web site: www.jrt.org.
Ran Avni, Artistic Director.
Description: Full-length comedies, dramas, musicals, and adaptations, with up to 10 cast members, relating to the Jewish experience. Pays varying rates. Enclose SASE.

THE JULIAN THEATRE

New College of California, 777 Valencia St., San Francisco, CA 94110. **Description:** Full-length comedies and dramas with a social statement. Send scene (5-10 pages), synopsis, cast description, and SASE. Pays on contractual basis. Responds in 2-9 months. Readings offered.

KUMU KAHUA THEATRE

46 Merchant St., Honolulu, HI 96813. 808-536-4222. Harry Wong III, Artistic Director. **Description:** Full-length plays, especially relevant to life in Hawaii. Prefers simple sets for arena productions. Submit resumé and synopsis. Pays $50 per performance. Readings. Contests.

LITTLE BROADWAY PRODUCTIONS

c/o Jill Shawn, P. O. Box 15068, N. Hollywood, CA 91615. **Description:** Musicals and other plays for children, by adult actors; 55 minutes, no intermission. Cast of 5-10. Submit manuscript with synopsis, return postcard, resumé, and SASE. Negotiable rates.

LOS ANGELES DESIGNERS' THEATRE

P.O. Box 1883, Studio City, CA 91614-0883. 323-650-9600. E-mail: ladesigners@juno.com. Richard Niederberg, Artistic Director. **Description:** Seeking new full-length plays: comedy, drama, musicals, adaptations. Can incorporate religious, social, or political themes, "street language," nudity, etc. No cast or set restrictions. Offers revisions/criticisms, contests. Looking to commission scripts on work-for-hire basis. Has produced over 400 original works since 1970.

LOVE CREEK PRODUCTIONS

162 Nesbit St., Weehawken, NJ 07087. E-mail: creekread@aol.com. **Description:** Seeking new plays for production: one-act and full-length. Cast: 6 or more characters for full-lengths. For Developmental Series, minimal production values. We welcome new authors, well-crafted scripts with responsible treatment of humanistic theme. Tips: One-acts have better chance for production. Contact: Cynthia Granville-Callahan.

THE MAGIC THEATRE

Fort Mason Ctr., Bldg. D, San Francisco, CA 94123. 415-441-8001. E-mail: magicthtre@aol.com. Laura Owens, Literary Manager. **Description:** Comedies and dramas, interested in political, non-linear, and multi-cultural work for mainstage productions. Query with synopsis, resumé, first 10-20 pages of script, and SASE; no unsolicited manuscripts. Pays varying rates.

MANHATTAN THEATRE CLUB

311 W. 43rd St., New York, NY 10036. 212-399-3000.
E-mail: lit@mtc-nyc.org. Web site: www.manhattantheatreclub.com.
Lynne Meadow, Artistic Director.
Description: Seeking new full-length new American plays: comedy, drama, musicals, adaptations. Sponsors MTC Playwriting Fellowships. Offers workshops/readings. Comprehensive play development programs. Contact: Christian Parker, Literary Manager.

MCCARTER THEATRE COMPANY

91 University Pl., Princeton, NJ 08540. 609-258-6500.
Web site: www.mccarter.org.
Emily Mann, Artistic Director.
Description: Seeking new full-length plays: comedies, dramas, adaptations. Contact: Literary Manager.

METROPOLITAN THEATRICAL SOCIETY

Box 56512, Washington, DC 20012.
Gaynelle Reed Lewis, Artistic Director.
Description: Realistic, full-length dramas, comedies, and musicals. Special interest in plays for multi-ethnic casts. Submit manuscript with SASE.

METROSTAGE

P.O. Box 329, Alexandria, VA 22313. 703-548-9044.
Web site: www.metrostage.com.
Carolyn Griffin, Artistic Director.
Description: Seeking new full-length plays in comedy, drama, small musicals. Cast: 4-8. Unit sets preferred. Workshops/readings offered. Interested only in plays with history of readings and development. SASE.

MILL MOUNTAIN THEATRE

One Market Sq., SE, Second Fl., Roanoke, VA 24011. 540-342-5749.
E-mail: outreach@millmountain.org. Web site: www.millmountain.org.
Jere Lee Hodgin, Artistic Director.
Description: Seeking full length and one-act new plays: comedy, drama, musicals, children's. Mill Mountain Theatre New Play competition. Centerpiece, one-act reading series. Tips: See guidelines at web site. Contact: Literary Coordinator.

MISSOURI REPERTORY THEATRE

4949 Cherry St., Kansas City, MO 64110.
E-mail: theatre@umkc.edu. Web site: www.missourireptheatre.org.
Felicia Londré, Artistic Director.
Description: Full-length comedies and dramas. Query with synopsis, cast list, resumé, and SAS postcard. Royalty. Responds in 6 months.

MUSIC-THEATRE GROUP
29 Bethune St., New York, NY 10014.
Description: Innovative works of music-theatre, to 90 minutes. Query only, with synopsis and SAS postcard. Submissions: September-December.

MUSICAL THEATRE WORKS
440 Lafayette St., New York, NY 10003.
Lonny Price, Artistic Director.
Description: Write for submission guidelines.

NATIONAL BLACK THEATRE
2033 Fifth Ave., Harlem, NY 10035.
Tunde Samuel.
Description: Drama, musicals, and children's plays. Scripts should reflect African and African-American lifestyle. Historical, inspirational, and ritualistic forms appreciated. Workshops and readings.

NATIONAL DRAMA SERVICE
127 Ninth Ave. N., MSN 158, Nashville, TN 37234.
E-mail: churchdrama@earthlink.net.
Description: Publishes dramatic material "that communicates the message of Christ . . . scripts that help even the smallest church enhance their ministry with drama." Scripts, 2-7 minutes long: drama in worship, puppets, clowns, Christian comedy, mime, movement, readers' theater, creative worship services, and monologues. Payment varies, on acceptance. Guidelines.

NATIONAL PLAYWRIGHTS CONFERENCE
Eugene O'Neill Theatre Center, 234 W. 44th St., Suite 901, New York, NY 10036.
212-382-2790.
James Houghton, Artistic Director.
Description: Annual competition for new stage plays and teleplays/screenplays for development during summer at Waterford, CT, location. Submission deadline: November 15. Send #10-size SASE in the fall for guidelines. Pays stipend of $1,000, plus travel/living expenses for conference in July. Send SASE for guidelines to Managing Director.

THE NEGRO ENSEMBLE COMPANY
165 W. 46th St., Ste. 409, New York, NY 10036.
Douglas Turner Ward, Artistic Director.
Description: Full-length comedies, dramas, musicals, and adaptations on the Black experience. Submit March-May. Pays on royalty basis. Enclose return postcard.

NEW ENSEMBLE ACTORS THEATRE
138 South Oxford Street, Suite 1D, Brooklyn, NY 11217. 718-398-4979.
E-mail: spmime@netzero.net.
Ms. Scottie Davis, Artistic Director.
Description: Not currently seeking new plays. Project of Salt & Pepper Mime Co., surreal, mimetic, sci-fi, fantasy.

NEW THEATRE, INC.
P.O. Box 173, Boston, MA 02117-0173.
Description: New full-length scripts for readings, workshop, and main stage productions. Include SASE.

NEW YORK ACTOR'S NETWORK
FAPC, 6753 Fourth Ave., Brooklyn, NY 11220.
Michelle Marotta, Artistic Director.
Description: One-act plays with 2-5 characters, very simple sets. No payment.

NEW YORK SHAKESPEARE FESTIVAL/
JOSEPH PAPP PUBLIC THEATER
425 Lafayette St., New York, NY 10003.
Shirley Fishman / Mervin P. Antonio, Artistic Director.
Description: Plays and translations, and adaptations. Submit sample dialogue with synopsis, cassette (for musicals), and SASE. Responds in 4-6 months.

NEW YORK STATE THEATRE INSTITUTE
155 River St., Troy, NY 12180.
Patricia Di Benedetto Snyder, Producing Artistic Director.
Description: Emphasis on new, full-length plays and musicals for family audiences. Query with synopsis and cast list. Payment varies.

ODYSSEY THEATRE ENSEMBLE
2055 S. Sepulveda Blvd., Los Angeles, CA 90025. 310-477-2055.
Web site: www.odysseytheatre.com.
Ron Sossi, Artistic Director.
Description: Seeking new full-length comedies, dramas, musicals, and adaptations: provocative subject matter, or plays that stretch and explore the possibilities of theater. Cast: limit to 10. Offers workshops/readings. Contact: Sally Essex-Lopresti, Literary Manager.

OLD GLOBE THEATRE
Simon Edison Center for Performing Arts, Box 2171, San Diego, CA 92112-2171.
Katie Smalheer, Artistic Director.
Description: Full-length comedies, dramas, and musicals. No unsolicited manuscripts. Submit through agent, or query with synopsis.

OLDCASTLE THEATRE COMPANY

Bennington Center for the Arts, P.O. Box 1555, Bennington, VT 05201.

Eric Peterson, Artistic Director.

Description: Full-length comedies, dramas, and musicals for small cast (up to 10). Submit synopsis and cast list in the winter. Responds in 6 months. Offers workshops and readings. Pays expenses for playwright to attend rehearsals. Royalty.

PAPER MILL PLAYHOUSE

Brookside Dr., Millburn, NJ 07041.

Maryan F. Stephens, Artistic Director.

Description: Full-length plays and musicals. Submit synopsis, resumé, and tape for musicals; responds in 4-6 months.

PENGUIN REPERTORY COMPANY

Box 91, Stony Point, Rockland County, NY 10980.

Joe Brancato, Artistic Director.

Description: Full-length comedies and dramas, cast size to 5. Submit script, resumé, and SASE. Payment varies.

PEOPLE'S LIGHT AND THEATRE COMPANY

39 Conestoga Rd., Malvern, PA 19355.

Alda Cortese, Artistic Director.

Description: Full-length comedies, dramas, adaptations. No unsolicited manuscripts; query with synopsis and 10 pages of script. Responds in 6 months. Payment negotiable.

PIER ONE THEATRE

Box 894, Homer, AK 99603-0894. 907-235-2333.

E-mail: lance@xyz.net. Web site: www.pieronetheatre.org.

Lance Petersen, Artistic Director.

Description: Seeking new full-length and one-act comedies, dramas, musicals, children's plays, and adaptations. Offers workshops/readings. Tips: Do not start the play with a phone call! No AIDS plays, new age plays; must have something wonderful and unique to offer.

PIONEER DRAMA SERVICE

P.O. Box 4267, Englewood, CO 80155. 303-779-4035.

E-mail: editors@pioneerdrama.com. Web site: www.pioneerdrama.com.

Steven Fendrich, Publisher.

Description: Publishes full-length and one-act plays, also musicals, melodramas, and children's theatre. No unproduced plays or plays with mostly male casts. Simple sets preferred. Query first. Royalty. Contact: Beth Somers, Submissions Editor.

PLAYHOUSE ON THE SQUARE
51 S. Cooper in Overton Sq., Memphis, TN 38104.
Jackie Nichols, Artistic Director.
Description: Full-length comedies, dramas; cast up to 15. Contest deadline: April for fall production. Pays fee.

PLAYS
P.O. Box 600160, Newton, MA 02460. 617-332-4063.
E-mail: /preston@playsmag.com. Web site: www.playsmag.com.
Elizabeth Preston, Artistic Director.
Description: "The drama magazine for young people." Publishes one-act plays, for production by people ages 7-17. Comedies, dramas, farces, skits, holiday plays. Also adaptations of classics, biographies, puppet plays, creative dramatics. No religious themes. Cast: at least 8 characters. Sets, within capabilities of amateur set designers (school teachers, students, volunteers). Tips: Read copy of magazine for feel for the kinds of plays we publish.

PLAYWRIGHTS HORIZONS
416 W. 42nd St., New York, NY 10036. 212-564-1235.
Web site: www.playwrightshorizons.org.
Sonya Sobieski, Literary Manager.
Description: Full-length, original comedies, dramas, and musicals by American authors. No one-acts or screenplays. Synopses discouraged; send script, resumé and SASE, include tape for musicals. Off-Broadway contract.

PLAYWRIGHTS' PLATFORM
Massachusetts College of Art, 164 Brayton Rd., Boston, MA 02135.
Web site: www.theatermirror.com.
George Sauer, Artistic Director.
Description: Full-length and one-act plays of all kinds. Script development workshops and public readings for Massachusetts playwrights only. Tips: Massachusetts residents only. No sexist or racist material.

POPE THEATRE COMPANY
262 S. Ocean Blvd., Manalapan, FL 33462.
J. Barry Lewis, Artistic Director.
Description: Full-length comedies, dramas, musicals, and children's plays. Query October-May with synopsis, cast list (up to 10 actors), resumé, and SASE. Royalty. Responds in 6 months.

POPLAR PIKE PLAYHOUSE
7653 Old Poplar Pike, Germantown, TN 38138. 901-755-7775.
E-mail: efblue@aol.com. Web site: www.ppp.org.
Frank Bluestein, Artistic Director.
Description: Full-length and one-act comedies, dramas, musicals, and children's

plays. We are in a high school; most plays feature high-school students, with characters that students can realistically portray and understand.

PORTLAND STAGE COMPANY
Box 1458, Portland, ME 04104. 207-774-1043.
E-mail: portstage@aol.com.
Lisa DiFranza, Literary Manager.
Description: No unsolicited material at this time.

PRINCETON REPERTORY COMPANY
44 Nassau St., Suite 350, Princeton, NJ 08542.
Victoria Liberatori, Artistic Director.
Description: One-act plays on classical subject only, considered for reading and/or workshop. Submit synopsis (2 pages only), cast list, resumé, and 3 pages of dialogue. Responds within 2 years.

THE PUERTO RICAN TRAVELING THEATRE
141 W. 94th St., New York, NY 10025.
Miriam Colon Valle, Artistic Director.
Description: Full-length and one-act comedies, dramas, and musicals; cast up to 8; simple sets. Prefer plays on contemporary Hispanic experience, with social, cultural, or psychological content. Payment negotiable.

THE RADIO PLAY
Public Media Foundation, 100 Boylston St., Suite 230, Boston, MA 02116.
Valerie Henderson, Artistic Director.
Description: Publishes original radio plays and radio dramatizations of American classics in the public domain, 28-29 pages, 30-minute program format. Query for dramatizations only. Send SASE for style sheet.

THE REPERTORY THEATRE OF ST. LOUIS
Box 191730, St. Louis, MO 63119.
E-mail: sgregg@repstl.org.
S. Gregg, Artistic Director.
Description: Query with brief synopsis, technical requirements, and cast size. Unsolicited manuscripts are returned unread.

ROUND HOUSE THEATRE
12210 Bushey Dr., #101, Silver Spring, MD 20902. 301-933-9530.
E-mail: dcrosby@round-house.org.
Jerry Whiddon, Artistic Director.
Description: Seeking new full-length plays in all areas. Cast: 8-10 actors max. Unit set preferred. Offers workshops/reading, revisions for New Voices series (November and June, readings of local playwrights). Contact: Danisha Crosby.

SAMUEL FRENCH, INC.
45 W. 25th St., New York, NY 10010.
Web site: www.samuelfrench.com.
Lawrence Harbison, Artistic Director.
Description: Publishes full-length plays and musicals. One-act plays, 20-45 minutes. Children's plays, 45-60 minutes. Stage plays. Unpublished writers considered. Query with complete manuscript; unsolicited and multiple queries okay. No fees.

SEATTLE REPERTORY THEATRE
155 Mercer St., Seattle, WA 98109.
Web site: www.seattlerep.org.
Sharon Ott, Artistic Director.
Description: Full-length comedies, dramas, and adaptations. No unsolicited submissions.

SINISTER WISDOM
P.O. Box 3252, Berkeley, CA 94703.
Margo Mercedes Rivera, Artistic Director.
Description: Quarterly, publishes one-act (15 pages or less) lesbian drama, that reflects diverse and multicultural experiences. Responds in 3-9 months; write for upcoming themes. SASE. Payment: in copies.

SOCIETY HILL PLAYHOUSE
507 S. 8th St., Philadelphia, PA 19147.
Web site: www.erols.com/shp.
Walter Vail, Artistic Director.
Description: Full-length dramas, comedies, and musicals, up to 6 cast members, simple set. Submit synopsis and SASE. Responds in 6 months. Nominal payment.

SOUTH COAST REPERTORY
P.O. Box 2197, Costa Mesa, CA 92628. 714-708-5500.
Web site: www.scr.org.
John Glore, Artistic Director.
Description: Full-length comedies, dramas, musicals, juveniles. Query with synopsis and resumé. Payment varies.

SOUTHERN APPALACHIAN REPERTORY THEATRE
P.O. Box 1720, Mars Hill, NC 28754. 828-689-1384.
E-mail: sart@mhc.edu. Web site: www.sartheatre.com.
Bill Gregg, Managing Director.
Description: Seeking new full-length plays: comedy, drama, and musicals that explore and celebrate culture, history, or life in Southern Appalachian region. No cast restrictions. Unit set, or suggestions if multi-location. Southern Appalachian Playwright's Conference in spring; 5 plays read and discussed; playwrights get room and board. One play may receive full production next season. First-time authors wel-

come. Tips: Avoid scripts that read like screenplays, and use of profanity for shock value only. Contact: Managing Director.

STAGE LEFT THEATRE
3408 N. Sheffield, Chicago, IL 60657. 773-883-8830.
E-mail: sltchicago@aol.com. Web site: http://members.aol.com/sltchicago.
Jessi D. Hill, Artistic Director.
Description: Produce plays on political and social issues: full-length comedies, dramas, and adaptations for cast of 1-12. Shows include post-show discussions. New authors welcomed. Offers workshops/readings. New-play development program, Downstage Left, send for guidelines. Contact: Literary Manager.

STAGE ONE: PROFESSIONAL THEATRE
FOR YOUNG AUDIENCES
5 Riverfront Plaza, 501 W. Main Street , Louisville, KY 40202. 502-589-5946.
E-mail: stageone@kca.org. Web site: www.stageone.org.
Moses Goldberg, Artistic Director.
Description: Seeking new children's plays, adaptations of classics and original plays for young audiences (ages 4-18). No restrictions on cast or set. Tips: Seek plays relevant to young people and their families, related to school curriculum, and classic tales of childhood, ancient and modern.

STAGES REPERTORY THEATRE
3201 Allen Pkwy., #101, Houston, TX 77019. 713-527-0220.
E-mail: stagestheatre.com. Web site: www.stagestheatre.com.
Rob Bundy, Artistic Director.
Description: Southwest Festival of New Plays. Divisions: Children's Theatre, Texas Playwrights, Women Playwrights, and Hispanic Playwrights. Seeking new plays: comedy and drama (full-length). Cast: 6-8 max. Unit set with multiple locations preferable. Tips: Not interested in realistic domestic dramas, prefer theatrically told stories.

STATE THEATER COMPANY
719 Congress Ave., Austin, TX 78701. 512-472-5143.
Scott Kanoff, Artistic Director.
Description: Seeking new full-length plays, comedy and drama. Annual Harvest Festival. Contact: John Walch.

STATE UNIVERSITY OF NEW YORK AT STONY BROOK
Theatre Arts Dept., Stony Brook, NY 11794.
Richard Dunham, Artistic Director.
Description: One-act and full-length comedies and dramas. Submit synopsis with resumé and SASE. No unsolicited manuscripts. Offers workshops and readings.

STUDIO ARENA THEATRE
710 Main St., Buffalo, NY 14202-1990.
Description: Comedies and dramas, cast up to 8. Interested in plays of theatrical/nonrealistic nature. Include synopsis, resumé, cast list, sample dialogue.

MARK TAPER FORUM
135 N. Grand Ave., Los Angeles, CA 90012. 213-972-8033.
E-mail: vshaskan@ctgla.org. Web site: www.taperahmanson.com.
Gordon Davidson, Artistic Director.
Description: Seeking new full-length plays. Annual New Work Festival, offering selected playwrights resources to work on their plays. Each play get at least one open public rehearsal in a small Los Angeles theater. Contact: Pier Carlo Talenti, Literary Manager.

THE TEN MINUTE MUSICALS PROJECT
Box 461194, W. Hollywood, CA 90046. 323-651-4899.
Michael Koppy, Producer.
Description: Currently seeking new plays: short 1-act musicals and special material (please describe), for cast up to 5 women and 5 men. No set restrictions. Tips: Start with a strong story, even it if means postponing work on music and lyrics until dramatic foundation is complete. Contact: Michael Koppy.

THEATER ARTISTS OF MARIN
Box 150473, San Rafael, CA 94915.
Charles Brousse.
Description: Full-length comedies, dramas, and musicals for a cast of 2-8. Submit complete script with SASE. Responds in 4-6 months. Three productions each year.

THEATER OF THE FIRST AMENDMENT
George Mason University, Institute of the Arts MSN 3E6, Fairfax, VA 22030.
Rick Davis, Artistic Director.
Description: Full-length and one-act comedies, drama, and adaptations. Send synopsis and resumé with return postcard.

THEATRE AMERICANA
Box 245, Altadena, CA 91003-0245.
Description: Full-length comedies and dramas, with American theme. No children's plays or musicals. Language and subject matter suitable for community audience. Send bound manuscript with cast list, resumé, and SASE, by February 1. No payment. Allow 3-6 months for reply. Limit: 2 entries per season.

THE THEATRE BUILDING/NEW TUNERS
1225 W. Belmont Ave., Chicago, IL 60657. 773-929-7367.
E-mail: tbturners@aol.com. Web site: www.adamczyk.com/newtuners.
John Sparks, Artistic Director.
Description: New musicals only, all styles, full length and one-act (10 min.), for children, young adults, opera and broadway audiences, etc. Writers workshop meets monthly (fee based). No restrictions on cast. No sets or lighting in developmental programming. Sponsors contests. Tips: Single author projects discouraged.

THE THEATRE ON THE SQUARE
450 Post St., San Francisco, CA 94102.
Jonathan Reinis, Artistic Director.
Description: Full-length comedies, dramas, and musicals for 15-person cast. Submit cast list and script with SASE. Responds in 30 days.

THEATRE/TEATRO
Bilingual Foundation of the Arts, 421 N. Ave., #19, Los Angeles, CA 90031.
Agustin Coppola, Artistic Director.
Description: Full-length plays about the Hispanic experience; small casts. Submit manuscript with SASE. Pays negotiable rates.

THEATREWORKS
1100 Hamilton Ct., Menlo Park, CA 94025.
Description: Full-length comedies, dramas, and musicals. Submit complete script or synopsis with SAS postcard and SASE, cast list, theatre resumé, production history. For musicals, include cassette of up to 6 songs, with lyrics. Responds in 4-5 months. Payment negotiable.

THEATREWORKS/USA
151 W. 26th St., 7th Fl., New York, NY 10011. 212-647-1100.
E-mail: info@theatreworksusa.org. Web site: www.theatreworksusa.org.
Barbara Pasternack, Artistic Director.
Description: Seeking new one-act (60-90 minute) plays and musicals for children's productions, celebrating history's heroes/heroines, or dramatizing historical event. Adaptations of fairy tales, literary classics, and contemporary children's literature. Literate, creative, entertaining, with something to say to young audience. Cast: 6 actors. Production must be tourable in 2 vans. Contact: Michael Alltop, Assistant Artistic Director.

WALNUT STREET THEATRE COMPANY
825 Walnut St., Philadelphia, PA 19107.
Beverly Elliott, Artistic Director.
Description: Mainstage: Full-length comedies, dramas, musicals, and popular, upbeat adaptations; also, plays for studio stage, cast of 1-4 . Submit 10-20 sample

pages with SAS postcard, character breakdown, synopsis. Musical submissions must include audio cassette or CD. Responds in 6 months with SASE. Payment varies.

THE WESTERN STAGE

156 Homestead Ave., Salinas, CA 93901.

Michael Roddy, Artistic Director.

Description: Ongoing submissions; send query. Prefers adaptations of works of literary significance and/or large cast shows. Two or more shows chosen to workshop yearly.

WOOLLY MAMMOTH THEATRE COMPANY

1401 Church St. N.W., Washington, DC 20005.

Jim Byrnes, Artistic Director.

Description: Looking for offbeat material, unusual writing. Unsolicited scripts accepted. Payment varies.

GREETING CARD PUBLISHERS

Companies selling greeting cards and novelty items (T-shirts, coffee mugs, buttons, etc.) often have their own specific requirements for the submission of ideas, verse, and artwork. In general, however, each verse or message should be typed double-space on a 3x5 or 4x6 card. Use only one side of the card, and be sure to put your name and address in the upper left-hand corner. Keep a copy of every verse or idea you send. (It's also advisable to keep a record of what you've submitted to each publisher.) Always enclose an SASE, and do not send out more than ten verses or ideas in a group to any one publisher. Never send original artwork unless a publisher indicates a definite interest in using your work.

AMBERLEY GREETING CARD COMPANY
11510 Goldcoast Dr., Cincinnati, OH 45249-1695. 513-489-2775.
E-mail: dcronstein@amberleygreeting.com. Web site: www.amberleygreeting.com.
Description: Humorous ideas for cards: birthday, illness, friendship, anniversary, congratulations, "miss you," etc. Short, humorous verse OK. SASE for guidelines. Pays $150. Rights: All. Contact: Dan Cronstein, Editor, or Chuck Marshall.

AMERICAN GREETINGS
One American Rd., Cleveland, OH 44144. 216-252-7300.
Web site: www.greetingcard.com.
Description: Send #10 SASE to receive Humorous Writing guidelines. Current need is for humor only. Contact: Kathleen McKay.

BLUE MOUNTAIN ARTS, INC.
P.O. Box 1007, Boulder, CO 80306.
Web site: www.bluemountain.com.
Description: Poetry for cards. Pays $200 per poem. Also sponsors annual Poetry contest with prizes up to $300. See web site for details.

BRILLIANT ENTERPRISES
117 W. Valerio St., Santa Barbara, CA 93101-2927.
Web site: www.ashleighbrilliant.com.
Description: Illustrated epigrams emphasizing truth, wit, universality, originality. Payment is $60. Rights: All. Payment: On acceptance. Contact: Ashleigh Brilliant.

COMSTOCK CARDS
600 S. Rock, Suite 15, Reno, NV 89502-4115. .
Web site: www.comstockcards.com.
Description: Adult humor, outrageous or sexual, for greeting cards, invitations, and notepads. SASE. Payment varies, on publication. Guidelines on web site. Contact: David Delacroix.

CONTENOVA GIFTS

879 Cranberry Ct., Oakville, Ont., Canada L6L 6J7.

Description: Catchy, humorous, and sentimental one-liners for ceramic gift mugs. Submit on 3x5 cards; up to 15 ideas at a time. Payment varies, on acceptance. Guidelines. Contact: Jeff Sinclair.

CURRENT, INC.

Box 2559, Colorado Springs, CO 80901-2559.

Description: Non-risqué birthday, woman-to-woman cards, and Post-It notes. SASE.

DAYSPRING GREETING CARDS

P.O. Box 1010, Siloam Springs, AR 72761.

E-mail: info@dayspring.com.

Description: Inspirational material for everyday occasions and most holidays. Currently only accepting free-lance copy submissions from published greeting card authors. Qualified writers should send samples of their published greeting cards (up to 5 cards or copies; the words "Previously Published" must be written on lower left corner of the mailing envelope containing the submissions). Payment is $50 on acceptance. Send SASE for guidelines, or email to and type in the word "write" for guidelines. Contact: Freelance Editor.

DESIGN DESIGN, INC.

P.O. Box 2266, Grand Rapids, MI 49501-2266.

Description: Short verses for both humorous and sentimental concepts for greeting cards. Everyday (birthday, get well, just for fun, etc.) and seasonal (Christmas, Valentine's Day, Easter, Mother's Day, Father's Day, Graduation, Halloween, Thanksgiving) material. Flat fee payment on publication. SASE.

DUCK & COVER

P.O. Box 21640, Oakland, CA 94620.

E-mail: duckcover@aol.com.

Description: We do not produce any greeting cards. However, we make buttons, magnets and stickers with fresh, original and outrageous slogans. Contact: Jim Buser, Editor.

EPHEMERA, INC.

P.O. Box 490, Phoenix, OR 97535. 541-535-4195.

E-mail: mail@ephemera-inc.com. Web site: www.ephemera-inc.com.

Description: Provocative, irreverent, and outrageously funny slogans for novelty buttons, magnets, and stickers. Submit typed list of slogans. SASE. Pays $40 per slogan. Looking for satirical slogans about pop culture, free speech, work attitudes, women's and men's issues, coffee, booze, pot, drugs, food, aging boomers, teens, gays and lesbians. Surprise us!

FRAVESSI GREETINGS, INC.

11 Edison Pl., Springfield, NJ 07081.
Description: Short verse, mostly humorous or sentimental; cards with witty prose. Christmas and everyday material. Pays varying rates, on acceptance.

FREEDOM GREETING CARDS

75 West St., Walpole, MA 02081.
Web site: www.freedomgreetings.com.
Description: Traditional and humorous verse and love messages. Inspirational poetry for all occasions. Pays negotiable rates, on acceptance. Query with SASE. Contact: Jay Levitt, Editorial Department.

GALLANT GREETINGS CORPORATION

2654 West Medill, Chicago, IL 60647.
Web site: www.gallantgreetings.com.
Description: Ideas for humorous and serious greeting cards.

HALLMARK CARDS, INC.

Box 419580, Mail Drop 288, Kansas City, MO 64141.
Web site: www.hallmark.com.
Description: Uses very little freelance.

KATE HARPER DESIGNS

P.O. Box 2112, Berkeley, CA 94702. .
E-mail: kateharp@aol.com.
Description: Contact via web site/e-mail only. Greeting card concepts desired: quotations with humor, wit about everyday life. Pay varies. Pays $25 for short children's quotes.

NOBLE WORKS

113 Clinton St., Hoboken, NJ 07030.
Description: Humorous greeting card ideas and copy. No smut, no verse, nothing sweet or sentimental. We like *Saturday Night Live*-style humor. Pays $150 per complete idea against royalties, on publication. (Other deals and licensing agreements available depending on artist and quality of work.) SASE. Contact: Christopher Noble.

OATMEAL STUDIOS GREETING CARD COMPANY

Box 138 TW, Rochester, VT 05767. 802-767-3171.
Web site: www.awoc.com/guidelines.
Description: Humorous ideas for all occasions. We pay $75 for each idea we purchase. Your ideas must be original! We look forward to seeing your work! Contact: Dawn Abraham, Editor.

OTHER MARKETS

PARAMOUNT CARDS

P.O. Box 6546, Providence, RI 02940-6546.

Description: Humorous, traditional, and inspirational card ideas for birthday, relative's birthday, friendship, romance, get well, Christmas, Valentine's Day, Easter, Mother's Day, Father's Day, and Graduation. Submit each idea (5-10 per submission) on 3x5 card with name and address on each. SASE. Payment varies, on acceptance.

PLUM GRAPHICS INC.

Prince Street Station, P.O. Box 136, New York, NY 10014. 212-337-0999. E-mail: plumgraphic@aol.com. Web site: http://plumgraphi@aol.com. **Description:** Humorous mostly, short (1-2 lines), SASE for guidelines. Contact: Michelle Reynoso.

RECYCLED PAPER PRODUCTS, INC.

3636 N. Broadway, Chicago, IL 60613-4488.

Description: Original copy that is hip, flip, and concise. Risqué material considered. Send up to 10 pieces; mock-up ideas (with type and color) preferred. Allow 12 weeks for response. Payment made if design tests well and is picked up for distribution. SASE for guidelines. Contact: Melinda Gordon.

REGENCY THERMOGRAPHERS

64 N. Conahan Dr., P.O. Box 2009, Hazelton, PA 18201.

Description: Quotations for wedding invitations; clever invitation verses for birthday parties and other special occasions. Pays $25 per quote/verse, on acceptance. Contact: Burt Dolgin, Editor.

ROCKSHOTS, INC.

20 S. Van Dam Street, 4th Floor, New York, NY 10013. 212-243-9661. Web site: www.rockshots.com.

Description: Humorous, soft line. Combination of sexy and humorous come-on type greeting; and "cute" insult cards. Card gag can adopt a sentimental style, then take an ironic twist and end on an offbeat note. No Sentimental or conventional material. Put gag lines on 8x11 paper with name, address, and phone and social security numbers in right corner, or individually on 3x5 cards. Submit 10 ideas/batch. Pays $50/gag line. Response: SASE required. Rights: Greeting Card. Payment: On acceptance. Contact: Bob Vesce, Editor.

SANGAMON COMPANY

Route 48 W., P.O. Box 410, Taylorville, IL 62568.

Description: SASE for guidelines to experienced freelancers only. Work on assignment. Pays competitive rates, on acceptance.

MARCEL SCHUMAN COMPANY

101 New Montgomery, 6th Fl., San Francisco, CA 94105. 415-284-0133. **Description:** Sincere, friendly and appropriate cards. Not just generic, polite

greetings—lighthearted sarcasm OK. Usually purchase particular occasions cards from freelancers. Also, fine art, whimsy, traditional, contemporary, photography, and humor. Payment is $125. Contact: Deanne Quinones.

SPS STUDIOS, INC.

P.O. Box 1007, Boulder, CO 80306. 303-449-0536.

E-mail: editorial@spsstudios.com.

Description: Poetry and prose about love, friendship, family, philosophies, etc. Also material for special occasions and holidays: birthdays, get well, Christmas, Valentine's Day, Easter, etc. Submit seasonal material 5 months in advance of holiday. No artwork. Include SASE. Pays $200 per poem. Rights: All Rights. Payment: On publication. Contact: Patti Wayant, Editorial Department.

SUNRISE PUBLICATIONS, INC.

P.O. Box 4699, Bloomington, IN 47402-4699.

E-mail: info@interart.com. Web site: www.interart.com.

Description: Original copy for holiday and everyday cards. Submit up to 15 verses, 1-4 lines, on 3x5 cards; simple, to-the-point ideas that could be serious, humorous, or light-hearted, but sincere, without being overly sentimental. Rhymed verse not generally used. Allow 3 months for response. One SASE for guidelines and one for return of your submission. Accepts email submissions. Pays standard rates.

VAGABOND CREATIONS, INC.

2560 Lance Dr., Dayton, OH 45409. 937-298-1124.

E-mail: vagabond@siscom.net. Web site: www.vagabondcreations.com.

Description: Greeting cards with graphics only on cover (no copy) and short punch line inside: birthday, everyday, Valentine's Day, Christmas, and graduation. Mildly risqué humor with double entendre acceptable. Ideas for illustrated theme stationery. Pays $20, on acceptance. **Tips:** Check publishers who are looking for freelance contributors. Do not send style of material that publisher cannot use. Response: SASE required. Rights: All. Payment: On acceptance. Contact: George F. Stanley, Jr.

CAROL WILSON FINE ARTS, INC.

P.O. Box 17394, Portland, OR 97217.

Description: Carol Wilson, Eds. Humorous copy for greeting cards. Query. Pays $75 or negotiated royalties, on publication. Guidelines. Contact: Gary Spector.

SYNDICATES

Syndicates buy material from writers and artists to sell to newspapers all over the country and the world. Authors are paid either a percentage of the gross proceeds or an outright fee. Of course, features by people well known in their fields have the best chance of being syndicated. In general, syndicates want columns that have been popular in a local newspaper or magazine. Since most syndicated fiction has been published previously in magazines or books, beginning fiction writers should try to sell their stories to magazines before submitting them to syndicates.

Always query syndicates before sending manuscripts, since their needs change frequently, and be sure to enclose SASEs with queries and manuscripts.

AGEVENTURE NEWS SERVICE

Demko Publishing, 21946 Pine Trace, Boca Raton, FL 33428. 561-482-6271.
E-mail: editor@demko.com. Web site: www.demko.com.
David Demko, Writer and Editor.
Description: Age Venture presents work to international audience of 3 million readers in 29 countries. Topics must address baby-boomer and retiree concerns. Submissions should be between 250-500 words; specify costs for use at time of submission. Submit manuscripts as e-mail text (no attached files).

AMPERSAND COMMUNICATIONS

2311 S. Bayshore Dr., Miami, FL 33133-4728. 305-285-2200.
E-mail: amprsnd@aol.com.
Web site: members.aol.com/amprsnd/ampersandcommunications.html.
George Leposky, Editor.
Description: Feature material for online use, and for newspapers, magazines, and special-interest publications. Sells content to end-users directly and through marketing agreements with other online syndication services. Topics include: book reviews, humor, business, medicine and health, business travel, pets, cooking, food, and wine, senior lifestyles, environmental issues, timesharing and vacation ownership, home improvement, travel. No unsolicited mss., query first.

ANTHONY ASSOCIATES

10355 Freshley Avenue, NE, Alliance, OH 44601. 330-821-4285.
Sally Neib, Editor.
Description: Book reviews on adult topics, gardening, and landscaping.

AP NEWSFEATURES

50 Rockefeller Plaza, New York, NY 10020. 212-621-1720.
Susan Clark, Corporate Communications.
Description: No unsolicited manuscripts. Feature columns on health, education, book reviews, careers, humor. 1,500 subscribers.

ARKIN MAGAZINE SYNDICATE

300 Bayview Dr., Suite A-8, N. Miami Beach, FL 33160. 305-949-9573.
Ms. Mitzi Roberg, Editorial Director.
Description: Articles, 750-2,200 words, for trade and professional magazines. Must have small-business slant, be written in layman's language, and offer solutions to business problems. Articles should apply to many businesses, not just a specific industry. No columns. Pays $.03 to $.10 a word, on acceptance. SASE required; query not necessary.

ARTHUR'S INTERNATIONAL

2613 High Range Drive, Las Vegas, NV 89134. 702-228-3731.
E-mail: arthurintl@aol.com.
Marvin C. Arthur, President.
Description: Short stories and fine arts. Submit unsolicited mss. in column or short story form, send SASE.

ASK THE BUILDER

3166 N. Farmcrest Dr., Cincinnati, OH 45213-1112. 513-531-9229.
E-mail: tim@askbuild.com. Web site: www.askthebuilder.com.
Tim Carter, Editor.
Description: Home improvement articles. Submit electronic press-release or product information via e-mail; lead with a 100-word (max.) summary of the press release. Color images for the *Ask the Builder* e-zine should be in .gif or .jpg format (width: 250 pixels; height: proportional; resolution: 72 dpi; send as e-mail attachment).

BUDDY BASCH FEATURE SYNDICATE

720 West End Avenue, No. 1216, New York, NY 10025-6299. 212-666-2300.
Buddy Basch, Publisher/Editor.
Description: Entertainment, travel, human interest, science and medical, food. Accepts little freelance, query with SASE; or send mss. with SASE.

BLACK CONSCIENCE SYNDICATION

308-A Deer Park Rd, Dix Hills, NY 11746. 631-462-3933.
E-mail: cldavis@suffolklib.ny.us.
Clyde Davis, President.
Description: All types of material covering black issues accepted (book reviews, poetry, cartoons, sports, music, and politics). Query with SASE.

CONTEMPORARY FEATURES SYNDICATE

P.O. Box 1258, Jackson, TN 38302-1258.
Mr. Lloyd Russell, Editor.
Description: Articles, 1,000-10,000 words: how-to, money savers, business, etc. Self-help pieces for small business. Pays from $25, on acceptance. Query.

COPLEY NEWS SERVICE

Box 120190, San Diego, CA 92112. 619-293-1818.

E-mail: infofax@copleynews.com. Web site: www.copleynews.com.

P. Gonzales, Vice President.

Description: Features columns on: music, books, cars, fashion, films, sports, gardening, photography, and other special interests. 1,500 subscribers. Accepts unsolicited mss.

HARRIS & ASSOCIATES FEATURES

15915 Caminito Aire Puro, San Diego, CA 92128. 858-485-9027.

E-mail: rhh1234@yahoo.com.

Dick Harris, Editor.

Description: Sports features; golf and golf travel; sports personalities. Maximum 2,500 words. Send one-page query first. Pay varies.

HISPANIC LINK NEWS SERVICE

1420 N St. N.W., Washington, DC 20005. 202-234-0280.

E-mail: zapoteco@aol.com.

Mr. Charles A. Ericksen, Editor.

Description: Trend articles, opinion and personal experience pieces, and general features with Hispanic focus, 650-700 words; editorial cartoons. Pays $25 for op-ed columns and cartoons, on acceptance. Send SASE for guidelines.

THE HOLLYWOOD INSIDE SYNDICATE

Box 49957, Los Angeles, CA 90049-0957. 818-784-5066.

E-mail: holywood@ez2.net. Web site: www.ez2.net/hollywood.

John Austin, Director.

Description: Anything on world-class celebrities, up to 1,500 words. Column items for internationally syndicated "Hollywood Inside" column. SASE required.

KING FEATURES SYNDICATE

235 E. 45th St., New York, NY 10017. 212-455-4000/800-526-5464.

E-mail: jdangel@hearst.com. Web site: www.kingfeatures.com.

Mr. Paul Eberhart, Executive Editor.

Description: Columns, comics. Does not buy individual articles; looking for ideas for nationally syndicated columns. Submit cover letter, 6 sample columns of 650 words each, bio sheet and any additional clips, and SASE. No simultaneous submissions. Send SASE for guidelines.

LISTENING INC

8716 Pine St., Gary, IN 46403. 219-938-6962.

E-mail: addup@crown.net.

Patricia Work Bennett, President.

Description: Articles and stories on nontraditional families, post-divorce, remarriage and children of divorce, school violence, Attention Deficit Disorder in adults. Query first.

LOS ANGELES TIMES SYNDICATE
145 S. Spring St., Los Angeles, CA 90012. 213-237-7987.
Web site: www.lats.com.
Timothy Lange, Executive Editor.
Description: Commentary, features, columns, editorial cartoons, comics, puzzles and games; news services, and online products. Send SASE for submission guidelines.

NATIONAL NEWS BUREAU
P.O. Box 43039, Philadelphia, PA 19129. 215-849-9016.
Harry Jay Katz, Editor.
Description: Articles, 500-1,500 words, interviews, consumer news, how-tos, travel pieces, reviews, entertainment pieces, features, etc. Pays on publication.

NEW DIMENSIONS RADIO
P.O. Box 569, Ukiah, CA 95482. 707-468-5215.
E-mail: ndradio@pacific.net. Web site: www.newdimensions.org.
Rose Holland, Associate Producer.
Description: Topics include social change, and the humanities and arts in everyday life. No unsolicited mss.; query first.

NEW YORK TIMES SYNDICATION SALES
122 E. 42nd St., 14th Floor, New York, NY 10168. 212-499-3300/800-972-3550.
E-mail: nytss@mcimail.com. Web site: www.nytimes.com.
Ms. Gloria Brown Anderson, Editor-in-Chief.
Description: Articles on international, seasonal, health, lifestyle, and entertainment topics, to 1,500 words (previously published or unpublished). Query with published article or tear sheet and SASE. No calls please. Pays 50% royalty on collected sales.

NEWSPAPER ENTERPRISE ASSOCIATION/
UNITED FEATURE SYNDICATE
200 Madison Ave., 4th Fl., New York, NY 10016. 212-293-8500/800-221-4816.
Rebecca Shannonhouse, Editor.
Description: National features and columns on news, politics, sports, business, entertainment, books, and lifestyles, for over 600 daily newspapers. Payment varies.

OCEANIC PRESS SERVICE
Seaview Business Park, 1030 Calle Cordillera, Unit #106, San Clemente, CA 92673.
Mr. Peter Carbone, Editor.
Description: Buys reprint rights for foreign markets, for previously published novels, self-help, and how-to books; interviews with celebrities; illustrated features on celebrities, family, health, beauty, personal relationships, etc.; cartoons, comic strips. Pays on acceptance; or 50% on acceptance, 50% on syndication. Query.

SINGER MEDIA CORP.

#106, 1030 Calle Cordillera, San Clemente, CA 92673.

Ms. Helen J. Lee, Editor.

Description: International syndication, some domestic. Subjects must be of global interest. Features: celebrity interviews and profiles, women's, health, fitness, self-help, business, computer, etc., all lengths; psychological quizzes; puzzles (no word puzzles), single-panel cartoons (with no bubbles), and games for children or adults. Pays 50% of sales.

TRIBUNE MEDIA SERVICES

435 N. Michigan Ave., #1500, Chicago, IL 60611. 312-222-4444, 800-245-6536.

E-mail: tms@tribune.com. Web site: www.tribune.com.

Fred Schecker, Editor.

Description: Continuing columns, comic strips, features, electronic databases, puzzles and word games. Query with clips.

UNITED PRESS INTERNATIONAL

1510 H St. N.W., Suite 600, Washington, DC 20005. 202-898-8000.

John O'Sullivan, Editor-in-Chief.

Description: Feature and audio service, news, news pictures. Accepts freelance photography.

UNIVERSAL PRESS SYNDICATE

4900 Main St., Suite 700, Kansas City, MO 64111. 816-932-6600.

Web site: www.uexpress.com.

Alan McDermott, Managing Editor.

Description: Articles for kiosk feature service, covering lifestyles, trends, health, fashion, parenting, business, humor, the home, entertainment, and personalities. Query. Payment varies.

WORLDWIDE MEDIA

27324 Camino Capistrano, Suite 211, Laguna Niguel, CA 92677. 949-582-6995.

E-mail: wwm@wwmedia.net. Web site: www.wwmedia.net.

Mayra Gomez / Helen J. Lee, Acquisitions Director.

Description: International newspaper syndicate servicing overseas publications. We look for articles, columns, and puzzles (previously published preferred) to be sold for reprint in foreign publications. Must have global appeal. No poetry. Query with SASE. Tips: We are looking for borderless and timeless articles that will be appropriate for usage by foreign publication. Queries: Preferred. E-queries: Yes. Unsolicited mss: Accepts. Response: Queries 30 days submissions 60-90 days, SASE required. Freelance Content: 80%. Rights: International syndication. Payment: On publication.

TELEVISION & FILM

Given the quantity of television programming on commercial, educational, and cable stations, plus the hundreds of major-studio and independent films released each year, freelance writers may feel this is a promising market. However, it is very competitive.

Several things may help a writer with good ideas and writing skills to break in. First, finding an agent who specializes in scripts is very helpful; most television or film producers will look at material submitted from recognized agents first before looking at other submissions. Another requirement is submitting the information in the correct format; writers must be prepared to learn the special techniques and conventions of scriptwriting, either by taking a workshop through a university or at a writers' conference. Also, there are a number of good books written on this subject, as well as computer programs designed to format scripts in the accepted manner.

Experience gained in playwriting for live theater is always valuable practice for producing good scripts with solid dramatic structure and appealing characters. Finally, developing industry contacts is often helpful; one place to begin is with local associations of scriptwriters. A beginning writer may sometimes be lucky enough to team up with a more experienced partner to work on a project and thereby start to develop the skills, experience, and credentials needed to improve and move to the next level.

AMERICAN FILM INSTITUTE
2021 N. Western Avenue, Los Angeles, CA 90027. 323-856-7600.
Description: Nonprofit film institute.

ANGEL FILMS
967 Hwy. 40, New Franklin, MO 65274-9778. 573-698-3900.
E-mail: angelfilm@aol.com.
Matthew Eastman, V.P. Production.
Description: Seeking projects that can be used to produce feature films and television animation for children. Query with SASE.

ARTISAN ENTERTAINMENT, INC.
2700 Colorado Avenue, 2nd Floor, Santa Monica, CA 90404. 310-449-9200.
Description: Develops, produces, markets, and distributes motion pictures domestically and through distributors internationally.

BIG EVENT PICTURES
11288 Ventura Blvd., #909, Studio City, CA 90025.
E-mail: bigevent1@hotmail.com.
Michael Cargile, President.
Description: Seeking all genres in film. Looking for unique stories with strong characters. Query with synopsis and SASE.

BKS ENTERTAINMENT
250 West 54th, Suite 807, New York, NY 10019. 212-765-5555.
Description: Develops television entertainment and distributes programming.

CINEMANOW, INC.
4553 Glencoe Ave., Ste. 380, Marina del Rey, CA 90292. 310-314-2000.
Description: Works with the Internet and other technologies to develop and distribute innovative film programs. Opportunities for freelancers.

COBBLESTONE FILMS
1484 Reeves St, Suite 203, Los Angeles, CA 90035.
E-mail: cstone@aol.com.
Jacque Adler, Producer.
Description: Seeking commercial/independent screenplays, good writing on any subject. Open to working with and developing ideas with writers. Prefers completed screenplays.

COMEDY CENTRAL
1775 Broadway, New York, NY 10019. 212-767-8600.
Description: 24-hour basic cable station with eclectic mix of original programming, including standup comedy, sketch comedy, basic television shows, and movies.

CORPORATION FOR PUBLIC BROADCASTING
901 "E" Street NW, Washington, DC 20004. 202-879-9600.
Description: Private nonprofit corporation. Promotes noncommercial public telecommunications services (television, radio, online. and digital) for the American people.

CREATIVE PLANET
5700 Wilshire Blvd., Suite 600, Los Angeles, CA 90036. 323-634-3400.
Description: Online news and information service for creative professionals in the entertainment industry.

WALT DISNEY COMPANY
500 South Buena Vista St., Burbank, CA 91521-7235. 818-558-2222.
Web site: www.disney.com.
Description: Film, animated features, television, theatre.

DLT ENTERTAINMENT
31 West 56th Street, New York, NY 10019. 212-245-4680.
Description: International producer of TV program for network, cable, and PBS.

E! ENTERTAINMENT TELEVISION
5750 Wilshire Blvd., Los Angeles, CA 90036. 323-954-2666.
Description: TV station specializing in programming on the entertainment scene.

FOX LATIN AMERICA CHANNEL
11833 Mississippi Ave., Los Angeles, CA 90025.
Description: Fox channel for to the growing Latin America audience.

RICHARD FRANKEL PRODUCTIONS
729 Seventh Avenue, 12th Floor, New York, NY 10019.
Description: Independent theatrical production and general management company.

GRANADA ENTERTAINMENT
11812 San Vicente Blvd., Suite 500, Los Angeles, CA 90049.
Description: Develops and produces movies and series for the U.S. television market.

GRB ENTERTAINMENT
13400 Riverside Drive, 3rd Floor, Sherman Oaks, CA 91423. 818-728-7600.
Description: Production company, many shows for the Discovery Channel.

HBO
2049 Century Park East, Suite #4100, Los Angeles, CA 90067. 310-201-9200.
Description: Premium cable-television network; some original productions.

JIM HENSON COMPANY
1416 N. La Brea, Hollywood, CA 90028. 323-960-4096.
Description: Developer of the Muppets and other animated feature movies and TV programs.

INDEPENDENT TELEVISION SERVICE
51 Federal Street, 1st Floor, San Francisco, CA 94107. 415-356-8383.
Description: ITVS finances independent films, and distributes and promotes them to PBS and public television.

LAKESHORE ENTERTAINMENT
5555 Melrose Ave., Hollywood, CA 90038. 323-956-4222.
Description: Major independent-film production and distribution company.

LIONS GATE ENTERTAINMENT
4553 Glencoe Avenue, Suite 200, Marina del Rey, CA 90292.
Description: Develops and produces feature films, television series and movies, mini-series, reality-based and animated programming.

LOCKWOOD FILMS
12569 Boston Dr., RR #41, London, Ontario N6H 5L2 Canada. 519-657-3994.
E-mail: mark.mccurdy@odyssey.on.ca.
Nancy Johnson, President.
Description: Seeking material for family entertainment, series, mini-series, movies of the week, specials. Send synopsis with resumé or sample scripts, include SASE.

MEDIACOM DEVELOPMENT CORP.
P.O. Box 6331 , Burbank, CA 91510-6331. 818-594-4089.
Felix Gerard, Director/Program Development.
Description: Looking for flexible, creative subject matter. Needs good, fresh projects from freelancers, on a specific topic (special and series) for pay TV and cable. Query.

MINDSTORM
1434 Sixth St., Suite 1, Santa Monica, CA 91401.
Karina Duffy, President.
Description: Seeking videotapes, script work that is unique, with good character development, for target audience in mid-20s or 30s. Looking for female-driven scripts (drama/comedy). Query with synopsis and resumé.

MOON CRESCENT STUDIOS
601 Nash Street, El Segundo, CA 90245. 310-524-4800.
Description: Independent film studio.

NASH ENTERTAINMENT
1483 N. Gower St., Bldg. 16, Hollywood, CA 90028. 323-468-4600.
Description: Produces reality specials and series for major networks and cable channels.

NEW CONCORDE
11600 San Vicente Blvd., Los Angeles, CA 90049. 310-820-6733.
Description: Independent film production and distribution company.

NEW REGENCY PRODUCTIONS
10201 W. Pico Blvd., Bldg. 12, Los Angeles, CA 90035. 310-369-000.
Description: Makes and distributes movies, television, and music.

ODYSSEY NETWORK
12700 Ventura Blvd., Ste. 200, Studio City, CA 91604. 818-755-2400.
Description: Cable TV provider of quality family entertainment.

ORBIT PICTURES
714 N. LaBrea Avenue, Hollywood, CA 90038. 213-525-2626.
Kevin Moreton, Vice President.
Description: Seeking stories in script form that are distinctive and well-written, to be the basis for feature-film projects: comedy, sci-fi, horror, and drama. Query with synopsis.

PAX COMMUNICATIONS CORPORATION
601 Clearwater Park Road, West Palm Beach, FL 33401. 561-659-4122.
Description: Family-entertainment TV, free of senseless violence.

PEARSON TELEVISION

2700 Colorado Ave., Ste. 450, Santa Monica, CA 90404. 310-255-4700.
Description: Largest independent international producer of television entertainment.

PLANET GRANDE PICTURES

23440 Civic Center Way, Ste. 104, Malibu, CA 90265. 310-317-1545.
Description: Full-service television/film company.

PORCHLIGHT ENTERTAINMENT

11777 Mississippi Ave., Los Angeles, CA 90025.
Description: Production, international distribution.

REEL LIFE WOMEN

10158 Hollow Glen Circle, Bel Air, CA 90077. 310-271-4722.
E-mail: reellifewomen@compuserve.com.
Joanne Parrent, Co-President.
Description: Seeking material for mass audience. Query with synopsis, resumé, SASE.

SHOWTIME NETWORKS

10880 Wilshire Blvd., Ste. 1600, Los Angeles, CA 90024.
Web site: www.showtimeonline.com.
Description: Cable channel featuring movies, sports specials, and original programming.

FRED SILVERMAN COMPANY

1648 Mandeville Cyn. Rd., Los Angeles, CA 90049. 310-471-4676.
Description: Media development company.

SPIRIT DANCE ENTERTAINMENT

1023 North Orange Drive, Los Angeles, CA 90038-2317. 323-512-7988.
E-mail: meridian39301@earthlink.net.
Robert Wheaton, Editor.
Description: Seeking scripts for feature-length films with a strong emotional base, well-developed characters. Considers material of almost any genre; welcomes music-driven material. Material should show the writer's passion for screenwriting and the material. Query with synopsis.

SUMMIT ENTERTAINMENT

1630 Stewart St., Ste 120, Santa Monica, CA 90404. 310-309-8400.
Description: International film distribution/production company.

SUNBOW ENTERTAINMENT

100 Fifth Avenue, 3rd Floor, New York, NY 10011.
Description: Division of Sony Wonder; develops and distributes quality children and family animation, plus live-action television.

TELEMUNDO NETWORK GROUP

2290 West 8th Avenue, Hialeah, FL 33010. 305-884-8200.

Description: Fastest growing Spanish-language television network. Features a wide range of programming, including novellas, talk shows, original sitcoms, etc.

TIM REID PRODUCTIONS

One New Millennium Drive, Petersburg, VA 23805. 804-957-4200.

E-mail: jareneef@nmstudios.com.

Jarene Fleming, Development Executive.

Description: Seeking multicultural TV movies portraying positive black images. Produces 2 films per year. Query with synopsis. No dysfunctional-family premises.

TIMELINE FILMS

11819 Wilshire Suite 205, Los Angeles, CA 90025. 310-268-0399.

Web site: www.timelinefilms.com.

Description: Produces documentaries for television, mainly about the film industry and the performing arts.

TURNER ENTERTAINMENT NETWORKS

1050 Techwood Drive, Atlanta, GA 30318. 404-885-4850.

Description: Involved with TBS, Cartoon Network, TNT, Turner Classic Movies, etc.

UNAPIX

15910 Ventura Blvd., 9th Fl., Encino, CA 91436. 818-981-8592.

Description: Global film, television, video distribution and production company.

WINTER FILMS

415 N. Camden Dr., Ste. 114, Beverly Hills, CA 90210. 310-288-0150.

Description: Independent motion-picture production company.

XENON PICTURES

1440 9th St., Santa Monica, CA 90401. 310-451-5510.

Description: Specializes in urban, Hispanic, martial arts, foreign and art-house films.

ZACHERY ENTERTAINMENT

273 S. Swall Drive, Beverly Hills, CA 90211-2612. 310-289-9788.

E-mail: zacharyent@aol.com.

David Miller, Development Associate.

Description: Seeking films for theatrical, network, and cable release. Audiences of all ages. Submit a 1-line description and short synopsis. Topic must be focused.

OTHER RESOURCES

AGENTS

As the number of book publishers that will consider only agented submissions grows, more writers are turning to agents to sell their manuscripts. The agents in the following list handle both literary and dramatic material. Included in each listing are such important details as type of material represented, submission procedure, and commission. Since agents derive their income from the sales of their clients' work, they must represent writers who are selling fairly regularly to good markets. Nonetheless, many of the agents listed here note they will consider unpublished writers. Always query an agent first, and enclose a self-addressed, stamped envelope; most agents will not respond without it. Do not send any manuscripts until the agent has asked you to do so; and be wary of agents who charge fees for reading manuscripts. All of the following agents have indicated they do not charge reading fees; however, some charge for copyright fees, manuscript retyping, photocopies, copies of books for use in the sale of other rights, and long distance calls.

To learn more about agents and their role in publishing, the Association of Authors' Representatives, Inc., publishes a canon of ethics as well as an up-to-date list of AAR members. Write to: Association of Authors' Representatives, P.O. Box 237201, Ansonia Station, New York, NY 10023, or visit their web site: www.aar-online.org.

Another good source which lists agents and their policies is Literary Market Place, a directory found in most libraries.

ABRAMS ARTISTS AGENCY
275 Seventh Ave., 26th Floor, New York, NY 10001. 646-486-4600.
Description: Plays and screenplays. Ave. 1,000 queries/submissions per year. Unpublished writers considered. Query with synopsis, up to 10 sample pages, bio/resumé, SASE required. No electronic queries. Multiple queries okay. Commission: 10% scripts. Fees: none. Contact: Charmaine Ferenczi.

BRET ADAMS LTD.
448 W. 44th St., New York, NY 10036.
Description: Screenplays, teleplays, stage plays, and musicals. Unproduced writers considered. Query with synopsis, bio, resumé, and SASE. Commission: 10%. Fees: none. Contact: Bruce Ostler, Bret Adams.

LEE ALLAN AGENCY
7464 N. 107 St., Milwaukee, WI 53224-3706. 414-357-7708.
E-mail: lmatt@execpc.com.
Description: All genres and subjects except poetry, anthologies, and textbooks. Genre fiction; science fiction, fantasy, mystery, horror, thrillers, men's adventure, historical, westerns, and mainstream. No short stories. Specializes in screenplays, film

and TV rights. No fax queries. No reading fees. 15% commission and required foreign rights or subagent fees; commissions and special fees for copying, overseas calls, shipping. Contact: Lee A. Matthias.

JAMES ALLEN LITERARY AGENT

538 East Harford St., P.O. Box 909, Milford, PA 18337. 570-296-6205.
E-mail: vkagency@pikeonline.net.
Description: Fiction and nonfiction. Special interests: speculative fiction, upscale women's fiction, fine mainstream, mysteries. Representatives in Hollywood and all principal foreign countries. No unsolicited mss. Send 2-page synopsis with cover letter first, with SASE. No reading fee. Submit outline. Handles film and TV rights through Renaissance Agency. Contact: Virginia Kidd.

MICHAEL AMATO AGENCY

1650 Broadway, Rm. 307, New York, NY 10019.
Description: Screenplays. Send query or complete manuscript. Commission: 10%. Fees: none.

MARCIA AMSTERDAM AGENCY

41 W. 82nd St., #9A, New York, NY 10024.
Description: Adult and young adult fiction; mainstream nonfiction. Screenplays and teleplays: comedy, romance, psychological suspense. Query with resumé, SASE; multiple queries okay; 3-week exclusive for requested submissions, 2 days to 2 weeks to respond to queries. Ave. 14,000 submissions per year; 5-6% unsolicited material accepted. Accepts unsolicited queries, but not manuscripts. Considers unpublished writers. No electronic queries. Considers multiple queries. Commission: 15% books; 10% screen or TV, 20% foreign. Fees: photocopying and shipping. Contact: Marcia Amsterdam.

AVATAR LITERARY AGENCY

4611 S. University Dr., Suite 438, Davie, FL 33328.
E-mail: avatar@reps.net.
Description: Fiction and nonfiction in all categories and genres, including collections of short stories and young adult novels. No other children's material; no poetry. Submit e-mail query; send hard copy with SASE; or send entire manuscript on diskette with SASE. Commission: 10% domestic; 15% foreign. Contact: K. Lisa Brodsky.

AXELROD AGENCY

54 Church St., Lenox, MA 01240. 413-637-2000.
E-mail: steve@axelrodagency.com.
Description: Fiction and nonfiction, film and TV rights, software. No unsolicited mss.; query first. No reading fee. Commissions: 10% domestic, 15% foreign. Contact: Steven Axelrod.

MALAGA BALDI LITERARY AGENCY

204 W. 84th St., Suite 3 C, New York, NY 10024. 212-579-5075.
E-mail: MBALDI@aol.com.
Description: Quality literary adult fiction and nonfiction. Ave. 1000s of queries/submissions per year; 2% of unsolicited material accepted. Considers unsolicited queries/manuscripts. Unpublished writers considered. Query first; if interested, will ask for proposal, outline, and sample pages for nonfiction, complete manuscript for fiction. SASE required. Response time: to 10 weeks. No electronic queries. Multiple queries okay. Commission: 15%. Fees: none. Contact: Malaga Baldi.

THE BALKIN AGENCY

P.O. Box 222, Amherst, MA 01004. 413-548-9835.
E-mail: balkin@crocker.com.
Description: Specializes in adult nonfiction, professional books, and college textbooks. No fiction. No unsolicited mss.; query first; submit outline and 1 sample chapter. No reading fee. 15% agency commission, 20% foreign rights. Contact: Rick Balkin.

LORETTA BARRETT BOOKS

101 Fifth Ave., New York, NY 10003. 212-242-3420.
Description: Specialize in fiction and nonfiction. Handle film and TV rights. No unsolicited mss.; query first with SASE. Submit outlines, sample chapters (nonfiction); synopsis, (fiction). No reading fee. Representatives on West Coast and in all major foreign countries. Contact: Loretta Barrett.

BERMAN, BOALS & FLYNN

208 W. 30th St., Suite 401, New York, NY 10001. 212-868-1068.
Description: Full-length stage plays, musicals. Considers unsolicited queries, but not manuscripts. Unpublished, unproduced writers considered only rarely, unless recommended by industry colleagues. Query with SASE, bio, and resumé. Commission: 10%. Fees: photocopying. Contact: Judy Boals.

REID BOATES LITERARY AGENCY

Box 328, 69 Cooks Crossroad, Pittstown, NJ 08867-0328. 908-730-8523.
E-mail: boatesliterary@aol.net.
Description: Adult mainstream fiction and nonfiction only. Agents in film and in all major foreign markets. Query first with SASE. Unpublished writers considered. No multiple queries or unsolicited manuscripts. Commission: 15%. Fees: none. Contact: Reid Boates.

BOOK DEALS, INC.

Civic Opera Bldg., 417 N. Sangamon St., Chicago, IL 60606. 312-491-0300.
E-mail: bookdeals@aol.com. Web site: www.bookdealsinc.com.
Description: General-interest adult fiction and nonfiction. Ave. 6,000 queries/submissions per year; less than 1% unsolicited material accepted. Considers unsolicited

queries, but not manuscripts. Considers unpublished writers with professional credentials, quality work. Query with lead, 2 sample chapters, and SASE. Responds: 2-3 weeks for queries, 4-6 weeks for submissions. Accepts electronic and multiple queries. Commission: 15% domestic, 20% foreign. Fees: copying, shipping. See web site for details. Contact: Caroline Carney.

BOOKSTOP LITERARY AGENCY
67 Meadow View Rd., Orinda, CA 94563. 925-254-2664.
Description: Juvenile and young adult fiction and nonfiction, also illustration for children's books. Unpublished writers considered. Mss. evaluation services available. No queries; send complete manuscript (fiction), sample chapters and outline (nonfiction). No reading fee. Commission: 15%. Fees: photocopying, shipping. Contact: Kendra Marcus.

GEORGES BORCHARDT, INC.
136 E. 57th St., New York, NY 10022. 212-753-5785.
Description: Fiction and nonfiction. No unsolicited mss. Handles film and TV rights, software. Commission: 15%.

BRANDT & BRANDT LITERARY AGENTS
1501 Broadway, New York, NY 10036. 212-840-5760.
Description: Fiction and nonfiction, film and TV rights; no original screenplays. No unsolicited mss.; query first. No reading fee. Agents in most foreign countries. Foreign rep: AM Heath & Co. Ltd. (UK). Contact: Carl D. Brandt, Gail Hochman.

HELEN BRANN AGENCY
94 Curtis Rd., Bridgewater, CT 06752. 860-354-9580.
Description: Adult fiction and nonfiction. Unpublished writers considered. No unsolicited mss., query first. No reading fee. Commission: 15%. Fees: none. Contact: Carol White.

ANDREA BROWN LITERARY AGENCY
P.O. Box 1027, Montara, CA 94037. 650-728-1783.
Description: Children's and young adult fiction and nonfiction only. Film and TV rights. Query with outline, sample pages, bio and resumé, and SASE; no faxes. Commission: 15% domestic; 20% foreign. Fees: none. Contact: Andrea Brown.

CURTIS BROWN LTD.
10 Astor Pl., New York, NY 10003. 212-473-5400.
Description: Handles general trade fiction and nonfiction, juvenile. No unsolicited mss.; query first with SASE. Submit outline or sample chapters. No reading fee. Other fees: photocopies, express mail, etc. Handles software, film and TV rights, multimedia. Reps in all major foreign countries. Contact: Peter L. Ginsberg, President.

KNOX BURGER ASSOCIATES

425 Madison Avenue, New York, NY 10011. 212-759-8600.
E-mail: kburger@haroldober.com.
Description: Adult fiction and nonfiction. No science fiction, fantasy, or romance. Highly selective. Unsolicited queries accepted, but not unsolicited manuscripts. Query with SASE. No multiple or electronic queries. Commission: 15%. Fees: photocopying. Contact: Knox Burger.

SHEREE BYKOFSKY ASSOCIATES, INC.

16 West 36th Street, New York, NY 10018.
Description: Adult nonfiction and fiction. Unpublished writers considered. Query with outline, up to 3 sample pages or proposal, and SASE. Multiple queries okay if noted as such. Commission: 15%. Fees: none.

MARTHA CASSELMAN

P.O. Box 342, Calistoga, CA 94515-0342. 707-942-4341.
Description: Trade nonfiction, food and cookbooks, no children's or young adult. No fiction, poetry, short stories. No unsolicited mss., query first (not by fax). Submit brief sample and synopsis (no simultaneous submissions) with SASE, query letter with SASE. No reading fee. Some expenses (copying, overnight mail). Contact: Martha Casselman, AAR.

JULIE CASTIGLIA AGENCY

1155 Camino del Mar, Suite 510, Del Mar, CA 92014. 858-755-8761.
Description: Specializes in ethnic, commercial, and literary fiction, science, biography, psychology, women's issues, business/finance, popular culture, health, and niche books. Submit synopsis and 2 chapters (fiction), outline or proposal plus 2 chapters (nonfiction). No phone queries. Handles TV and film rights. Major postal, copying, and other unusual expenses. No reading fee. Contact: Julie Castiglia, AAR.

RUTH COHEN, INC.

P.O. Box 7626, Menlo Park, CA 94025. 650-854-2054.
Description: Adult mysteries and women's fiction; quality juvenile fiction and nonfiction. Unpublished writers seriously considered. Query with first 10 pages, synopsis, bio and resumé, and SASE. Commission: 15%. Fees: some shipping, photocopying, foreign agent fees. Agents in Hollywood for film and TV rights. Contact: Ruth Cohen, AAR.

HY COHEN LITERARY AGENCY

P.O. Box 43770, Upper Montclair, NJ 07043-0770. 973-783-9494.
E-mail: cogency@home.com.
Description: Quality adult and young adult fiction and nonfiction. Ave. several hundred queries/submissions per year; few unsolicited material accepted. Considers unsolicited queries and manuscripts. Unpublished writers considered. Query with

SASE. Multiple submissions encouraged. Accepts electronic queries. Responds: several days to queries, 2 weeks to submissions. Commission: 10% domestic; 20% foreign. Fees: phone, photocopying, postage. Contact: Hy Cohen, Director.

COLUMBIA LITERARY ASSOCIATES
7902 Nottingham Way, Ellicott City, MD 21043. 410-465-1595.
Description: Commercial fiction (including mainstream novels, women's fiction, category and mainstream contemporary romances), also nonfiction (especially cookbooks). No historicals, literary fiction, horror, science fiction/fantasy, men's adventure, children's books, screenplays, short stories, or poetry. No unsolicited mss. Queries must include: SASE and first chapters, complete narrative synopsis, total mss. word count, project's submissions history. Contact: Linda Hayes, AAR.

DON CONGDON ASSOCIATES
156 Fifth Ave., Suite 625, New York, NY 10010. 212-645-1229.
E-mail: doncongdon@aol.com.
Description: Handles any and all trade books, for professional writers. Handle film and TV rights for regular clients. No unsolicited mss., query first with SASE. No reading fee. Contact: Don Congdon, Susan Ramer, AAR.

DOE COOVER AGENCY
P.O. Box 668, Winchester, MA 01890. 781-721-6000.
Description: Handles a broad range of nonfiction, including memoirs, biographies, business, social science, cooking and gardening. Also handles literary fiction, software, TV and film rights (only on agency projects). Ave. 250 queries/submissions per year; 2% unsolicited material accepted. Considers unsolicited queries, but not manuscripts;. Unpublished writers considered. Query with outline, sample pages, bio/resumé, SASE. Responds: 2 weeks. Multiple queries okay. No electronic queries. Commission: 15%. Fees: none. Contact: Frances Kennedy.

RICHARD CURTIS ASSOCIATES
171 E. 74th St., New York, NY 10021. 212-772-7363.
E-mail: jhackworth@curtisagency.com. Web site: www.curtisagency.com.
Description: Commercial adult nonfiction; commercial fiction by published authors. Ave. 3,000 submissions/queries per year; less than 1% unsolicited material accepted. Accepts unsolicited queries with SASE. No unsolicited manuscripts. No unproduced writers. Considers unpublished writers in nonfiction only. Query with bio/resumé and SASE. Responds: 4 weeks to queries. No electronic or multiple queries. Commission: 15% domestic; 20% foreign. Fees: some expenses for copying and shipping, for accepted work. Contact: Pamela Valvera.

DARHANSOFF & VERRILL LITERARY AGENCY
179 Franklin St., New York, NY 10013. 212-334-5980.
Description: Fiction and nonfiction, literary fiction, history, science, biography, pop culture and current affairs. No unsolicited mss., query first. Film and TV rights

handled by Los Angeles associates, Lynn Pleshette, Richard Green and UTA. Agents in many foreign countries. Contact: Liz Darhansoff, Leigh Feldman.

ELAINE DAVIE LITERARY AGENCY
620 Park Ave., Rochester, NY 14607.
Description: Adult fiction and nonfiction, specializes in popular/commercial novels by and for women, especially romance. Unpublished writers considered. Query with outline, sample pages or synopsis, and first 100 pages. SASE required. Multiple submissions okay. Commission: 15%. Fees: none. Contact: Elaine Davie.

SANDRA DIJKSTRA LITERARY AGENCY
PMB 515, 1155 Camino del Mar, Suite 515C, Del Mar, CA 92014. 858-755-3115.
E-mail: sdla@dijkstraagency.com.
Description: Adult literary and commercial fiction. Historical and inspirational nonfiction. Children's literature mysteries. 10% of unsolicited material accepted. Unsolicited queries and manuscripts not considered. Unpublished writers considered. Query with outline and bio/resumé. Submit first 50 pages and synopsis (fiction); proposal (nonfiction). SASE required. Responds in 4 weeks to queries, 6-8 weeks to submissions. No electronic queries. Multiple queries accepted. Commission: 15% domestic, 20% foreign. Fees: Clients billed for mailing and copy costs. Some editorial services for clients. Contact: Nicole Pitesa.

JONATHAN DOLGER AGENCY
49 E. 96th St., 9B, New York, NY 10128. 212-427-1853.
Description: Adult fiction and nonfiction; illustrated books. No unsolicited mss.; query first with SASE. Film and TV rights handled by Los Angeles associate. Agents in all principal foreign countries. Contact: Jonathan Dolger, Dee Ratterree.

DOUGLAS, GORMAN, ROTHACKER & WILHELM
1501 Broadway, Suite 703, New York, NY 10036.
Description: Screenplays and full-length teleplays. Query with 10-page synopsis, bio/resumé. Commission: 10%. Fees: none.

DWYER & O'GRADY, INC.
P.O. Box 239, East Lempster, NH 03605. 603-863-9347.
E-mail: donorth@srnet.com.
Description: Specializes in children's fiction with emphasis on picture books and middle grade/young adult readers, nonfiction. No unsolicited mss.; query by letter first. No telephone queries. Handles film and TV rights. No reading fee. Member: ABA, SCBWI, Society of Illustrators. Contact: Elizabeth O'Grady.

JANE DYSTEL LITERARY MANAGEMENT
One Union Square W., Suite 904, New York, NY 10003. 212-627-9100.
Web site: www.dystel.com.
Description: Adult and juvenile fiction and nonfiction. Ave. 15,000 queries/submis-

sions per year; 10% unsolicited material accepted. Considers unsolicited queries, but not manuscripts. Unpublished writers considered. Query with bio/resumé. Responds: 3 weeks to queries, 2 months to submissions. Accepts electronic queries. No multiple queries. Commission: 15% domestic, 19% foreign. Fees: none. Editorial feedback on projects chosen to represent.

EDUCATIONAL DESIGN SERVICES

P.O. Box 253, Wantaugh, NY 11793.
Description: Educational texts (K-12 only). Ave. 300 queries/submissions per year; 3% unsolicited material accepted. Considers unsolicited queries and manuscripts. Unpublished writers considered. Query with outline, sample pages or complete manuscript, bio/resumé, and SASE. No electronic queries. Considers multiple queries. Responds: 3-4 weeks for queries and submissions. Commission: 15% domestic, 25% foreign. Fees: none. Contact: Bertram L. Linder.

ETHAN ELLENBERG LITERARY AGENCY

548 Broadway, Suite #5E, New York, NY 10012. 212-431-4554.
E-mail: ellenbergagent@aol.com. Web site: www.ethanellenberg.com.
Description: Seeking established and new writers in wide range of genres. All commercial fiction: thrillers, mysteries, children's romance, women's fiction, ethnic, science fiction, fantasy, general fiction. Also, literary fiction with strong narrative. No poetry or short stories. Nonfiction: current affairs, health, science, psychology, cookbooks, new age, spirituality, pop-science, pop-culture, adventure, true crime, biography and memoir. Query with first 3 chapters, synopsis, SASE. Ave. 10,000 queries/submission per year; 5% unsolicited material accepted. Accepts unsolicited queries and manuscripts. Responds 1-2 weeks for queries, 4-6 weeks for submissions. No phone calls. Accepts electronic and multiple queries. Commission: 15% domestic; 20% foreign. No reading fees, some fees for copying, shipping. Contact: Ethan Ellenberg, Michael Psaltis.

ANN ELMO AGENCY

60 E. 42nd St., New York, NY 10165. 212-661-2880.
Description: Handles books, plays, movie and TV rights, and teenage books. No unsolicited mss.; query letters only. No reading fee. Agents in all European countries. Contact: Lettie Lee, Andree Abecassis, Mari Cronin.

FELICIA ETH

555 Bryant St., Suite 350, Palo Alto, CA 94301. 650-375-1276.
Description: Selective mainstream literary fiction; diverse nonfiction including psychology, health, and popular science, including women's issues, investigative journalism, and biography. No unsolicited mss., query first for fiction, proposal for nonfiction. Handles film and TV rights for clients' books only, through subagents in L.A. No reading fee. Foreign rights agents and reps in all major territories. Contact: Felicia Eth, AAR.

FARBER LITERARY AGENCY

14 E. 75th St., New York, NY 10021. 212-861-7075.
E-mail: farberlit@aol.com. Web site: www.donaldfarber.com.
Description: All original fiction and nonfiction, adult, young adult, and children; plays, some films. Considers unpublished writers and unsolicited queries. Query with outline, 3 chapters, SASE. Ave. 3,500 queries/submissions per year. Accepts unsolicited manuscripts. Responds: queries 3-5 days, submissions 1-3 weeks. Accepts electronic queries. Considers multiple queries. Commission: 15%, includes legal services of Donald C. Farber, entertainment attorney. No fees. Editorial services in exceptional cases, for a fee. Contact: Ann Farber.

JOYCE FLAHERTY

816 Lynda Ct., St. Louis, MO 63122. 314-966-3057.
Description: We accept only work of currently published authors of book-length manuscripts, who continue to write in their specialties. Adult fiction and nonfiction. No unsolicited mss.; preliminary letter or phone call first. Query with outline or synopsis, first chapter, and bio. Commission: 15% domestic; 30% foreign. Fees: none. Contact: Joyce A. Flaherty, John Flaherty, AAR.

FLANNERY LITERARY

1140 Wickfield Ct., Naperville, IL 60563-3300. 630-428-2682.
E-mail: flanlit@aol.com.
Description: Fiction and nonfiction for children and young adults, all genres, infant to college age. Accepts unsolicited queries/manuscripts. Unpublished writers considered. Query by letter only (no phone or fax queries); multiple queries okay, SASE required. Responds: 2 weeks for queries, 3-4 weeks for submissions. No electronic queries. Commission: 15% domestic, 20% foreign. Fees: none. Contact: Jennifer Flannery.

FOGELMAN LITERARY AGENCY

7515 Greenville Ave., Suite 712, Dallas, TX 75231. 214-361-9956.
E-mail: info@fogelman.com. Web site: www.fogelman.com.
Description: Adult romance and women's fiction. Commercial books of pop-culture. Published authors may call or submit a query (1-2 pages) with SASE. Handles TV and film rights. Commission: 15% domestic; 10% foreign. Fees: none. Contact: Linda M. Kruger.

ROBERT A. FREEDMAN DRAMATIC AGENCY

1501 Broadway, Suite 2310, New York, NY 10036. 212-840-5760.
Description: Screenplays, teleplays, and stage plays. No unsolicited mss.; send query first. Multiple queries okay. Commission: standard. No reading fees. Fees: photocopying. Contact: Robert A. Freedman, Selma Luttinger.

GELFMAN SCHNEIDER

250 W. 57th St., Suite 2515, New York, NY 10107. 212-245-1993.
E-mail: gslc@msn.com.
Description: Contemporary women's commercial fiction; literary and commercial fiction; mystery and suspense; some nonfiction. Ave. 2,000 queries/submissions per year. Considers unsolicited queries, not manuscripts. Unpublished writers considered. Query with outline, sample pages, and bio; SASE required. No electronic queries; by mail only. Responds in 4-6 weeks to queries. Responds to multiple queries. Commission: 15% domestic; 20% foreign; 15% film and dramatic. Fees: none. Contact: Cathy Gleason.

GEM LITERARY SERVICES

4717 Poe Rd., Medina, OH 44256.
Description: Fiction, all genres (no erotica), and nonfiction. Submit complete manuscript with SASE, short bio, and 2-5 page synopsis for fiction; chapter outline for nonfiction. Mark envelope: "Submission." Commission: 15% domestic; 20% foreign and film rights. Fees: none. Contact: Darla L. Pfenninger.

GOODMAN ASSOCIATES

500 West End Ave., New York, NY 10024. 212-873-4806.
Description: Adult book-length fiction and nonfiction. No plays, screenplays, poetry, textbooks, science fiction, children's books. Unpublished writers considered. No unsolicited mss.; query first with SASE. No reading fee. Handles film and TV rights for clients' materials. Reps in Hollywood and major foreign markets. Contact: Elise Simon Goodman.

GRAYBILL & ENGLISH

1920 N St. N.W., Suite 620, Washington, DC 20036. 202-861-0106.
Description: 20% adult fiction, 80% adult nonfiction. Nina Graybill: nonfiction, literary/commercial fiction. Lynn Whitakker: nonfiction, literary fiction, women's fiction, mystery. Elaine English: women's fiction, including romance (single titles), historical, contemporary. Jeff Kleinman: nonfiction, especially historical, literary/commercial fiction. Send query letter with bio, proposal or up to 3 sample chapters, and SASE. No unsolicited manuscripts. Ave. 3,000 queries/submissions per year; accepts 5-10% unsolicited material. Considers unpublished writers. Responds: 2-3 weeks to queries, up to 8 weeks for submissions. No electronic queries. Multiple queries okay. Commission: 15% domestic; 25% foreign. Fees: photocopying, shipping, etc. Members of AAR.

SANFORD J. GREENBURGER ASSOCIATES

55 Fifth Ave., 15th Fl., New York, NY 10003. 212-206-5600.
Web site: www.greenburger.com.
Description: All types of fiction and nonfiction, including sports books, health, business, psychology, parenting, science, biography, gay; juvenile books. Unpublished writers with strong credentials considered. Query with proposal, including sample

pages, bio, and SASE. Multiple queries okay. Considers unsolicited queries and manuscripts. Responds: queries and submissions, 4-6 weeks. Commission: 15% domestic;
20% foreign. Fees: photocopying. Contact: Heide Lange.

MAIA GREGORY ASSOCIATES
311 E. 72nd St., New York, NY 10021.
Description: Adult nonfiction and literary fiction only. Query with sample pages and
bio/resumé. No multiple queries. Commission: 15%. Fees: none. Contact: Maia
Gregory, Diana Delhi Gould.

CHARLOTTE GUSAY LITERARY AGENCY
10532 Blythe, Los Angeles, CA 90064. 310-559-0831.
E-mail: gusay1@aol.com. Web site: www.mediastudio.com/gusay.
Description: Adult/juvenile fiction, nonfiction, screenplays, books to film, young
adult material suitable for film. Ave. 2,000 queries/submissions per year. Accepts
unsolicited queries, but not manuscripts. Considers unpublished writers. Submit
1-page query only, with bio/resumé and SASE. Multiple queries discouraged.
Responds: 3-6 weeks for queries, 6-8 weeks for submissions. Commission: 15%. No
reading fees. If accepted, we share out-of-pocket expenses. Occasional nonfiction
book proposal consultation. Contact: Charlotte Gusay.

HARDEN CURTIS ASSOCIATES
850 Seventh Ave., Suite 405, New York, NY 10019.
Description: Stage plays. Query with bio and resumé, SASE; no multiple queries.
Commission: 10%. Fees: none. Not accepting new clients at this time.

JOY HARRIS LITERARY AGENCY
156 Fifth Ave., Suite 617, New York, NY 10010. 212-924-6269.
Description: Adult fiction and nonfiction. Submit outline or sample chapters. No
unsolicited mss.; query first with return postage. Film and TV rights. Agents in all
major territories. No fees. Contact: Joy Harris, AAR.

HEACOCK LITERARY AGENCY
1523 Sixth St., Suite 14, Santa Monica, CA 90401. 310-393-6227.
Description: Specializes in general nonfiction and fiction books. No unsolicited
mss.; query first with letter, and SASE. Submit outline and sample chapters. No
queries by fax accepted. No scripts. No reading fee. Other fees: postage, phone, copying, fax, packing. Contact: Rosalie Heacock.

JOHN L. HOCHMANN BOOKS
320 E. 58th St., New York, NY 10022-2220. 212-319-0505.
Description: Adult nonfiction, biography, history, textbooks for college courses with
heavy enrollment, gay/lesbian, popular medical, heath. Contact: Theodora Eagle.

BARBARA HOGENSON AGENCY

165 West End Ave., Suite 19-C, New York, NY 10023.
Description: Adult fiction, nonfiction. Screenplays, teleplays, and stage plays. Query with bio and synopsis, SASE. Multiple queries okay. Commission: 10% scripts; 15% books. Fees: none. Contact: Barbara Hogenson.

HULL HOUSE LITERARY AGENCY

240 E. 82nd St., New York, NY 10028. 212-988-0725.
Description: Commercial, literary, and mystery fiction; nonfiction: true crime, biographies, military history, art history. No unsolicited mss.; query first. Submit outline and sample chapters with SASE. No reading fee. Handle film and TV rights through Richard Green United Talent Agency. Contact: David Stewart Hull.

IMG BACH LITERARY AGENCY

22 E. 71st St., New York, NY 10021. 212-489-5400.
E-mail: ckrupp@imgworld.com.
Description: Specializes in fiction and nonfiction. No unsolicited mss.; query first with SASE. Handles film and TV rights. No reading fee. Foreign rep: Sophia Seidner. Contact: Julian Bach, Carolyn Krupp.

SHARON JARVIS & CO.

Toad Hall, Inc., RR2, Box 2090, Laceyville, PA 18623. 570-869-2942.
E-mail: toadhallco@aol.com. Web site: www.laceyville.com/toad-hall.
Description: Commercial adult fiction and nonfiction. No short material; books only. Ave. 500 queries/submissions per year; 1% of unsolicited material accepted. Unsolicited queries accepted, but not manuscripts. Unpublished writers considered. Query with bio or resumé, and outline or synopsis, SASE required. Responds: 2 weeks to queries, 3 months to submissions. No electronic queries or multiple queries. Commission: 15% domestic, extra 10-15% foreign. Fees: photocopying, shipping (books only), bank fees. Contact: Sharon Jarvis.

JCA LITERARY AGENCY

27 W. 20th St., Suite 1103, New York, NY 10011. 212-807-0888.
Description: Adult fiction and nonfiction. Unpublished writers considered. Query with sample pages; multiple queries okay. Commission: 15% domestic; 20% foreign. Fees: photocopying, shipping. "Be straightforward, to-the-point. Don't try to hype us or bury us in detail." No unsolicited manuscripts. No children's books, no screenplays. Contact: Jeff Gerecke, Tony Outhwaite, AAR.

NATASHA KERN LITERARY AGENCY

P.O. Box 2908, Portland, OR 97208-2908. 503-297-6190.
E-mail: nkla@teleport.com. Web site: www.natashakern.com.
Description: Full-service agency, commercial adult fiction and nonfiction books, represents bestselling authors, as well as beginners. Co-agents in Hollywood and all foreign markets. Nonfiction: health, natural science, investigative journalism, inspira-

tion, new age, psychology, self-help, parenting, gardening, celebrity bios, and business, also current, controversial, and women's issues. Fiction: specializes in thrillers, mysteries, mainstream women's fiction, historicals, romances. No horror, true crime, children's or young adult, short stories, poetry, scripts, software, sports, photography, cookbooks, gift books, scholarly works. Ave. 10,000 queries/submissions per year; 1% unsolicited material accepted. Considers unsolicited queries, but not manuscripts. Considers unpublished writers. Responds: 3-4 weeks for queries, 8 weeks for submissions. Considers electronic and multiple queries. Commission: 15% domestic; 10% foreign. Fees: none. Contact: Natasha Kern.

KIDDE, HOYT & PICARD
335 E. 51st St., New York, NY 10022. 212-755-9461.
Description: Mainstream fiction, literary fiction, romance, mysteries, and general nonfiction. Ave. 5,000 queries/submission per year; 1% unsolicited material accepted. Unpublished writers considered. Unsolicited queries considered, but not manuscripts. Query with 2-3 chapters and synopsis; include past writing experience and SASE. Multiple queries okay. Responds: 1 week to queries, 1 month to submissions. No electronic queries. Commission: 15% domestic; 20% foreign. Fees: photocopying. "Looking for exciting, witty, compelling characters, in psychologically suspenseful plot (fiction)—and the counterpart of that in nonfiction." Contact: Katharine Kidde, Laura Langlie.

KIRCHOFF/WOHLBERG, INC.
866 United Nations Plaza, Suite 525, New York, NY 10017. 212-644-2020.
Description: Children and young adult, nonfiction trade books only. No adult titles. No unsolicited mss. Query first with outline, sample chapter, SASE. No fees. Contact: Elizabeth J. Ford.

HARVEY KLINGER, INC.
301 W. 53rd St., New York, NY 10019. 212-581-7068.
Description: Mainstream adult fiction and nonfiction, literary and commercial. Unpublished writers considered. Query with outline, sample pages, and bio/resumé. No multiple queries; no phone calls or faxes. Ave. 5,000 queries per year; 1% unsolicited material accepted. No unsolicited manuscripts. Responds 4-6 weeks for queries and 2-3 months for submissions. SASE required. Commission: 15% domestic, 25% foreign. Fees: photocopying, shipping. "We critique clients' work carefully to get manuscript in best possible form before submitting to publishers." Contact: Harvey Klinger.

BARBARA S. KOUTS
P.O. Box 560, Bellport, NY 11713. 631-286-1278.
Description: Adult /children's fiction and nonfiction. Unpublished writers considered. Query with bio/resumé. Multiple queries okay. Ave. 1,500 queries per year; 10% unsolicited material accepted. Accepts unsolicited material, but not manuscripts. Considers unpublished writers. Responds: 1 week for queries, 6-8 weeks for submissions,

SASE required. No electronic queries. Multiple queries okay. Commission: 10%, 20% foreign. Contact: Barbara Kouts.

OTTO R. KOZAK LITERARY AGENCY

P.O. Box 152, Long Beach, NY 11561.
Description: Scripts only: female/family oriented stories, contemporary, with central heroine; freak comedies; good horror/suspense stories; docudramas based on true stories; socially relevant stories. Ave. 200 queries/submissions per year; 5% unsolicited material accepted. Considers unsolicited queries, but not manuscripts. Unpublished/unproduced writers considered. Query with outline, SASE required. Responds: 2 weeks to queries, 4 weeks to submissions. No electronic queries. Accepts multiple queries. Commission: 10%. Fees: none. Editorial services on occasion. Contact: Yitka Kozak.

EDITE KROLL

12 Grayhurst Pk., Portland, ME 04102. 207-773-4922.
Description: Feminist nonfiction; humor; children's fiction and picture books written and illustrated by artists. Unpublished writers considered. Query with outline, sample pages, a brief note about the author, and SASE; multiple queries okay. Keep queries brief; no phone or fax queries. Commission: 15% domestic; 20% foreign. Fees: photocopying. Contact: Edite Kroll.

PETER LAMPACK AGENCY

551 Fifth Ave., Suite 1613, New York, NY 10014. 212-687-9106.
E-mail: renboPLA@aol.com.
Description: Commercial and literary fiction; nonfiction by experts in a given field (especially autobiography, biography, law, finance, politics, history). No horror, sci-fi, westerns, romance. Handles motion picture/TV rights from book properties only. No original screenplays. Ave. 3,000 queries/submissions per year; less than 1% unsolicited material accepted. Considers unsolicited queries, but not manuscripts. Unpublished writers considered. Query should include the nature of the submission, plus author's credentials. Sample chapter, synopsis, SASE required, e-mail address if applicable. Responds: 2 weeks to queries and submissions. No electronic queries accepted. Multiple queries okay. Commission: 15% domestic; 20% foreign. Fees: none. Contact: Loren Soeiro.

THE LANTZ OFFICE

200 W. 57th Street, Suite 503, New York, NY 10019. 212-586-0200.
Description: Adult fiction and nonfiction. Stage plays. Query with bio and resumé; no multiple queries. Fees: none. Contact: Robert Lantz.

MAUREEN LASHER AGENCY

P.O. Box 888, Pacific Palisades, CA 90272. 310-459-8415.
E-mail: HL8LA@aol.com.
Description: Adult fiction and nonfiction books; handles film and TV rights. No

unsolicited mss.; query first with outline, sample pages (approx. 50), bio/resumé, SASE. No reading fee. Contact: Ann Cashman.

ELLEN LEVINE LITERARY AGENCY
15 E. 26th St., Suite 1801, New York, NY 10010. 212-889-0620.
Description: General fiction and nonfiction. Handles film and TV rights for clients only. No unsolicited mss.; query with SASE, then submit outline and sample chapters. No reading fees. Representatives in Hollywood. Contact: Diana Finch, Elizabeth Kaplan, AAR.

JOANNA LEWIS COLE
404 Riverside Dr., New York, NY 10025.
Description: Juvenile fiction and nonfiction, all ages. Unpublished writers considered. Send query letter with SASE; multiple queries okay. Commission 10-15%. Fees: none.

LICHTMAN, TRISTER, SINGER & ROSS
1666 Connecticut Ave. N.W., Suite 500, Washington, DC 20009.
Description: Adult nonfiction. Unpublished writers considered. Query with outline, sample pages, resumé, and SASE. Multiple queries okay. Commission: 15%. Fees: none. Contact: Gail Ross, Howard Yoon.

NANCY LOVE LITERARY AGENCY
250 E. 65th St., Suite 4A, New York, NY 10021. 212-980-3499.
Description: Adult nonfiction: health, self-help, parenting, medical, psychology, women's issues, memoirs (literary), current affairs, pop science. Popular reference if by an authority, with a fresh slant. Adult fiction: mysteries and thrillers only. Ave. 2,000 queries/submissions per year; 1% unsolicited material accepted. Considers unsolicited queries, but not manuscripts. Query with SASE. Responds: 4 weeks to queries. No electronic queries. Multiple submissions accepted. Commission: 15% domestic; 20% foreign. Fees: photocopying, overseas shipping. Editorial services: light editing, not in-depth rewrite or collaboration. "Looking for brands, authorities with a track record." Contact: Daniel Genis.

DONALD MAASS LITERARY AGENCY
157 W. 57th St., Suite 703, New York, NY 10019. 212-757-7755.
E-mail: dmala@mindspring.com.
Description: Fiction only. No unsolicited mss. Query first with SASE. Handles film and TV rights. No reading fee. Contact: Donald Maass.

GINA MACCOBY LITERARY AGENCY
P.O. Box 60, Chappaqua, NY 10514. 914-238-5630.
Description: Fiction and nonfiction for adults and children. Handles film and TV rights. No unsolicited mss.; query first with SASE. No reading fee. Agents in Hollywood and many foreign countries. Foreign rep: A.M. Heath & Co.

CAROL MANN LITERARY AGENCY

55 Fifth Ave., New York, NY 10003. 212-206-5635.

Description: Literary and commercial fiction, no genre fiction, general nonfiction. Sub-agents in Los Angeles and all foreign languages. No unsolicited mss.; query first for submissions. No reading fee. Handles film and TV rights for book clients only. Do not fax or e-mail query. Fiction: send synopsis, and bio; nonfiction, send outline, bio, and sample chapters; SASE required. Contact: Carol Mann.

MANUS ASSOCIATES

417 E. 57th St., Suite 5D, New York, NY 10022. 212-644-8020.
Web site: www.manuslit.com.

Description: General fiction and dramatic nonfiction books, TV and motion picture rights. No unsolicited mss.; query first with synopsis and first 30 pages. No reading fee. Representatives on West Coast and all major foreign countries; handles software only in connection with our books. Contact: Janet Wilkens Manus.

ELISABETH MARTON AGENCY

One Union Square W., Rm. 612, New York, NY 10003-3303.
Description: Plays only. Not considering new work at this time. Commission: 10%. Fees: none. Contact: Tonda Marton.

JED MATTES, INC.

2095 Broadway, #302, New York, NY 10023-2895. 212-595-5228.
E-mail: mattesinc@aol.com.

Description: Fiction and nonfiction. Handles film and TV rights. No unsolicited mss.; query first. No reading fee. Agents in many foreign countries. Foreign reps: Greene & Heaton Ltd. (UK); the Marsh Agency. Contact: Jed Mattes, Fred Morris.

HELMUT MEYER LITERARY AGENCY

330 E. 79th St., New York, NY 10021. 212-288-2421.
Description: Novel-length fiction; trade nonfiction and autobiographic material; foreign rights; motion picture and TV rights. No unsolicited mss.; query first by telephone. Submit outline and sample chapters with SASE. No reading fee. Representatives and agents in all major foreign countries. Contact: Helmut Meyer, Owner.

MICHAEL LARSEN/ELIZABETH POMADA

1029 Jones St., San Francisco, CA 94109. 415-673-0939.
E-mail: larsenpoma@aol.com. Web site: www.larsen-pomada.com.

Description: New voices and fresh ideas in literary/commercial fiction and nonfiction for adults. Ave. 5,000 queries/submission per year; 1% of unsolicited material accepted. Considers unsolicited queries. Unpublished writers welcome. Query (fiction) with first 10 pages, synopsis of finished work, and phone number. SASE required. For nonfiction, read and follow Michael's book *How to Write a Book Proposal,* then send by mail or e-mail the title or promotion plan. Responds in 6-8 weeks to queries, 4-6 weeks to submissions. No electronic queries. Multiple queries okay with notice. Commission: 15% domestic, 20% foreign. Fees: none. Contact: Elizabeth Pomada (fiction), Michael Larsen (nonfiction).

HENRY MORRISON, INC.
Box 235, Bedford Hills, NY 10507. 914-666-3500.
Description: Fiction and nonfiction, screenplays. Handles film and TV rights. Send query and outline first with SASE. No reading fee; fee for mss. copies, galleys, and bound books for foreign and domestic submissions. Contact: Henry Morrison, AAR.

MULTIMEDIA PRODUCT DEVELOPMENT
410 S. Michigan Ave., Suite 724, Chicago, IL 60605. 312-922-3063.
Description: Adult/juvenile fiction and general adult/juvenile nonfiction. Ave. 5,000 queries/submissions per year; little unsolicited material accepted. Considers unsolicited queries, but not manuscripts. Unpublished writers considered. Query with outline, sample pages, bio/resumé, and SASE. Responds: 72 hours queries, 6 weeks submissions. No electronic queries. Multiple queries okay. Commission: 15% domestic; 20% foreign. Fees: copying, foreign phone, fax, postage. Contact: Jane Jordan Browne, President.

JEAN V. NAGGAR LITERARY AGENCY
216 E. 75th St., New York, NY 10021. 212-794-1082.
Description: Strong adult mainstream fiction and nonfiction, from literary to commercial, with a good story told in a distinctive voice. Solid nonfiction; little self-help, no sports or politics. Ave. 6,000 queries/submission per year. Considers unsolicited queries, but not manuscripts. Considers some unpublished writers. Query with outline, SASE, bio, and resumé. No electronic or multiple queries. Responds: 48 hours to queries, several weeks for submissions. Commission: 15% domestic; 20% foreign. Fees: none. Contact: Jean Naggar, Frances Kuffel, Alice Tasman.

RUTH NATHAN AGENCY
53 E. 34th St., Suite 207, New York, NY 10016. 212-481-1185.
Description: Few illustrated books, fine art and decorative arts, biography in those areas, true crime, show business, medieval historical fiction (no fantasy). No unsolicited mss.; query first. Send 1-page outline and sample chapters. Fees: copying, Fed Ex, phone calls. Represented in Los Angeles by Renaissance Agency, and in most major foreign countries. No reading fee.

NEW ENGLAND PUBLISHING ASSOCIATES
P.O. Box 5, Chester, CT 06412. 860-345-7323.
Description: Editorial guidance, representation, and mss. development for book projects. Handles general interest nonfiction and nonfiction for adult market, particularly reference, true crime, biography, women's issues, current events, history, and politics. Query first; submit outline, table of contents with one-paragraph descriptions, author's bio, sample chapters. No reading fee; commissions only. Handle film

and TV rights through Renaissance Agency. Contact: Elizabeth Frost-Knappman, Edward W. Knappman.

BETSY NOLAN LITERARY AGENCY
224 W. 29th St., 15th Fl., New York, NY 10001. 212-967-8200.
E-mail: 74731.2172@compuserve.com.
Description: Adult nonfiction, especially popular psychology, child care, cookbooks, gardening, music books, African-American and Jewish issues. Some literary fiction. No unsolicited mss.; query first. Submit outline, no more than 3 sample chapters, author background. No reading fee. Commission: 15%. Contact: Betsy Nolan.

RICHARD PARKS AGENCY
138 E. 16th St., 5th floor, New York, NY 10003-3561. 212-254-9067.
Description: General trade adult nonfiction; fiction by referral only. Unpublished writers considered. Query with SASE; multiple queries okay if noted as such. No phone calls or faxed queries. Accepts unsolicited queries. Does not accept unsolicited manuscripts. Responds to queries: 2-4 weeks, 4-6 weeks for submissions. No electronic queries. Commission: 15% domestic; 20% foreign. Fees: photocopying. Contact: Richard Parks.

JAMES PETER ASSOCIATES
P.O. Box 670, Tenafly, NJ 07670. 201-568-0760.
E-mail: bertholtje@compuserve.com.
Description: Any adult nonfiction subject. Considers unsolicited queries, but not manuscripts. Unpublished writers considered. Query with outline, sample pages, and bio/resumé, SASE required. Responds: 2-3 weeks to queries. No electronic queries. Accepts multiple queries. Commission: 15% domestic; 20% foreign. Fees: none. Contact: Bert Holtje.

ALISON PICARD, LITERARY AGENT
P.O. Box 2000, Cotuit, MA 02635. 508-477-7192.
E-mail: ajpicard@aol.com.
Description: Adult fiction, nonfiction, and juvenile/young adult, screenplays. No poetry, short stories, or plays. Ave. 500 queries/submissions per year; 5% accepted. Considers unsolicited queries, but not manuscripts. Attach a partial list of clients and sales. Unpublished writers considered. Multiple queries okay. Responds: 1 weeks for queries, 2 months for submissions, SASE required. Accepts electronic queries. Commission: 15%. Fees: none. Contact: Alison Picard.

PINDER LANE & GARON-BROOKE ASSOCIATES
159 W. 53rd St., #14-E, New York, NY 10019. 212-489-0880.
Description: Fiction and nonfiction, film and TV rights. No unsolicited mss.; query first. No reading fee. Submit short synopsis. Representatives in Hollywood and all foreign markets. Contact: Dick Duane, Robert Thixton, Nancy Coffey.

SUSAN ANN PROTTER

110 W. 40th St., Suite 1408, New York, NY 10018. 212-840-0480.
Description: Fiction and nonfiction, health/medicine, how-to, mysteries, thrillers, science, science fiction, true crime, psychology, biography, photography, reference, self-help. No juveniles. No unsolicited mss.; query first with letter and SASE. No queries by phone or fax. No reading fee. Agents in Hollywood and all major foreign countries. Contact: Susan Ann Protter, AAR.

ROBERTA PRYOR, INC.

288 Titicus Rd., N. Salem, NY 10560.
Description: Adult fiction, nonfiction, current affairs, biographies, ecology. Unpublished writers considered. Query with outline, sample pages, and bio/resumé. Multiple queries okay. Commission: 10% domestic; 10% foreign and film. Fees: photocopying, Federal Express. "Some applicants feel a copywriter's approach, i.e., jacket copy come-on, will tickle our fancy. Not so."

RAINES & RAINES

71 Park Ave., Suite 4A, New York, NY 10016. 212-684-5160.
Description: Handles film and TV rights. No unsolicited mss.; query first with 1 page. No reading fee. Agents in all principal countries. Contact: Keith Korman, Joan Raines, Theron Raines.

JODY REIN BOOKS, INC.

7741 S. Ash Ct., Littleton, CO 80122. 303-694-4430.
E-mail: jreinbooks@aol.com.
Description: Commercial and narrative nonfiction, by writers with media contacts, experience, and expertise in their field. Also, outstanding works of literary fiction by award-winning short-story writers. Ave. 1,000 queries/submissions per year; less than 1% unsolicited material accepted. Considers unsolicited queries, but not manuscripts. Unpublished writers considered. Query with SASE. Responds: 2-4 weeks to queries, 4-6 weeks to submissions. No electronic queries. Considers multiple queries. Commission: 15% domestic; 25% foreign. Fees: copying, shipping. Contact: Alexandre Philippe.

RENAISSANCE AGENCY

9220 Sunset Blvd., Suite 302, Los Angeles, CA 90069. 310-858-5365.
E-mail: renaissance@earthlink.net.
Description: Commercial fiction and nonfiction. Handle film and TV rights; novels; plays. No unsolicited mss. Query first. Handles highly recommended manuscripts. Submit outline, sample chapters. No reading fee. 10% commission. Contact: Steven Fisher.

JANE ROTROSEN AGENCY

318 E. 51st St., New York, NY 10022. 212-593-4330.

E-mail: dcleary170@aol.com.

Description: Fiction and nonfiction. No unsolicited mss.; query first. Submit brief description. Handles film and TV rights. No reading fee. 15% commission in USA and Canada. Represented abroad and on the West Coast. Member: Authors Guild. Contact: Donald Cleary, Business Affairs. Contact: Jane Rotrosen, AAR.

PETER RUBIE LITERARY AGENCY

240 W. 35 St., Suite 500, New York, NY 10001. 212-279-1776.

E-mail: prubie@compuserve.com. Web site: www.prlit.com.

Description: Literate fiction and nonfiction, all types, for adults and juveniles. Seeks authors with strong writing backgrounds or recognized experts in their fields. No romance. Ave. 8,000 queries/submissions per year; 5% unsolicited material accepted. Considers unsolicited queries, but not manuscripts. Unpublished writers considered. Query with outline, sample pages, bio, and resumé, SASE required. Responds: 6-8 weeks to queries, 12-14 weeks to submissions. Considers electronic and multiple queries. Commission: 15% domestic; 20% foreign. Fees: copying, shipping. Contact: Peter Rubie, Jennifer Dechiora (children's), June Clark.

RUSSELL & VOLKENING

50 W. 29th St., Suite 7E, New York, NY 10001. 212-684-6050.

Description: General fiction and nonfiction, film and TV rights. No screenplays; no romance or science fiction. Submit outline and 2 sample chapters. No reading fee. Contact: Jennie Dunham, AAR.

SANDUM & ASSOCIATES

144 E. 84th St., New York, NY 10028. 212-737-2011.

Description: Primarily nonfiction and literary fiction. Query with sample pages and bio/resumé. Multiple queries okay. Commission: 15% domestic; 10% when foreign or TV/film subagents are used. New clients by referral only. Contact: Howard E. Sandum, Director.

SHUKAT COMPANY

340 W. 55th St., Suite 1A, New York, NY 10019-3744. 212-582-7614.

E-mail: staff@shukat.com.

Description: Represents writers for theatre, film, TV, book publishing. Personal management of composers, lyricists and directors. No unsolicited mss. Query first. Submit outline and sample chapters. No reading fee. Member AAR. Contact: Scott Shukat, Pat McLaughlin, Maribel Rivas.

ZACHARY SHUSTER LITERARY AGENCY

729 Boylston Street, 5th Floor, Boston, MA 02116. 617-262-2400.

Description: Commercial and literary adult fiction and nonfiction, biography, memoirs, business, psychology, and medicine. Ave. 2,000 queries/submissions per year; accepts less than 1% unsolicited material. Considers unpublished/unproduced writers. Query with sample pages (no more than 30 pages), SASE required. Do not fax queries. Responds: 1-2 months for queries, 2-4 months for submissions. No electronic queries. Multiple queries accepted. Commission: 15% domestic; 20% foreign. Fees: none.

BOBBE SIEGEL, RIGHTS LITERARY AGENT

41 W. 83rd St., New York, NY 10024. 212-877-4985.
Description: Adult fiction and nonfiction. No plays (dramatic or screen), romances, juvenile, humor, or short stories. Considers unsolicited queries, not manuscripts. Unpublished writers considered. Query; multiple queries okay. SASE required. Responds: 2-3 weeks for queries, 2-3 months for submissions. No electronic queries. Commission: 15% domestic; 10% foreign. Fees: none. Editorial services suggested if needed. Contact: Bobbe Siegel.

JACQUELINE SIMENAUER LITERARY AGENCY

P.O. Box 1039, Barnegat, NJ 08005. 941-390-9282.
Description: Nonfiction: medical, popular psychology, how-to/self-help, women's issues, health, alternative health concepts, spirituality, New Age, fitness, diet, nutrition, current issues, true crime, business, celebrities, reference, social issues. Fiction: literary and mainstream commercial. Query with outline, synopsis, and SASE. Multiple queries okay. Commission: 15% domestic; 20% foreign. Queries: required. E-queries: yes. Unsolicited mss: accepts. Contact: Jacqueline Simenauer (nonfiction), Fran Pardi (fiction).

F. JOSEPH SPIELER LITERARY AGENCY

154 W. 57th St., Rm. 135, New York, NY 10019. 212-663-3427.
Description: Adult nonfiction, literary fiction (no romance novels or thrillers). Ave. 1,000 queries/submissions per year; less than 1% unsolicited material accepted. Considers unsolicited queries, but not manuscripts. Unpublished writers considered. Query with outline, SASE (or material will not be returned); no multiple queries or electronic queries. Responds: 2 weeks to queries, 6-8 weeks to submissions. Commission: 15% domestic; 20% foreign. Fees: third-party charges (e.g., messengers, photocopying). Contact: Ada Muellner.

PHILIP G. SPITZER LITERARY AGENCY

50 Talmage Farm Ln., East Hampton, NY 11937. 516-329-3650.
E-mail: ji116981@aol.com. Phillip Spitzer, AAR.
Description: Adult fiction and nonfiction. Query. Literary fiction, suspense/mystery. Film and TV rights. No unsolicited mss.; query first with outline and sample chapters. No reading fee, copying fee. Foreign rights agents in all major markets.

WALES LITERARY AGENCY

108 Hayes St., Seattle, WA 98109. 206-284-7114.
E-mail: waleslit@aol.com.
Description: Mainstream and literary fiction and nonfiction. No unsolicited mss. Query first with SASE. Submit outline and sample chapter. No reading fee. Handles film and TV rights. Contact: Elizabeth Wales, Adrienne Reed.

JOHN A. WARE LITERARY AGENCY

392 Central Park W., New York, NY 10025. 212-866-4733.
Description: Adult fiction and nonfiction. Literate, accessible, noncategory fiction, plus thrillers and mysteries. Nonfiction: biography, history, current affairs, investigative journalism, social criticism, Americana and folklore, "bird's eye view" of phenomena, science, medicine, sports. Unpublished writers considered. Query letter only, with SASE; multiple queries okay. Ave. 2,000 queries per year; 1-2% unsolicited material accepted. Accepts unsolicited queries, but not manuscripts. No telephone or fax queries. Responds in 2 weeks to queries; as arranged to submissions. Accepts electronic queries. Commission: 15% domestic; 20% foreign. Fees: photocopying. Contact: John Ware.

WATKINS/LOOMIS AGENCY

133 E. 35th St., Suite One, New York, NY 10016. 212-532-0080.
Description: Adult literary fiction and nonfiction: biographies, memoirs, and others; cookbooks. No romance, self-help, or novelty books. Ave. 500 queries/submissions per year; 5% unsolicited material accepted. Considers unsolicited queries and manuscripts. Unpublished writers considered. Query letter with first 3 chapters for fiction; query letter plus synopsis for nonfiction; SASE required. We only accept submissions sent via regular mail (hard copy). Responds: 1 week for queries and 6 weeks for submissions. No electronic or multiple queries. Fees: none. Contact: Katherine Fausset.

SANDRA WATT & ASSOCIATES

1750 N. Sierra Bonita, Los Angeles, CA 90046. 323-851-1021.
E-mail: rondvart.
Description: Looking for well-written adult fiction and nonfiction. Ave. 200 queries/submissions per year; 2% of unsolicited material accepted. Accepts unsolicited manuscripts/not queries. Unpublished writers sometimes considered. Query with bio/resumé; SASE required. Responds: 1 weeks to queries, 3 weeks to submissions. No electronic queries. Accepts multiple queries. Commission: 15% domestic and foreign. Fees: none. Contact: Sandra Watt.

WIESER & WIESER

118 E. 25th St.,7th Fl., New York, NY 10010. 212-260-0860.
Description: Specializes in trade and mass market adult fiction and nonfiction books. Unpublished writers considered. Query with outline and bio/resumé. Submit

outline, 100 pages, SASE; no reading fee. Commission: 15%. Fees: photocopying, shipping. Contact: Olga Wieser, George Wieser, Jake Elwell.

WITHERSPOON ASSOCIATES
235 E. 31st St., New York, NY 10016. 212-889-8626.
Description: Adult fiction and nonfiction. Unpublished writers considered. Query with sample pages; no multiple queries. Handles film and TV. Commission: 15%. Fees: none. Contact: Kimberly Witherspoon.

ANN WRIGHT REPRESENTATIVES
165 W. 46th St., Suite 1105, New York, NY 10036-2501. 212-764-6770.
E-mail: danwrightlit@aol.com.
Description: Fiction and screenplays with strong film potential, varied subjects. Considers only queries or referrals, with SASE. Ave. 6,000 queries/submissions per year; 1-2% unsolicited material accepted. Considers unsolicited queries, but not manuscripts. Unpublished writers considered; specializes in encouraging new writers. Responds: 1-2 weeks to queries, 4-8 weeks for submissions. No electronic queries. Accepts multiple queries (agency only). Commission: 10% Film/TV; 10%-20% literary. Fees: photocopying, shipping. "Always open to new writers of screen material and to new authors of fiction with strong film potential." Contact: Dan Wright.

WRITERS HOUSE
21 W. 26th St., New York, NY 10010. 212-685-2400.
Description: Represents trade books of all types, fiction and nonfiction, including all rights; handles film and TV rights. No screenplays, teleplays, or software. Must send query first. No reading fee. Contact: Simon Lipskar.

WRITERS' PRODUCTIONS
P.O. Box 630, Westport, CT 06881. 203-227-8199.
Description: Literary quality fiction and nonfiction. Ave. 1,500 queries/submissions per year; not accepting new clients at this time. Query with SASE. Responds: 1 week to 1 month. No electronic queries. Commission: 15% domestic; 25% foreign, dramatic, multimedia, software sales, licensing, and merchandising. Contact: David L. Meth.

THE WRITERS SHOP
101 Fifth Ave., New York, NY 10003-1008. 212-255-6515.
Description: Literary adult fiction and nonfiction. Commercial fiction and nonfiction. Ave. 2,500 queries/submissions per year; 1% unsolicited material accepted. Considers unsolicited queries, but not manuscripts. Query with outline, sample pages, bio/resumé, and SASE. Multiple queries accepted. No electronic queries. Responds: 2 weeks. Commission: 15% domestic; 20% foreign. Fees: photocopying. "No fantasy, no illustrated work." Contact: Jennifer Rudolph Walsh, Jay Mandel.

SUSAN ZECKENDORF ASSOCIATES

171 W. 57th St., New York, NY 10019. 212-245-2928.
Description: Commercial fiction and nonfiction. Mysteries, thrillers, literary fiction, science, biography, health, parenting, social history, classical music. Ave. 3,000 queries/submissions per year; 2% of unsolicited material accepted. Considers unsolicited queries, but not manuscripts. Unpublished writers considered. Query with outline and bio/resumé, SASE required. Responds: 1 week to queries, 2 weeks to submissions. No electronic queries. Multiple queries accepted. Commission: 15% domestic; 20% foreign. Fees: photocopying. Offers some editorial suggestions. "We're a small agency providing individual attention." Contact: Susan Zeck.

STATE ARTS COUNCILS

State arts councils are a resource frequently overlooked by writers, but they offer useful services that can boost a writer's career. First of all, many offer cash awards of various sorts. One type of award is a "project" grant; that is, a specific award to complete a specified piece of work. These are awarded based on details of a proposal the individual author or a sponsoring arts group submits. The criteria for project grants are the quality of writing (based on sample poems or pages of fiction or nonfiction submitted), the clarity of the project, and some indication of community support, such as a letter of support from a community group. For instance, a project to publish an anthology of multicultural writers from your state might qualify for a grant. Other projects can be as diverse and creative as printing poems on placards to place in public transit vehicles, or on billboards or in other nontraditional venues.

The other type of cash support is a fellowship award. Many states offer awards for writers based on the general quality of their work. There is no "project" requirement; the money awarded is simply to further the author's career and is "unrestricted"; that is, it may be used for any purpose at all.

Arts councils have printed or online guidelines that give all the application information for grants and fellowships.

The review process often involves peer groups of writers, creative artists, and arts administrators from around the state. The important thing to know is that these panels constantly rotate their membership. Review is somewhat subjective; a panel that hated your work one year may love it the next. Don't give up applying for fellowships, in particular—which are the easiest to apply for—just because you did not win in the first year you applied. Keep sending in your 1-page form and 10 best poems (or whatever is requested) each year. You may be pleasantly surprised one year to be selected for a writing fellowship award.

For project grants, after you get a rough idea of your desired project, you may wish to call the arts council to talk briefly with a grants officer. This person may be able to help you think through some key elements of your project that will need to be covered in a proposal. Many arts councils also offer regional grants-writing workshops and sometimes fund local agencies that in turn offer awards to authors.

Finally, arts councils have a variety of other services, such as newsletters which publish information on regional and national prize competitions, requests for submissions for regional collections of writing, and so on.

All writers should contact their state agencies and get on their mailing list, to keep abreast of these valuable services.

ALABAMA STATE COUNCIL ON THE ARTS
201 Monroe St., Suite 110, Montgomery, AL 36130. 334-242-4076.
E-mail: staff@arts.state.al.us. Web site: staff@arts.state.al.us.
Description: Newsletter, workshops, conferences, and grants.
Contact: Albert B. Head, Director.

ALASKA STATE COUNCIL ON THE ARTS
411 W. 4th Ave., Suite 1E, Anchorage, AK 99501-2343. 907-267-6610.
E-mail: info@aksca.org. Web site: www.aksca.org. Helen Howarth, Director.
Description: Workshops, conferences, grants, roster, and newsletter.
Contact: Shannon Planchon.

ARIZONA COMMISSION ON THE ARTS
417 W. Roosevelt, Phoenix, AZ 85003. 602-255-5882.
E-mail: general@ArizonaArts.org. Web site: http://az.arts.asu.edu/artscomm.
Description: Newsletter, workshops, conference, grants, and fellowships.
Contact: Shelley Cohn, Public Information/Literature Director.

ARKANSAS ARTS COUNCIL
1500 Tower Bldg., 323 Center St., Little Rock, AR 72201. 501-324-9766.
E-mail: info@dah.state.ar.us. Web site: www.arkansasarts.com.
Description: Various programs for writers. See web site for details.
Contact: James E. Mitchell, Executive Director.

CALIFORNIA ARTS COUNCIL
1300 I St., Suite 930, Sacramento, CA 95814. 303-894-2617.
E-mail: cac@cwo.com. Web site: www.cac.ca.gov.
Description: Programs for writers. See web site for details.
Contact: Adam Gottlieb, Executive Director.

COLORADO COUNCIL ON THE ARTS
750 Pennsylvania St., Denver, CO 80203-3699. 303-894-2617.
E-mail: coloarts@state.co.us. Web site: www.coloarts.state.co.us.
Description: Newsletter and grants.
Contact: Nancy Sullivan, Fran Holden, Executive Director.

COMPAS: WRITERS & ARTISTS IN THE SCHOOLS
304 Landmark Center, 75 W. Fifth St., St. Paul, MN 55102. 651-292-3254.
Web site: www.compas.org.
Description: Various artist's and writer's programs. See web site for details.
Contact: Daniel Gabriel, Director.

CONNECTICUT COMMISSION ON THE ARTS
1 Financial Plaza, Hartford, CT 06103. 860-566-4770.
Description: Programs for writers. Write for more information.
Contact: John Ostrout, Executive Director.

DELAWARE DIVISION OF THE ARTS
Carvel State Bldg., 820 N. French St., Wilmington, DE 19801. 302-577-8278.
Web site: www.artsdel.org.

Description: See web site for details on the various programs.
Contact: Kristin Pleasanton, Art and Artist Services Coordinator.

FLORIDA ARTS COUNCIL
The Capitol, Tallahassee, FL 32399-0250.
Web site: www.dos.state.fl.us.
Description: Programs of all sorts; see web site for more information.
Contact: Ms. Peg Richardson, Director.

GEORGIA COUNCIL FOR THE ARTS
260 14th St. N.W., Suite 401, Atlanta, GA 30318. 404-685-2787.
Rick George, Interim Executive Director.
Description: Programs for writers.
Contact: Ann Davis, Grants Manager, Literature.

HAWAII STATE FOUNDATION ON CULTURE AND THE ARTS
44 Merchant St., Honolulu, HI 96813. 808-586-0300.
E-mail: sfca@sfca.state.hi.us. Web site: www.state.hi.us/sfca.
Description: A variety of programs available. See web site for details.

IDAHO COMMISSION ON THE ARTS
Box 83720, Boise, ID 83720-0008. 208-334-2119.
E-mail: cconley@ica.state.id.us. Web site: www2.state.id.us/arts.
Description: Variety of programs. Visit web site for more information.
Contact: Cort Conley, Director.

ILLINOIS ARTS COUNCIL
James R. Thompson Center, 100 W. Randolph, Suite 10-500, Chicago, IL 60601.
312-814-6750. E-mail: Susan@arts.state.il.us or info@arts.state.il.us.
Web site: www.state.il.us/agency/iac.
Description: Annual Fellowships in Poetry and Prose (Deadline, Dec. 1). Literary
Arts Award for authors published in nonprofit Illinois literary publications (Deadline,
March 1). Newsletter, workshops, grants, and prizes.
Contact: Rhoda Pierce, Director of Lit. Programs.

INDIANA ARTS COMMISSION
402 W. Washington St., Rm. 072, Indianapolis, IN 46204-2741. 317-232-1268.
Web site: www.state.in.us\iac\.
Description: Programs for writers and others. See web site for details.
Contact: Dorothy Ilgen, Executive Director.

INSTITUTO DE CULTURA PUERTORRIQUENA
P.O. Box 9024184, San Juan, PR 00902-4184. 787-724-3210.
E-mail: apoyo@icp.prstar.net. Web site: www.icp.prstar.net/programas/apoyo.
Description: Newsletter, workshops, conferences, grants, and prizes.

IOWA ARTS COUNCIL

600 E. Locust, Des Moines, IA 50319-0290. 515-282-6500.
Description: Programs for writers, artists, and others. Write for details.
Contact: Stephen Poole, Director.

KANSAS ARTS COMMISSION

700 S.W. Jackson, Suite 1004, Topeka, KS 66603-3761. 785-296-3335.
E-mail: KAC@arts.state.KS.US.
Web site: http://arts.state.KS.US.
Description: See web site for more information on specific programs.
Contact: Robert T. Burtch, Editor.

KENTUCKY ARTS COUNCIL

Old Capitol Annex, 300 West Broadway, Frankfort, KY 40601-1950. 502-564-3757.
E-mail: kyarts@mail.state.ky.us. Web site: www.kyarts.org.
Description: Various programs for writers. See web site for more information.
Contact: Gerri Combs, Executive Director.

LOUISIANA DIVISION OF THE ARTS

Box 44247, Baton Rouge, LA 70804. 225-342-8180.
E-mail: jborders@crt.state.la.us. Web site: www.crt.state.la.us.
Description: Workshops, conference, grants, and newsletter.
Contact: James Borders, Executive Director.

MAINE ARTS COMMISSION

25 State House Station, 55 Capitol Street, Augusta, ME 04333-0025. 207-287-2724.
E-mail: kathy.jones@state.me.us. Web site: www.mainearts.com.
Description: Newsletter, workshops, and grants.
Contact: Alden C. Wilson, Director.

MARYLAND STATE ARTS COUNCIL

175 W. Ostend St., Suite E, Baltimore, MD 21230. 410-767-6450.
E-mail: rturner@mdbusiness.state.md.us. Web site: www.msac.org.
Description: Literature Program: Grants, prizes, newsletter.
Contact: James Backas, Director.

MASSACHUSETTS CULTURAL COUNCIL

10 St. James Avenue, 3rd Floor, Boston, MA 02116. 617-727-3668.
E-mail: mcc@art.state.ma.us. Web site: www.massculturalcouncil.org.
Mary Kelley, Director.
Description: Newsletter and grants.
Contact: Charles Coe, Literature Coordinator.

MICHIGAN COUNCIL FOR ARTS AND CULTURAL AFFAIRS
525 W. Ottawa, P.O. Box 30705, Lansing, MI 48909-8205. 517-241-4011.
Web site: www.cis.state.mi.us.
Description: Various programs available. See web site for details.
Contact: Betty Boone, Executive Director.

MINNESOTA STATE ARTS BOARD
Park Square Court, 400 Sibley St., Suite 200, St. Paul, MN 55101-1928.
651-215-1600, 800-8MN-ARTS.
E-mail: msab@arts.state.mn.us. Web site: www.arts.state.mn.us.
Robert Booker, Executive Director.
Description: Newsletter, workshops, grants.
Contact: Amy Frimpong, Artist Assistance Program Associate.

MISSISSIPPI ARTS COMMISSION
239 N. Lamar St., Suite 207, Jackson, MS 39201. 601-359-6030.
Web site: www.arts.state.ms.us.
Description: Various programs for writers. See web site for information.
Contact: Lynn Adams Wilkins, Community Arts Director.

MISSOURI ARTS COUNCIL
Wainwright Office Complex, 111 N. 7th St., Suite 105, St. Louis, MO 63101-2188.
314-340-6845.
E-mail: dbruns@mail.state.mo.us. Web site: www.missouriartscouncil.org.
Description: Newsletter, conferences, grants.
Contact: Norce Boyd, Program Specialist, Music and Literature.

MONTANA ARTS COUNCIL
P.O. Box 202201, Helena, MT 59620-2201. 406-444-6430.
Web site: www.art.state.mt.us.
Description: Programs for writers and artists. See the web site for more information.
Contact: Arlynn Fishbaugh, Executive Director.

NEBRASKA ARTS COUNCIL
3838 Davenport St., Omaha, NE 68131-2329. 402-595-2122.
Web site: www.nebraskaartscouncil.org.
Description: Variety of programs. See web site for details.
Contact: Jennifer Severin, Executive Director.

NEVADA ARTS COUNCIL
716 N. Carson Street, Suite A, Carson City, NV 89703. 775-687-6680.
Web site: www.dmla.clan.lib.nv.us.
Description: Workshops, conferences, newsletter, and grants.
Contact: Susan Boskoff, Executive Director.

NEW HAMPSHIRE STATE COUNCIL ON THE ARTS

Phenix Hall, 40 N. Main St., Concord, NH 03301-4974. 603-271-2789.
E-mail: cobrian@nharts.state.nh.us. Web site: www.state.nh.us/nharts.
Rebecca Lawrence, Director.
Description: Newsletter, workshops, conference, grants, and prizes.
Contact: Catherine O'Brian, Artist Services Coordinator.

NEW JERSEY STATE COUNCIL ON THE ARTS

Artist Services, P.O. Box 306, Trenton, NJ 08625. 609-292-6130.
E-mail: Beth@arts.sos.state.nj.us. Web site: www.njartscouncil.org.
Description: Workshops, newsletter, conferences, grants.
Contact: Beth Vogel, Program Officer.

NEW MEXICO ARTS

P.O. Box 1450, Santa Fe, NM 8750187501. 505-827-6490.
E-mail: rforrest@oca.state.nm.us.
Description: Several programs.
Contact: Randy Forrester, Program Coordinator.

NEW YORK STATE COUNCIL ON THE ARTS

915 Broadway, New York, NY 10010. 212-387-7022.
E-mail: KMASTERSON@NYSCA.org. Web site: www.nysca.org.
Description: Variety of programs. See web site for more information.
Contact: Kathleen Masterson, Director, Literature Program.

NORTH CAROLINA ARTS COUNCIL

Dept. of Cultural Resources, Raleigh, NC 27699-4632. 919-733-2111 .
E-mail: debbie.mcgill@ncmail.net. Web site: www.ncarts.org.
Description: Newsletter, grants.
Contact: Deborah McGill, Literature Director.

NORTH DAKOTA COUNCIL ON THE ARTS

418 E. Broadway, Suite 70, Bismarck, ND 58501-4086. 701-328-3954.
E-mail: comserv@state.nd.us. Web site: www.discovernd.com/arts.
Description: Newsletter and grants.
Contact: Janine Webb, Director.

OHIO ARTS COUNCIL

727 E. Main St., Columbus, OH 43205-1796. 405-521-2931.
Web site: www.oac.state.oh.us.
Description: Visit the web site for information on writer's programs.
Contact: Bob Fox, Literature Program Coordinator.

OKLAHOMA ARTS COUNCIL

P.O. Box 52001-2001, Oklahoma City, OK 73152-2001. 405-521-2931.

E-mail: jennifer@arts.state.ok.us. Web site: www.state.ok.us/~arts.
Betty Price, Executive Director.
Description: Workshops, conferences, newsletters, grants.
Contact: Jennifer James.

OREGON ARTS COMMISSION
775 Summer St. N.E., Salem, OR 97310. 503-986-0082.
E-mail: oregon.artscomm@state.or.us. Web site: http://art.econ.state.or.us.
Description: Various programs. Visit the web site for details.
Contact: Assistant Director.

PENNSYLVANIA COUNCIL ON THE ARTS
Room 216, Finance Bldg., Harrisburg, PA 17120. 717-787-6883.
Web site: http://artsnet.org/pca/.
Description: See web site for more information.
Contact: James Woland, Literature Program.

RHODE ISLAND STATE COUNCIL ON THE ARTS
83 Park Street, 6th Floor, Providence, RI 02903-1037. 401-222-3880.
E-mail: randy@risca.state.ri.us. Web site: www.risca.state.ri.us.
Randall Rosenbaum, Executive Director.
Description: Workshops and grants.
Contact: Karolye Cunha.

SOUTH CAROLINA ARTS COMMISSION
1800 Gervais St., Columbia, SC 29201. 803-734-8696.
E-mail: goldstsa@arts.state.sc.us. Web site: www.state.sc.us/arts.
Description: Festivals, workshops and an artist's directory.
Contact: Sara June Goldstein, Director, Literary Arts Program.

SOUTH DAKOTA ARTS COUNCIL
800 Governors Dr., Pierre, SD 57501-2294. 605-773-3131.
E-mail: sdac@stlib.state.sd.us. Web site: www.sdarts.org.
Description: Workshops, conferences, grants, and newsletter.
Contact: Dennis Holub, Executive Director.

TENNESSEE ARTS COMMISSION
401 Charlotte Ave., Nashville, TN 37243-078037243-0780. 615-741-1701.
Web site: www.arts.state.tn.us.
Description: Variety of programs, grants. See web site for details.
Contact: Literary Arts Director.

TEXAS COMMISSION ON THE ARTS
P.O. Box 13406, Austin, TX 78711-3406. 512-463-5535.
E-mail: front.desk@arts.state.tx.us. Web site: www.arts.state.tx.us.

Description: Newsletter, workshops, conferences, grants.
Contact: Gaye Greever McElwain, Director of Marketing.

UTAH ARTS COUNCIL

617 E. South Temple, Salt Lake , UT 84102-1177. 801-236-7553.
Description: Programs for artists and writers. Write for more information.
Contact: Guy Lebeda, Literary Coordinator.

VERMONT ARTS COUNCIL

136 State St., Drawer 33, Montpelier, VT 05633-6001. 802-828-3291.
E-mail: info@arts.vca.state.vt.us. Web site: www.vermontartscouncil.org.
Description: Workshops, newsletter, conferences, grants.
Contact: Alexander L. Aldrich, Director of Artist Programs.

VIRGINIA COMMISSION FOR THE ARTS

223 Governor St., Lewis House, 2nd Fl, Richmond, VA 23219-2010. 804-225-3132.
E-mail: pbaggett.arts@state.va.us. Web site: www.artswire.org/vacomm.
Description: Workshops, conferences, and grants.
Contact: Peggy J. Baggett, Executive Director.

WASHINGTON STATE ARTS COMMISSION

234 E. 8th Ave., P.O. Box 42675, Olympia, WA 98504-2675. 360-586-2421.
E-mail: bitsyb@wsac.wa.gov. Web site: www.arts.wa.gov.
Kris Tucker, Director.
Description: Newsletter, workshops, grants (for nonprofits only, no individuals).
Contact: Bitsy Bidwell, Community Arts Development Manager.

WEST VIRGINIA DIVISION OF CULTURE & HISTORY

The Cultural Center, Capitol Complex, 1900 Kanawha Blvd. E., Charleston, WV
25305-0300. 304-558-0220.
E-mail: debbie.haught@wvculture.org. Web site: www.wvculture.org.
Description: Various programs. See web site for details.

WISCONSIN ARTS BOARD

101 E. Wilson St., 1st Floor, Madison, WI 53702. 608-266-0190.
E-mail: artsboard@arts.state.wi.us. Web site: www.arts.state.wi.us.
George Tzougros, Executive Director.
Description: Newsletter, workshops, conferences, and grants.
Contact: Mark Fraire.

WYOMING ARTS COUNCIL

2320 Capitol Ave., Cheyenne, WY 82002. 307-777-7742.
E-mail: mshay@missc.state.wy.us.
Description: Programs for artists and writers.
Contact: Michael Shay, Literature Program Manager.

COLONIES

Writers' colonies offer solitude and freedom from everyday distractions so that writers can concentrate on their work. Though some colonies are quite small, with space for just three or four writers at a time, others can provide accommodations for as many as thirty or forty. The length of a residency may vary, too, from a couple of weeks to five or six months. These programs have strict admissions policies, and writers must submit a formal application or letter of intent, a resumé, writing samples, and letters of recommendation. As an alternative to the traditional writers' colony, a few of the organizations listed offer writing rooms for writers who live nearby. Write for application information first, enclosing a stamped, self-addressed envelope. Residency fees are subject to change.

EDWARD F. ALBEE FOUNDATION

14 Harrison St., New York, NY 10013. 212-266-2020.
Mr. David Briggs, Secretary.
Description: On Long Island, "The Barn" (William Flanagan Memorial Creative Persons Center), offers 1-month residences to 12 writers each season, from June 1 to October 1. Criteria: talent and need. Applications (writing samples, project description, and resumé) are accepted January 1-April 1. No fees, but residents are responsible for their own food and travel expenses.

ALTOS DE CHAVÓN

2 W. 13th St., Rm. 707, New York, NY 10011. 212-229-5370.
Stephen D. Kaplan, Arts/Education Director.
Description: A nonprofit center for the arts in the Dominican Republic, for design innovation, international creative exchange, and the promotion of Dominican culture. Residencies average 12 weeks, offering emerging or established artists a chance to live and work in a setting of architectural and natural beauty. Note: the library is oriented toward the design profession; the apartments also accommodate university students. Two to three writers are chosen each year. Fee is $350/month for apartment with kitchenette; linen and cleaning services extra. Send a letter of interest, writing sample, and resumé. Deadline: July 15.

MARY ANDERSON CENTER FOR THE ARTS

101 St. Francis Dr., Mount St. Francis, IN 47146. 812-923-8602.
E-mail: maca@iglou.com.
Debra Carmody, Executive Director.
Description: Artists' residency and retreat is on the grounds of a Franciscan friary with 400 acres of rolling hills and woods. Space for 7 residents at a time, including private rooms, working space, and a visual artists' studio; meals are provided. Residencies of 1 week to 3 months, granted based on project proposal and artist's body of work; apply year-round (with $15 application fee). Daily fee: $30/day, can be reduced in some cases.

ATLANTIC CENTER FOR THE ARTS

1414 Art Center Ave., New Smyrna Beach, FL 32168. 904-427-6975, 800-393-6975. E-mail: program@atlanticcenterforthearts.org. Web site: www.atlantic-centerarts.org. Rachel Ward, Program Director.

Description: The center is on central Florida's east coast, with 67 acres of pristine land on tidal estuary. All buildings, connected by wooden walkways, are handicapped-accessible and air-conditioned. Offers unique environment for sharing ideas, learning, and collaborating on interdisciplinary projects. Master artists meet with talented artists for readings and critiques, with time for individual work. Residencies: 1-3 weeks. Fees: $100/week tuition, $25/day for housing (off-site, tuition-only plans available); financial aid is limited. Application deadlines vary.

BLUE MOUNTAIN CENTER

Blue Mountain Lake, NY 12812-0109. 518-352-7391. E-mail: bmcl@telenet.net. Harriet Barlow, Director.

Description: Hosts month-long residencies for artists and writers, mid-June to late October. For established fiction and nonfiction writers, poets, and playwrights whose work shows social and ecological concern (14 residents/per session). No fees for residency. No application form; send a brief biographical sketch, a plan for work at Blue Mountain, 5-10 slides or a writing sample (any length), indication of preference for early summer, late summer, or fall residence, and a $20 application fee (Attn: Admissions Committee). Contact: Ben Strader.

BYRDCLIFFE ARTS COLONY

Artists' Residency Program, Woodstock Guild, 34 Tinker St., Woodstock, NY 12498. 845-679-2079. E-mail: wguild@ulster.net. Web site: www.woodstockguild.org.

Description: The Villetta Inn, a 400-acre arts colony, offers private studios and separate bedrooms, a communal kitchen, and a peaceful environment for fiction writers, poets, playwrights, and visual artists. One-month residencies offered June to September. Fee: $500 per month, $5 application fee. Submit application, resumé, writing sample, and 2 letters of recommendation. Deadline: April 1. Send SASE for application. Contact: Catherine Callahan, Director.

CAMARGO FOUNDATION

125 Park Square Ct., 400 Sibley St., St. Paul, MN 55101-1982. 651-290-2237. E-mail: camargo@jeromefoln.org. Michael Pritina, Director.

Description: Maintains a center of studies in France for 9 scholars and graduate students each semester to pursue projects in humanities and social sciences on France and Francophone culture. Also, one artist, one composer, and one writer accepted each semester. Offers furnished apartments and a reference library in city of Cassis. Research should be at advanced stage and not require resources unavailable in Marseilles-Aix-Cassis region. Send application form, curriculum vitae, 3 letters of recommendation, and project description. Writers, artists, and composers must send work samples. Deadline: February 1. Contact: William Reichard.

CENTRUM

P.O. Box 1158, Port Townsend, WA 98368. 360-385-3102.
E-mail: ted@centrum.org. Web site: www.centrum.org.
Description: For writers and other creative artists, 1-week to 2-month residencies, September to May. Applicants selected by a peer jury receive free housing. Some stipends ($300 or less) available for Seattle area artists. Previous residents may return on a space-available basis for a rental fee. Deadline: August 19. Application fee, $10. Contact: Ted Senecal, Program Coordinator.

DJERASSI RESIDENT ARTISTS PROGRAM

2325 Bear Gulch Rd., Woodside, CA 94062. 650-747-1250.
E-mail: drap@djerassi.org. Web site: www.djerassi.org.
Description: Offers 4-week residencies, at no cost, to artists in literature (prose, poetry, drama, playwrights/screenwriters), choreography, music composition, visual arts, and media arts/new genres. Application fee: $25. Located in spectacular rural setting in Santa Cruz Mountains, 1 hour south of San Francisco. Postmark deadline for applications: February 15, for residency the following year. For application, send SASE, or visit web site.

DORLAND MOUNTAIN ARTS COLONY

P.O. Box 6, Temecula, CA 92593. 909-302-3837.
E-mail: dorland@ez2.net. Web site: www.ez2.net/dorland/.
Description: Dorland is a nature preserve and "retreat for creative people" in the Palomar Mountains of Southern California. "Without electricity, residents find a new, natural rhythm for their work." Novelists, playwrights, poets, nonfiction writers, composers, and visual artists are welcomed for residencies of 1-2 months. Fee: $300/month includes cottage, fuel, and firewood. Send SASE for application. Deadlines: March 1 and September 1. Contact: Karen Parrott, Director.

DORSET COLONY HOUSE

Box 510, Dorset, VT 05251. 802-867-2223.
E-mail: theatre@sover.net. Web site: www.theatredirectories.com.
John Nassivera, Director.
Description: Writers and playwrights (up to 8 at a time) are offered low-cost rooms with kitchen facilities at historic Colony House, for residencies of 2-3 weeks in the fall and spring. Applications accepted year-round. Fee: $120/week; financial aid is limited. For details, send SASE. Contact: Barbara Ax.

FINE ARTS WORK CENTER IN PROVINCETOWN

24 Pearl St., Provincetown, MA 02657. 508-487-9960.
E-mail: fawc@capecod.net. Web site: www.fawc.org.
Hunter O'Hanian, Executive Director.
Description: Fellowships (living and studio space, monthly stipends) offered at Fine Arts Work Center on Cape Cod, for fiction writers and poets to work independently. Residency are for 7 months (Oct. 1 to May 1) for 10 writers and 10 visual artists; no fees. Deadline: Dec. 1 for writers, Feb. 1 for visual artists. Send SASE for details. Contact: Melanie Braverman.

GLENESSENCE WRITERS COLONY

1447 West Ward Ave., Ridgecrest, CA 93555. 760-446-5894.
Description: Glenessence is a luxury villa in the Upper Mojave Desert (private rooms with bath, pool, spa, courtyard, shared kitchen, fitness center, and library). Children, pets, and smoking prohibited. Residencies for $565/month; meals not provided. Reservations on a first-come basis. Seasonal (January through May). Contact: Allison Swift, Director.

TYRONE GUTHRIE CENTRE

Annaghmakerrig, Newbliss, County Monaghan, Ireland. 353-47-54003.
E-mail: thetgc@indigo.ie. Web site: www.tyroneguthrie.ie.
Sheila Pratsche, Director.
Description: On a 450-acre forested estate, the center offers peace and seclusion to writers and other artists to allow them to work. All art forms represented. Residencies of 1-3 months throughout the year. Fee: £2,000/month; financial assistance available to Irish citizens only. Some longer-term self-catering houses in old farmyard are available at £300/week. Writers chosen based on c.v., samples of published work, and outline of intended project. Applications accepted year-round. Contact: Regina Doyle.

THE HAMBIDGE CENTER

P.O. Box 339, Rabun Gap, GA 30568. 706-746-5718.
E-mail: center@hambidge.org. Web site: www.hambidge.org.
Description: The center is on 600 pristine acres of quiet woods in north Georgia mountains. Eight private cottages available. All fellowships partially underwritten, residents contribute $125/week. Residencies of 2-8 weeks, year-round, for serious artists in all disciplines. Send SASE for application. Deadlines: Nov. 1 for May to October; May 1 for November to April.

HEADLANDS CENTER FOR THE ARTS

944 Fort Barry, Sausalito, CA 94965. 415-331-2787.
Description: On 13,000 acres of open coastal space, programs are available to residents of Ohio, New Jersey, North Carolina, and California. Application requirements vary by state. Deadline: June. Decisions announced October for residencies beginning February. No residency or application fees. Send SASE for details.

HEDGEBROOK

2197 E. Millman Rd., Langley, WA 98260. 360-321-4786.
E-mail: hedgebrk@whidbey.com. Web site: www.hedgebrook.org.
Linda Bowers, Director.
Description: Provides women writers, published or not, of all ages and from all cultural backgrounds, with a natural place to work. The retreat is on 33 acres of farmland and woods on Whidbey Island in Washington State. Each writer has her own cottage (6 available), with electricity and woodstove. A bathhouse serves all 6 cottages. Lunch brought to cottage in a basket; communal dinner. Limited travel scholarships available. Residencies: 1 week to 2 months. Stipend available for low income and 55 or older (without 4-year college degree). Contact: Denise Lee.

KALANI OCEANSIDE RETREAT CENTER

Artist-in-Residence Program
RR2, Box 4500 Beach Road, Pahoa, HI 96778. 808-965-7828, 800-800-6886.
E-mail: kalani@kalani.com. Web site: www.kalani.com.
Richard Koob, Program Coordinator.
Description: In a rural coastal setting of 113 botanical acres, Kalani Oceanside Retreat hosts and sponsors educational programs to bring together creative people from around the world in culturally and artistically stimulating environment. Housing with bathrooms, b/w darkroom, various studio spaces for performing and visual artists and writers. Residencies: 2 weeks to 2 months, available year-round. Fees: $50 to $105/day, meals available at extra fee. Applications accepted year-round. Contact: Rachel Gonzalez, G.M.

THE MACDOWELL COLONY

100 High St., Peterborough, NH 03458. 603-924-3886.
Description: Studios, room, and board for writers to work in a woodland setting. Stipend available, up to $1,000 depending on financial need. Selection is competitive. Apply by Jan. 15 for May through August; by April 15 for September through December; by Sept. 15 for January through April. Residencies: up to 8 weeks; 80-90 writers accepted each year. Send SASE for application. Contact: Pat Dodge, Admissions Coordinator.

JENNY McKEAN MOORE WRITER-IN-WASHINGTON

Dept. of English, The George Washington University, Washington, DC 20052.
E-mail: Faymos@gwu.edu.
Description: Fellowship for a writer to teach 2 paid semesters (salary: $48,000) at George Washington University. Teaching duties include a fiction workshop each semester for students from metropolitan community who may have had little formal education; and one class each semester for university students. Fiction and poetry alternate years. To apply, send letter, noting publications and other projects, extent of teaching experience, and other qualifications. Application must include resumé and 15-25 sample pages of your work. Deadline: Nov. 15.
Contact: Prof. Faye Moskowitz.

THE MILLAY COLONY FOR THE ARTS

444 East Hill Rd., P.O. Box 3, Austerlitz, NY 12017-0003. 518-392-3103.
E-mail: giles@millaycolony.org. Web site: www.millaycolony.org.
Description: At Steepletop (former home of Edna St. Vincent Millay), writers are provided studios, universally accessible living quarters, and meals at no cost. Residencies: 1 month. Applications reviewed by independent jurors, selection based on talent. Send for applications, or e-mail: application@millaycolony.org. Contact: Gail Giles, Director of Admissions.

MILLETT FARM: AN ART COLONY FOR WOMEN

295 Bowery, New York, NY 10003.
Description: Summer residencies for women writers and visual artists at picturesque tree farm in rural New York. For housing, all residents contribute 5 hours of work each weekday morning and $70/week for meals. Preference to writers who can stay all summer or at least 6 weeks. Also, 1-week master class ($500) available with Kate Millett. For details, send SASE. Contact: Kate Millett, Director.

MOLASSES POND WRITERS' RETREAT AND WORKSHOP

RR 1, Box 85C, Milbridge, ME 04658. 207-546-2506.
Description: Led by published authors who teach writing at University of New Hampshire, this 1-week workshop is held in June, with time for writing, as well as manuscript critique and writing classes. Up to 10 writers stay in a colonial farmhouse with private bed/work rooms for each, common areas for meals and classes. Fee: $450 (lodging, meals, and tuition). Applicants must be serious about their work. No children's literature or poetry. Submit statement of purpose and 15-20 pages of fiction or nonfiction between February 15 and March 1. Contact: Martha Barron Barrett and Sue Wheeler, Coordinators.

MONTANA ARTISTS REFUGE

P.O. Box 8, Basin, MT 59631. 406-225-3500.
E-mail: mtrefuge@pop.mcn.net. Web site: www.montanartistsrefuge.org.
Jennifer Pryor, Coordinator.
Description: In a rural environment, this artist nonresidency program offers living and studio space to self-directed artists, all disciplines. Writers can work with other artists or in solitude. Residencies, with kitchen facilities and private phone, from 3 months to 1 year; with rents $395-$550/month. One soundproof apartment available for writer or musician/composer. Financial aid available. Send SASE for details. Contact: Joy Lewis, Board President.

NEW YORK MILLS ARTS RETREAT
AND REGIONAL CULTURAL CENTER

24 N. Main Ave., New York Mills, MN 56567. 218-385-3339.
E-mail: nymills@uslink.net. Web site: www.kulcher.org.
Kent Scheer, Retreat Coordinator.
Description: For 5-7 emerging artists, writers, filmmakers, or musicians, during

9-month season. Each artist receives a stipend ($750-$1,500 for 2 to 4 weeks) from the Jerome Foundation. Participants live in a small house in the heart of this community of 1,000 people. Deadlines: April 1 and Oct. 1. Contact: Kayleen Roberts.

NORTHWOOD UNIVERSITY

Alden B. Dow Creativity Center, 4000 Whiting Dr., Midland, MI 48640-2398. 517-837-4478.
E-mail: creativity@northwood.edu. Web site: www.northwood.edu/abd.
Description: Fellowships for individuals to pursue project ideas without interruption. A project idea should be innovative, creative, with potential for impact in its field. Four 10-week residencies (early-June to mid-August) awarded yearly. Application fee: $10. A $750 stipend plus room and board are provided. No spouses or families. Deadline: Dec. 31.

OX-BOW

37 S. Wabash Ave., Chicago, IL 60603. 312-899-7455.
E-mail: oxbow@artic.edu. Web site: www.ox-bow.org.
Description: One-week residencies (mid-June to mid-August) for writers to reside and work in secluded, natural environment in Michigan. Fee: $390/week for room and board. Primarily for the visual arts, Ox-Bow nurtures the creative process through instruction, example, and community. Resident writers encouraged to present a reading of their work and to participate in the community life at Ox-Bow. For application, write or call. Deadline: May 14.

RAGDALE FOUNDATION

1260 N. Green Bay Rd., Lake Forest, IL 60045. 847-234-1063.
E-mail: ragdalel@aol.com. Web site: www.ragdale.org. Susan Tillett, Admissions.
Description: This Lake Forest estate, 30 miles north of Chicago on 55 acres of prairie, is now an artists' retreat for 3 visual artists, 1 composer, and 8 writers at a time. Allows time and peaceful space for writers to finish works in progress, to begin new works, to solve creative problems, and to experiment in new genres. Residencies: 2 weeks to 2 months. Fee: $15/day; some fee waivers available, based on financial need. Send SASE for details. Application fee: $20. Contact: Lisa LeVally.

SASKATCHEWAN WRITERS/ARTISTS COLONIES
AND INDIVIDUAL RETREATS

P.O. Box 3986, Regina, Saskatchewan S4P 3R9, Canada . 306-565-8785.
E-mail: skcolony@attglobal.net. Web site: www.skwriter.com/colonies.html.
Description: Rural St. Peter's Abbey, near Humboldt, offers a 6-week summer colony (July-August) and a 2-week winter colony in February; also, individual retreats (for Canadian residents only) offered year-round, for up to 3 residents at a time. Emma Lake, near Prince Albert, is the site of a 2-week colony in the summer. Fees: $150/week ($200 for non-members) at St. Peter's, $175/week ($225 for non-members) at Emma Lake. Dec. 1 deadline for winter colony; May 1 deadline for summer. Contact: Shelley Sopher, Colony Coordinator.

JOHN STEINBECK ROOM

Long Island University, Southampton College Library, Southampton, NY 11968. 631-287-8382. E-mail: library@southampton.liu.edu.

Description: At Long Island University, the John Steinbeck Room provides a basic research facility to writers with either a current book contract or a confirmed magazine assignment. The room is available for up to 6 months with one 6-month renewal allowed. Send SASE for application. Contact: Robert Gerbereux, Library Director.

THURBER HOUSE RESIDENCIES

c/o Thurber House, 77 Jefferson Ave., Columbus, OH 43215. 614-464-1032. E-mail: thhouse@thurberhouse.org. Web site: www.thurberhouse.org.

Description: Residencies in the restored home of James Thurber are awarded to journalists, poets, and playwrights. Residents work on their own writing projects, and in addition to other duties, teach a class at the Ohio State University. A stipend of $6,000 per quarter is provided. Deadline: Dec. 15, for letter of interest and curriculum vitae (for the following academic year). Contact: Michael J. Rosen, Literary Director.

TWO WHITE WOLVES RETREAT

P.O. Box 16727, Encino, CA 91416. 818-753-7754. E-mail: williamwallaceworldwide@yahoo.com.

Description: These retreats are self-contained areas with ponds and streams, on 150 acres in Canada and 5 acres in Missouri. Writers are welcome to apply for a residency, no time limit or residency fee. Application fee: $50.00. No hunting; this is a sanctuary for fauna, flora, and humans; all guests are caretakers of these beautiful areas. Send for a portfolio. Contact: Kate Alexander, Director.

UCROSS FOUNDATION

Residency Program, 30 Big Red Lane, Clearmont, WY 82835. 307-737-2291. E-mail: ucross@wyoming.com. Web site: ucrossfoundation.org.

Description: Residencies of 2-8 weeks, in the foothills of Big Horn Mountains of Wyoming, allow writers, artists, and scholars to concentrate on their work. Two residency sessions annually: February-June and August-December. No charge for room, board, or studio space. $20 application fee. Deadines: March 1 for the fall session; October 1 for the spring session. Send SASE for details. Contact: Sharon Dynak, Executive Director.

VERMONT STUDIO CENTER

P.O. Box 613, Johnson, VT 05656. 802-635-2727. E-mail: info@vscvt.org. Web site: www.vermontstudiocenter.org.

Description: Offers independent residencies of 4-12 weeks, year-round, for up to 12 writers of fiction, nonfiction, and poetry. All residents receive a private studio space, room, meals, and community interaction (24 painters, 12 sculptors, 2 printmakers), also optional readings and private conferences with prominent visiting writers. One-month residency fee: $3,200. Full fellowships, grants, and work-exchange aid are available. Deadlines: Feb. 15, June 15, and Sept. 30. Application fee: $25.

VILLA MONTALVO ARTIST RESIDENCY PROGRAM

P.O. Box 158, Saratoga, CA 95071. 408-961-5818.

E-mail: kfunk@villamontalvo.org. Web site: www.villamontalvo.org.

Description: Offers residencies of 1-3 months, in the foothills of Santa Cruz Mountains south of San Francisco, free of charge, to writers, visual artists, and composers. Several merit-based fellowships are available. Deadlines: Sept. 1 and March 1; send self-addressed label and first-class postage for two ounces to receive details and application. Application fee: $20. Contact: Kathryn Funk, Artist Residency Director.

VIRGINIA CENTER FOR THE CREATIVE ARTS

P.O. Box VCCA, Sweet Briar, VA 24595. 804-946-7236.

E-mail: vcca@vcca.com. Web site: www.vcca.com.

Description: A working retreat for writers, composers, and visual artists in Virginia's Blue Ridge Mountains. Residencies from 2 weeks to 2 months available year-round. Deadlines: 15th of Jan., May, and Sept.; about 300 residents accepted each year. Limited financial aid is available. Send SASE for details. Contact: Suny Monk, Executive Director.

THE WRITERS ROOM

10 Astor Pl., 6th Fl., New York, NY 10003. 212-254-6995.

E-mail: writersroom@writersroom.org. Web site: www.writersroom.org.

Donna Brodie, Executive Director.

Description: In the East Village, the Writers Room offers a quiet work space for all types of writers, at all stages of their careers. The Room holds 30 desks separated by partitions, a typing room with 5 desks, a kitchen, and a library. Open 24 hours/day, 365 days/year. There is a one-time $50 application fee (also, send 3 references); fees for a 3-month period include $185 for a "floater" desk. Part-time memberships at reduced rates available. Call, fax, or write for application (no visits without appointment), or visit web site. Currently a 2-year wait for full-time membership. Contact: Angela Patrinos.

THE WRITERS STUDIO

The Mercantile Library Association, 17 E. 47th St., New York, NY 10017.

212-755-6710. E-mail: mercantile_library@msn.com.

Harold Augenbraum, Director.

Description: A quiet place for writers to rent space to allow them to produce good work. A carrel, locker ($15 fee), small reference collection, electrical outlets, and membership in the Mercantile Library are available for $200 for 3 months. Submit application, resumé, and writing samples; applications considered year-round. Must have proof of previously published work and current contract with a publisher. Contact: Ann Keisman.

HELENE WURLITZER FOUNDATION OF NEW MEXICO

P.O. Box 1891, Taos, NM 87571. 505-758-2413.

E-mail: hwf@taosnet.com.

Michael A. Knight, Director.

Description: Rent-free, fully furnished houses, with free utilities, in Taos on 18-acre campus, offered to writers and artists in all media. Residency is usually 3 months, April 1 to Sept. 30, and on a limited basis October through March. Send SASE for application and guidelines. Deadline: Jan. 18 for following year. Contact: Noel Simmons, Office Manager.

YADDO

P.O. Box 395, Saratoga Springs, NY 12866-0395. 518-584-0746.

E-mail: yaddo@yaddo.org. Web site: www.yaddo.org.

Elaina Richardson, Program Coordinator.

Description: A 400-acre estate, with private bedrooms and studios for each visiting artist. All meals provided. Visual artists, writers, choreographers, film/video artists, performance artists, composers, and collaborators, working at a professional level, are invited for stays from 2 weeks to 2 months. No residency fee. Deadlines: Jan. 15 and Aug. 1. Application fee: $20. Send SASE for form. Contact: Candace Wait.

WRITERS' CONFERENCES

Each year, hundreds of writers' conferences are held across the country. The following list, arranged by state, represents a sampling of conferences; each listing includes the location of the conference, the month during which it is usually held, and the name and address of the person from whom specific information may be received. Writers are advised to write or e-mail directly to conference directors for full details, or check the web sites. Always enclose an SASE. Additional conferences are listed annually in the May issue of *The Writer* magazine (Kalmbach Publishing Co., 21027 Crossroads Circle, P.O. Box 1612, Waukesha, WI 53187-1612).

Writers' conferences are a great opportunity not only to develop writing skills in specific areas but also to meet and develop lasting friendships with other writers, as well as with agents and editors.

ALABAMA

SPRINGMINGLE '02!
Gulf Shores, Ala., February.
E-mail: joanbroerman@home.com.
Web site: http://members.home.net/southernbreeze.
Description: Immersion in the study and production of quality children's literature. "Offers a professional focus for writers and illustrators whose goal is to produce quality children's literature." Number of attendees: 80. Contact: Joan Broerman, Southern Breeze, P.O. Box 26282, Birmingham, AL 35260.

WRITING AND ILLUSTRATING FOR KIDS
Birmingham, Ala., October.
E-mail: joanbroerman@home.com.
Web site: http://members.home.net/southernbreeze.
Description: More than 30 workshops on craft, technique, and professional concerns. Private manuscript critiques available. Sponsored by Southern Breeze SCBWI. Number of attendees: 125. Contact: Joan Broerman, Southern Breeze, P.O. Box 26282, Birmingham, AL 35260.

ALASKA

SITKA SYMPOSIUM
Sitka, Alaska, June.
E-mail: island@ak.net. Web site: www.islandinstitutealaska.org.
Description: Gathering that puts written and oral traditions to the service of ideas.

Caters to a broad audience of writers and readers. Number of attendees: 55. Contact: Carolyn Servid, Island Institute, P.O. Box 2420, Sitka, AK 99835. 907-747-3794.

ARKANSAS

ARKANSAS WRITERS CONFERENCE
Little Rock, Ark., June.
Description: Workshops, lectures, and contests. Number of attendees: 200. Contact: Barbara Longstreth-Mulkey, 17 Red Maple Ct., Little Rock, AR 72211. 501-312-1747.

OZARK CREATIVE WRITERS CONFERENCE
Eureka Springs, Ark., October.
Description: Contest, talks by topnotch writers, editors, and publishers from all genres. Held in a "beautiful Victorian town in the Ozarks." Number of attendees: 150. Contact: Marcia Camp (conference) or Chrissy Willis (contest), 75 Robinwood Dr., Little Rock, AR 72227. 501-225-8619 (conference) or 501-228-9921 (contest).

CALIFORNIA

MEDOCINO COAST WRITERS CONFERENCE
Fort Bragg, Calif., June.
Web site: www.mcwcwritewhale.com
Description: A gathering of writers, agents, editors, and publishers, held at a college campus on the ocean. Workshops, lectures, consultations, and writing sessions on writing fiction, nonfiction, poetry, screenplays, and children's literature. Number of attendees: 99. Contact: Jan Boyd, Mendocino Coast Writers Conference, College of the Redwoods, 1211 Del Mar Dr., Fort Bragg CA 95437. 707-961-6248.

MICHAEL HAUGE'S SCREENWRITING FOR HOLLYWOOD
Los Angeles, Calif., July and October.
E-mail: mhauge@juno.com.
Description: "From Concept to Sale." Intensive seminar on the art, craft, and business of screenwriting, led by script consultant/screenwriter Michael Hauge. Contact: Hilltop Productions, P.O. Box 55728, Sherman Oaks, CA 91413. 800-477-1947.

SANTA BARBARA CHRISTIAN WRITERS CONFERENCE
Santa Barbara, Calif., October.
Description: Speakers, food, fellowship, and support. Held at Westmont College. For discount, reserve by Sept. 1. Number of attendees: 60-100. Contact: Rev. Opal Mae Dailey, P.O. Box 42429, Santa Barbara, CA 93140. 805-647-9162.

SANTA BARBARA WRITERS CONFERENCE

Santa Barbara, Calif., June.
Description: Week-long workshops in all genres. Held at Westmont College. Number of attendees: 400. Contact: Mary Conrad, SBWC, P.O. Box 304, Carpinteria, CA 93013. 805-684-2250.

COLORADO

ASPEN SUMMER WORDS WRITING RETREAT AND LITERARY FESTIVAL

Aspen, Colo., June.
E-mail: aspenwrite@aol. com. Web site: www.aspenwriters.org.
Description: Intensive study in small group workshops. Social activities, guest readings, and private meetings with agents and editors. Literary festival follows with lectures, industry talks, roundtable discussions, and readings. Number of attendees: 100. Contact: Julie Comins, P.O. Box 7726, Aspen, CO 81612. 800-925-2526.

COLORADO CHRISTIAN WRITERS CONFERENCE

Estes Park, Colo., May.
E-mail: mbagnull@aol.com. Web site: www.writehisanswer.com.
Description: Authors and editors offer continuing sessions and numerous workshops. Number of attendees: 200. Contact: Marlene Bagnull, 316 Blanchard Rd., Drexel Hill, PA 19026. 610-626-6833.

ROMANCE WRITERS OF AMERICA NATIONAL CONFERENCE

Denver, Colo., July.
E-mail: info@rwanational.com. Web site: www.rwanational.com.
Description: Denver will be the location of the 2002 annual event. More than 100 workshops on the craft and business of writing. Participants include published and aspiring romance novelists, literary agents, and publishing executives. Number of attendees: 2,000. Contact: Romance Writers of America, 3707 FM 1960 W, Suite 555, Houston, TX 77068. 281-440-6885.

PUBLISHING INSTITUTE AT THE UNIVERSITY OF DENVER

Denver, Colo., July-August.
E-mail: pzelarne@du.edu. Web site: www.du.edu/pi.
Description: For recent college graduates and career changers who seek careers in book publishing, and for those presently employed in the publishing field. Admission is selective. Number of attendees: 90. Contact: Pearlanne Zelarney, The Publishing Institute, 2075 S. University Blvd., D-114, Denver, CO 80210. 303-871-2570.

STEAMBOAT SPRINGS WRITERS CONFERENCE

Steamboat Springs, Colo., July.
E-mail: freiberger@compuserve.com.

Description: Readings, workshops, writing sessions, and social events. Number of attendees: 35-40. Contact: Harriet Freiberger, SSAC, P.O. Box 774284, Steamboat Springs, CO 80477. 970-879-8079.

CONNECTICUT

WESLEYAN WRITERS CONFERENCE
Middletown, Conn., June.
E-mail: agreene@wesleyan.edu. Web site: www.wesleyan.edu/writing/conferen.html.
Description: Seminars, workshops, lectures, readings, publishing panels, and manuscript consultations. Teaching fellowships and scholarships available in fiction, nonfiction, and poetry. Rolling admission. Number of attendees: 100. Contact: Anne Greene, Wesleyan Writers Conference, Wesleyan University, Middletown, CT 06459. 860-685-3604.

DISTRICT OF COLUMBIA

NEW MEDIA PUBLISHING: E-CHALLENGES, E-SSENTIALS
Washington, D.C., June.
E-mail: mail@edpress.org. Web site: www.edpress.org.
Description: Addresses a cross-section of educational publishing professionals. Workshops, critiques, and roundtables. Number of attendees: 300. Contact: Penni Starer, 510 Heron Dr., Suite 309, Logan Township, NJ 08085. 856-256-4610.

FLORIDA

KEY WEST LITERARY SEMINAR
Key West, Fla., January.
E-mail: mail@keywestliteraryseminar.org. Web site: www.keywestliteraryseminar.org.
Description: A premier literary gathering in a tropical setting. Each annual event features a selected topic and a number of prominent American authors. Readings, lectures, panel presentations, informal gatherings, and discussions. Contact: Alan Kelly Hamm, Administrative Offices, 4 Portside Lane, Searsport ME 04974.

WRITING THE REGION: MARJORIE KINNON RAWLINGS WRITERS WORKSHOP
Gainesville, Fla., June or July.
E-mail: shakes@ufl.edu.
Description: Sessions on fiction, nonfiction, poetry, travel writing, writing for children, publishing, editing, agents, and more. Evening activities, readings, and banquet, trip to Rawlings' home. Number of attendees: 100 or more. Contact: Norma Homan, P.O. Box 12246, Gainesville, FL 32604. 888-917-7001.

GEORGIA

SOUTHEASTERN WRITERS ASSOCIATION
WRITERS WORKSHOP
St. Simons Island, Ga., June.
E-mail: rube774@ CLDS.net. Web site: www.southeastern writers.com.
Description: Intensive study, manuscript critiques, entertaining speakers, and time to rekindle the creative spark. Held at Epworth-by-the-Sea. Number of attendees: 100. Contact: Harry Rubin, P.O. Box 774, Hinesville, GA 31310. 912-876-3118.

ILLINOIS

MISSISSIPPI VALLEY WRITERS CONFERENCE
Rock Island, Ill., June.
E-mail: KIMSEUSS@aol.com.
Description: Workshops cover topics such as Basics for Beginners, Poetry, Writing for Children, Marketing, Nonfiction, Novel Basics, and Photography. Manuscript critiques. Cash scholarships awarded based on manuscripts submitted. Held at Augustana College; room and board available. Number of attendees: 80. Contact: David R. Collins, 3403 45th St., Moline, IL 61265. 309-762-8985.

OF DARK & STORMY NIGHTS
Rolling Meadows, Ill., June.
E-mail: spurgeon mwa@juno.com.
Description: Concentrated workshop/conference for writers and would-be writers of mystery and true crime. Faculty includes published writers, publicists, agents, editors, police officers, and advanced forensic experts. Manuscript critiques. Number of attendees: 150 or more. Contact: Wiley W. (Bill) Spurgeon, Mystery Writers of America, Midwest Chapter, P.O. Box 1944, Muncie, IN 47308. 765-288-7402.

INDIANA

INDIANA UNIVERSITY WRITERS CONFERENCE
Bloomington, Ind., June.
E-mail: rrubinas@indiana.edu. Web site: http://php.indiana.edu/~iuwc.
Description: Classes, readings, and workshops. Faculty includes Beth Ann Fennelly, Jim Grimsley, Alyce Miller, Ernesto Quinonez, Alan Shapiro, and Jean Valentine. Reserve by May 11 for workshops, by June 19 for other events. Number of attendees: 125. Contact: Romayne Rubinas, IUWC, Ballantine Hall 464, 1020 E. Kirkwood, Bloomington, IN 47405. 812-855-1877.

MIDWEST WRITERS WORKSHOP
Muncie, Ind., July.
E-mail: earllconn@aol.com. Web site: www.midwestwriters.org.
Description: Intensive one-day workshops to improve your writing. Number of attendees: 100. Contact: Earl L. Conn, Midwest Writers Workshop, c/o Dept. of Journalism, Ball State University, Muncie, IN 47306. 765-285-5587.

ROPEWALK WRITERS RETREAT
New Harmony, Ind., June.
E-mail: lcleek@usi.edu. Web site: www.usi.edu/extserv/ropewalk.htm.
Description: Workshops, conference, and public events. Number of attendees: 50. Contact: Linda Cleek, USI Extended Services, 8600 University Blvd., Evansville, IN 47712. 812-464-1989.

IOWA

IOWA SUMMER WRITING FESTIVAL
Iowa City, Iowa, June or July
E-mail: iswfestival@uiowa.edu. Web site: www.uiowa.edu/~iswfest.
Description: Short-term, noncredit writing program for adults. 135 workshops across a spectrum of literary genres, including novel, short fiction, poetry, essay, screenwriting, and writing for children; workshops run for a week or a weekend. Housing is available. Contact: University of Iowa, Iowa Summer Writing Festival, 100 Oakdale Campus W310, Iowa City, IA 52242. 319-335-4160.

KANSAS

WRITERS WORKSHOP IN SCIENCE FICTION
Lawrence, Kan., June or July.
E-mail: jgunn@ukans.edu. Web site: http://falcon.cc.ukans.edu/~sfcenter
Description: Critiques and revision of submitted manuscripts, plus time for writing, study, consultation, and recreation. Number of attendees: 12. Contact: James Gunn, English Department, University of Kansas, Lawrence, KS 66045. 785-864-3380.

KENTUCKY

APPALACHIAN WRITERS WORKSHOP
Hindman, Ky., July or August.
E-mail: hss@tgtel.com. Web site: http://hindmansettlement.org.
Description: Presents and promotes writers and writing from the Appalachian region. Number of attendees: 80-90. Contact: Mike Mullins, Hindman Settlement School, P.O. Box 844, Hindman, KY 41822. 606-785-5475.

GO FICTION GETAWAY
Louisville, Ky., March.
E-mail: mary_odell@ ntr.net.
Description: "Spend an entire week making progress on your novel. And here are other writers to offer support." Reserve by early February for housing. Number of attendees: 40-50. Contact: Mary O'Dell, Green River Writers Inc., 703 Eastbridge Ct., Louisville, KY 40223. 502-245-4902.

GREEN RIVER WRITERS WORKSHOP WEEKEND & RETREAT
Louisville, Ky., July.
E-mail: mary_odell@ntr.net.
Description: Retreat for writers; peer encouragement and critiquing available. Number of attendees: 40. Contact: Mary O'Dell, Green River Writers Inc., 703 Eastbridge Ct., Louisville, KY 40223. 502-245-4902.

TOUCH OF SUCCESS WRITING SEMINARS
Glendale, Ky., October.
Web site: www.touchofsuccess.com.
Description: Work on leads for nonfiction magazine articles, query letters, photo captions, and book proposals. Led by author Bill Thomas. Reserve by September. Number of attendees: 8. Contact: Bill Thomas, Touch of Success Writing Seminars, P.O. Box 194, Lowell, FL 32663. 352-867-0463.

MAINE

STONECOAST WRITERS CONFERENCE
Freeport, Maine, July.
E-mail: summer@usm.maine.edu. Web site: www.usm.maine.edu/summer.
Description: Workshops in poetry, popular fiction, novels, short stories, and non-fiction. Faculty includes authors and editors known nationally for their publishing and teaching. Guest readings and special events. Number of attendees: 95. Contact: B. Lee Hope, 37 College Ave., Gorham, ME 04038. 207-780-5617.

WORKSHOP LEADERSHIP TRAINING: AMHERST WRITERS & ARTISTS METHOD
Amherst, Maine, July, October, November and April.
E-mail: pat@amherstwriters.com. Web site: www.amherstwriters.com.
Description: Intensive training led by Pat Schneider, author of *The Writer as an Artist: A New Approach to Writing Alone & With Others.* Events fill early. Number of attendees: 12. Contact: Pat Schneider, Amherst Writers & Artists, P.O. Box 1076, Amherst, ME 01004. 413-253-3307.

MARYLAND

ASSOCIATION FOR WOMEN IN COMMUNICATIONS
PROFESSIONAL CONFERENCE
Baltimore, Md., August.
E-mail: brenda@baymed.com. Web site: www.womcom.org.
Description: Workshops, keynote speakers, presentation of the Clarion Awards.
Contact: Brenda Gracely, Bay Media, Inc./ Association of Women in Communication,
780 Ritchie Hwy., Suite 28S, Severna Park, MD 21146. 410-647-8402.

MID-ATLANTIC CREATIVE NONFICTION
SUMMER WRITERS CONFERENCE
Baltimore, Md., August.
E-mail: nmack@goucher. edu. Web site: www.goucher.edu/cnf.
Description: Intensive workshops on the art and craft of creative nonfiction.
Number of attendees: 80. Contact: Noreen Mack, Goucher College, Center for
Graduate and Continuing Studies, 1021 Dulaney Valley Rd., Baltimore, MD 21204.
800-697-4646.

MASSACHUSETTS

CASTLE HILL WORKSHOPS
Truro, Mass., various dates.
E-mail: castlehill@capecod.net. Web site: www.castlehill.org.
Description: Series of writing workshops on poetry, playwriting, fiction, memoir,
and biography, held at the Truro Center for the Arts. Number of sessions per work-
shop varies. Ave. number of attendees: 10. Contact: Mary Stackhouse, Castle Hill,
P.O. Box 756, Truro, MA 02666. 508-349-7511.

CAPE COD WRITERS CONFERENCE
Cape Cod, Mass., Aug. 19-24.
E-mail: ccwc@capecod.net. Web site: www.capecod.net/writers.
Description: Classes in fiction, nonfiction, mystery, poetry, writing for children,
screenwriting, and other genres. Personal conferences and manuscript evaluations,
young writers workshop. Number of attendees: 150. Contact: Jacqueline M. Loring,
CCWC, Box 186, Barnstable, MA 02630. 508-375-0516.

MICHIGAN

CRITICAL CONNECTION FICTION WRITERS CONFERENCE
Ann Arbor, Mich., June.
E-mail: criticalconnection@hotmail.com. Web site: www.criticalconnection.org.
Description: Novel-writing instruction, fiction workshops, and seminars on getting

published. Number of attendees: 50. Contact: Keith Hood, Critical Connection Fiction Workshops, 3096 Williamsburg, Ann Arbor, MI 48108.

MIDLAND WRITERS CONFERENCE

Midland, Mich., June.
E-mail: ajarvis@midland-mi.org. Web site: www.gracedowlibrary.org.
Description: Forum for writers at all levels to exchange ideas with professionals. Workshop sessions and well-known keynote speaker. Number of attendees: 50-100. Contact: Ann C. Jarvis, Grace A. Dow Memorial Library, 1710 W. St. Andrews, Midland, MI 48640. 517-837-3435.

MIDWEST POETS & WRITERS CONFERENCE

Detroit, Mich., August or September.
Web site: www.BlackArts-Literature.org.
Description: 3-day gathering with workshops, guest speakers, panel discussions, manuscript critiques, seminars, and special events. Held in conjunction with Detroit's Montreux Jazz Festival. Contact: Heather Buchanan, Detroit Black Writer's Guild, P.O. Box 23100, Detroit, MI 48223. 313-897-2551.

WALLOON WRITERS RETREAT

Boyne City, Mich., September.
E-mail: johndlamb@ameritech.net. Web site: www.springfed.org.
Description: Workshops, readings, and panel discussions for writers and poets at all levels. Held at Walloon Lake. Number of attendees: 50-60. Contact: John D. Lamb, Springfed Arts, P.O. Box 304, Royal Oak, MI 48068. 248-589-3913.

WRITERS CONFERENCE AT OAKLAND UNIVERSITY

Rochester, Mich., October 19-20.
E-mail: gjboddy@oakland.edu. Web site: www.oakland.edu/contin-ed/writersconf.
Description: Private and group manuscript evaluations and numerous presentations by professionals. Number of attendees: 300. Contact: Gloria J. Boddy, 231 Varner Hall, Oakland University, Rochester, MI 48309. 248-370-4386.

MINNESOTA

INSIDE BOOKS

St. Joseph, Minn., July 15-20.
E-mail: insidebooks@csbsju.edu. Web site: www. csbsju.edu/literaryarts/insidebooks.
Description: Workshop focuses on small presses, literary magazines, and alternative publishing. Contact: Diane Calabria, Inside Books, College of St. Benedict, 37 S. College Ave., St. Joseph, MN 56374. 320-363-5247.

SPLIT ROCK ARTS PROGRAM
Duluth, Minn., July or August.
E-mail: srap@ cce.umn.edu. Web site: www.cce.umn.edu/splitrockarts.
Description: 40 intensive week-long residential workshops in visual and literary arts. Work with nationally renowned practicing writers, artists, and craftspeople. Number of attendees: 550. Contact: Vivien Oja, Split Rock Arts Program, University of Minnesota, 360 Coffey Hall, 1420 Eckles Ave., St. Paul, MN 55108. 612-625-8100.

MISSISSIPPI

NATCHEZ LITERARY AND CINEMA CELEBRATION
Natchez, Miss., February.
E-mail: carolyn.smith@colin.cc.ms.us. Web site: www.colin.cc.ms.us/nlcc.
Description: Lecture series with related activities. Number of attendees: 1,000+. Contact: Carolyn Vance Smith, P.O. Box 894, Natchez, MS 39121. 601-446-1208.

MONTANA

SAGEBRUSH WRITERS WORKSHOP
Big Timber, Mont., March.
E-mail: sagewriter@mcn.net.
Description: Workshops, manuscript critiques, guest speakers, and book sales and signings. Number of attendees: 30. Contact: Gwen Peterson, P.O. Box 1255, Big Timber, MT 59011. 406-932-4227.

NEW HAMPSHIRE

MOLASSES POND WRITERS RETREAT/WORKSHOP
Wakefield, N.H., June.
E-mail: mbarrett@nemaine.com.
Description: Manuscript critiques, classes, and time set aside for writing. Held at the 1780 Twin Farms Writing Center in New Hampshire's Lake Region. $450 fee covers lodging, all meals and workshops. Number of attendees: 10. Contact: Martha Barron Barrett, 36 Manning St., Portsmouth, NH 03801. 603-431-6306.

NEW ENGLAND WRITERS CONFERENCE
Hanover, N.H., July 21.
E-mail: newvtpoet@aol.com.
Description: Writers panel, seminars on poetry and prose, open readings, and book sales. Sponsored by the University Press of New England. Number of attendees: 150. Contact: Frank and Susan C. Anthony, P.O. Box 483, Windsor, VT 05089. 802-674-2315.

ODYSSEY FANTASY WRITING WORKSHOP
Manchester, N.H., June or July.
E-mail: jcavelos@sff.net. Web site: www.sff.net/odyssey.
Description: Intensive 6-week workshop for writers of fantasy, science fiction, and horror. Dorm housing and college credits are available. Number of attendees: 20. Contact: Jeanne Cavelos, Odyssey, 20 Levesque Ln., Mont Vernon, NH 03057. 603-673-6234.

NEW MEXICO

SOUTHWEST WRITERS ANNUAL CONFERENCE
Albuquerque, N.M., September.
Web site: www.southwestwriters.org.
Description: Large gathering of Southwest writers for workshops in all genres of writing fiction and nonfiction for adults and children, also manuscript critiques, meetings with agents and editors, social events, and writing sessions. Number of attendees: 300-500. Contact: Lori Johnson, Southwest Writers, 8200 Mountain Road NE, Suite 106, Albuquerque, NM 87100. 505-265-9485.

TAOS SUMMER WRITERS CONFERENCE
Taos, N.M., July.
E-mail: taosconf@unm.edu. Web site: www.unm.edu/~taosconf.
Description: Workshops on fiction, poetry, publishing, travel writing, and creative nonfiction. Readings, publishing panel, and a visit to the D.H. Lawrence Ranch. Walk-in registrations accepted, space permitting. Number of attendees: 120-150. Contact: Sharon Oard Warner, Humanities Bldg., Taos Summer Writers' Conference, University of New Mexico, Albuquerque, NM 87131. 505-277-6248.

NEW YORK

CATSKILL POETRY WORKSHOP
Oneonta, N.Y., June or July.
E-mail: frostc@hartwick.edu.
Web site: www. hartwick.edu/library/catskill/poetry.htm.
Description: Workshops, classes on craft, evening readings by staff and guest writers, and individual instruction. Opportunity for talented writers to apply themselves to the art and craft of poetry. Number of attendees: 30-40. Contact: Carol Frost, Hartwick College, 1 Hartwick Dr., Oneonta, NY 13820. 607-431-4448.

CHENANGO VALLEY WRITERS CONFERENCE
Hamilton, N.Y., June.
E-mail: mleone@ mail.colgate.edu.
Web site: http://clark.colgate.edu/cvwritersconference.

Description: Consultations, workshops, panel discussions, readings, and conversations. Number of attendees: 60. Contact: Matthew Leone, Office of Summer Programs, Colgate University, Hamilton, NY 13346. 315-228-7771.

CHILDREN'S BOOK WRITING & ILLUSTRATING WORKSHOPS

New York City, July.
E-mail: rqstudios@aol.com. Web site: www.rquackenbush.com.
Description: Focuses on picture books and middle-grade readers. Led by author/illustrator Robert Quackenbush. Number of attendees: 10. Contact: Robert Quackenbush Studios, 460 E. 79th St., New York, NY 10021. 212-744-3822.

HIGHLIGHTS FOUNDATION WRITERS WORKSHOP

Chautauqua, N.Y., July.
E-mail: contact@highlightsfoundation.org.
Description: Intense, week-long workshop geared to children's writers. Number of attendees: 100. Contact: Lori Lyons, Highlights Foundation, 814 Court St., Honesdale, PA 18431. 570-253-1192.

JEFFREY SWEET'S PLAYWRIGHTS RETREAT

Woodbourne, N.Y., August.
E-mail: artnewdir@aol.com. Web site: www.artisticnewdirections.org.
Description: Work on your play under the guidance of Jeffrey Sweet, whose techniques include the use of improvisation. Held in New York's Catskills region. Number of attendees: 10-12. Contact: Kristine Niven, Artistic New Directions, 250 W. 90th St. #15G, New York, NY 10024. 212-875-1857.

LAKE PLACID FILM FORUM

Lake Placid, N.Y., June.
E-mail: adkfilm@gisco.net. Web site: www.lakeplacid-filmforum.org.
Description: Gathering of writers, filmmakers, and film lovers to explore issues of content and the medium, share ideas and experiences, see films, attend readings, and relax. Reserve early for reduced fees. Number of attendees: 500+. Contact: Naj Wikoff, Lake Placid Film Forum, P.O. Box 489, Lake Placid, NY 12946. 518-523-3456.

REMEMBER THE MAGIC SUMMER CONFERENCE

Saratoga Springs, N.Y., August.
E-mail: dirhahn@aol.com. Web site: www.iwwg.com.
Description: Over 60 workshops for women writers presented daily. Held at Skidmore College. Number of attendees: 500. Contact: Hannelore Hahn, International Women's Writing Guild, P.O. Box 810, Gracie Sta., New York, NY 10028. 212-737-7536.

SUMMER IMPROV RETREAT

Woodbourne, N.Y., July or August.

E-mail: artnewdir@aol.com. Web site: www.artisticnewdirections.org.

Description: Provides a protected environment for creative growth in the inter-related disciplines of acting, improvisation, and playwriting. Number of attendees: 50-60. Contact: Kristine Niven, Artistic New Directions, 250 W. 90th St. #15G, New York, NY 10024. 212-875-1857.

THE WRITERS CONFERENCE

New York City, June.

Web site: www.mmce.edu.

Description: Advice on how to succeed as a writer from more than 60 distinguished authors, agents, and publicists. Contact: Writing Center, Marymount Manhattan College, 221 E. 71st St., New York, NY 10021. 212-774-0780.

NORTH CAROLINA

JOHN C. CAMPBELL FOLK SCHOOL

Brasstown, N.C., year-round events.

Web site: www.folkschool.com

Description: Offers 5-7 day courses in writing fiction, plays, autobiography and memoirs, poety, children's literature. Some workshops focus on regional Appalachian culture and writing. Located in a rural setting in the beautiful Blue Ridge Mountains. Contact: Publicity Director, John C. Campbell Folk School, 1 Folk School Road, Brasstown, NC 28902. 800-365-5724.

NORTH CAROLINA WRITERS NETWORK FALL CONFERENCE

Charlotte, N.C., November.

E-mail: mail@ncwriters.org. Web site: www.ncwriters.org.

Description: Workshops, panel discussions, manuscript "mart," and readings by established writers. Instruction and encouragement to writers at all levels. Number of attendees: 500. Contact: Shannon Woolfe, NCWN, P.O. Box 954, Carrboro, NC 27510. 919-967-9540.

NORTH DAKOTA

NATIONAL FEDERATION OF PRESS WOMEN CONFERENCE

Bismarck, N.D., September.

E-mail: presswomen@aol.com. Web site: www.nfpw.com.

Description: Professional development conference for professional writers. Number of attendees: 200. Contact: Carol Pierce, National Federation of Press Women, P.O. Box 5556, Arlington, VA 22205. 703-534-2500.

OHIO

ANTIOCH WRITERS WORKSHOP
Yellow Springs, Ohio, July.
Web site: www.antiochwritersworkshop.com
Description: Week-long sessions in poety, fiction, and nonfiction, with manuscript critiques and discussions on the writer's life. Includes ample time to interact with instructors on an informal basis. Contact: Mindy Carpenter, Antioch Writers' Workshop, P.O. Box 494, Yellow Springs, OH 45387. 877-914-3349.

THE WRITERS WORKSHOP
Gambier, Ohio, June or July.
Web site: www. kenyonreview.org.
Description: Intensive experience of workshops, individual writing, and readings in the wooded village of Gambier. Contact: Ellen Sheffield, *The Kenyon Review,* Sunset Cottage, Gambier, OH 43022. 740-427-5207.

OKLAHOMA

OKLAHOMA FALL ARTS INSTITUTE
Lone Wolf, Okla., October.
E-mail: okarts@okartinst.org. Web site: www.okartinst.org.
Description: Weekend of workshops led by nationally acclaimed writers at the Quartz Mountain Arts and Conference Center. Scholarships available for public school teachers and higher education professionals from Oklahoma. Number of attendees: 100. Contact: Lee Warren, 105 N. Hudson, Suite 101, Oklahoma City, OK 73102. 405-319-9019.

SHORT COURSE ON PROFESSIONAL WRITING
Norman, Okla., June.
E-mail: jmadisondavis@ou.edu. Web site: http://jmc.ou.edu.
Description: Practical tips on writing and publishing. Number of attendees: 200. Contact: J. Madison Davis, Gaylord College of Journalism, University of Oklahoma, Norman, OK 73019. 405-325-2721.

OREGON

ASHLAND WRITERS CONFERENCE
Ashland, Ore., July.
E-mail: awcore@aol.com. Web site: www. ashlandwriters.com.
Description: Workshops on poetry, fiction, and nonfiction. Private instructor conferences. Number of attendees: 112. Contact: Jonah Bornstein, 295 E. Main St. #5, Ashland, OR 97520. 541-482-2783.

WILLAMETTE WRITERS CONFERENCE
Portland, Ore., August.
E-mail: wilwrite@willamettewriters.com. Web site: www.willamettewriters.com.
Description: One-on-one sessions with agents, editors, and film producers. Workshops on writing fiction, genres, nonfiction, screenwriting, and young adult literature. Number of attendees: 350. Contact: Bill Johnson, 9045 SW Barbur Blvd., Suite 5A, Portland, OR 97219. 503-452-1592.

PENNSYLVANIA

BOYDS MILLS WRITING WORKSHOPS
Boyds Mills, Pa., Spring-Fall.
E-mail: maewain@highlights-corp.com.
Web site: www.boydsmillspress.com/currentevents/spotlight.html.
Description: Workshops for professional children's writers and illustrators, held in the scenic Pocono Mountains at Boyds Mills conference center, home of the Highlights founders. Contact: Margaret Ewain, Highlights Foundation, 814 Court St., Honesdale, PA 18431. 570-253-1192.

CHRISTIAN WRITERS CONFERENCE
Montrose, Pa., July.
E-mail: donna@montrosebible.org. Web site: www.montrosebible.org.
Description: Topics designed to help beginning and experienced writers. Manuscript critiques and editorial appointments. Held at the Montrose Bible Conference. Number of attendees: 80-100. Contact: Donna Kosik, Montrose Bible Conference, 5 Locust St., Montrose, PA 18801. 570-278-1001.

GREATER PHILADELPHIA CHRISTIAN WRITERS CONFERENCE
Glenside, Pa., August.
E-mail: mbagnull@aol.com. Web site: www.writehisanswer.com.
Description: Authors and editors offer continuing sessions and numerous workshops. Fellowship with other authors. Held at Beaver College. Number of attendees: 200. Contact: Marlene Bagnull, 316 Blanchard Rd., Drexel Hill, PA 19026. 610-626-6833.

LIGONIER VALLEY WRITERS CONFERENCE
Ligonier, Pa., July.
E-mail: sarshi@wpa.net.
Description: Courses on fiction, nonfiction, poetry, and specialties yet to be finalized. Workshops, seminars, and social events. Faculty readings. All ages and skill levels welcome. Number of attendees: 50. Contact: Sally Shirey, Ligonier Valley Writers, P.O. Box B, Ligonier, PA 15658. 724-537-3341.

PENNWRITERS CONFERENCE

Hershey, Pa., May.

E-mail: elizwrite8@aol.com. Web site: www.pennwriters.org.

Description: Workshops, panels, faculty consultations, and manuscript critiques. Number of attendees: 100 or more. Contact: Elizabeth Darrach, Pennwriters Annual Conference, 492 Letort Rd., Millersville, PA 17551. 717-871-9712.

PHILADELPHIA WRITERS CONFERENCE

Philadelphia, Pa., June.

Web site: http://pwcgold.com.

Description: 3-day gathering, with agent/editor sessions, panel discussions, manuscript critiques, contest with cash prizes. Contact: I. Murden, Philadelphia Writers Conference, 107 Newington Dr., Hatboro PA 19040-4508. 215-744-1417.

TENNESSEE

SEWANEE WRITERS CONFERENCE

Sewanee, Tenn., July

E-mail: cpeters@sewanee.edu. Web site: www.sewaneewriters.org.

Description: Instruction and criticism through workshops and lectures in fiction, poetry, and playwriting. Agents, editors, publishers, and others give readings, make presentations, and answer questions. Number of attendees: 105. Contact: Cheri Sedell Peters, 310 St. Luke's Hall, 735 University Ave., Sewanee, TN 37383. 931-598-1141.

TEXAS

AGENTS! AGENTS! AGENTS! & EDITORS TOO!

Austin, Texas, July.

E-mail: awl@writers league.org. Web site: www.writersleague.org.

Description: Meet and network with 10-20 literary agents and editors from both coasts. Panel discussions, small roundtable discussions, and private consultations. Number of attendees: 250. Contact: Jim Bob McMillan, Writers' League of Texas, 1501 W. 5th St., Suite E2, Austin, TX 78703. 512-499-8914.

INSIDE THE CHILDREN'S BOOK BIZ

Arlington, Texas, September

E-mail: sudden word@hotmail.com. Web site: janpeck.com/txcsbwi.htm.

Description: Manuscript critiques, "Pitch to the Pros" sessions with editors. Annual conference of the NC/NE Texas SCBWI. Contact: Vicki L. Perez, 1549 Bosque Dr., Garland, TX 75040. 972-272-9253.

TEXAS CHRISTIAN WRITERS CONFERENCE
Houston, August.
E-mail: martharexrogers@aol.com.
Description: Workshops on all aspects of writing. Door prizes, luncheon, contest. Send SASE for contest forms. Reserve by July 15. Number of attendees: 50. Contact: Martha Rogers, 6038 Greenmont, Houston, TX 77092. 713-686-7209.

UTAH

DESERT WRITERS WORKSHOP
Moab, Utah, spring to fall.
E-mail: cfiinfo@canyonlandsfieldinst.org. Web site: www.canyonlandsfieldinst.org.
Description: Participants work in poetry, nonfiction, or fiction with faculty member. Readings, instruction, critiques, private time to write, and nature hikes. In addition, learn about the fascinating geology and history of the Colorado Plateau region. Number of attendees: 20-35. Contact: Canyonlands Field Institute, P.O. Box 68, Moab, UT 84532. 800-860-5262 or 435-259-7750.

VERMONT

WILDBRANCH WORKSHOP IN OUTDOOR, NATURAL HISTORY, AND ENVIRONMENTAL WRITING
Craftsbury Common, Vt., June.
E-mail: wldbrnch@sterlingcollege.edu.
Web site: www.sterlingcollege.edu/wildbranch.htm.
Description: Workshops and daily options benefit writers interested in producing fiction, journalism, or personal essays that portray the natural world. Contact: David W. Brown, Dir., Wildbranch, Sterling College, Craftsbury Common, VT 05827. 800-648-3591.

VIRGINIA

HIGHLAND SUMMER CONFERENCE
Radford, Va., June.
E-mail: jasbury@radford.edu.
Description: Study and practice creative and expository writing within the context of regional culture, exploring the heritage, environment, and culture of the Appalachian Mountain region. Number of attendees: 25. Contact: Jo Ann Asbury, Radford Univ., Appalachian Regional Studies Center, Box 7014, Radford, VA 24142. 540-831-5366.

MALICE DOMESTIC XIV

Arlington, Va., May.

E-mail: Malice@erols.com. Web site: http://users.erols.com/malice.

Description: Mystery authors, fans, and others celebrate "mysteries of manners." Noted authors and experts featured in panels, sessions, and special programming. Contact: Malice Domestic XIV, P.O. Box 31137, Bethesda, MD 20824.

RAPPAHANNOCK FICTION WRITERS WORKSHOP

Tappahannock, Va., August.

E-mail: ficwriters@aol.com. Web site: http://members.aol.com/ficwriters/.

Description: Held on the campus of St. Margaret's School, located on the scenic Rappahannock River in the historic Tidewater region, the 4-day long workshops offer the chance to work closely with well-established writers. Includes ample time for writing and strolling along the river. Contact: Anne Wilson Gregory, Rappahannock Fiction Writers Workshop, P.O. Box 1157, Virginia Beach, VA 23451.

WASHINGTON

CENTRUM'S PORT TOWNSEND WRITERS CONFERENCE

Port Townsend, Wash., July.

E-mail: carla@centrum.org. Web site: www.centrum.org.

Description: Workshops, readings, and lectures. The Pacific Northwest's "premier literary conference." Held at the Fort Worden State Park Conference Center. Contact: Carla VanderVen, P.O. Box 1158, Port Townsend, WA 98368. 360-385-3102.

GIG HARBOR WRITERS CONFERENCE

Gig Harbor, Wash., May.

E-mail: kathmob@aol.com.

Description: Lecture and workshop sessions with an experienced and award-winning faculty. Contact: Kathleen O'Brien, Gig Harbor/Key Peninsula Cultural Arts Commission, P.O. Box 826, Gig Harbor, WA 98335.

WHIDBEY ISLAND WRITERS CONFERENCE

Langley, Wash., March.

E-mail: writers@whidbey.com. Web site: www.whidbey.com/writers.

Description: Fireside chats, intensive workshops, informative classes, hands-on writing sessions, and panel discussions with agents and editors. Covers fiction, non-fiction, poetry, screenwriting, children's writing, travel writing, magazine writing, self-publishing, and more. Number of attendees: 250. Contact: Celeste Mergens, 5456 Pleasant View Ln., Freeland, WA 98249. 360-331-6714.

WISCONSIN

GREEN LAKE WRITERS CONFERENCE
Green Lake, Wis., June or July.
E-mail: blythean@greenlake-aba.org. Web site: www.greenlake-aba.org.
Description: Week-long workshops, hour-long seminars, and informal critique groups. Gifted instructors in the areas of writing for children, poetry, inspirational and devotionals, and humor writing. Number of attendees: 60. Contact: Blythe Ann Cooper, Green Lake Conference Center, W2511 State Hwy. 23, Green Lake, WI 54941. 800-558-8898.

SCBWI WISCONSIN FALL RETREAT
Racine, Wis., October.
E-mail: aangel@aol.com.
Description: Editors, writers, and illustrators speak, critique manuscripts, and network with participants. Number of attendees: 50. Contact: Ann Angel, Society of Children's Book Writers & Illustrators, 15255 Turnberry Dr., Brookfield, WI 53005. 262-783-4890.

WYOMING

JACKSON HOLE WRITERS CONFERENCE
Jackson Hole, Wyo., June or July.
E-mail: kguille@ uwyo.edu.
Web site: http://ses.uwyo.edu/conferences/jacksonwriters.
Description: Programs relevant to fiction, screenwriting, and creative nonfiction: story structure, narrative thrust, character development, work habits, and business techniques. Agent and editor roundtable discussions. Setting is near the spectacular Tetons and Yellowstone National Park. Number of attendees: 75. Contact: Keith Guille, Conferences, P.O. Box 3972, Laramie, WY 82071. 307-766-2938.

CANADA

BANFF CENTRE FOR THE ARTS
Banff, Alberta, July.
E-mail: Arts_Info@banff centre.ab.ca.
Web site: www.banffcentre.ab.ca/writing.
Description: Revision of text, independent writing time, consultation with writers/editors. Readings and lectures, book launches, literary festivals, publishing symposiums. Open to those already producing works of literary merit. Located in the Canadian Rockies. Contact: Banff Centre for the Arts, Box 1020, Sta. 28, Banff, AB T0L 0C0. 800-565-9989 or 403-762-6180.

BLOODY WORDS

Toronto, Ont., June.

E-mail: soles@sff.net. Web site: www.bloodywords.com.

Description: Canada's only annual mystery conference for readers and writers of crime books. Workshop, panel discussions, readings, interviews, and award presentations. Number of attendees: 250. Contact: Caro Soles, 12 Roundwood Ct., Toronto, ON M1W 1Z2. 416-497-5293.

INTERNATIONAL

ART WORKSHOP INTERNATIONAL

Assisi, Italy, June or July.

E-mail: meshepley@aol.com or bk@artworkshopintl.com.

Web site: www. artworkshopintl.com.

Description: 2- to 6-week classes in art and writing with time for day trips, short-term travel, shopping and resting. Held in a 12th-century Umbrian hilltown. Number of attendees: 75. Contact: Michael Shepley, 36 W. Parker Ave., Maplewood, NJ 07040. 800-835-7454.

ART WORKSHOPS IN GUATEMALA

Antigua, Guatemala, November.

E-mail: info@artguat.org. Web site: www.artguat.org.

Description: Writing exercises, group readings, critiques, and time to write. Held in 17th-century Antigua, home to artists and language schools. Contact: Liza Fourre, 4758 Lyndale Ave. S, Minneapolis, MN 55409. 612-825-0747.

SAN MIGUEL POETRY WEEK

San Miguel de Allende, Gto., Mexico, early January.

E-mail: poetry week@aol.com.

Description: Poetry lectures and workshops. Top U.S. instructors and Mexican poets teach and read. Held in a preserved colonial town favored by artists, writers, and expatriates. Applicants judged based on their work. Number of attendees: 35. Contact: Jennifer Clement or Barbara Sibley, P.O. Box 171, Cooper Sta., New York, NY 10276. 212-439-5104.

WRITERS CONFERENCE AND BOOKFAIR

Winchester, Hampshire, England, June or July.

E-mail:writerconf@aol.com. Web site: www.gmp.co.uk/writers/conference.

Description: U.K.'s "foremost writers conference." Workshops, mini-courses, editor appointments, lectures, and seminars to help writers harness their creativity and develop technical skills. Number of attendees: 400-500. Contact: Barbara Large, M.B.E., Chinook, Southdown Rd., Shawford, Hampshire S021 2BY, England. 01962-712307.

ORGANIZATIONS

AMERICAN SOCIETY OF JOURNALISTS AND AUTHORS, INC.

1501 Broadway, Suite 302, New York, NY 10036. 212-997-0947.
E-mail: ASJA@compuserve.com. Web site: http://www.asja.org.
Alexandra Owens, Executive Director.
Description: A national organization of independent writers of nonfiction, promoting high standards of writing. ASJA offers extensive benefits: referral services, many discount services, and ways to explore professional issues and concerns with other writers; also produces a free electronic bulletin board for freelancers on contract issues in the new-media age. Members receive a monthly newsletter with confidential market information. Membership open to professional freelance writers of nonfiction; qualifications judged by the membership committee. Call or write for application details.

ASSOCIATED WRITING PROGRAMS

Tallwood House, Mail Stop 1E3, George Mason University, Fairfax, VA 22030.
703-993-4301. Web site: www.awpwriter.org.
Description: Nonprofit organization of teachers, writers, writing programs, and lovers of literature. Awards: for poetry, short fiction, and creative nonfiction; Thomas Dunne Books Award for novels; Praque Summer Seminars Fellowship Competition. Annual conferences. See web site for contest guidelines. Annual dues: $59 ($37 for students), $20 for subscription to *AWP Chronicle* only.

THE AUTHORS GUILD, INC.

330 W. 42nd St., 29th Fl., New York, NY 10036-6902. 212-563-5904.
E-mail: staff@authorsguild.org. Web site: www.authorsguild.org.
Description: The largest organization of published writers in America. Membership offers free reviews of publishing and agency contracts, access to group health insurance, and seminars on subjects of concern. Authors Guild also lobbies on behalf of authors on issues such as copyright, taxation, freedom of expression. A writer who has published a book in the last 7 years with an established publisher, or has published 3 articles in general-circulation periodicals in the prior 18 months is eligible for active membership. An unpublished writer with a contract offer may be eligible for associate membership. First-year annual dues: $90.

DRAMATISTS GUILD OF AMERICA

1501 Broadway, Suite 701, New York, NY 10036-3909. 212-398-9366 Ext. 11.
E-mail: membership@dramatistsguild.com. Web site: www.dramatistsguild.com.
Christopher Wilson, Executive Director.
Description: National professional association of playwrights, composers, and lyricists, working to protect author rights and to improve working conditions. Services include use of guild contracts; a toll-free number for members in need of business advice; discount tickets; access to health insurance programs and group term-life

insurance plan; many seminars. Frederick Loew room is available to members for readings and rehearsals at a nominal fee. Publishes *Dramatists Guild Resource Directory* and *The Dramatists Magazine*. All playwrights, produced or not, are eligible for membership. Annual dues: $125 (active), $75 (associate), $35 (student). Contact: Tom Epstein, Dir. of Membership Services.

INTERNATIONAL ASSOCIATION OF CRIME WRITERS

P.O. Box 8674, New York, NY 10116-8674. 212-243-8966.

E-mail: mfrisque@igc.org.

Mary A. Frizque, Director.

Description: Promotes communications among crime writers worldwide, encourages translation of crime writing into other languages, and defends authors against censorship. The North American branch of IACW also sponsors conferences, publishes quarterly newsletter, *Border Patrol,* and awards annual Hammett prize for literary excellence in crime writing (fiction or nonfiction) by U.S. or Canadian author. Membership open to published authors of crime fiction, nonfiction, and screenplays. Agents, editors, and booksellers are also eligible to apply. Annual dues: $50. Contact: Jim Weikart, President.

INTERNATIONAL WOMEN'S WRITING GUILD

Box 810, Gracie Station, New York, NY 10028-0082. 212-737-7536.

E-mail: iwwg@iwwg-com. Web site: www.iwwg.com.

Hannelore Hahn, Executive Director.

Description: A network for personal and professional empowerment of women through writing. Services include 6 issues of a 32-page newsletter, a list of literary agents, independent small presses, and publishing services, access to group health insurance plan, writing conferences, referral services, and events, including an annual summer conference at Skidmore College in Saratoga Springs, N.Y., regional writing clusters, and year-round supportive networking. Any woman may join regardless of portfolio. Annual dues: $45.

MIDWEST RADIO THEATRE WORKSHOP

915 E. Broadway, Columbia, MO 65201. 573-874-5676.

E-mail: mrtw@mrtw.org.

Sue Zizza, Director.

Description: The only national resource for American radio dramatists, offering referrals, technical assistance, educational materials, and workshops. MRTW coordinates an annual national radio script contest, publishes annual radio scriptbook, and distributes a script anthology with primer. Send SASE for details.

MYSTERY WRITERS OF AMERICA

17 E. 47th St., 6th Fl., New York, NY 10017. 212-888-8171.

Mary Beth Becker, Executive Director.

Description: Works to raise the prestige of mystery and detective writing, and to defend the rights and increase the income of all writers in mystery, detection, and fact-crime writing. Each year, presents the Edgar Allan Poe Awards for the best mystery writing in a variety of fields. Membership classes: "active" (open to any writer who has made a sale in mystery, suspense, or crime writing), "associate" (professionals in allied fields), "corresponding" (writers living outside the U.S.), and "affiliate" (unpublished writers). Annual dues: $65 ($32.50 for "corresponding").

NATIONAL ASSOCIATION OF SCIENCE WRITERS

P.O. Box 294, Greenlawn, NY 11740. 516-757-5664.
E-mail: diane@nasw.ORG. Web site: www.nasw.org.
Ms. Diane McGurgan, Executive Director.
Description: Promotes and helps improve the flow of accurate information about science through all media. Anyone actively engaged in the dissemination of science information is eligible to apply. Members must be principally involved in reporting on science through newspapers, magazines, TV, or other media that reach the public directly. Annual dues: $60, students $15.

NATIONAL CONFERENCE OF EDITORIAL WRITERS

6223 Executive Blvd., Rockville, MD 20852.
E-mail: ncewhqs@erols.com. Web site: www.ncew.org.
Description: A nonprofit organization, NCEW works to improve the quality of editorial pages and broadcast editorials, and to promote high standards among opinion writers and editors. Offers networking opportunities, regional meetings, page exchanges, foreign tours, educational opportunities and seminars, annual convention, and a subscription to quarterly journal, *The Masthead*. Membership is open to opinion writers and editors for general-circulation newspapers, radio or television stations, and syndicated columnists; teachers and students of journalism; and others who determine editorial policy. Annual dues (based on circulation or broadcast audience), $85-$150 (journalism educators: $75; students: $50).

THE NATIONAL LEAGUE OF AMERICAN PEN WOMEN

PEN Arts Building, 1300 17th St. N.W., Washington, DC 20036-1973.
202-785-1997. E-mail: NLAPW1@juno.com.
Web site: http://members.aol.com/penwomen/pen.htm.
Judith La Fourest, President.
Description: Promotes development of creative talents of professional women in the arts. Membership is through local branches, in categories of Art, Letters, and Music.

NATIONAL WRITERS ASSOCIATION

3140 S. Peoria, #295, Aurora, CO 80014. 303-841-0246.
E-mail: sandywrter@aol.com. Web site: www.nationalwriters.com.
Sandy Whelchel, Executive Director.
Description: Full-service organization assisting writers, from formatting a manuscript to assistance finding agents and publishers. Awards cash prizes in 5 contests each year. Published book contest, David R. Raffelock Award for Publishing

Excellence. Referral services, conferences, and financial assistance also offered. Annual dues: $65 Individual, $35 Student, $85 Professional.

NATIONAL WRITERS UNION

113 University Place, 6th Fl., New York, NY 10003. 212-254-0279. E-mail: nwu@nwu.org. Web site: www.nwu.org. Jonathan Tasini, President. **Description:** Works for equitable payment and fair treatment for freelance writers through collective action. Membership over 6,000, includes authors, poets, cartoonists, journalists, and technical writers in 17 chapters nationwide. Offers contract and agent information, group health insurance, press credentials, grievance handling, a quarterly magazine, and sample contracts and resource materials. Sponsors workshops and seminars. Membership open to writers who have published a book, play, 3 articles, 5 poems, a short story, or an equivalent amount of newsletter, publicity, technical, commercial, government, or institutional copy, or have written unpublished material and are actively seeking publication. Annual dues: $95-$210.

NEW DRAMATISTS

424 W. 44th St., New York, NY 10036. Todd London, Artistic Director. **Description:** Helps gifted playwrights to secure the time, space, and tools to develop their craft. Services include readings and workshops; a director-in-residence program; national script distribution for members; artist work spaces; international playwright exchange programs; script copying facilities; and a free ticket program. Membership open to residents of New York City and surrounding tri-state area. National memberships for those outside the area who spend time in NYC. Apply between July 15 and Sept. 15. No annual dues.

NORTHWEST PLAYWRIGHTS GUILD

318 S.W. Palatine Hill Rd., Portland, OR 97219. 503-452-4778. E-mail: bjscript@teleport.com. Web site: www.nwpg.org. Barbara Callander, Director. **Description:** Chapters in Portland (Oregon) and Seattle (Washington). Encourages the creation and production of new plays. Support through play development, staged readings, and networking for play competitions and production opportunities. Oregon chapter offers Page to Stage and Living Room Theater to help playwrights develop new work. Monthly and quarterly newsletters. Annual dues: $25. Contact: Bill Johnson, Office Manager.

OUTDOOR WRITERS ASSOCIATION OF AMERICA

121 Hickory Street, Suite 1, Missoula, MT 59801. 406-728-7434. E-mail: owaa@montana.com. Web site: www.owaa.org. Steve Wagner, Meeting Director. **Description:** A non-profit organization of outdoor communicators. Awards: Ham Brown Award, Jade of Chiefs, Excellence in Craft, Mountain of Jade Award, Jackie

Pfeiffer Memorial Award. Also, referral services and conferences. Dues: $100 individual, $40 student, $300 supporting.

PEN AMERICAN CENTER
568 Broadway, New York, NY 10012. 212-334-1660.
E-mail: pen@pen.org. Web site: www.pen.org.
Michael Roberts, Executive Director.
Description: One of over 130 centers worldwide of International PEN. Members are poets, playwrights, essayists, editors, and novelists, also literary translators and agents who have made a substantial contribution to the literary community. Main office in New York City; branches in Boston, Chicago, New Orleans, Portland, Oregon, and San Francisco. Programs and services include literary events and awards, outreach projects, assistance to writers in financial need, and international and domestic human-rights campaigns on behalf of literary figures imprisoned because of their writing. Membership open to writers who have published 2 books of literary merit, also editors, agents, playwrights, and translators who meet specific standards; apply to membership committee. Annual dues, $75. Contact: John Moprone.

THE PLAYWRIGHTS' CENTER
2301 Franklin Ave. E., Minneapolis, MN 55406. 612-332-7481.
E-mail: info@pwcenter.org. Web site: www.pwcenter.org.
Carlo Cuesta, Executive Director.
Description: Provides services to support playwrights and playwriting, nurtures artistic excellence and new visions, fosters initiative and leadership, practices cultural pluralism, discovers emerging artists, and connects playwrights with audiences. Annual awards: McKnight Residency and Commission, McKnight Advancement Grant, Jerome fellowships, Many Voices residencies, Many Voices Cultural Collaboration Grants. Members may apply for all programs and participate in special activities, including classes, outreach programs, and PlayLabs. Annual dues: $75 local individual, $30 student/senior, $40 low-income member, $40 member over 100 miles. Contact: Megan Monaghan, Playwright Services Dir.

POETRY SOCIETY OF AMERICA
15 Gramercy Park, New York, NY 10003. 212-254-9628.
Web site: www.poetrysociety.org.
Alice Quinn, Programs Associate.
Description: Seeks to raise awareness of poetry, to deepen understanding of it, and to encourage more people to read, listen to, and write poetry. Presents national series of readings including "Tributes in Libraries" and "Poetry in Public Places," and places posters on mass transit vehicles through "Poetry in Motion." Also offers annual contests for poetry, seminars, conferences, poetry festivals, and publishes a journal. Annual dues: from $40 ($25 for students). Contact: Brett Lauer.

POETS AND WRITERS

72 Spring St., New York, NY 10012. 212-226-3586.

Web site: www.pw.org.

Elliot Figman, Executive Director.

Description: Fosters the development of poets and fiction writers and promotes communication throughout the literary community. A non-membership organization, it offers information, a magazine for poets and writers, and a directory of American poets and fiction writers, also support for readings and workshops at varied venues.

ROMANCE WRITERS OF AMERICA

3707 FM 1960 West, Suite 555, Houston, TX 77068. 281-440-6885.

E-mail: info@rwanational.com. Web site: www.rwanational.com.

Allison Kelley, Executive Director.

Description: A nonprofit organization for published or unpublished writers interested in the field of romantic fiction. Offers conferences, and awards: RITA (for published romance novels), Golden Heart (for unpublished manuscripts). Annual dues, $75.

SCIENCE-FICTION AND FANTASY WRITERS OF AMERICA

532 La Guardia Pl., #632, New York, NY 10012-1428.

Robert J. Sawyer, President.

Description: Promotes the professional interests of science fiction and fantasy writers. Presents annual Nebula Award for excellence in the field; publishes the "Bulletin" and "SFWA Handbook" for members (also available to non-members). Any writer who has sold a work of science fiction or fantasy is eligible. Annual dues: $50 (active), $35 ("affiliate"), plus $10 installation fee; send for application.

SISTERS IN CRIME

P.O. Box 442124, Lawrence, KS 66044-8933.

E-mail: sistersincrime@juno.com. Web site: www.sistersincrime.org.

Barbara Burnett Smith, President.

Description: Fights discrimination against women in the mystery field, educates publishers and the public about inequalities in the treatment of female authors, and increases awareness of their contribution to the field. Membership open to all: writers, readers, editors, agents, booksellers, librarians. Publishes a quarterly newsletter and Books in Print membership directory. Annual dues: $35 (U.S.), $40 (foreign). Members interested in mysteries for young readers may join Mysteries for Minors (Katherine Hall Page, Chair, P.O. Box 442124, Lawrence, KS 66044-8933) at no extra cost.

SOCIETY OF AMERICAN TRAVEL WRITERS

4101 Lake Boone Trail, Suite 201, Raleigh, NC 27607. 919-787-5181.

Cathy Korr, Executive Director.

Description: Represents writers and other professionals who strive to provide travelers with accurate reports on destinations, facilities, and services. Active membership limited to travel writers and freelancers with a steady volume of published or distributed work about travel. Application fees: $250 (active), $500 (associate). Annual dues: $130 (active), $250 (associate).

SOCIETY OF CHILDREN'S BOOK WRITERS & ILLUSTRATORS
8271 Beverly Blvd., Los Angeles, CA 90048. 323-782-1010.
E-mail: scbwi@scbwi.org. Web site: www.scbwi.org.
Lin Oliver, Executive Director.
Description: A national organization of authors, editors, publishers, illustrators, librarians, and educators; for beginners and established professionals alike. Offers varied services: referrals, conferences, grants program. Full memberships open to anyone who has had at least 1 children's book or story published. Associate memberships open to all interested in children's literature. Annual dues: $50. Annual awards: Golden Kite Book Award, Magazine Merit Award.

SOCIETY OF ENVIRONMENTAL JOURNALISTS
P.O. Box 27280, Philadelphia, PA 19118. 215-836-9970.
E-mail: SEJ@SEJ.ORG. Web site: www.SEJ.org.
Beth Parke, Executive Director.
Description: Dedicated to improving the quality, accuracy, and visibility of environmental reporting. Serves 1,200 members with quarterly newsletter, national and regional conferences, web site, and membership directory. Annual dues: $40, $30 (student).

SOCIETY OF PROFESSIONAL JOURNALISTS
16 S. Jackson St., Greencastle, IN 46135-0077. 765-653-3333.
Web site: http://spj.org.
Description: Serves the interests of print, broadcast, and wire journalists (13,500 members and 300 chapters). Services: legal counsel on journalism issues, jobs-for-journalists career search newsletter, professional development seminars, and awards. Members receive *Quill*, a monthly magazine on current issues in the field. Also promotes programs on ethics and freedom of information. Annual dues: $70 (professional), $35 (student).

SONGWRITERS GUILD
1560 Broadway, Suite 1306, New York, NY 10036.
George Wurzbach, National Projects Director.
Description: Provides published and unpublished songwriters with sample contracts, reviews contracts, collects royalties from publishers, offers group health and life insurance plans, conducts workshops and critique sessions, and provides newsletter. Annual dues: $55 (associate), $70 and up (full member).

THEATRE COMMUNICATIONS GROUP
355 Lexington Ave., New York, NY 10017. 212-697-5230.
Web site: www.tcg.org.
Terence Nemeth, Vice President.
Description: National organization offers a wide array of services to strengthen,

nurture, and promote the not-for-profit American theatre (artistic and management programs, advocacy activities, and publications). Seeks to increase organizational efficiency of member theatres, encourages artistic talent and achievement, and promotes greater public appreciation for the field. Individual members receive *American Theatre* magazine. Annual dues: $35 (individual).

WESTERN WRITERS OF AMERICA

1012 Fair St., Franklin, TN 37064. 615-791-1444.
E-mail: Tncrutch@aol.com. Web site: www.westernwriters.org.
James A. Crutchfield, Managing Editor.
Description: Open to professional writers of fiction and nonfiction on the history and literature of the American West. Promotes distribution, readership, and appreciation of the West and its literature. Annual convention last week of June. Sponsors annual Spur Awards, Owen Wister Award, and Medicine Pipe Bearer's Award for published work and produced screenplays. Annual dues: $75.

WRITERS GUILD OF AMERICA, EAST

555 W. 57th St., New York, NY 10019. 212-767-7800.
Web site: www.wgaeast.org.
Mona Mangan, Executive Director.
Description: See Writer's Guild of America, West.

WRITERS GUILD OF AMERICA, WEST

7000 W. 3rd St., Los Angeles, CA 90048. 213-951-4000.
Web site: www.wga.org.
Brian Walton, Executive Director.
Description: Writers Guild of America (East and West) represents writers in motion pictures, broadcast, cable, and new media industries, including news and entertainment. To qualify for membership, a writer must meet requirements for employment or sale of material. Basic dues: $25/quarter. Also, quarterly dues based on percentage of the member's earnings in any of the fields over which the guild has jurisdiction. Initiation fee: $1,500 for WGAE (writers living east of the Mississippi), $2,500 for WGAW (for those west of the Mississippi).

WRITERS INFORMATION NETWORK

P.O. Box 11337, Bainbridge Island, WA 98110. 206-842-9103.
E-mail: writersinfonetwork@juno.com. Web site: www.bluejaypub.com/win.
Elaine Wright Colvin, Director.
Description: Provides a link between Christian writers and the religious publishing industry. Publishes *WIN-Informer*, magazine of industry news and trends, market reports, professional advice on marketing, ethics, contracts, editor relations, writing problems and concerns, author/speaker referral services. Annual dues: $35.

PRIZES & AWARDS

Writers seeking the thrill of competition should review this list of literary prize offers, many designed to promote the as-yet-unpublished author. Most of the competitions listed here are for unpublished manuscripts and usually offer publication in addition to a cash prize. The prestige that comes with winning one of the more established awards can do much to further a writer's career, as editors, publishers, and agents are likely to consider the future work of the prize winner more closely.

There are hundreds of literary contests open to writers in all genres, and the following list covers a representative number of them. The summaries given below are intended merely as guides; since submission requirements are more detailed than space allows, writers should send an SASE for complete guidelines before entering any contest. Writers are also advised to check the monthly "Prize Offerings" column of *The Writer* magazine (Kalmbach Publishing Co., 21027 Crossroads Circle, P.O. Box 1612, Waukesha, WI 53187-1612) for additional contest listings and up-to-date contest requirements. Deadlines are annual unless otherwise noted.

ACADEMY FOUNDATION OF THE ACADEMY OF MOTION PICTURES ARTS AND SCIENCES

Don and Gee Nicholl Fellowships in Screenwriting, 8849 Wilshire Blvd., Beverly Hills, CA 90211. 310-247-3000.
E-mail: nicholl@oscars.org. Web site: www.oscars.org/nicholl.
Description: Original feature film screenplay, appr. 100-130 pages. No translations. Entry fee: $30. Deadline: May 1. Prizes: Up to 5 fellowships of $30,000 each. See web site for application form.

ACADEMY OF AMERICAN POETS

Walt Whitman Award, 584 Broadway, Suite 1208, New York, NY 10012-3250. 212-274-0343.
E-mail: academy@poets.org. Web site: www.poets.org.
Description: Award of $5,000 plus publication, and a 1-month residency at Vermont Studio Center, for a book-length poetry manuscript by a poet who has not yet published a volume of poetry. Deadline: November 15. $20 entry fee.

ACTORS THEATRE OF LOUISVILLE

Ten-Minute Play Contest, 316 W. Main St., Louisville, KY 40202-4218.
Description: A prize of $1,000, for a previously unproduced 10-page script. Deadline: December 1.

AMERICAN ACADEMY OF ARTS AND LETTERS

Richard Rogers Awards, 633 W. 155th St, New York, NY 10032.
Description: Offers subsidized productions or staged readings in New York City by a nonprofit theater for a musical, play with music, thematic review, or any comparable work. Deadline: November 1.

AMERICAN ANTIQUARIAN SOCIETY

Fellowships for Historical Research, 185 Salisbury St., Worcester, MA 01609. John B. Hench, Director.
Description: At least 3 fellowships, for creative and performing artists, writers, filmmakers, and journalists, for research on pre-20th century American history. Residencies 4-8 weeks; travel expenses and stipends of $1,200 per month. Write for guidelines. Deadline: October.

AMERICAN MARKETS NEWSLETTERS

American Markets Newsletter Competition, 1974 46th Ave., San Francisco, CA 94116.
Description: Fiction and nonfiction to 2,000 words, both published and unpublished. All entries will be considered for worldwide syndication. Deadline: July 31. Entry fee: AMN subscribers, $6 for 1 entry, $9 for 2 entries; non subscribers, $7.50/entry. Prizes: $150; $40; $30.

AMERICAN-SCANDINAVIAN FOUNDATION

ASF Translation Prize, 58 Park Ave., New York, NY 10016. 212-249-3444.
E-mail: agyongy@amscan.org. Web site: www.amscan.org.
Description: Translations of literary prose (50+ pages) or poetry (25+ pages) originally written in Danish, Finnish, Icelandic, Norwegian, or Swedish. SASE or e-mail for guidelines. Entry fee: none. Deadline: June 1. Prizes: $2,000, publication of excerpt and medallion; $500.

ANHINGA PRESS

Anhinga Prize for Poetry, P.O. Box 10595 , Tallahassee, FL 32302-0595. 850-521-9920.
E-mail: info@anhinga.org. Web site: www.anhinga.org.
Description: A $2,000 prize, for an unpublished full-length collection of poetry, 48-72 pages, by a poet who has published no more than one full-length collection. Deadline: March 15. Entry fee.

ASSOCIATED WRITING PROGRAMS

AWP/Thomas Dunne Books Novel Award and AWP Award Series, Tallwood House, Mail Stop 1E3, George Mason University, Fairfax, VA 22030.
E-mail: awpchron@mason.gmu.edu. Web site: www.awpwriter.org.
Description: Open to all authors writing in English. Only book-length manuscripts are eligible: for poetry, 48 pages minimum text; short story collections and creative nonfiction, 150-300 manuscript pages; novels at least 60,000 words. Send a business-size SASE for guidelines. $10,000 advance against earnings for novel; $2,000 honorarium for poetry, short fiction and nonfiction. Deadline: submissions must be postmarked between Jan. 1 and Feb. 28. $20 entry fee. ($10 if AWP member).

ASSOCIATION OF JEWISH LIBRARIES

315 Maitland Ave., Teaneck, NJ 07666. 201-862-0312.
E-mail: rkglasser@aol.com. Web site: www.jewishlibraries.org.
Rachel Glasser, Coordinator.
Description: Sydney Taylor Manuscript Competition. Stories must have a positive Jewish focus. Deadline: January 1st. No entry fee.

BANKS CHANNEL BOOKS

Carolina Novel Award, P.O. Box 4446, Wilmington, NC 28406.
Description: Awards $1,000 advance, plus publication, for an original, unpublished novel by a North or South Carolina writer. Deadline: July 31 of even-numbered years. Entry fee.

BANTAM DOUBLEDAY DELL BOOKS FOR YOUNG READERS

Marguerite de Angeli Prize, Dept. BFYR, 1540 Broadway, New York, NY 10036. 212-782-9000.
Web site: www.randomhouse.com/kids.
Description: Awards $1,500, plus $3,500 advance against royalties, for a middle-grade fiction manuscript that explores the diversity of the American experience. Open to U.S. and Canadian writers who have not previously published a novel for middle-grade readers. Deadline: June 30.

BARNARD COLLEGE

New Women Poets Prize, Columbia University, 3009 Broadway, New York, NY 10027.
Description: A prize of $1,500, and publication by Beacon Press, for an unpublished poetry manuscript, 50-100 pages, by a female poet who has never published a book of poetry. Deadline: October 15.

THE BELLINGHAM REVIEW

Western Washington University, MS-9053, Bellingham, WA 98225.
Web site: www.wwu.edu/bhreview.
Description: Tobias Wolff Award in Fiction: prizes of $500 plus publication, $250, $100, for short story or novel excerpt. Deadline: March 1. Annie Dillard Award in Nonfiction: prizes of $500 plus publication, $250, $100, for previously unpublished essays. Deadline: March 1. 49th Parallel Poetry Award: publication and prizes of $500, $250, $100. Deadline: November 30. Entry fees.

BEVERLY HILLS THEATRE GUILD

Julie Harris Playwright Award, 2815 N. Beachwood Dr., Los Angeles, CA 90068-1923. 323-465-2703.
Marcella Meharg, Director.
Description: Offers prize of $5,000, $2,000, and $1,000 for an unpublished full-length play. Deadline: November 1.

BIRMINGHAM-SOUTHERN COLLEGE

Hackney Literary Awards, Box 549003, Birmingham, AL 35254. 205-226-4921. E-mail: D.C.Wilson@bsc.edu. Web site: www.bsc.edu.

Martha Ross, Director.

Description: Awards, open to writers nationwide, presented as part of Birmingham-Southern College "Writing Today" Conference. Awards $5,000 in annual prizes for poetry and short fiction (in national and state categories), plus a $5,000 prize for an unpublished novel. Write for details.

BLUE MOUNTAIN CENTER

Richard J. Margolis Award, 294 Washington St., Suite 610, Boston, MA 02108.

Description: Awarded annually to a promising journalist or essayist whose work combines warmth, humor, wisdom, and a concern with social issues. Apply with up to 30 pages of published or unpublished work. Deadline: July 1. Prize: $4,000 grant and 1-month residency at the Blue Mountain Center in the Adirondacks. Include short bio., description of current and anticipated work, 3 writing samples.

BOISE STATE UNIVERSITY

Rocky Mountain Artists' Book Competition, Hemingway Western Studies Center, Boise, ID 83725.

Description: A prize of $500, and publication, for up to 3 books. Manuscripts (text and/or visual material) and proposals considered for short-run printing of books on public issues concerning the Inter-Mountain West. Deadline: year-round.

BOSTON REVIEW

Poetry Contest, MIT, E53-407, Cambridge, MA 02139. 617-253-3642. Web site: http://bostonreview.mit.edu.

Description: Annual poetry contest for original, unpublished poems, 5 poems, to 10 pages. Awards $1,000, plus publication. Submit 2 copies. Deadline: June 1. Entry fee: $15. Prize: $1,000 and publication.

BOX TURTLE PRESS

Mudfish Poetry Prize, 184 Franklin St., New York, NY 10013. 212-219-9278. Jill Hoffman, Director.

Description: Awards $500, plus publication. Deadline: April 30. Entry fee.

ARCH AND BRUCE BROWN FOUNDATION

P.O. Box 45231, Phoenix, AZ 85064.

Description: Offers $1,000 grants for gay and lesbian-positive fiction. Deadline: May 31.

BUCKNELL UNIVERSITY

Philip Roth Residence in Creative Writing, Stadler Center for Poetry, Lewisburg, PA 17837.

Cynthia Hogue, Director.

Description: Awards fall residency (studio, lodging, meals) and $1,000 stipend, for a writer, over 21, not currently enrolled in a university, to work on a first or second book. Awarded in odd-numbered years to a fiction writer, and in even-numbered years to a poet. Deadline: March 1.

CASE WESTERN RESERVE UNIVERSITY

Marc A. Klein Playwriting Award, Dept. of Theater Arts, 10900 Euclid Ave., Cleveland, OH 44106-7077. 216-368-4868.

E-mail: ksg@po.cwru.edu.

Description: A prize of $1,000, plus production, for an original, previously unproduced full-length play by a student currently enrolled at an American university or college. Deadline: May 15.

CENTER FOR BOOK ARTS

Poetry Chapbook Prize, Center for Book Arts, 626 Broadway, 5th Floor, New York, NY 10012.

Description: Offers $1,000, publication, and a public reading for poetry manuscript, to 500 lines. Deadline: December 31. Entry fee.

THE CENTER FOR WRITERS

Mississippi Review Prize, University of Southern Mississippi, P.O. Box 5144, Hattiesburg, MS 39406. 601-266-4321.

E-mail: rief@netdoor.com. Web site: http://orca.otr.usm.edu.mrw.

Description: Short stories to 4,000 words. 3 poems to 10 pages total. Place contact information on first page. Entry fee: $15. Deadline: May 31. Prizes: $1,000 in 2 categories—short story and poem.

CHELSEA AWARDS

Chelsea Awards, P.O. Box 773, Cooper Station, New York, NY 10276-0773.

Description: Awards for Fiction and Poetry. Prizes: $1,000 each, plus publication. Traditional and experimental fiction, previously unpublished, up to 30 typed pages or 7,500 words. Deadlines: June 15 (fiction), Dec. 15 (poetry). Entry fee: $10, includes discounted subscription.

THE CHICAGO TRIBUNE

Nelson Algren Awards, Chicago Tribune, 435 N. Michigan Ave., Chicago, IL 60611.

Description: A first prize of $5,000, and 3 runner-up prizes of $1,000, for outstanding unpublished short stories, 2,500-10,000 words, by American writers. Deadline: Feb. 1.

CHICKEN SOUP FOR THE WRITER'S SOUL

P.O. Box 30880, Santa Barbara, CA 93130. 805-563-2945.

Web site: www.chickensoup.com.

Description: Original essays, short stories, and poems up to 1,200 words that are uplifting, inspiring, and present a positive viewpoint. Open to U.S. residents only. Winner will receive hotel, airfare and paid entrance to the Maui Writer's Conference and story will be considered for publication in the *Chicken Soup* book series. Deadline: March 1. No entry fee.

CLAREMONT GRADUATE UNIVERSITY

Kingsley Tufts Poetry Awards and Kate Tufts Discovery Award, 160 E. 10th St., Claremont, CA 91711. 909-621-8974.

Web site: www.cgu.edu/commun/tuftsent.html.

Betty A. Terrell, Awards Administrator.

Description: Kingsley Tufts Poetry Award, $100,000 for an American poet. Kate Tufts Discovery Award, $10,000, for an emerging poet whose work shows extraordinary promise. Deadline: Sept. 15. No entry fee.

CLEVELAND STATE UNIVERSITY POETRY CENTER

Poetry Center Prize, Dept. of English, Rhodes Tower, Rm. 1815, Cleveland, OH 44115-2440. 216-687-3986.

E-mail: poetrycenter@csuohio.edu.

Web site: www.ims.csuohio.edu/poetrycenter.html.

Description: An award of $1,000, and publication, for a previously unpublished book-length volume of poetry. Deadline: March 1. Entry fee.

COALITION FOR THE ADVANCEMENT OF JEWISH EDUCATION

David Dornstein Memorial Creative Writing Contest, 261 W. 35th St., Floor 12A, New York, NY 10001.

Description: Prizes of $700, $200, and $100, and publication, for the 3 best original, previously unpublished short stories, to 5,000 words, on a Jewish theme or topic, by writers age 18-35. Deadline: Dec. 31.

COLONIAL PLAYERS

Promising Playwright Award, 98 Tower Dr., Stevensville, MD 21666.

Description: A prize of $750, plus possible production, for the best full-length play by a resident of MD, DC, VA, WV, DE, or PA. Deadline: Dec. 31 of even-numbered years.

COLORADO STATE UNIVERSITY

Colorado Prize for Poetry, *Colorado Review*, Dept. of English, Fort Collins, CO 80523.

Description: A prize of $1,500, plus publication, for a book-length collection of original poems. Deadline: Jan. 10. Entry fee.

COMMUNITY CHILDREN'S THEATRE OF KANSAS CITY
8021 E. 129th Terrace, Grandview, MO 64030.
Blanche Sellens, Director.
Description: A prize of $500, plus production, for the best play, up to 1 hour long, to be performed by adults for elementary school audiences. Deadline: Jan. 31.

COMMUNITY WRITERS ASSOCIATION
CWA Writing Contest, P.O. Box 12, Newport, RI 02840-0001.
Description: A prize of $500, for short stories, to 2,000 words, and poetry, any length. Deadline: June 1. Entry fee.

CONNECTICUT POETRY SOCIETY
Joseph E. Brodine Poetry Contest, P.O. Box 4053, Waterbury, CT 06704.
203-753-7815.
E-mail: wtarzia@nvctc5comment.edu.
Web site: http://hometown.aol.com/ctpoetrysociety.
Description: Original, unpublished poetry up to 40 lines, maximum of 5 poems. Send 2 copies of each poem, one with name and address in upper right-hand corner. SASE for results. Deadline: July 31. Entry fee: $2/poem. Prize: $150; $100; $50 plus publication.

EUGENE V. DEBS FOUNDATION
Bryant Spann Memorial Prize, Indiana State University, Dept. of History, Terre Haute, IN 47809.
Description: A prize of $1,000, for a published or unpublished article or essay on themes relating to social protest or human equality. Deadline: April 30.

DELACORTE PRESS/RANDOM HOUSE INC.
Marguerite De Angeli Contest, 1540 Broadway, New York, NY 10036.
Web site: www.randomhouse.com.
Description: Contemporary or historical fiction manuscripts, 40-144 pages for readers ages 7-10. Open to U.S. and Canadian writers who have not previously published a novel for middle-grade readers. SASE for return and SASE for notification. Deadline: June 30. No entry fee. Prize: $1,500 cash, $3,500 advance and publication.

THE DOUGLAS COLLEGE REVIEW
Event Creative Nonfiction Contest, P.O. Box 2503, New Westminister, BC V3L 5B2.
604-527-5293.
E-mail: event@douglas.bc.ca. Web site: http://event.douglas.bc.ca.
Description: Creative nonfiction up to 5,000 words, typed and double-spaced. Entry fee: $25 (includes a subscription to Event magazine.) Deadline: April 15. Prizes: Three $500 plus publication.

DRURY COLLEGE

Playwriting Contest, 900 N. Benton Ave., Springfield, MO 65802. 417-873-7430. E-mail: sasher@drury.edu. Web site: www.drury.edu/academics/playatt.html. Sandy Asher, Director. **Description:** Writer-in-Residence. Prizes of $300 and two $150 honorable mentions, plus possible production (Open Eye Theatre), for original, previously unproduced one-act plays. Deadline: Dec. 1 of even-numbered years.

DUBUQUE FINE ARTS PLAYERS

One-Act Playwriting Contest, 330 Clarke Dr., Dubuque, IA 52001. 319-588-0646. E-mail: snakelady@mwci.net. Web site: www.community.iowa.com/ic/oneactplaycontest. Jennifer G. Stabenow, Contest Coordinator. **Description:** Prizes of $600, $300, and $200, plus full production of all winners if possible. Seeking original one-act plays of up to 40 minutes. Deadline: Jan. 31. Entry fee: $10.

DUKE UNIVERSITY PRESS

1317 W. Pettigrew Street, Durham, NC 27705. 919-660-3663. E-mail: alexad@duke.edu. Web site: http://cds.aas.duke,edu/1-t/. Tom Rankin, Center's Director. **Description:** A grant of up to $10,000, for a writer and photographer working together in the formative stages of a documentary project to ultimately result in a publishable work. Collaborative submissions on any subject are welcome. Deadline: Jan. 31. (accepts submissions only during month of January). See web site for details. Contact: Alexa Dilworth, Award Administrator.

ELF: ECLECTIC LITERARY FORUM

Ruth Cable Memorial Prize, P.O. Box 392, Tonawanda, NY 14150. **Description:** Awards of $500 and three $50 prizes, for poems up to 50 lines. Short Fiction Prize awards, $500 plus publication, and two $50 prizes for stories, to 3,500 words. Deadline: March 31. Fiction deadline: August 31. Entry fee.

EMPORIA STATE UNIVERSITY

Bluestem Award, English Dept., Emporia State Univ., Emporia, KS 66801-5087. 316-341-5216. E-mail: bluestem@esumail.emporia.edu. Web site: bluestem@emporia.edu. Philip Heldrich, Director. **Description:** A prize of $1,000, plus publication, for a previously unpublished book of poems in English by a U.S. author. Deadline: March 1st. Entry fee: $18. Contact: Any Sage Webb.

FLORIDA FREELANCE WRITER'S ASSOCIATION

CNW/FFWA Florida State Writing Competition, P.O. Box A, North Stratford, NH 03590. 603-922-8338.

Description: Categories include fiction, nonfiction, children's and poetry. SASE for guidelines and entry form. No entry fee. Deadline march 15. Prizes $100-$500. Contact: Dana K. Cassell.

THE FLORIDA REVIEW

Editors' Awards, Dept. of English, Univ. of Central Florida , Orlando, FL 32816-0001. 407-823-2038.

Web site: www.pegasus.cc.ucf.edu/~english/floridareview/home.htm.

Description: Unpublished fiction and memoirs to 10,000 words, poetry to 40 lines. SASE. Entry fee: $10. Prizes: Three $500 awards.

FLORIDA STUDIO THEATRE

Shorts Contest, 1241 N. Palm Ave., Sarasota, FL 34236. 941-366-9017.

E-mail: james@fst2000.org.

Christian Angermann, Director.

Description: Short scripts, songs, and other performance pieces on a given theme are eligible for a prize of $500. Deadline: Feb. 15.

THE FORMALIST

Howard Nemerov Sonnet Award, 320 Hunter Dr., Evansville, IN 47711.

Description: Offers $1,000 prize, plus publication, for previously unpublished, original sonnet. Deadline: June 15. Entry fee.

FOUR WAY BOOKS

Intro Prize in Poetry, P.O. Box 535, Village Station, New York, NY 10014. 212-619-1105.

E-mail: four_way_editors@yahoo.com. Web site: www.fourway.com.

Martha Rhodes, Director.

Description: Different prizes annually, cash honorarium and book publication. Deadline: March 31. Entry fee. Contact: K. Clarke, Contest Coordinator.

JOHN GASSNER MEMORIAL PLAYWRITING AWARD

The New England Theatre Conference, Northeastern University, 360 Huntington Ave., Boston, MA 02115.

E-mail: netc@world.std.com.

Description: New, unpublished full-length plays that have not been produced by a professional or Equity company. Open to New England residents and NETC members. SASE. Entry fee: $10. Deadline: April 15. Prizes: $1,000 and $500.

GENERAL FOUNDATION OF WOMAN'S CLUBS

Jane Cunningham CROLY/GFWC Print Journalism Contest, 1734 N St. NW, Washington, DC 20036. 202-347-3168.

E-mail: gfwc@gfwc.org. Web site: www.gfwc.org.

Description: Submit 3 stories published in the previous year to demonstrate a concern for the rights and advancement of women, an awareness of women's sensitivity and strength, and/or an attempt to counteract sexism. Deadline: March 1. Entry fee: $50. $1,000 Prize. Contact: Sally Kranz.

GEORGE MASON UNIVERSITY

Greg Grummer Award in Poetry, 4400 Univ. Dr., Fairfax, VA 22030-4444.

Description: A prize of $500, plus publication, for an outstanding previously unpublished poem. Deadline: Dec. 15. Entry fee.

GEORGE WASHINGTON UNIVERSITY

Jenny McKean Moore, Writer-in-Washington, Dept. of English, Washington, D.C. 20052.

Description: A salaried teaching position for 2 semesters, for a creative writer (various mediums in alternate years) with "significant publications and a demonstrated commitment to teaching. Need not have conventional academic credentials." Deadline: Nov. 15.

THE GEORGETOWN REVIEW

Fiction and Poetry Contest, P.O. Box 6309, Southern Station, Hattiesburg, MS 39406-6309.

Description: A prize of $1,000, for a short story of no more than 25 pages or 6,500 words; and $500, for a single poem, any length. Includes publication and subscription. Deadline: Oct. 1. Entry fee.

GEORGIA POETRY SOCIETY

Edward Davin Vickers Poetry Contest, 3822 Clubhouse Pl., Gainesville, GA 30501. 770-531-9473.

Description: Original, unpublished poetry. Send 2 copies of each poem with contest name in upper right-hand corner, entry name and address on 1 copy only. Deadline: July 15. Entry fee: $5 for 1 poem, $1 for each additional poem. Prizes: $250, $100; $50.

GLIMMER TRAIN PRESS

Semiannual Short Story Award for New Writers, 710 S.W. Madison St., #504, Portland, OR 97205. 503-221-0836.

Web site: www.glimmertrain.com.

Description: Prizes of $1,200 (plus publication), $500, and $300, for stories of 1,200-7,500 words by writers whose fiction has never appeared in a nationally distributed publication. Deadlines: March 31; Sept. 30. Entry fee.

GREENFIELD REVIEW LITERARY CENTER
North American Native Authors First Book Awards, P.O. Box 308, 2 Middle Grove Rd., Greenfield Center, NY 12833.
Joseph Bruchac, Director.
Description: Prizes of $500, plus publication, for poetry (64-100 pages), and prose (200-300 pages, fiction or nonfiction), by Native Americans of American Indian, Aleut, Inuit, or Metis ancestry, who have not yet published a book. Deadline: March 15.

GROLIER POETRY PRIZE
6 Plympton St., Cambridge, MA 02138. 617-547-4648.
Web site: www.grolier-poetry.com.
Description: Two $150 honorariums, for poetry manuscripts of up to 10 double-spaced pages, including no more than 5 previously unpublished poems, by writers who have not yet published a book of poems. Deadline: May 1. Entry fee.

HEEKIN GROUP FOUNDATION
Fiction Fellowships Competition, Box 1534, Sisters, OR 97759.
Description: Awards fellowships to beginning career writers: two $1,500 Tara Fellowships in Short Fiction; two $3,000 James Fellowships for Novel in Progress; a $2,000 Mary Molloy Fellowship for Juvenile Novel in Progress (address H.G.F., P.O. Box 209, Middlebury, VT 05753); and a $2,000 Cuchulain Fellowhip for Rhetoric (Essay). Writers who have never published a novel, a children's novel, more than 5 short stories in national publication, or an essay are eligible to enter. Deadline: Dec. 1. Entry fee.

HELICON NINE EDITIONS
Literary Prizes, 3607 Pennsylvania, Kansas City, MO 64111.
Description: Marianne Moore Poetry Prize: $1,000, for an original unpublished poetry manuscript of at least 48 pages. Willa Cather Fiction Prize: $1,000, for an original novella or short story collection, from 150-300 pages. Deadline: May 1. Entry fee.

HIGHLIGHTS FOR CHILDREN
Highlights for Children Fiction Contest, 803 Church St., Honesdale, PA 18431. 570-253-1080.
Description: Annual contest with a different theme each year. Write for more information. Stories for beginning readers to 500 words, for others up to 900 words. No stories that glorify war, crime or violence. SASE. Three winners receive $1000 each and publication in Highlights. Deadline: February 28. No entry fee.

KNOXVILLE WRITER'S GUILD
Peter Taylor Prize for the Novel, P.O. Box 2565, Knoxville, TN 37901.
Web site: www.knoxvillewritersguild.org.
Description: Unpublished novels of 40,000 words or more. SASE. See web site for details. Entry fee: $20. Deadline: April 30. Prize: $1,000 plus publication. Contact: Brian Griffin.

LAKE AFFECT MAGAZINE

Lake Affect Short Story Contest, 165 Park Ave., Rochester, NY 14609. E-mail: laffect@pop3.frontiernet.net. **Description:** Stories up to 2,500 words. Deadline: March 31. Entry fee: $10. First prize, $300 and publication in Lake Affect Magazine. Honorable mentions receive a $25 gift certificate from Barnes & Noble.

LOTUS PRESS

Naomi Long Madgett Poetry Award, P.O. Box 21607, Detroit, MI 48221. 313-861-1280. E-mail: lotuspress@aol.com. **Description:** Submit book-length manuscripts, 60-80 pages. By African-American poets only. Submit 3 copies. SASE or e-mail us for guidelines. Entry fee: $15. Prize: $500 plus publication.

MID-LIST PRESS

Mid-List Press First Series Award, 4324 12th Ave. S., Minneapolis, MN 54407. 612-822-3733. E-mail: guide@midlist.org. Web site: www.midlist.org. **Description:** Unpublished novels, poetry, short fiction, and creative nonfiction. Fiction and nonfiction manuscripts must be at least 50,000 words; poetry at least 60 pages. See web site for more information. SASE. Deadline: July 1. Entry fee: $20. Prize: Publication and advance against royalties in 4 categories.

MIDWEST WRITING CENTER

Mississippi Valley Poetry Contest, P.O. Box 3188, Rock Island, IL 61204. 319-359-1057. **Description:** Up to 5 unpublished poems, to 50 lines each. Nine categories. K-12 poets encouraged. Deadline: April 1. Entry fee: $3 (students) and $5 (adults). Total prizes $1,500-$1,700. Contact: Max Molleston.

MOONLIGHT & MAGNOLIA FICTION WRITING CONTEST

P.O. Box 180489, Richland, MS 39218-0489. 601-932-6670. E-mail: Hoover59@aol.com. **Description:** Annual competition for science fiction, fantasy and horror stories. Open to unpublished writers or those who have not published more than two stories in a national, 5,000+ circulation magazine. Submissions must be unpublished and not under contract. Stories up to 10,000 words. SASE. Entry fee: $7.50 per story, $2.50 per each additional story (3 entries per contest maximum). Prizes: $250 first prize, $100 second prize and $50 third prize. Deadline: October 31st.

NATIONAL LEAGUE OF AMERICAN PEN WOMEN
Dorothy Daniels Honorary Writing Awards, P.O. Box 1485, Simi Valley, CA 93062.
Description: Original, unpublished poetry to 50 lines, fiction to 2,000 words and nonfiction to 1,500 words. SASE. Deadline: July 30. Entry fee: $3/poem; $5/fiction or nonfiction entry. Prizes; $100 in 3 categories.

NEW ENGLAND POETRY CLUB
c/o Virginia Thayer, 11 Puritan Road, Arlington, MA 02476-7710.
Virginia Thayer, Director.
Description: Various prizes, for original, unpublished poems in English. Submit poems in duplicate, name on one only. Mark with name of contest. $1,000 for Varoujan prize, $250 for Mumford, Houghton prizes. $500 for Sheila Matton prize for book published in last 2 years. Send SASE for details. No fee for members paying $25 in dues, or students.

THE NEW ENGLAND THEATRE CONFERENCE
Aurand Harris Memorial Playwriting Award, Northeastern University,
360 Huntington Ave., Boston, MA 02115.
E-mail: netc@world.std.com.
Description: New, unpublished full-length plays for young audiences. Open to New England residents and NETC members. SASE. Entry fee: $20. Deadline: May 1. Prizes: $1,000 and $500.

NEW ISSUES POETRY/WESTERN MICHIGAN UNIVERSITY
The Green Rose Prize in Poetry, Western Michigan University, 1201 Oliver St., Kalamazoo, MI 49008.
Description: Open to poets who have had one or more full-length collections of poetry published, the winner receives a prize of $1,000 plus publication. Deadline: September 30. Entry fee.

NEW LETTERS
New Letters Literary Awards, University of Missouri-Kansas, University House, 5101 Rockhill Rd., Kansas City, MO 64110. 816-235-1168.
E-mail: ezraa@umkc.edu. Web site: www.umkc.edu/newsletters.
Description: Three categories: fiction (short story), poetry and creative nonfiction. SASE or see web site for guidelines. Deadline: May 18. Entry fee: $10. Prizes: $1,000 and publication.

NEW YORK UNIVERSITY PRESS
New York University Press Prizes, 70 Washington Sq. S., 2nd Fl.,New York, NY 10012-1091.
Description: Awards $1,000 plus publication to a book-length poetry manuscript and a book-length fiction manuscript. Deadline: May 1.

NIMROD INTERNATIONAL JOURNAL

Nimrod/Hardman Awards, 600 S. College Ave., Tulsa, OK 74104-3189.
Description: Katherine Anne Porter Prize offers prizes of $2,000 and $1,000 for fiction, to 7,500 words. Pablo Neruda Prize: offers prizes of $2,000 and $1,000 for one long poem or a selection of poems. Deadline: April 15. Entry fees.

NORTH CAROLINA WRITERS' NETWORK

International Literature Prizes, 3501 Hwy. 54 West, Studio C, Chapel Hill, NC 27516.
Description: Thomas Wolfe Fiction Prize: offers $500 for a previously unpublished short story or novel excerpt. Deadline: August 31. Paul Green Playwrights Prize: offers $500 for a previously unproduced, unpublished play. Deadline: September 30. Randall Jarrell Poetry Prize: offers $500 for a previously unpublished poem. Deadline: November 1. Entry fees.

NORTHEASTERN UNIVERSITY PRESS

Samuel French Morse Poetry Prize, English Dept., 406 Holmes Hall, Northeastern Univ., Boston, MA 02115.
Description: Offers $1,000 plus publication for a full-length poetry manuscript by a U.S. poet who has published no more than one book of poems. Deadline: August 1 (for inquiries); September 15 (for entries). Entry fee. Contact: Prof. Guy Rotella, Chairman.

NORTHERN KENTUCKY UNIVERSITY

Y.E.S. New Play Festival, Dept. of Theatre, FA 227, Nunn Dr., Highland Hts., KY 41099-1007.
Description: Awards three $400 prizes plus production for previously unproduced full-length plays and musicals. Deadline: October 31 (of even-numbered years). Contact: Sandra Forman, Project Dir.

NORTHERN MICHIGAN UNIVERSITY

Mildred & Albert Panowski Playwriting Competition, Forest Roberts Theatre, Northern Michigan Univ., 1401 Presque Isle Ave., Marquette, MI 49855-5364.
Description: Awards $2,000, plus production for an original, full-length, previously unproduced and unpublished play. Deadline: November 20.

NUCLEAR AGE PEACE FOUNDATION

Barbara Mandigo Kelly Peace Prize, PMB 121, 1187 Coast Village Rd., Ste. 1, Santa Barbara, CA 93108.
E-mail: wagingpeace@napf.org. Web site: www.wagingpeace.org.
Description: Original, unpublished poetry. Open to all writers. Deadline: July 1. Entry fees: $5 for 1 poem, $10 for 2-3 poems, none for youth entries. Prizes: $1,000 for adults, $200 for ages 13-18; $200 for under age 12.

O'NEILL THEATER CENTER
National Playwrights Conference, 234 W. 44th St., Suite 901, New York, NY 10036. **Description:** Offers stipend, staged readings, and room and board at the conference, for new stage and television plays. Deadline: December 1. Entry fee. Contact: Mary F. McCabe.

OFF CENTER THEATER
Women Playwright's Festival,Tampa Bay Performing Arts Center, P.O. Box 518, Tampa, FL 33601. **Description:** A $1,000 prize, production, and travel are offered for the best play about women, written by a woman; runner up receives staged reading. Deadline: September 15. Entry fee.

OHIO UNIVERSITY PRESS
Hollis Summers Poetry Prize, Scott Quadrangle, Athens, OH 45701. **Description:** A $500 prize plus publication is awarded for an original collection of poetry, 60 to 95 pages. Deadline: October 31. Entry fee.

OLD DOMINION UNIVERSITY
Vassar Miller Prize in Poetry, c/o English Dept., Old Dominion University, Norfolk, VA 23529. **Description:** Awards $1,000 plus publication by the University of North Texas Press for an original, unpublished poetry manuscript, 50 to 80 pages. Deadline: November 30. Entry fee. Contact: Scott Cairns, Series Ed.

PASSAGES NORTH
Elinor Benedict Poetry Prize, Dept. of English, Northern Michigan Univ., 1401 Presque Isle Ave., Marquette, MI 49855. **Description:** $500 prize for unpublished poem. Deadline: December 1. Entry fee.

PATHWAY PRODUCTIONS
National Playwriting Contest, 9561 E. Daines Dr., Temple City, CA 91780. E-mail: PathWayPro@earthlink.net **Description:** Awards $200 plus a workshop production to plays for and about teenagers. Deadline April 1.

PEN AMERICAN CENTER
PEN Writers Fund, 568 Broadway, New York, NY 10012. **Description:** Grants and interest-free loans of up to $500 are available to published writers or produced playwrights facing unanticipated financial emergencies. If the emergency is due to HIV- and AIDS-related illness, professional writers and editors qualify through the Fund for Writers and Editors with AIDS; all decisions are confidential. Deadline: year-round. Contact: India Amos, Writers Fund Coordinator.

PEN AMERICAN CENTER

PEN Writing Awards for Prisoners, 568 Broadway, New York, 10012.
Description: County, state, and federal prisoners are eligible to enter one unpublished manuscript, to 5,000 words, in each of these categories: fiction, drama, and nonfiction. Prisoners may submit up to 10 poems (any form) in the poetry category (to 20 pages total) in the poetry category. Prizes of $100, $50, and $25 are awarded in each category. Deadline: September 1.

PEREGRINE SMITH POETRY SERIES

Gibbs Smith, Publisher, P.O. Box 667, Layton, UT 84041.
Description: Offers a $500 prize plus publication for a previously unpublished 64-page poetry manuscript. Deadline: April 30. Entry fee.

PETERLOO POETS

Open Competition, 2 Kelly Gardens, Calstock, Cornwall PL18 9SA, U.K.
Description: Prizes totalling 5,100 British pounds, including a grand prize of £4,000 plus publication, are awarded for poems of up to 40 lines. Deadline: March 1.

PHILADELPHIA FESTIVAL OF WORLD CINEMA

"Set in Philadelphia" Screenwriting Competition, 3701 Chestnut St., Philadelphia, PA 19104-3195.
Description: A $5,000 prize is awarded for the best screenplay, 85 to 130 pages, set primarily in the greater Philadelphia area. Deadline: January 1. Entry fee.

PIG IRON PRESS

Kenneth Patchen Competition, P.O. Box 237, Youngstown, OH 44501.
Description: Awards paperback publication, $500, and 20 copies of the winning manuscript of fiction (in even-numbered years) and poetry (in odd-numbered years). Deadline: December 31. Entry fee.

PIONEER DRAMA SERVICE

Shubert Fendrich Memorial Playwriting Contest, P.O. Box 4267, Englewood, CO 80155-4267.
Description: A prize of publication plus a $1,000 advance is offered for a previously produced, though unpublished, full-length play suitable for community theater. Deadline: March 1.

PIRATE'S ALLEY FAULKNER SOCIETY

William Faulkner Creative Writing Competition, 624 Pirate's Alley, New Orleans, LA 70116. 504-586-1612.
E-mail: faulkner@aol.com. Web site: www.wordsandmusic.org.
Description: Unpublished works of fiction, nonfiction or poetry. SASE or see web site for guidelines and entry form. Deadline: April 1. Entry fees: $10-$35. Prizes $250-$7,500.

PLAYBOY
College Fiction Contest, 680 N. Lake Shore Dr., Chicago, IL 60611.
Description: Prizes of $3,000 plus publication, and $500, are offered for a short story, up to 25 pages, by a college student. Deadline: January 1.

THE PLAYWRIGHTS' CENTER
Jerome Fellowships, 2301 Franklin Ave. E., Minneapolis, MN 55406.
Description: Five emerging playwrights are offered a $7,000 stipend and 12-month residency; housing and travel are not provided. Deadline: September 16.

POCKETS
Fiction Contest, P.O. Box 189, Nashville, TN 37202-0189.
Description: A $1,000 prize goes to the author of the winning 1,000- to 1,600-word story for children in grades 1 to 6. Deadline: August 15. Contact: Lynn W. Gilliam, Assoc. Ed.

POETRY CENTER AT PASSAIC COUNTY COMMUNITY COLLEGE
Allen Ginsberg Poetry Awards, 1 College Blvd., Patterson, NJ 07505. 973-684-6555. Web site: www.pccc.cc.nj.us/poetry.
Description: Up to 5 previously unpublished poems, up to 2 pages each. Send 4 copies of each entry. Do not submit poems that imitate Allen Ginsberg's work. SASE. Deadline: April 1. Entry fee: $13. Prizes: $1,000, $200, and $100. Contact: Maria Mazziotti Gillan.

POETS AND PATRONS OF CHICAGO
Poets and Patrons of Chicago, 1206 Hutchings, Glenview, IL 60025.
Description: Prizes are $75 and $25 for original, unpublished poems of up to 40 lines. Deadline: September 1. Contact: Agnes Wathall Tatera.

POETS CLUB OF CHICAGO
130 Windsor Park Dr., C-323, Carol Stream, IL 60188.
Description: Shakespearean/Petrarchan Sonnet Contest, with prizes of $50, $35, and $15. Deadline: September 1. Conctac: LaVone Holt.

PRISM INTERNATIONAL
Short Fiction Contest, Creative Writing Dept., Univ. of B.C., E462-1866 Main Mall, Vancouver, B.C., V6T 1Z1.
Description: Publication, a $2,000 first prize, and five $200 prizes are awarded for stories of up to 25 pages. Deadline: December 31. Entry fee.

RIVER CITY
Writing Awards in Fiction, Dept. of English, Univ. of Memphis, Memphis, TN 38152.
Description: Awards of $2,000 plus publication, $500, and $300 are offered for previously unpublished short stories, to 7,500 words. Deadline: December 1. Entry fee.

ROME ART & COMMUNITY CENTER

Milton Dorfman Poetry Prize, 308 W. Bloomfield St., Rome, NY 13440.
Description: Offers prizes of $500, $200, and $100 for the best original, unpublished poems. Deadline: November 1. Entry fee.

ST. MARTIN'S PRESS/PRIVATE EYE NOVEL CONTEST

PWA Contest,175 Fifth Ave., New York, NY 10010.
Description: Co-sponsored by Private Eye Writers of America. The writer of the best first private eye novel, from 60,000 words, receives publication plus $10,000 against royalties. Deadline: August 1.

SARABANDE BOOKS

Poetry and Short Fiction Prizes, P.O. Box 4999, Louisville, KY 40204.
Description: Prizes are $2,000, publication, and a standard royalty contract in the competition for the Kathryn A. Morton Prize in Poetry (for a collection of poems, from 48 pages) and the Mary McCarthy Prize in Short Fiction (for a collection of short stories or novellas, 150 to 300 pages). Deadline: February 15. Entry fee.

SHENANARTS

Shenandoah International Playwrights Retreat, Rt. 5, Box 167-F, Staunton, VA 24401.
Description: Full fellowships are offered to playwrights to attend the four-week retreat held each August. Each year the retreat focuses on plays having to do with a specific region of the world. Deadline: February 1.

SIENA COLLEGE

International Playwrights' Competition, Siena College, 515 Loudon Rd., Loudonville, NY 12211-1462.
Description: Offers $2,000 plus campus residency expenses for the winning full-length script; no musicals. Deadline: June 30 (of even-numbered years).

SILVERFISH REVIEW PRESS

The Gerald Cable Book Award, P.O. Box 3541, Eugene, OR 97403.
Description: Awards $1,000 plus publication to a book-length manuscript of poetry by an author not yet published as a full-length collection. Deadline: November 1.

SNAKE NATION PRESS

Fiction and Poetry Contests, 110 #2 W. Force St.,Valdosta, GA 31601.
Description: Violet Reed Haas Prize: Offers publication plus $500 for a previously unpublished book of poetry, 50 to 75 pages. Deadline: January 15. *Snake Nation Review* Contest Issues: Prizes are publication plus $300, $200, and $100 for short stories; $100, $75, and $50 for poems. Deadlines: April 1; September 1. Entry fee. Contact: Nancy Phillips.

SONORA REVIEW
Contests, Univ. of Arizona, Dept. of English, Tucson, AZ 85721.
Description: Poetry, Nonfiction Contest: offers $250 plus publication for the best poem; $100 plus publication for the best nonfiction. Deadline: July 1 for poetry and nonfiction. Short Story Contest: offers $250 plus publication for the best short story. Deadline: December 1. Entry fees.

S.C. PLAYWRIGHTS CENTER
S.C. Playwrights Center, 1001 Bat St., Ste 101, Beaufort, SC 29902. 843-986-0589.
Description: Submit 3 copies of a play in play format with a synopsis. Reading time should be 30-90 minutes. No previous productions, musicals, or translations; must be original with a maximum of 8 characters. SASE for details. Selected playwrights will attend the Annual South Carolina Playwrights Conference. $10 reading fee. Deadline: Feb. 15.

THE SOUTHERN ANTHOLOGY
The Southern Prize, 2851 Johnston St., #123, Lafayette, LA 70503.
Description: A prize of $600 and publication are awarded for the best original, previously unpublished short story or novel excerpt, up to 7,500 words, or poem. Deadline: May 30. Entry fee.

SOUTHERN POETRY REVIEW
Guy Owen Poetry Prize, Southern Poetry Review, Advancement Studies Dept., Central Piedmont Community College, Charlotte, NC 28235.
Description: A prize of publication plus $500 is awarded for the best original, previously unpublished poem. Deadline: April 30. Entry fee. Contact: Ken McLaurin, Ed.

SOW'S EAR CHAPBOOK COMPETITION
Sow's Ear Poetry Review, 19535 Pleasant View Dr., Abingson, CA 24211. 540-628-2651.
E-mail: richman@preferred.com.
Description: Send 22-26 pages of poetry, 1 poem per page. Previously published poems OK if writer holds the publication rights. Deadline: May 1. Entry fee: $10. Prizes: $1,000 and publication; $200 and $100.

SPOON RIVER POETRY PRIZE
Dept. of English Publication Unit, Illinois State University, Normal, IL 61790.
Web site: www.litline.org/spoon/spooncontest.html..
Description: Submit 2 copies of 3 unpublished poems, up to 10 pages total. SASE. Entry fee: $15. Deadline: April 15. Prize: $1,000.

ANN STANFORD POETRY PRIZE

Professional Writing Program, University of Southern California, WPH 404, Los Angeles, CA 90089. 213-740-3252.
E-mail: mpw@mizar.exc.edu.
Description: Up to 5 unpublished poems; SASE. Entry fee: $10. Prizes: $1,000, $200, and $100 plus publication. Deadline: April 15.

STATE UNIVERSITY OF NEW YORK AT FARMINGDALE

Paumanok Poetry Award, English Dept., Knapp Hall, SUNY Farmingdale, Farmingdale, NY 11735.
Description: Prizes of $1,000 and two $500 prizes are offered for entries of three to five poems. Deadline: September 15. Entry fee.

STATE UNIVERSITY OF NEW YORK AT STONY BROOK

Short Fiction Prize, Dept. of English, Humanities Bldg., State Univ., Stony Brook, NY 11794-5350.
Description: A prize of $1,000 is offered for the best short story, up to 5,000 words, written by an undergraduate currently enrolled full-time in an American or Canadian college. Deadline: February 28. Contact: Carolyn McGrath.

STORY LINE PRESS

Nicholas Roerich Poetry Prize, Three Oaks Farm, P.O. Box 1240, Ashland, OR 97520-0055.
Description: A prize of $1,000 plus publication is awarded for an original book of poetry by a poet who has never before published a book of poetry. Deadline: October 31. Entry fee.

SYRACUSE UNIVERSITY PRESS

John Ben Snow Prize, 1600 Jamesville Ave., Syracuse, NY 13244-5160.
Description: Awards a $1,500 advance, plus publication, for an unpublished book-length nonfiction manuscript about New York State, especially upstate or central New York. Deadline: December 31.

TANTALUS MAGAZINE

Tantalus Poetry Contest, P.O. Box 189, Clarion, PA 16214.
E-mail: submissions@tantalusmagazine.com. Web site:www.tantalusmagazine.com.
Description: Original, previously unpublished poetry. Submissions must be hard copy and have name and address. Entry fee of $2 per poem. First prize $500; second prize $200; third prize $100. All entries will be reviewed for consideration of publication in the magazine. Deadline: March 1.

TEN MINUTE MUSICALS PROJECT

P.O. Box 461194, W. Hollywood, CA 90046.
Description: Prod. Musicals of 7 to 20 minutes are eligible for a $250 advance against royalties and musical anthology productions at theaters in the U.S. and Canada. Deadline: August 31. Contact: Michael Koppy.

DAVID THOMAS CHARITABLE TRUST

Open Competitions, P.O. Box 4, Nairn IV12 4HU, Scotland, UK.
Description: The trust sponsors a number of theme-based poetry and short story contests open to beginning writers, with prizes ranging from £25 to £1,200. Deadline: varies. Entry fee.

TRITON COLLEGE

Salute to the Arts Poetry Contest, 2000 Fifth Ave., River Grove, IL 60171.
Description: Winning original, unpublished poems, to 60 lines, on designated themes, are published by Triton College. Deadline: April 1.

UNICO NATIONAL

Ella T. Grasso Literary Award Contest, 72 Burroughs Pl., Bloomfield, NJ 07003.
Description: A prize of $1,000 is awarded for the best essay or short story, 1,500 to 2,000 words, on the Italian-American experience; two $250 prizes also awarded. Deadline: April 1.

U.S. NAVAL INSTITUTE

Arleigh Burke Essay Contest, *Proceedings Magazine*, 291 Wood Rd., Annapolis, MD 21402-5034.
Awards prizes of $3,000, $2,000, and $1,000 plus publication, for essays on the advancement of professional, literary, or scientific knowledge in the naval or maritime services, and the advancement of the knowledge of sea power. Deadline: December 31. Also sponsors several smaller contests; deadlines vary.

UNIVERSITIES WEST PRESS

Emily Dickinson Award in Poetry, Universities West Press, P.O. Box 22310, Flagstaff, AZ 86002-2310.
Description: A prize of $1,000 plus publication is awarded for an unpublished poem. Deadline: August 31. Entry fee.

UNIVERSITY OF AKRON PRESS

Akron Poetry Prize, 374 B Bierce Library, Akron, OH 44325. 877-UAPRESS.
E-mail: uapress@uakron.edu. Web site: www.akron.edu/uapress/poetry.html.
Description: Unbound manuscripts, 60-100 pages. Include list of previously published poems. Entries must be postmarked between May 15-June 30th. SASE. Entry fee: $25. Prize: $1,000 and publication.

UNIVERSITY OF CALIFORNIA-IRVINE
Chicano/Latino Literary Contest, Dept. of Spanish and Portuguese, UCI, Irvine, CA 92697-5275.
Description: A first prize of $1,000 plus publication, and prizes of $500 and $250 are awarded in alternating years for poetry, drama, novels, and short stories. Deadline: April 30. Contact: Alejandro Morales, Dir.

UNIVERSITY OF GEORGIA PRESS
Flannery O'Connor Award for Short Fiction, Univ. of Georgia Press, 330 Research Dr., Athens, GA 30602-4901.
Description: Two prizes of $1,000 plus publication are awarded for book-length collections of short fiction. Deadline: July 31. Entry fees.

UNIVERSITY OF GEORGIA PRESS CONTEMPORARY POETRY SERIES
Athens, GA 30602-4901.
Description: Offers publication of manuscripts from poets who have published at least one volume of poetry. Deadline: January 31. Publication of book-length poetry manuscripts is offered to poets who have never had a book of poems published. Deadline: September 30. Entry fee.

UNIVERSITY OF HAWAII AT MANOA
Kumu Kahua Playwriting Contest, Dept. of Drama and Theatre, 1770 East-West Rd., Honolulu, HI 96822.
Description: Awards $500 and $400 for full-length plays on the Hawaiian experience; $200 for plays on any topic. Also conducts contest for plays written by Hawaiian residents. Deadline: January 1.

UNIVERSITY OF IOWA
Iowa Publication Awards for Short Fiction, Iowa Writers' Workshop, 102 Dey House, Iowa City, IA 52242-1000.
Description: The John Simmons Short Fiction Award and the Iowa Short Fiction Award, both for unpublished full-length collections of short stories, offer publication under a standard contract. Deadline: September 30.

UNIVERSITY OF IOWA PRESS
Iowa Poetry Prize, 100 Kuhl House, Iowa City, IA 52242.
Web site: www.uiowa.edu/~uipress.
Description: Book-length collection of poems, written originally in English 50-100 manuscript pages. Open to new as well as established poets. Deadline: April 30. Entry fee: $15. Prize: Publication.

UNIVERSITY OF MASSACHUSETTS PRESS
Juniper Prize, Amherst, MA 01003.
Description: Offers a prize of $1,000 plus publication for a book-length manuscript

of poetry; awarded in odd-numbered years to writers who have never published a book of poetry, and in even-numbered years to writers who have published a book or chapbook of poetry. Deadline: September 30. Entry fee.

UNIVERSITY OF NEBRASKA-OMAHA
Awards in Poetry and Fiction, *The Nebraska Review*, Univ. of Nebraska-Omaha, Omaha, NE 68182-0324. **Description:** Offers $500 each plus publication to the winning short story (to 5,000 words) and the winning poem (or group of poems). Deadline: November 30. Entry fee.

UNIVERSITY OF NEBRASKA PRESS
North American Indian Prose Award, 312 N. 14th St., Lincoln, NE 68588-0484. Previously unpublished book-length manuscripts of biography, autobiography, - history, literary criticism, and essays will be judged for originality, literary merit, and familiarity with North American Indian life. A $1,000 advance and publication are offered. Deadline: July 1.

UNIVERSITY OF PITTSBURGH PRESS
3347 Forbes Ave., Pittsburgh, PA 15261. **Description:** Agnes Lynch Starrett Poetry Prize: offers $3,000 plus publication in the Pitt Poetry Series for a book-length collection of poems by a poet who has not yet published a volume of poetry. Deadline: April 30. Entry fee. Drue Heinz Literature Prize: offers $10,000 plus publication and royalty contract for an unpublished collection of short stories or novellas, 150 to 300 pages, by a writer who has previously published a book-length collection of fiction or at least three short stories or novellas in nationally distributed magazines. Deadline: June 30.

UNIVERSITY OF SOUTHERN CALIFORNIA
Ann Stanford Poetry Prize, Master of Professional Writing Program, WPH 404, Univ. of Southern California, Los Angeles, CA 90089-4034. **Description:** Publication plus prizes of $750, $250, and $100 are awarded; submit up to five poems. Deadline: April 15. Entry fee.

UTAH STATE UNIVERSITY PRESS
May Swenson Poetry Award, Utah State Univ. Press, Logan, UT 84322-7800. **Description:** Awards $750, plus publication and royalties to a collection of poems, 50 to 100 pages. Deadline: September 30. Entry fee.

VETERANS OF FOREIGN WARS
Voice of Democracy Audio Essay Competition, VFW National Headquarters, 406 W. 34th St., Kansas City, MO 64111. **Description:** Several national scholarships totalling over $120,000 are awarded to high school students for short, tape-recorded essays. Themes change annually. Deadline: November 1.

THE WORD WORKS

Washington Prize, P.O. Box 42164, Washington, DC 20015. 703-256-9275. E-mail: editor@wordworksdc.com. Web site: www.wordworksdc.com. **Description:** Original poetry by a living American writer. Send 48-64 page manuscripts with name, address, phone number, and signature on title page only. Include table of contents, acknowledgments page and brief bio. No mss are returned. Deadline: March 1. Entry fee: $20. All entrants receive a copy of the winning book. $1,500 award for the winner and publication.

YALE UNIVERSITY PRESS

Yale Series of Younger Poets Prize, Box 209040, Yale Sta., New Haven, CT 06520. **Description:** Series publication is awarded for a book-length manuscript of poetry written by a poet under 40 who has not previously published a volume of poems. Deadline: February 29. Entry fee.

GLOSSARY

Advance—The amount a publisher pays a writer before a book is published; it is deducted from the royalties earned from sales of the finished book.

Agented material—Submissions from literary or dramatic agents to a publisher. Some publishing companies accept agented material only.

All rights—Some magazines purchase all rights to the material they publish, which means that they can use it as they wish, as many times as they wish. They cannot purchase all rights unless the writer gives them written permission to do so.

Assignment—A contract, written or oral, between an editor and writer, confirming that the writer will complete a specific project by a certain date, and for a certain fee.

B&W—Abbreviation for black-and-white photographs.

Book outline—Chapter-by-chapter summary of a book, frequently in paragraph form, allowing an editor to evaluate the book's content, tone, and pacing, and determine whether he or she wants to see the entire manuscript for possible publication.

Book packager—Company that puts together all the elements of a book, from initial concept to writing, publishing, and marketing it. Also called **book producer** or **book developer.**

Byline—Author's name as it appears on a published piece.

Clips—Copies of a writer's published work, often used by editors to evaluate the writer's talent.

Column inch—One inch of a typeset column; often serves as a basis for payment.

Contributor's copies—Copies of a publication sent to a writer whose work is included in it.

Copy editing—Line-by-line editing to correct errors in spelling, grammar, and punctuation, and inconsistencies in style. Differs from **content editing,** which evaluates flow, logic, and overall message.

Copy—Manuscript pages before they are set into type.

Copyright—Legal protection of creative works from unauthorized use. Under the law, copyright is secured automatically when the work is set down for the first time in written or recorded form.

Cover letter—A brief letter that accompanies a manuscript or book proposal. A cover letter is not a query letter (see definition, page 887).

Deadline—The date on which a written work is due at the editor's office, agreed to by author and editor.

Draft—A complete version of an article, story, or book. First drafts are often called **rough drafts.**

Electronic rights—Refers to the use of an article in electronic form, rather than hard-copy formats. The term is not very precise, and it is a good idea to pin down exactly what the publisher means by electronic rights, and consider what rights are reasonable to allow considering the fee, advance, or royalty amount being offered.

Fair use—A provision of the copyright law allowing brief passages of copyrighted material to be quoted without infringing on the owner's rights.

Feature—An article that is generally longer than a news story and whose main focus is an issue, trend, or person.

Filler—Brief item used to fill out a newspaper or magazine column; could be a news item, joke, anecdote, or puzzle.

First serial rights—The right of a magazine or newspaper to publish a work for the first time in any periodical. After that, all rights revert to the writer.

FNASR (First North American Serial Rights)—This refers to the specific right to use an author's work in a serial periodical, in North America, for its first appearance. Thereafter, rights to reprint the work remain with the author.

Ghostwriter—Author of books, articles, and speeches that are credited to someone else.

Glossy—Black-and-white photo with a shiny, rather than a matte, finish.

Hard copy—The printed copy of material written on a computer.

Honorarium—A modest, token fee paid by a publication to an author in gratitude for a submission.

International reply coupon (IRC)—Included with any correspondence or submission to a foreign publication; allows the editor to reply by mail without incurring cost.

Internet rights—See also electronic rights. This refers to the rights to post an author's work on a website, and possibly to distribute or allow the distribution of the article further via the Internet.

Kill fee—Fee paid for an article that was assigned but subsequently not published; usually a percentage of the amount that would have been paid if the work had been published.

Lead time—Time between the planning of a magazine or book and its publication date.

Libel—A false accusation or published statement that causes a person embarrassment, loss of income, or damage to reputation.

Little magazines—Publications with limited circulation whose content often deals with literature or politics.

Mass market—Books appealing to a very large segment of the reading public and often sold in such outlets as drugstores, supermarkets, etc.

Masthead—A listing of the names and titles of a publication's staff members.

Ms—Abbreviation for manuscript; mss is the plural abbreviation.

Multiple submissions—Also called **simultaneous submissions.** Complete manuscripts sent simultaneously to different publications. Once universally discouraged by editors, the practice is gaining more acceptance, though some still frown on it. **Multiple queries** are generally accepted, however, since reading them requires less of an investment in time on the editor's part.

NA (North American)—sometimes appears as 1st NA; refers the right to publish the North American appearance of a piece of work, leaving the author free to market other appearances of the same work elsewhere.

No recent report—This indicates that we do not have sufficient recent information to verify the listing shown; the listing given being the same as that which appeared in the previous year's *Handbook*. Each such listing will be removed from the *Handbook* in the following year unless verified.

On speculation—Editor agrees to consider a work for publication "on speculation," without any guarantee that he or she will ultimately buy the work.

One-time rights—Editor buys manuscript from writer and agrees to publish it one time, after which the rights revert to the author for subsequent sales.

Op-ed—A newspaper piece, usually printed opposite the editorial page, that expresses a personal viewpoint on a timely news item.

Over-the-transom—Describes the submission of unsolicited material by a free-lance writer; the term harks back to the time when mail was delivered through the open window above an office door.

Payment on acceptance—Payment to writer when manuscript is submitted.

Payment on publication—Payment to writer when manuscript is published.

Pen name—A name other than his or her legal name that an author uses on written work.

Public domain—Published material that is available for use without permission, either because it was never copyrighted or because its copyright term is expired. Works published at least 75 years ago are considered in the public domain.

Q-and-A format—One type of presentation for an interview article, in which questions are printed, followed by the interviewee's answers.

Query letter—A letter—usually no longer than one page—in which a writer proposes an article idea to an editor.

Rejection slip—A printed note in which a publication indicates that it is not interested in a submission.

Reporting time—The weeks or months it takes for an editor to evaluate a submission.

Reprint rights—The legal right of a magazine or newspaper to print an article, story, or poem after it has already appeared elsewhere.

Royalty—A percentage of the amount received from retail sales of a book, paid to the author by the publisher. For hardcovers, the royalty is generally 10% on the first 5,000 copies sold; 12½% on the next 5,000 sold; 15% thereafter. Paperback royalties range from 4% to 8%, depending on whether it's a trade or mass-market book.

SASE—Self-addressed, stamped envelope, required with all submissions that the author wishes returned—either for return of material or (if you don't need material returned) for editor's reply.

Slush pile—The stack of unsolicited manuscripts in an editor's office.

Tear sheets—The pages of a magazine or newspaper on which an author's work is published.

Unsolicited submission—A manuscript that an editor did not specifically ask to see.

Vanity publisher—Also called **subsidy publisher.** A publishing company that charges an author all costs of printing his or her book. No reputable book publisher operates on this subsidy basis.

Web rights—See Internet rights.

Work for hire—When a work is written on a "for hire" basis, all rights in it become the property of the publisher. Though the work-for-hire clause applies mostly to work done by regular employees of a company, some editors offer work-for-hire agreements to free lancers. Think carefully before signing such agreements, however, since by doing so you will essentially be signing away your rights and will not be able to try to resell your work on your own.

Worldwide—Refers to the right to publish an article anywhere in the world (however, this right may be limited by other wording in a contract to publication in the English language only, or in-print only, or in electronic form only, etc.).

Writers guidelines—A formal statement of a publication's editorial needs, payment schedule, deadlines, and other essential information.

INDEX